Contents

Student Edition Answers

Workbook Answers

Math in Focus
Student Edition Answers
Grade 4

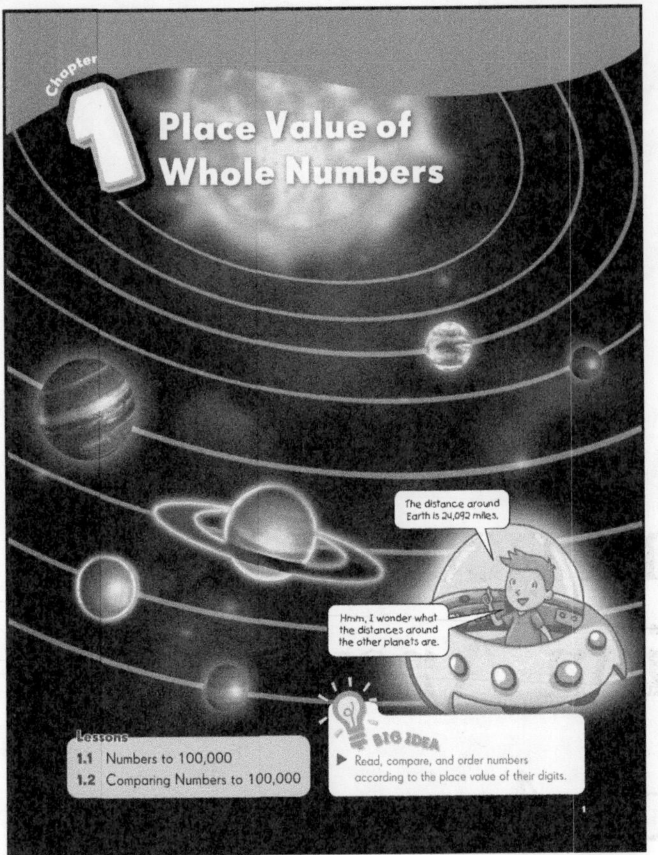

Chapter 1

Place Value of Whole Numbers

The distance around Earth is 24,092 miles.

Hmm, I wonder what the distances around the other planets are.

Lessons

1.1 Numbers to 100,000

1.2 Comparing Numbers to 100,000

BIG IDEA

▶ Read, compare, and order numbers according to the place value of their digits.

1

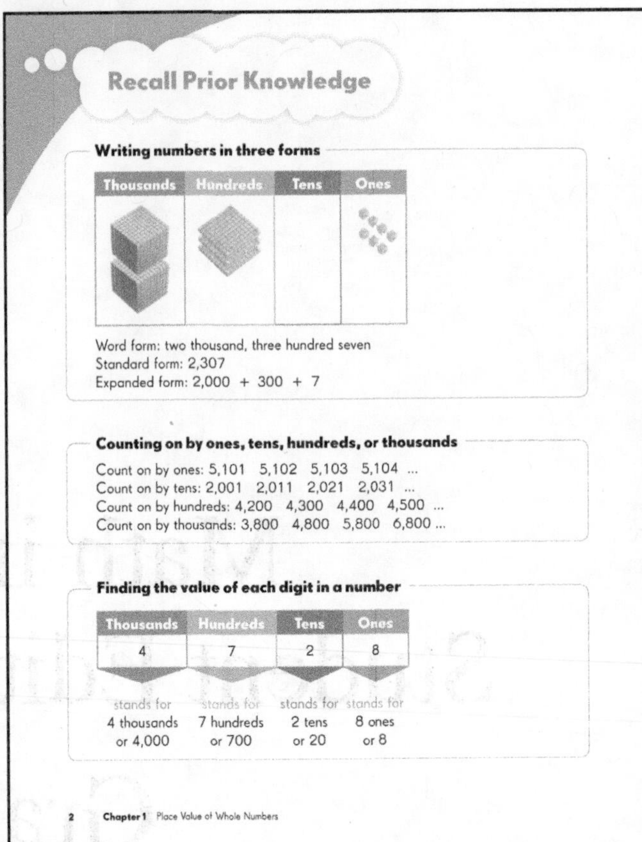

Recall Prior Knowledge

Writing numbers in three forms

Thousands	Hundreds	Tens	Ones

Word form: two thousand, three hundred seven
Standard form: 2,307
Expanded form: 2,000 + 300 + 7

Counting on by ones, tens, hundreds, or thousands

Count on by ones: 5,101 5,102 5,103 5,104 ...
Count on by tens: 2,001 2,011 2,021 2,031 ...
Count on by hundreds: 4,200 4,300 4,400 4,500 ...
Count on by thousands: 3,800 4,800 5,800 6,800 ...

Finding the value of each digit in a number

Thousands	Hundreds	Tens	Ones
4	7	2	8
stands for 4 thousands or 4,000	stands for 7 hundreds or 700	stands for 2 tens or 20	stands for 8 ones or 8

2 Chapter 1 Place Value of Whole Numbers

Comparing numbers using a place-value chart

	Thousands	Hundreds	Tens	Ones
2,910	2	9	1	0
2,688	2	6	8	8

First, compare the thousands. They are the same.
Then, compare the hundreds. 9 hundreds is greater than 6 hundreds.
So, 2,910 is greater than 2,688.

Completing a pattern by finding the rule

+ 200 + 200

4,182 4,382 4,582 ? 4,982

Add 200 to 4,582 to get 4,782.
Check your answer by adding 200 to 4,782. You will get 4,982.
So, the rule is to add 200 to a number to get the next number in the pattern.

✔Quick Check

Express each number in word form.

1. 5,691 five thousand, six hundred ninety-one
2. 9,056 nine thousand, fifty-six

Express each number in standard form.

3. two thousand, three hundred seven 2,307
4. six thousand, twelve 6,012

Chapter 1 Place Value of Whole Numbers 3

Express each number in expanded form.

5. 6,432 = 6,000 + 400 + 30 + 2
6. 3,805 = 3,000 + 800 + 5

Continue each number pattern. Count on by ones, tens, hundreds, or thousands.

7. 5,500 5,600 5,700 5,800
8. 9,077 9,078 9,079 9,080
9. 5,320 6,320 7,320 8,320

Complete.

In 5,628,

10. The digit 6 is in the ______ place. hundreds
11. The value of the digit 5 is ______. 5,000
12. The digit 2 stands for ______. 2 tens or 20

Compare the numbers.

13. Which is greater, 3,819 or 3,918? 3,918
14. Which is less, 7,052 or 936? 936
15. Which is the greatest, 3,625, 4,130, or 4,031? 4,130

Continue or complete each number pattern. Then state the rule.

16. 6,385 6,395 6,405 6,415

Rule: Add 10 to a number to get the next number in the pattern.

17. 7,821 7,521 7,221 6,921

Rule: Subtract 300 from a number to get the next number in the pattern.

4 Chapter 1 Place Value of Whole Numbers

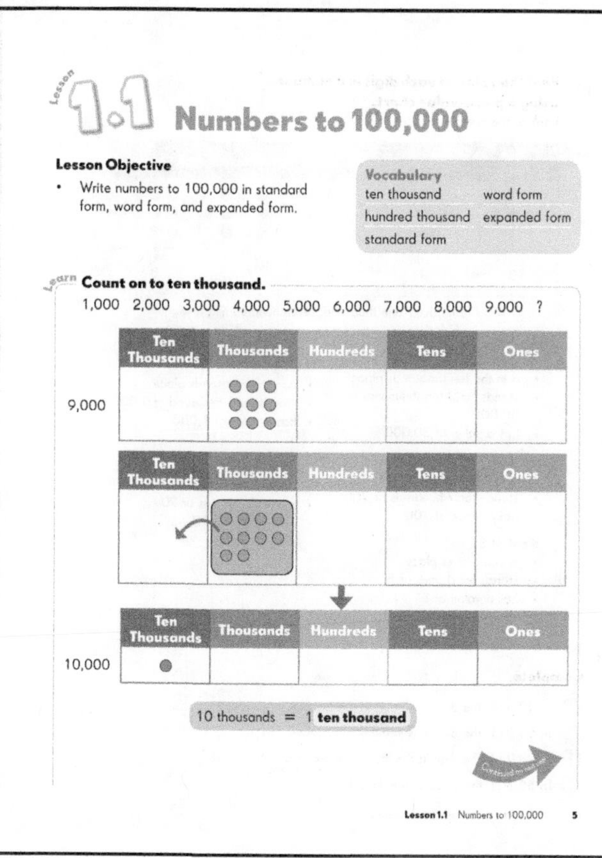

Lesson 1.1 **Numbers to 100,000**

Lesson Objective

- Write numbers to 100,000 in standard form, word form, and expanded form.

Vocabulary
ten thousand | word form
hundred thousand | expanded form
standard form

Learn **Count on to ten thousand.**

1,000 2,000 3,000 4,000 5,000 6,000 7,000 8,000 9,000 ?

	Ten Thousands	Thousands	Hundreds	Tens	Ones
9,000					

Ten Thousands	Thousands	Hundreds	Tens	Ones

	Ten Thousands	Thousands	Hundreds	Tens	Ones
10,000					

10 thousands = 1 **ten thousand**

Continued on next page

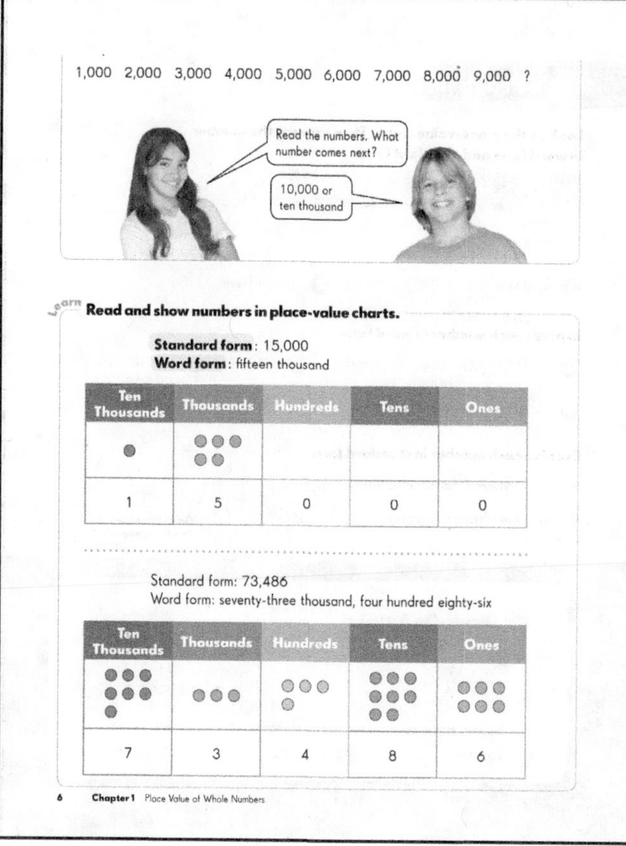

1,000 2,000 3,000 4,000 5,000 6,000 7,000 8,000 9,000 ?

Read the numbers. What number comes next?
10,000 or ten thousand

Learn **Read and show numbers in place-value charts.**

Standard form: 15,000
Word form: fifteen thousand

Ten Thousands	Thousands	Hundreds	Tens	Ones
1	5	0	0	0

Standard form: 73,486
Word form: seventy-three thousand, four hundred eighty-six

Ten Thousands	Thousands	Hundreds	Tens	Ones
7	3	4	8	6

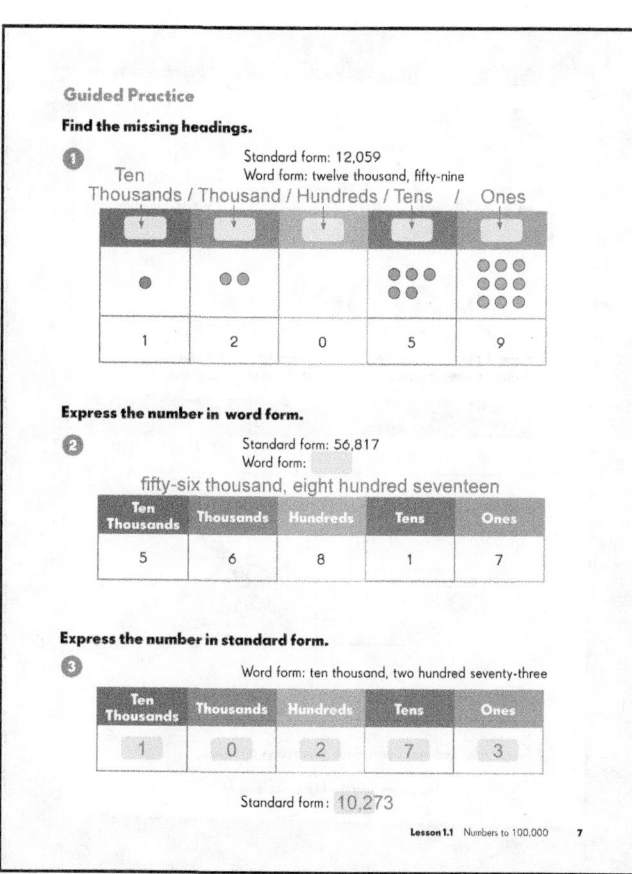

Guided Practice

Find the missing headings.

1. Standard form: 12,059
Word form: twelve thousand, fifty-nine

Ten Thousands	Thousand	Hundreds	Tens	Ones
1	2	0	5	9

Express the number in word form.

2. Standard form: 56,817
Word form: fifty-six thousand, eight hundred seventeen

Ten Thousands	Thousands	Hundreds	Tens	Ones
5	6	8	1	7

Express the number in standard form.

3. Word form: ten thousand, two hundred seventy-three

Ten Thousands	Thousands	Hundreds	Tens	Ones
1	0	2	7	3

Standard form: 10,273

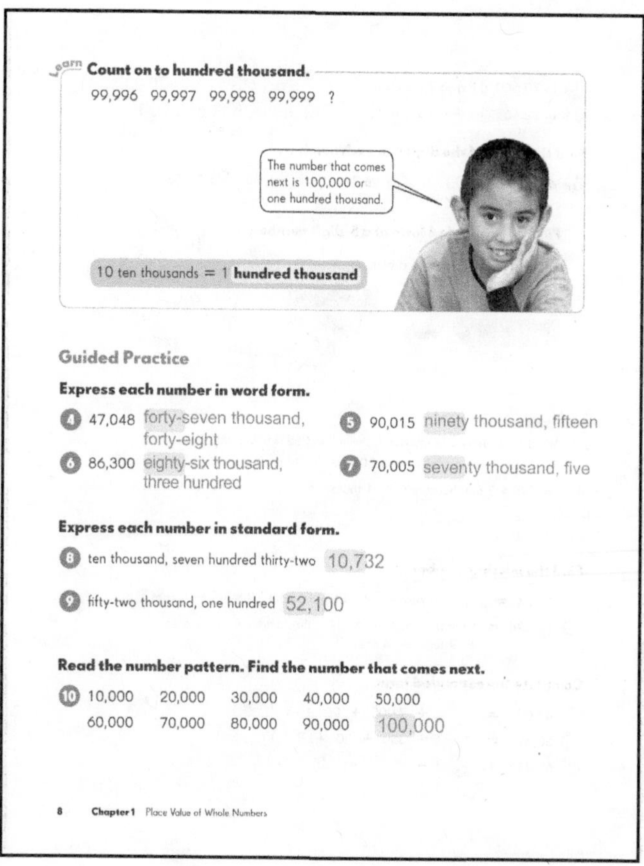

Learn **Count on to hundred thousand.**

99,996 99,997 99,998 99,999 ?

The number that comes next is 100,000 or one hundred thousand.

10 ten thousands = 1 **hundred thousand**

Guided Practice

Express each number in word form.

4. 47,048 forty-seven thousand, forty-eight
5. 90,015 ninety thousand, fifteen
6. 86,300 eighty-six thousand, three hundred
7. 70,005 seventy thousand, five

Express each number in standard form.

8. ten thousand, seven hundred thirty-two 10,732
9. fifty-two thousand, one hundred 52,100

Read the number pattern. Find the number that comes next.

10. 10,000 20,000 30,000 40,000 50,000
60,000 70,000 80,000 90,000 100,000

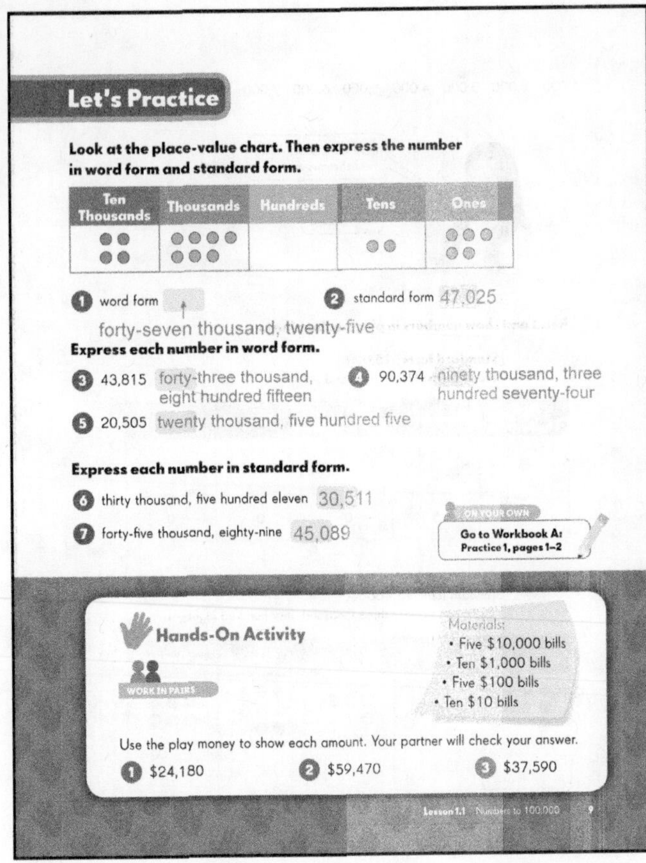

Let's Practice
Look at the place-value chart. Then express the number in word form and standard form.
Ten Thousands | Thousands | Hundreds | Tens | Ones
1 word form forty-seven thousand, twenty-five
2 standard form 47,025
Express each number in word form.
3 43,815 forty-three thousand, eight hundred fifteen
4 90,374 ninety thousand, three hundred seventy-four
5 20,505 twenty thousand, five hundred five
Express each number in standard form.
6 thirty thousand, five hundred eleven 30,511
7 forty-five thousand, eighty-nine 45,089
ON YOUR OWN
Go to Workbook A: Practice 1, pages 1–2
Hands-On Activity
WORK IN PAIRS
Materials:
• Five $10,000 bills
• Ten $1,000 bills
• Five $100 bills
• Ten $10 bills
Use the play money to show each amount. Your partner will check your answer.
1 $24,180
2 $59,470
3 $37,590
Lesson 1.1 Numbers to 100,000 9

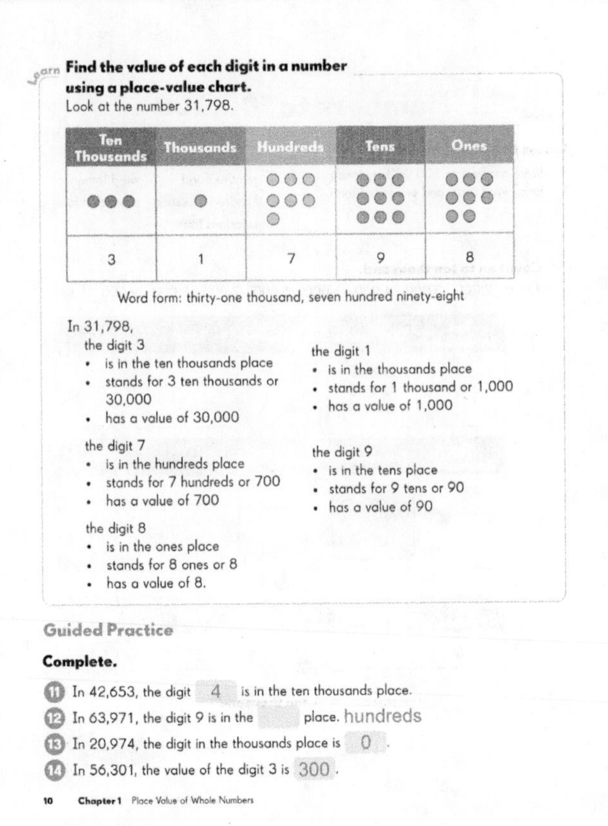

Learn Find the value of each digit in a number using a place-value chart.
Look at the number 31,798.
Ten Thousands | Thousands | Hundreds | Tens | Ones
3 | 1 | 7 | 9 | 8
Word form: thirty-one thousand, seven hundred ninety-eight
In 31,798,
the digit 3
• is in the ten thousands place
• stands for 3 ten thousands or 30,000
• has a value of 30,000
the digit 1
• is in the thousands place
• stands for 1 thousand or 1,000
• has a value of 1,000
the digit 7
• is in the hundreds place
• stands for 7 hundreds or 700
• has a value of 700
the digit 9
• is in the tens place
• stands for 9 tens or 90
• has a value of 90
the digit 8
• is in the ones place
• stands for 8 ones or 8
• has a value of 8.
Guided Practice
Complete.
11 In 42,653, the digit 4 is in the ten thousands place.
12 In 63,971, the digit 9 is in the hundreds place.
13 In 20,974, the digit in the thousands place is 0.
14 In 56,301, the value of the digit 3 is 300.
10 Chapter 1 Place Value of Whole Numbers

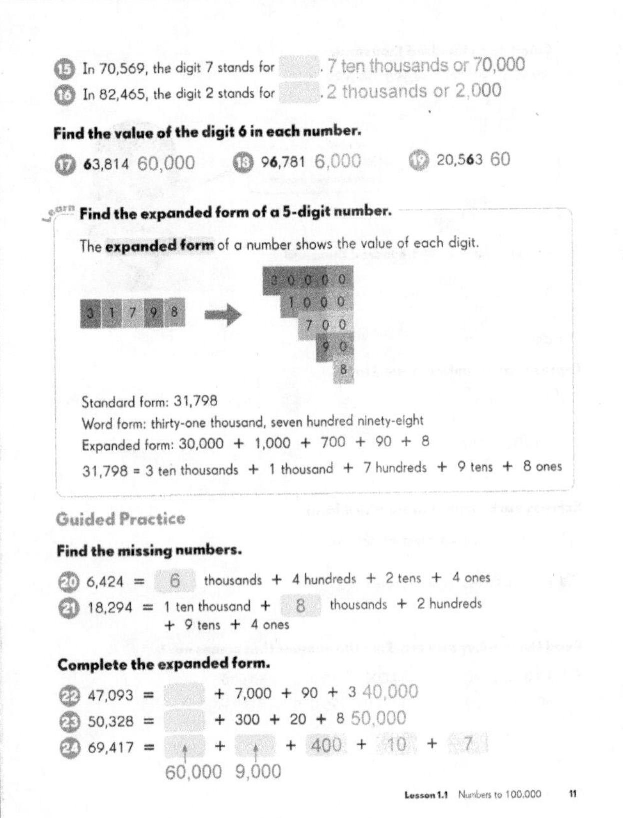

15 In 70,569, the digit 7 stands for 7 ten thousands or 70,000.
16 In 82,465, the digit 2 stands for 2 thousands or 2,000.
Find the value of the digit 6 in each number.
17 63,814 60,000
18 96,781 6,000
19 20,563 60
Learn Find the expanded form of a 5-digit number.
The expanded form of a number shows the value of each digit.
3 1 7 9 8
30000
1000
700
90
8
Standard form: 31,798
Word form: thirty-one thousand, seven hundred ninety-eight
Expanded form: 30,000 + 1,000 + 700 + 90 + 8
31,798 = 3 ten thousands + 1 thousand + 7 hundreds + 9 tens + 8 ones
Guided Practice
Find the missing numbers.
20 6,424 = 6 thousands + 4 hundreds + 2 tens + 4 ones
21 18,294 = 1 ten thousand + 8 thousands + 2 hundreds + 9 tens + 4 ones
Complete the expanded form.
22 47,093 = 40,000 + 7,000 + 90 + 3
23 50,328 = 50,000 + 300 + 20 + 8
24 69,417 = 60,000 + 9,000 + 400 + 10 + 7
Lesson 1.1 Numbers to 100,000 11

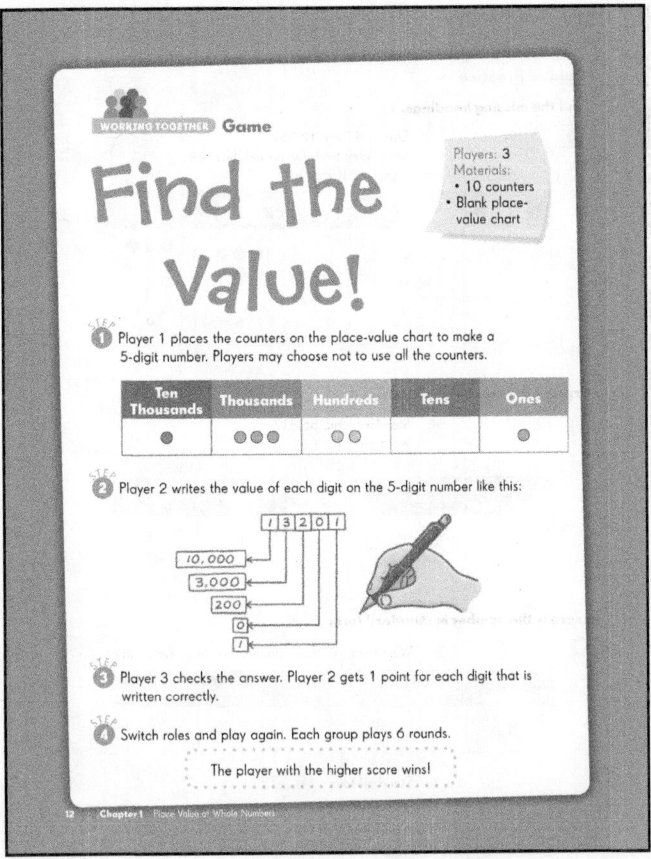

WORKING TOGETHER Game
Find the Value!
Players: 3
Materials:
• 10 counters
• Blank place-value chart
STEP 1 Player 1 places the counters on the place-value chart to make a 5-digit number. Players may choose not to use all the counters.
Ten Thousands | Thousands | Hundreds | Tens | Ones
STEP 2 Player 2 writes the value of each digit on the 5-digit number like this:
1 3 2 0 1
10,000
3,000
200
0
1
STEP 3 Player 3 checks the answer. Player 2 gets 1 point for each digit that is written correctly.
STEP 4 Switch roles and play again. Each group plays 6 rounds.
The player with the higher score wins!
12 Chapter 1 Place Value of Whole Numbers

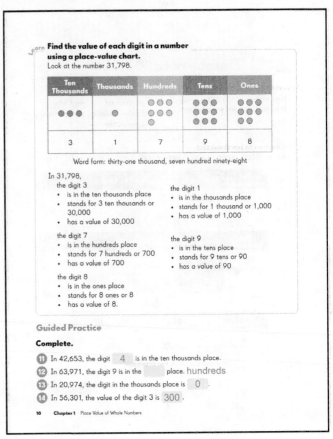

Let's Practice

Complete.

1. In 20,675, the digit 0 is in the ____ place. thousands
2. In 76,501, the digit 5 is in the hundreds place.
3. In 39,472, the digit 7 is in the tens place, and the digit 3 is in the ten thousands place.

Find the value of the digit 5 in each number.

4. 27,0**5**8 50
5. 8**5**,027 5,000
6. **5**2,708 50,000

Find the missing numbers.

7. 40,925 = 40,000 + 900 + 20 + 5
8. 32,176 = 3 ten thousands + 2 thousands + 1 hundred + 7 tens + 6 ones
9. 63,602 = 6 ten thousands + 3 thousands + 6 hundreds + 2 ones
10. 94,057 = 94 thousands + 5 tens + 7 ones

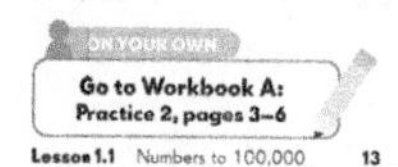

Lesson 1.2 Comparing Numbers to 100,000

Lesson Objectives

- Compare and order numbers to 100,000.
- Identify how much more or less one number is than another number.
- Find the rule in a number pattern.

Vocabulary
greater than (>) greatest
less than (<) least
more than order

Learn **Compare 5-digit numbers using greater than and less than.**

Which number is greater, 93,085 or 76,105?

Ten Thousands	Thousands	Hundreds	Tens	Ones
9	3	0	8	5
7	6	1	0	5

Compare the number of ten thousands in the two numbers.
9 ten thousands is greater than 7 ten thousands.

So, 93,085 is greater than 76,105.
93,085 > 76,105

Which number is less, 36,520 or 37,859?

Ten Thousands	Thousands	Hundreds	Tens	Ones
3	6	5	2	0
3	7	8	5	9

First, compare the number of ten thousands in the two numbers.
They are the same.
Then, compare the number of thousands in the two numbers.
6 thousands is less than 7 thousands.

So, 36,520 is less than 37,859.
36,520 < 37,859

Guided Practice

Compare the numbers. Write > or <.

1. 90,847 > 69,948
2. 64,515 < 65,500
3. 31,256 < 31,265
4. 19,283 < 19,289
5. 42,100 > 41,002
6. 16,935 > 16,918

Learn **Order 5-digit numbers from greatest to least.**

Order 62,357, 9,638, and 28,986 from greatest to least.

Ten Thousands	Thousands	Hundreds	Tens	Ones
6	2	3	5	7
	9	6	3	8
2	8	9	8	6

Compare the number of ten thousands in each number.
6 ten thousands is greater than 0 ten thousands and 2 ten thousands.
62,357 is the greatest number.

2 ten thousands is greater than 0 ten thousands.
9,638 is the least number.

So, the numbers in order from greatest to least are:
62,357 28,986 9,638

Guided Practice

Order the numbers from least to greatest.

7. 9,456 73,842 30,512 9,456 30,512 73,842
8. 41,325 31,425 51,324 14,325 14,325 31,425 41,325 51,324
9. 27,084 20,784 27,840 20,874 20,784 20,874 27,084 27,840

Learn **Compare 5-digit numbers using more than.**

Look at the numbers in the place-value chart.

Ten Thousands	Thousands	Hundreds	Tens	Ones
6	5	1	2	3
6	7	1	2	3

First, compare the number of ten thousands in the two numbers.
They are the same.
Then, compare the number of thousands in the two numbers.
65,123 is 2,000 less than 67,123.
2,000 more than 65,123 is 67,123.

Guided Practice

Look at the numbers in the place-value chart. Complete.

Ten Thousands	Thousands	Hundreds	Tens	Ones
3	7	6	2	5
	7	6	2	5

10. 30,000 more than 7,625 is ____. 37,625
11. ____ is 30,000 less than 37,625. 7,625

Find the missing numbers.

12. 30,000 less than 34,200 is ____. 4,200
13. ____ is 20,000 more than 53. 20,053
14. 100 more than 58,967 is ____. 59,067

Find the rule for each number pattern. Then continue or complete the pattern.

15. 2,985 2,885 2,785 2,685 2,585 2,485 Subtract 100.
16. 97,642 77,642 57,642 37,642 Subtract 20,000.
17. 24,701 26,702 28,703 30,704 32,705 Add 2,001.
18. 18,079 20,079 20,279 22,279 22,479 24,479 24,679 26,679 Add 2,000. Then add 200.

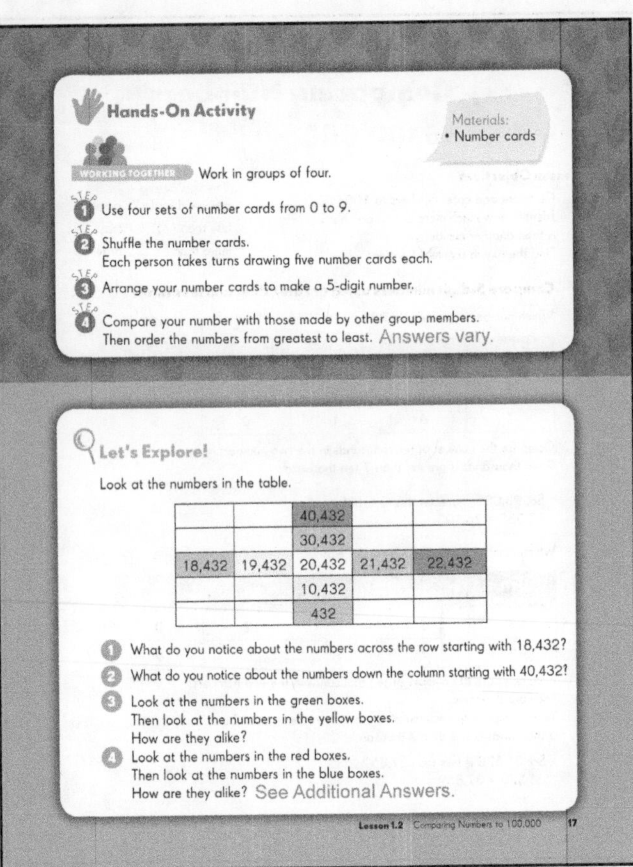

Hands-On Activity

Materials:
- Number cards

WORKING TOGETHER Work in groups of four.

1. Use four sets of number cards from 0 to 9.
2. Shuffle the number cards. Each person takes turns drawing five number cards each.
3. Arrange your number cards to make a 5-digit number.
4. Compare your number with those made by other group members. Then order the numbers from greatest to least. Answers vary.

Let's Explore!

Look at the numbers in the table.

		40,432		
		30,432		
18,432	19,432	20,432	21,432	22,432
		10,432		
		432		

1. What do you notice about the numbers across the row starting with 18,432?
2. What do you notice about the numbers down the column starting with 40,432?
3. Look at the numbers in the green boxes. Then look at the numbers in the yellow boxes. How are they alike?
4. Look at the numbers in the red boxes. Then look at the numbers in the blue boxes. How are they alike? See Additional Answers.

Lesson 1.2 Comparing Numbers to 100,000 17

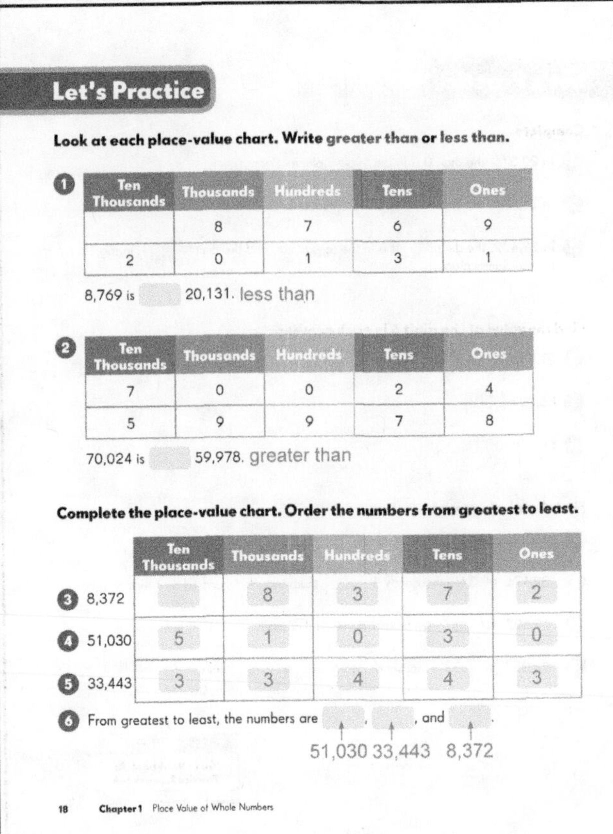

Let's Practice

Look at each place-value chart. Write greater than or less than.

1.

Ten Thousands	Thousands	Hundreds	Tens	Ones
	8	7	6	9
2	0	1	3	1

8,769 is ___ 20,131. less than

2.

Ten Thousands	Thousands	Hundreds	Tens	Ones
7	0	0	2	4
5	9	9	7	8

70,024 is ___ 59,978. greater than

Complete the place-value chart. Order the numbers from greatest to least.

	Ten Thousands	Thousands	Hundreds	Tens	Ones
3. 8,372		8	3	7	2
4. 51,030	5	1	0	3	0
5. 33,443	3	3	4	4	3

6. From greatest to least, the numbers are ___, ___, and ___.
51,030 33,443 8,372

18 Chapter 1 Place Value of Whole Numbers

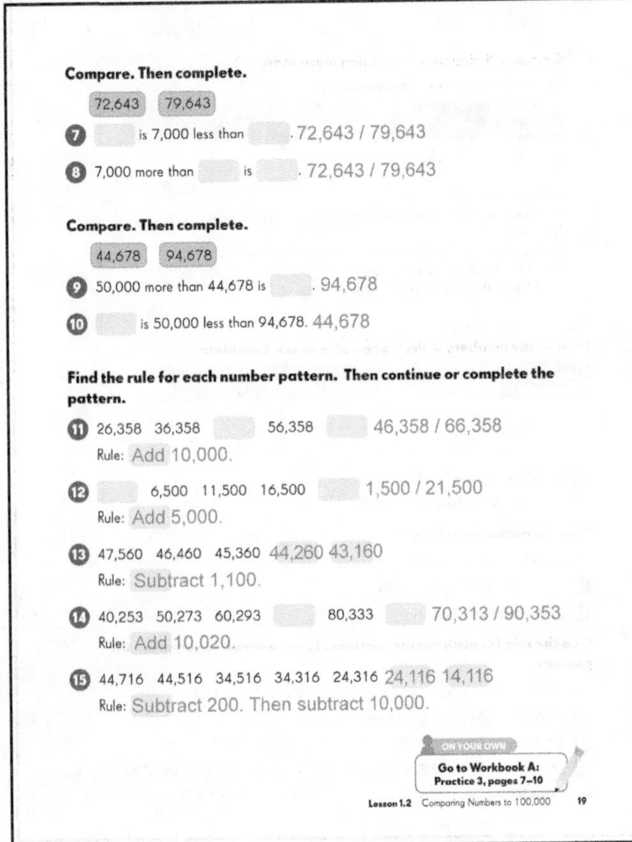

Compare. Then complete.

72,643 79,643

7. ___ is 7,000 less than ___. 72,643 / 79,643
8. 7,000 more than ___ is ___. 72,643 / 79,643

Compare. Then complete.

44,678 94,678

9. 50,000 more than 44,678 is ___. 94,678
10. ___ is 50,000 less than 94,678. 44,678

Find the rule for each number pattern. Then continue or complete the pattern.

11. 26,358 36,358 ___ 56,358 ___ 46,358 / 66,358
Rule: Add 10,000.
12. ___ 6,500 11,500 16,500 ___ 1,500 / 21,500
Rule: Add 5,000.
13. 47,560 46,460 45,360 44,260 43,160
Rule: Subtract 1,100.
14. 40,253 50,273 60,293 ___ 80,333 ___ 70,313 / 90,353
Rule: Add 10,020.
15. 44,716 44,516 34,516 34,316 24,316 24,116 14,116
Rule: Subtract 200. Then subtract 10,000.

ON YOUR OWN
Go to Workbook A: Practice 3, pages 7–10

Lesson 1.2 Comparing Numbers to 100,000 19

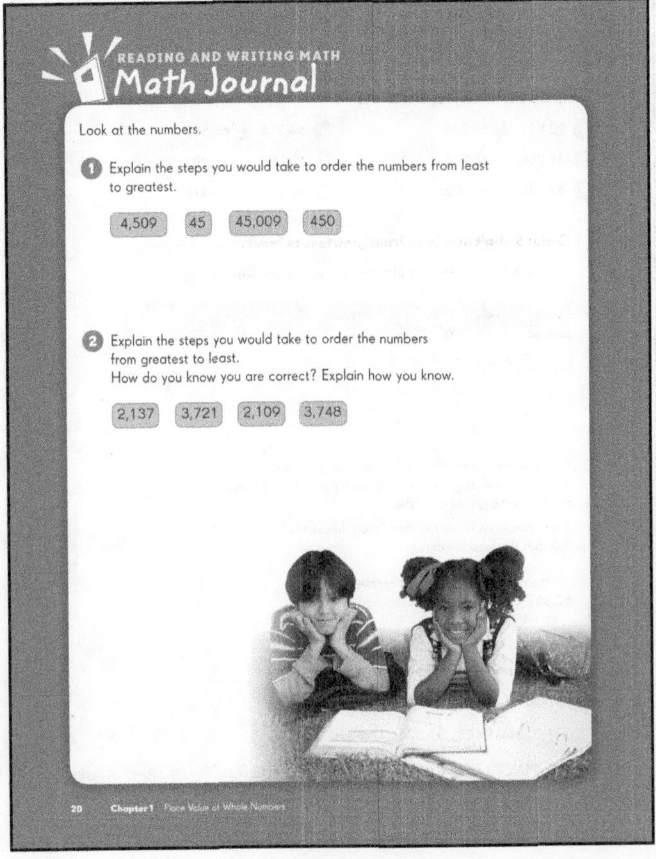

READING AND WRITING MATH
Math Journal

Look at the numbers.

1. Explain the steps you would take to order the numbers from least to greatest.

4,509 45 45,009 450

2. Explain the steps you would take to order the numbers from greatest to least. How do you know you are correct? Explain how you know.

2,137 3,721 2,109 3,748

20 Chapter 1 Place Value of Whole Numbers

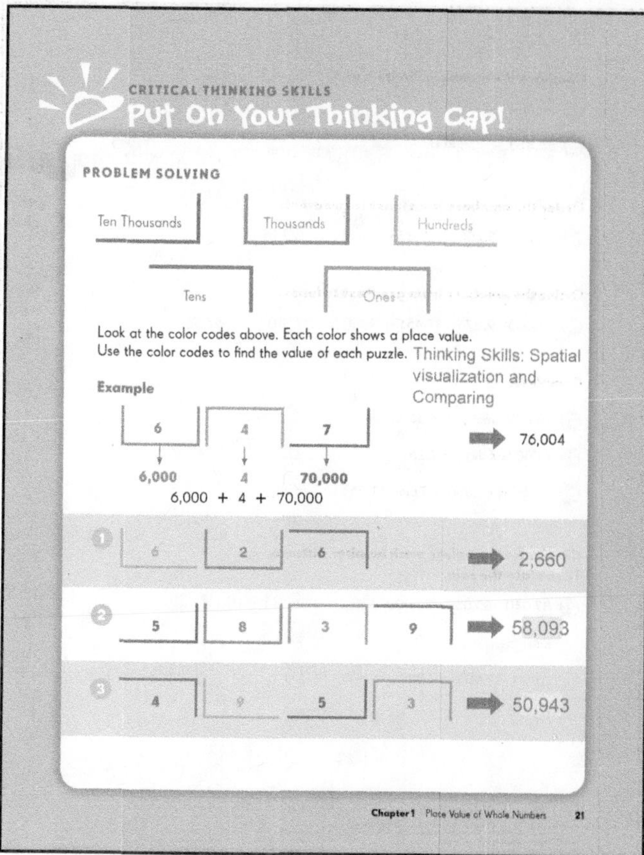

CRITICAL THINKING SKILLS

Put On Your Thinking Cap!

PROBLEM SOLVING

Ten Thousands | Thousands | Hundreds

Tens | Ones

Look at the color codes above. Each color shows a place value.
Use the color codes to find the value of each puzzle. Thinking Skills: Spatial visualization and Comparing

Example

6 | 4 | 7 → 76,004

6,000 4 70,000

6,000 + 4 + 70,000

1. 6 | 2 | 6 → 2,660
2. 5 | 8 | 3 | 9 → 58,093
3. 4 | 9 | 5 | 3 → 50,943

Chapter 1 Place Value of Whole Numbers 21

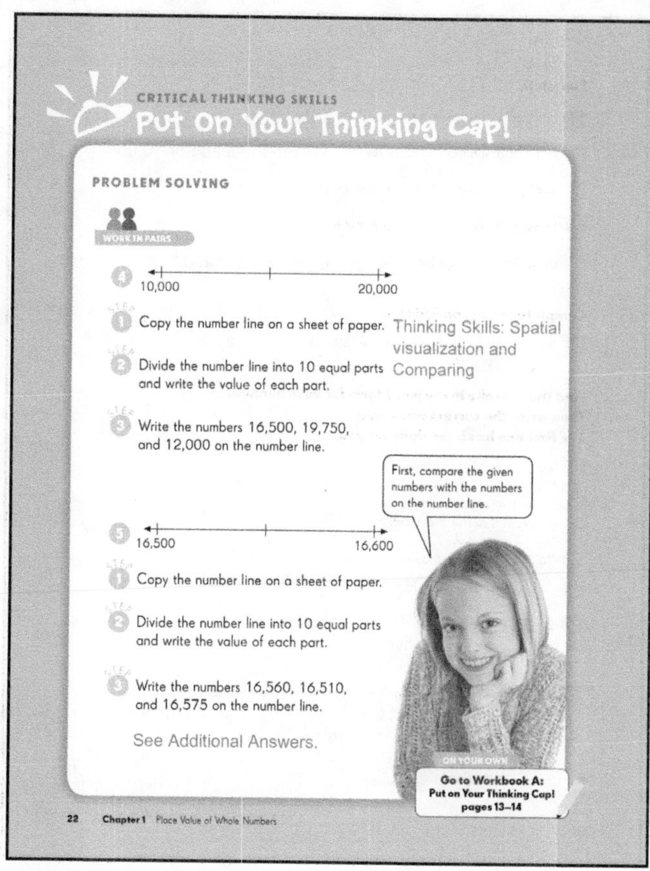

CRITICAL THINKING SKILLS

Put On Your Thinking Cap!

PROBLEM SOLVING

WORK IN PAIRS

4. 10,000 ——— 20,000

STEP 1 Copy the number line on a sheet of paper. Thinking Skills: Spatial visualization and Comparing

STEP 2 Divide the number line into 10 equal parts and write the value of each part.

STEP 3 Write the numbers 16,500, 19,750, and 12,000 on the number line.

First, compare the given numbers with the numbers on the number line.

5. 16,500 ——— 16,600

STEP 1 Copy the number line on a sheet of paper.

STEP 2 Divide the number line into 10 equal parts and write the value of each part.

STEP 3 Write the numbers 16,560, 16,510, and 16,575 on the number line.

See Additional Answers.

ON YOUR OWN

Go to Workbook A: Put on Your Thinking Cap! pages 13–14

22 Chapter 1 Place Value of Whole Numbers

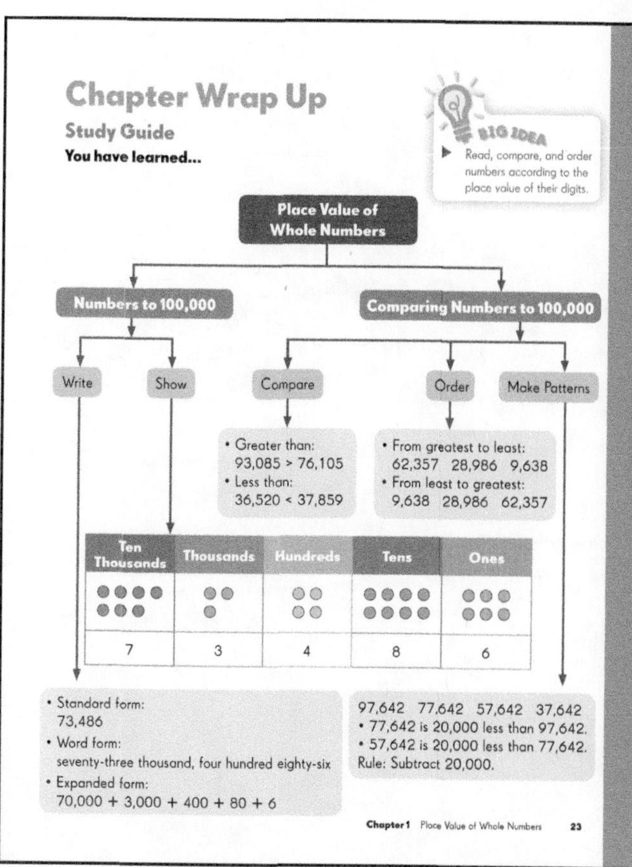

Chapter Wrap Up

Study Guide

You have learned...

BIG IDEA

Read, compare, and order numbers according to the place value of their digits.

Place Value of Whole Numbers

Numbers to 100,000: Write, Show

Comparing Numbers to 100,000: Compare, Order, Make Patterns

- Greater than: 93,085 > 76,105
- Less than: 36,520 < 37,859

- From greatest to least: 62,357 28,986 9,638
- From least to greatest: 9,638 28,986 62,357

Ten Thousands	Thousands	Hundreds	Tens	Ones
7	3	4	8	6

- Standard form: 73,486
- Word form: seventy-three thousand, four hundred eighty-six
- Expanded form: 70,000 + 3,000 + 400 + 80 + 6

97,642 77,642 57,642 37,642
- 77,642 is 20,000 less than 97,642.
- 57,642 is 20,000 less than 77,642.

Rule: Subtract 20,000.

Chapter 1 Place Value of Whole Numbers 23

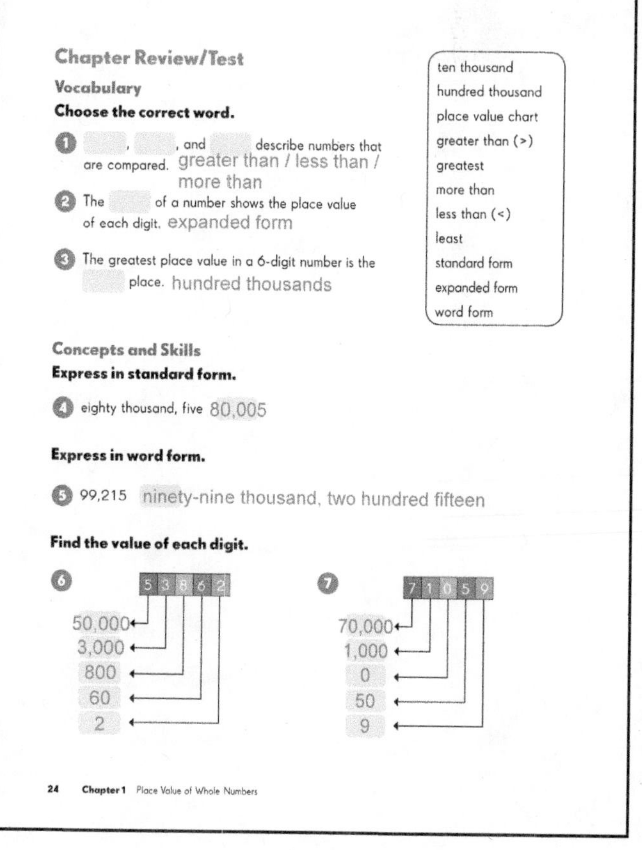

Chapter Review/Test

Vocabulary

Choose the correct word.

ten thousand
hundred thousand
place value chart
greater than (>)
greatest
more than
less than (<)
least
standard form
expanded form
word form

1. ___, ___, and ___ describe numbers that are compared. greater than / less than / more than
2. The ___ of a number shows the place value of each digit. expanded form
3. The greatest place value in a 6-digit number is the ___ place. hundred thousands

Concepts and Skills

Express in standard form.

4. eighty thousand, five 80,005

Express in word form.

5. 99,215 ninety-nine thousand, two hundred fifteen

Find the value of each digit.

6. 5 3 8 6 2 → 50,000; 3,000; 800; 60; 2
7. 7 1 0 5 9 → 70,000; 1,000; 0; 50; 9

24 Chapter 1 Place Value of Whole Numbers

Complete.

8. In 45,876, the value of the digit 5 is ___. 5,000
9. In 12,083, the digit 1 stands for ___. 1 ten thousand or 10,000
10. In 67,210, the digit 2 stands for 200.
11. In 39,813, the digit 1 is in the tens place.
12. In 52,981, the digit 5 is in the ___ place. ten thousands

Complete the expanded form.

13. 86,322 = ___ + 6,000 + 300 + 20 + 2
80,000

Find the mistake in the word form for each number.
Then write the correct answer.
The first one has been done for you.

Example
12,005
Word form: twelve thousand, hundred
Correct answer: twelve thousand, hundred five

14. 76,300 seven thousand, six hundred three hundred
seventy-six thousand, three hundred

15. 25,709 twenty-five thousand, seventy-nine
twenty-five thousand, seven hundred nine

16. 68,217 sixty-eight ten thousand, two hundred seventeen
sixty-eight thousand, two hundred seventeen

Compare the numbers. Write < or >.

17. 10,589 > 9,875
18. 56,410 < 58,400

Order the numbers from least to greatest.

19. 70,250 50,000 29,875 29,875 50,000 70,250

Order the numbers from greatest to least.

20. 81,005 9,875 37,451 81,005 37,451 9,875

Complete.

21. 10,000 greater than 56,877 is ___. 66,877
22. 2,000 less than 16,025 is ___. 14,025
23. 1,256 is 40,000 less than 41,256.

Continue or complete each number pattern.
Then state the rule.

24. 87,040 85,030 83,020 ___ ___ 81,010 / 79,000
Rule: Subtract 2,010.

25. 5,600 10,600 10,800 15,800 16,000 ___ ___ 21,000/21,200
Rule: Add 5,000. Then add 200.

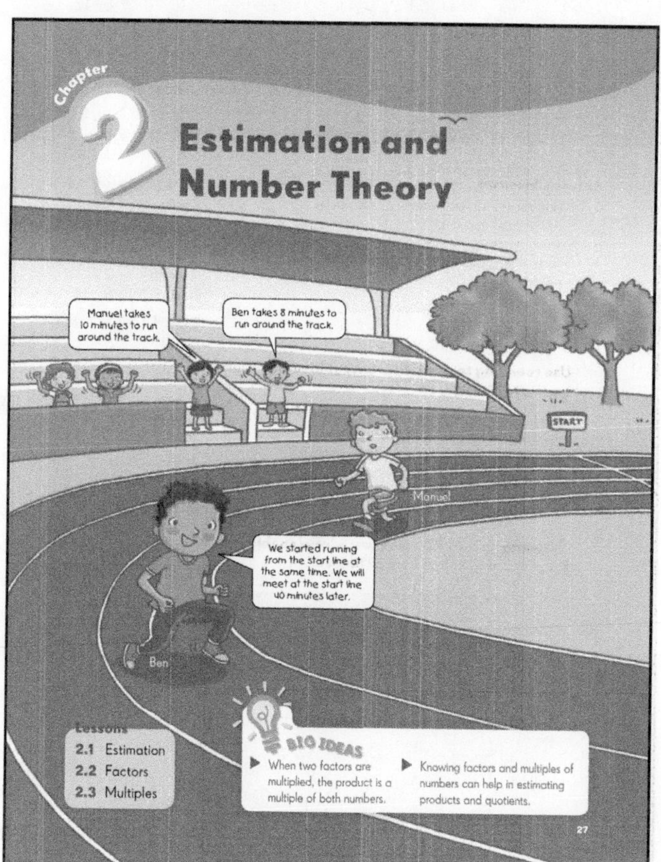
Chapter 2

Estimation and Number Theory

Manuel takes 10 minutes to run around the track.
Ben takes 8 minutes to run around the track.
START
Manuel
We started running from the start line at the same time. We will meet at the start line 40 minutes later.
Ben

Lessons
2.1 Estimation
2.2 Factors
2.3 Multiples

BIG IDEAS
▶ When two factors are multiplied, the product is a multiple of both numbers.
▶ Knowing factors and multiples of numbers can help in estimating products and quotients.

27

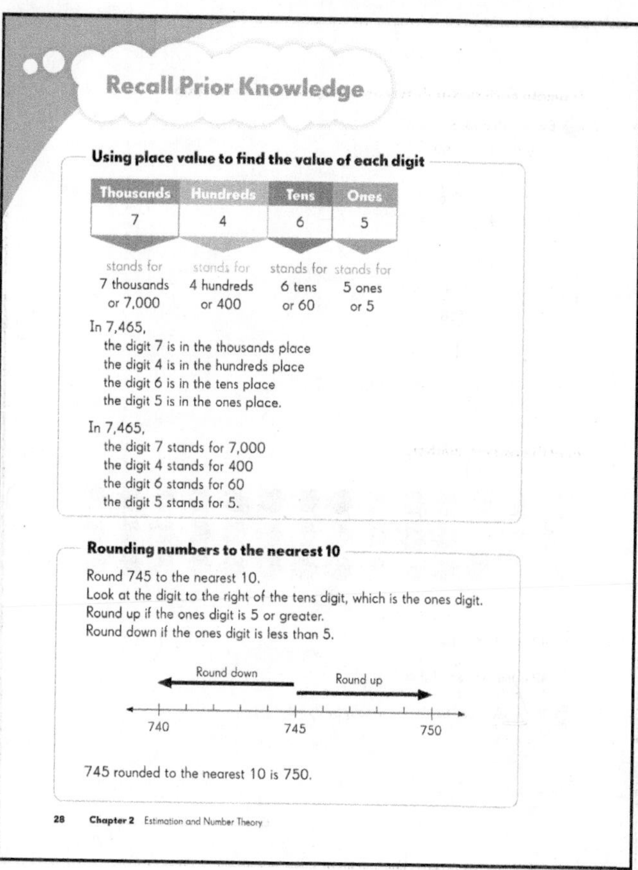
Recall Prior Knowledge

Using place value to find the value of each digit

Thousands	Hundreds	Tens	Ones
7	4	6	5
stands for 7 thousands or 7,000	stands for 4 hundreds or 400	stands for 6 tens or 60	stands for 5 ones or 5

In 7,465,
the digit 7 is in the thousands place
the digit 4 is in the hundreds place
the digit 6 is in the tens place
the digit 5 is in the ones place.

In 7,465,
the digit 7 stands for 7,000
the digit 4 stands for 400
the digit 6 stands for 60
the digit 5 stands for 5.

Rounding numbers to the nearest 10

Round 745 to the nearest 10.
Look at the digit to the right of the tens digit, which is the ones digit.
Round up if the ones digit is 5 or greater.
Round down if the ones digit is less than 5.

Round down — Round up
740 — 745 — 750

745 rounded to the nearest 10 is 750.

28 **Chapter 2** Estimation and Number Theory

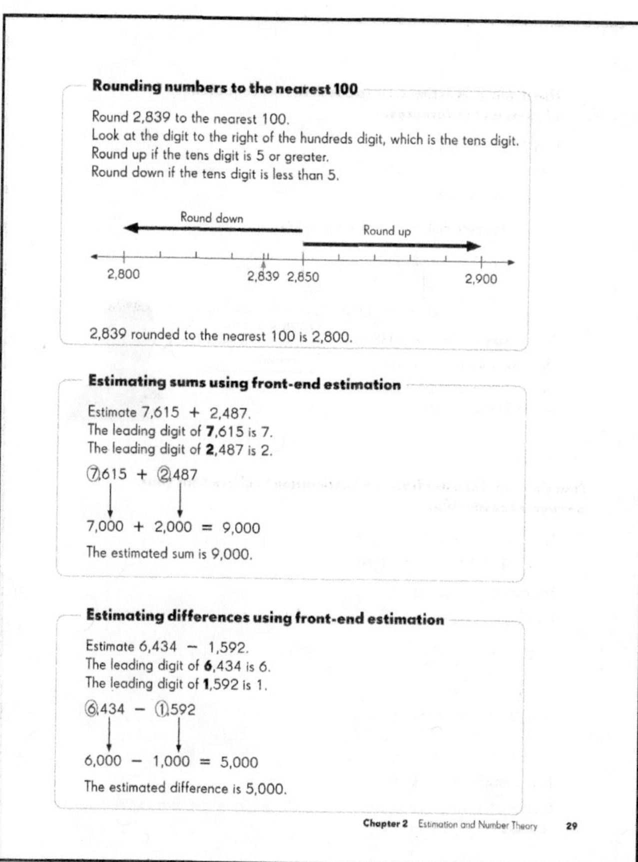
Rounding numbers to the nearest 100

Round 2,839 to the nearest 100.
Look at the digit to the right of the hundreds digit, which is the tens digit.
Round up if the tens digit is 5 or greater.
Round down if the tens digit is less than 5.

Round down — Round up
2,800 — 2,839 2,850 — 2,900

2,839 rounded to the nearest 100 is 2,800.

Estimating sums using front-end estimation

Estimate 7,615 + 2,487.
The leading digit of **7**,615 is 7.
The leading digit of **2**,487 is 2.

(7)615 + (2)487

7,000 + 2,000 = 9,000
The estimated sum is 9,000.

Estimating differences using front-end estimation

Estimate 6,434 − 1,592.
The leading digit of **6**,434 is 6.
The leading digit of **1**,592 is 1.

(6)434 − (1)592

6,000 − 1,000 = 5,000
The estimated difference is 5,000.

Chapter 2 Estimation and Number Theory 29

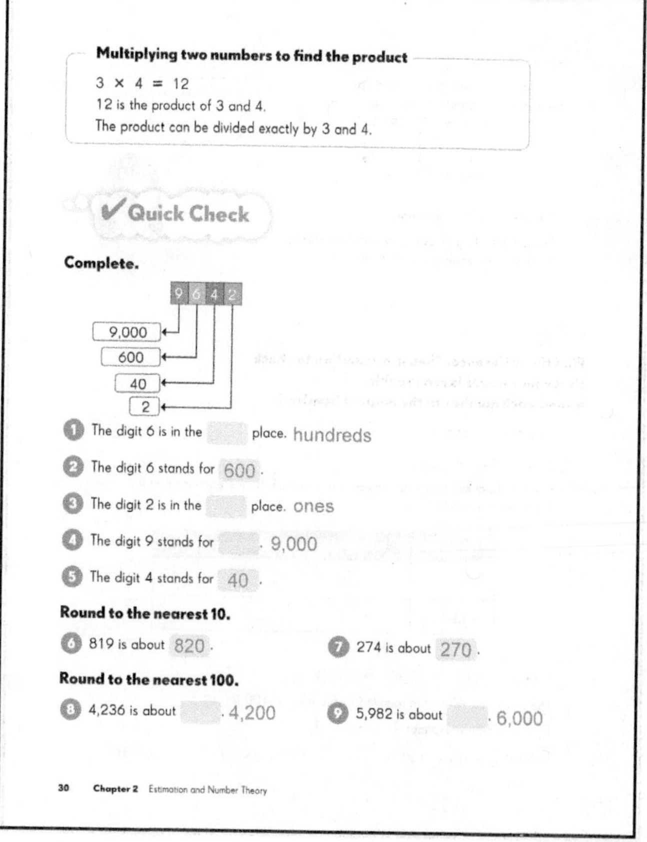
Multiplying two numbers to find the product

3 × 4 = 12
12 is the product of 3 and 4.
The product can be divided exactly by 3 and 4.

✓Quick Check

Complete.

9 6 4 2
9,000
600
40
2

1. The digit 6 is in the ___ place. hundreds
2. The digit 6 stands for 600.
3. The digit 2 is in the ___ place. ones
4. The digit 9 stands for ___. 9,000
5. The digit 4 stands for 40.

Round to the nearest 10.

6. 819 is about 820.
7. 274 is about 270.

Round to the nearest 100.

8. 4,236 is about ___. 4,200
9. 5,982 is about ___. 6,000

30 **Chapter 2** Estimation and Number Theory

Estimate each sum or difference using front-end estimation.

10. Estimate 5,833 + 3,689.

5,833 + 3,689

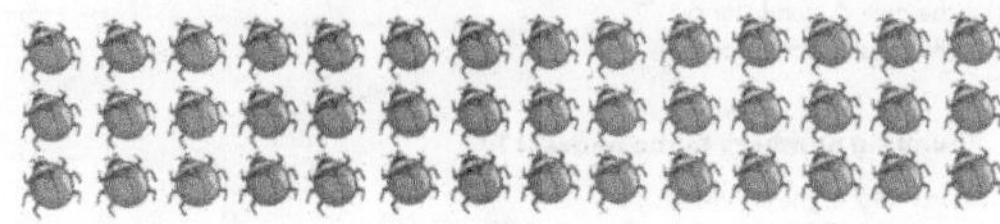

5,000 + 3,000 = 8,000

11. Estimate 5,673 − 2,568.

5,673 − 2,568

5,000 − 2,000 = 3,000

Find the correct numbers.

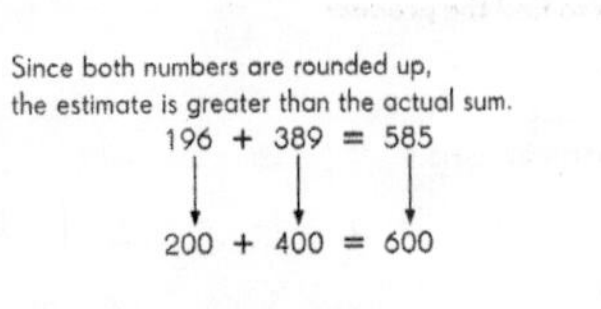

12. 42 = 3 × 14

13. 42 is the product of 3 and 14.

14. The product can be divided exactly by 3 and 14.

Lesson 2.1 Estimation

Lesson Objectives

- Round numbers to estimate sums, differences, products, and quotients.
- Estimate to check that an answer is reasonable.
- Decide whether an estimate or an exact answer is needed.

Vocabulary
estimate
reasonable
front-end estimation
rounding
product
quotient

Learn **Use rounding to check the reasonableness of sums and differences.**

Eva's Market sold 196 jars of grape jelly in September. In October, the market sold 389 jars. How many jars of grape jelly did they sell over the two months?

196 + 389 = 585

The market sold 585 jars of grape jelly altogether.

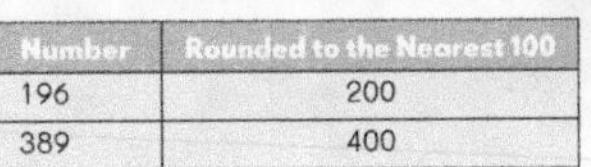

Estimate to check that the answer is **reasonable**.
Round each number to the nearest hundred.

Number	Rounded to the Nearest 100
196	200
389	400

Add: 200 + 400 = 600

The estimated sum rounded to the nearest 100 is 600.

Since both numbers are rounded up, the estimate is greater than the actual sum.

196 + 389 = 585

200 + 400 = 600

The answer 585 is reasonable.

The same method of estimation can be used to check the reasonableness of differences.

The actual sum is close to the estimate. So, the sum is reasonable.

Guided Practice

Find the difference. Then use rounding to check that your answer is reasonable.
Round each number to the nearest hundred.

1. Find 786 − 453.

786 − 453 = 333

Estimate to check that your answer is reasonable. Round each number to the nearest hundred.

Number	Rounded to the Nearest 100
786	800
453	500

Subtract: 800 − 500 = 300

The estimated difference rounded to the nearest 100 is 300.

Is your answer reasonable?

Explain: 333 is close to 300. So the answer is reasonable.

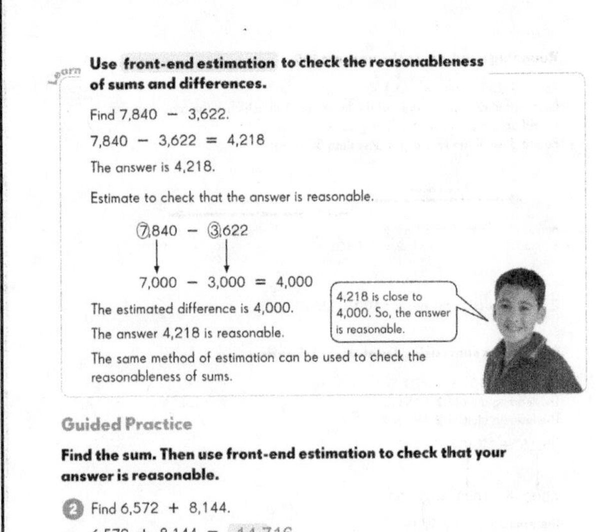

Learn **Use front-end estimation to check the reasonableness of sums and differences.**

Find 7,840 − 3,622.

7,840 − 3,622 = 4,218

The answer is 4,218.

Estimate to check that the answer is reasonable.

(7),840 − (3),622

7,000 − 3,000 = 4,000

The estimated difference is 4,000.

The answer 4,218 is reasonable.

4,218 is close to 4,000. So, the answer is reasonable.

The same method of estimation can be used to check the reasonableness of sums.

Guided Practice

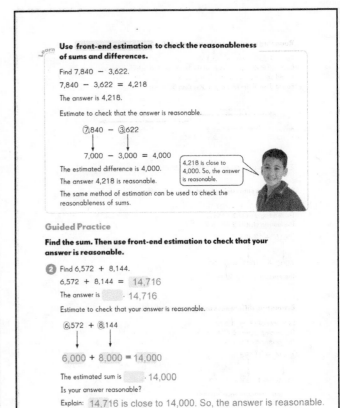

Find the sum. Then use front-end estimation to check that your answer is reasonable.

2. Find 6,572 + 8,144.

6,572 + 8,144 = 14,716

The answer is 14,716.

Estimate to check that your answer is reasonable.

(6),572 + (8),144

6,000 + 8,000 = 14,000

The estimated sum is 14,000.

Is your answer reasonable?

Explain: 14,716 is close to 14,000. So, the answer is reasonable.

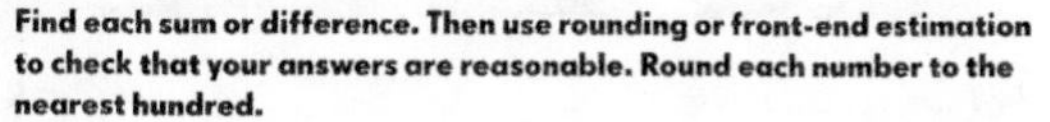

Find each sum or difference. Then use rounding or front-end estimation to check that your answers are reasonable. Round each number to the nearest hundred.

3. 5,426 + 3,210 = 8,636; Methods vary.
4. 8,475 − 3,356 = 5,119; Methods vary.
5. 9,633 + 4,250 = 13,883; Methods vary.
6. 16,862 − 12,551 = 4,311; Methods vary.

Learn Use rounding to check the reasonableness of products.

Santos bought 2 cartons of single cup coffee pods, each containing 326 coffee pods.
Find the total number of coffee pods in the cartons.

326 × 2 = 652

The total number of coffee pods is 652.

Estimate to check that the answer is reasonable.

Round 326 to the nearest hundred and multiply by 2.

Number	Rounded to the Nearest 100 × 2
326	300 × 2 = 600

The estimated product rounded to the nearest 100 is 600.

The answer 652 is reasonable.

652 is close to 600, so the answer is reasonable.

Since 326 is rounded down, the estimate is less than the actual product.

326 × 2 = 652
↓ ↓
300 × 2 = 600

Guided Practice

Find the product. Then use rounding to check that your answer is reasonable. Round the 3-digit number to the nearest hundred.

7. Find 242 × 4.

242 × 4 = 968

The answer is 968.

Estimate to check that your answer is reasonable.

Round 242 to the nearest hundred and multiply by 4.

Number	Rounded to the Nearest 100 × 4
242	200 × 4 = 800

The estimated product rounded to the nearest 100 is 800.

Is your answer reasonable?

Explain: 968 is close to 800. So, the answer is reasonable.

Learn Use front-end estimation to check the reasonableness of products.

Find 134 × 5.

134 × 5 = 670

The answer is 670.

Estimate to check that the answer is reasonable.
Multiply the value of the digits in the greatest place of each number.

(1)34 × 5
↓
100 × 5 = 500

1 hundred × 5 = 5 hundreds or 500

The estimated product is 500.

The answer 670 is reasonable.

670 is close to 500. So, the answer is reasonable.

Guided Practice

Find the product. Then use front-end estimation to check that your answer is reasonable.

8. Find 471 × 2.

471 × 2 = 942

The answer is 942.

Estimate to check that your answer is reasonable.

(4)71 × 2
↓ ↓
400 × 2 = 800

The estimated product is 800.

Is your answer reasonable?

Explain: 942 is close to 800. So, the answer is reasonable.

Learn Use related multiplication facts to check the reasonableness of quotients.

Novak bought a box of 72 building blocks. He shared the blocks equally with his 2 friends. How many blocks did each of them get?

72 ÷ 3 = 24

Each of them got 24 blocks.

Use related multiplication facts to check that your answer is reasonable. Since division is the opposite of multiplication, find a multiple of 3 that is close to 7.

3 × 2 = 6 3 × 20 = 60
3 × 3 = 9 3 × 30 = 90

72 is closer to 60 than to 90.

So, 72 ÷ 3 is about 60 ÷ 3.

60 ÷ 3 = 20

The estimated quotient is 20.
The answer 24 is reasonable.

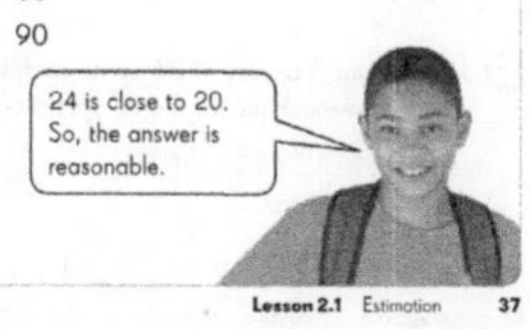
24 is close to 20. So, the answer is reasonable.

Guided Practice

Find each quotient. Then use related multiplication facts to check that your answers are reasonable.

9. Find 92 ÷ 2.

92 ÷ 2 = 46

The answer is 46.

Use related multiplication facts to check that your answer is reasonable. Since division is the opposite of multiplication, find a multiple of 2 that is close to 9.

2 × 40 = 80 2 × 50 = 100

92 is closer to 100 than to 80.

So, 92 ÷ 2 is about 100 ÷ 2.

100 ÷ 2 = 50

The estimated quotient is 50.

Is your answer reasonable?

Explain: 46 is close to 50. So, the answer is reasonable.

10. Find 76 ÷ 4.

76 ÷ 4 = 19

The answer is 19.

Use related multiplication facts to check that your answer is reasonable. Since division is the opposite of multiplication, find a multiple of 4 that is close to 7.

4 × 10 = 40 4 × 20 = 80

76 is closer to 80 than to 40.

So, 76 ÷ 4 is about 80 ÷ 4.

80 ÷ 4 = 20

The estimated quotient is 20.

Is your answer reasonable?

Explain: 19 is close to 20. So, the answer is reasonable.

11 Find 85 ÷ 5.

85 ÷ 5 = 17

The answer is 17.

Use related multiplication facts to check that your answer is reasonable.
Since division is the opposite of multiplication, find a multiple of 5 that is close to 8.

5 × 10 = 50

5 × 20 = 100

85 is closer to 100 than to 50.

So, 85 ÷ 5 is about 100 ÷ 5.

100 ÷ 5 = 20

The estimated quotient is 20.

Is your answer reasonable?

Explain: 17 is close to 20. So, the answer is reasonable.

Find each product or quotient. Then use one of the methods above to check that your answers are reasonable.

12 123 × 7 = 861
Estimate: Answers vary.
Is your answer reasonable?
Explain: Answers vary.

13 54 ÷ 3 = 18
Estimate: Answers vary.
Is your answer reasonable?
Explain: Answers vary.

14 323 × 3 = 969
Estimate: Answers vary.
Is your answer reasonable?
Explain: Answers vary.

15 96 ÷ 4 = 24
Estimate: Answers vary.
Is your answer reasonable?
Explain: Answers vary.

Let's Explore!

Use two methods to estimate.

Example

Estimate 73 ÷ 8.

Method 1

73 is close to 72.
So, 73 ÷ 8 ⟶ 72 ÷ 8 = 9.

Method 2

8 × 8 = 64
8 × 9 = 72
8 × 10 = 80
8 × 9 = 72 is the closest to 73, so the estimated quotient is 9.

Example

Estimate 9 × 26.

Method 1

9 is close to 10.
So, 9 × 26 ⟶ 10 × 26 = 260.

Method 2

9 × 26 ⟶ 9 × 25 = 225

Method 3

9 × 26 ⟶ 10 × 25 = 250

1 658 ÷ 8
Answers vary.

2 6 × 52
Answers vary.

Learn **Decide whether to find an estimate or an exact answer.**

The Senior Citizen Committee has raised $1,000 for the Senior Center.
Is $1,000 enough to buy the items shown?
Decide if you need an exact answer or an estimate.

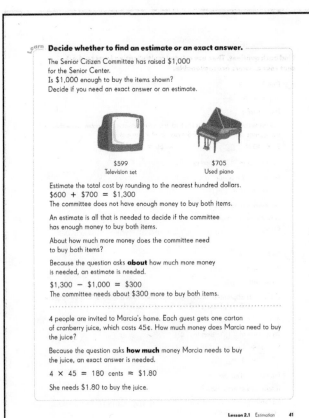

$599
Television set

$705
Used piano

Estimate the total cost by rounding to the nearest hundred dollars.
$600 + $700 = $1,300
The committee does not have enough money to buy both items.

An estimate is all that is needed to decide if the committee has enough money to buy both items.

About how much more money does the committee need to buy both items?

Because the question asks **about** how much more money is needed, an estimate is needed.

$1,300 − $1,000 = $300
The committee needs about $300 more to buy both items.

4 people are invited to Marcia's home. Each guest gets one carton of cranberry juice, which costs 45¢. How much money does Marcia need to buy the juice?

Because the question asks **how much** money Marcia needs to buy the juice, an exact answer is needed.

4 × 45 = 180 cents = $1.80

She needs $1.80 to buy the juice.

Guided Practice

Solve. Decide whether to find an estimate or an exact answer.

16 The table shows the number of dogs that were adopted in a state within a year.

Dogs Adopted in a Year	Number
Mixed-breed adults	12,760
Pure-bred adults	17,432
Puppies	20,979

How many dogs were adopted altogether that year?

Exact answer: 51,171

17 Mr. Sousa has $250. He wants to spend $63 on a sweatshirt, $45 on running shoes, and $120 on sports gear.
Does he have enough money?

Estimate: $210
Yes, he has enough money.

18 A family has 7 people. Each person is supposed to drink $\frac{7}{8}$ quart of water every day. About how much water is needed for the whole family each day?

Estimate: 7 quarts

19 Kerry bought 15 roasted chickens. Each chicken cost $6. Find the total amount Kerry spent on the chickens.

Exact answer: $90

20 Joel bought 3 apples at 26 cents each and 4 oranges at 32 cents each. About how much money did he spend on the apples and oranges?

Estimate: 210 cents

Let's Practice

Find each sum or difference. Then use rounding or front-end estimation to check that your answers are reasonable. Round each number to the nearest hundred.

1. 536 + 289 + 109 = 934
2. 320 + 478 + 215 = 1,013
3. 8,530 − 1,286 = 7,244
4. 7,271 + 1,335 = 8,606
5. 26,235 − 1,451 = 24,784
6. 15,422 + 13,130 = 28,552
7. 18,726 + 29,343 = 48,069
8. 31,540 − 24,622 = 6,918

Estimated values vary for Exercises 1-8.

Find each product. Then use rounding or front-end estimation to check your answers. Round the 3-digit number to the nearest hundred.

9. 232 × 4 = 928; The estimated value is 800.
10. 148 × 5 = 740; The estimated value is 500.
11. 212 × 3 = 636; The estimated value is 600.
12. 498 × 2 = 996; The estimated value is 1,000.

Find each quotient. Then use related multiplication facts to check your answers.

13. 42 ÷ 3 = 14
14. 56 ÷ 2 = 28
15. 80 ÷ 5 = 16
16. 88 ÷ 4 = 22

Estimated values vary for Exercises 13-16.

Solve. Decide whether to find an estimate or an exact answer.

17. A rectangular lawn is 11 meters long and 4 meters wide. About how many square meters of grass sod is needed to cover the entire lawn?
Estimate: 40 square meters.

18. A rectangular courtyard is 12 feet long and 8 feet wide. A tile is 2 feet long and 2 feet wide. How many tiles are needed to pave the courtyard?
Exact answer: 24 tiles

Go to Workbook A: Practice 1, pages 15–20

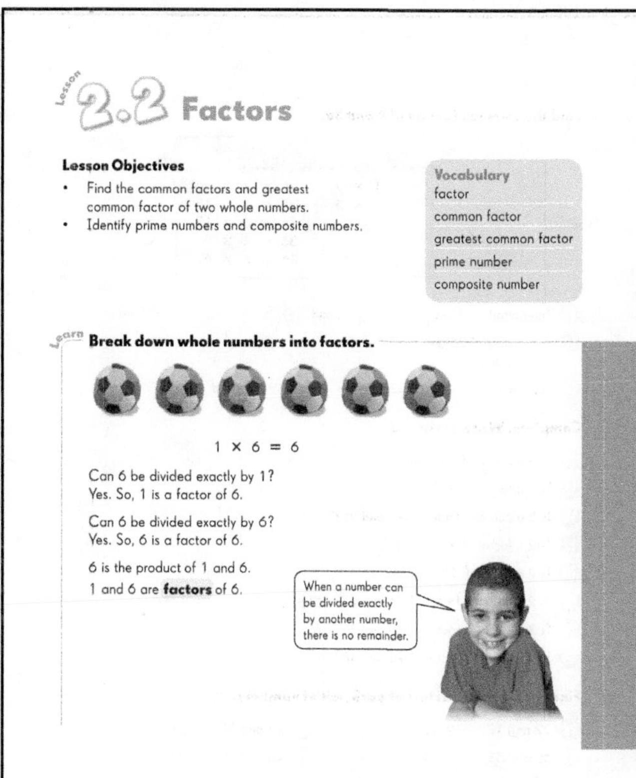

Lesson 2.2 Factors

Lesson Objectives

- Find the common factors and greatest common factor of two whole numbers.
- Identify prime numbers and composite numbers.

Vocabulary
factor
common factor
greatest common factor
prime number
composite number

Learn **Break down whole numbers into factors.**

1 × 6 = 6

Can 6 be divided exactly by 1?
Yes. So, 1 is a factor of 6.

Can 6 be divided exactly by 6?
Yes. So, 6 is a factor of 6.

6 is the product of 1 and 6.
1 and 6 are **factors** of 6.

When a number can be divided exactly by another number, there is no remainder.

Chapter 2

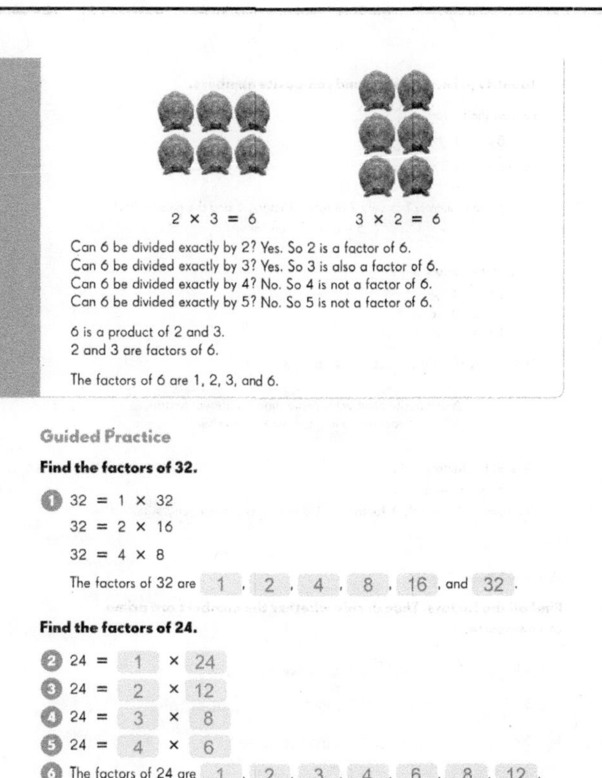

2 × 3 = 6 3 × 2 = 6

Can 6 be divided exactly by 2? Yes. So 2 is a factor of 6.
Can 6 be divided exactly by 3? Yes. So 3 is also a factor of 6.
Can 6 be divided exactly by 4? No. So 4 is not a factor of 6.
Can 6 be divided exactly by 5? No. So 5 is not a factor of 6.

6 is a product of 2 and 3.
2 and 3 are factors of 6.

The factors of 6 are 1, 2, 3, and 6.

Guided Practice

Find the factors of 32.

1. 32 = 1 × 32
32 = 2 × 16
32 = 4 × 8
The factors of 32 are 1, 2, 4, 8, 16, and 32.

Find the factors of 24.

2. 24 = 1 × 24
3. 24 = 2 × 12
4. 24 = 3 × 8
5. 24 = 4 × 6
6. The factors of 24 are 1, 2, 3, 4, 6, 8, 12, and 24.

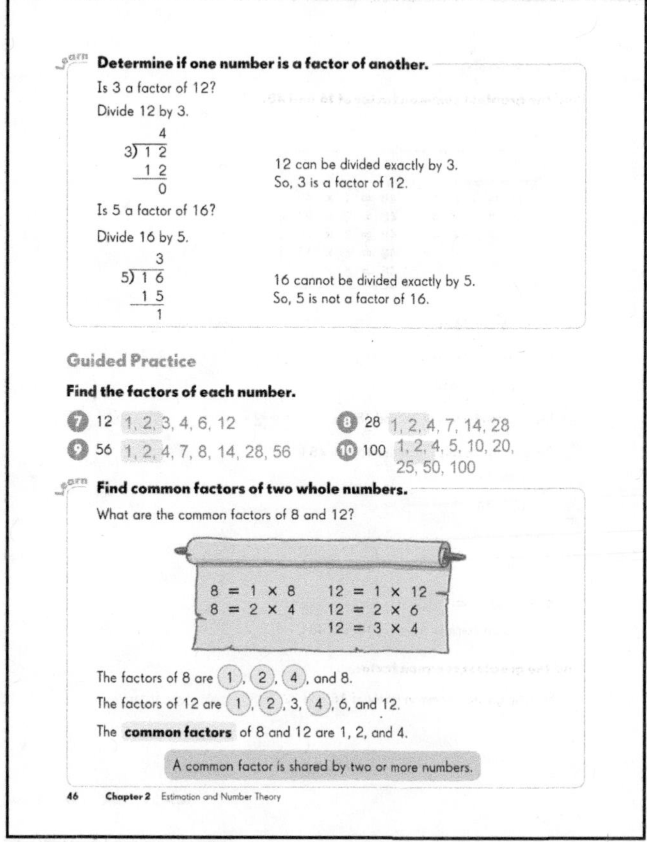

Learn **Determine if one number is a factor of another.**

Is 3 a factor of 12?
Divide 12 by 3.

$$\begin{array}{r} 4 \\ 3\overline{)12} \\ \underline{12} \\ 0 \end{array}$$

12 can be divided exactly by 3.
So, 3 is a factor of 12.

Is 5 a factor of 16?

Divide 16 by 5.

$$\begin{array}{r} 3 \\ 5\overline{)16} \\ \underline{15} \\ 1 \end{array}$$

16 cannot be divided exactly by 5.
So, 5 is not a factor of 16.

Guided Practice

Find the factors of each number.

7. 12 1, 2, 3, 4, 6, 12
8. 28 1, 2, 4, 7, 14, 28
9. 56 1, 2, 4, 7, 8, 14, 28, 56
10. 100 1, 2, 4, 5, 10, 20, 25, 50, 100

Learn **Find common factors of two whole numbers.**

What are the common factors of 8 and 12?

8 = 1 × 8
8 = 2 × 4

12 = 1 × 12
12 = 2 × 6
12 = 3 × 4

The factors of 8 are 1, 2, 4, and 8.
The factors of 12 are 1, 2, 3, 4, 6, and 12.
The **common factors** of 8 and 12 are 1, 2, and 4.

A common factor is shared by two or more numbers.

Chapter 2

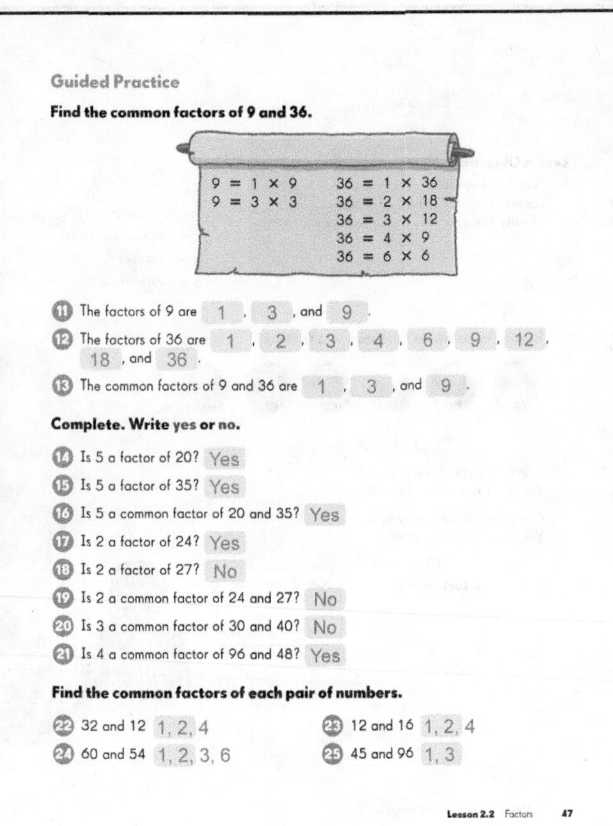

Guided Practice

Find the common factors of 9 and 36.

9 = 1 × 9
9 = 3 × 3

36 = 1 × 36
36 = 2 × 18
36 = 3 × 12
36 = 4 × 9
36 = 6 × 6

11. The factors of 9 are 1, 3, and 9.
12. The factors of 36 are 1, 2, 3, 4, 6, 9, 12, 18, and 36.
13. The common factors of 9 and 36 are 1, 3, and 9.

Complete. Write yes or no.

14. Is 5 a factor of 20? Yes
15. Is 5 a factor of 35? Yes
16. Is 5 a common factor of 20 and 35? Yes
17. Is 2 a factor of 24? Yes
18. Is 2 a factor of 27? No
19. Is 2 a common factor of 24 and 27? No
20. Is 3 a common factor of 30 and 40? No
21. Is 4 a common factor of 96 and 48? Yes

Find the common factors of each pair of numbers.

22. 32 and 12 1, 2, 4
23. 12 and 16 1, 2, 4
24. 60 and 54 1, 2, 3, 6
25. 45 and 96 1, 3

Lesson 2.2 Factors 47

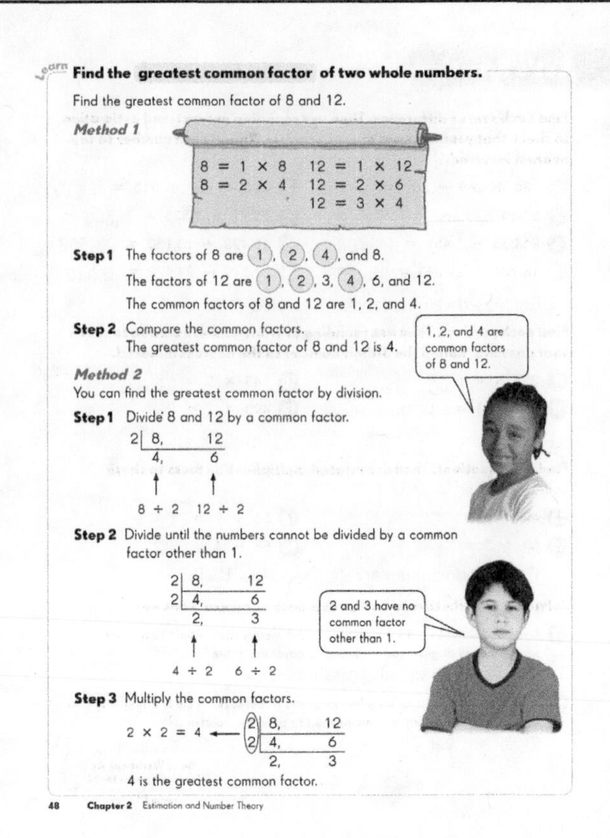

Learn **Find the greatest common factor of two whole numbers.**

Find the greatest common factor of 8 and 12.

Method 1

8 = 1 × 8
8 = 2 × 4

12 = 1 × 12
12 = 2 × 6
12 = 3 × 4

Step 1 The factors of 8 are (1), (2), (4), and 8.
The factors of 12 are (1), (2), 3, (4), 6, and 12.
The common factors of 8 and 12 are 1, 2, and 4.

Step 2 Compare the common factors.
The greatest common factor of 8 and 12 is 4.

1, 2, and 4 are common factors of 8 and 12.

Method 2

You can find the greatest common factor by division.

Step 1 Divide 8 and 12 by a common factor.

2 | 8, 12
4, 6

8 ÷ 2 12 ÷ 2

Step 2 Divide until the numbers cannot be divided by a common factor other than 1.

2 | 8, 12
2 | 4, 6
2, 3

4 ÷ 2 6 ÷ 2

2 and 3 have no common factor other than 1.

Step 3 Multiply the common factors.

2 × 2 = 4 ← (2) | 8, 12
(2) | 4, 6
2, 3

4 is the greatest common factor.

48 Chapter 2 Estimation and Number Theory

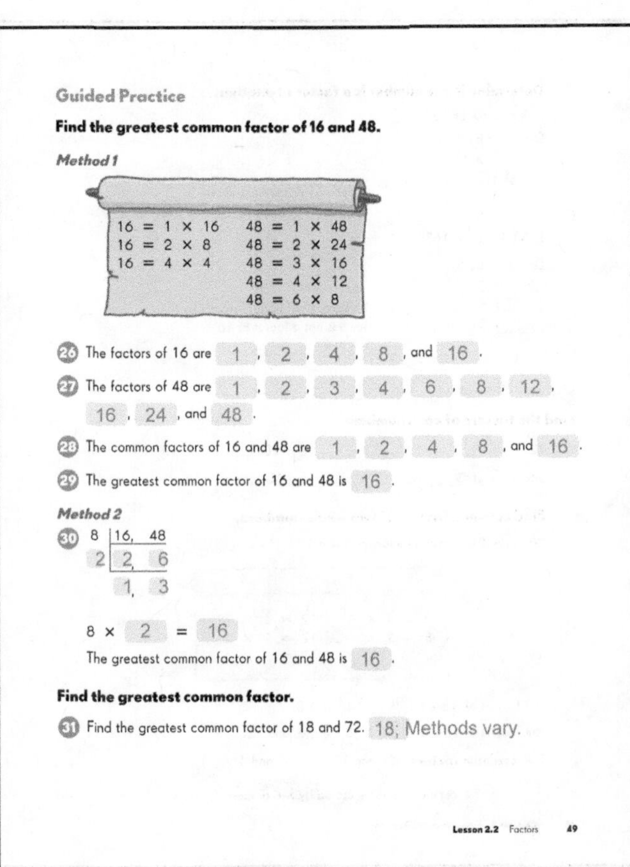

Guided Practice

Find the greatest common factor of 16 and 48.

Method 1

16 = 1 × 16
16 = 2 × 8
16 = 4 × 4

48 = 1 × 48
48 = 2 × 24
48 = 3 × 16
48 = 4 × 12
48 = 6 × 8

26. The factors of 16 are 1, 2, 4, 8, and 16.
27. The factors of 48 are 1, 2, 3, 4, 6, 8, 12, 16, 24, and 48.
28. The common factors of 16 and 48 are 1, 2, 4, 8, and 16.
29. The greatest common factor of 16 and 48 is 16.

Method 2

30. 8 | 16, 48
2 | 2, 6
1, 3

8 × 2 = 16

The greatest common factor of 16 and 48 is 16.

Find the greatest common factor.

31. Find the greatest common factor of 18 and 72. 18; Methods vary.

Lesson 2.2 Factors 49

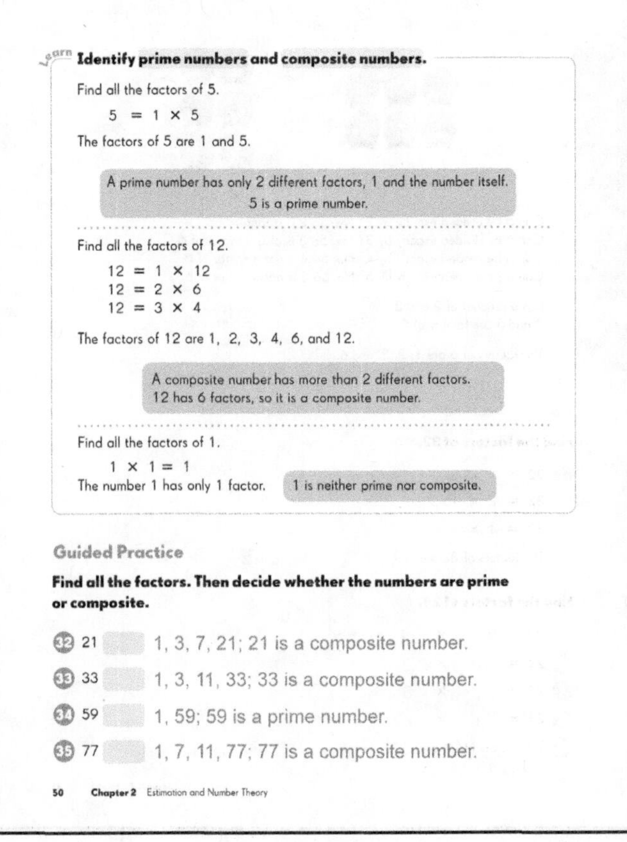

Learn **Identify prime numbers and composite numbers.**

Find all the factors of 5.

5 = 1 × 5

The factors of 5 are 1 and 5.

A prime number has only 2 different factors, 1 and the number itself.
5 is a prime number.

Find all the factors of 12.

12 = 1 × 12
12 = 2 × 6
12 = 3 × 4

The factors of 12 are 1, 2, 3, 4, 6, and 12.

A composite number has more than 2 different factors.
12 has 6 factors, so it is a composite number.

Find all the factors of 1.

1 × 1 = 1

The number 1 has only 1 factor. 1 is neither prime nor composite.

Guided Practice

Find all the factors. Then decide whether the numbers are prime or composite.

32. 21 1, 3, 7, 21; 21 is a composite number.
33. 33 1, 3, 11, 33; 33 is a composite number.
34. 59 1, 59; 59 is a prime number.
35. 77 1, 7, 11, 77; 77 is a composite number.

50 Chapter 2 Estimation and Number Theory

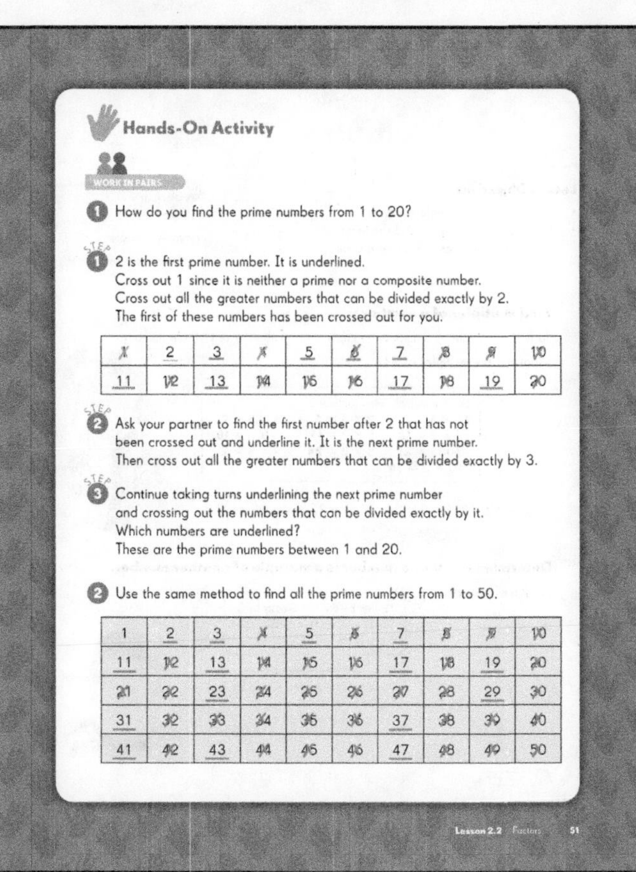

Hands-On Activity

WORK IN PAIRS

1 How do you find the prime numbers from 1 to 20?

STEP 1 2 is the first prime number. It is underlined.
Cross out 1 since it is neither a prime nor a composite number.
Cross out all the greater numbers that can be divided exactly by 2.
The first of these numbers has been crossed out for you.

1	2	3	4	5	6	7	8	9	10
11	12	13	14	15	16	17	18	19	20

STEP 2 Ask your partner to find the first number after 2 that has not been crossed out and underline it. It is the next prime number. Then cross out all the greater numbers that can be divided exactly by 3.

STEP 3 Continue taking turns underlining the next prime number and crossing out the numbers that can be divided exactly by it. Which numbers are underlined?
These are the prime numbers between 1 and 20.

2 Use the same method to find all the prime numbers from 1 to 50.

1	2	3	4	5	6	7	8	9	10
11	12	13	14	15	16	17	18	19	20
21	22	23	24	25	26	27	28	29	30
31	32	33	34	35	36	37	38	39	40
41	42	43	44	45	46	47	48	49	50

Lesson 2.2 Factors 51

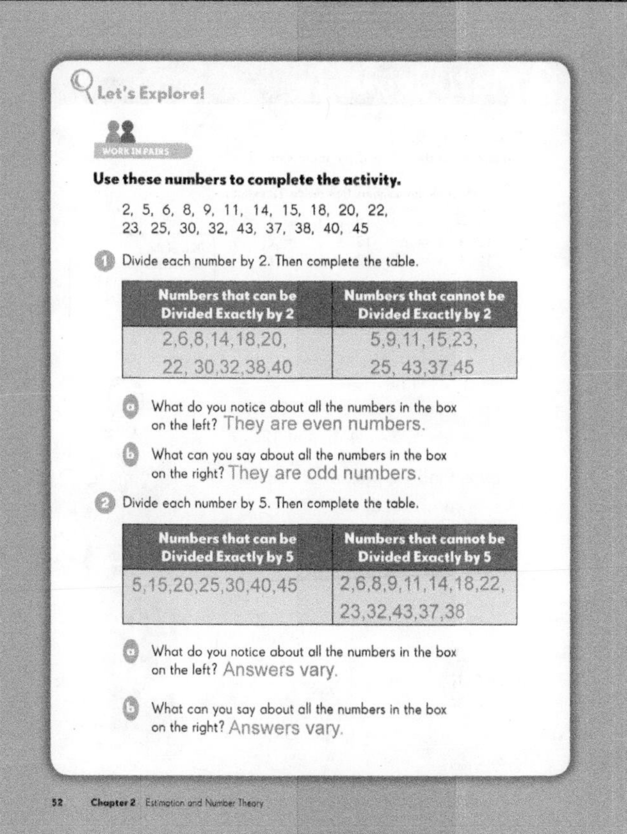

Let's Explore!

WORK IN PAIRS

Use these numbers to complete the activity.

2, 5, 6, 8, 9, 11, 14, 15, 18, 20, 22,
23, 25, 30, 32, 43, 37, 38, 40, 45

1 Divide each number by 2. Then complete the table.

Numbers that can be Divided Exactly by 2	Numbers that cannot be Divided Exactly by 2
2,6,8,14,18,20, 22, 30,32,38,40	5,9,11,15,23, 25, 43,37,45

a What do you notice about all the numbers in the box on the left? They are even numbers.

b What can you say about all the numbers in the box on the right? They are odd numbers.

2 Divide each number by 5. Then complete the table.

Numbers that can be Divided Exactly by 5	Numbers that cannot be Divided Exactly by 5
5,15,20,25,30,40,45	2,6,8,9,11,14,18,22, 23,32,43,37,38

a What do you notice about all the numbers in the box on the left? Answers vary.

b What can you say about all the numbers in the box on the right? Answers vary.

52 Chapter 2 Estimation and Number Theory

Let's Practice

Think about multiplication and division. Then find the missing numbers.

1 28 = 1 × 28
28 ÷ 1 = 28

2 28 = 2 × 14
28 ÷ 2 = 14

3 28 = 4 × 7
28 ÷ 4 = 7

4 The factors of 28 are 1, 2, 4, 7, 14, and 28.

Find all the factors of 42.

5 42 = 1 × 42

6 42 = 2 × 21

7 42 = 3 × 14

8 42 = 6 × 7

9 The factors of 42 are 1, 2, 3, 6, 7, 14, 21, and 42.

Complete.

10 The factors of 8 are 1, 2, 4, and 8.

11 The factors of 24 are 1, 2, 3, 4, 6, 8, 12, and 24.

12 The common factors of 8 and 24 are 1, 2, 4, and 8.

13 The greatest common factor of 8 and 24 is 8.

14 The factors of 52 are 1, 2, 4, 13, 26, and 52.

15 The common factors of 24 and 52 are 1, 2, and 4.

16 The greatest common factor of 24 and 52 is 4.

Lesson 2.2 Factors 53

Answer each question.

6, 14, 15, 20, 23, 25, 28, 32, 33, 35, 39

17 Which of these numbers have 2 as a factor? 6, 14, 20, 28, 32

18 Which of these numbers have 5 as a factor? 15, 20, 25, 35

Find a possible number which has only these factors.

Factors of a Number

	Factors	Number
19	1, 2, 3, and 6	6
20	1, 2, 5, and 10	10

Complete.

21 Find all the prime numbers from 1 to 10. 2,3,5,7

22 Find all the prime numbers for each set of numbers. Complete the table.

Prime Numbers

1 to 16	16 to 32	32 to 48
2,3,5,7,11, and 13	17,19,23, 29, and 31	37, 41, 43, and 47

Which set has more prime numbers? Numbers 1 to 16

Solve.

23 Julia's birthday is on 3/7/1998. Using the digits from her birthday, form three 2-digit prime numbers, and three 2-digit composite numbers.
Answers vary. Sample answer:
Prime numbers: 13,17,19.
Composite numbers: 18, 38, 93

ON YOUR OWN
Go to Workbook A: Practice 2, pages 21–26

54 Chapter 2 Estimation and Number Theory

Chapter 2

Chapter 2

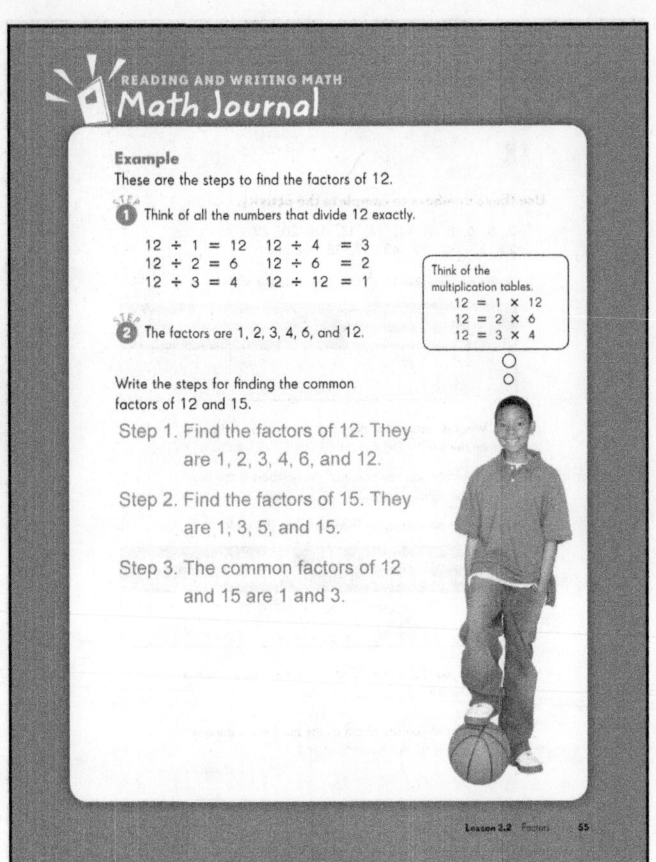

READING AND WRITING MATH

Math Journal

Example

These are the steps to find the factors of 12.

Step 1 Think of all the numbers that divide 12 exactly.

$12 \div 1 = 12$ $12 \div 4 = 3$
$12 \div 2 = 6$ $12 \div 6 = 2$
$12 \div 3 = 4$ $12 \div 12 = 1$

Think of the multiplication tables.
$12 = 1 \times 12$
$12 = 2 \times 6$
$12 = 3 \times 4$

Step 2 The factors are 1, 2, 3, 4, 6, and 12.

Write the steps for finding the common factors of 12 and 15.

Step 1. Find the factors of 12. They are 1, 2, 3, 4, 6, and 12.

Step 2. Find the factors of 15. They are 1, 3, 5, and 15.

Step 3. The common factors of 12 and 15 are 1 and 3.

Lesson 2.2 Factors 55

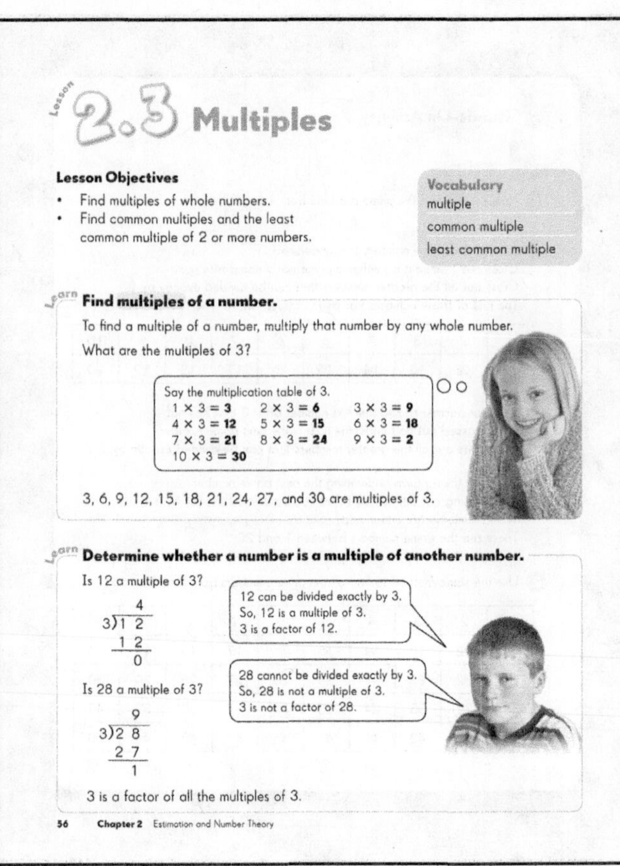

Lesson 2.3 Multiples

Lesson Objectives

- Find multiples of whole numbers.
- Find common multiples and the least common multiple of 2 or more numbers.

Vocabulary
multiple
common multiple
least common multiple

Learn **Find multiples of a number.**

To find a multiple of a number, multiply that number by any whole number.

What are the multiples of 3?

Say the multiplication table of 3.
$1 \times 3 = \mathbf{3}$ $2 \times 3 = \mathbf{6}$ $3 \times 3 = \mathbf{9}$
$4 \times 3 = \mathbf{12}$ $5 \times 3 = \mathbf{15}$ $6 \times 3 = \mathbf{18}$
$7 \times 3 = \mathbf{21}$ $8 \times 3 = \mathbf{24}$ $9 \times 3 = \mathbf{2}$
$10 \times 3 = \mathbf{30}$

3, 6, 9, 12, 15, 18, 21, 24, 27, and 30 are multiples of 3.

Learn **Determine whether a number is a multiple of another number.**

Is 12 a multiple of 3?

$$\begin{array}{r} 4 \\ 3\overline{)12} \\ \underline{12} \\ 0 \end{array}$$

12 can be divided exactly by 3.
So, 12 is a multiple of 3.
3 is a factor of 12.

Is 28 a multiple of 3?

$$\begin{array}{r} 9 \\ 3\overline{)28} \\ \underline{27} \\ 1 \end{array}$$

28 cannot be divided exactly by 3.
So, 28 is not a multiple of 3.
3 is not a factor of 28.

3 is a factor of all the multiples of 3.

56 Chapter 2 Estimation and Number Theory

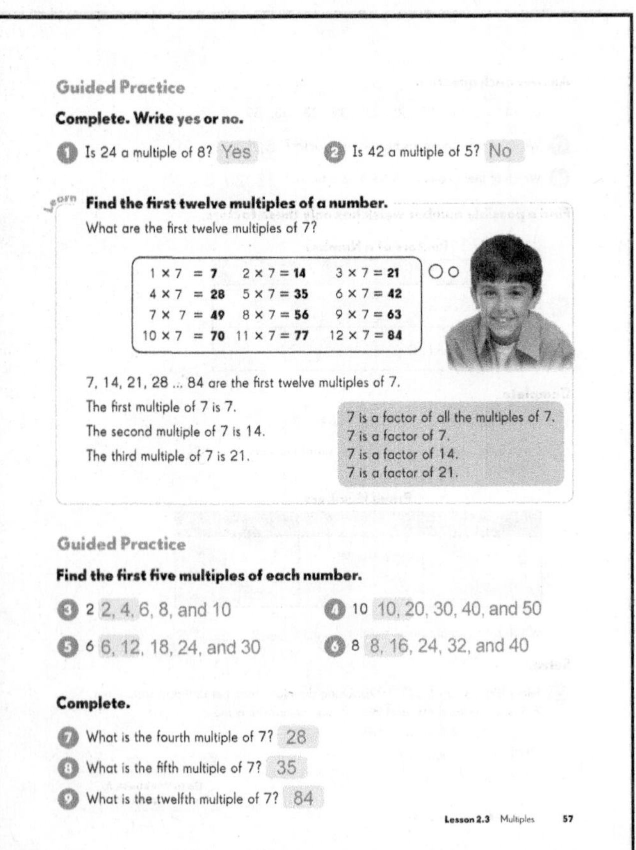

Guided Practice

Complete. Write yes or no.

1. Is 24 a multiple of 8? Yes
2. Is 42 a multiple of 5? No

Learn **Find the first twelve multiples of a number.**

What are the first twelve multiples of 7?

$1 \times 7 = \mathbf{7}$ $2 \times 7 = \mathbf{14}$ $3 \times 7 = \mathbf{21}$
$4 \times 7 = \mathbf{28}$ $5 \times 7 = \mathbf{35}$ $6 \times 7 = \mathbf{42}$
$7 \times 7 = \mathbf{49}$ $8 \times 7 = \mathbf{56}$ $9 \times 7 = \mathbf{63}$
$10 \times 7 = \mathbf{70}$ $11 \times 7 = \mathbf{77}$ $12 \times 7 = \mathbf{84}$

7, 14, 21, 28 ... 84 are the first twelve multiples of 7.

The first multiple of 7 is 7.
The second multiple of 7 is 14.
The third multiple of 7 is 21.

7 is a factor of all the multiples of 7.
7 is a factor of 7.
7 is a factor of 14.
7 is a factor of 21.

Guided Practice

Find the first five multiples of each number.

3. 2 2, 4, 6, 8, and 10
4. 10 10, 20, 30, 40, and 50
5. 6 6, 12, 18, 24, and 30
6. 8 8, 16, 24, 32, and 40

Complete.

7. What is the fourth multiple of 7? 28
8. What is the fifth multiple of 7? 35
9. What is the twelfth multiple of 7? 84

Lesson 2.3 Multiples 57

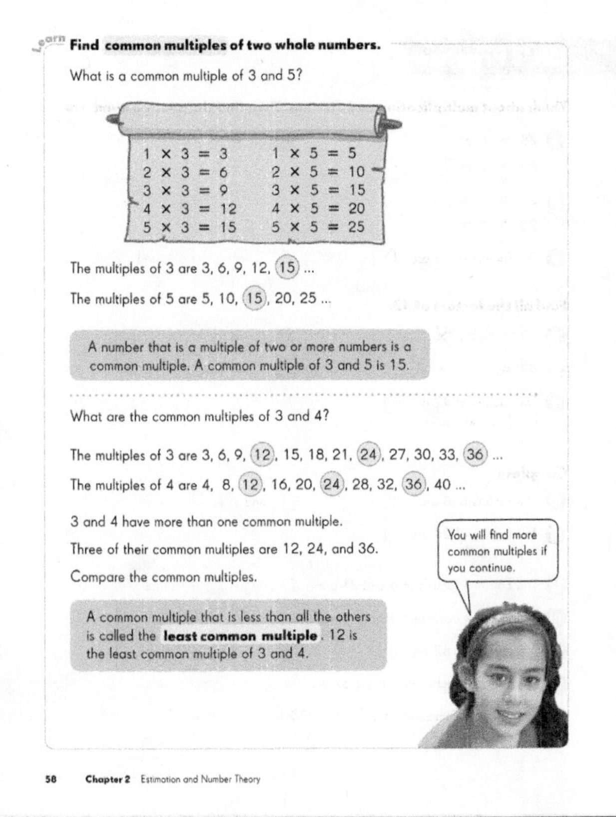

Learn **Find common multiples of two whole numbers.**

What is a common multiple of 3 and 5?

$1 \times 3 = 3$ $1 \times 5 = 5$
$2 \times 3 = 6$ $2 \times 5 = 10$
$3 \times 3 = 9$ $3 \times 5 = 15$
$4 \times 3 = 12$ $4 \times 5 = 20$
$5 \times 3 = 15$ $5 \times 5 = 25$

The multiples of 3 are 3, 6, 9, 12, (15) ...

The multiples of 5 are 5, 10, (15), 20, 25 ...

A number that is a multiple of two or more numbers is a common multiple. A common multiple of 3 and 5 is 15.

What are the common multiples of 3 and 4?

The multiples of 3 are 3, 6, 9, (12), 15, 18, 21, (24), 27, 30, 33, (36) ...

The multiples of 4 are 4, 8, (12), 16, 20, (24), 28, 32, (36), 40 ...

3 and 4 have more than one common multiple.

Three of their common multiples are 12, 24, and 36.

Compare the common multiples.

You will find more common multiples if you continue.

A common multiple that is less than all the others is called the **least common multiple**. 12 is the least common multiple of 3 and 4.

58 Chapter 2 Estimation and Number Theory

Guided Practice

List the first twelve multiples of 4 and 6. Then find the common multiples of 4 and 6 from the first twelve multiples.

10. The first twelve multiples of 4 are 4, 8, 12, 16, 20, 24, 28, 32, 36, 40, 44 and 48.

11. The first twelve multiples of 6 are 6, 12, 18, 24, 30, 36, 42, 48, 54, 60, 66 and 72.

12. From the list of twelve multiples, the common multiples of 4 and 6 are 12, 24, 36, and 48.

13. The least common multiple of 4 and 6 is 12.

Complete.

14. List the first twelve multiples of 5 and 8. From the list, find a common multiple of 5 and 8. 40

Find a common multiple of each pair of numbers. Answers vary.

15. 3 and 4 12
16. 5 and 4 20
17. 2 and 7 14

Solve.

18. 15 and 30 are common multiples of 5 and X. X is a 1-digit number. X is not 1. What number is X? 3

19. Make a list of the multiples of 3 and 7. Find the first three common multiples of 3 and 7. Which is the least common multiple?

The common multiples of 3 and 7 are 21, 42, and 63.
The least common multiple of 3 and 7 is 21.

Learn Find the least common multiple of two whole numbers.

Find the least common multiple of 30 and 48.

2	30,	48
3	15,	24
	5,	8

5 and 8 have no common factor other than 1.

Multiply the four factors.

$2 \times 3 \times 5 \times 8 = 240$

So, 240 is the least common multiple of 30 and 48.

Divide 30 and 48 until they cannot be divided by a common factor other than 1.

Guided Practice

Find the least common multiple of each pair of numbers using the division method.

20. 12 and 26

2	12,	26
	6,	13

The least common multiple of 12 and 26 is 156.

21. 15 and 21

3	15,	21
	5,	7

The least common multiple of 15 and 21 is 105.

Let's Practice

Find the first five multiples of each number.

1. 9 9, 18, 27, 36, 45
2. 7 7, 14, 21, 28, 35

Find the numbers in the box that are multiples of each given number.

6 16 18 27 36 42 63

3. 4 16, 36
4. 9 18, 27, 36, 63

Complete.

5. List the first twelve multiples of 6 and 8. From the list, find the common multiples of 6 and 8. 24, 48, 72

Solve.

Here is a list of numbers. Circle the multiples of 5. Two of the multiples of 5 are common multiples of 5 and X.

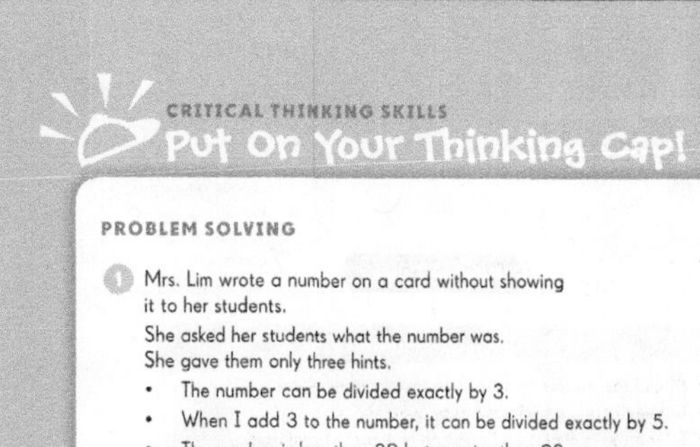

6. What number is X? 3
7. From the list, what are the common multiples of 5 and X? 15 and 45

Find the least common multiple of each pair of numbers.

8. 4 and 9 36
9. 5 and 8 40
10. 12 and 56 168

Solve.

11. 12 is the least common multiple of 4 and X. Find three possible values of X. 3, 6, and 12

ON YOUR OWN
Go to Workbook A: Practice 3, pages 27–30

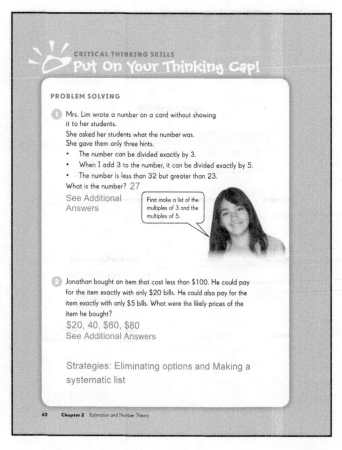

CRITICAL THINKING SKILLS
Put On Your Thinking Cap!

PROBLEM SOLVING

1. Mrs. Lim wrote a number on a card without showing it to her students.
She asked her students what the number was.
She gave them only three hints.
   - The number can be divided exactly by 3.
   - When I add 3 to the number, it can be divided exactly by 5.
   - The number is less than 32 but greater than 23.

What is the number? 27
See Additional Answers

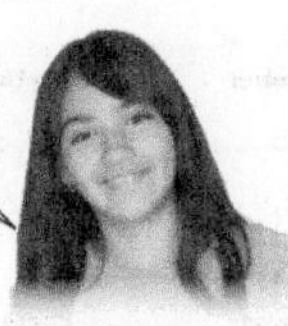

First make a list of the multiples of 3 and the multiples of 5.

2. Jonathan bought an item that cost less than $100. He could pay for the item exactly with only $20 bills. He could also pay for the item exactly with only $5 bills. What were the likely prices of the item he bought?
$20, 40, $60, $80
See Additional Answers

Strategies: Eliminating options and Making a systematic list

Chapter 2

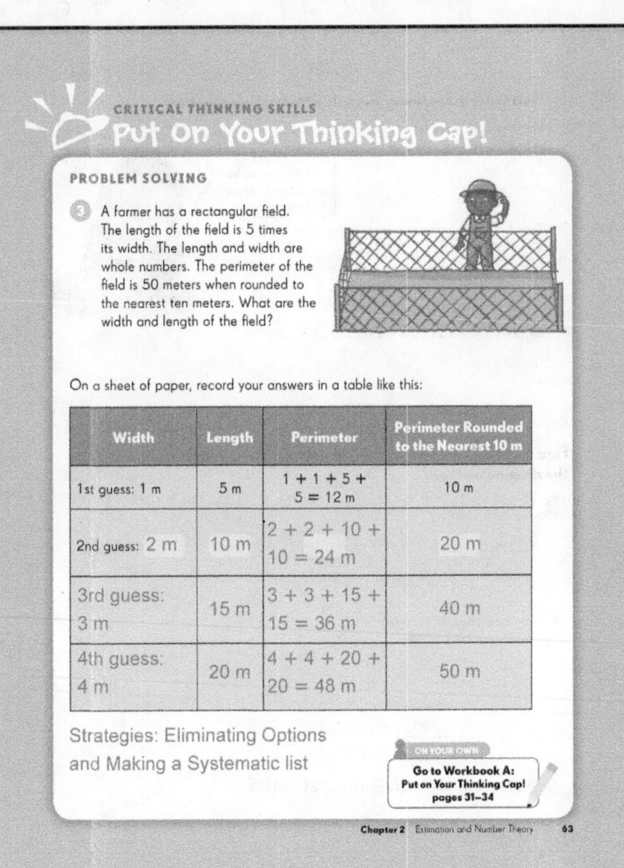

CRITICAL THINKING SKILLS

Put On Your Thinking Cap!

PROBLEM SOLVING

3 A farmer has a rectangular field. The length of the field is 5 times its width. The length and width are whole numbers. The perimeter of the field is 50 meters when rounded to the nearest ten meters. What are the width and length of the field?

On a sheet of paper, record your answers in a table like this:

Width	Length	Perimeter	Perimeter Rounded to the Nearest 10 m
1st guess: 1 m	5 m	1 + 1 + 5 + 5 = 12 m	10 m
2nd guess: 2 m	10 m	2 + 2 + 10 + 10 = 24 m	20 m
3rd guess: 3 m	15 m	3 + 3 + 15 + 15 = 36 m	40 m
4th guess: 4 m	20 m	4 + 4 + 20 + 20 = 48 m	50 m

Strategies: Eliminating Options and Making a Systematic list

ON YOUR OWN

Go to Workbook A: Put on Your Thinking Cap! pages 31–34

Chapter 2 Estimation and Number Theory 63

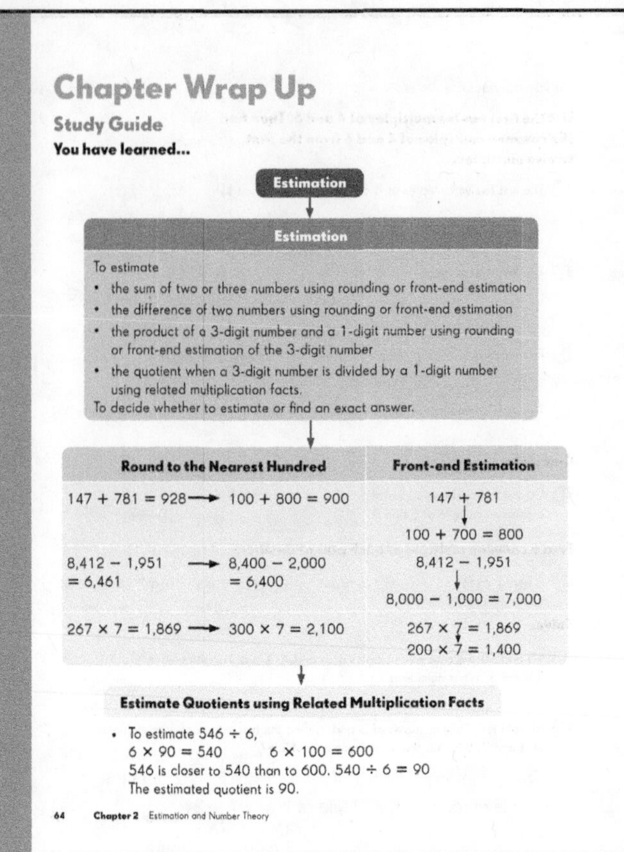

Chapter Wrap Up

Study Guide

You have learned...

Estimation

Estimation

To estimate

- the sum of two or three numbers using rounding or front-end estimation
- the difference of two numbers using rounding or front-end estimation
- the product of a 3-digit number and a 1-digit number using rounding or front-end estimation of the 3-digit number
- the quotient when a 3-digit number is divided by a 1-digit number using related multiplication facts.

To decide whether to estimate or find an exact answer.

Round to the Nearest Hundred		Front-end Estimation
147 + 781 = 928 →	100 + 800 = 900	147 + 781 ↓ 100 + 700 = 800
8,412 − 1,951 = 6,461 →	8,400 − 2,000 = 6,400	8,412 − 1,951 ↓ 8,000 − 1,000 = 7,000
267 × 7 = 1,869 →	300 × 7 = 2,100	267 × 7 = 1,869 ↓ 200 × 7 = 1,400

Estimate Quotients using Related Multiplication Facts

- To estimate 546 ÷ 6,
  6 × 90 = 540 6 × 100 = 600
  546 is closer to 540 than to 600. 540 ÷ 6 = 90
  The estimated quotient is 90.

64 Chapter 2 Estimation and Number Theory

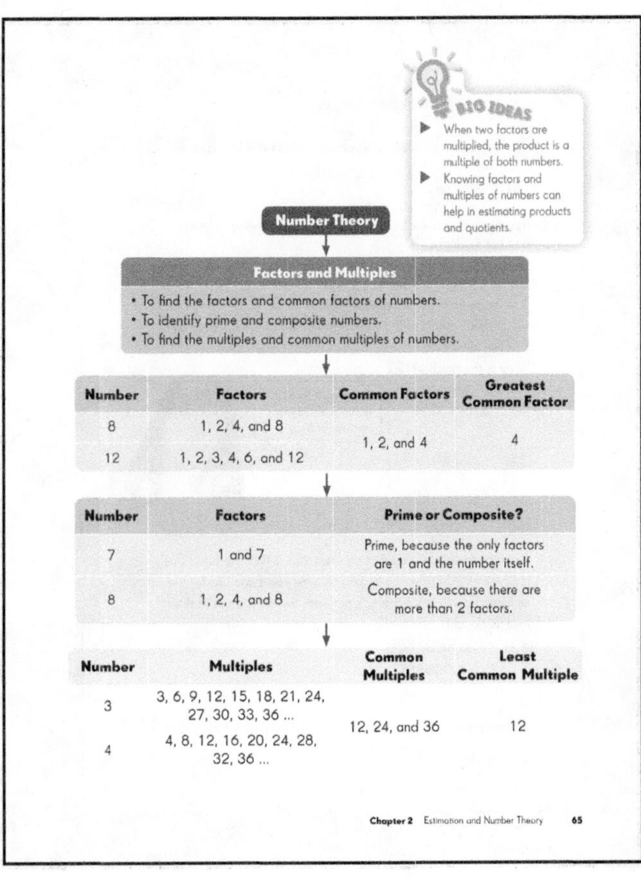

BIG IDEAS

- When two factors are multiplied, the product is a multiple of both numbers.
- Knowing factors and multiples of numbers can help in estimating products and quotients.

Number Theory

Factors and Multiples

- To find the factors and common factors of numbers.
- To identify prime and composite numbers.
- To find the multiples and common multiples of numbers.

Number	Factors	Common Factors	Greatest Common Factor
8	1, 2, 4, and 8	1, 2, and 4	4
12	1, 2, 3, 4, 6, and 12		

Number	Factors	Prime or Composite?
7	1 and 7	Prime, because the only factors are 1 and the number itself.
8	1, 2, 4, and 8	Composite, because there are more than 2 factors.

Number	Multiples	Common Multiples	Least Common Multiple
3	3, 6, 9, 12, 15, 18, 21, 24, 27, 30, 33, 36 ...	12, 24, and 36	12
4	4, 8, 12, 16, 20, 24, 28, 32, 36 ...		

Chapter 2 Estimation and Number Theory 65

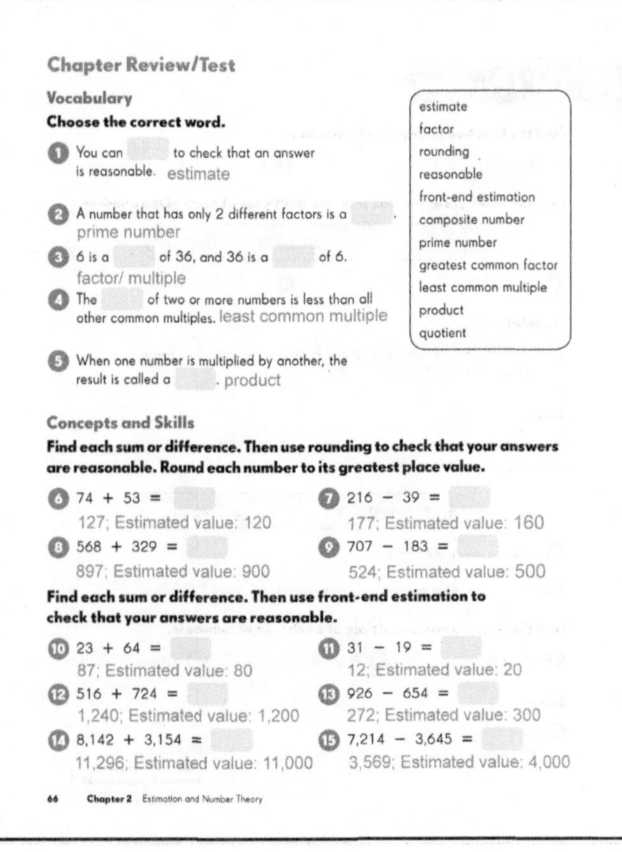

Chapter Review/Test

Vocabulary

Choose the correct word.

estimate
factor
rounding
reasonable
front-end estimation
composite number
prime number
greatest common factor
least common multiple
product
quotient

1 You can ___ to check that an answer is reasonable. estimate

2 A number that has only 2 different factors is a ___. prime number

3 6 is a ___ of 36, and 36 is a ___ of 6. factor/ multiple

4 The ___ of two or more numbers is less than all other common multiples. least common multiple

5 When one number is multiplied by another, the result is called a ___. product

Concepts and Skills

Find each sum or difference. Then use rounding to check that your answers are reasonable. Round each number to its greatest place value.

6 74 + 53 = ___ 127; Estimated value: 120

7 216 − 39 = ___ 177; Estimated value: 160

8 568 + 329 = ___ 897; Estimated value: 900

9 707 − 183 = ___ 524; Estimated value: 500

Find each sum or difference. Then use front-end estimation to check that your answers are reasonable.

10 23 + 64 = ___ 87; Estimated value: 80

11 31 − 19 = ___ 12; Estimated value: 20

12 516 + 724 = ___ 1,240; Estimated value: 1,200

13 926 − 654 = ___ 272; Estimated value: 300

14 8,142 + 3,154 = ___ 11,296; Estimated value: 11,000

15 7,214 − 3,645 = ___ 3,569; Estimated value: 4,000

66 Chapter 2 Estimation and Number Theory

Find each product or quotient. Then estimate to check that your answers are reasonable.

16 42 × 3 = 126
17 231 × 4 = 924
18 93 ÷ 3 = 31
19 70 ÷ 5 = 14

Estimated values vary for Exercises 16-19.

Complete. Then estimate to check that your answers are reasonable.

20 8,012 + 1,569 = 9,581
21 568 − 127 = 441
22 3,516 − 1,657 = 1,859
23 59 × 6 = 354
24 72 ÷ 3 = 24
25 78 × 5 = 390
26 84 ÷ 2 = 42
27 44 × 8 = 352
28 56 ÷ 4 = 14
29 96 ÷ 3 = 32
30 109 × 7 = 763
31 95 ÷ 5 = 19

Estimated values vary for Exercises 20-31.

Find the factors of each number.

32 16 1, 2, 4, 8, and 16

33 36 1, 2, 3, 4, 6, 9, 12, 18, and 36

Complete.

34 Find the common factors of 16 and 36 1, 2, and 4

35 The greatest common factor of 16 and 36 is 4.

Find the first eight multiples of each number.

36 4 4, 8, 12, 16, 20, 24, 28, 32

37 5 5, 10, 15, 20, 25, 30, 35, 40

Complete.

38 Find a common multiple of 4 and 5. Answers vary. Sample answer: 20, 40, and 60.

39 The least common multiple of 4 and 5 is 20.

Find the factors of each number. Then list the prime numbers and composite numbers.

23 32 9 1,851 37 79

40 Prime numbers 23, 37, 79

Composite numbers 9, 32, 1,851

Problem Solving

Solve. Decide whether to find the estimate or the exact answer.

41 Jared has 98 oranges. He packs them into 4 crates. How many oranges does he have left over? Exact answer: 2 oranges

42 There are 147 erasers, 215 pencils, and 327 pens in a stationery shop. About how many erasers, pencils and pens are there altogether? Estimate: 600

43 A tourist agency is expecting 83 visitors in a week. Each of the agency's cars can carry 4 passengers. How many cars will be needed for all the visitors?
Exact answer: 21 cars

44 Ms. Clarkson has $315 to spend on kitchen appliances. She has to choose between two of three options; a microwave for $220, a coffee machine for $83, and a waffle maker for $98. Should she buy the microwave and the coffee machine, or the microwave and the waffle maker?
Exact answer; She should buy the microwave and the coffee machine.

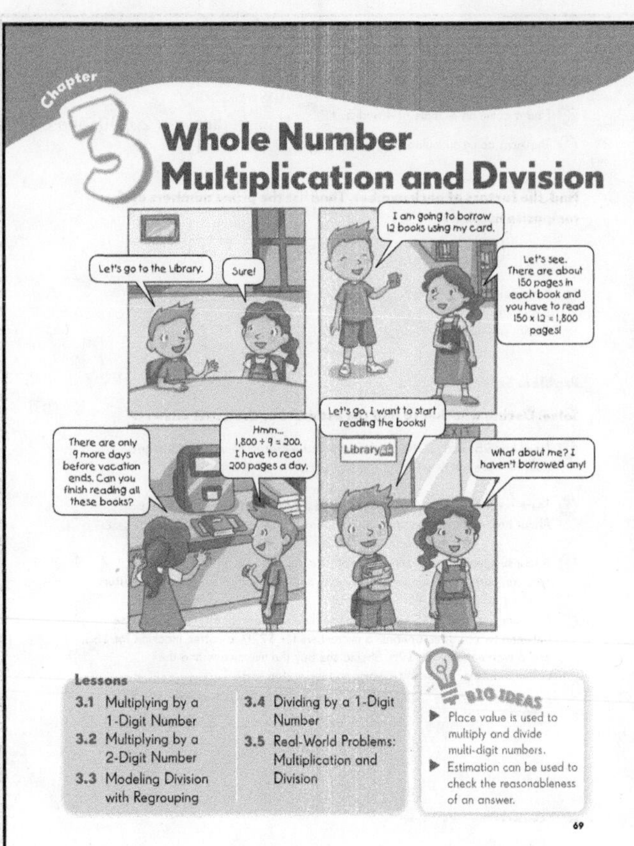

Chapter 3
Whole Number Multiplication and Division

Lessons

- **3.1** Multiplying by a 1-Digit Number
- **3.2** Multiplying by a 2-Digit Number
- **3.3** Modeling Division with Regrouping
- **3.4** Dividing by a 1-Digit Number
- **3.5** Real-World Problems: Multiplication and Division

BIG IDEAS

- ▶ Place value is used to multiply and divide multi-digit numbers.
- ▶ Estimation can be used to check the reasonableness of an answer.

69

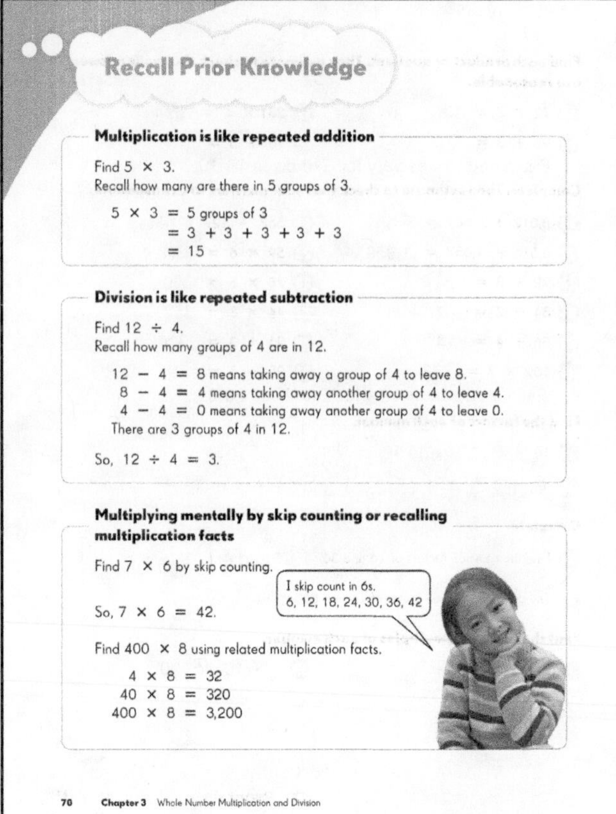

Recall Prior Knowledge

Multiplication is like repeated addition

Find 5 × 3.
Recall how many are there in 5 groups of 3.

$5 \times 3 = 5$ groups of 3
$= 3 + 3 + 3 + 3 + 3$
$= 15$

Division is like repeated subtraction

Find 12 ÷ 4.
Recall how many groups of 4 are in 12.

$12 - 4 = 8$ means taking away a group of 4 to leave 8.
$8 - 4 = 4$ means taking away another group of 4 to leave 4.
$4 - 4 = 0$ means taking away another group of 4 to leave 0.
There are 3 groups of 4 in 12.

So, $12 \div 4 = 3$.

Multiplying mentally by skip counting or recalling multiplication facts

Find 7 × 6 by skip counting.

So, $7 \times 6 = 42$.

Find 400 × 8 using related multiplication facts.

$4 \times 8 = 32$
$40 \times 8 = 320$
$400 \times 8 = 3{,}200$

70 Chapter 3 Whole Number Multiplication and Division

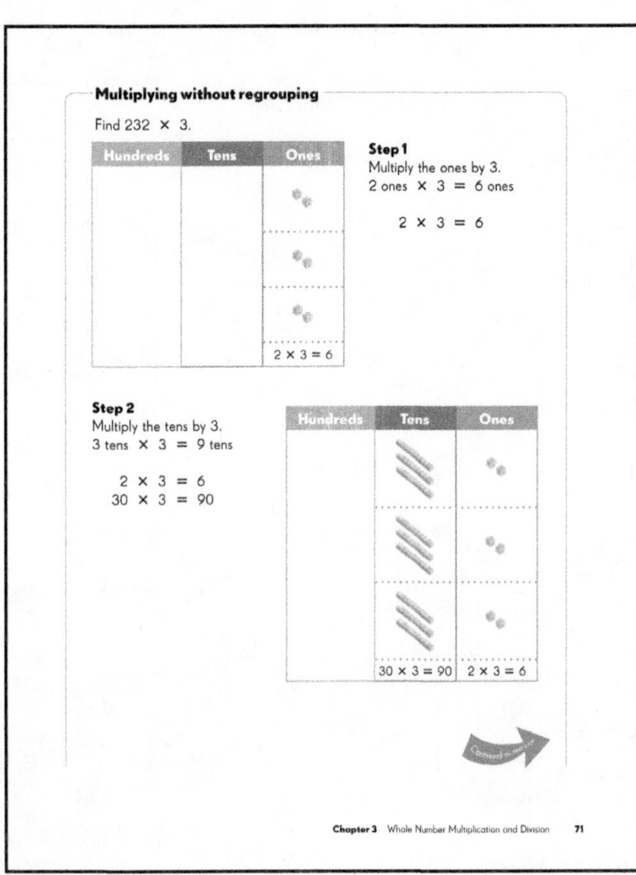

Multiplying without regrouping

Find 232 × 3.

Hundreds	Tens	Ones
		2 × 3 = 6

Step 1
Multiply the ones by 3.
2 ones × 3 = 6 ones

$2 \times 3 = 6$

Step 2
Multiply the tens by 3.
3 tens × 3 = 9 tens

$2 \times 3 = 6$
$30 \times 3 = 90$

Hundreds	Tens	Ones
	30 × 3 = 90	2 × 3 = 6

Chapter 3 Whole Number Multiplication and Division 71

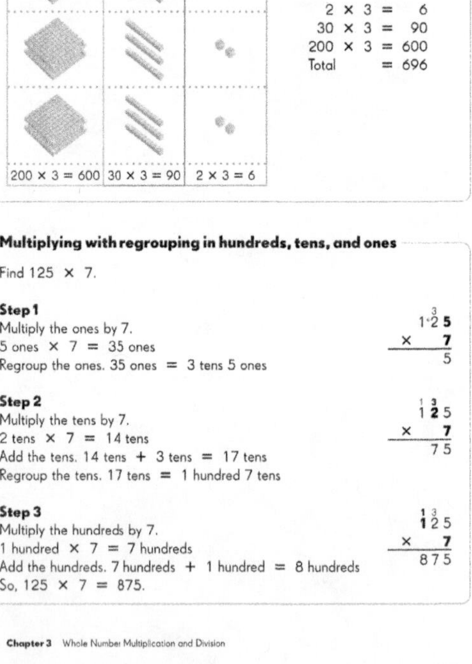

Hundreds	Tens	Ones
200 × 3 = 600	30 × 3 = 90	2 × 3 = 6

Step 3
Multiply the hundreds by 3.
2 hundreds × 3
= 6 hundreds

$2 \times 3 = 6$
$30 \times 3 = 90$
$200 \times 3 = 600$
Total $= 696$

Multiplying with regrouping in hundreds, tens, and ones

Find 125 × 7.

Step 1
Multiply the ones by 7.
5 ones × 7 = 35 ones
Regroup the ones. 35 ones = 3 tens 5 ones

$$\begin{array}{r} {}^{3}\\ 125 \\ \times\ \ 7 \\ \hline 5 \end{array}$$

Step 2
Multiply the tens by 7.
2 tens × 7 = 14 tens
Add the tens. 14 tens + 3 tens = 17 tens
Regroup the tens. 17 tens = 1 hundred 7 tens

$$\begin{array}{r} {}^{1\,3}\\ 125 \\ \times\ \ 7 \\ \hline 75 \end{array}$$

Step 3
Multiply the hundreds by 7.
1 hundred × 7 = 7 hundreds
Add the hundreds. 7 hundreds + 1 hundred = 8 hundreds
So, 125 × 7 = 875.

$$\begin{array}{r} {}^{1\,3}\\ 125 \\ \times\ \ 7 \\ \hline 875 \end{array}$$

72 Chapter 3 Whole Number Multiplication and Division

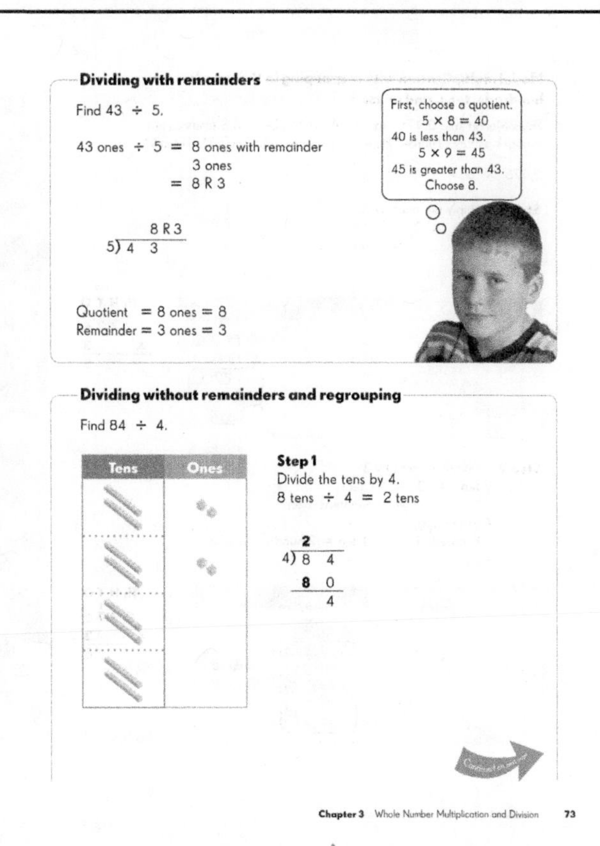

Dividing with remainders

Find 43 ÷ 5.

43 ones ÷ 5 = 8 ones with remainder 3 ones
= 8 R 3

$$5\overline{)4\ 3}\quad 8\ R\ 3$$

Quotient = 8 ones = 8
Remainder = 3 ones = 3

First, choose a quotient.
5 × 8 = 40
40 is less than 43.
5 × 9 = 45
45 is greater than 43.
Choose 8.

Dividing without remainders and regrouping

Find 84 ÷ 4.

Tens	Ones

Step 1
Divide the tens by 4.
8 tens ÷ 4 = 2 tens

```
     2
 4)8 4
   8 0
     4
```

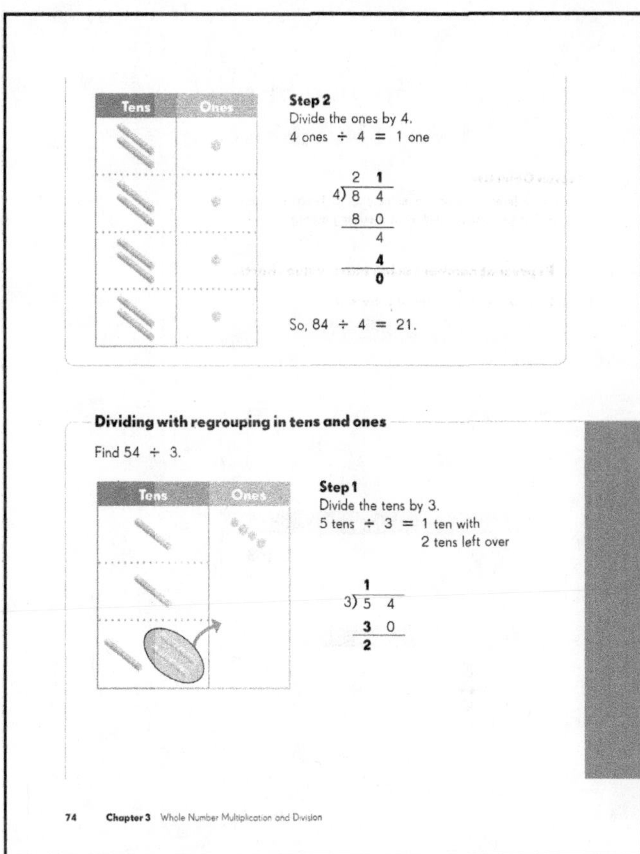

Tens	Ones

Step 2
Divide the ones by 4.
4 ones ÷ 4 = 1 one

```
     2 1
 4)8 4
   8 0
     4
     4
     0
```

So, 84 ÷ 4 = 21.

Dividing with regrouping in tens and ones

Find 54 ÷ 3.

Tens	Ones

Step 1
Divide the tens by 3.
5 tens ÷ 3 = 1 ten with 2 tens left over

```
     1
 3)5 4
   3 0
   2
```

Chapter 3

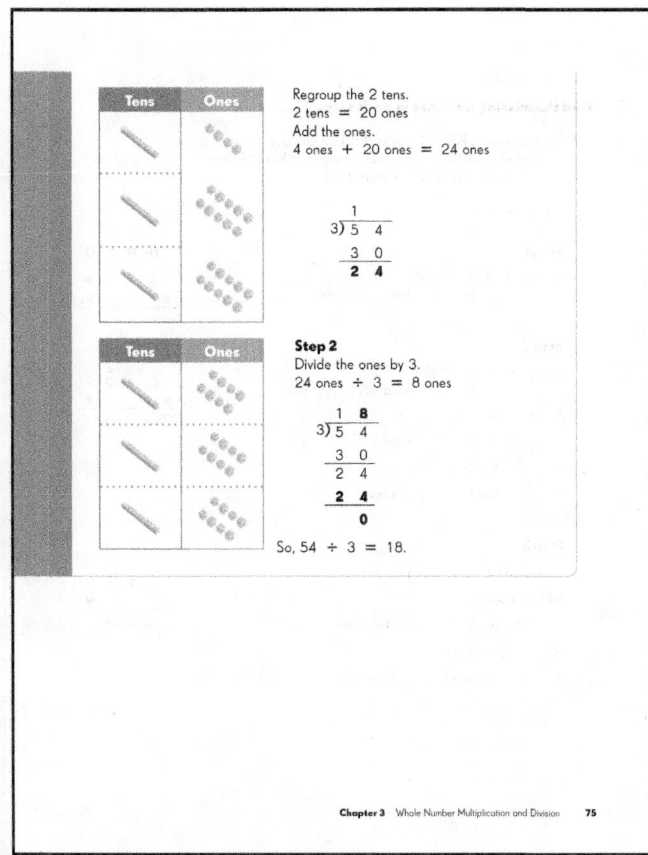

Tens	Ones

Regroup the 2 tens.
2 tens = 20 ones
Add the ones.
4 ones + 20 ones = 24 ones

```
     1
 3)5 4
   3 0
   2 4
```

Tens	Ones

Step 2
Divide the ones by 3.
24 ones ÷ 3 = 8 ones

```
     1 8
 3)5 4
   3 0
   2 4
   2 4
     0
```

So, 54 ÷ 3 = 18.

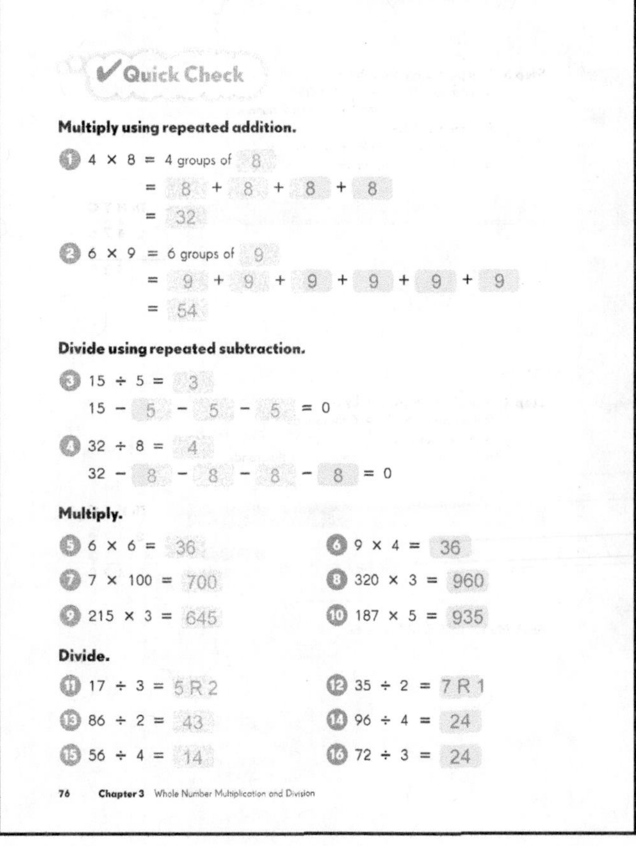

✔ Quick Check

Multiply using repeated addition.

1. 4 × 8 = 4 groups of 8
= 8 + 8 + 8 + 8
= 32

2. 6 × 9 = 6 groups of 9
= 9 + 9 + 9 + 9 + 9 + 9
= 54

Divide using repeated subtraction.

3. 15 ÷ 5 = 3
15 − 5 − 5 − 5 = 0

4. 32 ÷ 8 = 4
32 − 8 − 8 − 8 − 8 = 0

Multiply.

5. 6 × 6 = 36
6. 9 × 4 = 36
7. 7 × 100 = 700
8. 320 × 3 = 960
9. 215 × 3 = 645
10. 187 × 5 = 935

Divide.

11. 17 ÷ 3 = 5 R 2
12. 35 ÷ 2 = 7 R 1
13. 86 ÷ 2 = 43
14. 96 ÷ 4 = 24
15. 56 ÷ 4 = 14
16. 72 ÷ 3 = 24

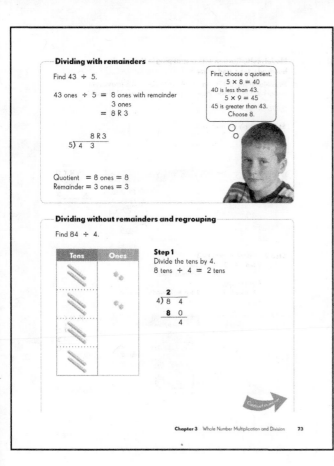

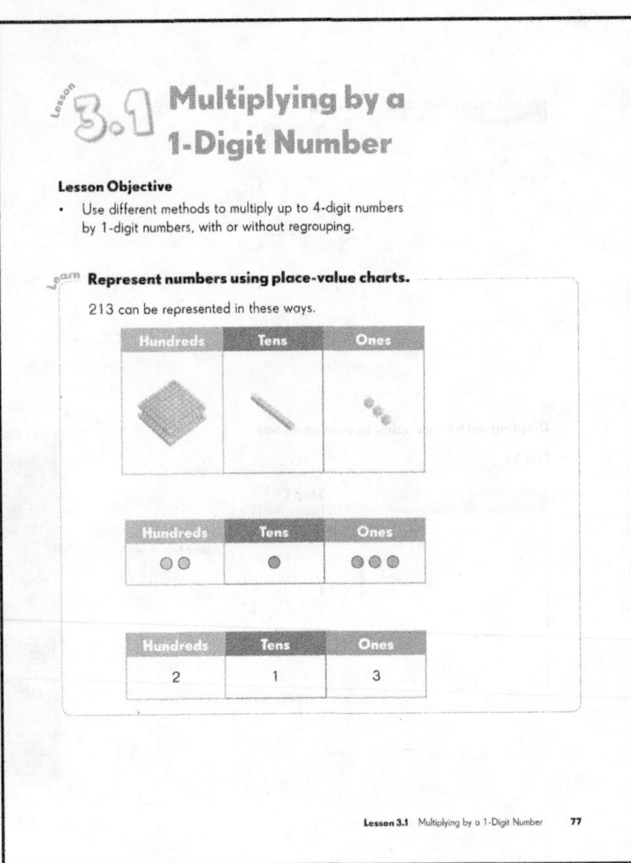

Lesson 3.1 Multiplying by a 1-Digit Number

Lesson Objective

- Use different methods to multiply up to 4-digit numbers by 1-digit numbers, with or without regrouping.

Learn: Represent numbers using place-value charts.

213 can be represented in these ways.

Hundreds	Tens	Ones
(1 hundred flat)	(1 ten rod)	(3 ones cubes)

Hundreds	Tens	Ones
●●	●	●●●

Hundreds	Tens	Ones
2	1	3

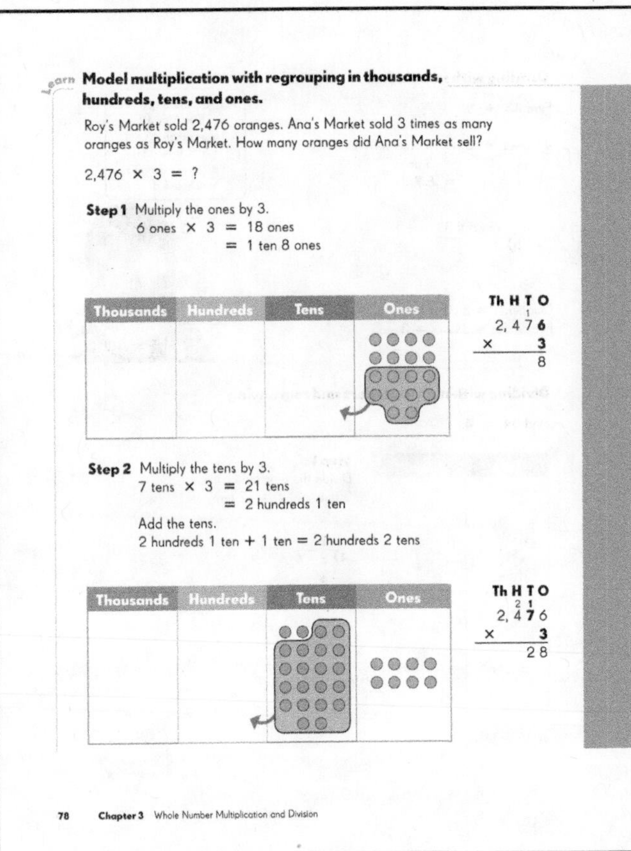

Learn: Model multiplication with regrouping in thousands, hundreds, tens, and ones.

Roy's Market sold 2,476 oranges. Ana's Market sold 3 times as many oranges as Roy's Market. How many oranges did Ana's Market sell?

2,476 × 3 = ?

Step 1 Multiply the ones by 3.
6 ones × 3 = 18 ones
= 1 ten 8 ones

Thousands	Hundreds	Tens	Ones
			●●●● ●●●● (18 ones, 10 regrouped)

Th H T O
2,476 (regrouped 1 above tens)
× 3
8

Step 2 Multiply the tens by 3.
7 tens × 3 = 21 tens
= 2 hundreds 1 ten
Add the tens.
2 hundreds 1 ten + 1 ten = 2 hundreds 2 tens

Thousands	Hundreds	Tens	Ones
		(21 tens, 20 regrouped)	●●●● ●●●●

Th H T O
2,476 (regrouped 2 1)
× 3
28

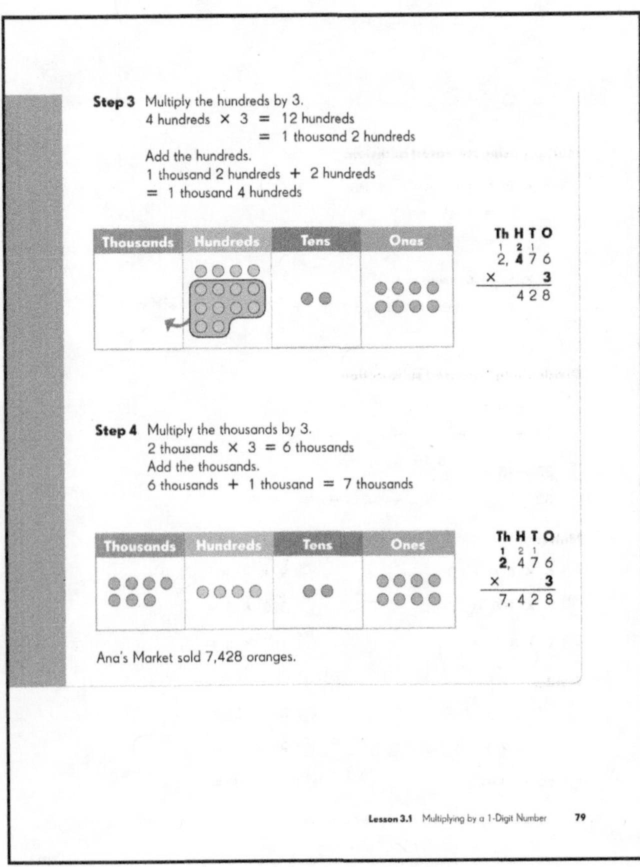

Step 3 Multiply the hundreds by 3.
4 hundreds × 3 = 12 hundreds
= 1 thousand 2 hundreds
Add the hundreds.
1 thousand 2 hundreds + 2 hundreds
= 1 thousand 4 hundreds

Thousands	Hundreds	Tens	Ones
	(14 hundreds, 10 regrouped)	●●	●●●● ●●●●

Th H T O
2,476 (regrouped 1 2 1)
× 3
428

Step 4 Multiply the thousands by 3.
2 thousands × 3 = 6 thousands
Add the thousands.
6 thousands + 1 thousand = 7 thousands

Thousands	Hundreds	Tens	Ones
●●●● ●●●	●●●●	●●	●●●● ●●●●

Th H T O
2,476 (regrouped 1 2 1)
× 3
7,428

Ana's Market sold 7,428 oranges.

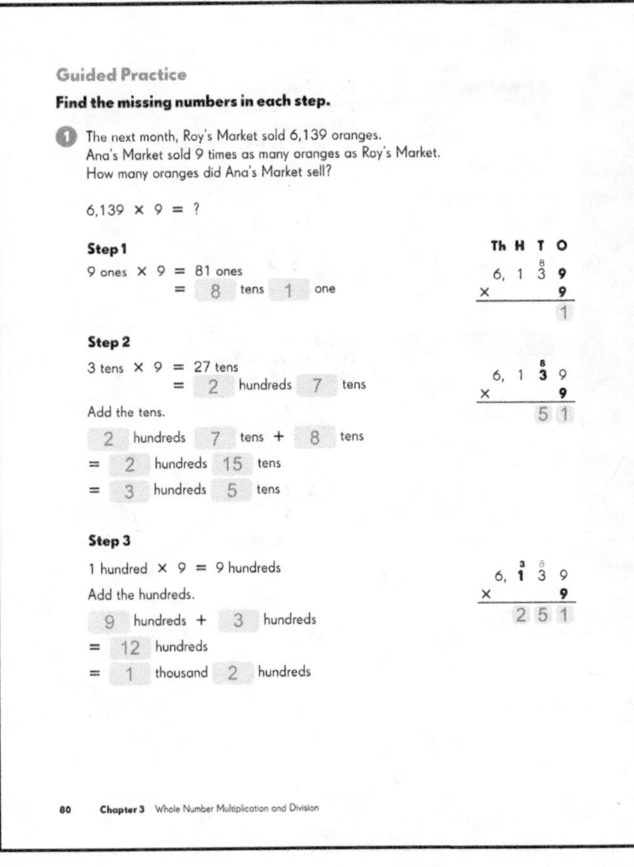

Guided Practice

Find the missing numbers in each step.

1. The next month, Roy's Market sold 6,139 oranges. Ana's Market sold 9 times as many oranges as Roy's Market. How many oranges did Ana's Market sell?

6,139 × 9 = ?

Step 1
9 ones × 9 = 81 ones
= 8 tens 1 one

Th H T O
6, 1 3 9 (regrouped 8)
× 9
1

Step 2
3 tens × 9 = 27 tens
= 2 hundreds 7 tens
Add the tens.
2 hundreds 7 tens + 8 tens
= 2 hundreds 15 tens
= 3 hundreds 5 tens

6, 1 3 9 (regrouped 8)
× 9
5 1

Step 3
1 hundred × 9 = 9 hundreds
Add the hundreds.
9 hundreds + 3 hundreds
= 12 hundreds
= 1 thousand 2 hundreds

6, 1 3 9 (regrouped 3 8)
× 9
2 5 1

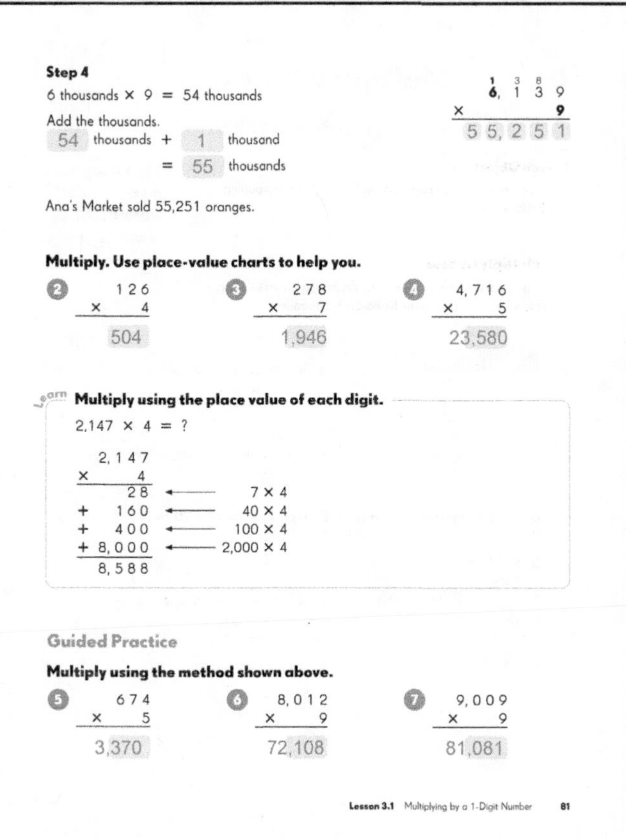

Step 4

6 thousands × 9 = 54 thousands

Add the thousands.

54 thousands + 1 thousand

= 55 thousands

$$\begin{array}{r} \scriptstyle 1\ \ 3\ \ 8 \\ 6,139 \\ \times \quad\ 9 \\ \hline 55,251 \end{array}$$

Ana's Market sold 55,251 oranges.

Multiply. Use place-value charts to help you.

2. 126 × 4 = 504
3. 278 × 7 = 1,946
4. 4,716 × 5 = 23,580

Learn **Multiply using the place value of each digit.**

2,147 × 4 = ?

$$\begin{array}{rl} 2,147 & \\ \times \quad\ \ 4 & \\ \hline 28 & \leftarrow 7 \times 4 \\ +\ \ 160 & \leftarrow 40 \times 4 \\ +\ \ 400 & \leftarrow 100 \times 4 \\ +\ 8,000 & \leftarrow 2,000 \times 4 \\ \hline 8,588 & \end{array}$$

Guided Practice

Multiply using the method shown above.

5. 674 × 5 = 3,370
6. 8,012 × 9 = 72,108
7. 9,009 × 9 = 81,081

Lesson 3.1 Multiplying by a 1-Digit Number 81

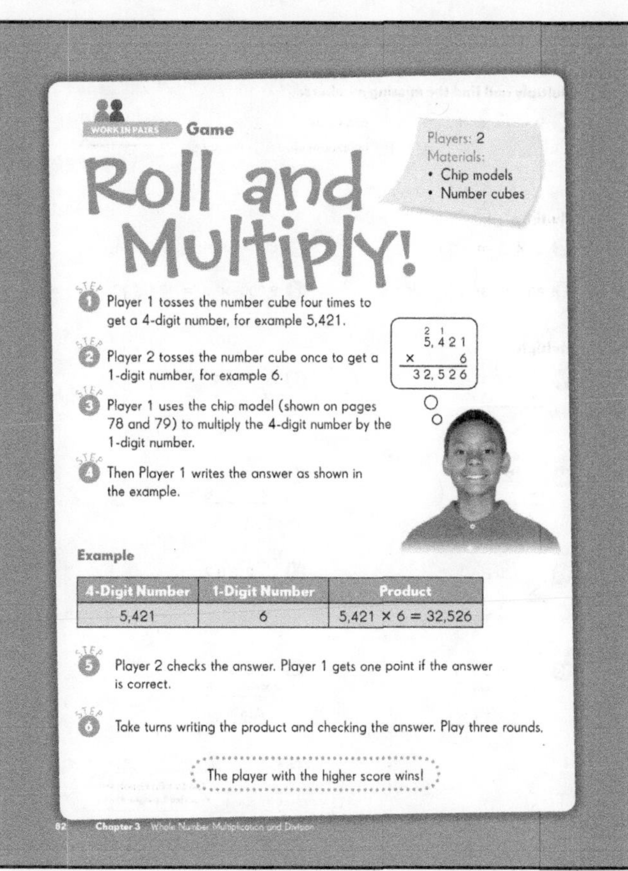

WORK IN PAIRS **Game**

Roll and Multiply!

Players: 2

Materials:
- Chip models
- Number cubes

STEP 1 Player 1 tosses the number cube four times to get a 4-digit number, for example 5,421.

STEP 2 Player 2 tosses the number cube once to get a 1-digit number, for example 6.

STEP 3 Player 1 uses the chip model (shown on pages 78 and 79) to multiply the 4-digit number by the 1-digit number.

STEP 4 Then Player 1 writes the answer as shown in the example.

$$\begin{array}{r} \scriptstyle 2\ 1\ \ \ \ \\ 5,421 \\ \times \qquad 6 \\ \hline 32,526 \end{array}$$

Example

4-Digit Number	1-Digit Number	Product
5,421	6	5,421 × 6 = 32,526

STEP 5 Player 2 checks the answer. Player 1 gets one point if the answer is correct.

STEP 6 Take turns writing the product and checking the answer. Play three rounds.

The player with the higher score wins!

82 Chapter 3 Whole Number Multiplication and Division

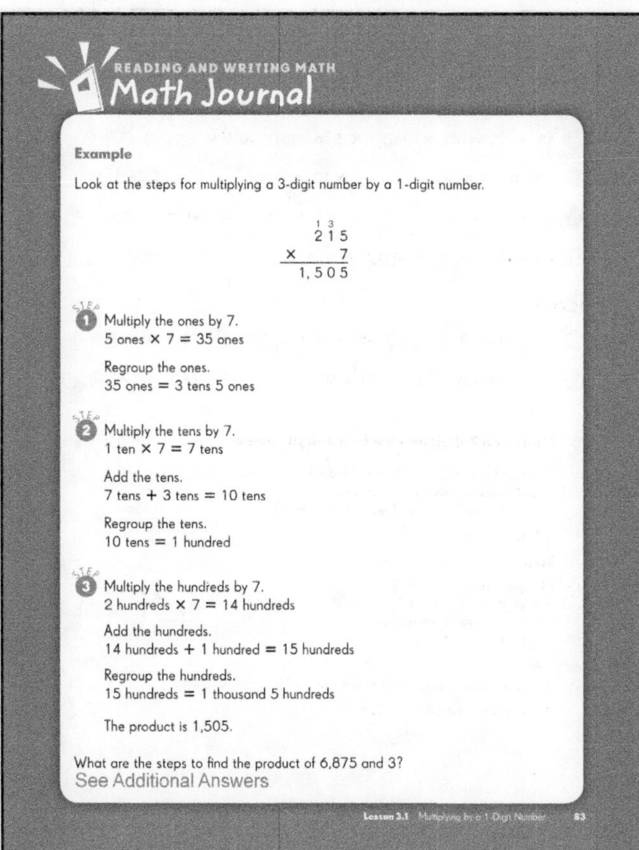

READING AND WRITING MATH

Math Journal

Example

Look at the steps for multiplying a 3-digit number by a 1-digit number.

$$\begin{array}{r} \scriptstyle 1\ 3\ \ \\ 215 \\ \times \quad\ 7 \\ \hline 1,505 \end{array}$$

STEP 1 Multiply the ones by 7.
5 ones × 7 = 35 ones

Regroup the ones.
35 ones = 3 tens 5 ones

STEP 2 Multiply the tens by 7.
1 ten × 7 = 7 tens

Add the tens.
7 tens + 3 tens = 10 tens

Regroup the tens.
10 tens = 1 hundred

STEP 3 Multiply the hundreds by 7.
2 hundreds × 7 = 14 hundreds

Add the hundreds.
14 hundreds + 1 hundred = 15 hundreds

Regroup the hundreds.
15 hundreds = 1 thousand 5 hundreds

The product is 1,505.

What are the steps to find the product of 6,875 and 3?
See Additional Answers

Lesson 3.1 Multiplying by a 1-Digit Number 83

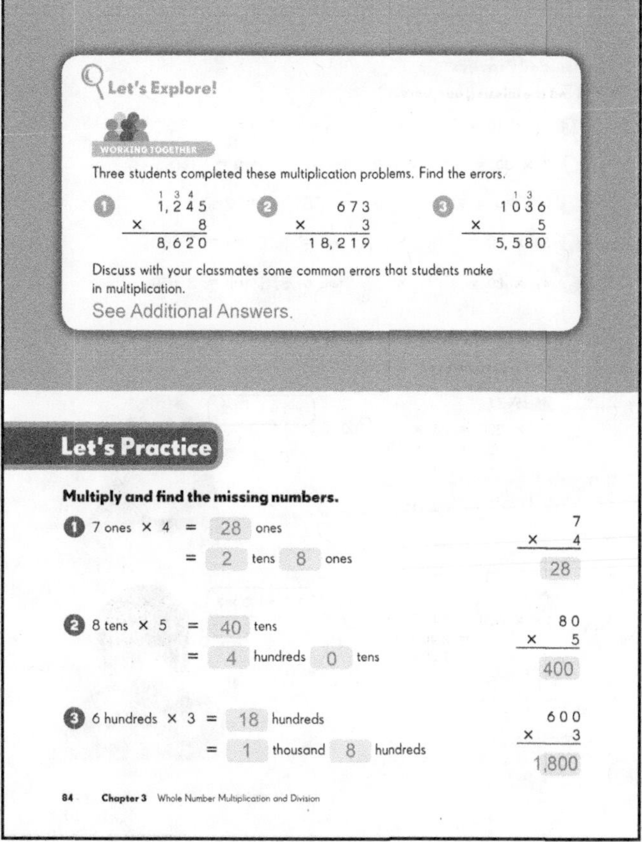

Let's Explore!

WORKING TOGETHER

Three students completed these multiplication problems. Find the errors.

1. $\begin{array}{r} \scriptstyle 1\ 3\ 4\ \ \\ 1,245 \\ \times \qquad 8 \\ \hline 8,620 \end{array}$
2. $\begin{array}{r} 673 \\ \times \quad 3 \\ \hline 18,219 \end{array}$
3. $\begin{array}{r} \scriptstyle 1\ 3\ \ \\ 1036 \\ \times \quad\ 5 \\ \hline 5,580 \end{array}$

Discuss with your classmates some common errors that students make in multiplication.
See Additional Answers.

Let's Practice

Multiply and find the missing numbers.

1. 7 ones × 4 = 28 ones
   = 2 tens 8 ones
   7 × 4 = 28
2. 8 tens × 5 = 40 tens
   = 4 hundreds 0 tens
   80 × 5 = 400
3. 6 hundreds × 3 = 18 hundreds
   = 1 thousand 8 hundreds
   600 × 3 = 1,800

84 Chapter 3 Whole Number Multiplication and Division

Chapter 3

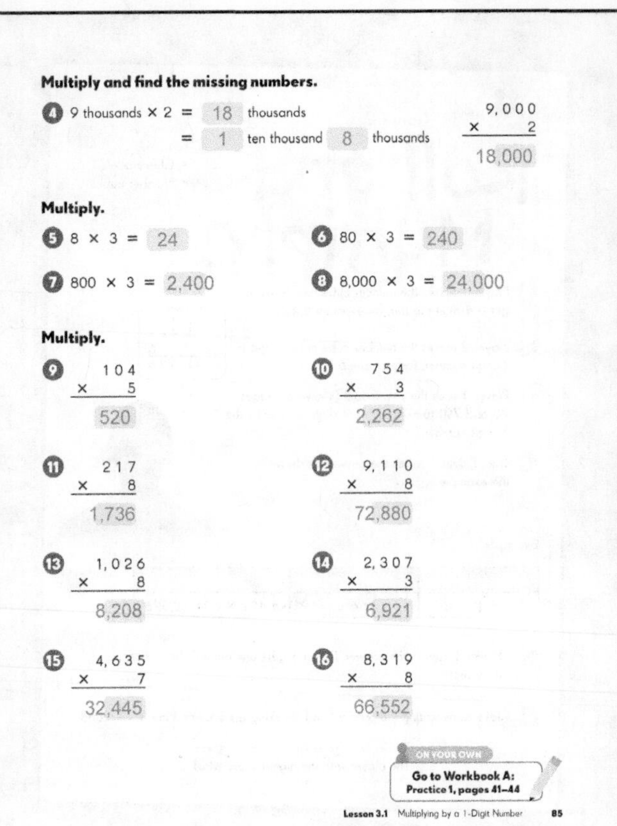

Chapter 3

Multiply and find the missing numbers.

4. 9 thousands × 2 = 18 thousands
   = 1 ten thousand 8 thousands

$$\begin{array}{r} 9,000 \\ \times \quad 2 \\ \hline 18,000 \end{array}$$

Multiply.

5. 8 × 3 = 24
6. 80 × 3 = 240
7. 800 × 3 = 2,400
8. 8,000 × 3 = 24,000

Multiply.

9. $\begin{array}{r} 104 \\ \times \quad 5 \\ \hline 520 \end{array}$
10. $\begin{array}{r} 754 \\ \times \quad 3 \\ \hline 2,262 \end{array}$
11. $\begin{array}{r} 217 \\ \times \quad 8 \\ \hline 1,736 \end{array}$
12. $\begin{array}{r} 9,110 \\ \times \quad 8 \\ \hline 72,880 \end{array}$
13. $\begin{array}{r} 1,026 \\ \times \quad 8 \\ \hline 8,208 \end{array}$
14. $\begin{array}{r} 2,307 \\ \times \quad 3 \\ \hline 6,921 \end{array}$
15. $\begin{array}{r} 4,635 \\ \times \quad 7 \\ \hline 32,445 \end{array}$
16. $\begin{array}{r} 8,319 \\ \times \quad 8 \\ \hline 66,552 \end{array}$

ON YOUR OWN
Go to Workbook A: Practice 1, pages 41–44

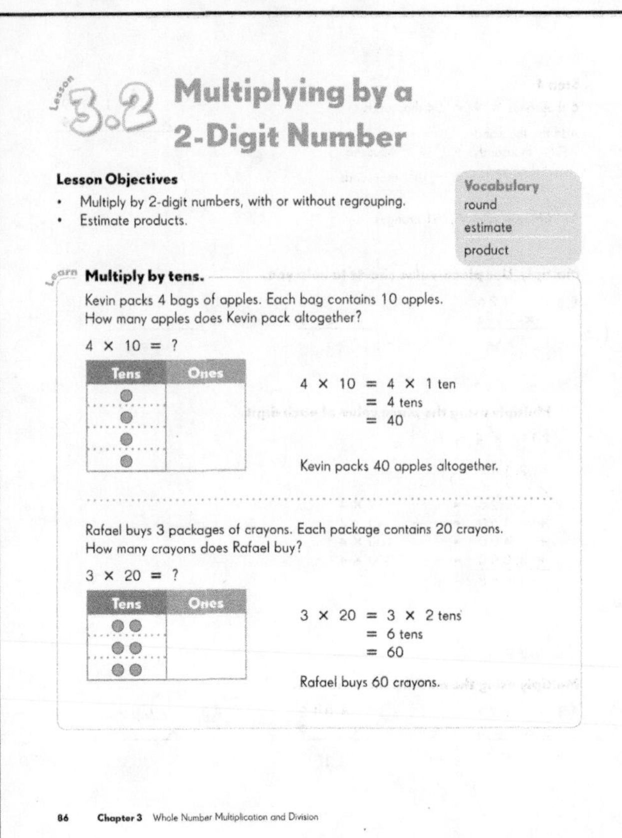

Lesson 3.2 Multiplying by a 2-Digit Number

Lesson Objectives
- Multiply by 2-digit numbers, with or without regrouping.
- Estimate products.

Vocabulary
round
estimate
product

Learn: Multiply by tens.

Kevin packs 4 bags of apples. Each bag contains 10 apples.
How many apples does Kevin pack altogether?

4 × 10 = ?

Tens	Ones
● ● ● ●	

4 × 10 = 4 × 1 ten
= 4 tens
= 40

Kevin packs 40 apples altogether.

Rafael buys 3 packages of crayons. Each package contains 20 crayons.
How many crayons does Rafael buy?

3 × 20 = ?

Tens	Ones
●● ●● ●●	

3 × 20 = 3 × 2 tens
= 6 tens
= 60

Rafael buys 60 crayons.

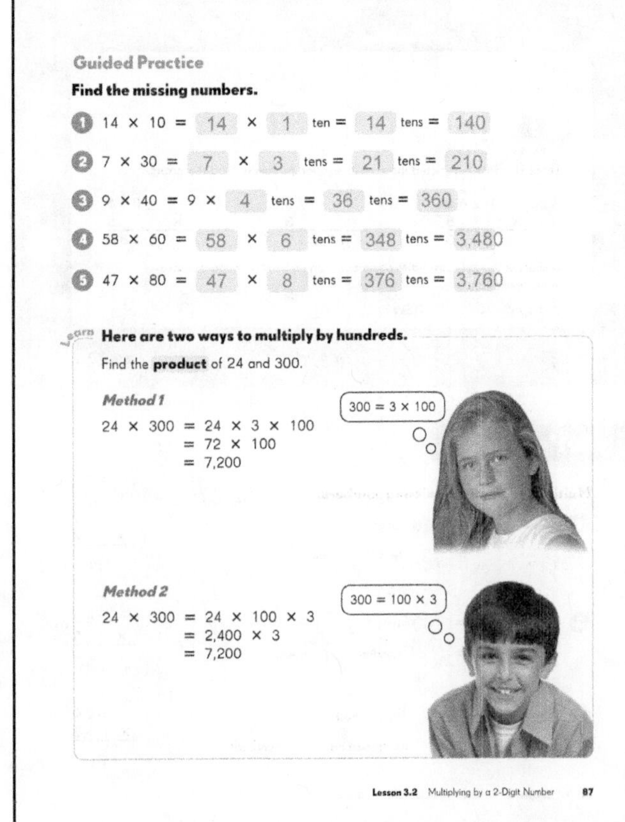

Guided Practice

Find the missing numbers.

1. 14 × 10 = 14 × 1 ten = 14 tens = 140
2. 7 × 30 = 7 × 3 tens = 21 tens = 210
3. 9 × 40 = 9 × 4 tens = 36 tens = 360
4. 58 × 60 = 58 × 6 tens = 348 tens = 3,480
5. 47 × 80 = 47 × 8 tens = 376 tens = 3,760

Learn: Here are two ways to multiply by hundreds.

Find the **product** of 24 and 300.

Method 1

24 × 300 = 24 × 3 × 100
= 72 × 100
= 7,200

300 = 3 × 100

Method 2

24 × 300 = 24 × 100 × 3
= 2,400 × 3
= 7,200

300 = 100 × 3

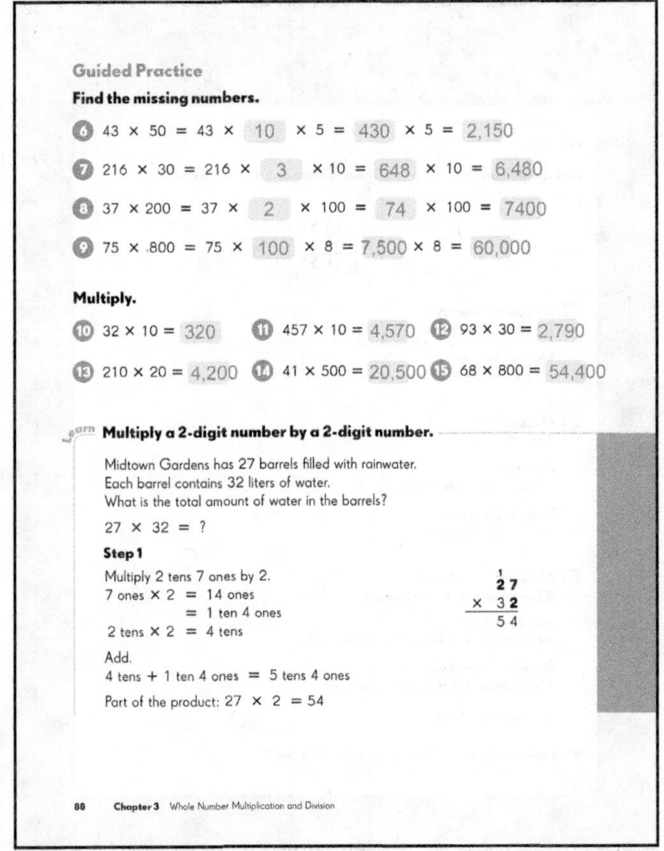

Guided Practice

Find the missing numbers.

6. 43 × 50 = 43 × 10 × 5 = 430 × 5 = 2,150
7. 216 × 30 = 216 × 3 × 10 = 648 × 10 = 6,480
8. 37 × 200 = 37 × 2 × 100 = 74 × 100 = 7400
9. 75 × 800 = 75 × 100 × 8 = 7,500 × 8 = 60,000

Multiply.

10. 32 × 10 = 320
11. 457 × 10 = 4,570
12. 93 × 30 = 2,790
13. 210 × 20 = 4,200
14. 41 × 500 = 20,500
15. 68 × 800 = 54,400

Learn: Multiply a 2-digit number by a 2-digit number.

Midtown Gardens has 27 barrels filled with rainwater.
Each barrel contains 32 liters of water.
What is the total amount of water in the barrels?

27 × 32 = ?

Step 1

Multiply 2 tens 7 ones by 2.
7 ones × 2 = 14 ones
= 1 ten 4 ones
2 tens × 2 = 4 tens

Add.
4 tens + 1 ten 4 ones = 5 tens 4 ones

Part of the product: 27 × 2 = 54

$$\begin{array}{r} {}^{1}\\ 27 \\ \times \ 32 \\ \hline 54 \end{array}$$

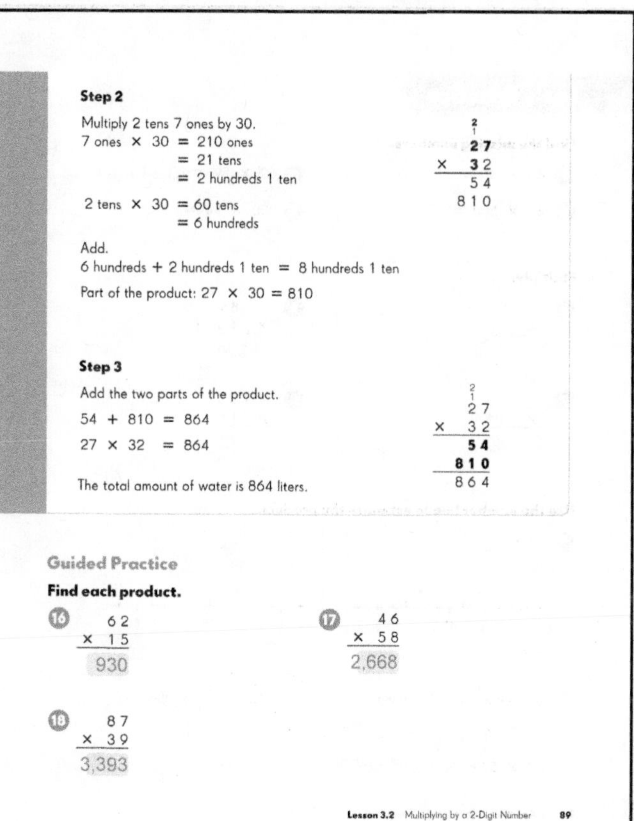

Step 2

Multiply 2 tens 7 ones by 30.

7 ones × 30 = 210 ones
= 21 tens
= 2 hundreds 1 ten

2 tens × 30 = 60 tens
= 6 hundreds

Add.

6 hundreds + 2 hundreds 1 ten = 8 hundreds 1 ten

Part of the product: 27 × 30 = 810

```
    2
    2 7
×   3 2
    5 4
  8 1 0
```

Step 3

Add the two parts of the product.

54 + 810 = 864

27 × 32 = 864

The total amount of water is 864 liters.

```
    2
    2 7
×   3 2
    5 4
  8 1 0
  8 6 4
```

Guided Practice

Find each product.

16. 62 × 15 = 930

17. 46 × 58 = 2,668

18. 87 × 39 = 3,393

Lesson 3.2 Multiplying by a 2-Digit Number 89

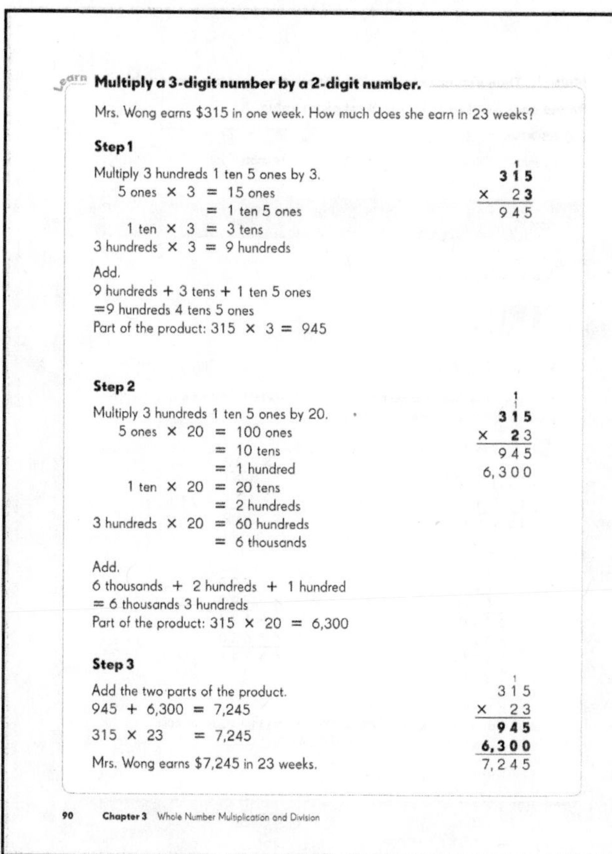

Learn Multiply a 3-digit number by a 2-digit number.

Mrs. Wong earns $315 in one week. How much does she earn in 23 weeks?

Step 1

Multiply 3 hundreds 1 ten 5 ones by 3.

5 ones × 3 = 15 ones
= 1 ten 5 ones

1 ten × 3 = 3 tens

3 hundreds × 3 = 9 hundreds

Add.

9 hundreds + 3 tens + 1 ten 5 ones
=9 hundreds 4 tens 5 ones

Part of the product: 315 × 3 = 945

```
    1
  3 1 5
×   2 3
  9 4 5
```

Step 2

Multiply 3 hundreds 1 ten 5 ones by 20.

5 ones × 20 = 100 ones
= 10 tens
= 1 hundred

1 ten × 20 = 20 tens
= 2 hundreds

3 hundreds × 20 = 60 hundreds
= 6 thousands

Add.

6 thousands + 2 hundreds + 1 hundred
= 6 thousands 3 hundreds

Part of the product: 315 × 20 = 6,300

```
      1
    3 1 5
×     2 3
    9 4 5
 6, 3 0 0
```

Step 3

Add the two parts of the product.

945 + 6,300 = 7,245

315 × 23 = 7,245

Mrs. Wong earns $7,245 in 23 weeks.

```
      1
    3 1 5
×     2 3
    9 4 5
 6, 3 0 0
 7, 2 4 5
```

90 Chapter 3 Whole Number Multiplication and Division

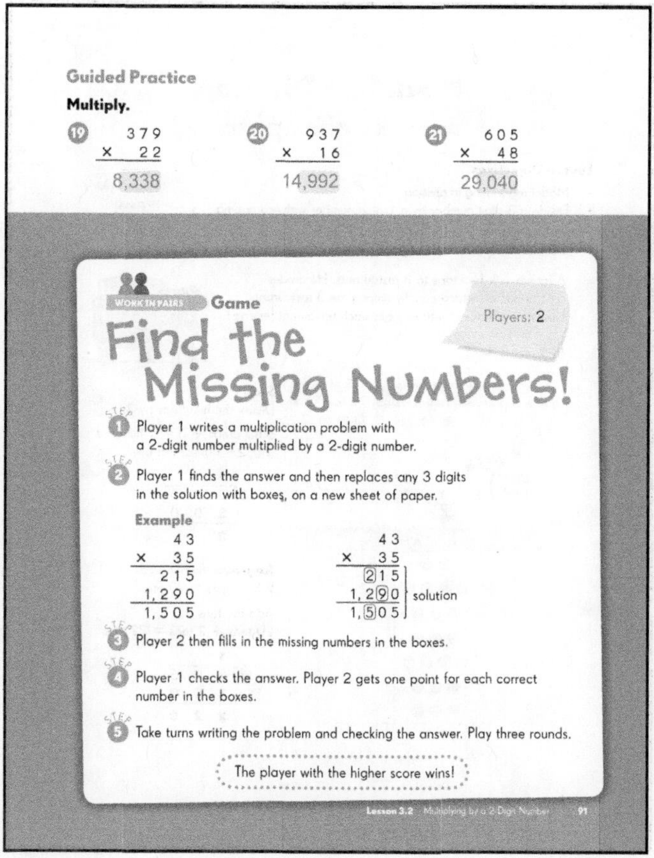

Guided Practice

Multiply.

19. 379 × 22 = 8,338

20. 937 × 16 = 14,992

21. 605 × 48 = 29,040

WORK IN PAIRS **Game**

Players: 2

Find the Missing Numbers!

1. Player 1 writes a multiplication problem with a 2-digit number multiplied by a 2-digit number.
2. Player 1 finds the answer and then replaces any 3 digits in the solution with boxes, on a new sheet of paper.

Example

```
      4 3              4 3
×     3 5        ×     3 5
    2 1 5            [2]1 5
 1, 2 9 0         1, 2[9]0   solution
 1, 5 0 5         1,[5]0 5
```

3. Player 2 then fills in the missing numbers in the boxes.
4. Player 1 checks the answer. Player 2 gets one point for each correct number in the boxes.
5. Take turns writing the problem and checking the answer. Play three rounds.

The player with the higher score wins!

Lesson 3.2 Multiplying by a 2-Digit Number 91

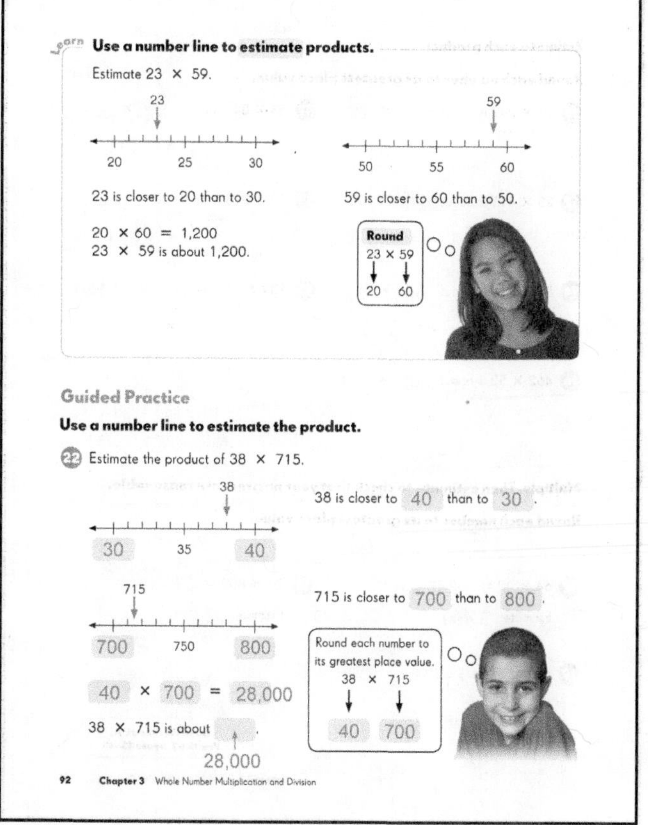

Learn Use a number line to estimate products.

Estimate 23 × 59.

23 is closer to 20 than to 30.

59 is closer to 60 than to 50.

20 × 60 = 1,200

23 × 59 is about 1,200.

Guided Practice

Use a number line to estimate the product.

22. Estimate the product of 38 × 715.

38 is closer to 40 than to 30.

715 is closer to 700 than to 800.

40 × 700 = 28,000

38 × 715 is about 28,000.

92 Chapter 3 Whole Number Multiplication and Division

Chapter 3

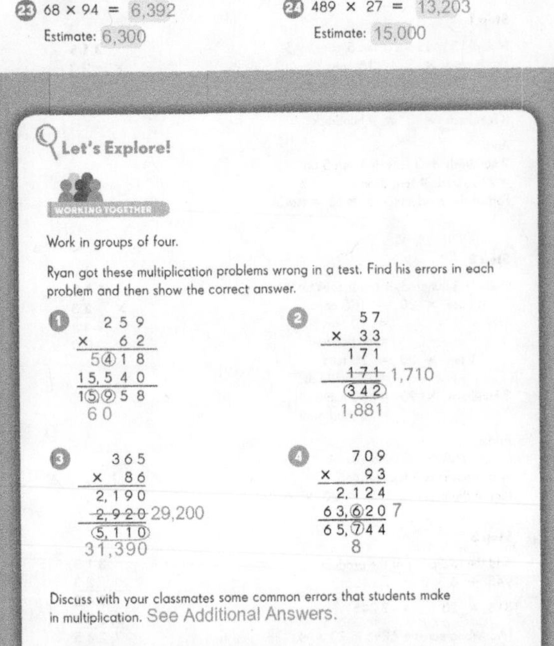

Multiply. Then estimate to check that your answers are reasonable.

Round each number to its greatest place value.

23. 68 × 94 = 6,392
Estimate: 6,300

24. 489 × 27 = 13,203
Estimate: 15,000

Let's Explore!

WORKING TOGETHER

Work in groups of four.

Ryan got these multiplication problems wrong in a test. Find his errors in each problem and then show the correct answer.

1. 259 × 62 — 5④18; 15,540; 1⑤⑨58 — corrections: 6 0
2. 57 × 33 — 171; ~~171~~ 1,710; ③④② — 1,881
3. 365 × 86 — 2,190; ~~2,920~~ 29,200; ⑤,1 1 0 — 31,390
4. 709 × 93 — 2,124; 63,⑥20 7; 65,⑦44 — 8

Discuss with your classmates some common errors that students make in multiplication. See Additional Answers.

Lesson 3.2 Multiplying by a 2-Digit Number 93

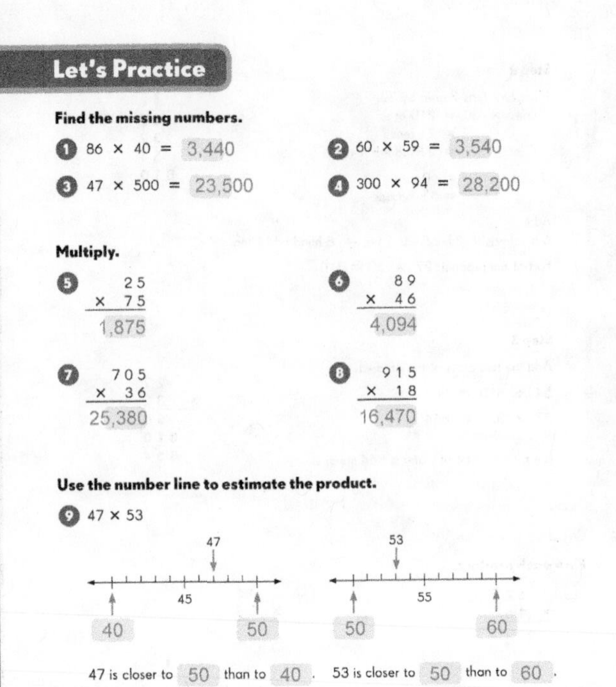

Let's Practice

Find the missing numbers.

1. 86 × 40 = 3,440
2. 60 × 59 = 3,540
3. 47 × 500 = 23,500
4. 300 × 94 = 28,200

Multiply.

5. 25 × 75 = 1,875
6. 89 × 46 = 4,094
7. 705 × 36 = 25,380
8. 915 × 18 = 16,470

Use the number line to estimate the product.

9. 47 × 53

47 is closer to 50 than to 40. 53 is closer to 50 than to 60.

50 × 50 = 2,500

47 × 53 is about 2,500.

94 Chapter 3 Whole Number Multiplication and Division

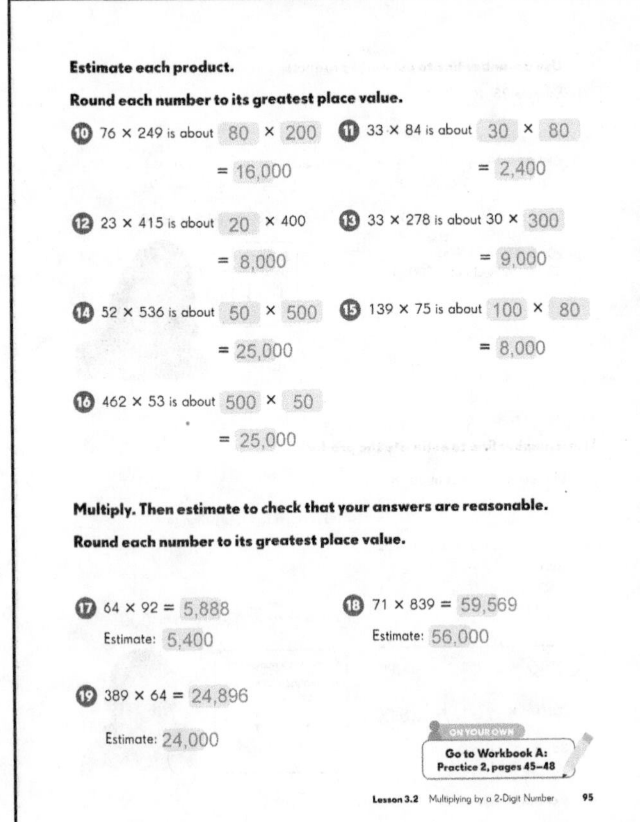

Estimate each product.

Round each number to its greatest place value.

10. 76 × 249 is about 80 × 200 = 16,000
11. 33 × 84 is about 30 × 80 = 2,400
12. 23 × 415 is about 20 × 400 = 8,000
13. 33 × 278 is about 30 × 300 = 9,000
14. 52 × 536 is about 50 × 500 = 25,000
15. 139 × 75 is about 100 × 80 = 8,000
16. 462 × 53 is about 500 × 50 = 25,000

Multiply. Then estimate to check that your answers are reasonable.

Round each number to its greatest place value.

17. 64 × 92 = 5,888
Estimate: 5,400

18. 71 × 839 = 59,569
Estimate: 56,000

19. 389 × 64 = 24,896
Estimate: 24,000

ON YOUR OWN
Go to Workbook A: Practice 2, pages 45–48

Lesson 3.2 Multiplying by a 2-Digit Number 95

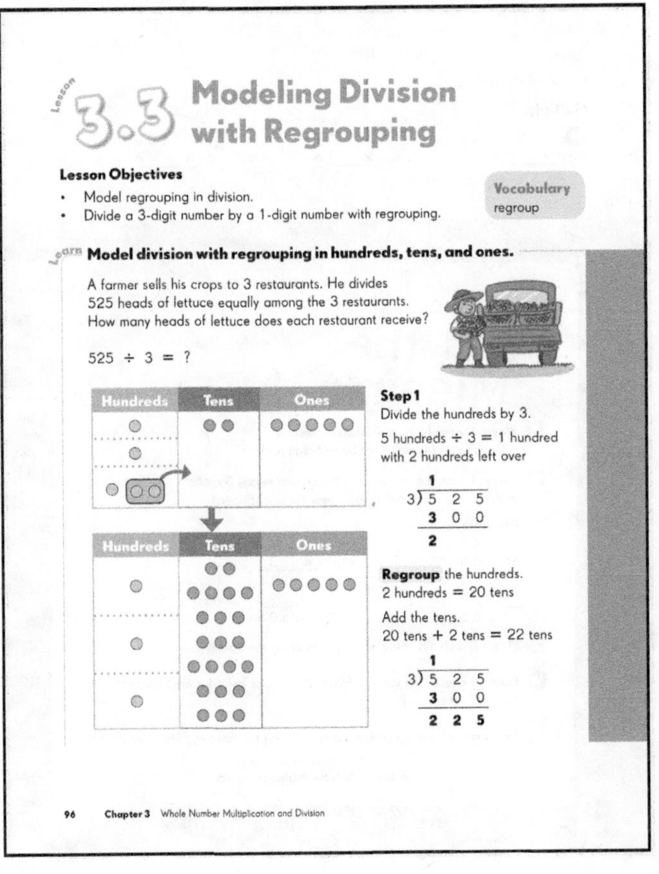

Lesson 3.3 Modeling Division with Regrouping

Lesson Objectives

- Model regrouping in division.
- Divide a 3-digit number by a 1-digit number with regrouping.

Vocabulary
regroup

Learn Model division with regrouping in hundreds, tens, and ones.

A farmer sells his crops to 3 restaurants. He divides 525 heads of lettuce equally among the 3 restaurants. How many heads of lettuce does each restaurant receive?

525 ÷ 3 = ?

Step 1
Divide the hundreds by 3.
5 hundreds ÷ 3 = 1 hundred with 2 hundreds left over

$$\begin{array}{r} 1 \\ 3\overline{)525} \\ \underline{300} \\ 2 \end{array}$$

Regroup the hundreds.
2 hundreds = 20 tens
Add the tens.
20 tens + 2 tens = 22 tens

$$\begin{array}{r} 1 \\ 3\overline{)525} \\ \underline{300} \\ 225 \end{array}$$

96 Chapter 3 Whole Number Multiplication and Division

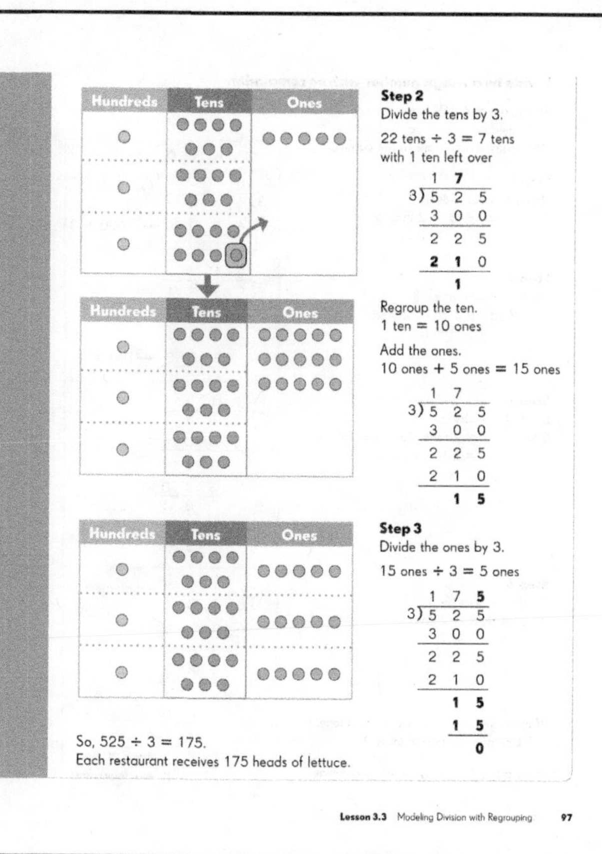

Hundreds	Tens	Ones

Step 2
Divide the tens by 3.
22 tens ÷ 3 = 7 tens with 1 ten left over

$$\begin{array}{r} 17 \\ 3\overline{)525} \\ \underline{300} \\ 225 \\ \underline{210} \\ 1 \end{array}$$

Regroup the ten.
1 ten = 10 ones
Add the ones.
10 ones + 5 ones = 15 ones

$$\begin{array}{r} 17 \\ 3\overline{)525} \\ \underline{300} \\ 225 \\ \underline{210} \\ 15 \end{array}$$

Step 3
Divide the ones by 3.
15 ones ÷ 3 = 5 ones

$$\begin{array}{r} 175 \\ 3\overline{)525} \\ \underline{300} \\ 225 \\ \underline{210} \\ 15 \\ \underline{15} \\ 0 \end{array}$$

So, 525 ÷ 3 = 175.
Each restaurant receives 175 heads of lettuce.

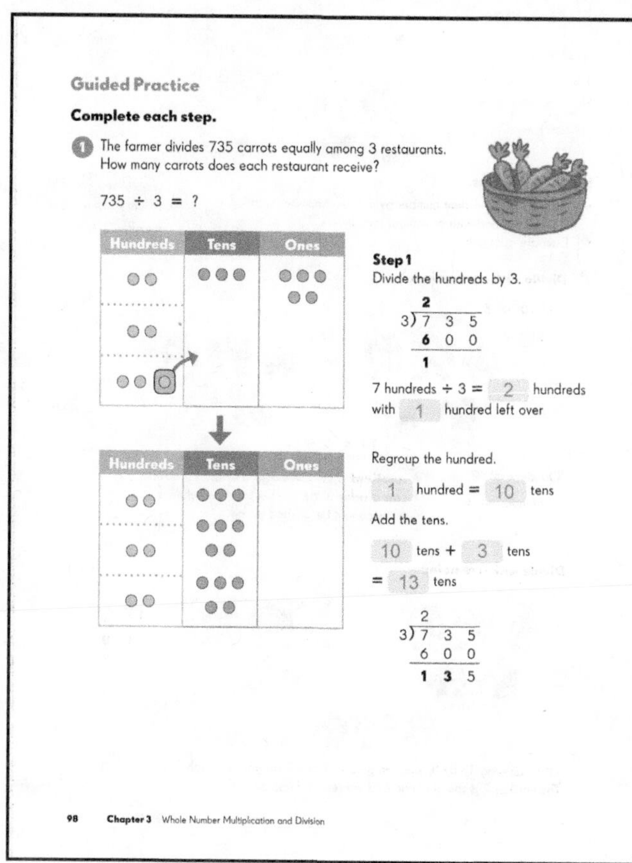

Guided Practice

Complete each step.

1. The farmer divides 735 carrots equally among 3 restaurants. How many carrots does each restaurant receive?

735 ÷ 3 = ?

Step 1
Divide the hundreds by 3.

$$\begin{array}{r} 2 \\ 3\overline{)735} \\ \underline{600} \\ 1 \end{array}$$

7 hundreds ÷ 3 = 2 hundreds with 1 hundred left over

Regroup the hundred.
1 hundred = 10 tens
Add the tens.
10 tens + 3 tens
= 13 tens

$$\begin{array}{r} 2 \\ 3\overline{)735} \\ \underline{600} \\ 135 \end{array}$$

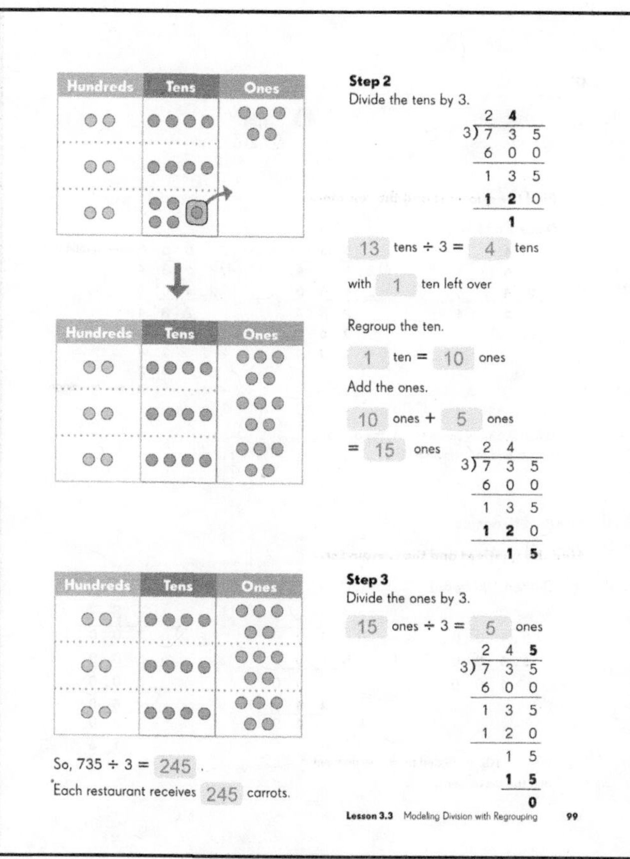

Step 2
Divide the tens by 3.

$$\begin{array}{r} 24 \\ 3\overline{)735} \\ \underline{600} \\ 135 \\ \underline{120} \\ 1 \end{array}$$

13 tens ÷ 3 = 4 tens
with 1 ten left over

Regroup the ten.
1 ten = 10 ones
Add the ones.
10 ones + 5 ones
= 15 ones

$$\begin{array}{r} 24 \\ 3\overline{)735} \\ \underline{600} \\ 135 \\ \underline{120} \\ 15 \end{array}$$

Step 3
Divide the ones by 3.
15 ones ÷ 3 = 5 ones

$$\begin{array}{r} 245 \\ 3\overline{)735} \\ \underline{600} \\ 135 \\ \underline{120} \\ 15 \\ \underline{15} \\ 0 \end{array}$$

So, 735 ÷ 3 = 245.
Each restaurant receives 245 carrots.

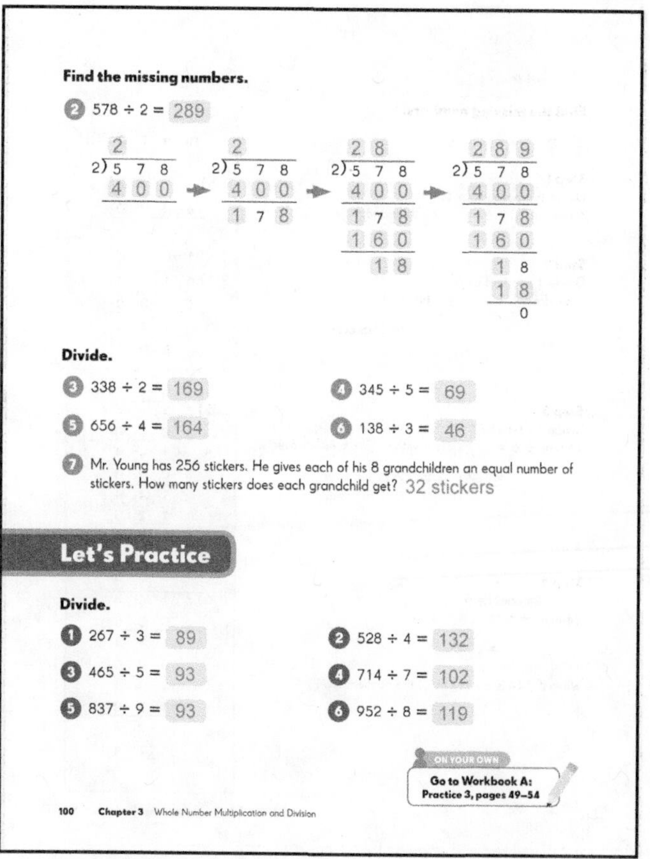

Find the missing numbers.

2. 578 ÷ 2 = 289

$$\begin{array}{r} 2 \\ 2\overline{)578} \\ \underline{400} \end{array} \rightarrow \begin{array}{r} 2 \\ 2\overline{)578} \\ \underline{400} \\ 178 \end{array} \rightarrow \begin{array}{r} 28 \\ 2\overline{)578} \\ \underline{400} \\ 178 \\ \underline{160} \\ 18 \end{array} \rightarrow \begin{array}{r} 289 \\ 2\overline{)578} \\ \underline{400} \\ 178 \\ \underline{160} \\ 18 \\ \underline{18} \\ 0 \end{array}$$

Divide.

3. 338 ÷ 2 = 169
4. 345 ÷ 5 = 69
5. 656 ÷ 4 = 164
6. 138 ÷ 3 = 46
7. Mr. Young has 256 stickers. He gives each of his 8 grandchildren an equal number of stickers. How many stickers does each grandchild get? 32 stickers

Let's Practice

Divide.

1. 267 ÷ 3 = 89
2. 528 ÷ 4 = 132
3. 465 ÷ 5 = 93
4. 714 ÷ 7 = 102
5. 837 ÷ 9 = 93
6. 952 ÷ 8 = 119

ON YOUR OWN
Go to Workbook A: Practice 3, pages 49–54

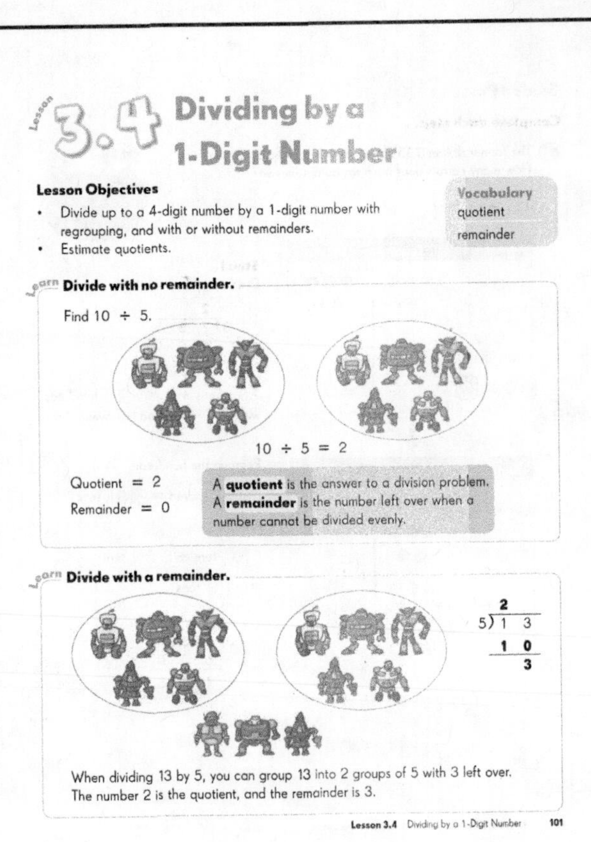

Lesson 3.4 Dividing by a 1-Digit Number

Lesson Objectives
- Divide up to a 4-digit number by a 1-digit number with regrouping, and with or without remainders.
- Estimate quotients.

Vocabulary
quotient
remainder

Learn Divide with no remainder.

Find 10 ÷ 5.

10 ÷ 5 = 2

Quotient = 2
Remainder = 0

A **quotient** is the answer to a division problem.
A **remainder** is the number left over when a number cannot be divided evenly.

Learn Divide with a remainder.

```
   2
5)1 3
  1 0
    3
```

When dividing 13 by 5, you can group 13 into 2 groups of 5 with 3 left over.
The number 2 is the quotient, and the remainder is 3.

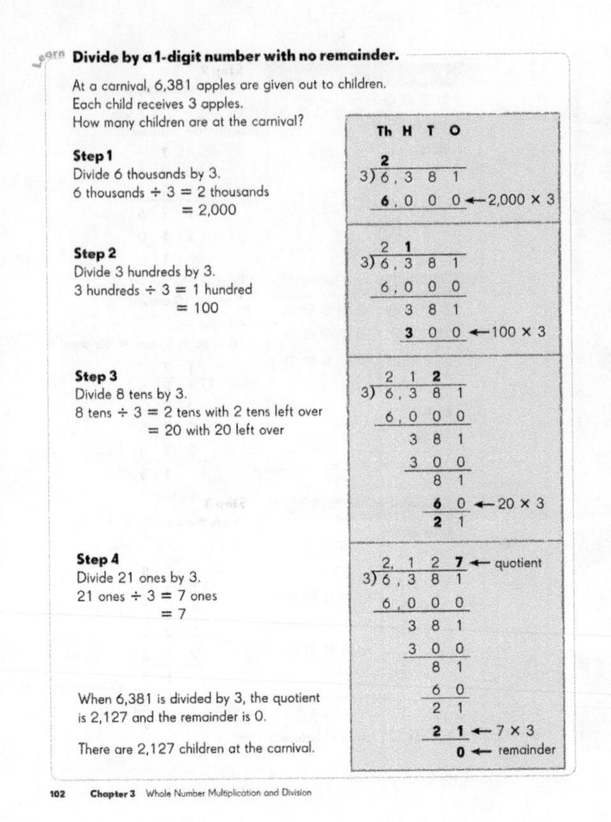

Learn Divide by a 1-digit number with no remainder.

At a carnival, 6,381 apples are given out to children.
Each child receives 3 apples.
How many children are at the carnival?

Step 1
Divide 6 thousands by 3.
6 thousands ÷ 3 = 2 thousands
= 2,000

```
Th H T O
   2
3)6,3 8 1
  6,0 0 0  ← 2,000 × 3
```

Step 2
Divide 3 hundreds by 3.
3 hundreds ÷ 3 = 1 hundred
= 100

```
   2 1
3)6,3 8 1
  6,0 0 0
    3 8 1
    3 0 0  ← 100 × 3
```

Step 3
Divide 8 tens by 3.
8 tens ÷ 3 = 2 tens with 2 tens left over
= 20 with 20 left over

```
   2 1 2
3)6,3 8 1
  6,0 0 0
    3 8 1
    3 0 0
      8 1
      6 0  ← 20 × 3
      2 1
```

Step 4
Divide 21 ones by 3.
21 ones ÷ 3 = 7 ones
= 7

```
   2,1 2 7  ← quotient
3)6,3 8 1
  6,0 0 0
    3 8 1
    3 0 0
      8 1
      6 0
      2 1
      2 1  ← 7 × 3
        0  ← remainder
```

When 6,381 is divided by 3, the quotient is 2,127 and the remainder is 0.

There are 2,127 children at the carnival.

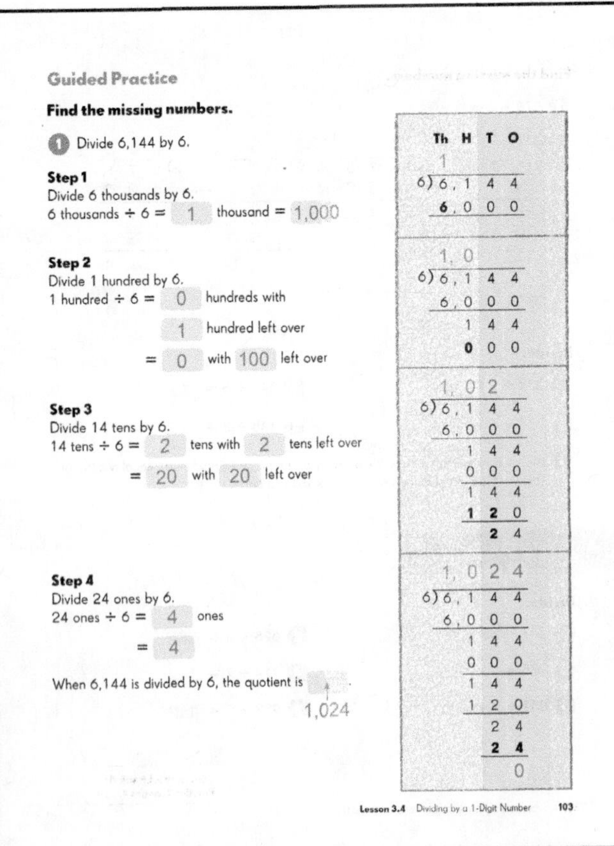

Guided Practice

Find the missing numbers.

1 Divide 6,144 by 6.

Step 1
Divide 6 thousands by 6.
6 thousands ÷ 6 = 1 thousand = 1,000

```
Th H T O
   1
6)6,1 4 4
  6,0 0 0
```

Step 2
Divide 1 hundred by 6.
1 hundred ÷ 6 = 0 hundreds with
1 hundred left over
= 0 with 100 left over

```
   1,0
6)6,1 4 4
  6,0 0 0
    1 4 4
    0 0 0
```

Step 3
Divide 14 tens by 6.
14 tens ÷ 6 = 2 tens with 2 tens left over
= 20 with 20 left over

```
   1,0 2
6)6,1 4 4
  6,0 0 0
    1 4 4
    0 0 0
    1 4 4
    1 2 0
      2 4
```

Step 4
Divide 24 ones by 6.
24 ones ÷ 6 = 4 ones
= 4

When 6,144 is divided by 6, the quotient is 1,024.

```
   1,0 2 4
6)6,1 4 4
  6,0 0 0
    1 4 4
    0 0 0
    1 4 4
    1 2 0
      2 4
      2 4
        0
```


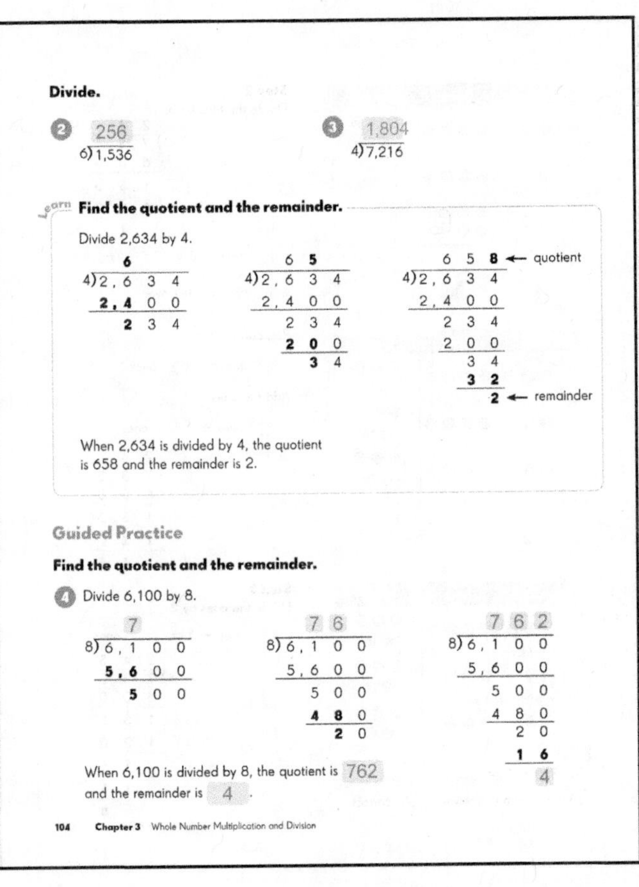

Divide.

2 6)1,536 = 256

3 4)7,216 = 1,804

Learn Find the quotient and the remainder.

Divide 2,634 by 4.

```
   6
4)2,6 3 4
  2,4 0 0
    2 3 4
```

```
   6 5
4)2,6 3 4
  2,4 0 0
    2 3 4
    2 0 0
      3 4
```

```
   6 5 8  ← quotient
4)2,6 3 4
  2,4 0 0
    2 3 4
    2 0 0
      3 4
      3 2
        2  ← remainder
```

When 2,634 is divided by 4, the quotient is 658 and the remainder is 2.

Guided Practice

Find the quotient and the remainder.

4 Divide 6,100 by 8.

```
   7
8)6,1 0 0
  5,6 0 0
    5 0 0
```

```
   7 6
8)6,1 0 0
  5,6 0 0
    5 0 0
    4 8 0
      2 0
```

```
   7 6 2
8)6,1 0 0
  5,6 0 0
    5 0 0
    4 8 0
      2 0
      1 6
        4
```

When 6,100 is divided by 8, the quotient is 762 and the remainder is 4.

Divide. Find each quotient (Q) and remainder (R).

5. 5,608 ÷ 6
   Q = 934 R = 4
6. 2,117 ÷ 7
   Q = 302 R = 3
7. 4,135 ÷ 3
   Q = 1,378 R = 1
8. 4,165 ÷ 5
   Q = 833 R = 0
9. 3,796 ÷ 9
   Q = 421 R = 7
10. 5,084 ÷ 7
   Q = 726 R = 2

Find each quotient and remainder.

11. 4)423 = 105 R 3
12. 9)1,803 = 200 R 3

Learn: Estimate quotients using related multiplication facts.

Find 438 ÷ 5.

438 (number line: 400, 450, 500)

Related multiplication facts:
5 × 8 = 40 5 × 9 = 45
438 ÷ 5 is about 450 ÷ 5.
The estimated quotient is 90.

5 × 80 = 400
5 × 90 = 450
438 is closer to 450 than to 400.

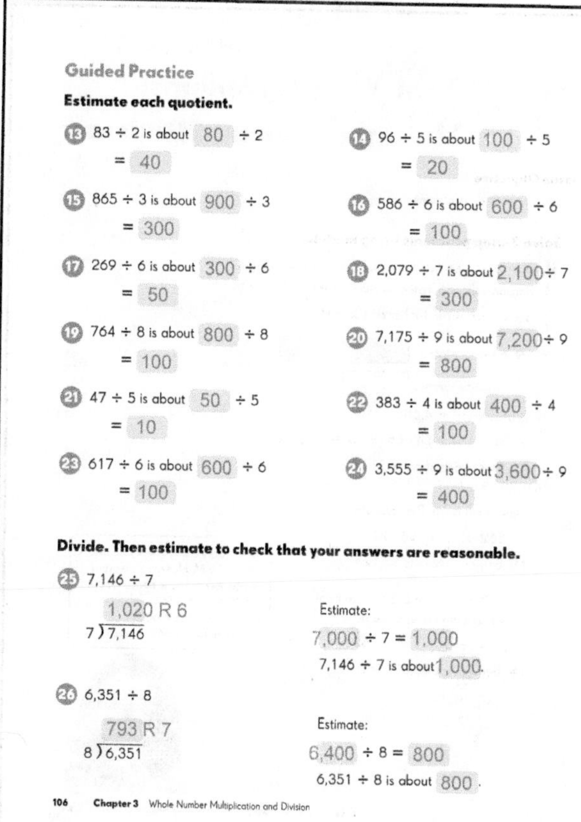

Guided Practice

Estimate each quotient.

13. 83 ÷ 2 is about 80 ÷ 2 = 40
14. 96 ÷ 5 is about 100 ÷ 5 = 20
15. 865 ÷ 3 is about 900 ÷ 3 = 300
16. 586 ÷ 6 is about 600 ÷ 6 = 100
17. 269 ÷ 6 is about 300 ÷ 6 = 50
18. 2,079 ÷ 7 is about 2,100 ÷ 7 = 300
19. 764 ÷ 8 is about 800 ÷ 8 = 100
20. 7,175 ÷ 9 is about 7,200 ÷ 9 = 800
21. 47 ÷ 5 is about 50 ÷ 5 = 10
22. 383 ÷ 4 is about 400 ÷ 4 = 100
23. 617 ÷ 6 is about 600 ÷ 6 = 100
24. 3,555 ÷ 9 is about 3,600 ÷ 9 = 400

Divide. Then estimate to check that your answers are reasonable.

25. 7,146 ÷ 7
   7)7,146 = 1,020 R 6
   Estimate:
   7,000 ÷ 7 = 1,000
   7,146 ÷ 7 is about 1,000.
26. 6,351 ÷ 8
   8)6,351 = 793 R 7
   Estimate:
   6,400 ÷ 8 = 800
   6,351 ÷ 8 is about 800.

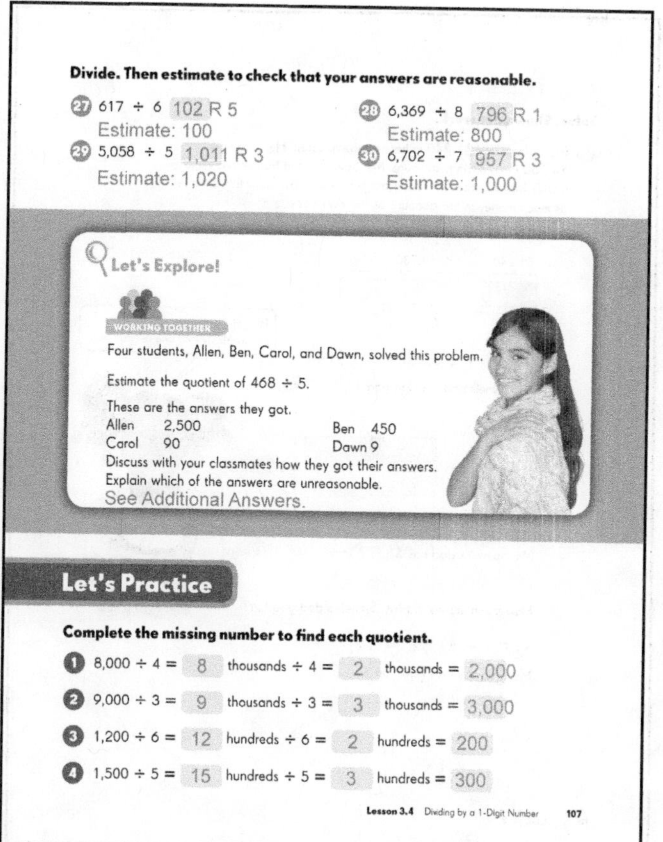

Divide. Then estimate to check that your answers are reasonable.

27. 617 ÷ 6 102 R 5
   Estimate: 100
28. 6,369 ÷ 8 796 R 1
   Estimate: 800
29. 5,058 ÷ 5 1,011 R 3
   Estimate: 1,020
30. 6,702 ÷ 7 957 R 3
   Estimate: 1,000

Let's Explore!

WORKING TOGETHER

Four students, Allen, Ben, Carol, and Dawn, solved this problem.

Estimate the quotient of 468 ÷ 5.

These are the answers they got.

Allen 2,500 Ben 450
Carol 90 Dawn 9

Discuss with your classmates how they got their answers.
Explain which of the answers are unreasonable.
See Additional Answers.

Let's Practice

Complete the missing number to find each quotient.

1. 8,000 ÷ 4 = 8 thousands ÷ 4 = 2 thousands = 2,000
2. 9,000 ÷ 3 = 9 thousands ÷ 3 = 3 thousands = 3,000
3. 1,200 ÷ 6 = 12 hundreds ÷ 6 = 2 hundreds = 200
4. 1,500 ÷ 5 = 15 hundreds ÷ 5 = 3 hundreds = 300

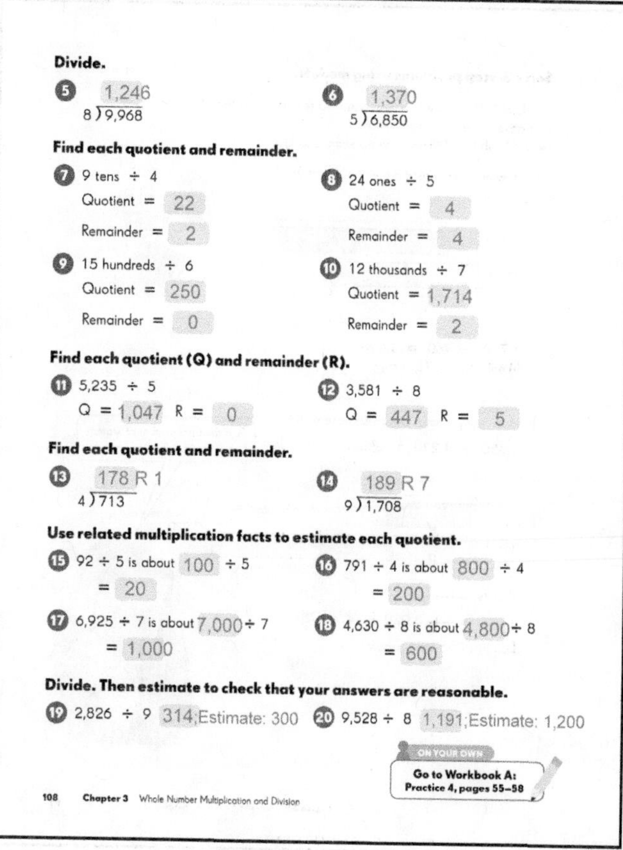

Divide.

5. 8)9,968 = 1,246
6. 5)6,850 = 1,370

Find each quotient and remainder.

7. 9 tens ÷ 4
   Quotient = 22
   Remainder = 2
8. 24 ones ÷ 5
   Quotient = 4
   Remainder = 4
9. 15 hundreds ÷ 6
   Quotient = 250
   Remainder = 0
10. 12 thousands ÷ 7
   Quotient = 1,714
   Remainder = 2

Find each quotient (Q) and remainder (R).

11. 5,235 ÷ 5
   Q = 1,047 R = 0
12. 3,581 ÷ 8
   Q = 447 R = 5

Find each quotient and remainder.

13. 4)713 = 178 R 1
14. 9)1,708 = 189 R 7

Use related multiplication facts to estimate each quotient.

15. 92 ÷ 5 is about 100 ÷ 5 = 20
16. 791 ÷ 4 is about 800 ÷ 4 = 200
17. 6,925 ÷ 7 is about 7,000 ÷ 7 = 1,000
18. 4,630 ÷ 8 is about 4,800 ÷ 8 = 600

Divide. Then estimate to check that your answers are reasonable.

19. 2,826 ÷ 9 314; Estimate: 300
20. 9,528 ÷ 8 1,191; Estimate: 1,200

ON YOUR OWN
Go to Workbook A: Practice 4, pages 55–58

Chapter 3

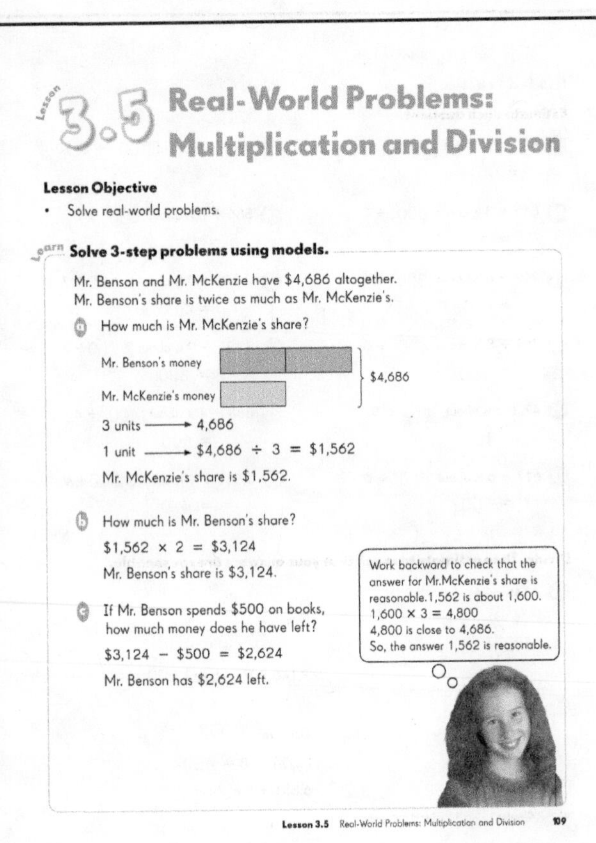

Lesson 3.5 Real-World Problems: Multiplication and Division

Lesson Objective

- Solve real-world problems.

Learn Solve 3-step problems using models.

Mr. Benson and Mr. McKenzie have $4,686 altogether.
Mr. Benson's share is twice as much as Mr. McKenzie's.

a) How much is Mr. McKenzie's share?

Mr. Benson's money
Mr. McKenzie's money
$4,686

3 units ⟶ 4,686
1 unit ⟶ $4,686 ÷ 3 = $1,562
Mr. McKenzie's share is $1,562.

b) How much is Mr. Benson's share?
$1,562 × 2 = $3,124
Mr. Benson's share is $3,124.

c) If Mr. Benson spends $500 on books, how much money does he have left?
$3,124 − $500 = $2,624
Mr. Benson has $2,624 left.

Work backward to check that the answer for Mr.McKenzie's share is reasonable. 1,562 is about 1,600.
1,600 × 3 = 4,800
4,800 is close to 4,686.
So, the answer 1,562 is reasonable.

Lesson 3.5 Real-World Problems: Multiplication and Division 109

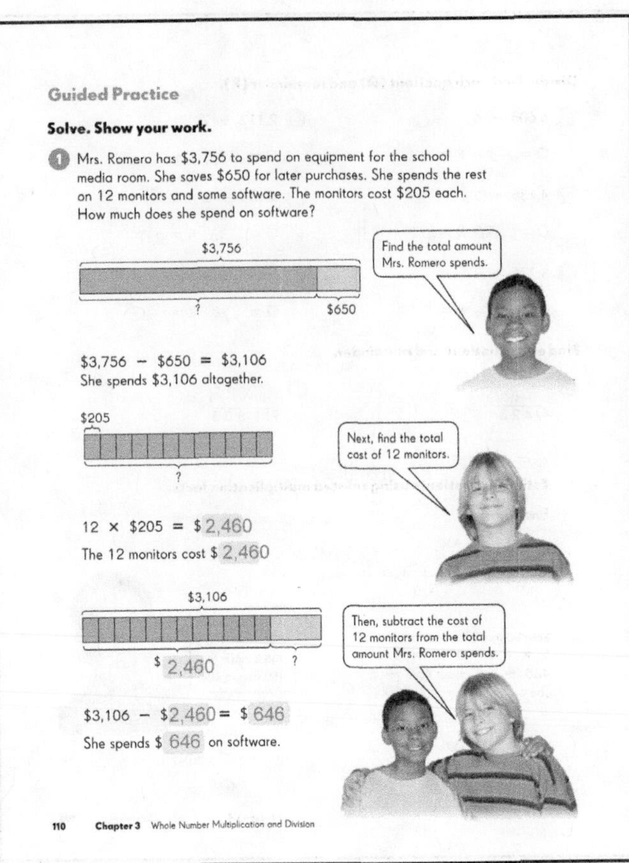

Guided Practice

Solve. Show your work.

1. Mrs. Romero has $3,756 to spend on equipment for the school media room. She saves $650 for later purchases. She spends the rest on 12 monitors and some software. The monitors cost $205 each. How much does she spend on software?

$3,756
?
$650
Find the total amount Mrs. Romero spends.

$3,756 − $650 = $3,106
She spends $3,106 altogether.

$205
?
Next, find the total cost of 12 monitors.

12 × $205 = $ 2,460
The 12 monitors cost $ 2,460

$3,106
$ 2,460
?
Then, subtract the cost of 12 monitors from the total amount Mrs. Romero spends.

$3,106 − $2,460 = $ 646
She spends $ 646 on software.

110 Chapter 3 Whole Number Multiplication and Division

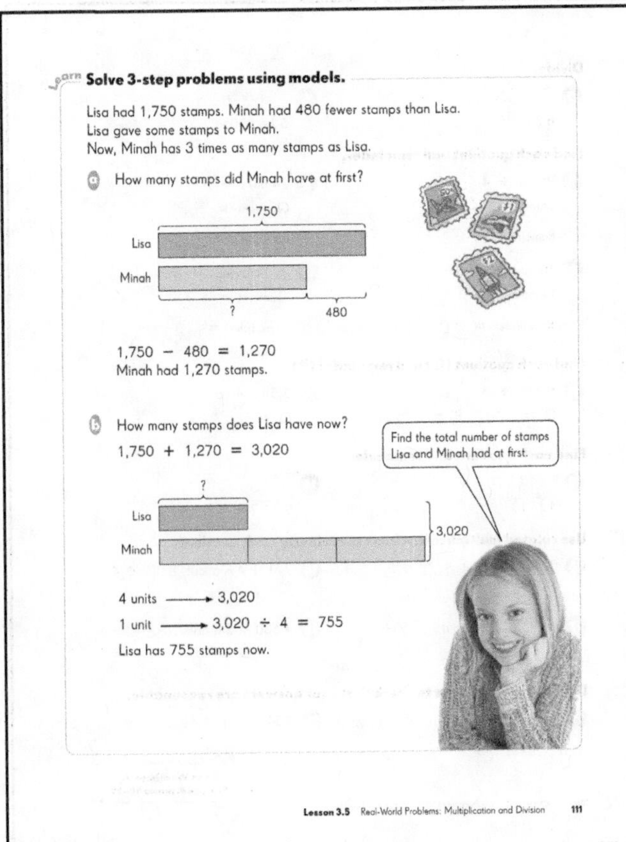

Learn Solve 3-step problems using models.

Lisa had 1,750 stamps. Minah had 480 fewer stamps than Lisa.
Lisa gave some stamps to Minah.
Now, Minah has 3 times as many stamps as Lisa.

a) How many stamps did Minah have at first?

1,750
Lisa
Minah
?
480

1,750 − 480 = 1,270
Minah had 1,270 stamps.

b) How many stamps does Lisa have now?
1,750 + 1,270 = 3,020

Find the total number of stamps Lisa and Minah had at first.
?
Lisa
Minah
3,020

4 units ⟶ 3,020
1 unit ⟶ 3,020 ÷ 4 = 755
Lisa has 755 stamps now.

Lesson 3.5 Real-World Problems: Multiplication and Division 111

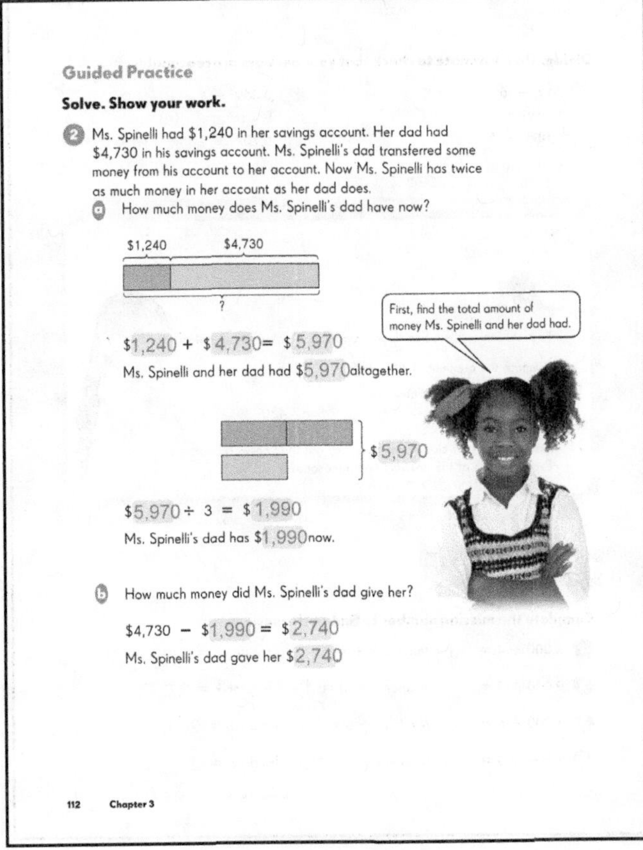

Guided Practice

Solve. Show your work.

2. Ms. Spinelli had $1,240 in her savings account. Her dad had $4,730 in his savings account. Ms. Spinelli's dad transferred some money from his account to her account. Now Ms. Spinelli has twice as much money in her account as her dad does.

a) How much money does Ms. Spinelli's dad have now?

$1,240
$4,730
?
First, find the total amount of money Ms. Spinelli and her dad had.

$1,240 + $4,730 = $5,970
Ms. Spinelli and her dad had $5,970 altogether.

$5,970

$5,970 ÷ 3 = $1,990
Ms. Spinelli's dad has $1,990 now.

b) How much money did Ms. Spinelli's dad give her?
$4,730 − $1,990 = $2,740
Ms. Spinelli's dad gave her $2,740

112 Chapter 3

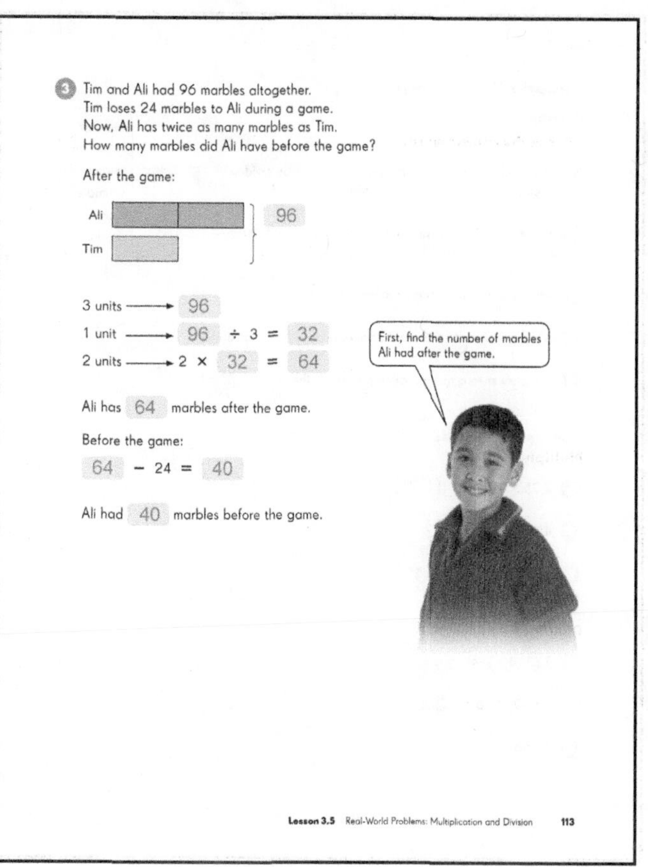

3. Tim and Ali had 96 marbles altogether.
Tim loses 24 marbles to Ali during a game.
Now, Ali has twice as many marbles as Tim.
How many marbles did Ali have before the game?

After the game:

Ali
Tim
96

3 units → 96
1 unit → 96 ÷ 3 = 32
2 units → 2 × 32 = 64

First, find the number of marbles Ali had after the game.

Ali has 64 marbles after the game.

Before the game:

64 − 24 = 40

Ali had 40 marbles before the game.

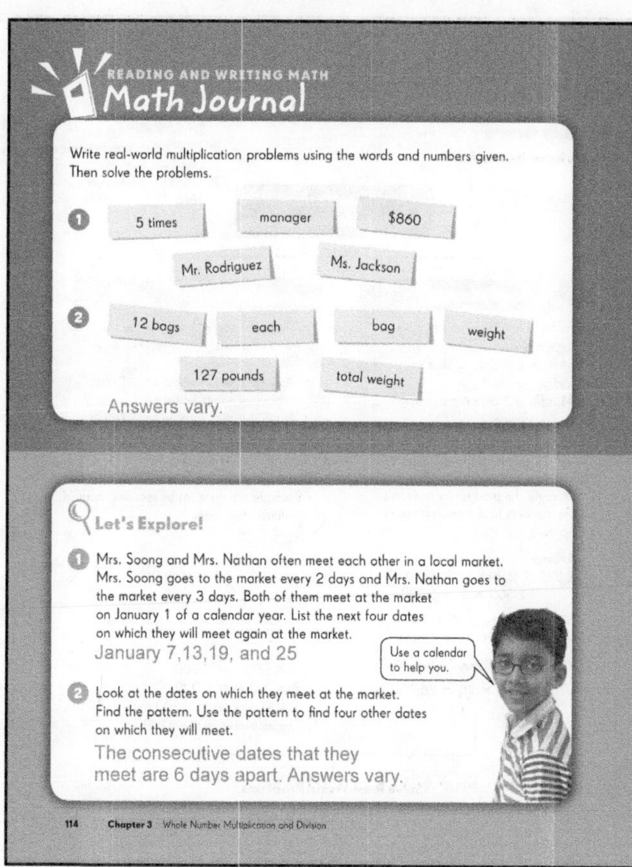

READING AND WRITING MATH

Math Journal

Write real-world multiplication problems using the words and numbers given. Then solve the problems.

1. 5 times | manager | $860 | Mr. Rodriguez | Ms. Jackson
2. 12 bags | each | bag | weight | 127 pounds | total weight

Answers vary.

Let's Explore!

1. Mrs. Soong and Mrs. Nathan often meet each other in a local market. Mrs. Soong goes to the market every 2 days and Mrs. Nathan goes to the market every 3 days. Both of them meet at the market on January 1 of a calendar year. List the next four dates on which they will meet again at the market.
January 7,13,19, and 25

Use a calendar to help you.

2. Look at the dates on which they meet at the market. Find the pattern. Use the pattern to find four other dates on which they will meet.
The consecutive dates that they meet are 6 days apart. Answers vary.

Chapter 3

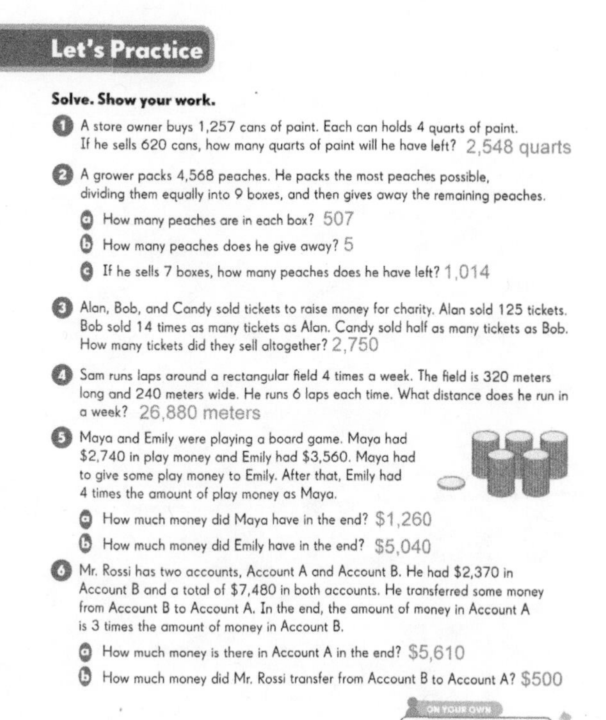

Let's Practice

Solve. Show your work.

1. A store owner buys 1,257 cans of paint. Each can holds 4 quarts of paint. If he sells 620 cans, how many quarts of paint will he have left? 2,548 quarts
2. A grower packs 4,568 peaches. He packs the most peaches possible, dividing them equally into 9 boxes, and then gives away the remaining peaches.
   a. How many peaches are in each box? 507
   b. How many peaches does he give away? 5
   c. If he sells 7 boxes, how many peaches does he have left? 1,014
3. Alan, Bob, and Candy sold tickets to raise money for charity. Alan sold 125 tickets. Bob sold 14 times as many tickets as Alan. Candy sold half as many tickets as Bob. How many tickets did they sell altogether? 2,750
4. Sam runs laps around a rectangular field 4 times a week. The field is 320 meters long and 240 meters wide. He runs 6 laps each time. What distance does he run in a week? 26,880 meters
5. Maya and Emily were playing a board game. Maya had $2,740 in play money and Emily had $3,560. Maya had to give some play money to Emily. After that, Emily had 4 times the amount of play money as Maya.
   a. How much money did Maya have in the end? $1,260
   b. How much money did Emily have in the end? $5,040
6. Mr. Rossi has two accounts, Account A and Account B. He had $2,370 in Account B and a total of $7,480 in both accounts. He transferred some money from Account B to Account A. In the end, the amount of money in Account A is 3 times the amount of money in Account B.
   a. How much money is there in Account A in the end? $5,610
   b. How much money did Mr. Rossi transfer from Account B to Account A? $500

ON YOUR OWN
Go to Workbook A: Practice 5, pages 59–62

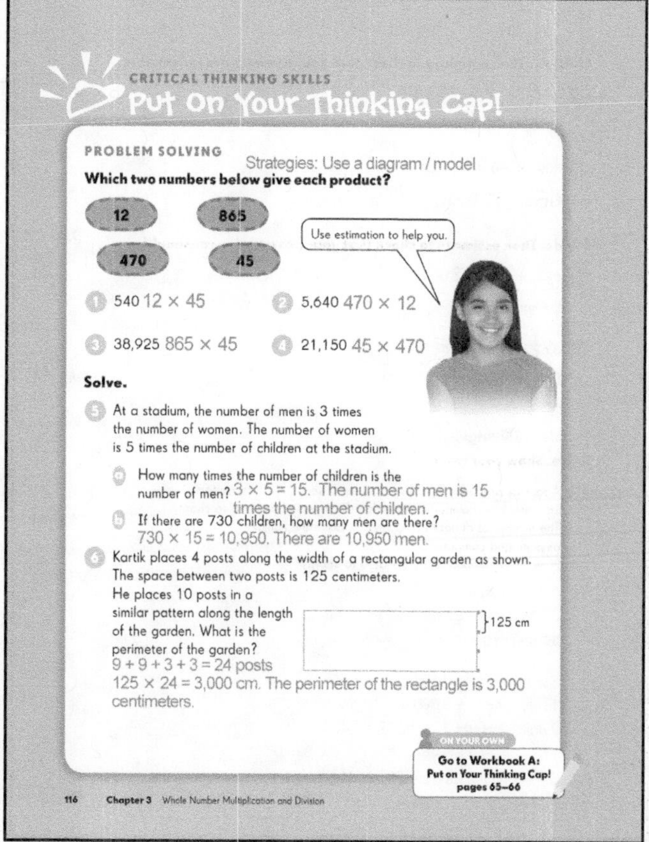

CRITICAL THINKING SKILLS

Put On Your Thinking Cap!

PROBLEM SOLVING

Strategies: Use a diagram / model

Which two numbers below give each product?

12 | 865 | 470 | 45

Use estimation to help you.

1. 540 12 × 45
2. 5,640 470 × 12
3. 38,925 865 × 45
4. 21,150 45 × 470

Solve.

5. At a stadium, the number of men is 3 times the number of women. The number of women is 5 times the number of children at the stadium.
   a. How many times the number of children is the number of men? 3 × 5 = 15. The number of men is 15 times the number of children.
   b. If there are 730 children, how many men are there?
   730 × 15 = 10,950. There are 10,950 men.
6. Kartik places 4 posts along the width of a rectangular garden as shown. The space between two posts is 125 centimeters. He places 10 posts in a similar pattern along the length of the garden. What is the perimeter of the garden?

125 cm

9 + 9 + 3 + 3 = 24 posts
125 × 24 = 3,000 cm. The perimeter of the rectangle is 3,000 centimeters.

ON YOUR OWN
Go to Workbook A: Put on Your Thinking Cap! pages 65–66

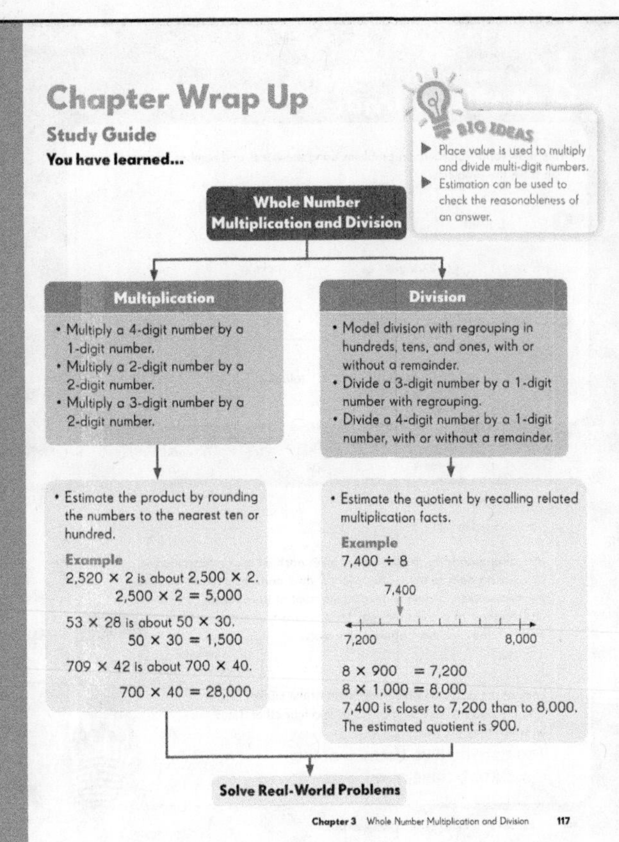

Chapter Wrap Up

Study Guide

You have learned...

BIG IDEAS

- Place value is used to multiply and divide multi-digit numbers.
- Estimation can be used to check the reasonableness of an answer.

Whole Number Multiplication and Division

Multiplication

- Multiply a 4-digit number by a 1-digit number.
- Multiply a 2-digit number by a 2-digit number.
- Multiply a 3-digit number by a 2-digit number.

- Estimate the product by rounding the numbers to the nearest ten or hundred.

Example

2,520 × 2 is about 2,500 × 2.
2,500 × 2 = 5,000

53 × 28 is about 50 × 30.
50 × 30 = 1,500

709 × 42 is about 700 × 40.
700 × 40 = 28,000

Division

- Model division with regrouping in hundreds, tens, and ones, with or without a remainder.
- Divide a 3-digit number by a 1-digit number with regrouping.
- Divide a 4-digit number by a 1-digit number, with or without a remainder.

- Estimate the quotient by recalling related multiplication facts.

Example

7,400 ÷ 8

8 × 900 = 7,200
8 × 1,000 = 8,000
7,400 is closer to 7,200 than to 8,000.
The estimated quotient is 900.

Solve Real-World Problems

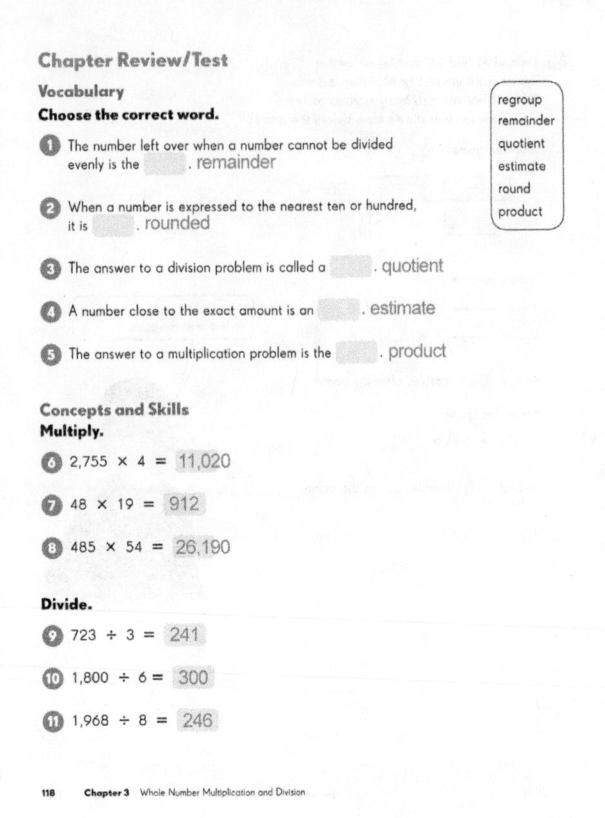

Chapter Review/Test

Vocabulary

Choose the correct word.

regroup
remainder
quotient
estimate
round
product

1. The number left over when a number cannot be divided evenly is the ______. remainder
2. When a number is expressed to the nearest ten or hundred, it is ______. rounded
3. The answer to a division problem is called a ______. quotient
4. A number close to the exact amount is an ______. estimate
5. The answer to a multiplication problem is the ______. product

Concepts and Skills

Multiply.

6. 2,755 × 4 = 11,020
7. 48 × 19 = 912
8. 485 × 54 = 26,190

Divide.

9. 723 ÷ 3 = 241
10. 1,800 ÷ 6 = 300
11. 1,968 ÷ 8 = 246

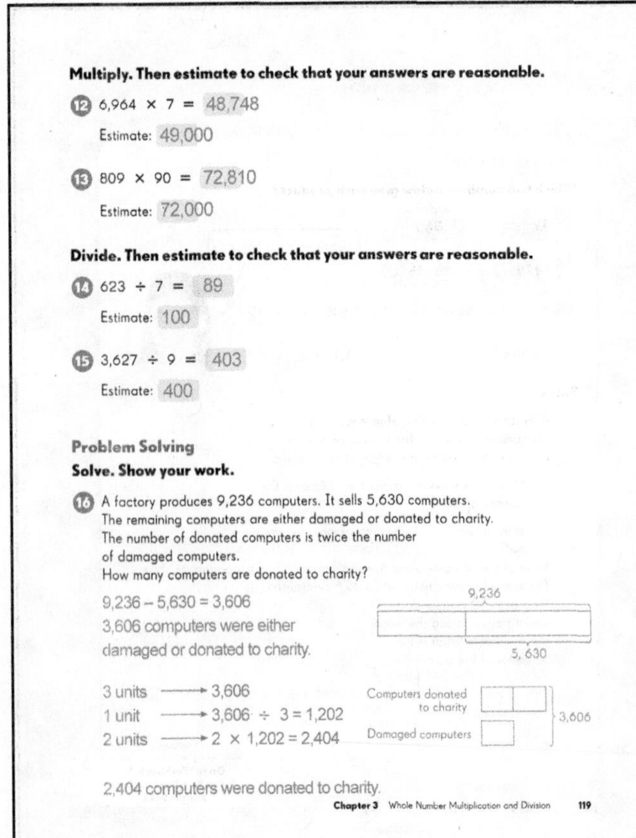

Multiply. Then estimate to check that your answers are reasonable.

12. 6,964 × 7 = 48,748
    Estimate: 49,000
13. 809 × 90 = 72,810
    Estimate: 72,000

Divide. Then estimate to check that your answers are reasonable.

14. 623 ÷ 7 = 89
    Estimate: 100
15. 3,627 ÷ 9 = 403
    Estimate: 400

Problem Solving

Solve. Show your work.

16. A factory produces 9,236 computers. It sells 5,630 computers. The remaining computers are either damaged or donated to charity. The number of donated computers is twice the number of damaged computers.
    How many computers are donated to charity?

9,236 – 5,630 = 3,606
3,606 computers were either damaged or donated to charity.

3 units ⟶ 3,606
1 unit ⟶ 3,606 ÷ 3 = 1,202
2 units ⟶ 2 × 1,202 = 2,404

2,404 computers were donated to charity.

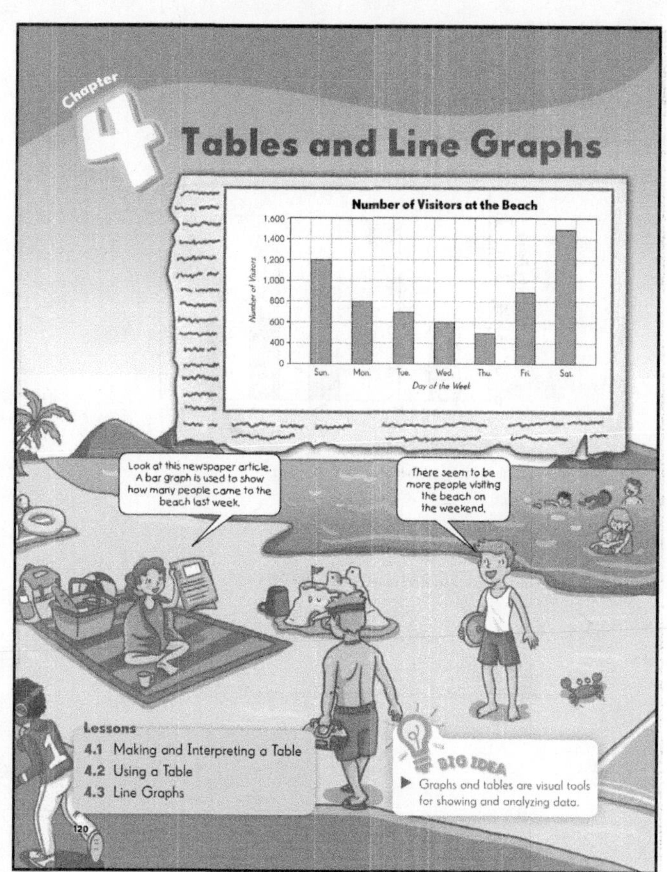

Chapter 4

Tables and Line Graphs

Lessons

BIG IDEA

▶ Graphs and tables are visual tools for showing and analyzing data.

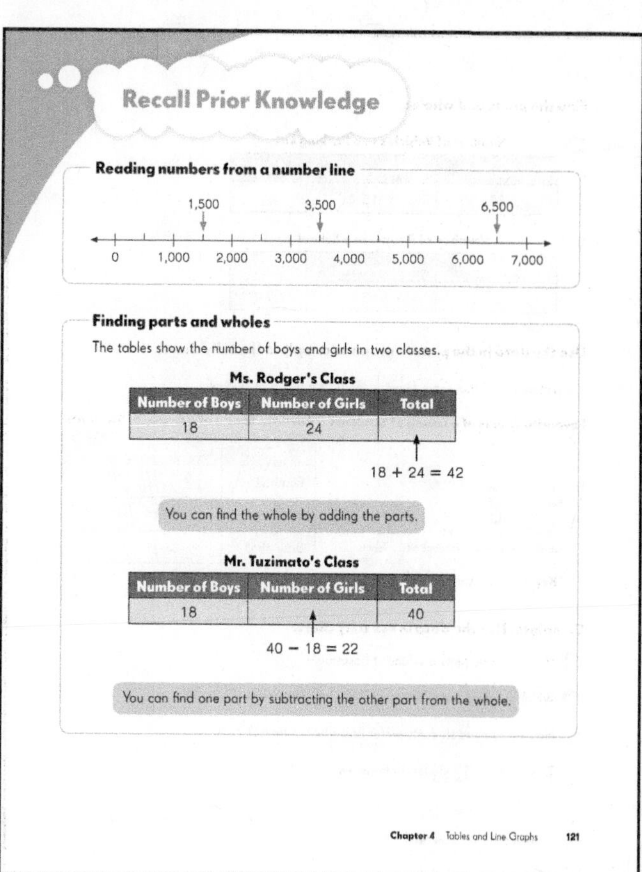

Recall Prior Knowledge

Reading numbers from a number line

Finding parts and wholes

The tables show the number of boys and girls in two classes.

Ms. Rodger's Class

Number of Boys	Number of Girls	Total
18	24	

18 + 24 = 42

You can find the whole by adding the parts.

Mr. Tuzimato's Class

Number of Boys	Number of Girls	Total
18		40

40 − 18 = 22

You can find one part by subtracting the other part from the whole.

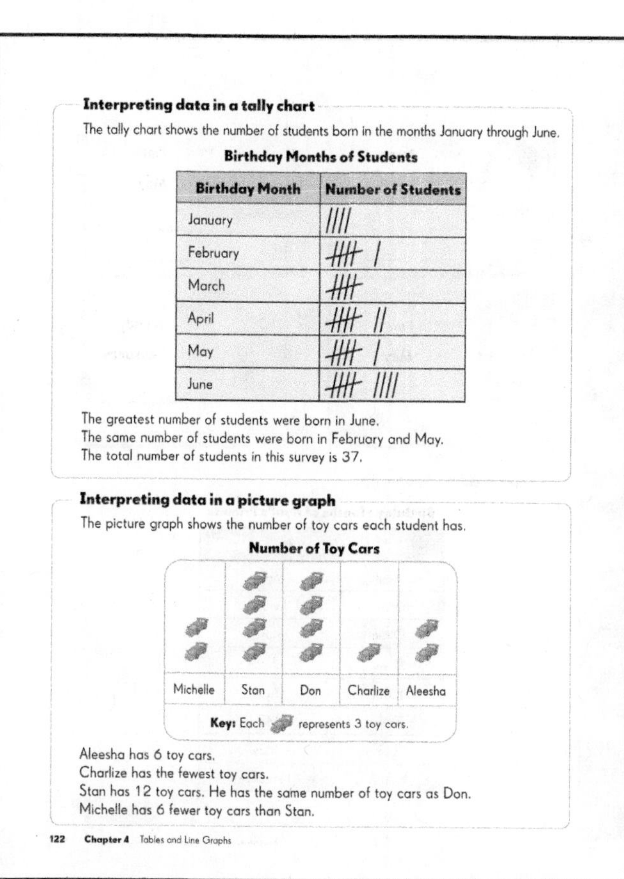

Interpreting data in a tally chart

The tally chart shows the number of students born in the months January through June.

Birthday Months of Students

Birthday Month	Number of Students
January	////
February	~~////~~ /
March	~~////~~
April	~~////~~ //
May	~~////~~ /
June	~~////~~ ////

The greatest number of students were born in June.
The same number of students were born in February and May.
The total number of students in this survey is 37.

Interpreting data in a picture graph

The picture graph shows the number of toy cars each student has.

Number of Toy Cars

Aleesha has 6 toy cars.
Charlize has the fewest toy cars.
Stan has 12 toy cars. He has the same number of toy cars as Don.
Michelle has 6 fewer toy cars than Stan.

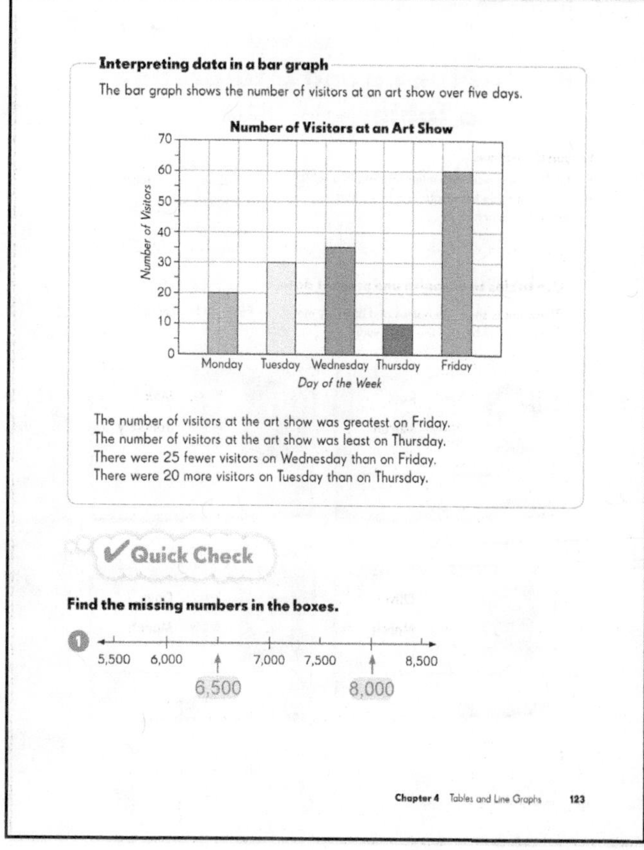

Interpreting data in a bar graph

The bar graph shows the number of visitors at an art show over five days.

The number of visitors at the art show was greatest on Friday.
The number of visitors at the art show was least on Thursday.
There were 25 fewer visitors on Wednesday than on Friday.
There were 20 more visitors on Tuesday than on Thursday.

Quick Check

Find the missing numbers in the boxes.

1 5,500 6,000 ? 7,000 7,500 ? 8,500

6,500 8,000

Chapter 4

Find the parts and wholes.

2 Number of Vehicles in a Parking Lot

Cars	Motorcycles	Total
32	15	47

3 Number of People in a School

Students	Teachers	Total
1,279	63	1,342

Use the data in the picture graph to complete the tally chart.

The picture graph shows the favorite sports of a group of students.

Favourite Sports of a Group of Students

Football | Baseball | Basketball | Tennis

Key: Each represents 2 students.

Favorite Sports of a Group of Students

Sport	Number of Students
Football	𝍸 I
Baseball	𝍸 𝍸
Basketball	𝍸 III
Tennis	II

Complete. Use the data in the tally chart.

4 How many students are fans of basketball? 8

5 Which sport do the greatest number of students prefer? Baseball

6 How many more students prefer basketball to tennis? 6

7 There are 26 students altogether.

Complete. Use the data in the bar graph.

The bar graph shows the number of fundraising tickets sold by some volunteers.

Fundraising Tickets Sold by Volunteers

Number of Tickets: 0, 5, 10, 15, 20, 25, 30, 35

Volunteer: Steven, Michael, Jill, Zach, Rahul

8 Who sold the greatest number of tickets? Rahul

9 Who sold the least number of tickets? Jill

10 How many fewer tickets did Steven sell than Rahul? 18

11 Which two volunteers sold a difference of 1 ticket? Michael, Zach

12 How many tickets did the five volunteers sell altogether? 107

Lesson 4.1

Making and Interpreting a Table

Lesson Objectives

- Collect, organize, and interpret data in a table.
- Create a table from data in a tally chart and a bar graph.

Vocabulary
data table
tally chart

Learn **Use tables to organize and present data.**

These cards show the names and birthday months of Raul and his friends. They were all born in the same year.

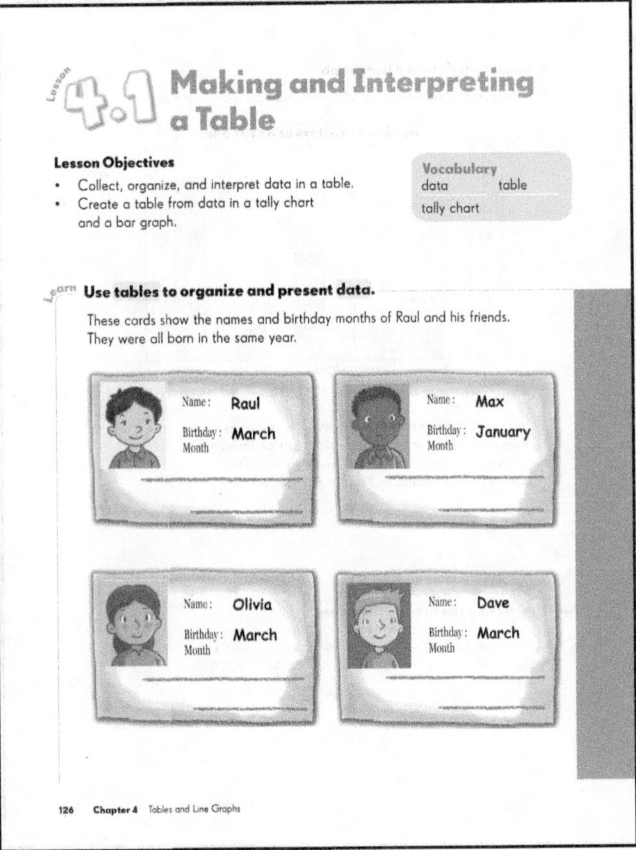

Name: Raul
Birthday Month: March
Name: Max
Birthday Month: January
Name: Olivia
Birthday Month: March
Name: Dave
Birthday Month: March

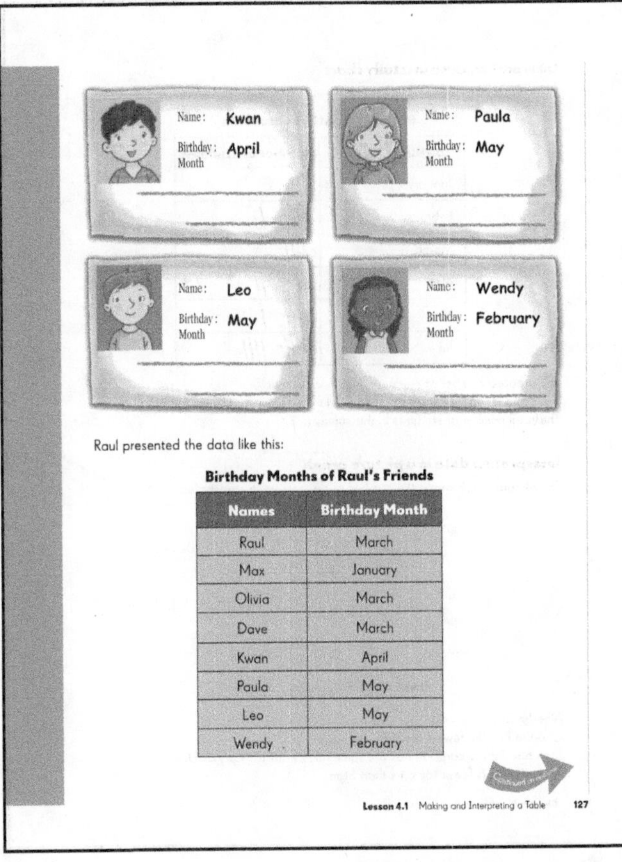

Raul presented the data like this:

Birthday Months of Raul's Friends

Names	Birthday Month
Raul	March
Max	January
Olivia	March
Dave	March
Kwan	April
Paula	May
Leo	May
Wendy	February

Continued on next page

Raul then used a **tally chart** to record what he had found.

Birthday Months of Raul's Friends

Birthday Month	January	February	March	April	May
Tally	/	/	///	/	//

Raul counted the tally marks to find the number of friends whose birthdays fell in each month. Then he presented the data in a table.

Birthday Months of Raul's Friends

Birthday Month	Number of Friends
January	1
February	1
March	3
April	1
May	2

2 of Raul's friends were born in May.
The month with the most number of birthdays is March.
There were 2 more friends born in March than in January.
Raul collected data from 7 friends in total, excluding himself.

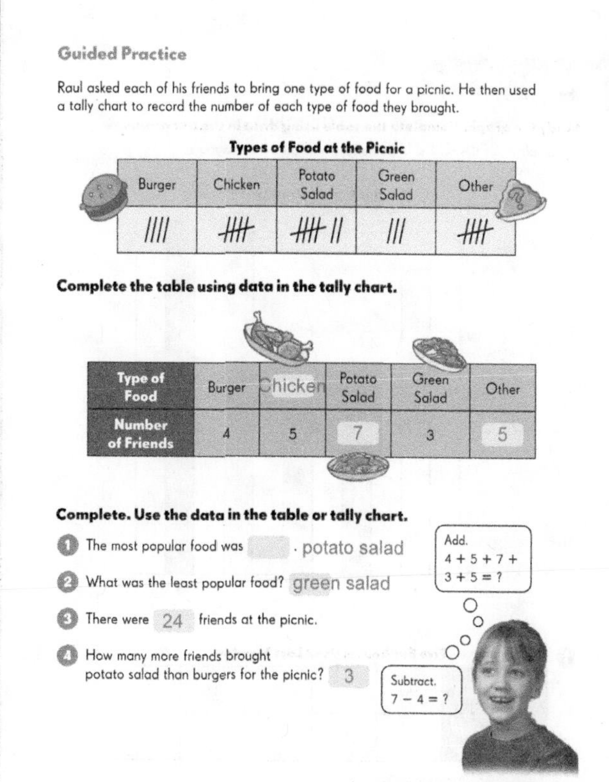

Guided Practice

Raul asked each of his friends to bring one type of food for a picnic. He then used a tally chart to record the number of each type of food they brought.

Types of Food at the Picnic

Burger	Chicken	Potato Salad	Green Salad	Other
////	~~////~~	~~////~~ //	///	~~////~~

Complete the table using data in the tally chart.

Type of Food	Burger	Chicken	Potato Salad	Green Salad	Other
Number of Friends	4	5	7	3	5

Complete. Use the data in the table or tally chart.

1. The most popular food was ____. potato salad
2. What was the least popular food? green salad
3. There were 24 friends at the picnic.
4. How many more friends brought potato salad than burgers for the picnic? 3

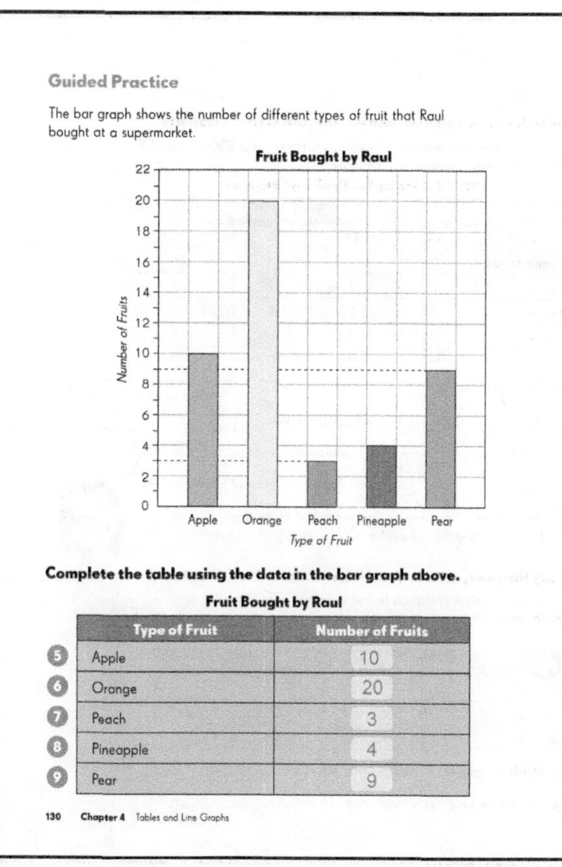

Guided Practice

The bar graph shows the number of different types of fruit that Raul bought at a supermarket.

Complete the table using the data in the bar graph above.

Fruit Bought by Raul

	Type of Fruit	Number of Fruits
5	Apple	10
6	Orange	20
7	Peach	3
8	Pineapple	4
9	Pear	9

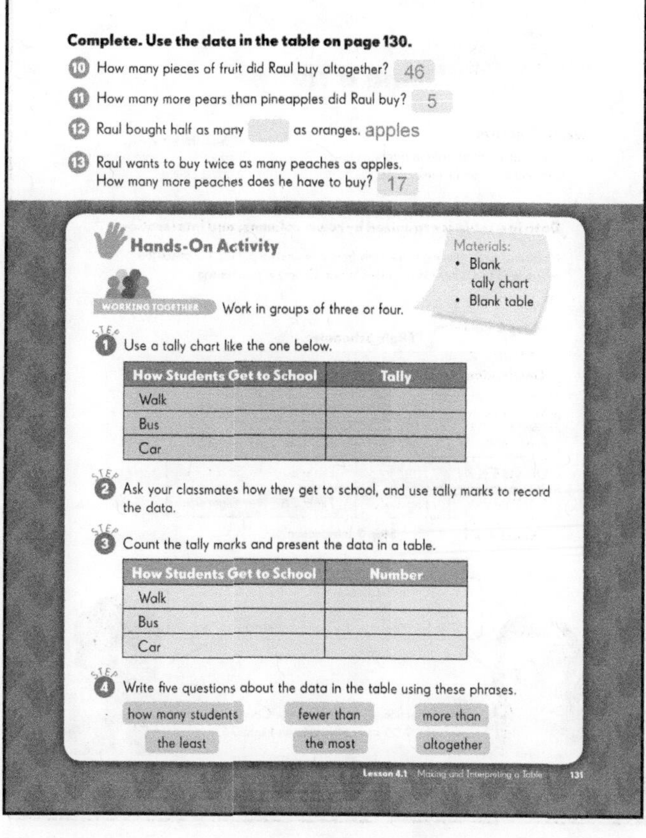

Complete. Use the data in the table on page 130.

10. How many pieces of fruit did Raul buy altogether? 46
11. How many more pears than pineapples did Raul buy? 5
12. Raul bought half as many ____ as oranges. apples
13. Raul wants to buy twice as many peaches as apples. How many more peaches does he have to buy? 17

Hands-On Activity

Materials:
- Blank tally chart
- Blank table

WORKING TOGETHER Work in groups of three or four.

STEP 1 Use a tally chart like the one below.

How Students Get to School	Tally
Walk	
Bus	
Car	

STEP 2 Ask your classmates how they get to school, and use tally marks to record the data.

STEP 3 Count the tally marks and present the data in a table.

How Students Get to School	Number
Walk	
Bus	
Car	

STEP 4 Write five questions about the data in the table using these phrases.

how many students | fewer than | more than | the least | the most | altogether

Chapter 4

Let's Practice

Study the graph. Complete the table using data in the bar graph.

The graph shows the number of passengers who used five bus routes last Monday.

Five Bus Routes Used Last Monday

Number of Passengers: 0, 100, 200, 300, 400, 500, 600

Bus Route: A, B, C, D, E

1 **Five Bus Routes Used Last Monday**

Bus Route	A	B	C	D	E
Number of Passengers	500	260	280	560	580

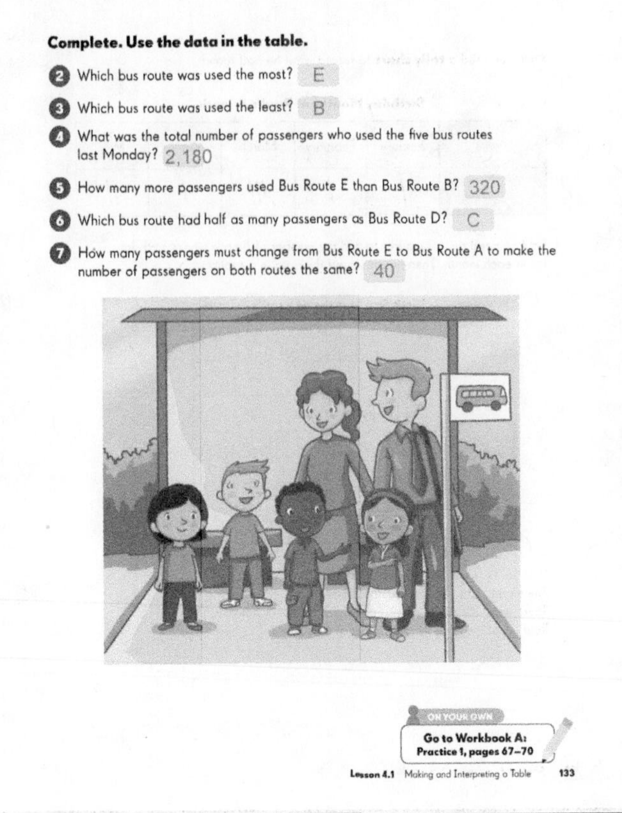

Complete. Use the data in the table.

2 Which bus route was used the most? E

3 Which bus route was used the least? B

4 What was the total number of passengers who used the five bus routes last Monday? 2,180

5 How many more passengers used Bus Route E than Bus Route B? 320

6 Which bus route had half as many passengers as Bus Route D? C

7 How many passengers must change from Bus Route E to Bus Route A to make the number of passengers on both routes the same? 40

ON YOUR OWN

Go to Workbook A: Practice 1, pages 67–70

Lesson 4.1 Making and Interpreting a Table 133

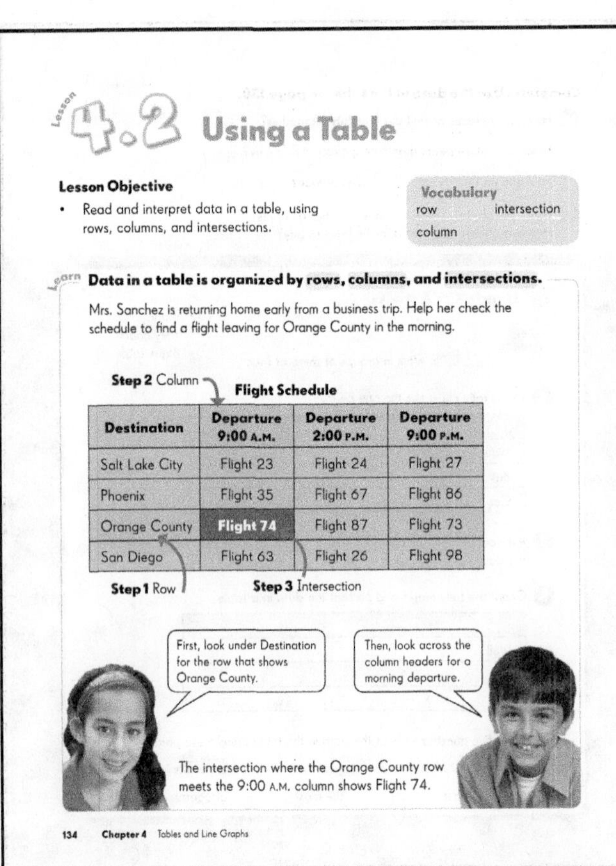

Lesson

4.2 Using a Table

Lesson Objective

- Read and interpret data in a table, using rows, columns, and intersections.

Vocabulary
row
intersection
column

Learn **Data in a table is organized by rows, columns, and intersections.**

Mrs. Sanchez is returning home early from a business trip. Help her check the schedule to find a flight leaving for Orange County in the morning.

Step 2 Column

Flight Schedule

Destination	Departure 9:00 A.M.	Departure 2:00 P.M.	Departure 9:00 P.M.
Salt Lake City	Flight 23	Flight 24	Flight 27
Phoenix	Flight 35	Flight 67	Flight 86
Orange County	Flight 74	Flight 87	Flight 73
San Diego	Flight 63	Flight 26	Flight 98

Step 1 Row

Step 3 Intersection

First, look under Destination for the row that shows Orange County.
Then, look across the column headers for a morning departure.
The intersection where the Orange County row meets the 9:00 A.M. column shows Flight 74.

134 Chapter 4 Tables and Line Graphs

Guided Practice

Study the rows, columns, and intersections. Then complete.

The number of medals won by top ranking countries in the 2006 Winter Olympics held in Turin, Italy is recorded in the table.

Medals Won by Top Ranking Countries

Country	Gold	Silver	Bronze	Total Number
Germany	11	12	6	29
United States	9	9	7	25
Austria	9	7	7	23
Russia	8	6	8	22
Canada	7	10	7	24

Source: www.abc.net.au/winterolympics/2006/fullmedal-tally.htm

1 The United States won 9 silver medals.

2 Russia won a total of 22 medals altogether.

3 Austria won 2 fewer gold medals than Germany.

4 ___, ___, and ___ won the same number of bronze medals. Austria / Canada / United States

5 The number 11 appears at the intersection of the row for ___ and the column for ___. Germany gold medals

Where does the row for the United States intersect with the column for silver medals?

Study the rows, columns, and intersections. Then complete.

A food court surveys customers to find out which type of food is most popular among three age groups of people.

Popular Types of Food

Age Group	Fast Food	Italian	Mexican	Chinese
Under 12	54	21	16	9
From 12 to 18	34	24	29	13
Over 18	11	35	26	28

6 The least number of children under the age of 12 eat ___ food. Chinese

7 The greatest number of adults over 18 eat ___ food. Italian

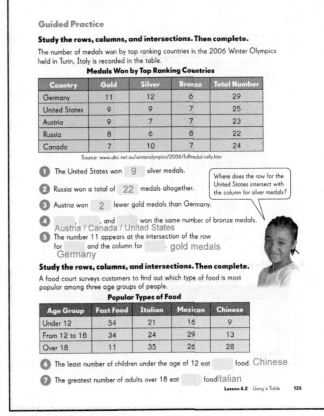

8 The difference between the number of children under 12 who prefer Italian food to Mexican food is 5.

9 The difference between the number of students in the 12 to 18 age group who prefer fast food to Chinese food is 21.

10 The number of adults who prefer Mexican and Chinese food altogether is 54.

Complete the table to answer the questions below.

Rebecca made this table to show the birthdays of her classmates in the months from January to June. All her classmates were born in the same year.
Help Rebecca complete the table.

Birthday Months of Rebecca's Classmates

Birthday Month	Number of Boys	Number of Girls	Total Number
January	2	3	5
February	4	2	6
March	1	2	3
April	5	0	5
May	4	2	6
June	4	3	7
Total	20	12	32

11 How many classmates were born in May and June? 13

12 How many classmates were born in these six months? 32

13 Which month has the greatest number of birthdays? June

14 Rebecca is the youngest among those born in March.

a How many of her classmates born from January to June are older than Rebecca? 13

b How many of her classmates born from January to June are younger than Rebecca? 18

Complete the table to answer the questions below.

The table shows the number of dimes and quarters that five students collected during the first hour of a fundraising event.

Dimes and Quarters Collected at a Fundraising Event

Student	Dimes		Quarters		Total Amount
	Number of Coins Collected	Amount Collected	Number of Coins Collected	Amount Collected	
Ryan	12	$1.20	18	$4.50	$5.70
Janice	15	$1.50	16	$4.00	$5.50
Steve	20	$2.00	10	$2.50	$4.50
Selma	13	$1.30	12	$3.00	$4.30
Ying	6	$0.60	25	$6.25	$6.85
Total	66	$6.60	81	$20.25	$26.85

15 Selma collected a total of $4.30.

16 Who collected the greatest amount of money? Ying

17 Who collected the greatest number of coins? Janice and Ying

18 How much more did Ying collect than Janice? $ 1.35

19 How much less did Steve collect than Janice? $ 1.00

20 How much more must Ryan collect to match the amount that Ying has collected? $ 1.15

Talk to your classmates to find out their favorite colors.
Record your findings. Then make a table on a computer to show the data you have collected. Present your table to the class.

Guided Practice

Complete the table to answer the questions below.

The table shows the number of bottles of water and juice sold at each booth during a fall festival.

Bottles Sold at a Fall Festival

Booth	Water (50¢ each)		Juice (80¢ each)		Total Amount
	Number of Bottles Sold	Amount Collected	Number of Bottles Sold	Amount Collected	
A	25	$12.50	20	$16.00	$28.50
B	25	$12.50	10	$ 8	$20.50
C	12	$ 6	5	$ 4	$ 10
D	30	$ 15	15	$ 12	$ 27
Total	92	$ 46	50	$ 40	$ 86

21 Which booth collected the most money? Booth A

22 Which booth collected the least money? Booth C

23 Which booths sold the greatest number of bottles of water and juice? Booths A and D

24 Which booth sold the least number of bottles of water and juice? Booth C

Suggest why this booth sold the least number of bottles of water and juice.
Answers vary.

Let's Practice

Complete the table and answer the questions below.

The table shows Ms. Frey's students' favorite colors.

Favorite Colors of Ms. Frey's Students

Color	Number of Boys	Number of Girls	Total Number
Red	2	4	6
Blue	2	3	5
Green	3	2	5
Yellow	2	2	4
Total	9	11	20

1 The number 6 appears in the intersection of the row for Red and the column for Total Number.

2 The number at the intersection of the row for Green and the column for Number of Boys is 3.

3 Which color is least popular among the students? Yellow

4 Which color is most popular among the girls? Red

5 How many more girls than boys like red? 2

6 Are there fewer students who like green than red? Yes
If so, how many fewer? 1

7 What is the total number of boys in the class? 9

8 How many students are there in the class altogether? 20

Lesson 4.3 Line Graphs

Lesson Objectives
- Make, read, and interpret line graphs.
- Choose an appropriate graph to display a given data set.

Vocabulary
line graph
vertical axis
horizontal axis

Learn **Read a line graph to find out how data changes over time.**

The table shows the temperature at different times of the day at a school.

Temperature at a School

Time	7 A.M.	8 A.M.	9 A.M.	10 A.M.	11 A.M.	12 P.M.
Temperature (°F)	70	74	78	84	88	90

The data in the table can also be shown in this line graph.

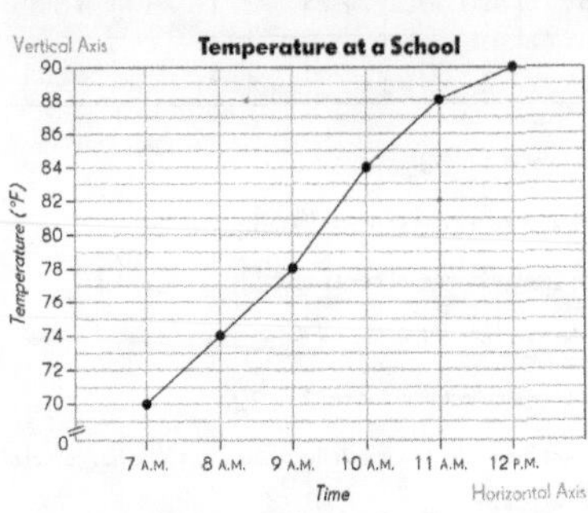

What is the temperature at 11:00 A.M.?

Step 1 Find 11:00 A.M. along the **horizontal axis** (green line).

Step 2 Move up until you meet a point on the graph.

Step 3 From that point on the graph, move left until you meet the **vertical axis** (pink line).

Step 4 The point on the scale, or vertical axis (pink line) is 88°F.

The temperature at 11:00 A.M. is 88°F.

The red lines track the path of steps 1 to 4. This is how you read the temperature at different times.

At what time was the temperature 74°F.?

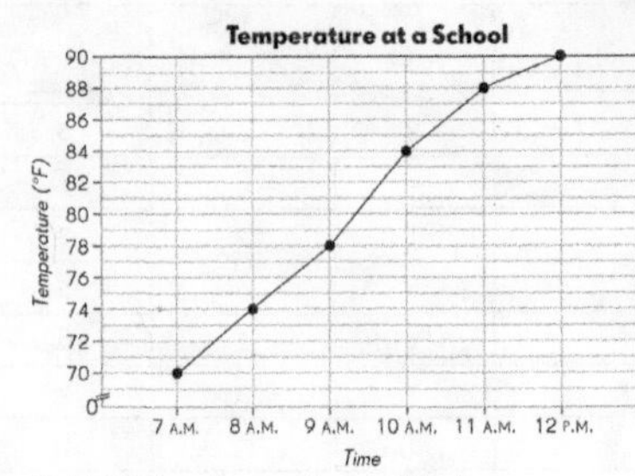

Step 1 Find 74°F along the vertical axis (pink line).

Step 2 Move right until you meet a point on the graph.

Step 3 From that point on the graph, move down until you meet the horizontal axis (green line).

Step 4 The point on the horizontal axis (green line) is 8:00 A.M.

The temperature was 74°F at 8:00 A.M.

The blue lines track the path of steps 1 to 4. This is how you find the time at which the temperature was a given value.

Guided Practice

Complete. Use the data in the line graph.

The table and line graph show the distance from Ryan's home during the first seven minutes of a bus trip.

Distance from Ryan's Home

Time after Bus Trip Begins (min)	1	2	3	4	5	6	7
Distance from Ryan's Home (m)	250	750	1,250	1,500	1,500	2,500	2,000

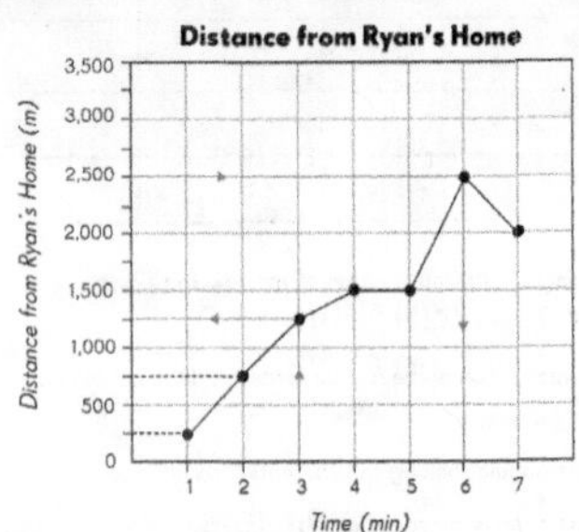

1. How far is Ryan from his home after 3 minutes on the bus? 1,250 m
2. After 6 minutes on the bus, Ryan is 2,500 meters from his home.
3. The bus stopped at a bus stop between the fourth and fifth minute.
4. What was the increase in distance from Ryan's home from the first to the third minute? 1,000 m
5. After how many minutes of its journey did the bus turn around and travel in the direction of Ryan's home? 6
6. During which 1-minute interval was the bus moving the fastest?
   Between the fifth and the sixth minute.

Complete. Use data from the line graph.

The line graph shows the cost of a type of wire sold in a hardware store.

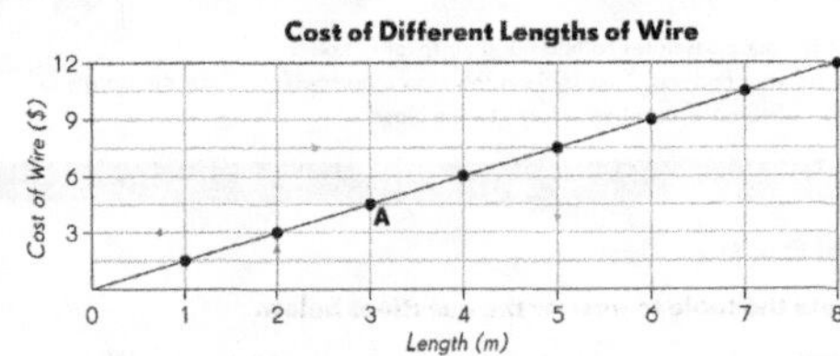

7. a. The graph shows that 2 meters of wire cost $ 3.00.
   b. The graph also shows that when the cost is $7.50, the length of the wire is 5 meters.
8. a. 4 meters of wire cost $ 6.
   b. 8 meters of wire cost $ 12.

The graph is a straight line.

9. a. When the cost is $9.00, the length of the wire is 6 meters.
   b. When the cost is $10.50, the length of the wire is 7 meters.
10. Find the length and cost of a wire at point A on the graph.
    At point A, the length of the wire is 3 meters.
    The cost of the wire at point A is $ 4.50.
11. Use the graph to find the missing numbers below. What is the increase in the cost of the wire for every 1 meter increase in length?

	1 m	1 m	1 m	1 m	Increase in length of wire
Length (m)	1	2	3	4	5
Cost ($)	1.50	3	4.50	6	7.50
	$1.50	$1.50	$1.50	$1.50	Increase in cost of wire

For every 1 meter increase in length, the cost of the wire increases by $ 1.50.

Complete. Use data from the line graph.

The line graph shows the length of a spring when various masses are hung on it.

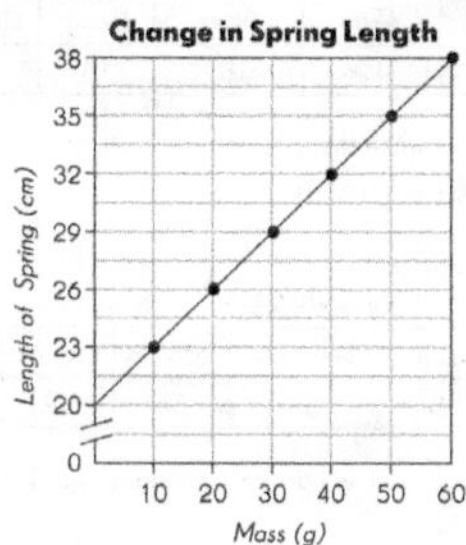

Change in Spring Length
Length of Spring (cm)
38
35
32
29
26
23
20
0
10 20 30 40 50 60
Mass (g)

12. What is the length of the spring when it is not stretched? 20 cm

13. What is the length of the spring when these masses are hung on it?
  a. 10 grams 23 cm
  b. 30 grams 29 cm
  c. 40 grams 32 cm
  d. 50 grams 35 cm

14. What is the mass hung on the spring when its length is
  a. 26 centimeters? 20 g
  b. 38 centimeters? 60 g

15. Compare the original length of the spring to its length when different masses are hung on it.
  a. By how many centimeters is the spring stretched when a mass of 60 grams is hung on it? 18 cm
  b. If the spring is stretched by 15 centimeters, what is the mass that is hung on it? 50 g

144 **Chapter 4** Tables and Line Graphs

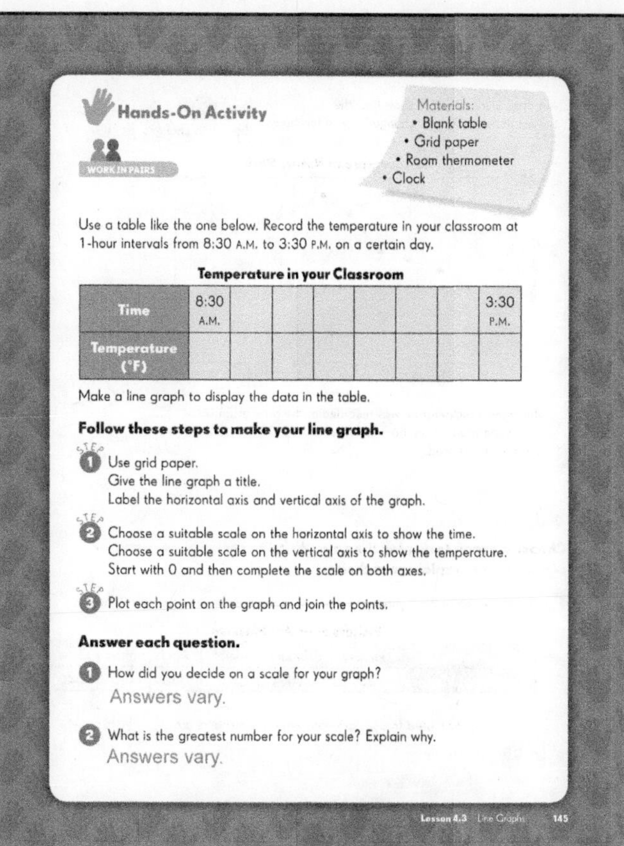

Hands-On Activity

WORK IN PAIRS

Materials:
- Blank table
- Grid paper
- Room thermometer
- Clock

Use a table like the one below. Record the temperature in your classroom at 1-hour intervals from 8:30 A.M. to 3:30 P.M. on a certain day.

Temperature in Your Classroom

Time	8:30 A.M.							3:30 P.M.
Temperature (°F)								

Make a line graph to display the data in the table.

Follow these steps to make your line graph.

STEP 1 Use grid paper.
Give the line graph a title.
Label the horizontal axis and vertical axis of the graph.

STEP 2 Choose a suitable scale on the horizontal axis to show the time.
Choose a suitable scale on the vertical axis to show the temperature.
Start with 0 and then complete the scale on both axes.

STEP 3 Plot each point on the graph and join the points.

Answer each question.

1. How did you decide on a scale for your graph?
Answers vary.

2. What is the greatest number for your scale? Explain why.
Answers vary.

Lesson 4.3 Line Graphs 145

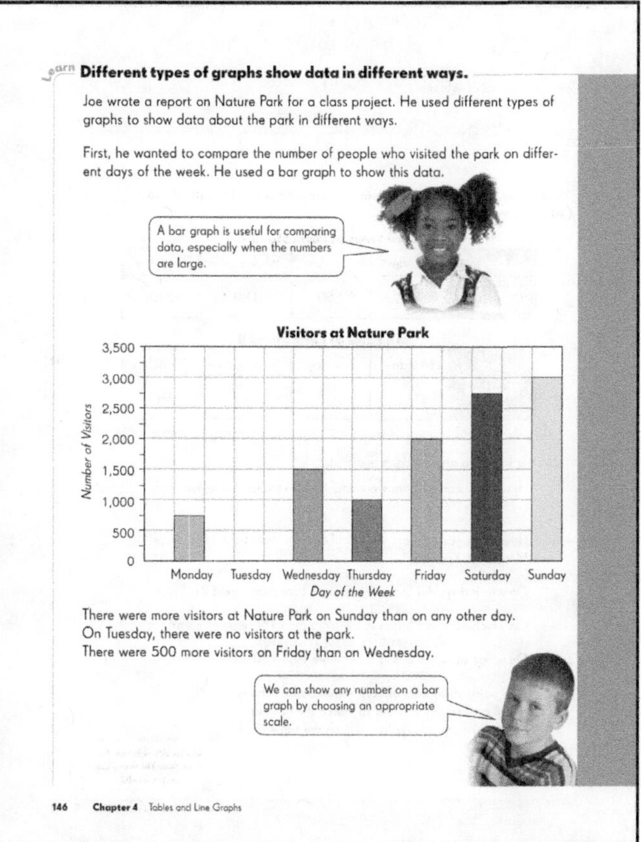

Learn **Different types of graphs show data in different ways.**

Joe wrote a report on Nature Park for a class project. He used different types of graphs to show data about the park in different ways.

First, he wanted to compare the number of people who visited the park on different days of the week. He used a bar graph to show this data.

A bar graph is useful for comparing data, especially when the numbers are large.
Visitors at Nature Park
Number of Visitors
3,500
3,000
2,500
2,000
1,500
1,000
500
0
Monday Tuesday Wednesday Thursday Friday Saturday Sunday
Day of the Week

There were more visitors at Nature Park on Sunday than on any other day.
On Tuesday, there were no visitors at the park.
There were 500 more visitors on Friday than on Wednesday.

We can show any number on a bar graph by choosing an appropriate scale.

146 **Chapter 4** Tables and Line Graphs

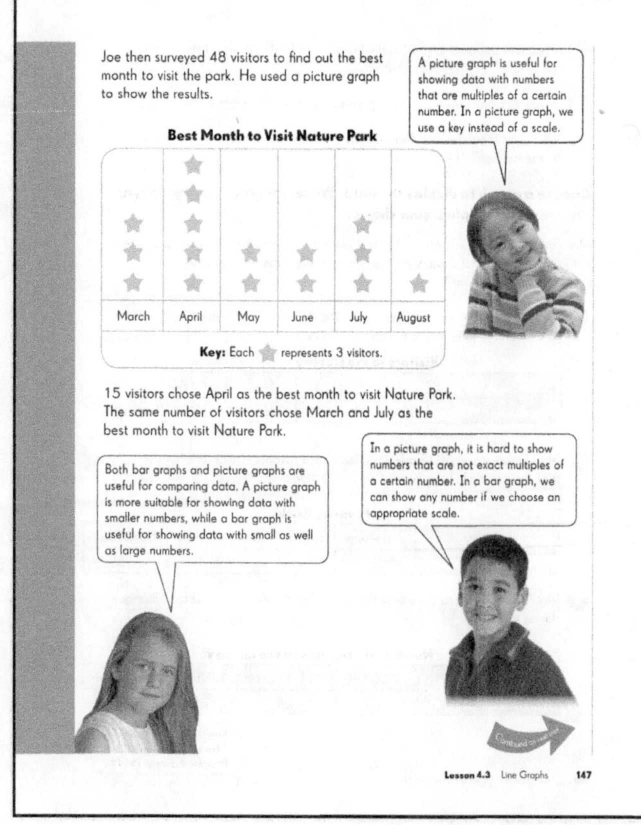

Joe then surveyed 48 visitors to find out the best month to visit the park. He used a picture graph to show the results.

A picture graph is useful for showing data with numbers that are multiples of a certain number. In a picture graph, we use a key instead of a scale.
Best Month to Visit Nature Park
March
April
May
June
July
August
Key: Each ★ represents 3 visitors.

15 visitors chose April as the best month to visit Nature Park.
The same number of visitors chose March and July as the best month to visit Nature Park.

Both bar graphs and picture graphs are useful for comparing data. A picture graph is more suitable for showing data with smaller numbers, while a bar graph is useful for showing data with small as well as large numbers.
In a picture graph, it is hard to show numbers that are not exact multiples of a certain number. In a bar graph, we can show any number if we choose an appropriate scale.
Continued on next page

Lesson 4.3 Line Graphs 147

Chapter 4

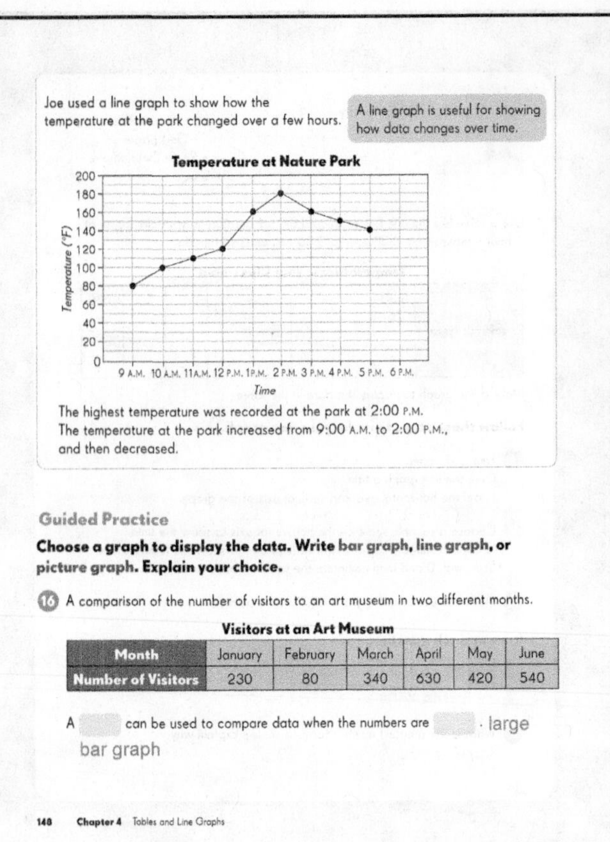

Joe used a line graph to show how the temperature at the park changed over a few hours.

A line graph is useful for showing how data changes over time.

Temperature at Nature Park

The highest temperature was recorded at the park at 2:00 P.M.
The temperature at the park increased from 9:00 A.M. to 2:00 P.M., and then decreased.

Guided Practice

Choose a graph to display the data. Write bar graph, line graph, or picture graph. Explain your choice.

16 A comparison of the number of visitors to an art museum in two different months.

Visitors at an Art Museum

Month	January	February	March	April	May	June
Number of Visitors	230	80	340	630	420	540

A ____ can be used to compare data when the numbers are ____. large
bar graph

17 Number of books read by some students each month.

Number of Books Read by Students

Student	Andy	Brian	Doug	Candy
Number of Books	12	8	16	4

A ____ can be used when the numbers are small, and are multiples of a certain number. picture graph

18 Pete's weight over five months.

Pete's Weight

Month	January	February	March	April	May
Weight (lb)	50	53	54	52	51

A ____ can be used to show how data changes over time.
line graph

Let's Practice

Complete. Use data from the line graph.

The line graph shows the height of a balloon above the ground between 1:00 P.M. and 6:00 P.M. on Monday.

Change in Height of Balloon

Height of Balloon (m): 40, 45, 50, 55, 60
Time: 1 P.M., 2 P.M., 3 P.M., 4 P.M., 5 P.M., 6 P.M.

1 What was the height of the balloon at (a) 1:00 P.M. 40 m (b) 5:00 P.M.? 52.5 m

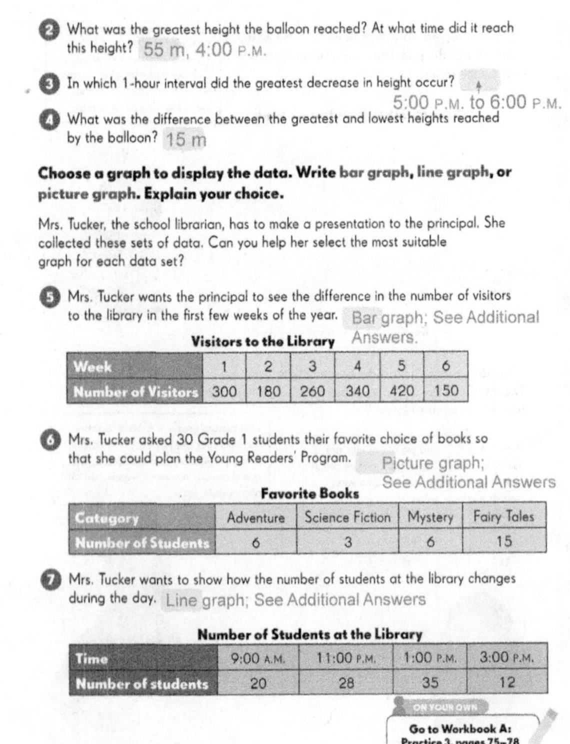

2 What was the greatest height the balloon reached? At what time did it reach this height? 55 m, 4:00 P.M.

3 In which 1-hour interval did the greatest decrease in height occur?
5:00 P.M. to 6:00 P.M.

4 What was the difference between the greatest and lowest heights reached by the balloon? 15 m

Choose a graph to display the data. Write bar graph, line graph, or picture graph. Explain your choice.

Mrs. Tucker, the school librarian, has to make a presentation to the principal. She collected these sets of data. Can you help her select the most suitable graph for each data set?

5 Mrs. Tucker wants the principal to see the difference in the number of visitors to the library in the first few weeks of the year. Bar graph; See Additional Answers.

Visitors to the Library

Week	1	2	3	4	5	6
Number of Visitors	300	180	260	340	420	150

6 Mrs. Tucker asked 30 Grade 1 students their favorite choice of books so that she could plan the Young Readers' Program. Picture graph; See Additional Answers

Favorite Books

Category	Adventure	Science Fiction	Mystery	Fairy Tales
Number of Students	6	3	6	15

7 Mrs. Tucker wants to show how the number of students at the library changes during the day. Line graph; See Additional Answers

Number of Students at the Library

Time	9:00 A.M.	11:00 P.M.	1:00 P.M.	3:00 P.M.
Number of students	20	28	35	12

ON YOUR OWN
Go to Workbook A: Practice 3, pages 75–78

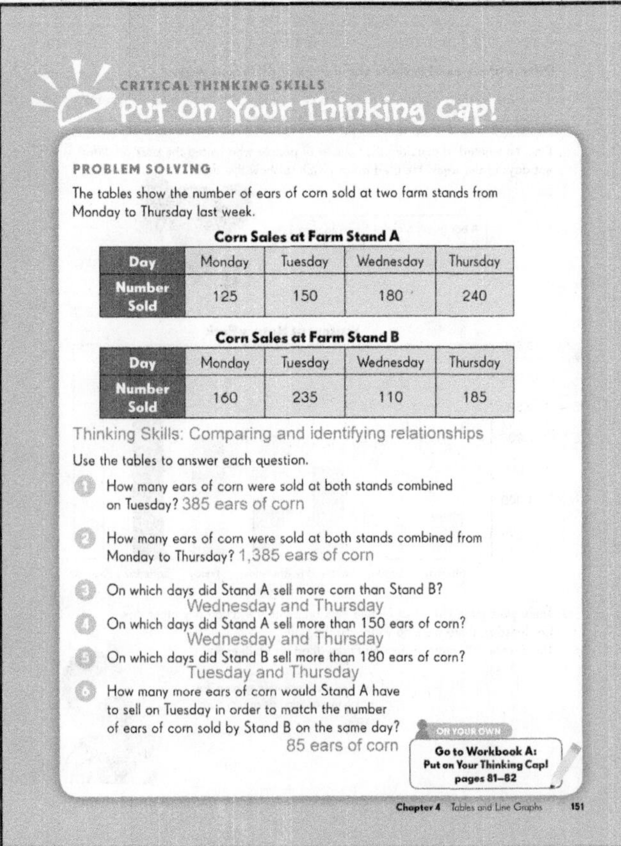

CRITICAL THINKING SKILLS

Put On Your Thinking Cap!

PROBLEM SOLVING

The tables show the number of ears of corn sold at two farm stands from Monday to Thursday last week.

Corn Sales at Farm Stand A

Day	Monday	Tuesday	Wednesday	Thursday
Number Sold	125	150	180	240

Corn Sales at Farm Stand B

Day	Monday	Tuesday	Wednesday	Thursday
Number Sold	160	235	110	185

Thinking Skills: Comparing and identifying relationships

Use the tables to answer each question.

1 How many ears of corn were sold at both stands combined on Tuesday? 385 ears of corn

2 How many ears of corn were sold at both stands combined from Monday to Thursday? 1,385 ears of corn

3 On which days did Stand A sell more corn than Stand B?
Wednesday and Thursday

4 On which days did Stand A sell more than 150 ears of corn?
Wednesday and Thursday

5 On which days did Stand B sell more than 180 ears of corn?
Tuesday and Thursday

6 How many more ears of corn would Stand A have to sell on Tuesday in order to match the number of ears of corn sold by Stand B on the same day?
85 ears of corn

ON YOUR OWN
Go to Workbook A: Put on Your Thinking Cap! pages 81–82

Chapter Wrap Up

Study Guide

You have learned...

Make and Interpret a Table

Make a table from data provided in the form of a tally chart or bar graph.

Example

Bicycle Sales

Day	Tally
Monday	~~////~~
Tuesday	~~////~~ /
Wednesday	~~////~~ ~~////~~
Thursday	/
Friday	///

Bicycle Sales

Day	Bicycle Sales
Monday	5
Tuesday	6
Wednesday	10
Thursday	1
Friday	3

- On Wednesday, 4 more bicycles were sold than on Tuesday.
- Twice as many bicycles were sold on Tuesday than on Friday.

Using a Table

Data in a table is organized by rows, columns, and intersections.

Favorite Sports of a Group of Students

Sport	Number of Boys	Number of Girls	Total Number
Football	10	6	16
Basketball	12	8	20
Swimming	9	11	20

- 2 more girls than boys like swimming.
- The total number of students who like basketball is 20.

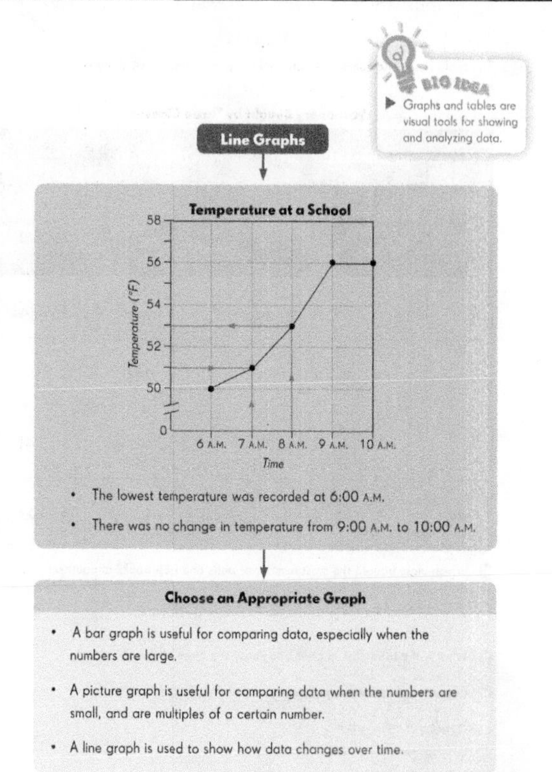

- The lowest temperature was recorded at 6:00 A.M.
- There was no change in temperature from 9:00 A.M. to 10:00 A.M.

Choose an Appropriate Graph

- A bar graph is useful for comparing data, especially when the numbers are large.
- A picture graph is useful for comparing data when the numbers are small, and are multiples of a certain number.
- A line graph is used to show how data changes over time.

Chapter Review/Test

Vocabulary

Choose the correct word.

table
tally chart
row
column
intersection
horizontal axis
vertical axis
line graph

1. In a table, the place where a row and a column meet is called an ____. intersection
2. A ____ organizes data in groups of 5. tally chart
3. A ____ shows how data changes over time. line graph

Concepts and Skills

Solve. Show your work.

4. The bar graph shows the number of people from each New England state participating in a tournament.

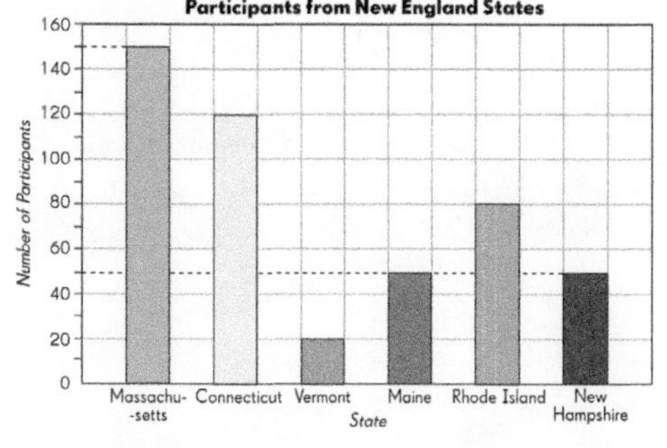

a. Use the data from the bar graph to complete the table.

State	Number of Participants
Massachusetts	150
Connecticut	120
Vermont	20
Maine	50
Rhode Island	80
New Hampshire	50

b. How many participants were from Connecticut? 120

c. Which state sent the most number of participants? Massachusetts

d. Which states sent the same number of participants? Maine and New Hampshire

e. How many fewer participants did Vermont send than Rhode Island? 60

f. How many more participants should Maine send to equal the number of participants from Connecticut? 70

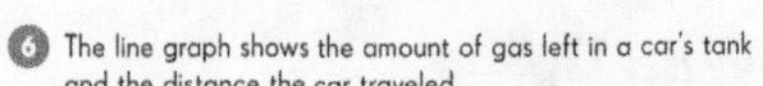

5 The table shows the number of notebooks and pens bought by three classes in a school.

Stationery Bought by Three Classes

Class	Notebooks ($2 each)		Pens (80¢ each)		Total Cost
	Number of Notebooks Bought	Cost	Number of Pens Bought	Cost	
A	12	$ 24	6	$4.80	$28.80
B	15	$ 30	10	$8.00	$ 38
C	8	$16.00	8	$6.40	$22.40
Total	35	$ 70	24	$19.20	$89.20

a Which class bought the most number of pens and notebooks altogether? Class B

b Which class spent the least amount of money on stationery? Class C

c What is the total cost of pens bought by the three classes? $19.20

d Class A spent more money on notebooks than on pens.

How much more was it? $19.20

6 The line graph shows the amount of gas left in a car's tank and the distance the car traveled.

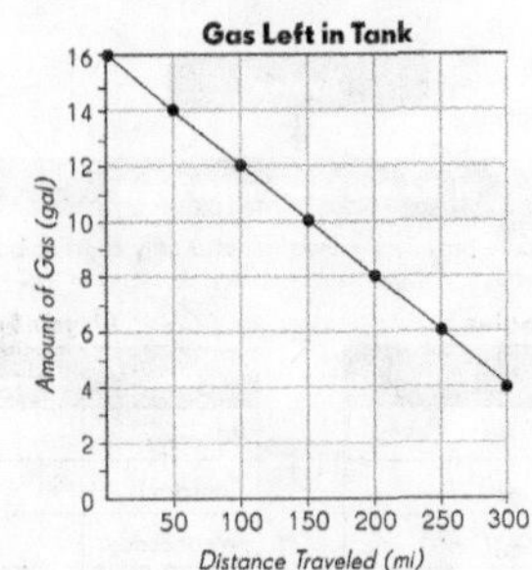

a How much gas was in the car's tank at

i the start of the trip? 16 gal

ii the end of the trip? 4 gal

b How much gas was used for

i the first 50 miles traveled? 2 gal

ii the second 50 miles traveled? 2 gal

iii the third 50 miles traveled? 2 gal

iv the fourth 50 miles traveled? 2 gal

c Look at your answers in Exercise 6b.

i How far can this car travel on 2 gallons of gas? 50 mi

ii How far can it travel on 1 gallon of gas? 25 mi

7 The line graph shows the number of people in line at a post office from 9:00 A.M. to 3:00 P.M.

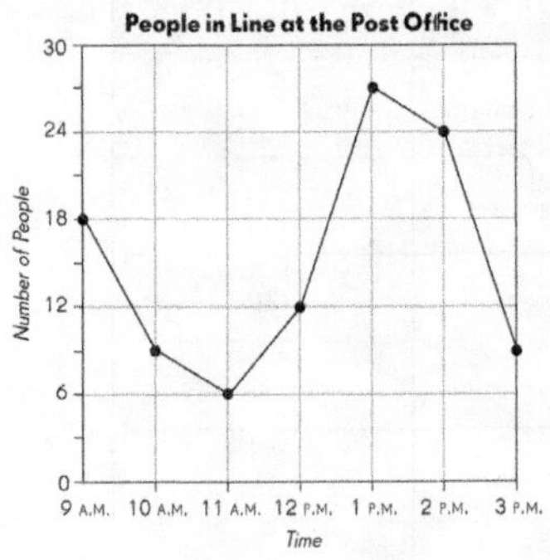

a At what time was the line the shortest? 11:00 A.M.

b At what time was the line the longest? 1:00 P.M.

c i What was the decrease in the number of people in the line from 10:00 A.M. to 11:00 A.M.? 3

ii In which 1-hour interval did the line decrease by the same number of people as from 10:00 A.M. to 11:00 A.M.? 1:00 P.M. to 2:00 P.M.

d What would be the best time to use this post office? State a reason for your answer. 11:00 A.M.; because the line is the shortest.

Chapter 4

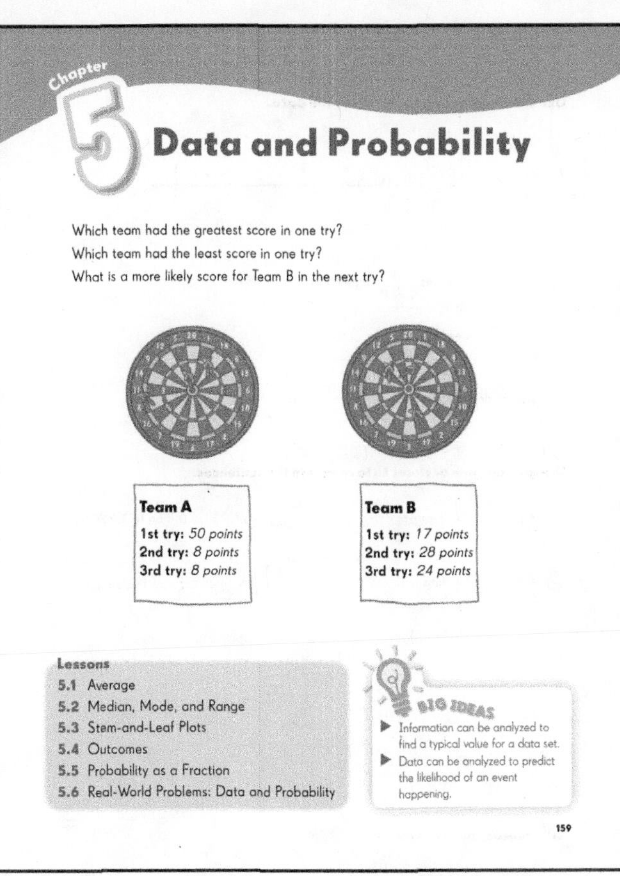
Chapter 5

Data and Probability

Which team had the greatest score in one try?
Which team had the least score in one try?
What is a more likely score for Team B in the next try?

Team A
1st try: *50 points*
2nd try: *8 points*
3rd try: *8 points*

Team B
1st try: *17 points*
2nd try: *28 points*
3rd try: *24 points*

Lessons
5.1 Average
5.2 Median, Mode, and Range
5.3 Stem-and-Leaf Plots
5.4 Outcomes
5.5 Probability as a Fraction
5.6 Real-World Problems: Data and Probability

BIG IDEAS
- Information can be analyzed to find a typical value for a data set.
- Data can be analyzed to predict the likelihood of an event happening.

159

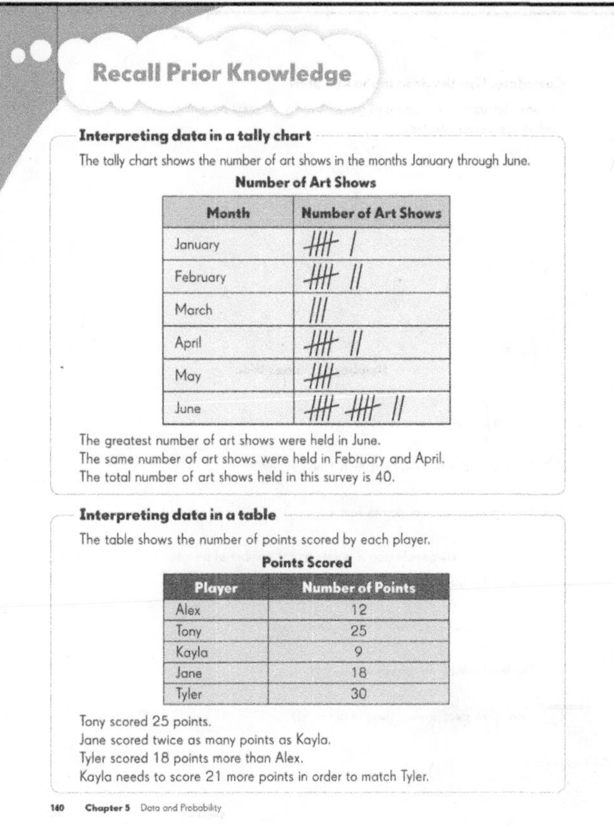
Recall Prior Knowledge

Interpreting data in a tally chart

The tally chart shows the number of art shows in the months January through June.

Number of Art Shows

Month	Number of Art Shows
January	~~||||~~ |
February	~~||||~~ ||
March	|||
April	~~||||~~ ||
May	~~||||~~
June	~~||||~~ ~~||||~~ ||

The greatest number of art shows were held in June.
The same number of art shows were held in February and April.
The total number of art shows held in this survey is 40.

Interpreting data in a table

The table shows the number of points scored by each player.

Points Scored

Player	Number of Points
Alex	12
Tony	25
Kayla	9
Jane	18
Tyler	30

Tony scored 25 points.
Jane scored twice as many points as Kayla.
Tyler scored 18 points more than Alex.
Kayla needs to score 21 more points in order to match Tyler.

140 **Chapter 5** Data and Probability

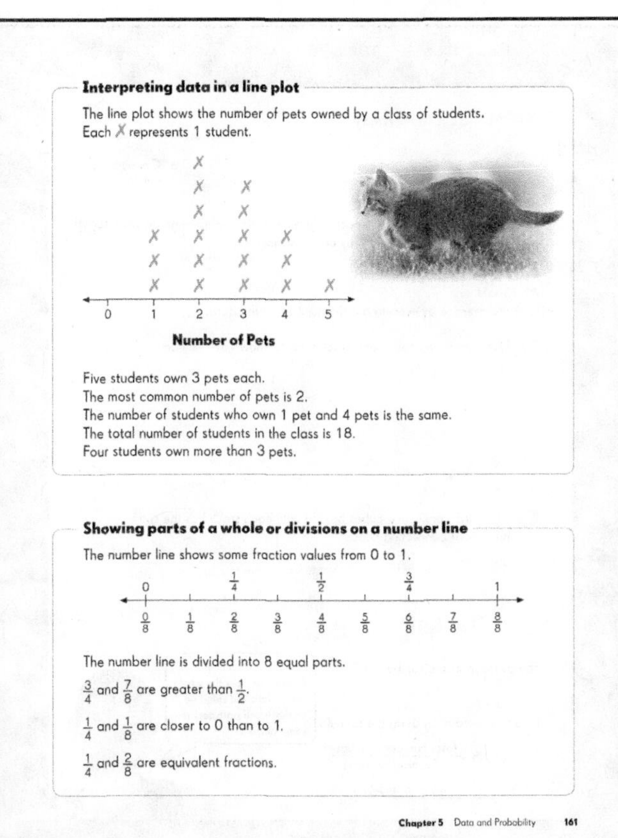
Interpreting data in a line plot

The line plot shows the number of pets owned by a class of students.
Each X represents 1 student.

Five students own 3 pets each.
The most common number of pets is 2.
The number of students who own 1 pet and 4 pets is the same.
The total number of students in the class is 18.
Four students own more than 3 pets.

Showing parts of a whole or divisions on a number line

The number line shows some fraction values from 0 to 1.

The number line is divided into 8 equal parts.
$\frac{3}{4}$ and $\frac{7}{8}$ are greater than $\frac{1}{2}$.
$\frac{1}{4}$ and $\frac{1}{8}$ are closer to 0 than to 1.
$\frac{1}{4}$ and $\frac{2}{8}$ are equivalent fractions.

Chapter 5 Data and Probability 161

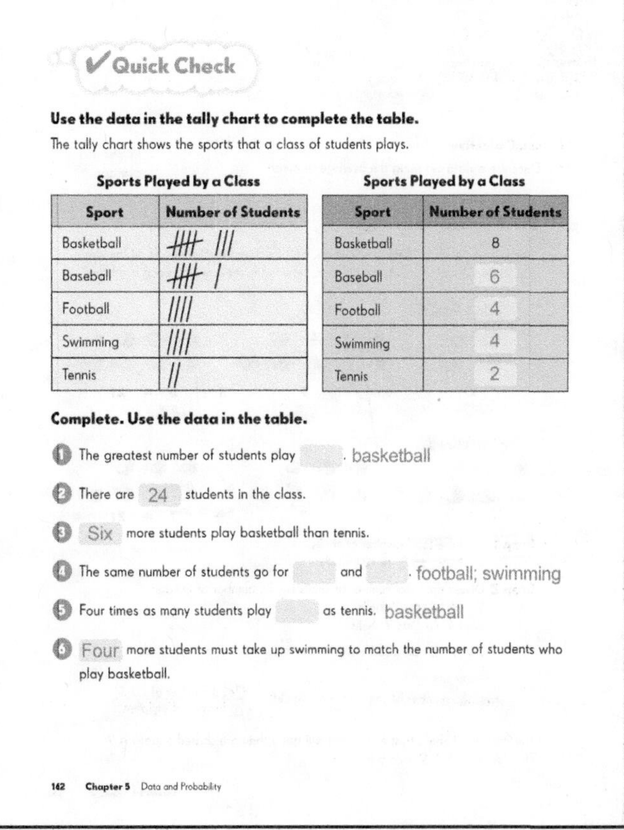
✔Quick Check

Use the data in the tally chart to complete the table.

The tally chart shows the sports that a class of students plays.

Sports Played by a Class

Sport	Number of Students
Basketball	~~||||~~ |||
Baseball	~~||||~~ |
Football	||||
Swimming	||||
Tennis	||

Sports Played by a Class

Sport	Number of Students
Basketball	8
Baseball	6
Football	4
Swimming	4
Tennis	2

Complete. Use the data in the table.

1. The greatest number of students play ____. basketball
2. There are 24 students in the class.
3. Six more students play basketball than tennis.
4. The same number of students go for ____ and ____. football; swimming
5. Four times as many students play ____ as tennis. basketball
6. Four more students must take up swimming to match the number of students who play basketball.

142 **Chapter 5** Data and Probability

Chapter 5

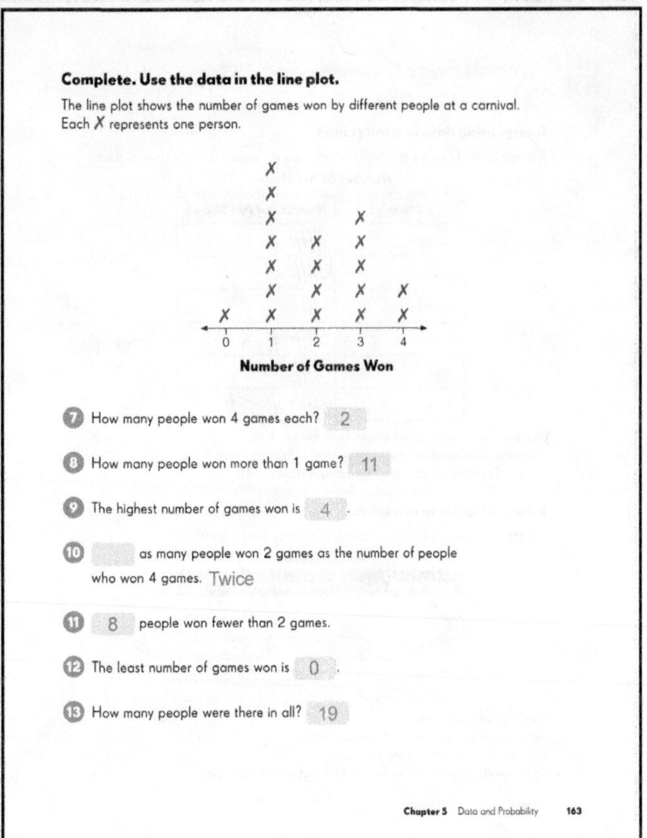

Complete. Use the data in the line plot.

The line plot shows the number of games won by different people at a carnival. Each X represents one person.

7. How many people won 4 games each? 2

8. How many people won more than 1 game? 11

9. The highest number of games won is 4.

10. ____ as many people won 2 games as the number of people who won 4 games. Twice

11. 8 people won fewer than 2 games.

12. The least number of games won is 0.

13. How many people were there in all? 19

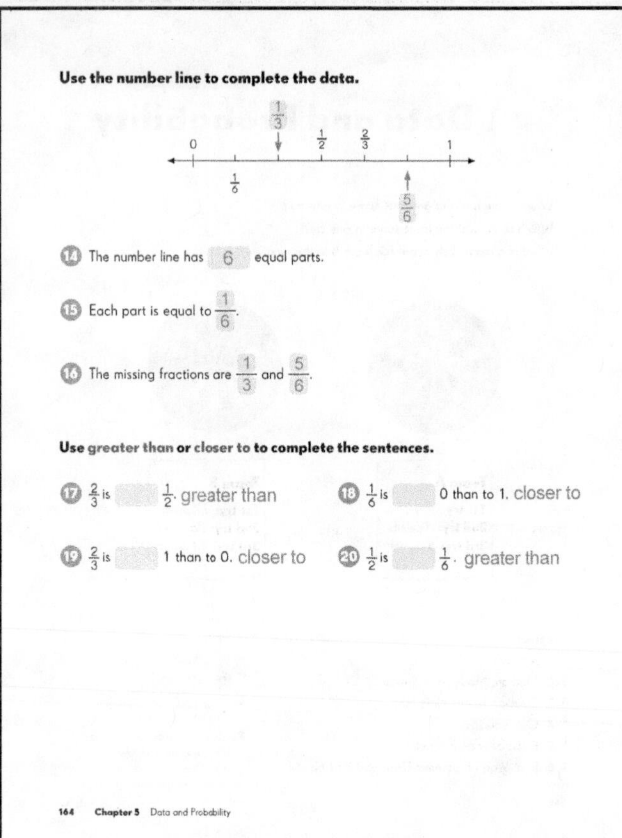

Use the number line to complete the data.

14. The number line has 6 equal parts.

15. Each part is equal to $\frac{1}{6}$.

16. The missing fractions are $\frac{1}{3}$ and $\frac{5}{6}$.

Use greater than or closer to to complete the sentences.

17. $\frac{2}{3}$ is ____ $\frac{1}{2}$. greater than

18. $\frac{1}{6}$ is ____ 0 than to 1. closer to

19. $\frac{2}{3}$ is ____ 1 than to 0. closer to

20. $\frac{1}{2}$ is ____ $\frac{1}{6}$. greater than

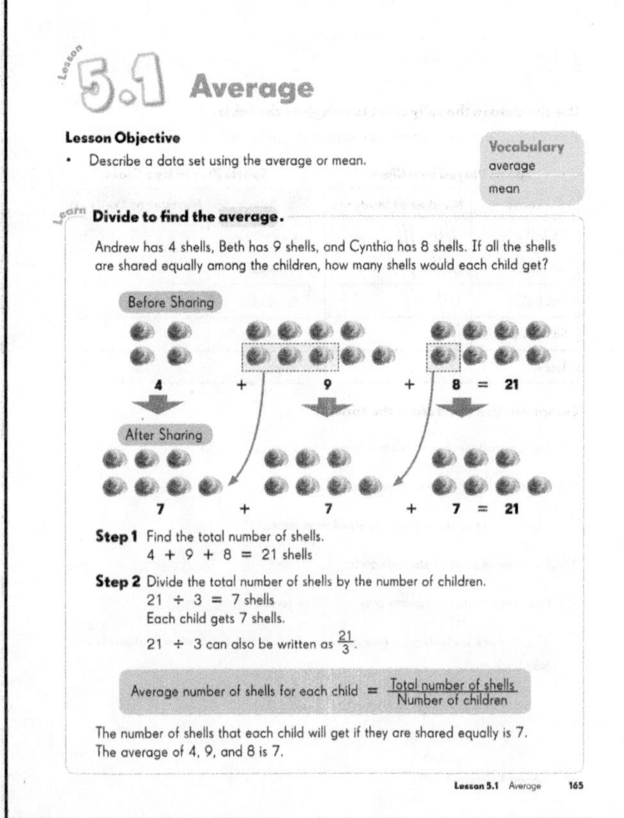

Lesson 5.1 Average

Lesson Objective

- Describe a data set using the average or mean.

Vocabulary
average
mean

Learn Divide to find the average.

Andrew has 4 shells, Beth has 9 shells, and Cynthia has 8 shells. If all the shells are shared equally among the children, how many shells would each child get?

Step 1 Find the total number of shells.
4 + 9 + 8 = 21 shells

Step 2 Divide the total number of shells by the number of children.
21 ÷ 3 = 7 shells
Each child gets 7 shells.

21 ÷ 3 can also be written as $\frac{21}{3}$.

$$\text{Average number of shells for each child} = \frac{\text{Total number of shells}}{\text{Number of children}}$$

The number of shells that each child will get if they are shared equally is 7.
The average of 4, 9, and 8 is 7.

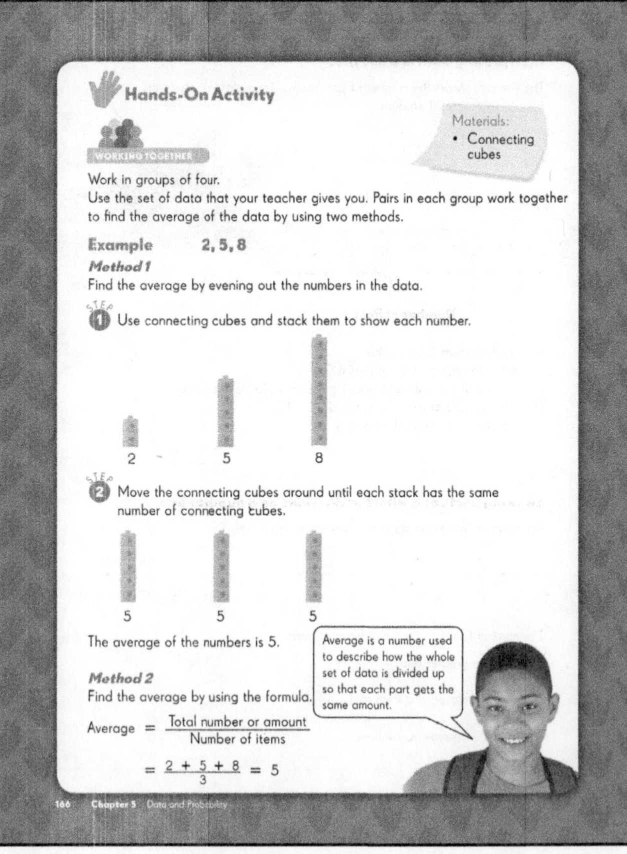

Hands-On Activity

Materials:
- Connecting cubes

WORKING TOGETHER

Work in groups of four.
Use the set of data that your teacher gives you. Pairs in each group work together to find the average of the data by using two methods.

Example 2, 5, 8

Method 1

Find the average by evening out the numbers in the data.

STEP 1 Use connecting cubes and stack them to show each number.

STEP 2 Move the connecting cubes around until each stack has the same number of connecting cubes.

The average of the numbers is 5.

Method 2

Find the average by using the formula.

$$\text{Average} = \frac{\text{Total number or amount}}{\text{Number of items}}$$

$$= \frac{2 + 5 + 8}{3} = 5$$

Chapter 5

Guided Practice

Find the average.

1. Four students sold stickers for charity. The table shows the number of stickers each student sold.

Number of Stickers Sold for Charity

Name	Number of Stickers
Abe	12
Bette	20
Carlo	16
Diana	28

What is the average number of stickers that each student sold?

$$\text{Average number of stickers sold by each student} = \frac{\text{Total number of stickers sold}}{\text{Number of students}}$$

Total = 12 + 20 + 16 + 28 = 76

Average = 76 ÷ 4 = 19

The average number of stickers that each student sold is 19.

Learn **Another word for average is mean.**

These are the scores Lila, Jody, and Chris got on an English test.

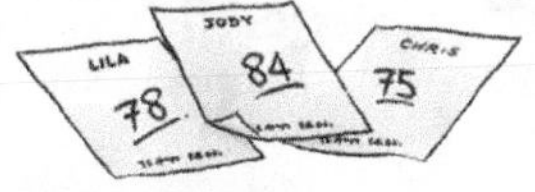

$$\text{Mean or average} = \frac{\text{Total number or amount}}{\text{Number of items}}$$

What is the total of the 3 scores?

Total score = 78 + 84 + 75
= 237

The total score that Lila, Jody, and Chris got is 237.

What is their mean score?

Mean score = 237 ÷ 3
= 79

Their mean score is 79.

For data sets that do not have very high or very low numbers, the mean or average gives a good description of the data.

Guided Practice

Find the mean or average.

A farmer has 5 dogs whose weights are 28 pounds, 34 pounds, 56 pounds, 42 pounds, and 60 pounds.

2. What is the total weight of the 5 dogs?

Total weight = 28 + 34 + 56 + 42 + 60
= 220 lb

The total weight of the 5 dogs is 220 pounds.

3. What is the mean weight of the 5 dogs?

Mean weight = 220 ÷ 5
= 44 lb

The mean weight of the 5 dogs is 44 pounds.

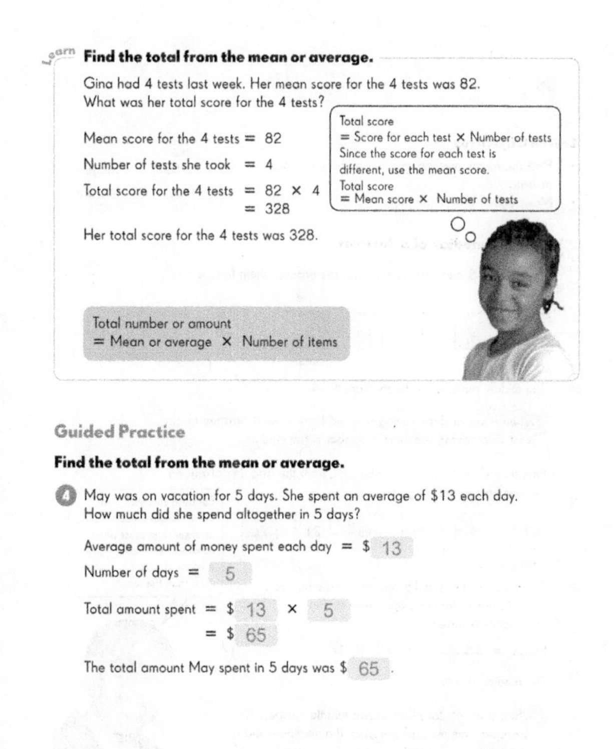

Learn **Find the total from the mean or average.**

Gina had 4 tests last week. Her mean score for the 4 tests was 82. What was her total score for the 4 tests?

Mean score for the 4 tests = 82

Number of tests she took = 4

Total score for the 4 tests = 82 × 4
= 328

Her total score for the 4 tests was 328.

Total score
= Score for each test × Number of tests
Since the score for each test is different, use the mean score.
Total score
= Mean score × Number of tests

Total number or amount
= Mean or average × Number of items

Guided Practice

Find the total from the mean or average.

4. May was on vacation for 5 days. She spent an average of $13 each day. How much did she spend altogether in 5 days?

Average amount of money spent each day = $ 13

Number of days = 5

Total amount spent = $ 13 × 5
= $ 65

The total amount May spent in 5 days was $ 65.

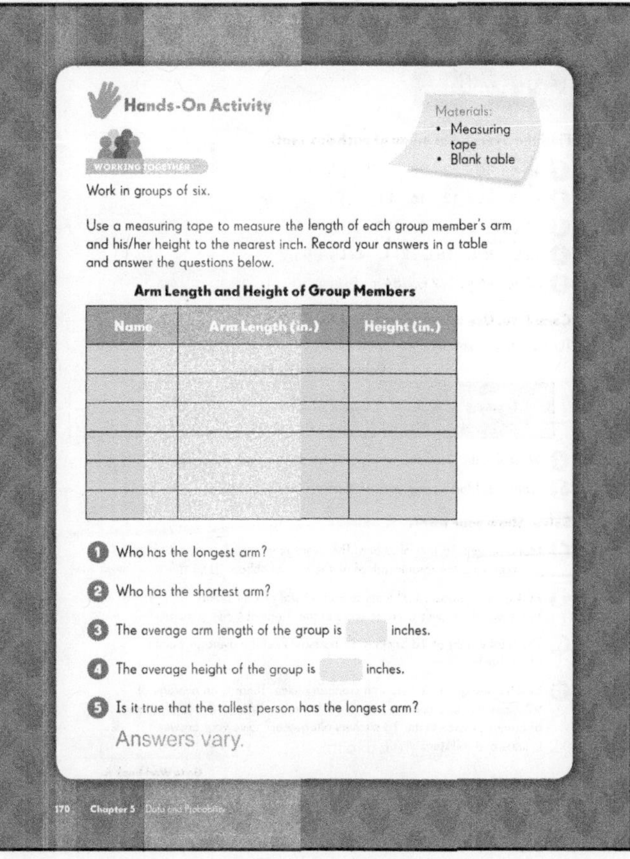

Hands-On Activity

WORKING TOGETHER

Materials:
- Measuring tape
- Blank table

Work in groups of six.

Use a measuring tape to measure the length of each group member's arm and his/her height to the nearest inch. Record your answers in a table and answer the questions below.

Arm Length and Height of Group Members

Name	Arm Length (in.)	Height (in.)

1. Who has the longest arm?
2. Who has the shortest arm?
3. The average arm length of the group is ___ inches.
4. The average height of the group is ___ inches.
5. Is it true that the tallest person has the longest arm?

Answers vary.

Chapter 5

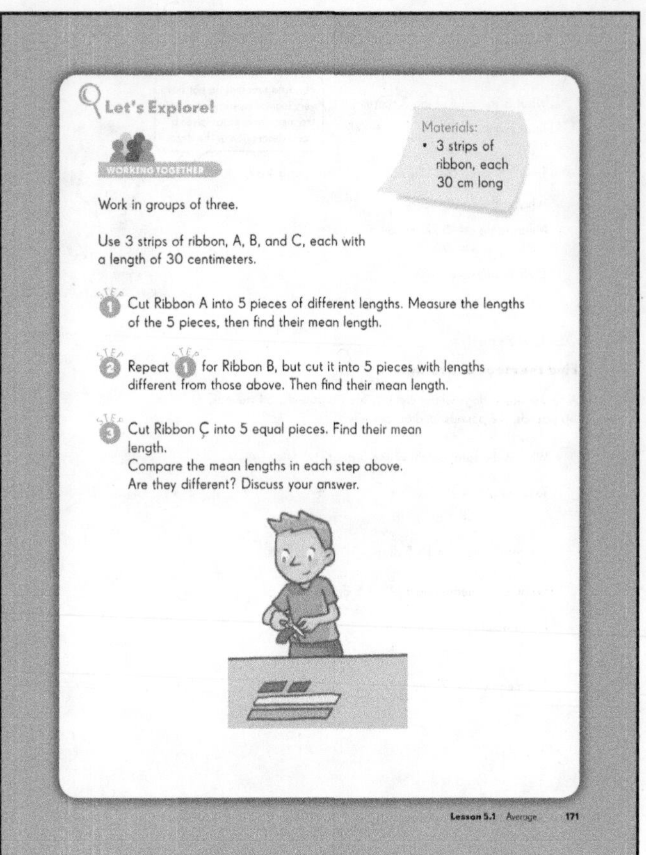

Let's Explore!

WORKING TOGETHER

Materials:
- 3 strips of ribbon, each 30 cm long

Work in groups of three.

Use 3 strips of ribbon, A, B, and C, each with a length of 30 centimeters.

STEP 1 Cut Ribbon A into 5 pieces of different lengths. Measure the lengths of the 5 pieces, then find their mean length.

STEP 2 Repeat STEP 1 for Ribbon B, but cut it into 5 pieces with lengths different from those above. Then find their mean length.

STEP 3 Cut Ribbon C into 5 equal pieces. Find their mean length.
Compare the mean lengths in each step above.
Are they different? Discuss your answer.

Lesson 5.1 Average 171

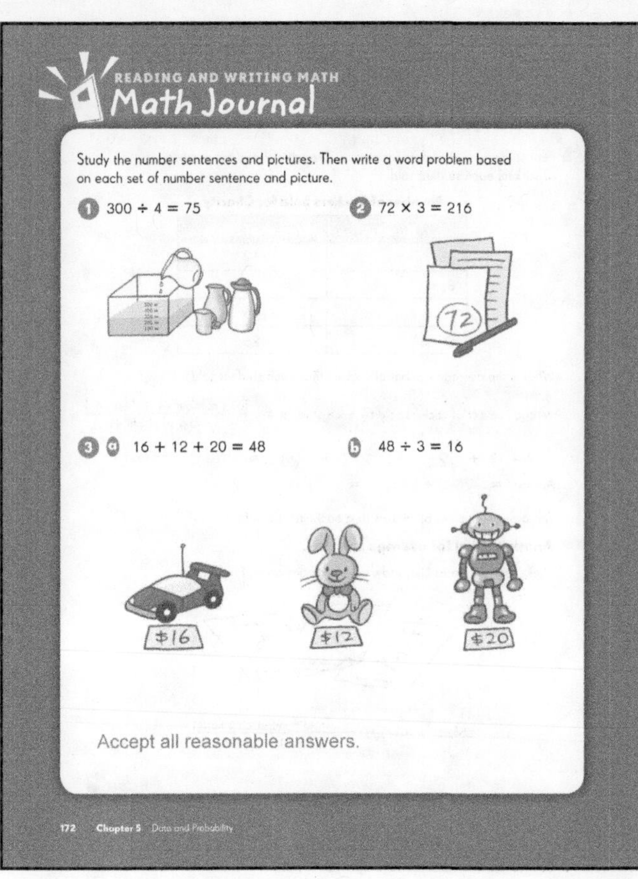

READING AND WRITING MATH

Math Journal

Study the number sentences and pictures. Then write a word problem based on each set of number sentence and picture.

1. $300 \div 4 = 75$
2. $72 \times 3 = 216$

3. a. $16 + 12 + 20 = 48$ b. $48 \div 3 = 16$

Accept all reasonable answers.

172 Chapter 5 Data and Probability

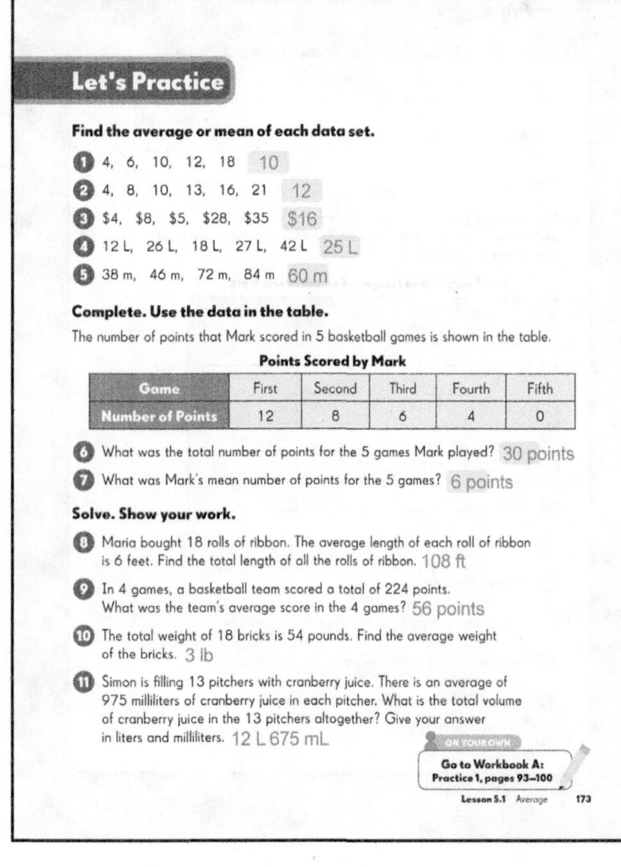

Chapter 5

Let's Practice

Find the average or mean of each data set.

1. 4, 6, 10, 12, 18 10
2. 4, 8, 10, 13, 16, 21 12
3. $4, $8, $5, $28, $35 $16
4. 12 L, 26 L, 18 L, 27 L, 42 L 25 L
5. 38 m, 46 m, 72 m, 84 m 60 m

Complete. Use the data in the table.

The number of points that Mark scored in 5 basketball games is shown in the table.

Points Scored by Mark

Game	First	Second	Third	Fourth	Fifth
Number of Points	12	8	6	4	0

6. What was the total number of points for the 5 games Mark played? 30 points
7. What was Mark's mean number of points for the 5 games? 6 points

Solve. Show your work.

8. Maria bought 18 rolls of ribbon. The average length of each roll of ribbon is 6 feet. Find the total length of all the rolls of ribbon. 108 ft
9. In 4 games, a basketball team scored a total of 224 points. What was the team's average score in the 4 games? 56 points
10. The total weight of 18 bricks is 54 pounds. Find the average weight of the bricks. 3 lb
11. Simon is filling 13 pitchers with cranberry juice. There is an average of 975 milliliters of cranberry juice in each pitcher. What is the total volume of cranberry juice in the 13 pitchers altogether? Give your answer in liters and milliliters. 12 L 675 mL

ON YOUR OWN
Go to Workbook A: Practice 1, pages 93–100

Lesson 5.1 Average 173

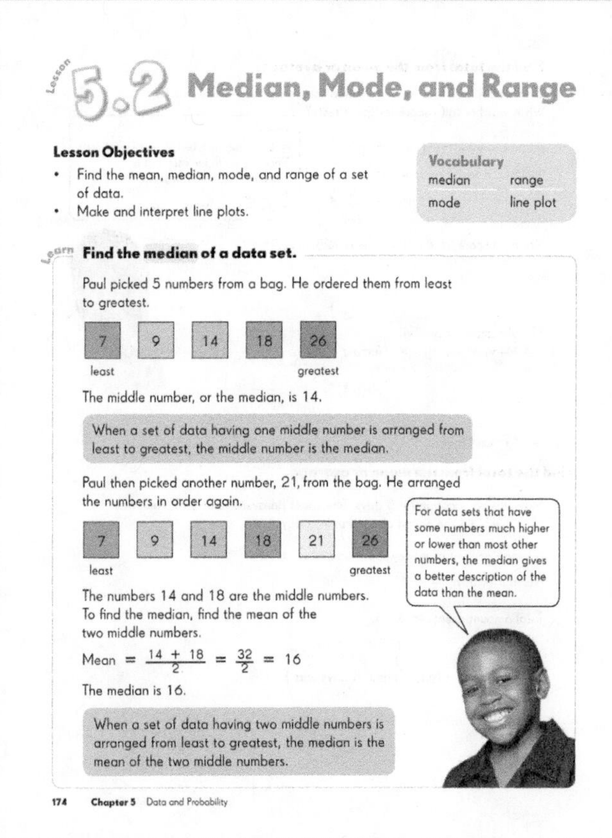

Lesson 5.2 Median, Mode, and Range

Lesson Objectives
- Find the mean, median, mode, and range of a set of data.
- Make and interpret line plots.

Vocabulary
median range
mode line plot

Learn Find the median of a data set.

Paul picked 5 numbers from a bag. He ordered them from least to greatest.

7 9 14 18 26
least greatest

The middle number, or the median, is 14.

When a set of data having one middle number is arranged from least to greatest, the middle number is the median.

Paul then picked another number, 21, from the bag. He arranged the numbers in order again.

7 9 14 18 21 26
least greatest

The numbers 14 and 18 are the middle numbers. To find the median, find the mean of the two middle numbers.

Mean $= \frac{14 + 18}{2} = \frac{32}{2} = 16$

The median is 16.

When a set of data having two middle numbers is arranged from least to greatest, the median is the mean of the two middle numbers.

For data sets that have some numbers much higher or lower than most other numbers, the median gives a better description of the data than the mean.

174 Chapter 5 Data and Probability

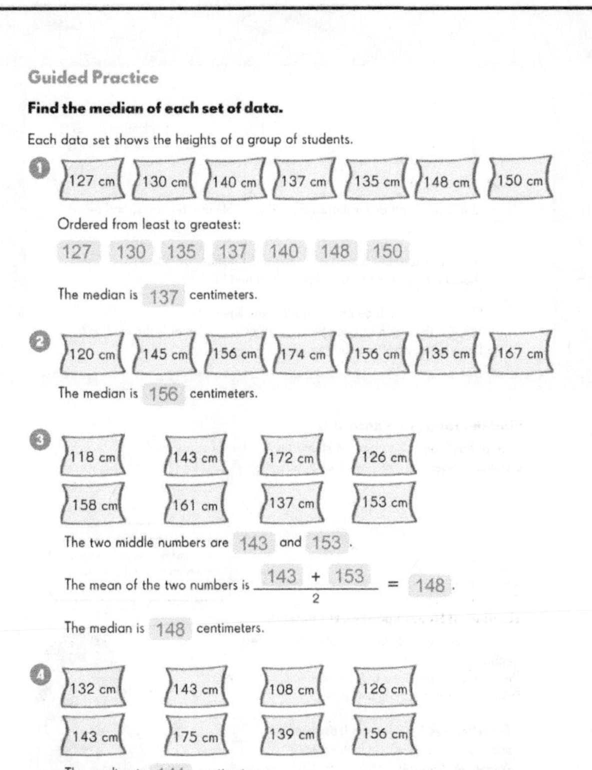

Guided Practice

Find the median of each set of data.

Each data set shows the heights of a group of students.

1. 127 cm, 130 cm, 140 cm, 137 cm, 135 cm, 148 cm, 150 cm

Ordered from least to greatest:

127 130 135 137 140 148 150

The median is 137 centimeters.

2. 120 cm, 145 cm, 156 cm, 174 cm, 156 cm, 135 cm, 167 cm

The median is 156 centimeters.

3. 118 cm, 143 cm, 172 cm, 126 cm, 158 cm, 161 cm, 137 cm, 153 cm

The two middle numbers are 143 and 153.

The mean of the two numbers is $\frac{143 + 153}{2} = 148$.

The median is 148 centimeters.

4. 132 cm, 143 cm, 108 cm, 126 cm, 143 cm, 175 cm, 139 cm, 156 cm

The median is 141 centimeters.

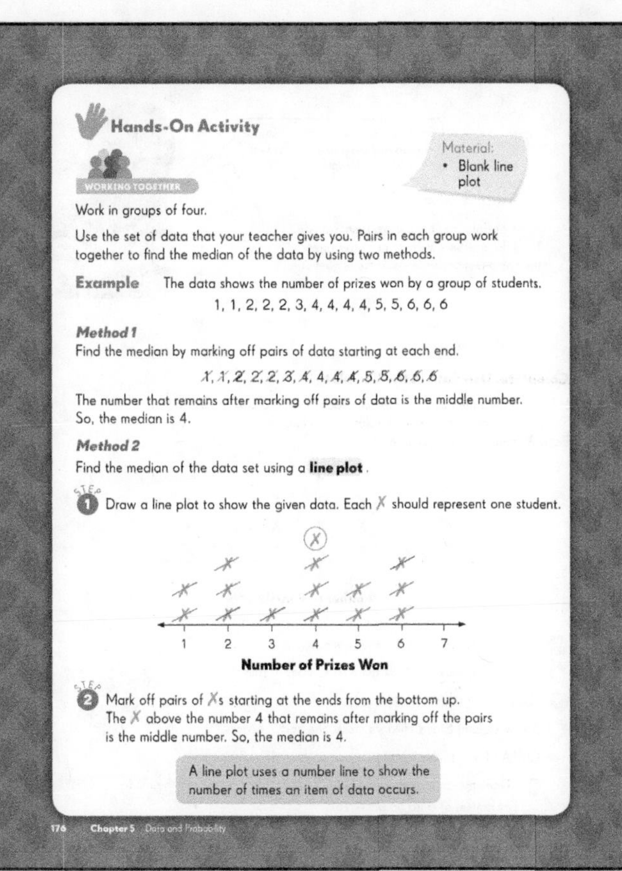

Hands-On Activity

WORKING TOGETHER

Material:
- Blank line plot

Work in groups of four.

Use the set of data that your teacher gives you. Pairs in each group work together to find the median of the data by using two methods.

Example The data shows the number of prizes won by a group of students.

1, 1, 2, 2, 2, 3, 4, 4, 4, 4, 5, 5, 6, 6, 6

Method 1

Find the median by marking off pairs of data starting at each end.

~~1~~, ~~1~~, ~~2~~, ~~2~~, ~~2~~, ~~3~~, ~~4~~, 4, ~~4~~, ~~4~~, ~~5~~, ~~5~~, ~~6~~, ~~6~~, ~~6~~

The number that remains after marking off pairs of data is the middle number. So, the median is 4.

Method 2

Find the median of the data set using a **line plot**.

STEP 1 Draw a line plot to show the given data. Each X should represent one student.

STEP 2 Mark off pairs of Xs starting at the ends from the bottom up. The X above the number 4 that remains after marking off the pairs is the middle number. So, the median is 4.

A line plot uses a number line to show the number of times an item of data occurs.

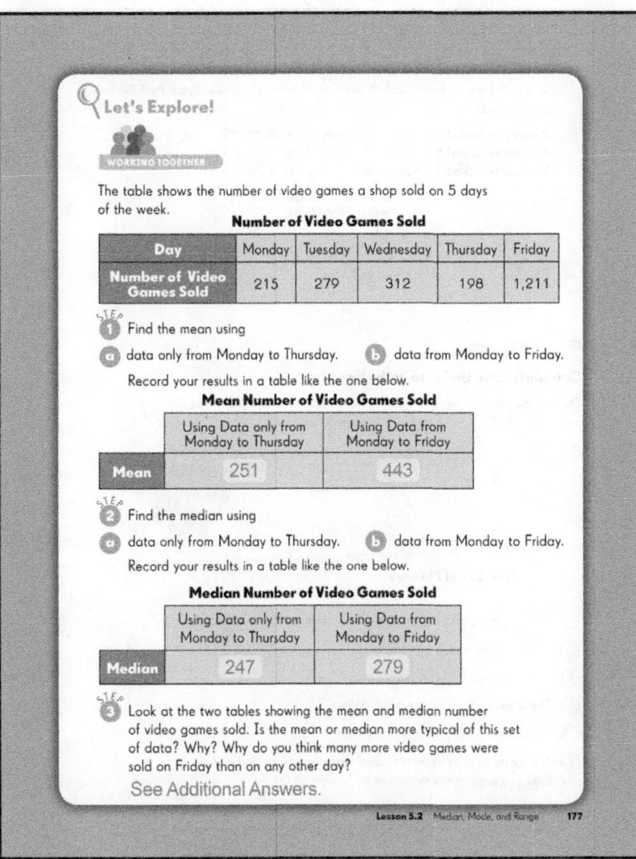

Let's Explore!

WORKING TOGETHER

The table shows the number of video games a shop sold on 5 days of the week.

Number of Video Games Sold

Day	Monday	Tuesday	Wednesday	Thursday	Friday
Number of Video Games Sold	215	279	312	198	1,211

STEP 1 Find the mean using

a. data only from Monday to Thursday. b. data from Monday to Friday.

Record your results in a table like the one below.

Mean Number of Video Games Sold

	Using Data only from Monday to Thursday	Using Data from Monday to Friday
Mean	251	443

STEP 2 Find the median using

a. data only from Monday to Thursday. b. data from Monday to Friday.

Record your results in a table like the one below.

Median Number of Video Games Sold

	Using Data only from Monday to Thursday	Using Data from Monday to Friday
Median	247	279

STEP 3 Look at the two tables showing the mean and median number of video games sold. Is the mean or median more typical of this set of data? Why? Why do you think many more video games were sold on Friday than on any other day?

See Additional Answers.

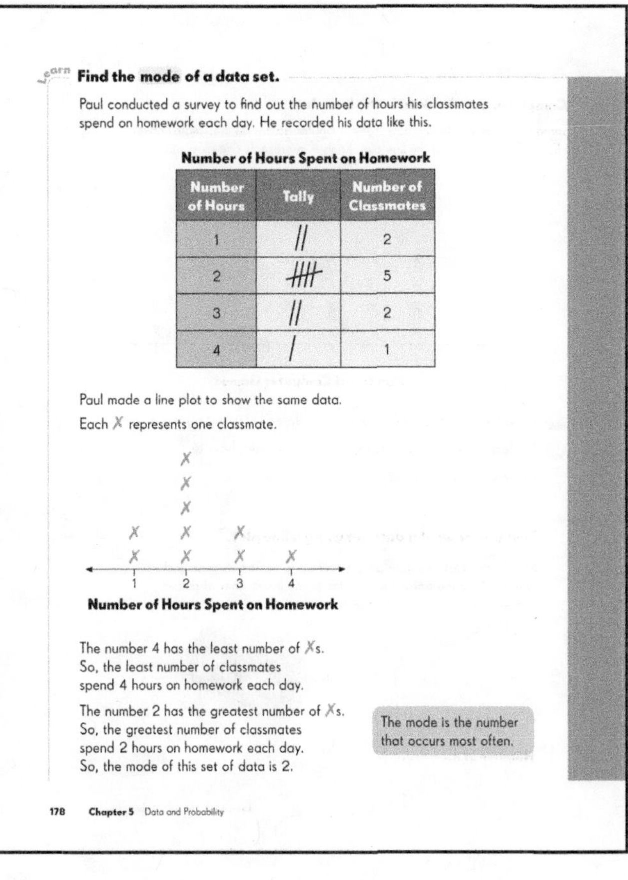

Learn Find the mode of a data set.

Paul conducted a survey to find out the number of hours his classmates spend on homework each day. He recorded his data like this.

Number of Hours Spent on Homework

Number of Hours	Tally	Number of Classmates
1	//	2
2	~~////~~	5
3	//	2
4	/	1

Paul made a line plot to show the same data.

Each X represents one classmate.

The number 4 has the least number of Xs. So, the least number of classmates spend 4 hours on homework each day.

The number 2 has the greatest number of Xs. So, the greatest number of classmates spend 2 hours on homework each day. So, the mode of this set of data is 2.

The mode is the number that occurs most often.

Chapter 5

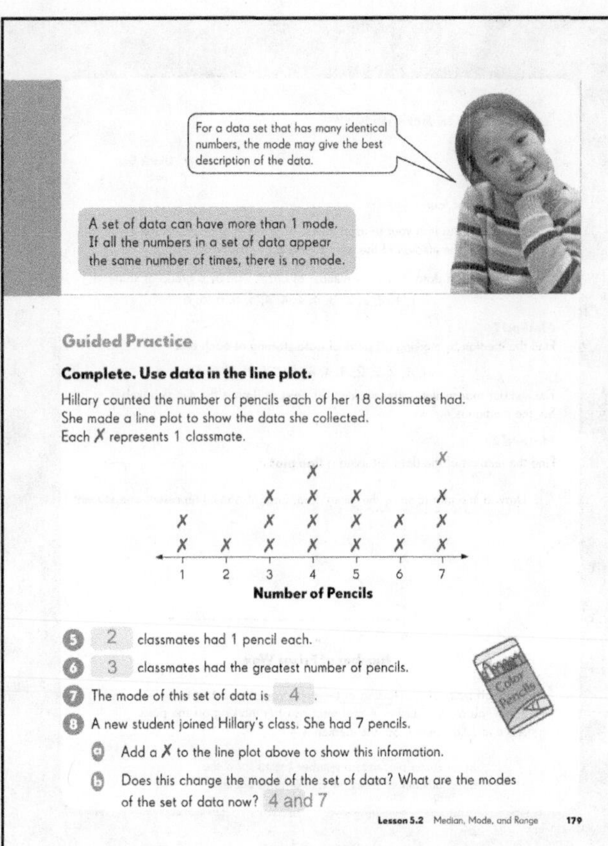

For a data set that has many identical numbers, the mode may give the best description of the data.

A set of data can have more than 1 mode. If all the numbers in a set of data appear the same number of times, there is no mode.

Guided Practice

Complete. Use data in the line plot.

Hillary counted the number of pencils each of her 18 classmates had. She made a line plot to show the data she collected. Each ✗ represents 1 classmate.

Number of Pencils

5. 2 classmates had 1 pencil each.
6. 3 classmates had the greatest number of pencils.
7. The mode of this set of data is 4.
8. A new student joined Hillary's class. She had 7 pencils.
   a. Add a ✗ to the line plot above to show this information.
   b. Does this change the mode of the set of data? What are the modes of the set of data now? 4 and 7

Lesson 5.2 Median, Mode, and Range 179

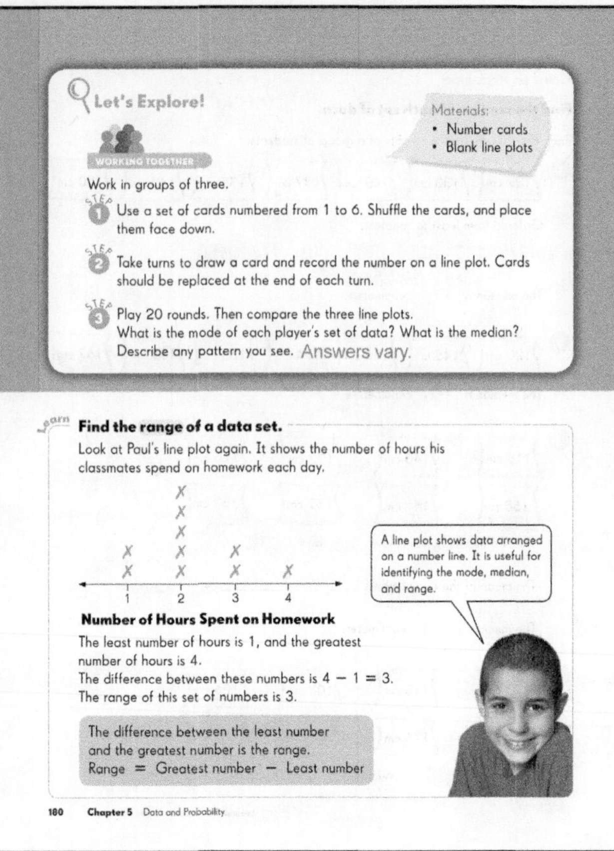

Let's Explore!

Materials:
- Number cards
- Blank line plots

WORKING TOGETHER

Work in groups of three.

STEP 1 Use a set of cards numbered from 1 to 6. Shuffle the cards, and place them face down.

STEP 2 Take turns to draw a card and record the number on a line plot. Cards should be replaced at the end of each turn.

STEP 3 Play 20 rounds. Then compare the three line plots. What is the mode of each player's set of data? What is the median? Describe any pattern you see. Answers vary.

Learn Find the range of a data set.

Look at Paul's line plot again. It shows the number of hours his classmates spend on homework each day.

Number of Hours Spent on Homework

A line plot shows data arranged on a number line. It is useful for identifying the mode, median, and range.

The least number of hours is 1, and the greatest number of hours is 4.
The difference between these numbers is $4 - 1 = 3$.
The range of this set of numbers is 3.

The difference between the least number and the greatest number is the range.
Range = Greatest number − Least number

180 Chapter 5 Data and Probability

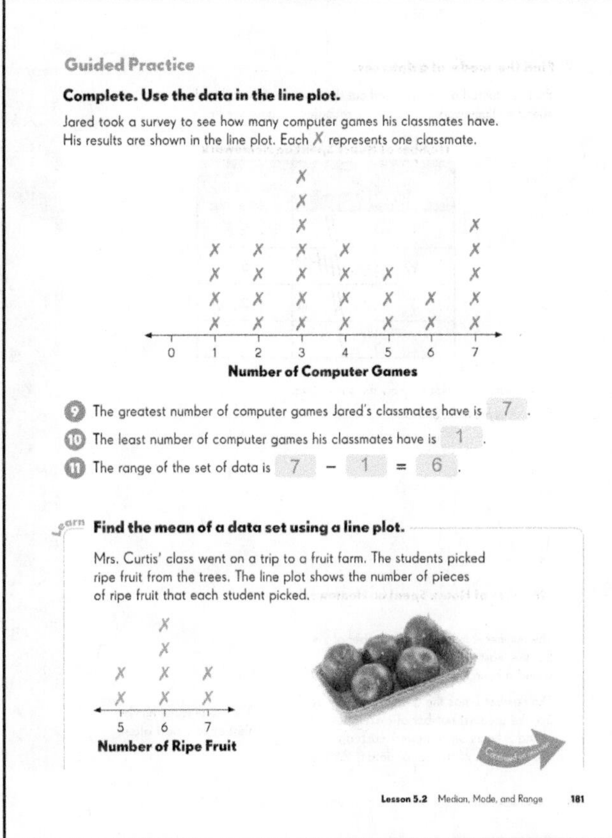

Guided Practice

Complete. Use the data in the line plot.

Jared took a survey to see how many computer games his classmates have. His results are shown in the line plot. Each ✗ represents one classmate.

Number of Computer Games

9. The greatest number of computer games Jared's classmates have is 7.
10. The least number of computer games his classmates have is 1.
11. The range of the set of data is 7 − 1 = 6.

Learn Find the mean of a data set using a line plot.

Mrs. Curtis' class went on a trip to a fruit farm. The students picked ripe fruit from the trees. The line plot shows the number of pieces of ripe fruit that each student picked.

Number of Ripe Fruit

Lesson 5.2 Median, Mode, and Range 181

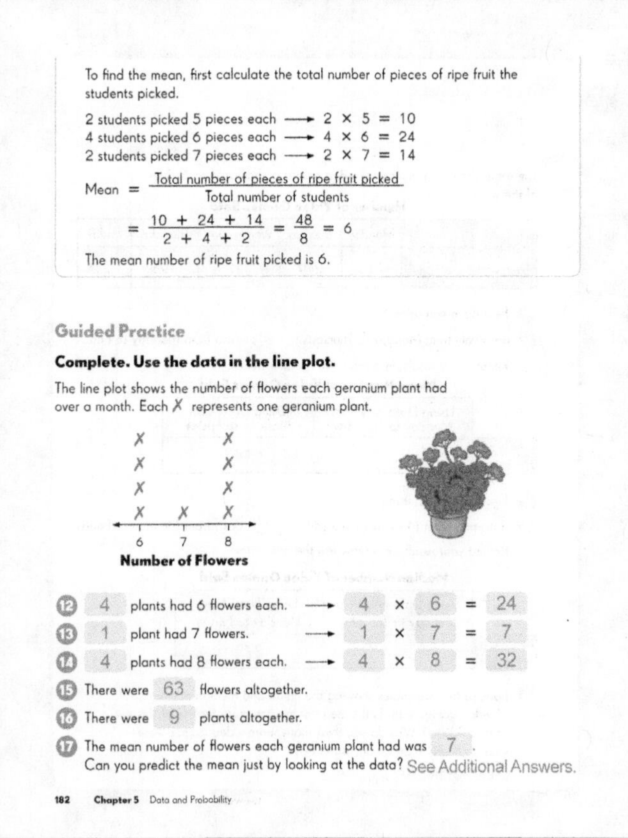

To find the mean, first calculate the total number of pieces of ripe fruit the students picked.

2 students picked 5 pieces each ⟶ $2 \times 5 = 10$
4 students picked 6 pieces each ⟶ $4 \times 6 = 24$
2 students picked 7 pieces each ⟶ $2 \times 7 = 14$

$$\text{Mean} = \frac{\text{Total number of pieces of ripe fruit picked}}{\text{Total number of students}} = \frac{10 + 24 + 14}{2 + 4 + 2} = \frac{48}{8} = 6$$

The mean number of ripe fruit picked is 6.

Guided Practice

Complete. Use the data in the line plot.

The line plot shows the number of flowers each geranium plant had over a month. Each ✗ represents one geranium plant.

Number of Flowers

12. 4 plants had 6 flowers each. ⟶ $4 \times 6 = 24$
13. 1 plant had 7 flowers. ⟶ $1 \times 7 = 7$
14. 4 plants had 8 flowers each. ⟶ $4 \times 8 = 32$
15. There were 63 flowers altogether.
16. There were 9 plants altogether.
17. The mean number of flowers each geranium plant had was 7. Can you predict the mean just by looking at the data? See Additional Answers.

182 Chapter 5 Data and Probability

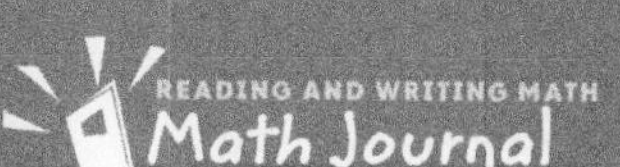

The set of numbers is arranged in order.

2, 4, 6, 12, 12, 18, 20, 32

Are the statements below true or false? If the statement is false, explain how to change the numbers or words to make it true.

1. The mode of the data set is 12 because it appears twice. True
2. There is no median for this set of data because the set of numbers is even and there is no middle number. See Additional Answers.
3. The mean and median of this set of data are the same. See Additional Answers.

Let's Practice

Find the median.

The table shows the temperature at noon from Monday to Saturday.

Temperature in Fahrenheit (°F)

	Monday	Tuesday	Wednesday	Thursday	Friday	Saturday
Week 1	39°	47°	39°	52°	28°	55°
Week 2	32°	66°	47°	54°	68°	48°

1. The median temperature in Week 1 is 43 °F.
2. The median temperature in Week 2 is 51 °F.

Lesson 5.2 Median, Mode, and Range 183

Complete. Use the data in the line plot.

The line plot shows the number of players who scored 2, 3, or 4 goals in their matches.
Each X represents one player.

Club A — Goals Scored (2, 3, 4)

Club B — Goals Scored (2, 3, 4)

3. How many players were goal scorers in each club? Club A: 9; Club B: 10
4. What is the median number of goals scored by the players in
   a. Club A? 3
   b. Club B? 3

Complete. Use the data in the line plot.

Mr. Gupta sells fabric. The line plot shows the lengths of fabric his customers bought in one afternoon.

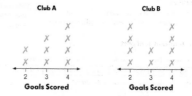

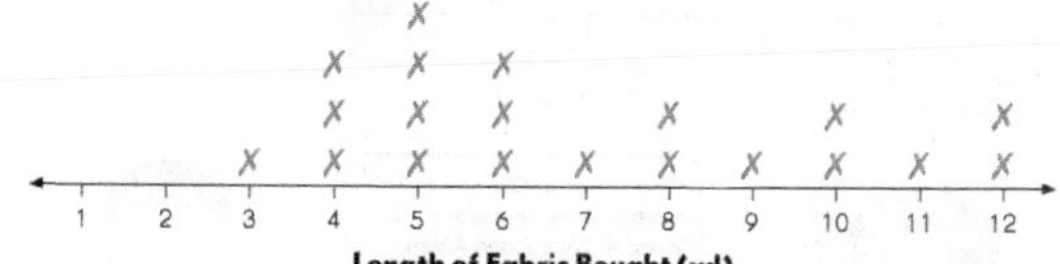

5. What is the range of the lengths of fabric bought? 9 yd
6. What is the mode of the set of data? Is the mode typical of this set of data? 5 yd; See Additional Answers.

184 Chapter 5 Data and Probability

7. What is the median of the set of data? Is the median typical of this set of data? 6yd; See Additional Answers.
8. What is the mean of this set of data? Is the mean typical of this set of data? 7 yd; See Additional Answers.
9. a. At the end of the day, another customer buys 196 yards of fabric. What is the mean, median, and mode of the new data set? See Additional Answers.
   b. Do the new mean, median, and mode seem typical of the data set? See Additional Answers.

Make a line plot to show the data. Use your line plot to answer each question.

A group of children went fishing at a neighborhood creek. They counted and weighed the fish they caught. The tally chart shows this data.

Number of Fish Caught

Weight of Fish (lb)	Tally	Number
1	///	3
2	~~////~~ /	6
3	////	4
4	/	1
5	/	1

10. How many fish were caught altogether? 15
11. What is the range of the weight of fish caught? 4 lb
12. What is the mode of the set of data? 2 lb
13. What is the median of the set of data? 2 lb

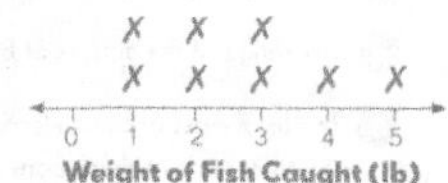

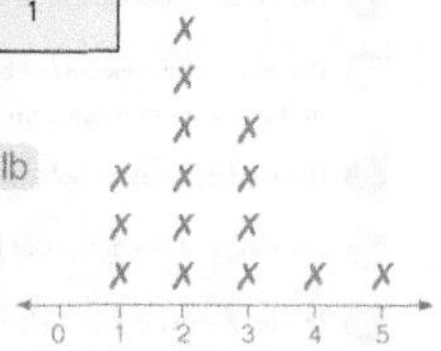

Lesson 5.2 Median, Mode, and Range 185

Complete. Use the data in the line plot.

Members of a running club recorded the number of marathons they ran in a line plot.

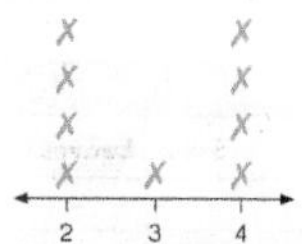

14. What is the total number of marathons the club members have run altogether? 27
15. Can you find the mean without calculating? Why? Evening out the Xs on the line plot shows that the mean is 3.

Use the table to find each median.

Dakota counted the number of falling meteors in the sky during the August meteor showers for three years.

August Meteor Showers for Three Years

	Day 1	Day 2	Day 3	Day 4	Day 5	Day 6
Year 1	45	43	31	38	49	53
Year 2	55	40	45	49	51	58
Year 3	42	39	36	34	35	36

16. The median number of meteors in Year 1 is 44.
17. The median number of meteors in Year 2 is 50.
18. The median number of meteors in Year 3 is 36.
19. The greatest median number of meteors was recorded in Year 2.
20. The difference between the greatest and the least median number of meteors is 14.
21. The median number of meteors recorded on Day 5 is 49.

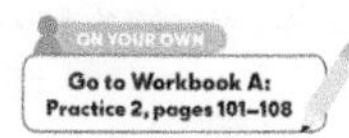

ON YOUR OWN
Go to Workbook A: Practice 2, pages 101–108

186 Chapter 5 Data and Probability

Chapter 5

Lesson 5.3 Stem-and-Leaf Plots

Lesson Objectives
- Organize and represent data in a stem-and-leaf plot.
- Use a stem-and-leaf plot to find median, mode, and range.

Vocabulary
stem-and-leaf plot
outlier

Learn Make a stem-and-leaf plot.

These are the grades that ten students scored on a math assignment.

71 58 56 69 42 72 64 56 44 88

Make a stem-and-leaf-plot to organize the data.

Step 1
Order the grades from least to greatest.

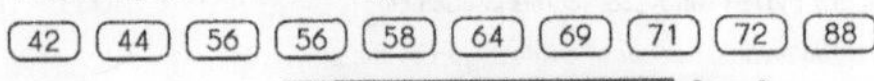

42 44 56 56 58 64 69 71 72 88

Step 2
Put the digits in tens place in the 'stem' column.

Math Assignment Grades

Stem	Leaves
4	2 4
5	6 6 8
6	4 9
7	1 2
8	8

4 | 2 = 42

Step 3
Put the digits in ones place in the 'leaves' column.

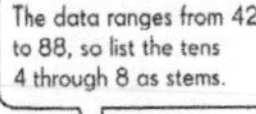

The data ranges from 42 to 88, so list the tens 4 through 8 as stems.

For the grades 42 and 44, the numbers in the ones place are 2 and 4. Write 2 and 4 side by side in the leaves column to represent the ones place for both 42 and 44. Order the numbers in the 'leaves' column from least to greatest.

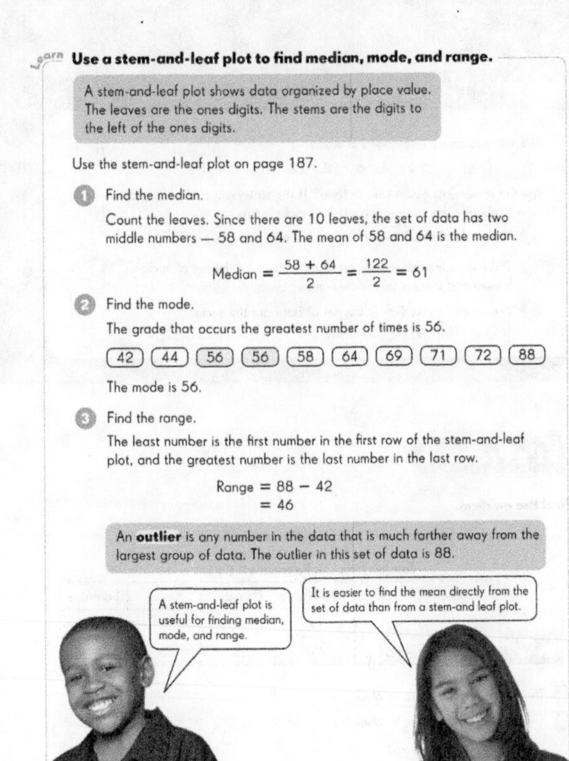

Learn Use a stem-and-leaf plot to find median, mode, and range.

A stem-and-leaf plot shows data organized by place value. The leaves are the ones digits. The stems are the digits to the left of the ones digits.

Use the stem-and-leaf plot on page 187.

1. Find the median.
   Count the leaves. Since there are 10 leaves, the set of data has two middle numbers — 58 and 64. The mean of 58 and 64 is the median.

$$\text{Median} = \frac{58 + 64}{2} = \frac{122}{2} = 61$$

2. Find the mode.
   The grade that occurs the greatest number of times is 56.

   42 44 56 56 58 64 69 71 72 88

   The mode is 56.

3. Find the range.
   The least number is the first number in the first row of the stem-and-leaf plot, and the greatest number is the last number in the last row.

$$\text{Range} = 88 - 42 = 46$$

An **outlier** is any number in the data that is much farther away from the largest group of data. The outlier in this set of data is 88.

Guided Practice

Complete. Use the data in the stem-and-leaf plot.

The stem-and-leaf plot shows the weights of some crates of potatoes at a supermarket.

Weight of Crates (lb)

Stem	Leaves
2	5
3	0 4 4 7
4	8
5	2 8
6	9

2 | 5 = 25

1. For the number 58, 5 is in the stem column, and 8 is in the leaves column.
2. The stem 3 has 4 leaves.
3. The weight that appears most often is 34 pounds. The mode is 34 pounds.
4. The median of the set of data is 37 pounds.
5. The greatest weight of a crate of potatoes is 69 pounds.
6. The least weight of a crate of potatoes is 25 pounds.
7. The difference between the least and the greatest weight of a crate of potatoes is 44 pounds. The range of the set of data is 44 pounds.
8. The total weight of all the crates of potatoes is 387 pounds.

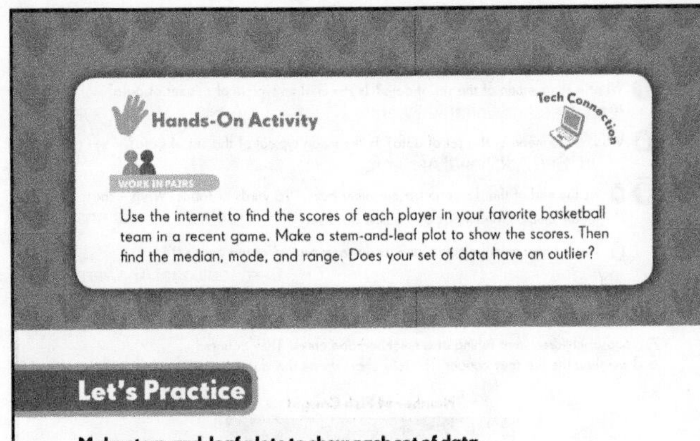

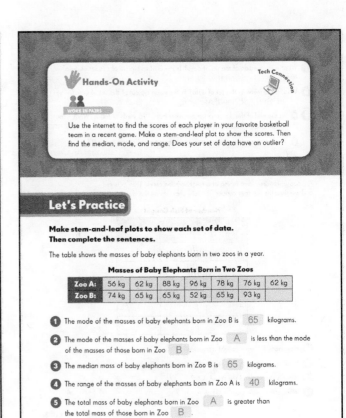

Hands-On Activity

Tech Connection

WORK IN PAIRS

Use the internet to find the scores of each player in your favorite basketball team in a recent game. Make a stem-and-leaf plot to show the scores. Then find the median, mode, and range. Does your set of data have an outlier?

Let's Practice

Make stem-and-leaf plots to show each set of data. Then complete the sentences.

The table shows the masses of baby elephants born in two zoos in a year.

Masses of Baby Elephants Born in Two Zoos

Zoo A:	56 kg	62 kg	88 kg	96 kg	78 kg	76 kg	62 kg
Zoo B:	74 kg	65 kg	65 kg	52 kg	65 kg	93 kg	

1. The mode of the masses of baby elephants born in Zoo B is 65 kilograms.
2. The mode of the masses of baby elephants born in Zoo A is less than the mode of the masses of those born in Zoo B.
3. The median mass of baby elephants born in Zoo B is 65 kilograms.
4. The range of the masses of baby elephants born in Zoo A is 40 kilograms.
5. The total mass of baby elephants born in Zoo A is greater than the total mass of those born in Zoo B.

The table shows the number of crafts a group of students made for a fair.

Number of Crafts Made

Student	Number of Crafts
Rachel	51
Cheyenne	44
Stella	64
Alisha	38
Michelle	44
Jordan	32
Andrew	47
Jen	40

6 The range of the set of data is 32.

7 The mode of the set of data is 44.

8 The median of the set of data is 44.

9 There are 2 leaves for the place value of 3 tens.

10 There are 4 leaves for the place value of 4 tens.

ON YOUR OWN

Go to Workbook A: Practice 3, pages 109–112

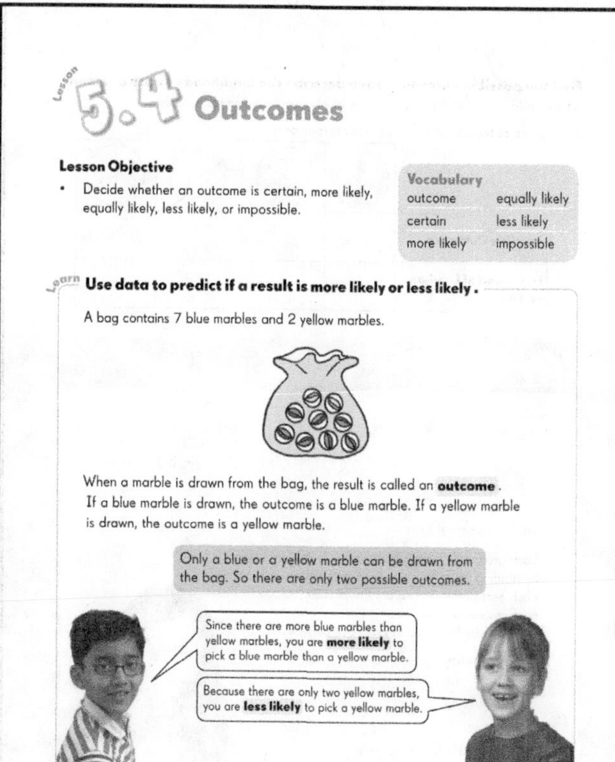

Lesson 5.4 Outcomes

Lesson Objective

- Decide whether an outcome is certain, more likely, equally likely, less likely, or impossible.

Vocabulary

outcome	equally likely
certain	less likely
more likely	impossible

Learn Use data to predict if a result is more likely or less likely.

A bag contains 7 blue marbles and 2 yellow marbles.

When a marble is drawn from the bag, the result is called an **outcome**. If a blue marble is drawn, the outcome is a blue marble. If a yellow marble is drawn, the outcome is a yellow marble.

Only a blue or a yellow marble can be drawn from the bag. So there are only two possible outcomes.

Since there are more blue marbles than yellow marbles, you are **more likely** to pick a blue marble than a yellow marble.
Because there are only two yellow marbles, you are **less likely** to pick a yellow marble.

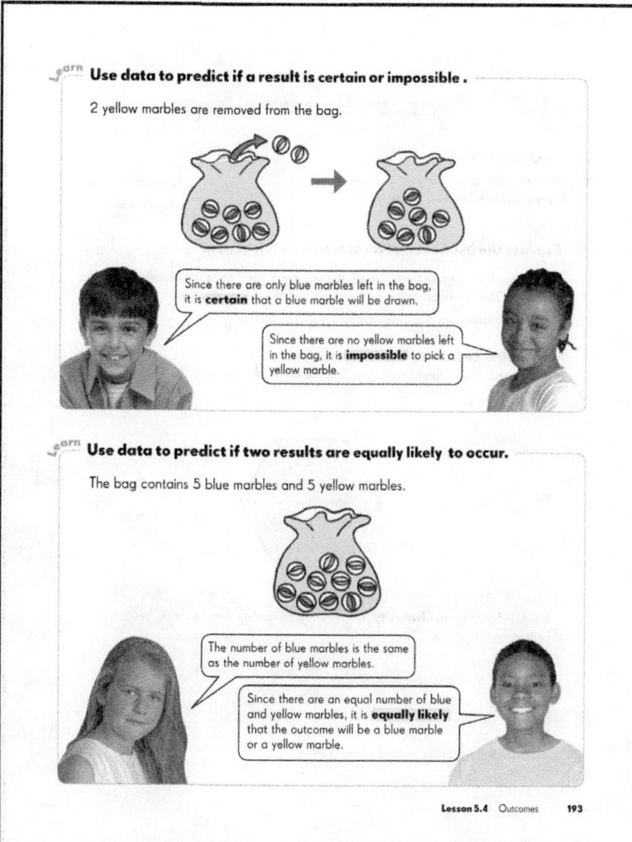

Learn Use data to predict if a result is certain or impossible.

2 yellow marbles are removed from the bag.

Since there are only blue marbles left in the bag, it is **certain** that a blue marble will be drawn.
Since there are no yellow marbles left in the bag, it is **impossible** to pick a yellow marble.

Learn Use data to predict if two results are equally likely to occur.

The bag contains 5 blue marbles and 5 yellow marbles.

The number of blue marbles is the same as the number of yellow marbles.
Since there are an equal number of blue and yellow marbles, it is **equally likely** that the outcome will be a blue marble or a yellow marble.

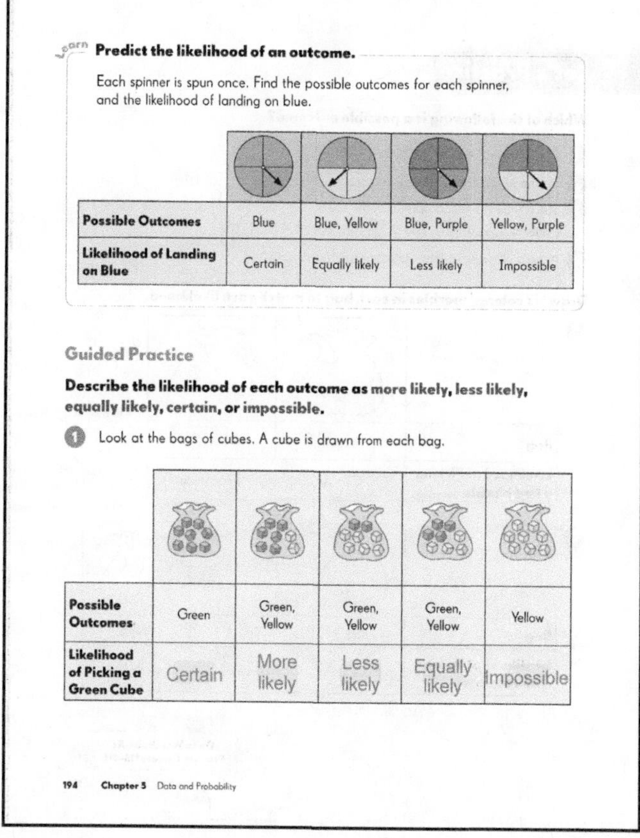

Learn Predict the likelihood of an outcome.

Each spinner is spun once. Find the possible outcomes for each spinner, and the likelihood of landing on blue.

	Spinner 1	Spinner 2	Spinner 3	Spinner 4
Possible Outcomes	Blue	Blue, Yellow	Blue, Purple	Yellow, Purple
Likelihood of Landing on Blue	Certain	Equally likely	Less likely	Impossible

Guided Practice

Describe the likelihood of each outcome as more likely, less likely, equally likely, certain, or impossible.

1 Look at the bags of cubes. A cube is drawn from each bag.

	Bag 1	Bag 2	Bag 3	Bag 4	Bag 5
Possible Outcomes	Green	Green, Yellow	Green, Yellow	Green, Yellow	Yellow
Likelihood of Picking a Green Cube	Certain	More likely	Less likely	Equally likely	Impossible

Chapter 5

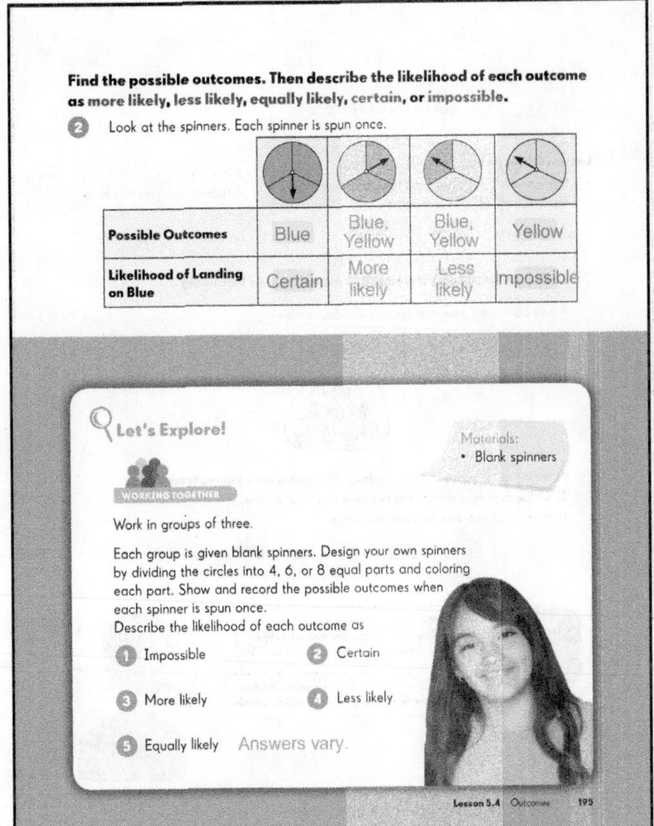

Find the possible outcomes. Then describe the likelihood of each outcome as more likely, less likely, equally likely, certain, or impossible.

2 Look at the spinners. Each spinner is spun once.

	Spinner 1	Spinner 2	Spinner 3	Spinner 4
Possible Outcomes	Blue	Blue, Yellow	Blue, Yellow	Yellow
Likelihood of Landing on Blue	Certain	More likely	Less likely	Impossible

Let's Explore!

WORKING TOGETHER

Materials:
- Blank spinners

Work in groups of three.

Each group is given blank spinners. Design your own spinners by dividing the circles into 4, 6, or 8 equal parts and coloring each part. Show and record the possible outcomes when each spinner is spun once.
Describe the likelihood of each outcome as

1 Impossible
2 Certain
3 More likely
4 Less likely
5 Equally likely

Answers vary.

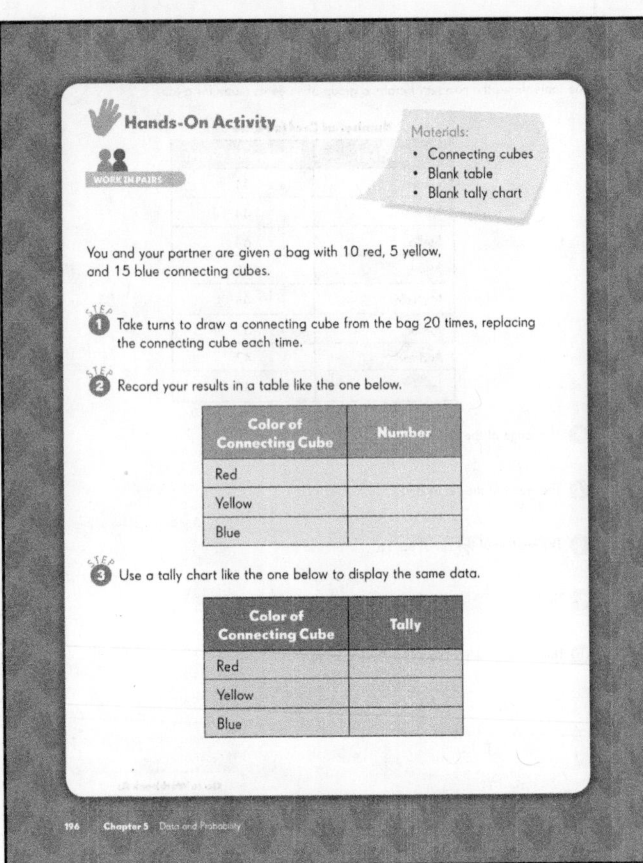

Hands-On Activity

WORK IN PAIRS

Materials:
- Connecting cubes
- Blank table
- Blank tally chart

You and your partner are given a bag with 10 red, 5 yellow, and 15 blue connecting cubes.

STEP 1 Take turns to draw a connecting cube from the bag 20 times, replacing the connecting cube each time.

STEP 2 Record your results in a table like the one below.

Color of Connecting Cube	Number
Red	
Yellow	
Blue	

STEP 3 Use a tally chart like the one below to display the same data.

Color of Connecting Cube	Tally
Red	
Yellow	
Blue	

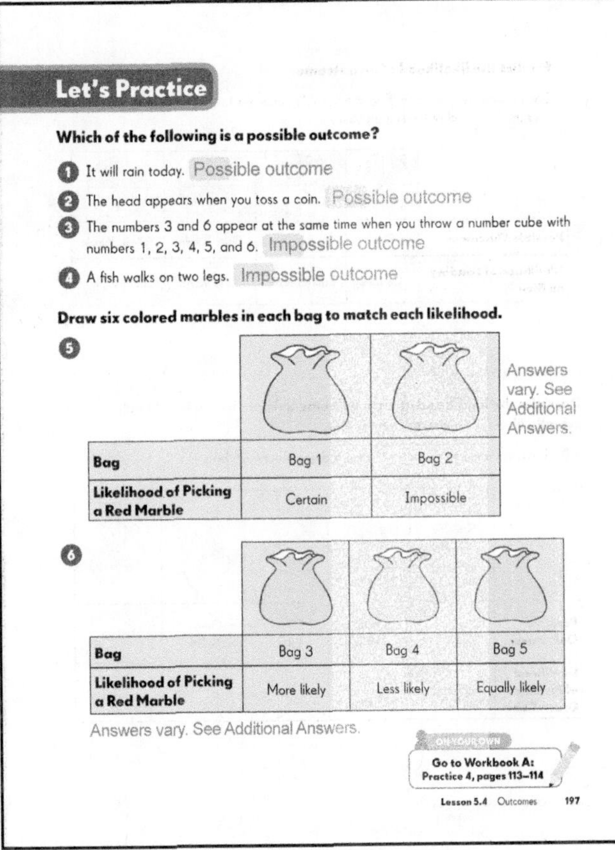

Let's Practice

Which of the following is a possible outcome?

1 It will rain today. Possible outcome

2 The head appears when you toss a coin. Possible outcome

3 The numbers 3 and 6 appear at the same time when you throw a number cube with numbers 1, 2, 3, 4, 5, and 6. Impossible outcome

4 A fish walks on two legs. Impossible outcome

Draw six colored marbles in each bag to match each likelihood.

5

Bag	Bag 1	Bag 2
Likelihood of Picking a Red Marble	Certain	Impossible

Answers vary. See Additional Answers.

6

Bag	Bag 3	Bag 4	Bag 5
Likelihood of Picking a Red Marble	More likely	Less likely	Equally likely

Answers vary. See Additional Answers.

ON YOUR OWN

Go to Workbook A: Practice 4, pages 113–114

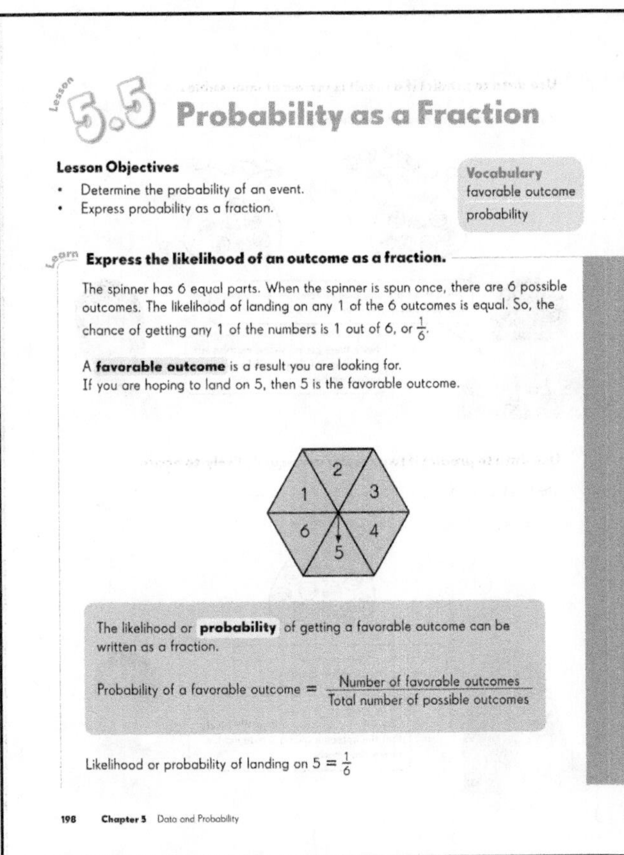

Lesson 5.5

Probability as a Fraction

Lesson Objectives
- Determine the probability of an event.
- Express probability as a fraction.

Vocabulary
favorable outcome
probability

Learn **Express the likelihood of an outcome as a fraction.**

The spinner has 6 equal parts. When the spinner is spun once, there are 6 possible outcomes. The likelihood of landing on any 1 of the 6 outcomes is equal. So, the chance of getting any 1 of the numbers is 1 out of 6, or $\frac{1}{6}$.

A **favorable outcome** is a result you are looking for.
If you are hoping to land on 5, then 5 is the favorable outcome.

The likelihood or **probability** of getting a favorable outcome can be written as a fraction.

$$\text{Probability of a favorable outcome} = \frac{\text{Number of favorable outcomes}}{\text{Total number of possible outcomes}}$$

Likelihood or probability of landing on 5 $= \frac{1}{6}$

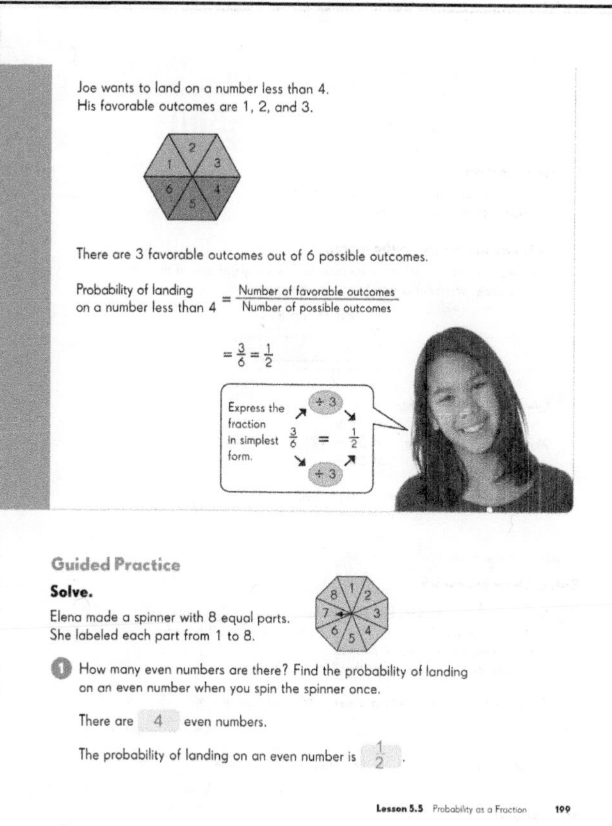
Joe wants to land on a number less than 4.
His favorable outcomes are 1, 2, and 3.

There are 3 favorable outcomes out of 6 possible outcomes.

Probability of landing on a number less than 4 $= \frac{\text{Number of favorable outcomes}}{\text{Number of possible outcomes}}$

$= \frac{3}{6} = \frac{1}{2}$

Express the fraction $\frac{3}{6}$ in simplest form. $\frac{3}{6} = \frac{1}{2}$ (÷ 3, ÷ 3)

Guided Practice

Solve.

Elena made a spinner with 8 equal parts.
She labeled each part from 1 to 8.

1. How many even numbers are there? Find the probability of landing on an even number when you spin the spinner once.

There are 4 even numbers.

The probability of landing on an even number is $\frac{1}{2}$.

Lesson 5.5 Probability as a Fraction 199

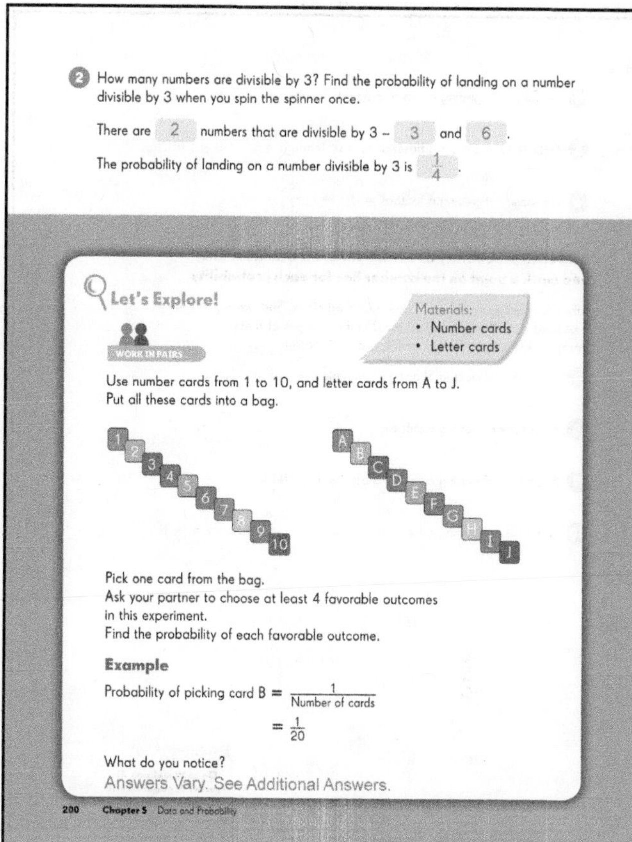
2. How many numbers are divisible by 3? Find the probability of landing on a number divisible by 3 when you spin the spinner once.

There are 2 numbers that are divisible by 3 – 3 and 6.

The probability of landing on a number divisible by 3 is $\frac{1}{4}$.

Let's Explore!

WORK IN PAIRS

Materials:
- Number cards
- Letter cards

Use number cards from 1 to 10, and letter cards from A to J.
Put all these cards into a bag.

Pick one card from the bag.
Ask your partner to choose at least 4 favorable outcomes in this experiment.
Find the probability of each favorable outcome.

Example

Probability of picking card B $= \frac{1}{\text{Number of cards}}$

$= \frac{1}{20}$

What do you notice?
Answers Vary. See Additional Answers.

200 Chapter 5 Data and Probability

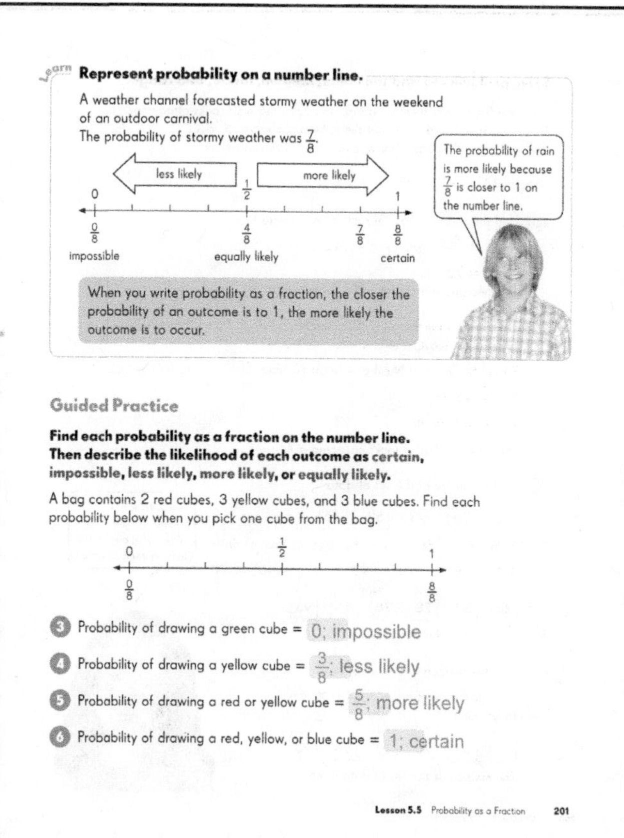
Represent probability on a number line.

A weather channel forecasted stormy weather on the weekend of an outdoor carnival.
The probability of stormy weather was $\frac{7}{8}$.

less likely — more likely

0, $\frac{1}{2}$, 1

$\frac{0}{8}$ impossible, $\frac{4}{8}$ equally likely, $\frac{7}{8}$, $\frac{8}{8}$ certain

The probability of rain is more likely because $\frac{7}{8}$ is closer to 1 on the number line.

When you write probability as a fraction, the closer the probability of an outcome is to 1, the more likely the outcome is to occur.

Guided Practice

Find each probability as a fraction on the number line. Then describe the likelihood of each outcome as certain, impossible, less likely, more likely, or equally likely.

A bag contains 2 red cubes, 3 yellow cubes, and 3 blue cubes. Find each probability below when you pick one cube from the bag.

3. Probability of drawing a green cube = 0; impossible
4. Probability of drawing a yellow cube = $\frac{3}{8}$; less likely
5. Probability of drawing a red or yellow cube = $\frac{5}{8}$; more likely
6. Probability of drawing a red, yellow, or blue cube = 1; certain

Lesson 5.5 Probability as a Fraction 201

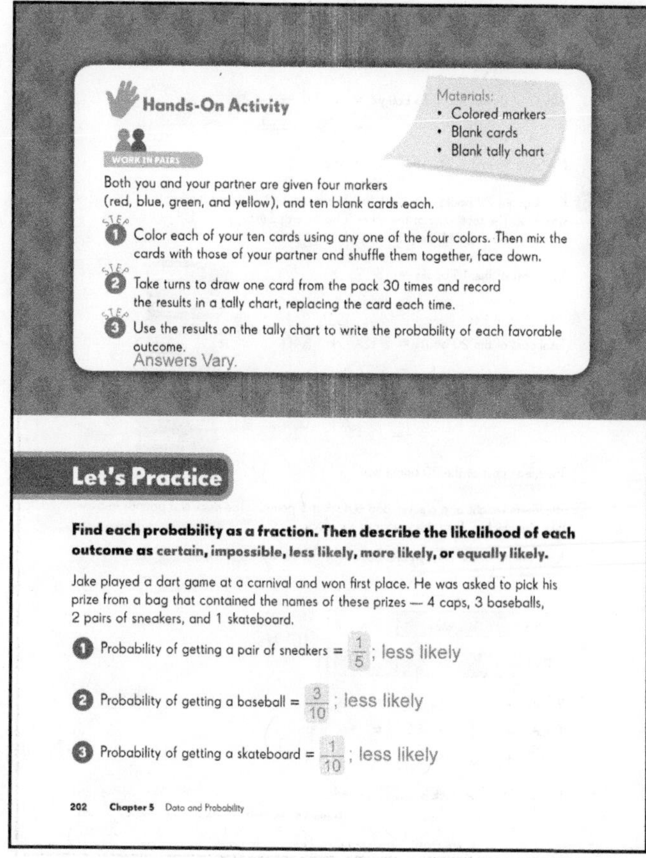
Hands-On Activity

WORK IN PAIRS

Materials:
- Colored markers
- Blank cards
- Blank tally chart

Both you and your partner are given four markers (red, blue, green, and yellow), and ten blank cards each.

STEP 1 Color each of your ten cards using any one of the four colors. Then mix the cards with those of your partner and shuffle them together, face down.

STEP 2 Take turns to draw one card from the pack 30 times and record the results in a tally chart, replacing the card each time.

STEP 3 Use the results on the tally chart to write the probability of each favorable outcome.
Answers Vary.

Let's Practice

Find each probability as a fraction. Then describe the likelihood of each outcome as certain, impossible, less likely, more likely, or equally likely.

Jake played a dart game at a carnival and won first place. He was asked to pick his prize from a bag that contained the names of these prizes — 4 caps, 3 baseballs, 2 pairs of sneakers, and 1 skateboard.

1. Probability of getting a pair of sneakers = $\frac{1}{5}$; less likely
2. Probability of getting a baseball = $\frac{3}{10}$; less likely
3. Probability of getting a skateboard = $\frac{1}{10}$; less likely

202 Chapter 5 Data and Probability

Chapter 5

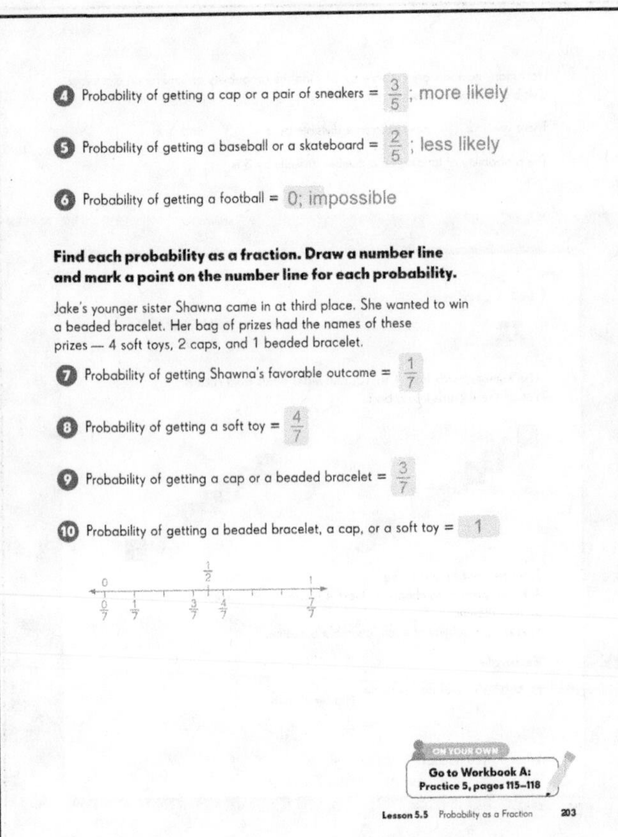

4 Probability of getting a cap or a pair of sneakers = $\frac{3}{5}$; more likely

5 Probability of getting a baseball or a skateboard = $\frac{2}{5}$; less likely

6 Probability of getting a football = 0; impossible

Find each probability as a fraction. Draw a number line and mark a point on the number line for each probability.

Jake's younger sister Shawna came in at third place. She wanted to win a beaded bracelet. Her bag of prizes had the names of these prizes — 4 soft toys, 2 caps, and 1 beaded bracelet.

7 Probability of getting Shawna's favorable outcome = $\frac{1}{7}$

8 Probability of getting a soft toy = $\frac{4}{7}$

9 Probability of getting a cap or a beaded bracelet = $\frac{3}{7}$

10 Probability of getting a beaded bracelet, a cap, or a soft toy = 1

ON YOUR OWN
Go to Workbook A: Practice 5, pages 115–118

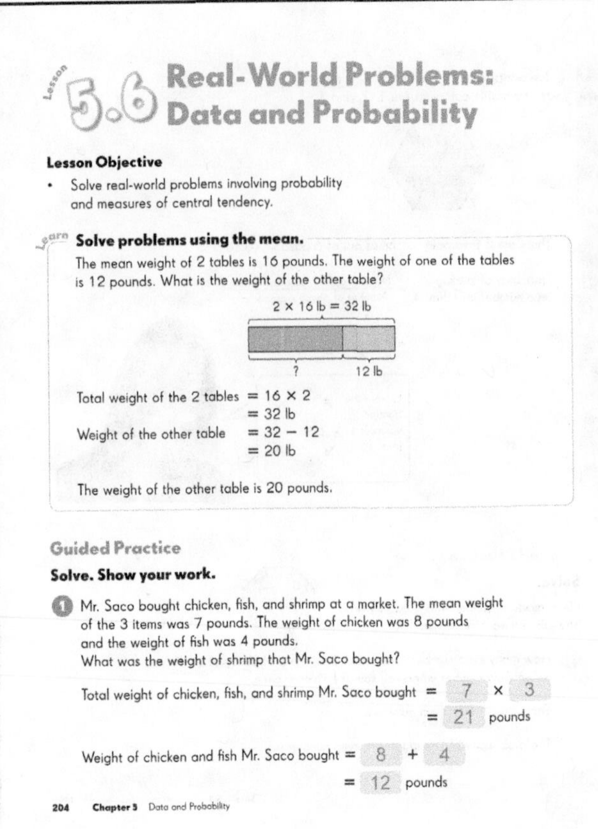

Lesson 5.6 Real-World Problems: Data and Probability

Lesson Objective

- Solve real-world problems involving probability and measures of central tendency.

Learn Solve problems using the mean.

The mean weight of 2 tables is 16 pounds. The weight of one of the tables is 12 pounds. What is the weight of the other table?

Total weight of the 2 tables = 16 × 2
= 32 lb

Weight of the other table = 32 − 12
= 20 lb

The weight of the other table is 20 pounds.

Guided Practice

Solve. Show your work.

1 Mr. Saco bought chicken, fish, and shrimp at a market. The mean weight of the 3 items was 7 pounds. The weight of chicken was 8 pounds and the weight of fish was 4 pounds.
What was the weight of shrimp that Mr. Saco bought?

Total weight of chicken, fish, and shrimp Mr. Saco bought = 7 × 3
= 21 pounds

Weight of chicken and fish Mr. Saco bought = 8 + 4
= 12 pounds

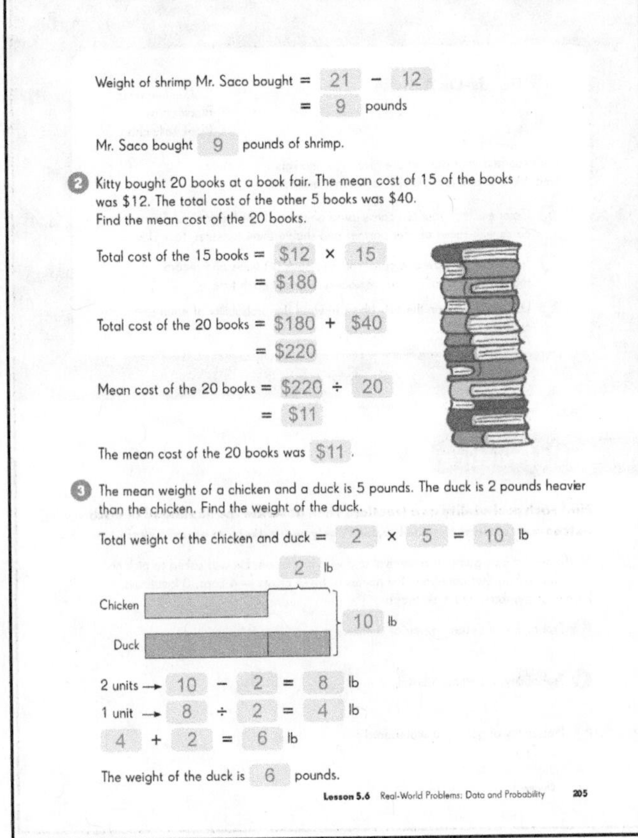

Weight of shrimp Mr. Saco bought = 21 − 12
= 9 pounds

Mr. Saco bought 9 pounds of shrimp.

2 Kitty bought 20 books at a book fair. The mean cost of 15 of the books was $12. The total cost of the other 5 books was $40.
Find the mean cost of the 20 books.

Total cost of the 15 books = $12 × 15
= $180

Total cost of the 20 books = $180 + $40
= $220

Mean cost of the 20 books = $220 ÷ 20
= $11

The mean cost of the 20 books was $11.

3 The mean weight of a chicken and a duck is 5 pounds. The duck is 2 pounds heavier than the chicken. Find the weight of the duck.

Total weight of the chicken and duck = 2 × 5 = 10 lb

2 units → 10 − 2 = 8 lb

1 unit → 8 ÷ 2 = 4 lb

4 + 2 = 6 lb

The weight of the duck is 6 pounds.

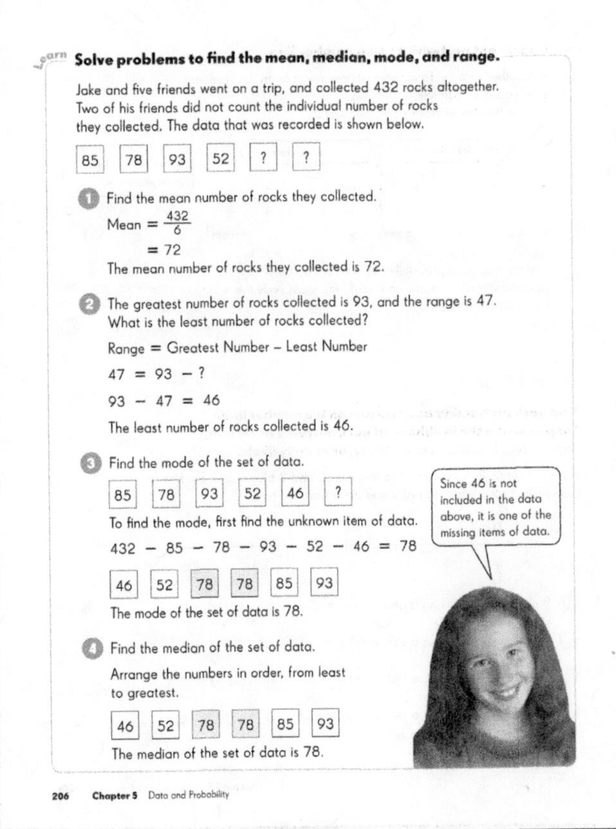

Learn Solve problems to find the mean, median, mode, and range.

Jake and five friends went on a trip, and collected 432 rocks altogether. Two of his friends did not count the individual number of rocks they collected. The data that was recorded is shown below.

85 | 78 | 93 | 52 | ? | ?

1 Find the mean number of rocks they collected.

Mean = $\frac{432}{6}$
= 72

The mean number of rocks they collected is 72.

2 The greatest number of rocks collected is 93, and the range is 47. What is the least number of rocks collected?

Range = Greatest Number – Least Number

47 = 93 − ?

93 − 47 = 46

The least number of rocks collected is 46.

3 Find the mode of the set of data.

85 | 78 | 93 | 52 | 46 | ?

To find the mode, first find the unknown item of data.

432 − 85 − 78 − 93 − 52 − 46 = 78

46 | 52 | 78 | 78 | 85 | 93

The mode of the set of data is 78.

Since 46 is not included in the data above, it is one of the missing items of data.

4 Find the median of the set of data.

Arrange the numbers in order, from least to greatest.

46 | 52 | 78 | 78 | 85 | 93

The median of the set of data is 78.

Chapter 5

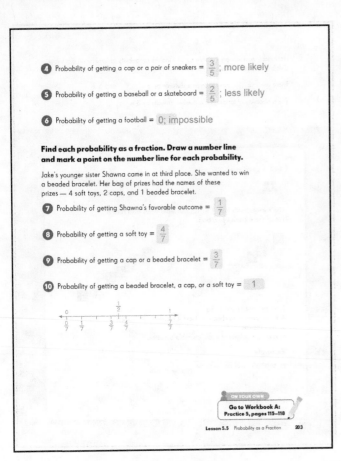

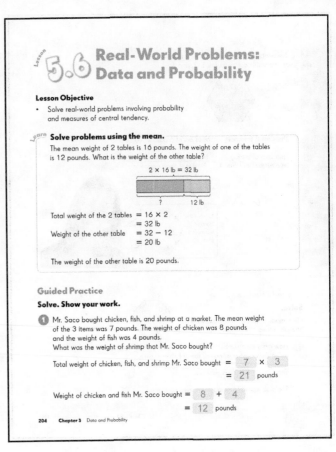

Guided Practice

Solve. Show your work.

4. A farmer weighed and recorded his crop of pumpkins to the nearest pound as shown in the line plot.

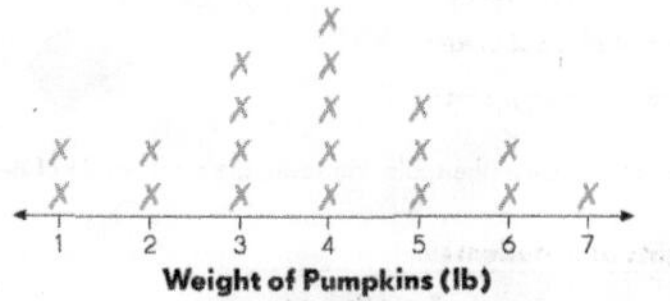

Weight of Pumpkins (lb)

a. What is the mode of the set of data? 4 lb

b. What is the median of the set of data? 4 lb

c. The farmer sold the 4-lb pumpkins at $6 each, the 5-lb pumpkins at $8 each, and the 6-lb pumpkins at $10 each. He kept the rest of the pumpkins. How much money did he earn from the sale? $74

5. In a mini-bowling competition of four frames per player, Sean scored the following in the first three frames.

Sean's Bowling Score

Frame 1	Frame 2	Frame 3	Frame 4
17	28	25	?

a. How many points must he score in the next frame so that he can achieve a mean score of 25? 30 points

b. How many points must he score in the next frame so that the range of the set of data is 12? Find both possible answers. 29 points; 16 points

Learn Solve problems using a stem-and-leaf plot.

A kindergarten class counted the number of carrots each of its 9 rabbits ate over six months. The stem-and-leaf plot shows the data.

Number of Carrots	
Stem	**Leaves**
5	7 ?
6	3 5 8
7	0 4 4
9	1

5|7 = 57

1. If the mean number of carrots each rabbit ate was 69, find the total number of carrots the rabbits ate over 6 months.

Total number of carrots the rabbits ate over 6 months = 69 × 9
= 621

The rabbits ate 621 carrots over 6 months.

2. Complete the stem-and-leaf plot by filling in the missing item of data.

621 − 57 − 63 − 65 − 68 − 70 − 74 − 74 − 91 = 59

The missing item of data is 59.

3. Find the mode of the set of data.

The mode of the set of data is 74.

4. Find the median of the set of data.

The median of the set of data is 68.

5. Find the range of the set of data.

The range of the set of data is 91 − 57 = 34.

6. What is the outlier?

The number farthest from the others is 91. The outlier is 91.

Guided Practice

Solve. Show your work.

6. The stem-and-leaf plot shows the lengths of 8 ribbons in inches.

Length of Ribbons (in.)	
Stem	**Leaves**
2	6 8
3	5 6 6 9
4	3
5	3

2|6 = 26

a. Which length is the outlier? 53 in.

b. Find the stem which has only even numbers in its leaves column. 2 for 20

c. Change some data to make the mode 26 without changing the sum of the lengths. Answers vary. See Additional Answers.

Learn Solve problems by predicting the likelihood of an outcome.

Jayne has a spinner divided into 12 equal parts. There are 5 yellow parts, 3 green parts, and the remaining 4 parts are blue and red.

1. Jayne spins the spinner once. What color is she most likely to spin?
The color with the greatest number of parts is yellow.
She is most likely to spin yellow.

2. The spinner is equally likely to spin green and one other color. The most unlikely outcome is blue.
Draw the spinner with the correct colored parts.

3. Jayne colored one of the yellow parts green. What is the likelihood she will spin red now? Does this change the color she is least likely to spin?
There are now 4 yellow parts, 4 green parts, 3 red parts, and 1 blue part. She is unlikely to spin red. The color she is least likely to spin is still blue.

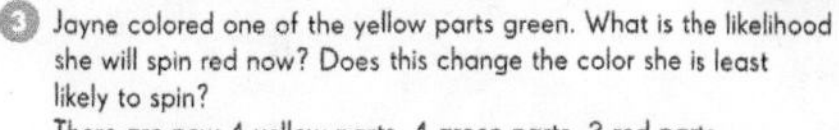

Guided Practice

Solve. Show your work.

7. A bag contains 15 marbles, of which 6 are red, 5 are blue, and 4 are green. Charlene draws two marbles from the bag.

a. If the first marble she draws is red, what is the likelihood that the second marble is blue or red? Equally likely

b. Charlene returns the first two marbles to the bag, and adds two more marbles. She then draws another marble from the bag. What color are the new marbles if each of the following is true?

i. The marble she draws is equally likely to be green or red. Green

ii. The marble she draws is most likely to be red. 2 red or 1 red, 1 green or 1 red, 1 blue

iii. The marble she draws is equally likely to be green or blue. 1 red, 1 green

Learn Solve problems by finding probability as a fraction.

A choir of 32 singers performs at a concert. There are 11 sopranos, 9 tenors, 6 bass, and 6 altos.

After the performance, a singer is randomly chosen to perform a solo.

1. What is the probability that the singer chosen is an alto?

The probability that the singer chosen is an alto is $\frac{6}{32} = \frac{3}{16}$.

Chapter 5

7. What is the probability that the singer chosen is a soprano or a tenor?

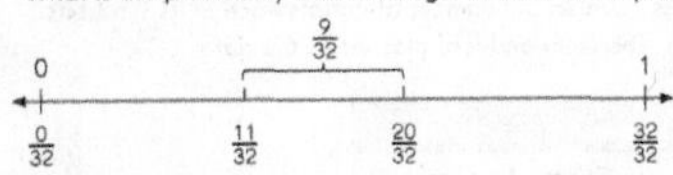

11 + 9 = 20

The probability that the singer chosen is a soprano or a tenor is $\frac{20}{32} = \frac{5}{8}$.

Guided Practice

Solve. Show your work.

8. Eighteen students go into a classroom. Eleven of them are girls. Find each probability as a fraction when the recess bell is rung.

   a. The first student to come out is a girl. $\frac{11}{18}$

   b. The first student to come out is a boy. $\frac{7}{18}$

   c. If the first student to come out is a girl, find the probability that the next student to come out is a boy. $\frac{7}{17}$

   d. The probability of the second student to come out being a girl is $\frac{11}{17}$. Was the first student a boy or a girl? Boy

9. A bag has 6 green marbles and 4 orange marbles. Find the least number of marbles of either color you would add to make the probability of picking an orange marble

   a. $\frac{1}{2}$ 2 orange marbles

   b. $\frac{1}{3}$ 2 green marbles

Let's Practice

Solve. Show your work.

1. Mandy bought a turkey burger and a chicken burger. The mean cost of the 2 burgers was \$6. The turkey burger cost \$5.

   a. What was the total cost of the 2 burgers? \$12

   b. How much did the chicken burger cost? \$7

2. The weights of 5 students are shown in the table. However, the total weight of the girls was left out.

Weights of 5 Students

	Students	Total Weight
Girls	Linda, Elsie	?
Boys	Alvin, Chris, George	105 kg

The mean weight of the 5 students is 31 kilograms.

   a. Find the total weight of the girls. 50 kg

   b. Find the mean weight of the girls. 25 kg

3. Ace Transport has a fleet of 10 trucks. The 7 small trucks use a mean amount of 28 gallons of gas each day. The 3 large trucks use a total amount of 114 gallons each day. What is the mean amount of gas used each day by all 10 trucks? 31 gal

4. Mr. and Mrs. Soong's mean salary is \$2,730. Mrs. Soong earns \$230 less than Mr. Soong. How much does each of them earn?
Mr. Soong's salary = \$2,845; Mrs. Soong's salary = \$2,615

5. Hisham bought 2 action figures at a mean weight of 1,240 grams. The first action figure weighed 80 grams more than the second action figure. What was the weight of the lighter action figure? 1,200 g

6. Katrina sold 4 times as many apples as Bess at a school fair. Both of them sold an average of 285 apples. How many apples did Katrina sell? 456

7. Matt and his 4 friends collect baseball cards. They have 325 cards altogether. These are the number of baseball cards that 3 of the boys have.

   53 73 50 ? ?

   a. Find the mean number of cards they have. 65

   b. Matt has the largest collection. He has 100 cards. The range of the set of data is 51. What is the smallest collection? 49

   c. Jose adds his cards to their collection. There are now 6 friends with 360 cards altogether. What is the range of this new set of data? 65

8. A teacher counted the number of peanut butter and jelly sandwiches each of his students had for lunch over a school term. One item of data is missing.

Number of Sandwiches

Stem	Leaves
1	? 6
2	2 2 4 5
3	2 3
4	0 1

1 | 6 = 16

   a. The mean number of sandwiches each student had was 27. Find the total number of sandwiches. 270

   b. What is the missing number in the stem-and-leaf plot? 15

   c. Find the mode of the set of data. 22

   d. Find the range of the set of data. 26

   e. If one of the students was randomly selected, what is the probability that the student had 22 sandwiches? $\frac{1}{5}$

9. A box has 10 number cards. The cards are numbered 1 to 10. Ann draws a card from the box.

   a. What is the probability that she draws an even number? $\frac{1}{2}$

   b. What is the probability that she draws an odd number that is divisible by 3? $\frac{1}{5}$

10. A bag contains 1 red cube and 8 blue cubes. Nick picks a cube from the bag.

   a. What is the probability that he picks a red cube? $\frac{1}{9}$

   b. If Nick puts the cube back into the bag and picks a cube from the bag again, what is the probability that the second cube is red? $\frac{1}{9}$

   c. If Nick does not put the first cube back and picks a cube from the bag again, what is the probability that the second cube is red? 0

11. A group of 12 boys, 18 girls, and some adults went to the circus. At a show, 1 of the spectators was randomly selected to perform with the clown. The probability that an adult was selected was $\frac{1}{4}$.

   a. How many adults were there? 10

   b. What is the probability that a girl was selected? $\frac{9}{20}$

12. A group of students count the number of times the letter A appears in their names. The data is shown in the line plot. Each X represents one student.

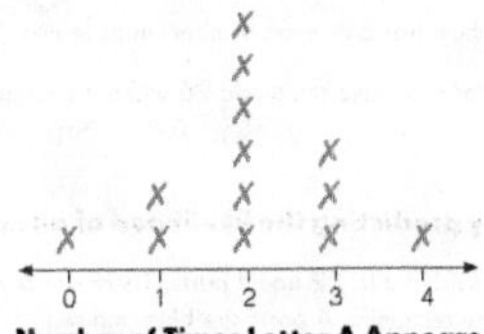

   a. What is the total number of students in the group? 13

   b. What is the mode of this set of data? Is the mode typical of this set of data? See Additional Answers.

ON YOUR OWN
Go to Workbook A: Practice 6, pages 119–131

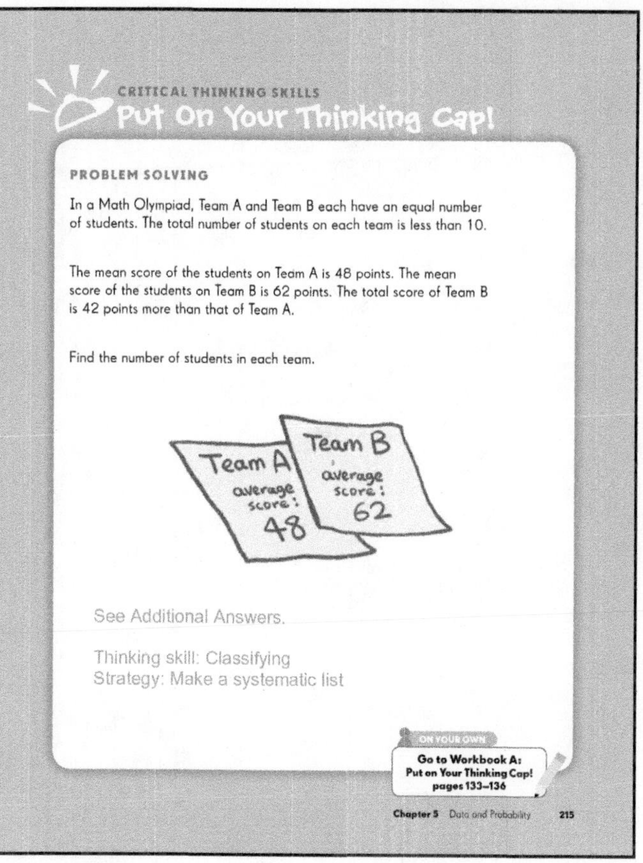

CRITICAL THINKING SKILLS

Put On Your Thinking Cap!

PROBLEM SOLVING

In a Math Olympiad, Team A and Team B each have an equal number of students. The total number of students on each team is less than 10.

The mean score of the students on Team A is 48 points. The mean score of the students on Team B is 62 points. The total score of Team B is 42 points more than that of Team A.

Find the number of students in each team.

See Additional Answers.

Thinking skill: Classifying
Strategy: Make a systematic list

ON YOUR OWN
Go to Workbook A: Put on Your Thinking Cap! pages 133–136

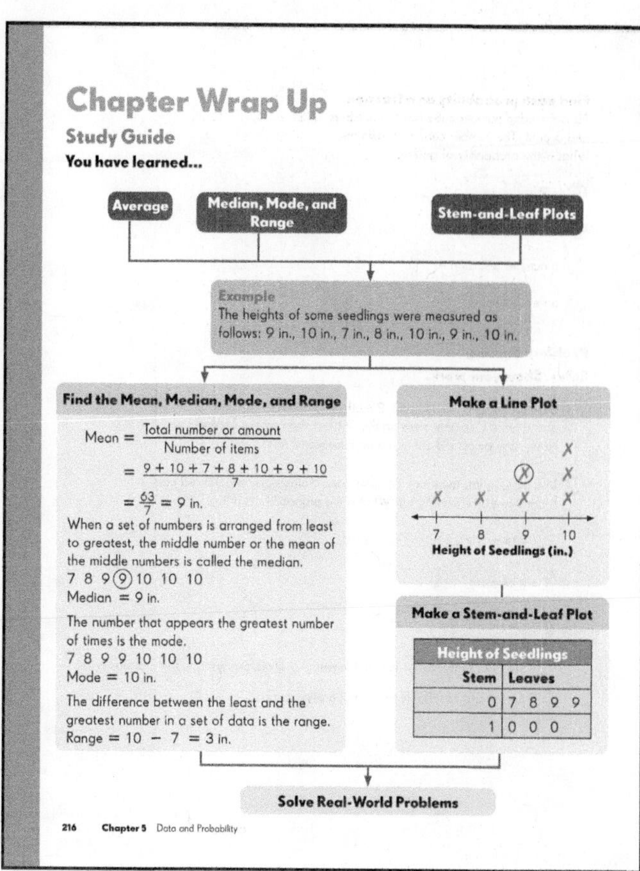

Chapter Wrap Up

Study Guide

You have learned...

Example
The heights of some seedlings were measured as follows: 9 in., 10 in., 7 in., 8 in., 10 in., 9 in., 10 in.

Find the Mean, Median, Mode, and Range

$$\text{Mean} = \frac{\text{Total number or amount}}{\text{Number of items}}$$

$$= \frac{9 + 10 + 7 + 8 + 10 + 9 + 10}{7}$$

$$= \frac{63}{7} = 9 \text{ in.}$$

When a set of numbers is arranged from least to greatest, the middle number or the mean of the middle numbers is called the median.

7 8 9 (9) 10 10 10
Median = 9 in.

The number that appears the greatest number of times is the mode.

7 8 9 9 10 10 10
Mode = 10 in.

The difference between the least and the greatest number in a set of data is the range.
Range = 10 − 7 = 3 in.

Make a Line Plot

Make a Stem-and-Leaf Plot

Height of Seedlings	
Stem	Leaves
0	7 8 9 9
1	0 0 0

Solve Real-World Problems

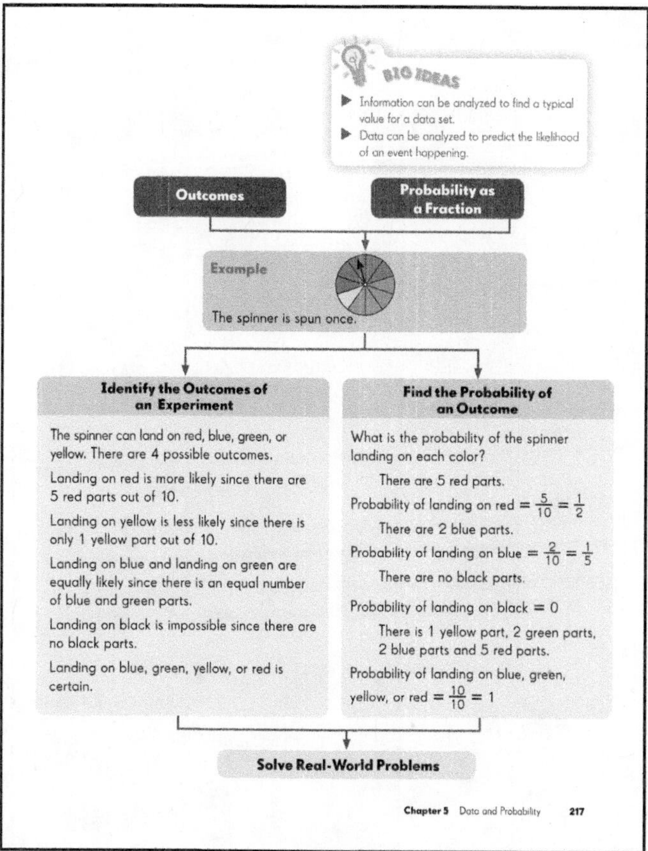

BIG IDEAS

- Information can be analyzed to find a typical value for a data set.
- Data can be analyzed to predict the likelihood of an event happening.

Example
The spinner is spun once.

Identify the Outcomes of an Experiment

The spinner can land on red, blue, green, or yellow. There are 4 possible outcomes.

Landing on red is more likely since there are 5 red parts out of 10.

Landing on yellow is less likely since there is only 1 yellow part out of 10.

Landing on blue and landing on green are equally likely since there is an equal number of blue and green parts.

Landing on black is impossible since there are no black parts.

Landing on blue, green, yellow, or red is certain.

Find the Probability of an Outcome

What is the probability of the spinner landing on each color?

There are 5 red parts.
Probability of landing on red $= \frac{5}{10} = \frac{1}{2}$

There are 2 blue parts.
Probability of landing on blue $= \frac{2}{10} = \frac{1}{5}$

There are no black parts.
Probability of landing on black = 0

There is 1 yellow part, 2 green parts, 2 blue parts and 5 red parts.
Probability of landing on blue, green, yellow, or red $= \frac{10}{10} = 1$

Solve Real-World Problems

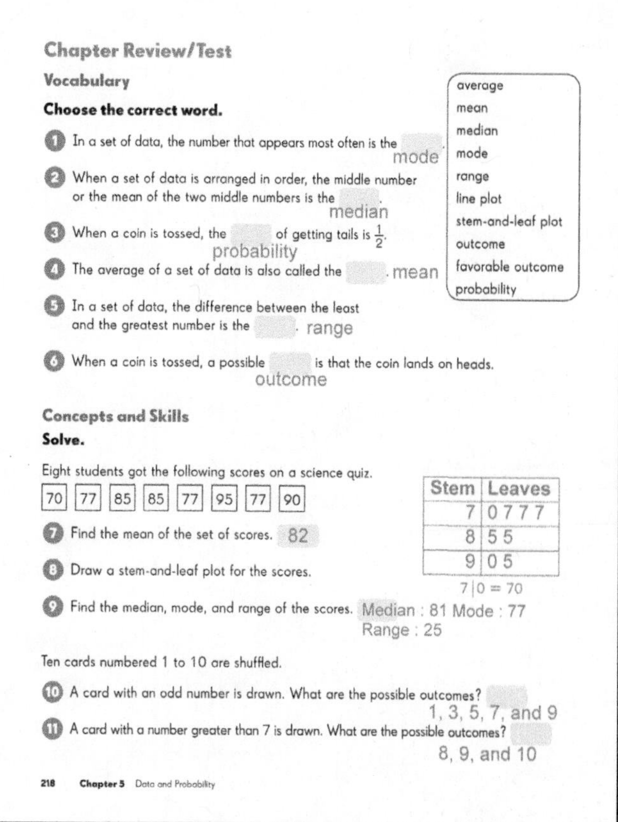

Chapter Review/Test

Vocabulary

Choose the correct word.

average
mean
median
mode
range
line plot
stem-and-leaf plot
outcome
favorable outcome
probability

1. In a set of data, the number that appears most often is the ___. mode
2. When a set of data is arranged in order, the middle number or the mean of the two middle numbers is the ___. median
3. When a coin is tossed, the ___ of getting tails is $\frac{1}{2}$. probability
4. The average of a set of data is also called the ___. mean
5. In a set of data, the difference between the least and the greatest number is the ___. range
6. When a coin is tossed, a possible ___ is that the coin lands on heads. outcome

Concepts and Skills

Solve.

Eight students got the following scores on a science quiz.

70 77 85 85 77 95 77 90

7. Find the mean of the set of scores. 82
8. Draw a stem-and-leaf plot for the scores.

Stem	Leaves
7	0 7 7 7
8	5 5
9	0 5

7 | 0 = 70

9. Find the median, mode, and range of the scores. Median : 81 Mode : 77 Range : 25

Ten cards numbered 1 to 10 are shuffled.

10. A card with an odd number is drawn. What are the possible outcomes? 1, 3, 5, 7, and 9
11. A card with a number greater than 7 is drawn. What are the possible outcomes? 8, 9, and 10

Chapter 5

Find each probability as a fraction.
An eight-sided number cube has the numbers 1, 2, 3, 4, 5, 6, 7, and 8 on it. The number cube is thrown once.
What is the probability of getting

12 a 2? $\frac{1}{8}$

13 a 2 or a 5? $\frac{1}{4}$

14 a number less than 4? $\frac{3}{8}$

15 an even number? $\frac{1}{2}$

Problem Solving

Solve. Show your work.

16 During one term, Rachel took 2 mathematics tests. Her mean score was 75. She scored 12 points more on the first test than on the second test. How many points did she score on the second test? 69

17 In a parking lot, there are 16 silver cars, 8 blue cars, and 10 red cars. A car leaves the parking lot. What is the probability that it is

a a silver car? $\frac{8}{17}$

b a blue car? $\frac{4}{17}$

c a red car? $\frac{5}{17}$

d Suppose that the first car that leaves is a silver car. What is the probability that the second car that leaves is not a silver car? $\frac{18}{33}$

Chapter 5 Data and Probability 219

Chapter 5

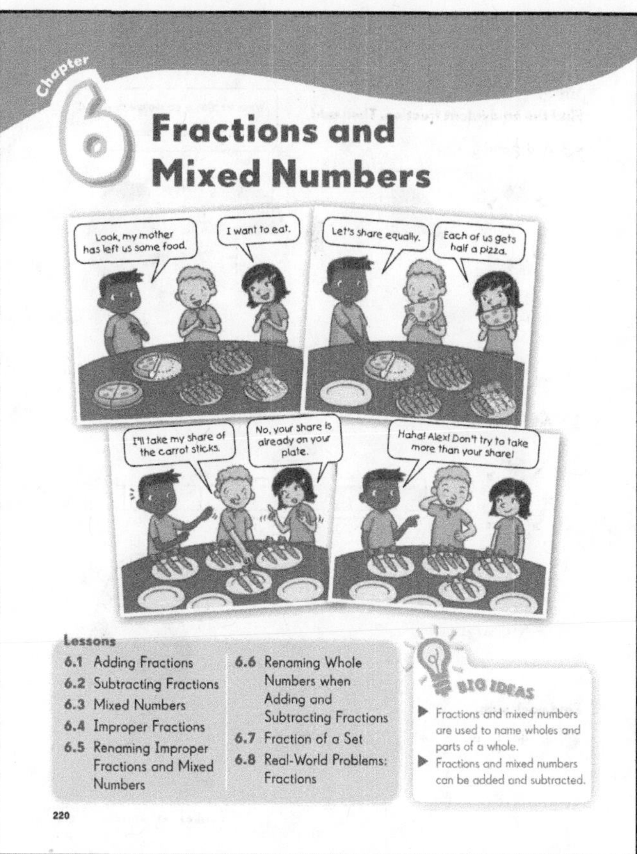

Chapter 6

Fractions and Mixed Numbers

Lessons

BIG IDEAS

- Fractions and mixed numbers are used to name wholes and parts of a whole.
- Fractions and mixed numbers can be added and subtracted.

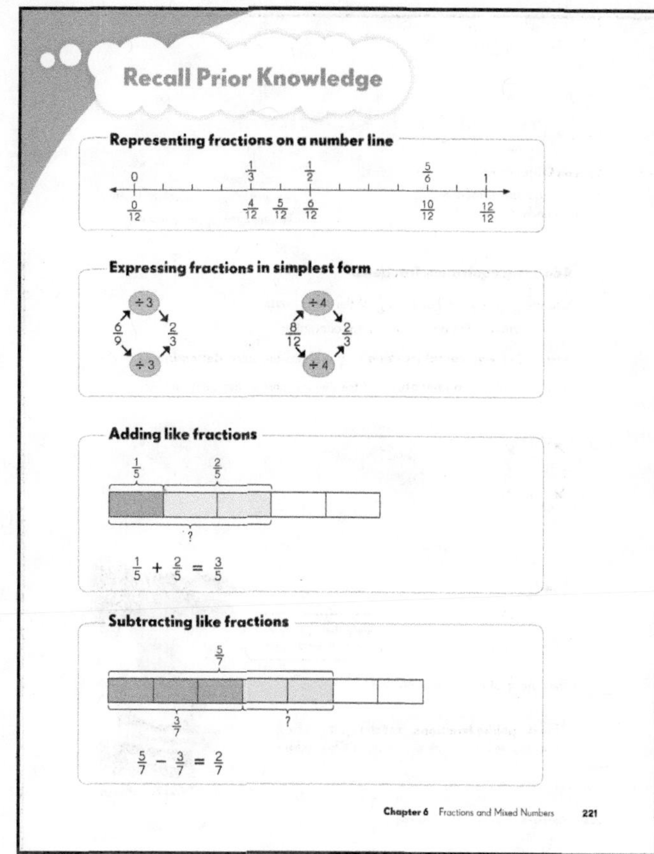

Recall Prior Knowledge

Representing fractions on a number line

Expressing fractions in simplest form

Adding like fractions

$\frac{1}{5} + \frac{2}{5} = \frac{3}{5}$

Subtracting like fractions

$\frac{5}{7} - \frac{3}{7} = \frac{2}{7}$

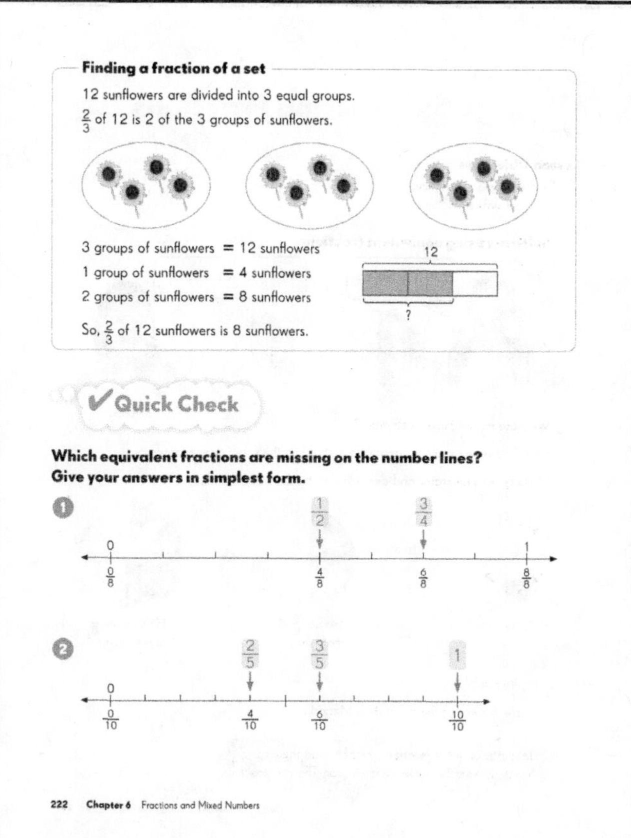

Finding a fraction of a set

12 sunflowers are divided into 3 equal groups.

$\frac{2}{3}$ of 12 is 2 of the 3 groups of sunflowers.

3 groups of sunflowers = 12 sunflowers

1 group of sunflowers = 4 sunflowers

2 groups of sunflowers = 8 sunflowers

So, $\frac{2}{3}$ of 12 sunflowers is 8 sunflowers.

Quick Check

Which equivalent fractions are missing on the number lines? Give your answers in simplest form.

1

2

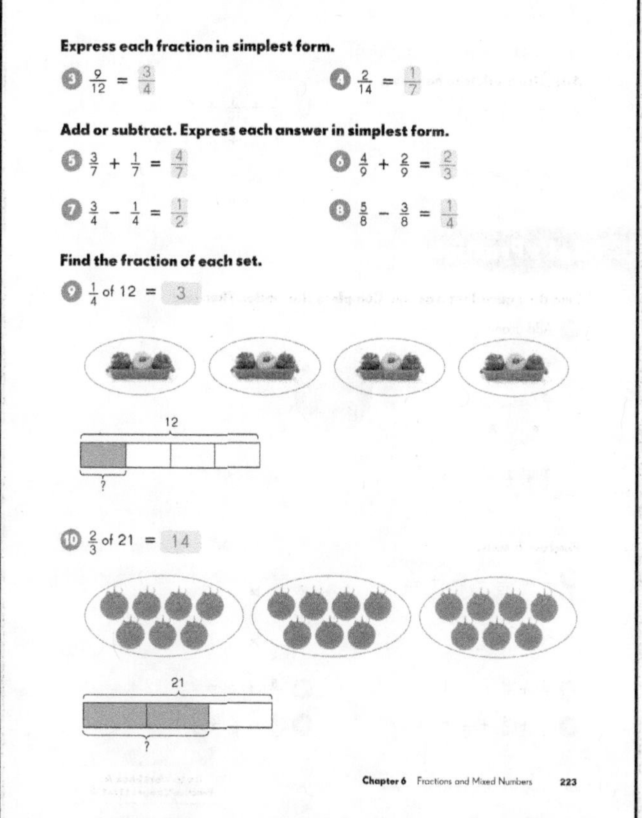

Express each fraction in simplest form.

3 $\frac{9}{12} = \frac{3}{4}$

4 $\frac{2}{14} = \frac{1}{7}$

Add or subtract. Express each answer in simplest form.

5 $\frac{3}{7} + \frac{1}{7} = \frac{4}{7}$

6 $\frac{4}{9} + \frac{2}{9} = \frac{2}{3}$

7 $\frac{3}{4} - \frac{1}{4} = \frac{1}{2}$

8 $\frac{5}{8} - \frac{3}{8} = \frac{1}{4}$

Find the fraction of each set.

9 $\frac{1}{4}$ of 12 = 3

10 $\frac{2}{3}$ of 21 = 14

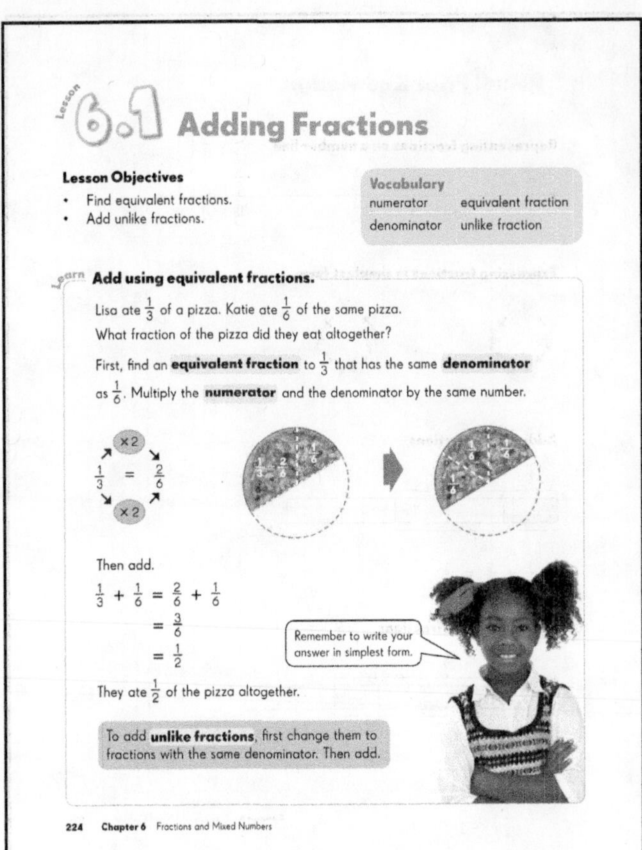

Lesson 6.1 Adding Fractions

Lesson Objectives
- Find equivalent fractions.
- Add unlike fractions.

Vocabulary
numerator, equivalent fraction, denominator, unlike fraction

Learn: Add using equivalent fractions.

Lisa ate $\frac{1}{3}$ of a pizza. Katie ate $\frac{1}{6}$ of the same pizza.
What fraction of the pizza did they eat altogether?

First, find an **equivalent fraction** to $\frac{1}{3}$ that has the same **denominator** as $\frac{1}{6}$. Multiply the **numerator** and the denominator by the same number.

$\frac{1}{3} = \frac{2}{6}$ (×2)

Then add.

$\frac{1}{3} + \frac{1}{6} = \frac{2}{6} + \frac{1}{6}$
$= \frac{3}{6}$
$= \frac{1}{2}$

Remember to write your answer in simplest form.

They ate $\frac{1}{2}$ of the pizza altogether.

To add **unlike fractions**, first change them to fractions with the same denominator. Then add.

224 Chapter 6 Fractions and Mixed Numbers

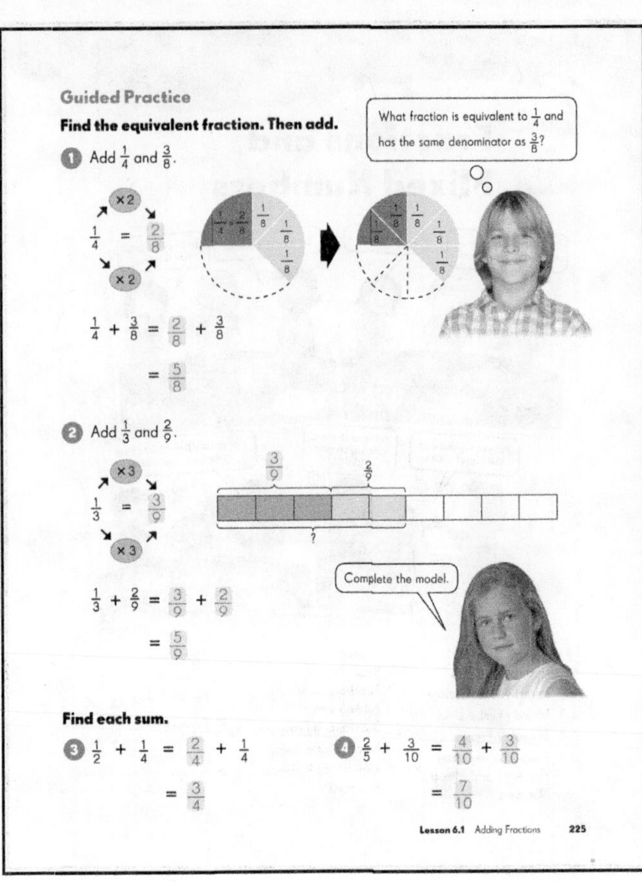

Guided Practice

Find the equivalent fraction. Then add.

What fraction is equivalent to $\frac{1}{4}$ and has the same denominator as $\frac{3}{8}$?

1. Add $\frac{1}{4}$ and $\frac{3}{8}$.

$\frac{1}{4} = \frac{2}{8}$ (×2)

$\frac{1}{4} + \frac{3}{8} = \frac{2}{8} + \frac{3}{8}$
$= \frac{5}{8}$

2. Add $\frac{1}{3}$ and $\frac{2}{9}$.

$\frac{1}{3} = \frac{3}{9}$ (×3)

$\frac{1}{3} + \frac{2}{9} = \frac{3}{9} + \frac{2}{9}$
$= \frac{5}{9}$

Complete the model.

Find each sum.

3. $\frac{1}{2} + \frac{1}{4} = \frac{2}{4} + \frac{1}{4}$
$= \frac{3}{4}$

4. $\frac{2}{5} + \frac{3}{10} = \frac{4}{10} + \frac{3}{10}$
$= \frac{7}{10}$

Lesson 6.1 Adding Fractions 225

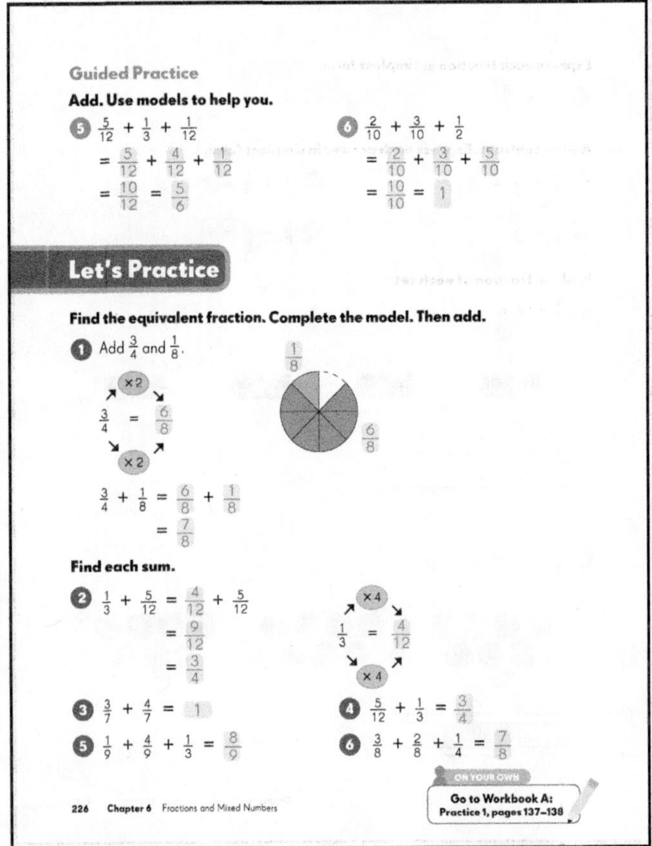

Guided Practice

Add. Use models to help you.

5. $\frac{5}{12} + \frac{1}{3} + \frac{1}{12}$
$= \frac{5}{12} + \frac{4}{12} + \frac{1}{12}$
$= \frac{10}{12} = \frac{5}{6}$

6. $\frac{2}{10} + \frac{3}{10} + \frac{1}{2}$
$= \frac{2}{10} + \frac{3}{10} + \frac{5}{10}$
$= \frac{10}{10} = 1$

Let's Practice

Find the equivalent fraction. Complete the model. Then add.

1. Add $\frac{3}{4}$ and $\frac{1}{8}$.

$\frac{3}{4} = \frac{6}{8}$ (×2)

$\frac{3}{4} + \frac{1}{8} = \frac{6}{8} + \frac{1}{8}$
$= \frac{7}{8}$

Find each sum.

2. $\frac{1}{3} + \frac{5}{12} = \frac{4}{12} + \frac{5}{12}$
$= \frac{9}{12}$
$= \frac{3}{4}$

$\frac{1}{3} = \frac{4}{12}$ (×4)

3. $\frac{3}{7} + \frac{4}{7} = 1$

4. $\frac{5}{12} + \frac{1}{3} = \frac{3}{4}$

5. $\frac{1}{9} + \frac{4}{9} + \frac{1}{3} = \frac{8}{9}$

6. $\frac{3}{8} + \frac{2}{8} + \frac{1}{4} = \frac{7}{8}$

ON YOUR OWN
Go to Workbook A: Practice 1, pages 137–138

226 Chapter 6 Fractions and Mixed Numbers

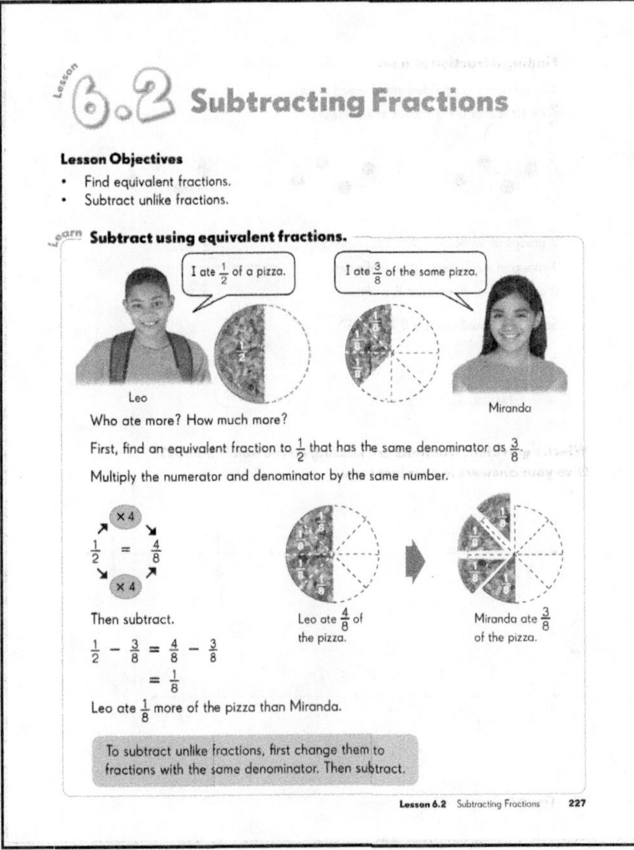

Lesson 6.2 Subtracting Fractions

Lesson Objectives
- Find equivalent fractions.
- Subtract unlike fractions.

Learn: Subtract using equivalent fractions.

I ate $\frac{1}{2}$ of a pizza.
I ate $\frac{3}{8}$ of the same pizza.
Leo
Miranda

Who ate more? How much more?

First, find an equivalent fraction to $\frac{1}{2}$ that has the same denominator as $\frac{3}{8}$.
Multiply the numerator and denominator by the same number.

$\frac{1}{2} = \frac{4}{8}$ (×4)

Leo ate $\frac{4}{8}$ of the pizza.
Miranda ate $\frac{3}{8}$ of the pizza.

Then subtract.

$\frac{1}{2} - \frac{3}{8} = \frac{4}{8} - \frac{3}{8}$
$= \frac{1}{8}$

Leo ate $\frac{1}{8}$ more of the pizza than Miranda.

To subtract unlike fractions, first change them to fractions with the same denominator. Then subtract.

Lesson 6.2 Subtracting Fractions 227

Chapter 6

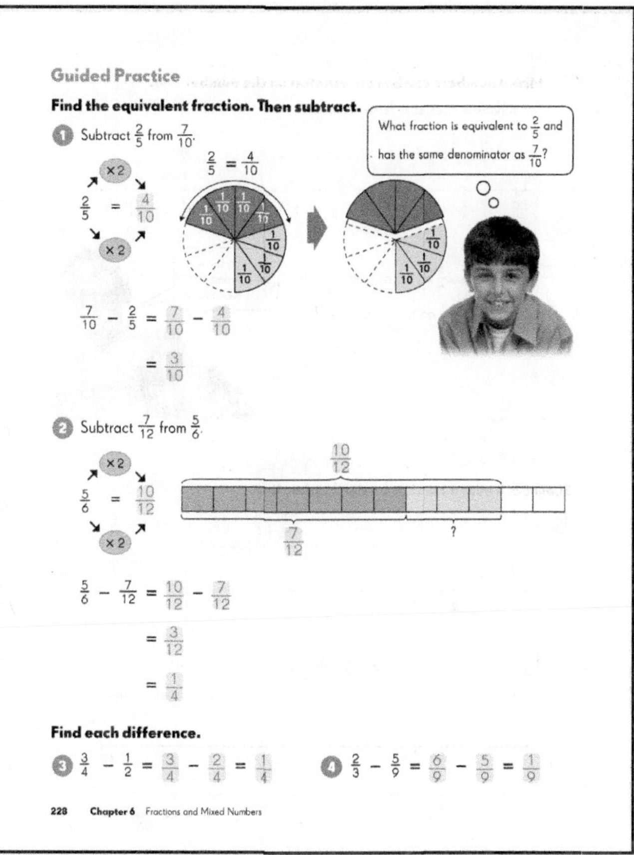
Guided Practice

Find the equivalent fraction. Then subtract.

1 Subtract $\frac{2}{5}$ from $\frac{7}{10}$.

$\frac{2}{5} = \frac{4}{10}$ (×2)

$\frac{7}{10} - \frac{2}{5} = \frac{7}{10} - \frac{4}{10}$

$= \frac{3}{10}$

2 Subtract $\frac{7}{12}$ from $\frac{5}{6}$.

$\frac{5}{6} = \frac{10}{12}$ (×2)

$\frac{5}{6} - \frac{7}{12} = \frac{10}{12} - \frac{7}{12}$

$= \frac{3}{12}$

$= \frac{1}{4}$

Find each difference.

3 $\frac{3}{4} - \frac{1}{2} = \frac{3}{4} - \frac{2}{4} = \frac{1}{4}$

4 $\frac{2}{3} - \frac{5}{9} = \frac{6}{9} - \frac{5}{9} = \frac{1}{9}$

228 **Chapter 6** Fractions and Mixed Numbers

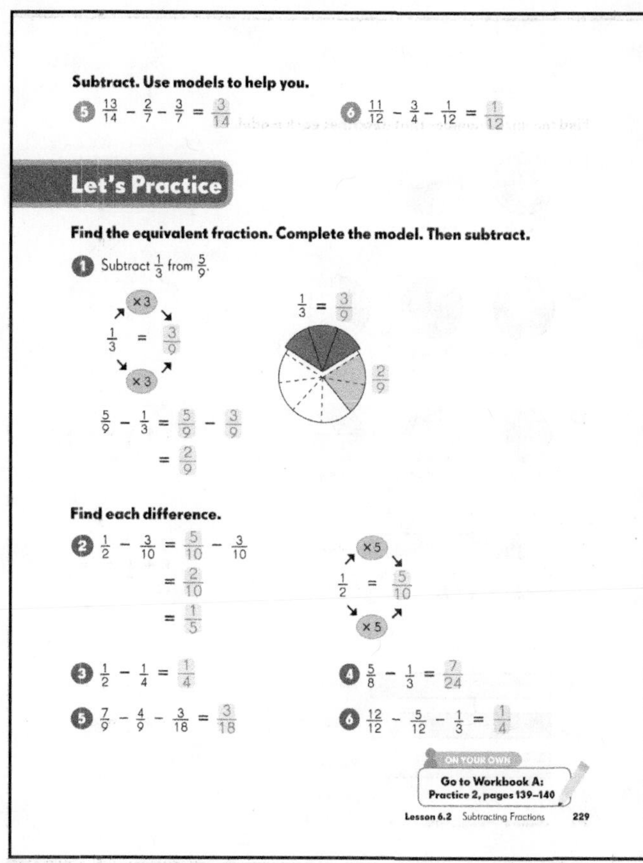
Subtract. Use models to help you.

5 $\frac{13}{14} - \frac{2}{7} - \frac{3}{7} = \frac{3}{14}$

6 $\frac{11}{12} - \frac{3}{4} - \frac{1}{12} = \frac{1}{12}$

Let's Practice

Find the equivalent fraction. Complete the model. Then subtract.

1 Subtract $\frac{1}{3}$ from $\frac{5}{9}$.

$\frac{1}{3} = \frac{3}{9}$ (×3)

$\frac{5}{9} - \frac{1}{3} = \frac{5}{9} - \frac{3}{9}$

$= \frac{2}{9}$

Find each difference.

2 $\frac{1}{2} - \frac{3}{10} = \frac{5}{10} - \frac{3}{10}$

$= \frac{2}{10}$

$= \frac{1}{5}$

$\frac{1}{2} = \frac{5}{10}$ (×5)

3 $\frac{1}{2} - \frac{1}{4} = \frac{1}{4}$

4 $\frac{5}{8} - \frac{1}{3} = \frac{7}{24}$

5 $\frac{7}{9} - \frac{4}{9} - \frac{3}{18} = \frac{3}{18}$

6 $\frac{12}{12} - \frac{5}{12} - \frac{1}{3} = \frac{1}{4}$

ON YOUR OWN

Go to Workbook A: Practice 2, pages 139–140

Lesson 6.2 Subtracting Fractions 229

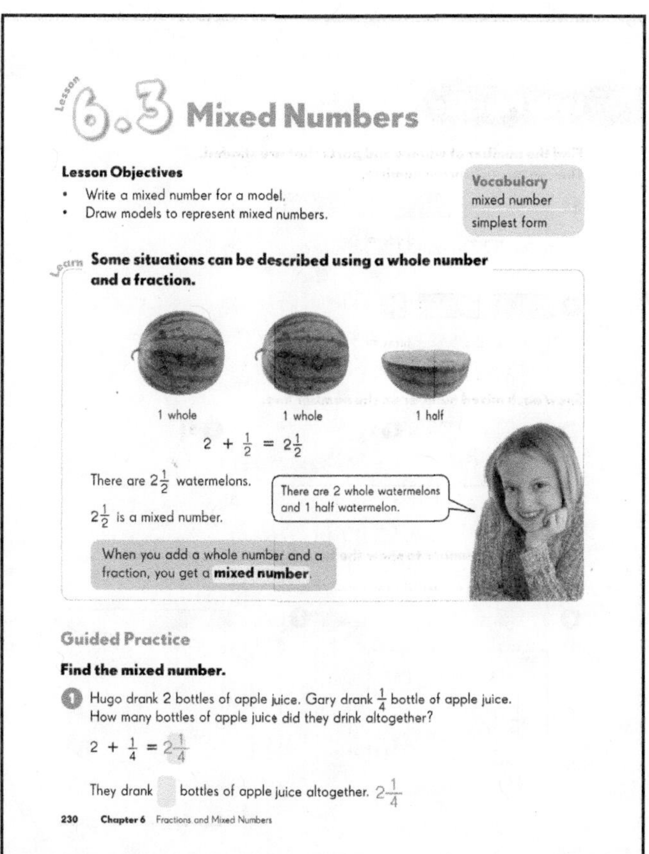
Lesson 6.3 Mixed Numbers

Lesson Objectives

- Write a mixed number for a model.
- Draw models to represent mixed numbers.

Vocabulary
mixed number
simplest form

Learn **Some situations can be described using a whole number and a fraction.**

1 whole 1 whole 1 half

$2 + \frac{1}{2} = 2\frac{1}{2}$

There are $2\frac{1}{2}$ watermelons.

$2\frac{1}{2}$ is a mixed number.

There are 2 whole watermelons and 1 half watermelon.

When you add a whole number and a fraction, you get a **mixed number**.

Guided Practice

Find the mixed number.

1 Hugo drank 2 bottles of apple juice. Gary drank $\frac{1}{4}$ bottle of apple juice. How many bottles of apple juice did they drink altogether?

$2 + \frac{1}{4} = 2\frac{1}{4}$

They drank ___ bottles of apple juice altogether. $2\frac{1}{4}$

230 **Chapter 6** Fractions and Mixed Numbers

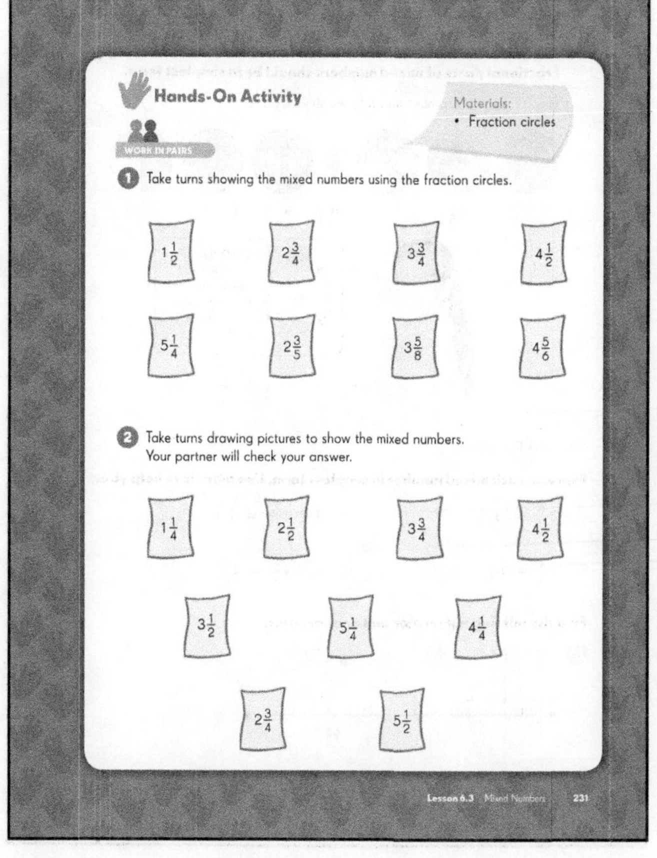
Hands-On Activity

Materials:
- Fraction circles

WORK IN PAIRS

1 Take turns showing the mixed numbers using the fraction circles.

$1\frac{1}{2}$ $2\frac{3}{4}$ $3\frac{3}{4}$ $4\frac{1}{2}$

$5\frac{1}{4}$ $2\frac{3}{5}$ $3\frac{5}{8}$ $4\frac{5}{6}$

2 Take turns drawing pictures to show the mixed numbers. Your partner will check your answer.

$1\frac{1}{4}$ $2\frac{1}{2}$ $3\frac{3}{4}$ $4\frac{1}{2}$

$3\frac{1}{2}$ $5\frac{1}{4}$ $4\frac{1}{4}$

$2\frac{3}{4}$ $5\frac{1}{2}$

Lesson 6.3 Mixed Numbers 231

Chapter 6

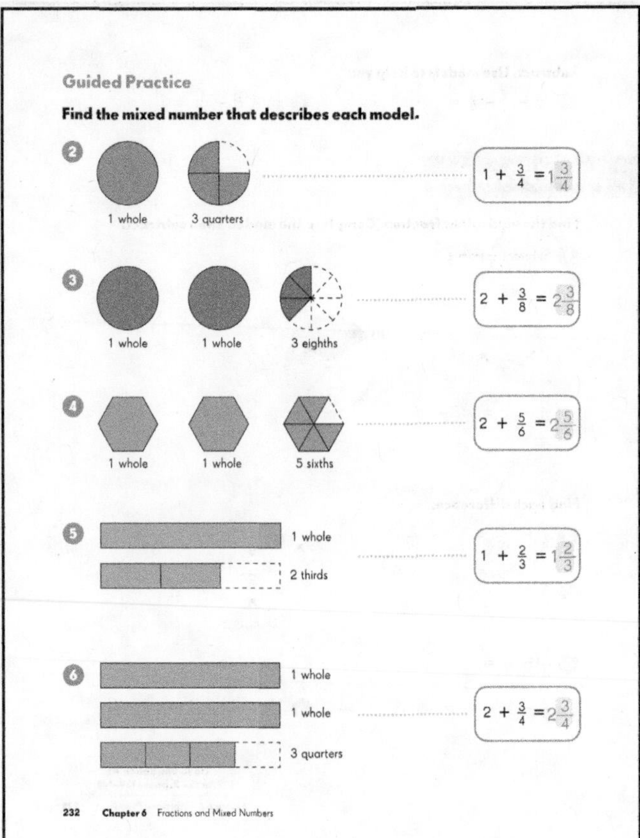

Guided Practice

Find the mixed number that describes each model.

2. 1 whole, 3 quarters — $1 + \frac{3}{4} = 1\frac{3}{4}$

3. 1 whole, 1 whole, 3 eighths — $2 + \frac{3}{8} = 2\frac{3}{8}$

4. 1 whole, 1 whole, 5 sixths — $2 + \frac{5}{6} = 2\frac{5}{6}$

5. 1 whole, 2 thirds — $1 + \frac{2}{3} = 1\frac{2}{3}$

6. 1 whole, 1 whole, 3 quarters — $2 + \frac{3}{4} = 2\frac{3}{4}$

232 Chapter 6 Fractions and Mixed Numbers

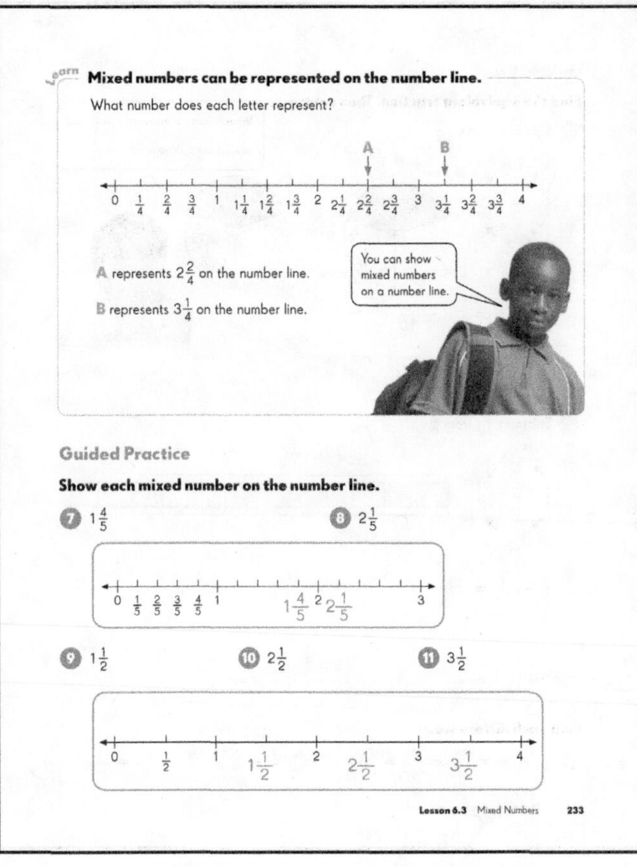

Learn Mixed numbers can be represented on the number line.

What number does each letter represent?

A represents $2\frac{2}{4}$ on the number line.

B represents $3\frac{1}{4}$ on the number line.

You can show mixed numbers on a number line.

Guided Practice

Show each mixed number on the number line.

7. $1\frac{4}{5}$ 8. $2\frac{1}{5}$

9. $1\frac{1}{2}$ 10. $2\frac{1}{2}$ 11. $3\frac{1}{2}$

Lesson 6.3 Mixed Numbers 233

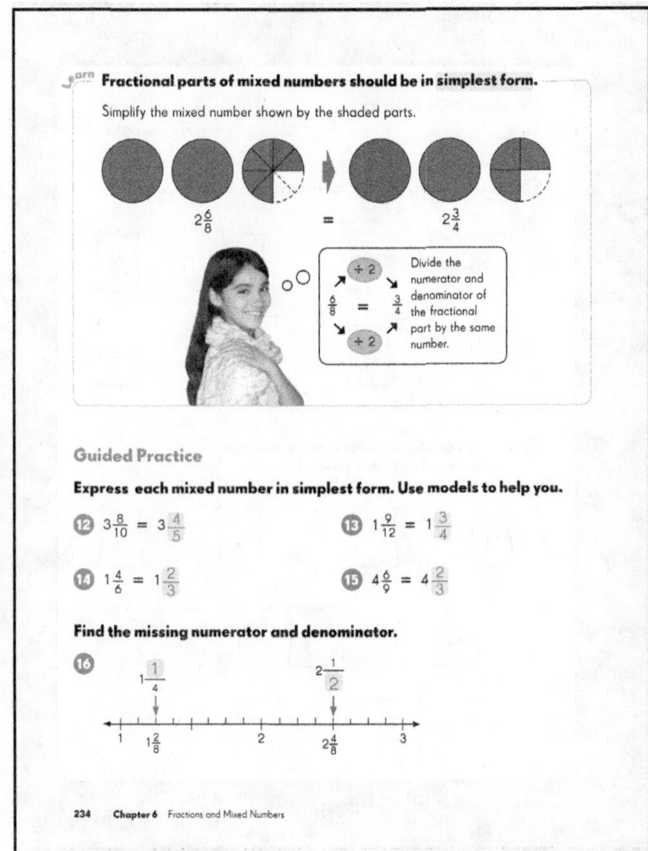

Learn Fractional parts of mixed numbers should be in simplest form.

Simplify the mixed number shown by the shaded parts.

$2\frac{6}{8} = 2\frac{3}{4}$

$\frac{6}{8} = \frac{3}{4}$ (÷ 2)
Divide the numerator and denominator of the fractional part by the same number.

Guided Practice

Express each mixed number in simplest form. Use models to help you.

12. $3\frac{8}{10} = 3\frac{4}{5}$ 13. $1\frac{9}{12} = 1\frac{3}{4}$

14. $1\frac{4}{6} = 1\frac{2}{3}$ 15. $4\frac{6}{9} = 4\frac{2}{3}$

Find the missing numerator and denominator.

16. $1\frac{1}{4}$ ($1\frac{2}{8}$), $2\frac{1}{2}$ ($2\frac{4}{8}$)

234 Chapter 6 Fractions and Mixed Numbers

Chapter 6

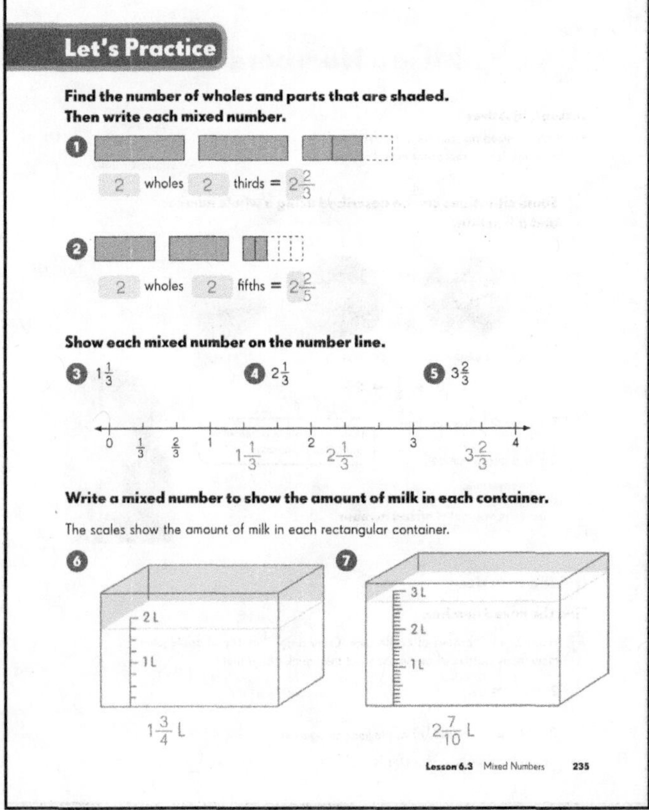

Let's Practice

Find the number of wholes and parts that are shaded. Then write each mixed number.

1. 2 wholes 2 thirds = $2\frac{2}{3}$

2. 2 wholes 2 fifths = $2\frac{2}{5}$

Show each mixed number on the number line.

3. $1\frac{1}{3}$ 4. $2\frac{1}{3}$ 5. $3\frac{2}{3}$

Write a mixed number to show the amount of milk in each container.

The scales show the amount of milk in each rectangular container.

6. $1\frac{3}{4}$ L

7. $2\frac{7}{10}$ L

Lesson 6.3 Mixed Numbers 235

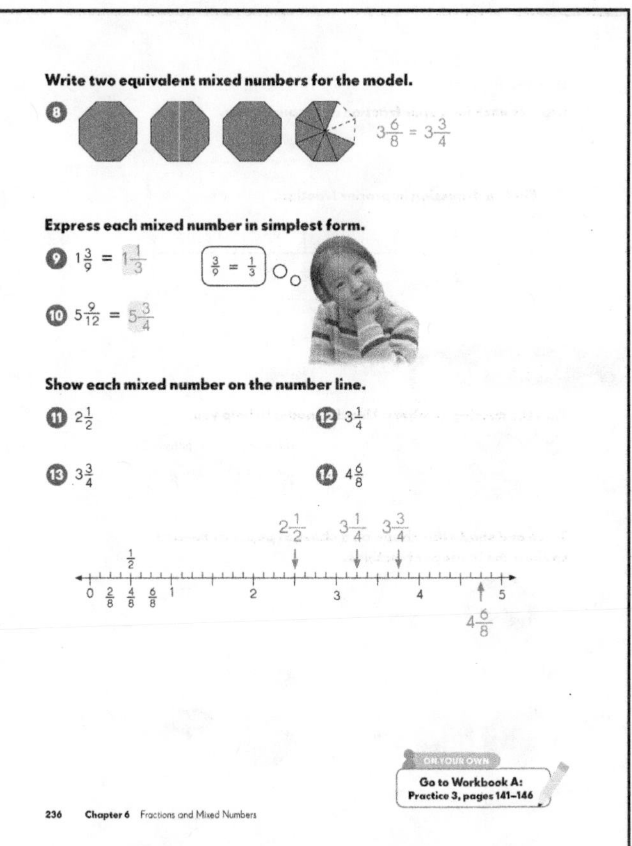

Write two equivalent mixed numbers for the model.

8. $3\frac{6}{8} = 3\frac{3}{4}$

Express each mixed number in simplest form.

9. $1\frac{3}{9} = 1\frac{1}{3}$

$\frac{3}{9} = \frac{1}{3}$

10. $5\frac{9}{12} = 5\frac{3}{4}$

Show each mixed number on the number line.

11. $2\frac{1}{2}$

12. $3\frac{1}{4}$

13. $3\frac{3}{4}$

14. $4\frac{6}{8}$

ON YOUR OWN

Go to Workbook A: Practice 3, pages 141–146

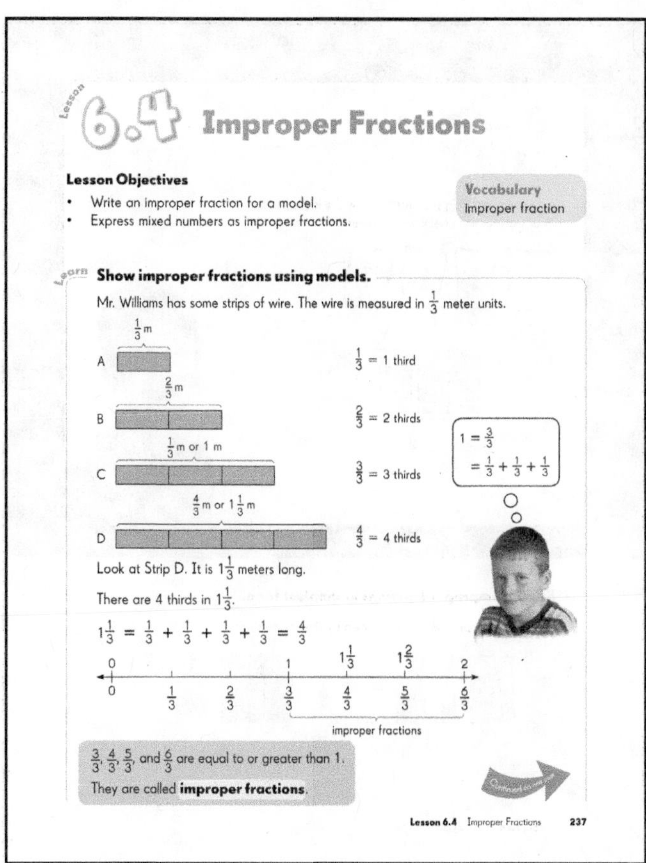

Lesson

6.4 Improper Fractions

Lesson Objectives

- Write an improper fraction for a model.
- Express mixed numbers as improper fractions.

Vocabulary
improper fraction

Learn

Show improper fractions using models.

Mr. Williams has some strips of wire. The wire is measured in $\frac{1}{3}$ meter units.

Look at Strip D. It is $1\frac{1}{3}$ meters long.

There are 4 thirds in $1\frac{1}{3}$.

$1\frac{1}{3} = \frac{1}{3} + \frac{1}{3} + \frac{1}{3} + \frac{1}{3} = \frac{4}{3}$

$\frac{3}{3}$, $\frac{4}{3}$, $\frac{5}{3}$, and $\frac{6}{3}$ are equal to or greater than 1.
They are called **improper fractions**.

Continued on next page

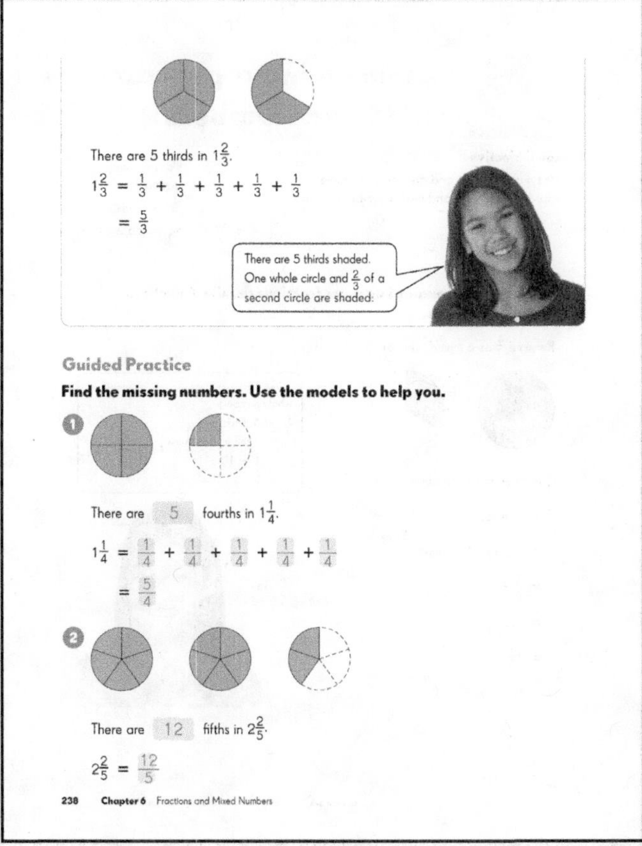

There are 5 thirds in $1\frac{2}{3}$.

$1\frac{2}{3} = \frac{1}{3} + \frac{1}{3} + \frac{1}{3} + \frac{1}{3} + \frac{1}{3}$

$= \frac{5}{3}$

There are 5 thirds shaded. One whole circle and $\frac{2}{3}$ of a second circle are shaded.

Guided Practice

Find the missing numbers. Use the models to help you.

1. There are 5 fourths in $1\frac{1}{4}$.

$1\frac{1}{4} = \frac{1}{4} + \frac{1}{4} + \frac{1}{4} + \frac{1}{4} + \frac{1}{4}$

$= \frac{5}{4}$

2. There are 12 fifths in $2\frac{2}{5}$.

$2\frac{2}{5} = \frac{12}{5}$

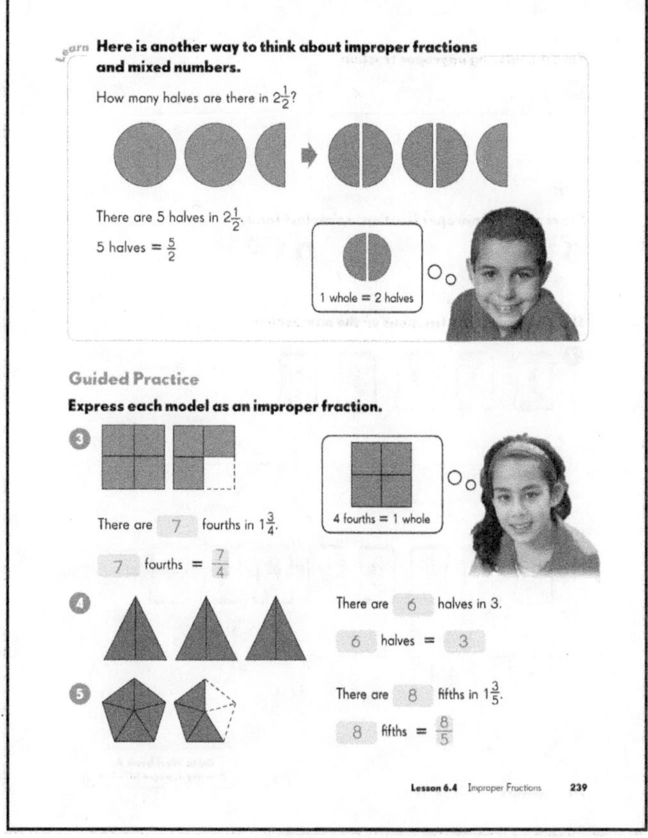

Learn

Here is another way to think about improper fractions and mixed numbers.

How many halves are there in $2\frac{1}{2}$?

There are 5 halves in $2\frac{1}{2}$.

5 halves = $\frac{5}{2}$

Guided Practice

Express each model as an improper fraction.

3. There are 7 fourths in $1\frac{3}{4}$.

7 fourths = $\frac{7}{4}$

4. There are 6 halves in 3.

6 halves = 3

5. There are 8 fifths in $1\frac{3}{5}$.

8 fifths = $\frac{8}{5}$

Chapter 6

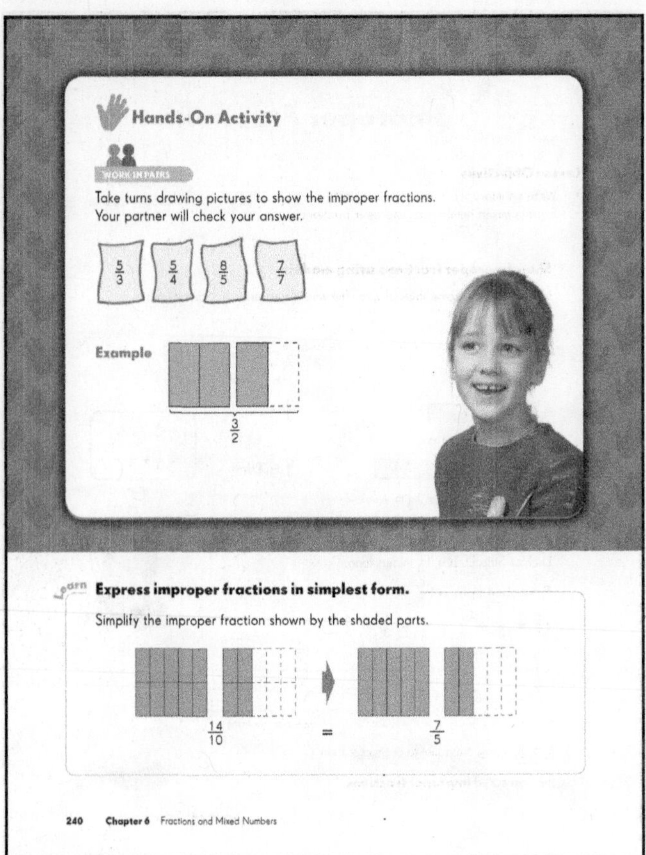

Hands-On Activity

WORK IN PAIRS

Take turns drawing pictures to show the improper fractions. Your partner will check your answer.

$\frac{5}{3}$ $\frac{5}{4}$ $\frac{8}{5}$ $\frac{7}{7}$

Example

$\frac{3}{2}$

Learn **Express improper fractions in simplest form.**

Simplify the improper fraction shown by the shaded parts.

$\frac{14}{10} = \frac{7}{5}$

240 **Chapter 6** Fractions and Mixed Numbers

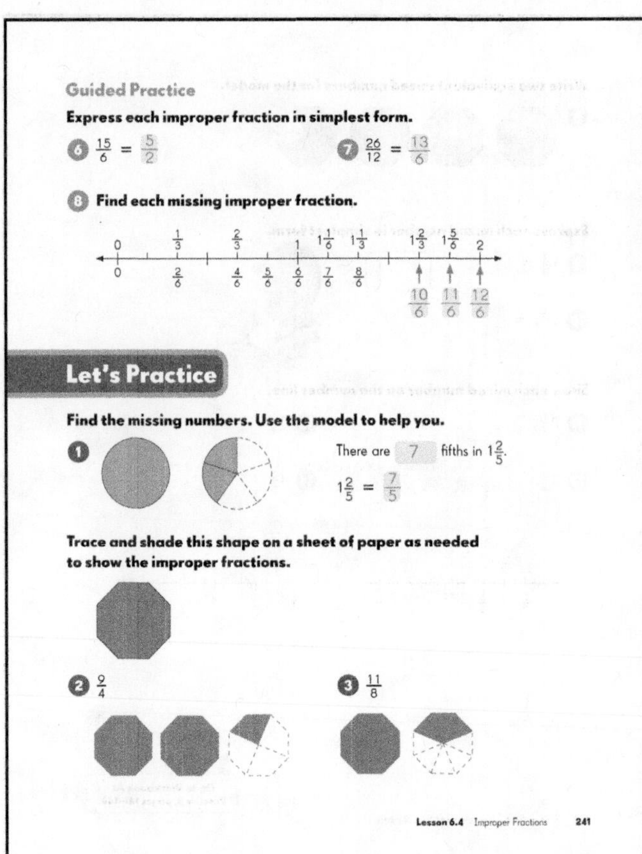

Guided Practice

Express each improper fraction in simplest form.

6. $\frac{15}{6} = \frac{5}{2}$

7. $\frac{26}{12} = \frac{13}{6}$

8. **Find each missing improper fraction.**

Number line (top): 0, $\frac{1}{3}$, $\frac{2}{3}$, 1, $1\frac{1}{6}$, $1\frac{1}{3}$, $1\frac{2}{3}$, $1\frac{5}{6}$, 2

Number line (bottom): 0, $\frac{2}{6}$, $\frac{4}{6}$, $\frac{5}{6}$, $\frac{6}{6}$, $\frac{7}{6}$, $\frac{8}{6}$, $\frac{10}{6}$, $\frac{11}{6}$, $\frac{12}{6}$

Let's Practice

Find the missing numbers. Use the model to help you.

1. There are 7 fifths in $1\frac{2}{5}$.

$1\frac{2}{5} = \frac{7}{5}$

Trace and shade this shape on a sheet of paper as needed to show the improper fractions.

2. $\frac{9}{4}$

3. $\frac{11}{8}$

Lesson 6.4 Improper Fractions 241

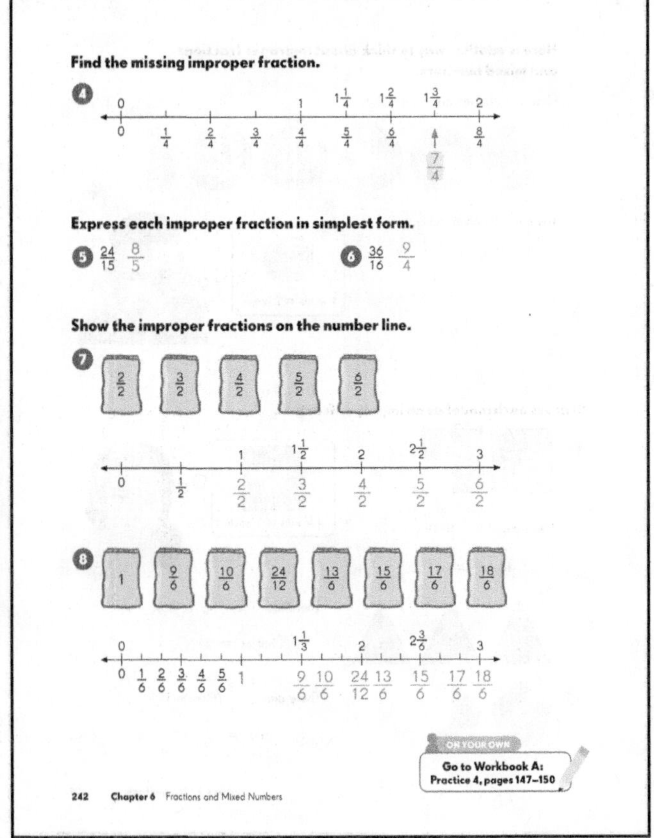

Find the missing improper fraction.

4. Number line (top): 0, 1, $1\frac{1}{4}$, $1\frac{2}{4}$, $1\frac{3}{4}$, 2

Number line (bottom): 0, $\frac{1}{4}$, $\frac{2}{4}$, $\frac{3}{4}$, $\frac{4}{4}$, $\frac{5}{4}$, $\frac{6}{4}$, $\frac{7}{4}$, $\frac{8}{4}$

Express each improper fraction in simplest form.

5. $\frac{24}{15}$ $\frac{8}{5}$

6. $\frac{36}{16}$ $\frac{9}{4}$

Show the improper fractions on the number line.

7. $\frac{2}{2}$ $\frac{3}{2}$ $\frac{4}{2}$ $\frac{5}{2}$ $\frac{6}{2}$

Number line (top): 0, 1, $1\frac{1}{2}$, 2, $2\frac{1}{2}$, 3

Number line (bottom): 0, $\frac{1}{2}$, $\frac{2}{2}$, $\frac{3}{2}$, $\frac{4}{2}$, $\frac{5}{2}$, $\frac{6}{2}$

8. 1 $\frac{9}{6}$ $\frac{10}{6}$ $\frac{24}{12}$ $\frac{13}{6}$ $\frac{15}{6}$ $\frac{17}{6}$ $\frac{18}{6}$

Number line (top): 0, $1\frac{1}{3}$, 2, $2\frac{3}{6}$, 3

Number line (bottom): 0, $\frac{1}{6}$, $\frac{2}{6}$, $\frac{3}{6}$, $\frac{4}{6}$, $\frac{5}{6}$, 1, $\frac{9}{6}$, $\frac{10}{6}$, $\frac{24}{12}$, $\frac{13}{6}$, $\frac{15}{6}$, $\frac{17}{6}$, $\frac{18}{6}$

ON YOUR OWN

Go to Workbook A: Practice 4, pages 147–150

242 **Chapter 6** Fractions and Mixed Numbers

Chapter 6

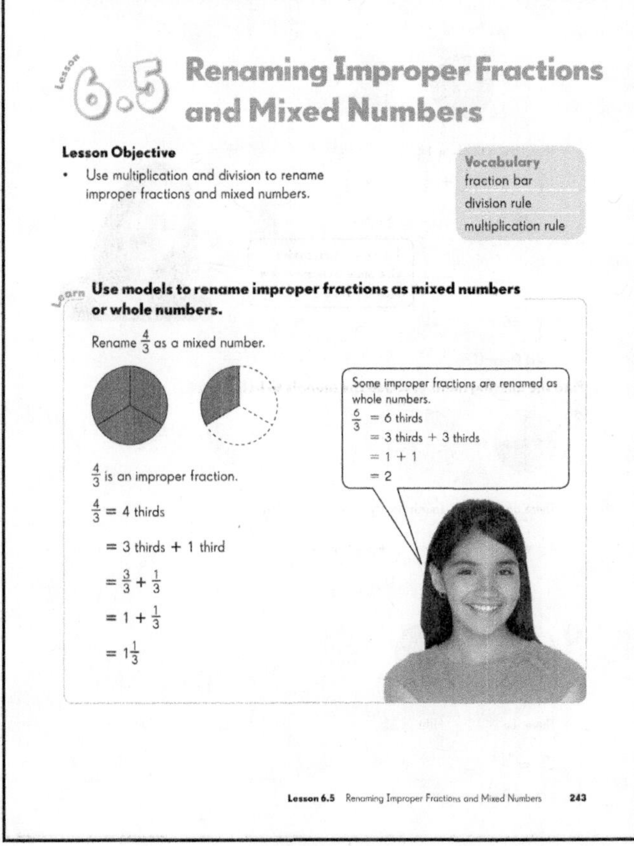

Lesson 6.5 **Renaming Improper Fractions and Mixed Numbers**

Lesson Objective

- Use multiplication and division to rename improper fractions and mixed numbers.

Vocabulary
fraction bar
division rule
multiplication rule

Learn **Use models to rename improper fractions as mixed numbers or whole numbers.**

Rename $\frac{4}{3}$ as a mixed number.

$\frac{4}{3}$ is an improper fraction.

$\frac{4}{3}$ = 4 thirds

= 3 thirds + 1 third

$= \frac{3}{3} + \frac{1}{3}$

$= 1 + \frac{1}{3}$

$= 1\frac{1}{3}$

Some improper fractions are renamed as whole numbers.
$\frac{6}{3}$ = 6 thirds
= 3 thirds + 3 thirds
= 1 + 1
= 2

Lesson 6.5 Renaming Improper Fractions and Mixed Numbers 243

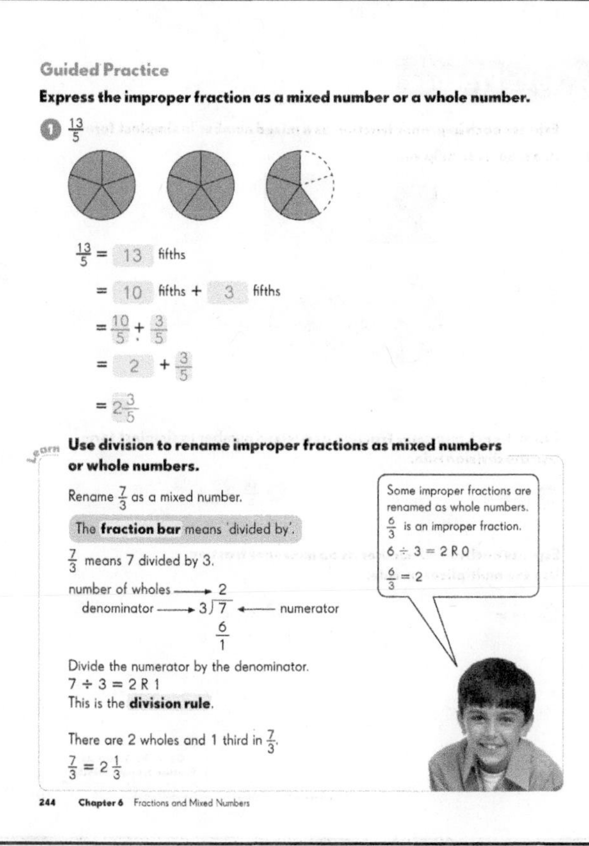

Guided Practice

Express the improper fraction as a mixed number or a whole number.

1. $\frac{13}{5}$

$\frac{13}{5}$ = 13 fifths

= 10 fifths + 3 fifths

$= \frac{10}{5} + \frac{3}{5}$

$= 2 + \frac{3}{5}$

$= 2\frac{3}{5}$

Learn **Use division to rename improper fractions as mixed numbers or whole numbers.**

Rename $\frac{7}{3}$ as a mixed number.

The **fraction bar** means 'divided by'.

$\frac{7}{3}$ means 7 divided by 3.

number of wholes → 2
denominator → $3\overline{)7}$ ← numerator
6
1

Divide the numerator by the denominator.
$7 \div 3 = 2$ R 1
This is the **division rule**.

There are 2 wholes and 1 third in $\frac{7}{3}$.
$\frac{7}{3} = 2\frac{1}{3}$

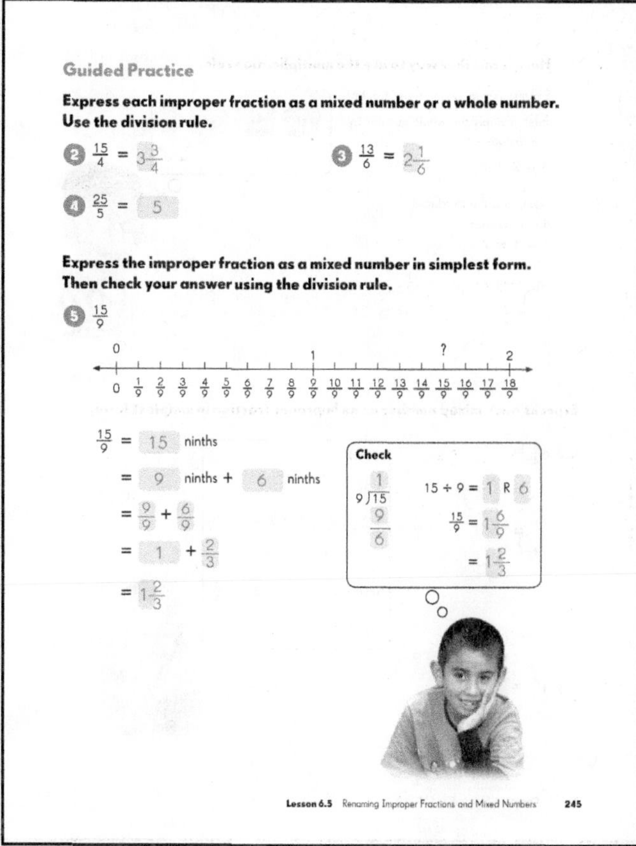

Guided Practice

Express each improper fraction as a mixed number or a whole number. Use the division rule.

2. $\frac{15}{4} = 3\frac{3}{4}$
3. $\frac{13}{6} = 2\frac{1}{6}$
4. $\frac{25}{5} = 5$

Express the improper fraction as a mixed number in simplest form. Then check your answer using the division rule.

5. $\frac{15}{9}$

$\frac{15}{9}$ = 15 ninths

= 9 ninths + 6 ninths

$= \frac{9}{9} + \frac{6}{9}$

$= 1 + \frac{2}{3}$

$= 1\frac{2}{3}$

Check
$9\overline{)15}$ = 1, 9, 6
$15 \div 9 = 1$ R 6
$\frac{15}{9} = 1\frac{6}{9}$
$= 1\frac{2}{3}$

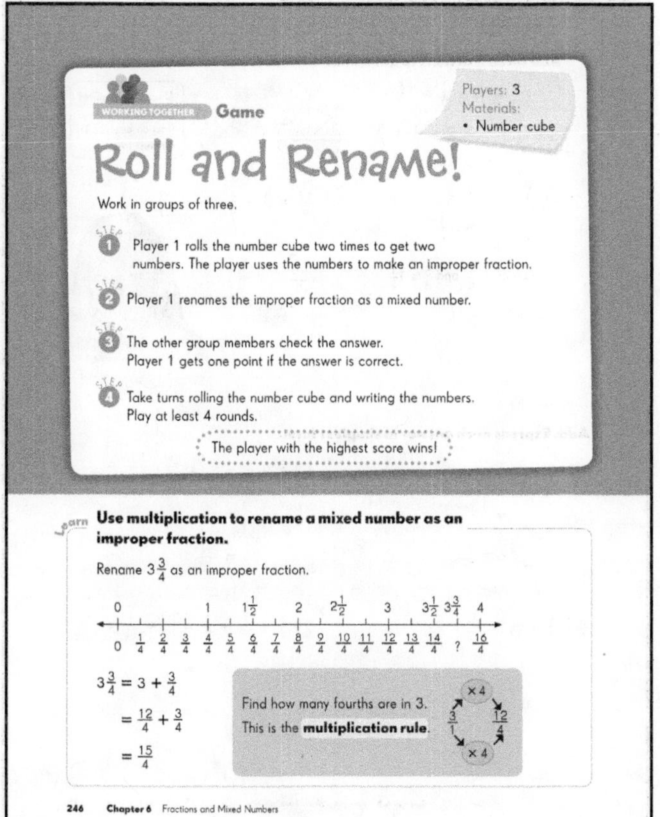

WORKING TOGETHER **Game**

Players: 3
Materials:
• Number cube

Roll and Rename!

Work in groups of three.

1. Player 1 rolls the number cube two times to get two numbers. The player uses the numbers to make an improper fraction.
2. Player 1 renames the improper fraction as a mixed number.
3. The other group members check the answer. Player 1 gets one point if the answer is correct.
4. Take turns rolling the number cube and writing the numbers. Play at least 4 rounds.

The player with the highest score wins!

Learn **Use multiplication to rename a mixed number as an improper fraction.**

Rename $3\frac{3}{4}$ as an improper fraction.

$3\frac{3}{4} = 3 + \frac{3}{4}$

$= \frac{12}{4} + \frac{3}{4}$

$= \frac{15}{4}$

Find how many fourths are in 3.
This is the **multiplication rule**.

$\frac{3}{1} = \frac{12}{4}$ (×4)

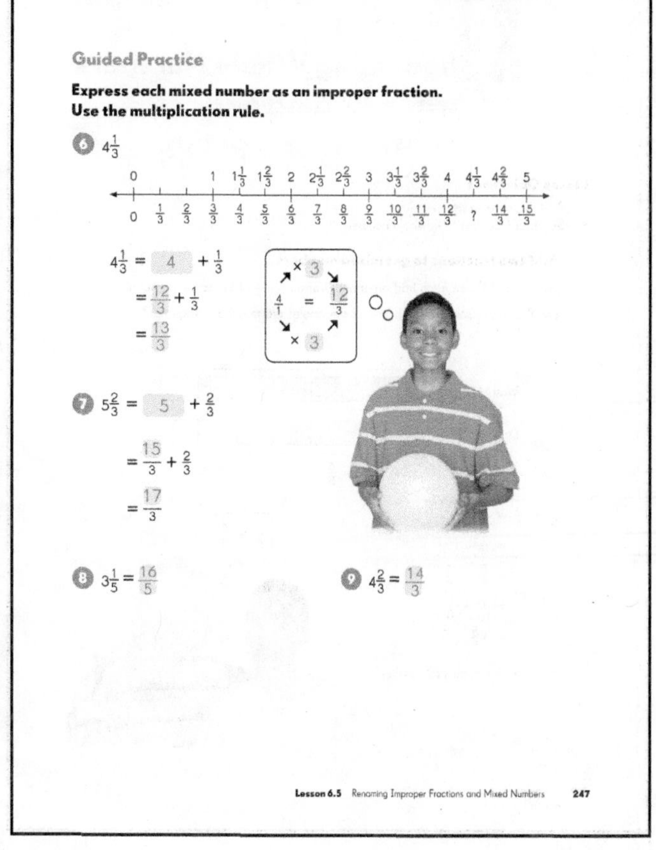

Guided Practice

Express each mixed number as an improper fraction. Use the multiplication rule.

6. $4\frac{1}{3}$

$4\frac{1}{3} = 4 + \frac{1}{3}$

$= \frac{12}{3} + \frac{1}{3}$

$= \frac{13}{3}$

$\frac{4}{1} = \frac{12}{3}$ (×3)

7. $5\frac{2}{3} = 5 + \frac{2}{3}$

$= \frac{15}{3} + \frac{2}{3}$

$= \frac{17}{3}$

8. $3\frac{1}{5} = \frac{16}{5}$
9. $4\frac{2}{3} = \frac{14}{3}$

Chapter 6

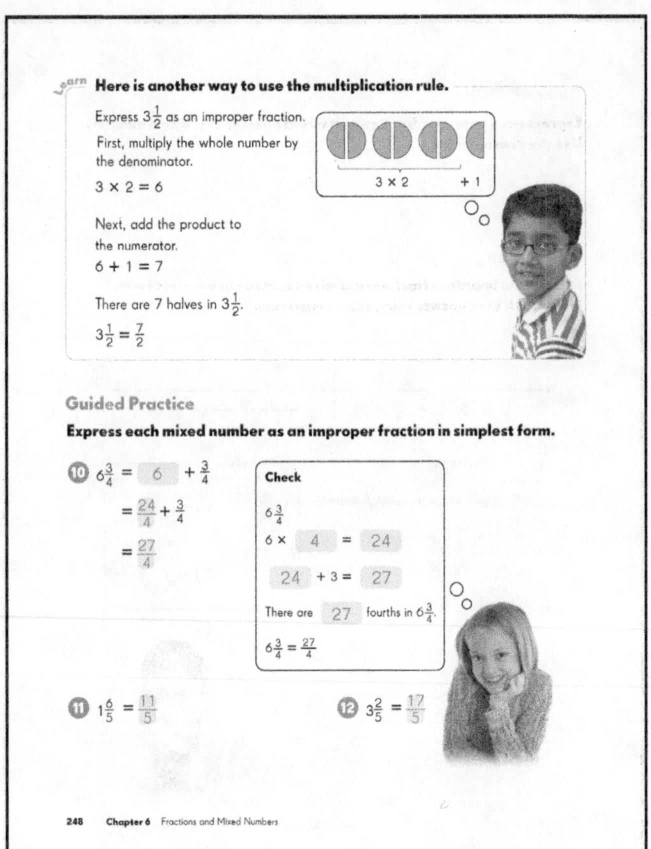

Learn **Here is another way to use the multiplication rule.**

Express $3\frac{1}{2}$ as an improper fraction.

First, multiply the whole number by the denominator.

$3 \times 2 = 6$

Next, add the product to the numerator.

$6 + 1 = 7$

There are 7 halves in $3\frac{1}{2}$.

$3\frac{1}{2} = \frac{7}{2}$

Guided Practice

Express each mixed number as an improper fraction in simplest form.

10. $6\frac{3}{4} = 6 + \frac{3}{4}$
$= \frac{24}{4} + \frac{3}{4}$
$= \frac{27}{4}$

Check

$6\frac{3}{4}$

$6 \times 4 = 24$

$24 + 3 = 27$

There are 27 fourths in $6\frac{3}{4}$.

$6\frac{3}{4} = \frac{27}{4}$

11. $1\frac{6}{5} = \frac{11}{5}$

12. $3\frac{2}{5} = \frac{17}{5}$

248 **Chapter 6** Fractions and Mixed Numbers

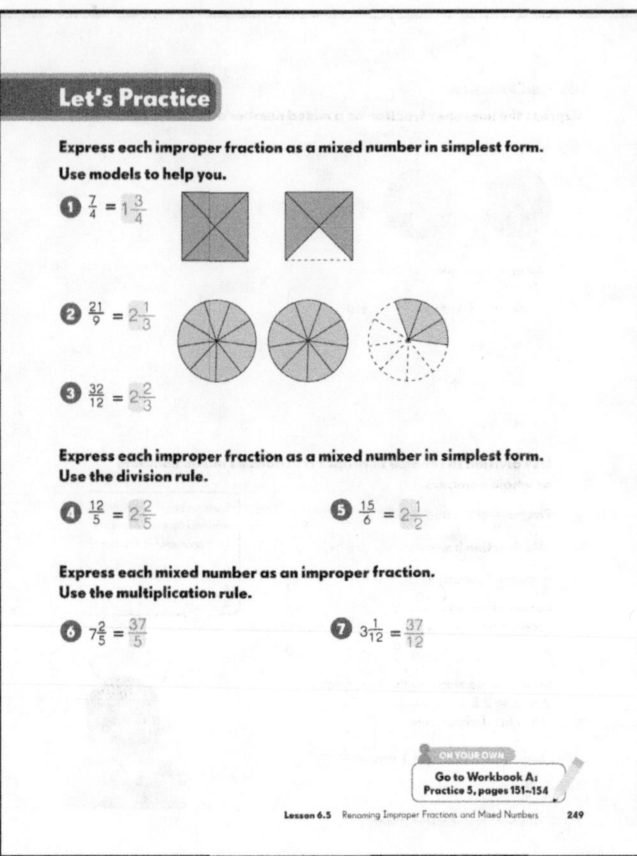

Let's Practice

Express each improper fraction as a mixed number in simplest form. Use models to help you.

1. $\frac{7}{4} = 1\frac{3}{4}$
2. $\frac{21}{9} = 2\frac{1}{3}$
3. $\frac{32}{12} = 2\frac{2}{3}$

Express each improper fraction as a mixed number in simplest form. Use the division rule.

4. $\frac{12}{5} = 2\frac{2}{5}$
5. $\frac{15}{6} = 2\frac{1}{2}$

Express each mixed number as an improper fraction. Use the multiplication rule.

6. $7\frac{2}{5} = \frac{37}{5}$
7. $3\frac{1}{12} = \frac{37}{12}$

ON YOUR OWN

Go to Workbook A: Practice 5, pages 151–154

Lesson 6.5 Renaming Improper Fractions and Mixed Numbers 249

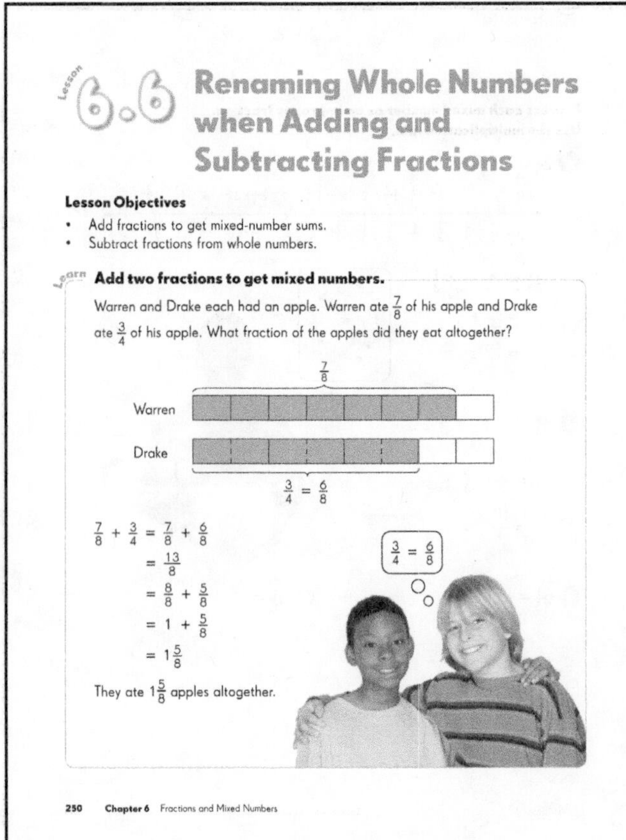

Lesson 6.6

Renaming Whole Numbers when Adding and Subtracting Fractions

Lesson Objectives

- Add fractions to get mixed-number sums.
- Subtract fractions from whole numbers.

Learn **Add two fractions to get mixed numbers.**

Warren and Drake each had an apple. Warren ate $\frac{7}{8}$ of his apple and Drake ate $\frac{3}{4}$ of his apple. What fraction of the apples did they eat altogether?

$\frac{7}{8} + \frac{3}{4} = \frac{7}{8} + \frac{6}{8}$
$= \frac{13}{8}$
$= \frac{8}{8} + \frac{5}{8}$
$= 1 + \frac{5}{8}$
$= 1\frac{5}{8}$

They ate $1\frac{5}{8}$ apples altogether.

Chapter 6

250 **Chapter 6** Fractions and Mixed Numbers

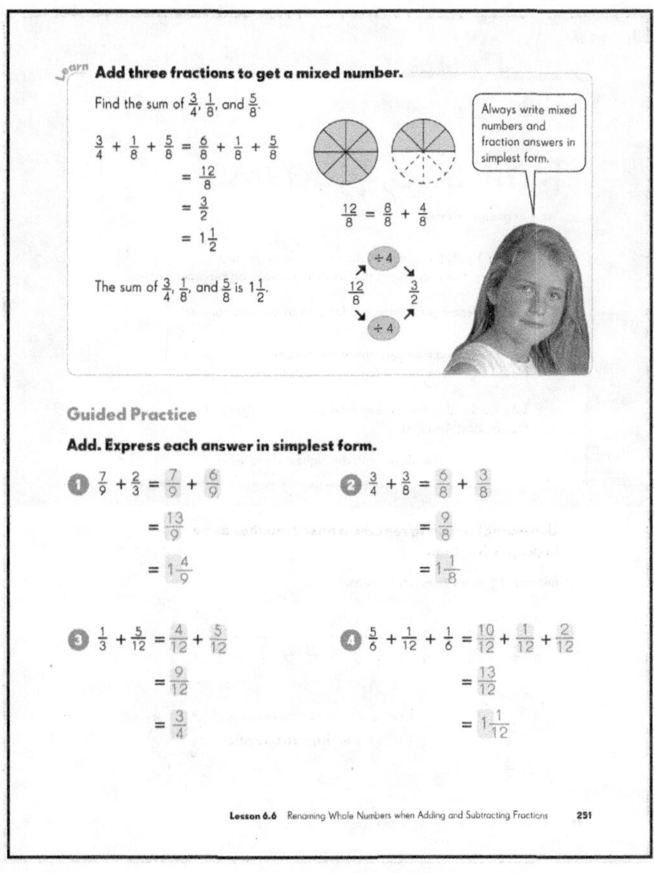

Learn **Add three fractions to get a mixed number.**

Find the sum of $\frac{3}{4}$, $\frac{1}{8}$, and $\frac{5}{8}$.

$\frac{3}{4} + \frac{1}{8} + \frac{5}{8} = \frac{6}{8} + \frac{1}{8} + \frac{5}{8}$
$= \frac{12}{8}$
$= \frac{3}{2}$
$= 1\frac{1}{2}$

$\frac{12}{8} = \frac{8}{8} + \frac{4}{8}$
÷ 4
$\frac{12}{8}$ $\frac{3}{2}$
÷ 4
Always write mixed numbers and fraction answers in simplest form.

The sum of $\frac{3}{4}$, $\frac{1}{8}$, and $\frac{5}{8}$ is $1\frac{1}{2}$.

Guided Practice

Add. Express each answer in simplest form.

1. $\frac{7}{9} + \frac{2}{3} = \frac{7}{9} + \frac{6}{9}$
$= \frac{13}{9}$
$= 1\frac{4}{9}$

2. $\frac{3}{4} + \frac{3}{8} = \frac{6}{8} + \frac{3}{8}$
$= \frac{9}{8}$
$= 1\frac{1}{8}$

3. $\frac{1}{3} + \frac{5}{12} = \frac{4}{12} + \frac{5}{12}$
$= \frac{9}{12}$
$= \frac{3}{4}$

4. $\frac{5}{6} + \frac{1}{12} + \frac{1}{6} = \frac{10}{12} + \frac{1}{12} + \frac{2}{12}$
$= \frac{13}{12}$
$= 1\frac{1}{12}$

Lesson 6.6 Renaming Whole Numbers when Adding and Subtracting Fractions 251

Learn Subtract fractions from whole numbers.

Rosita had 3 pretzel rods. She ate $\frac{4}{9}$ of one pretzel rod.
What fraction of the pretzel rods are left?

Method 1

$3 - \frac{4}{9} = 2\frac{9}{9} - \frac{4}{9}$

$= 2\frac{5}{9}$

Method 2

$3 - \frac{4}{9} = \frac{27}{9} - \frac{4}{9}$

$= \frac{23}{9}$

$= 2\frac{5}{9}$

$9\overline{)23}$ = 2 R 5 (23 − 18 = 5)

There are $2\frac{5}{9}$ pretzel rods left.

252 Chapter 6 Fractions and Mixed Numbers

Guided Practice

Find the difference.

5. 2 and $\frac{3}{8}$.

Method 1

$2 - \frac{3}{8} = 1\frac{8}{8} - \frac{3}{8}$

$= 1\frac{5}{8}$

Method 2

$2 - \frac{3}{8} = \frac{16}{8} - \frac{3}{8}$

$= \frac{13}{8}$

$= 1\frac{5}{8}$

6. 5 and $\frac{7}{8}$

$\frac{5}{1} = \frac{40}{8}$ (×8)

$\frac{40}{8} - \frac{7}{8} = \frac{33}{8}$

$= 4\frac{1}{8}$

Lesson 6.6 Renaming Whole Numbers when Adding and Subtracting Fractions 253

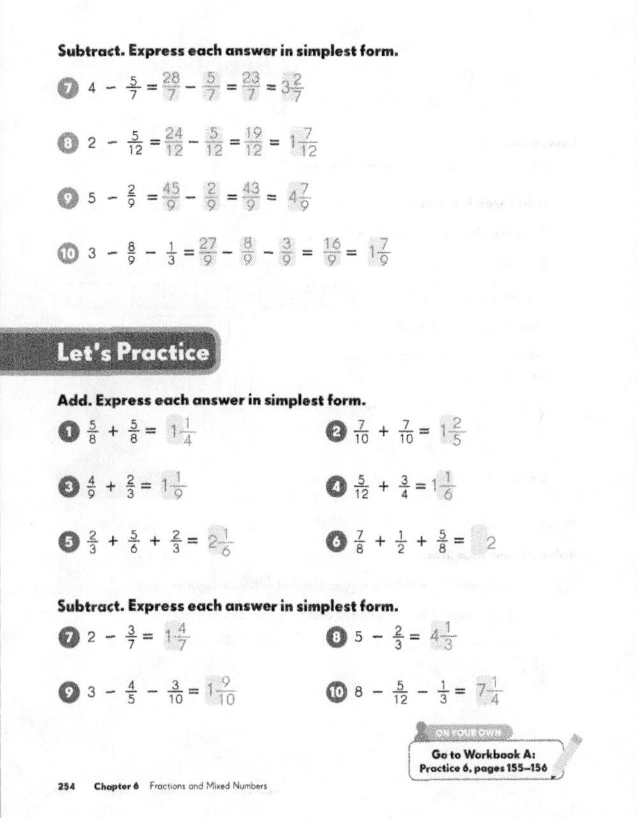

Subtract. Express each answer in simplest form.

7. $4 - \frac{5}{7} = \frac{28}{7} - \frac{5}{7} = \frac{23}{7} = 3\frac{2}{7}$

8. $2 - \frac{5}{12} = \frac{24}{12} - \frac{5}{12} = \frac{19}{12} = 1\frac{7}{12}$

9. $5 - \frac{2}{9} = \frac{45}{9} - \frac{2}{9} = \frac{43}{9} = 4\frac{7}{9}$

10. $3 - \frac{8}{9} - \frac{1}{3} = \frac{27}{9} - \frac{8}{9} - \frac{3}{9} = \frac{16}{9} = 1\frac{7}{9}$

Let's Practice

Add. Express each answer in simplest form.

1. $\frac{5}{8} + \frac{5}{8} = 1\frac{1}{4}$
2. $\frac{7}{10} + \frac{7}{10} = 1\frac{2}{5}$
3. $\frac{4}{9} + \frac{2}{3} = 1\frac{1}{9}$
4. $\frac{5}{12} + \frac{3}{4} = 1\frac{1}{6}$
5. $\frac{2}{3} + \frac{5}{6} + \frac{2}{3} = 2\frac{1}{6}$
6. $\frac{7}{8} + \frac{1}{2} + \frac{5}{8} = 2$

Subtract. Express each answer in simplest form.

7. $2 - \frac{3}{7} = 1\frac{4}{7}$
8. $5 - \frac{2}{3} = 4\frac{1}{3}$
9. $3 - \frac{4}{5} - \frac{3}{10} = 1\frac{9}{10}$
10. $8 - \frac{5}{12} - \frac{1}{3} = 7\frac{1}{4}$

ON YOUR OWN
Go to Workbook A: Practice 6, pages 155–156

254 Chapter 6 Fractions and Mixed Numbers

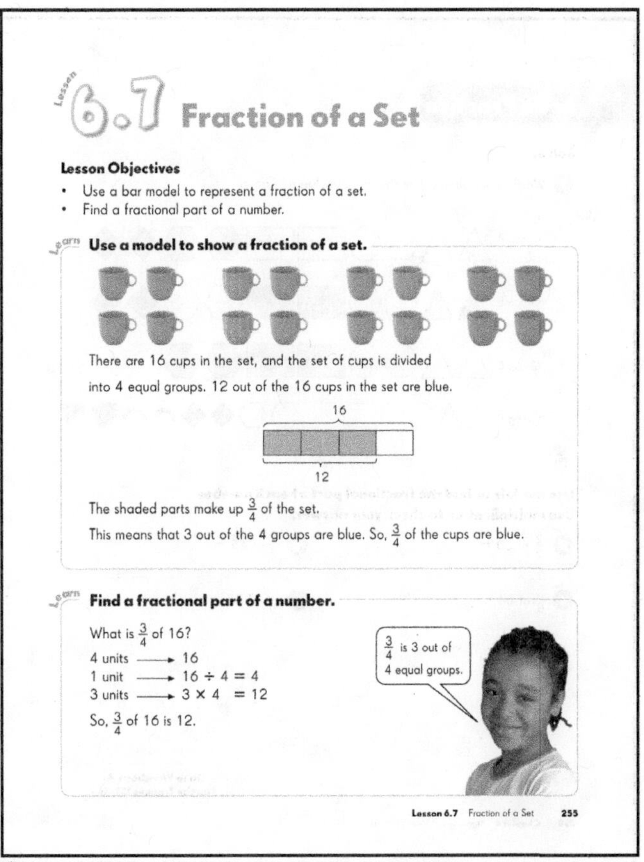

Lesson 6.7 Fraction of a Set

Lesson Objectives

- Use a bar model to represent a fraction of a set.
- Find a fractional part of a number.

Learn Use a model to show a fraction of a set.

There are 16 cups in the set, and the set of cups is divided into 4 equal groups. 12 out of the 16 cups in the set are blue.

The shaded parts make up $\frac{3}{4}$ of the set.

This means that 3 out of the 4 groups are blue. So, $\frac{3}{4}$ of the cups are blue.

Learn Find a fractional part of a number.

What is $\frac{3}{4}$ of 16?

4 units ⟶ 16

1 unit ⟶ 16 ÷ 4 = 4

3 units ⟶ 3 × 4 = 12

So, $\frac{3}{4}$ of 16 is 12.

Lesson 6.7 Fraction of a Set 255

Chapter 6

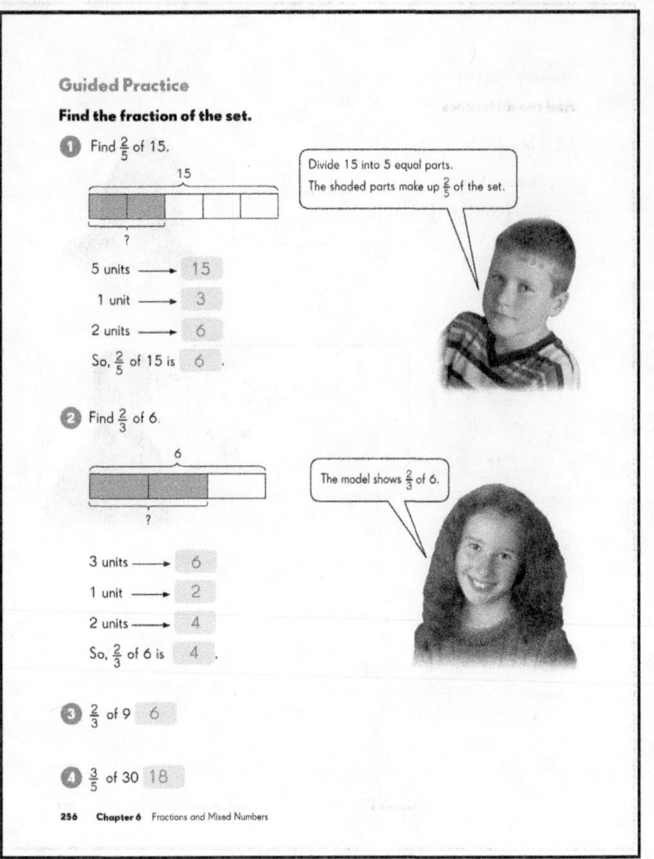
Guided Practice

Find the fraction of the set.

1. Find $\frac{2}{5}$ of 15.

15
?
Divide 15 into 5 equal parts.
The shaded parts make up $\frac{2}{5}$ of the set.

5 units → 15

1 unit → 3

2 units → 6

So, $\frac{2}{5}$ of 15 is 6.

2. Find $\frac{2}{3}$ of 6.

3 units → 6

1 unit → 2

2 units → 4

So, $\frac{2}{3}$ of 6 is 4.

3. $\frac{2}{3}$ of 9 6

4. $\frac{3}{5}$ of 30 18

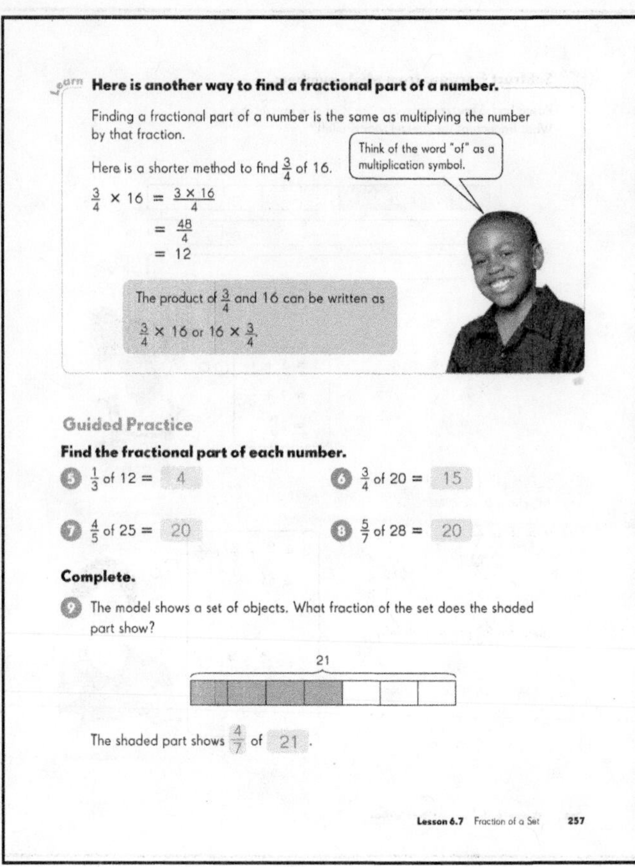
Learn: Here is another way to find a fractional part of a number.

Finding a fractional part of a number is the same as multiplying the number by that fraction.

Think of the word "of" as a multiplication symbol.

Here is a shorter method to find $\frac{3}{4}$ of 16.

$$\frac{3}{4} \times 16 = \frac{3 \times 16}{4} = \frac{48}{4} = 12$$

The product of $\frac{3}{4}$ and 16 can be written as $\frac{3}{4} \times 16$ or $16 \times \frac{3}{4}$.

Guided Practice

Find the fractional part of each number.

5. $\frac{1}{3}$ of 12 = 4

6. $\frac{3}{4}$ of 20 = 15

7. $\frac{4}{5}$ of 25 = 20

8. $\frac{5}{7}$ of 28 = 20

Complete.

9. The model shows a set of objects. What fraction of the set does the shaded part show?

The shaded part shows $\frac{4}{7}$ of 21.

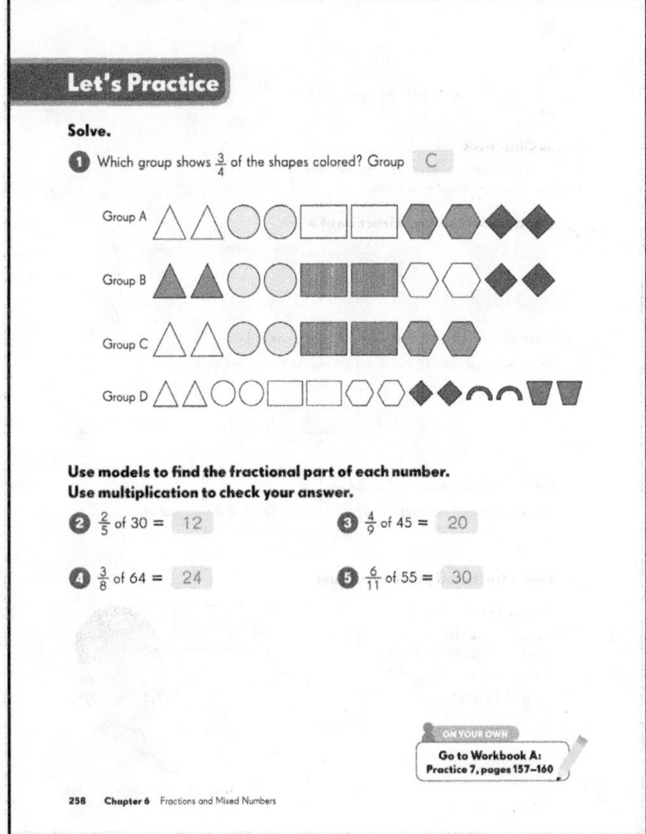
Let's Practice

Solve.

1. Which group shows $\frac{3}{4}$ of the shapes colored? Group C

Use models to find the fractional part of each number.
Use multiplication to check your answer.

2. $\frac{2}{5}$ of 30 = 12

3. $\frac{4}{9}$ of 45 = 20

4. $\frac{3}{8}$ of 64 = 24

5. $\frac{6}{11}$ of 55 = 30

ON YOUR OWN
Go to Workbook A: Practice 7, pages 157–160

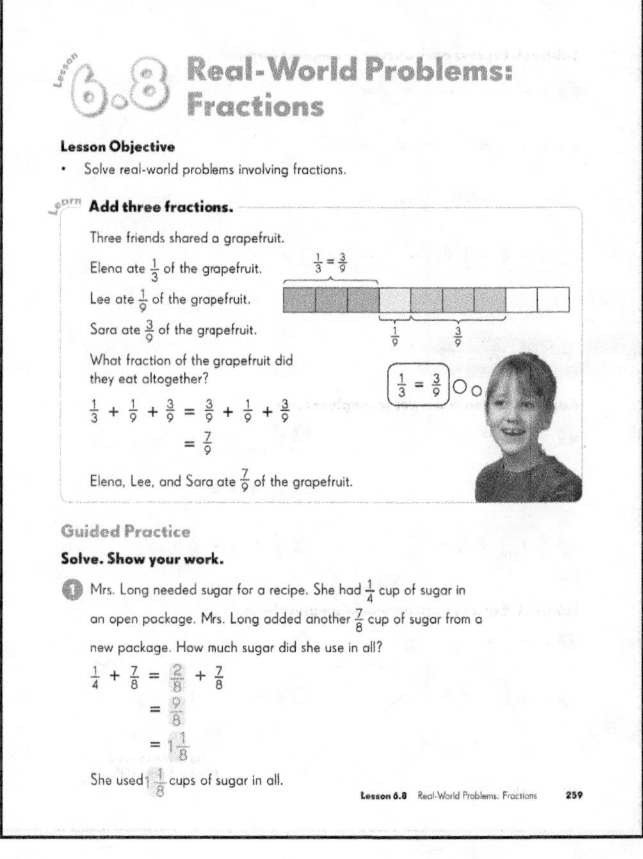
Lesson 6.8 Real-World Problems: Fractions

Lesson Objective

- Solve real-world problems involving fractions.

Learn: Add three fractions.

Three friends shared a grapefruit.

Elena ate $\frac{1}{3}$ of the grapefruit.

Lee ate $\frac{1}{9}$ of the grapefruit.

Sara ate $\frac{3}{9}$ of the grapefruit.

What fraction of the grapefruit did they eat altogether?

$$\frac{1}{3} + \frac{1}{9} + \frac{3}{9} = \frac{3}{9} + \frac{1}{9} + \frac{3}{9} = \frac{7}{9}$$

Elena, Lee, and Sara ate $\frac{7}{9}$ of the grapefruit.

Guided Practice

Solve. Show your work.

1. Mrs. Long needed sugar for a recipe. She had $\frac{1}{4}$ cup of sugar in an open package. Mrs. Long added another $\frac{7}{8}$ cup of sugar from a new package. How much sugar did she use in all?

$$\frac{1}{4} + \frac{7}{8} = \frac{2}{8} + \frac{7}{8} = \frac{9}{8} = 1\frac{1}{8}$$

She used $1\frac{1}{8}$ cups of sugar in all.

2 Sean, Roger, and Damon each drank different amounts of milk one day.

Sean drank $\frac{5}{6}$ quart of milk. Roger drank $\frac{7}{12}$ quart of milk and Damon drank $\frac{11}{12}$ quart of milk.

How much milk did they drink altogether?

$\frac{5}{6} + \frac{7}{12} + \frac{11}{12} = \frac{10}{12} + \frac{7}{12} + \frac{11}{12}$

$= \frac{28}{12}$

$= 2\frac{4}{12}$

$= 2\frac{1}{3}$

They drank $2\frac{1}{3}$ quarts of milk altogether.

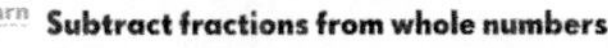

Learn Subtract fractions from whole numbers.

Cheryl and Dennis made a pumpkin pie.

Cheryl ate $\frac{2}{5}$ of the pie.

Dennis ate $\frac{3}{10}$ of the pie.

$\frac{10}{10}$

$\frac{2}{5} = \frac{4}{10}$ $\frac{3}{10}$

What fraction of the pumpkin pie was left?

$1 - \frac{2}{5} - \frac{3}{10} = \frac{10}{10} - \frac{4}{10} - \frac{3}{10}$

$= \frac{3}{10}$

$\frac{2}{5} = \frac{4}{10}$

$\frac{3}{10}$ of the pumpkin pie was left.

A craft store has a 9-yard spool of ribbon. In the morning, a customer buys $\frac{1}{5}$ yard of ribbon from the spool. In the afternoon, another customer buys $\frac{7}{10}$ yard of ribbon from the spool. How much ribbon is left?

Method 1

$9 - \frac{1}{5} - \frac{7}{10} = 8\frac{10}{10} - \frac{1}{5} - \frac{7}{10}$

$= 8\frac{10}{10} - \frac{2}{10} - \frac{7}{10}$

$= 8\frac{1}{10}$

Method 2

$\frac{1}{5} + \frac{7}{10} = \frac{2}{10} + \frac{7}{10}$

$= \frac{9}{10}$

$9 - \frac{9}{10} = 8\frac{10}{10} - \frac{9}{10}$

$= 8\frac{1}{10}$

$8\frac{1}{10}$ yards of ribbon are left.

Guided Practice

Solve. Show your work.

3 Terry had to travel 12 miles from Town A to Town B. He traveled $\frac{5}{8}$ miles by bus. Then he traveled another $\frac{1}{4}$ miles by car just before the car broke down. How far was he from Town B when the car broke down?

Method 1

$12 - \frac{5}{8} - \frac{1}{4} = 11\frac{8}{8} - \frac{5}{8} - \frac{1}{4}$

$= 11\frac{8}{8} - \frac{5}{8} - \frac{2}{8}$

$= 11\frac{1}{8}$

Method 2

$\frac{5}{8} + \frac{1}{4} = \frac{5}{8} + \frac{2}{8}$

$= \frac{7}{8}$

$12 - \frac{7}{8} = 11\frac{8}{8} - \frac{7}{8}$

$= 11\frac{1}{8}$

He was $11\frac{1}{8}$ miles from Town B when the car broke down.

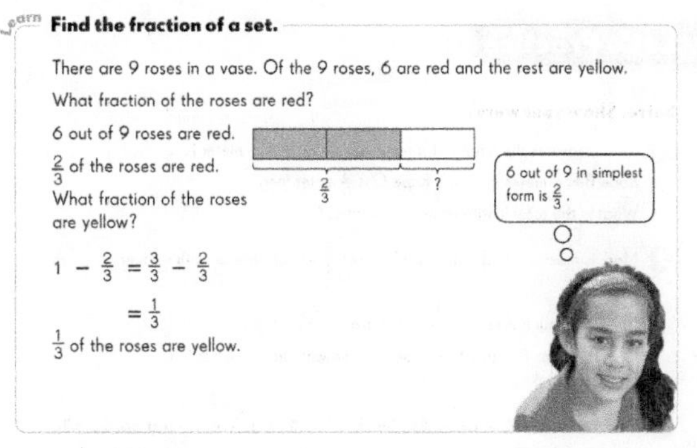

Learn Find the fraction of a set.

There are 9 roses in a vase. Of the 9 roses, 6 are red and the rest are yellow.

What fraction of the roses are red?

6 out of 9 roses are red.

$\frac{2}{3}$ of the roses are red.

$\frac{2}{3}$?

What fraction of the roses are yellow?

6 out of 9 in simplest form is $\frac{2}{3}$.

$1 - \frac{2}{3} = \frac{3}{3} - \frac{2}{3}$

$= \frac{1}{3}$

$\frac{1}{3}$ of the roses are yellow.

Guided Practice

Solve. Show your work.

4 Alma had a 1-meter length of string. She cut off an 18-centimeter piece.

a What fraction of the string is cut off?

18 out of 100 is $\frac{18}{100}$.

$\frac{18}{100} = \frac{9}{50}$

$\frac{9}{50}$ of the string is cut off.

Convert 1 meter to 100 centimeters.

b What fraction of the string is left?

$1 - \frac{9}{50} = \frac{50}{50} - \frac{9}{50} = \frac{41}{50}$

$\frac{41}{50}$ of the string is left.

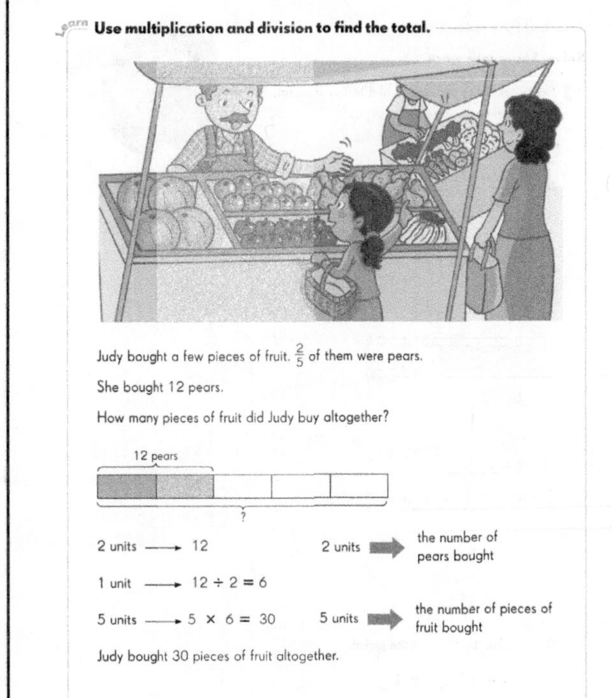

Learn Use multiplication and division to find the total.

Judy bought a few pieces of fruit. $\frac{2}{5}$ of them were pears.

She bought 12 pears.

How many pieces of fruit did Judy buy altogether?

12 pears

?

2 units → 12

2 units ➡ the number of pears bought

1 unit → $12 \div 2 = 6$

5 units → $5 \times 6 = 30$

5 units ➡ the number of pieces of fruit bought

Judy bought 30 pieces of fruit altogether.

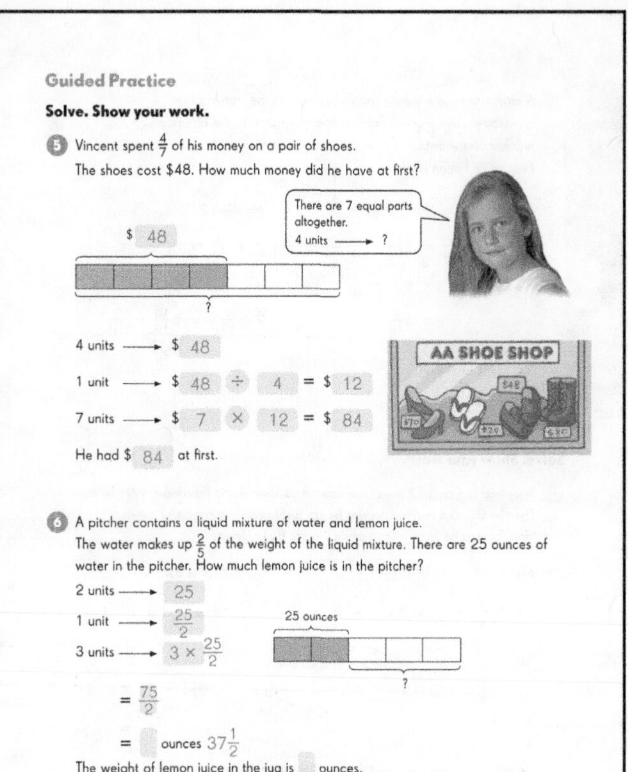

Guided Practice

Solve. Show your work.

5. Vincent spent $\frac{4}{7}$ of his money on a pair of shoes. The shoes cost \$48. How much money did he have at first?

4 units → \$ 48

1 unit → \$ 48 ÷ 4 = \$ 12

7 units → \$ 7 × 12 = \$ 84

He had \$ 84 at first.

6. A pitcher contains a liquid mixture of water and lemon juice. The water makes up $\frac{2}{5}$ of the weight of the liquid mixture. There are 25 ounces of water in the pitcher. How much lemon juice is in the pitcher?

2 units → 25

1 unit → $\frac{25}{2}$

3 units → $3 \times \frac{25}{2}$

$= \frac{75}{2}$

= ounces $37\frac{1}{2}$

The weight of lemon juice in the jug is $37\frac{1}{2}$ ounces.

264 **Chapter 6** Fractions and Mixed Numbers

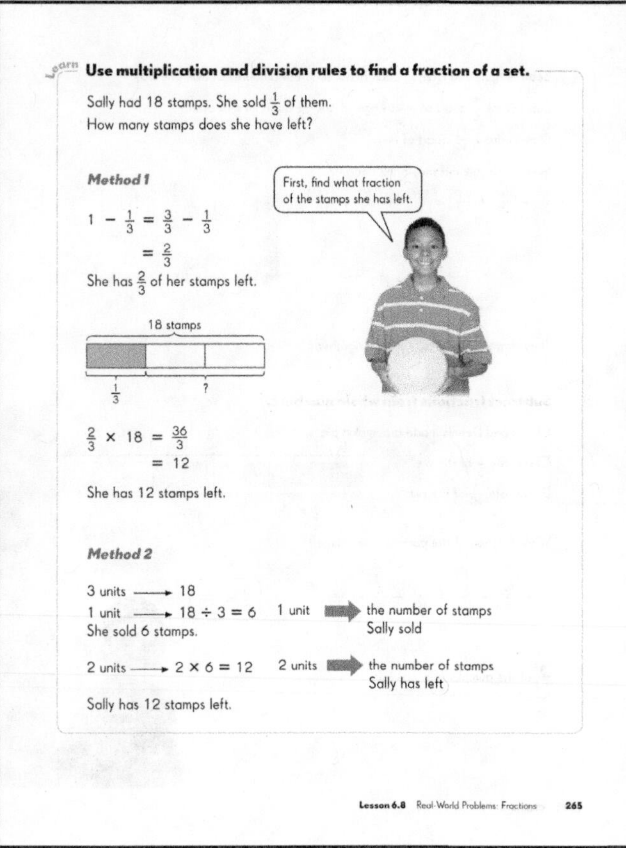

Learn: Use multiplication and division rules to find a fraction of a set.

Sally had 18 stamps. She sold $\frac{1}{3}$ of them. How many stamps does she have left?

Method 1

$1 - \frac{1}{3} = \frac{3}{3} - \frac{1}{3}$

$= \frac{2}{3}$

She has $\frac{2}{3}$ of her stamps left.

$\frac{2}{3} \times 18 = \frac{36}{3}$

$= 12$

She has 12 stamps left.

Method 2

3 units → 18

1 unit → 18 ÷ 3 = 6

She sold 6 stamps.

1 unit ➡ the number of stamps Sally sold

2 units → 2 × 6 = 12

2 units ➡ the number of stamps Sally has left

Sally has 12 stamps left.

Lesson 6.8 Real-World Problems: Fractions 265

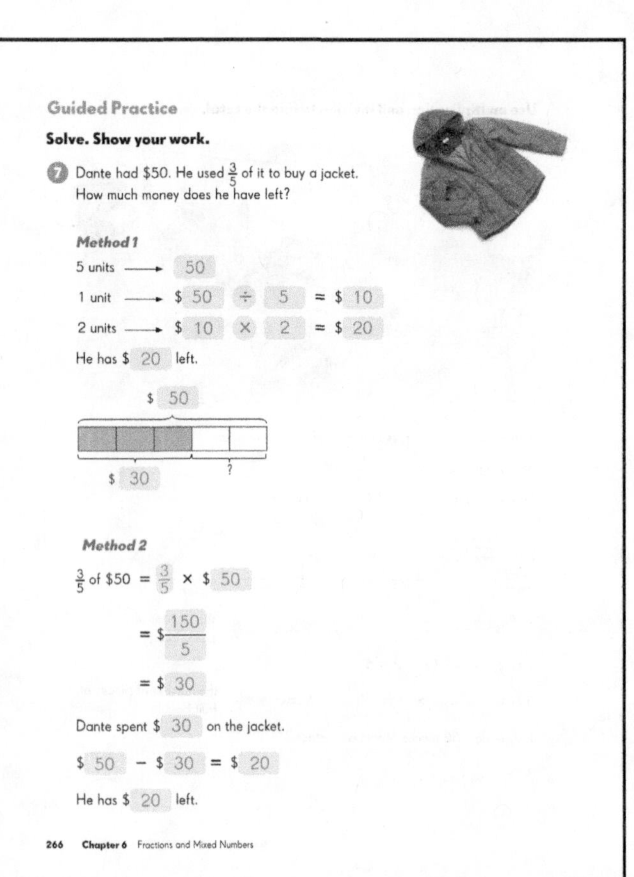

Guided Practice

Solve. Show your work.

7. Dante had \$50. He used $\frac{3}{5}$ of it to buy a jacket. How much money does he have left?

Method 1

5 units → 50

1 unit → \$ 50 ÷ 5 = \$ 10

2 units → \$ 10 × 2 = \$ 20

He has \$ 20 left.

Method 2

$\frac{3}{5}$ of \$50 = $\frac{3}{5}$ × \$ 50

= \$ $\frac{150}{5}$

= \$ 30

Dante spent \$ 30 on the jacket.

\$ 50 − \$ 30 = \$ 20

He has \$ 20 left.

266 **Chapter 6** Fractions and Mixed Numbers

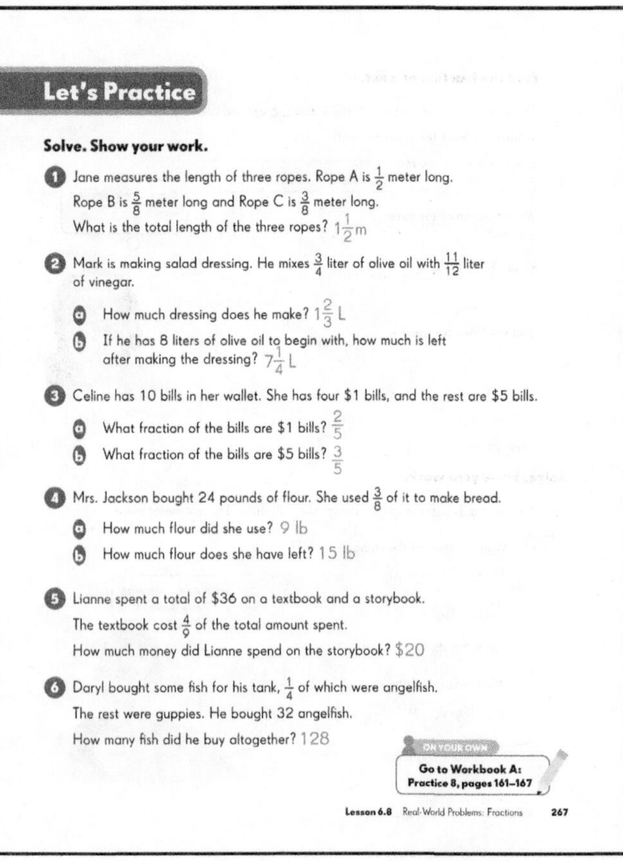

Let's Practice

Solve. Show your work.

1. Jane measures the length of three ropes. Rope A is $\frac{1}{2}$ meter long. Rope B is $\frac{5}{8}$ meter long and Rope C is $\frac{3}{8}$ meter long. What is the total length of the three ropes? $1\frac{1}{2}$ m

2. Mark is making salad dressing. He mixes $\frac{3}{4}$ liter of olive oil with $\frac{11}{12}$ liter of vinegar.
   a. How much dressing does he make? $1\frac{2}{3}$ L
   b. If he has 8 liters of olive oil to begin with, how much is left after making the dressing? $7\frac{1}{4}$ L

3. Celine has 10 bills in her wallet. She has four \$1 bills, and the rest are \$5 bills.
   a. What fraction of the bills are \$1 bills? $\frac{2}{5}$
   b. What fraction of the bills are \$5 bills? $\frac{3}{5}$

4. Mrs. Jackson bought 24 pounds of flour. She used $\frac{3}{8}$ of it to make bread.
   a. How much flour did she use? 9 lb
   b. How much flour does she have left? 15 lb

5. Lianne spent a total of \$36 on a textbook and a storybook. The textbook cost $\frac{4}{9}$ of the total amount spent. How much money did Lianne spend on the storybook? \$20

6. Daryl bought some fish for his tank, $\frac{1}{4}$ of which were angelfish. The rest were guppies. He bought 32 angelfish. How many fish did he buy altogether? 128

ON YOUR OWN
Go to Workbook A: Practice 8, pages 161–167

Lesson 6.8 Real-World Problems: Fractions 267

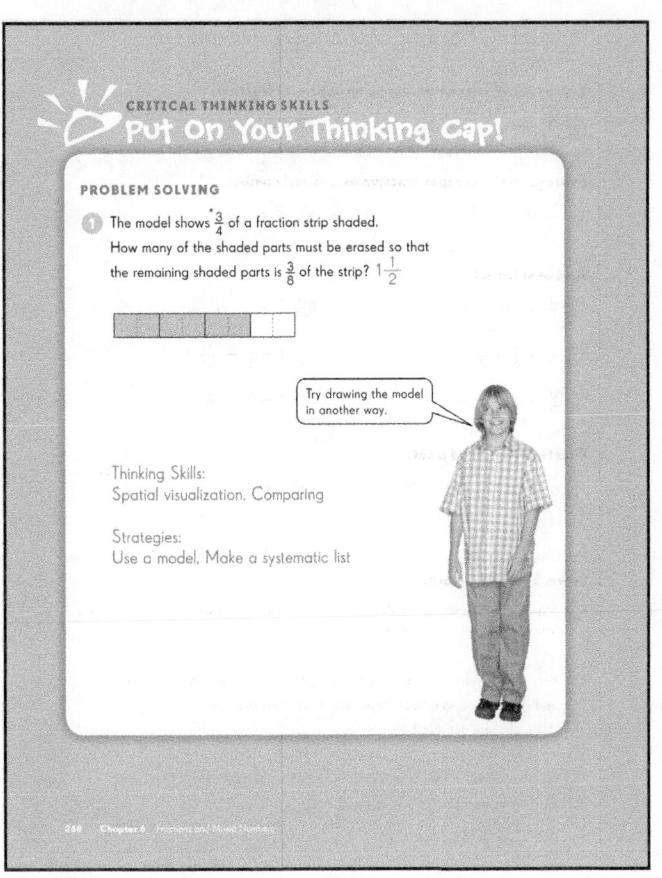

CRITICAL THINKING SKILLS

Put On Your Thinking Cap!

PROBLEM SOLVING

1 The model shows $\frac{3}{4}$ of a fraction strip shaded.
How many of the shaded parts must be erased so that the remaining shaded parts is $\frac{3}{8}$ of the strip? $1\frac{1}{2}$

Thinking Skills:
Spatial visualization, Comparing

Strategies:
Use a model, Make a systematic list

268 Chapter 6 Fractions and Mixed Numbers

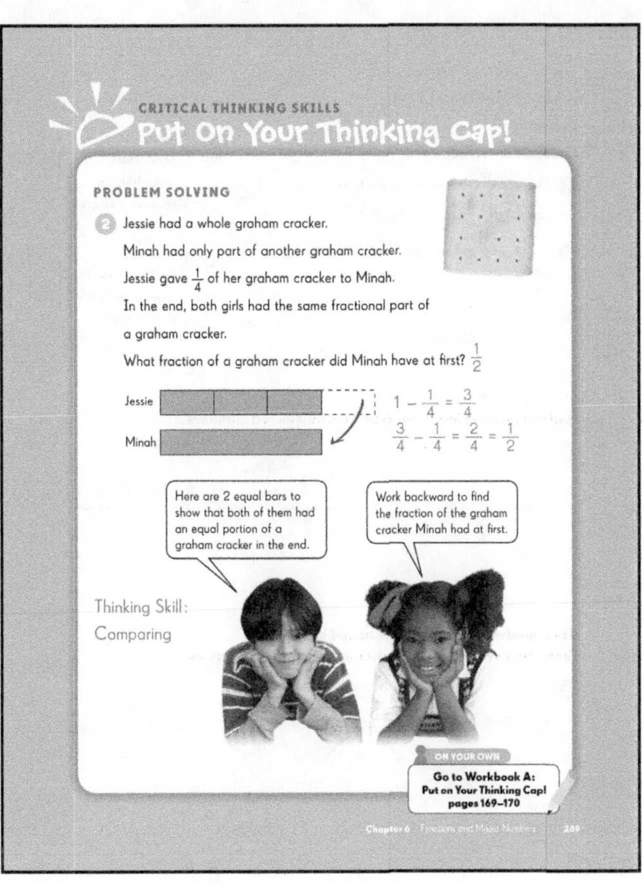

CRITICAL THINKING SKILLS

Put On Your Thinking Cap!

PROBLEM SOLVING

2 Jessie had a whole graham cracker.
Minah had only part of another graham cracker.
Jessie gave $\frac{1}{4}$ of her graham cracker to Minah.
In the end, both girls had the same fractional part of a graham cracker.
What fraction of a graham cracker did Minah have at first? $\frac{1}{2}$

Thinking Skill:
Comparing

ON YOUR OWN
Go to Workbook A: Put on Your Thinking Cap! pages 169–170

Chapter 6 Fractions and Mixed Numbers 269

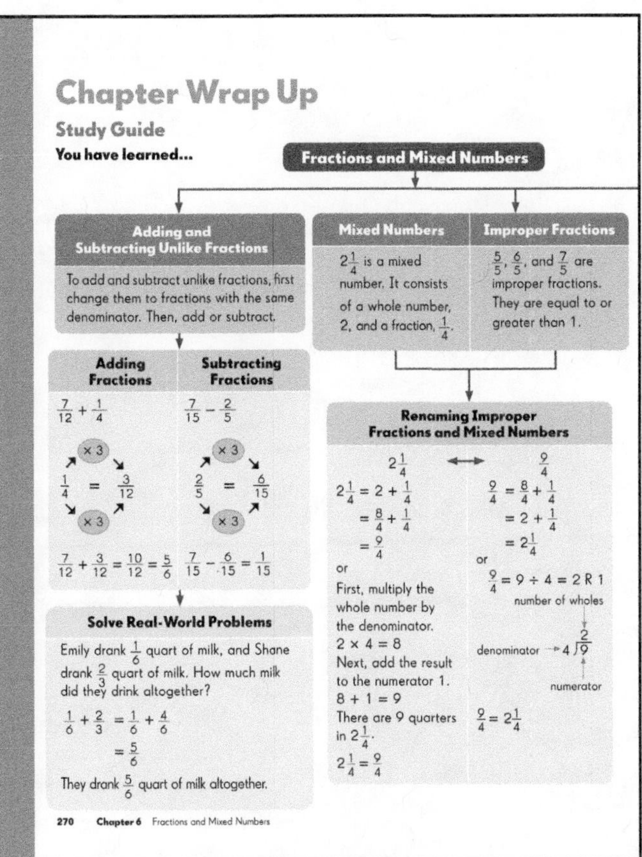

Chapter Wrap Up

Study Guide

You have learned...

Fractions and Mixed Numbers

Adding and Subtracting Unlike Fractions

To add and subtract unlike fractions, first change them to fractions with the same denominator. Then, add or subtract.

Adding Fractions

$\frac{7}{12} + \frac{1}{4}$

$\frac{1}{4} = \frac{3}{12}$ (× 3)

$\frac{7}{12} + \frac{3}{12} = \frac{10}{12} = \frac{5}{6}$

Subtracting Fractions

$\frac{7}{15} - \frac{2}{5}$

$\frac{2}{5} = \frac{6}{15}$ (× 3)

$\frac{7}{15} - \frac{6}{15} = \frac{1}{15}$

Solve Real-World Problems

Emily drank $\frac{1}{6}$ quart of milk, and Shane drank $\frac{2}{3}$ quart of milk. How much milk did they drink altogether?

$\frac{1}{6} + \frac{2}{3} = \frac{1}{6} + \frac{4}{6}$
$= \frac{5}{6}$

They drank $\frac{5}{6}$ quart of milk altogether.

Mixed Numbers

$2\frac{1}{4}$ is a mixed number. It consists of a whole number, 2, and a fraction, $\frac{1}{4}$.

Improper Fractions

$\frac{5}{5}$, $\frac{6}{5}$, and $\frac{7}{5}$ are improper fractions. They are equal to or greater than 1.

Renaming Improper Fractions and Mixed Numbers

$2\frac{1}{4} \longleftrightarrow \frac{9}{4}$

$2\frac{1}{4} = 2 + \frac{1}{4}$
$= \frac{8}{4} + \frac{1}{4}$
$= \frac{9}{4}$

or

First, multiply the whole number by the denominator.
$2 \times 4 = 8$
Next, add the result to the numerator 1.
$8 + 1 = 9$
There are 9 quarters in $2\frac{1}{4}$.
$2\frac{1}{4} = \frac{9}{4}$

$\frac{9}{4} = \frac{8}{4} + \frac{1}{4}$
$= 2 + \frac{1}{4}$
$= 2\frac{1}{4}$

or

$\frac{9}{4} = 9 \div 4 = 2 \text{ R } 1$

number of wholes: 2; denominator: 4; numerator: 1 ($4\overline{)9}$)

$\frac{9}{4} = 2\frac{1}{4}$

270 Chapter 6 Fractions and Mixed Numbers

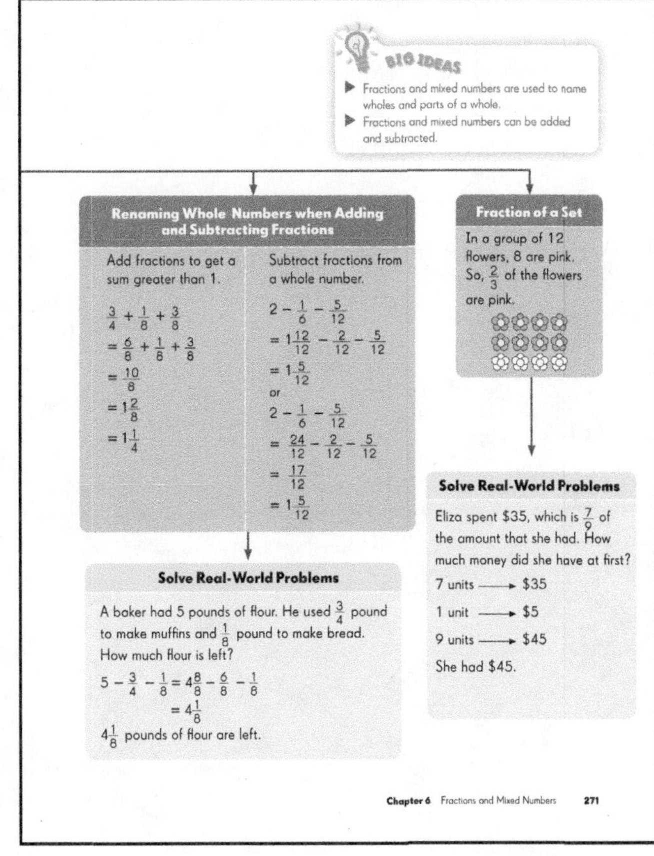

BIG IDEAS

- Fractions and mixed numbers are used to name wholes and parts of a whole.
- Fractions and mixed numbers can be added and subtracted.

Renaming Whole Numbers when Adding and Subtracting Fractions

Add fractions to get a sum greater than 1.

$\frac{3}{4} + \frac{1}{8} + \frac{3}{8}$
$= \frac{6}{8} + \frac{1}{8} + \frac{3}{8}$
$= \frac{10}{8}$
$= 1\frac{2}{8}$
$= 1\frac{1}{4}$

Subtract fractions from a whole number.

$2 - \frac{1}{6} - \frac{5}{12}$
$= 1\frac{12}{12} - \frac{2}{12} - \frac{5}{12}$
$= 1\frac{5}{12}$

or

$2 - \frac{1}{6} - \frac{5}{12}$
$= \frac{24}{12} - \frac{2}{12} - \frac{5}{12}$
$= \frac{17}{12}$
$= 1\frac{5}{12}$

Solve Real-World Problems

A baker had 5 pounds of flour. He used $\frac{3}{4}$ pound to make muffins and $\frac{1}{8}$ pound to make bread. How much flour is left?

$5 - \frac{3}{4} - \frac{1}{8} = 4\frac{8}{8} - \frac{6}{8} - \frac{1}{8}$
$= 4\frac{1}{8}$

$4\frac{1}{8}$ pounds of flour are left.

Fraction of a Set

In a group of 12 flowers, 8 are pink. So, $\frac{2}{3}$ of the flowers are pink.

Solve Real-World Problems

Eliza spent \$35, which is $\frac{7}{9}$ of the amount that she had. How much money did she have at first?

7 units → \$35
1 unit → \$5
9 units → \$45

She had \$45.

Chapter 6 Fractions and Mixed Numbers 271

Chapter 6

Chapter Review/Test

Vocabulary

Choose the correct word.

numerator
denominator
unlike fractions
equivalent fraction
fraction bar
mixed number
improper fraction
multiplication rule
division rule

1. The numerator appears above the fraction bar, and the denominator appears below it.
2. Two fractions that have different denominators are called unlike fractions.
3. The multiplication rule is used to rename a mixed number as an improper fraction.

Concepts and Skills

Find the missing improper fractions and mixed numbers.

4. 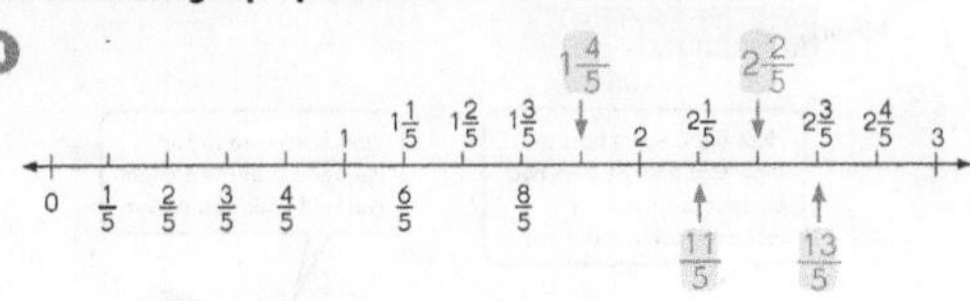

Answers: $1\frac{4}{5}$, $2\frac{2}{5}$, $\frac{11}{5}$, $\frac{13}{5}$

Use a model to represent the mixed number. Then express the mixed number as an improper fraction.

5. $2\frac{1}{2}$

There are 5 halves in $2\frac{1}{2}$.

$2\frac{1}{2} = \frac{5}{2}$

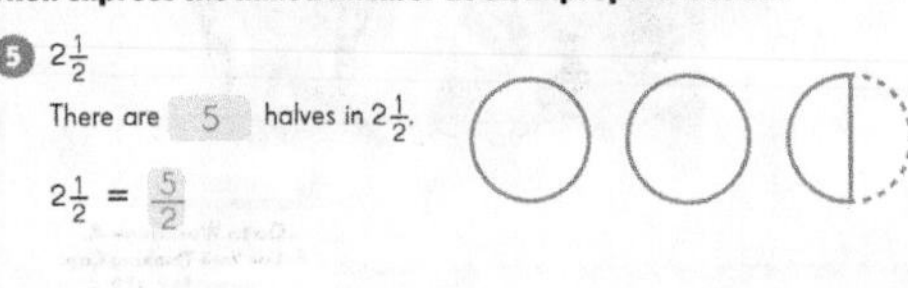

Express each mixed number as an improper fraction.

6. $3\frac{1}{4} = \frac{13}{4}$
7. $2\frac{1}{3} = \frac{7}{3}$

Express each improper fraction as a mixed number.

8. $\frac{7}{4} = 1\frac{3}{4}$
9. $\frac{9}{2} = 4\frac{1}{2}$

Add or subtract.

10. $\frac{4}{5} + \frac{3}{10} = 1\frac{1}{10}$
11. $\frac{5}{7} - \frac{1}{14} = \frac{9}{14}$
12. $\frac{1}{3} + \frac{5}{6} + \frac{2}{3} = 1\frac{5}{6}$
13. $1 - \frac{2}{5} - \frac{1}{10} = \frac{1}{2}$
14. $\frac{4}{9} + \frac{2}{3} + \frac{1}{3} = 1\frac{4}{9}$
15. $3 - \frac{5}{6} - \frac{1}{12} = 2\frac{1}{12}$

Find the fraction of a set.

16. $\frac{5}{6}$ of 48 = 40
17. $\frac{4}{7}$ of 49 = 28

Problem Solving

Solve. Show your work.

18. Mary has 18 beads, and 6 of them are red. The rest are blue. What fraction of the beads are blue? $\frac{2}{3}$

19. Rory spends $\frac{1}{5}$ hour cleaning the table, $\frac{3}{10}$ hour washing dishes, and $\frac{4}{5}$ hour reading a book. How many hours does she spend doing all these activities? $1\frac{3}{10}$ h

20. John has \$24. He uses $\frac{2}{3}$ of his money to buy a pair of shoes. How much money is left? \$8

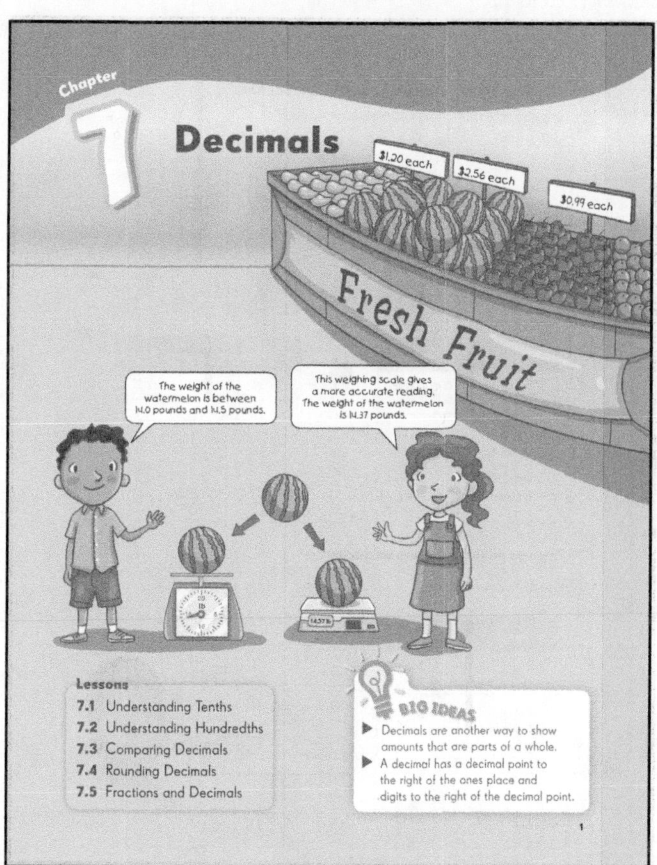

Chapter 7

Decimals

Lessons

- **7.1** Understanding Tenths
- **7.2** Understanding Hundredths
- **7.3** Comparing Decimals
- **7.4** Rounding Decimals
- **7.5** Fractions and Decimals

BIG IDEAS

- Decimals are another way to show amounts that are parts of a whole.
- A decimal has a decimal point to the right of the ones place and digits to the right of the decimal point.

1

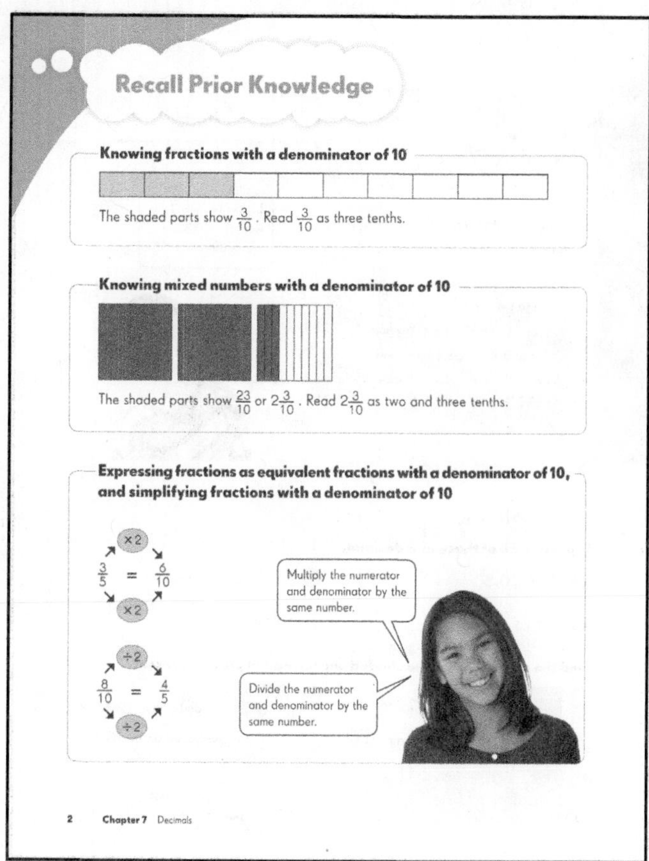

Recall Prior Knowledge

Knowing fractions with a denominator of 10

The shaded parts show $\frac{3}{10}$. Read $\frac{3}{10}$ as three tenths.

Knowing mixed numbers with a denominator of 10

The shaded parts show $\frac{23}{10}$ or $2\frac{3}{10}$. Read $2\frac{3}{10}$ as two and three tenths.

Expressing fractions as equivalent fractions with a denominator of 10, and simplifying fractions with a denominator of 10

$\frac{3}{5} = \frac{6}{10}$ (×2)

Multiply the numerator and denominator by the same number.

$\frac{8}{10} = \frac{4}{5}$ (÷2)

Divide the numerator and denominator by the same number.

2 Chapter 7 Decimals

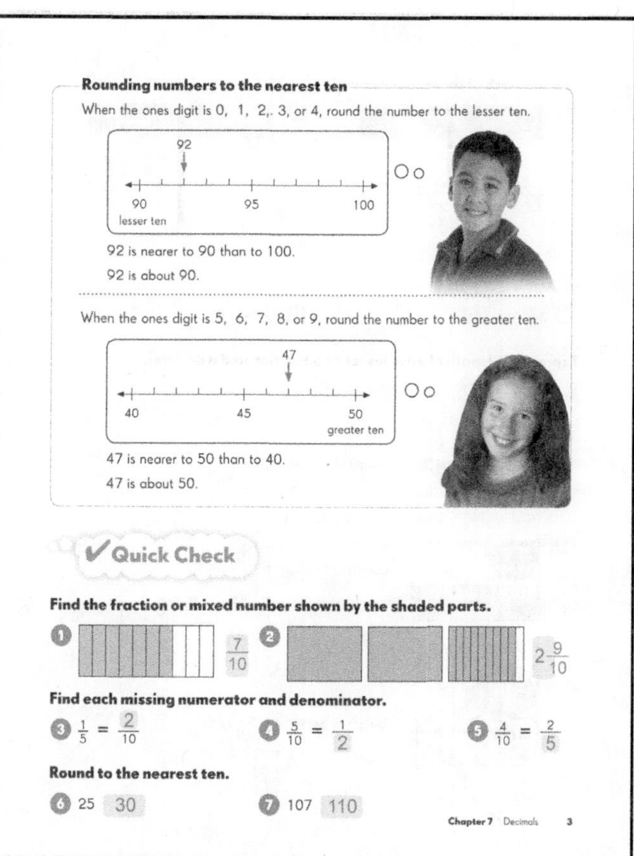

Rounding numbers to the nearest ten

When the ones digit is 0, 1, 2, 3, or 4, round the number to the lesser ten.

92 is nearer to 90 than to 100.

92 is about 90.

When the ones digit is 5, 6, 7, 8, or 9, round the number to the greater ten.

47 is nearer to 50 than to 40.

47 is about 50.

Quick Check

Find the fraction or mixed number shown by the shaded parts.

1. $\frac{7}{10}$
2. $2\frac{9}{10}$

Find each missing numerator and denominator.

3. $\frac{1}{5} = \frac{2}{10}$
4. $\frac{5}{10} = \frac{1}{2}$
5. $\frac{4}{10} = \frac{2}{5}$

Round to the nearest ten.

6. 25 30
7. 107 110

Chapter 7 Decimals 3

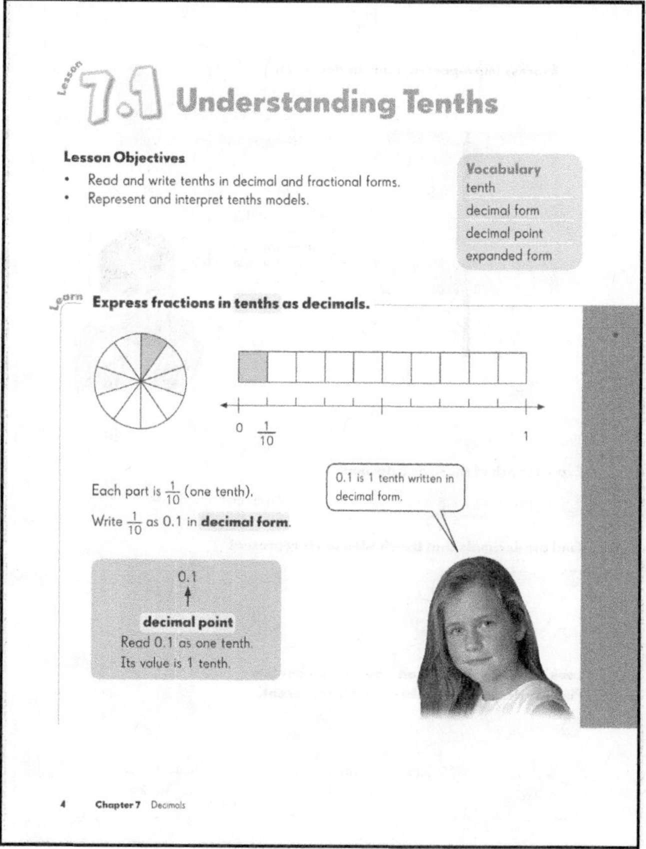

Lesson

7.1 Understanding Tenths

Lesson Objectives

- Read and write tenths in decimal and fractional forms.
- Represent and interpret tenths models.

Vocabulary
tenth
decimal form
decimal point
expanded form

Learn **Express fractions in tenths as decimals.**

Each part is $\frac{1}{10}$ (one tenth).

Write $\frac{1}{10}$ as 0.1 in **decimal form**.

0.1 is 1 tenth written in decimal form.

0.1

decimal point

Read 0.1 as one tenth.

Its value is 1 tenth.

4 Chapter 7 Decimals

Chapter 7

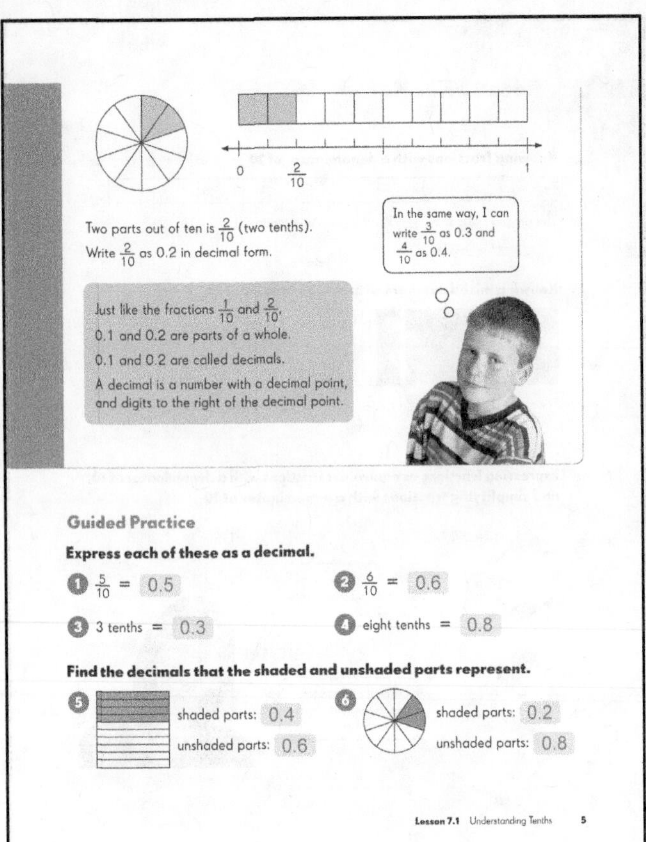

Two parts out of ten is $\frac{2}{10}$ (two tenths).
Write $\frac{2}{10}$ as 0.2 in decimal form.

In the same way, I can write $\frac{3}{10}$ as 0.3 and $\frac{4}{10}$ as 0.4.

Just like the fractions $\frac{1}{10}$ and $\frac{2}{10}$,
0.1 and 0.2 are parts of a whole.
0.1 and 0.2 are called decimals.
A decimal is a number with a decimal point, and digits to the right of the decimal point.

Guided Practice

Express each of these as a decimal.

1. $\frac{5}{10}$ = 0.5
2. $\frac{6}{10}$ = 0.6
3. 3 tenths = 0.3
4. eight tenths = 0.8

Find the decimals that the shaded and unshaded parts represent.

5. shaded parts: 0.4 unshaded parts: 0.6
6. shaded parts: 0.2 unshaded parts: 0.8

Lesson 7.1 Understanding Tenths 5

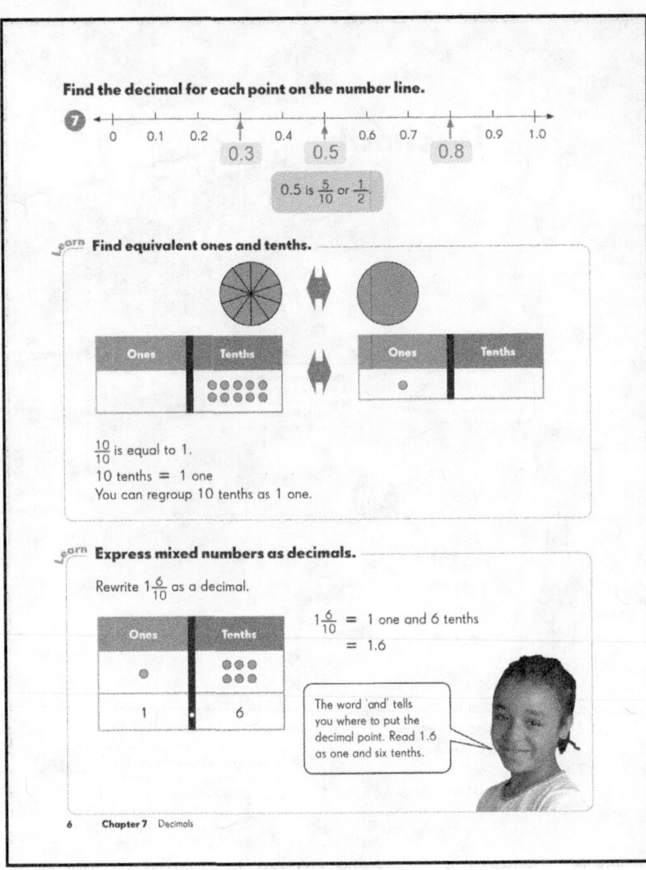

Find the decimal for each point on the number line.

7. 0 0.1 0.2 0.4 0.6 0.7 0.9 1.0
0.3 0.5 0.8
0.5 is $\frac{5}{10}$ or $\frac{1}{2}$

Learn Find equivalent ones and tenths.

Ones	Tenths
	●●●●● ●●●●●

Ones	Tenths
●	

$\frac{10}{10}$ is equal to 1.
10 tenths = 1 one
You can regroup 10 tenths as 1 one.

Learn Express mixed numbers as decimals.

Rewrite $1\frac{6}{10}$ as a decimal.

Ones	Tenths
●	●●● ●●●
1	6

$1\frac{6}{10}$ = 1 one and 6 tenths
= 1.6

The word 'and' tells you where to put the decimal point. Read 1.6 as one and six tenths.

6 Chapter 7 Decimals

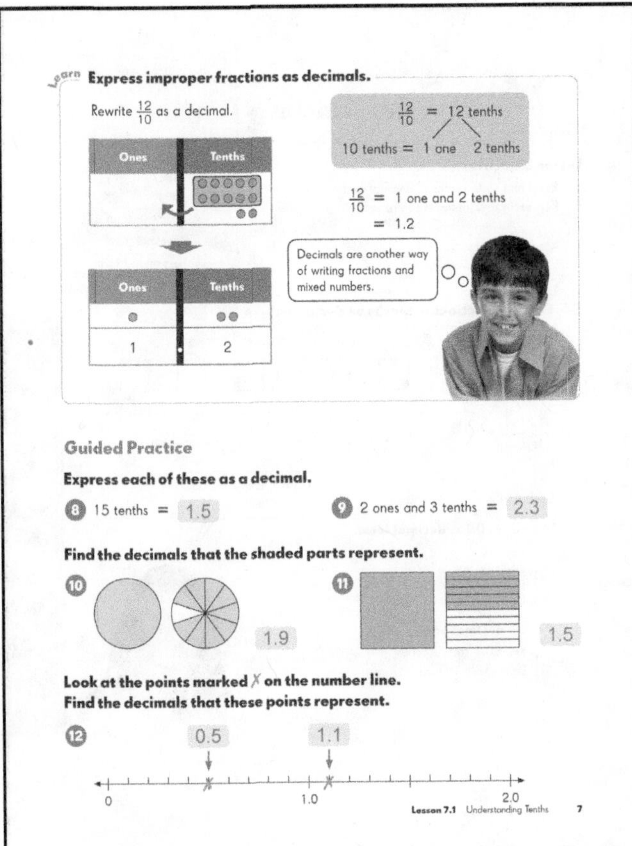

Learn Express improper fractions as decimals.

Rewrite $\frac{12}{10}$ as a decimal.

Ones	Tenths
	●●●●● ●●●●● ●●

Ones	Tenths
●	●●
1	2

$\frac{12}{10}$ = 12 tenths
10 tenths = 1 one 2 tenths

$\frac{12}{10}$ = 1 one and 2 tenths
= 1.2

Decimals are another way of writing fractions and mixed numbers.

Guided Practice

Express each of these as a decimal.

8. 15 tenths = 1.5
9. 2 ones and 3 tenths = 2.3

Find the decimals that the shaded parts represent.

10. 1.9
11. 1.5

Look at the points marked X on the number line. Find the decimals that these points represent.

12. 0.5 1.1
0 1.0 2.0

Lesson 7.1 Understanding Tenths 7

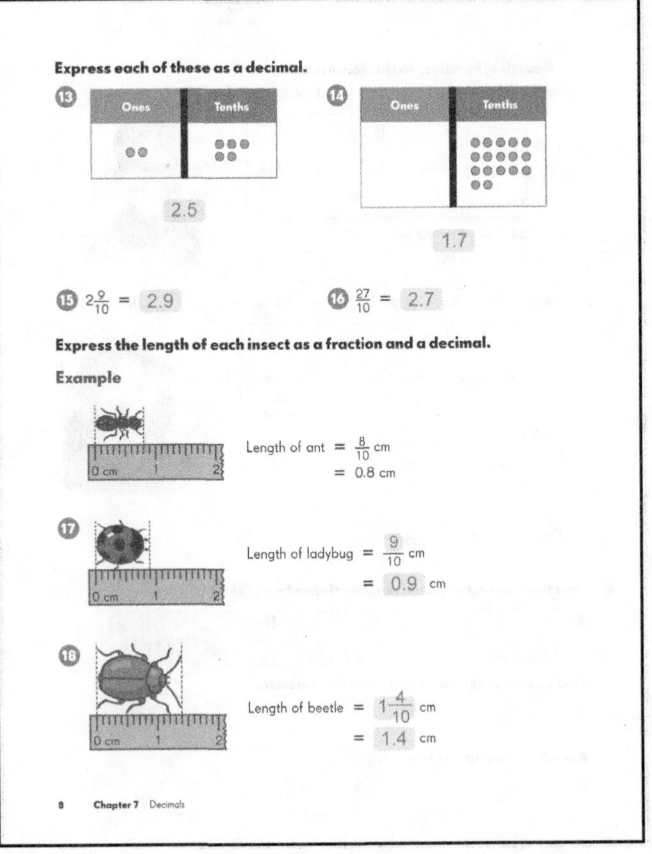

Express each of these as a decimal.

13.

Ones	Tenths
●●	●●● ●●

2.5

14.

Ones	Tenths
	●●●●● ●●●●● ●●●●● ●●

1.7

15. $2\frac{9}{10}$ = 2.9
16. $\frac{27}{10}$ = 2.7

Express the length of each insect as a fraction and a decimal.

Example

Length of ant = $\frac{8}{10}$ cm
= 0.8 cm

17. Length of ladybug = $\frac{9}{10}$ cm
= 0.9 cm

18. Length of beetle = $1\frac{4}{10}$ cm
= 1.4 cm

8 Chapter 7 Decimals

Express the total amount of water as a mixed number and a decimal.

19

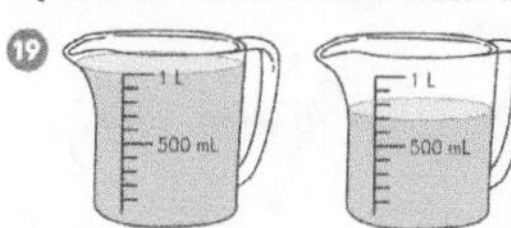

Total amount of water $= 1\frac{7}{10}$ L

$=$ 1.7 L

Express each decimal as tenths.

20 0.9 = 9 tenths

21 0.7 = 7 tenths

22 1.1 = 11 tenths

23 4.3 = 43 tenths

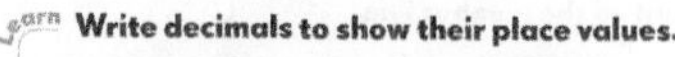

Learn Write decimals to show their place values.

Tens	Ones	Tenths
4	2	3

42.3 = 4 tens + 2 ones + 3 tenths
= 40 + 2 + 0.3
= $40 + 2 + \frac{3}{10}$

$40 + 2 + \frac{3}{10}$ is called the **expanded form** of a decimal.

Guided Practice

Find the missing numbers in expanded form.

24 76.4 = 7 tens + 6 ones + 4 tenths
= 70 + 6 + 0.4
= $70 + 6 + \frac{4}{10}$

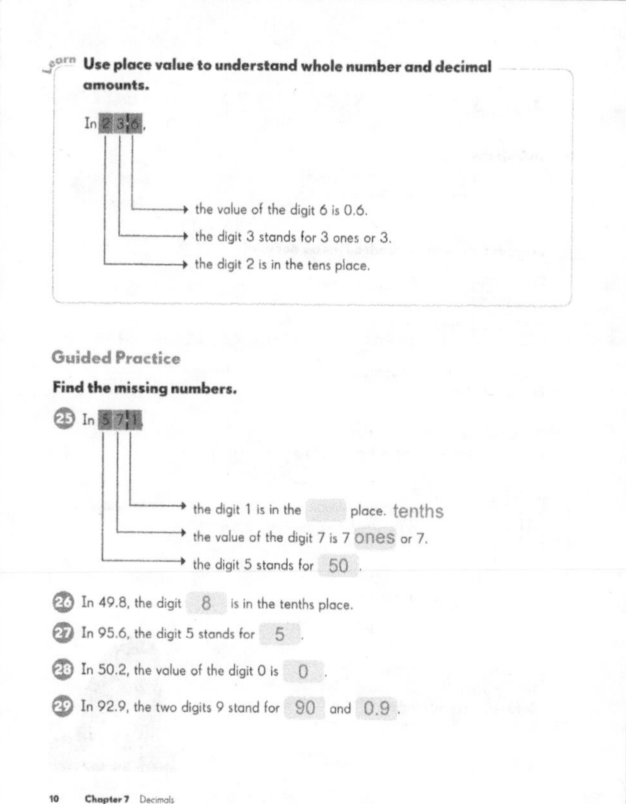

Learn Use place value to understand whole number and decimal amounts.

In 23.6,

the value of the digit 6 is 0.6.
the digit 3 stands for 3 ones or 3.
the digit 2 is in the tens place.

Guided Practice

Find the missing numbers.

25 In 57.1,

the digit 1 is in the tenths place.
the value of the digit 7 is 7 ones or 7.
the digit 5 stands for 50.

26 In 49.8, the digit 8 is in the tenths place.

27 In 95.6, the digit 5 stands for 5.

28 In 50.2, the value of the digit 0 is 0.

29 In 92.9, the two digits 9 stand for 90 and 0.9.

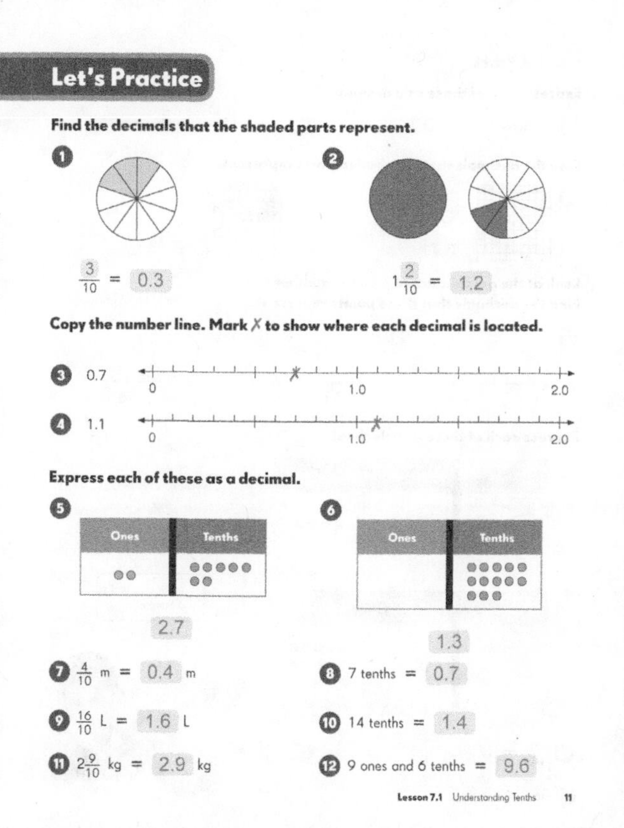

Let's Practice

Find the decimals that the shaded parts represent.

1 $\frac{3}{10}$ = 0.3

2 $1\frac{2}{10}$ = 1.2

Copy the number line. Mark X to show where each decimal is located.

3 0.7 (number line 0, 1.0, 2.0)

4 1.1 (number line 0, 1.0, 2.0)

Express each of these as a decimal.

5

Ones	Tenths
●●	●●●●● ●●

2.7

6

Ones	Tenths
	●●●●● ●●●●● ●●●

1.3

7 $\frac{4}{10}$ m = 0.4 m

8 7 tenths = 0.7

9 $\frac{16}{10}$ L = 1.6 L

10 14 tenths = 1.4

11 $2\frac{9}{10}$ kg = 2.9 kg

12 9 ones and 6 tenths = 9.6

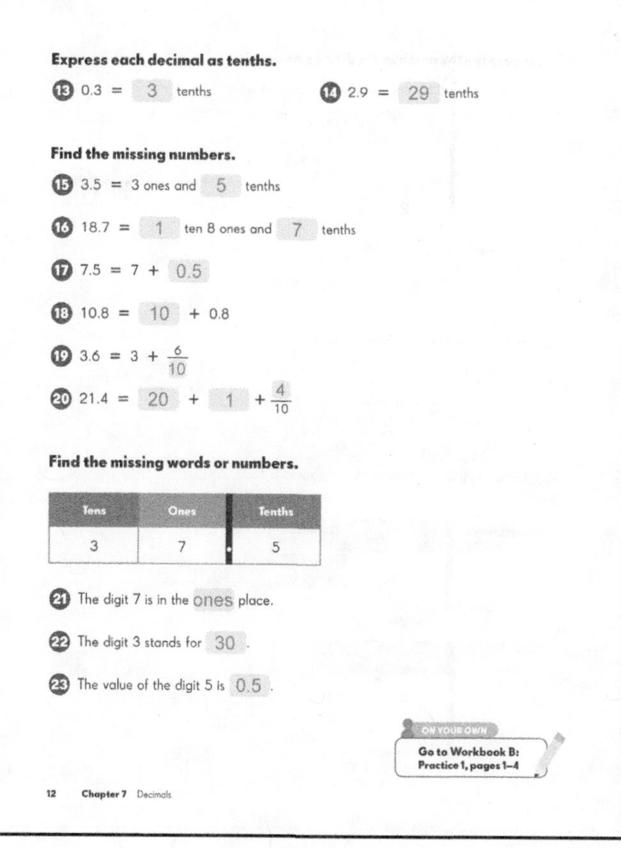

Express each decimal as tenths.

13 0.3 = 3 tenths

14 2.9 = 29 tenths

Find the missing numbers.

15 3.5 = 3 ones and 5 tenths

16 18.7 = 1 ten 8 ones and 7 tenths

17 7.5 = 7 + 0.5

18 10.8 = 10 + 0.8

19 $3.6 = 3 + \frac{6}{10}$

20 $21.4 = 20 + 1 + \frac{4}{10}$

Find the missing words or numbers.

Tens	Ones	Tenths
3	7	5

21 The digit 7 is in the ones place.

22 The digit 3 stands for 30.

23 The value of the digit 5 is 0.5.

ON YOUR OWN
Go to Workbook B: Practice 1, pages 1–4

Chapter 7

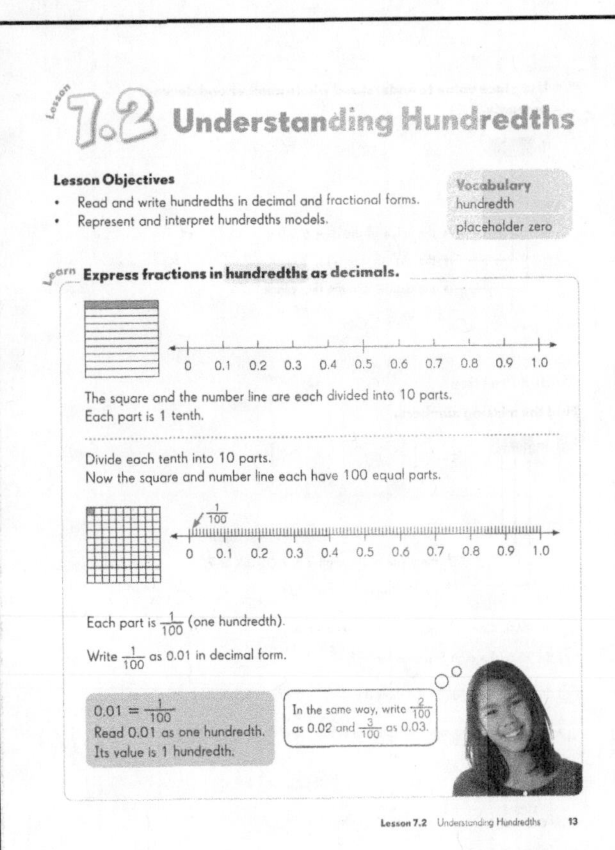

Lesson **7.2** **Understanding Hundredths**

Lesson Objectives
- Read and write hundredths in decimal and fractional forms.
- Represent and interpret hundredths models.

Vocabulary
hundredth
placeholder zero

Learn **Express fractions in hundredths as decimals.**

0 0.1 0.2 0.3 0.4 0.5 0.6 0.7 0.8 0.9 1.0

The square and the number line are each divided into 10 parts.
Each part is 1 tenth.

Divide each tenth into 10 parts.
Now the square and number line each have 100 equal parts.

$\frac{1}{100}$

0 0.1 0.2 0.3 0.4 0.5 0.6 0.7 0.8 0.9 1.0

Each part is $\frac{1}{100}$ (one hundredth).

Write $\frac{1}{100}$ as 0.01 in decimal form.

$0.01 = \frac{1}{100}$
Read 0.01 as one hundredth.
Its value is 1 hundredth.

In the same way, write $\frac{2}{100}$ as 0.02 and $\frac{3}{100}$ as 0.03.

Lesson 7.2 Understanding Hundredths 13

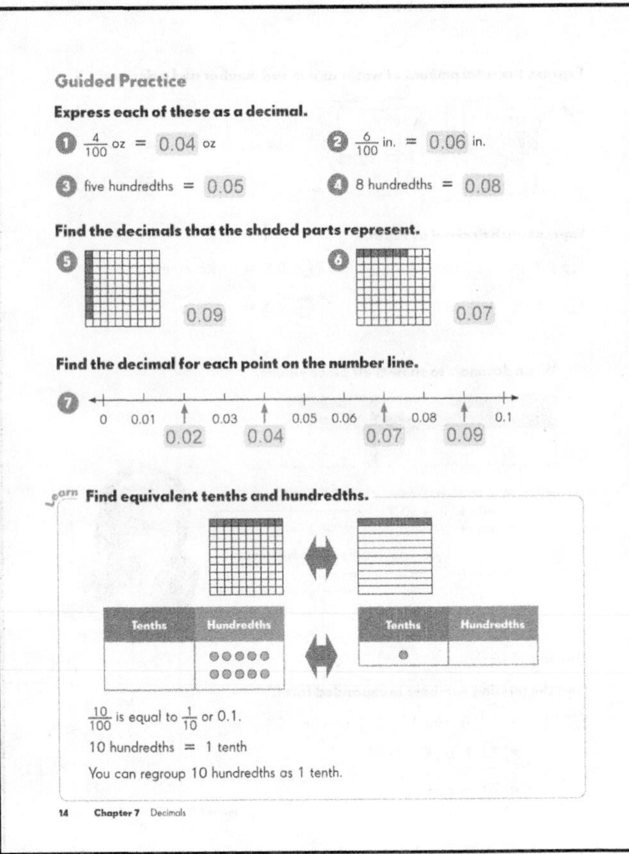

Guided Practice

Express each of these as a decimal.

1. $\frac{4}{100}$ oz = 0.04 oz
2. $\frac{6}{100}$ in. = 0.06 in.
3. five hundredths = 0.05
4. 8 hundredths = 0.08

Find the decimals that the shaded parts represent.

5. 0.09
6. 0.07

Find the decimal for each point on the number line.

7. 0 0.01 0.03 0.05 0.06 0.08 0.1
0.02 0.04 0.07 0.09

Learn **Find equivalent tenths and hundredths.**

Tenths	Hundredths
	●●●●● ●●●●●

Tenths	Hundredths
●	

$\frac{10}{100}$ is equal to $\frac{1}{10}$ or 0.1.
10 hundredths = 1 tenth
You can regroup 10 hundredths as 1 tenth.

14 Chapter 7 Decimals

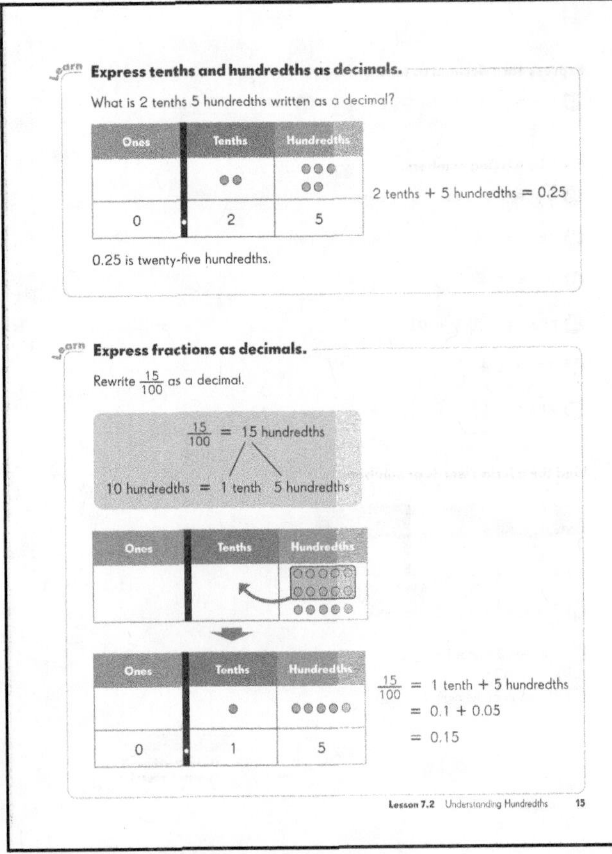

Learn **Express tenths and hundredths as decimals.**

What is 2 tenths 5 hundredths written as a decimal?

Ones	Tenths	Hundredths
	●●	●●● ●●
0	2	5

2 tenths + 5 hundredths = 0.25

0.25 is twenty-five hundredths.

Learn **Express fractions as decimals.**

Rewrite $\frac{15}{100}$ as a decimal.

$\frac{15}{100}$ = 15 hundredths
10 hundredths = 1 tenth 5 hundredths

Ones	Tenths	Hundredths
		●●●●● ●●●●● ●●●●●

Ones	Tenths	Hundredths
	●	●●●●●
0	1	5

$\frac{15}{100}$ = 1 tenth + 5 hundredths
= 0.1 + 0.05
= 0.15

Lesson 7.2 Understanding Hundredths 15

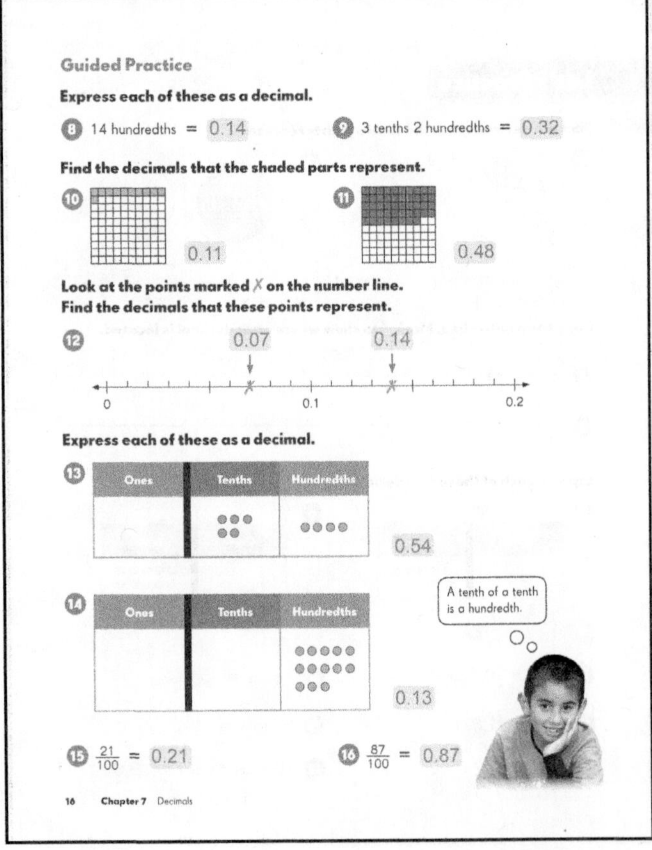

Guided Practice

Express each of these as a decimal.

8. 14 hundredths = 0.14
9. 3 tenths 2 hundredths = 0.32

Find the decimals that the shaded parts represent.

10. 0.11
11. 0.48

Look at the points marked X on the number line.
Find the decimals that these points represent.

12. 0.07 0.14
0 0.1 0.2

Express each of these as a decimal.

13.

Ones	Tenths	Hundredths
	●●● ●●	●●●●

0.54

14.

Ones	Tenths	Hundredths
		●●●●● ●●●●● ●●●

0.13

A tenth of a tenth is a hundredth.

15. $\frac{21}{100}$ = 0.21
16. $\frac{87}{100}$ = 0.87

16 Chapter 7 Decimals

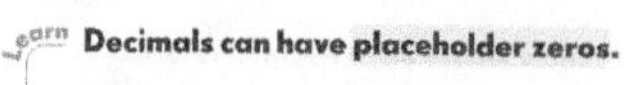

Decimals can have placeholder zeros.

Does 0.90 have the same value as 0.9?

$0.90 = \frac{90}{100}$
$= \frac{9}{10}$
$= 0.9$

$\frac{90}{100} = \frac{9}{10}$ (÷10)

Express ones, tenths, and hundredths as decimals.

What is 2 ones and 4 tenths 7 hundredths written as a decimal?

Ones	Tenths	Hundredths
●●	●●●●	●●●●● ●●

2 ones and 4 tenths 7 hundredths
= 2 ones and 47 hundredths
= 2.47

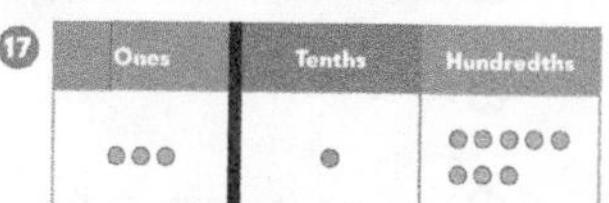

Guided Practice

Express each of these as a decimal.

17

Ones	Tenths	Hundredths
●●●	●	●●●●● ●●●

3.18

18 4 ones and 9 tenths 1 hundredth = 4.91

Find the decimal that the shaded parts represent.

19

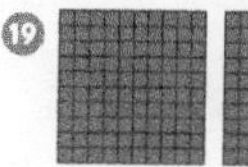
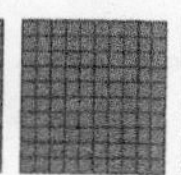
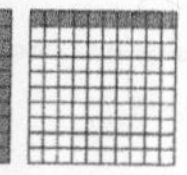

2.10

Look at the points marked ✗ on the number line.
Find the decimals that these points represent.

20

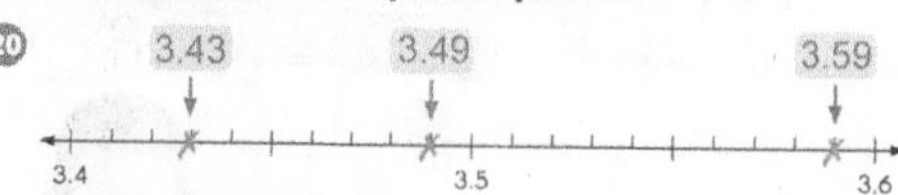

Express mixed numbers as decimals.

Rewrite $1\frac{53}{100}$ as a decimal.

Ones	Tenths	Hundredths
●	●●●●●	●●●
1	5	3

$1\frac{53}{100}$ = 1 one and 5 tenths 3 hundredths
= 1 one and 53 hundredths
= 1.53

Express improper fractions as decimals.

Rewrite $\frac{147}{100}$ as a decimal.

$\frac{147}{100}$ = 1 one and 47 hundredths
= 1.47

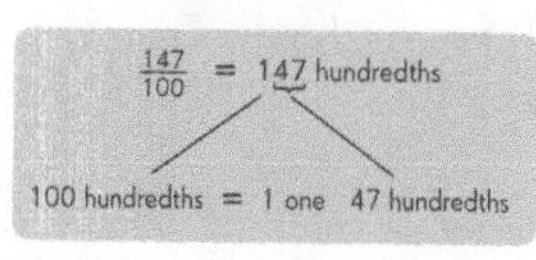

Guided Practice

Express each fraction or mixed number as a decimal.

21 $2\frac{75}{100}$ = 2.75

22 $\frac{103}{100}$ = 1.03

23 $3\frac{16}{100}$ L = 3.16 L

24 $\frac{204}{100}$ km = 2.04 km

Express each decimal as hundredths.

25 0.03 = 3 hundredths

26 0.31 = 31 hundredths

27 6.17 = 617 hundredths

28 2.09 = 209 hundredths

Write decimals to show their place values.

Tens	Ones	Tenths	Hundredths
7	8	4	1

78.41 = 7 tens + 8 ones + 4 tenths + 1 hundredth
= 70 + 8 + 0.4 + 0.01
= $70 + 8 + \frac{4}{10} + \frac{1}{100}$

Guided Practice

Find the missing numbers in the expanded form.

29 20.39 = 2 tens + 0 ones + 3 tenths + 9 hundredths
= 20 + 0.3 + 0.09
= $20 + \frac{3}{10} + \frac{9}{100}$

Use place value to understand whole number and decimal amounts.

In 3.47,
the value of the digit 7 is 0.07.
the digit 4 stands for 4 tenths or 0.4.
the digit 3 is in the ones place.

Guided Practice

Find the missing words or numbers.

30 In 5.18, the digit 1 is in the tenths place.

31 In 2.59, the value of the digit 9 is 0.09.

32 In 82.03, the value of the digit 8 is 80.

Use decimals to write dollars and cents.

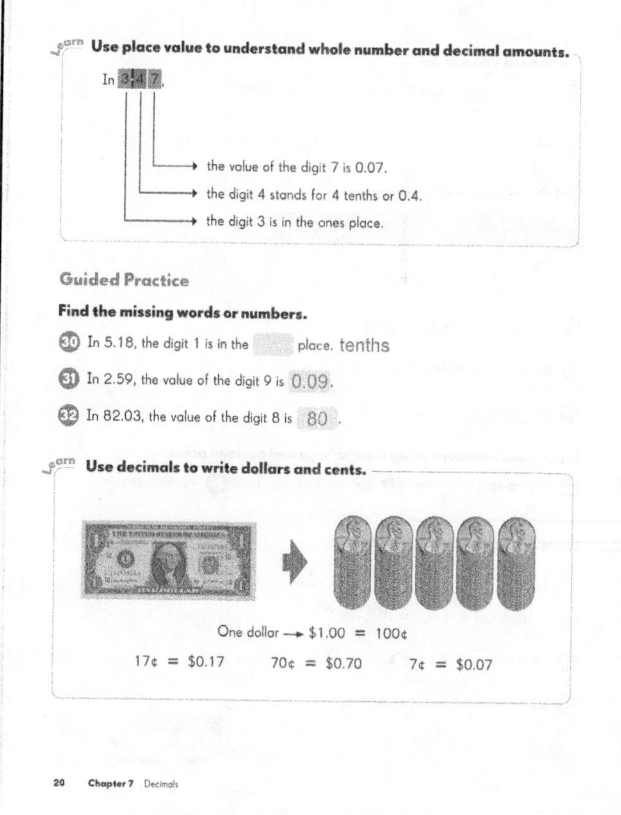

Chapter 7

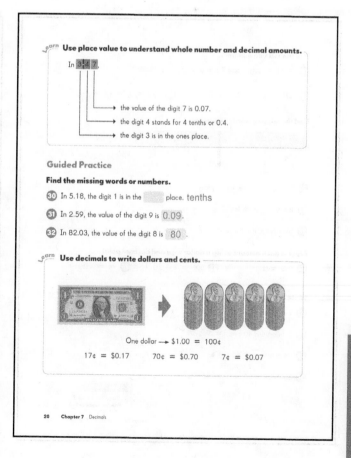

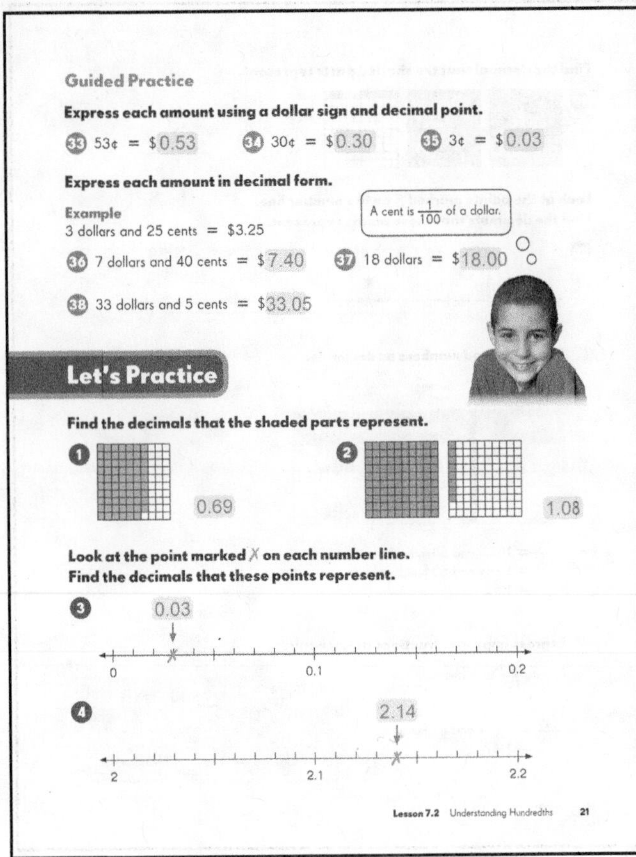

Guided Practice

Express each amount using a dollar sign and decimal point.

33 53¢ = $0.53 34 30¢ = $0.30 35 3¢ = $0.03

Express each amount in decimal form.

Example
3 dollars and 25 cents = $3.25

A cent is $\frac{1}{100}$ of a dollar.

36 7 dollars and 40 cents = $7.40 37 18 dollars = $18.00

38 33 dollars and 5 cents = $33.05

Let's Practice

Find the decimals that the shaded parts represent.

1 0.69 2 1.08

Look at the point marked X on each number line.
Find the decimals that these points represent.

3 0.03 (number line: 0, 0.1, 0.2)

4 2.14 (number line: 2, 2.1, 2.2)

Lesson 7.2 Understanding Hundredths 21

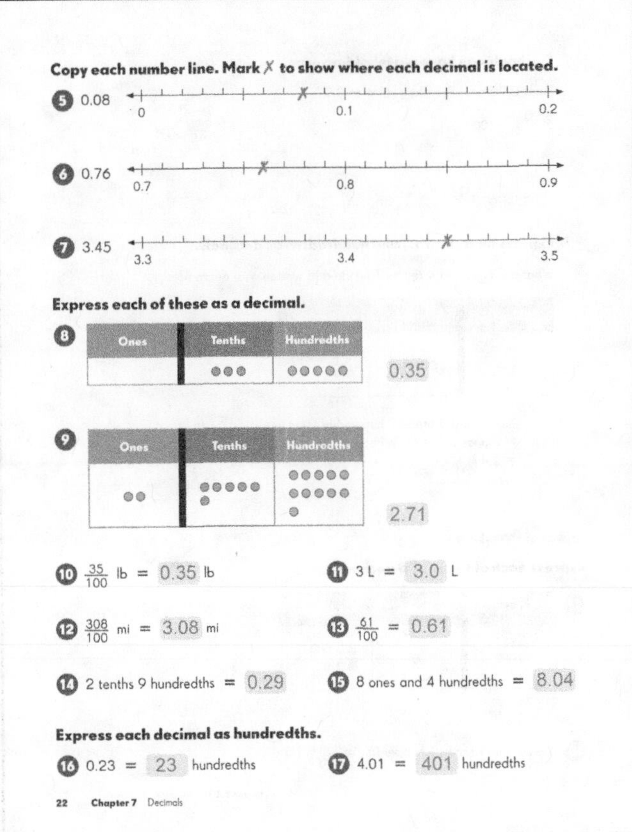

Copy each number line. Mark X to show where each decimal is located.

5 0.08 (number line: 0, 0.1, 0.2)

6 0.76 (number line: 0.7, 0.8, 0.9)

7 3.45 (number line: 3.3, 3.4, 3.5)

Express each of these as a decimal.

8

Ones	Tenths	Hundredths
	●●●	●●●●●

0.35

9

Ones	Tenths	Hundredths
●●	●●●●● ●●●	●●●●● ●●●●● ●

2.71

10 $\frac{35}{100}$ lb = 0.35 lb 11 3 L = 3.0 L

12 $\frac{308}{100}$ mi = 3.08 mi 13 $\frac{61}{100}$ = 0.61

14 2 tenths 9 hundredths = 0.29 15 8 ones and 4 hundredths = 8.04

Express each decimal as hundredths.

16 0.23 = 23 hundredths 17 4.01 = 401 hundredths

22 Chapter 7 Decimals

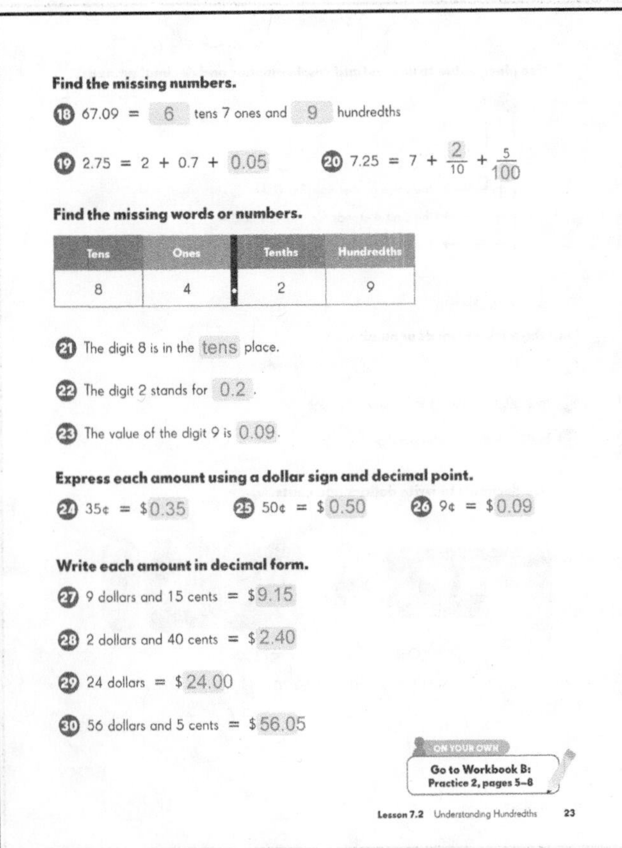

Find the missing numbers.

18 67.09 = 6 tens 7 ones and 9 hundredths

19 2.75 = 2 + 0.7 + 0.05 20 7.25 = 7 + $\frac{2}{10}$ + $\frac{5}{100}$

Find the missing words or numbers.

Tens	Ones	Tenths	Hundredths
8	4	2	9

21 The digit 8 is in the tens place.

22 The digit 2 stands for 0.2.

23 The value of the digit 9 is 0.09.

Express each amount using a dollar sign and decimal point.

24 35¢ = $0.35 25 50¢ = $0.50 26 9¢ = $0.09

Write each amount in decimal form.

27 9 dollars and 15 cents = $9.15

28 2 dollars and 40 cents = $2.40

29 24 dollars = $24.00

30 56 dollars and 5 cents = $56.05

ON YOUR OWN
Go to Workbook B: Practice 2, pages 5–8

Lesson 7.2 Understanding Hundredths 23

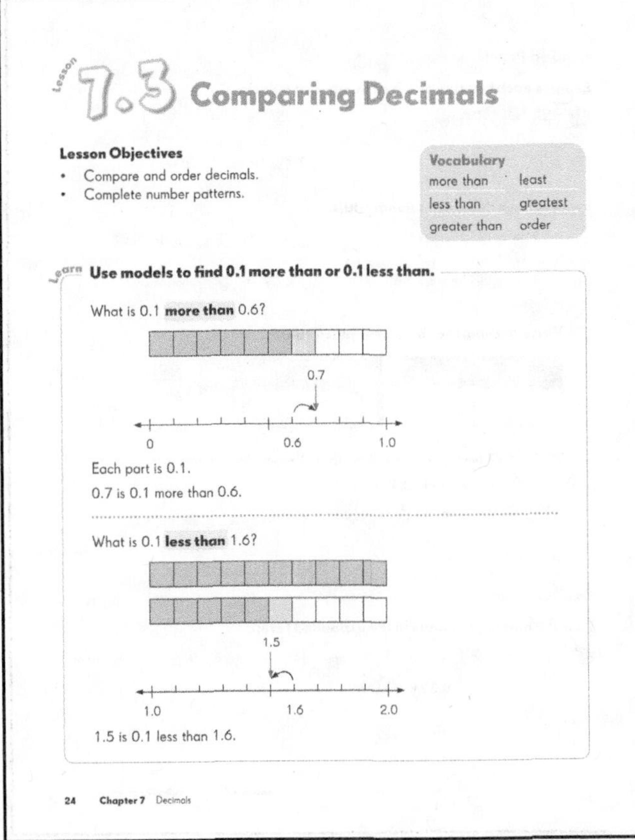

Lesson 7.3 Comparing Decimals

Lesson Objectives
- Compare and order decimals.
- Complete number patterns.

Vocabulary
more than least
less than greatest
greater than order

Learn **Use models to find 0.1 more than or 0.1 less than.**

What is 0.1 **more than** 0.6?

0.7 (number line: 0, 0.6, 1.0)

Each part is 0.1.
0.7 is 0.1 more than 0.6.

What is 0.1 **less than** 1.6?

1.5 (number line: 1.0, 1.6, 2.0)

1.5 is 0.1 less than 1.6.

24 Chapter 7 Decimals

Chapter 7

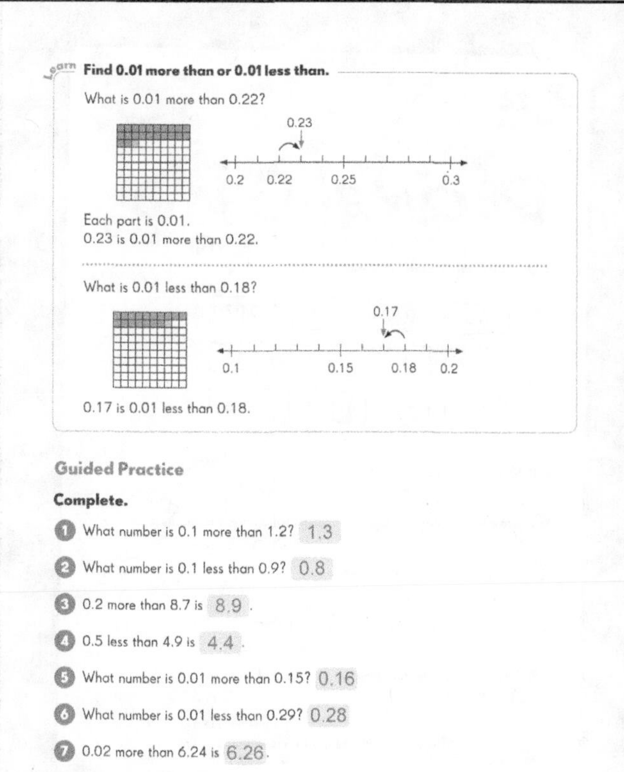

Learn **Find 0.01 more than or 0.01 less than.**

What is 0.01 more than 0.22?

0.23

0.2 0.22 0.25 0.3

Each part is 0.01.
0.23 is 0.01 more than 0.22.

What is 0.01 less than 0.18?

0.17

0.1 0.15 0.18 0.2

0.17 is 0.01 less than 0.18.

Guided Practice

Complete.

1. What number is 0.1 more than 1.2? 1.3
2. What number is 0.1 less than 0.9? 0.8
3. 0.2 more than 8.7 is 8.9.
4. 0.5 less than 4.9 is 4.4.
5. What number is 0.01 more than 0.15? 0.16
6. What number is 0.01 less than 0.29? 0.28
7. 0.02 more than 6.24 is 6.26.
8. 0.04 less than 7.16 is 7.12.

Lesson 7.3 Comparing Decimals 25

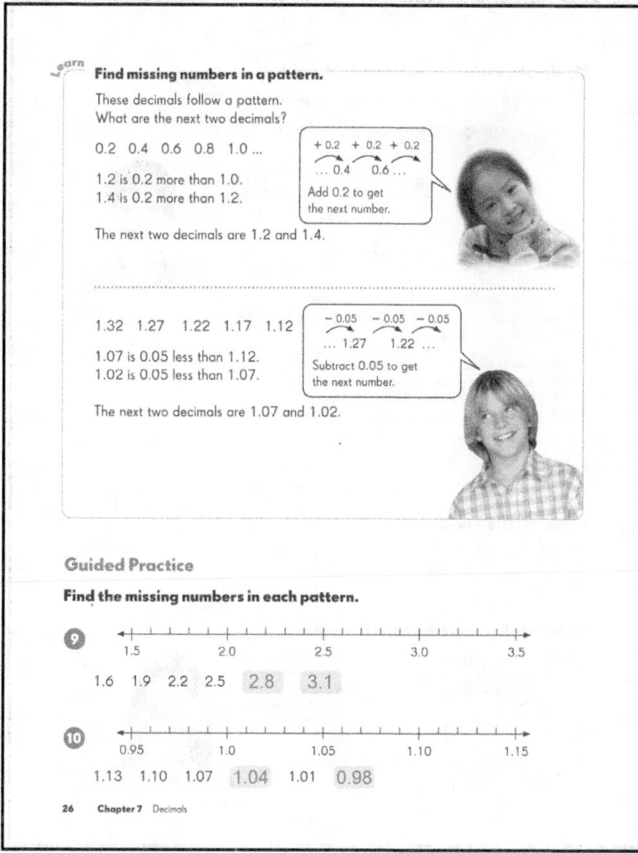

Learn **Find missing numbers in a pattern.**

These decimals follow a pattern.
What are the next two decimals?

0.2 0.4 0.6 0.8 1.0 ...

1.2 is 0.2 more than 1.0.
1.4 is 0.2 more than 1.2.

+ 0.2 + 0.2 + 0.2
... 0.4 0.6 ...
Add 0.2 to get the next number.

The next two decimals are 1.2 and 1.4.

1.32 1.27 1.22 1.17 1.12

1.07 is 0.05 less than 1.12.
1.02 is 0.05 less than 1.07.

− 0.05 − 0.05 − 0.05
... 1.27 1.22 ...
Subtract 0.05 to get the next number.

The next two decimals are 1.07 and 1.02.

Guided Practice

Find the missing numbers in each pattern.

9. 1.5 2.0 2.5 3.0 3.5

1.6 1.9 2.2 2.5 2.8 3.1

10. 0.95 1.0 1.05 1.10 1.15

1.13 1.10 1.07 1.04 1.01 0.98

26 Chapter 7 Decimals

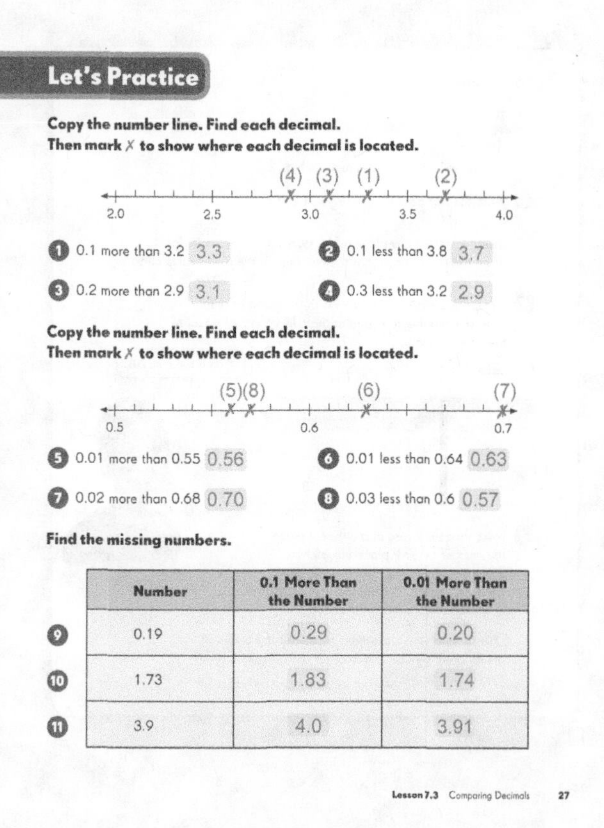

Let's Practice

Copy the number line. Find each decimal.
Then mark ✗ to show where each decimal is located.

(4) (3) (1) (2)

2.0 2.5 3.0 3.5 4.0

1. 0.1 more than 3.2 3.3
2. 0.1 less than 3.8 3.7
3. 0.2 more than 2.9 3.1
4. 0.3 less than 3.2 2.9

Copy the number line. Find each decimal.
Then mark ✗ to show where each decimal is located.

(5)(8) (6) (7)

0.5 0.6 0.7

5. 0.01 more than 0.55 0.56
6. 0.01 less than 0.64 0.63
7. 0.02 more than 0.68 0.70
8. 0.03 less than 0.6 0.57

Find the missing numbers.

	Number	0.1 More Than the Number	0.01 More Than the Number
9	0.19	0.29	0.20
10	1.73	1.83	1.74
11	3.9	4.0	3.91

Lesson 7.3 Comparing Decimals 27

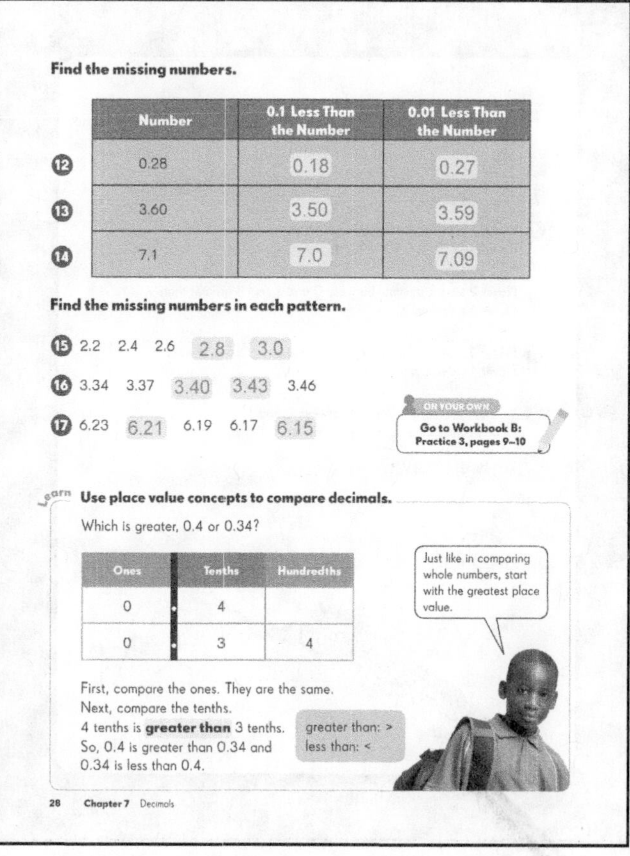

Find the missing numbers.

	Number	0.1 Less Than the Number	0.01 Less Than the Number
12	0.28	0.18	0.27
13	3.60	3.50	3.59
14	7.1	7.0	7.09

Find the missing numbers in each pattern.

15. 2.2 2.4 2.6 2.8 3.0
16. 3.34 3.37 3.40 3.43 3.46
17. 6.23 6.21 6.19 6.17 6.15

ON YOUR OWN
Go to Workbook B: Practice 3, pages 9–10

Learn **Use place value concepts to compare decimals.**

Which is greater, 0.4 or 0.34?

Ones	Tenths	Hundredths
0	4	
0	3	4

Just like in comparing whole numbers, start with the greatest place value.

First, compare the ones. They are the same.
Next, compare the tenths.
4 tenths is **greater than** 3 tenths.
So, 0.4 is greater than 0.34 and 0.34 is less than 0.4.

greater than: >
less than: <

28 Chapter 7 Decimals

Chapter 7

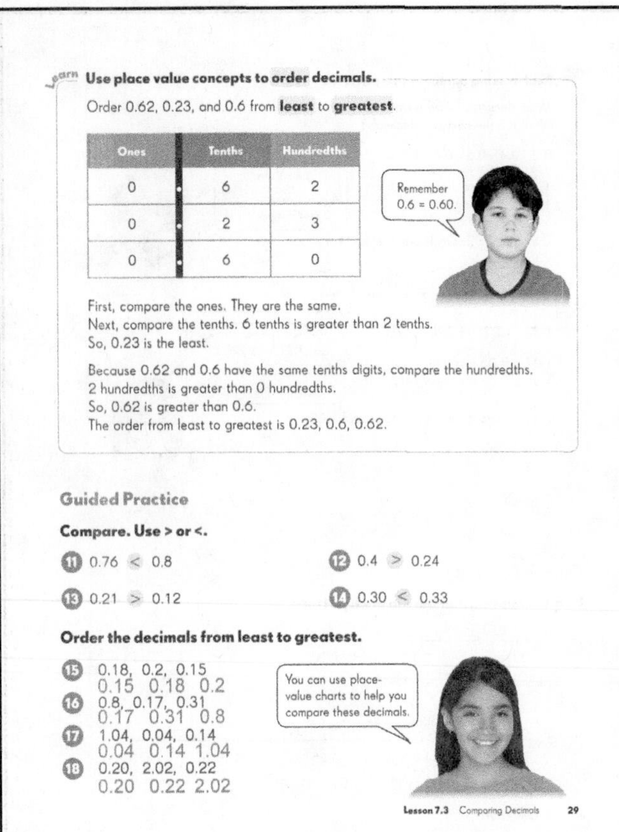

Learn Use place value concepts to order decimals.

Order 0.62, 0.23, and 0.6 from **least** to **greatest**.

Ones	Tenths	Hundredths
0	6	2
0	2	3
0	6	0

Remember 0.6 = 0.60.

First, compare the ones. They are the same.
Next, compare the tenths. 6 tenths is greater than 2 tenths.
So, 0.23 is the least.

Because 0.62 and 0.6 have the same tenths digits, compare the hundredths.
2 hundredths is greater than 0 hundredths.
So, 0.62 is greater than 0.6.
The order from least to greatest is 0.23, 0.6, 0.62.

Guided Practice

Compare. Use > or <.

11. 0.76 < 0.8
12. 0.4 > 0.24
13. 0.21 > 0.12
14. 0.30 < 0.33

Order the decimals from least to greatest.

15. 0.18, 0.2, 0.15 — 0.15 0.18 0.2
16. 0.8, 0.17, 0.31 — 0.17 0.31 0.8
17. 1.04, 0.04, 0.14 — 0.04 0.14 1.04
18. 0.20, 2.02, 0.22 — 0.20 0.22 2.02

You can use place-value charts to help you compare these decimals.

Lesson 7.3 Comparing Decimals 29

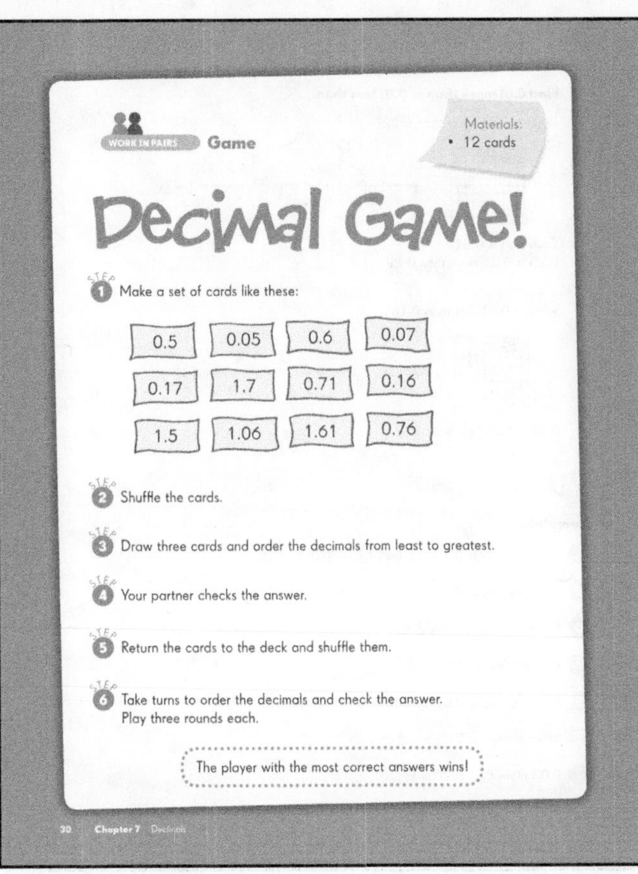

WORK IN PAIRS **Game**

Materials:
- 12 cards

Decimal Game!

STEP 1 Make a set of cards like these:

0.5	0.05	0.6	0.07
0.17	1.7	0.71	0.16
1.5	1.06	1.61	0.76

STEP 2 Shuffle the cards.

STEP 3 Draw three cards and order the decimals from least to greatest.

STEP 4 Your partner checks the answer.

STEP 5 Return the cards to the deck and shuffle them.

STEP 6 Take turns to order the decimals and check the answer. Play three rounds each.

The player with the most correct answers wins!

30 Chapter 7 Decimals

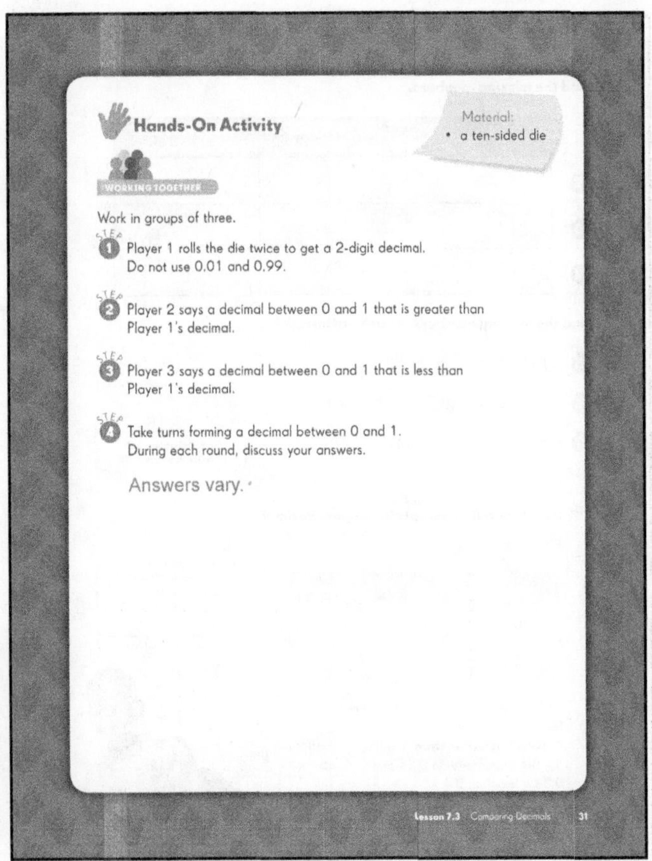

Hands-On Activity

Material:
- a ten-sided die

WORKING TOGETHER

Work in groups of three.

STEP 1 Player 1 rolls the die twice to get a 2-digit decimal. Do not use 0.01 and 0.99.

STEP 2 Player 2 says a decimal between 0 and 1 that is greater than Player 1's decimal.

STEP 3 Player 3 says a decimal between 0 and 1 that is less than Player 1's decimal.

STEP 4 Take turns forming a decimal between 0 and 1. During each round, discuss your answers.

Answers vary.

Lesson 7.3 Comparing Decimals 31

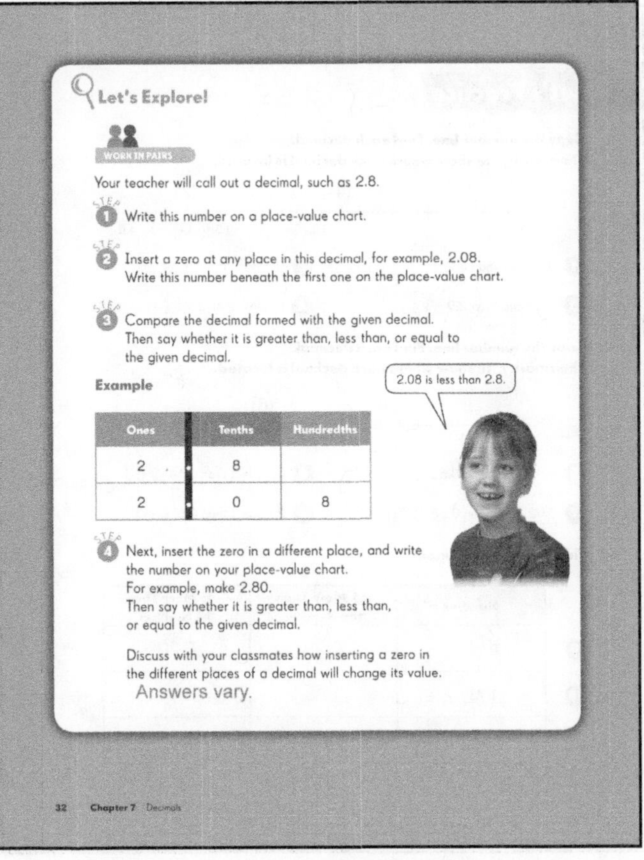

Let's Explore!

WORK IN PAIRS

Your teacher will call out a decimal, such as 2.8.

STEP 1 Write this number on a place-value chart.

STEP 2 Insert a zero at any place in this decimal, for example, 2.08. Write this number beneath the first one on the place-value chart.

STEP 3 Compare the decimal formed with the given decimal. Then say whether it is greater than, less than, or equal to the given decimal.

Example

Ones	Tenths	Hundredths
2	8	
2	0	8

2.08 is less than 2.8.

STEP 4 Next, insert the zero in a different place, and write the number on your place-value chart. For example, make 2.80. Then say whether it is greater than, less than, or equal to the given decimal.

Discuss with your classmates how inserting a zero in the different places of a decimal will change its value.

Answers vary.

32 Chapter 7 Decimals

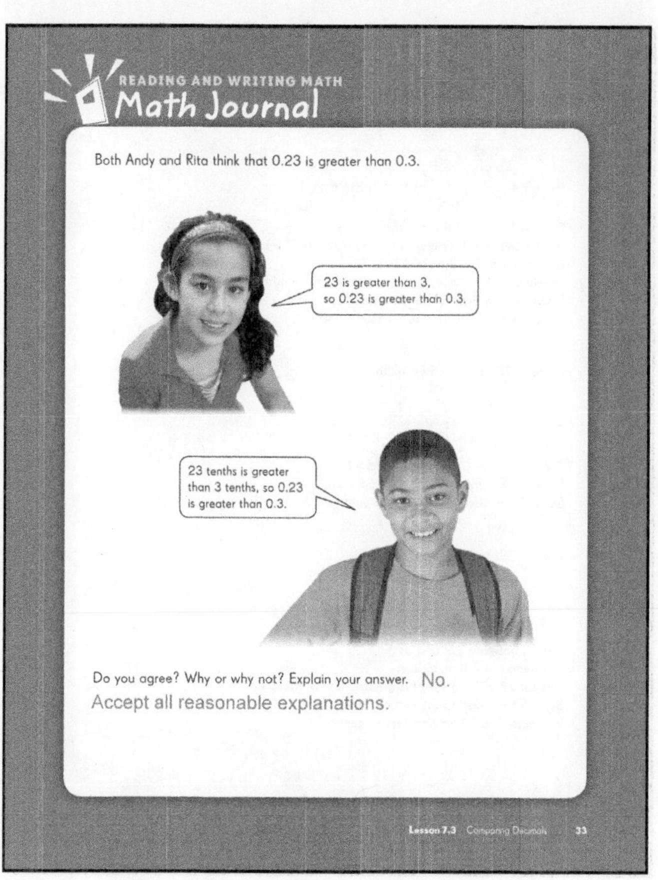
READING AND WRITING MATH

Math Journal

Both Andy and Rita think that 0.23 is greater than 0.3.

23 is greater than 3, so 0.23 is greater than 0.3.
23 tenths is greater than 3 tenths, so 0.23 is greater than 0.3.

Do you agree? Why or why not? Explain your answer. No.
Accept all reasonable explanations.

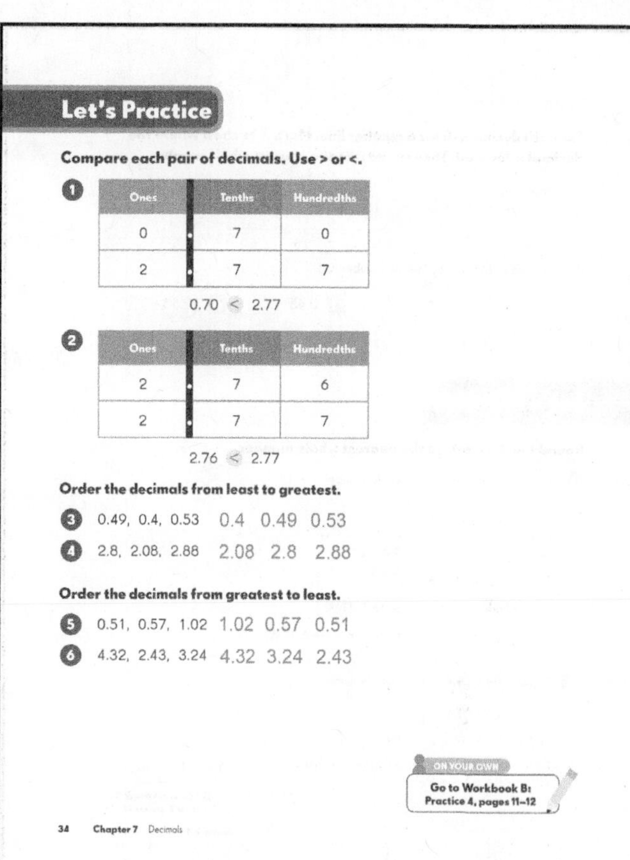

Let's Practice

Compare each pair of decimals. Use > or <.

1

Ones	Tenths	Hundredths
0	7	0
2	7	7

0.70 < 2.77

2

Ones	Tenths	Hundredths
2	7	6
2	7	7

2.76 < 2.77

Order the decimals from least to greatest.

3. 0.49, 0.4, 0.53 0.4 0.49 0.53
4. 2.8, 2.08, 2.88 2.08 2.8 2.88

Order the decimals from greatest to least.

5. 0.51, 0.57, 1.02 1.02 0.57 0.51
6. 4.32, 2.43, 3.24 4.32 3.24 2.43

ON YOUR OWN
Go to Workbook B: Practice 4, pages 11–12

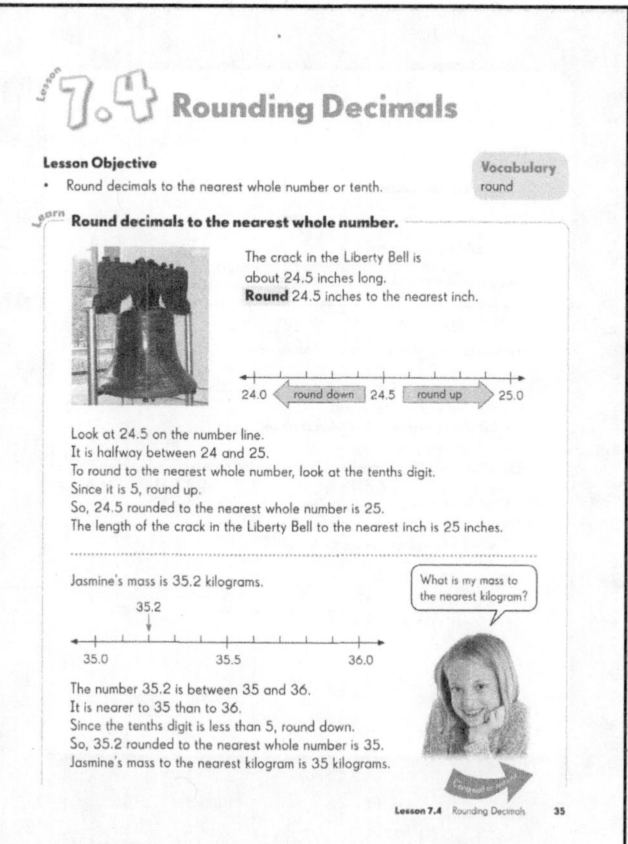

Lesson 7.4 Rounding Decimals

Lesson Objective

- Round decimals to the nearest whole number or tenth.

Vocabulary
round

Learn Round decimals to the nearest whole number.

The crack in the Liberty Bell is about 24.5 inches long.
Round 24.5 inches to the nearest inch.

24.0 round down 24.5 round up 25.0

Look at 24.5 on the number line.
It is halfway between 24 and 25.
To round to the nearest whole number, look at the tenths digit.
Since it is 5, round up.
So, 24.5 rounded to the nearest whole number is 25.
The length of the crack in the Liberty Bell to the nearest inch is 25 inches.

Jasmine's mass is 35.2 kilograms.

What is my mass to the nearest kilogram?
35.2
35.0 35.5 36.0

The number 35.2 is between 35 and 36.
It is nearer to 35 than to 36.
Since the tenths digit is less than 5, round down.
So, 35.2 rounded to the nearest whole number is 35.
Jasmine's mass to the nearest kilogram is 35 kilograms.

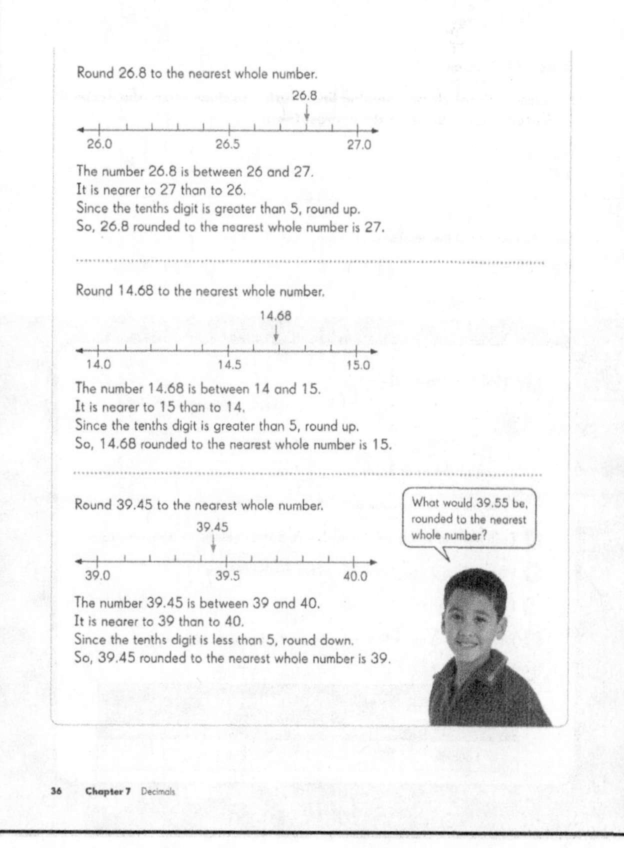

Round 26.8 to the nearest whole number.

26.8
26.0 26.5 27.0

The number 26.8 is between 26 and 27.
It is nearer to 27 than to 26.
Since the tenths digit is greater than 5, round up.
So, 26.8 rounded to the nearest whole number is 27.

Round 14.68 to the nearest whole number.

14.68
14.0 14.5 15.0

The number 14.68 is between 14 and 15.
It is nearer to 15 than to 14.
Since the tenths digit is greater than 5, round up.
So, 14.68 rounded to the nearest whole number is 15.

Round 39.45 to the nearest whole number.

39.45
39.0 39.5 40.0
What would 39.55 be, rounded to the nearest whole number?

The number 39.45 is between 39 and 40.
It is nearer to 39 than to 40.
Since the tenths digit is less than 5, round down.
So, 39.45 rounded to the nearest whole number is 39.

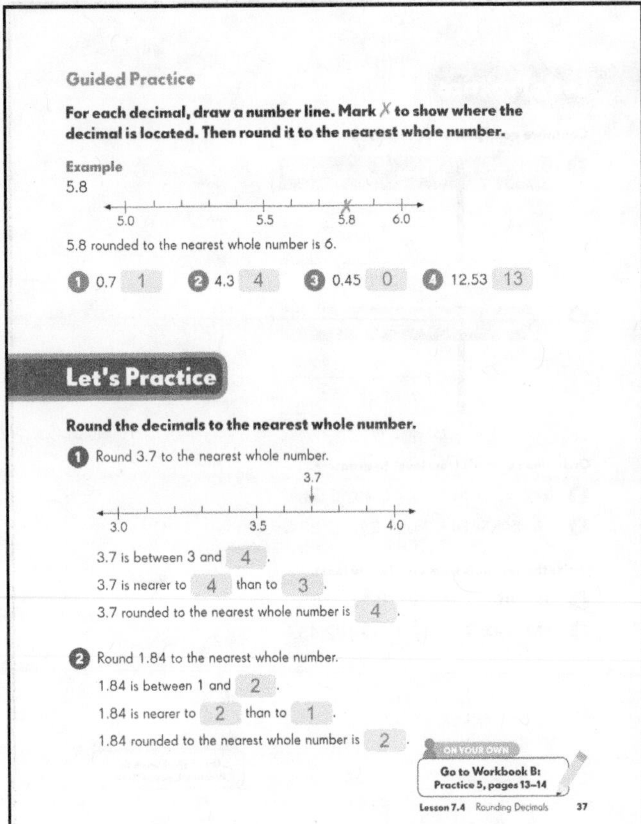

Guided Practice

For each decimal, draw a number line. Mark X to show where the decimal is located. Then round it to the nearest whole number.

Example
5.8

5.0 5.5 5.8 6.0

5.8 rounded to the nearest whole number is 6.

1. 0.7 **1** 2. 4.3 **4** 3. 0.45 **0** 4. 12.53 **13**

Let's Practice

Round the decimals to the nearest whole number.

1. Round 3.7 to the nearest whole number.

   3.7
   3.0 3.5 4.0

   3.7 is between 3 and **4**.
   3.7 is nearer to **4** than to **3**.
   3.7 rounded to the nearest whole number is **4**.

2. Round 1.84 to the nearest whole number.

   1.84 is between 1 and **2**.
   1.84 is nearer to **2** than to **1**.
   1.84 rounded to the nearest whole number is **2**.

ON YOUR OWN
Go to Workbook B: Practice 5, pages 13–14

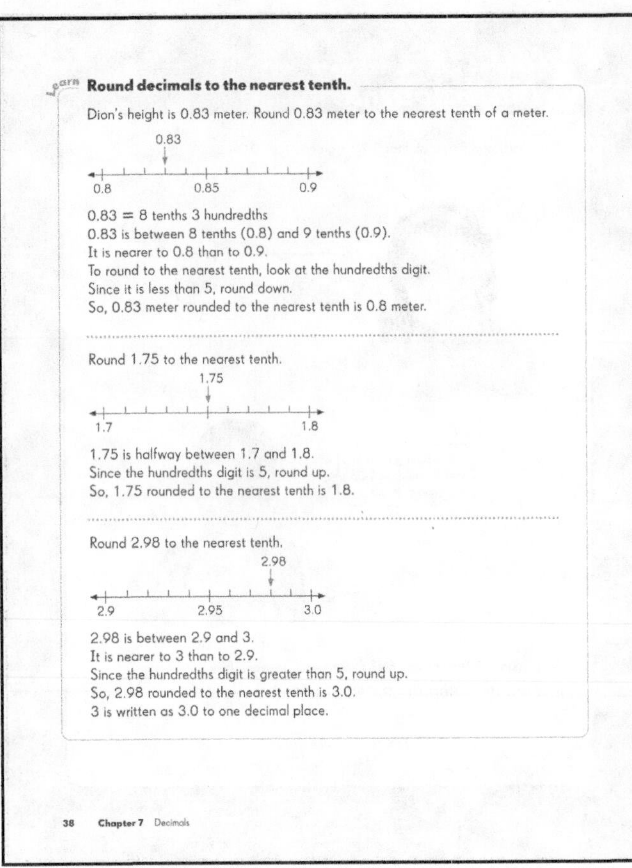

Learn Round decimals to the nearest tenth.

Dion's height is 0.83 meter. Round 0.83 meter to the nearest tenth of a meter.

0.83
0.8 0.85 0.9

0.83 = 8 tenths 3 hundredths
0.83 is between 8 tenths (0.8) and 9 tenths (0.9).
It is nearer to 0.8 than to 0.9.
To round to the nearest tenth, look at the hundredths digit.
Since it is less than 5, round down.
So, 0.83 meter rounded to the nearest tenth is 0.8 meter.

Round 1.75 to the nearest tenth.

1.75
1.7 1.8

1.75 is halfway between 1.7 and 1.8.
Since the hundredths digit is 5, round up.
So, 1.75 rounded to the nearest tenth is 1.8.

Round 2.98 to the nearest tenth.

2.98
2.9 2.95 3.0

2.98 is between 2.9 and 3.
It is nearer to 3 than to 2.9.
Since the hundredths digit is greater than 5, round up.
So, 2.98 rounded to the nearest tenth is 3.0.
3 is written as 3.0 to one decimal place.

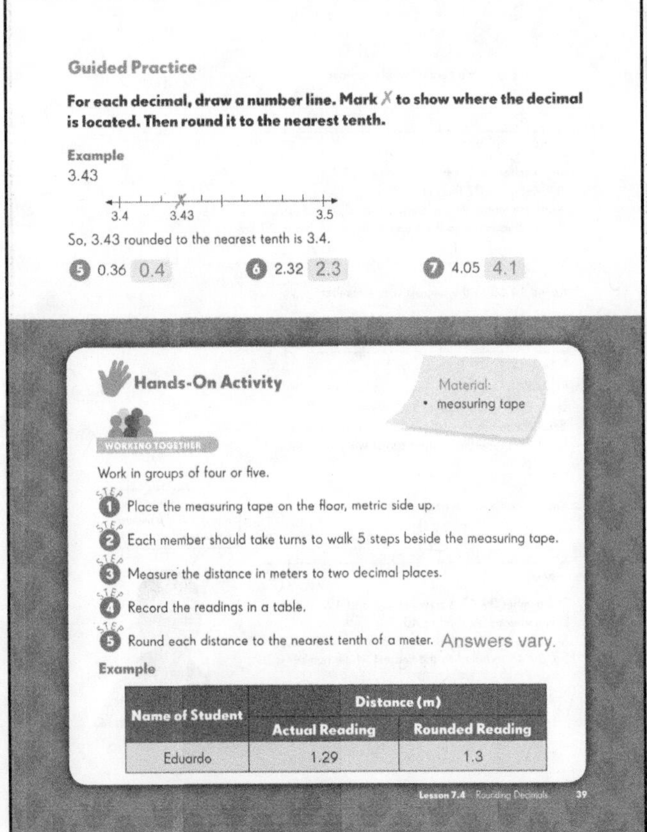

Guided Practice

For each decimal, draw a number line. Mark X to show where the decimal is located. Then round it to the nearest tenth.

Example
3.43

3.4 3.43 3.5

So, 3.43 rounded to the nearest tenth is 3.4.

5. 0.36 **0.4** 6. 2.32 **2.3** 7. 4.05 **4.1**

Hands-On Activity

Material:
- measuring tape

WORKING TOGETHER

Work in groups of four or five.

STEP 1 Place the measuring tape on the floor, metric side up.
STEP 2 Each member should take turns to walk 5 steps beside the measuring tape.
STEP 3 Measure the distance in meters to two decimal places.
STEP 4 Record the readings in a table.
STEP 5 Round each distance to the nearest tenth of a meter. **Answers vary.**

Example

Name of Student	Distance (m)	
	Actual Reading	Rounded Reading
Eduardo	1.29	1.3

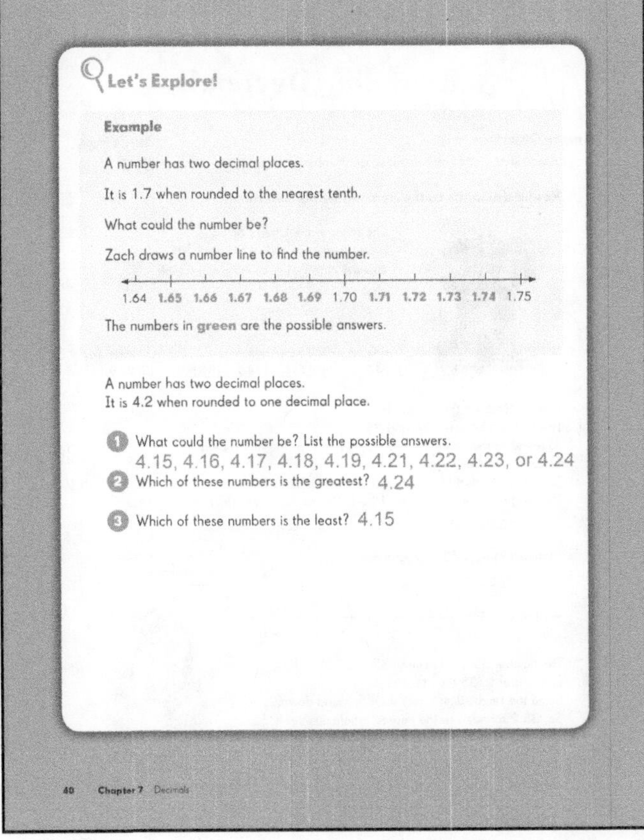

Let's Explore!

Example

A number has two decimal places.

It is 1.7 when rounded to the nearest tenth.

What could the number be?

Zach draws a number line to find the number.

1.64 1.65 1.66 1.67 1.68 1.69 1.70 1.71 1.72 1.73 1.74 1.75

The numbers in green are the possible answers.

A number has two decimal places.
It is 4.2 when rounded to one decimal place.

1. What could the number be? List the possible answers.
   4.15, 4.16, 4.17, 4.18, 4.19, 4.21, 4.22, 4.23, or 4.24
2. Which of these numbers is the greatest? **4.24**
3. Which of these numbers is the least? **4.15**

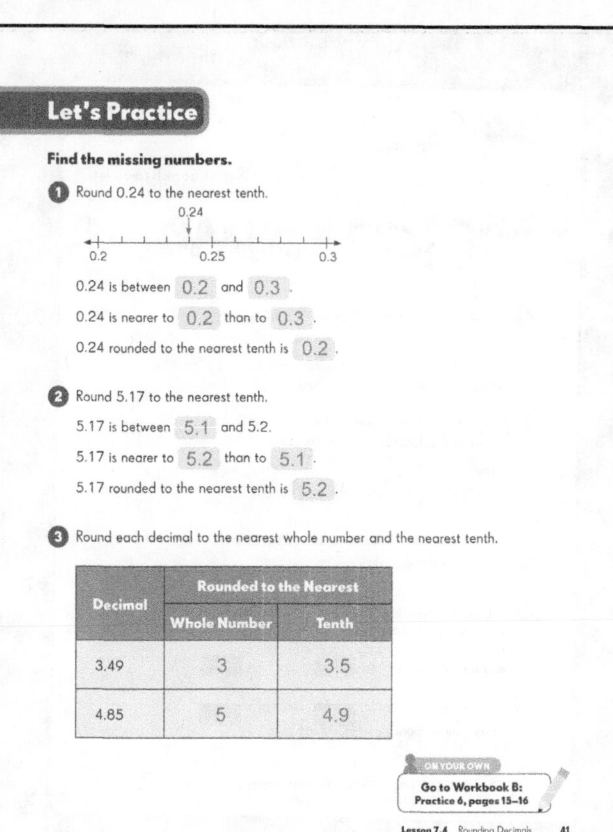
Let's Practice

Find the missing numbers.

1. Round 0.24 to the nearest tenth.

0.24 is between 0.2 and 0.3.

0.24 is nearer to 0.2 than to 0.3.

0.24 rounded to the nearest tenth is 0.2.

2. Round 5.17 to the nearest tenth.

5.17 is between 5.1 and 5.2.

5.17 is nearer to 5.2 than to 5.1.

5.17 rounded to the nearest tenth is 5.2.

3. Round each decimal to the nearest whole number and the nearest tenth.

Decimal	Rounded to the Nearest	
	Whole Number	Tenth
3.49	3	3.5
4.85	5	4.9

ON YOUR OWN
Go to Workbook B: Practice 6, pages 15–16

Lesson 7.4 Rounding Decimals 41

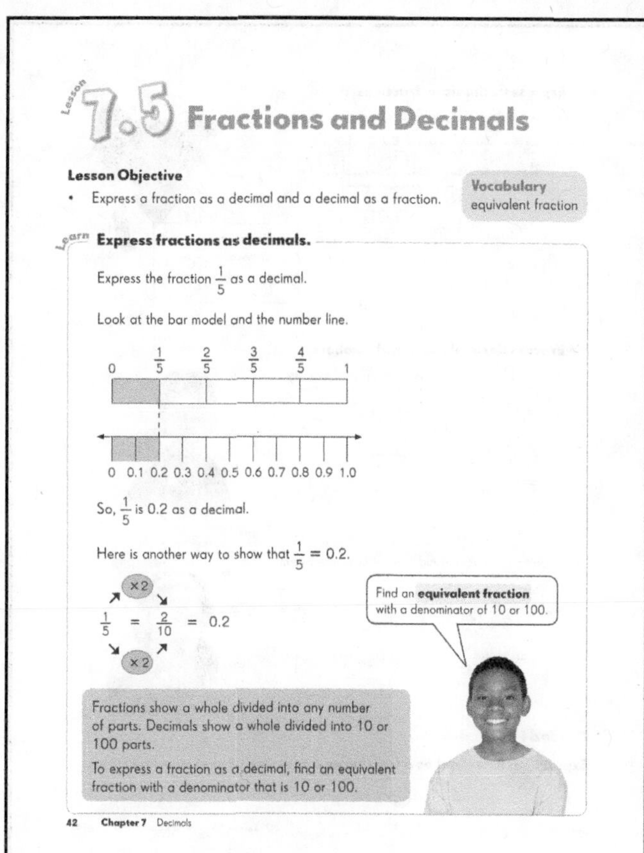
Lesson 7.5 Fractions and Decimals

Lesson Objective

- Express a fraction as a decimal and a decimal as a fraction.

Vocabulary
equivalent fraction

Learn Express fractions as decimals.

Express the fraction $\frac{1}{5}$ as a decimal.

Look at the bar model and the number line.

So, $\frac{1}{5}$ is 0.2 as a decimal.

Here is another way to show that $\frac{1}{5} = 0.2$.

$\frac{1}{5} = \frac{2}{10} = 0.2$ (×2)

Fractions show a whole divided into any number of parts. Decimals show a whole divided into 10 or 100 parts.

To express a fraction as a decimal, find an equivalent fraction with a denominator that is 10 or 100.

42 Chapter 7 Decimals

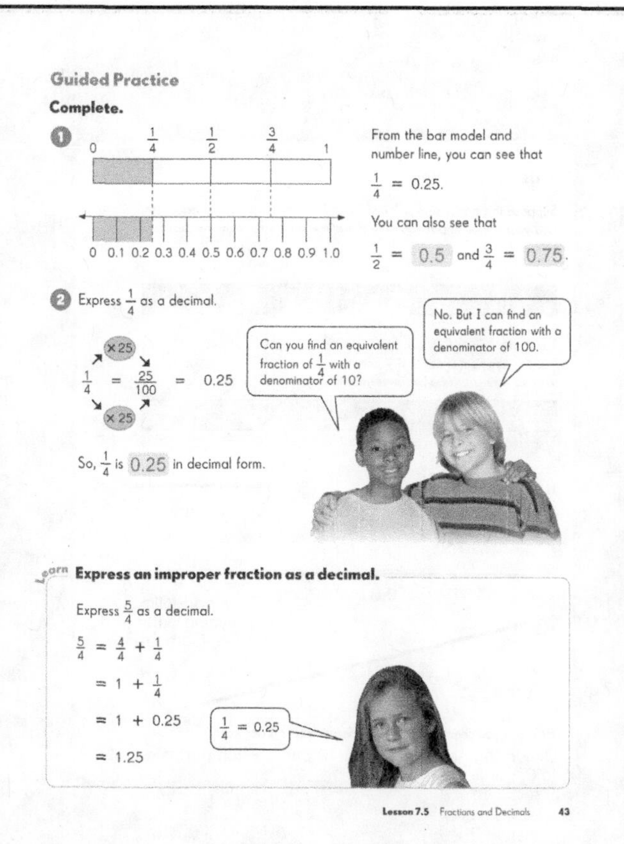
Guided Practice

Complete.

1.

From the bar model and number line, you can see that

$\frac{1}{4} = 0.25$.

You can also see that

$\frac{1}{2} =$ 0.5 and $\frac{3}{4} =$ 0.75.

2. Express $\frac{1}{4}$ as a decimal.

$\frac{1}{4} = \frac{25}{100} = 0.25$ (×25)

Can you find an equivalent fraction of $\frac{1}{4}$ with a denominator of 10?
No. But I can find an equivalent fraction with a denominator of 100.

So, $\frac{1}{4}$ is 0.25 in decimal form.

Learn Express an improper fraction as a decimal.

Express $\frac{5}{4}$ as a decimal.

$\frac{5}{4} = \frac{4}{4} + \frac{1}{4}$

$= 1 + \frac{1}{4}$

$= 1 + 0.25$

$= 1.25$

Lesson 7.5 Fractions and Decimals 43

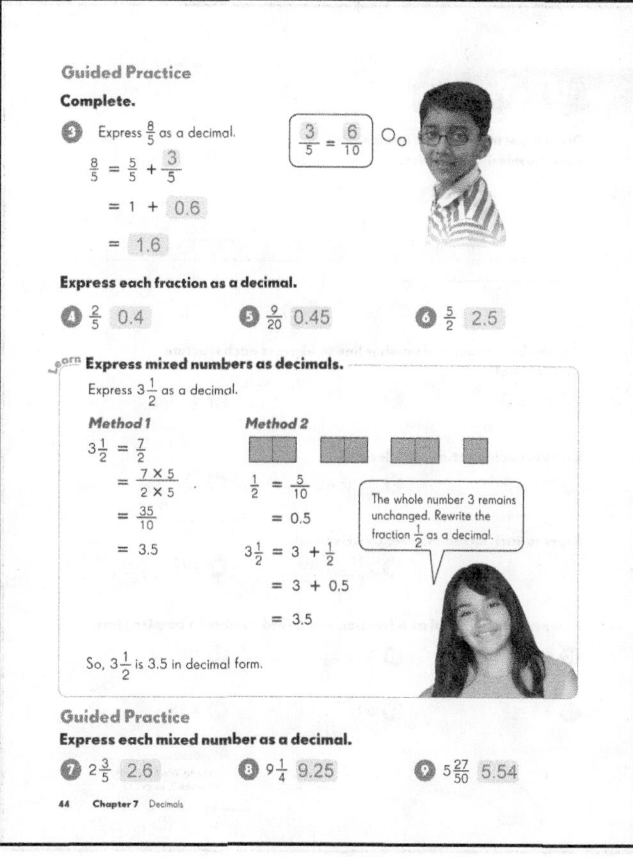
Guided Practice

Complete.

3. Express $\frac{8}{5}$ as a decimal.

$\frac{8}{5} = \frac{5}{5} + \frac{3}{5}$

$= 1 +$ 0.6

$=$ 1.6

Express each fraction as a decimal.

4. $\frac{2}{5}$ 0.4
5. $\frac{9}{20}$ 0.45
6. $\frac{5}{2}$ 2.5

Learn Express mixed numbers as decimals.

Express $3\frac{1}{2}$ as a decimal.

Method 1

$3\frac{1}{2} = \frac{7}{2}$

$= \frac{7 \times 5}{2 \times 5}$

$= \frac{35}{10}$

$= 3.5$

Method 2

$\frac{1}{2} = \frac{5}{10}$

$= 0.5$

$3\frac{1}{2} = 3 + \frac{1}{2}$

$= 3 + 0.5$

$= 3.5$

The whole number 3 remains unchanged. Rewrite the fraction $\frac{1}{2}$ as a decimal.

So, $3\frac{1}{2}$ is 3.5 in decimal form.

Guided Practice

Express each mixed number as a decimal.

7. $2\frac{3}{5}$ 2.6
8. $9\frac{1}{4}$ 9.25
9. $5\frac{27}{50}$ 5.54

44 Chapter 7 Decimals

Chapter 7

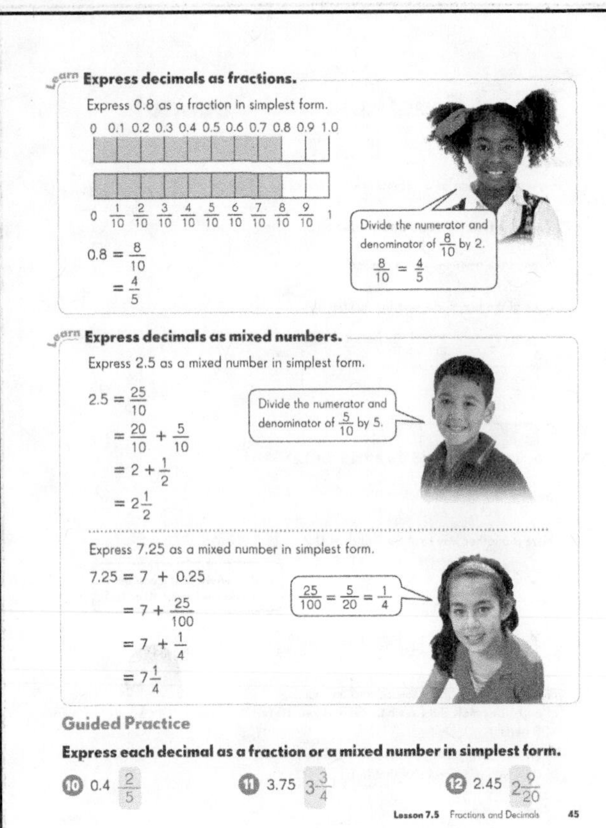

Learn **Express decimals as fractions.**

Express 0.8 as a fraction in simplest form.

0 0.1 0.2 0.3 0.4 0.5 0.6 0.7 0.8 0.9 1.0

0 $\frac{1}{10}$ $\frac{2}{10}$ $\frac{3}{10}$ $\frac{4}{10}$ $\frac{5}{10}$ $\frac{6}{10}$ $\frac{7}{10}$ $\frac{8}{10}$ $\frac{9}{10}$ 1

$0.8 = \frac{8}{10}$

$= \frac{4}{5}$

Divide the numerator and denominator of $\frac{8}{10}$ by 2.

$\frac{8}{10} = \frac{4}{5}$

Learn **Express decimals as mixed numbers.**

Express 2.5 as a mixed number in simplest form.

$2.5 = \frac{25}{10}$

$= \frac{20}{10} + \frac{5}{10}$

$= 2 + \frac{1}{2}$

$= 2\frac{1}{2}$

Divide the numerator and denominator of $\frac{5}{10}$ by 5.

Express 7.25 as a mixed number in simplest form.

$7.25 = 7 + 0.25$

$= 7 + \frac{25}{100}$

$= 7 + \frac{1}{4}$

$= 7\frac{1}{4}$

$\frac{25}{100} = \frac{5}{20} = \frac{1}{4}$

Guided Practice

Express each decimal as a fraction or a mixed number in simplest form.

10. 0.4 $\frac{2}{5}$ 11. 3.75 $3\frac{3}{4}$ 12. 2.45 $2\frac{9}{20}$

Lesson 7.5 Fractions and Decimals 45

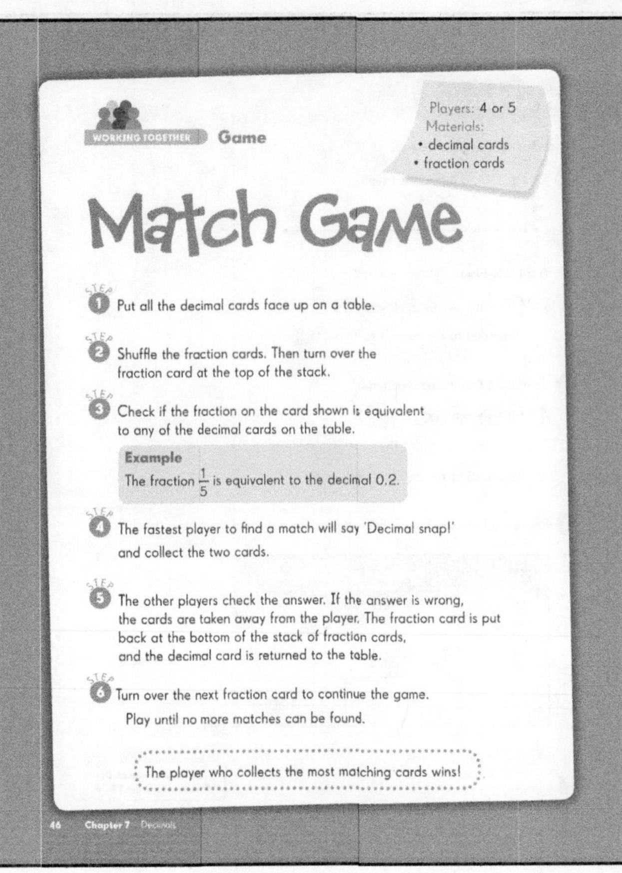

WORKING TOGETHER **Game**

Players: 4 or 5

Materials:
- decimal cards
- fraction cards

Match Game

STEP 1 Put all the decimal cards face up on a table.

STEP 2 Shuffle the fraction cards. Then turn over the fraction card at the top of the stack.

STEP 3 Check if the fraction on the card shown is equivalent to any of the decimal cards on the table.

Example

The fraction $\frac{1}{5}$ is equivalent to the decimal 0.2.

STEP 4 The fastest player to find a match will say 'Decimal snap!' and collect the two cards.

STEP 5 The other players check the answer. If the answer is wrong, the cards are taken away from the player. The fraction card is put back at the bottom of the stack of fraction cards, and the decimal card is returned to the table.

STEP 6 Turn over the next fraction card to continue the game. Play until no more matches can be found.

The player who collects the most matching cards wins!

46 Chapter 7 Decimals

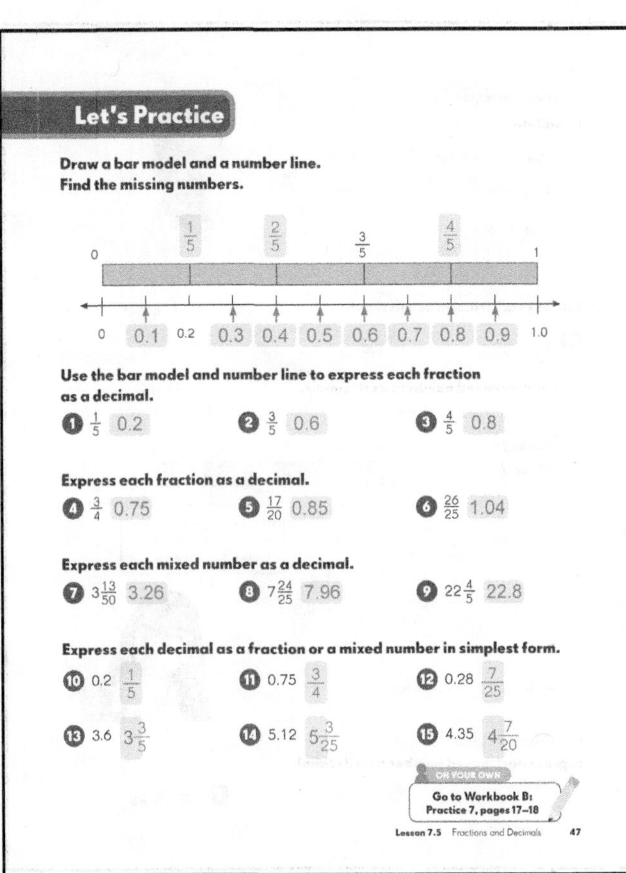

Let's Practice

Draw a bar model and a number line. Find the missing numbers.

0 $\frac{1}{5}$ $\frac{2}{5}$ $\frac{3}{5}$ $\frac{4}{5}$ 1

0 0.1 0.2 0.3 0.4 0.5 0.6 0.7 0.8 0.9 1.0

Use the bar model and number line to express each fraction as a decimal.

1. $\frac{1}{5}$ 0.2 2. $\frac{3}{5}$ 0.6 3. $\frac{4}{5}$ 0.8

Express each fraction as a decimal.

4. $\frac{3}{4}$ 0.75 5. $\frac{17}{20}$ 0.85 6. $\frac{26}{25}$ 1.04

Express each mixed number as a decimal.

7. $3\frac{13}{50}$ 3.26 8. $7\frac{24}{25}$ 7.96 9. $22\frac{4}{5}$ 22.8

Express each decimal as a fraction or a mixed number in simplest form.

10. 0.2 $\frac{1}{5}$ 11. 0.75 $\frac{3}{4}$ 12. 0.28 $\frac{7}{25}$

13. 3.6 $3\frac{3}{5}$ 14. 5.12 $5\frac{3}{25}$ 15. 4.35 $4\frac{7}{20}$

ON YOUR OWN
Go to Workbook B: Practice 7, pages 17–18

Lesson 7.5 Fractions and Decimals 47

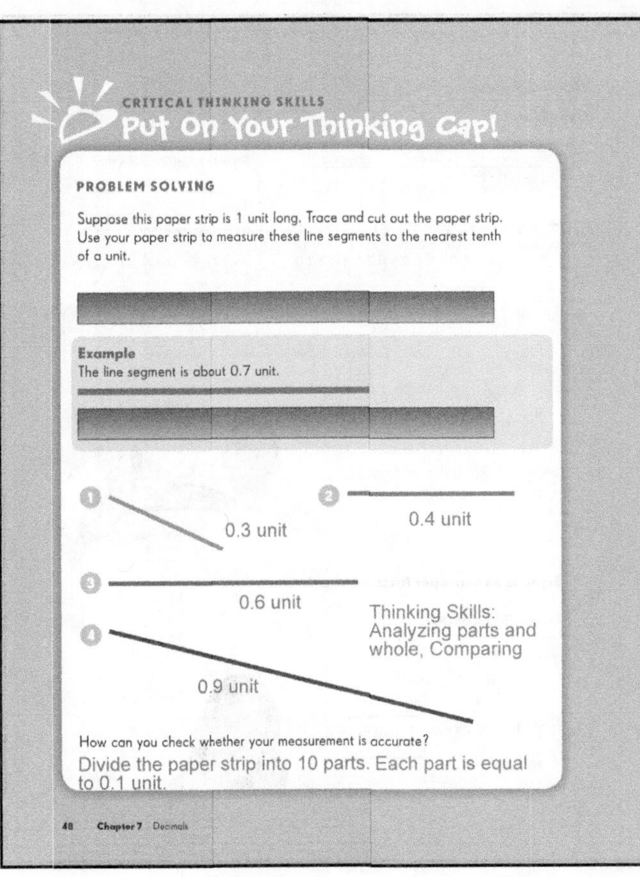

CRITICAL THINKING SKILLS

Put On Your Thinking Cap!

PROBLEM SOLVING

Suppose this paper strip is 1 unit long. Trace and cut out the paper strip. Use your paper strip to measure these line segments to the nearest tenth of a unit.

Example

The line segment is about 0.7 unit.

1. 0.3 unit
2. 0.4 unit
3. 0.6 unit
4. 0.9 unit

Thinking Skills: Analyzing parts and whole, Comparing

How can you check whether your measurement is accurate?

Divide the paper strip into 10 parts. Each part is equal to 0.1 unit.

48 Chapter 7 Decimals

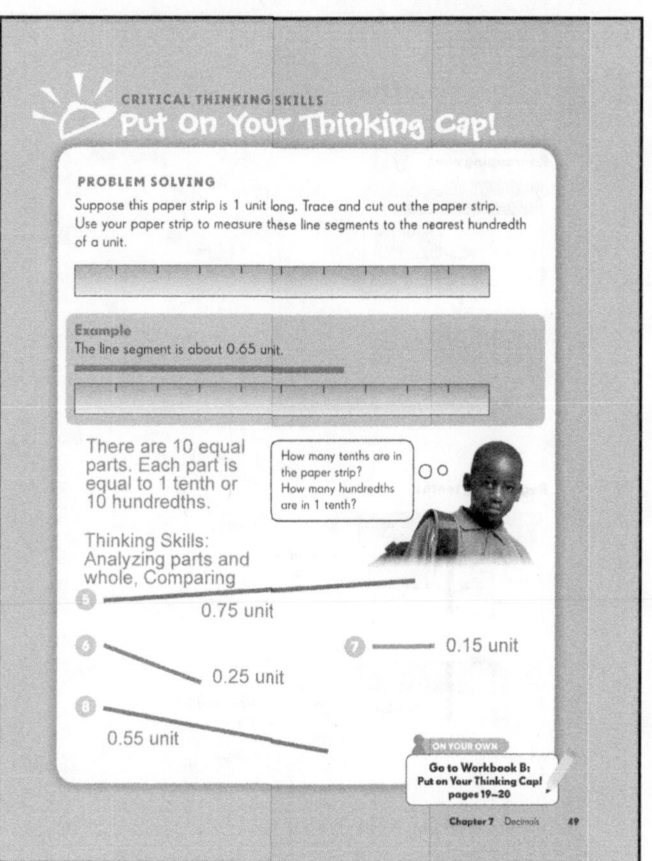

CRITICAL THINKING SKILLS

Put On Your Thinking Cap!

PROBLEM SOLVING

Suppose this paper strip is 1 unit long. Trace and cut out the paper strip. Use your paper strip to measure these line segments to the nearest hundredth of a unit.

Example

The line segment is about 0.65 unit.

There are 10 equal parts. Each part is equal to 1 tenth or 10 hundredths.

How many tenths are in the paper strip? How many hundredths are in 1 tenth?

Thinking Skills: Analyzing parts and whole, Comparing

5 0.75 unit

6 0.25 unit

7 0.15 unit

8 0.55 unit

ON YOUR OWN

Go to Workbook B: Put on Your Thinking Cap! pages 19–20

Chapter 7 Decimals 49

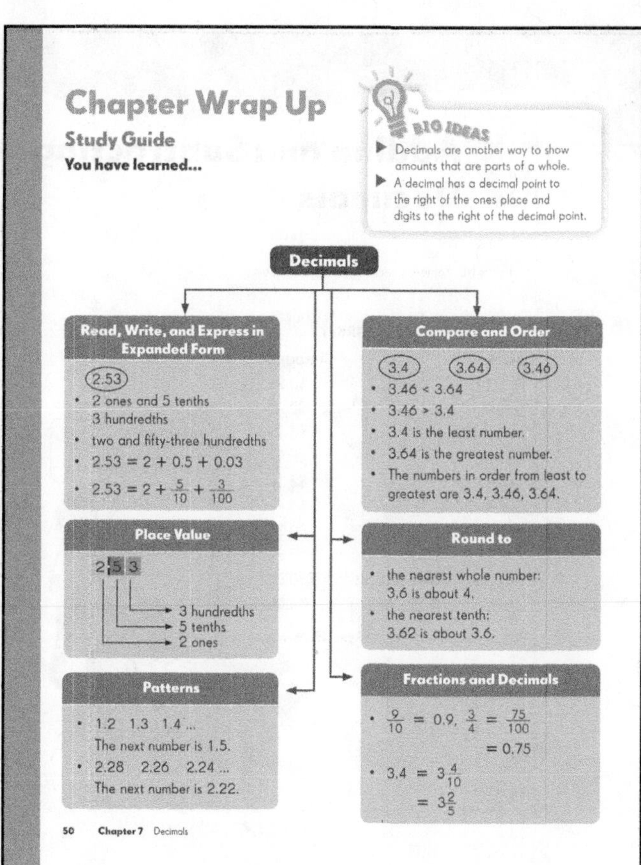

Chapter Wrap Up

Study Guide

You have learned...

BIG IDEAS

- Decimals are another way to show amounts that are parts of a whole.
- A decimal has a decimal point to the right of the ones place and digits to the right of the decimal point.

Decimals

Read, Write, and Express in Expanded Form

(2.53)

- 2 ones and 5 tenths 3 hundredths
- two and fifty-three hundredths
- 2.53 = 2 + 0.5 + 0.03
- $2.53 = 2 + \frac{5}{10} + \frac{3}{100}$

Place Value

2.5 3

3 hundredths
5 tenths
2 ones

Patterns

- 1.2 1.3 1.4 ...
  The next number is 1.5.
- 2.28 2.26 2.24 ...
  The next number is 2.22.

Compare and Order

(3.4) (3.64) (3.46)

- 3.46 < 3.64
- 3.46 > 3.4
- 3.4 is the least number.
- 3.64 is the greatest number.
- The numbers in order from least to greatest are 3.4, 3.46, 3.64.

Round to

- the nearest whole number:
  3.6 is about 4.
- the nearest tenth:
  3.62 is about 3.6.

Fractions and Decimals

- $\frac{9}{10} = 0.9$, $\frac{3}{4} = \frac{75}{100} = 0.75$
- $3.4 = 3\frac{4}{10} = 3\frac{2}{5}$

50 Chapter 7 Decimals

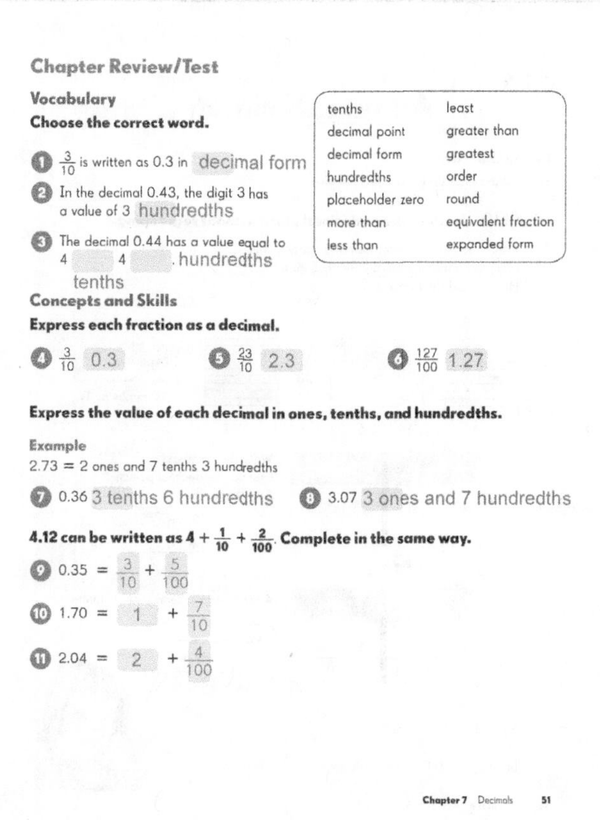

Chapter Review/Test

Vocabulary

Choose the correct word.

tenths	least
decimal point	greater than
decimal form	greatest
hundredths	order
placeholder zero	round
more than	equivalent fraction
less than	expanded form

1 $\frac{3}{10}$ is written as 0.3 in decimal form

2 In the decimal 0.43, the digit 3 has a value of 3 hundredths

3 The decimal 0.44 has a value equal to 4 tenths 4 hundredths

Concepts and Skills

Express each fraction as a decimal.

4 $\frac{3}{10}$ 0.3 5 $\frac{23}{10}$ 2.3 6 $\frac{127}{100}$ 1.27

Express the value of each decimal in ones, tenths, and hundredths.

Example

2.73 = 2 ones and 7 tenths 3 hundredths

7 0.36 3 tenths 6 hundredths 8 3.07 3 ones and 7 hundredths

4.12 can be written as $4 + \frac{1}{10} + \frac{2}{100}$. Complete in the same way.

9 $0.35 = \frac{3}{10} + \frac{5}{100}$

10 $1.70 = 1 + \frac{7}{10}$

11 $2.04 = 2 + \frac{4}{100}$

Chapter 7 Decimals 51

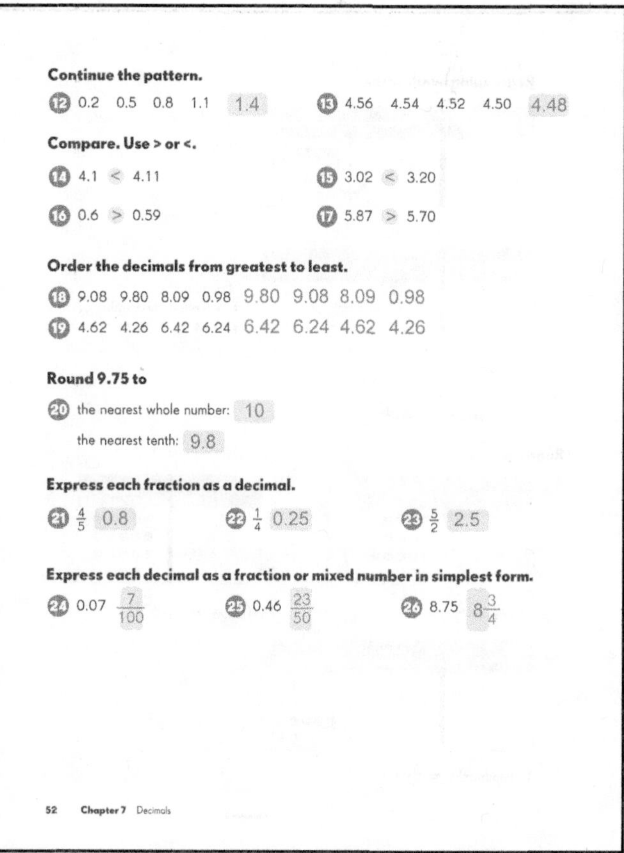

Continue the pattern.

12 0.2 0.5 0.8 1.1 1.4 13 4.56 4.54 4.52 4.50 4.48

Compare. Use > or <.

14 4.1 < 4.11 15 3.02 < 3.20

16 0.6 > 0.59 17 5.87 > 5.70

Order the decimals from greatest to least.

18 9.08 9.80 8.09 0.98 9.80 9.08 8.09 0.98

19 4.62 4.26 6.42 6.24 6.42 6.24 4.62 4.26

Round 9.75 to

20 the nearest whole number: 10

the nearest tenth: 9.8

Express each fraction as a decimal.

21 $\frac{4}{5}$ 0.8 22 $\frac{1}{4}$ 0.25 23 $\frac{5}{2}$ 2.5

Express each decimal as a fraction or mixed number in simplest form.

24 0.07 $\frac{7}{100}$ 25 0.46 $\frac{23}{50}$ 26 8.75 $8\frac{3}{4}$

52 Chapter 7 Decimals

Chapter 7

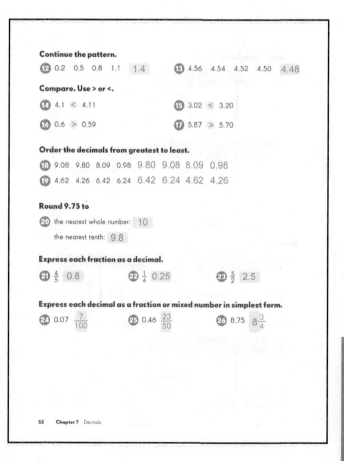

Chapter 8

Adding and Subtracting Decimals

This is Mr. Romero's receipt from a supermarket.

SUPER SAVE MARKET

Item	Amount
Broccoli	$3.38
Lettuce	$2.98
Grapefruit	$0.99
Chicken	$6.87
Tomato	$3.18
Grapes	$4.47
Apples	$3.87
Total	$25.74
Cash Payment	$30.00
Change	$4.26

Thank you for shopping at Super Save Market.

Add to find the total. Subtract to find the amount of change.
$30.00 − $25.74 = $4.26
I received $4.26 change.

Lessons

BIG IDEA

▶ Decimals can be added and subtracted in the same ways as whole numbers.

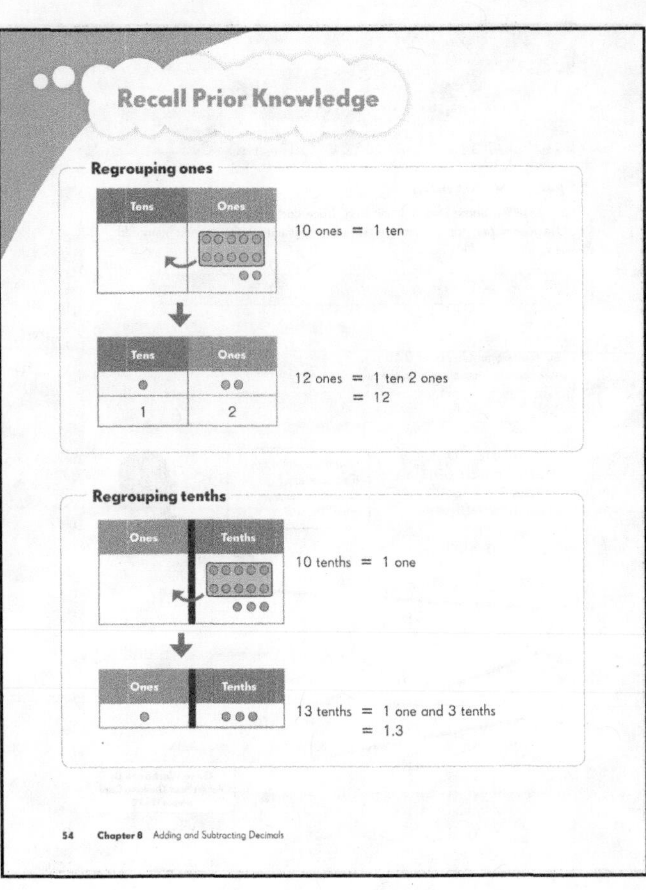

Recall Prior Knowledge

Regrouping ones

10 ones = 1 ten

Tens	Ones
1	2

12 ones = 1 ten 2 ones
= 12

Regrouping tenths

10 tenths = 1 one

13 tenths = 1 one and 3 tenths
= 1.3

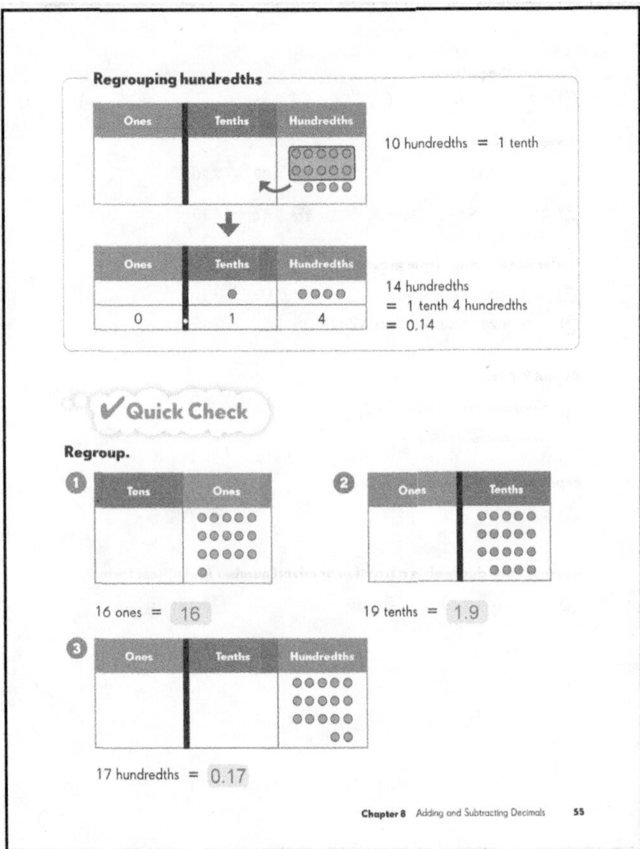

Regrouping hundredths

10 hundredths = 1 tenth

Ones	Tenths	Hundredths
0	1	4

14 hundredths
= 1 tenth 4 hundredths
= 0.14

✔ Quick Check

Regroup.

1. 16 ones = 16
2. 19 tenths = 1.9
3. 17 hundredths = 0.17

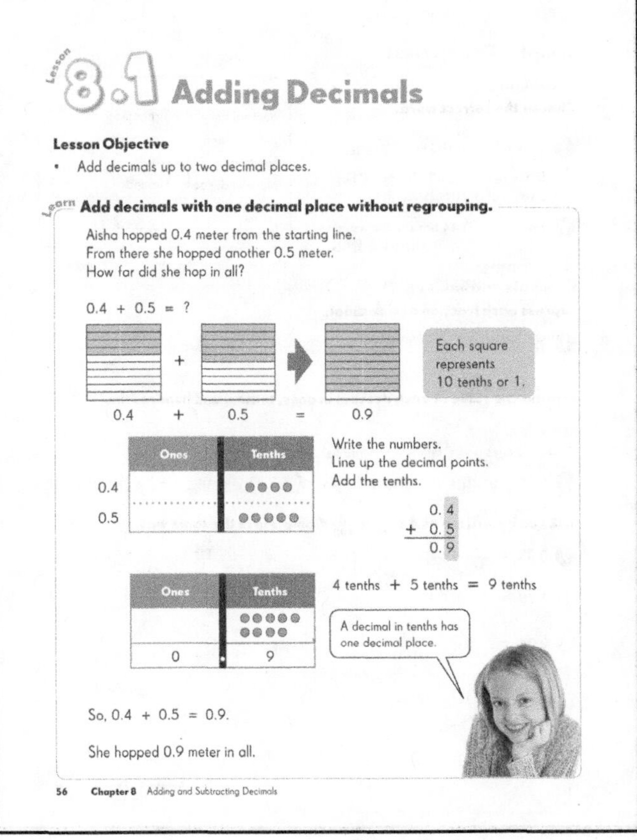

Lesson

8.1 Adding Decimals

Lesson Objective

- Add decimals up to two decimal places.

Learn **Add decimals with one decimal place without regrouping.**

Aisha hopped 0.4 meter from the starting line.
From there she hopped another 0.5 meter.
How far did she hop in all?

0.4 + 0.5 = ?

0.4 + 0.5 = 0.9

Each square represents 10 tenths or 1.

Write the numbers.
Line up the decimal points.
Add the tenths.

$$\begin{array}{r} 0.4 \\ +\ 0.5 \\ \hline 0.9 \end{array}$$

4 tenths + 5 tenths = 9 tenths

Ones	Tenths
0	9

A decimal in tenths has one decimal place.

So, 0.4 + 0.5 = 0.9.

She hopped 0.9 meter in all.

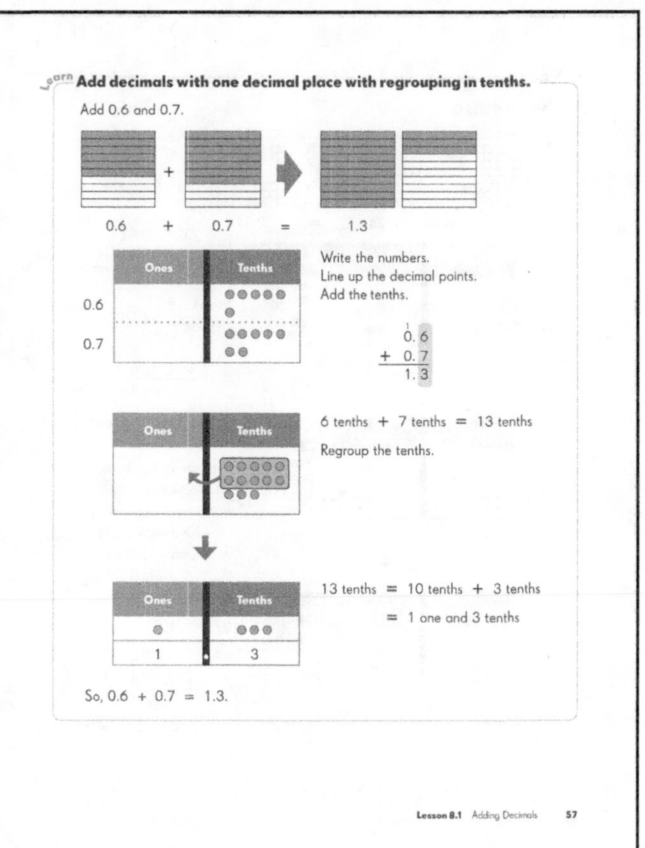

Learn **Add decimals with one decimal place with regrouping in tenths.**

Add 0.6 and 0.7.

0.6 + 0.7 = 1.3

	Ones	Tenths
0.6		●●●●● ●
0.7		●●●●● ●●

Write the numbers.
Line up the decimal points.
Add the tenths.

$$\begin{array}{r} \overset{1}{0}.6 \\ +\ 0.7 \\ \hline 1.3 \end{array}$$

6 tenths + 7 tenths = 13 tenths

Regroup the tenths.

Ones	Tenths
●	●●●
1	3

13 tenths = 10 tenths + 3 tenths
= 1 one and 3 tenths

So, 0.6 + 0.7 = 1.3.

Lesson 8.1 Adding Decimals 57

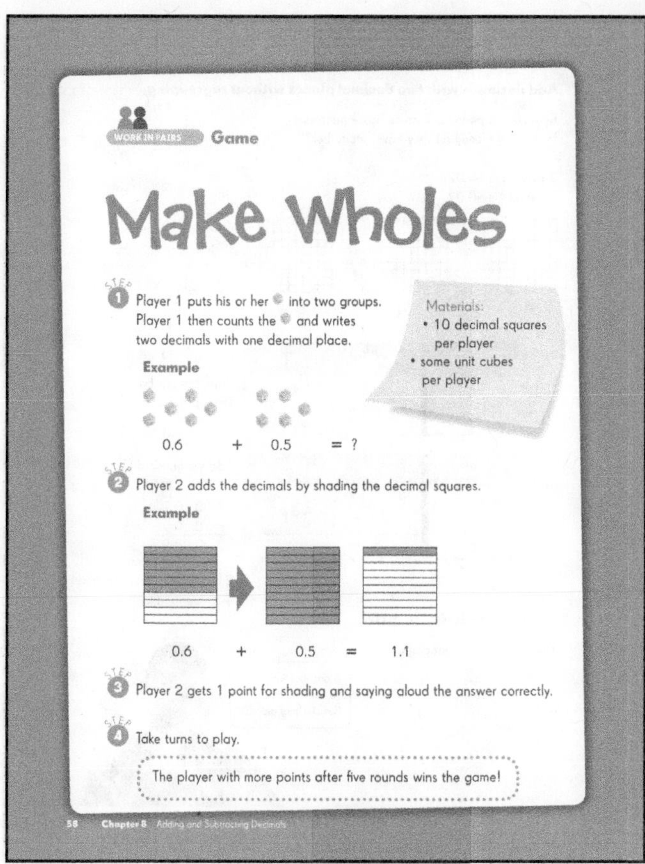

WORK IN PAIRS Game

Make Wholes

STEP 1 Player 1 puts his or her ● into two groups. Player 1 then counts the ● and writes two decimals with one decimal place.

Materials:
- 10 decimal squares per player
- some unit cubes per player

Example

0.6 + 0.5 = ?

STEP 2 Player 2 adds the decimals by shading the decimal squares.

Example

0.6 + 0.5 = 1.1

STEP 3 Player 2 gets 1 point for shading and saying aloud the answer correctly.

STEP 4 Take turns to play.

The player with more points after five rounds wins the game!

58 Chapter 8 Adding and Subtracting Decimals

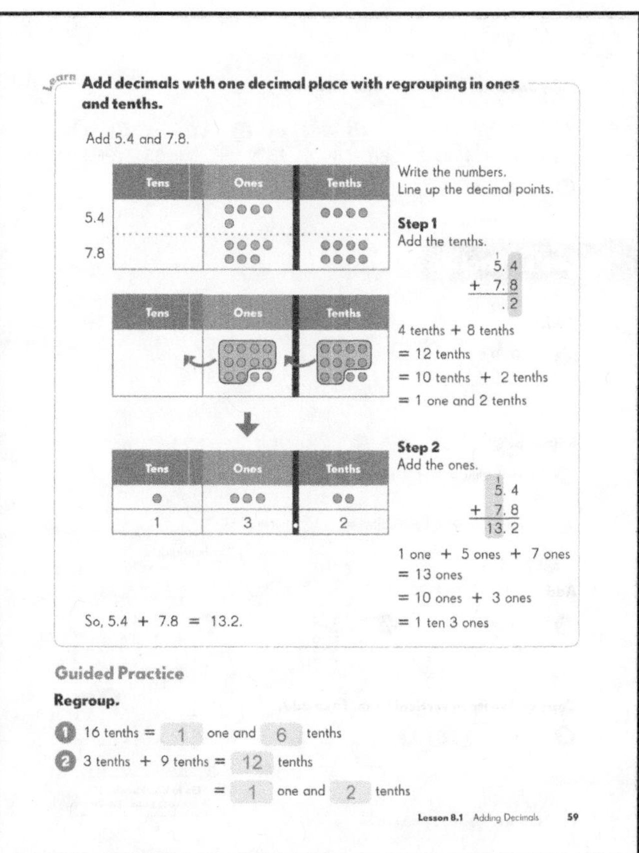

Learn **Add decimals with one decimal place with regrouping in ones and tenths.**

Add 5.4 and 7.8.

	Tens	Ones	Tenths
5.4		●●●●●	●●●●
7.8		●●●●●●●	●●●●●●●●

Write the numbers.
Line up the decimal points.

Step 1
Add the tenths.

$$\begin{array}{r} \overset{1}{5}.4 \\ +\ 7.8 \\ \hline .2 \end{array}$$

4 tenths + 8 tenths
= 12 tenths
= 10 tenths + 2 tenths
= 1 one and 2 tenths

Tens	Ones	Tenths
●	●●●	●●
1	3	2

Step 2
Add the ones.

$$\begin{array}{r} \overset{1}{5}.4 \\ +\ 7.8 \\ \hline 13.2 \end{array}$$

1 one + 5 ones + 7 ones
= 13 ones
= 10 ones + 3 ones
= 1 ten 3 ones

So, 5.4 + 7.8 = 13.2.

Guided Practice

Regroup.

1. 16 tenths = 1 one and 6 tenths
2. 3 tenths + 9 tenths = 12 tenths
   = 1 one and 2 tenths

Lesson 8.1 Adding Decimals 59

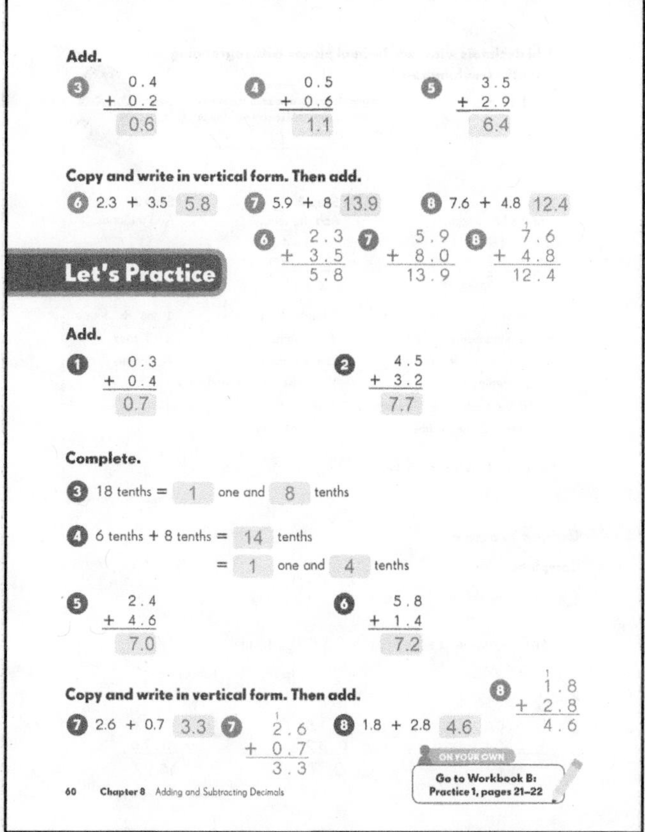

Add.

3. 0.4 + 0.2 = 0.6
4. 0.5 + 0.6 = 1.1
5. 3.5 + 2.9 = 6.4

Copy and write in vertical form. Then add.

6. 2.3 + 3.5 = 5.8
7. 5.9 + 8 = 13.9
8. 7.6 + 4.8 = 12.4

$$\begin{array}{r} 2.3 \\ +\ 3.5 \\ \hline 5.8 \end{array} \qquad \begin{array}{r} 5.9 \\ +\ 8.0 \\ \hline 13.9 \end{array} \qquad \begin{array}{r} 7.6 \\ +\ 4.8 \\ \hline 12.4 \end{array}$$

Let's Practice

Add.

1. 0.3 + 0.4 = 0.7
2. 4.5 + 3.2 = 7.7

Complete.

3. 18 tenths = 1 one and 8 tenths
4. 6 tenths + 8 tenths = 14 tenths
   = 1 one and 4 tenths
5. 2.4 + 4.6 = 7.0
6. 5.8 + 1.4 = 7.2

Copy and write in vertical form. Then add.

7. 2.6 + 0.7 = 3.3
8. 1.8 + 2.8 = 4.6

$$\begin{array}{r} \overset{1}{2}.6 \\ +\ 0.7 \\ \hline 3.3 \end{array} \qquad \begin{array}{r} \overset{1}{1}.8 \\ +\ 2.8 \\ \hline 4.6 \end{array}$$

ON YOUR OWN
Go to Workbook B: Practice 1, pages 21–22

60 Chapter 8 Adding and Subtracting Decimals

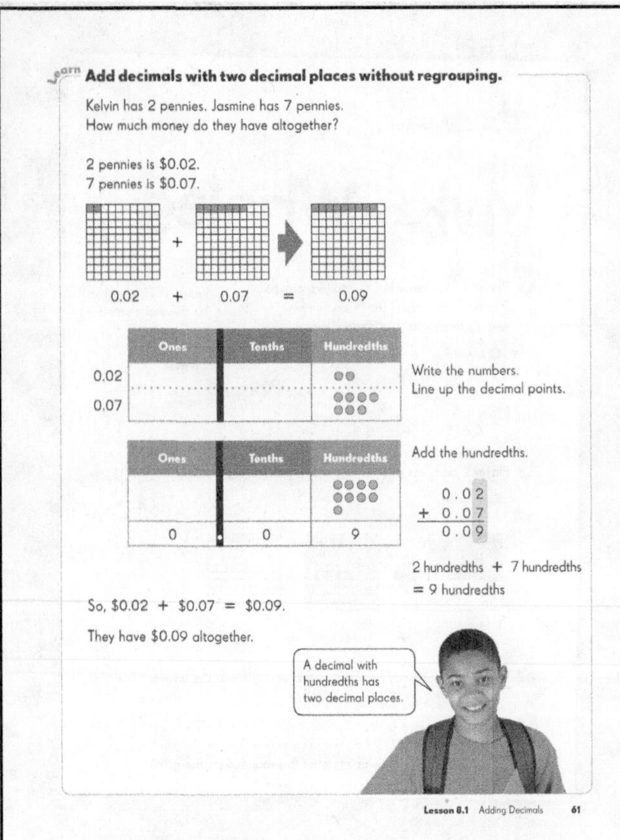

Learn Add decimals with two decimal places without regrouping.

Kelvin has 2 pennies. Jasmine has 7 pennies.
How much money do they have altogether?

2 pennies is \$0.02.
7 pennies is \$0.07.

0.02 + 0.07 = 0.09

	Ones	Tenths	Hundredths
0.02			●●
0.07			●●●●●●●

Write the numbers.
Line up the decimal points.

Ones	Tenths	Hundredths
		●●●●●●●●●
0	0	9

Add the hundredths.

$$\begin{array}{r} 0.02 \\ +\ 0.07 \\ \hline 0.09 \end{array}$$

2 hundredths + 7 hundredths
= 9 hundredths

So, \$0.02 + \$0.07 = \$0.09.

They have \$0.09 altogether.

A decimal with hundredths has two decimal places.

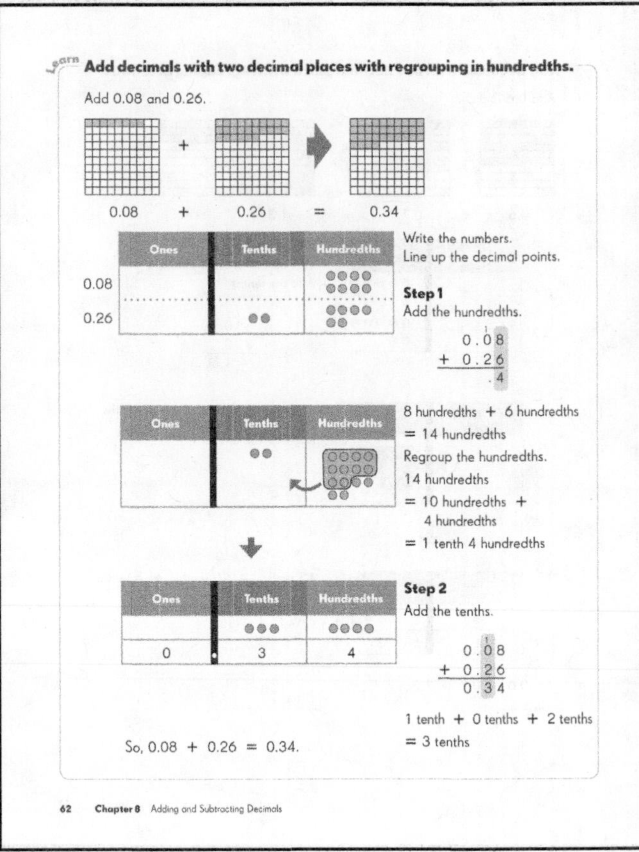

Learn Add decimals with two decimal places with regrouping in hundredths.

Add 0.08 and 0.26.

0.08 + 0.26 = 0.34

	Ones	Tenths	Hundredths
0.08			●●●●●●●●
0.26		●●	●●●●●●

Write the numbers.
Line up the decimal points.

Step 1
Add the hundredths.

$$\begin{array}{r} \overset{1}{0}.08 \\ +\ 0.26 \\ \hline .\ 4 \end{array}$$

Ones	Tenths	Hundredths
	●●	●●●●●●●●●●●●●●

8 hundredths + 6 hundredths
= 14 hundredths
Regroup the hundredths.
14 hundredths
= 10 hundredths +
4 hundredths
= 1 tenth 4 hundredths

Ones	Tenths	Hundredths
	●●●	●●●●
0	3	4

Step 2
Add the tenths.

$$\begin{array}{r} 0.08 \\ +\ 0.26 \\ \hline 0.34 \end{array}$$

1 tenth + 0 tenths + 2 tenths
= 3 tenths

So, 0.08 + 0.26 = 0.34.

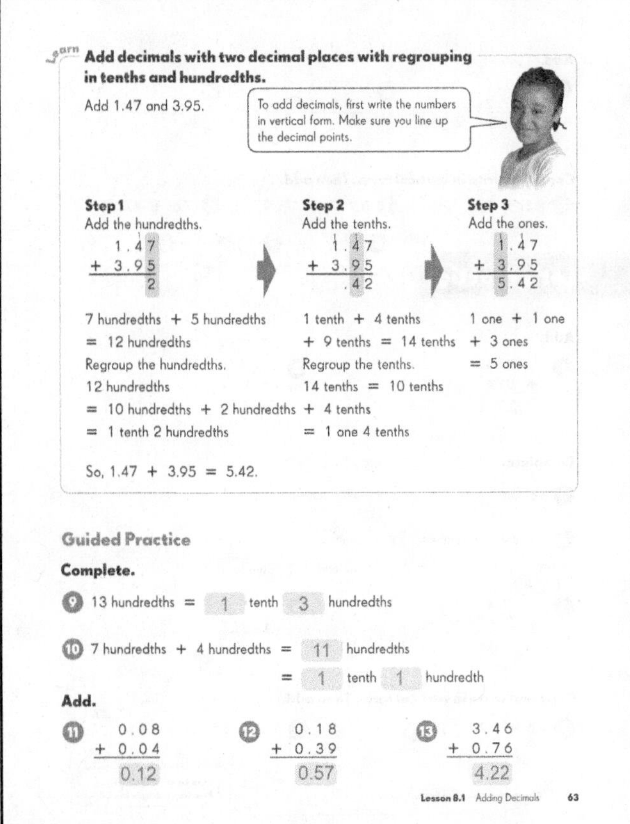

Learn Add decimals with two decimal places with regrouping in tenths and hundredths.

Add 1.47 and 3.95.

To add decimals, first write the numbers in vertical form. Make sure you line up the decimal points.

Step 1
Add the hundredths.

$$\begin{array}{r} 1.47 \\ +\ 3.95 \\ \hline 2 \end{array}$$

7 hundredths + 5 hundredths
= 12 hundredths
Regroup the hundredths.
12 hundredths
= 10 hundredths + 2 hundredths
= 1 tenth 2 hundredths

Step 2
Add the tenths.

$$\begin{array}{r} 1.47 \\ +\ 3.95 \\ \hline .42 \end{array}$$

1 tenth + 4 tenths
+ 9 tenths = 14 tenths
Regroup the tenths.
14 tenths = 10 tenths
+ 4 tenths
= 1 one 4 tenths

Step 3
Add the ones.

$$\begin{array}{r} 1.47 \\ +\ 3.95 \\ \hline 5.42 \end{array}$$

1 one + 1 one
+ 3 ones
= 5 ones

So, 1.47 + 3.95 = 5.42.

Guided Practice

Complete.

9. 13 hundredths = 1 tenth 3 hundredths

10. 7 hundredths + 4 hundredths = 11 hundredths
= 1 tenth 1 hundredth

Add.

11. 0.08 + 0.04 = 0.12

12. 0.18 + 0.39 = 0.57

13. 3.46 + 0.76 = 4.22

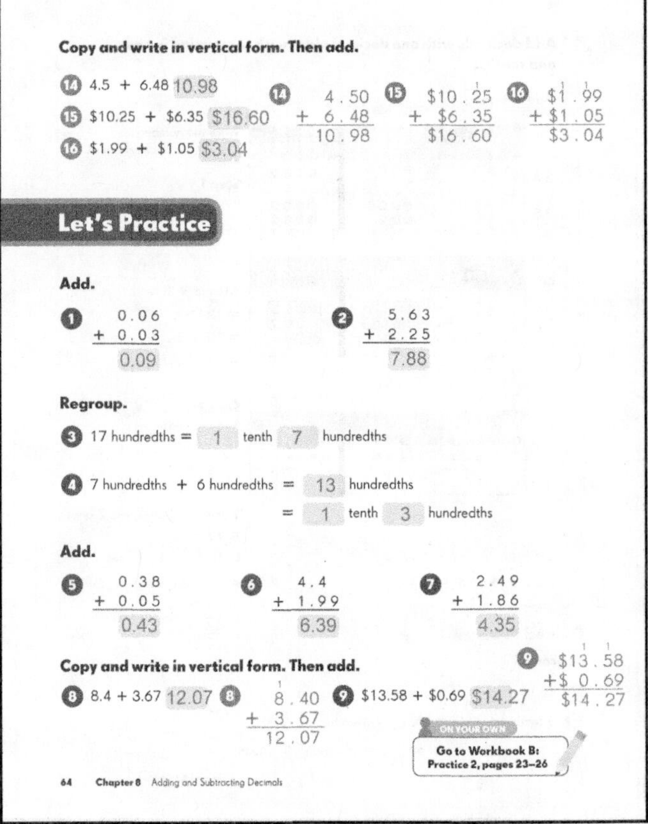

Copy and write in vertical form. Then add.

14. 4.5 + 6.48 10.98

15. \$10.25 + \$6.35 \$16.60

16. \$1.99 + \$1.05 \$3.04

$$\begin{array}{r} 4.50 \\ +\ 6.48 \\ \hline 10.98 \end{array} \qquad \begin{array}{r} \$10.25 \\ +\ \$6.35 \\ \hline \$16.60 \end{array} \qquad \begin{array}{r} \$1.99 \\ +\ \$1.05 \\ \hline \$3.04 \end{array}$$

Let's Practice

Add.

1. 0.06 + 0.03 = 0.09

2. 5.63 + 2.25 = 7.88

Regroup.

3. 17 hundredths = 1 tenth 7 hundredths

4. 7 hundredths + 6 hundredths = 13 hundredths
= 1 tenth 3 hundredths

Add.

5. 0.38 + 0.05 = 0.43

6. 4.4 + 1.99 = 6.39

7. 2.49 + 1.86 = 4.35

Copy and write in vertical form. Then add.

8. 8.4 + 3.67 12.07

$$\begin{array}{r} 8.40 \\ +\ 3.67 \\ \hline 12.07 \end{array}$$

9. \$13.58 + \$0.69 \$14.27

$$\begin{array}{r} \$13.58 \\ +\ \$0.69 \\ \hline \$14.27 \end{array}$$

ON YOUR OWN
Go to Workbook B: Practice 2, pages 23–26

Lesson 8.2 Subtracting Decimals

Lesson Objective

- Subtract decimals up to two decimal places.

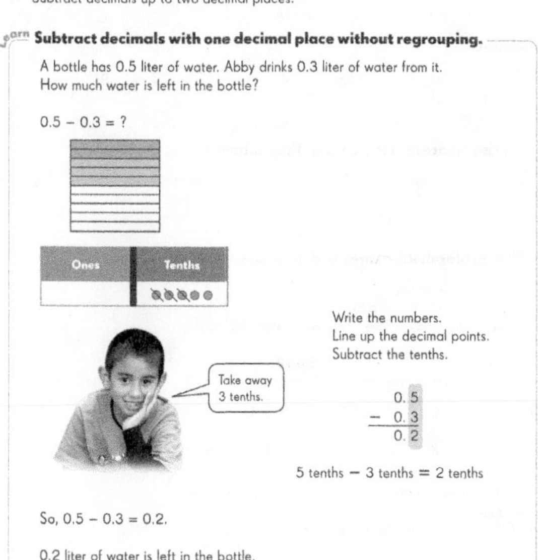

Learn Subtract decimals with one decimal place without regrouping.

A bottle has 0.5 liter of water. Abby drinks 0.3 liter of water from it.
How much water is left in the bottle?

0.5 − 0.3 = ?

Ones	Tenths
	●●●●●

Take away 3 tenths.

Write the numbers.
Line up the decimal points.
Subtract the tenths.

$$\begin{array}{r} 0.5 \\ -\ 0.3 \\ \hline 0.2 \end{array}$$

5 tenths − 3 tenths = 2 tenths

So, 0.5 − 0.3 = 0.2.

0.2 liter of water is left in the bottle.

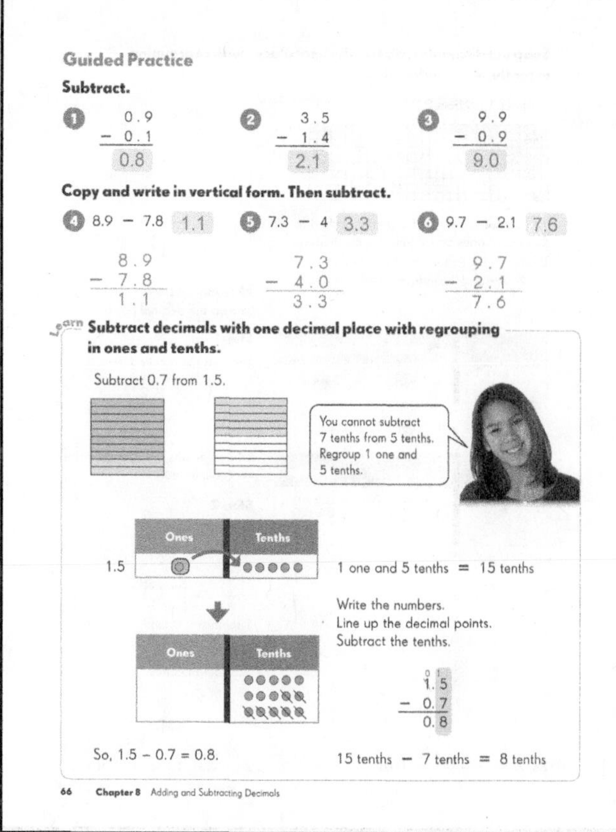

Guided Practice

Subtract.

1. $\begin{array}{r} 0.9 \\ -\ 0.1 \\ \hline 0.8 \end{array}$
2. $\begin{array}{r} 3.5 \\ -\ 1.4 \\ \hline 2.1 \end{array}$
3. $\begin{array}{r} 9.9 \\ -\ 0.9 \\ \hline 9.0 \end{array}$

Copy and write in vertical form. Then subtract.

4. 8.9 − 7.8 **1.1** $\begin{array}{r} 8.9 \\ -\ 7.8 \\ \hline 1.1 \end{array}$
5. 7.3 − 4 **3.3** $\begin{array}{r} 7.3 \\ -\ 4.0 \\ \hline 3.3 \end{array}$
6. 9.7 − 2.1 **7.6** $\begin{array}{r} 9.7 \\ -\ 2.1 \\ \hline 7.6 \end{array}$

Learn Subtract decimals with one decimal place with regrouping in ones and tenths.

Subtract 0.7 from 1.5.

You cannot subtract 7 tenths from 5 tenths. Regroup 1 one and 5 tenths.

	Ones	Tenths
1.5	●	●●●●●

1 one and 5 tenths = 15 tenths

Write the numbers.
Line up the decimal points.
Subtract the tenths.

$$\begin{array}{r} \overset{0}{1}.\overset{1}{5} \\ -\ 0.7 \\ \hline 0.8 \end{array}$$

So, 1.5 − 0.7 = 0.8.

15 tenths − 7 tenths = 8 tenths

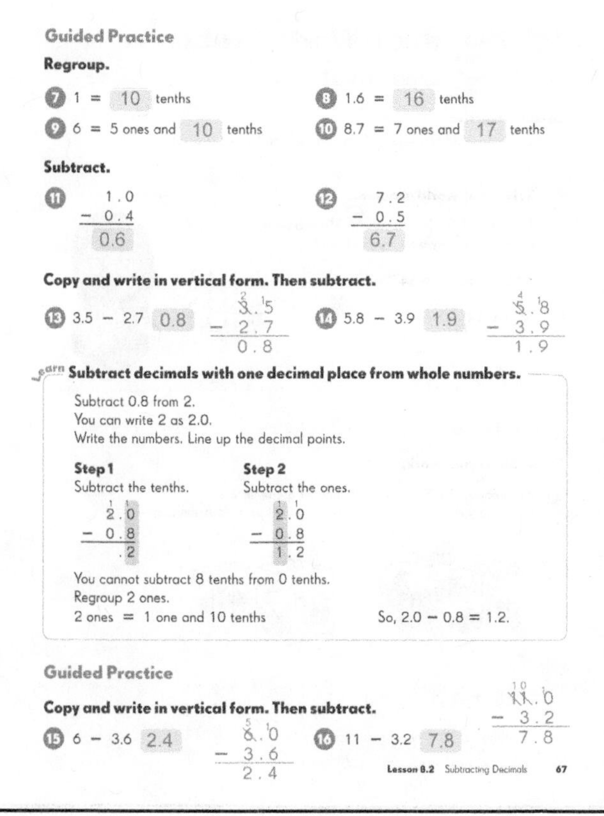

Guided Practice

Regroup.

7. 1 = **10** tenths
8. 1.6 = **16** tenths
9. 6 = 5 ones and **10** tenths
10. 8.7 = 7 ones and **17** tenths

Subtract.

11. $\begin{array}{r} 1.0 \\ -\ 0.4 \\ \hline 0.6 \end{array}$
12. $\begin{array}{r} 7.2 \\ -\ 0.5 \\ \hline 6.7 \end{array}$

Copy and write in vertical form. Then subtract.

13. 3.5 − 2.7 **0.8** $\begin{array}{r} 3.5 \\ -\ 2.7 \\ \hline 0.8 \end{array}$
14. 5.8 − 3.9 **1.9** $\begin{array}{r} 5.8 \\ -\ 3.9 \\ \hline 1.9 \end{array}$

Learn Subtract decimals with one decimal place from whole numbers.

Subtract 0.8 from 2.
You can write 2 as 2.0.
Write the numbers. Line up the decimal points.

Step 1
Subtract the tenths.

$$\begin{array}{r} 2.0 \\ -\ 0.8 \\ \hline .2 \end{array}$$

Step 2
Subtract the ones.

$$\begin{array}{r} 2.0 \\ -\ 0.8 \\ \hline 1.2 \end{array}$$

You cannot subtract 8 tenths from 0 tenths.
Regroup 2 ones.
2 ones = 1 one and 10 tenths

So, 2.0 − 0.8 = 1.2.

Guided Practice

Copy and write in vertical form. Then subtract.

15. 6 − 3.6 **2.4** $\begin{array}{r} 6.0 \\ -\ 3.6 \\ \hline 2.4 \end{array}$
16. 11 − 3.2 **7.8** $\begin{array}{r} 11.0 \\ -\ 3.2 \\ \hline 7.8 \end{array}$

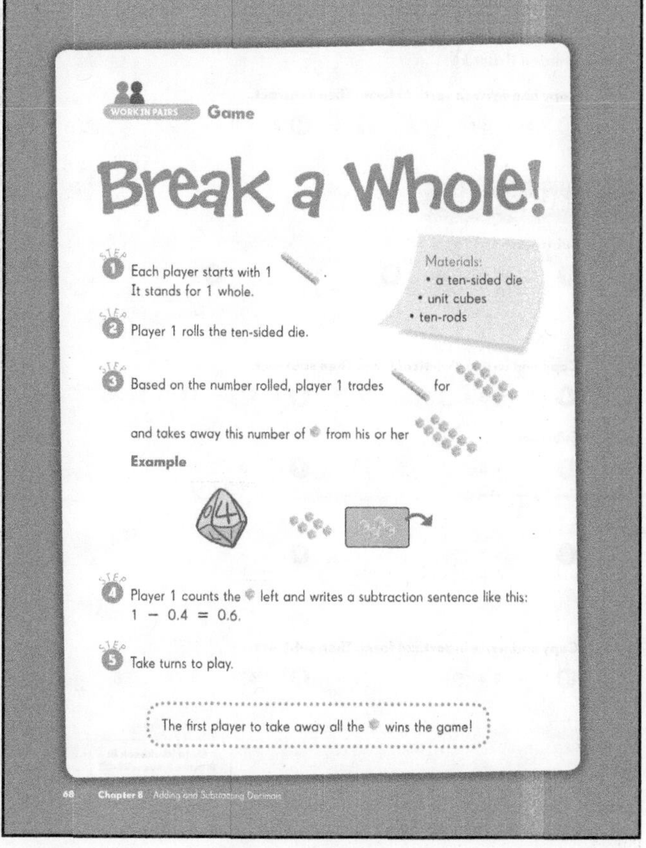

WORK IN PAIRS **Game**

Break a Whole!

Materials:
- a ten-sided die
- unit cubes
- ten-rods

1. Each player starts with 1 ten-rod. It stands for 1 whole.
2. Player 1 rolls the ten-sided die.
3. Based on the number rolled, player 1 trades the ten-rod for ten unit cubes and takes away this number of cubes from his or her ten unit cubes.

Example

4. Player 1 counts the cubes left and writes a subtraction sentence like this:
1 − 0.4 = 0.6.
5. Take turns to play.

The first player to take away all the cubes wins the game!

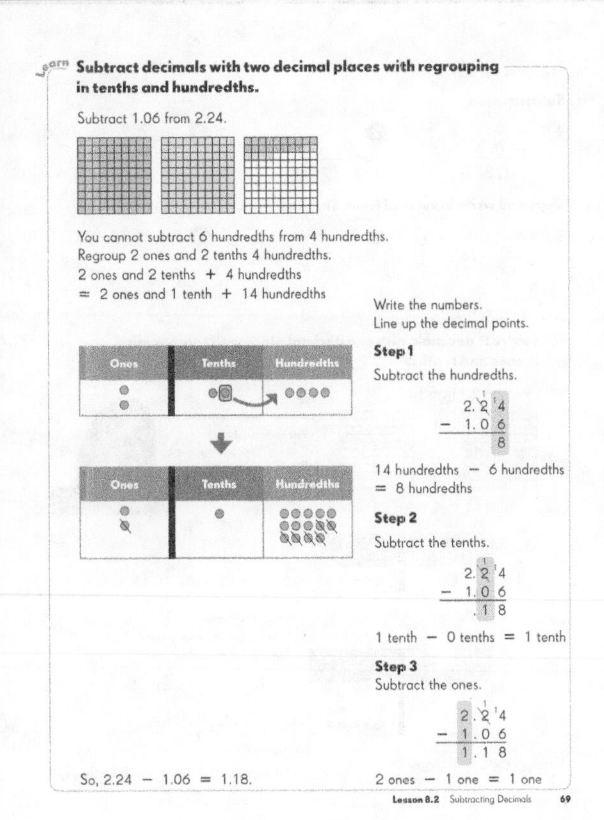

Learn **Subtract decimals with two decimal places with regrouping in tenths and hundredths.**

Subtract 1.06 from 2.24.

You cannot subtract 6 hundredths from 4 hundredths.
Regroup 2 ones and 2 tenths 4 hundredths.
2 ones and 2 tenths + 4 hundredths
= 2 ones and 1 tenth + 14 hundredths

Write the numbers.
Line up the decimal points.

Ones	Tenths	Hundredths

Step 1
Subtract the hundredths.

2.2 4
− 1.0 6
8

14 hundredths − 6 hundredths = 8 hundredths

Step 2
Subtract the tenths.

2.2 4
− 1.0 6
.1 8

1 tenth − 0 tenths = 1 tenth

Step 3
Subtract the ones.

2.2 4
− 1.0 6
1.1 8

So, 2.24 − 1.06 = 1.18.

2 ones − 1 one = 1 one

Lesson 8.2 Subtracting Decimals 69

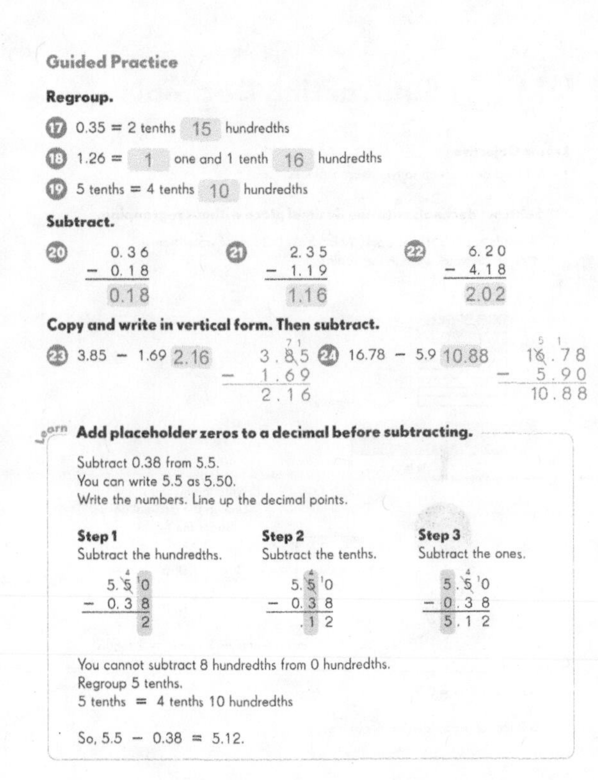

Guided Practice

Regroup.

17 0.35 = 2 tenths 15 hundredths

18 1.26 = 1 one and 1 tenth 16 hundredths

19 5 tenths = 4 tenths 10 hundredths

Subtract.

20 0.36 − 0.18 = 0.18

21 2.35 − 1.19 = 1.16

22 6.20 − 4.18 = 2.02

Copy and write in vertical form. Then subtract.

23 3.85 − 1.69 2.16

3.8 5
− 1.6 9
2.1 6

24 16.78 − 5.9 10.88

16.7 8
− 5.9 0
10.8 8

Learn **Add placeholder zeros to a decimal before subtracting.**

Subtract 0.38 from 5.5.
You can write 5.5 as 5.50.
Write the numbers. Line up the decimal points.

Step 1
Subtract the hundredths.

5.5 0
− 0.3 8
2

Step 2
Subtract the tenths.

5.5 0
− 0.3 8
.1 2

Step 3
Subtract the ones.

5.5 0
− 0.3 8
5.1 2

You cannot subtract 8 hundredths from 0 hundredths.
Regroup 5 tenths.
5 tenths = 4 tenths 10 hundredths

So, 5.5 − 0.38 = 5.12.

70 Chapter 8 Adding and Subtracting Decimals

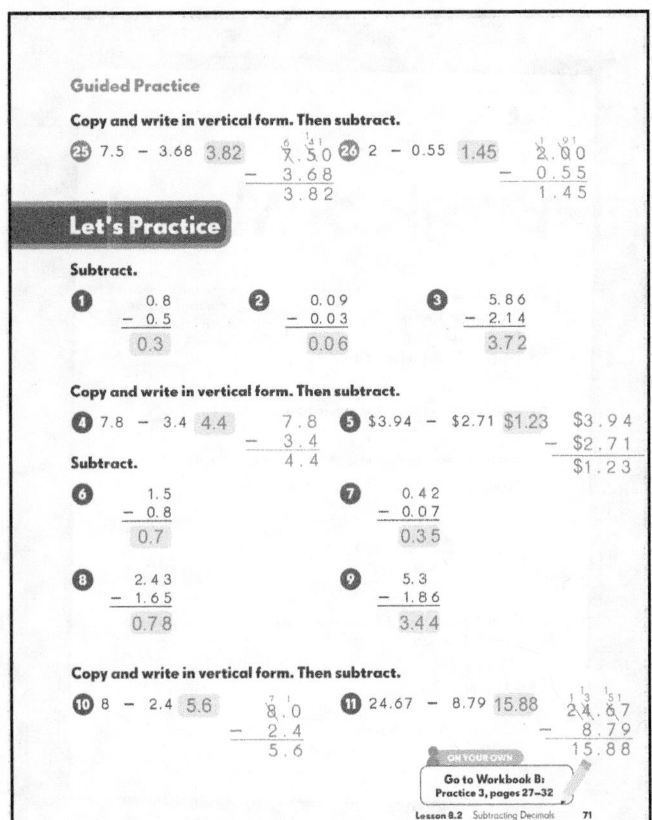

Guided Practice

Copy and write in vertical form. Then subtract.

25 7.5 − 3.68 3.82

7.5 0
− 3.6 8
3.8 2

26 2 − 0.55 1.45

2.0 0
− 0.5 5
1.4 5

Let's Practice

Subtract.

1 0.8 − 0.5 = 0.3

2 0.09 − 0.03 = 0.06

3 5.86 − 2.14 = 3.72

Copy and write in vertical form. Then subtract.

4 7.8 − 3.4 4.4

7.8
− 3.4
4.4

5 $3.94 − $2.71 $1.23

$3.9 4
− $2.7 1
$1.2 3

Subtract.

6 1.5 − 0.8 = 0.7

7 0.42 − 0.07 = 0.35

8 2.43 − 1.65 = 0.78

9 5.3 − 1.86 = 3.44

Copy and write in vertical form. Then subtract.

10 8 − 2.4 5.6

8.0
− 2.4
5.6

11 24.67 − 8.79 15.88

24.6 7
− 8.7 9
15.8 8

ON YOUR OWN
Go to Workbook B: Practice 3, pages 27–32

Lesson 8.2 Subtracting Decimals 71

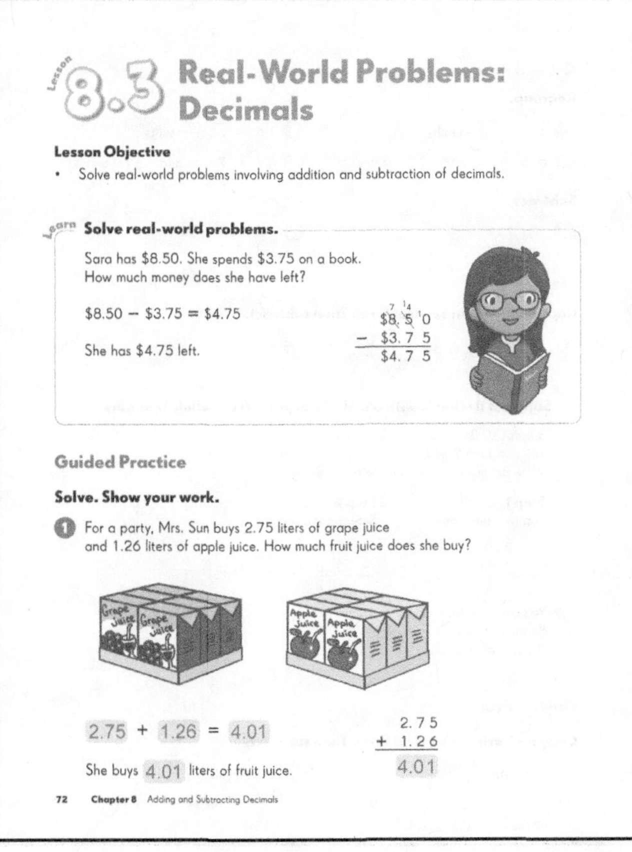

Lesson 8.3 Real-World Problems: Decimals

Lesson Objective

- Solve real-world problems involving addition and subtraction of decimals.

Learn **Solve real-world problems.**

Sara has $8.50. She spends $3.75 on a book.
How much money does she have left?

$8.50 − $3.75 = $4.75

$8.5 0
− $3.7 5
$4.7 5

She has $4.75 left.

Guided Practice

Solve. Show your work.

1 For a party, Mrs. Sun buys 2.75 liters of grape juice and 1.26 liters of apple juice. How much fruit juice does she buy?

2.75 + 1.26 = 4.01

2.7 5
+ 1.2 6
4.0 1

She buys 4.01 liters of fruit juice.

72 Chapter 8 Adding and Subtracting Decimals

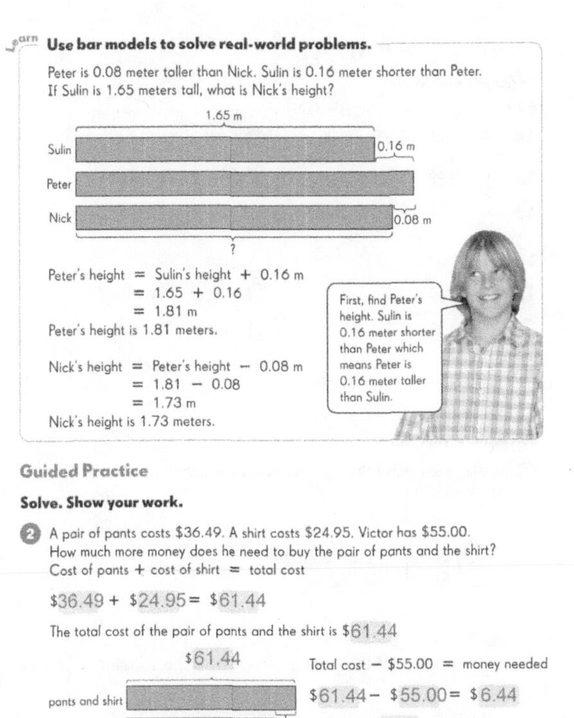

Learn **Use bar models to solve real-world problems.**

Peter is 0.08 meter taller than Nick. Sulin is 0.16 meter shorter than Peter. If Sulin is 1.65 meters tall, what is Nick's height?

Peter's height = Sulin's height + 0.16 m
= 1.65 + 0.16
= 1.81 m

Peter's height is 1.81 meters.

Nick's height = Peter's height − 0.08 m
= 1.81 − 0.08
= 1.73 m

Nick's height is 1.73 meters.

Guided Practice

Solve. Show your work.

2. A pair of pants costs $36.49. A shirt costs $24.95. Victor has $55.00. How much more money does he need to buy the pair of pants and the shirt?

Cost of pants + cost of shirt = total cost

$36.49 + $24.95 = $61.44

The total cost of the pair of pants and the shirt is $61.44

Total cost − $55.00 = money needed

$61.44 − $55.00 = $6.44

He needs $6.44 more to buy the pair of pants and the shirt.

Lesson 8.3 Real-World Problems: Decimals 73

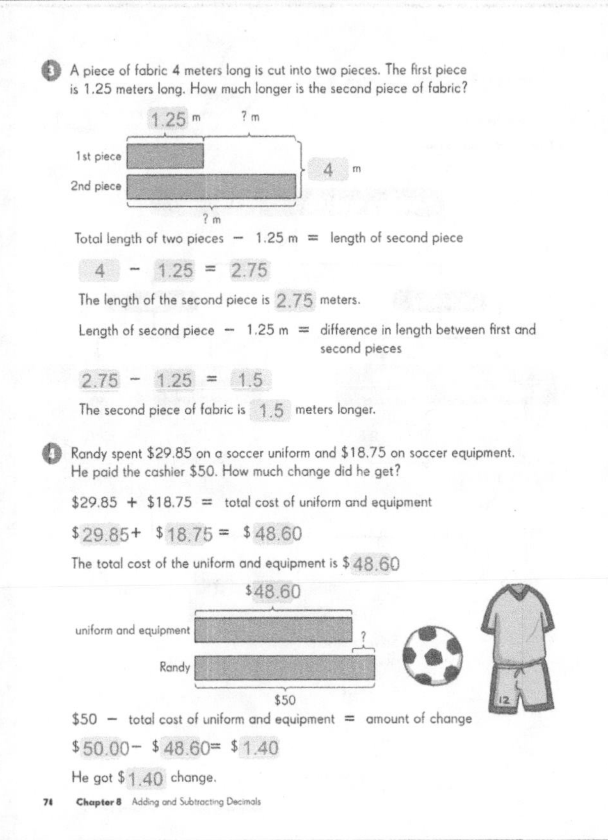

3. A piece of fabric 4 meters long is cut into two pieces. The first piece is 1.25 meters long. How much longer is the second piece of fabric?

Total length of two pieces − 1.25 m = length of second piece

4 − 1.25 = 2.75

The length of the second piece is 2.75 meters.

Length of second piece − 1.25 m = difference in length between first and second pieces

2.75 − 1.25 = 1.5

The second piece of fabric is 1.5 meters longer.

4. Randy spent $29.85 on a soccer uniform and $18.75 on soccer equipment. He paid the cashier $50. How much change did he get?

$29.85 + $18.75 = total cost of uniform and equipment

$29.85 + $18.75 = $48.60

The total cost of the uniform and equipment is $48.60

$50 − total cost of uniform and equipment = amount of change

$50.00 − $48.60 = $1.40

He got $1.40 change.

74 Chapter 8 Adding and Subtracting Decimals

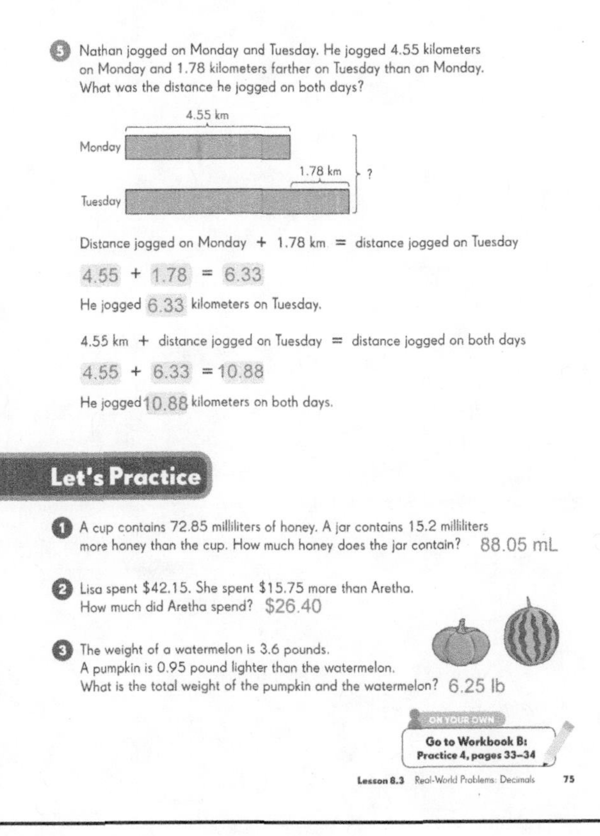

5. Nathan jogged on Monday and Tuesday. He jogged 4.55 kilometers on Monday and 1.78 kilometers farther on Tuesday than on Monday. What was the distance he jogged on both days?

Distance jogged on Monday + 1.78 km = distance jogged on Tuesday

4.55 + 1.78 = 6.33

He jogged 6.33 kilometers on Tuesday.

4.55 km + distance jogged on Tuesday = distance jogged on both days

4.55 + 6.33 = 10.88

He jogged 10.88 kilometers on both days.

Let's Practice

1. A cup contains 72.85 milliliters of honey. A jar contains 15.2 milliliters more honey than the cup. How much honey does the jar contain? 88.05 mL
2. Lisa spent $42.15. She spent $15.75 more than Aretha. How much did Aretha spend? $26.40
3. The weight of a watermelon is 3.6 pounds. A pumpkin is 0.95 pound lighter than the watermelon. What is the total weight of the pumpkin and the watermelon? 6.25 lb

ON YOUR OWN
Go to Workbook B: Practice 4, pages 33–34

Lesson 8.3 Real-World Problems: Decimals 75

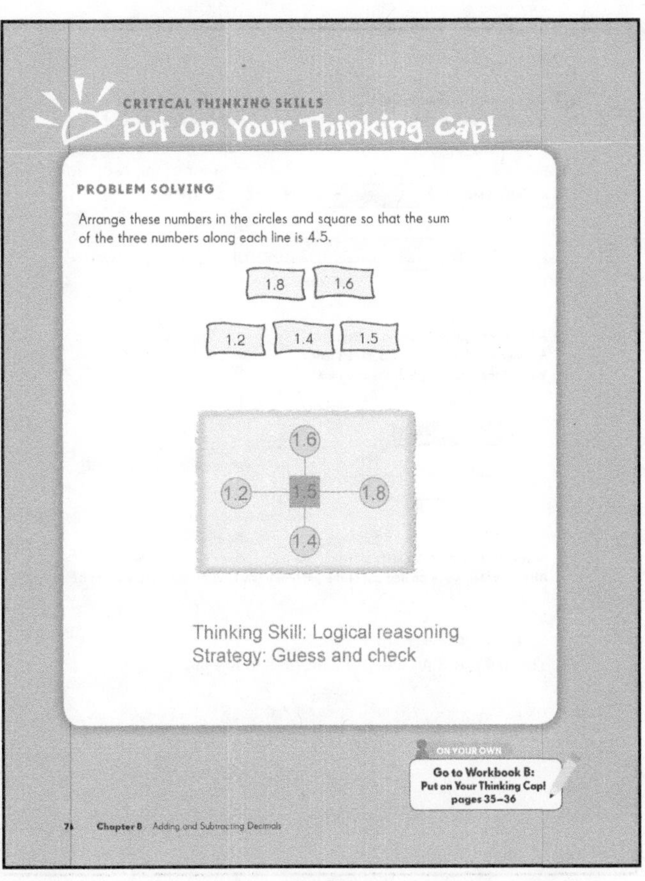

CRITICAL THINKING SKILLS

Put On Your Thinking Cap!

PROBLEM SOLVING

Arrange these numbers in the circles and square so that the sum of the three numbers along each line is 4.5.

Thinking Skill: Logical reasoning
Strategy: Guess and check

ON YOUR OWN
Go to Workbook B: Put on Your Thinking Cap! pages 35–36

76 Chapter 8 Adding and Subtracting Decimals

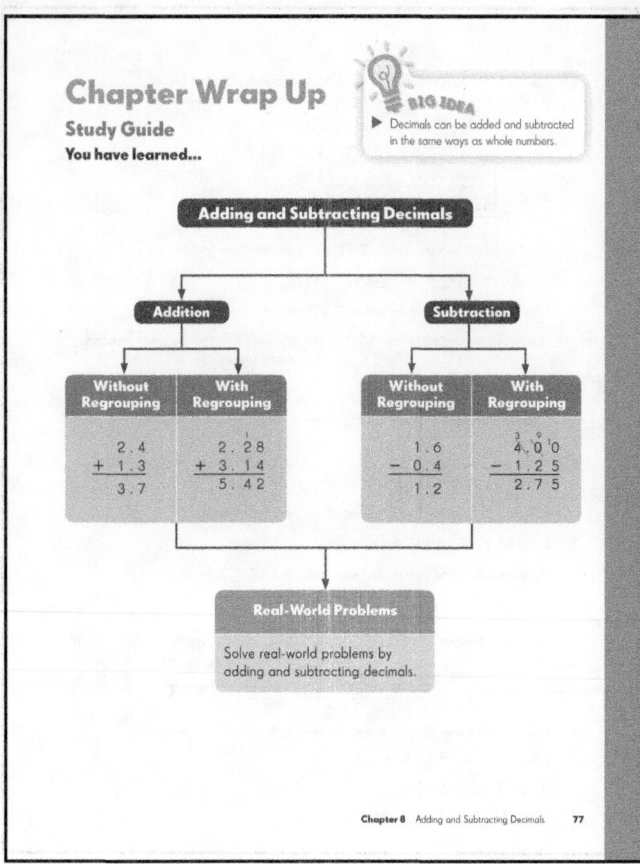

Chapter Wrap Up

Study Guide

You have learned...

BIG IDEA

▶ Decimals can be added and subtracted in the same ways as whole numbers.

Adding and Subtracting Decimals

Addition

Without Regrouping	With Regrouping
2.4 + 1.3 = 3.7	2.28 + 3.14 = 5.42

Subtraction

Without Regrouping	With Regrouping
1.6 − 0.4 = 1.2	4.00 − 1.25 = 2.75

Real-World Problems

Solve real-world problems by adding and subtracting decimals.

Chapter 8 Adding and Subtracting Decimals 77

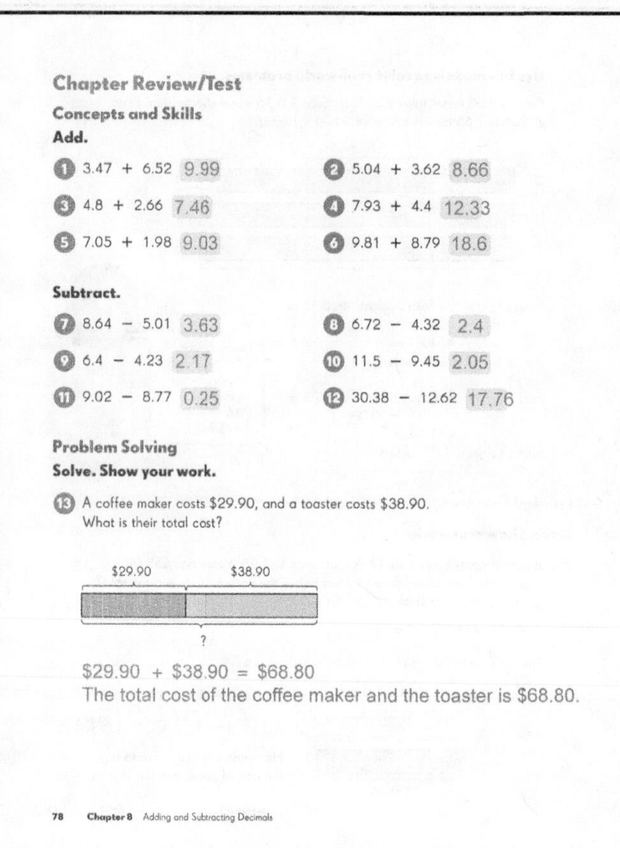

Chapter Review/Test

Concepts and Skills

Add.

1. 3.47 + 6.52 9.99
2. 5.04 + 3.62 8.66
3. 4.8 + 2.66 7.46
4. 7.93 + 4.4 12.33
5. 7.05 + 1.98 9.03
6. 9.81 + 8.79 18.6

Subtract.

7. 8.64 − 5.01 3.63
8. 6.72 − 4.32 2.4
9. 6.4 − 4.23 2.17
10. 11.5 − 9.45 2.05
11. 9.02 − 8.77 0.25
12. 30.38 − 12.62 17.76

Problem Solving

Solve. Show your work.

13. A coffee maker costs $29.90, and a toaster costs $38.90. What is their total cost?

$29.90 + $38.90 = $68.80

The total cost of the coffee maker and the toaster is $68.80.

78 **Chapter 8** Adding and Subtracting Decimals

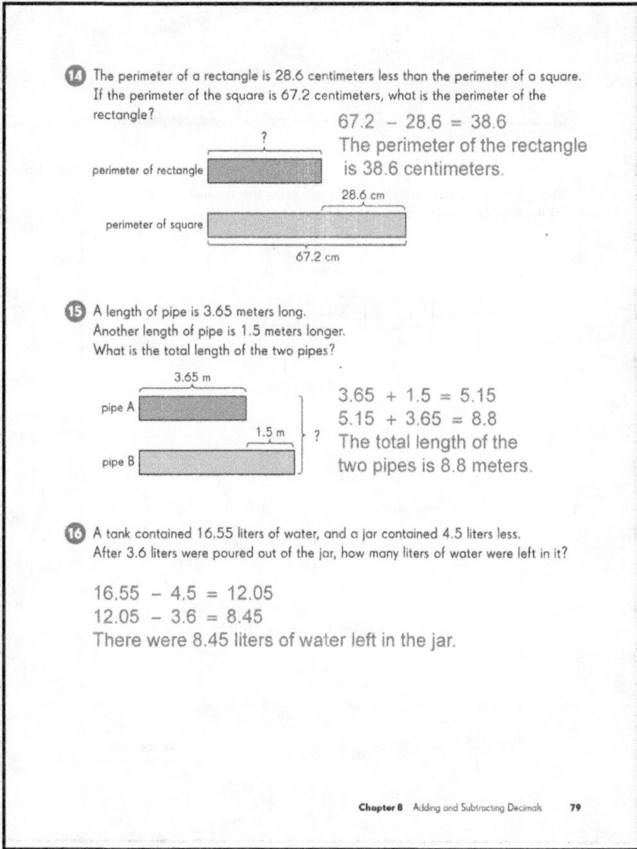

14. The perimeter of a rectangle is 28.6 centimeters less than the perimeter of a square. If the perimeter of the square is 67.2 centimeters, what is the perimeter of the rectangle?

67.2 − 28.6 = 38.6

The perimeter of the rectangle is 38.6 centimeters.

15. A length of pipe is 3.65 meters long. Another length of pipe is 1.5 meters longer. What is the total length of the two pipes?

3.65 + 1.5 = 5.15

5.15 + 3.65 = 8.8

The total length of the two pipes is 8.8 meters.

16. A tank contained 16.55 liters of water, and a jar contained 4.5 liters less. After 3.6 liters were poured out of the jar, how many liters of water were left in it?

16.55 − 4.5 = 12.05

12.05 − 3.6 = 8.45

There were 8.45 liters of water left in the jar.

Chapter 8 Adding and Subtracting Decimals 79

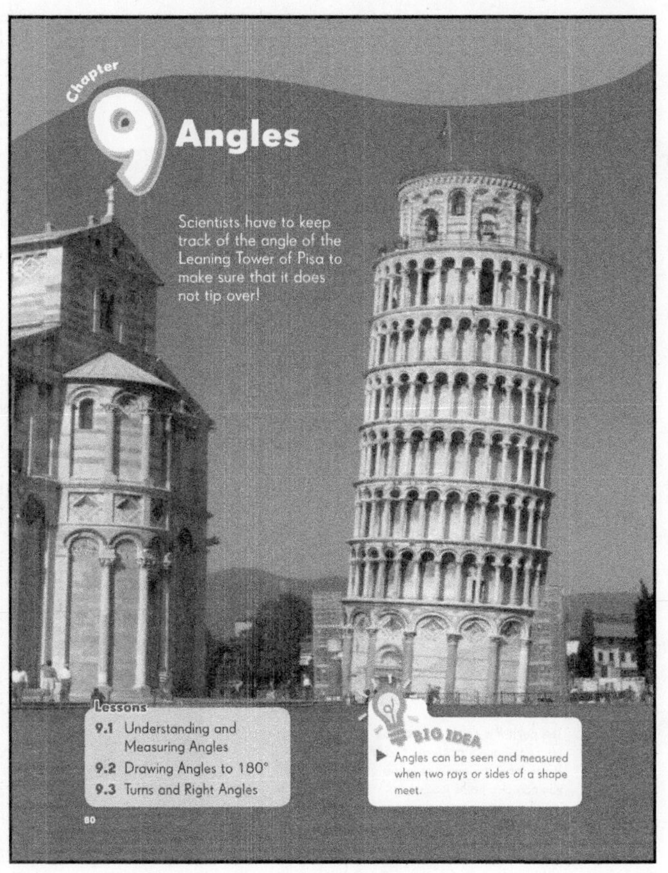

Chapter 9 Angles

Scientists have to keep track of the angle of the Leaning Tower of Pisa to make sure that it does not tip over!

Lessons
9.1 Understanding and Measuring Angles
9.2 Drawing Angles to 180°
9.3 Turns and Right Angles

BIG IDEA
▶ Angles can be seen and measured when two rays or sides of a shape meet.

80

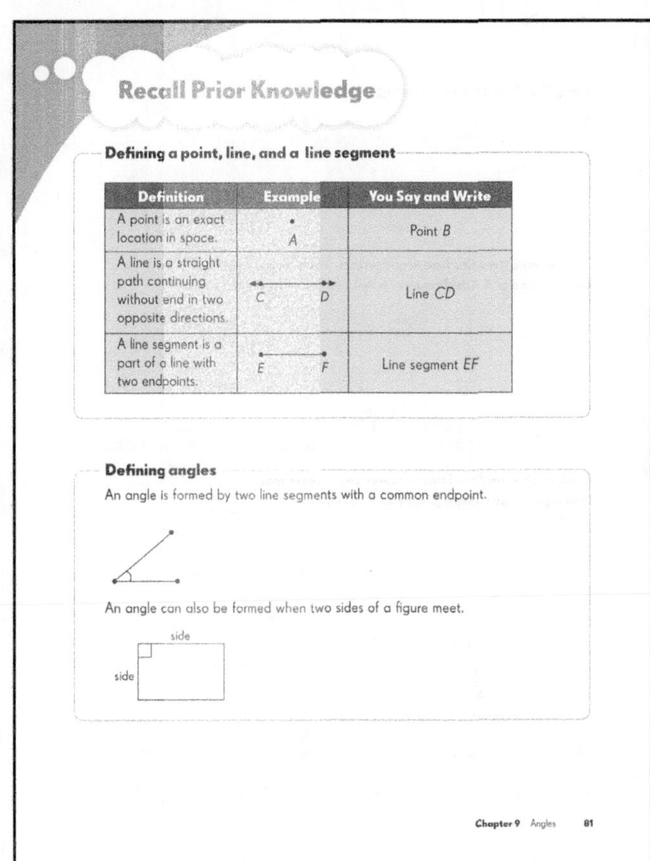

Recall Prior Knowledge

Defining a point, line, and a line segment

Definition	Example	You Say and Write
A point is an exact location in space.	• A	Point *B*
A line is a straight path continuing without end in two opposite directions.	C D	Line *CD*
A line segment is a part of a line with two endpoints.	E F	Line segment *EF*

Defining angles

An angle is formed by two line segments with a common endpoint.

An angle can also be formed when two sides of a figure meet.

Chapter 9 Angles 81

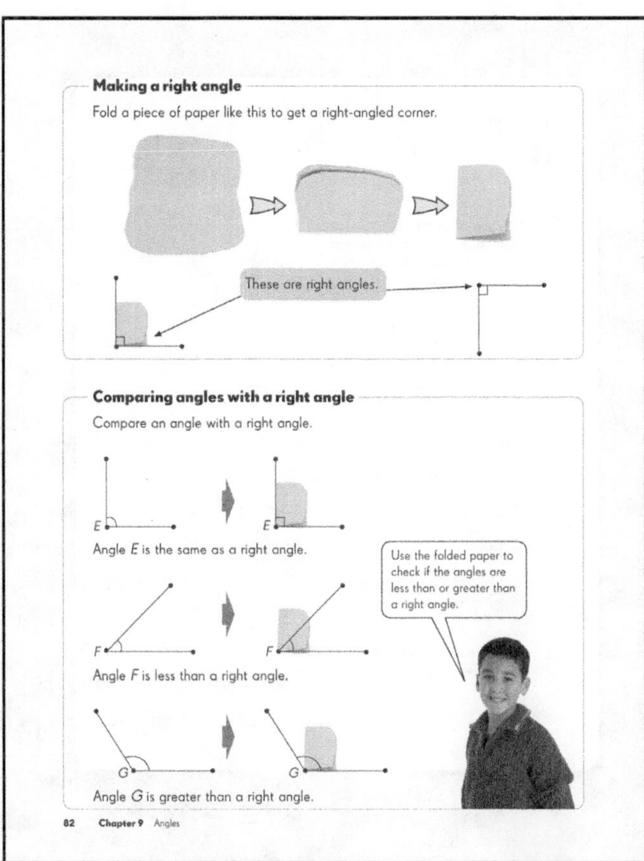

Making a right angle

Fold a piece of paper like this to get a right-angled corner.

Comparing angles with a right angle

Compare an angle with a right angle.

Angle *E* is the same as a right angle.

Angle *F* is less than a right angle.

Angle *G* is greater than a right angle.

82 Chapter 9 Angles

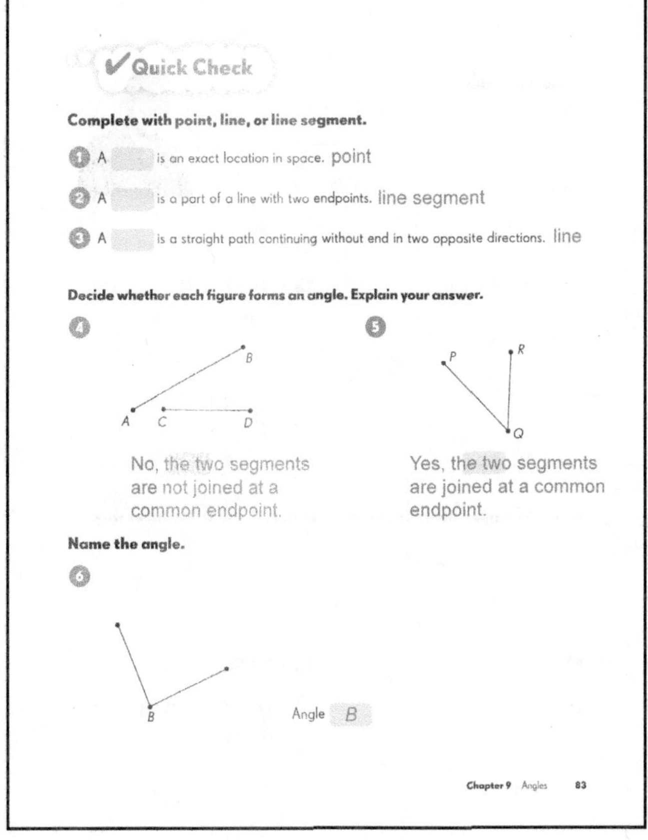

✔ Quick Check

Complete with point, line, or line segment.

1. A ____ is an exact location in space. point
2. A ____ is a part of a line with two endpoints. line segment
3. A ____ is a straight path continuing without end in two opposite directions. line

Decide whether each figure forms an angle. Explain your answer.

4.
No, the two segments are not joined at a common endpoint.

5.
Yes, the two segments are joined at a common endpoint.

Name the angle.

6.
Angle B

Chapter 9 Angles 83

Chapter 9

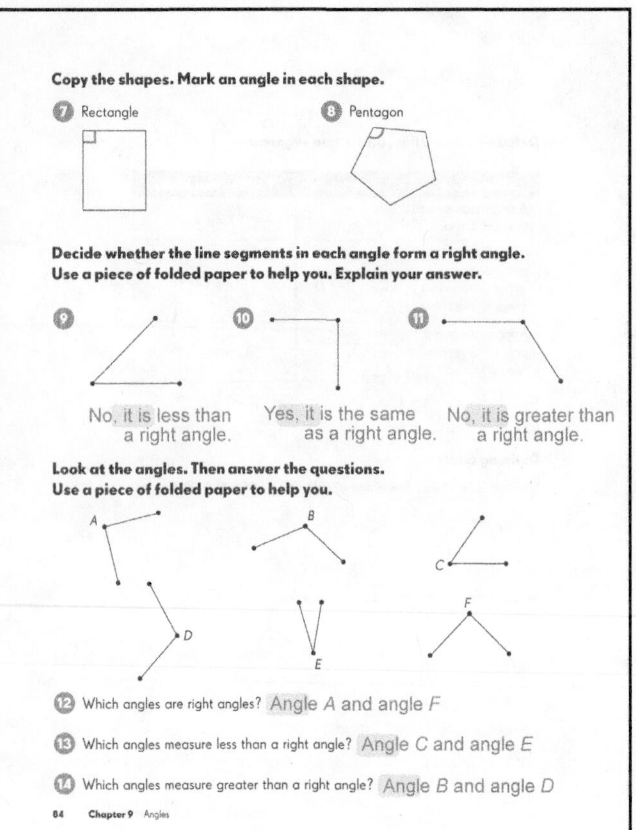
Copy the shapes. Mark an angle in each shape.

7 Rectangle

8 Pentagon

Decide whether the line segments in each angle form a right angle. Use a piece of folded paper to help you. Explain your answer.

9 No, it is less than a right angle.

10 Yes, it is the same as a right angle.

11 No, it is greater than a right angle.

Look at the angles. Then answer the questions. Use a piece of folded paper to help you.

12 Which angles are right angles? Angle *A* and angle *F*

13 Which angles measure less than a right angle? Angle *C* and angle *E*

14 Which angles measure greater than a right angle? Angle *B* and angle *D*

84 Chapter 9 Angles

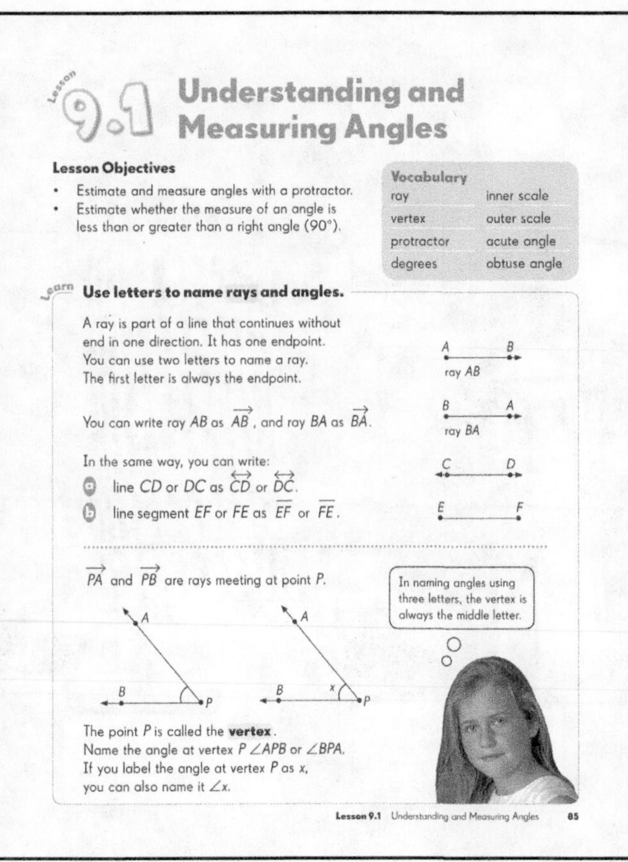
Lesson 9.1 Understanding and Measuring Angles

Lesson Objectives

- Estimate and measure angles with a protractor.
- Estimate whether the measure of an angle is less than or greater than a right angle (90°).

Vocabulary

ray	inner scale
vertex	outer scale
protractor	acute angle
degrees	obtuse angle

Learn Use letters to name rays and angles.

A ray is part of a line that continues without end in one direction. It has one endpoint. You can use two letters to name a ray. The first letter is always the endpoint.

You can write ray *AB* as $\overrightarrow{AB}$, and ray *BA* as $\overrightarrow{BA}$.

In the same way, you can write:

a line *CD* or *DC* as $\overleftrightarrow{CD}$ or $\overleftrightarrow{DC}$.

b line segment *EF* or *FE* as $\overline{EF}$ or $\overline{FE}$.

$\overrightarrow{PA}$ and $\overrightarrow{PB}$ are rays meeting at point *P*.

In naming angles using three letters, the vertex is always the middle letter.

The point *P* is called the **vertex**.
Name the angle at vertex *P* ∠*APB* or ∠*BPA*.
If you label the angle at vertex *P* as *x*, you can also name it ∠*x*.

Lesson 9.1 Understanding and Measuring Angles 85

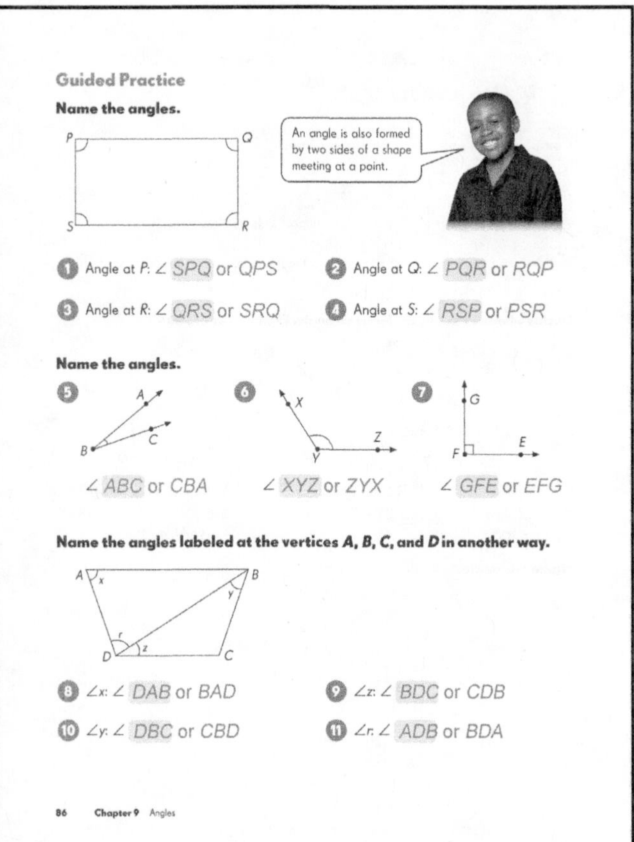
Guided Practice

Name the angles.

An angle is also formed by two sides of a shape meeting at a point.

1 Angle at *P*: ∠ SPQ or QPS

2 Angle at *Q*: ∠ PQR or RQP

3 Angle at *R*: ∠ QRS or SRQ

4 Angle at *S*: ∠ RSP or PSR

Name the angles.

5 ∠ ABC or CBA

6 ∠ XYZ or ZYX

7 ∠ GFE or EFG

Name the angles labeled at the vertices *A*, *B*, *C*, and *D* in another way.

8 ∠*x*: ∠ DAB or BAD

9 ∠*z*: ∠ BDC or CDB

10 ∠*y*: ∠ DBC or CBD

11 ∠*r*: ∠ ADB or BDA

86 Chapter 9 Angles

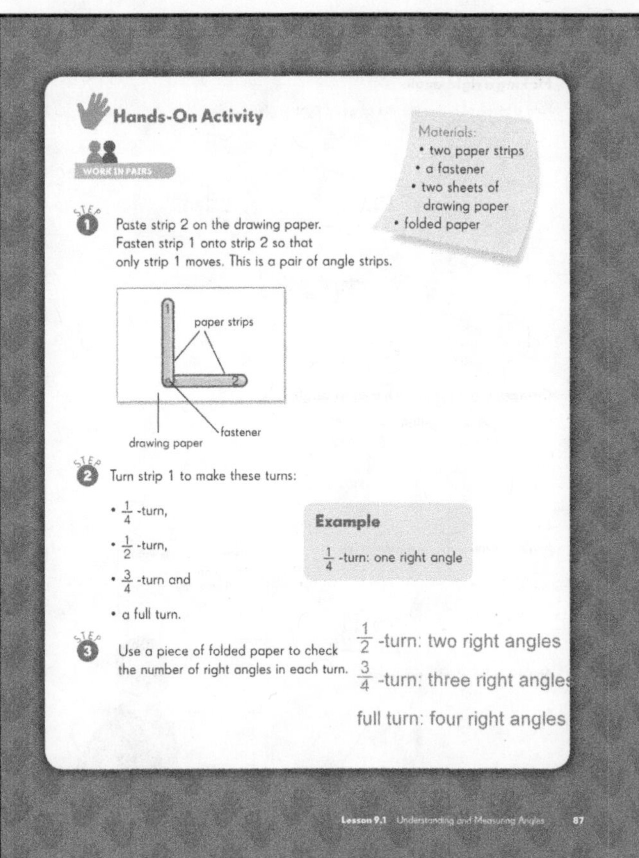
Hands-On Activity

WORK IN PAIRS

Materials:
- two paper strips
- a fastener
- two sheets of drawing paper
- folded paper

STEP 1 Paste strip 2 on the drawing paper. Fasten strip 1 onto strip 2 so that only strip 1 moves. This is a pair of angle strips.

STEP 2 Turn strip 1 to make these turns:

- $\frac{1}{4}$ -turn,
- $\frac{1}{2}$ -turn,
- $\frac{3}{4}$ -turn and
- a full turn.

Example

$\frac{1}{4}$ -turn: one right angle

STEP 3 Use a piece of folded paper to check the number of right angles in each turn.

$\frac{1}{2}$ -turn: two right angles

$\frac{3}{4}$ -turn: three right angles

full turn: four right angles

Lesson 9.1 Understanding and Measuring Angles 87

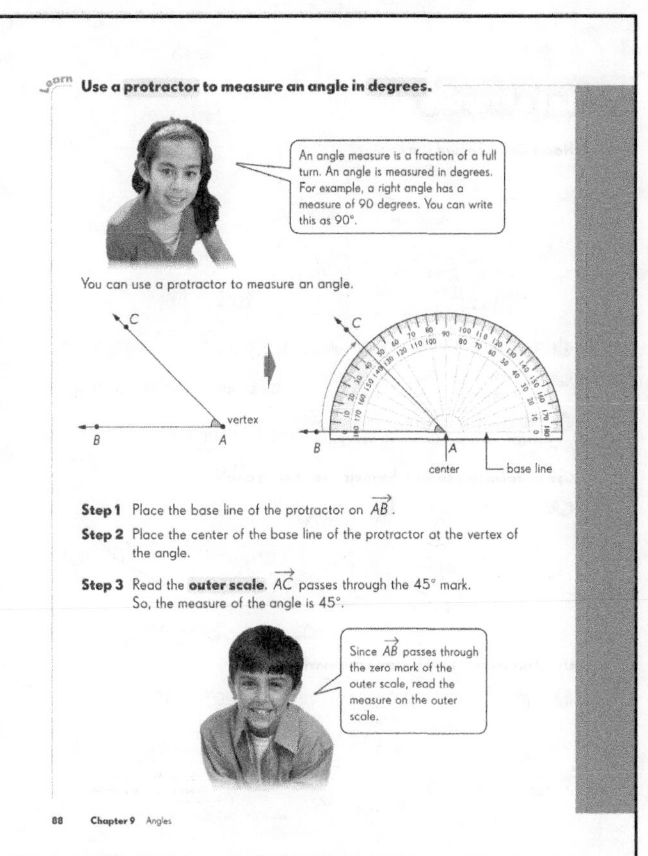

Learn **Use a protractor to measure an angle in degrees.**

An angle measure is a fraction of a full turn. An angle is measured in degrees. For example, a right angle has a measure of 90 degrees. You can write this as 90°.

You can use a protractor to measure an angle.

Step 1 Place the base line of the protractor on $\overrightarrow{AB}$.

Step 2 Place the center of the base line of the protractor at the vertex of the angle.

Step 3 Read the **outer scale**. $\overrightarrow{AC}$ passes through the 45° mark. So, the measure of the angle is 45°.

Since $\overrightarrow{AB}$ passes through the zero mark of the outer scale, read the measure on the outer scale.

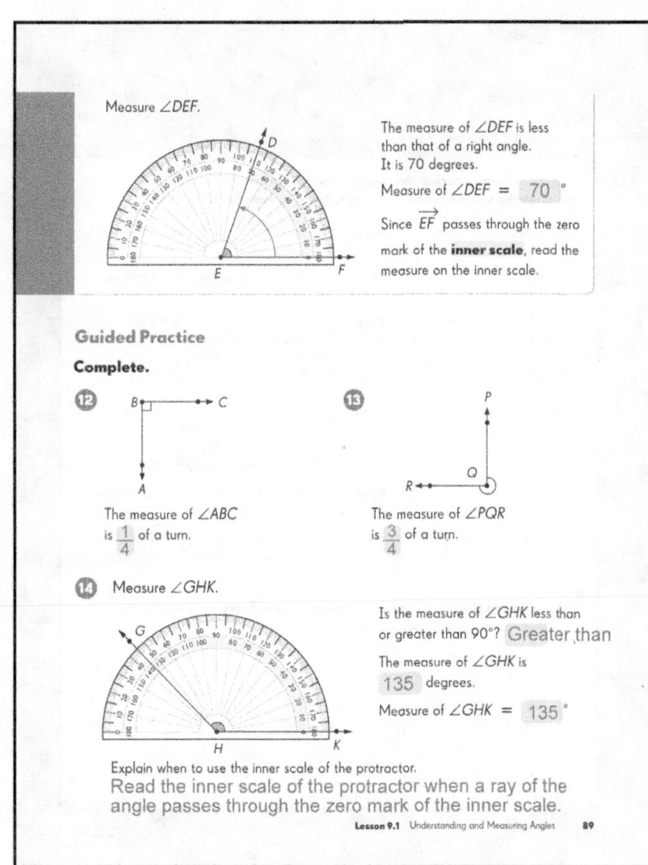

Measure ∠DEF.

The measure of ∠DEF is less than that of a right angle. It is 70 degrees.

Measure of ∠DEF = 70 °

Since $\overrightarrow{EF}$ passes through the zero mark of the **inner scale**, read the measure on the inner scale.

Guided Practice

Complete.

12 The measure of ∠ABC is $\frac{1}{4}$ of a turn.

13 The measure of ∠PQR is $\frac{3}{4}$ of a turn.

14 Measure ∠GHK.

Is the measure of ∠GHK less than or greater than 90°? Greater than

The measure of ∠GHK is 135 degrees.

Measure of ∠GHK = 135 °

Explain when to use the inner scale of the protractor.
Read the inner scale of the protractor when a ray of the angle passes through the zero mark of the inner scale.

Chapter 9

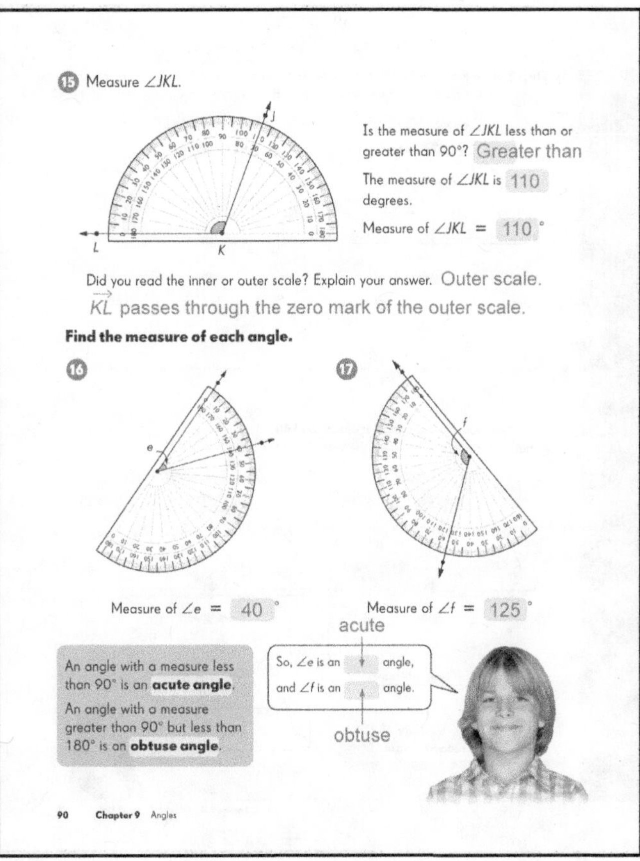

15 Measure ∠JKL.

Is the measure of ∠JKL less than or greater than 90°? Greater than

The measure of ∠JKL is 110 degrees.

Measure of ∠JKL = 110 °

Did you read the inner or outer scale? Explain your answer. Outer scale. $\overrightarrow{KL}$ passes through the zero mark of the outer scale.

Find the measure of each angle.

16 Measure of ∠e = 40 °

17 Measure of ∠f = 125 °

An angle with a measure less than 90° is an **acute angle**.

An angle with a measure greater than 90° but less than 180° is an **obtuse angle**.

So, ∠e is an acute angle, and ∠f is an obtuse angle.

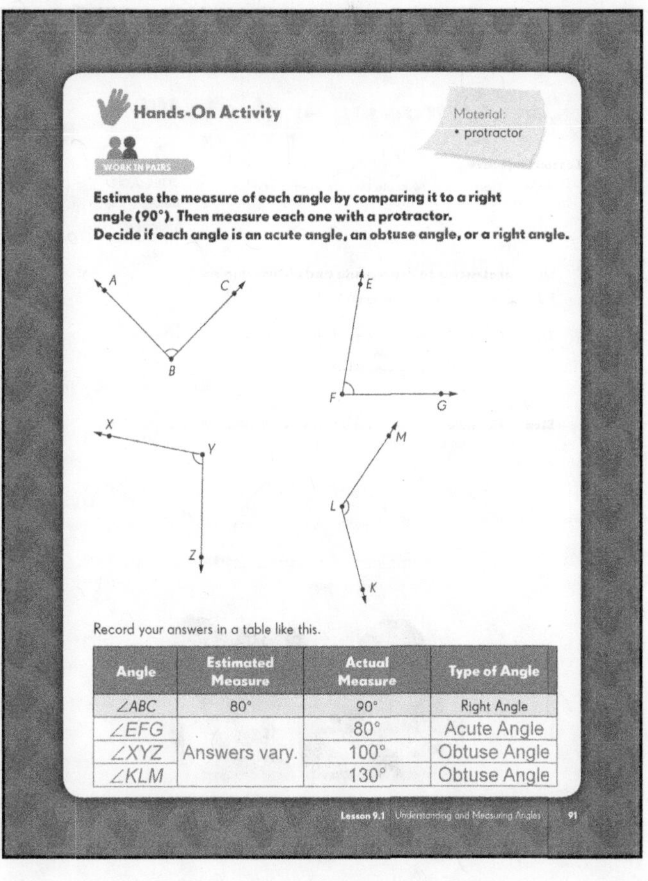

Hands-On Activity

Material:
• protractor

WORK IN PAIRS

Estimate the measure of each angle by comparing it to a right angle (90°). Then measure each one with a protractor.
Decide if each angle is an acute angle, an obtuse angle, or a right angle.

Record your answers in a table like this.

Angle	Estimated Measure	Actual Measure	Type of Angle
∠ABC	80°	90°	Right Angle
∠EFG	Answers vary.	80°	Acute Angle
∠XYZ		100°	Obtuse Angle
∠KLM		130°	Obtuse Angle

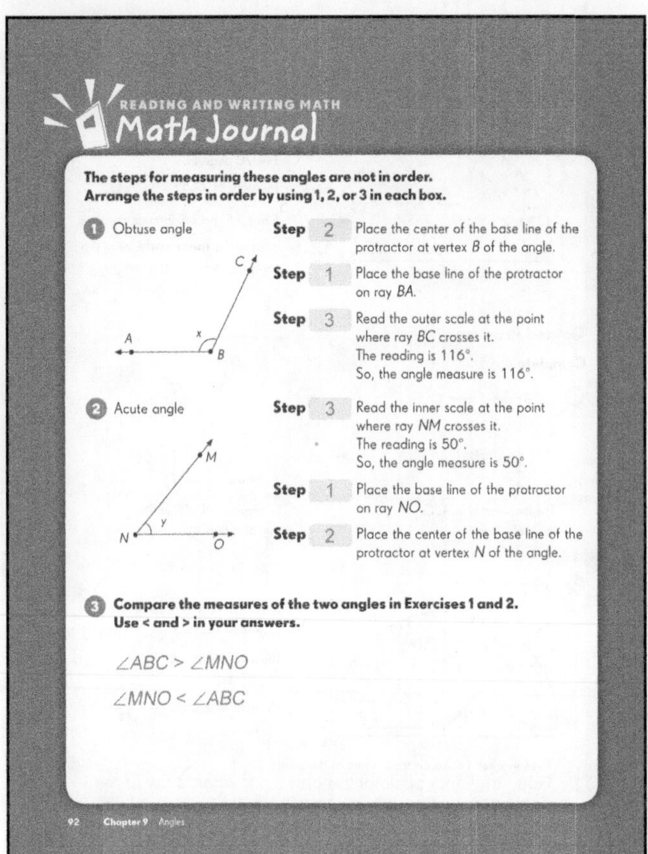

READING AND WRITING MATH

Math Journal

The steps for measuring these angles are not in order. Arrange the steps in order by using 1, 2, or 3 in each box.

1. Obtuse angle

Step 2 Place the center of the base line of the protractor at vertex *B* of the angle.

Step 1 Place the base line of the protractor on ray *BA*.

Step 3 Read the outer scale at the point where ray *BC* crosses it. The reading is 116°. So, the angle measure is 116°.

2. Acute angle

Step 3 Read the inner scale at the point where ray *NM* crosses it. The reading is 50°. So, the angle measure is 50°.

Step 1 Place the base line of the protractor on ray *NO*.

Step 2 Place the center of the base line of the protractor at vertex *N* of the angle.

3. **Compare the measures of the two angles in Exercises 1 and 2. Use < and > in your answers.**

∠ABC > ∠MNO

∠MNO < ∠ABC

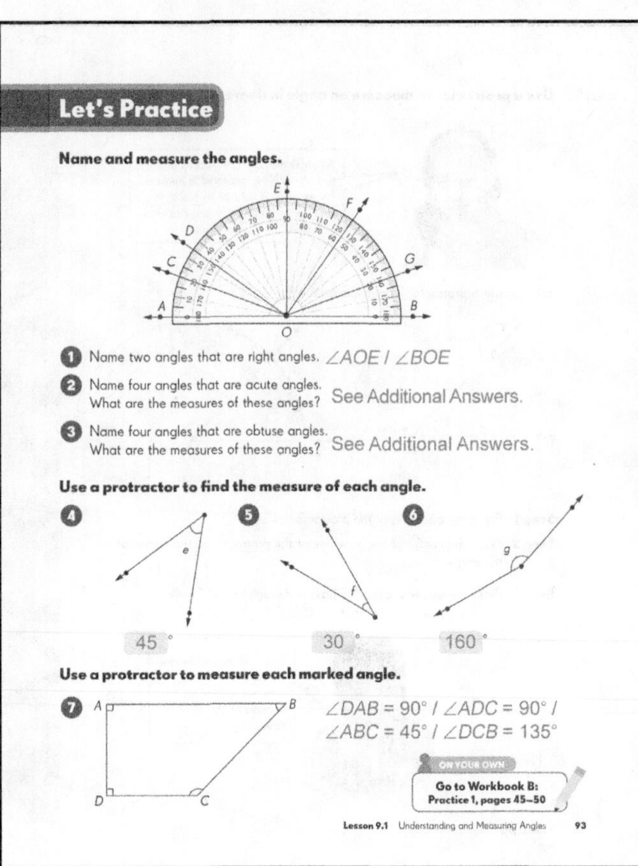

Let's Practice

Name and measure the angles.

1. Name two angles that are right angles. ∠AOE / ∠BOE
2. Name four angles that are acute angles. What are the measures of these angles? See Additional Answers.
3. Name four angles that are obtuse angles. What are the measures of these angles? See Additional Answers.

Use a protractor to find the measure of each angle.

4. *e* 45°
5. *f* 30°
6. *g* 160°

Use a protractor to measure each marked angle.

7. A B C D

∠DAB = 90° / ∠ADC = 90° / ∠ABC = 45° / ∠DCB = 135°

ON YOUR OWN

Go to Workbook B: Practice 1, pages 45–50

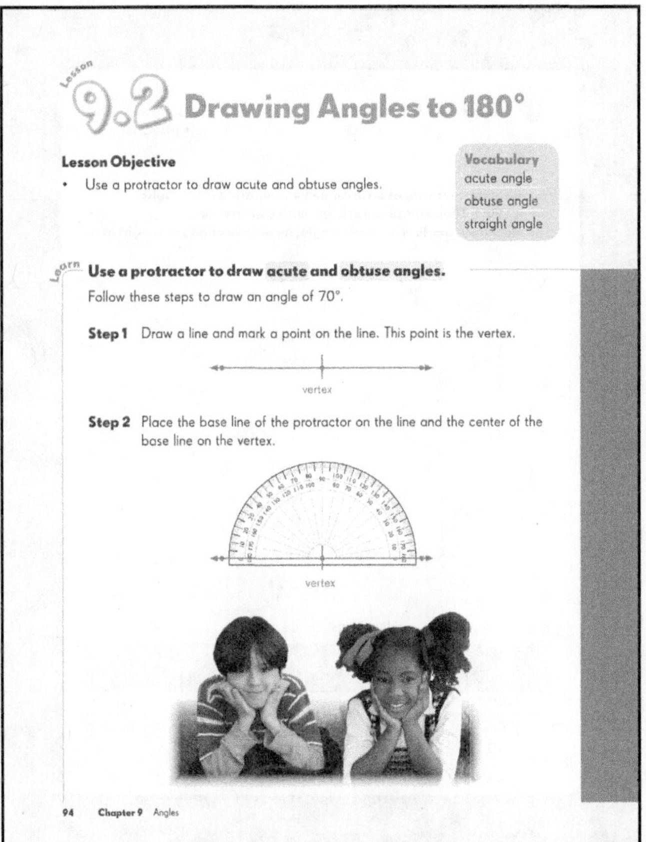

Lesson

9.2 Drawing Angles to 180°

Lesson Objective

- Use a protractor to draw acute and obtuse angles.

Vocabulary
acute angle
obtuse angle
straight angle

Learn **Use a protractor to draw acute and obtuse angles.**

Follow these steps to draw an angle of 70°.

Step 1 Draw a line and mark a point on the line. This point is the vertex.

Step 2 Place the base line of the protractor on the line and the center of the base line on the vertex.

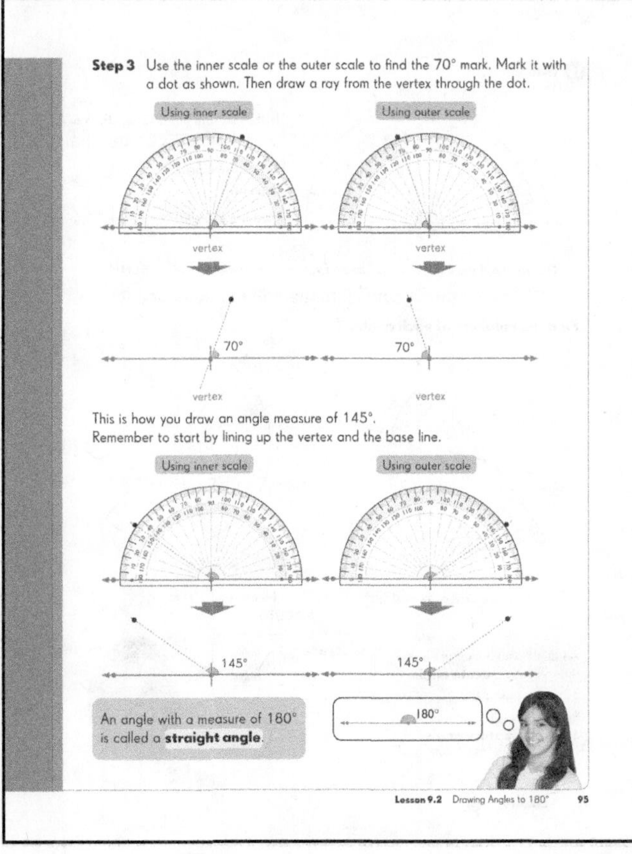

Step 3 Use the inner scale or the outer scale to find the 70° mark. Mark it with a dot as shown. Then draw a ray from the vertex through the dot.

This is how you draw an angle measure of 145°. Remember to start by lining up the vertex and the base line.

An angle with a measure of 180° is called a **straight angle**.

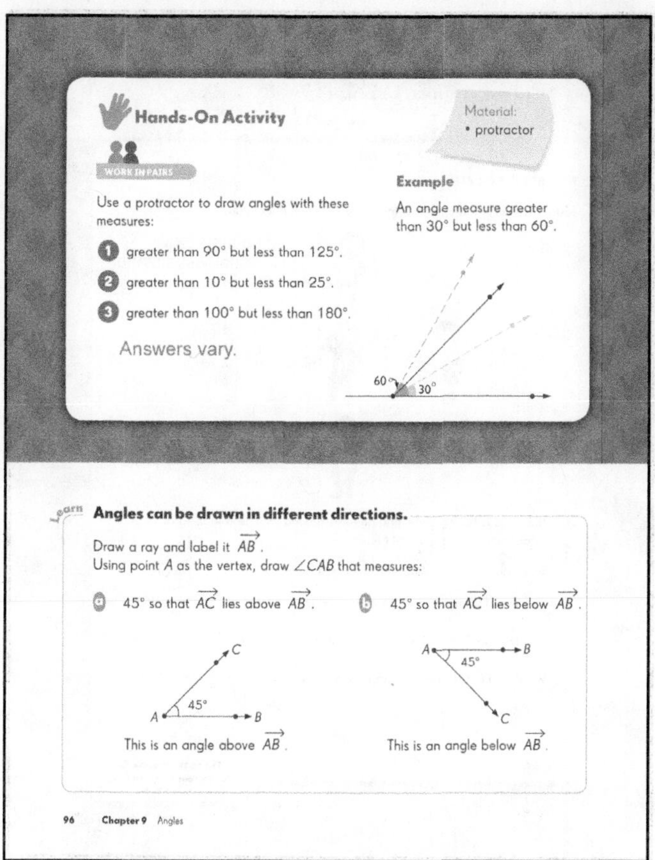

Hands-On Activity

Material:
• protractor

WORK IN PAIRS

Use a protractor to draw angles with these measures:

1. greater than 90° but less than 125°.
2. greater than 10° but less than 25°.
3. greater than 100° but less than 180°.

Answers vary.

Example

An angle measure greater than 30° but less than 60°.

60°
30°

Learn Angles can be drawn in different directions.

Draw a ray and label it $\overrightarrow{AB}$.
Using point A as the vertex, draw $\angle CAB$ that measures:

a. 45° so that $\overrightarrow{AC}$ lies above $\overrightarrow{AB}$.

This is an angle above $\overrightarrow{AB}$.

b. 45° so that $\overrightarrow{AC}$ lies below $\overrightarrow{AB}$.

This is an angle below $\overrightarrow{AB}$.

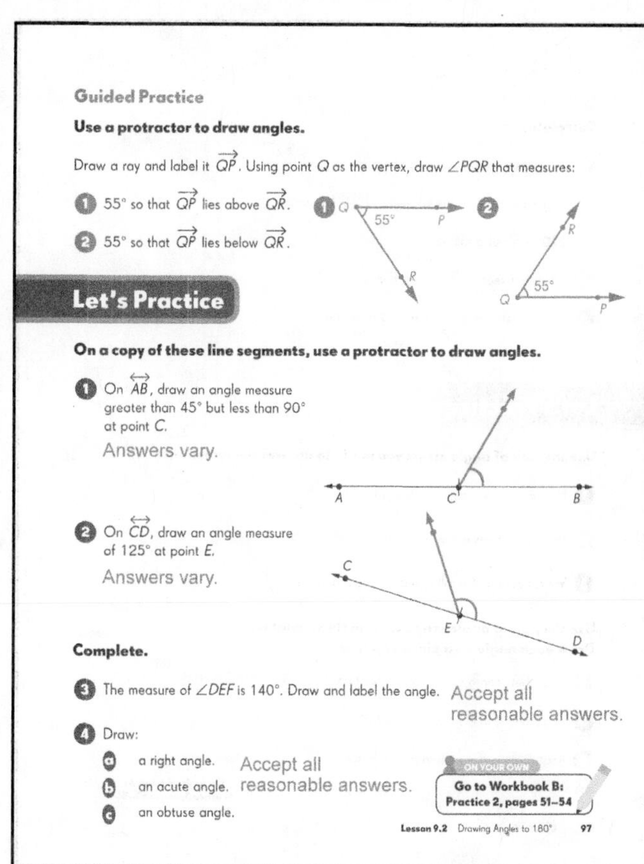

Guided Practice

Use a protractor to draw angles.

Draw a ray and label it $\overrightarrow{QP}$. Using point Q as the vertex, draw $\angle PQR$ that measures:

1. 55° so that $\overrightarrow{QP}$ lies above $\overrightarrow{QR}$.
2. 55° so that $\overrightarrow{QP}$ lies below $\overrightarrow{QR}$.

Let's Practice

On a copy of these line segments, use a protractor to draw angles.

1. On $\overleftrightarrow{AB}$, draw an angle measure greater than 45° but less than 90° at point C.
   Answers vary.
2. On $\overleftrightarrow{CD}$, draw an angle measure of 125° at point E.
   Answers vary.

Complete.

3. The measure of $\angle DEF$ is 140°. Draw and label the angle. Accept all reasonable answers.
4. Draw:
   a. a right angle.
   b. an acute angle.
   c. an obtuse angle.
   Accept all reasonable answers.

ON YOUR OWN
Go to Workbook B: Practice 2, pages 51–54

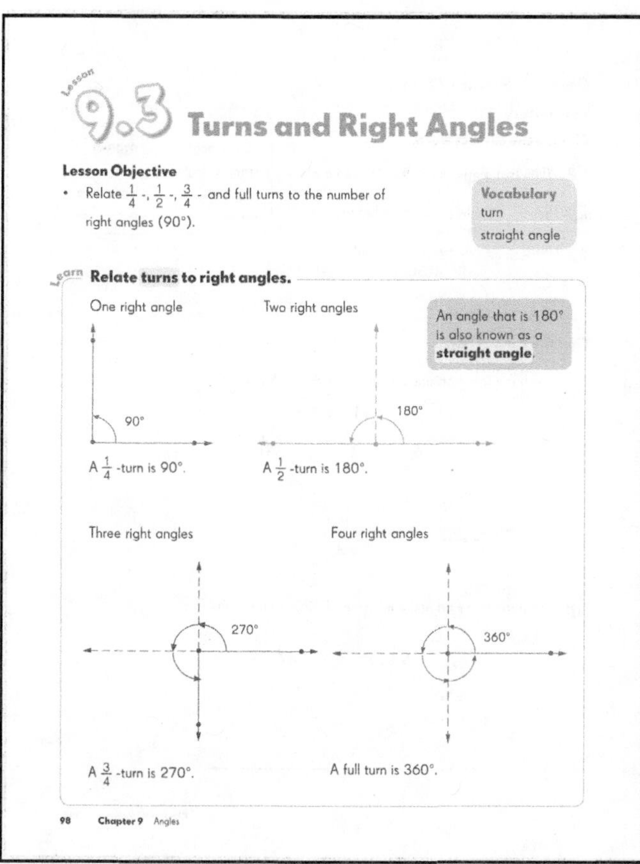

Lesson 9.3 Turns and Right Angles

Lesson Objective

- Relate $\frac{1}{4}$-, $\frac{1}{2}$-, $\frac{3}{4}$- and full turns to the number of right angles (90°).

Vocabulary
turn
straight angle

Learn Relate turns to right angles.

One right angle

A $\frac{1}{4}$-turn is 90°.

Two right angles

A $\frac{1}{2}$-turn is 180°.

An angle that is 180° is also known as a **straight angle**.

Three right angles

A $\frac{3}{4}$-turn is 270°.

Four right angles

A full turn is 360°.

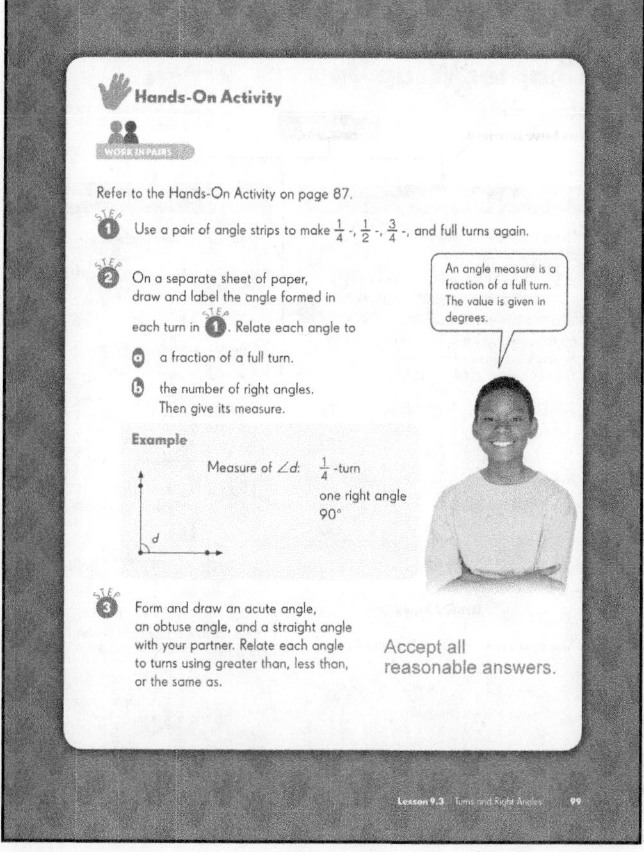

Hands-On Activity

WORK IN PAIRS

Refer to the Hands-On Activity on page 87.

STEP 1 Use a pair of angle strips to make $\frac{1}{4}$-, $\frac{1}{2}$-, $\frac{3}{4}$-, and full turns again.

STEP 2 On a separate sheet of paper, draw and label the angle formed in each turn in STEP 1. Relate each angle to

a. a fraction of a full turn.
b. the number of right angles. Then give its measure.

An angle measure is a fraction of a full turn. The value is given in degrees.

Example

Measure of $\angle d$: $\frac{1}{4}$-turn
one right angle
90°

STEP 3 Form and draw an acute angle, an obtuse angle, and a straight angle with your partner. Relate each angle to turns using greater than, less than, or the same as.

Accept all reasonable answers.

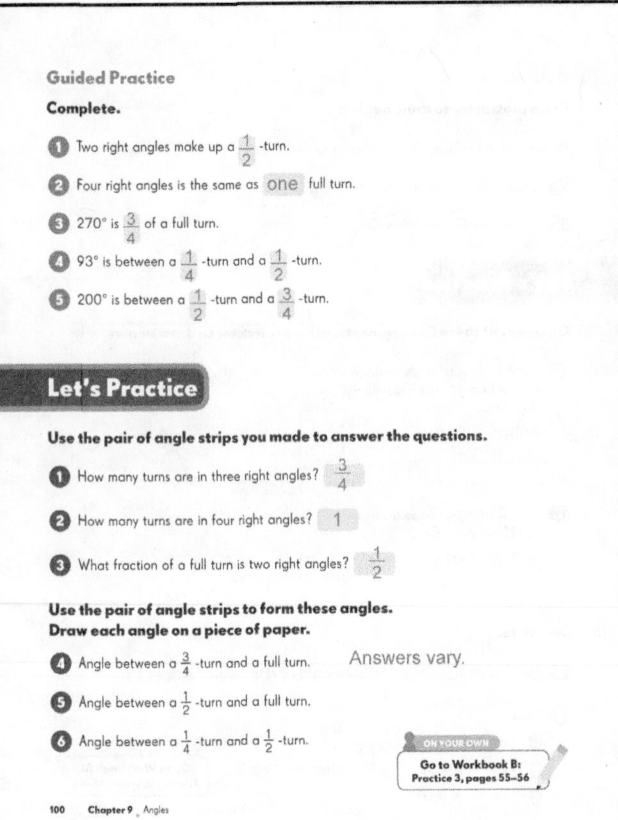

Guided Practice

Complete.

1. Two right angles make up a $\frac{1}{2}$-turn.
2. Four right angles is the same as one full turn.
3. 270° is $\frac{3}{4}$ of a full turn.
4. 93° is between a $\frac{1}{4}$-turn and a $\frac{1}{2}$-turn.
5. 200° is between a $\frac{1}{2}$-turn and a $\frac{3}{4}$-turn.

Let's Practice

Use the pair of angle strips you made to answer the questions.

1. How many turns are in three right angles? $\frac{3}{4}$
2. How many turns are in four right angles? 1
3. What fraction of a full turn is two right angles? $\frac{1}{2}$

Use the pair of angle strips to form these angles. Draw each angle on a piece of paper.

4. Angle between a $\frac{3}{4}$-turn and a full turn. Answers vary.
5. Angle between a $\frac{1}{2}$-turn and a full turn.
6. Angle between a $\frac{1}{4}$-turn and a $\frac{1}{2}$-turn.

ON YOUR OWN
Go to Workbook B: Practice 3, pages 55–56

100 Chapter 9 Angles

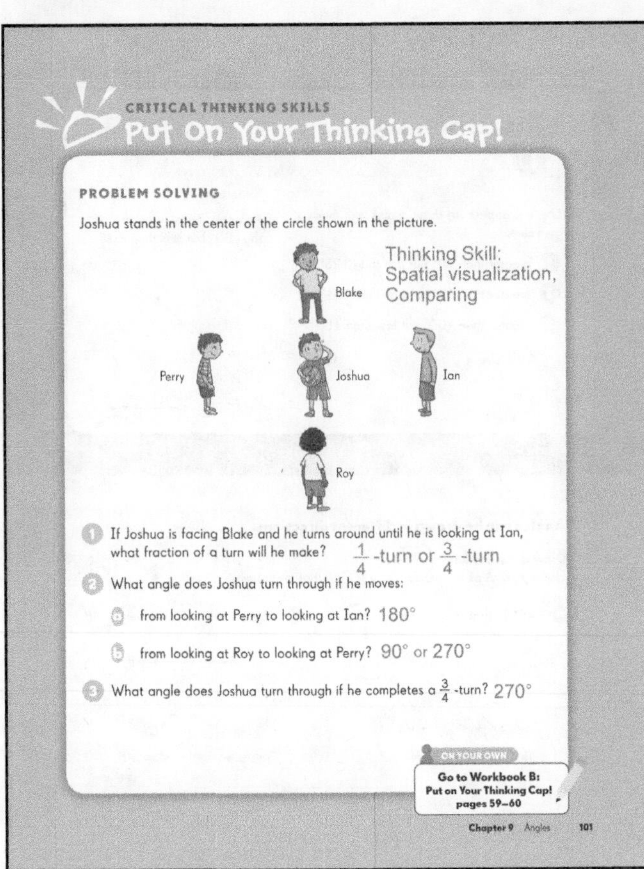

CRITICAL THINKING SKILLS

Put On Your Thinking Cap!

PROBLEM SOLVING

Joshua stands in the center of the circle shown in the picture.

Thinking Skill: Spatial visualization, Comparing

1. If Joshua is facing Blake and he turns around until he is looking at Ian, what fraction of a turn will he make? $\frac{1}{4}$-turn or $\frac{3}{4}$-turn
2. What angle does Joshua turn through if he moves:
   a. from looking at Perry to looking at Ian? 180°
   b. from looking at Roy to looking at Perry? 90° or 270°
3. What angle does Joshua turn through if he completes a $\frac{3}{4}$-turn? 270°

ON YOUR OWN
Go to Workbook B: Put on Your Thinking Cap! pages 59–60

Chapter 9 Angles 101

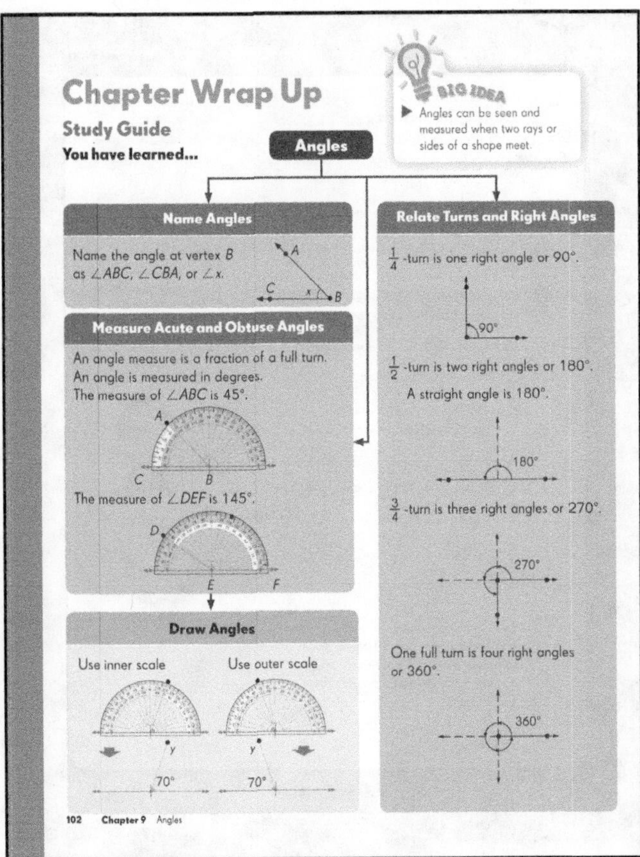

Chapter Wrap Up

Study Guide

You have learned...

BIG IDEA
▶ Angles can be seen and measured when two rays or sides of a shape meet.

Angles

Name Angles

Name the angle at vertex B as ∠ABC, ∠CBA, or ∠x.

Measure Acute and Obtuse Angles

An angle measure is a fraction of a full turn.
An angle is measured in degrees.
The measure of ∠ABC is 45°.

The measure of ∠DEF is 145°.

Draw Angles

Use inner scale　Use outer scale

Relate Turns and Right Angles

$\frac{1}{4}$-turn is one right angle or 90°.

$\frac{1}{2}$-turn is two right angles or 180°.
A straight angle is 180°.

$\frac{3}{4}$-turn is three right angles or 270°.

One full turn is four right angles or 360°.

102 Chapter 9 Angles

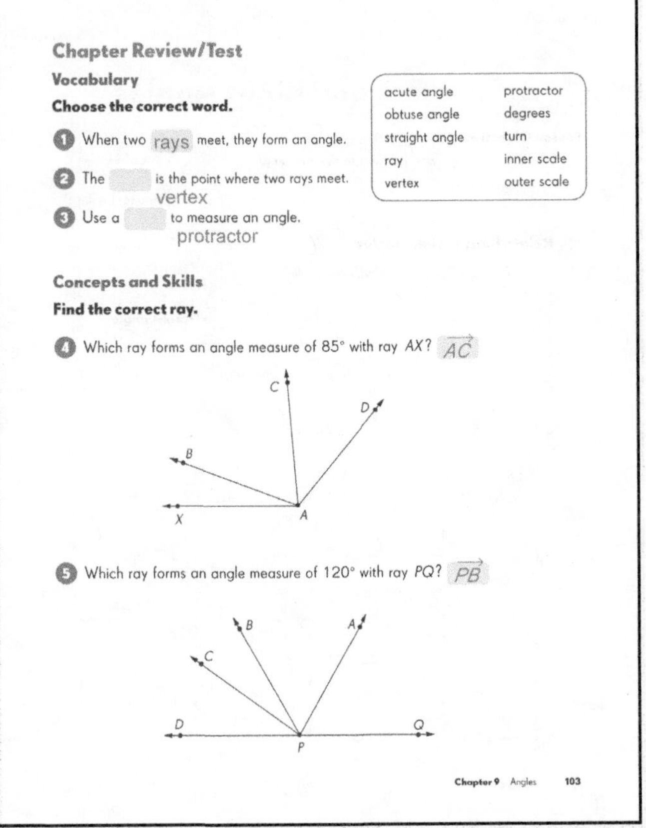

Chapter Review/Test

Vocabulary

Choose the correct word.

acute angle	protractor
obtuse angle	degrees
straight angle	turn
ray	inner scale
vertex	outer scale

1. When two rays meet, they form an angle.
2. The vertex is the point where two rays meet.
3. Use a protractor to measure an angle.

Concepts and Skills

Find the correct ray.

4. Which ray forms an angle measure of 85° with ray AX? $\overrightarrow{AC}$
5. Which ray forms an angle measure of 120° with ray PQ? $\overrightarrow{PB}$

Chapter 9 Angles 103

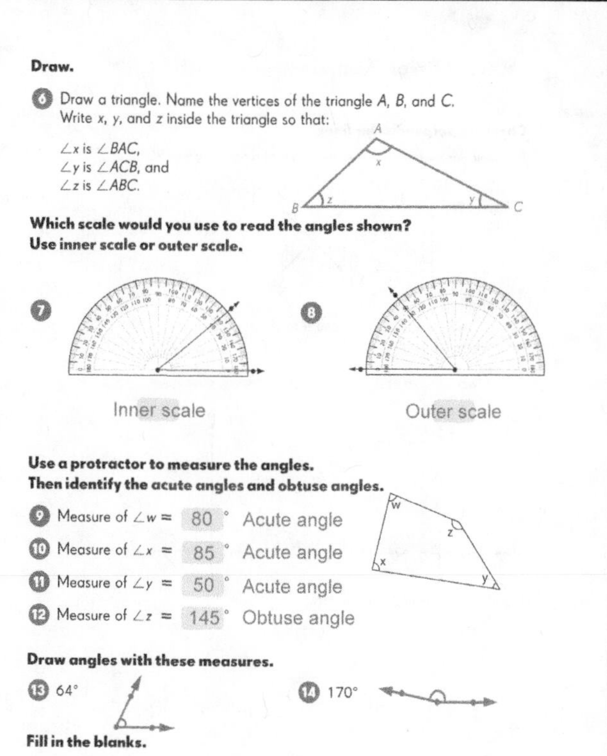

Draw.

6 Draw a triangle. Name the vertices of the triangle *A*, *B*, and *C*. Write *x*, *y*, and *z* inside the triangle so that:

$\angle x$ is $\angle BAC$,
$\angle y$ is $\angle ACB$, and
$\angle z$ is $\angle ABC$.

Which scale would you use to read the angles shown? Use inner scale or outer scale.

7 Inner scale

8 Outer scale

Use a protractor to measure the angles. Then identify the acute angles and obtuse angles.

9 Measure of $\angle w$ = 80° Acute angle

10 Measure of $\angle x$ = 85° Acute angle

11 Measure of $\angle y$ = 50° Acute angle

12 Measure of $\angle z$ = 145° Obtuse angle

Draw angles with these measures.

13 64°

14 170°

Fill in the blanks.

15 $\frac{3}{4}$-turn is 270°.

16 90° is $\frac{1}{4}$-turn.

17 One full turn is 360°.

104 **Chapter 9** Angles

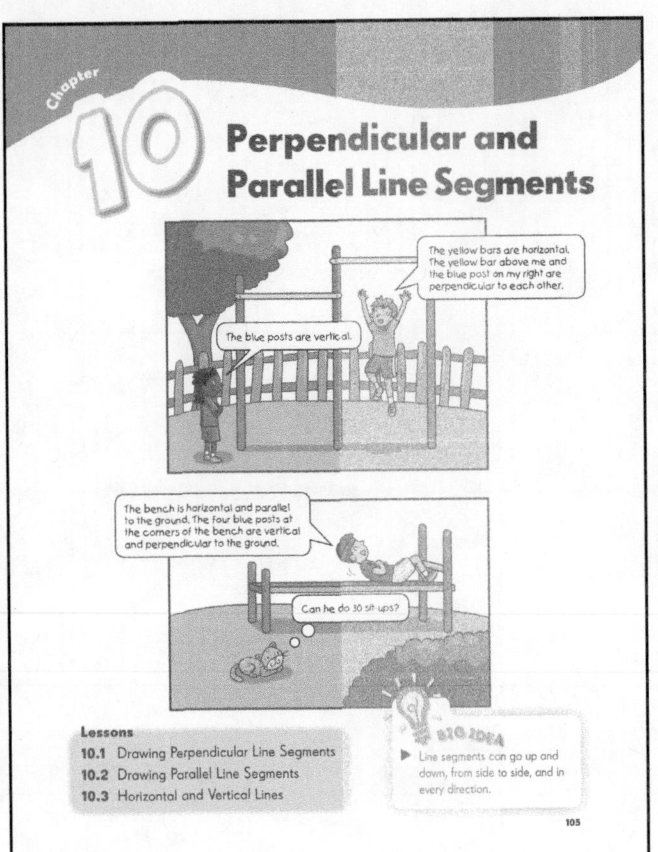
Chapter
10
Perpendicular and Parallel Line Segments
The yellow bars are horizontal. The yellow bar above me and the blue post on my right are perpendicular to each other.
The blue posts are vertical.
The bench is horizontal and parallel to the ground. The four blue posts at the corners of the bench are vertical and perpendicular to the ground.
Can he do 30 sit-ups?
Lessons
10.1 Drawing Perpendicular Line Segments
10.2 Drawing Parallel Line Segments
10.3 Horizontal and Vertical Lines
BIG IDEA
Line segments can go up and down, from side to side, and in every direction.
105

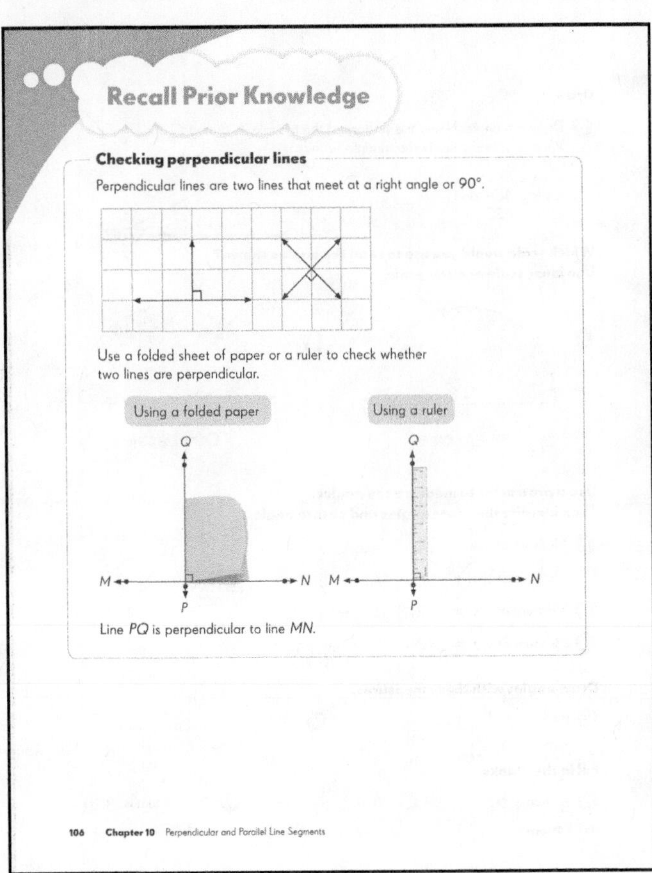
Recall Prior Knowledge
Checking perpendicular lines
Perpendicular lines are two lines that meet at a right angle or 90°.
Use a folded sheet of paper or a ruler to check whether two lines are perpendicular.
Using a folded paper
Using a ruler
Q
P
M
N
Line PQ is perpendicular to line MN.
106 Chapter 10 Perpendicular and Parallel Line Segments

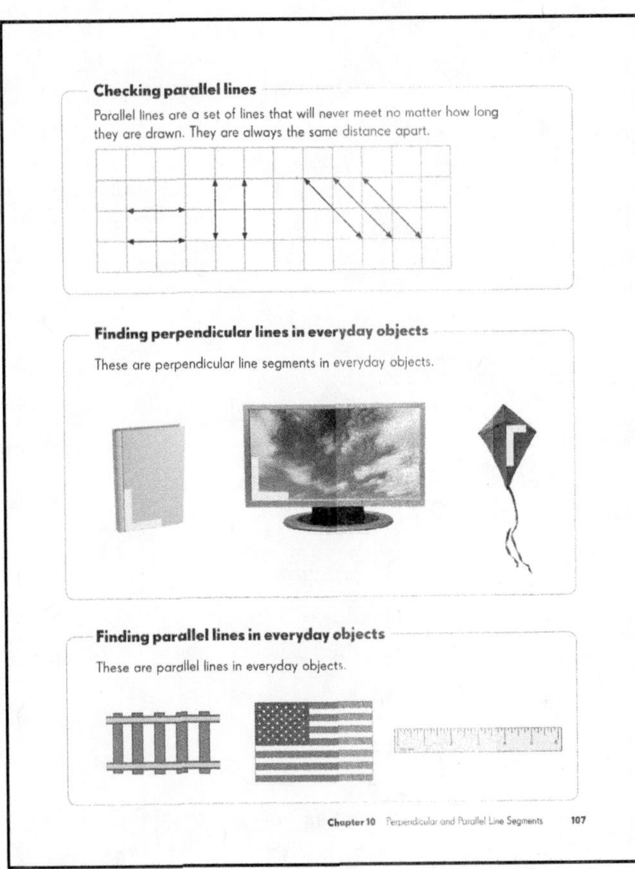
Checking parallel lines
Parallel lines are a set of lines that will never meet no matter how long they are drawn. They are always the same distance apart.
Finding perpendicular lines in everyday objects
These are perpendicular line segments in everyday objects.
Finding parallel lines in everyday objects
These are parallel lines in everyday objects.
Chapter 10 Perpendicular and Parallel Line Segments 107

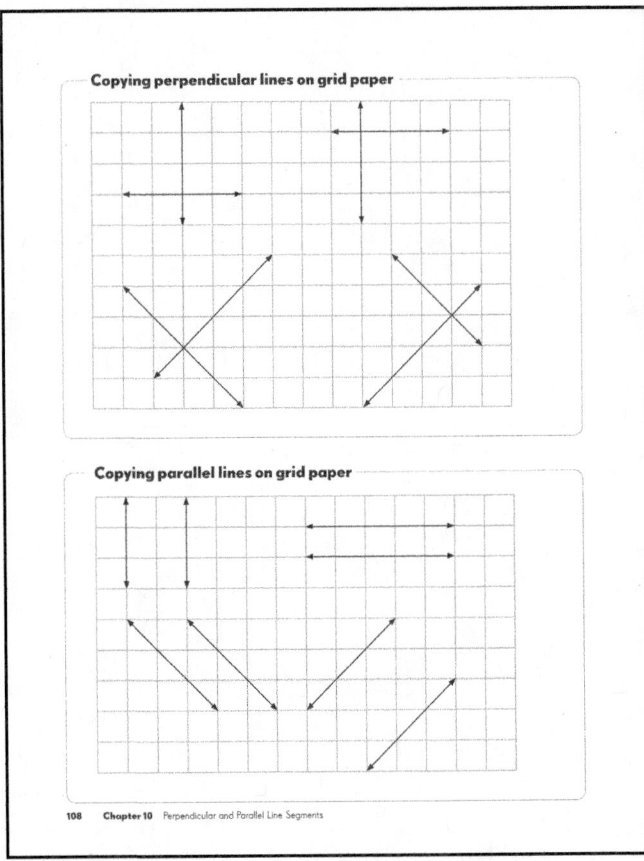
Copying perpendicular lines on grid paper
Copying parallel lines on grid paper
108 Chapter 10 Perpendicular and Parallel Line Segments

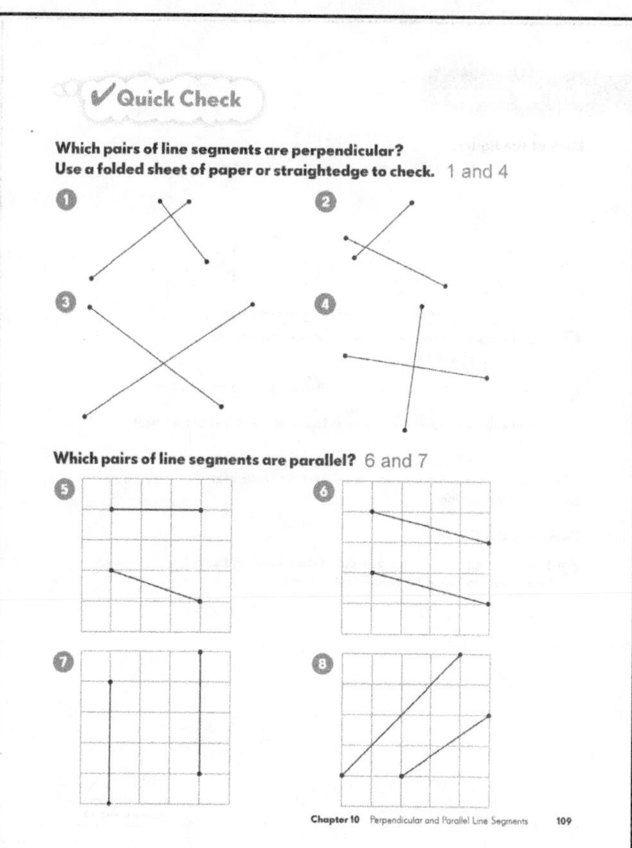

✔ Quick Check

Which pairs of line segments are perpendicular?
Use a folded sheet of paper or straightedge to check. 1 and 4

1
2
3
4

Which pairs of line segments are parallel? 6 and 7

5
6
7
8

Chapter 10 Perpendicular and Parallel Line Segments 109

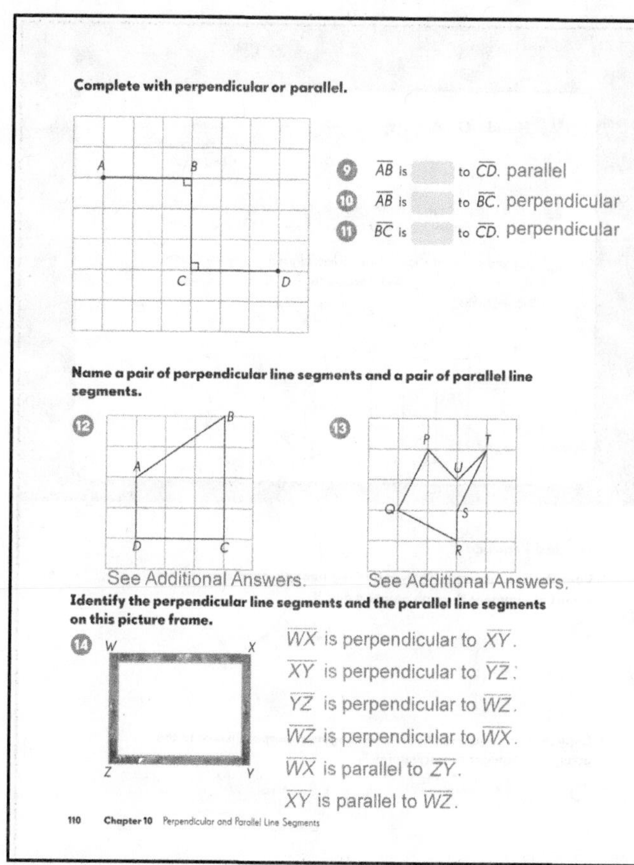

Complete with perpendicular or parallel.

9. $\overline{AB}$ is ___ to $\overline{CD}$. parallel
10. $\overline{AB}$ is ___ to $\overline{BC}$. perpendicular
11. $\overline{BC}$ is ___ to $\overline{CD}$. perpendicular

Name a pair of perpendicular line segments and a pair of parallel line segments.

12. See Additional Answers.

13. See Additional Answers.

Identify the perpendicular line segments and the parallel line segments on this picture frame.

14.

$\overline{WX}$ is perpendicular to $\overline{XY}$.
$\overline{XY}$ is perpendicular to $\overline{YZ}$.
$\overline{YZ}$ is perpendicular to $\overline{WZ}$.
$\overline{WZ}$ is perpendicular to $\overline{WX}$.
$\overline{WX}$ is parallel to $\overline{ZY}$.
$\overline{XY}$ is parallel to $\overline{WZ}$.

110 Chapter 10 Perpendicular and Parallel Line Segments

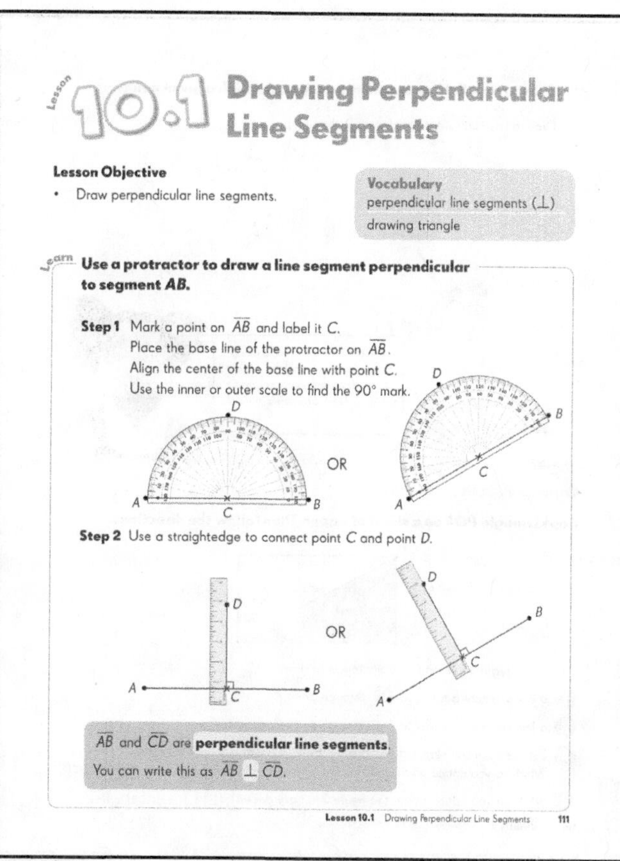

Lesson

10.1 Drawing Perpendicular Line Segments

Lesson Objective

- Draw perpendicular line segments.

Vocabulary
perpendicular line segments (⊥)
drawing triangle

Learn **Use a protractor to draw a line segment perpendicular to segment *AB*.**

Step 1 Mark a point on $\overline{AB}$ and label it *C*.
Place the base line of the protractor on $\overline{AB}$.
Align the center of the base line with point *C*.
Use the inner or outer scale to find the 90° mark.

OR

Step 2 Use a straightedge to connect point *C* and point *D*.

OR

$\overline{AB}$ and $\overline{CD}$ are **perpendicular line segments**.
You can write this as $\overline{AB} \perp \overline{CD}$.

Lesson 10.1 Drawing Perpendicular Line Segments 111

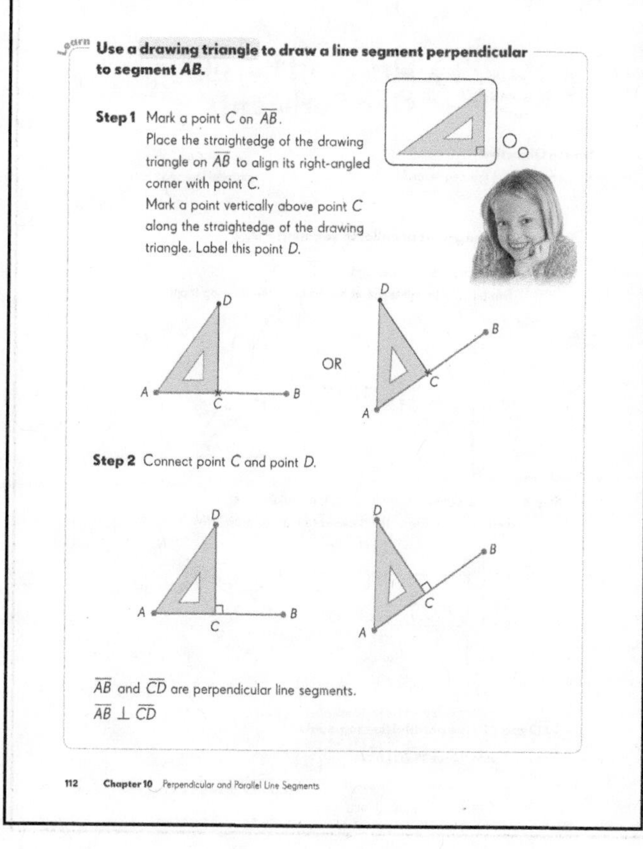

Learn **Use a drawing triangle to draw a line segment perpendicular to segment *AB*.**

Step 1 Mark a point *C* on $\overline{AB}$.
Place the straightedge of the drawing triangle on $\overline{AB}$ to align its right-angled corner with point *C*.
Mark a point vertically above point *C* along the straightedge of the drawing triangle. Label this point *D*.

OR

Step 2 Connect point *C* and point *D*.

$\overline{AB}$ and $\overline{CD}$ are perpendicular line segments.
$\overline{AB} \perp \overline{CD}$

112 Chapter 10 Perpendicular and Parallel Line Segments

Chapter 10

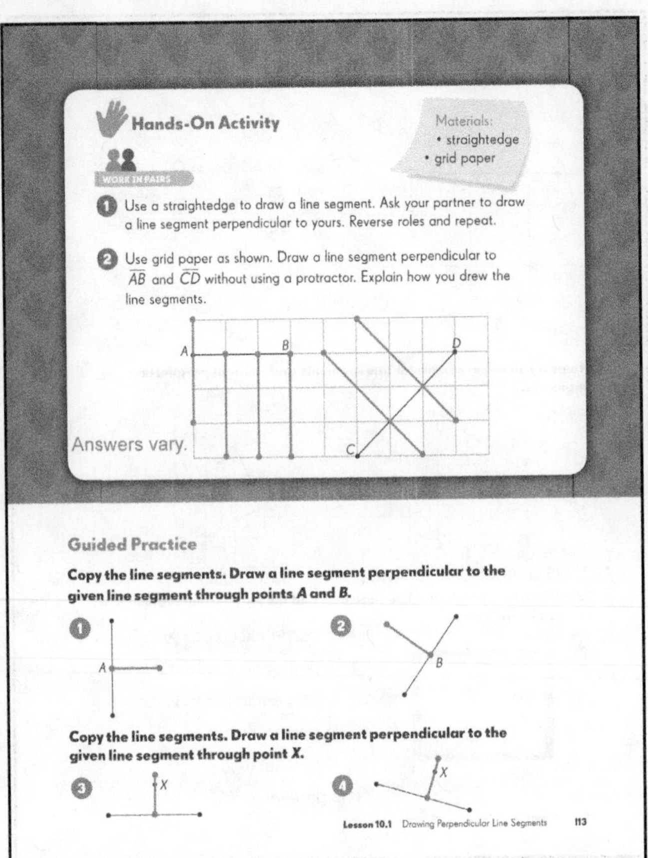
Hands-On Activity
Materials:
• straightedge
• grid paper
WORK IN PAIRS
1 Use a straightedge to draw a line segment. Ask your partner to draw a line segment perpendicular to yours. Reverse roles and repeat.
2 Use grid paper as shown. Draw a line segment perpendicular to $\overline{AB}$ and $\overline{CD}$ without using a protractor. Explain how you drew the line segments.
Answers vary.
Guided Practice
Copy the line segments. Draw a line segment perpendicular to the given line segment through points A and B.
Copy the line segments. Draw a line segment perpendicular to the given line segment through point X.
Lesson 10.1 Drawing Perpendicular Line Segments 113

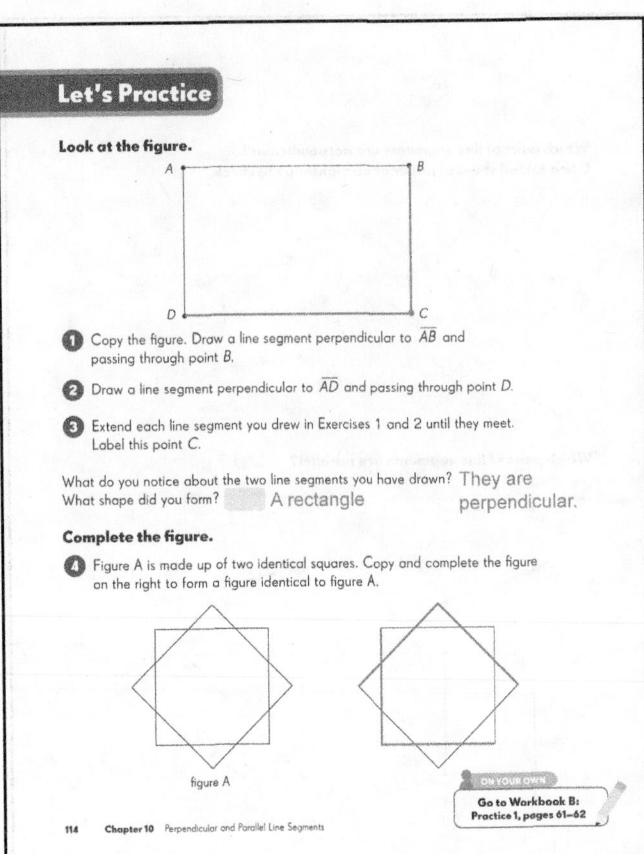
Let's Practice
Look at the figure.
1 Copy the figure. Draw a line segment perpendicular to $\overline{AB}$ and passing through point B.
2 Draw a line segment perpendicular to $\overline{AD}$ and passing through point D.
3 Extend each line segment you drew in Exercises 1 and 2 until they meet. Label this point C.
What do you notice about the two line segments you have drawn? They are perpendicular.
What shape did you form? A rectangle
Complete the figure.
4 Figure A is made up of two identical squares. Copy and complete the figure on the right to form a figure identical to figure A.
figure A
ON YOUR OWN
Go to Workbook B: Practice 1, pages 61–62
114 Chapter 10 Perpendicular and Parallel Line Segments

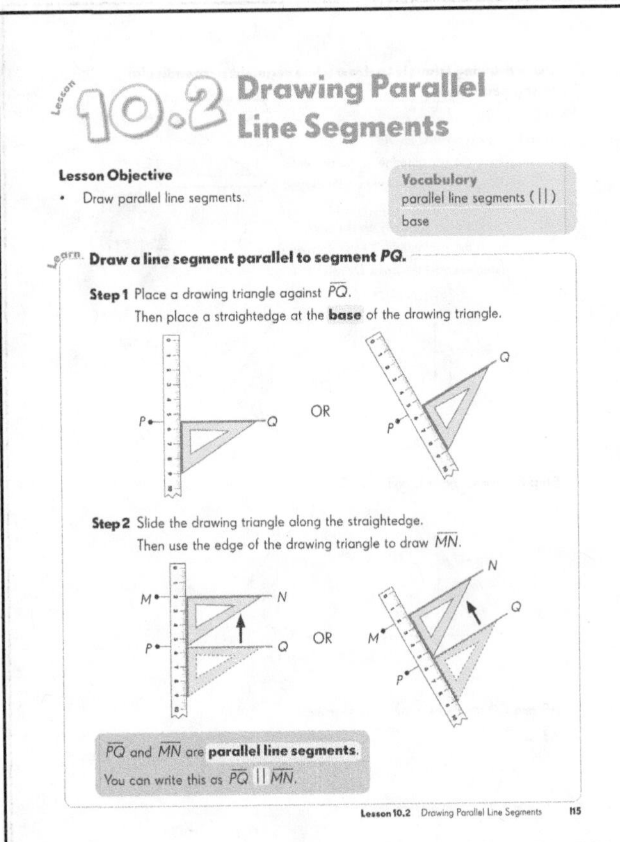
Lesson 10.2 Drawing Parallel Line Segments
Lesson Objective
• Draw parallel line segments.
Vocabulary
parallel line segments (||)
base
Learn Draw a line segment parallel to segment PQ.
Step 1 Place a drawing triangle against $\overline{PQ}$.
Then place a straightedge at the base of the drawing triangle.
Step 2 Slide the drawing triangle along the straightedge.
Then use the edge of the drawing triangle to draw $\overline{MN}$.
$\overline{PQ}$ and $\overline{MN}$ are parallel line segments.
You can write this as $\overline{PQ} \parallel \overline{MN}$.
Lesson 10.2 Drawing Parallel Line Segments 115

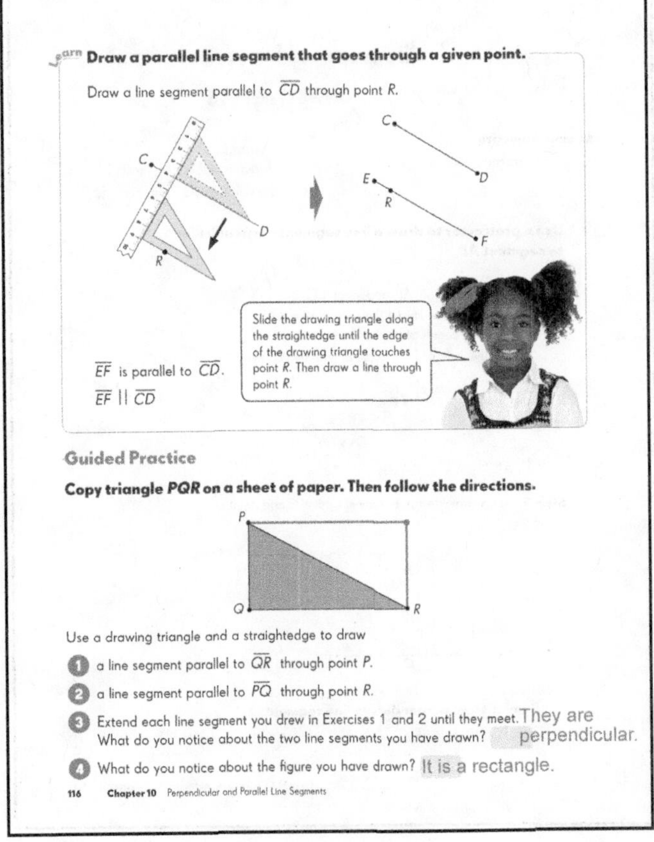
Learn Draw a parallel line segment that goes through a given point.
Draw a line segment parallel to $\overline{CD}$ through point R.
Slide the drawing triangle along the straightedge until the edge of the drawing triangle touches point R. Then draw a line through point R.
$\overline{EF}$ is parallel to $\overline{CD}$.
$\overline{EF} \parallel \overline{CD}$
Guided Practice
Copy triangle PQR on a sheet of paper. Then follow the directions.
Use a drawing triangle and a straightedge to draw
1 a line segment parallel to $\overline{QR}$ through point P.
2 a line segment parallel to $\overline{PQ}$ through point R.
3 Extend each line segment you drew in Exercises 1 and 2 until they meet. What do you notice about the two line segments you have drawn? They are perpendicular.
4 What do you notice about the figure you have drawn? It is a rectangle.
116 Chapter 10 Perpendicular and Parallel Line Segments

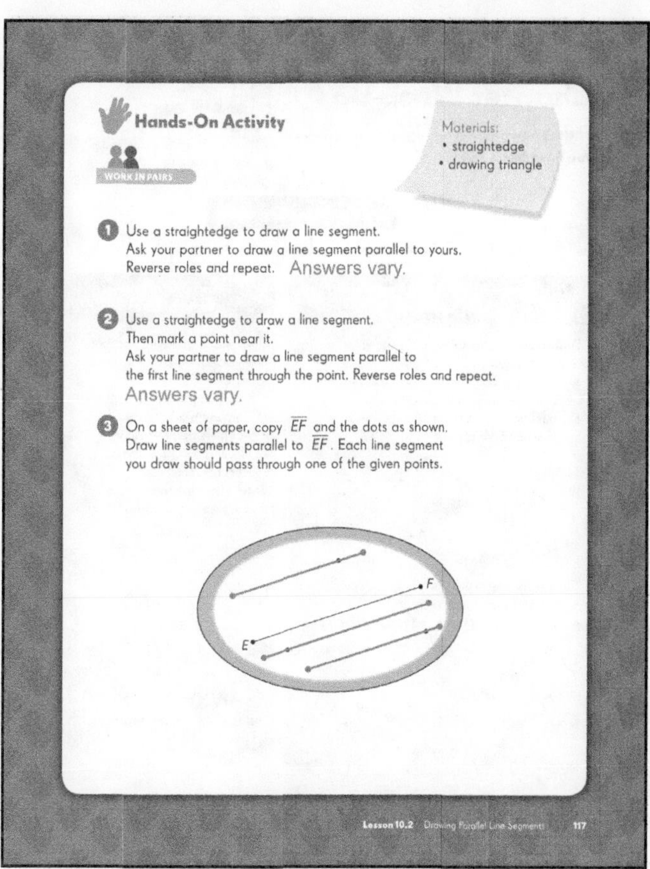
Hands-On Activity

WORK IN PAIRS

Materials:
- straightedge
- drawing triangle

1. Use a straightedge to draw a line segment.
Ask your partner to draw a line segment parallel to yours.
Reverse roles and repeat. Answers vary.

2. Use a straightedge to draw a line segment.
Then mark a point near it.
Ask your partner to draw a line segment parallel to the first line segment through the point. Reverse roles and repeat.
Answers vary.

3. On a sheet of paper, copy $\overline{EF}$ and the dots as shown.
Draw line segments parallel to $\overline{EF}$. Each line segment you draw should pass through one of the given points.

Lesson 10.2 Drawing Parallel Line Segments 117

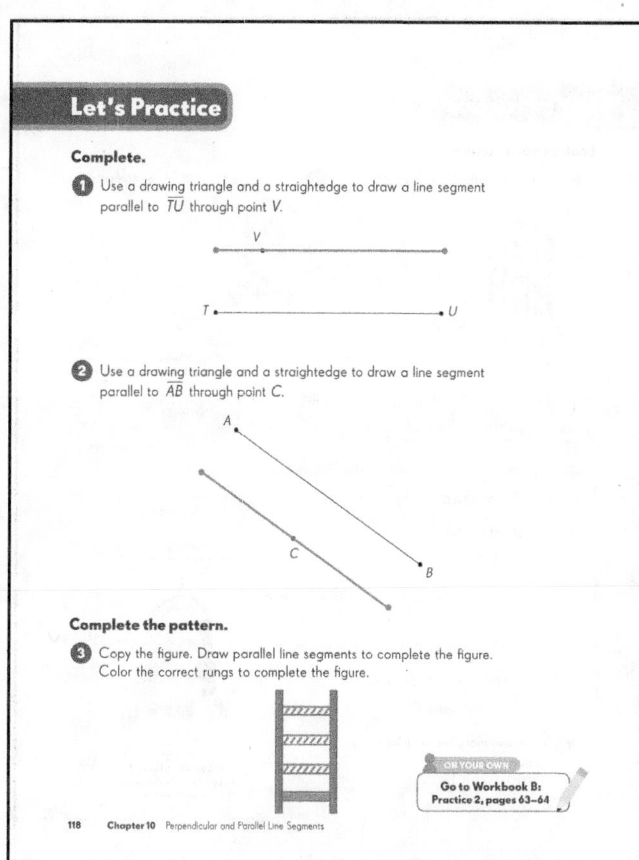
Let's Practice

Complete.

1. Use a drawing triangle and a straightedge to draw a line segment parallel to $\overline{TU}$ through point V.

2. Use a drawing triangle and a straightedge to draw a line segment parallel to $\overline{AB}$ through point C.

Complete the pattern.

3. Copy the figure. Draw parallel line segments to complete the figure.
Color the correct rungs to complete the figure.

ON YOUR OWN
Go to Workbook B: Practice 2, pages 63–64

118 Chapter 10 Perpendicular and Parallel Line Segments

Chapter 10

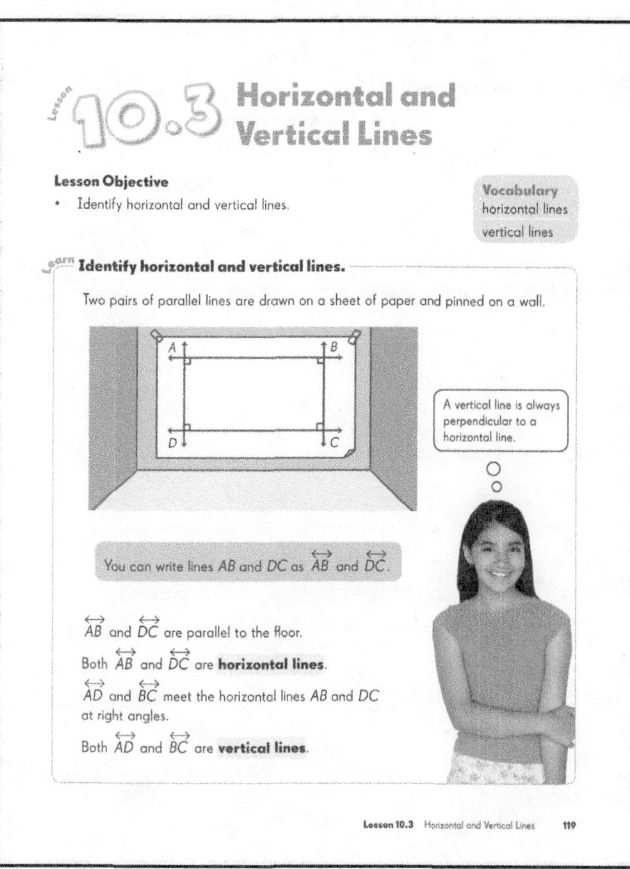
Lesson 10.3 Horizontal and Vertical Lines

Lesson Objective
- Identify horizontal and vertical lines.

Vocabulary
horizontal lines
vertical lines

Learn **Identify horizontal and vertical lines.**

Two pairs of parallel lines are drawn on a sheet of paper and pinned on a wall.

You can write lines AB and DC as $\overleftrightarrow{AB}$ and $\overleftrightarrow{DC}$.

$\overleftrightarrow{AB}$ and $\overleftrightarrow{DC}$ are parallel to the floor.
Both $\overleftrightarrow{AB}$ and $\overleftrightarrow{DC}$ are **horizontal lines**.
$\overleftrightarrow{AD}$ and $\overleftrightarrow{BC}$ meet the horizontal lines AB and DC at right angles.
Both $\overleftrightarrow{AD}$ and $\overleftrightarrow{BC}$ are **vertical lines**.

Lesson 10.3 Horizontal and Vertical Lines 119

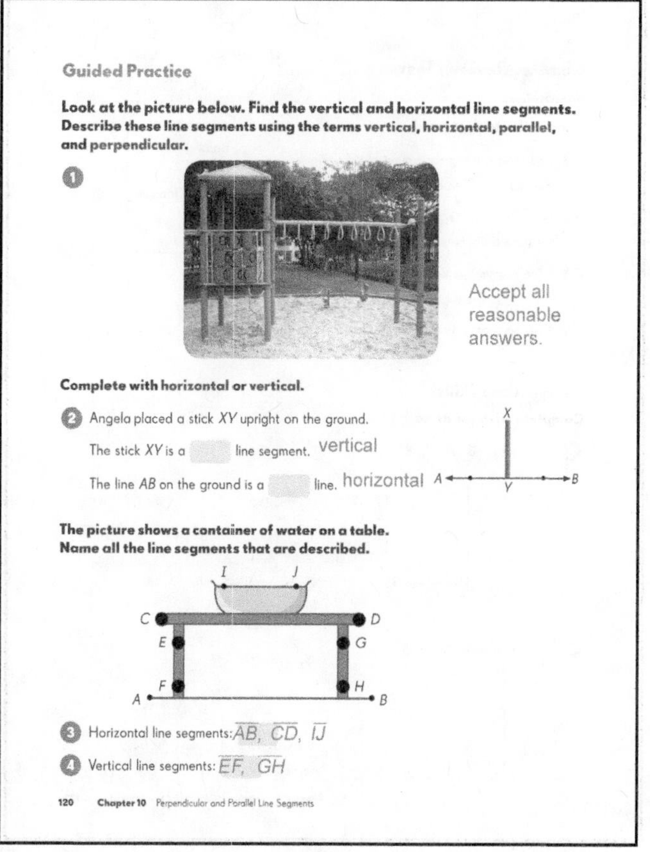
Guided Practice

Look at the picture below. Find the vertical and horizontal line segments. Describe these line segments using the terms vertical, horizontal, parallel, and perpendicular.

1. Accept all reasonable answers.

Complete with horizontal or vertical.

2. Angela placed a stick XY upright on the ground.
The stick XY is a vertical line segment.
The line AB on the ground is a horizontal line.

The picture shows a container of water on a table. Name all the line segments that are described.

3. Horizontal line segments: $\overline{AB}$, $\overline{CD}$, $\overline{IJ}$
4. Vertical line segments: $\overline{EF}$, $\overline{GH}$

120 Chapter 10 Perpendicular and Parallel Line Segments

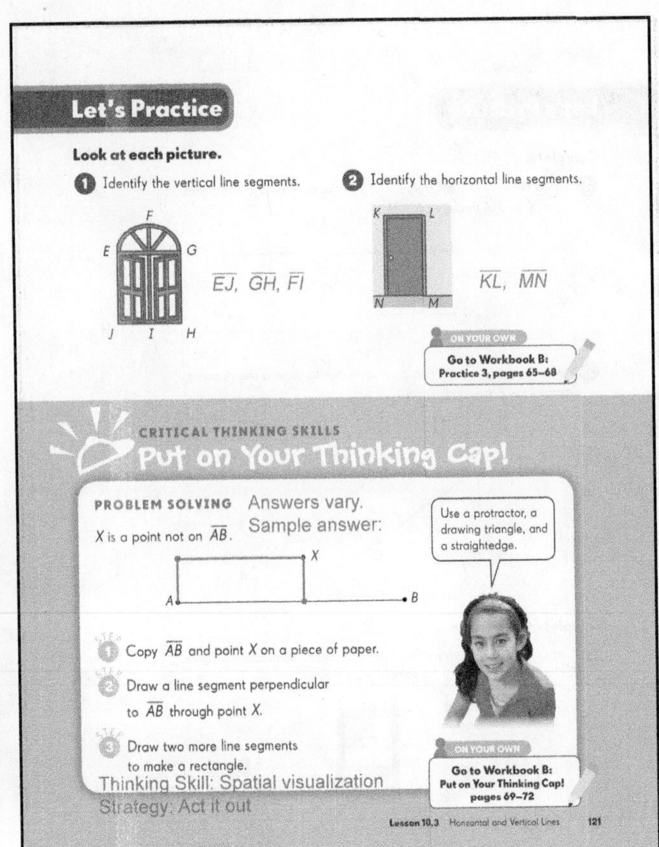

Let's Practice

Look at each picture.

1. Identify the vertical line segments.

$\overline{EJ}$, $\overline{GH}$, $\overline{FI}$

2. Identify the horizontal line segments.

$\overline{KL}$, $\overline{MN}$

ON YOUR OWN

Go to Workbook B: Practice 3, pages 65–68

CRITICAL THINKING SKILLS

Put on Your Thinking Cap!

PROBLEM SOLVING Answers vary. Sample answer:

X is a point not on $\overline{AB}$.

1. Copy $\overline{AB}$ and point *X* on a piece of paper.
2. Draw a line segment perpendicular to $\overline{AB}$ through point *X*.
3. Draw two more line segments to make a rectangle.

Thinking Skill: Spatial visualization

Strategy: Act it out

ON YOUR OWN

Go to Workbook B: Put on Your Thinking Cap! pages 69–72

Lesson 10.3 Horizontal and Vertical Lines 121

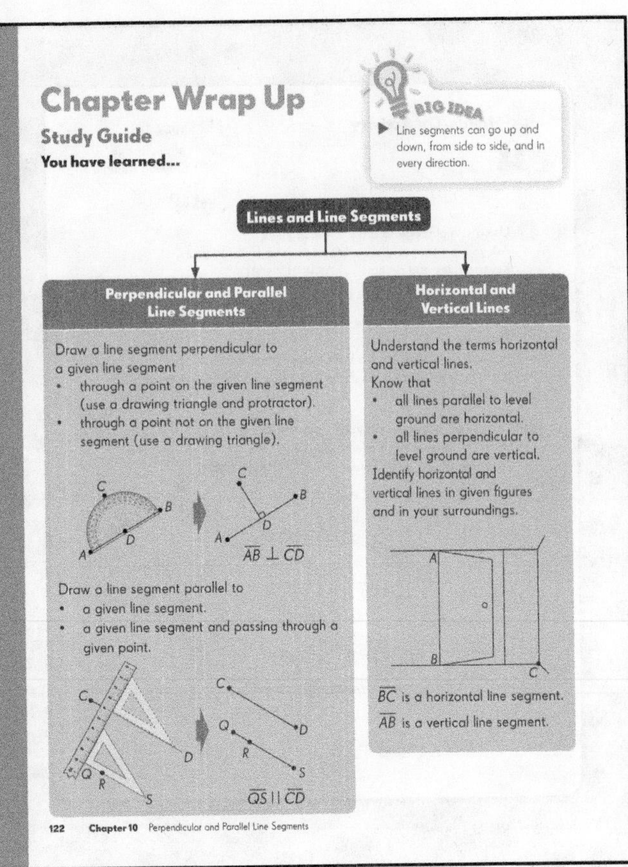

Chapter Wrap Up

Study Guide

You have learned...

BIG IDEA

▶ Line segments can go up and down, from side to side, and in every direction.

Lines and Line Segments

Perpendicular and Parallel Line Segments

Draw a line segment perpendicular to a given line segment

- through a point on the given line segment (use a drawing triangle and protractor).
- through a point not on the given line segment (use a drawing triangle).

Draw a line segment parallel to

- a given line segment.
- a given line segment and passing through a given point.

Horizontal and Vertical Lines

Understand the terms horizontal and vertical lines.

Know that

- all lines parallel to level ground are horizontal.
- all lines perpendicular to level ground are vertical.

Identify horizontal and vertical lines in given figures and in your surroundings.

$\overline{BC}$ is a horizontal line segment.

$\overline{AB}$ is a vertical line segment.

122 Chapter 10 Perpendicular and Parallel Line Segments

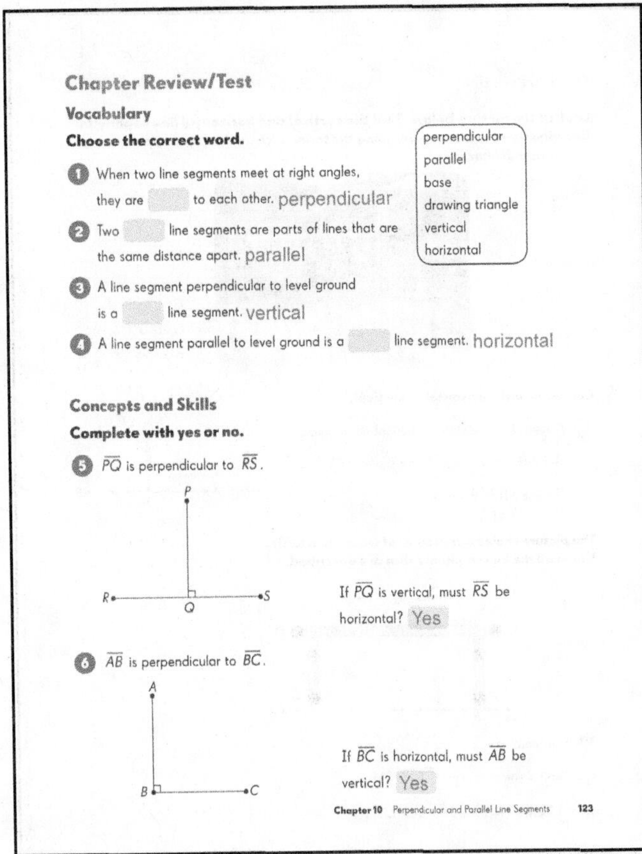

Chapter Review/Test

Vocabulary

Choose the correct word.

perpendicular
parallel
base
drawing triangle
vertical
horizontal

1. When two line segments meet at right angles, they are ___ to each other. perpendicular
2. Two ___ line segments are parts of lines that are the same distance apart. parallel
3. A line segment perpendicular to level ground is a ___ line segment. vertical
4. A line segment parallel to level ground is a ___ line segment. horizontal

Concepts and Skills

Complete with yes or no.

5. $\overline{PQ}$ is perpendicular to $\overline{RS}$.

If $\overline{PQ}$ is vertical, must $\overline{RS}$ be horizontal? Yes

6. $\overline{AB}$ is perpendicular to $\overline{BC}$.

If $\overline{BC}$ is horizontal, must $\overline{AB}$ be vertical? Yes

Chapter 10 Perpendicular and Parallel Line Segments 123

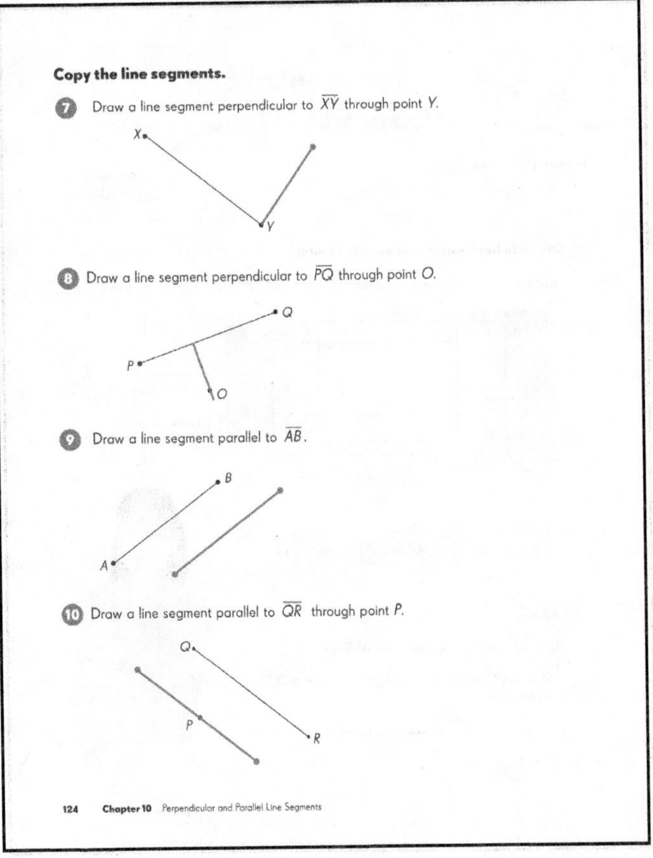

Copy the line segments.

7. Draw a line segment perpendicular to $\overline{XY}$ through point *Y*.

8. Draw a line segment perpendicular to $\overline{PQ}$ through point *O*.

9. Draw a line segment parallel to $\overline{AB}$.

10. Draw a line segment parallel to $\overline{QR}$ through point *P*.

124 Chapter 10 Perpendicular and Parallel Line Segments

Chapter 10

Chapter 11
Squares and Rectangles

Lessons
11.1 Squares and Rectangles
11.2 Properties of Squares and Rectangles

BIG IDEA
▶ Squares and rectangles are four-sided figures with special properties.

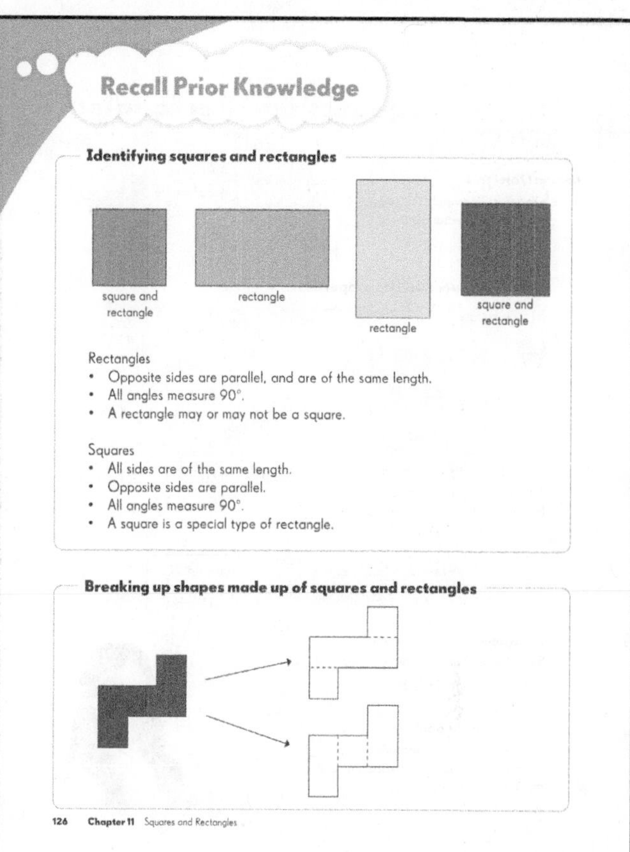

Recall Prior Knowledge

Identifying squares and rectangles

Rectangles
- Opposite sides are parallel, and are of the same length.
- All angles measure 90°.
- A rectangle may or may not be a square.

Squares
- All sides are of the same length.
- Opposite sides are parallel.
- All angles measure 90°.
- A square is a special type of rectangle.

Breaking up shapes made up of squares and rectangles

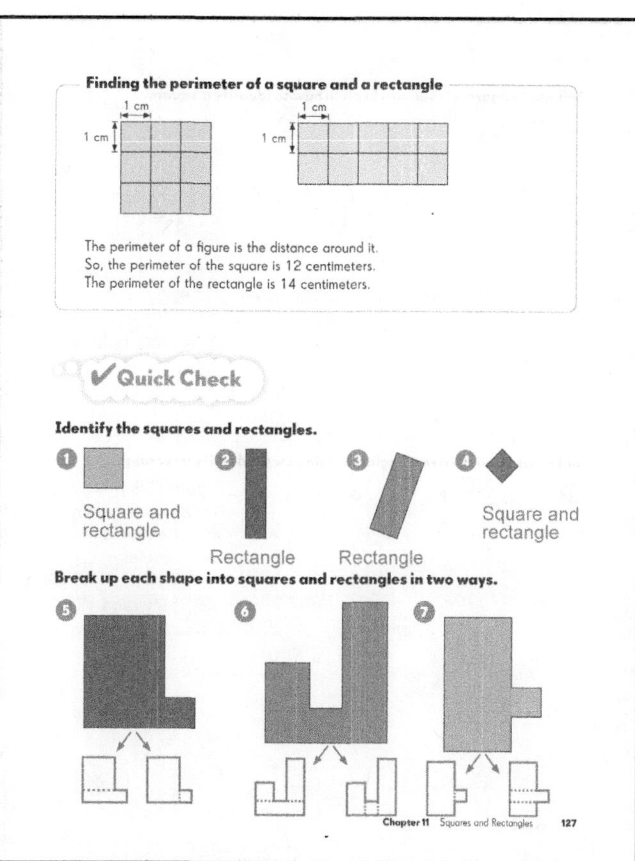

Finding the perimeter of a square and a rectangle

The perimeter of a figure is the distance around it.
So, the perimeter of the square is 12 centimeters.
The perimeter of the rectangle is 14 centimeters.

✔ Quick Check

Identify the squares and rectangles.

1. Square and rectangle
2. Rectangle
3. Rectangle
4. Square and rectangle

Break up each shape into squares and rectangles in two ways.

5.
6.
7.

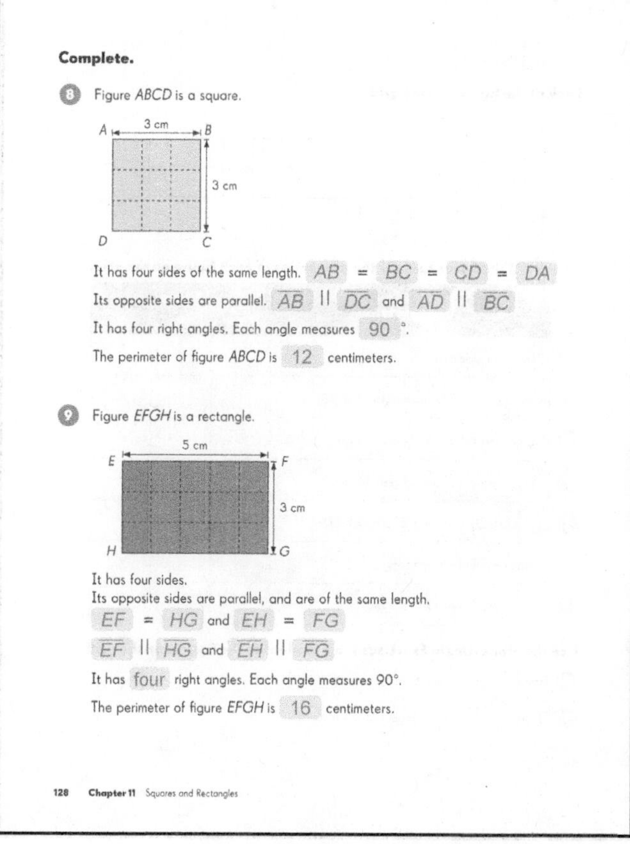

Complete.

8. Figure *ABCD* is a square.

It has four sides of the same length. AB = BC = CD = DA
Its opposite sides are parallel. $\overline{AB}$ || $\overline{DC}$ and $\overline{AD}$ || $\overline{BC}$
It has four right angles. Each angle measures 90 °.
The perimeter of figure *ABCD* is 12 centimeters.

9. Figure *EFGH* is a rectangle.

It has four sides.
Its opposite sides are parallel, and are of the same length.
EF = HG and EH = FG
$\overline{EF}$ || $\overline{HG}$ and $\overline{EH}$ || $\overline{FG}$
It has four right angles. Each angle measures 90°.
The perimeter of figure *EFGH* is 16 centimeters.

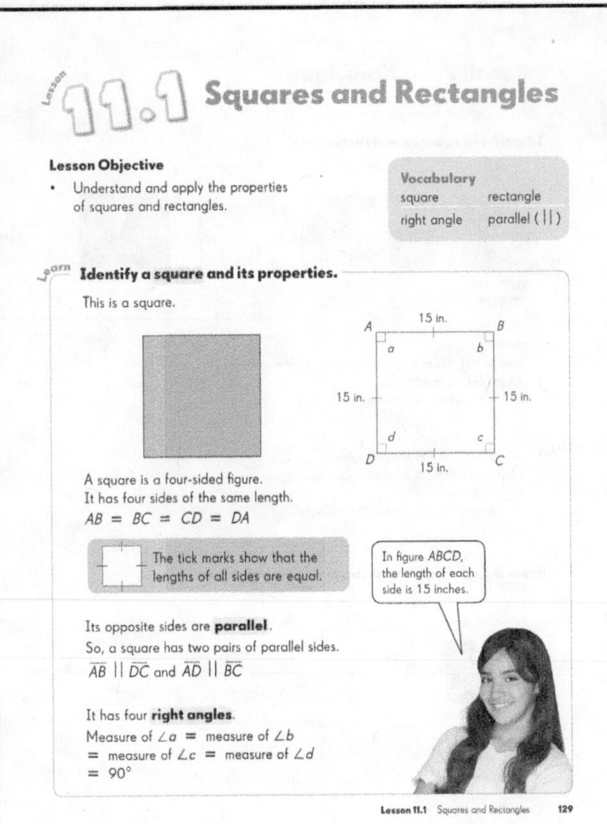

Lesson

11.1 Squares and Rectangles

Lesson Objective

- Understand and apply the properties of squares and rectangles.

Vocabulary
square　rectangle
right angle　parallel (||)

Learn **Identify a square and its properties.**

This is a square.

A square is a four-sided figure.
It has four sides of the same length.
$AB = BC = CD = DA$

The tick marks show that the lengths of all sides are equal.

In figure ABCD, the length of each side is 15 inches.

Its opposite sides are **parallel**.
So, a square has two pairs of parallel sides.
$\overline{AB} \parallel \overline{DC}$ and $\overline{AD} \parallel \overline{BC}$

It has four **right angles**.
Measure of $\angle a$ = measure of $\angle b$
= measure of $\angle c$ = measure of $\angle d$
= 90°

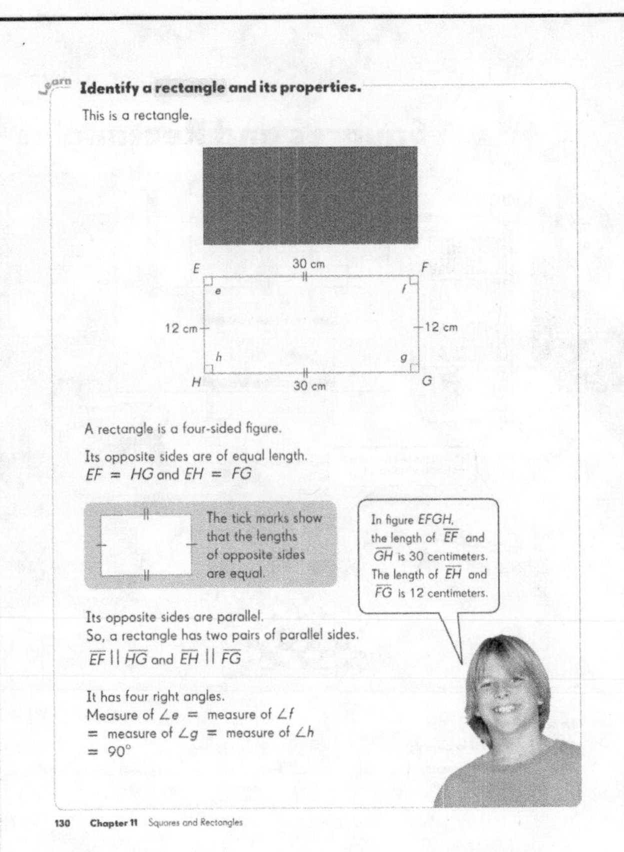

Learn **Identify a rectangle and its properties.**

This is a rectangle.

A rectangle is a four-sided figure.

Its opposite sides are of equal length.
$EF = HG$ and $EH = FG$

The tick marks show that the lengths of opposite sides are equal.

In figure EFGH, the length of EF and GH is 30 centimeters. The length of EH and FG is 12 centimeters.

Its opposite sides are parallel.
So, a rectangle has two pairs of parallel sides.
$\overline{EF} \parallel \overline{HG}$ and $\overline{EH} \parallel \overline{FG}$

It has four right angles.
Measure of $\angle e$ = measure of $\angle f$
= measure of $\angle g$ = measure of $\angle h$
= 90°

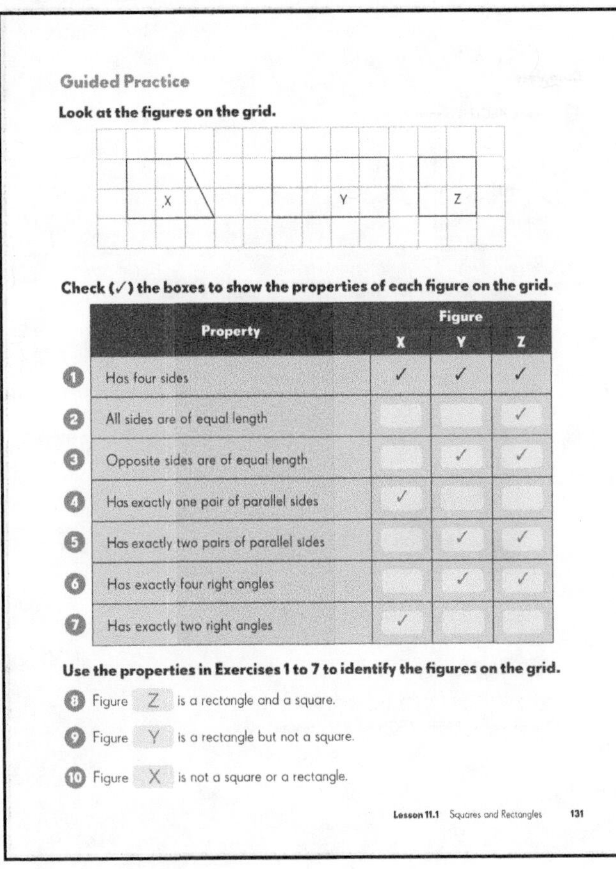

Guided Practice

Look at the figures on the grid.

Check (✓) the boxes to show the properties of each figure on the grid.

	Property	Figure X	Figure Y	Figure Z
1	Has four sides	✓	✓	✓
2	All sides are of equal length			✓
3	Opposite sides are of equal length		✓	✓
4	Has exactly one pair of parallel sides	✓		
5	Has exactly two pairs of parallel sides		✓	✓
6	Has exactly four right angles		✓	✓
7	Has exactly two right angles	✓		

Use the properties in Exercises 1 to 7 to identify the figures on the grid.

8. Figure Z is a rectangle and a square.
9. Figure Y is a rectangle but not a square.
10. Figure X is not a square or a rectangle.

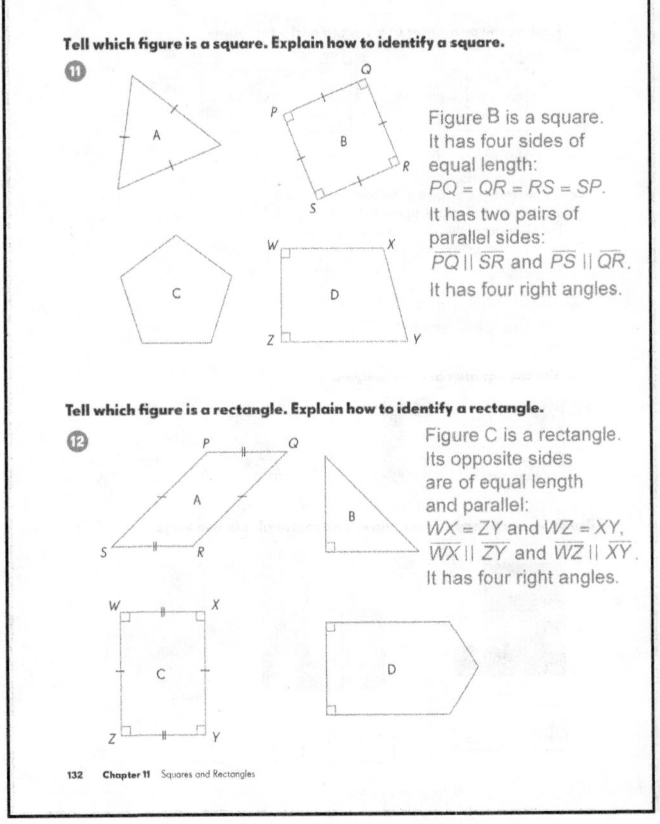

Tell which figure is a square. Explain how to identify a square.

11.

Figure B is a square.
It has four sides of equal length:
$PQ = QR = RS = SP$.
It has two pairs of parallel sides:
$\overline{PQ} \parallel \overline{SR}$ and $\overline{PS} \parallel \overline{QR}$.
It has four right angles.

Tell which figure is a rectangle. Explain how to identify a rectangle.

12.

Figure C is a rectangle.
Its opposite sides are of equal length and parallel:
$WX = ZY$ and $WZ = XY$,
$\overline{WX} \parallel \overline{ZY}$ and $\overline{WZ} \parallel \overline{XY}$.
It has four right angles.

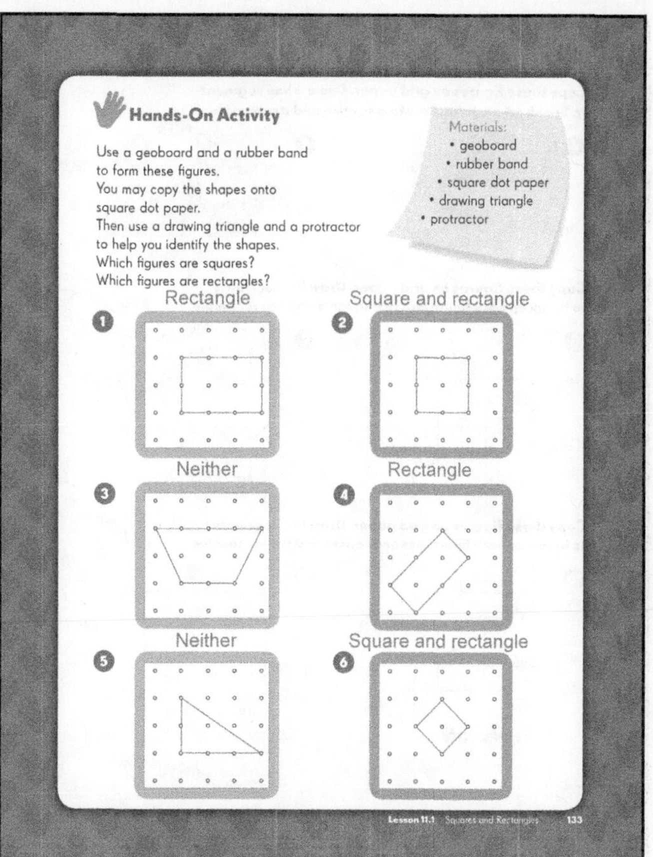

Hands-On Activity

Materials:
- geoboard
- rubber band
- square dot paper
- drawing triangle
- protractor

Use a geoboard and a rubber band to form these figures.
You may copy the shapes onto square dot paper.
Then use a drawing triangle and a protractor to help you identify the shapes.
Which figures are squares?
Which figures are rectangles?

1. Rectangle
2. Square and rectangle
3. Neither
4. Rectangle
5. Neither
6. Square and rectangle

Lesson 11.1 Squares and Rectangles 133

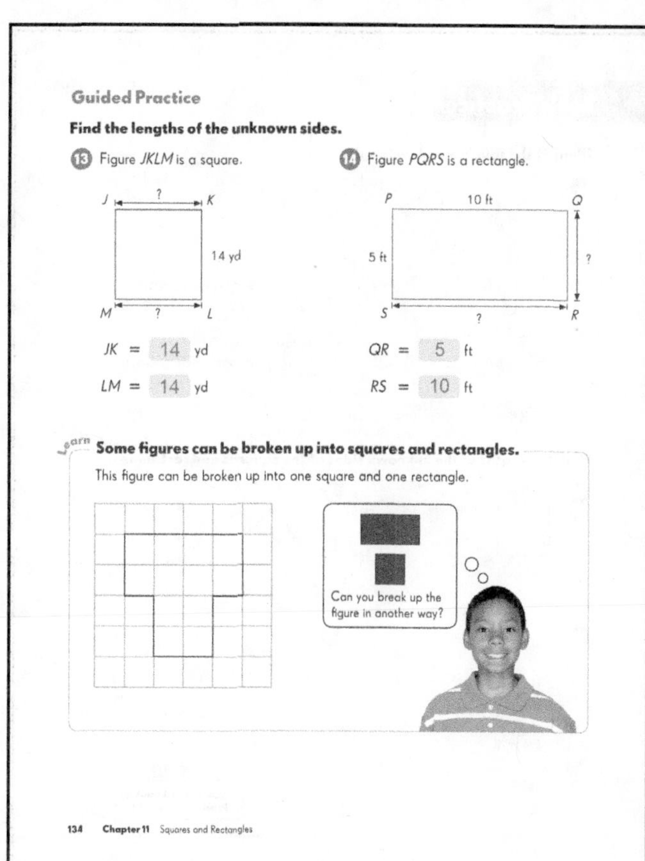

Guided Practice

Find the lengths of the unknown sides.

13. Figure *JKLM* is a square.

JK = 14 yd

LM = 14 yd

14. Figure *PQRS* is a rectangle.

QR = 5 ft

RS = 10 ft

Some figures can be broken up into squares and rectangles.

This figure can be broken up into one square and one rectangle.

134 Chapter 11 Squares and Rectangles

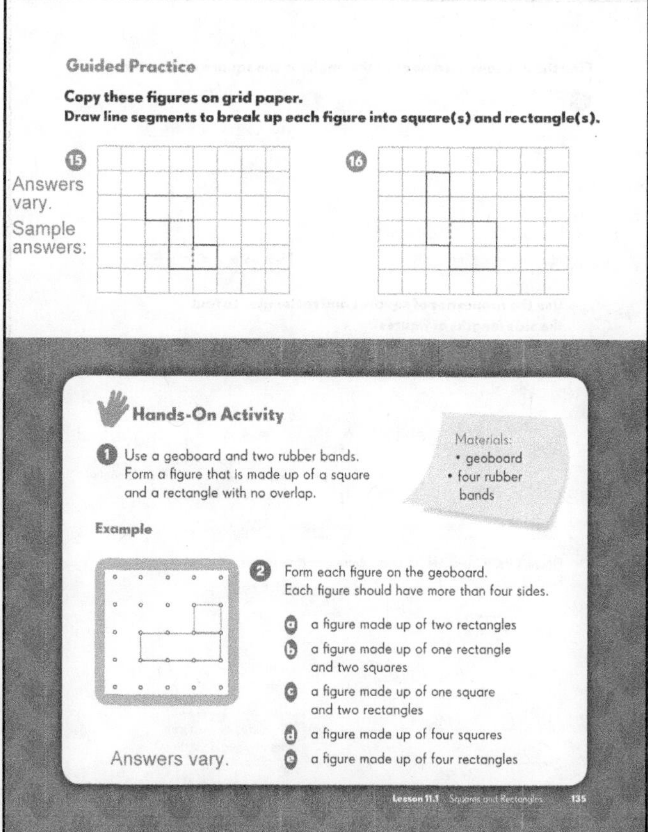

Guided Practice

Copy these figures on grid paper.
Draw line segments to break up each figure into square(s) and rectangle(s).

15. Answers vary. Sample answers:

16.

Hands-On Activity

Materials:
- geoboard
- four rubber bands

1. Use a geoboard and two rubber bands. Form a figure that is made up of a square and a rectangle with no overlap.

Example

2. Form each figure on the geoboard. Each figure should have more than four sides.
   a. a figure made up of two rectangles
   b. a figure made up of one rectangle and two squares
   c. a figure made up of one square and two rectangles
   d. a figure made up of four squares
   e. a figure made up of four rectangles

Answers vary.

Lesson 11.1 Squares and Rectangles 135

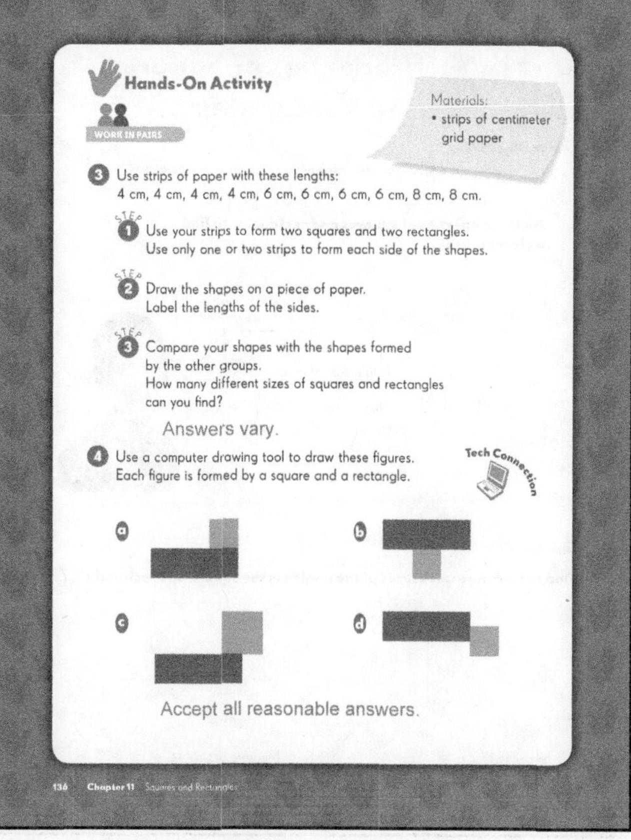

Hands-On Activity

WORK IN PAIRS

Materials:
- strips of centimeter grid paper

3. Use strips of paper with these lengths:
   4 cm, 4 cm, 4 cm, 4 cm, 6 cm, 6 cm, 6 cm, 6 cm, 8 cm, 8 cm.

   STEP 1 Use your strips to form two squares and two rectangles. Use only one or two strips to form each side of the shapes.

   STEP 2 Draw the shapes on a piece of paper. Label the lengths of the sides.

   STEP 3 Compare your shapes with the shapes formed by the other groups. How many different sizes of squares and rectangles can you find?

   Answers vary.

4. Use a computer drawing tool to draw these figures. Each figure is formed by a square and a rectangle.

Tech Connection

a. b. c. d.

Accept all reasonable answers.

136 Chapter 11 Squares and Rectangles

Chapter 11

Chapter 11

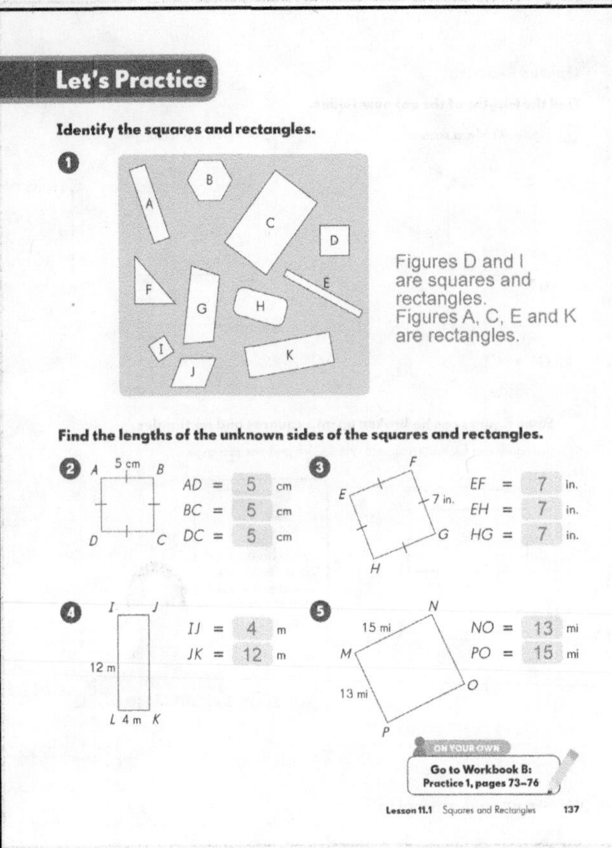

Let's Practice

Identify the squares and rectangles.

1

Figures D and I are squares and rectangles.
Figures A, C, E and K are rectangles.

Find the lengths of the unknown sides of the squares and rectangles.

2 (A, B, C, D; 5 cm)
AD = 5 cm
BC = 5 cm
DC = 5 cm

3 (E, F, G, H; 7 in.)
EF = 7 in.
EH = 7 in.
HG = 7 in.

4 (I, J, K, L; 12 m, 4 m)
IJ = 4 m
JK = 12 m

5 (M, N, O, P; 15 mi, 13 mi)
NO = 13 mi
PO = 15 mi

ON YOUR OWN
Go to Workbook B: Practice 1, pages 73–76

Lesson 11.1 Squares and Rectangles 137

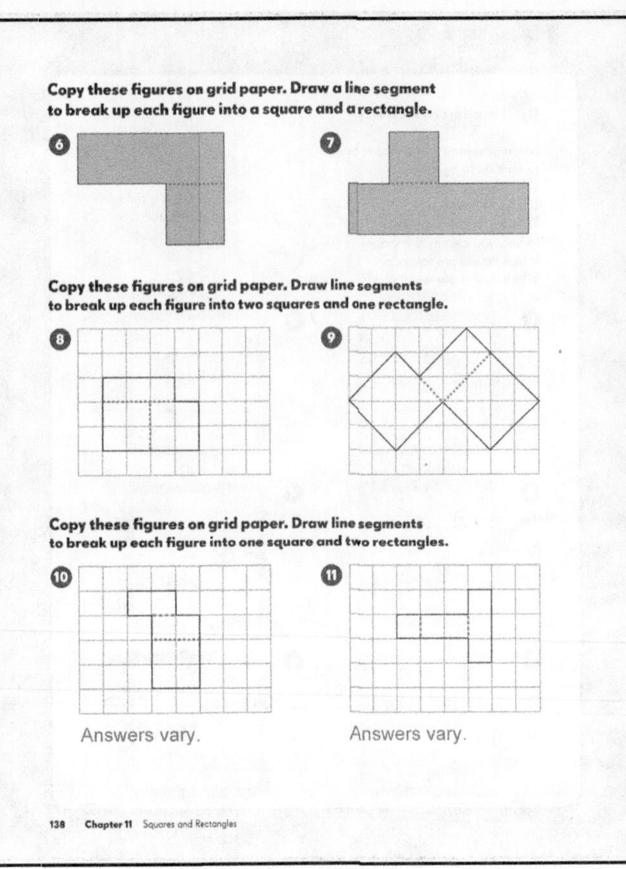

Copy these figures on grid paper. Draw a line segment to break up each figure into a square and a rectangle.

6

7

Copy these figures on grid paper. Draw line segments to break up each figure into two squares and one rectangle.

8

9

Copy these figures on grid paper. Draw line segments to break up each figure into one square and two rectangles.

10

11

Answers vary.

Answers vary.

138 Chapter 11 Squares and Rectangles

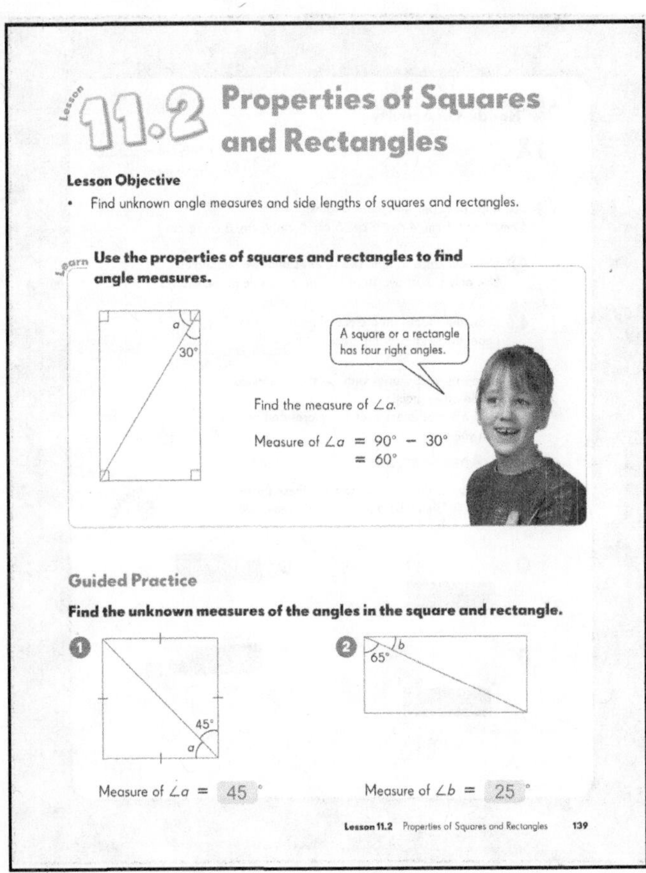

Lesson

11.2 Properties of Squares and Rectangles

Lesson Objective

- Find unknown angle measures and side lengths of squares and rectangles.

Learn **Use the properties of squares and rectangles to find angle measures.**

Find the measure of ∠a.

Measure of ∠a = 90° − 30°
= 60°

Guided Practice

Find the unknown measures of the angles in the square and rectangle.

1

Measure of ∠a = 45°

2

Measure of ∠b = 25°

Lesson 11.2 Properties of Squares and Rectangles 139

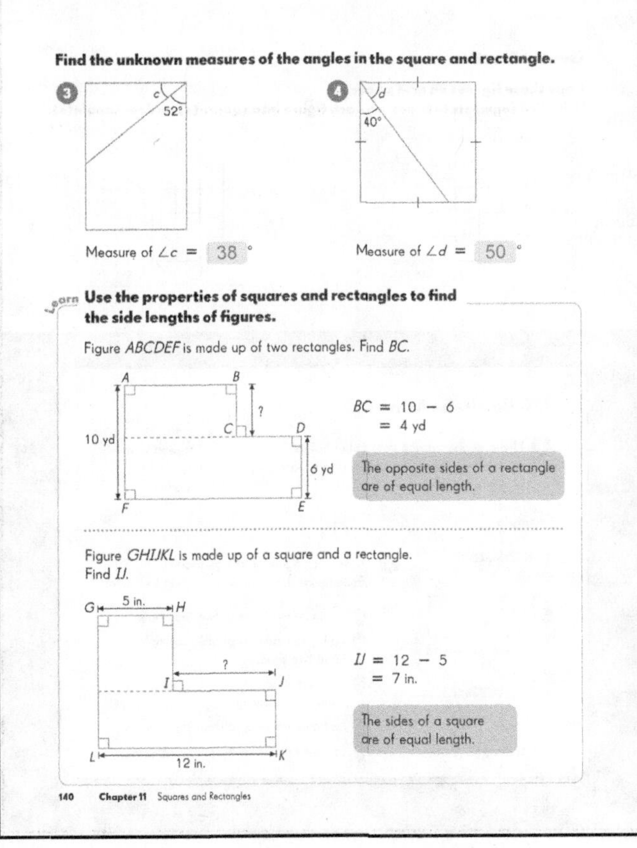

Find the unknown measures of the angles in the square and rectangle.

3

Measure of ∠c = 38°

4

Measure of ∠d = 50°

Learn **Use the properties of squares and rectangles to find the side lengths of figures.**

Figure *ABCDEF* is made up of two rectangles. Find *BC*.

BC = 10 − 6
= 4 yd

The opposite sides of a rectangle are of equal length.

Figure *GHIJKL* is made up of a square and a rectangle.
Find *IJ*.

IJ = 12 − 5
= 7 in.

The sides of a square are of equal length.

140 Chapter 11 Squares and Rectangles

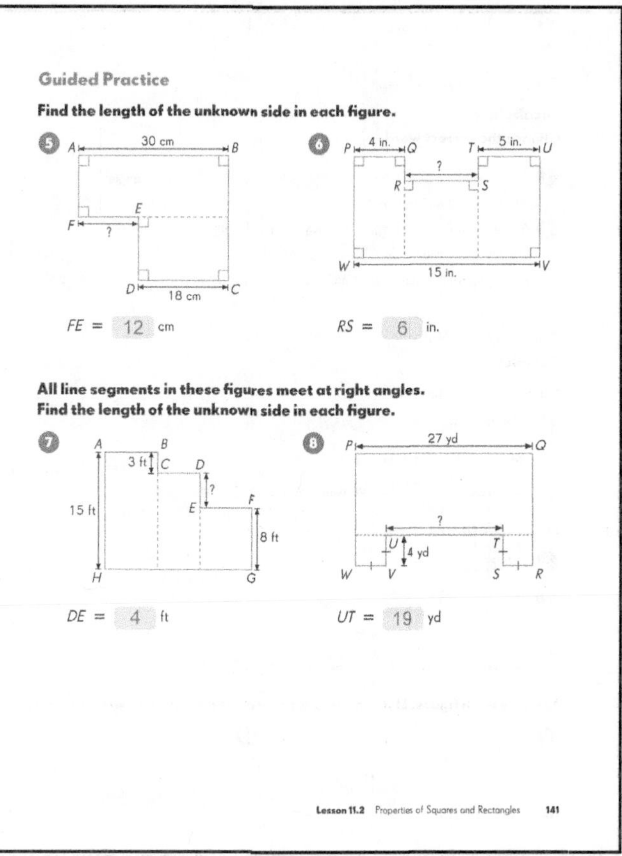
Guided Practice
Find the length of the unknown side in each figure.
FE = 12 cm
RS = 6 in.
All line segments in these figures meet at right angles.
Find the length of the unknown side in each figure.
DE = 4 ft
UT = 19 yd
Lesson 11.2 Properties of Squares and Rectangles 141

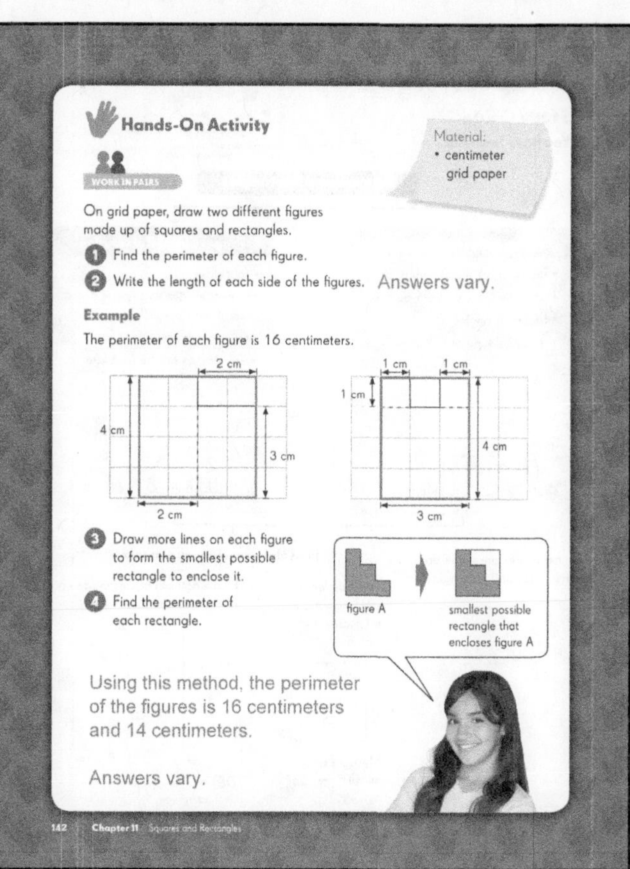
Hands-On Activity
Material:
• centimeter grid paper
On grid paper, draw two different figures made up of squares and rectangles.
1 Find the perimeter of each figure.
2 Write the length of each side of the figures. Answers vary.
Example
The perimeter of each figure is 16 centimeters.
3 Draw more lines on each figure to form the smallest possible rectangle to enclose it.
4 Find the perimeter of each rectangle.
figure A
smallest possible rectangle that encloses figure A
Using this method, the perimeter of the figures is 16 centimeters and 14 centimeters.
Answers vary.
142 Chapter 11 Squares and Rectangles

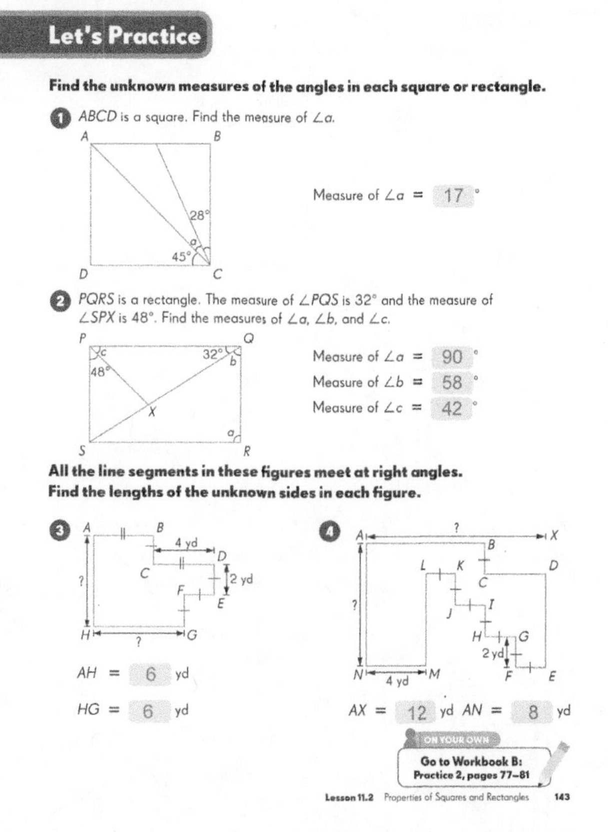
Let's Practice
Find the unknown measures of the angles in each square or rectangle.
1 ABCD is a square. Find the measure of ∠a.
Measure of ∠a = 17°
2 PQRS is a rectangle. The measure of ∠PQS is 32° and the measure of ∠SPX is 48°. Find the measures of ∠a, ∠b, and ∠c.
Measure of ∠a = 90°
Measure of ∠b = 58°
Measure of ∠c = 42°
All the line segments in these figures meet at right angles.
Find the lengths of the unknown sides in each figure.
AH = 6 yd
HG = 6 yd
AX = 12 yd AN = 8 yd
Go to Workbook B: Practice 2, pages 77–81
Lesson 11.2 Properties of Squares and Rectangles 143

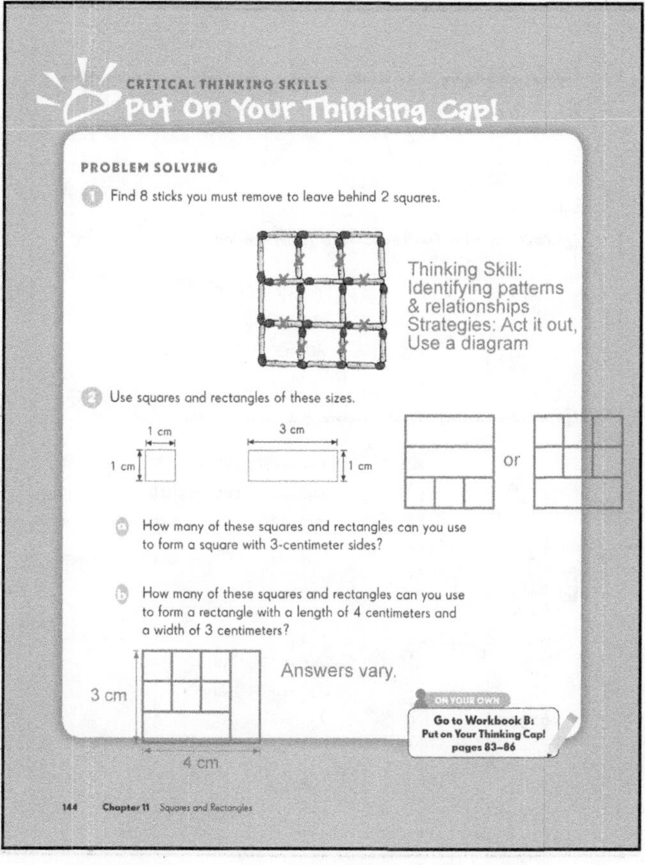
CRITICAL THINKING SKILLS
Put On Your Thinking Cap!
PROBLEM SOLVING
1 Find 8 sticks you must remove to leave behind 2 squares.
Thinking Skill: Identifying patterns & relationships
Strategies: Act it out, Use a diagram
2 Use squares and rectangles of these sizes.
a How many of these squares and rectangles can you use to form a square with 3-centimeter sides?
b How many of these squares and rectangles can you use to form a rectangle with a length of 4 centimeters and a width of 3 centimeters?
Answers vary.
Go to Workbook B: Put on Your Thinking Cap! pages 83–86
144 Chapter 11 Squares and Rectangles

Chapter 11

Chapter 11

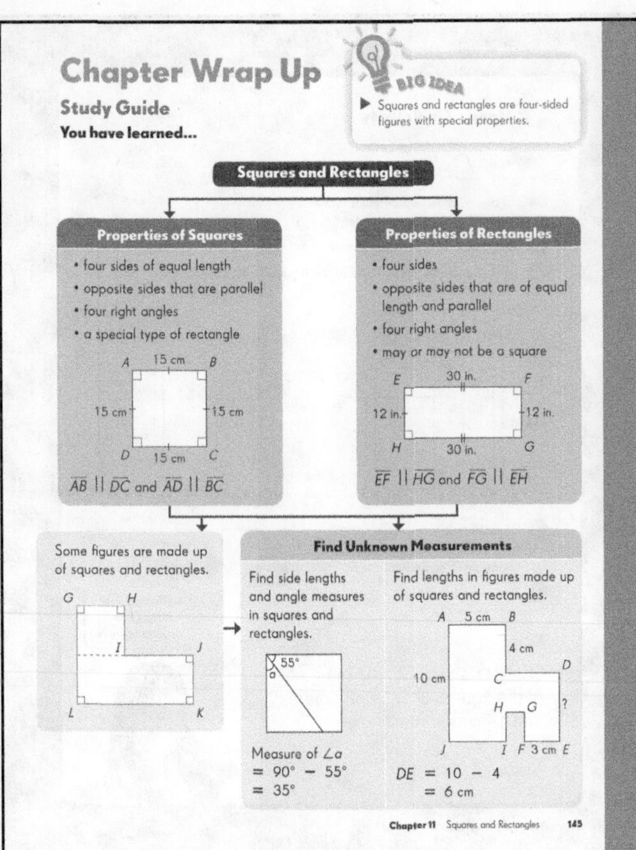

Chapter Wrap Up

Study Guide

You have learned...

BIG IDEA

▶ Squares and rectangles are four-sided figures with special properties.

Squares and Rectangles

Properties of Squares

- four sides of equal length
- opposite sides that are parallel
- four right angles
- a special type of rectangle

A 15 cm B, 15 cm, 15 cm, D 15 cm C

$\overline{AB} \parallel \overline{DC}$ and $\overline{AD} \parallel \overline{BC}$

Properties of Rectangles

- four sides
- opposite sides that are of equal length and parallel
- four right angles
- may or may not be a square

E 30 in. F, 12 in., 12 in., H 30 in. G

$\overline{EF} \parallel \overline{HG}$ and $\overline{FG} \parallel \overline{EH}$

Some figures are made up of squares and rectangles.

G H I J L K

Find Unknown Measurements

Find side lengths and angle measures in squares and rectangles.

55°, a

Measure of $\angle a$
$= 90° - 55°$
$= 35°$

Find lengths in figures made up of squares and rectangles.

A 5 cm B, 4 cm, 10 cm, C, D, H G, ?, J, I F 3 cm E

$DE = 10 - 4$
$= 6$ cm

Chapter 11 Squares and Rectangles 145

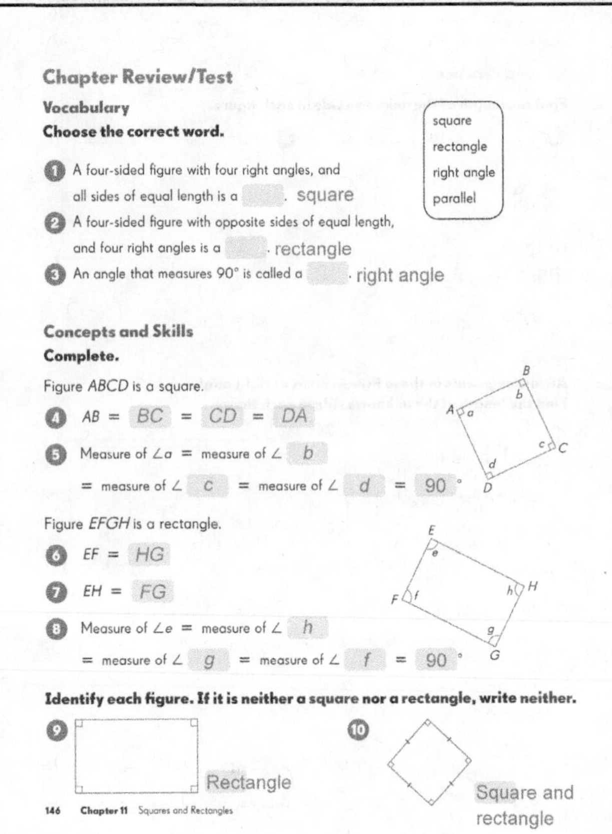

Chapter Review/Test

Vocabulary

Choose the correct word.

square / rectangle / right angle / parallel

1. A four-sided figure with four right angles, and all sides of equal length is a ____. square
2. A four-sided figure with opposite sides of equal length, and four right angles is a ____. rectangle
3. An angle that measures 90° is called a ____. right angle

Concepts and Skills

Complete.

Figure *ABCD* is a square.

4. AB = BC = CD = DA
5. Measure of $\angle a$ = measure of $\angle$ b = measure of $\angle$ c = measure of $\angle$ d = 90°

Figure *EFGH* is a rectangle.

6. EF = HG
7. EH = FG
8. Measure of $\angle e$ = measure of $\angle$ h = measure of $\angle$ g = measure of $\angle$ f = 90°

Identify each figure. If it is neither a square nor a rectangle, write neither.

9. Rectangle
10. Square and rectangle

146 Chapter 11 Squares and Rectangles

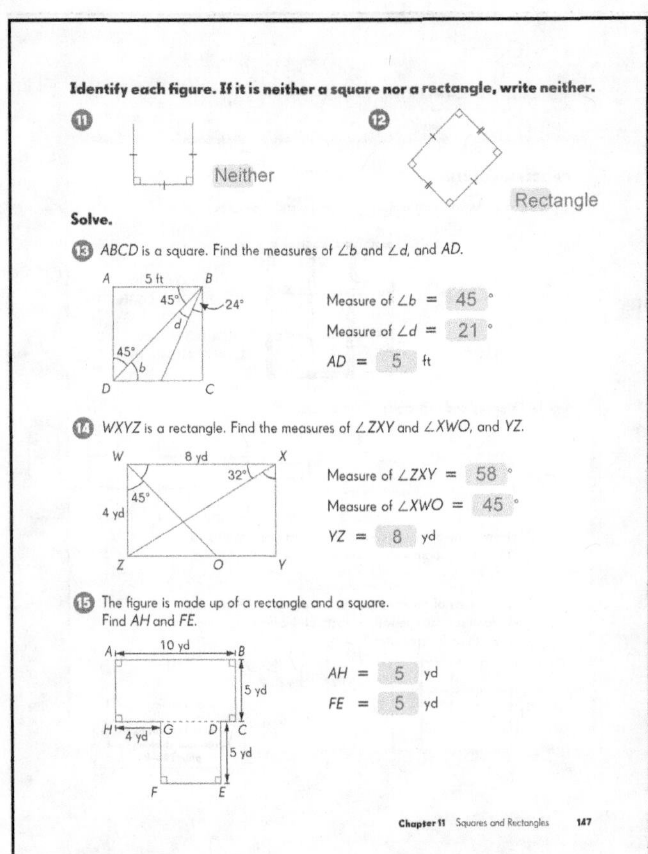

Identify each figure. If it is neither a square nor a rectangle, write neither.

11. Neither
12. Rectangle

Solve.

13. *ABCD* is a square. Find the measures of $\angle b$ and $\angle d$, and AD.

A 5 ft B, 45°, 24°, d, 45°, b, D C

Measure of $\angle b$ = 45°
Measure of $\angle d$ = 21°
AD = 5 ft

14. *WXYZ* is a rectangle. Find the measures of $\angle ZXY$ and $\angle XWO$, and YZ.

W 8 yd X, 32°, 45°, 4 yd, Z O Y

Measure of $\angle ZXY$ = 58°
Measure of $\angle XWO$ = 45°
YZ = 8 yd

15. The figure is made up of a rectangle and a square. Find AH and FE.

A 10 yd B, 5 yd, H 4 yd G, D C, 5 yd, F E

AH = 5 yd
FE = 5 yd

Chapter 11 Squares and Rectangles 147

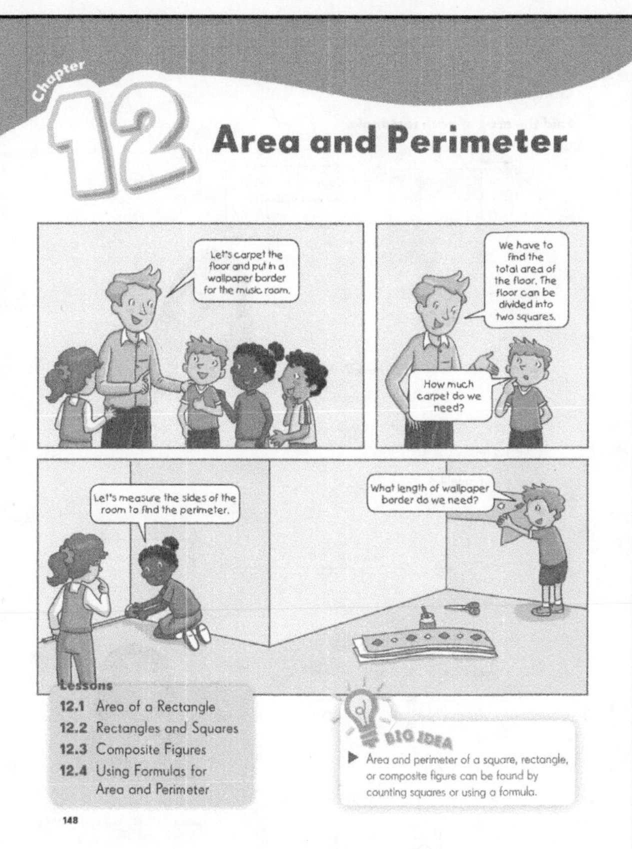

Chapter 12

Area and Perimeter

Let's carpet the floor and put in a wallpaper border for the music room.
We have to find the total area of the floor. The floor can be divided into two squares.
How much carpet do we need?
Let's measure the sides of the room to find the perimeter.
What length of wallpaper border do we need?

Lessons

BIG IDEA

▶ Area and perimeter of a square, rectangle, or composite figure can be found by counting squares or using a formula.

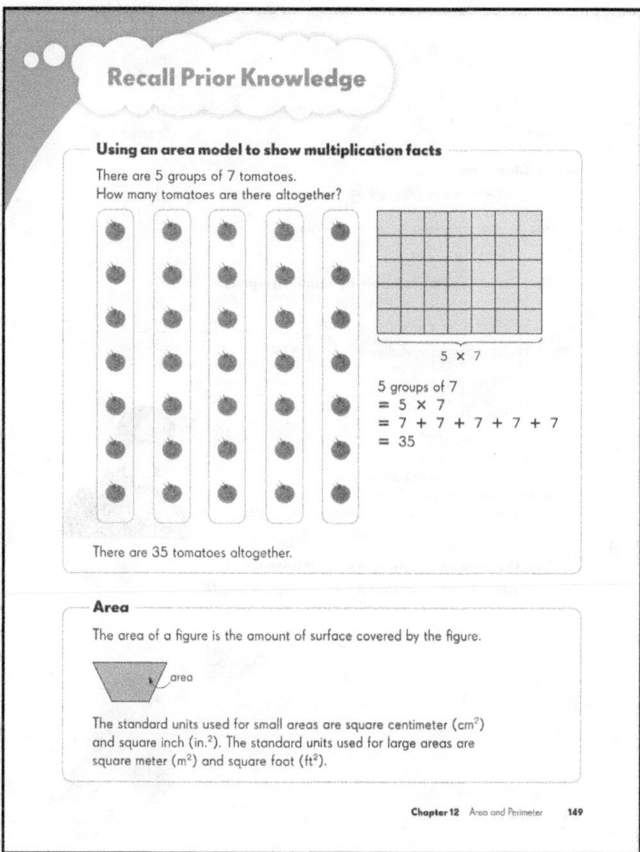

Recall Prior Knowledge

Using an area model to show multiplication facts

There are 5 groups of 7 tomatoes.
How many tomatoes are there altogether?

5 groups of 7
= 5 × 7
= 7 + 7 + 7 + 7 + 7
= 35

There are 35 tomatoes altogether.

Area

The area of a figure is the amount of surface covered by the figure.

The standard units used for small areas are square centimeter (cm^2) and square inch ($in.^2$). The standard units used for large areas are square meter (m^2) and square foot (ft^2).

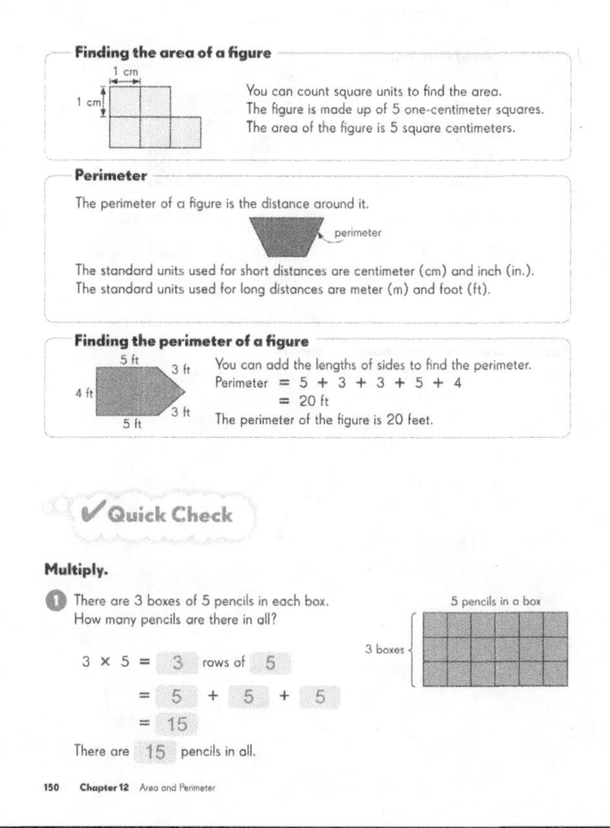

Finding the area of a figure

You can count square units to find the area.
The figure is made up of 5 one-centimeter squares.
The area of the figure is 5 square centimeters.

Perimeter

The perimeter of a figure is the distance around it.

The standard units used for short distances are centimeter (cm) and inch (in.).
The standard units used for long distances are meter (m) and foot (ft).

Finding the perimeter of a figure

You can add the lengths of sides to find the perimeter.
Perimeter = 5 + 3 + 3 + 5 + 4
= 20 ft
The perimeter of the figure is 20 feet.

Quick Check

Multiply.

1. There are 3 boxes of 5 pencils in each box.
How many pencils are there in all?

3 × 5 = 3 rows of 5
= 5 + 5 + 5
= 15

There are 15 pencils in all.

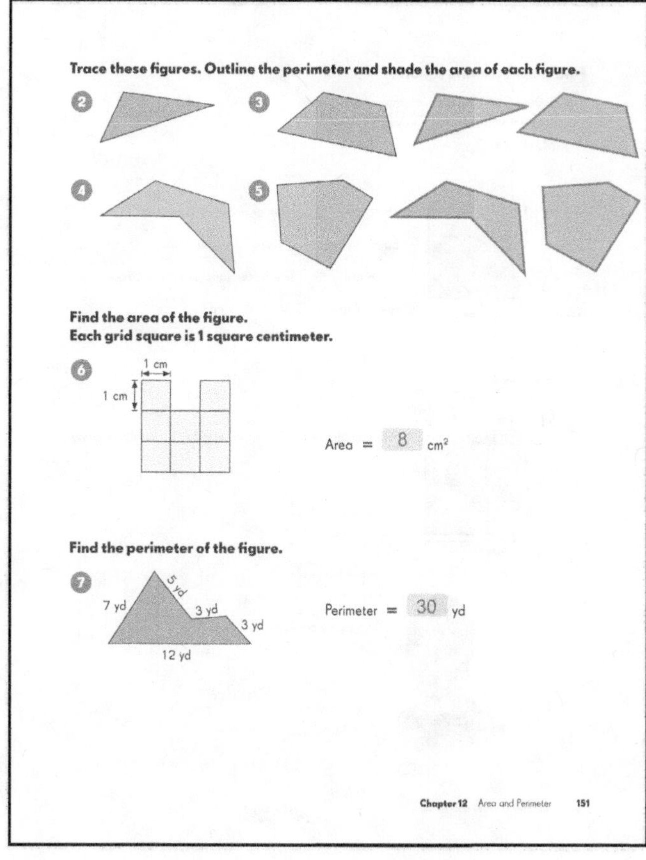

Trace these figures. Outline the perimeter and shade the area of each figure.

2 3 4 5

Find the area of the figure.
Each grid square is 1 square centimeter.

6

Area = 8 cm^2

Find the perimeter of the figure.

7

Perimeter = 30 yd

Chapter 12

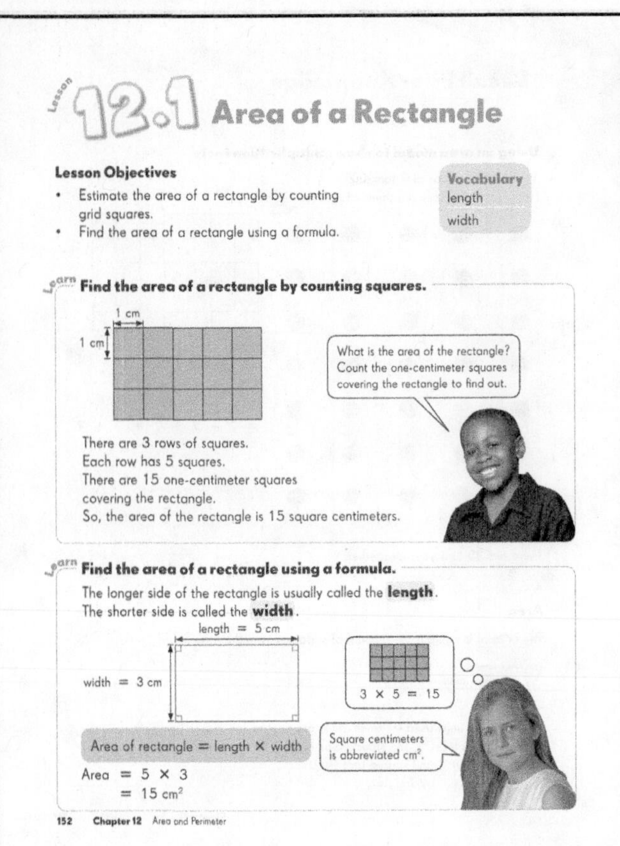

Lesson 12.1 Area of a Rectangle

Lesson Objectives

- Estimate the area of a rectangle by counting grid squares.
- Find the area of a rectangle using a formula.

Vocabulary
length
width

Learn **Find the area of a rectangle by counting squares.**

There are 3 rows of squares.
Each row has 5 squares.
There are 15 one-centimeter squares covering the rectangle.
So, the area of the rectangle is 15 square centimeters.

Learn **Find the area of a rectangle using a formula.**

The longer side of the rectangle is usually called the **length**.
The shorter side is called the **width**.

Area of rectangle = length × width

Area = 5 × 3
= 15 cm²

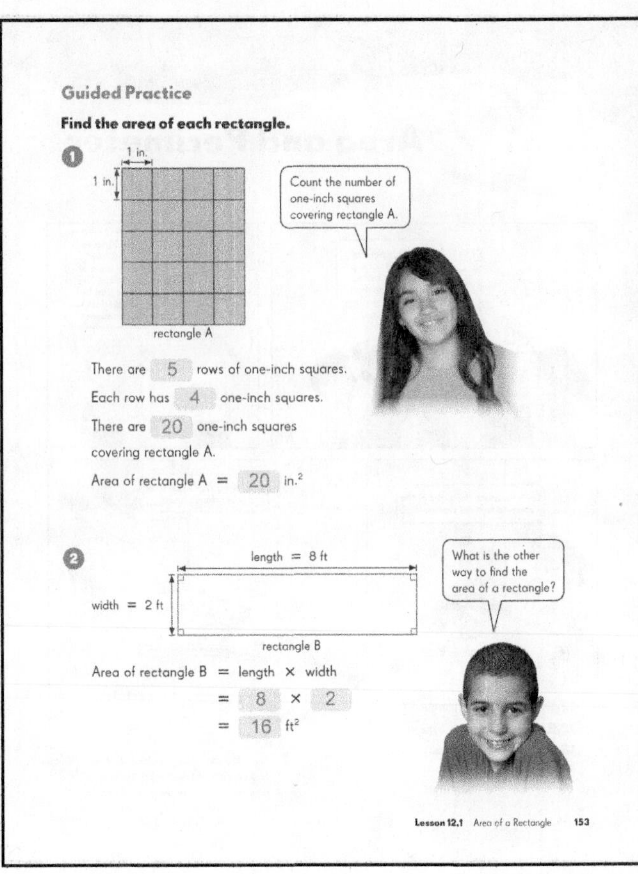

Guided Practice

Find the area of each rectangle.

1

There are 5 rows of one-inch squares.
Each row has 4 one-inch squares.
There are 20 one-inch squares covering rectangle A.
Area of rectangle A = 20 in.²

2

Area of rectangle B = length × width
= 8 × 2
= 16 ft²

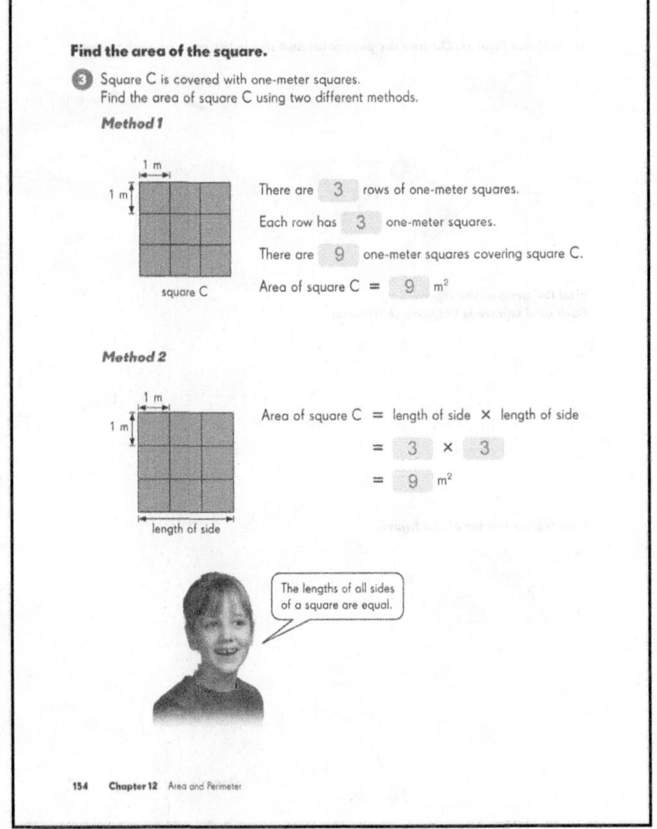

Find the area of the square.

3 Square C is covered with one-meter squares.
Find the area of square C using two different methods.

Method 1

There are 3 rows of one-meter squares.
Each row has 3 one-meter squares.
There are 9 one-meter squares covering square C.
Area of square C = 9 m²

Method 2

Area of square C = length of side × length of side
= 3 × 3
= 9 m²

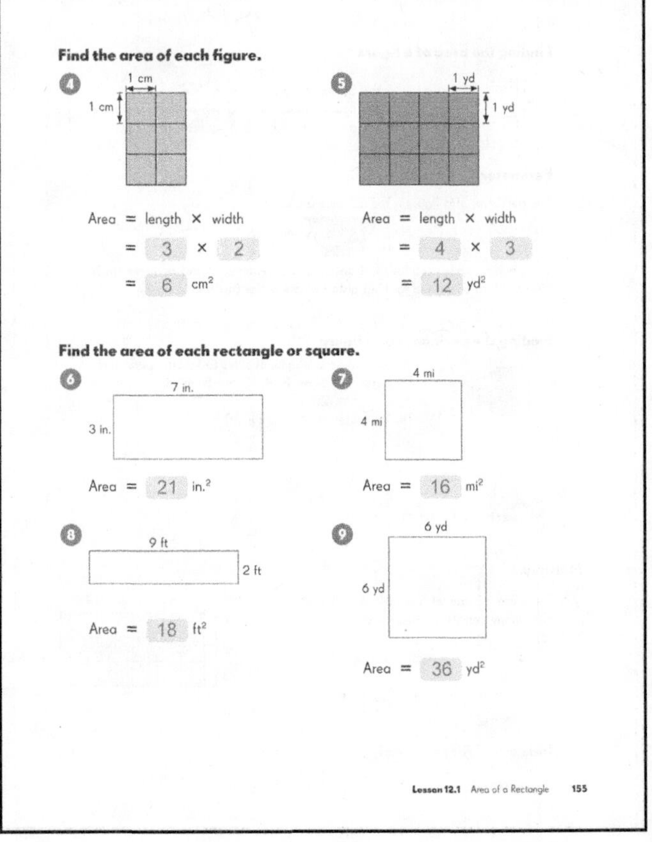

Find the area of each figure.

4

Area = length × width
= 3 × 2
= 6 cm²

5

Area = length × width
= 4 × 3
= 12 yd²

Find the area of each rectangle or square.

6

Area = 21 in.²

7

Area = 16 mi²

8

Area = 18 ft²

9

Area = 36 yd²

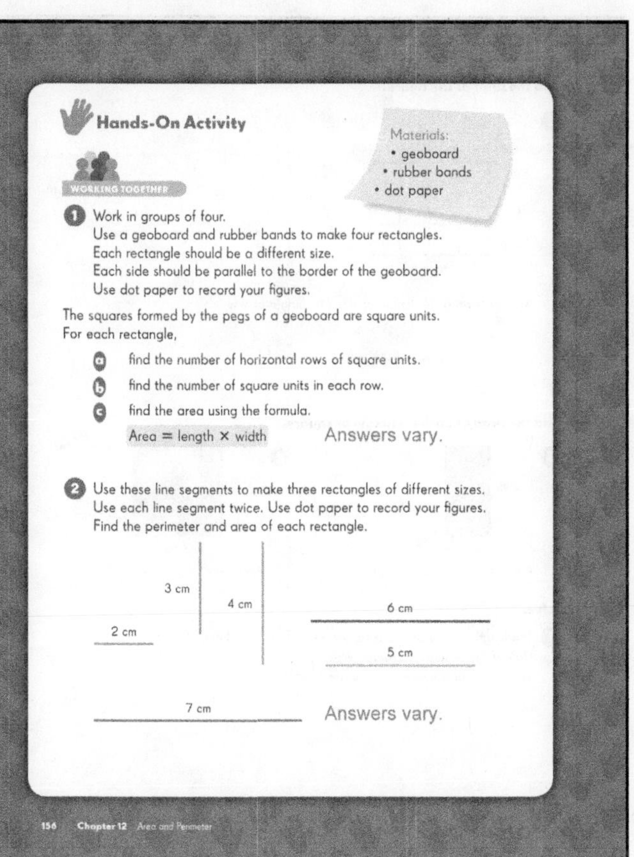

Hands-On Activity

WORKING TOGETHER

Materials:
- geoboard
- rubber bands
- dot paper

1. Work in groups of four.
Use a geoboard and rubber bands to make four rectangles.
Each rectangle should be a different size.
Each side should be parallel to the border of the geoboard.
Use dot paper to record your figures.

The squares formed by the pegs of a geoboard are square units.
For each rectangle,

a. find the number of horizontal rows of square units.
b. find the number of square units in each row.
c. find the area using the formula.
Area = length × width   Answers vary.

2. Use these line segments to make three rectangles of different sizes.
Use each line segment twice. Use dot paper to record your figures.
Find the perimeter and area of each rectangle.

Answers vary.

156 Chapter 12 Area and Perimeter

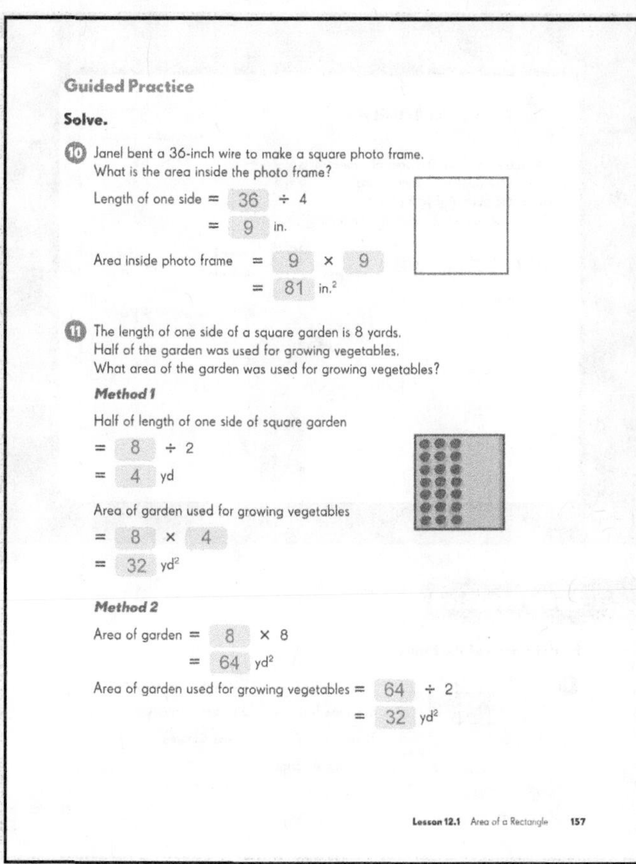

Guided Practice

Solve.

10. Janel bent a 36-inch wire to make a square photo frame.
What is the area inside the photo frame?

Length of one side = 36 ÷ 4
= 9 in.

Area inside photo frame = 9 × 9
= 81 in.^{2}

11. The length of one side of a square garden is 8 yards.
Half of the garden was used for growing vegetables.
What area of the garden was used for growing vegetables?

Method 1

Half of length of one side of square garden
= 8 ÷ 2
= 4 yd

Area of garden used for growing vegetables
= 8 × 4
= 32 yd^2

Method 2

Area of garden = 8 × 8
= 64 yd^2

Area of garden used for growing vegetables = 64 ÷ 2
= 32 yd^2

Lesson 12.1 Area of a Rectangle 157

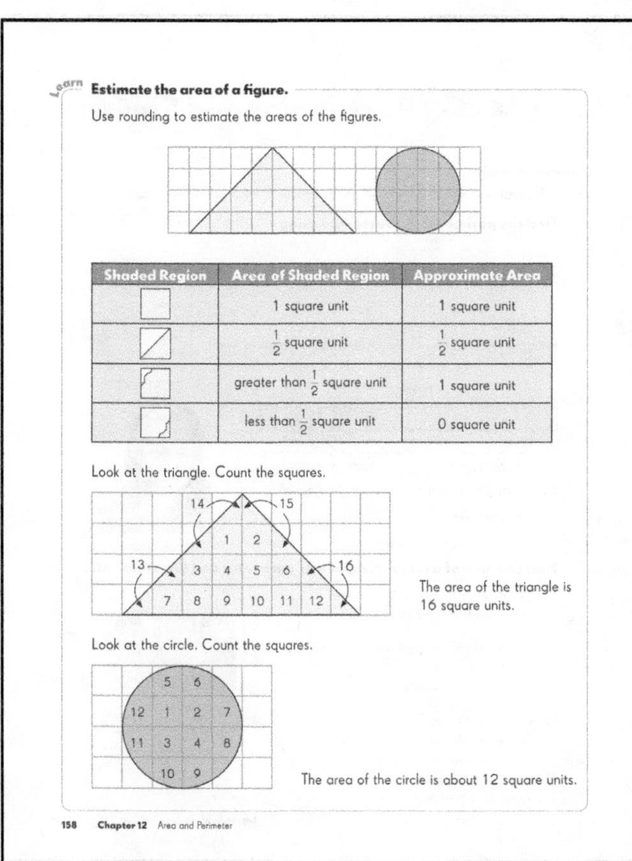

Learn: Estimate the area of a figure.

Use rounding to estimate the areas of the figures.

Shaded Region	Area of Shaded Region	Approximate Area
	1 square unit	1 square unit
	$\frac{1}{2}$ square unit	$\frac{1}{2}$ square unit
	greater than $\frac{1}{2}$ square unit	1 square unit
	less than $\frac{1}{2}$ square unit	0 square unit

Look at the triangle. Count the squares.

The area of the triangle is 16 square units.

Look at the circle. Count the squares.

The area of the circle is about 12 square units.

158 Chapter 12 Area and Perimeter

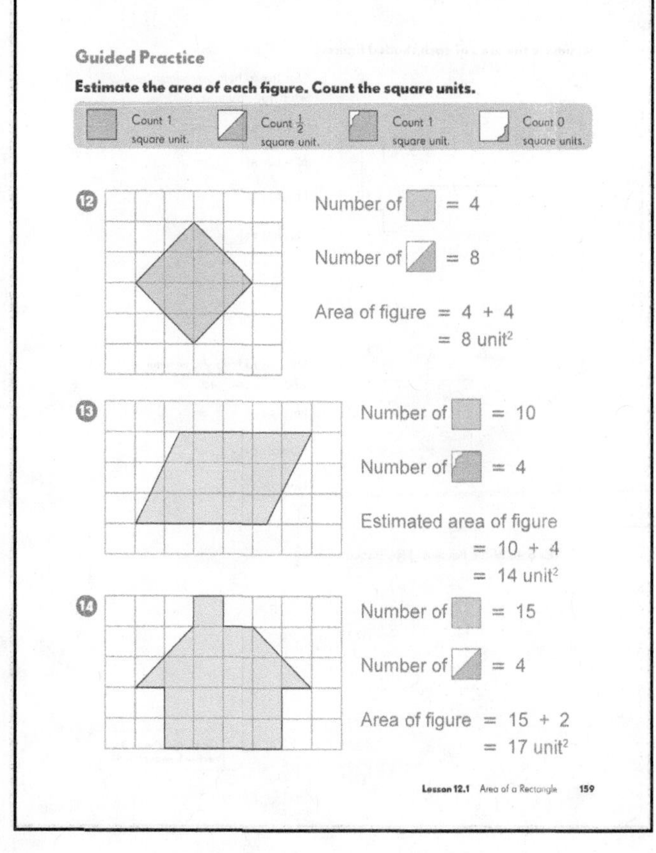

Guided Practice

Estimate the area of each figure. Count the square units.

Count 1 square unit. Count $\frac{1}{2}$ square unit. Count 1 square unit. Count 0 square units.

12. Number of (full squares) = 4
Number of (half squares) = 8
Area of figure = 4 + 4
= 8 unit^2

13. Number of (full squares) = 10
Number of (more than half squares) = 4
Estimated area of figure
= 10 + 4
= 14 unit^2

14. Number of (full squares) = 15
Number of (half squares) = 4
Area of figure = 15 + 2
= 17 unit^2

Lesson 12.1 Area of a Rectangle 159

Chapter 12

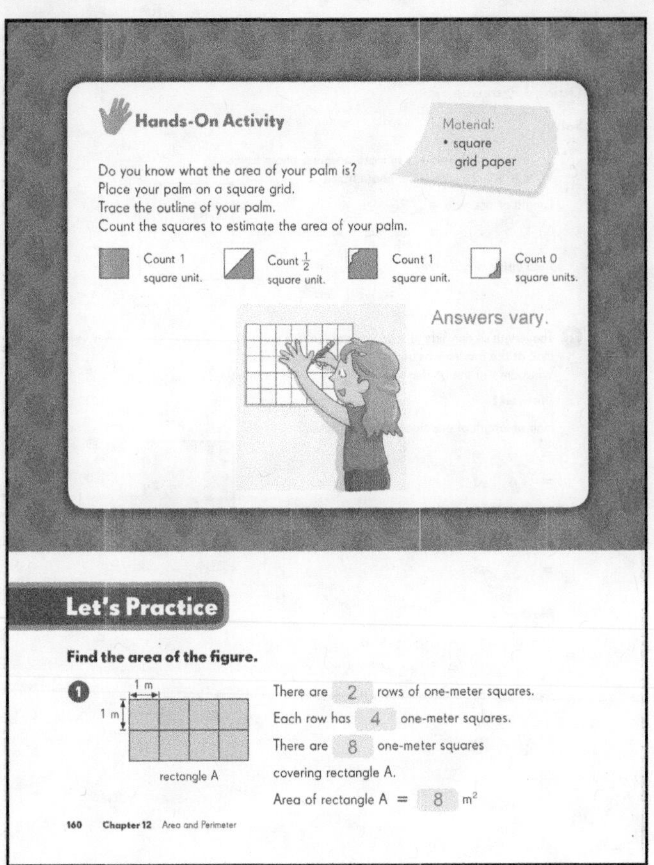

Hands-On Activity

Material:
- square grid paper

Do you know what the area of your palm is?
Place your palm on a square grid.
Trace the outline of your palm.
Count the squares to estimate the area of your palm.

Count 1 square unit. Count $\frac{1}{2}$ square unit. Count 1 square unit. Count 0 square units.

Answers vary.

Let's Practice

Find the area of the figure.

1. There are 2 rows of one-meter squares.
Each row has 4 one-meter squares.
There are 8 one-meter squares covering rectangle A.
Area of rectangle A = 8 m^2

160 Chapter 12 Area and Perimeter

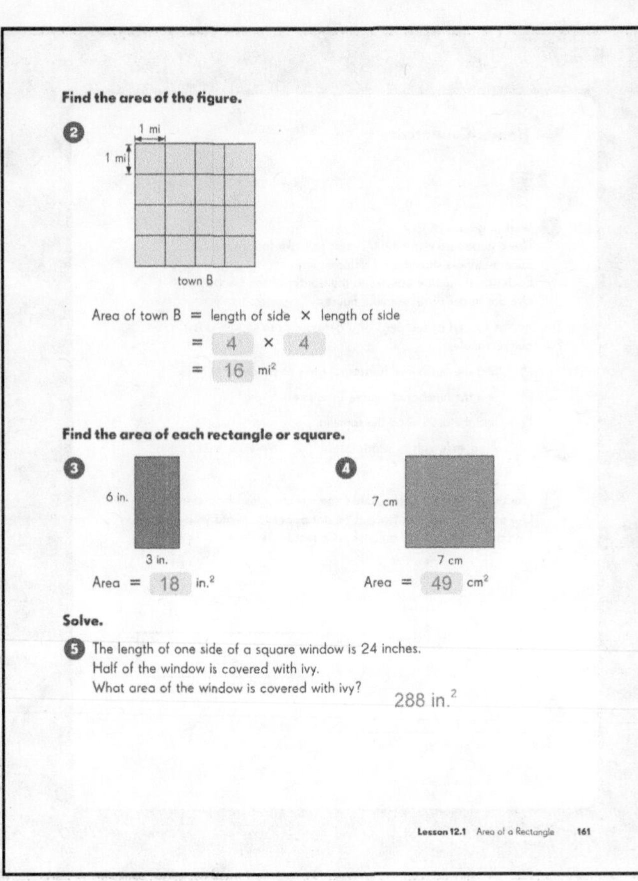

Find the area of the figure.

2.

Area of town B = length of side × length of side
= 4 × 4
= 16 mi^2

Find the area of each rectangle or square.

3. Area = 18 $in.^2$

4. Area = 49 cm^2

Solve.

5. The length of one side of a square window is 24 inches.
Half of the window is covered with ivy.
What area of the window is covered with ivy?

288 $in.^2$

Lesson 12.1 Area of a Rectangle 161

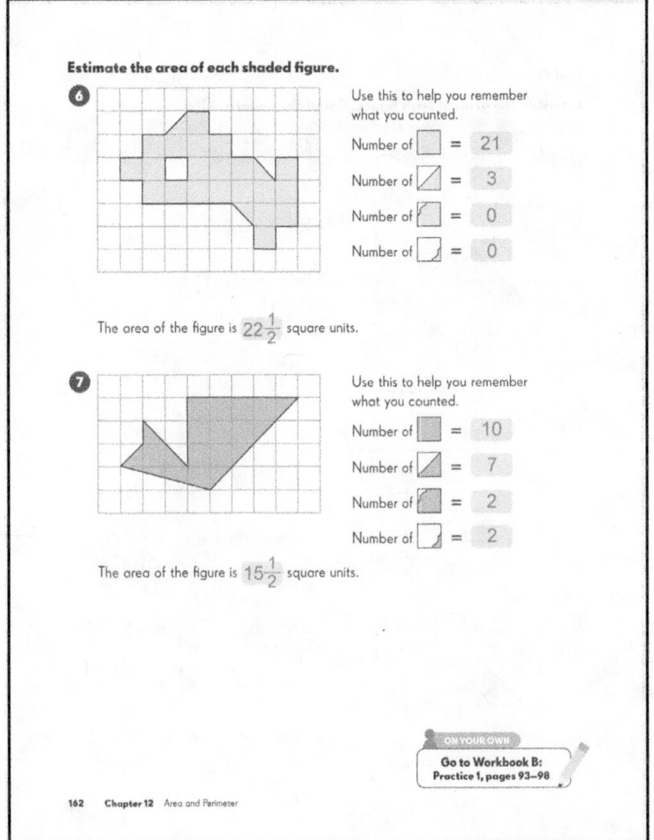

Estimate the area of each shaded figure.

6. Use this to help you remember what you counted.

Number of [full square] = 21
Number of [half square] = 3
Number of [more than half] = 0
Number of [less than half] = 0

The area of the figure is $22\frac{1}{2}$ square units.

7. Use this to help you remember what you counted.

Number of [full square] = 10
Number of [half square] = 7
Number of [more than half] = 2
Number of [less than half] = 2

The area of the figure is $15\frac{1}{2}$ square units.

ON YOUR OWN
Go to Workbook B: Practice 1, pages 93–98

162 Chapter 12 Area and Perimeter

Chapter 12

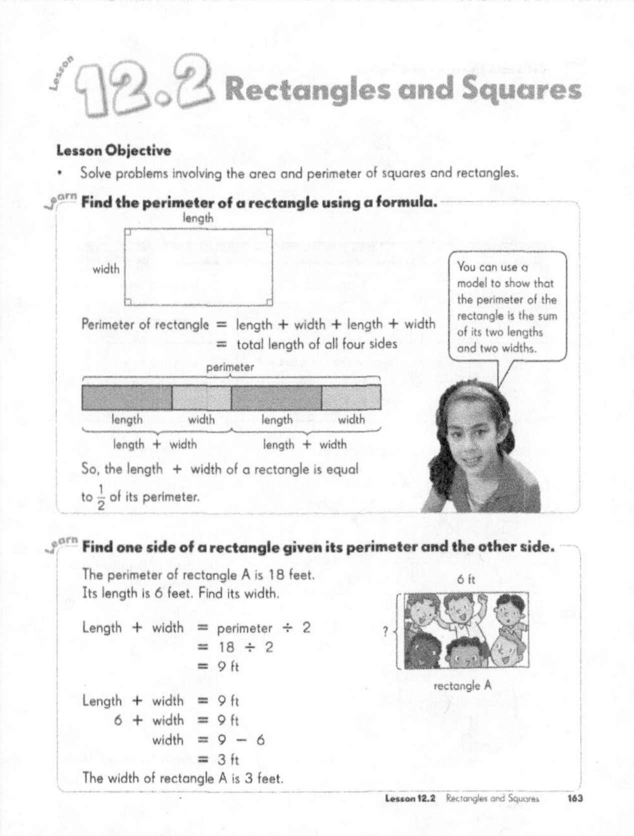

Lesson 12.2 Rectangles and Squares

Lesson Objective

- Solve problems involving the area and perimeter of squares and rectangles.

Learn Find the perimeter of a rectangle using a formula.

Perimeter of rectangle = length + width + length + width
= total length of all four sides

So, the length + width of a rectangle is equal to $\frac{1}{2}$ of its perimeter.

Learn Find one side of a rectangle given its perimeter and the other side.

The perimeter of rectangle A is 18 feet.
Its length is 6 feet. Find its width.

Length + width = perimeter ÷ 2
= 18 ÷ 2
= 9 ft

Length + width = 9 ft
6 + width = 9 ft
width = 9 − 6
= 3 ft

The width of rectangle A is 3 feet.

Lesson 12.2 Rectangles and Squares 163

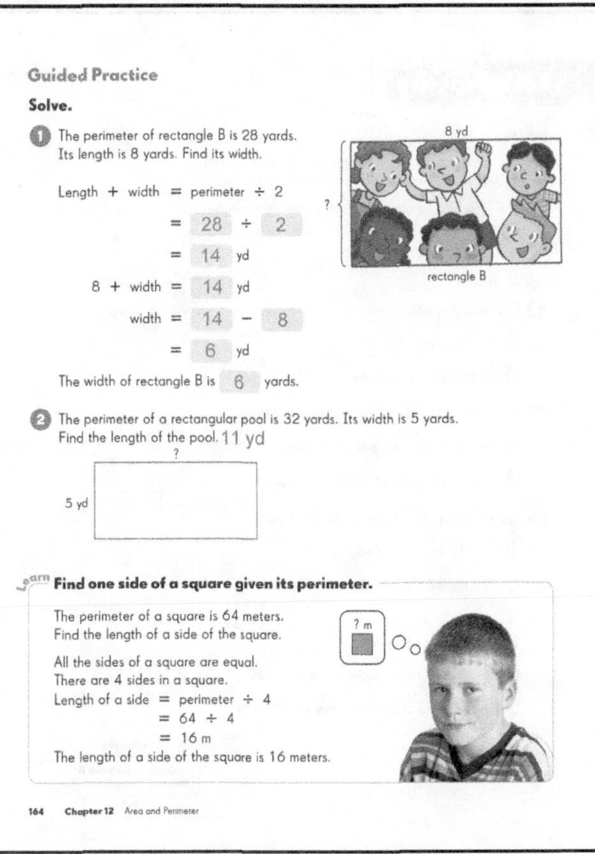

Guided Practice

Solve.

1. The perimeter of rectangle B is 28 yards. Its length is 8 yards. Find its width.

Length + width = perimeter ÷ 2
= 28 ÷ 2
= 14 yd
8 + width = 14 yd
width = 14 − 8
= 6 yd

The width of rectangle B is 6 yards.

2. The perimeter of a rectangular pool is 32 yards. Its width is 5 yards. Find the length of the pool. 11 yd

Learn Find one side of a square given its perimeter.

The perimeter of a square is 64 meters.
Find the length of a side of the square.

All the sides of a square are equal.
There are 4 sides in a square.
Length of a side = perimeter ÷ 4
= 64 ÷ 4
= 16 m
The length of a side of the square is 16 meters.

164 Chapter 12 Area and Perimeter

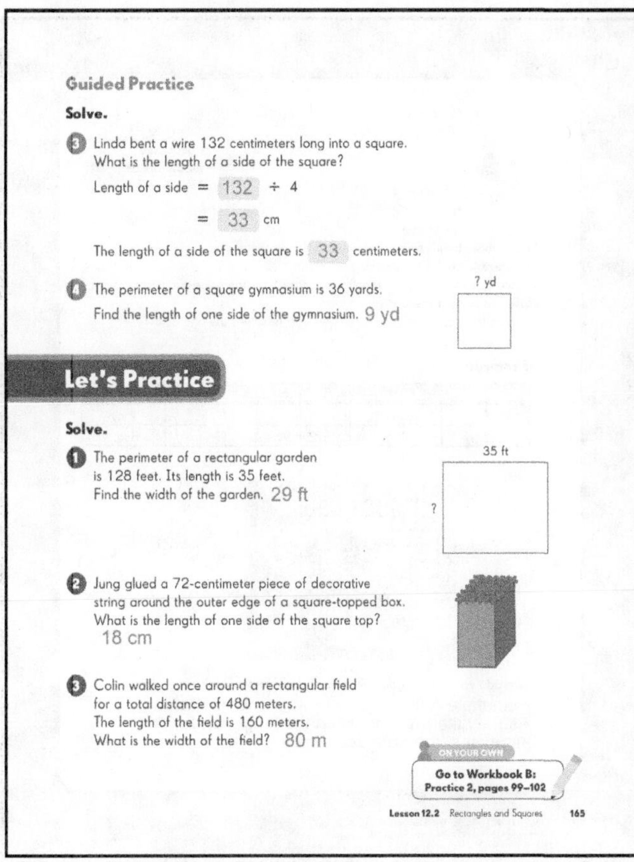

Guided Practice

Solve.

3. Linda bent a wire 132 centimeters long into a square. What is the length of a side of the square?

Length of a side = 132 ÷ 4
= 33 cm

The length of a side of the square is 33 centimeters.

4. The perimeter of a square gymnasium is 36 yards. Find the length of one side of the gymnasium. 9 yd

Let's Practice

Solve.

1. The perimeter of a rectangular garden is 128 feet. Its length is 35 feet. Find the width of the garden. 29 ft

2. Jung glued a 72-centimeter piece of decorative string around the outer edge of a square-topped box. What is the length of one side of the square top? 18 cm

3. Colin walked once around a rectangular field for a total distance of 480 meters. The length of the field is 160 meters. What is the width of the field? 80 m

ON YOUR OWN
Go to Workbook B: Practice 2, pages 99–102

Lesson 12.2 Rectangles and Squares 165

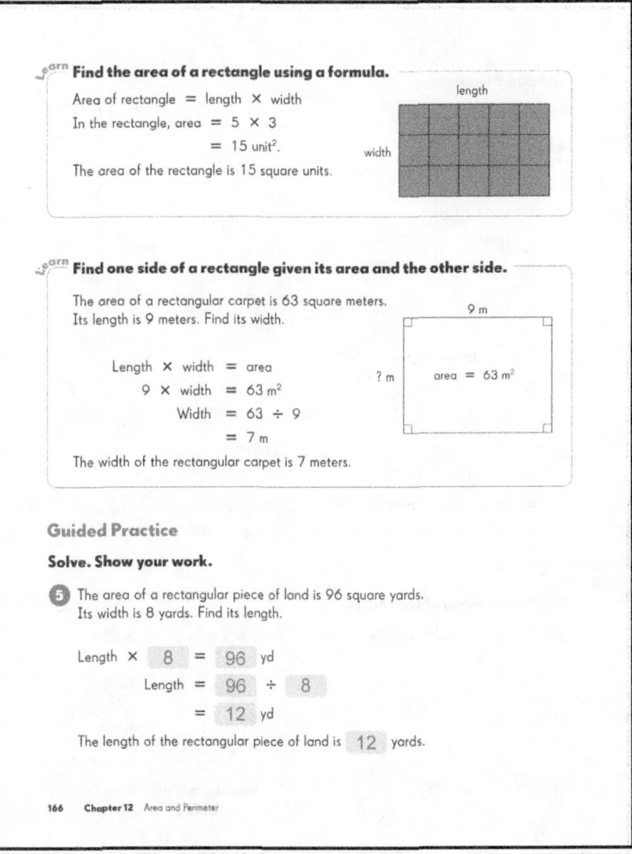

Learn Find the area of a rectangle using a formula.

Area of rectangle = length × width
In the rectangle, area = 5 × 3
= 15 unit².
The area of the rectangle is 15 square units.

Learn Find one side of a rectangle given its area and the other side.

The area of a rectangular carpet is 63 square meters. Its length is 9 meters. Find its width.

Length × width = area
9 × width = 63 m²
Width = 63 ÷ 9
= 7 m
The width of the rectangular carpet is 7 meters.

Guided Practice

Solve. Show your work.

5. The area of a rectangular piece of land is 96 square yards. Its width is 8 yards. Find its length.

Length × 8 = 96 yd
Length = 96 ÷ 8
= 12 yd

The length of the rectangular piece of land is 12 yards.

166 Chapter 12 Area and Perimeter

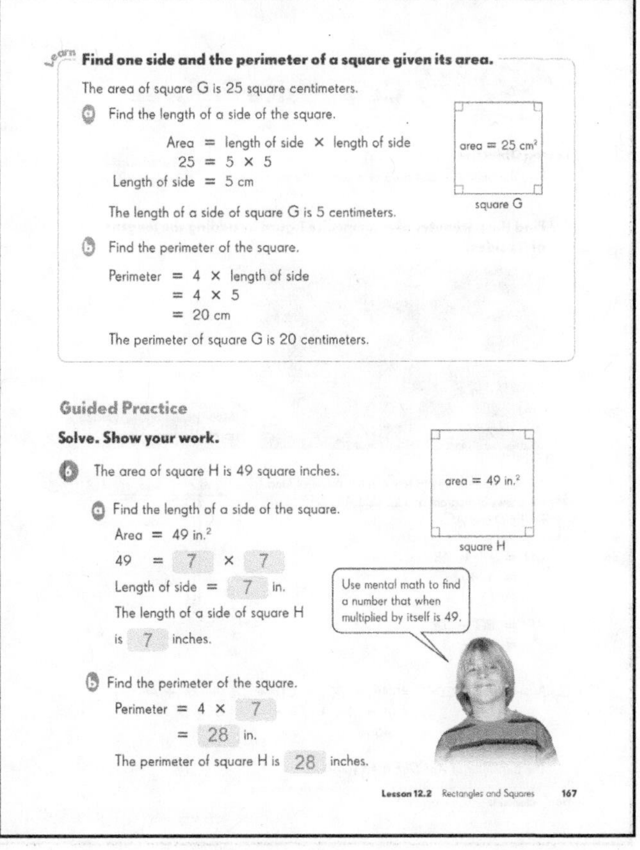

Learn Find one side and the perimeter of a square given its area.

The area of square G is 25 square centimeters.

a. Find the length of a side of the square.

Area = length of side × length of side
25 = 5 × 5
Length of side = 5 cm

The length of a side of square G is 5 centimeters.

b. Find the perimeter of the square.

Perimeter = 4 × length of side
= 4 × 5
= 20 cm

The perimeter of square G is 20 centimeters.

Guided Practice

Solve. Show your work.

6. The area of square H is 49 square inches.

a. Find the length of a side of the square.

Area = 49 in.²
49 = 7 × 7
Length of side = 7 in.
The length of a side of square H is 7 inches.

b. Find the perimeter of the square.

Perimeter = 4 × 7
= 28 in.

The perimeter of square H is 28 inches.

Lesson 12.2 Rectangles and Squares 167

Chapter 12

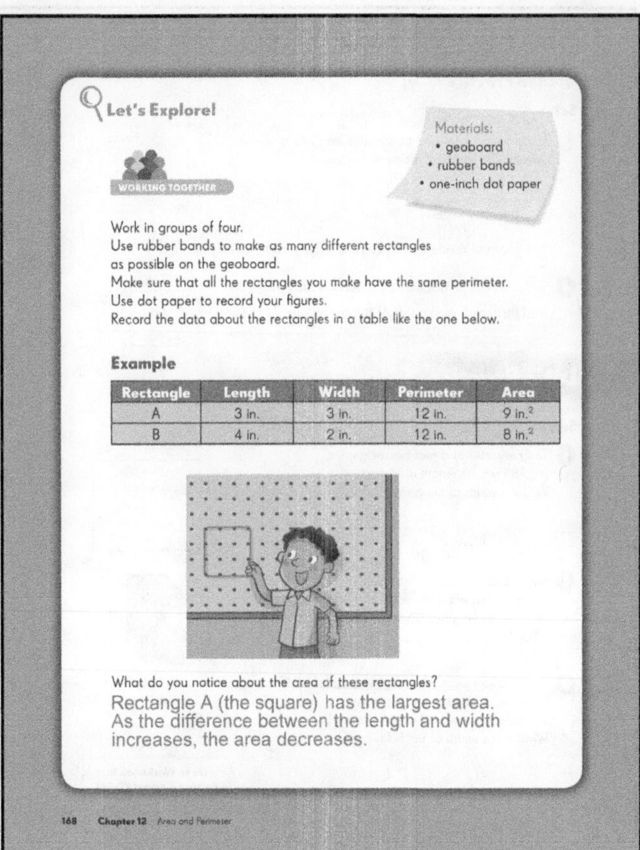

Let's Explore!

WORKING TOGETHER

Materials:
- geoboard
- rubber bands
- one-inch dot paper

Work in groups of four.
Use rubber bands to make as many different rectangles as possible on the geoboard.
Make sure that all the rectangles you make have the same perimeter.
Use dot paper to record your figures.
Record the data about the rectangles in a table like the one below.

Example

Rectangle	Length	Width	Perimeter	Area
A	3 in.	3 in.	12 in.	9 in.^{2}
B	4 in.	2 in.	12 in.	8 in.^{2}

What do you notice about the area of these rectangles?
Rectangle A (the square) has the largest area. As the difference between the length and width increases, the area decreases.

168 **Chapter 12** Area and Perimeter

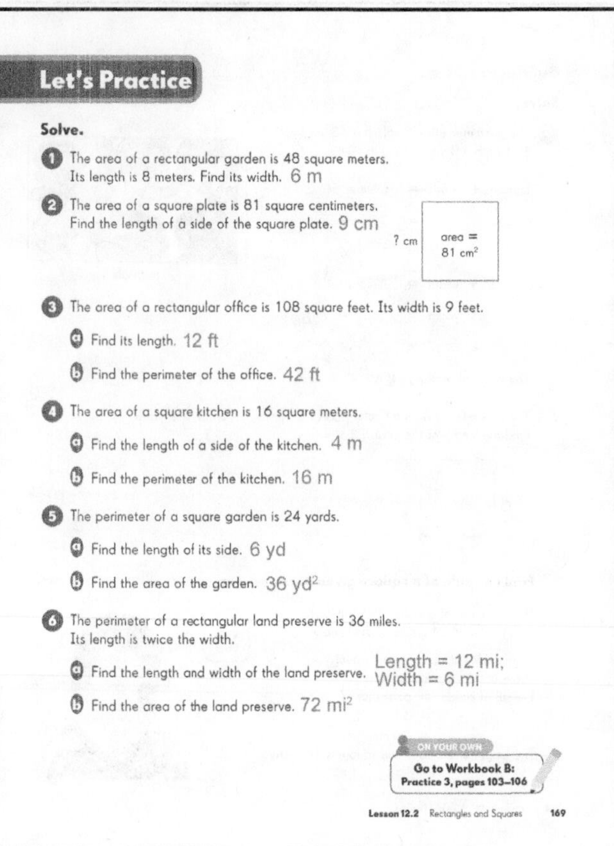

Let's Practice

Solve.

1. The area of a rectangular garden is 48 square meters. Its length is 8 meters. Find its width. 6 m
2. The area of a square plate is 81 square centimeters. Find the length of a side of the square plate. 9 cm
   (? cm; area = 81 cm^2)
3. The area of a rectangular office is 108 square feet. Its width is 9 feet.
   a. Find its length. 12 ft
   b. Find the perimeter of the office. 42 ft
4. The area of a square kitchen is 16 square meters.
   a. Find the length of a side of the kitchen. 4 m
   b. Find the perimeter of the kitchen. 16 m
5. The perimeter of a square garden is 24 yards.
   a. Find the length of its side. 6 yd
   b. Find the area of the garden. 36 yd^2
6. The perimeter of a rectangular land preserve is 36 miles. Its length is twice the width.
   a. Find the length and width of the land preserve. Length = 12 mi; Width = 6 mi
   b. Find the area of the land preserve. 72 mi^2

ON YOUR OWN
Go to Workbook B: Practice 3, pages 103–106

Lesson 12.2 Rectangles and Squares **169**

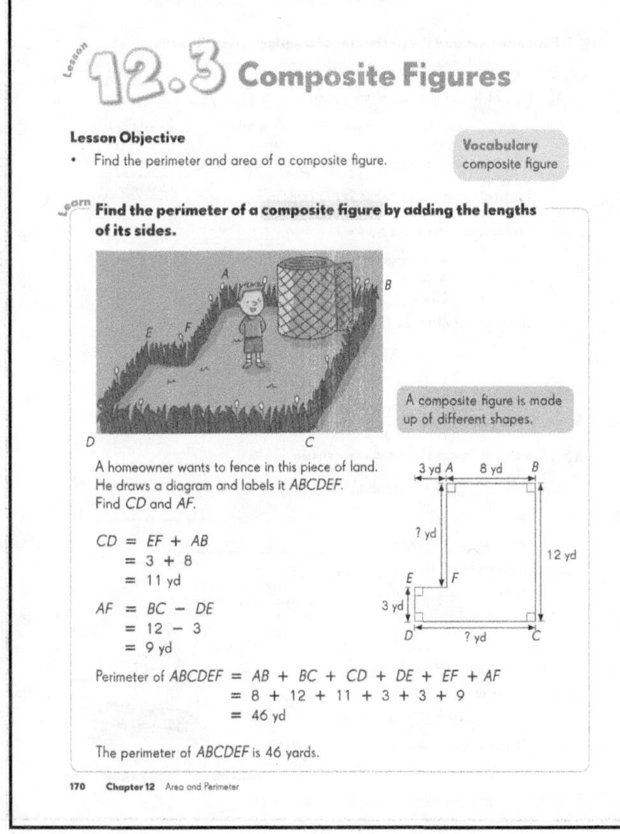

Lesson

12.3 Composite Figures

Lesson Objective
- Find the perimeter and area of a composite figure.

Vocabulary
composite figure

Learn

Find the perimeter of a composite figure by adding the lengths of its sides.

A composite figure is made up of different shapes.

A homeowner wants to fence in this piece of land. He draws a diagram and labels it *ABCDEF*. Find *CD* and *AF*.

CD = *EF* + *AB*
= 3 + 8
= 11 yd

AF = *BC* − *DE*
= 12 − 3
= 9 yd

Perimeter of *ABCDEF* = *AB* + *BC* + *CD* + *DE* + *EF* + *AF*
= 8 + 12 + 11 + 3 + 3 + 9
= 46 yd

The perimeter of *ABCDEF* is 46 yards.

170 **Chapter 12** Area and Perimeter

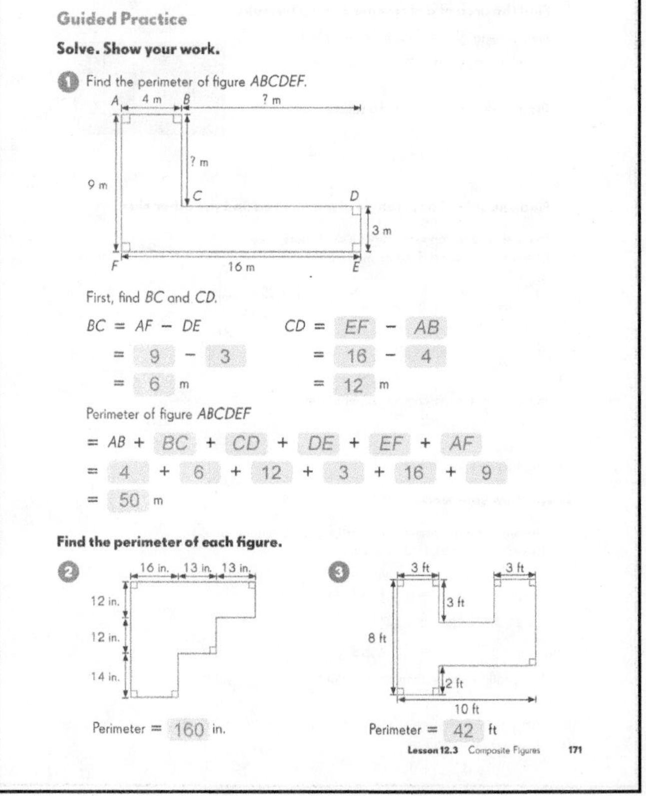

Guided Practice

Solve. Show your work.

1. Find the perimeter of figure *ABCDEF*.

First, find *BC* and *CD*.

BC = *AF* − *DE*
= 9 − 3
= 6 m

CD = *EF* − *AB*
= 16 − 4
= 12 m

Perimeter of figure *ABCDEF*
= *AB* + *BC* + *CD* + *DE* + *EF* + *AF*
= 4 + 6 + 12 + 3 + 16 + 9
= 50 m

Find the perimeter of each figure.

2.

Perimeter = 160 in.

3.

Perimeter = 42 ft

Lesson 12.3 Composite Figures **171**

Chapter 12

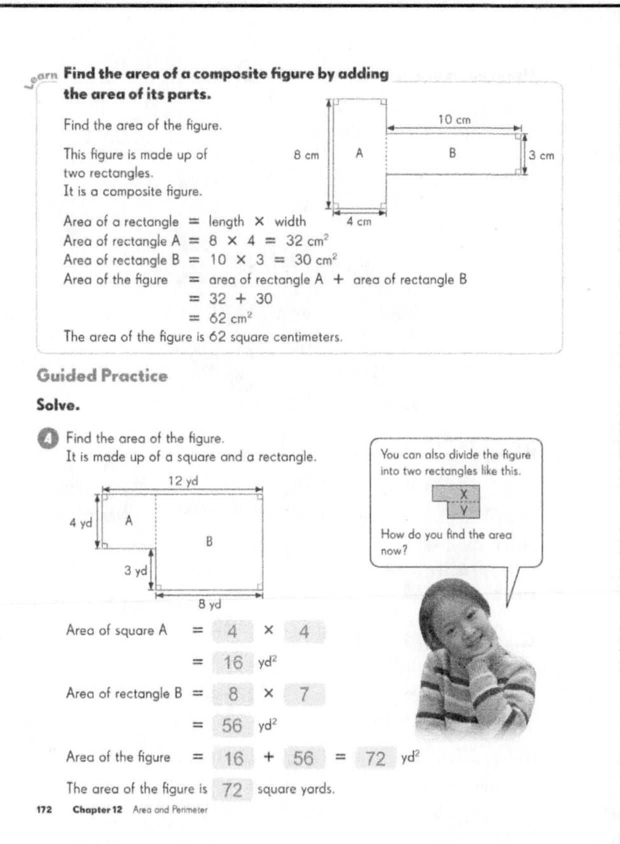

Learn: Find the area of a composite figure by adding the area of its parts.

Find the area of the figure.

This figure is made up of two rectangles.
It is a composite figure.

Area of a rectangle = length × width
Area of rectangle A = 8 × 4 = 32 cm^2
Area of rectangle B = 10 × 3 = 30 cm^2
Area of the figure = area of rectangle A + area of rectangle B
= 32 + 30
= 62 cm^2

The area of the figure is 62 square centimeters.

Guided Practice

Solve.

4. Find the area of the figure.
It is made up of a square and a rectangle.

Area of square A = 4 × 4
= 16 yd^2
Area of rectangle B = 8 × 7
= 56 yd^2
Area of the figure = 16 + 56 = 72 yd^2

The area of the figure is 72 square yards.

172 **Chapter 12** Area and Perimeter

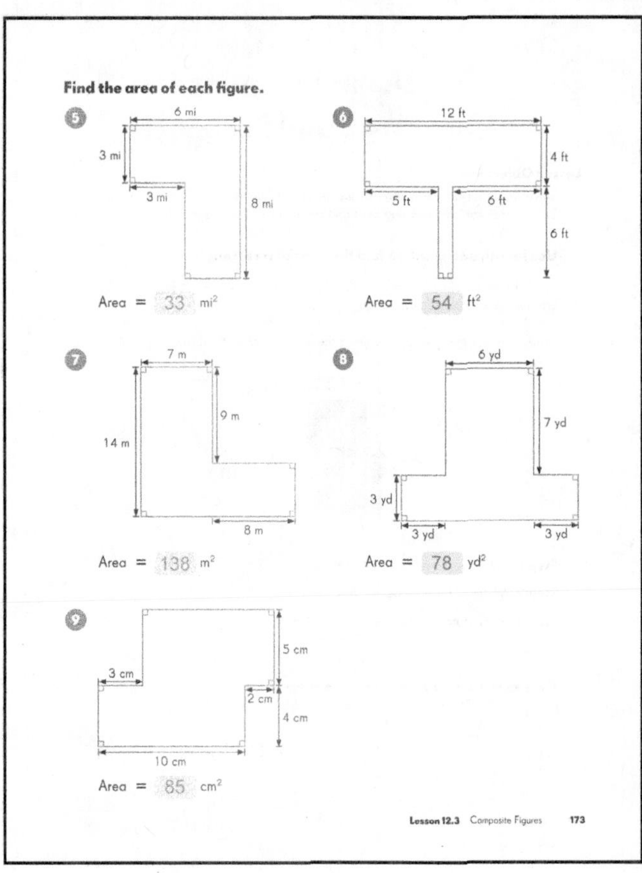

Find the area of each figure.

5.
Area = 33 mi^2

6.
Area = 54 ft^2

7.
Area = 138 m^2

8.
Area = 78 yd^2

9.
Area = 85 cm^2

Lesson 12.3 Composite Figures 173

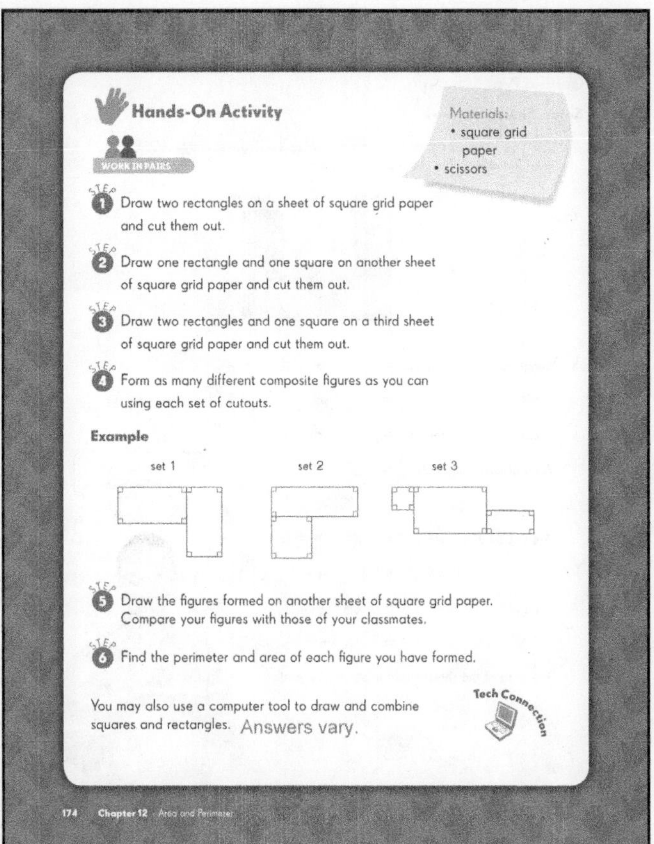

Hands-On Activity

WORK IN PAIRS

Materials:
- square grid paper
- scissors

STEP 1 Draw two rectangles on a sheet of square grid paper and cut them out.

STEP 2 Draw one rectangle and one square on another sheet of square grid paper and cut them out.

STEP 3 Draw two rectangles and one square on a third sheet of square grid paper and cut them out.

STEP 4 Form as many different composite figures as you can using each set of cutouts.

Example

STEP 5 Draw the figures formed on another sheet of square grid paper. Compare your figures with those of your classmates.

STEP 6 Find the perimeter and area of each figure you have formed.

You may also use a computer tool to draw and combine squares and rectangles. Answers vary.

Tech Connection

174 **Chapter 12** Area and Perimeter

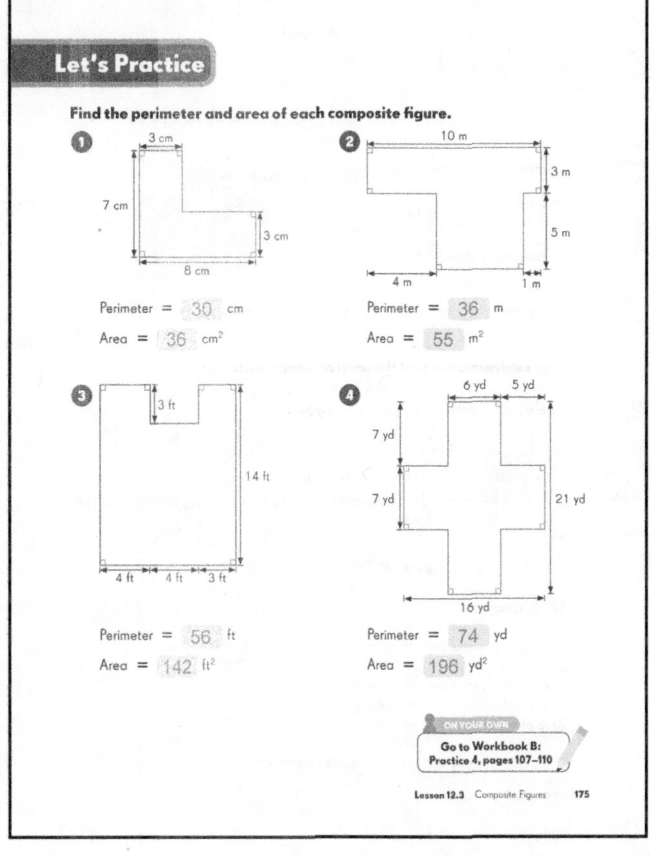

Let's Practice

Find the perimeter and area of each composite figure.

1.
Perimeter = 30 cm
Area = 36 cm^2

2.
Perimeter = 36 m
Area = 55 m^2

3.
Perimeter = 56 ft
Area = 142 ft^2

4.
Perimeter = 74 yd
Area = 196 yd^2

ON YOUR OWN
Go to Workbook B: Practice 4, pages 107–110

Lesson 12.3 Composite Figures 175

Chapter 12

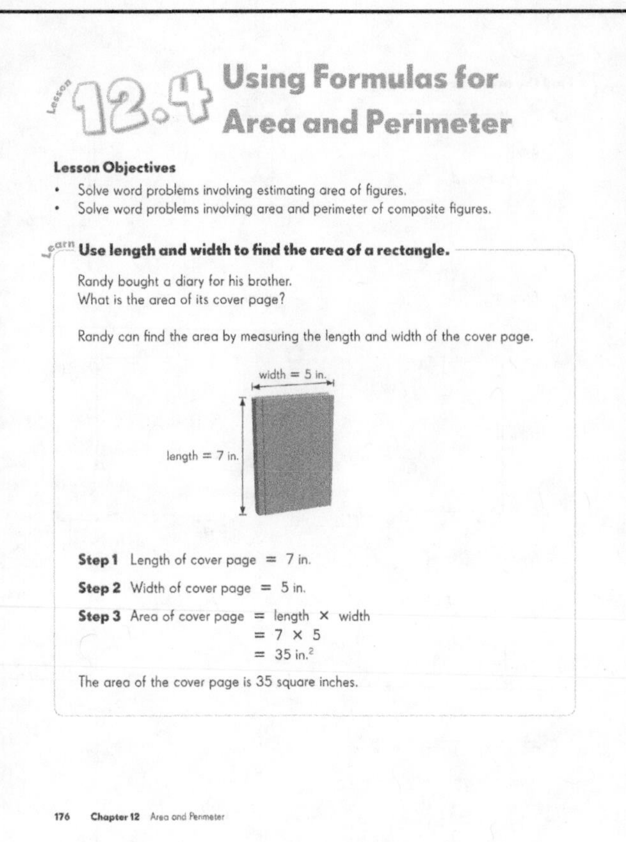

Lesson 12.4 Using Formulas for Area and Perimeter

Lesson Objectives

- Solve word problems involving estimating area of figures.
- Solve word problems involving area and perimeter of composite figures.

Learn Use length and width to find the area of a rectangle.

Randy bought a diary for his brother.
What is the area of its cover page?

Randy can find the area by measuring the length and width of the cover page.

Step 1 Length of cover page = 7 in.

Step 2 Width of cover page = 5 in.

Step 3 Area of cover page = length × width
= 7 × 5
= 35 $in.^2$

The area of the cover page is 35 square inches.

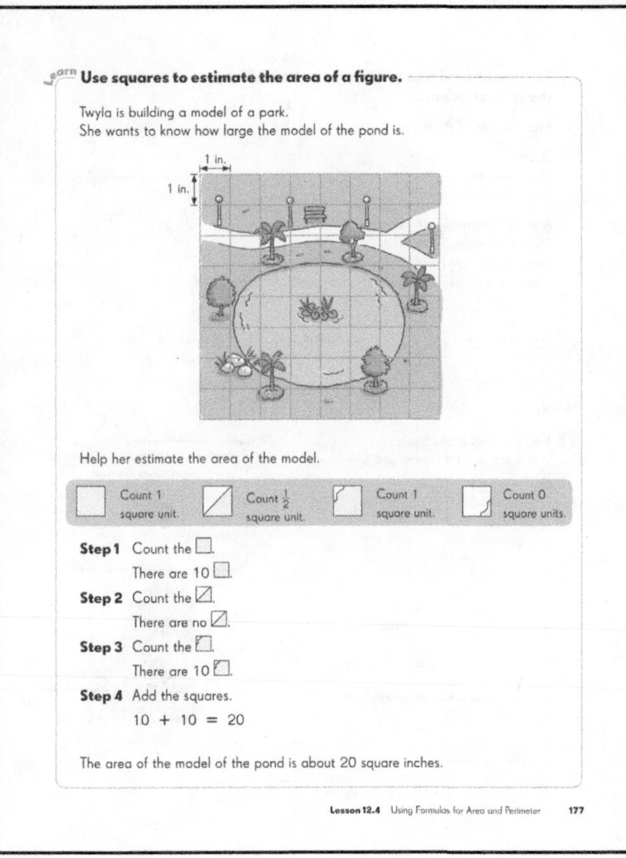

Learn Use squares to estimate the area of a figure.

Twyla is building a model of a park.
She wants to know how large the model of the pond is.

Help her estimate the area of the model.

☐	Count 1 square unit.	◺	Count $\frac{1}{2}$ square unit.	☐	Count 1 square unit.	☐	Count 0 square units.

Step 1 Count the ☐.
There are 10 ☐.

Step 2 Count the ◺.
There are no ◺.

Step 3 Count the ☐.
There are 10 ☐.

Step 4 Add the squares.
10 + 10 = 20

The area of the model of the pond is about 20 square inches.

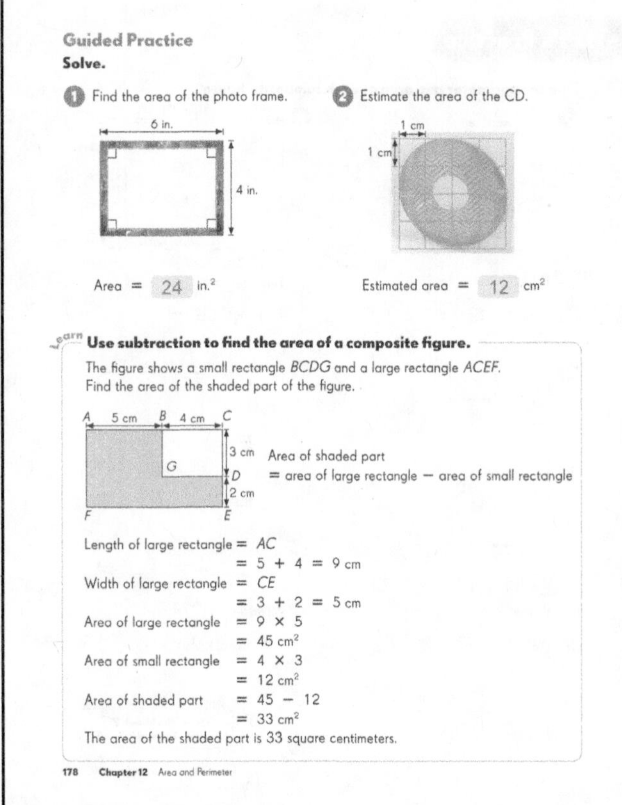

Guided Practice

Solve.

1. Find the area of the photo frame.

Area = 24 $in.^2$

2. Estimate the area of the CD.

Estimated area = 12 cm^2

Learn Use subtraction to find the area of a composite figure.

The figure shows a small rectangle *BCDG* and a large rectangle *ACEF*.
Find the area of the shaded part of the figure.

Area of shaded part
= area of large rectangle − area of small rectangle

Length of large rectangle = *AC*
= 5 + 4 = 9 cm

Width of large rectangle = *CE*
= 3 + 2 = 5 cm

Area of large rectangle = 9 × 5
= 45 cm^2

Area of small rectangle = 4 × 3
= 12 cm^2

Area of shaded part = 45 − 12
= 33 cm^2

The area of the shaded part is 33 square centimeters.

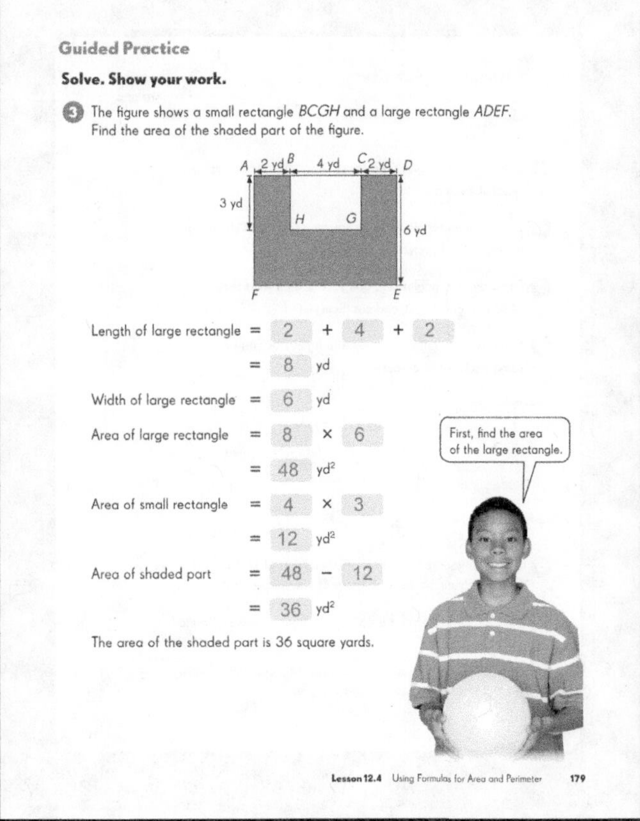

Guided Practice

Solve. Show your work.

3. The figure shows a small rectangle *BCGH* and a large rectangle *ADEF*.
Find the area of the shaded part of the figure.

Length of large rectangle = 2 + 4 + 2
= 8 yd

Width of large rectangle = 6 yd

Area of large rectangle = 8 × 6
= 48 yd^2

Area of small rectangle = 4 × 3
= 12 yd^2

Area of shaded part = 48 − 12
= 36 yd^2

The area of the shaded part is 36 square yards.

First, find the area of the large rectangle.

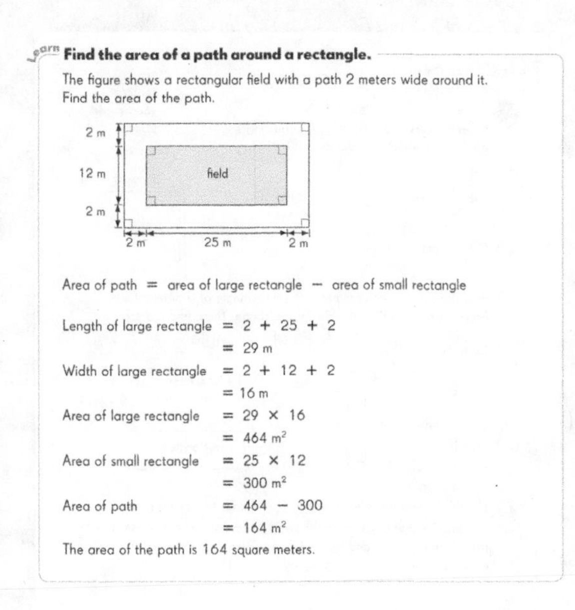

Learn Find the area of a path around a rectangle.

The figure shows a rectangular field with a path 2 meters wide around it.
Find the area of the path.

Area of path = area of large rectangle − area of small rectangle

Length of large rectangle = 2 + 25 + 2
= 29 m

Width of large rectangle = 2 + 12 + 2
= 16 m

Area of large rectangle = 29 × 16
= 464 m^2

Area of small rectangle = 25 × 12
= 300 m^2

Area of path = 464 − 300
= 164 m^2

The area of the path is 164 square meters.

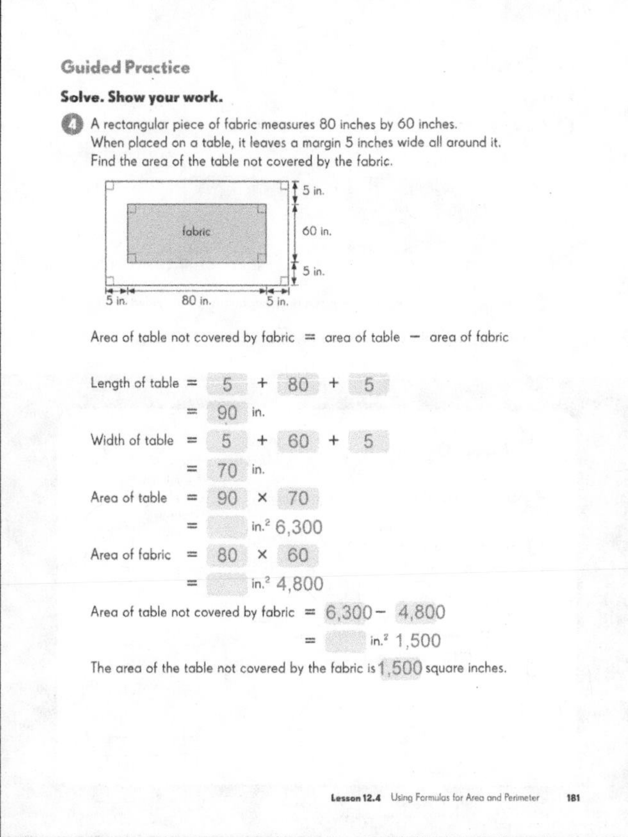

Guided Practice

Solve. Show your work.

4. A rectangular piece of fabric measures 80 inches by 60 inches.
When placed on a table, it leaves a margin 5 inches wide all around it.
Find the area of the table not covered by the fabric.

Area of table not covered by fabric = area of table − area of fabric

Length of table = 5 + 80 + 5
= 90 in.

Width of table = 5 + 60 + 5
= 70 in.

Area of table = 90 × 70
= in.² 6,300

Area of fabric = 80 × 60
= in.² 4,800

Area of table not covered by fabric = 6,300 − 4,800
= in.² 1,500

The area of the table not covered by the fabric is 1,500 square inches.

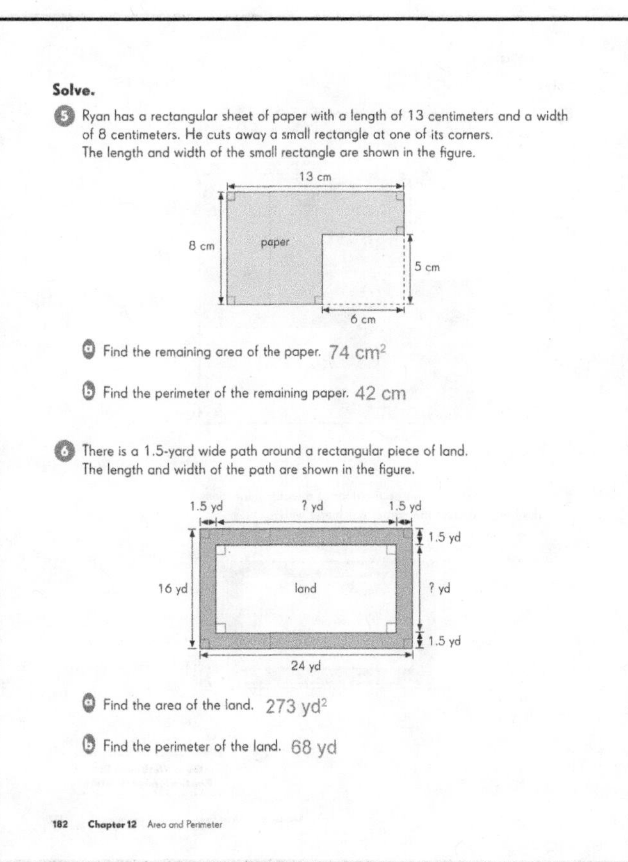

Solve.

5. Ryan has a rectangular sheet of paper with a length of 13 centimeters and a width of 8 centimeters. He cuts away a small rectangle at one of its corners.
The length and width of the small rectangle are shown in the figure.

a. Find the remaining area of the paper. 74 cm^2

b. Find the perimeter of the remaining paper. 42 cm

6. There is a 1.5-yard wide path around a rectangular piece of land.
The length and width of the path are shown in the figure.

a. Find the area of the land. 273 yd^2

b. Find the perimeter of the land. 68 yd

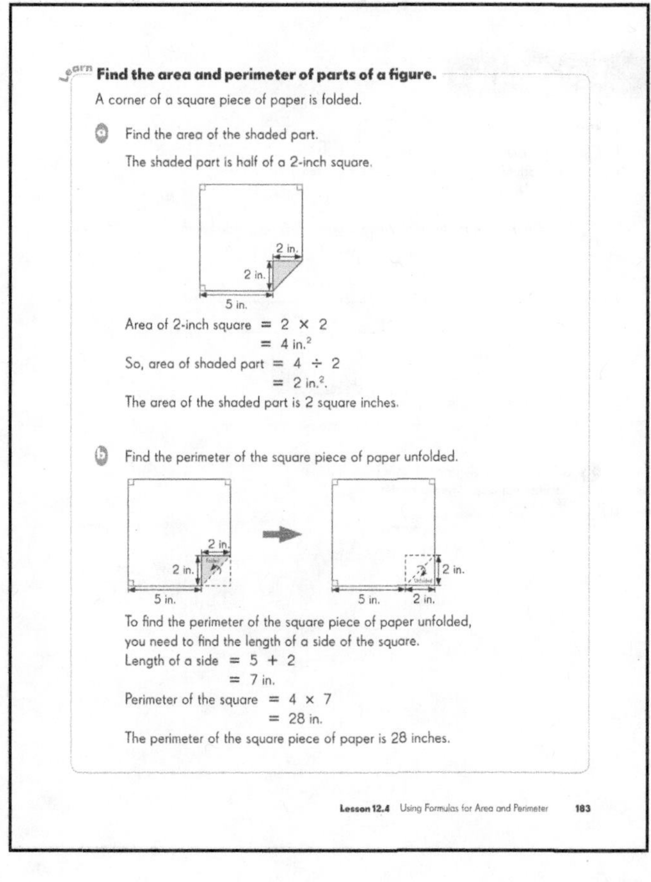

Learn Find the area and perimeter of parts of a figure.

A corner of a square piece of paper is folded.

a. Find the area of the shaded part.

The shaded part is half of a 2-inch square.

Area of 2-inch square = 2 × 2
= 4 in.²

So, area of shaded part = 4 ÷ 2
= 2 in.².

The area of the shaded part is 2 square inches.

b. Find the perimeter of the square piece of paper unfolded.

To find the perimeter of the square piece of paper unfolded, you need to find the length of a side of the square.

Length of a side = 5 + 2
= 7 in.

Perimeter of the square = 4 × 7
= 28 in.

The perimeter of the square piece of paper is 28 inches.

Chapter 12

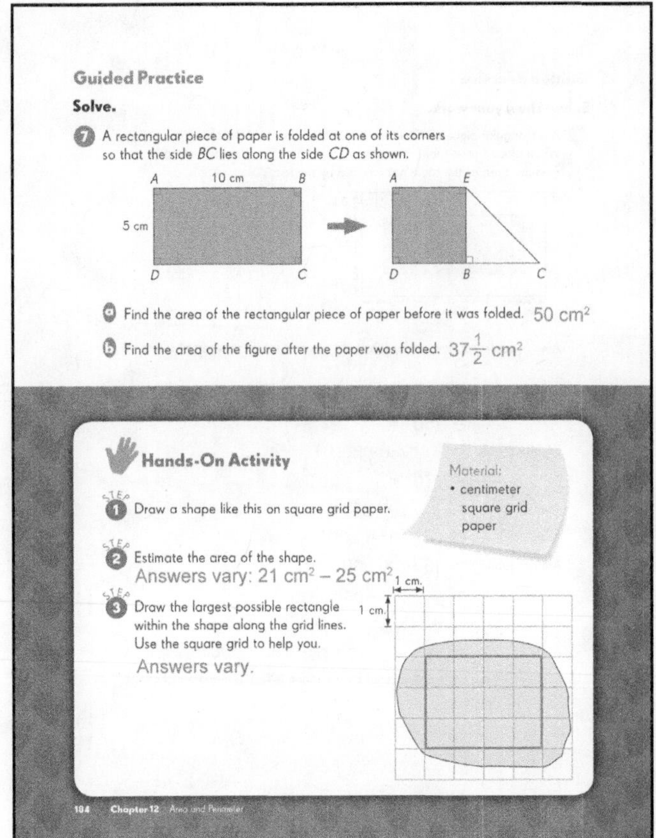

Guided Practice

Solve.

7. A rectangular piece of paper is folded at one of its corners so that the side *BC* lies along the side *CD* as shown.

a. Find the area of the rectangular piece of paper before it was folded. 50 cm^2

b. Find the area of the figure after the paper was folded. $37\frac{1}{2}$ cm^2

Hands-On Activity

Material:
- centimeter square grid paper

STEP 1. Draw a shape like this on square grid paper.

STEP 2. Estimate the area of the shape.
Answers vary: 21 cm^2 – 25 cm^2

STEP 3. Draw the largest possible rectangle within the shape along the grid lines. Use the square grid to help you.
Answers vary.

184 Chapter 12 Area and Perimeter

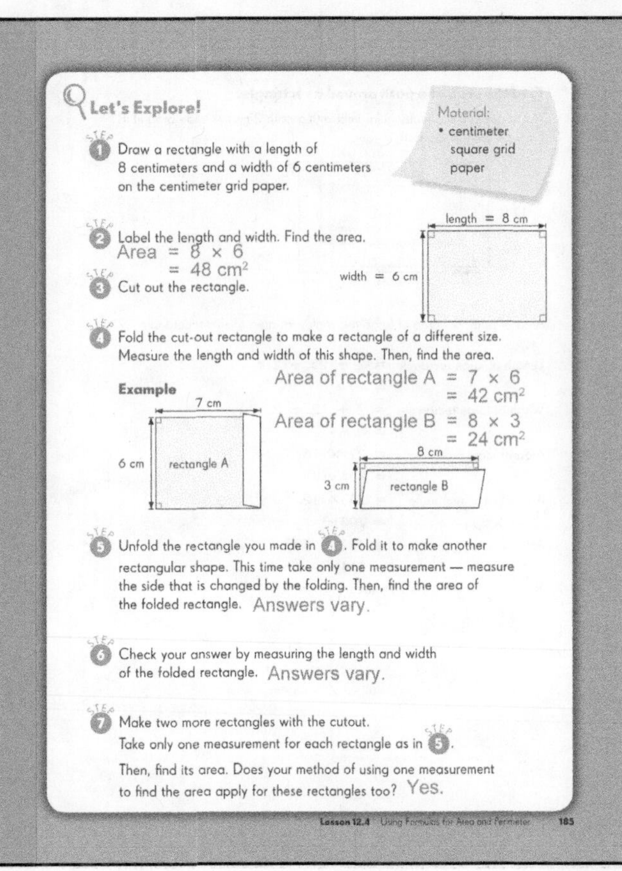

Let's Explore!

Material:
- centimeter square grid paper

STEP 1. Draw a rectangle with a length of 8 centimeters and a width of 6 centimeters on the centimeter grid paper.

STEP 2. Label the length and width. Find the area.
Area = 8 × 6
= 48 cm^2

STEP 3. Cut out the rectangle.

STEP 4. Fold the cut-out rectangle to make a rectangle of a different size. Measure the length and width of this shape. Then, find the area.

Example

Area of rectangle A = 7 × 6
= 42 cm^2

Area of rectangle B = 8 × 3
= 24 cm^2

STEP 5. Unfold the rectangle you made in 4. Fold it to make another rectangular shape. This time take only one measurement — measure the side that is changed by the folding. Then, find the area of the folded rectangle. Answers vary.

STEP 6. Check your answer by measuring the length and width of the folded rectangle. Answers vary.

STEP 7. Make two more rectangles with the cutout. Take only one measurement for each rectangle as in 5. Then, find its area. Does your method of using one measurement to find the area apply for these rectangles too? Yes.

Lesson 12.4 Using Formulas for Area and Perimeter 185

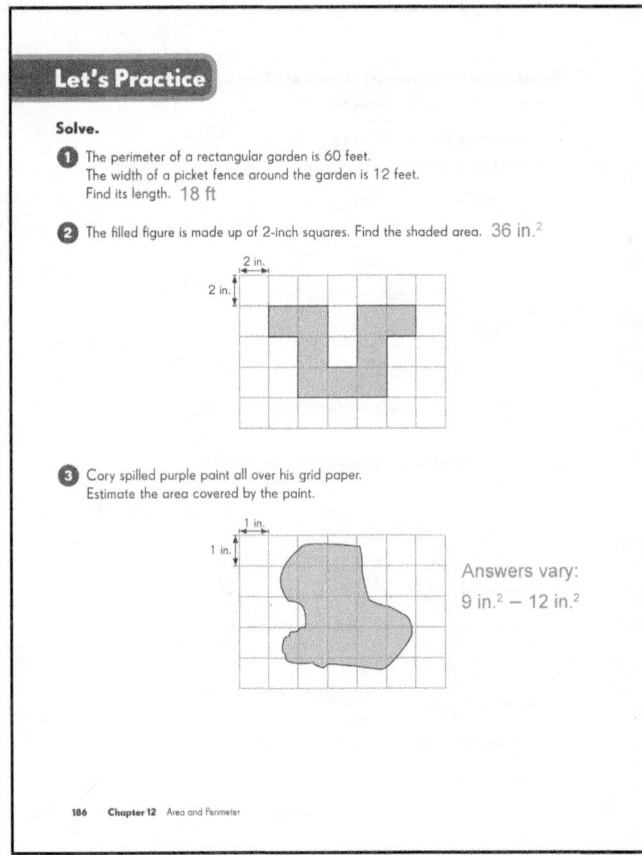

Let's Practice

Chapter 12

Solve.

1. The perimeter of a rectangular garden is 60 feet. The width of a picket fence around the garden is 12 feet. Find its length. 18 ft

2. The filled figure is made up of 2-inch squares. Find the shaded area. 36 $in.^2$

3. Cory spilled purple paint all over his grid paper. Estimate the area covered by the paint.

Answers vary: 9 $in.^2$ – 12 $in.^2$

186 Chapter 12 Area and Perimeter

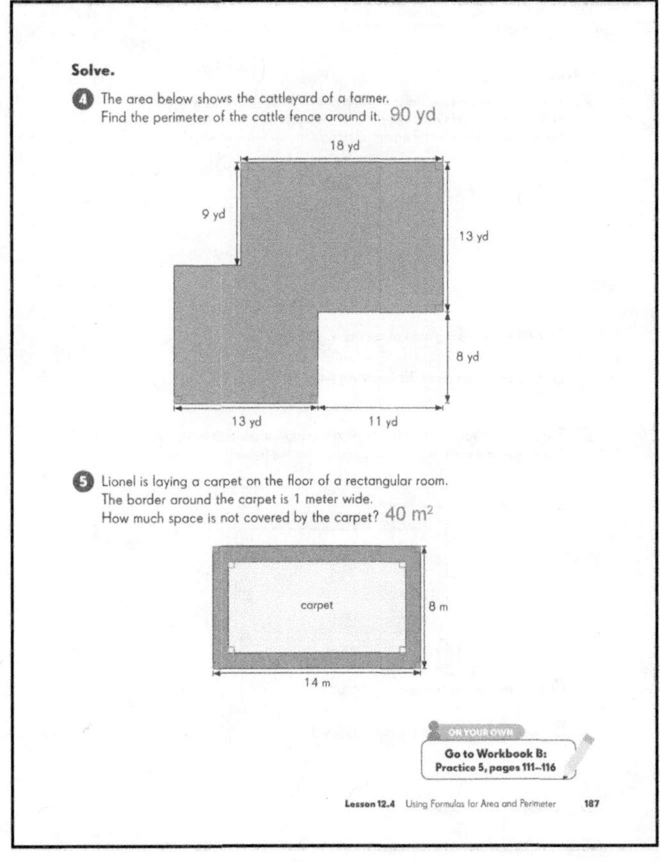

Solve.

4. The area below shows the cattleyard of a farmer. Find the perimeter of the cattle fence around it. 90 yd

5. Lionel is laying a carpet on the floor of a rectangular room. The border around the carpet is 1 meter wide. How much space is not covered by the carpet? 40 m^2

ON YOUR OWN
Go to Workbook B: Practice 5, pages 111–116

Lesson 12.4 Using Formulas for Area and Perimeter 187

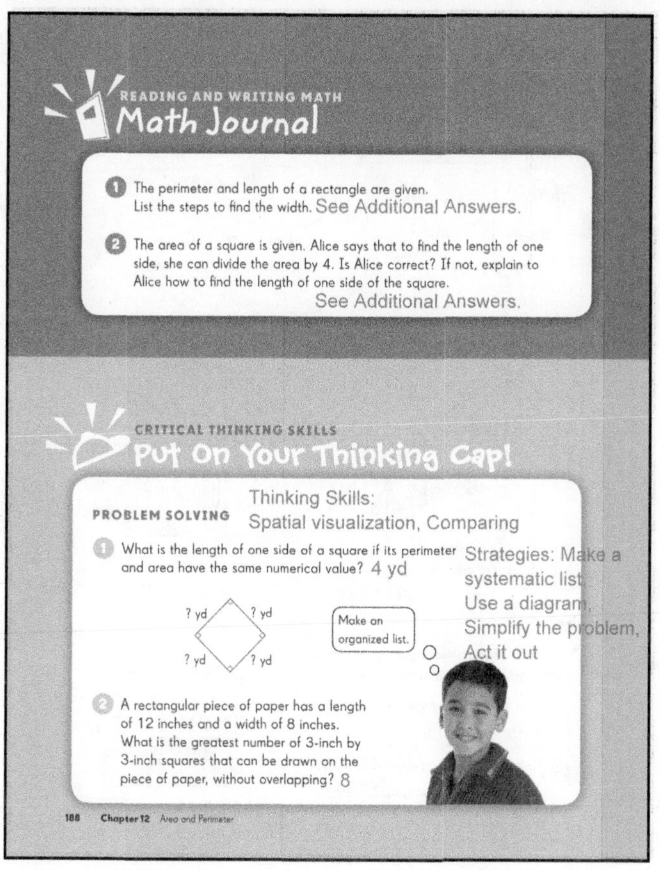

READING AND WRITING MATH

Math Journal

1. The perimeter and length of a rectangle are given. List the steps to find the width. See Additional Answers.
2. The area of a square is given. Alice says that to find the length of one side, she can divide the area by 4. Is Alice correct? If not, explain to Alice how to find the length of one side of the square. See Additional Answers.

CRITICAL THINKING SKILLS

Put On Your Thinking Cap!

PROBLEM SOLVING

Thinking Skills: Spatial visualization, Comparing

Strategies: Make a systematic list, Use a diagram, Simplify the problem, Act it out

1. What is the length of one side of a square if its perimeter and area have the same numerical value? 4 yd

2. A rectangular piece of paper has a length of 12 inches and a width of 8 inches. What is the greatest number of 3-inch by 3-inch squares that can be drawn on the piece of paper, without overlapping? 8

188 Chapter 12 Area and Perimeter

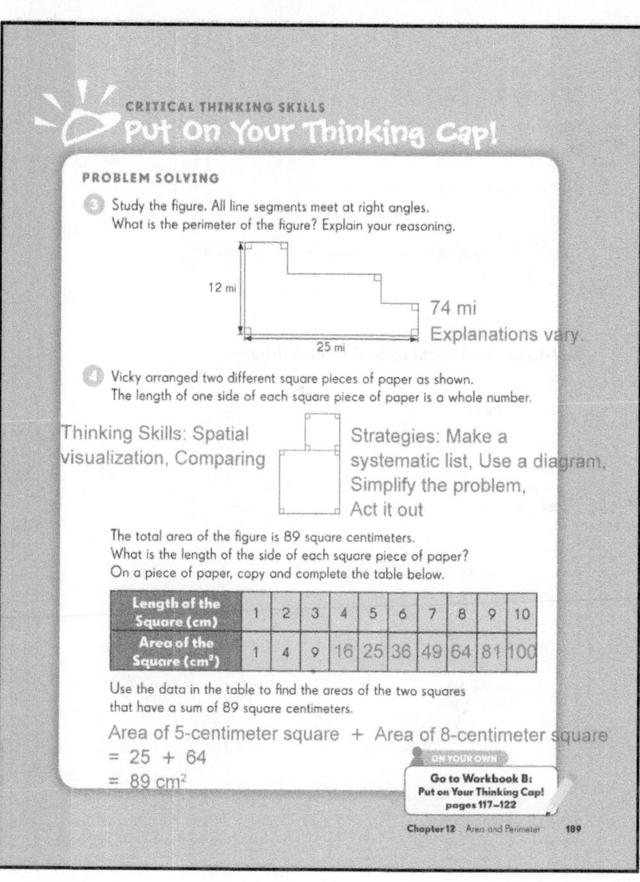

CRITICAL THINKING SKILLS

Put On Your Thinking Cap!

PROBLEM SOLVING

3. Study the figure. All line segments meet at right angles. What is the perimeter of the figure? Explain your reasoning.

74 mi

Explanations vary.

4. Vicky arranged two different square pieces of paper as shown. The length of one side of each square piece of paper is a whole number.

Thinking Skills: Spatial visualization, Comparing

Strategies: Make a systematic list, Use a diagram, Simplify the problem, Act it out

The total area of the figure is 89 square centimeters. What is the length of the side of each square piece of paper? On a piece of paper, copy and complete the table below.

Length of the Square (cm)	1	2	3	4	5	6	7	8	9	10
Area of the Square (cm^2)	1	4	9	16	25	36	49	64	81	100

Use the data in the table to find the areas of the two squares that have a sum of 89 square centimeters.

Area of 5-centimeter square + Area of 8-centimeter square
= 25 + 64
= 89 cm^2

ON YOUR OWN

Go to Workbook B: Put on Your Thinking Cap! pages 117–122

Chapter 12 Area and Perimeter 189

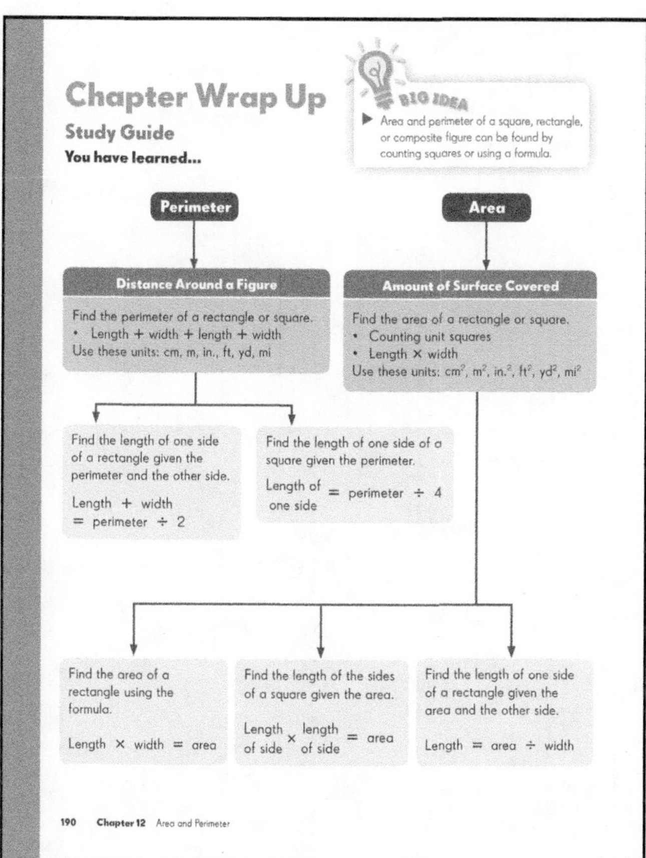

Chapter Wrap Up

Study Guide

You have learned...

BIG IDEA

▶ Area and perimeter of a square, rectangle, or composite figure can be found by counting squares or using a formula.

Perimeter

Distance Around a Figure

Find the perimeter of a rectangle or square.
- Length + width + length + width

Use these units: cm, m, in., ft, yd, mi

Find the length of one side of a rectangle given the perimeter and the other side.

Length + width = perimeter ÷ 2

Find the length of one side of a square given the perimeter.

Length of one side = perimeter ÷ 4

Area

Amount of Surface Covered

Find the area of a rectangle or square.
- Counting unit squares
- Length × width

Use these units: cm^2, m^2, $in.^2$, ft^2, yd^2, mi^2

Find the area of a rectangle using the formula.

Length × width = area

Find the length of the sides of a square given the area.

Length of side × length of side = area

Find the length of one side of a rectangle given the area and the other side.

Length = area ÷ width

190 Chapter 12 Area and Perimeter

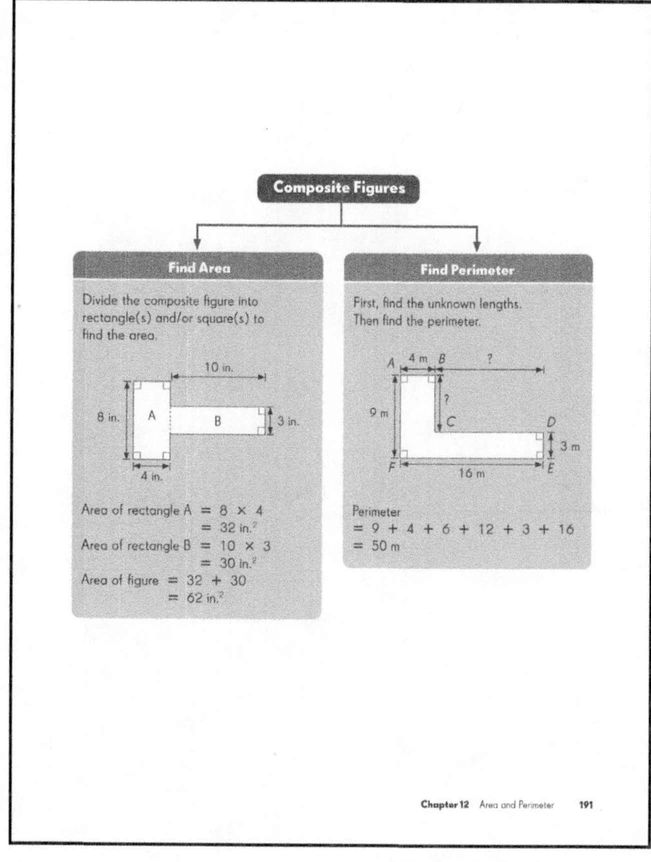

Composite Figures

Find Area

Divide the composite figure into rectangle(s) and/or square(s) to find the area.

Area of rectangle A = 8 × 4
= 32 $in.^2$

Area of rectangle B = 10 × 3
= 30 $in.^2$

Area of figure = 32 + 30
= 62 $in.^2$

Find Perimeter

First, find the unknown lengths. Then find the perimeter.

Perimeter
= 9 + 4 + 6 + 12 + 3 + 16
= 50 m

Chapter 12 Area and Perimeter 191

Chapter 12

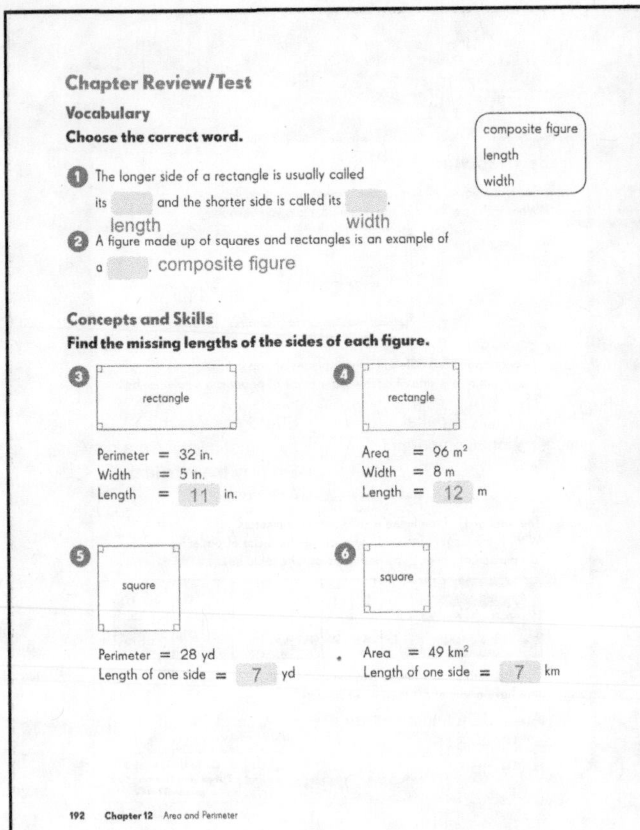

Chapter Review/Test
Vocabulary
Choose the correct word.
composite figure
length
width
The longer side of a rectangle is usually called its length and the shorter side is called its width.
A figure made up of squares and rectangles is an example of a composite figure.
Concepts and Skills
Find the missing lengths of the sides of each figure.
rectangle
Perimeter = 32 in.
Width = 5 in.
Length = 11 in.
rectangle
Area = 96 m²
Width = 8 m
Length = 12 m
square
Perimeter = 28 yd
Length of one side = 7 yd
square
Area = 49 km²
Length of one side = 7 km
192 Chapter 12 Area and Perimeter

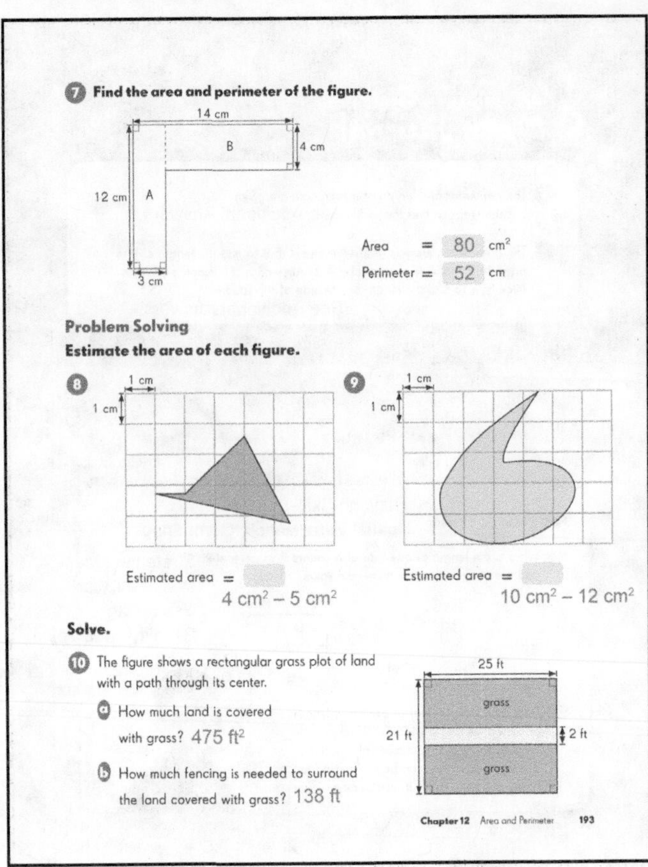

Find the area and perimeter of the figure.
14 cm
B
4 cm
12 cm
A
3 cm
Area = 80 cm²
Perimeter = 52 cm
Problem Solving
Estimate the area of each figure.
1 cm
1 cm
Estimated area = 4 cm² – 5 cm²
Estimated area = 10 cm² – 12 cm²
Solve.
The figure shows a rectangular grass plot of land with a path through its center.
How much land is covered with grass? 475 ft²
How much fencing is needed to surround the land covered with grass? 138 ft
25 ft
grass
21 ft
2 ft
grass
Chapter 12 Area and Perimeter 193

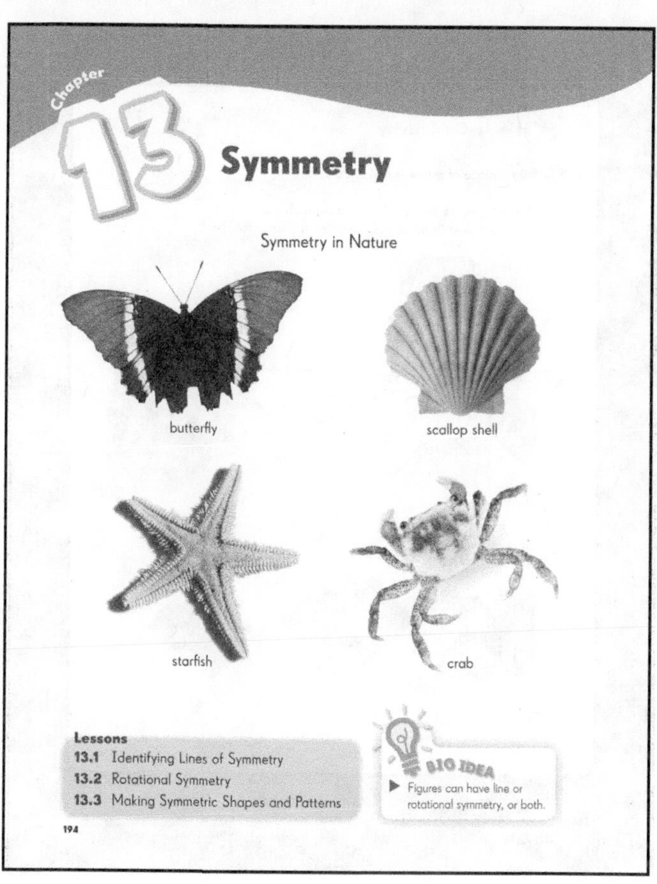
Chapter 13 Symmetry

Symmetry in Nature

Lessons

BIG IDEA
▶ Figures can have line or rotational symmetry, or both.

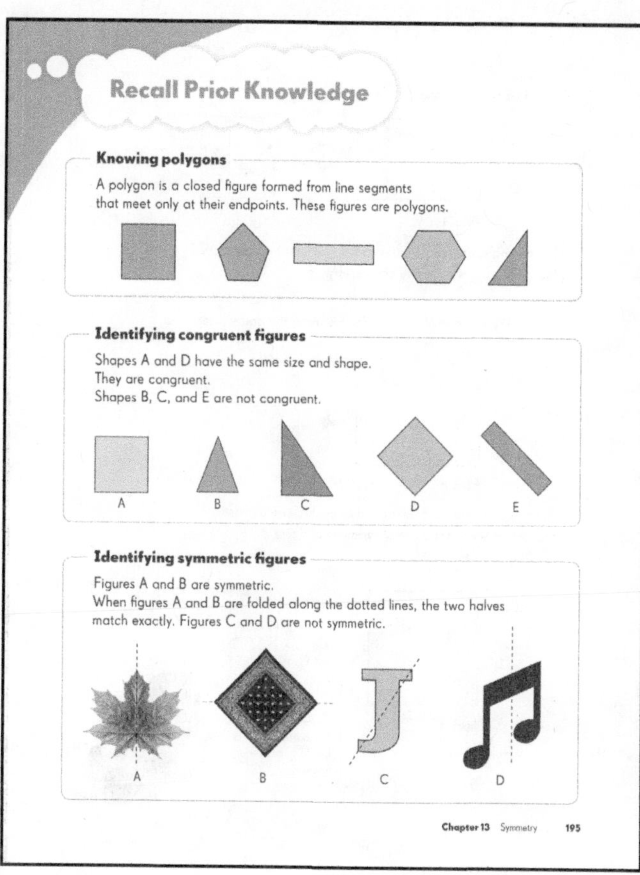
Recall Prior Knowledge

Knowing polygons

A polygon is a closed figure formed from line segments that meet only at their endpoints. These figures are polygons.

Identifying congruent figures

Shapes A and D have the same size and shape.
They are congruent.
Shapes B, C, and E are not congruent.

Identifying symmetric figures

Figures A and B are symmetric.
When figures A and B are folded along the dotted lines, the two halves match exactly. Figures C and D are not symmetric.

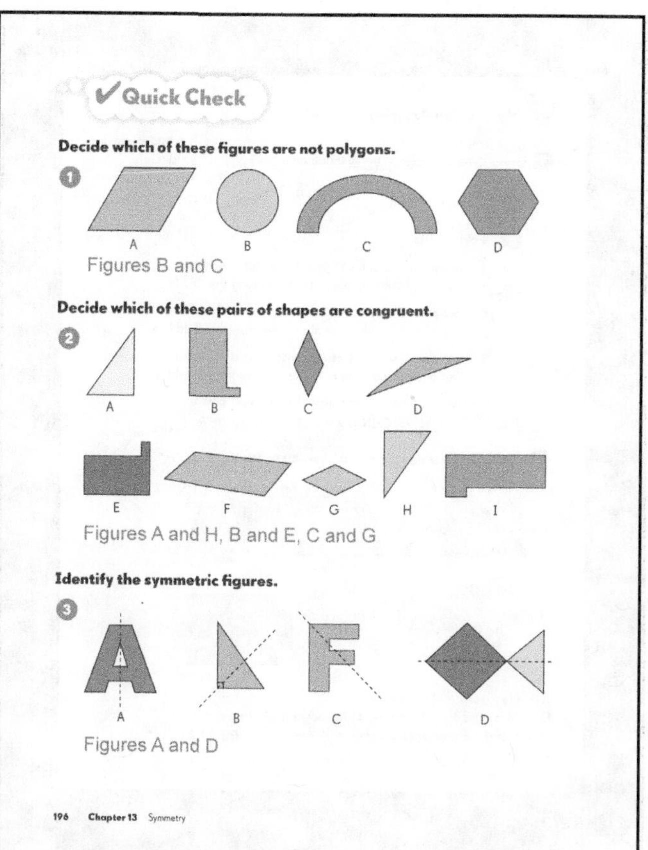
✔Quick Check

Decide which of these figures are not polygons.

1 A B C D

Figures B and C

Decide which of these pairs of shapes are congruent.

2 A B C D E F G H I

Figures A and H, B and E, C and G

Identify the symmetric figures.

3 A B C D

Figures A and D

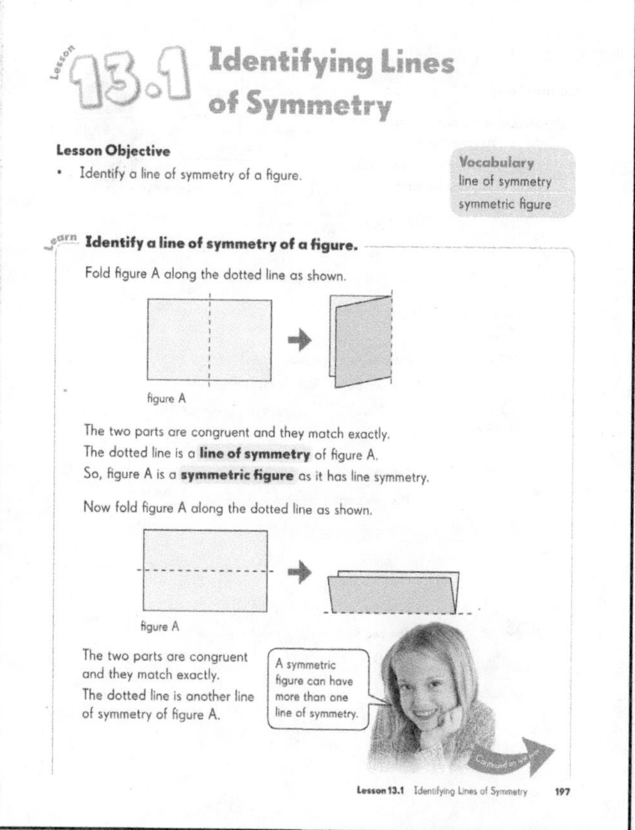
Lesson 13.1 Identifying Lines of Symmetry

Lesson Objective
- Identify a line of symmetry of a figure.

Vocabulary
line of symmetry
symmetric figure

Learn Identify a line of symmetry of a figure.

Fold figure A along the dotted line as shown.

The two parts are congruent and they match exactly.
The dotted line is a **line of symmetry** of figure A.
So, figure A is a **symmetric figure** as it has line symmetry.

Now fold figure A along the dotted line as shown.

The two parts are congruent and they match exactly.
The dotted line is another line of symmetry of figure A.

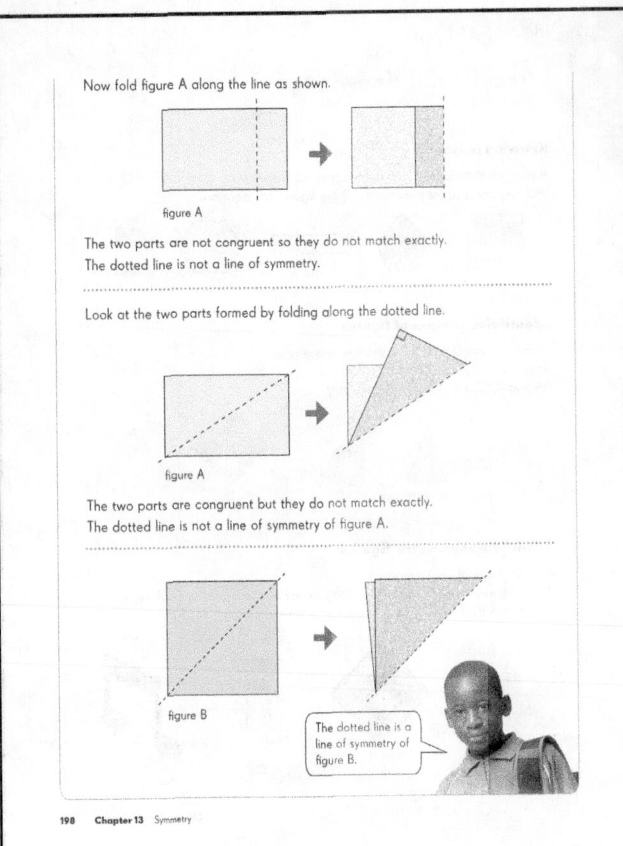

Now fold figure A along the line as shown.

figure A

The two parts are not congruent so they do not match exactly.
The dotted line is not a line of symmetry.

Look at the two parts formed by folding along the dotted line.

figure A

The two parts are congruent but they do not match exactly.
The dotted line is not a line of symmetry of figure A.

figure B

The dotted line is a line of symmetry of figure B.

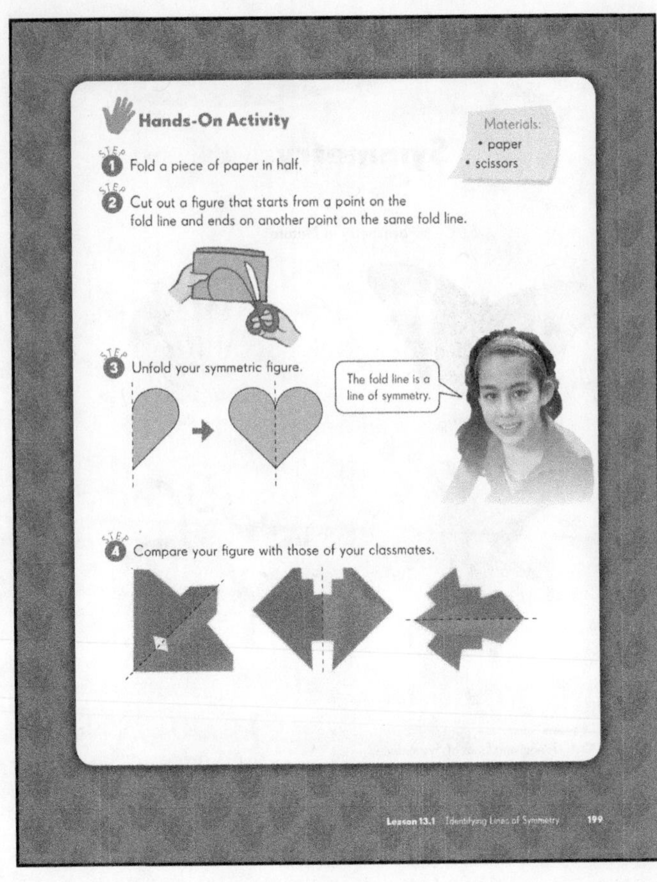

Hands-On Activity

Materials:
- paper
- scissors

STEP 1 Fold a piece of paper in half.

STEP 2 Cut out a figure that starts from a point on the fold line and ends on another point on the same fold line.

STEP 3 Unfold your symmetric figure.

The fold line is a line of symmetry.

STEP 4 Compare your figure with those of your classmates.

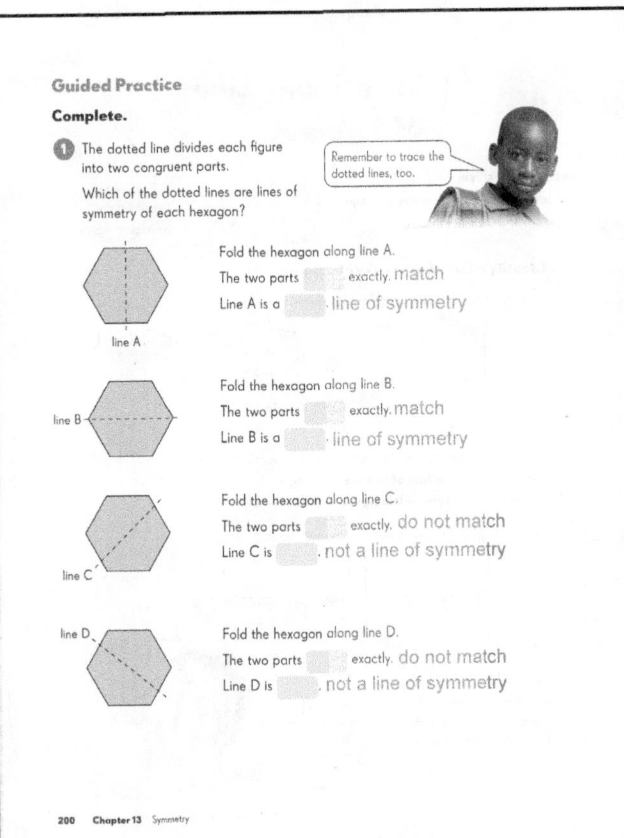

Guided Practice

Complete.

1 The dotted line divides each figure into two congruent parts.
Which of the dotted lines are lines of symmetry of each hexagon?

Remember to trace the dotted lines, too.

line A

Fold the hexagon along line A.
The two parts ___ exactly. match
Line A is a ___. line of symmetry

line B

Fold the hexagon along line B.
The two parts ___ exactly. match
Line B is a ___. line of symmetry

line C

Fold the hexagon along line C.
The two parts ___ exactly. do not match
Line C is ___. not a line of symmetry

line D

Fold the hexagon along line D.
The two parts ___ exactly. do not match
Line D is ___. not a line of symmetry

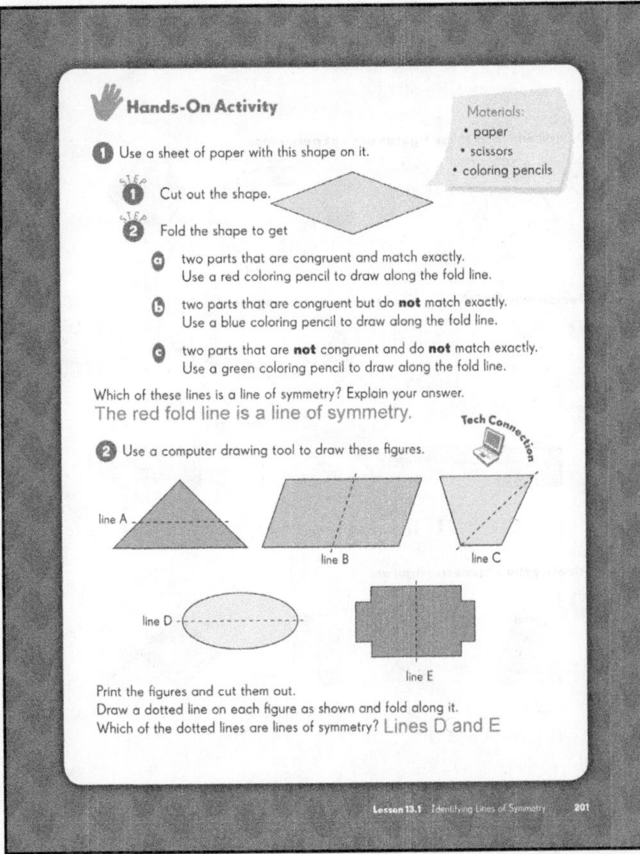

Hands-On Activity

Materials:
- paper
- scissors
- coloring pencils

1 Use a sheet of paper with this shape on it.

STEP 1 Cut out the shape.

STEP 2 Fold the shape to get

a two parts that are congruent and match exactly.
Use a red coloring pencil to draw along the fold line.

b two parts that are congruent but do **not** match exactly.
Use a blue coloring pencil to draw along the fold line.

c two parts that are **not** congruent and do **not** match exactly.
Use a green coloring pencil to draw along the fold line.

Which of these lines is a line of symmetry? Explain your answer.
The red fold line is a line of symmetry.

Tech Connection

2 Use a computer drawing tool to draw these figures.

line A line B line C line D line E

Print the figures and cut them out.
Draw a dotted line on each figure as shown and fold along it.
Which of the dotted lines are lines of symmetry? Lines D and E

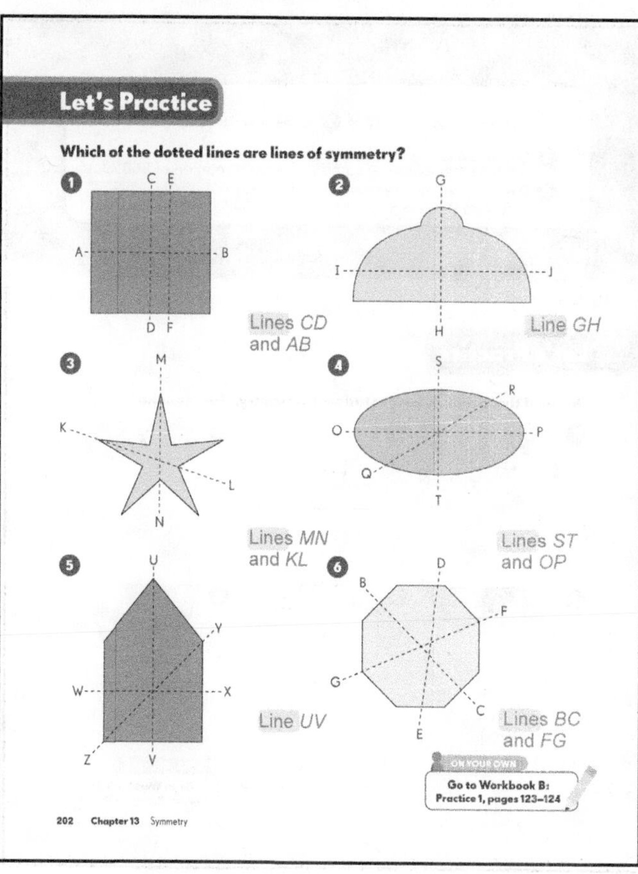

Let's Practice

Which of the dotted lines are lines of symmetry?

1. Lines *CD* and *AB*
2. Line *GH*
3. Lines *MN* and *KL*
4. Lines *ST* and *OP*
5. Line *UV*
6. Lines *BC* and *FG*

ON YOUR OWN

Go to Workbook B: Practice 1, pages 123–124

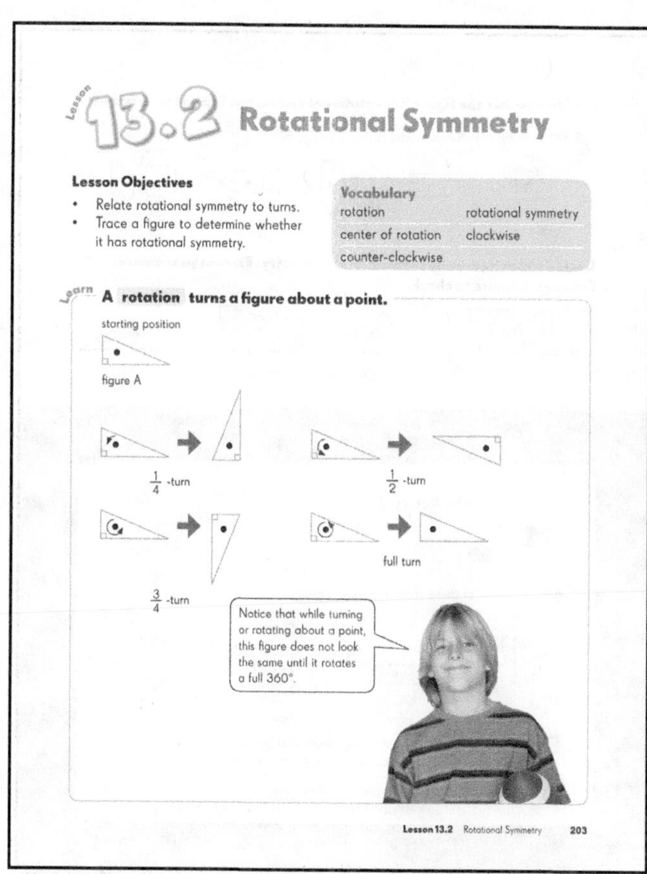

Lesson 13.2 Rotational Symmetry

Lesson Objectives

- Relate rotational symmetry to turns.
- Trace a figure to determine whether it has rotational symmetry.

Vocabulary

rotation	rotational symmetry
center of rotation	clockwise
counter-clockwise	

Learn A rotation turns a figure about a point.

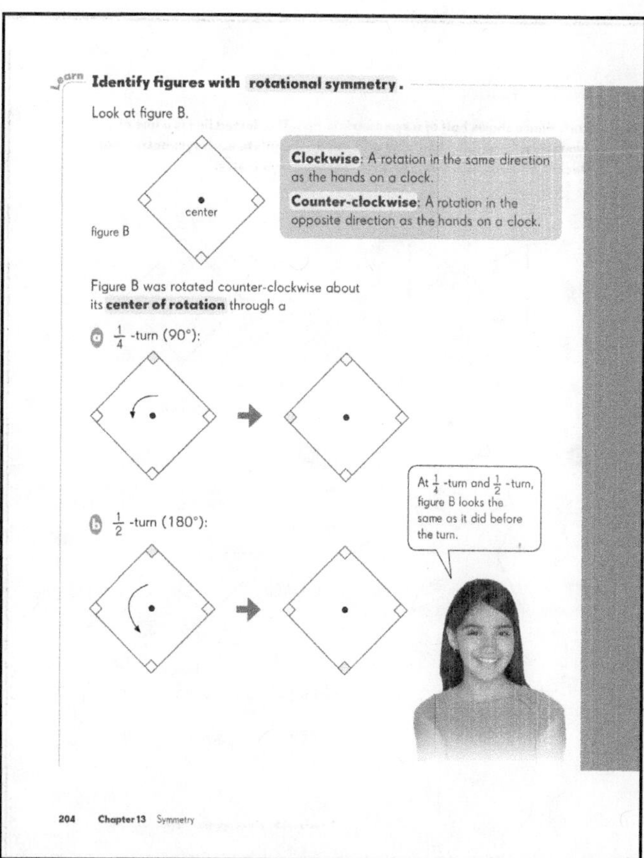

Notice that while turning or rotating about a point, this figure does not look the same until it rotates a full 360°.

Learn Identify figures with rotational symmetry.

Look at figure B.

Clockwise: A rotation in the same direction as the hands on a clock.

Counter-clockwise: A rotation in the opposite direction as the hands on a clock.

Figure B was rotated counter-clockwise about its **center of rotation** through a

a. $\frac{1}{4}$-turn (90°):

b. $\frac{1}{2}$-turn (180°):

At $\frac{1}{4}$-turn and $\frac{1}{2}$-turn, figure B looks the same as it did before the turn.

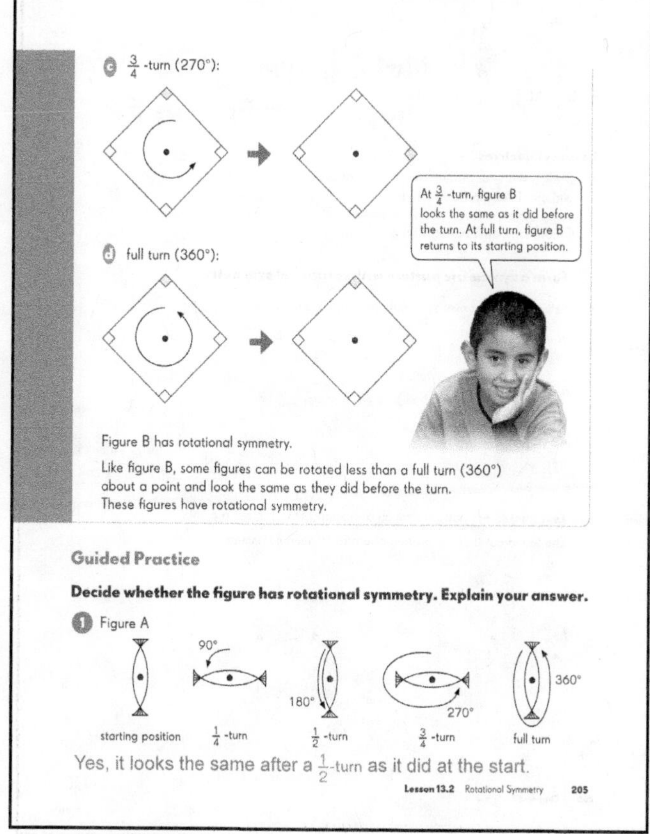

c. $\frac{3}{4}$-turn (270°):

d. full turn (360°):

At $\frac{3}{4}$-turn, figure B looks the same as it did before the turn. At full turn, figure B returns to its starting position.

Figure B has rotational symmetry.

Like figure B, some figures can be rotated less than a full turn (360°) about a point and look the same as they did before the turn. These figures have rotational symmetry.

Guided Practice

Decide whether the figure has rotational symmetry. Explain your answer.

1. Figure A

Yes, it looks the same after a $\frac{1}{2}$-turn as it did at the start.

Chapter 13

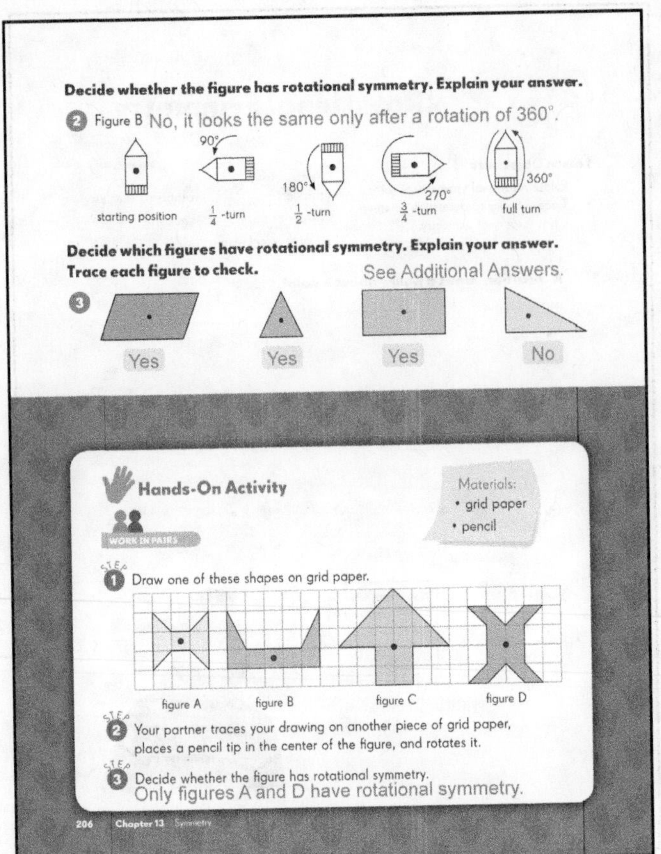

Decide whether the figure has rotational symmetry. Explain your answer.

2 Figure B No, it looks the same only after a rotation of 360°.

Decide which figures have rotational symmetry. Explain your answer. Trace each figure to check. See Additional Answers.

3 Yes Yes Yes No

Hands-On Activity

WORK IN PAIRS

Materials:
- grid paper
- pencil

STEP 1 Draw one of these shapes on grid paper.

STEP 2 Your partner traces your drawing on another piece of grid paper, places a pencil tip in the center of the figure, and rotates it.

STEP 3 Decide whether the figure has rotational symmetry.
Only figures A and D have rotational symmetry.

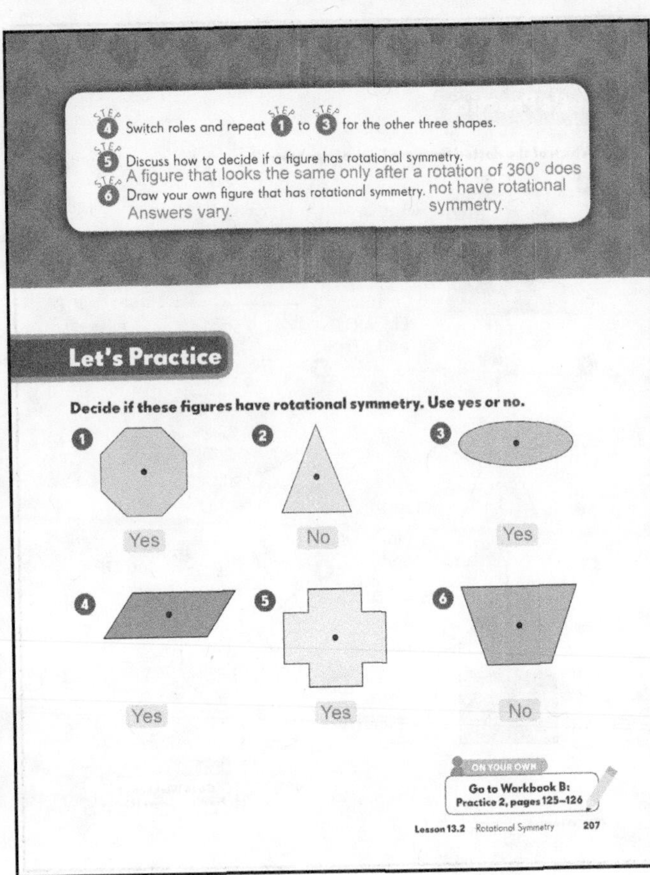

STEP 4 Switch roles and repeat STEP 1 to STEP 3 for the other three shapes.

STEP 5 Discuss how to decide if a figure has rotational symmetry.
A figure that looks the same only after a rotation of 360° does not have rotational symmetry.

STEP 6 Draw your own figure that has rotational symmetry.
Answers vary.

Let's Practice

Decide if these figures have rotational symmetry. Use yes or no.

1 Yes
2 No
3 Yes
4 Yes
5 Yes
6 No

ON YOUR OWN

Go to Workbook B: Practice 2, pages 125–126

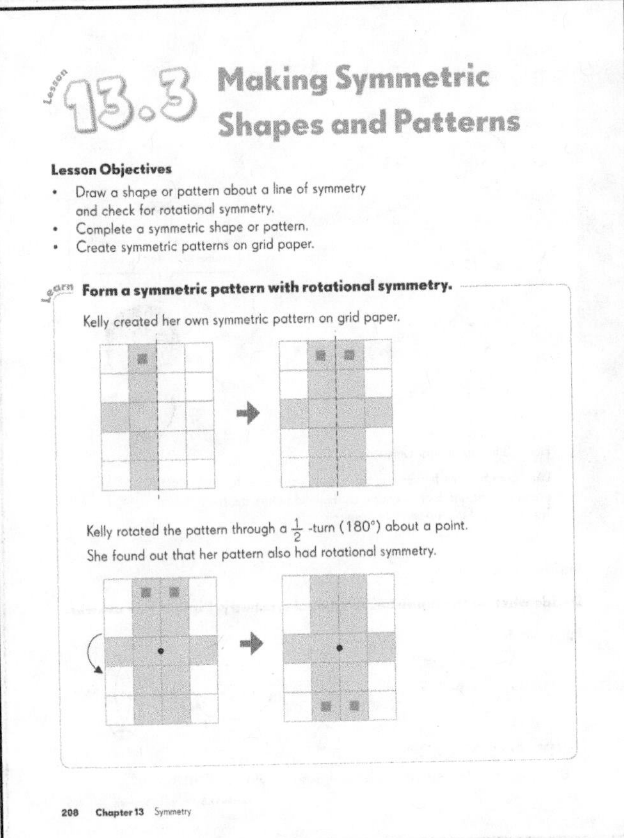

Lesson 13.3 Making Symmetric Shapes and Patterns

Lesson Objectives

- Draw a shape or pattern about a line of symmetry and check for rotational symmetry.
- Complete a symmetric shape or pattern.
- Create symmetric patterns on grid paper.

Learn **Form a symmetric pattern with rotational symmetry.**

Kelly created her own symmetric pattern on grid paper.

Kelly rotated the pattern through a $\frac{1}{2}$-turn (180°) about a point.
She found out that her pattern also had rotational symmetry.

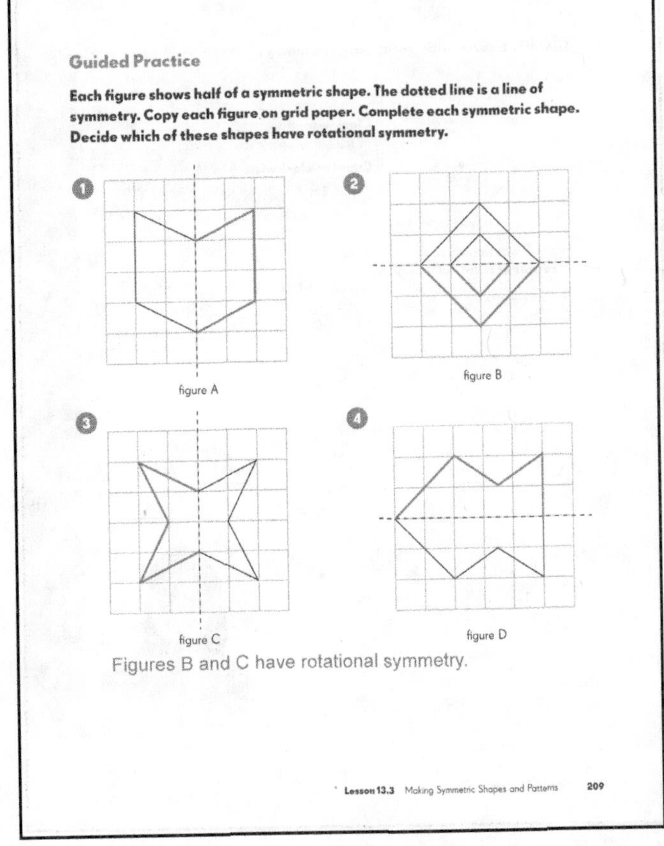

Guided Practice

Each figure shows half of a symmetric shape. The dotted line is a line of symmetry. Copy each figure on grid paper. Complete each symmetric shape. Decide which of these shapes have rotational symmetry.

1 figure A

2 figure B

3 figure C

4 figure D

Figures B and C have rotational symmetry.

Chapter 13

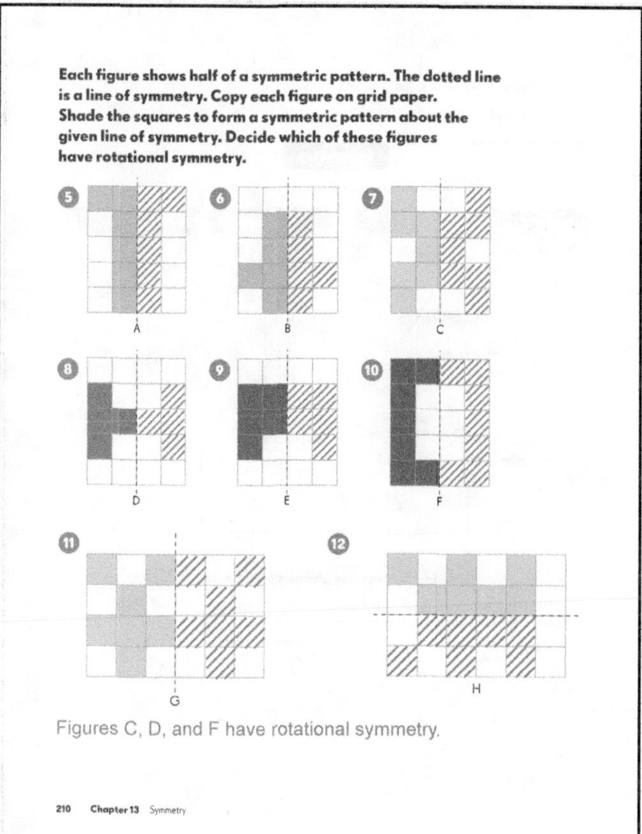

Each figure shows half of a symmetric pattern. The dotted line is a line of symmetry. Copy each figure on grid paper. Shade the squares to form a symmetric pattern about the given line of symmetry. Decide which of these figures have rotational symmetry.

5 A 6 B 7 C

8 D 9 E 10 F

11 G 12 H

Figures C, D, and F have rotational symmetry.

210 **Chapter 13** Symmetry

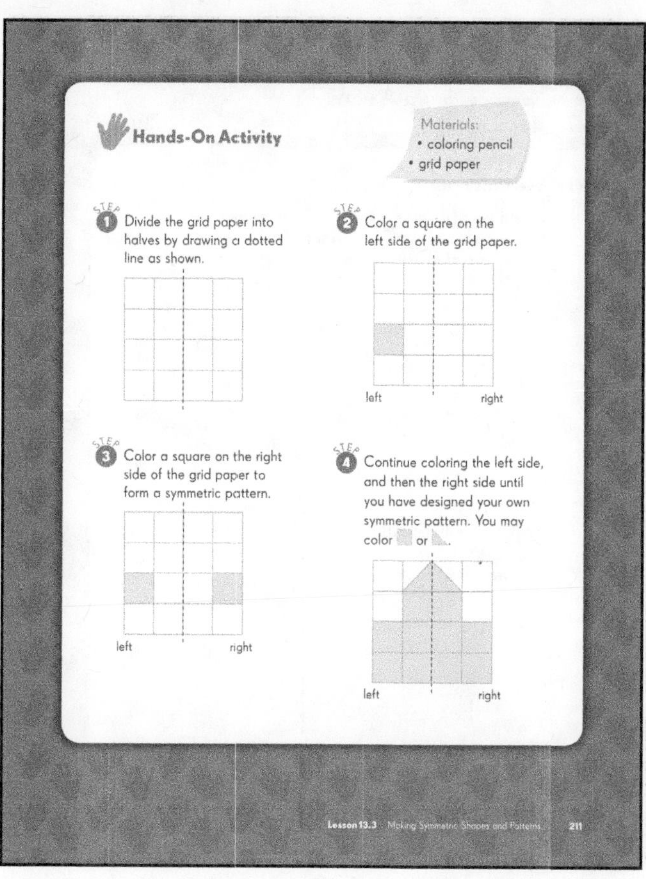

Hands-On Activity

Materials:
- coloring pencil
- grid paper

STEP 1 Divide the grid paper into halves by drawing a dotted line as shown.

STEP 2 Color a square on the left side of the grid paper.

left right

STEP 3 Color a square on the right side of the grid paper to form a symmetric pattern.

left right

STEP 4 Continue coloring the left side, and then the right side until you have designed your own symmetric pattern. You may color or .

left right

Lesson 13.3 Making Symmetric Shapes and Patterns **211**

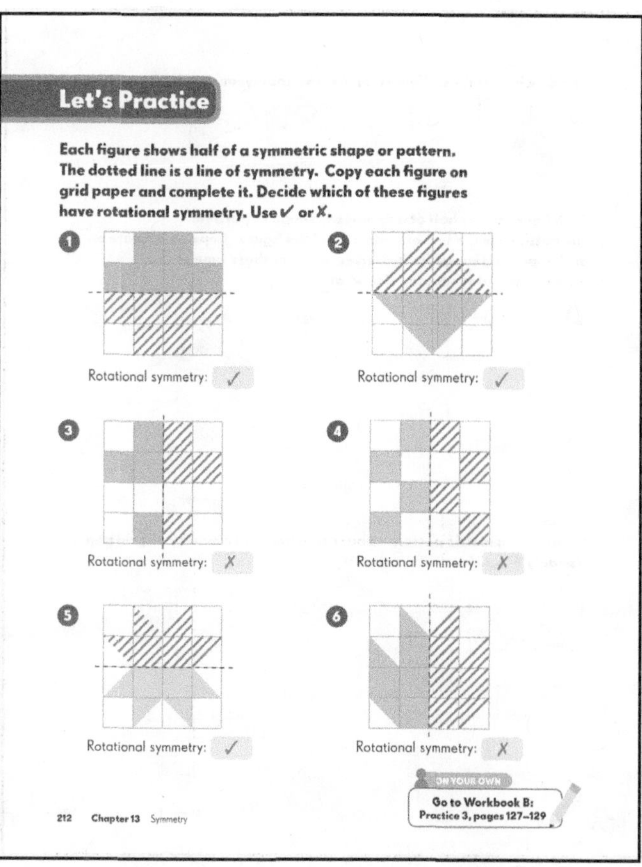

Let's Practice

Each figure shows half of a symmetric shape or pattern. The dotted line is a line of symmetry. Copy each figure on grid paper and complete it. Decide which of these figures have rotational symmetry. Use ✓ or ✗.

1 Rotational symmetry: ✓

2 Rotational symmetry: ✓

3 Rotational symmetry: ✗

4 Rotational symmetry: ✗

5 Rotational symmetry: ✓

6 Rotational symmetry: ✗

ON YOUR OWN
Go to Workbook B: Practice 3, pages 127–129

212 **Chapter 13** Symmetry

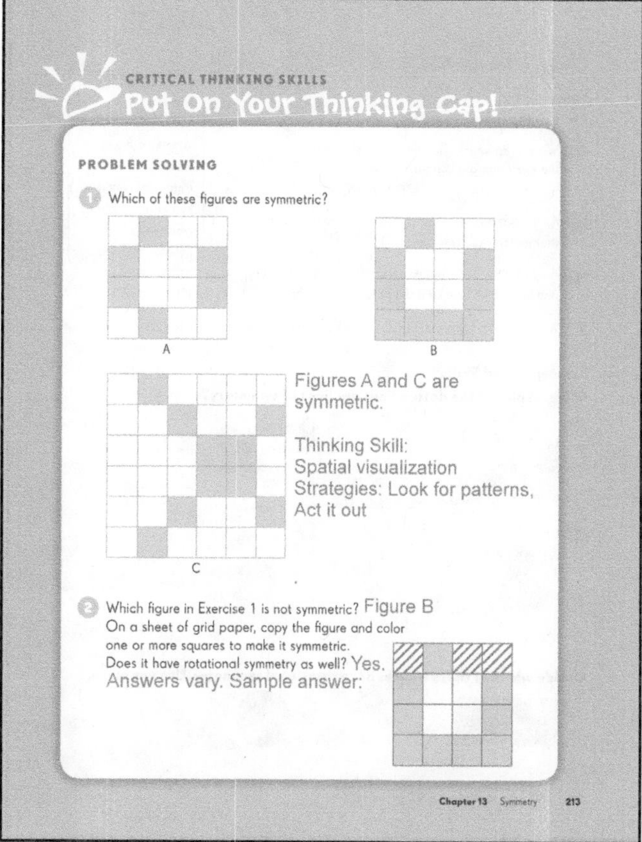

CRITICAL THINKING SKILLS
Put On Your Thinking Cap!

PROBLEM SOLVING

1 Which of these figures are symmetric?

A B C

Figures A and C are symmetric.

Thinking Skill:
Spatial visualization
Strategies: Look for patterns, Act it out

2 Which figure in Exercise 1 is not symmetric? Figure B
On a sheet of grid paper, copy the figure and color one or more squares to make it symmetric.
Does it have rotational symmetry as well? Yes.
Answers vary. Sample answer:

Chapter 13 Symmetry **213**

Chapter 13

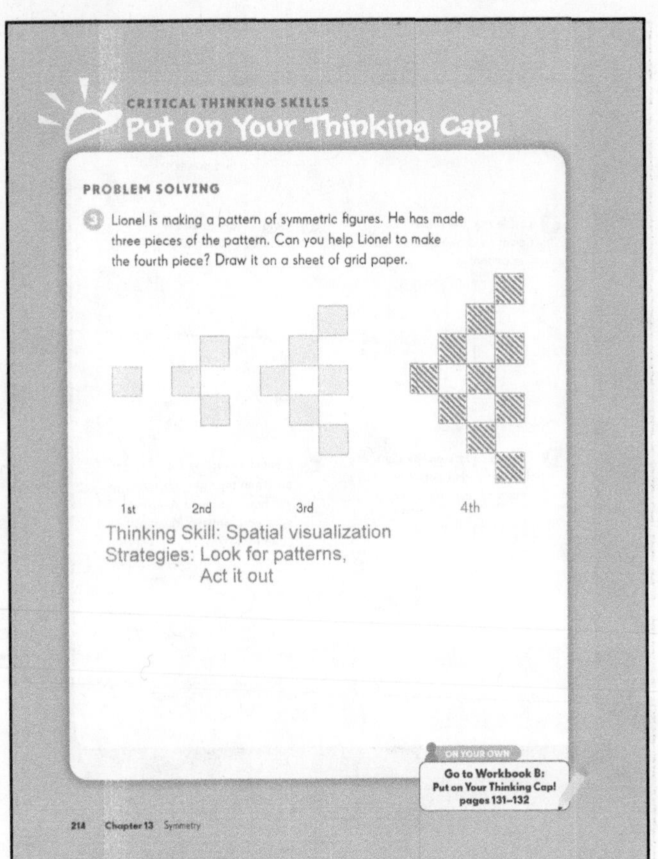
CRITICAL THINKING SKILLS
Put On Your Thinking Cap!
PROBLEM SOLVING
Lionel is making a pattern of symmetric figures. He has made three pieces of the pattern. Can you help Lionel to make the fourth piece? Draw it on a sheet of grid paper.
1st
2nd
3rd
4th
Thinking Skill: Spatial visualization
Strategies: Look for patterns,
Act it out
ON YOUR OWN
Go to Workbook B: Put on Your Thinking Cap! pages 131–132
214 Chapter 13 Symmetry

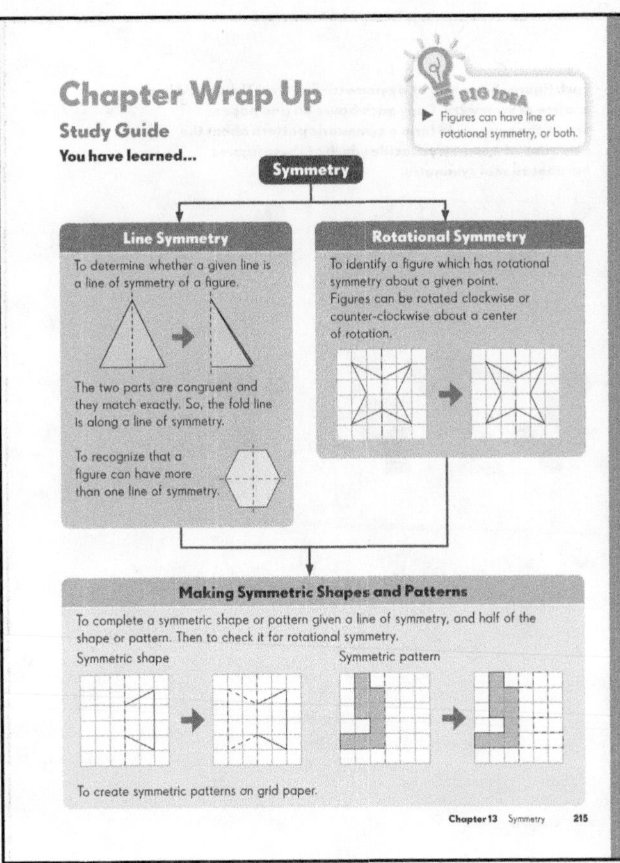
Chapter Wrap Up
Study Guide
You have learned...
BIG IDEA
Figures can have line or rotational symmetry, or both.
Symmetry
Line Symmetry
To determine whether a given line is a line of symmetry of a figure.
The two parts are congruent and they match exactly. So, the fold line is along a line of symmetry.
To recognize that a figure can have more than one line of symmetry.
Rotational Symmetry
To identify a figure which has rotational symmetry about a given point.
Figures can be rotated clockwise or counter-clockwise about a center of rotation.
Making Symmetric Shapes and Patterns
To complete a symmetric shape or pattern given a line of symmetry, and half of the shape or pattern. Then to check it for rotational symmetry.
Symmetric shape
Symmetric pattern
To create symmetric patterns on grid paper.
Chapter 13 Symmetry 215

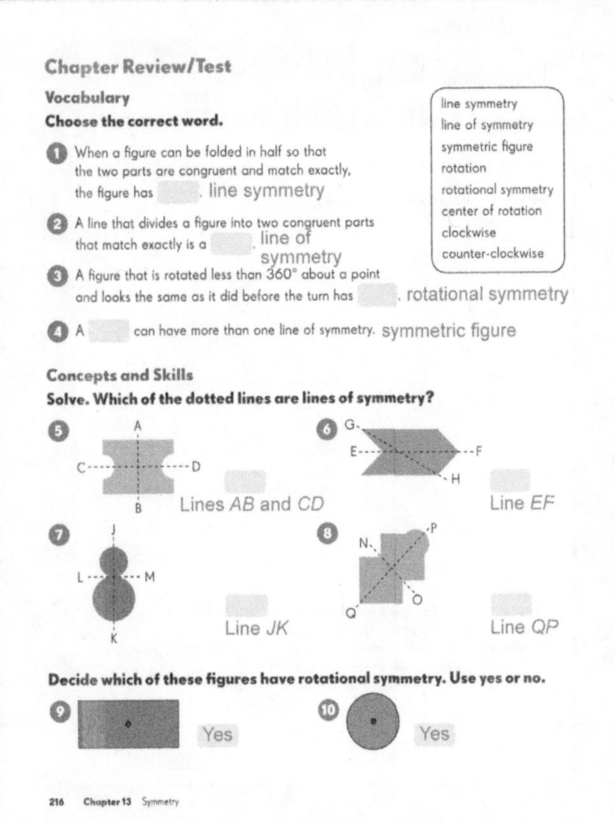
Chapter Review/Test
Vocabulary
Choose the correct word.
line symmetry
line of symmetry
symmetric figure
rotation
rotational symmetry
center of rotation
clockwise
counter-clockwise
1 When a figure can be folded in half so that the two parts are congruent and match exactly, the figure has ___. line symmetry
2 A line that divides a figure into two congruent parts that match exactly is a ___. line of symmetry
3 A figure that is rotated less than 360° about a point and looks the same as it did before the turn has ___. rotational symmetry
4 A ___ can have more than one line of symmetry. symmetric figure
Concepts and Skills
Solve. Which of the dotted lines are lines of symmetry?
5 Lines AB and CD
6 Line EF
7 Line JK
8 Line QP
Decide which of these figures have rotational symmetry. Use yes or no.
9 Yes
10 Yes
216 Chapter 13 Symmetry

Chapter 13

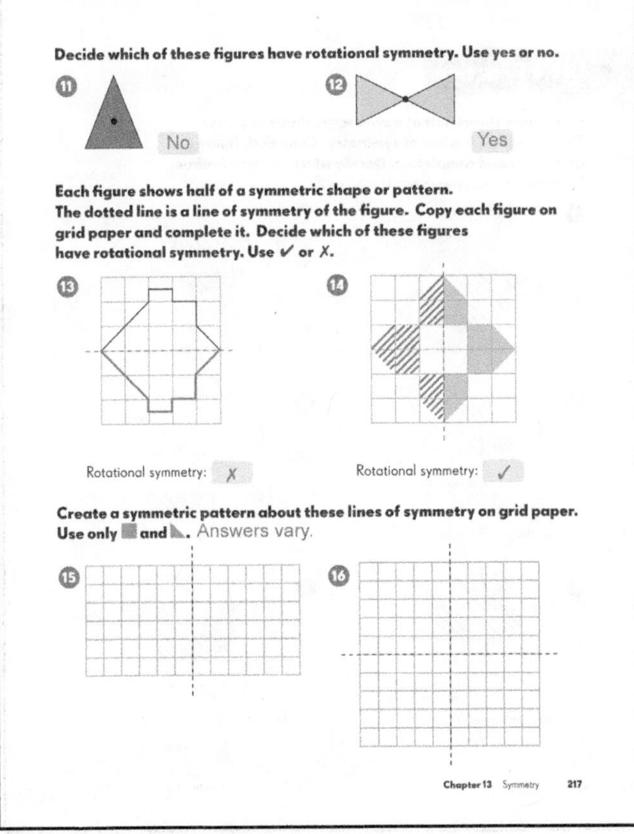
Decide which of these figures have rotational symmetry. Use yes or no.
11 No
12 Yes
Each figure shows half of a symmetric shape or pattern. The dotted line is a line of symmetry of the figure. Copy each figure on grid paper and complete it. Decide which of these figures have rotational symmetry. Use ✓ or ✗.
13 Rotational symmetry: ✗
14 Rotational symmetry: ✓
Create a symmetric pattern about these lines of symmetry on grid paper. Use only ■ and ◣. Answers vary.
15
16
Chapter 13 Symmetry 217

Chapter

14 Tessellations

Lessons

14.1 Identifying Tessellations

14.2 More Tessellations

BIG IDEA

▶ A tessellation is made when a shape (or shapes) is repeated, covering a plane (or surface) without gaps or overlaps to form patterns.

218

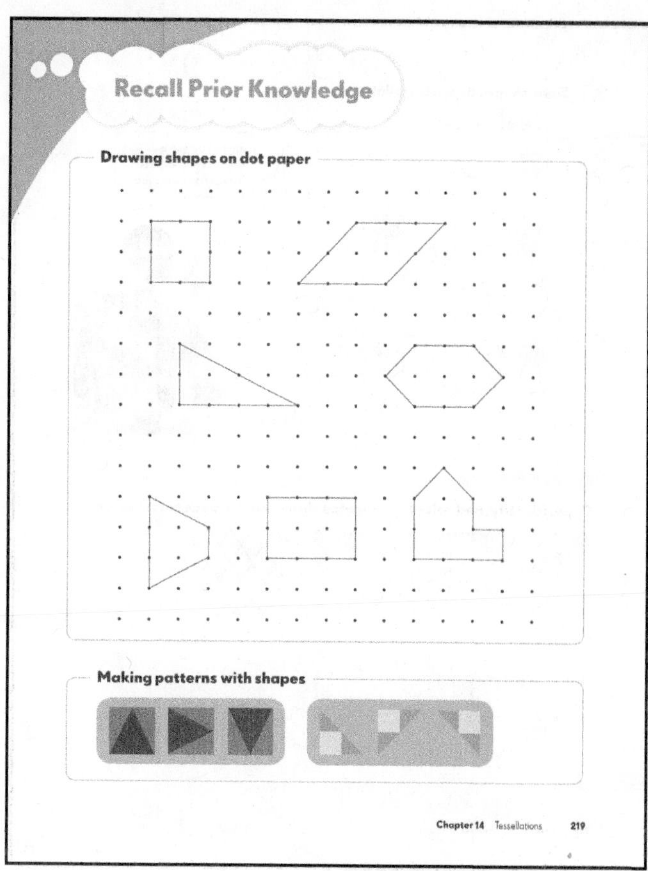
Recall Prior Knowledge

Drawing shapes on dot paper

Making patterns with shapes

Chapter 14 Tessellations 219

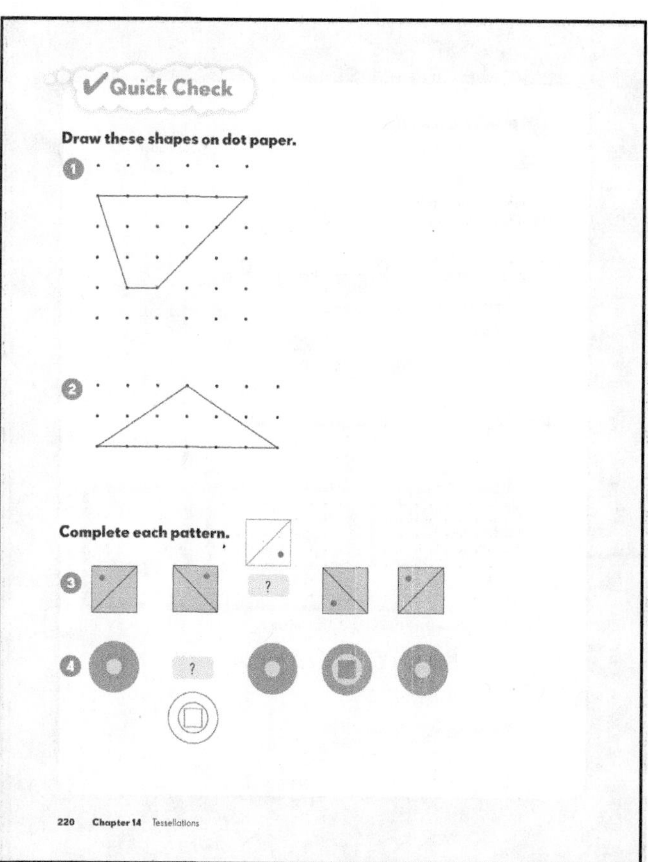
✔ Quick Check

Draw these shapes on dot paper.

1

2

Complete each pattern.

3 ?

4 ?

220 Chapter 14 Tessellations

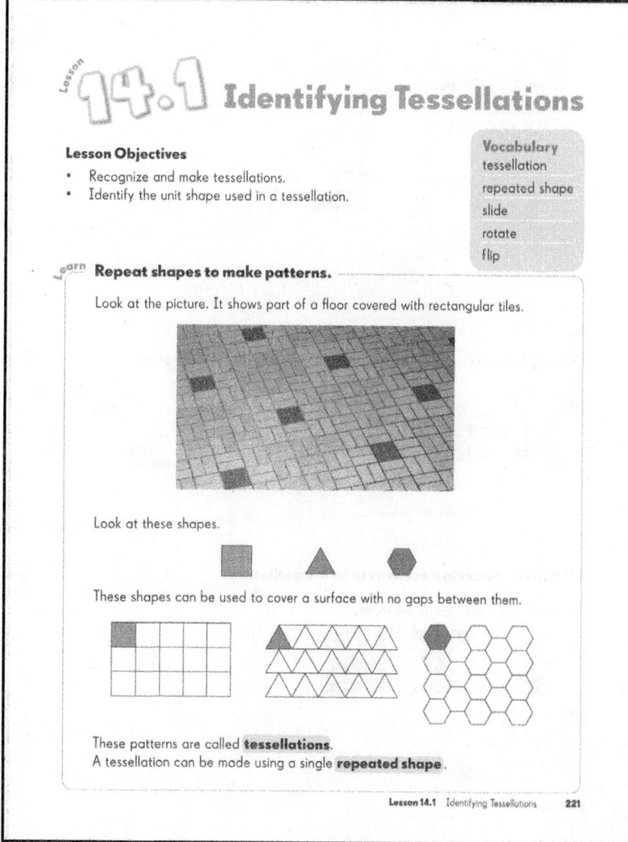
Lesson

14.1 Identifying Tessellations

Lesson Objectives

- Recognize and make tessellations.
- Identify the unit shape used in a tessellation.

Vocabulary
tessellation
repeated shape
slide
rotate
flip

Learn **Repeat shapes to make patterns.**

Look at the picture. It shows part of a floor covered with rectangular tiles.

Look at these shapes.

These shapes can be used to cover a surface with no gaps between them.

These patterns are called **tessellations**.
A tessellation can be made using a single **repeated shape**.

Lesson 14.1 Identifying Tessellations 221

Chapter 14

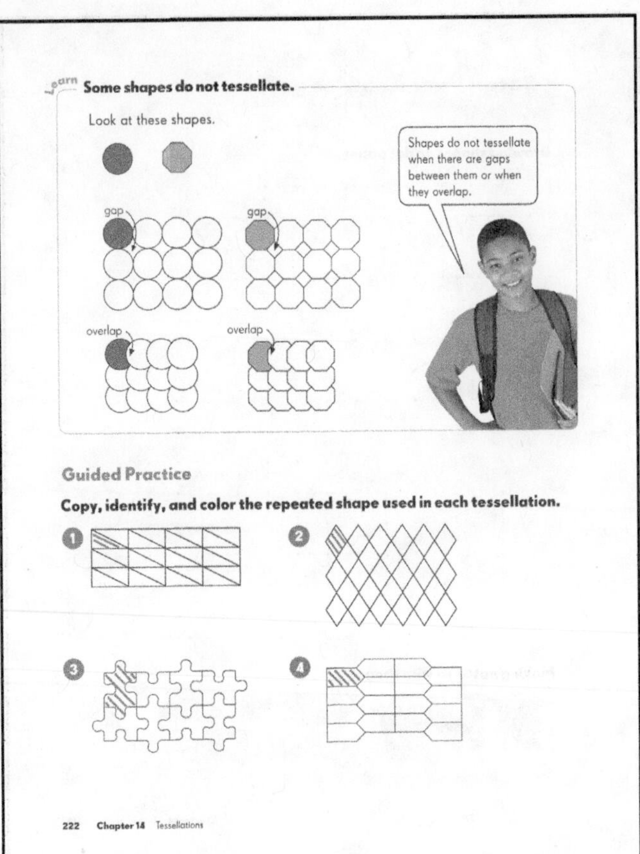

Learn Some shapes do not tessellate.

Look at these shapes.

Shapes do not tessellate when there are gaps between them or when they overlap.
gap
gap
overlap
overlap

Guided Practice

Copy, identify, and color the repeated shape used in each tessellation.

1

2

3

4

222 Chapter 14 Tessellations

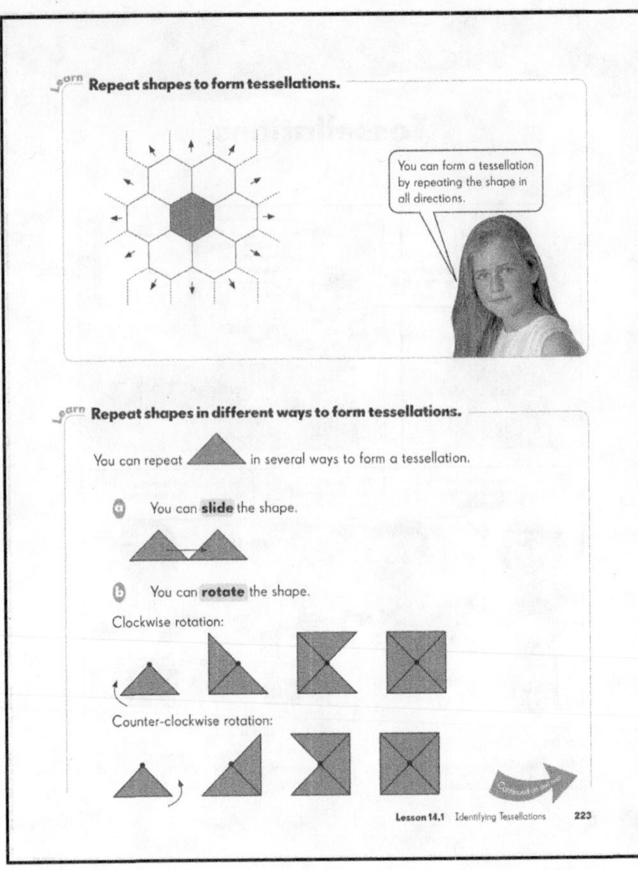

Learn Repeat shapes to form tessellations.

You can form a tessellation by repeating the shape in all directions.

Learn Repeat shapes in different ways to form tessellations.

You can repeat [triangle] in several ways to form a tessellation.

a You can **slide** the shape.

b You can **rotate** the shape.

Clockwise rotation:

Counter-clockwise rotation:

Lesson 14.1 Identifying Tessellations 223

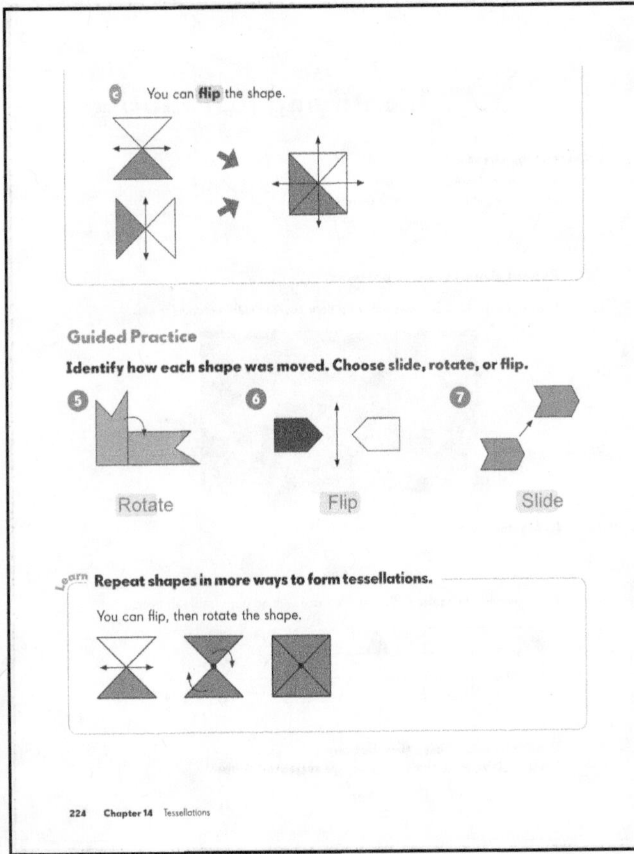

c You can **flip** the shape.

Guided Practice

Identify how each shape was moved. Choose slide, rotate, or flip.

5 Rotate

6 Flip

7 Slide

Learn Repeat shapes in more ways to form tessellations.

You can flip, then rotate the shape.

224 Chapter 14 Tessellations

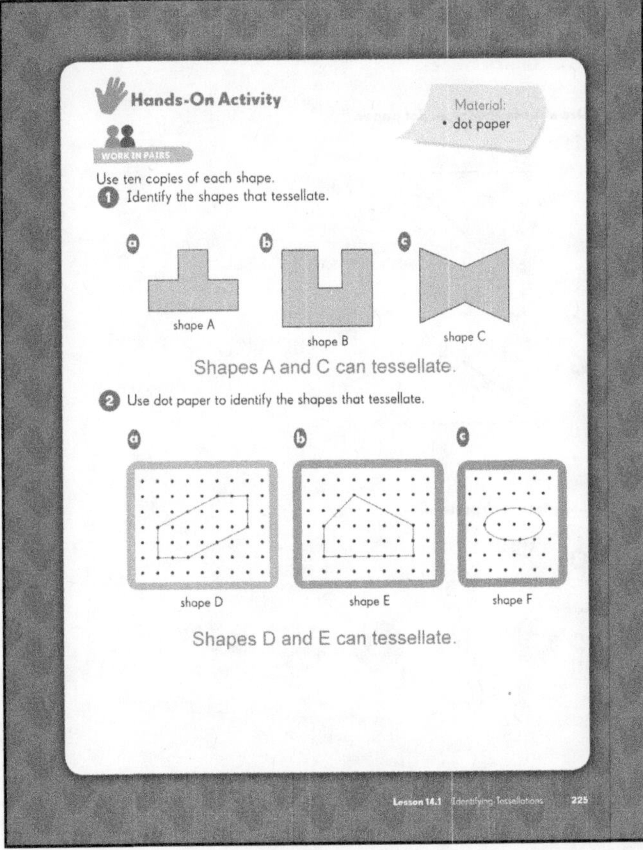

Hands-On Activity

WORK IN PAIRS

Material:
- dot paper

Use ten copies of each shape.

1 Identify the shapes that tessellate.

a shape A

b shape B

c shape C

Shapes A and C can tessellate.

2 Use dot paper to identify the shapes that tessellate.

a shape D

b shape E

c shape F

Shapes D and E can tessellate.

Lesson 14.1 Identifying Tessellations 225

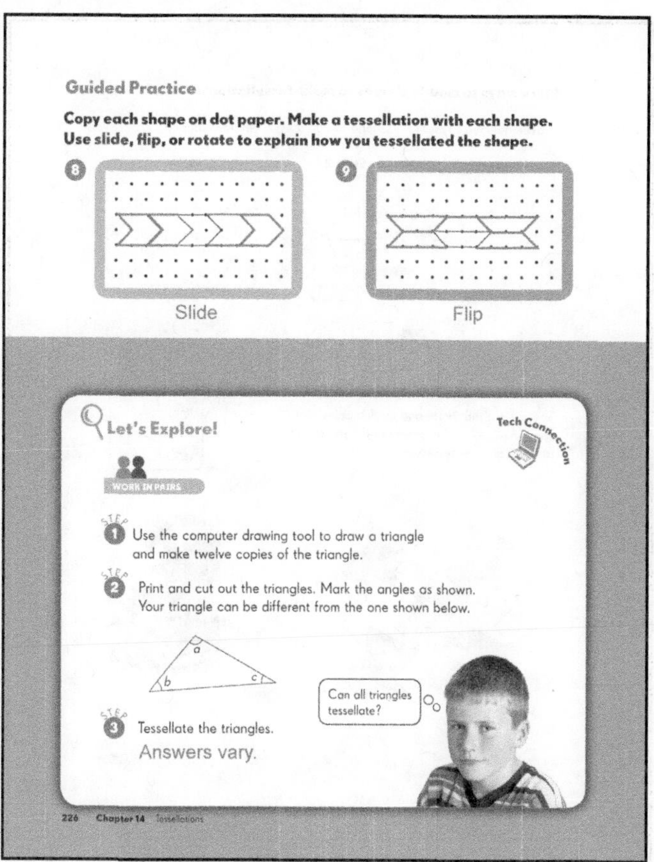

Guided Practice

Copy each shape on dot paper. Make a tessellation with each shape. Use slide, flip, or rotate to explain how you tessellated the shape.

8 Slide

9 Flip

Let's Explore!

Tech Connection

WORK IN PAIRS

STEP 1 Use the computer drawing tool to draw a triangle and make twelve copies of the triangle.

STEP 2 Print and cut out the triangles. Mark the angles as shown. Your triangle can be different from the one shown below.

a
b
c
Can all triangles tessellate?

STEP 3 Tessellate the triangles.

Answers vary.

226 Chapter 14 Tessellations

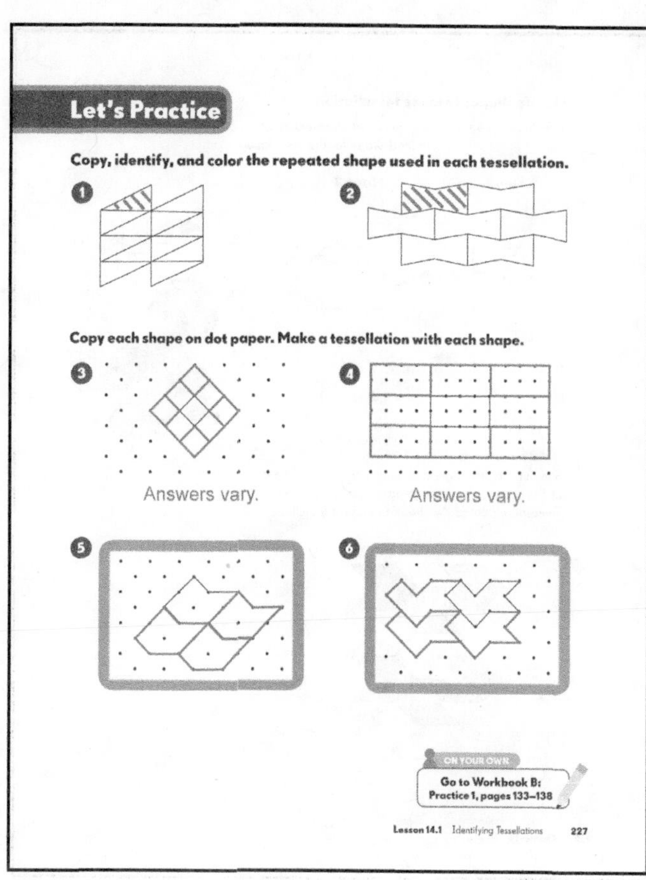

Let's Practice

Copy, identify, and color the repeated shape used in each tessellation.

1

2

Copy each shape on dot paper. Make a tessellation with each shape.

3 Answers vary.

4 Answers vary.

5

6

ON YOUR OWN

Go to Workbook B: Practice 1, pages 133–138

Lesson 14.1 Identifying Tessellations 227

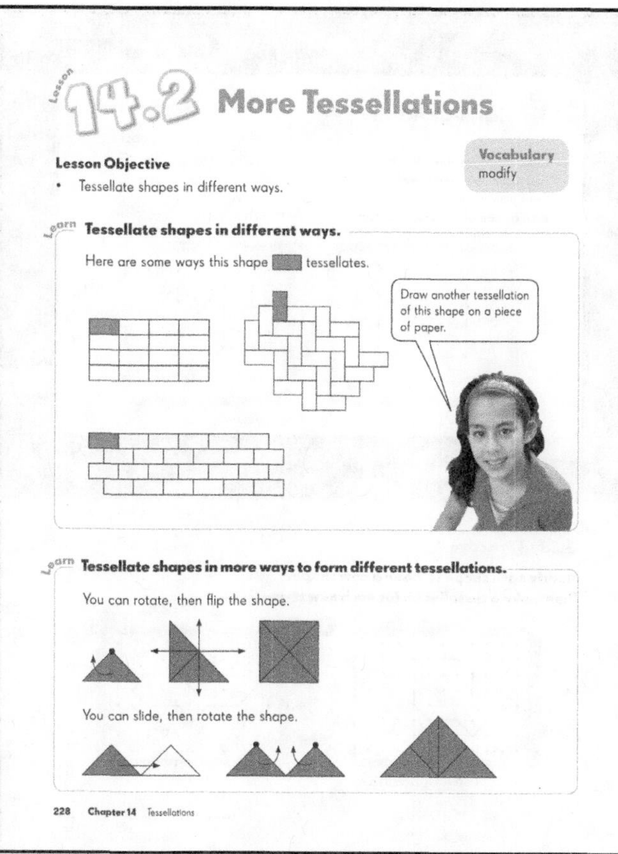

Lesson 14.2

More Tessellations

Lesson Objective

- Tessellate shapes in different ways.

Vocabulary
modify

Learn **Tessellate shapes in different ways.**

Here are some ways this shape tessellates.

Draw another tessellation of this shape on a piece of paper.

Learn **Tessellate shapes in more ways to form different tessellations.**

You can rotate, then flip the shape.

You can slide, then rotate the shape.

228 Chapter 14 Tessellations

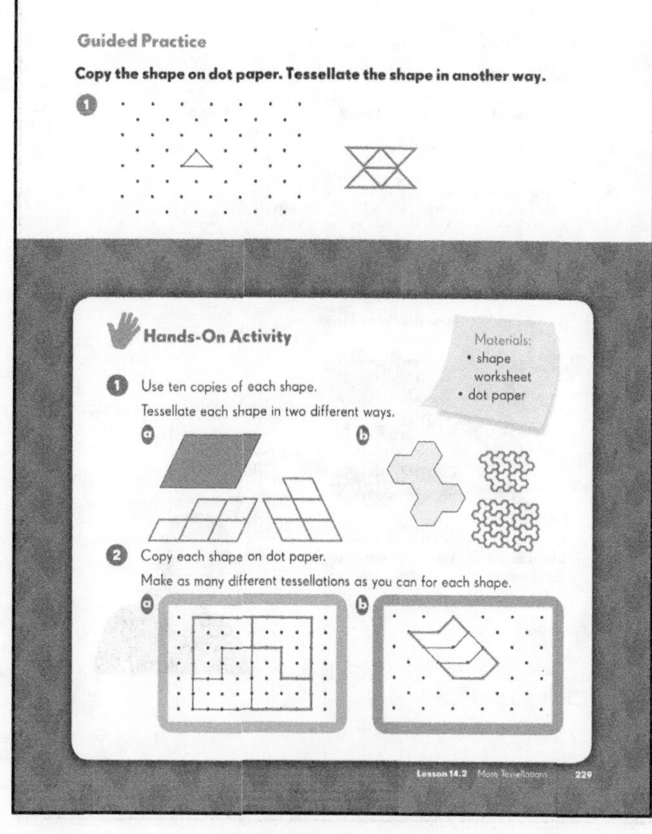

Guided Practice

Copy the shape on dot paper. Tessellate the shape in another way.

1

Hands-On Activity

Materials:
- shape worksheet
- dot paper

1 Use ten copies of each shape. Tessellate each shape in two different ways.

a

b

2 Copy each shape on dot paper. Make as many different tessellations as you can for each shape.

a

b

Lesson 14.2 More Tessellations 229

Chapter 14

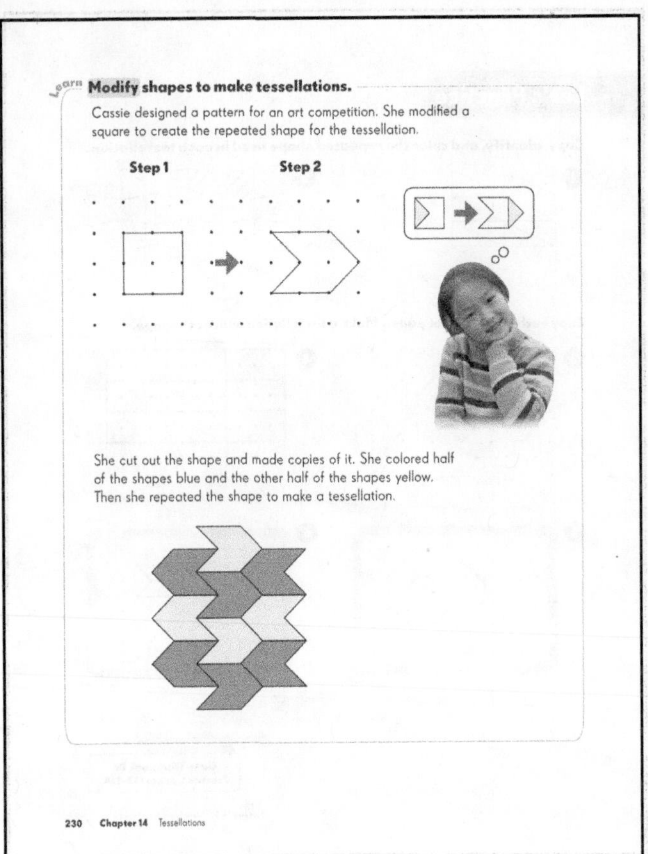
Learn **Modify shapes to make tessellations.**

Cassie designed a pattern for an art competition. She modified a square to create the repeated shape for the tessellation.

Step 1 **Step 2**

She cut out the shape and made copies of it. She colored half of the shapes blue and the other half of the shapes yellow. Then she repeated the shape to make a tessellation.

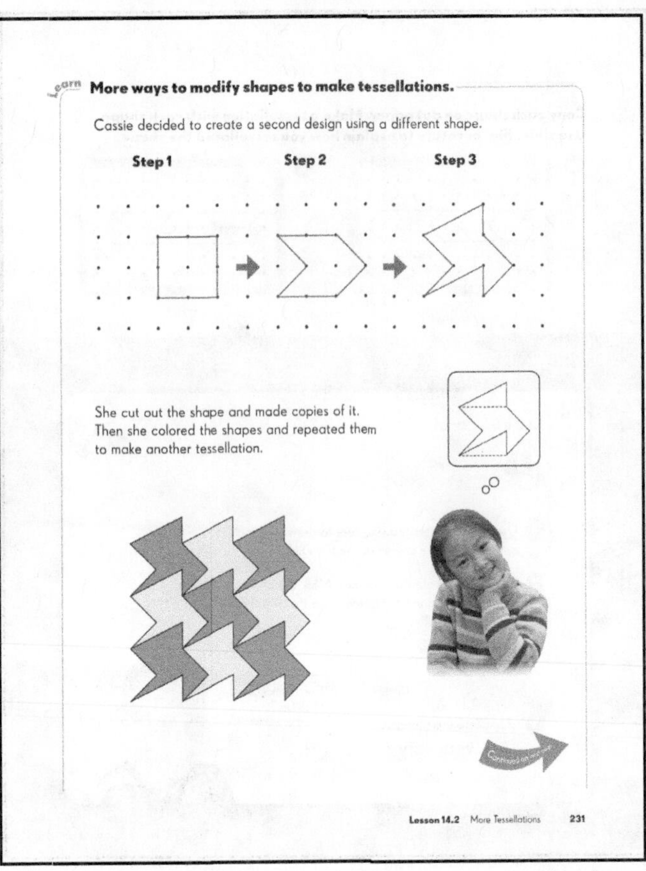
Learn **More ways to modify shapes to make tessellations.**

Cassie decided to create a second design using a different shape.

Step 1 **Step 2** **Step 3**

She cut out the shape and made copies of it. Then she colored the shapes and repeated them to make another tessellation.

Continued on next page

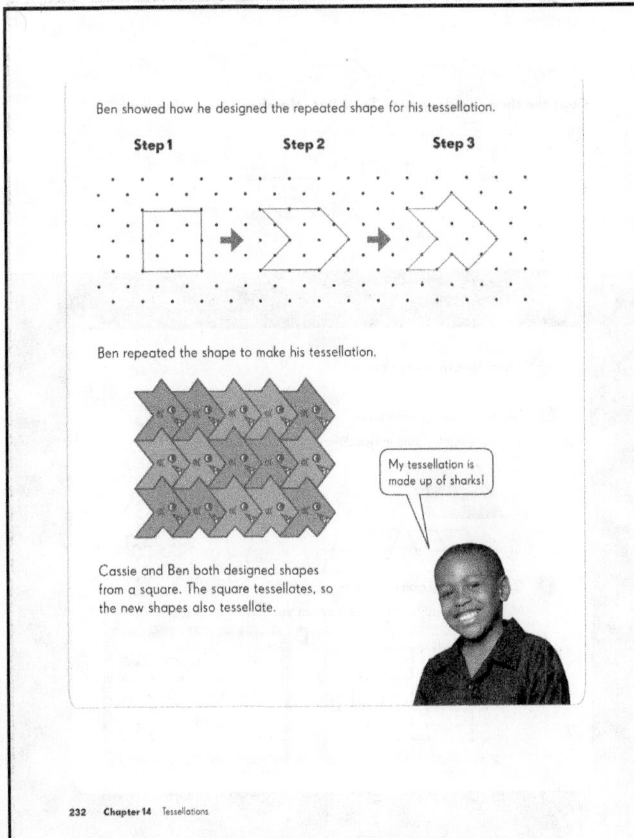
Ben showed how he designed the repeated shape for his tessellation.

Step 1 **Step 2** **Step 3**

Ben repeated the shape to make his tessellation.

My tessellation is made up of sharks!

Cassie and Ben both designed shapes from a square. The square tessellates, so the new shapes also tessellate.

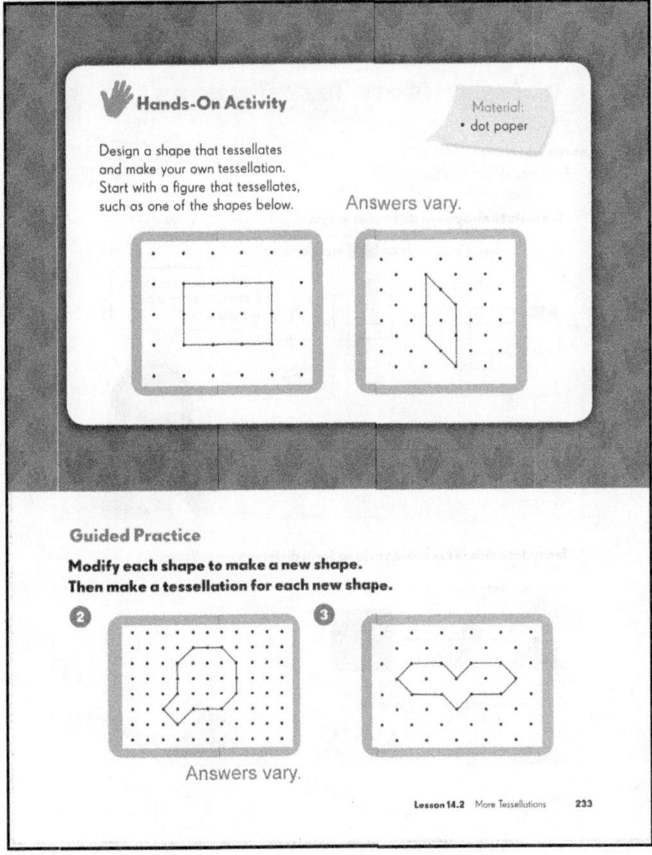
Hands-On Activity

Material:
• dot paper

Design a shape that tessellates and make your own tessellation. Start with a figure that tessellates, such as one of the shapes below.

Answers vary.

Guided Practice

Modify each shape to make a new shape. Then make a tessellation for each new shape.

2

3

Answers vary.

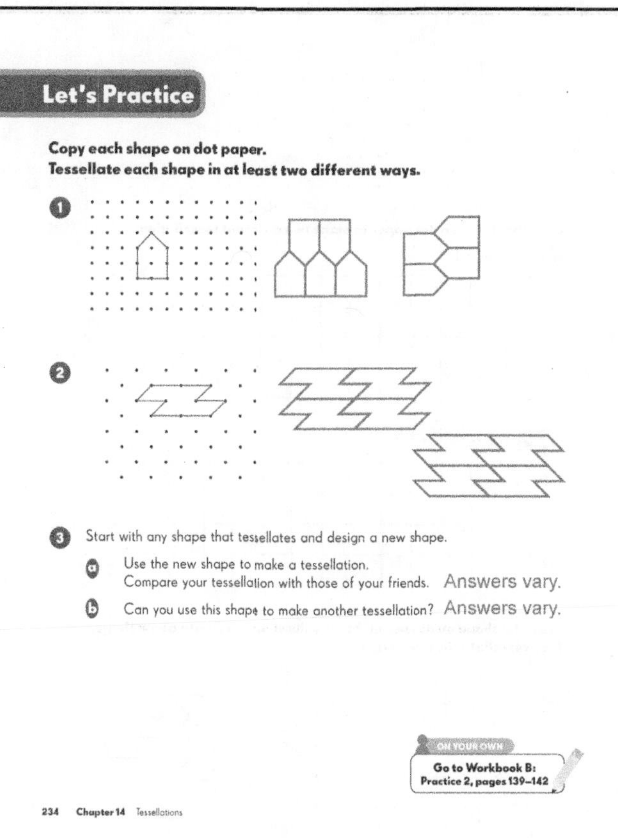

Let's Practice

Copy each shape on dot paper.
Tessellate each shape in at least two different ways.

1

2

3 Start with any shape that tessellates and design a new shape.

a Use the new shape to make a tessellation. Compare your tessellation with those of your friends. Answers vary.

b Can you use this shape to make another tessellation? Answers vary.

ON YOUR OWN
Go to Workbook B: Practice 2, pages 139–142

234 Chapter 14 Tessellations

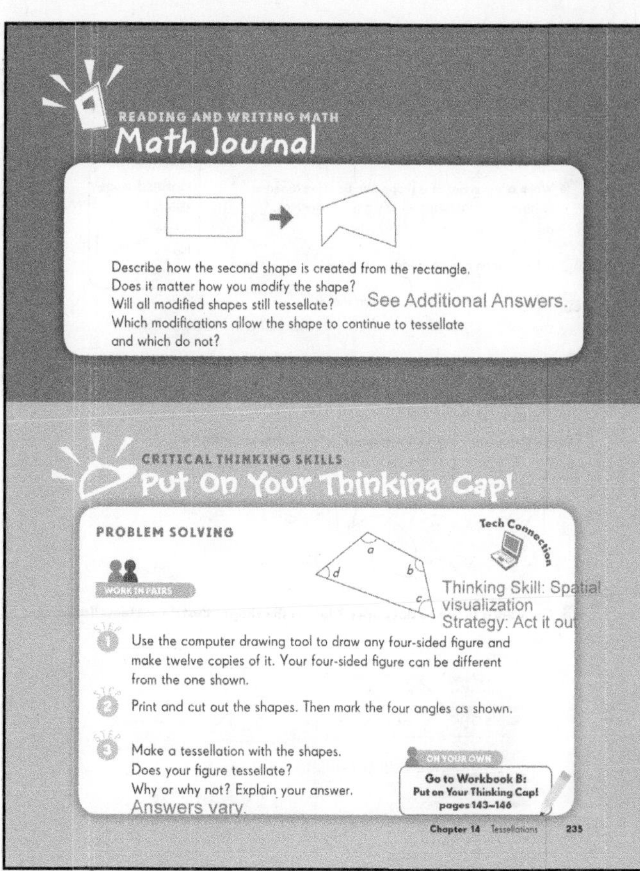

READING AND WRITING MATH

Math Journal

Describe how the second shape is created from the rectangle.
Does it matter how you modify the shape?
Will all modified shapes still tessellate? See Additional Answers.
Which modifications allow the shape to continue to tessellate and which do not?

CRITICAL THINKING SKILLS

Put On Your Thinking Cap!

PROBLEM SOLVING

WORK IN PAIRS

Tech Connection

Thinking Skill: Spatial visualization
Strategy: Act it out

1 Use the computer drawing tool to draw any four-sided figure and make twelve copies of it. Your four-sided figure can be different from the one shown.

2 Print and cut out the shapes. Then mark the four angles as shown.

3 Make a tessellation with the shapes. Does your figure tessellate? Why or why not? Explain your answer.
Answers vary.

ON YOUR OWN
Go to Workbook B: Put on Your Thinking Cap! pages 143–146

Chapter 14 Tessellations 235

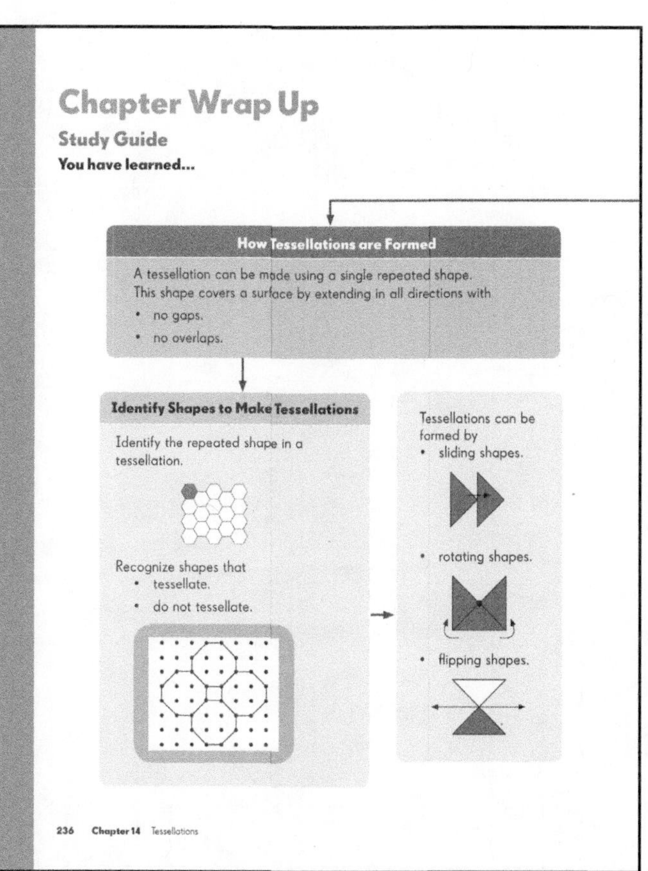

Chapter Wrap Up

Study Guide

You have learned...

How Tessellations are Formed

A tessellation can be made using a single repeated shape.
This shape covers a surface by extending in all directions with
- no gaps.
- no overlaps.

Identify Shapes to Make Tessellations

Identify the repeated shape in a tessellation.

Recognize shapes that
- tessellate.
- do not tessellate.

Tessellations can be formed by
- sliding shapes.
- rotating shapes.
- flipping shapes.

236 Chapter 14 Tessellations

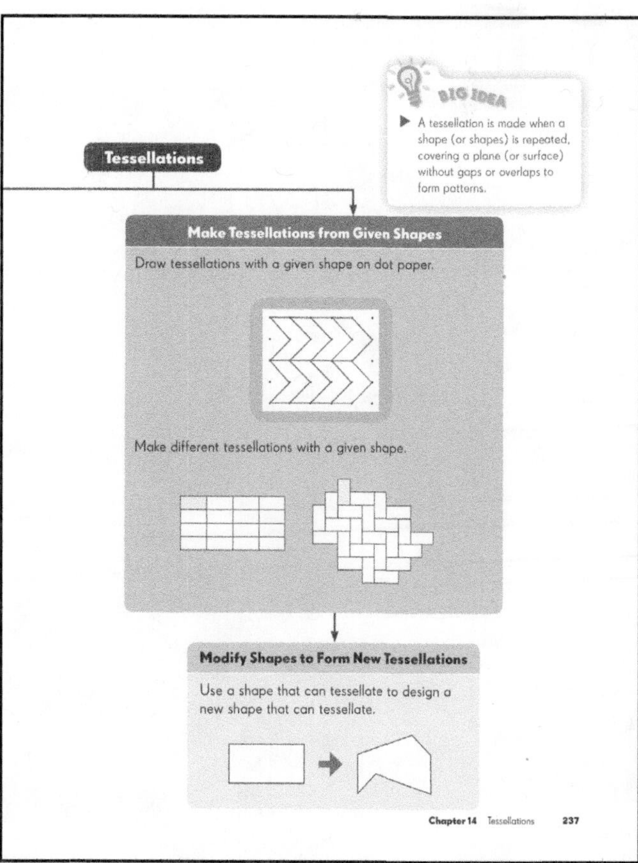

Tessellations

BIG IDEA
▶ A tessellation is made when a shape (or shapes) is repeated, covering a plane (or surface) without gaps or overlaps to form patterns.

Make Tessellations from Given Shapes

Draw tessellations with a given shape on dot paper.

Make different tessellations with a given shape.

Modify Shapes to Form New Tessellations

Use a shape that can tessellate to design a new shape that can tessellate.

Chapter 14 Tessellations 237

Chapter 14

Chapter Review/Test

Vocabulary

Choose the correct word.

tessellation
repeated shape
slide
rotate
flip
modify

1. When any number of a shape can be fitted together to cover a surface without any gaps or overlaps, a ____ is formed. tessellation
2. A tessellation can be made using a single ____ shape. repeated
3. To form a tessellation with a given shape, you can ____ or ____ or ____ it. flip / slide / rotate
4. You can ____ a repeated shape to create a new shape that can tessellate. modify

Concepts and Skills

Identify the repeated shape used to form this tessellation.

5.

6. **Copy each shape on dot paper. Identify the shapes that do not tessellate.**

a. This shape can tessellate.

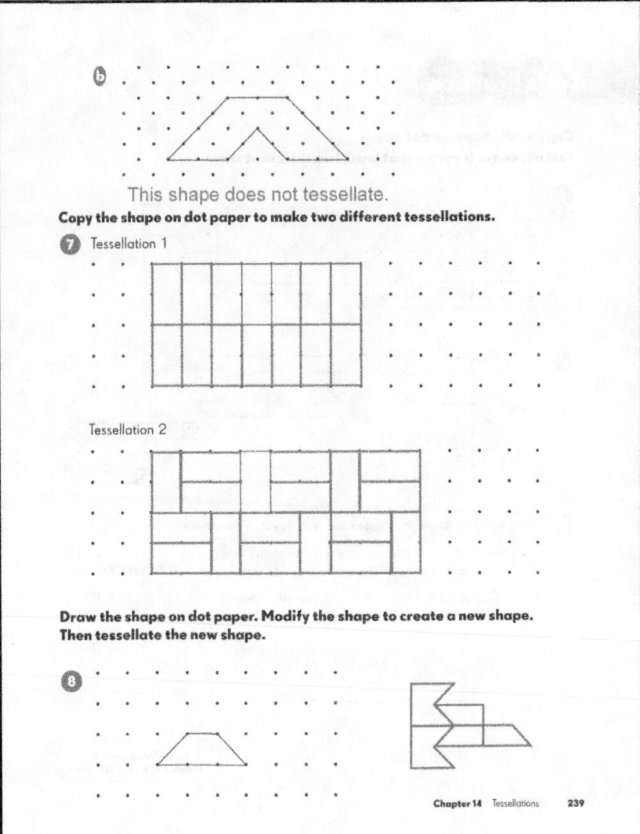

b. This shape does not tessellate.

Copy the shape on dot paper to make two different tessellations.

7. Tessellation 1

Tessellation 2

Draw the shape on dot paper. Modify the shape to create a new shape. Then tessellate the new shape.

8.

Math in Focus
Workbook Answers
Grade 4

Name: ______________________ Date: ______________

Chapter 1 Place Value of Whole Numbers

Practice 1 Numbers to 100,000

Write each number in standard form.

Example
seventy-two thousand, four hundred sixty — 72,460

1. seventy thousand, eight hundred twenty-three — 70,823
2. sixty-two thousand, four hundred eighteen — 62,418
3. ninety-seven thousand, four hundred — 97,400
4. thirty thousand, eleven — 30,011

Write each number in word form.

Example
56,548 — fifty-six thousand, five hundred forty-eight

5. 12,021 — twelve thousand, twenty-one
6. 70,009 — seventy thousand, nine
7. 40,807 — forty thousand, eight hundred seven

© 2009 Marshall Cavendish International (Singapore) Private Limited

Count on and fill in the blanks.

8. 81,000 82,000 83,000 84,000 85,000
9. 30,000 40,000 50,000 60,000 70,000
10. 10,000 15,000 20,000 25,000 30,000

Write the missing words and digits for each number.

Example
two thousand, five hundred twelve — 2,51 2

11. sixty-one thousand, one — 6 1,001
12. twenty-four thousand, three hundred ten — 24,3 1 0
13. forty-five thousand, two hundred six — 4 5 ,206
14. thirty-six thousand, one hundred eighty-nine — 36, 1 89

Make each 5-digit number using all the cards. Do not begin a number with '0'.

5 7 2 0 9

15. An odd number: Answers vary, but will end with 5, 7, or 9.
16. An even number: Answers vary, but will end with 0 or 2.
17. A number with zero in the hundreds place: Answers vary, but the middle number will be a 0.
18. A number beginning with the greatest digit: Answers vary, but will begin with 9.
19. A number with 2 in the tens place and 5 in the ones place: 79,025 70,925 90,725 97,025
20. A number ending with 7: Answers vary, but will end with 7.

© 2009 Marshall Cavendish International (Singapore) Private Limited

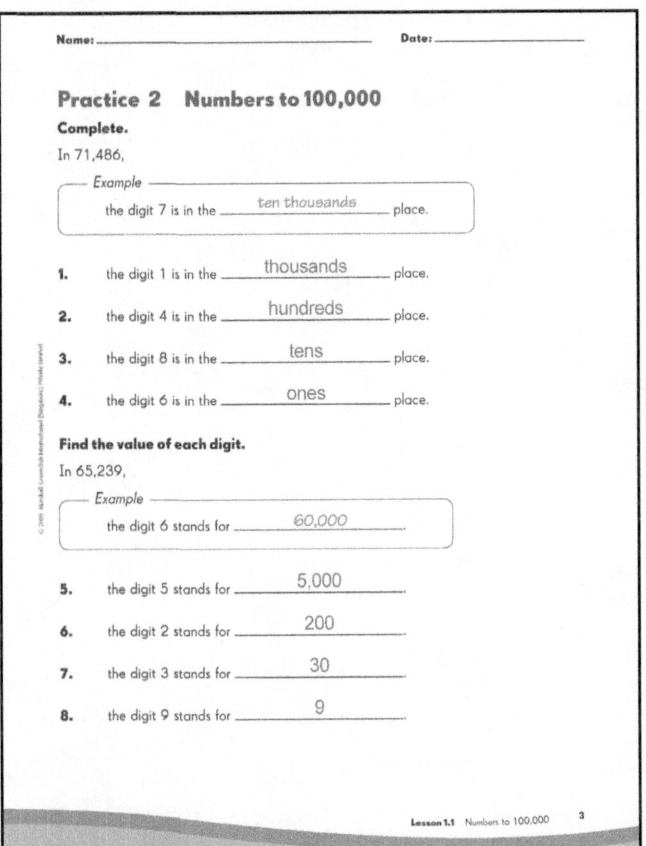

Name: ______________________ Date: ______________

Practice 2 Numbers to 100,000

Complete.

In 71,486,

Example
the digit 7 is in the ten thousands place.

1. the digit 1 is in the thousands place.
2. the digit 4 is in the hundreds place.
3. the digit 8 is in the tens place.
4. the digit 6 is in the ones place.

Find the value of each digit.

In 65,239,

Example
the digit 6 stands for 60,000.

5. the digit 5 stands for 5,000.
6. the digit 2 stands for 200.
7. the digit 3 stands for 30.
8. the digit 9 stands for 9.

© 2009 Marshall Cavendish International (Singapore) Private Limited

Write each number using the clues.

9.
The value of the digit 1 is 100.
The value of the digit 5 is 50.
The value of the digit 3 is 3.
The value of the digit 4 is 40,000.
The value of the digit 2 is 2,000.

The number is 42,153.

10.
The digit 4 is in the hundreds place.
The digit 2 is in the ten thousands place.
The digit 9 is in the tens place.
The digit 0 is in the ones place.
The digit 5 is in the thousands place.

The number is 25,490.

Write the missing numbers and words.

Example
In 36,172,
the digit 2 stands for 2 ones.
the digit 6 is in the thousands place.
the digit in the ten thousands place is 3.
the value of the digit 7 is 70.
the digit 1 is in the hundreds place and its value is 100.

© 2009 Marshall Cavendish International (Singapore) Private Limited

Name: ______ Date: ______

Write the missing numbers and words.

In 52,814,

11. the digit 4 stands for 4 ones.
12. the digit 1 is in the tens place.
13. the digit in the ten thousands place is 5
14. the value of the digit 8 is 800
15. the digit 2 is in the thousands place and its value is 2,000

Complete.

Example
38,295 = 3 ten thousands + 8 thousands + 2 hundreds + 9 tens + 5 ones

16. 72,439 = 7 ten thousands + 2 thousands + 4 hundreds + 3 tens + 9 ones
17. 99,088 = 9 ten thousands + 9 thousands + 0 hundreds + 8 tens + 8 ones

© 2009 Marshall Cavendish International (Singapore) Private Limited

Complete the expanded form.

Example
51,476 = 50,000 + 1,000 + 400 + 70 + 6

18. 36,427 = 30,000 + 6,000 + 400 + 20 + 7
19. 17,503 = 10,000 + 7,000 + 500 + 3
20. 45,080 = 40,000 + 5,000 + 80
21. 20,000 + 6,000 + 20 + 5 = 26,025
22. 5 + 60 + 80,000 = 80,065

Solve.

23. Color the puzzle pieces that show the answers in Exercises 18 to 22.

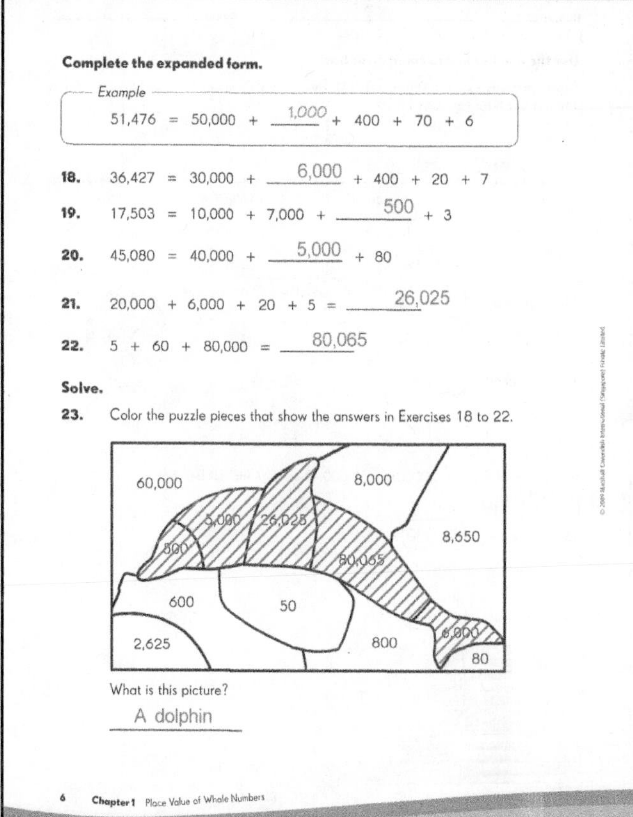

What is this picture?
A dolphin

© 2009 Marshall Cavendish International (Singapore) Private Limited

Name: ______ Date: ______

Practice 3 Comparing Numbers to 100,000

Write > or < in each ◯.

Example
15,408 (>) 12,508

> means greater than.
< means less than.

1. 63,809 (>) 36,908
2. 86,415 (<) 86,591
3. 45,638 (>) 8,594
4. 60,960 (<) 69,999

Compare the eight numbers in Exercises 1 to 4.

5. Which number is the greatest? 86,591
6. Which number is the least? 8,594

Order these numbers.

Example
Begin with the least:
52,081 63,456 51,125
51,125 52,081 63,456

Begin with the greatest:
76,332 74,236 81,152
81,152 76,332 74,236

© 2009 Marshall Cavendish International (Singapore) Private Limited

Order these numbers.

7. Begin with the least:
97,136 79,631 96,137
79,631 96,137 97,136

8. Begin with the greatest:
80,000 9,469 81,074
81,074 80,000 9,469

Write the missing numbers.

Example
1,000 more than 82,586 is 83,586.
17,312 is 40,000 less than 57,312.

9. 10,000 more than 56,821 is 66,821.
10. 29,895 is 50,000 less than 79,895.
11. 2,000 less than 18,563 is 16,563.
12. 51,200 is 3,000 more than 48,200.

© 2009 Marshall Cavendish International (Singapore) Private Limited

Name: ____________________ Date: ____________

Use the number line to count on or back.

Count on in steps of 4,000 from 20,000. Then write the number that you land on. The first one has been done for you.

20,000 30,000 40,000 50,000

13. 1 step (24,000)

I landed on 24,000 after 1 step.

14. 3 steps (32,000)

Count back in steps of 3,000 from 50,000. Then write the number that you land on.

15. 6 steps (32,000)

16. 8 steps (26,000)

© 2009 Marshall Cavendish International (Singapore) Private Limited

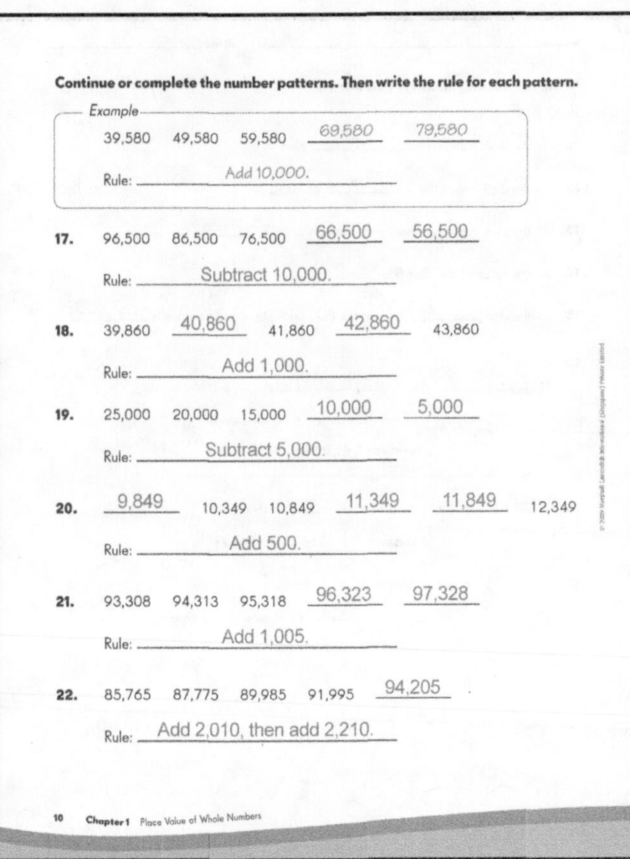

Continue or complete the number patterns. Then write the rule for each pattern.

Example

39,580 49,580 59,580 69,580 79,580

Rule: Add 10,000.

17. 96,500 86,500 76,500 66,500 56,500

Rule: Subtract 10,000.

18. 39,860 40,860 41,860 42,860 43,860

Rule: Add 1,000.

19. 25,000 20,000 15,000 10,000 5,000

Rule: Subtract 5,000.

20. 9,849 10,349 10,849 11,349 11,849 12,349

Rule: Add 500.

21. 93,308 94,313 95,318 96,323 97,328

Rule: Add 1,005.

22. 85,765 87,775 89,985 91,995 94,205

Rule: Add 2,010, then add 2,210.

© 2009 Marshall Cavendish International (Singapore) Private Limited

Name: ____________________ Date: ____________

Math Journal

1. Kim wrote these statements about the three numbers shown here. Do you agree? Explain why or why not.

85,691

85,945

3,869

3,869 is less than 85,945.

85,691 is greater than 85,945.

The number 3,869 has only 4 digits, so it is less than 85,945.

The number 85,691 has 6 in the hundreds place, but the number 85,945 has 9 in the hundreds place.

Hence, 85,945 is greater than 85,691.

2. Sam continued this number pattern. Do you agree? Explain why or why not.

5,400 10,400 10,600 15,600 15,800 (20,800)

His answer is correct.

The rule for this number pattern is add 5,000, then add 200.

Sam added 5,000 to 15,800, to get 20,800.

© 2009 Marshall Cavendish International (Singapore) Private Limited

3. Read the example. Then write your own 5-digit number and clues. Ask a friend or family member to solve your puzzle.

Example

45,870

The digit 5 is in the thousands place.

The value of the digit 7 is 70.

The digit in the hundreds place is 10 − 2.

The digit in the ten thousands place is 1 less than the digit in the thousands place.

The digit in the ones place is 0.

Number: Answers vary.

Clues: Answers vary.

© 2009 Marshall Cavendish International (Singapore) Private Limited

Name: ______________________ Date: ______________

Put On Your Thinking Cap!

Challenging Practice

Complete.

A 5-digit number is made up of different digits that are all odd numbers.

1. What is the greatest possible number? 97,531
2. What is the value of the digit in the hundreds place? 500

Continue the pattern.

3. 412 427 442 457 472 487 502

Fill in the blanks.

4. What is 3 ten thousands + 14 tens + 16 ones? 30,156
5. 7 thousands = 69 hundreds 10 tens

Thinking skills:
Identifying patterns and relationships

Answer these questions.

In 7(5), 8[5]9,

6. what is the value of the digit 5 in the ◯? 5,000
7. what is the value of the digit 5 in the □? 50
8. what is the difference between the answers in **Exercises 6 and 7**? 4,950
9. In 5◯, 2[7]8, the difference between the values of the digits in the ◯ and the □ is 8,930. What is the digit in the ◯? 9

© 2009 Marshall Cavendish International (Singapore) Private Limited

Put On Your Thinking Cap!

Problem Solving

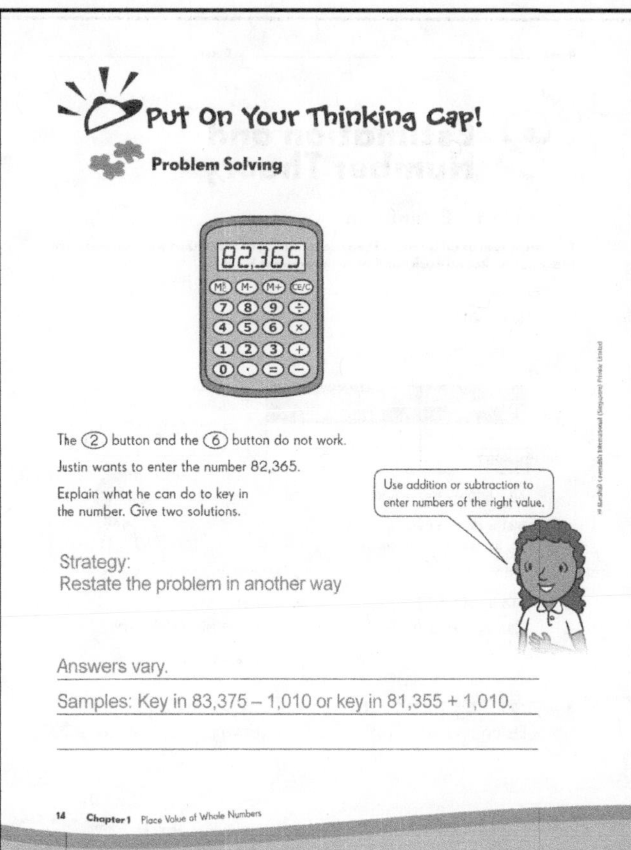

82,365
Use addition or subtraction to enter numbers of the right value.

The (2) button and the (6) button do not work.

Justin wants to enter the number 82,365.

Explain what he can do to key in the number. Give two solutions.

Strategy:
Restate the problem in another way

Answers vary.

Samples: Key in 83,375 – 1,010 or key in 81,355 + 1,010.

© Marshall Cavendish International (Singapore) Private Limited

Chapter 2

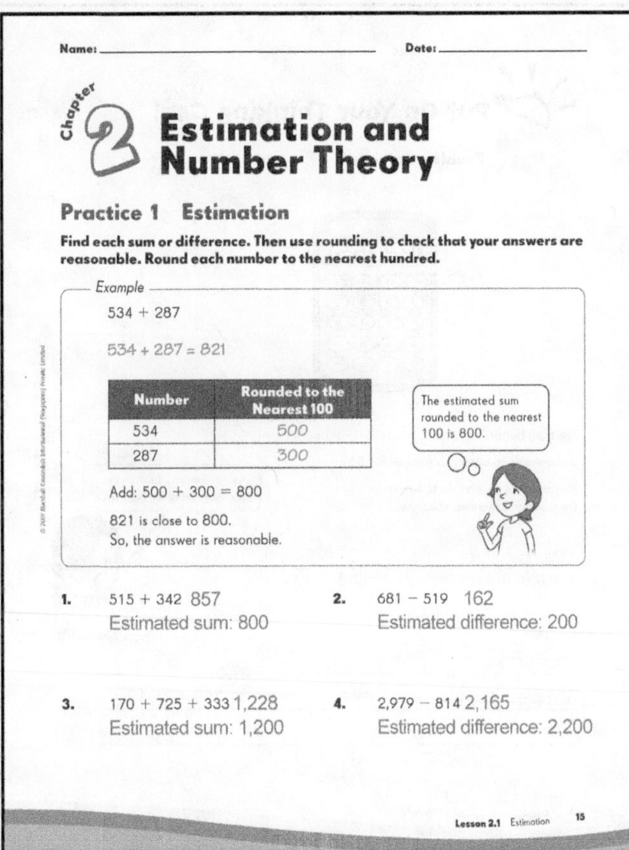

Name: ______________________ Date: ______________

Chapter 2 Estimation and Number Theory

Practice 1 Estimation

Find each sum or difference. Then use rounding to check that your answers are reasonable. Round each number to the nearest hundred.

Example

534 + 287

534 + 287 = 821

Number	Rounded to the Nearest 100
534	500
287	300

The estimated sum rounded to the nearest 100 is 800.

Add: 500 + 300 = 800

821 is close to 800.
So, the answer is reasonable.

1. 515 + 342 857
Estimated sum: 800

2. 681 − 519 162
Estimated difference: 200

3. 170 + 725 + 333 1,228
Estimated sum: 1,200

4. 2,979 − 814 2,165
Estimated difference: 2,200

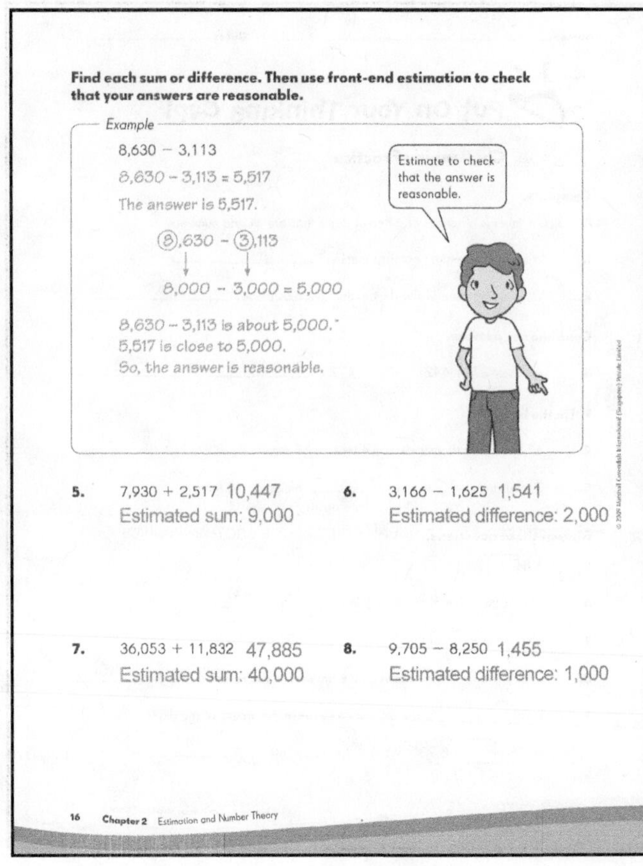

Find each sum or difference. Then use front-end estimation to check that your answers are reasonable.

Example

8,630 − 3,113

8,630 − 3,113 = 5,517

The answer is 5,517.

Estimate to check that the answer is reasonable.

(8),630 − (3),113

8,000 − 3,000 = 5,000

8,630 − 3,113 is about 5,000.
5,517 is close to 5,000.
So, the answer is reasonable.

5. 7,930 + 2,517 10,447
Estimated sum: 9,000

6. 3,166 − 1,625 1,541
Estimated difference: 2,000

7. 36,053 + 11,832 47,885
Estimated sum: 40,000

8. 9,705 − 8,250 1,455
Estimated difference: 1,000

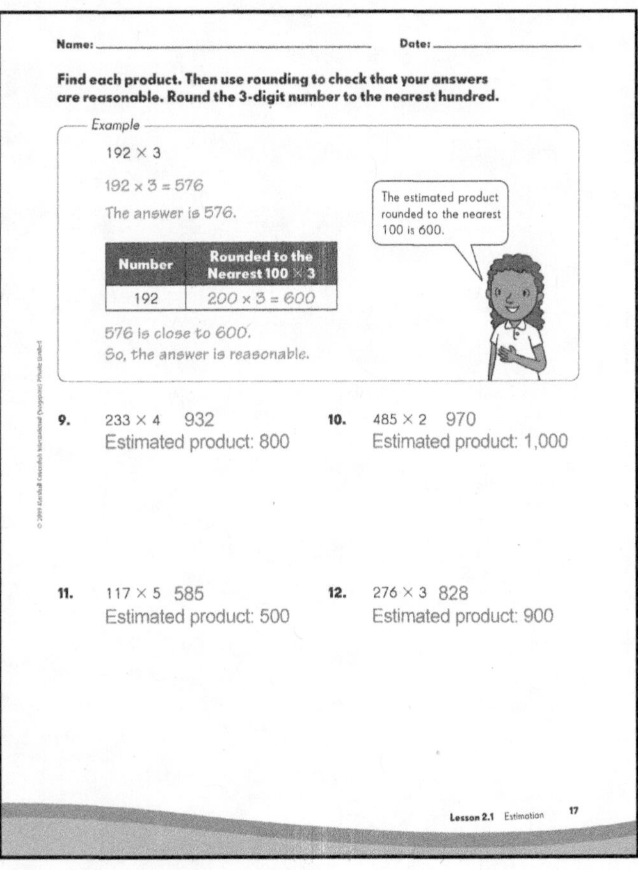

Name: ______________________ Date: ______________

Find each product. Then use rounding to check that your answers are reasonable. Round the 3-digit number to the nearest hundred.

Example

192 × 3

192 × 3 = 576

The answer is 576.

The estimated product rounded to the nearest 100 is 600.

Number	Rounded to the Nearest 100 × 3
192	200 × 3 = 600

576 is close to 600.
So, the answer is reasonable.

9. 233 × 4 932
Estimated product: 800

10. 485 × 2 970
Estimated product: 1,000

11. 117 × 5 585
Estimated product: 500

12. 276 × 3 828
Estimated product: 900

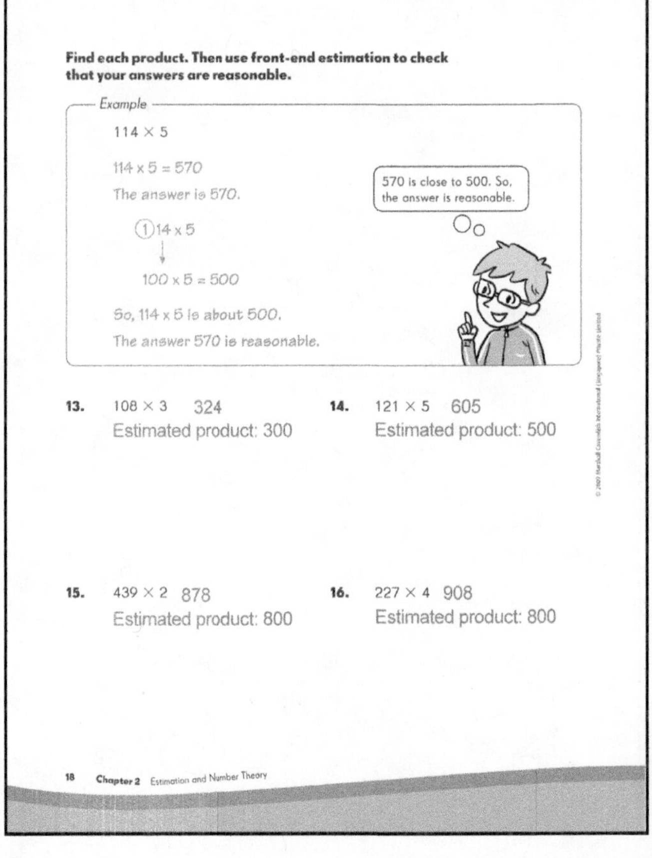

Find each product. Then use front-end estimation to check that your answers are reasonable.

Example

114 × 5

114 × 5 = 570

The answer is 570.

570 is close to 500. So, the answer is reasonable.

(1)14 × 5

100 × 5 = 500

So, 114 × 5 is about 500.
The answer 570 is reasonable.

13. 108 × 3 324
Estimated product: 300

14. 121 × 5 605
Estimated product: 500

15. 439 × 2 878
Estimated product: 800

16. 227 × 4 908
Estimated product: 800

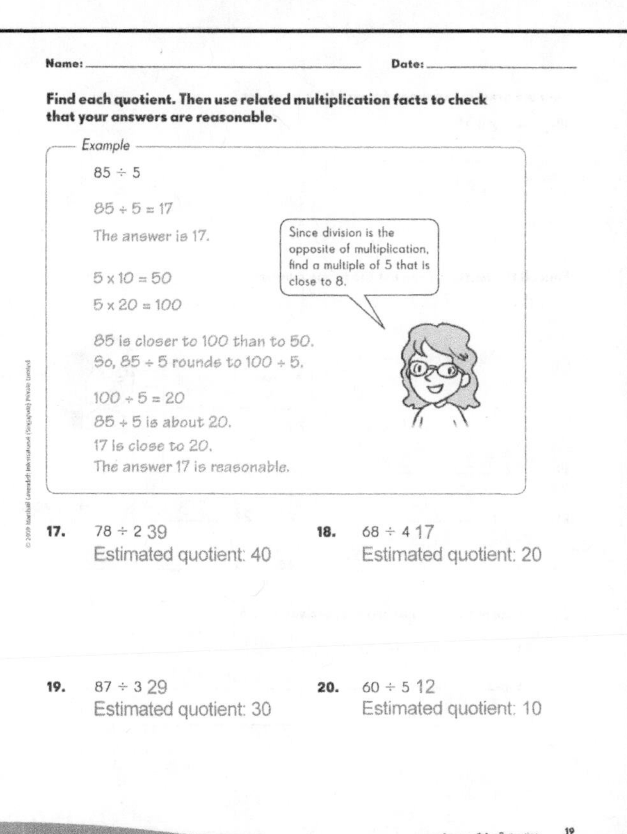

Name: ______________________ Date: ______________

Find each quotient. Then use related multiplication facts to check that your answers are reasonable.

Example

85 ÷ 5

85 ÷ 5 = 17

The answer is 17.

5 x 10 = 50

5 x 20 = 100

85 is closer to 100 than to 50.
So, 85 ÷ 5 rounds to 100 ÷ 5.

100 ÷ 5 = 20

85 ÷ 5 is about 20.

17 is close to 20.

The answer 17 is reasonable.

Since division is the opposite of multiplication, find a multiple of 5 that is close to 8.

17. 78 ÷ 2 39
Estimated quotient: 40

18. 68 ÷ 4 17
Estimated quotient: 20

19. 87 ÷ 3 29
Estimated quotient: 30

20. 60 ÷ 5 12
Estimated quotient: 10

© 2009 Marshall Cavendish International (Singapore) Private Limited

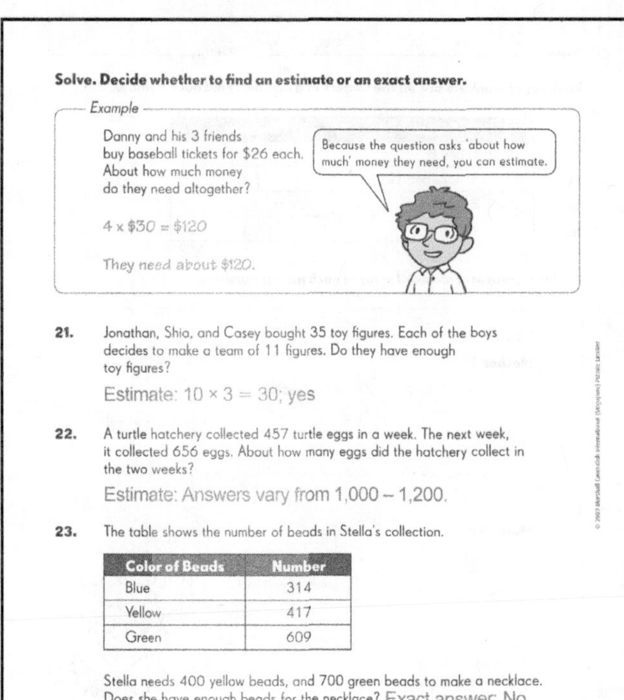

Solve. Decide whether to find an estimate or an exact answer.

Example

Danny and his 3 friends buy baseball tickets for $26 each. About how much money do they need altogether?

4 x $30 = $120

They need about $120.

Because the question asks 'about how much' money they need, you can estimate.

21. Jonathan, Shio, and Casey bought 35 toy figures. Each of the boys decides to make a team of 11 figures. Do they have enough toy figures?

Estimate: 10 × 3 = 30; yes

22. A turtle hatchery collected 457 turtle eggs in a week. The next week, it collected 656 eggs. About how many eggs did the hatchery collect in the two weeks?

Estimate: Answers vary from 1,000 – 1,200.

23. The table shows the number of beads in Stella's collection.

Color of Beads	Number
Blue	314
Yellow	417
Green	609

Stella needs 400 yellow beads, and 700 green beads to make a necklace. Does she have enough beads for the necklace? Exact answer: No

© 2009 Marshall Cavendish International (Singapore) Private Limited

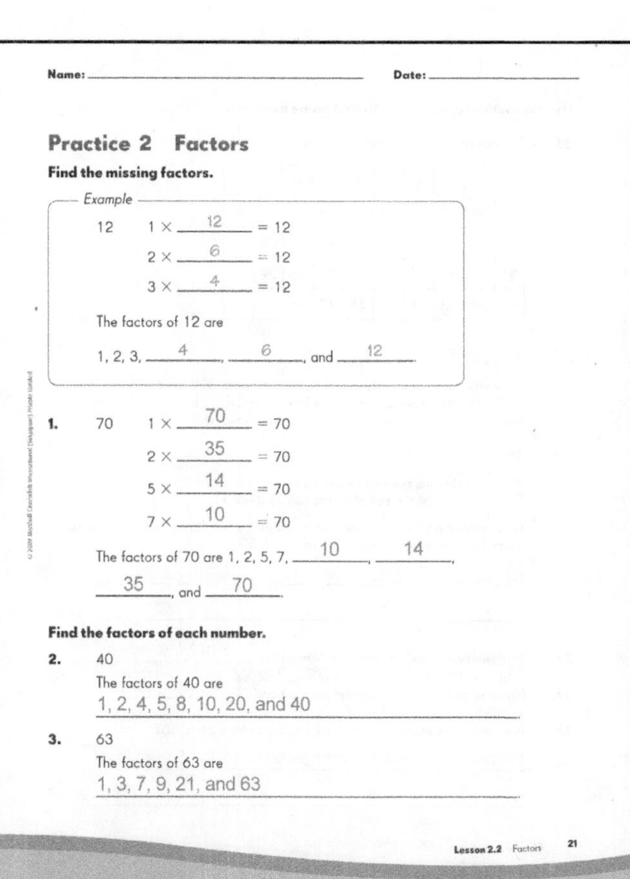

Name: ______________________ Date: ______________

Practice 2 Factors

Find the missing factors.

Example

12
1 × 12 = 12
2 × 6 = 12
3 × 4 = 12

The factors of 12 are
1, 2, 3, 4, 6, and 12.

1. 70
1 × 70 = 70
2 × 35 = 70
5 × 14 = 70
7 × 10 = 70

The factors of 70 are 1, 2, 5, 7, 10, 14, 35, and 70.

Find the factors of each number.

2. 40
The factors of 40 are
1, 2, 4, 5, 8, 10, 20, and 40

3. 63
The factors of 63 are
1, 3, 7, 9, 21, and 63

© 2009 Marshall Cavendish International (Singapore) Private Limited

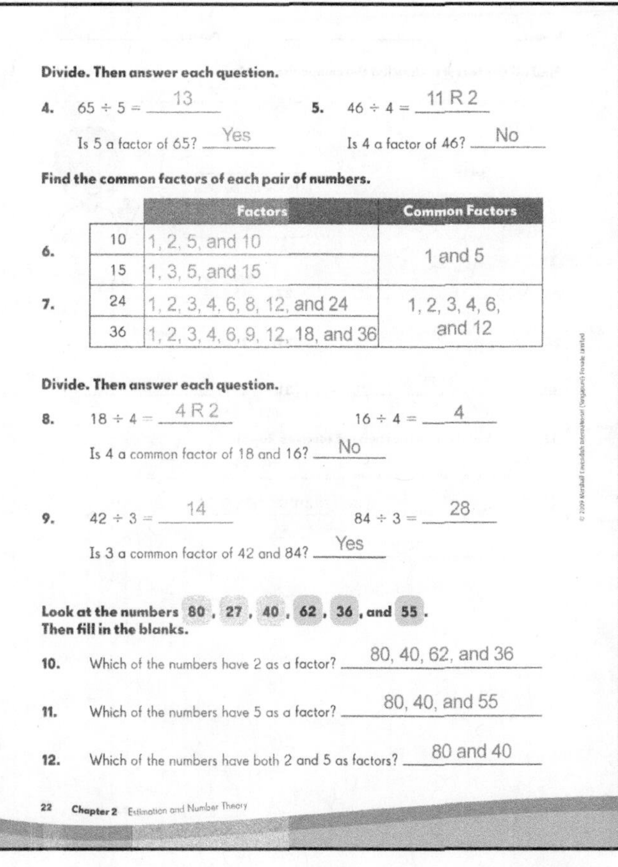

Divide. Then answer each question.

4. 65 ÷ 5 = 13
Is 5 a factor of 65? Yes

5. 46 ÷ 4 = 11 R 2
Is 4 a factor of 46? No

Find the common factors of each pair of numbers.

		Factors	Common Factors
6.	10	1, 2, 5, and 10	1 and 5
	15	1, 3, 5, and 15	
7.	24	1, 2, 3, 4, 6, 8, 12, and 24	1, 2, 3, 4, 6, and 12
	36	1, 2, 3, 4, 6, 9, 12, 18, and 36	

Divide. Then answer each question.

8. 18 ÷ 4 = 4 R 2 16 ÷ 4 = 4
Is 4 a common factor of 18 and 16? No

9. 42 ÷ 3 = 14 84 ÷ 3 = 28
Is 3 a common factor of 42 and 84? Yes

Look at the numbers 80, 27, 40, 62, 36, and 55. Then fill in the blanks.

10. Which of the numbers have 2 as a factor? 80, 40, 62, and 36

11. Which of the numbers have 5 as a factor? 80, 40, and 55

12. Which of the numbers have both 2 and 5 as factors? 80 and 40

© 2009 Marshall Cavendish International (Singapore) Private Limited

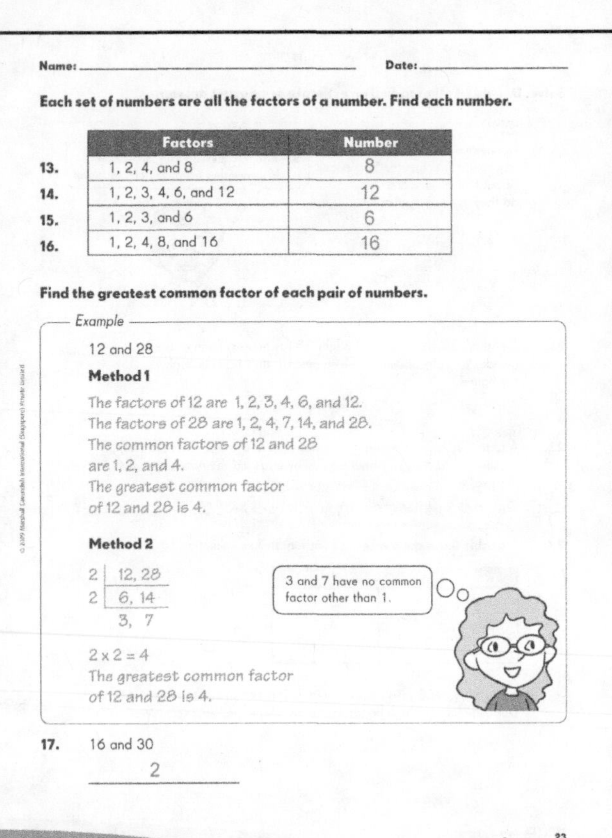
Name: ______________________ Date: ______________

Each set of numbers are all the factors of a number. Find each number.

	Factors	Number
13.	1, 2, 4, and 8	8
14.	1, 2, 3, 4, 6, and 12	12
15.	1, 2, 3, and 6	6
16.	1, 2, 4, 8, and 16	16

Find the greatest common factor of each pair of numbers.

Example

12 and 28

Method 1

The factors of 12 are 1, 2, 3, 4, 6, and 12.
The factors of 28 are 1, 2, 4, 7, 14, and 28.
The common factors of 12 and 28 are 1, 2, and 4.
The greatest common factor of 12 and 28 is 4.

Method 2

2 | 12, 28
2 | 6, 14
3, 7

$2 \times 2 = 4$
The greatest common factor of 12 and 28 is 4.

3 and 7 have no common factor other than 1.

17. 16 and 30

2

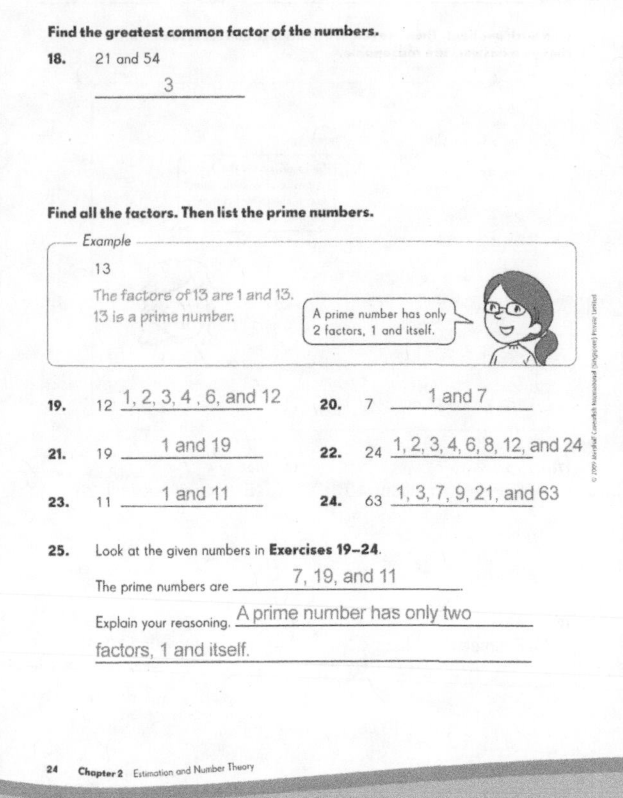
Find the greatest common factor of the numbers.

18. 21 and 54

3

Find all the factors. Then list the prime numbers.

Example

13

The factors of 13 are 1 and 13.
13 is a prime number.

A prime number has only 2 factors, 1 and itself.

19. 12 1, 2, 3, 4, 6, and 12

20. 7 1 and 7

21. 19 1 and 19

22. 24 1, 2, 3, 4, 6, 8, 12, and 24

23. 11 1 and 11

24. 63 1, 3, 7, 9, 21, and 63

25. Look at the given numbers in **Exercises 19–24**.

The prime numbers are 7, 19, and 11

Explain your reasoning. A prime number has only two factors, 1 and itself.

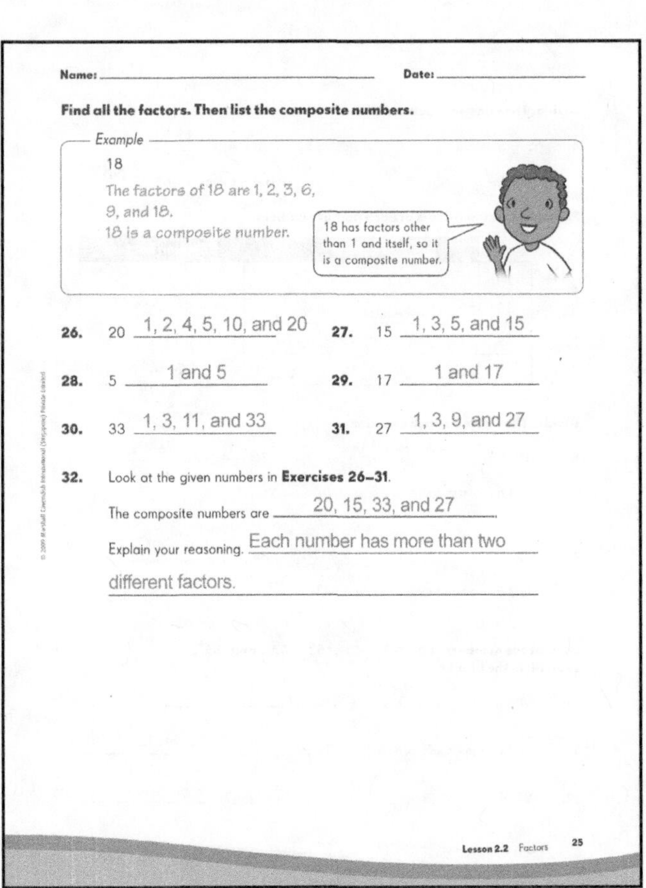
Name: ______________________ Date: ______________

Find all the factors. Then list the composite numbers.

Example

18

The factors of 18 are 1, 2, 3, 6, 9, and 18.
18 is a composite number.

18 has factors other than 1 and itself, so it is a composite number.

26. 20 1, 2, 4, 5, 10, and 20

27. 15 1, 3, 5, and 15

28. 5 1 and 5

29. 17 1 and 17

30. 33 1, 3, 11, and 33

31. 27 1, 3, 9, and 27

32. Look at the given numbers in **Exercises 26–31**.

The composite numbers are 20, 15, 33, and 27

Explain your reasoning. Each number has more than two different factors.

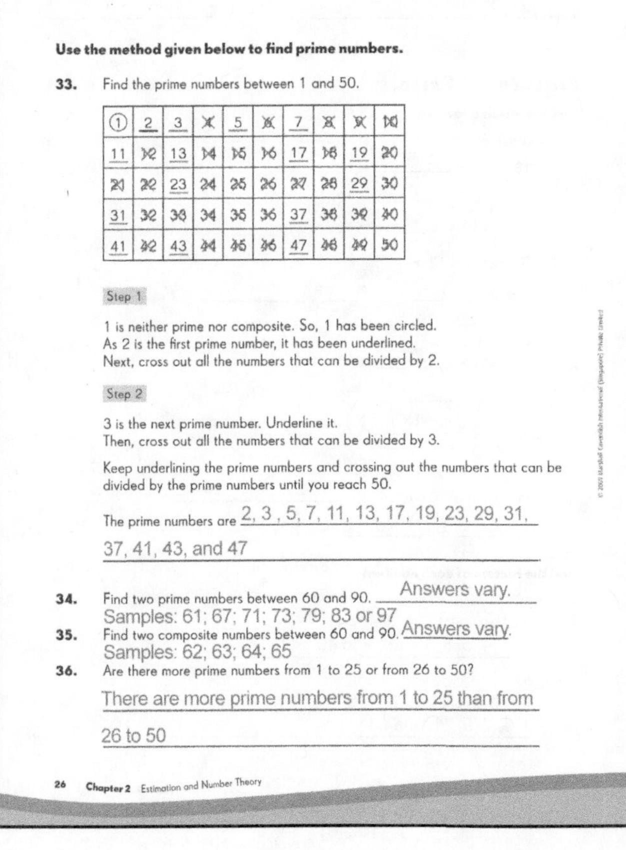
Use the method given below to find prime numbers.

33. Find the prime numbers between 1 and 50.

①	2	3	~~4~~	5	~~6~~	7	~~8~~	~~9~~	~~10~~
11	~~12~~	13	~~14~~	~~15~~	~~16~~	17	~~18~~	19	~~20~~
~~21~~	~~22~~	23	~~24~~	~~25~~	~~26~~	~~27~~	~~28~~	29	~~30~~
31	~~32~~	~~33~~	~~34~~	~~35~~	~~36~~	37	~~38~~	~~39~~	~~40~~
41	~~42~~	43	~~44~~	~~45~~	~~46~~	47	~~48~~	~~49~~	~~50~~

Step 1

1 is neither prime nor composite. So, 1 has been circled.
As 2 is the first prime number, it has been underlined.
Next, cross out all the numbers that can be divided by 2.

Step 2

3 is the next prime number. Underline it.
Then, cross out all the numbers that can be divided by 3.

Keep underlining the prime numbers and crossing out the numbers that can be divided by the prime numbers until you reach 50.

The prime numbers are 2, 3, 5, 7, 11, 13, 17, 19, 23, 29, 31, 37, 41, 43, and 47

34. Find two prime numbers between 60 and 90. Answers vary.
Samples: 61; 67; 71; 73; 79; 83 or 97

35. Find two composite numbers between 60 and 90. Answers vary.
Samples: 62; 63; 64; 65

36. Are there more prime numbers from 1 to 25 or from 26 to 50?

There are more prime numbers from 1 to 25 than from 26 to 50

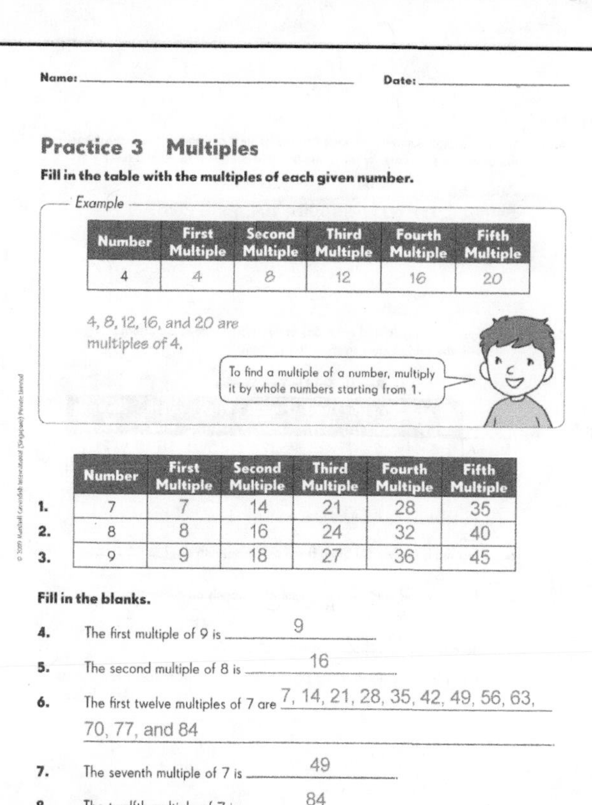

Name: __________ Date: __________

Practice 3 Multiples

Fill in the table with the multiples of each given number.

Example

Number	First Multiple	Second Multiple	Third Multiple	Fourth Multiple	Fifth Multiple
4	4	8	12	16	20

4, 8, 12, 16, and 20 are multiples of 4.

To find a multiple of a number, multiply it by whole numbers starting from 1.

	Number	First Multiple	Second Multiple	Third Multiple	Fourth Multiple	Fifth Multiple
1.	7	7	14	21	28	35
2.	8	8	16	24	32	40
3.	9	9	18	27	36	45

Fill in the blanks.

4. The first multiple of 9 is 9

5. The second multiple of 8 is 16

6. The first twelve multiples of 7 are 7, 14, 21, 28, 35, 42, 49, 56, 63, 70, 77, and 84

7. The seventh multiple of 7 is 49

8. The twelfth multiple of 7 is 84

© 2009 [illegible]

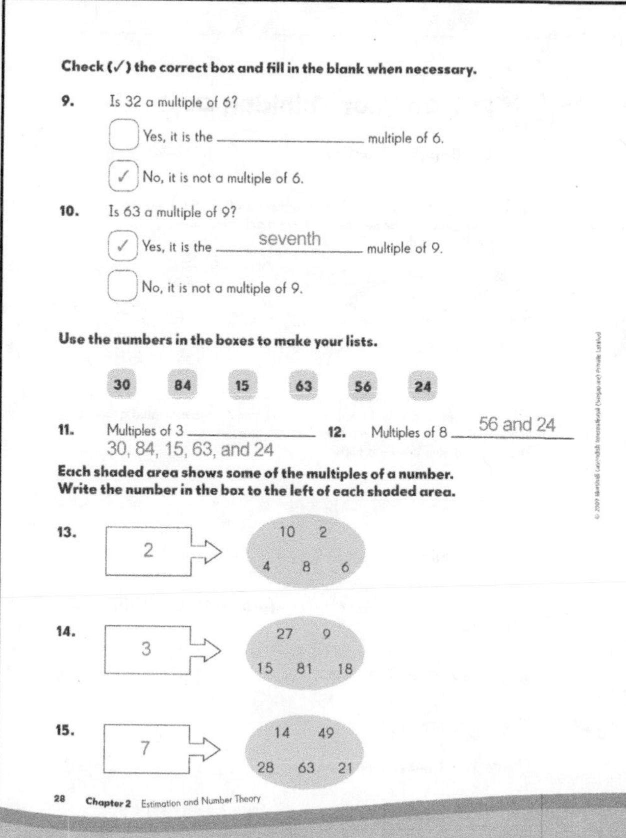

Check (✓) the correct box and fill in the blank when necessary.

9. Is 32 a multiple of 6?

☐ Yes, it is the ______ multiple of 6.

☑ No, it is not a multiple of 6.

10. Is 63 a multiple of 9?

☑ Yes, it is the seventh multiple of 9.

☐ No, it is not a multiple of 9.

Use the numbers in the boxes to make your lists.

30 84 15 63 56 24

11. Multiples of 3 30, 84, 15, 63, and 24

12. Multiples of 8 56 and 24

Each shaded area shows some of the multiples of a number. Write the number in the box to the left of each shaded area.

13. 2 → 10 2 4 8 6

14. 3 → 27 9 15 81 18

15. 7 → 14 49 28 63 21

© 2009 [illegible]

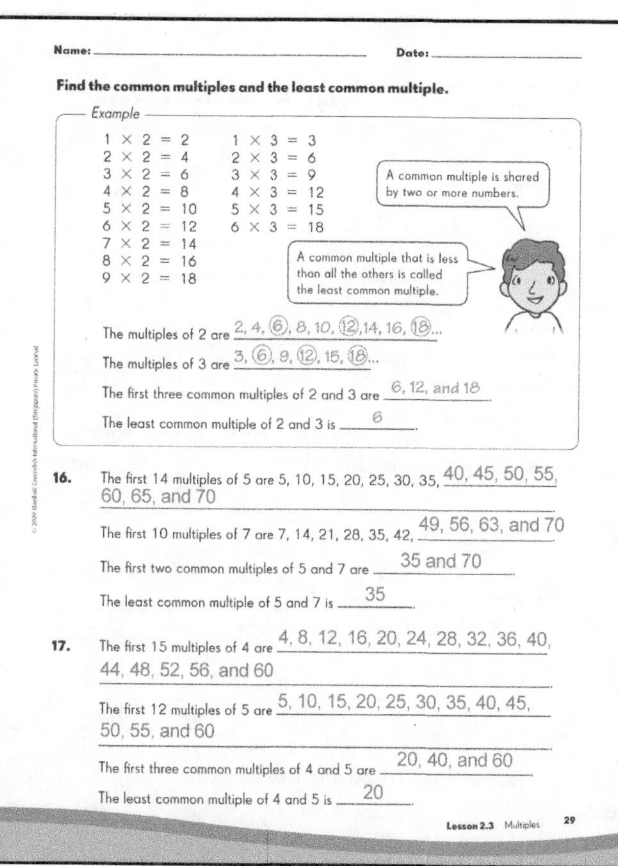

Name: __________ Date: __________

Find the common multiples and the least common multiple.

Example

1 × 2 = 2
2 × 2 = 4
3 × 2 = 6
4 × 2 = 8
5 × 2 = 10
6 × 2 = 12
7 × 2 = 14
8 × 2 = 16
9 × 2 = 18

1 × 3 = 3
2 × 3 = 6
3 × 3 = 9
4 × 3 = 12
5 × 3 = 15
6 × 3 = 18

A common multiple is shared by two or more numbers.
A common multiple that is less than all the others is called the least common multiple.

The multiples of 2 are 2, 4, (6), 8, 10, (12), 14, 16, (18)...

The multiples of 3 are 3, (6), 9, (12), 15, (18)...

The first three common multiples of 2 and 3 are 6, 12, and 18

The least common multiple of 2 and 3 is 6

16. The first 14 multiples of 5 are 5, 10, 15, 20, 25, 30, 35, 40, 45, 50, 55, 60, 65, and 70

The first 10 multiples of 7 are 7, 14, 21, 28, 35, 42, 49, 56, 63, and 70

The first two common multiples of 5 and 7 are 35 and 70

The least common multiple of 5 and 7 is 35

17. The first 15 multiples of 4 are 4, 8, 12, 16, 20, 24, 28, 32, 36, 40, 44, 48, 52, 56, and 60

The first 12 multiples of 5 are 5, 10, 15, 20, 25, 30, 35, 40, 45, 50, 55, and 60

The first three common multiples of 4 and 5 are 20, 40, and 60

The least common multiple of 4 and 5 is 20

© 2009 [illegible]

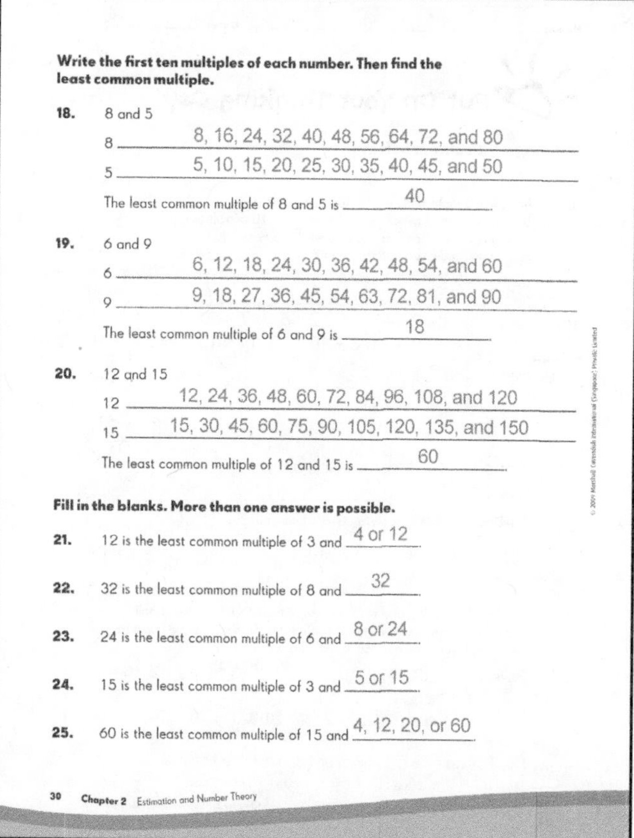

Write the first ten multiples of each number. Then find the least common multiple.

18. 8 and 5

8 8, 16, 24, 32, 40, 48, 56, 64, 72, and 80

5 5, 10, 15, 20, 25, 30, 35, 40, 45, and 50

The least common multiple of 8 and 5 is 40

19. 6 and 9

6 6, 12, 18, 24, 30, 36, 42, 48, 54, and 60

9 9, 18, 27, 36, 45, 54, 63, 72, 81, and 90

The least common multiple of 6 and 9 is 18

20. 12 and 15

12 12, 24, 36, 48, 60, 72, 84, 96, 108, and 120

15 15, 30, 45, 60, 75, 90, 105, 120, 135, and 150

The least common multiple of 12 and 15 is 60

Fill in the blanks. More than one answer is possible.

21. 12 is the least common multiple of 3 and 4 or 12

22. 32 is the least common multiple of 8 and 32

23. 24 is the least common multiple of 6 and 8 or 24

24. 15 is the least common multiple of 3 and 5 or 15

25. 60 is the least common multiple of 15 and 4, 12, 20, or 60

© 2009 [illegible]

Chapter 2

Name: ______________________ Date: ______________

Put On Your Thinking Cap!

Challenging Practice

1. The estimated difference between two numbers is 60. Find two numbers that when rounded to the nearest ten, have a difference of 60. Use the numbers in the box.

135	128	61	141	74	56

140 (130) 60 140 (70) 60

The two numbers are 128 and 74.

2. When a 3-digit number is divided by a 1-digit number, the estimated quotient is 50. Think of two possible numbers that can give this quotient. Then check if your answer is correct.

Answers vary.
Sample: 399 ÷ 8 rounds to 400 ÷ 8 = 50

Thinking skill: Identifying relationships

3. A given number is a multiple of 4. It is between 6 and 15. It is a factor of 16. What is the number?

Numbers between 6 and 15: 7, (8), 9, 10, 11, 12, 13, 14
Multiples of 4: 4, (8), 12 ...
Factors of 16: 1, 2, 4, (8), 16
The number is 8.

Strategy: Make a systematic list

© 2009 Marshall Cavendish International (Singapore) Private Limited

4. When a 3-digit number is rounded to the nearest ten and to the nearest hundred, the answer is the same. What is one possible number that fits this rule?

Answers vary.
Samples: The numbers 100 – 104, 195 – 204, 295 – 304, ... 995 – 999.

5. The number of bagels sold each day in two stores follows a pattern. Complete the table below to show this pattern.

Bagels Sold in Two Stores

	First Day	Second Day	Third Day	Fourth Day	Fifth Day	Sixth Day	Seventh Day
Store A	3	6	9	12	15	18	21
Store B	4	8	12	16	20	24	28

Fill in the blanks using the data from the table above.

a. How many bagels did Store B sell on the seventh day? 28

b. The two stores sold the same number of bagels on different days. Which were the days?

Store A: fourth day Store B: third day

Thinking Skill: Identifying patterns and relationships

© 2009 Marshall Cavendish International (Singapore) Private Limited

Name: ______________________ Date: ______________

Put On Your Thinking Cap!

Problem Solving

1. Mr. Chan bought some pencils for a group of students. If he gives them 2 pencils each, he will have 10 pencils left. If he gives them 3 pencils each, he will have none left. How many students are in the group?

No. of Pupils	2	4	7	10
(Multiples of 2) + 10	2 × 2 = 4 4 + 10 = 14	4 × 2 = 8 8 + 10 = 18	7 × 2 = 14 14 + 10 = 24	10 × 2 = 20 20 + 10 = 30
Multiples of 3	2 × 3 = 6	4 × 3 = 12	7 × 3 = 21	10 × 3 = 30

There are 10 students in the group.

Strategy: Make a systematic list

2. On the opening day at a toy store, every third customer gets a ball and every fourth customer gets a stuffed animal. Sixty people come to the store. How many get both a ball and a stuffed animal?

Balls: 3, 6, 9, (12), 15, 18, 21, (24), 27, 30, 33, (36), 39, 42, 45, (48), 51, 54, 57, (60)
Stuffed animals: 4, 8, (12), 16, 20, (24), 28, 32, (36), 40, 44, (48), 52, 56, (60)
There are 5 common multiples.
So, 5 customers get both a ball and a stuffed animal.

© 2009 Marshall Cavendish International (Singapore) Private Limited

3. A square table can seat 4 people. How many square tables are needed to seat 26 people if the tables are put together?

Hint:

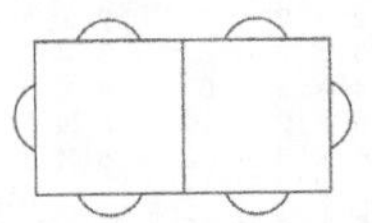

1 table can seat 4 people. 2 tables can seat 6 people.

Method 1

Remove 2 seats at the ends.

26 – 2 = 24.
24 ÷ 2 = 12 tables, as the people sit opposite each other.

Method 2

No. of Tables	No. of People
1	4
2	6
3	8
4	10
5	12
6	14
7	16
8	18
9	20
10	22
11	24
12	26

12 tables are needed to seat 26 people.

Strategies: Use a diagram, Make a systematic list

© 2009 Marshall Cavendish International (Singapore) Private Limited

Name: ______________________ Date: ______________

Cumulative Review
for Chapters 1 and 2

Concepts and Skills

Write each number in standard form. *(Lesson 1.1)*

1. forty-eight thousand, six 48,006
2. one hundred thousand 100,000
3. sixty-nine thousand, two hundred eleven 69,211

© 2009 Marshall Cavendish International (Singapore) Private Limited

Write each number in word form. *(Lesson 1.1)*

4. 53,900 fifty-three thousand, nine hundred
5. 16,658 sixteen thousand, six hundred fifty-eight
6. 20,306 twenty thousand, three hundred six

Fill in the blank to write the number in expanded form. *(Lesson 1.1)*

7. 13,901 = 10,000 + 3,000 + 900 + 1

Fill in the blanks. *(Lesson 1.2)*

8. 100 more than 26,542 is 26,642.
9. 78,923 is 100 less than 79,023.

Circle the number that is greater. *(Lesson 1.2)*

10. (12,630) or 6,238
11. 45,200 or (45,496)
12. 62,529 or (69,522)
13. (90,236) or 87,415

Circle the number that is less. *(Lesson 1.2)*

14. (6,563) or 48,200
15. (67,186) or 67,254
16. 74,258 or (71,852)
17. 96,125 or (69,521)

Write the set of numbers in order from least to greatest. *(Lesson 1.2)*

18. 8,654 56,207 68,543 56,719

8,654 56,207 56,719 68,543

© 2009 Marshall Cavendish International (Singapore) Private Limited

Continue or complete each number pattern. *(Lesson 1.2)*

19. 11,500 11,000 10,500 10,000 9,500
20. 63,800 64,100 64,400 64,700 65,000
21. 27,852 29,853 31,854 33,855 35,856

Find each sum or difference. Then use rounding to check that your answers are reasonable. *(Lesson 2.1)*

22. 522 − 389 133
Estimated difference: 100

23. 456 + 790 1,246
Estimated sum: 1,300

Name: ______________________ Date: ______________

Find each sum or difference. Then use front-end estimation to check that your answers are reasonable. *(Lesson 2.1)*

24. 432 + 759 1,191
Estimated sum: 1,100

25. 816 − 532 284
Estimated difference: 300

Find each product. Then use rounding to check that your answers are reasonable. *(Lesson 2.1)*

26. 383 × 2 766
Estimated product: 800

27. 241 × 4 964
Estimated product: 800

© 2009 Marshall Cavendish International (Singapore) Private Limited

Find each product. Then use front-end estimation to check that your answers are reasonable. *(Lesson 2.1)*

28. 308 × 3 924
Estimated product: 900

29. 126 × 5 630
Estimated product: 500

Find each quotient. Then use related multiplication facts to check that your answers are reasonable. *(Lesson 2.1)*

30. 92 ÷ 4 23
Estimated quotient: 20

31. 78 ÷ 3 29
Estimated quotient: 30

Find the factors of each number. *(Lesson 2.2)*

32. 36 1, 2, 3, 4, 6, 9, 12, 18, and 36
33. 40 1, 2, 4, 5, 8, 10, 20, and 40
34. 96 1, 2, 3, 4, 6, 8, 12, 16, 24, 32, 48, and 96

© 2009 Marshall Cavendish International (Singapore) Private Limited

Find the common factors of each pair of numbers. *(Lesson 2.2)*

35. 36 and 40
1, 2, and 4

36. 40 and 96
1, 2, 4, and 8

Find the greatest common factor of each pair of numbers. *(Lesson 2.2)*

37. 30 and 16
2

38. 48 and 18
6

Name: ________ Date: ________

Find the prime and composite numbers. *(Lesson 2.2)*

47 | 31 | 92 | 63 | 57 | 135

39. The prime numbers are 47 and 31

40. The composite numbers are 92, 63, 57, and 135

List the first eight multiples of each number. *(Lesson 2.3)*

41. 4 4, 8, 12, 16, 20, 24, 28, and 32

42. 6 6, 12, 18, 24, 30, 36, 42, and 48

43. 9 9, 18, 27, 36, 45, 54, 63, and 72

Find the first two common multiples of each pair of numbers. *(Lesson 2.3)*

44. 4 and 6
12 and 24

45. 6 and 9
18 and 36

Find the least common multiple of each pair of numbers. *(Lesson 2.3)*

46. 8 and 12
24

47. 27 and 36
108

Problem Solving

Solve. Show your work.

48. Make a 5-digit number using these clues.
The digit in the thousands place is 5.
The value of the digit in the ten thousands place is 20,000.
The digit in the tens place is 8.
One of the digits is a 0 and it is next to the digit 8.
The digit in the ones place is 2 less than the digit in the tens place.

The number is 2 5, 0 8 6.

49. 3,219 milliliters of water and 185 milliliters of orange syrup are mixed to make orange juice. About how much orange juice will there be?
Answers vary.
Accept 3,400mL; 3,100mL.

50. An empty parking lot has 300 spaces.
215 cars and 89 SUVs drive into the parking lot.
How many vehicles do not have parking spaces?
4 vehicles

51. Find a 2-digit number less than 50 using these clues.
It can be divided by 4 exactly.
When 4 is added to it, it can be divided by 5 exactly.

The number is 36.

52. Finch divides 12 peaches and 18 nectarines into the same number of equal groups. How many possible groups of each fruit can he make? How many are in each group?
Accept:
2 groups of 6 peaches and 2 groups of 9 nectarine;
3 groups of 4 peaches and 3 groups of 6 nectarine;
6 groups of 2 peaches and 6 groups of 3 nectarine

Name: ______________________ Date: ______________

Chapter 3 Whole Number Multiplication and Division

Practice 1 Multiplying by a 1-Digit Number

Multiply 962 by 6 and find the missing numbers.

Example

Step 1 2 ones × 6 = 12 ones
= 1 ten 2 ones

$\begin{array}{r} 2 \\ \times\ 6 \\ \hline 12 \end{array}$

1. Step 2 6 tens × 6 = 36 tens
= 3 hundreds 6 tens

$\begin{array}{r} 60 \\ \times\ 6 \\ \hline 360 \end{array}$

2. Step 3 9 hundreds × 6 = 54 hundreds
= 5 thousands 4 hundreds

$\begin{array}{r} 900 \\ \times\ 6 \\ \hline 5,400 \end{array}$

3. $\begin{array}{r} 962 \\ \times\ 6 \\ \hline 12 \\ 360 \\ 5,400 \\ \hline 5,772 \end{array}$

12 ← 2 ones × 6
360 ← 6 tens × 6
5,400 ← 9 hundreds × 6

© 2009 Marshall Cavendish International (Singapore) Private Limited

Multiply 9,086 by 7 and find the missing numbers.

4. Step 1 6 ones × 7 = 42 ones
= 4 tens 2 ones

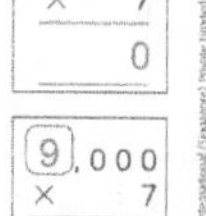

$\begin{array}{r} 6 \\ \times\ 7 \\ \hline 42 \end{array}$

5. Step 2 8 tens × 7 = 56 tens
= 5 hundreds 6 tens

$\begin{array}{r} 80 \\ \times\ 7 \\ \hline 560 \end{array}$

6. Step 3 0 hundreds × 7 = 0 hundreds

$\begin{array}{r} 000 \\ \times\ 7 \\ \hline 0 \end{array}$

7. Step 4 9 thousands × 7 = 63 thousands
= 6 ten thousands 3 thousands

$\begin{array}{r} 9,000 \\ \times\ 7 \\ \hline 63,000 \end{array}$

8. $\begin{array}{r} 9,086 \\ \times\ 7 \\ \hline 42 \\ 560 \\ 000 \\ 63,000 \\ \hline 63,602 \end{array}$

42 ← 6 ones × 7
560 ← 8 tens × 7
000 ← 0 hundreds × 7
63,000 ← 9 thousands × 7

© 2009 Marshall Cavendish International (Singapore) Private Limited

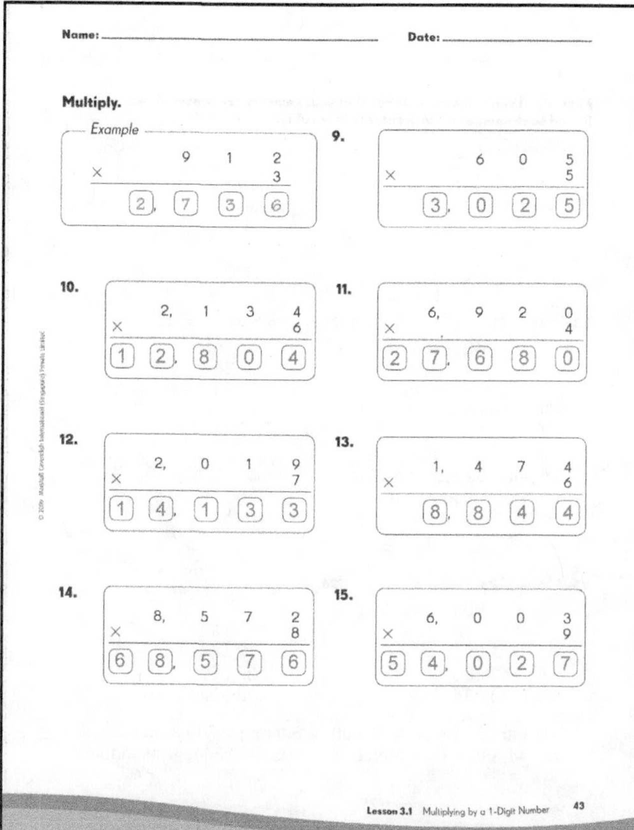

Name: ______________________ Date: ______________

Multiply.

Example $\begin{array}{r} 912 \\ \times\ 3 \\ \hline 2,736 \end{array}$

9. $\begin{array}{r} 605 \\ \times\ 5 \\ \hline 3,025 \end{array}$

10. $\begin{array}{r} 2,134 \\ \times\ 6 \\ \hline 12,804 \end{array}$

11. $\begin{array}{r} 6,920 \\ \times\ 4 \\ \hline 27,680 \end{array}$

12. $\begin{array}{r} 2,019 \\ \times\ 7 \\ \hline 14,133 \end{array}$

13. $\begin{array}{r} 1,474 \\ \times\ 6 \\ \hline 8,844 \end{array}$

14. $\begin{array}{r} 8,572 \\ \times\ 8 \\ \hline 68,576 \end{array}$

15. $\begin{array}{r} 6,003 \\ \times\ 9 \\ \hline 54,027 \end{array}$

© 2009 Marshall Cavendish International (Singapore) Private Limited

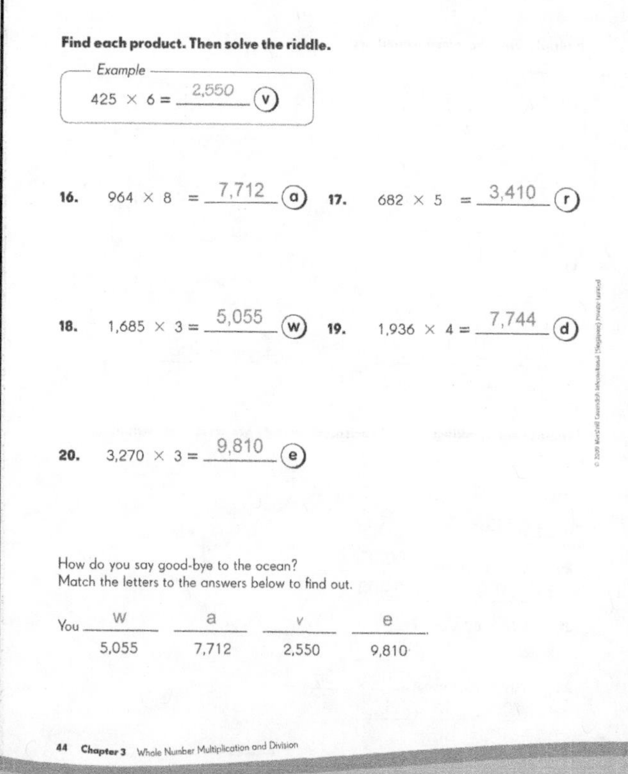

Find each product. Then solve the riddle.

Example 425 × 6 = 2,550 (v)

16. 964 × 8 = 7,712 (a)
17. 682 × 5 = 3,410 (r)
18. 1,685 × 3 = 5,055 (w)
19. 1,936 × 4 = 7,744 (d)
20. 3,270 × 3 = 9,810 (e)

How do you say good-bye to the ocean?
Match the letters to the answers below to find out.

You w a v e
5,055 7,712 2,550 9,810

© 2009 Marshall Cavendish International (Singapore) Private Limited

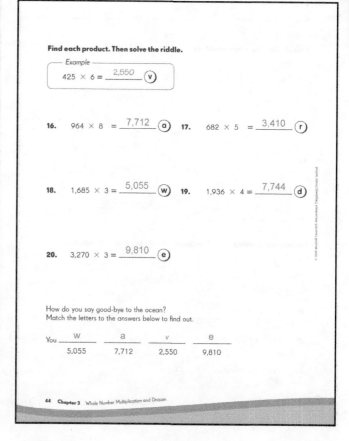

Chapter 3

Name: ______________________ Date: ______________________

Practice 2 Multiplying by a 2-Digit Number

Write the missing numbers. Then solve the riddle.

Example

15 × 10 = 150 (r)   63 × 10 = 630 (e)

1. 5 × 60 = 5 × 6 tens
= 30 tens
= 300 (n)

2. 16 × 20 = 16 × 2 tens
= 32 tens
= 320 (i)

3. 33 × 40 = 33 × 4 tens
= 132 tens
= 1,320 (l)

4. 29 × 30 = 29 × 3 tens
= 87 tens
= 870 (u)

5. 41 × 60 = 41 × 6 × 10
= 246 × 10
= 2,460 (B)

6. 96 × 40 = 96 × 10 × 4
= 960 × 4
= 3,840 (j)

7. 618 × 50
= 618 × 5 × 10
= 3,090 × 10
= 30,900 (o)

8. 752 × 70
= 752 × 10 × 7
= 7,520 × 7
= 52,640 (d)

What is the French word that has the same meaning as 'hello'?
Match the letters to the products below to find out.

B	o	n	j	o	u	r
2,460	30,900	300	3,840	30,900	870	150

© 2009 Marshall Cavendish International (Singapore) Private Limited

Find each product.

9. 42 × 10 = 420

10. 786 × 10 = 7,860

11. 16 × 5 = 80
16 × 50 = 800

12. 137 × 6 = 822
137 × 60 = 8,220

13. 23 × 4 = 92
23 × 40 = 920

14. 405 × 9 = 3,645
405 × 90 = 36,450

Find each product.

15. 70 × 800
7 × 8 = 56
7 × 80 = 560
7 × 800 = 5,600
So, 70 × 800 = 56,000

16. 300 × 90
3 × 9 = 27
3 × 90 = 270
30 × 90 = 2,700
So, 300 × 90 = 27,000.

© 2009 Marshall Cavendish International (Singapore) Private Limited

Name: ______________________ Date: ______________________

Multiply. Find the missing numbers.

Example

		6	7
×		3	5
	3	3	5
2,	0	1	0
2,	3	4	5

17.

		6	1
×		8	6
	3	6	6
4,	8	8	0
5,	2	4	6

18.

		8	7	2
	×		6	2
	1,	7	4	4
5	2,	3	2	0
5	4,	0	6	4

19.

		7	0	9
	×		4	9
	6,	3	8	1
2	8,	3	6	0
3	4,	7	4	1

Estimate each product. Round each number to its greatest place value.

Example

67 × 35 is about 70 × 40
70 × 40 = 2,800

20. 61 × 86 is about 60 × 90
60 × 90 = 5,400

21. 872 × 62 is about 900 × 60
900 × 60 = 54,000

22. 709 × 49 is about 700 × 50
700 × 50 = 35,000

© 2009 Marshall Cavendish International (Singapore) Private Limited

Multiply. Then estimate to check that your answers are reasonable. Round each number to its greatest place value.

Example

14 × 18 = 252

```
    14
  × 18
   112
   140
   252
```

14 is about 10.
18 is about 20.
Estimate:
10 × 20 = 200

252 is close to 200. So, the answer is reasonable.

23. 48 × 21 = 1,008

```
     48
  ×  21
     48
    960
  1,008
```

Estimate: 50 × 20 = 1,000
Yes, 1,008 is reasonable.

24. 196 × 34 = 6,664

```
    196
  ×  34
    784
  5,880
  6,664
```

Estimate: 200 × 30 = 6,000
Yes, 6,664 is reasonable.

25. 608 × 73 = 44,384

```
     608
  ×   73
   1,824
  42,560
  44,384
```

Estimate: 600 × 70 = 42,000
Yes, 44,384 is reasonable.

26. 721 × 54 = 38,934

```
     721
  ×   54
   2,884
  36,050
  38,934
```

Estimate: 700 × 50 = 35,000
Yes, 38,934 is reasonable.

© 2009 Marshall Cavendish International (Singapore) Private Limited

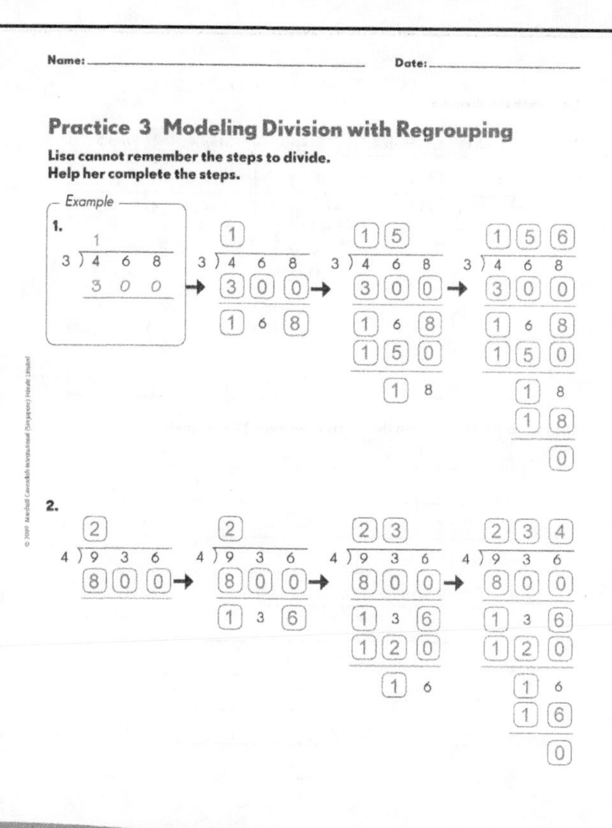

Name: ______ Date: ______

Practice 3 Modeling Division with Regrouping

Lisa cannot remember the steps to divide.
Help her complete the steps.

Example

1.

$3\overline{)468}$: 1; 3 0 0 → 1; 3 0 0; 1 6 8 → 1 5; 3 0 0; 1 6 8; 1 5 0; 1 8 → 1 5 6; 3 0 0; 1 6 8; 1 5 0; 1 8; 1 8; 0

2.

$4\overline{)936}$: 2; 8 0 0 → 2; 8 0 0; 1 3 6 → 2 3; 8 0 0; 1 3 6; 1 2 0; 1 6 → 2 3 4; 8 0 0; 1 3 6; 1 2 0; 1 6; 1 6; 0

Lesson 3.3 Modeling Division with Regrouping 49

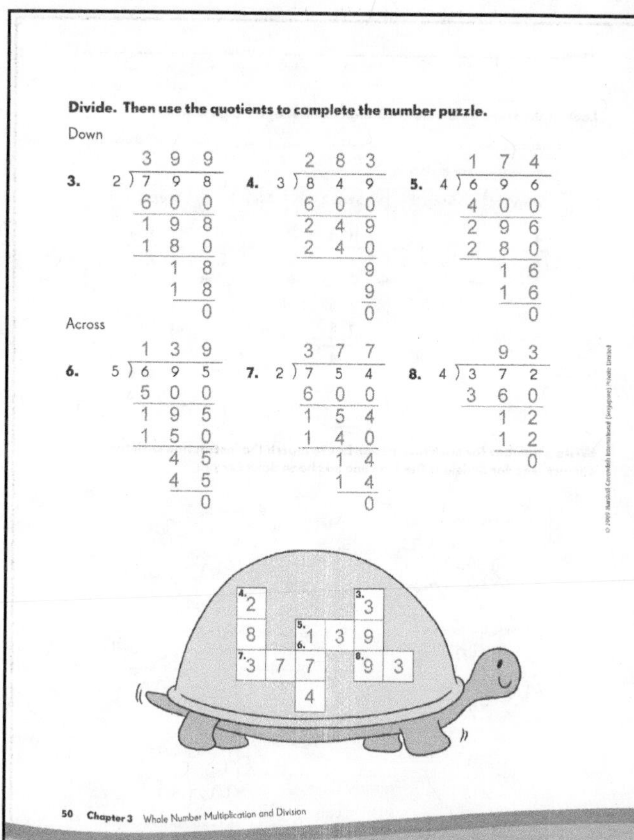

Divide. Then use the quotients to complete the number puzzle.

Down

3. $2\overline{)798}$ = 399: 6 0 0; 1 9 8; 1 8 0; 1 8; 1 8; 0

4. $3\overline{)849}$ = 283: 6 0 0; 2 4 9; 2 4 0; 9; 9; 0

5. $4\overline{)696}$ = 174: 4 0 0; 2 9 6; 2 8 0; 1 6; 1 6; 0

Across

6. $5\overline{)695}$ = 139: 5 0 0; 1 9 5; 1 5 0; 4 5; 4 5; 0

7. $2\overline{)754}$ = 377: 6 0 0; 1 5 4; 1 4 0; 1 4; 1 4; 0

8. $4\overline{)372}$ = 93: 3 6 0; 1 2; 1 2; 0

50 Chapter 3 Whole Number Multiplication and Division

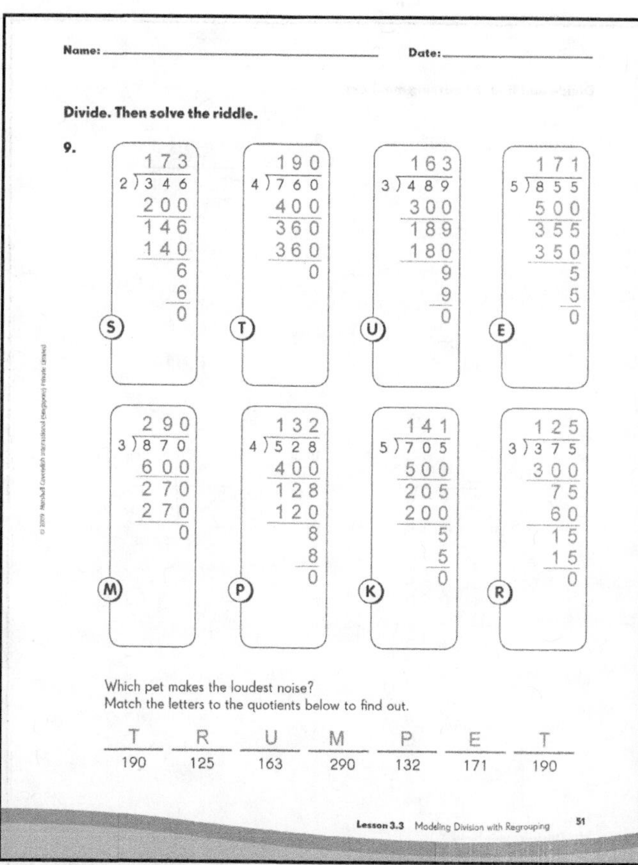

Name: ______ Date: ______

Divide. Then solve the riddle.

9.

S: $2\overline{)346}$ = 173: 2 0 0; 1 4 6; 1 4 0; 6; 6; 0

T: $4\overline{)760}$ = 190: 4 0 0; 3 6 0; 3 6 0; 0

U: $3\overline{)489}$ = 163: 3 0 0; 1 8 9; 1 8 0; 9; 9; 0

E: $5\overline{)855}$ = 171: 5 0 0; 3 5 5; 3 5 0; 5; 5; 0

M: $3\overline{)870}$ = 290: 6 0 0; 2 7 0; 2 7 0; 0

P: $4\overline{)528}$ = 132: 4 0 0; 1 2 8; 1 2 0; 8; 8; 0

K: $5\overline{)705}$ = 141: 5 0 0; 2 0 5; 2 0 0; 5; 5; 0

R: $3\overline{)375}$ = 125: 3 0 0; 7 5; 6 0; 1 5; 1 5; 0

Which pet makes the loudest noise?
Match the letters to the quotients below to find out.

T	R	U	M	P	E	T
190	125	163	290	132	171	190

Lesson 3.3 Modeling Division with Regrouping 51

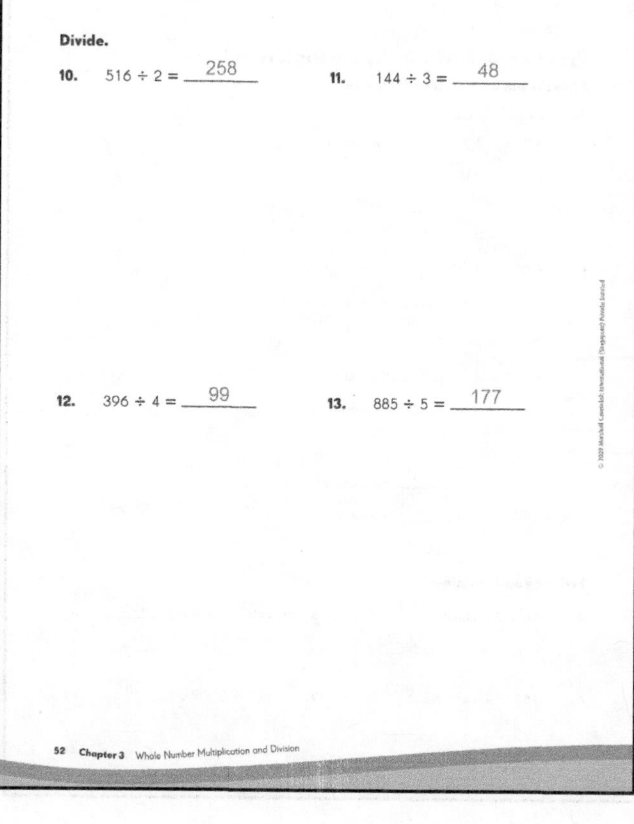

Divide.

10. 516 ÷ 2 = 258

11. 144 ÷ 3 = 48

12. 396 ÷ 4 = 99

13. 885 ÷ 5 = 177

52 Chapter 3 Whole Number Multiplication and Division

Chapter 3

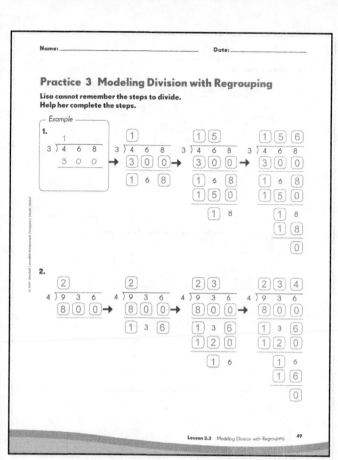

Chapter 3

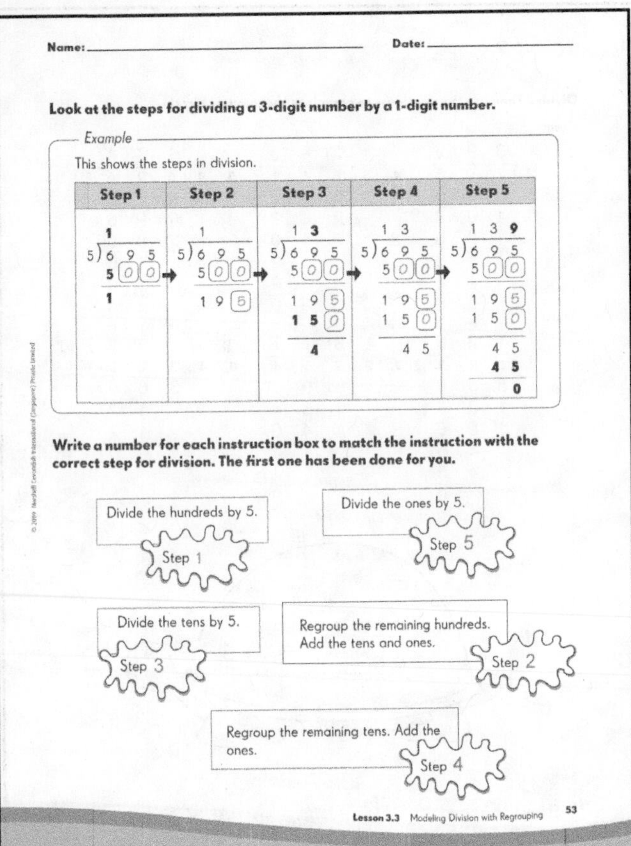
Name: ____________________ Date: ____________

Look at the steps for dividing a 3-digit number by a 1-digit number.

Example

This shows the steps in division.

Step 1	Step 2	Step 3	Step 4	Step 5
1 5) 6 9 5 5 0 0 1	1 5) 6 9 5 5 0 0 1 9 5	1 3 5) 6 9 5 5 0 0 1 9 5 1 5 0 4	1 3 5) 6 9 5 5 0 0 1 9 5 1 5 0 4 5	1 3 9 5) 6 9 5 5 0 0 1 9 5 1 5 0 4 5 4 5 0

Write a number for each instruction box to match the instruction with the correct step for division. The first one has been done for you.

Divide the hundreds by 5. — Step 1

Divide the ones by 5. — Step 5

Divide the tens by 5. — Step 3

Regroup the remaining hundreds. Add the tens and ones. — Step 2

Regroup the remaining tens. Add the ones. — Step 4

© 2009 Marshall Cavendish International (Singapore) Private Limited

Lesson 3.3 Modeling Division with Regrouping 53

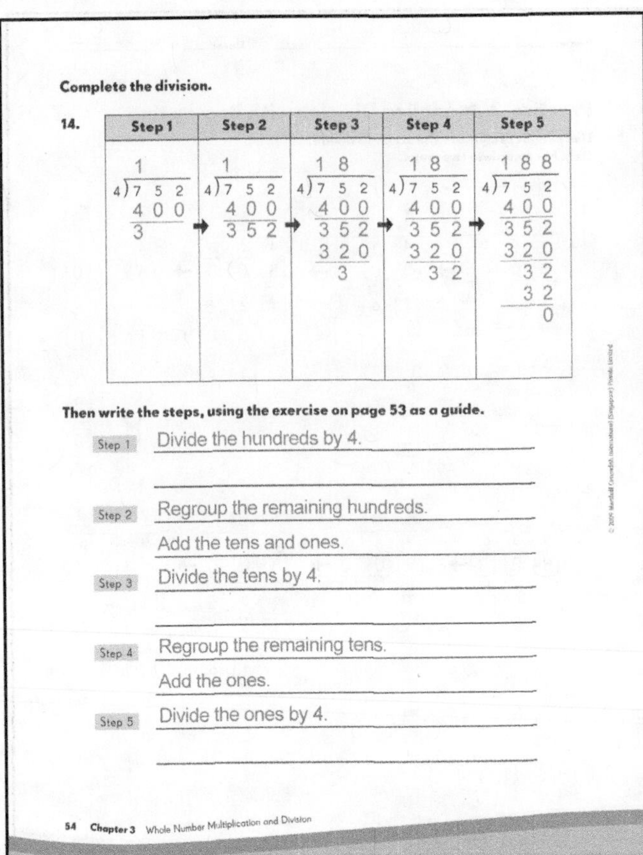
Complete the division.

14.

Step 1	Step 2	Step 3	Step 4	Step 5
1 4) 7 5 2 4 0 0 3	1 4) 7 5 2 4 0 0 3 5 2	1 8 4) 7 5 2 4 0 0 3 5 2 3 2 0 3	1 8 4) 7 5 2 4 0 0 3 5 2 3 2 0 3 2	1 8 8 4) 7 5 2 4 0 0 3 5 2 3 2 0 3 2 3 2 0

Then write the steps, using the exercise on page 53 as a guide.

Step 1 Divide the hundreds by 4.

Step 2 Regroup the remaining hundreds. Add the tens and ones.

Step 3 Divide the tens by 4.

Step 4 Regroup the remaining tens. Add the ones.

Step 5 Divide the ones by 4.

© 2009 Marshall Cavendish International (Singapore) Private Limited

54 Chapter 3 Whole Number Multiplication and Division

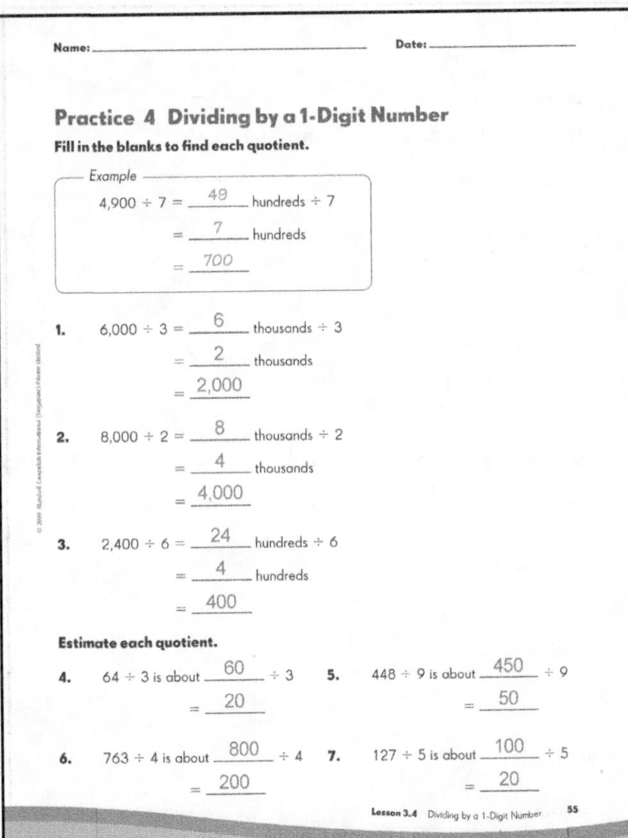
Name: ____________________ Date: ____________

Practice 4 Dividing by a 1-Digit Number

Fill in the blanks to find each quotient.

Example

4,900 ÷ 7 = 49 hundreds ÷ 7
= 7 hundreds
= 700

1. 6,000 ÷ 3 = 6 thousands ÷ 3
= 2 thousands
= 2,000

2. 8,000 ÷ 2 = 8 thousands ÷ 2
= 4 thousands
= 4,000

3. 2,400 ÷ 6 = 24 hundreds ÷ 6
= 4 hundreds
= 400

Estimate each quotient.

4. 64 ÷ 3 is about 60 ÷ 3
= 20

5. 448 ÷ 9 is about 450 ÷ 9
= 50

6. 763 ÷ 4 is about 800 ÷ 4
= 200

7. 127 ÷ 5 is about 100 ÷ 5
= 20

© 2009 Marshall Cavendish International (Singapore) Private Limited

Lesson 3.4 Dividing by a 1-Digit Number 55

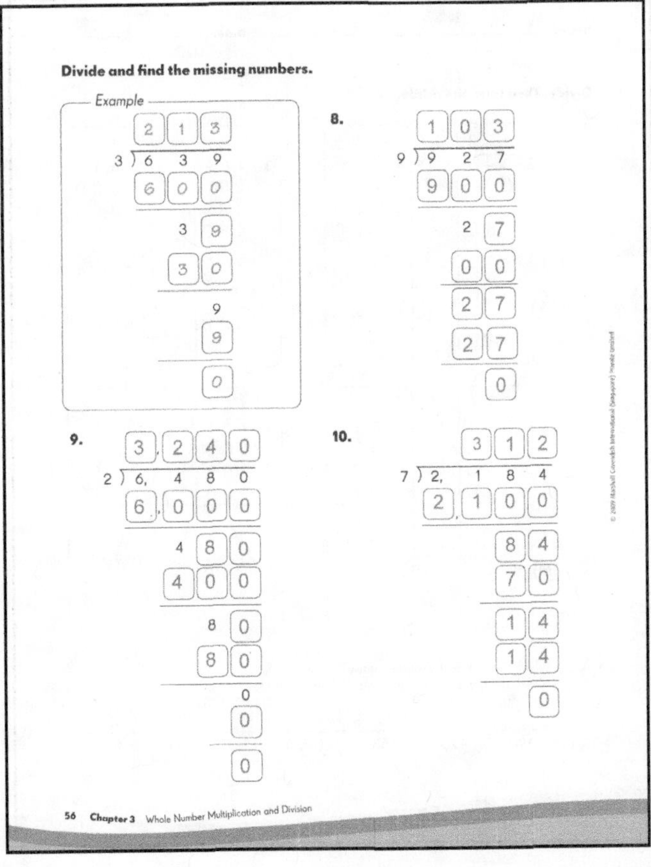
Divide and find the missing numbers.

Example

2 1 3
3) 6 3 9
6 0 0
3 9
3 0
9
9
0

8.

1 0 3
9) 9 2 7
9 0 0
2 7
0 0
2 7
2 7
0

9.

3,2 4 0
2) 6,4 8 0
6,0 0 0
4 8 0
4 0 0
8 0
8 0
0
0
0

10.

3 1 2
7) 2,1 8 4
2,1 0 0
8 4
7 0
1 4
1 4
0

© 2009 Marshall Cavendish International (Singapore) Private Limited

56 Chapter 3 Whole Number Multiplication and Division

Name: ______________________ Date: ______________

Divide. Then estimate to check that your answers are reasonable.

Example

```
       6  9  9
9 ) 6, 2  9  1
    5, 4  0  0
       8  9  1
       8  1  0
          8  1
          8  1
             0
```

Estimate:
6,291 is about 6,300.
6,300 ÷ 9 = 700

11.

```
       9  0  5
4 ) 3, 6  2  0
```

Estimate:
3,620 is about 3,600.
3,600 ÷ 4 = 900

12.

```
       4  0  1
7 ) 2, 8  0  7
```

Estimate:
2,807 is about 2,800.
2,800 ÷ 7 = 400

13.

```
       3  0  7
6 ) 1, 8  4  2
```

Estimate:
1,842 is about 1,800.
1,800 ÷ 6 = 300

© 2009 Marshall Cavendish International (Singapore) Private Limited

Find each quotient. Then estimate to check that your answers are reasonable.

Example

1,144 ÷ 9 = 127 R 1

```
       1  2  7 R1
9 ) 1, 1  4  4
       9  0  0
       2  4  4
       1  8  0
          6  4
          6  3
             1
```

Estimate: 1,144 ÷ 9 is about 900 ÷ 9 = 100.
The answer 127 R 1 is reasonable.

14. 6,514 ÷ 4 = 1,628 R 2

```
    1, 6  2  8 R2
4 ) 6, 5  1  4
```

6,514 ÷ 4 is about
6,000 ÷ 4 = 1,500.
The answer 1,628 R 2
is reasonable.

15. 1,340 ÷ 7 = 191 R 3

```
       1  9  1 R3
7 ) 1, 3  4  0
```

1,340 ÷ 7 is about
1,400 ÷ 7 = 200.
The answer 191 R 3
is reasonable.

16. 9,346 ÷ 8 = 1,168 R 2

```
    1, 1  6  8 R2
8 ) 9, 3  4  6
```

9,346 ÷ 8 is about
8,000 ÷ 8 = 1,000.
The answer 1,168 R 2
is reasonable.

© 2009 Marshall Cavendish International (Singapore) Private Limited

Name: ______________________ Date: ______________

Practice 5 Real-World Problems: Multiplication and Division

Solve. Show your work.

Example

A company has 4,059 people. Their names are listed in alphabetical order and then divided into groups of 5.

How many groups of 5 names are there and how many names are left?

4,059 ÷ 5 = 811 R 4
There are 811 groups of 5 names, and 4 names are left.

If the number of men in the company is 600 times the number of names left, how many men are there in the company?

600 × 4 = 2,400
There are 2,400 men in the company.

1. Factory A produces 326 sweaters in a day. Factory B produces 107 more sweaters a day than Factory A.

a. How many sweaters does Factory B produce in a day?

326 + 107 = 433
Factory B produces 433 sweaters a day.

b. How many sweaters do the two factories produce in 68 days?

433 + 326 = 759
759 × 68 = 51,612
The factories produce 51,612 sweaters in 68 days.

© 2009 Marshall Cavendish International (Singapore) Private Limited

2. In her shop, Lee had a piece of fabric measuring 150 meters. A customer asked her to sew 10 cushion covers, each requiring 3 meters of fabric. Another customer bought 21 meters of the same fabric. How much fabric does she have left?

10 × 3 = 30
150 – 30 = 120
120 – 21 = 99
She has 99 meters of fabric left.

3. A bakery produces 3,000 loaves of bread.
The bread is delivered to 75 stores.
Of the 75 stores, 67 receive 2,000 loaves of bread altogether.
The remaining stores receive an equal number of loaves of bread.
How many loaves does each of the remaining stores receive?

75 – 67 = 8
3,000 – 2,000 = 1,000
1,000 ÷ 8 = 125
Each of the remaining stores receives 125 loaves.

© 2009 Marshall Cavendish International (Singapore) Private Limited

Chapter 3

Name: ______________________ Date: ______________

4. Before lunch, Cindy packed 850 oranges, and Glen packed 470 fewer oranges than Cindy. Glen went home after lunch, but Cindy went back to work. That afternoon, Cindy packed 3 times as many oranges as Glen had packed in the morning.

a. How many oranges did Glen pack?
850 – 470 = 380
Glen packed 380 oranges.

b. How many oranges did Cindy pack altogether?
3 × 380 = 1,140
850 + 1,140 = 1,990
Cindy packed 1,990 oranges altogether.

c. Cindy packed the oranges in bags of 5.
How many bags of oranges did Cindy pack?
1,990 ÷ 5 = 398
She packed 398 bags.

5. Ms. Edstrom had a budget of $1,500 to spend on a table and 6 chairs.
The total price was $249 under her budget amount.
The table cost 3 times as much as a chair.
What was the price of the table?
$1,500 – $249 = $1,251
$1,251 ÷ 9 = $139
$139 × 3 = $417
The price of the table was $417.

© 2009 Marshall Cavendish International (Singapore) Private Limited

6. Kamala had 5,026 grams of flour in a canister. She bought a 4,157-gram bag of flour. She poured some flour from the bag to the canister. As a result, the mass of the flour in the canister is now twice the mass of the flour left in the bag. How much flour is in the bag now?

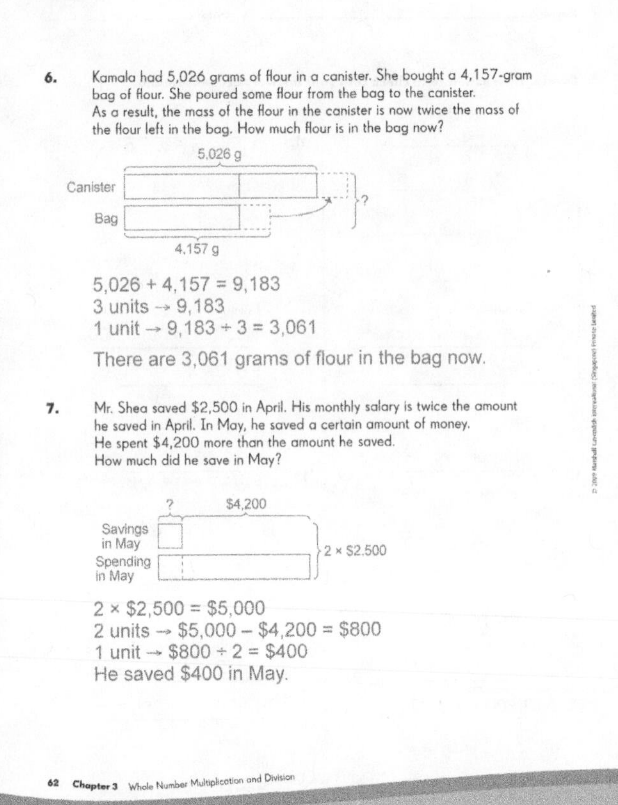

5,026 + 4,157 = 9,183
3 units → 9,183
1 unit → 9,183 ÷ 3 = 3,061
There are 3,061 grams of flour in the bag now.

7. Mr. Shea saved $2,500 in April. His monthly salary is twice the amount he saved in April. In May, he saved a certain amount of money.
He spent $4,200 more than the amount he saved.
How much did he save in May?

? $4,200
Savings in May
Spending in May
2 × $2,500

2 × $2,500 = $5,000
2 units → $5,000 – $4,200 = $800
1 unit → $800 ÷ 2 = $400
He saved $400 in May.

© 2009 Marshall Cavendish International (Singapore) Private Limited

Chapter 3

Name: ______________________ Date: ______________

Math Journal

Look at each problem. Use estimation to explain why the answers are not reasonable.

Example
5,268 × 8 = 2,144
Explain.
5,268 is about 5,000
5,000 × 8 = 40,000.
So the answer is too small.

1. 725 × 6 = 700
Explain.
725 is about 700.
700 × 6 = 4,200.
So the answer is too small.

2. 497 × 21 = 1,291
Explain.
497 is about 500 and 21 is about 20.
500 × 20 = 10,000.
So the answer is too small.

© 2009 Marshall Cavendish International (Singapore) Private Limited

Use estimation to explain why the answer is not reasonable.

3. 6,021 ÷ 3 = 207
Explain.
6,000 is close to 6021.
6,000 ÷ 3 = 2,000.
So the answer is too small.

Solve. Show your work.

4. Look at the number sentence.
72 ÷ 6 = 12
How would you use this to find the missing quotient?
7,200 ÷ 6 = ☐
7,200 = 72 hundreds
72 hundreds ÷ 6 = 12 hundreds
= 1,200

© 2009 Marshall Cavendish International (Singapore) Private Limited

Name: _______________ Date: _______________

Challenging Practice

Charlie has 1,243 stamps. He gives away 12 stamps. His father gives him 415 stamps. He divides as many stamps as possible equally among 4 albums.

1. How many stamps did he place in each album?

   1,243 – 12 = 1,231
   1,231 + 415 = 1,646
   1,646 ÷ 4 = 411 R2
   He placed 411 stamps in each album.

2. Based on your answer in **Exercise 1**, how many stamps are left over?

   2 stamps are left over.

Thinking skills: Identifying relationships; Sequencing

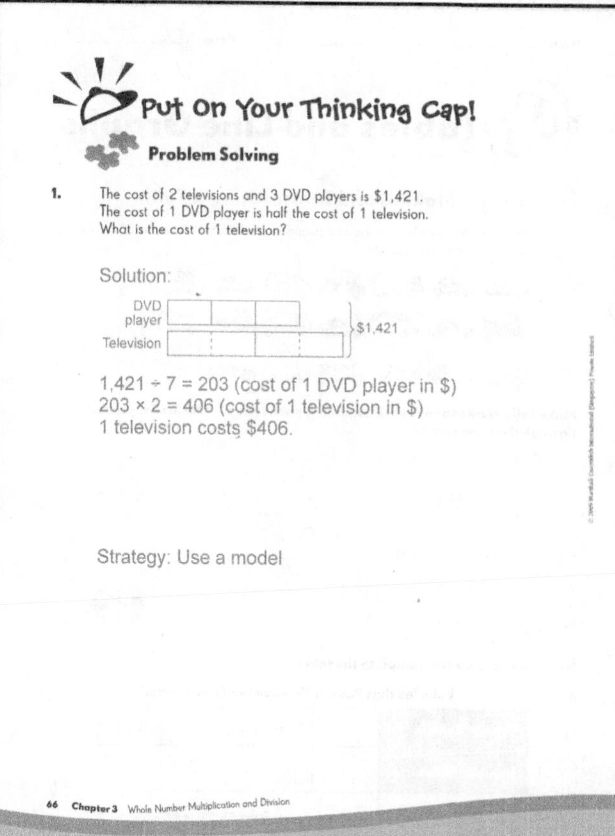

Put On Your Thinking Cap!
Problem Solving
1. The cost of 2 televisions and 3 DVD players is $1,421.
The cost of 1 DVD player is half the cost of 1 television.
What is the cost of 1 television?
Solution:
DVD player
Television
$1,421
1,421 ÷ 7 = 203 (cost of 1 DVD player in $)
203 × 2 = 406 (cost of 1 television in $)
1 television costs $406.
Strategy: Use a model
66 Chapter 3 Whole Number Multiplication and Division

Chapter 3

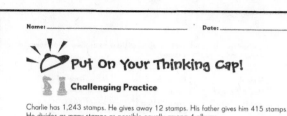

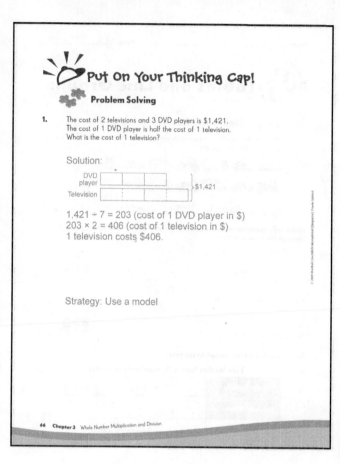

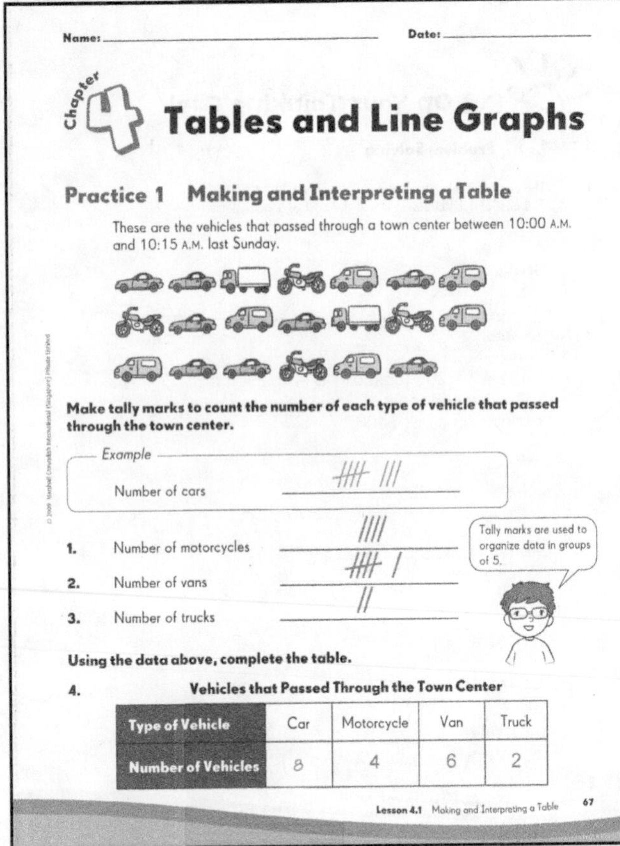

Name: ______________________ Date: ______________

Chapter 4

Tables and Line Graphs

Practice 1 Making and Interpreting a Table

These are the vehicles that passed through a town center between 10:00 A.M. and 10:15 A.M. last Sunday.

Make tally marks to count the number of each type of vehicle that passed through the town center.

Example

Number of cars ____𝍸 |||____

1. Number of motorcycles ____||||____
2. Number of vans ____𝍸 |____
3. Number of trucks ____||____

Tally marks are used to organize data in groups of 5.

Using the data above, complete the table.

4. **Vehicles that Passed Through the Town Center**

Type of Vehicle	Car	Motorcycle	Van	Truck
Number of Vehicles	8	4	6	2

The school nurse keeps the health records of all the students. These cards show the height and weight of nine students.

Name: Pablo Height: 62 in. Weight: 114 lb	Name: Grant Height: 59 in. Weight: 110 lb	Name: Tamara Height: 55 in. Weight: 103 lb
Name: John Height: 55 in. Weight: 114 lb	Name: Mei Li Height: 59 in. Weight: 103 lb	Name: Pauline Height: 62 in. Weight: 92 lb
Name: Nita Height: 55 in. Weight: 103 lb	Name: Evan Height: 51 in. Weight: 84 lb	Name: Samantha Height: 55 in. Weight: 92 lb

Complete. Use the data on the cards.

5. **Height of Students**

Height (in.)	Number of Students
51	1
55	4
59	2
62	2

Weight of Students

Weight (lb)	Number of Students
84	1
92	2
103	3
110	1
114	2

Name: ______________________ Date: ______________

Jane used tally marks to record the number of pets adopted from an animal shelter in a week.

Pets Adopted from an Animal Shelter

Pet	Tally
Guinea Pigs	𝍸 ||||
Hamsters	𝍸 𝍸 𝍸
White Mice	𝍸 𝍸 𝍸 |||
Rabbits	𝍸

Complete. Use the data in the tally chart.

6. **Pets Adopted from an Animal Shelter**

Pet	Number of Pets Adopted
Guinea Pigs	9
Hamsters	15
White Mice	18
Rabbits	5

Complete. Use the data in the table.

7. ____18____ white mice were adopted.
8. ____9____ guinea pigs were adopted.
9. ____9____ more white mice than guinea pigs were adopted.
10. Three times as many ____hamsters____ as ____rabbits____ were adopted.
11. The pets that were adopted most often from the animal shelter were ____white mice____

Gary has a coin collection. The bar graph shows the number of coins he collected from different countries.

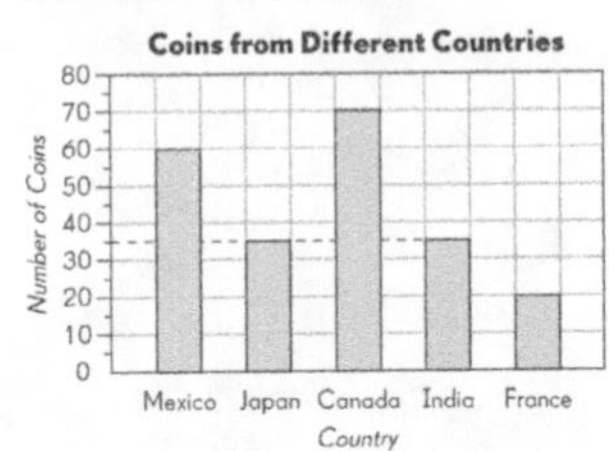

Use the data in the graph to complete the table. Then use the data in the table to complete the sentences.

12. **Coins from Different Countries**

Country	Number of Coins
Mexico	60
Japan	35
Canada	70
India	35
France	20

13. Gary has the same number of coins from ____Japan____ and ____India____.
14. Gary has half as many coins from Japan as he has from ____Canada____.
15. He has ____25____ more coins from Mexico than from India.
16. Gary gave away all his coins from Canada. He now has the greatest number of coins from ____Mexico____.

Chapter 4

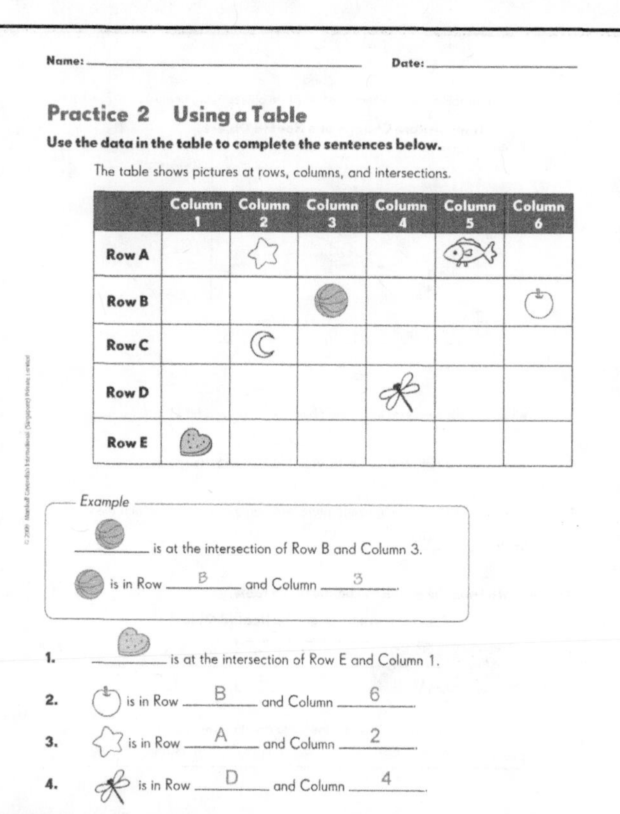

Name: ______________________ Date: ______________

Practice 2 Using a Table

Use the data in the table to complete the sentences below.

The table shows pictures at rows, columns, and intersections.

	Column 1	Column 2	Column 3	Column 4	Column 5	Column 6
Row A						
Row B						
Row C						
Row D						
Row E						

Example

______ is at the intersection of Row B and Column 3.

is in Row B and Column 3.

1. ______ is at the intersection of Row E and Column 1.
2. is in Row B and Column 6.
3. is in Row A and Column 2.
4. is in Row D and Column 4.

© 2009 Marshall Cavendish International (Singapore) Private Limited

The table shows part of Bill's class schedule from Monday through Wednesday.

Bill's Schedule

Time	Monday	Tuesday	Wednesday
09:00 A.M. – 10:00 A.M.	Science	Math	History
10:00 A.M. – 11:00 A.M.	Math	Geography	Science
11:00 A.M. – 12:00 P.M.	English	Science	Math
12:00 P.M. – 1:00 P.M.	Lunch	Lunch	Lunch

Use the table to answer the questions.

5. What class does Bill have between 10:00 A.M. and 11:00 A.M. on Mondays? Math
6. What class does Bill have between 9:00 A.M. and 10:00 A.M. on Wednesdays? History
7. His lunch break on Wednesday is between 12:00 P.M. and 1:00 P.M.
8. His Math class on Wednesday is between 11:00 A.M. and 12:00 P.M.
9. His Geography class on Tuesday is between 10:00 A.M. and 11:00 A.M.

© 2009 Marshall Cavendish International (Singapore) Private Limited

Name: ______________________ Date: ______________

Maria and Vinny collected stamps from three different countries: Singapore, Malaysia, and Thailand. The number of stamps collected is shown in the table below.

Stamps Collected

Collector	Singapore	Malaysia	Thailand
Maria	15	42	23
Vinny	31	18	29
Total	46	60	52

Complete the table, and answer the questions.

10. How many Thailand stamps did Vinny collect? 29
11. How many Thailand stamps did Maria and Vinny collect altogether? 52
12. How many more Malaysia stamps than Singapore stamps did Maria and Vinny collect altogether? 14
13. Who collected more stamps: Maria or Vinny? Maria
14. How many stamps did they collect altogether? 158

© 2009 Marshall Cavendish International (Singapore) Private Limited

The table shows the number of quarters and nickels that five students saved.

Quarters and Nickels Saved

	Quarters (25¢)		Nickels (5¢)		
Name	**Number of Coins Collected**	**Amount Saved ($)**	**Number of Coins Collected**	**Amount Saved ($)**	**Total Amount Saved ($)**
Amy	16	4.00	20	1.00	5.00
Bernard	10	2.50	7	0.35	2.85
Chin	18	4.50	25	1.25	5.75
Dawn	21	5.25	9	0.45	5.70
Ernest	15	3.75	15	0.75	4.50

Complete the table, and answer the questions.

15. Who saved the greatest amount? Chin
16. Who saved the least amount? Bernard
17. How many more coins did Chin collect than Ernest? 13
18. How much more must Bernard save in order to have the same amount as Dawn? $2.85
19. Which two students saved a total of less than $7.50? How much less? Bernard and Ernest, $.15
20. Which two students collected the same number of coins? Dawn and Ernest
21. Of the two students in **Exercise 20**, who saved more money? How much more? Dawn saved $1.20 more than Ernest.

© 2009 Marshall Cavendish International (Singapore) Private Limited

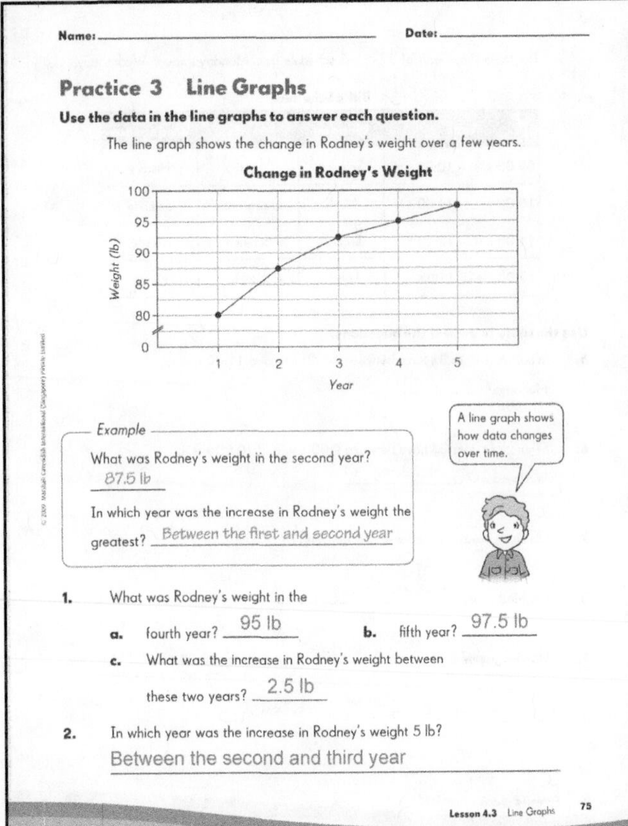

Name: ______________ Date: ______________

Practice 3 Line Graphs

Use the data in the line graphs to answer each question.

The line graph shows the change in Rodney's weight over a few years.

Example

What was Rodney's weight in the second year? 87.5 lb

In which year was the increase in Rodney's weight the greatest? Between the first and second year

A line graph shows how data changes over time.

1. What was Rodney's weight in the
   - **a.** fourth year? 95 lb
   - **b.** fifth year? 97.5 lb
   - **c.** What was the increase in Rodney's weight between these two years? 2.5 lb
2. In which year was the increase in Rodney's weight 5 lb? Between the second and third year

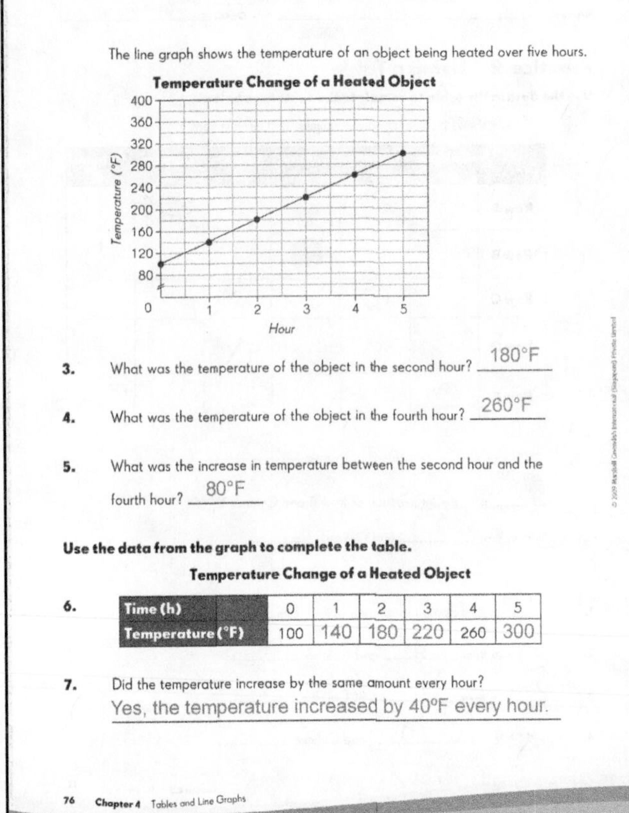

The line graph shows the temperature of an object being heated over five hours.

3. What was the temperature of the object in the second hour? 180°F
4. What was the temperature of the object in the fourth hour? 260°F
5. What was the increase in temperature between the second hour and the fourth hour? 80°F

Use the data from the graph to complete the table.

Temperature Change of a Heated Object

6.

Time (h)	0	1	2	3	4	5
Temperature (°F)	100	140	180	220	260	300

7. Did the temperature increase by the same amount every hour? Yes, the temperature increased by 40°F every hour.

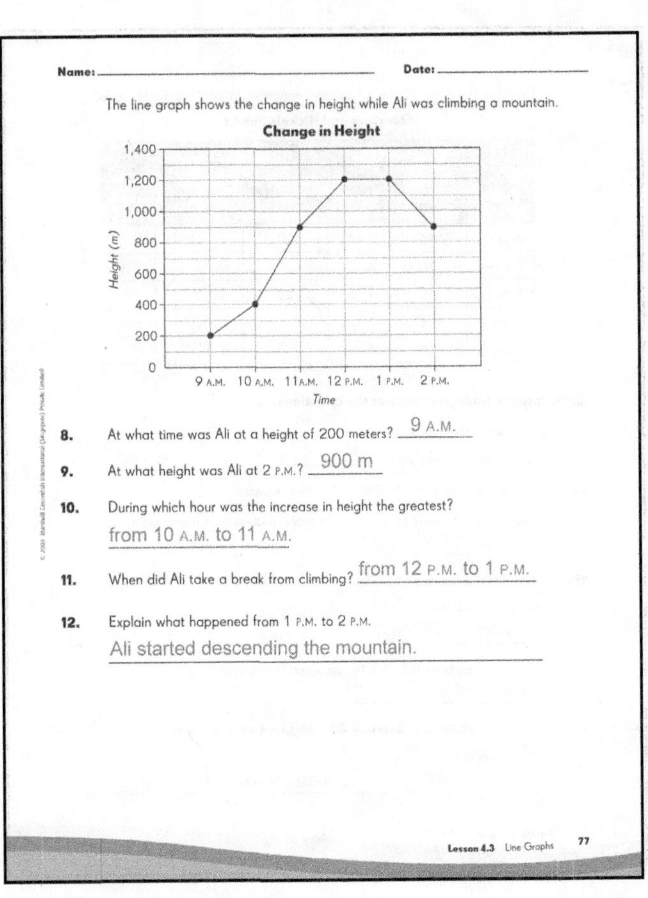

Name: ______________ Date: ______________

The line graph shows the change in height while Ali was climbing a mountain.

8. At what time was Ali at a height of 200 meters? 9 A.M.
9. At what height was Ali at 2 P.M.? 900 m
10. During which hour was the increase in height the greatest? from 10 A.M. to 11 A.M.
11. When did Ali take a break from climbing? from 12 P.M. to 1 P.M.
12. Explain what happened from 1 P.M. to 2 P.M. Ali started descending the mountain.

Choose an appropriate graph to display the data. Write *bar graph, line graph,* or *picture graph.* Explain your choice.

13. Anna recorded the rainfall amounts (in centimeters) in each month from January to June.
    Bar graph; A bar graph is used to compare data especially when the numbers are large.
14. Jim organized a party for 20 of his friends. He recorded the number of friends who liked each flavor of ice-cream — vanilla, strawberry, and chocolate. 4 friends liked vanilla ice-cream, 8 friends liked strawberry ice-cream, and 8 friends liked chocolate ice-cream.
    Picture graph or bar graph; In this case, a picture graph may be preferred as the number of friends is not very large and all the numbers are multiples of 4.
15. Temperature change of water (in °F) when it is heated over 20 minutes.
    Line graph; A line graph is used to show how data changes over time.
16. Level of water remaining in a leaking tank recorded over four hours.
    Line graph; A line graph is used to show how data changes over time.

© 2009 Marshall Cavendish International (Singapore) Private Limited

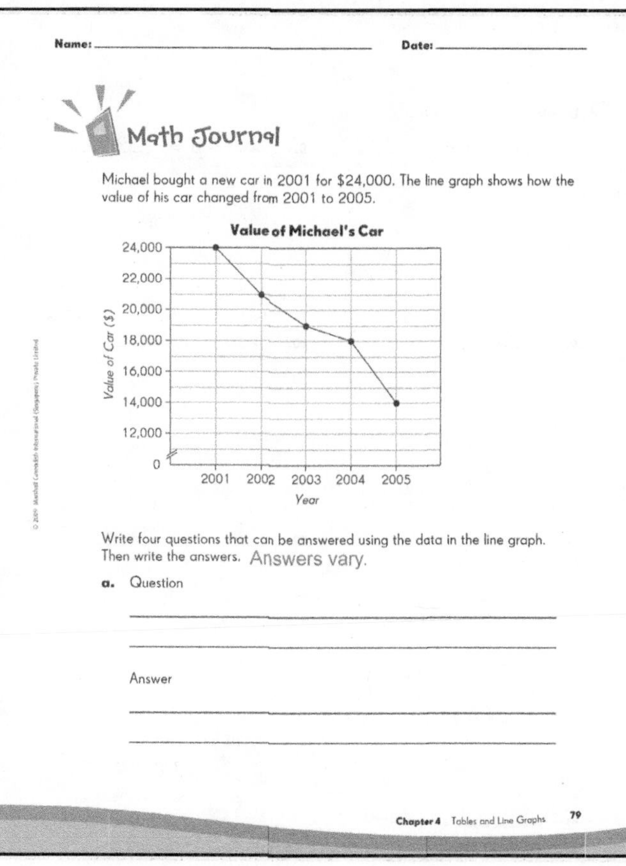

Name: ______________________ Date: ______________

Math Journal

Michael bought a new car in 2001 for $24,000. The line graph shows how the value of his car changed from 2001 to 2005.

Write four questions that can be answered using the data in the line graph. Then write the answers. Answers vary.

a. Question

Answer

b. Question

Answer

c. Question

Answer

d. Question

Answer

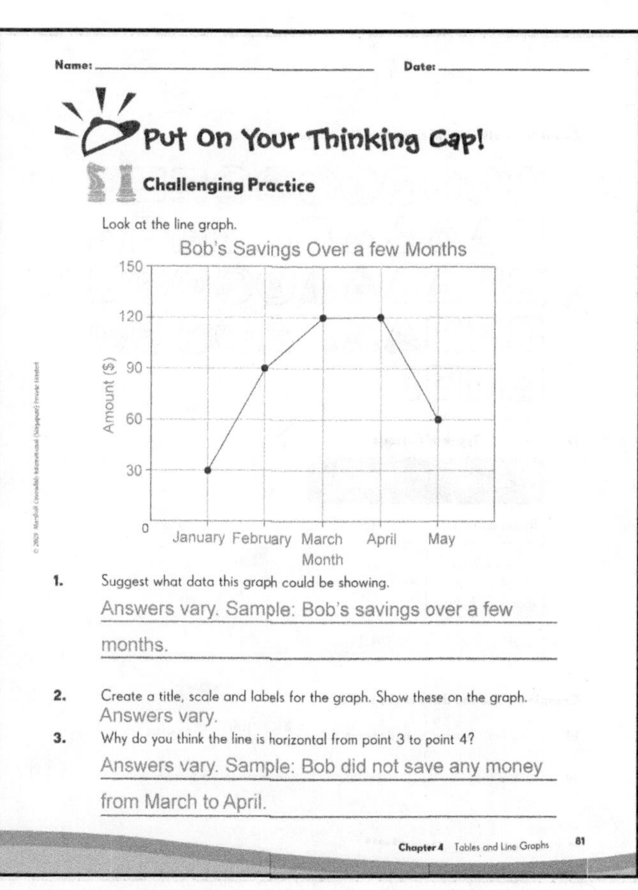

Name: ______________________ Date: ______________

Put On Your Thinking Cap!

Challenging Practice

Look at the line graph.

1. Suggest what data this graph could be showing.
   Answers vary. Sample: Bob's savings over a few months.
2. Create a title, scale and labels for the graph. Show these on the graph.
   Answers vary.
3. Why do you think the line is horizontal from point 3 to point 4?
   Answers vary. Sample: Bob did not save any money from March to April.

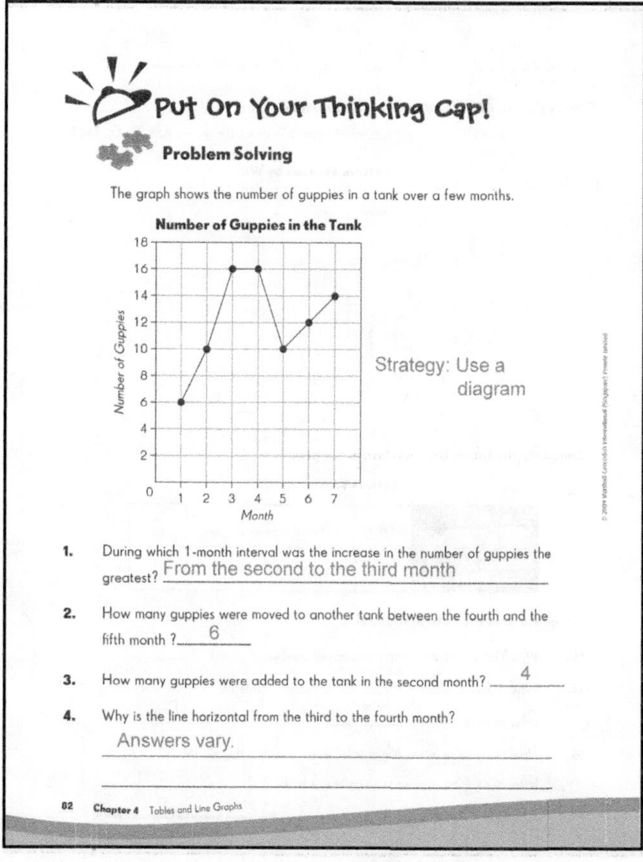

Put On Your Thinking Cap!

Problem Solving

The graph shows the number of guppies in a tank over a few months.

1. During which 1-month interval was the increase in the number of guppies the greatest? From the second to the third month
2. How many guppies were moved to another tank between the fourth and the fifth month? 6
3. How many guppies were added to the tank in the second month? 4
4. Why is the line horizontal from the third to the fourth month?
   Answers vary.

Chapter 4

Name: ______________________ Date: ______________

Cumulative Review for Chapters 3 and 4

Concepts and Skills

Multiply. *(Lessons 3.1 and 3.2)*

1. 27 × 8 = 216
2. 7,365 × 9 = 66,285
3. 94 × 67 = 6,298
4. 827 × 61 = 50,447
5. 625 × 29 = 18,125
6. 944 × 38 = 35,872

Divide. *(Lessons 3.3 and 3.4)*

7. 216 ÷ 3 = 72
8. 432 ÷ 8 = 54
9. 5,520 ÷ 6 = 920
10. 2,828 ÷ 7 = 404
11. 5,398 ÷ 5 = 1,079 R 3
12. 7,436 ÷ 7 = 1,062 R 2

Name: ______________________ Date: ______________

Study the bar graph and answer the questions. *(Lesson 4.1)*

The bar graph shows the number of times Will wrote the letters A, B, C, D, and E on a paper.

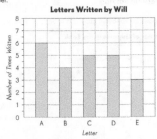

Letters Written by Will

Letter	Number of Times Written
A	6
B	4
C	5
D	5
E	3

Complete the table. Use the data in the graph.

13. **Letters Written by Will**

Letter	A	B	C	D	E
Number of Times Written	6	4	5	5	3

Complete. Use the data in the table.

14. Which letter did Will write the greatest number of times? A
15. How many more letter 'A's did Will write than the letter he wrote the least number of times? 3
16. How many more letter 'A's must be written so that the number of letter 'A's will be 3 times the number of letter 'B's? 6

Count the buttons and complete the table. *(Lesson 4.1)*

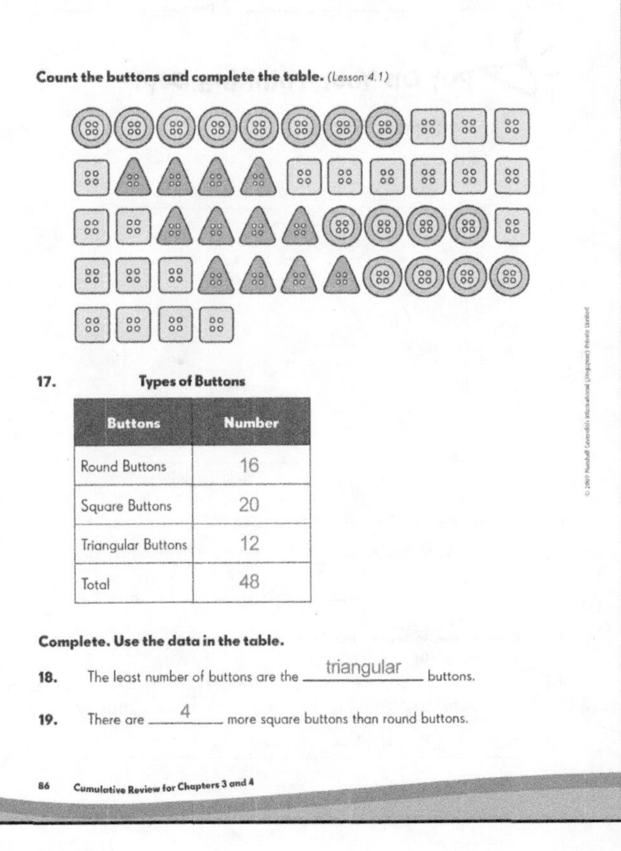

17. **Types of Buttons**

Buttons	Number
Round Buttons	16
Square Buttons	20
Triangular Buttons	12
Total	48

Complete. Use the data in the table.

18. The least number of buttons are the triangular buttons.
19. There are 4 more square buttons than round buttons.

Name: ______________________ Date: ______________

Complete the table by finding the rows, columns, and intersections. *(Lesson 4.2)*

The table shows the types of sandwiches ordered by a group of students at lunchtime.

20. **Sandwiches Ordered by Students**

Types of Sandwiches	Boys	Girls	Total
Chicken	6	4	10
Roast Beef	12	18	30
Tuna	7	8	15
Grilled Vegetables	3	18	21

Complete. Use the data in the table.

21. How many students ordered roast beef? 30

22. Find the number that should appear in the intersection for 'Tuna' and 'Girls'. 8

23. In which column does the number '7' appear? Boys

24. In which row does the number '6' appear? Chicken

25. The number '4' appears in the intersection of the column for Girls and the row for Chicken.

Complete the table by finding the rows, columns, and intersections. *(Lesson 4.2)*

The table shows the 50-cent and 20-cent toys that three friends bought for party favors.

26.

Name	50-cent Toys		20-cent Toys		Total Cost
	Number	Cost	Number	Cost	
Ashin	5	$2.50	9	$1.80	$4.30
Benjamin	6	$3.00	7	$1.40	$4.40
Cara	4	$2.00	8	$1.60	$3.60

Complete. Use the data in the table.

27. Who bought the most toys? Ashin

28. Who spent the most on the toys? Benjamin

29. How much more did Benjamin spend than Cara? $0.80

30. How much did they spend on 20-cent toys altogether? $4.80

31. How much more did they spend on 50-cent toys than on 20-cent toys? $2.70

Name: ______________________ Date: ______________

Complete. Use the data in the line graph. *(Lesson 4.3)*

The graph shows the amount of water in a leaking tank over 7 hours.

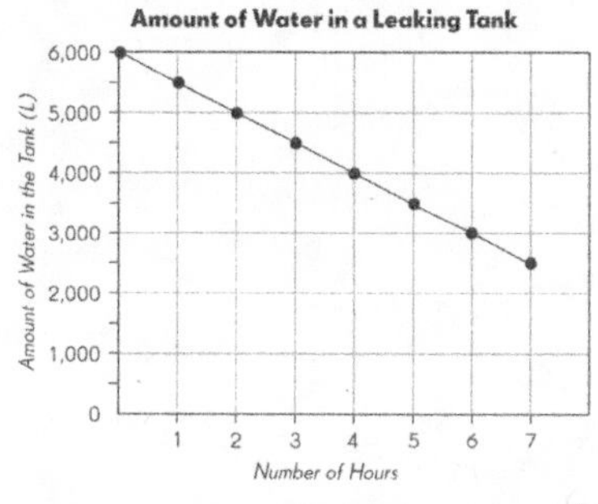

32. What was the amount of water in the tank at the start? 6,000 L

33. What was the amount of water in the tank after 7 hours? 2,500 L

34. After how many hours was the amount of water in the tank half that at the start? 6 hours

35. The owner of the tank paid a fine of $1 for every 8 liters of water lost. How much would the fine be after 4 hours? $250

Complete. Use the data in the line graph. *(Lesson 4.3)*

The line graph shows the change in water level in a tank over 6 minutes.

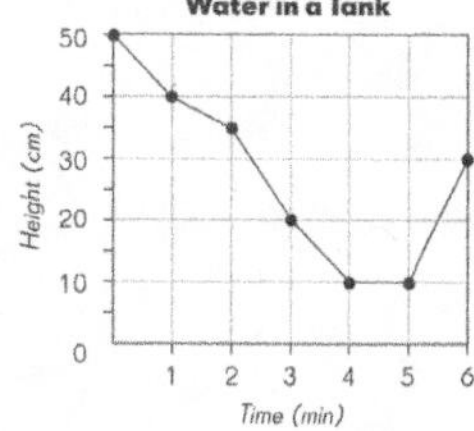

36. What was the height of the water after

a. 2 minutes? 35 cm **b.** $3\frac{1}{2}$ minutes? 15 cm

37. What was the decrease in the height of the water from the first to the second minute? 5 cm

38. During which 1-minute interval did the water level decrease the most? From the second minute to the third minute.

39. During which 1-minute interval did the water level increase by 20 centimeters? From the fifth minute to the sixth minute.

40. Was the tank ever empty? No

If the tank were ever empty, how would you tell from the graph? The line graph would decrease to 0 at that time.

Chapters 3-4 Review

Name: ____________________ Date: ____________

Problem Solving

Solve. Show your work.

41. Mr. Suarez has $2,760 to buy family meals for the local food pantry.

a. What is the greatest number of family meals he can buy if each meal costs $9?

2,760 ÷ 9 = 306 R 6

The greatest number of meals he can buy is 306.

b. How much money would he have left after buying the meals?

He would have $6 left after buying the meals.

42. A grocer bought two bags of dried fruit. One bag contained 4,950 ounces of fruit and the other bag contained 2,730 ounces of fruit. He repacked the fruit equally into 8 smaller packets. What was the weight of the fruit in each packet?

4,950 + 2,730 = 7,680 oz

7,680 ÷ 8 = 960 oz

The weight of the fruit in each packet was 960 oz.

Cumulative Review for Chapters 3 and 4 91

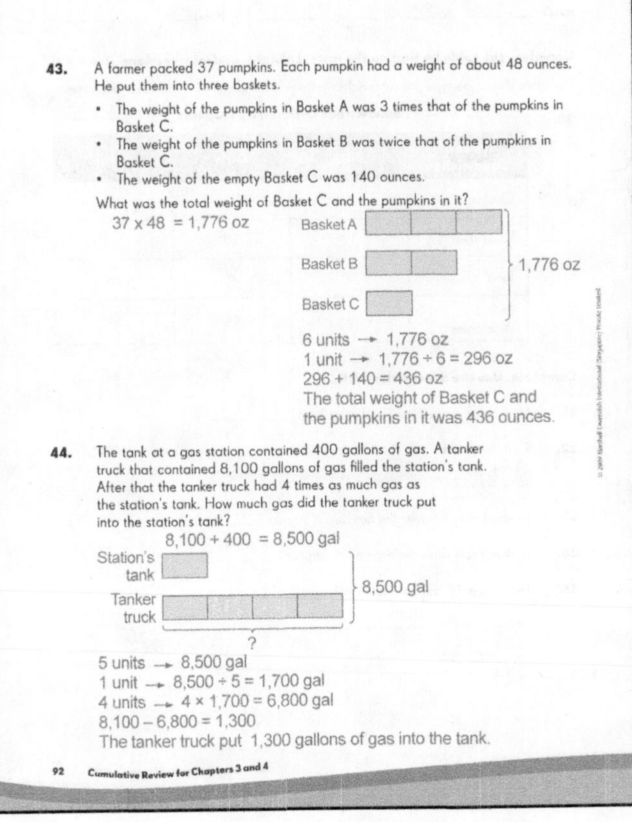

43. A farmer packed 37 pumpkins. Each pumpkin had a weight of about 48 ounces. He put them into three baskets.

- The weight of the pumpkins in Basket A was 3 times that of the pumpkins in Basket C.
- The weight of the pumpkins in Basket B was twice that of the pumpkins in Basket C.
- The weight of the empty Basket C was 140 ounces.

What was the total weight of Basket C and the pumpkins in it?

37 x 48 = 1,776 oz

6 units → 1,776 oz

1 unit → 1,776 ÷ 6 = 296 oz

296 + 140 = 436 oz

The total weight of Basket C and the pumpkins in it was 436 ounces.

44. The tank at a gas station contained 400 gallons of gas. A tanker truck that contained 8,100 gallons of gas filled the station's tank. After that the tanker truck had 4 times as much gas as the station's tank. How much gas did the tanker truck put into the station's tank?

8,100 + 400 = 8,500 gal

5 units → 8,500 gal

1 unit → 8,500 ÷ 5 = 1,700 gal

4 units → 4 × 1,700 = 6,800 gal

8,100 – 6,800 = 1,300

The tanker truck put 1,300 gallons of gas into the tank.

92 Cumulative Review for Chapters 3 and 4

Name: ______________________ Date: ______________

Chapter 5 Data and Probability

Practice 1 Average

Find the mean or average of each set of data.

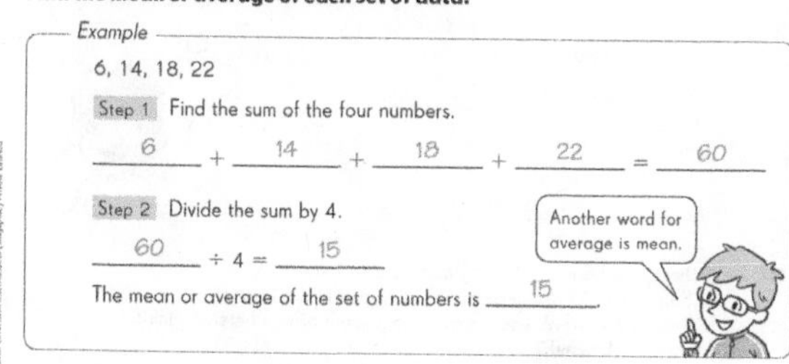

Example
6, 14, 18, 22
Step 1 Find the sum of the four numbers.
6 + 14 + 18 + 22 = 60
Step 2 Divide the sum by 4.
60 ÷ 4 = 15
The mean or average of the set of numbers is 15.
Another word for average is mean.

1. Here are the weights of 5 pieces of luggage at an airport.
   14 lb, 18 lb, 21 lb, 27 lb, 30 lb

   Step 1 Find the total weight of all the pieces of luggage.

   14 + 18 + 21 + 27 + 30

   = 110 lb

   Step 2 Divide the total by 5.

   110 ÷ 5 = 22 lb

   What is the average weight of the pieces of luggage? 22 lb

Find the mean of each set of data.

2. 37, 0, 67, 44

   Total = 37 + 0 + 67 + 44
   = 148
   Mean = 148 ÷ 4
   = 37

3. \$8, \$12, \$15, \$29

   Total = 8 + 12 + 15 + 29
   = \$64
   Mean = 64 ÷ 4
   = \$16

4. 15 pt, 21 pt, 34 pt, 48 pt, 52 pt

   Total = 15 + 21 + 34 + 48 + 52
   = 170 pt
   Mean = 170 ÷ 5
   = 34 pt

Name: ______________________ Date: ______________

5. 28 yd, 61 yd, 19 yd, 43 yd, 89 yd, 126 yd

   Total = 28 + 61 + 19 + 43 + 89 + 126
   = 366 yd
   Mean = 366 ÷ 6
   = 61 yd

6. 55 lb, 246 lb, 100 lb, 34 lb, 95 lb, 460 lb

   Total = 55 + 246 + 100 + 34 + 95 + 460
   = 990 lb
   Mean = 990 ÷ 6
   = 165 lb

Complete. Use the data in the table.

The table shows the distances Wayne jogged on 5 days.

Distances Wayne Jogged on Five Days

Day	Distance Jogged
Monday	3 km
Tuesday	2 km
Wednesday	4 km
Thursday	5 km
Friday	6 km

7. How many kilometers did he jog altogether?

   3 + 2 + 4 + 5 + 6 = 20

   Wayne jogged 20 kilometers altogether.

8. On average, how many kilometers did he jog each day?

   20 ÷ 5 = 4

   On average, Wayne jogged 4 kilometers each day.

Name: ________________ Date: ________________

Complete. Use the data in the table.

The table shows the number of trophies a school collected over 6 years.

Trophies Collected Over Six Years

Year	Number of Trophies Collected
1	15
2	9
3	12
4	18
5	20
6	22

9. What is the total number of trophies collected in 6 years?

15 + 9 + 12 + 18 + 20 + 22 = 96

The total number of trophies collected in 6 years is 96.

10. What is the average number of trophies collected each year?

96 ÷ 6 = 16

The average number of trophies collected each year is 16.

Solve. Show your work.

Example

Mrs. Lim made 6,250 milliliters of orange juice and poured it into 5 containers. Find the mean amount of juice in each container.

6,250 ÷ 5 = 1,250 mL

Mean = $\frac{\text{Total number or amount}}{\text{Number of items}}$

The mean amount of juice in each container is 1,250 mL.

11. A chess club began accepting members on January 1. By September 30 of the same year, the club had a total of 504 members. What was the average number of members who joined the club each month?

There are 9 months from January 1 to September 30.

504 ÷ 9 = 56

The average number of members who joined the club each month was 56.

Name: ________________ Date: ________________

Solve. Show your work.

Example

The average number of goals scored by a soccer team in a game was 4. The team played a total of 22 games. What was the total number of goals scored by the team?

4 × 22 = 88 goals

Total score = Average score × Number of games

The total number of goals scored by the team was 88.

12. The mean length of the sides of a triangular plot of land is 18 yards. What is its perimeter?

A triangular plot of land has 3 sides.

3 × 18 = 54 m

Its perimeter is 54 meters.

Solve. Show your work.

13. There are 12 peaches in a carton. The mean mass of all the peaches is 175 grams. What is their total mass?

12 × 175 = 2,100 g

The total mass of the peaches is 2,100 grams.

14. Alicia sews costumes for a school play. She takes an average of 86 minutes to sew each costume. How long would she take to sew 16 of these costumes?

16 × 86 = 1,376 min

Alicia would take 1,376 minutes to sew 16 of these costumes.

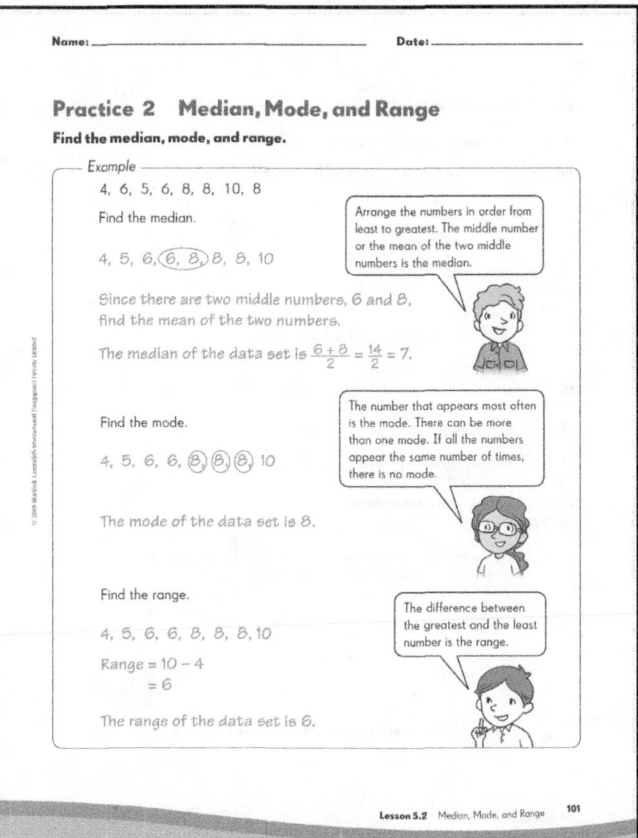

Name: ______________ Date: ______________

Practice 2 Median, Mode, and Range

Find the median, mode, and range.

Example

4, 6, 5, 6, 8, 8, 10, 8

Find the median.

4, 5, 6, (6, 8), 8, 8, 10

Since there are two middle numbers, 6 and 8, find the mean of the two numbers.

The median of the data set is $\frac{6+8}{2} = \frac{14}{2} = 7$.

Arrange the numbers in order from least to greatest. The middle number or the mean of the two middle numbers is the median.

Find the mode.

4, 5, 6, 6, (8), (8), (8), 10

The mode of the data set is 8.

The number that appears most often is the mode. There can be more than one mode. If all the numbers appear the same number of times, there is no mode.

Find the range.

4, 5, 6, 6, 8, 8, 8, 10

Range = 10 − 4
= 6

The range of the data set is 6.

The difference between the greatest and the least number is the range.

Lesson 5.2 Median, Mode, and Range 101

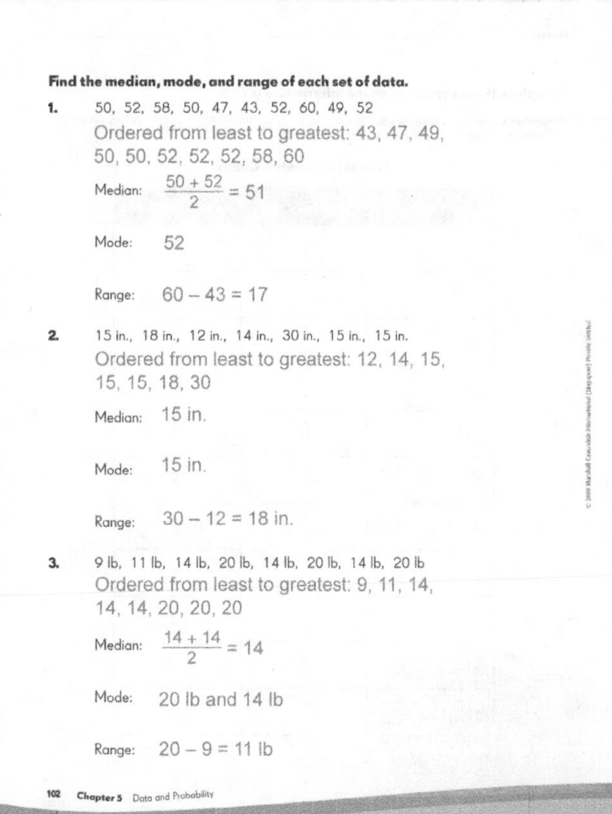

Find the median, mode, and range of each set of data.

1. 50, 52, 58, 50, 47, 43, 52, 60, 49, 52
   Ordered from least to greatest: 43, 47, 49, 50, 50, 52, 52, 52, 58, 60
   Median: $\frac{50 + 52}{2} = 51$
   Mode: 52
   Range: 60 − 43 = 17

2. 15 in., 18 in., 12 in., 14 in., 30 in., 15 in., 15 in.
   Ordered from least to greatest: 12, 14, 15, 15, 15, 18, 30
   Median: 15 in.
   Mode: 15 in.
   Range: 30 − 12 = 18 in.

3. 9 lb, 11 lb, 14 lb, 20 lb, 14 lb, 20 lb, 14 lb, 20 lb
   Ordered from least to greatest: 9, 11, 14, 14, 14, 20, 20, 20
   Median: $\frac{14 + 14}{2} = 14$
   Mode: 20 lb and 14 lb
   Range: 20 − 9 = 11 lb

102 Chapter 5 Data and Probability

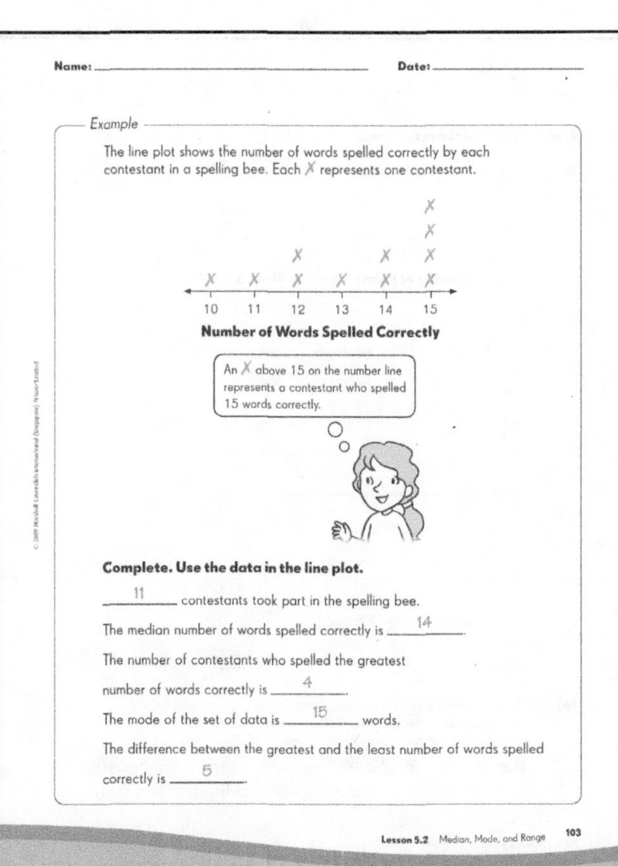

Name: ______________ Date: ______________

Example

The line plot shows the number of words spelled correctly by each contestant in a spelling bee. Each X represents one contestant.

10 11 12 13 14 15
Number of Words Spelled Correctly
An X above 15 on the number line represents a contestant who spelled 15 words correctly.

Complete. Use the data in the line plot.

11 contestants took part in the spelling bee.

The median number of words spelled correctly is 14.

The number of contestants who spelled the greatest number of words correctly is 4.

The mode of the set of data is 15 words.

The difference between the greatest and the least number of words spelled correctly is 5.

Lesson 5.2 Median, Mode, and Range 103

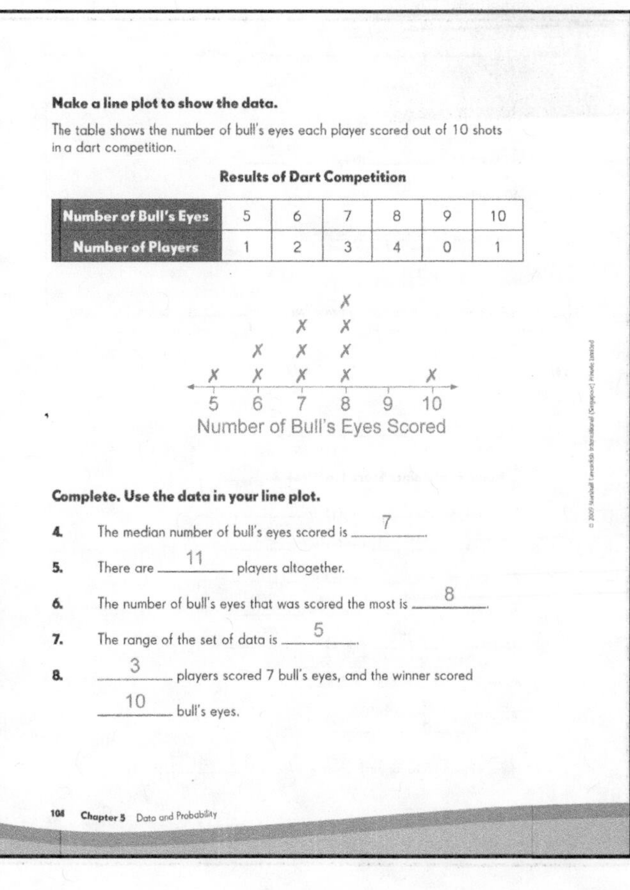

Make a line plot to show the data.

The table shows the number of bull's eyes each player scored out of 10 shots in a dart competition.

Results of Dart Competition

Number of Bull's Eyes	5	6	7	8	9	10
Number of Players	1	2	3	4	0	1

5 6 7 8 9 10
Number of Bull's Eyes Scored

Complete. Use the data in your line plot.

4. The median number of bull's eyes scored is 7.
5. There are 11 players altogether.
6. The number of bull's eyes that was scored the most is 8.
7. The range of the set of data is 5.
8. 3 players scored 7 bull's eyes, and the winner scored 10 bull's eyes.

104 Chapter 5 Data and Probability

Chapter 5

Name: ______________________ Date: ______________

Complete the table based on the information given.

A number cube has six faces numbered 1 to 6. John tossed two number cubes several times and added the numbers each time.

Sum of the Number Cubes

Total	Tally	Number of Times
2	/	1
3		0
4	//	2
5	/	1
6	//	2
7	////	4
8	//	2
9	/	1
10		0
11	/	1
12		0

© 2020 Marshall Cavendish International (Singapore) Private Limited

Complete. Use the data in the table.

9. John threw the two number cubes 14 times altogether.

10. Make a line plot to show the total for each toss.

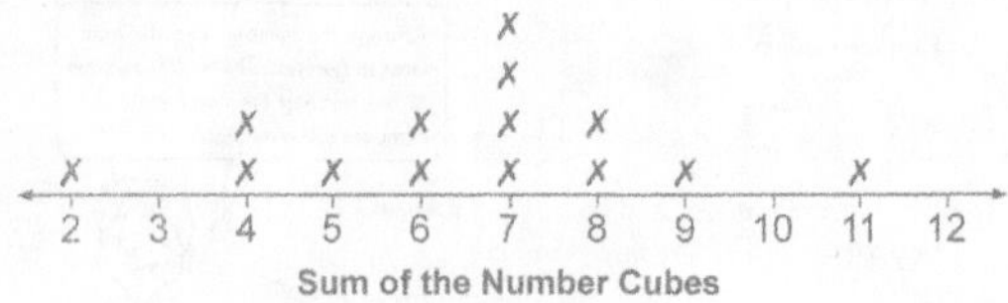

11. The median of the set of data is 7.

12. The mode of the set of data is 7.

13. The range of the set of data is 9.

Find the mean of each set of data.

Example

Haley made a line plot to show the number of points she scored in a computer math game over three weeks.

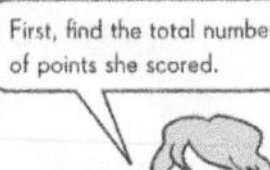

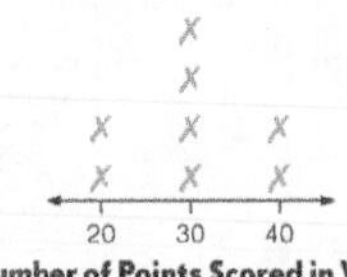

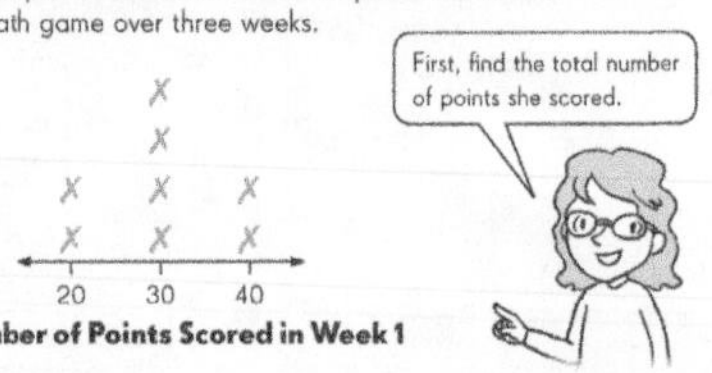

Number of Points Scored in Week 1

© 2020 Marshall Cavendish International (Singapore) Private Limited

Name: ______________________ Date: ______________

20 points × 2 times = 40

30 points × 4 times = 120

40 points × 2 times = 80

Mean = $\frac{\text{Total number of points scored}}{\text{Number of times played}}$

$= \frac{40 + 120 + 80}{2 + 4 + 2} = \frac{240}{8} = 30$

Haley's mean score for each game in Week 1 is 30 points.

14.

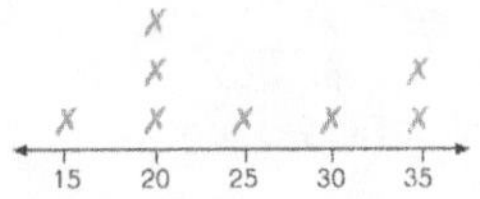

X at 15: 1; 20: 3; 25: 1; 30: 1; 35: 2

15 20 25 30 35

Number of Points Scored in Week 2

15 points × 1 time(s) = 15

20 points × 3 time(s) = 60

25 points × 1 time(s) = 25

30 points × 1 time(s) = 30

35 points × 2 time(s) = 70

Mean = $\frac{15 + 60 + 25 + 30 + 70}{1 + 3 + 1 + 1 + 2}$

$= \frac{200}{8} = 25$

Haley's mean score for each game in Week 2 is 25 points.

© 2020 Marshall Cavendish International (Singapore) Private Limited

Find the mean of the set of data.

15.

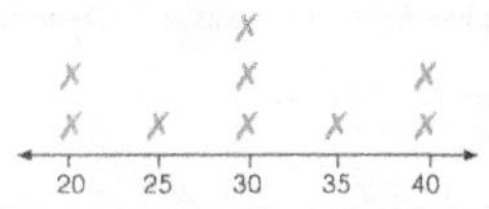

20 25 30 35 40

Number of Points Scored in Week 3

20 points × 2 time(s) = 40

25 points × 1 time(s) = 25

30 points × 3 time(s) = 90

35 points × 1 time(s) = 35

40 points × 2 time(s) = 80

Mean = $\frac{40 + 25 + 90 + 35 + 80}{2 + 1 + 3 + 1 + 2}$

$= \frac{270}{9}$

$= 30$

Haley's mean score for each game in Week 3 is 30 points.

16. Compare the line plots for Weeks 2 and 3. Can you tell which data set has a greater mean just by looking at the line plots? What part of the line plot makes you think that?

The line plot for Week 3 has a greater mean, because it has more Xs on the higher end of the number line.

© 2020 Marshall Cavendish International (Singapore) Private Limited

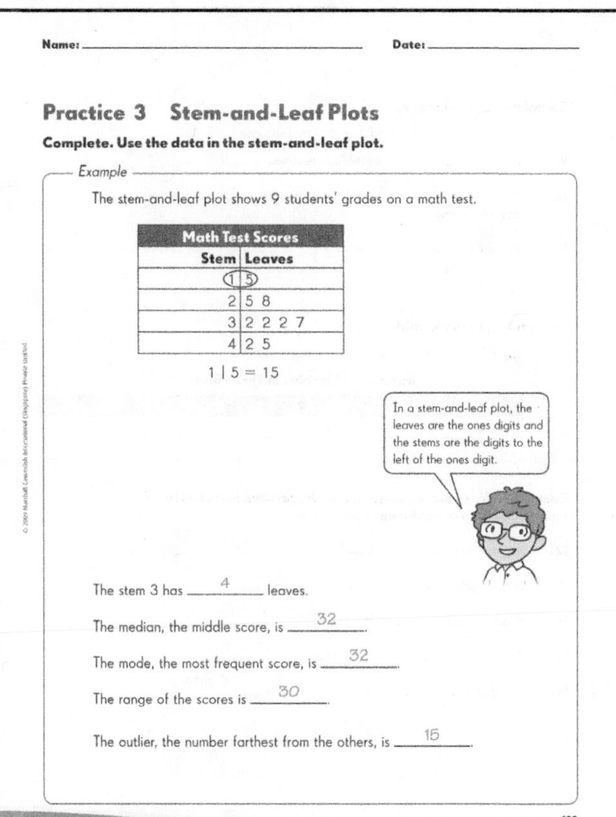

Name: ____________ Date: ____________

Practice 3 Stem-and-Leaf Plots

Complete. Use the data in the stem-and-leaf plot.

Example

The stem-and-leaf plot shows 9 students' grades on a math test.

Math Test Scores	
Stem	**Leaves**
1	5
2	5 8
3	2 2 2 7
4	2 5

1 | 5 = 15

In a stem-and-leaf plot, the leaves are the ones digits and the stems are the digits to the left of the ones digit.

The stem 3 has 4 leaves.

The median, the middle score, is 32.

The mode, the most frequent score, is 32.

The range of the scores is 30.

The outlier, the number farthest from the others, is 15.

Lesson 5.3 Stem-and-Leaf Plots 109

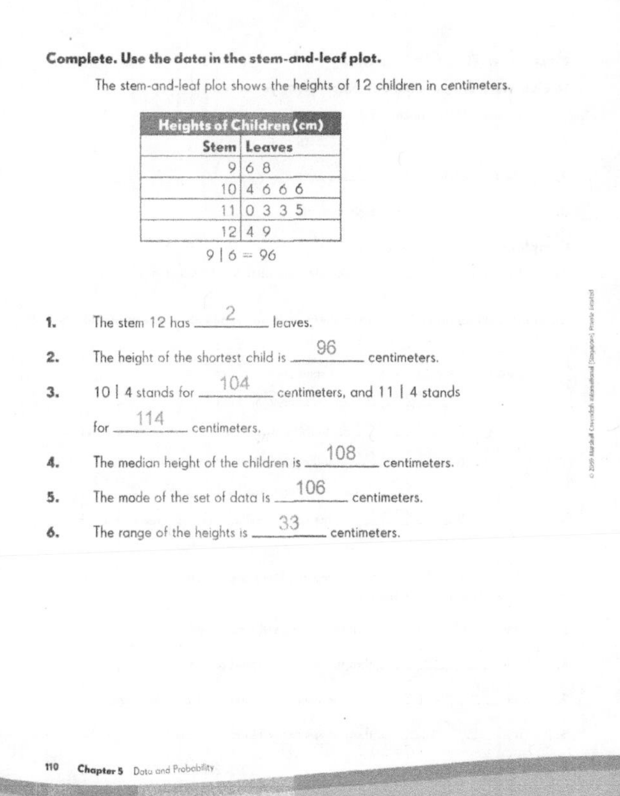

Complete. Use the data in the stem-and-leaf plot.

The stem-and-leaf plot shows the heights of 12 children in centimeters.

Heights of Children (cm)	
Stem	**Leaves**
9	6 8
10	4 6 6 6
11	0 3 3 5
12	4 9

9 | 6 = 96

1. The stem 12 has 2 leaves.
2. The height of the shortest child is 96 centimeters.
3. 10 | 4 stands for 104 centimeters, and 11 | 4 stands for 114 centimeters.
4. The median height of the children is 108 centimeters.
5. The mode of the set of data is 106 centimeters.
6. The range of the heights is 33 centimeters.

110 Chapter 5 Data and Probability

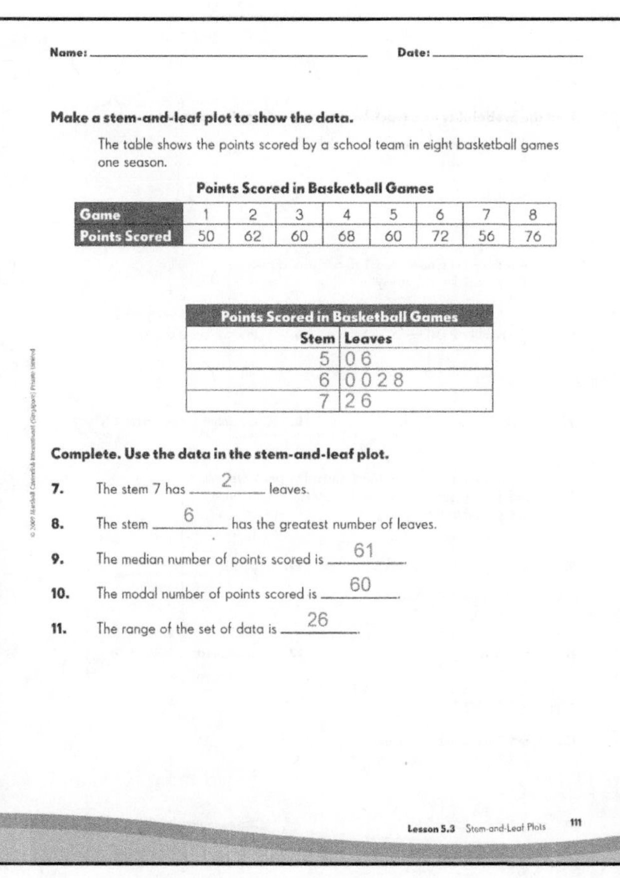

Name: ____________ Date: ____________

Make a stem-and-leaf plot to show the data.

The table shows the points scored by a school team in eight basketball games one season.

Points Scored in Basketball Games

Game	1	2	3	4	5	6	7	8
Points Scored	50	62	60	68	60	72	56	76

Points Scored in Basketball Games	
Stem	**Leaves**
5	0 6
6	0 0 2 8
7	2 6

Complete. Use the data in the stem-and-leaf plot.

7. The stem 7 has 2 leaves.
8. The stem 6 has the greatest number of leaves.
9. The median number of points scored is 61.
10. The modal number of points scored is 60.
11. The range of the set of data is 26.

Lesson 5.3 Stem-and-Leaf Plots 111

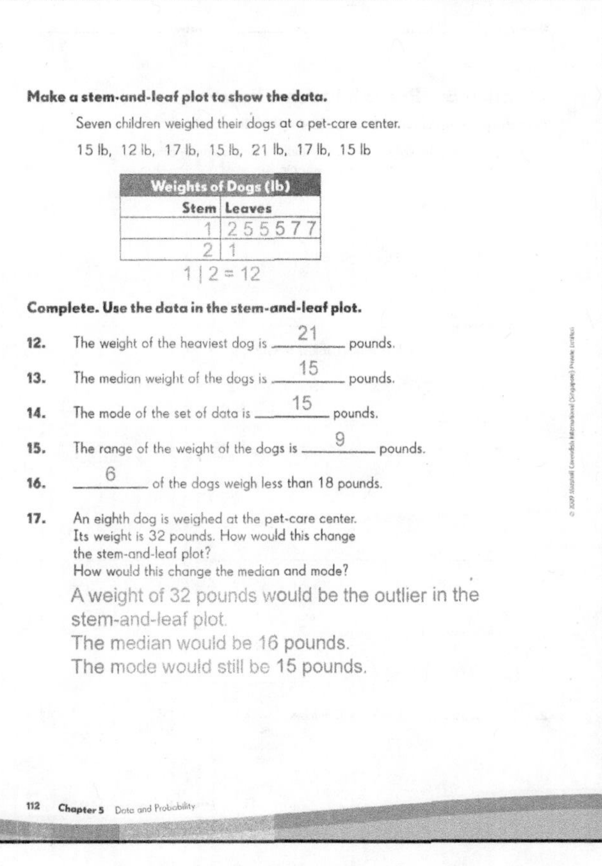

Make a stem-and-leaf plot to show the data.

Seven children weighed their dogs at a pet-care center.

15 lb, 12 lb, 17 lb, 15 lb, 21 lb, 17 lb, 15 lb

Weights of Dogs (lb)	
Stem	**Leaves**
1	2 5 5 5 7 7
2	1

1 | 2 = 12

Complete. Use the data in the stem-and-leaf plot.

12. The weight of the heaviest dog is 21 pounds.
13. The median weight of the dogs is 15 pounds.
14. The mode of the set of data is 15 pounds.
15. The range of the weight of the dogs is 9 pounds.
16. 6 of the dogs weigh less than 18 pounds.
17. An eighth dog is weighed at the pet-care center. Its weight is 32 pounds. How would this change the stem-and-leaf plot? How would this change the median and mode?

A weight of 32 pounds would be the outlier in the stem-and-leaf plot.
The median would be 16 pounds.
The mode would still be 15 pounds.

112 Chapter 5 Data and Probability

Chapter 5

Name: ______________________ Date: ______________

Practice 4 Outcomes

Decide which are possible outcomes. Write *yes* or *no*.

A coin is tossed once.

1. The coin lands on heads. Yes
2. The coin lands on tails. Yes
3. The coin lands on both heads and tails. No

Complete.

4. There are 2 possible outcomes when you toss a coin.

Complete. Write *more likely, less likely, certain, impossible,* or *equally likely*.

Example

Look at the spinner. Suppose it is spun once.

It is more likely that the spinner will land on red.

It is equally likely that the spinner will land on green or on purple.

It is impossible that the spinner will land on yellow.

It is less likely that the spinner will land on green.

It is certain that the spinner will land on red, green, or purple.

A spinner is divided into four equal parts. The parts are red, blue, yellow, and green. The spinner is spun once.

5. It is less likely that the spinner will land on red.
6. It is certain that the spinner will land on red, blue, yellow, or green.
7. It is equally likely that the spinner will land on blue or on green.
8. It is impossible that the spinner will land on purple.

Complete each sentence.

A number cube numbered 1 to 6 is tossed once.

9. There are 6 possible outcomes.
10. The number cube lands with an even number on top. There are 3 possible outcomes.
11. The number cube lands with a number less than 3 on top. There are 2 possible outcomes.

Study the data in the table.

Three bags each contain eight colored marbles.

Number of Marbles in Three Bags

Color of Marbles	Bag A	Bag B	Bag C
Green	4	6	8
Red	4	2	0

Complete. Write *more likely, less likely, certain, impossible,* or *equally likely* to describe each outcome.

12. A green marble is drawn from Bag B. More likely
13. A red marble is drawn from Bag B. Less likely
14. A green marble is drawn from Bag C. Certain
15. A red marble is drawn from Bag C. Impossible
16. A red or green marble is drawn from Bag B. Certain

Name: ______________________ Date: ______________

Practice 5 Probability as a Fraction

Find the probability as a fraction in simplest form.

Jake spins the spinner once. He wants to land on these numbers. What is the probability of a favorable outcome?

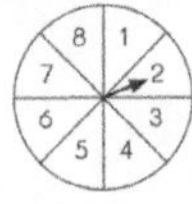

Example

He wants to land on a number less than 3.

There are 2 favorable outcomes: 1 and 2

There are 8 possible outcomes: 1, 2, 3, 4, 5, 6, 7, and 8

$$\text{Probability of a favorable outcome} = \frac{\text{Number of favorable outcomes}}{\text{Number of possible outcomes}} = \frac{2}{8} = \frac{1}{4}$$

1. He wants to land on the number 7. $\frac{1}{8}$
2. He wants to land on an odd number. 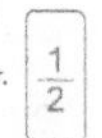 $\frac{1}{2}$

Find the probability as a fraction in simplest form for each outcome.

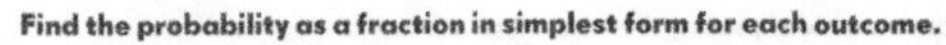

A coin is tossed once. The probability of getting

3. heads is $\frac{1}{2}$.
4. tails is $\frac{1}{2}$.

A number cube numbered 1 to 6 is tossed once. The probability of getting

5. the number 2 is $\frac{1}{6}$.
6. the number 0 is 0.
7. an even number is $\frac{1}{2}$.
8. a number greater than 4 is $\frac{1}{3}$.

A circular spinner has 4 equal parts. The parts are colored red, blue, green, and yellow. The spinner is spun once. The probability of landing on

9. red is $\frac{1}{4}$.
10. blue is $\frac{1}{4}$.
11. purple is 0.
12. green, red, or yellow is $\frac{3}{4}$.
13. red, blue, green, or yellow is $\frac{4}{4}$ or 1

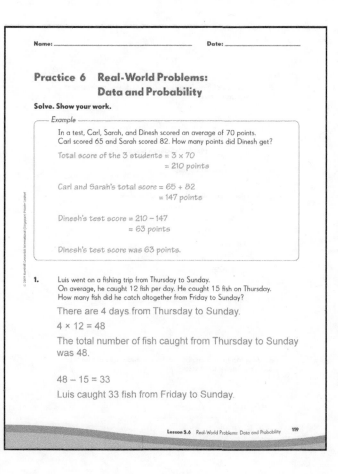

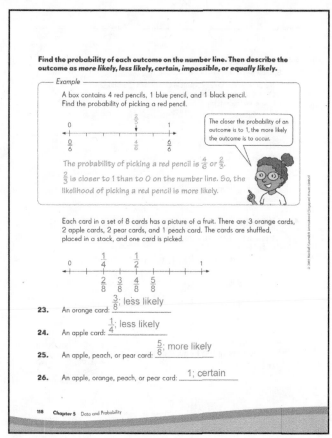

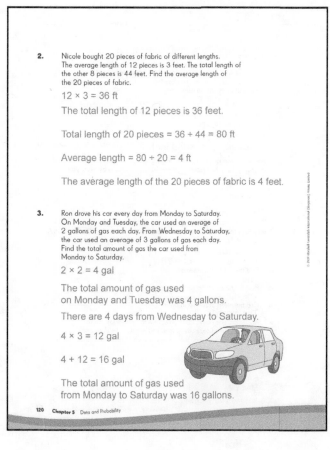

Name: ______________________ Date: ______________

Find the probability as a fraction in simplest form for each outcome.

A bag contains 10 discs numbered 1 to 10. A disc is drawn from the bag. The probability of drawing

14. the number 10 is $\frac{1}{10}$.

15. a number less than 5 is $\frac{2}{5}$.

16. an odd number is $\frac{1}{2}$.

17. a number divisible by 3 is $\frac{3}{10}$.

18. a number greater than 8 is $\frac{1}{5}$.

19. the number 12 is 0.

A bag contains 3 white marbles, 3 blue marbles, and 6 red marbles. A marble is drawn from the bag. The probability of getting

20. a white marble is $\frac{1}{4}$.

21. a blue marble is $\frac{1}{4}$.

22. Which is more likely: drawing a red marble or drawing a blue marble? Explain.

There are 6 red marbles and 3 blue marbles.

The probability of drawing a red marble is $\frac{1}{2}$, and the probability of drawing a blue marble is $\frac{1}{4}$.

Therefore, it is more likely that a red marble will be drawn.

© 2009 Marshall Cavendish International (Singapore) Private Limited

Find the probability of each outcome on the number line. Then describe the outcome as *more likely, less likely, certain, impossible,* or *equally likely.*

Example

A box contains 4 red pencils, 1 blue pencil, and 1 black pencil. Find the probability of picking a red pencil.

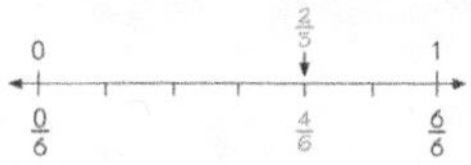

0
$\frac{2}{3}$
1
$\frac{0}{6}$
$\frac{4}{6}$
$\frac{6}{6}$

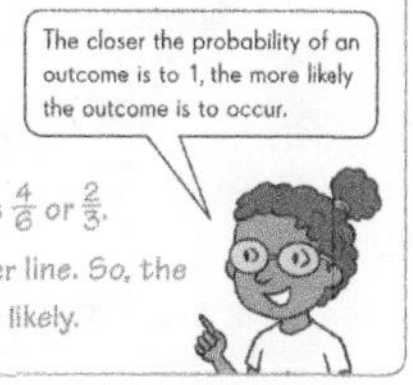

The closer the probability of an outcome is to 1, the more likely the outcome is to occur.

The probability of picking a red pencil is $\frac{4}{6}$ or $\frac{2}{3}$.

$\frac{2}{3}$ is closer to 1 than to 0 on the number line. So, the likelihood of picking a red pencil is more likely.

Each card in a set of 8 cards has a picture of a fruit. There are 3 orange cards, 2 apple cards, 2 pear cards, and 1 peach card. The cards are shuffled, placed in a stack, and one card is picked.

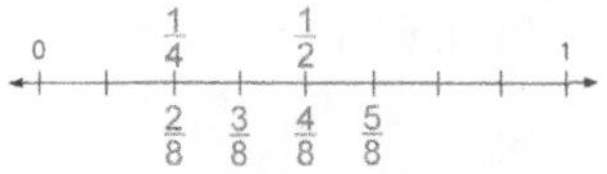

0
$\frac{1}{4}$
$\frac{1}{2}$
1
$\frac{2}{8}$
$\frac{3}{8}$
$\frac{4}{8}$
$\frac{5}{8}$

23. An orange card: $\frac{3}{8}$; less likely

24. An apple card: $\frac{1}{4}$; less likely

25. An apple, peach, or pear card: $\frac{5}{8}$; more likely

26. An apple, orange, peach, or pear card: 1; certain

© 2009 Marshall Cavendish International (Singapore) Private Limited

Name: ______________________ Date: ______________

Practice 6 Real-World Problems: Data and Probability

Solve. Show your work.

Example

In a test, Carl, Sarah, and Dinesh scored an average of 70 points. Carl scored 65 and Sarah scored 82. How many points did Dinesh get?

Total score of the 3 students = 3 × 70
= 210 points

Carl and Sarah's total score = 65 + 82
= 147 points

Dinesh's test score = 210 − 147
= 63 points

Dinesh's test score was 63 points.

1. Luis went on a fishing trip from Thursday to Sunday. On average, he caught 12 fish per day. He caught 15 fish on Thursday. How many fish did he catch altogether from Friday to Sunday?

There are 4 days from Thursday to Sunday.

4 × 12 = 48

The total number of fish caught from Thursday to Sunday was 48.

48 − 15 = 33

Luis caught 33 fish from Friday to Sunday.

© 2009 Marshall Cavendish International (Singapore) Private Limited

2. Nicole bought 20 pieces of fabric of different lengths. The average length of 12 pieces is 3 feet. The total length of the other 8 pieces is 44 feet. Find the average length of the 20 pieces of fabric.

12 × 3 = 36 ft

The total length of 12 pieces is 36 feet.

Total length of 20 pieces = 36 + 44 = 80 ft

Average length = 80 ÷ 20 = 4 ft

The average length of the 20 pieces of fabric is 4 feet.

3. Ron drove his car every day from Monday to Saturday. On Monday and Tuesday, the car used an average of 2 gallons of gas each day. From Wednesday to Saturday, the car used an average of 3 gallons of gas each day. Find the total amount of gas the car used from Monday to Saturday.

2 × 2 = 4 gal

The total amount of gas used on Monday and Tuesday was 4 gallons.

There are 4 days from Wednesday to Saturday.

4 × 3 = 12 gal

4 + 12 = 16 gal

The total amount of gas used from Monday to Saturday was 16 gallons.

© 2009 Marshall Cavendish International (Singapore) Private Limited

Chapter 5

Name: ______________________ Date: ______________

Solve. Show your work. Use bar models to help you.

Example

The average number of students in Class A and Class B is 24.
Class A has 4 more students than Class B.
How many students are there in each class?

Total number of students in both classes = 2 x 24 = 48
48 − 4 = 44
44 ÷ 2 = 22 students
22 + 4 = 26 students

Class A, Class B, 48, 4

Class A has 26 students, and Class B has 22 students.

4. Mrs. Johnson buys 2 chickens. The average weight of the 2 chickens is 4 pounds. One of the chickens is 2 pounds heavier than the other. What is the weight of the heavier chicken?

Total weight of 2 chickens = 2 x 4 = 8 lb

8 − 2 = 6 lb

6 ÷ 2 = 3 lb

3 + 2 = 5 lb

8 lb, 2 lb

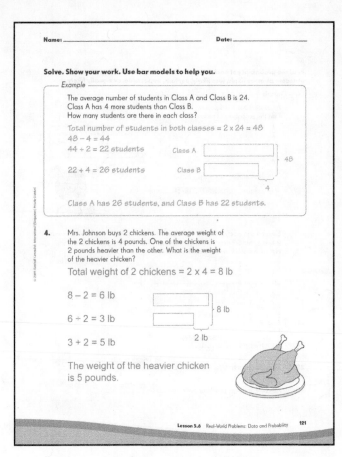

The weight of the heavier chicken is 5 pounds.

© 2009 Marshall Cavendish International (Singapore) Private Limited

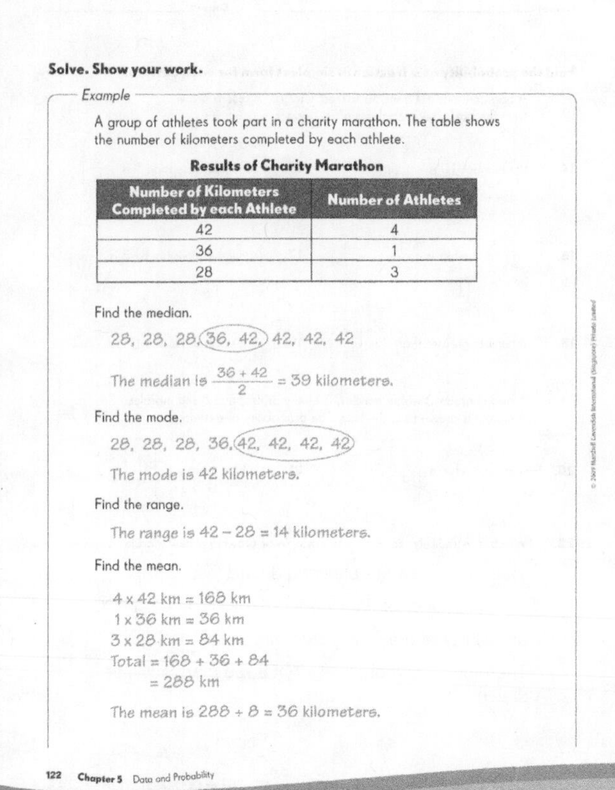

Solve. Show your work.

Example

A group of athletes took part in a charity marathon. The table shows the number of kilometers completed by each athlete.

Results of Charity Marathon

Number of Kilometers Completed by each Athlete	Number of Athletes
42	4
36	1
28	3

Find the median.

28, 28, 28, 36, 42, 42, 42, 42

The median is $\frac{36 + 42}{2}$ = 39 kilometers.

Find the mode.

28, 28, 28, 36, 42, 42, 42, 42

The mode is 42 kilometers.

Find the range.

The range is 42 − 28 = 14 kilometers.

Find the mean.

4 x 42 km = 168 km
1 x 36 km = 36 km
3 x 28 km = 84 km
Total = 168 + 36 + 84
= 288 km

The mean is 288 ÷ 8 = 36 kilometers.

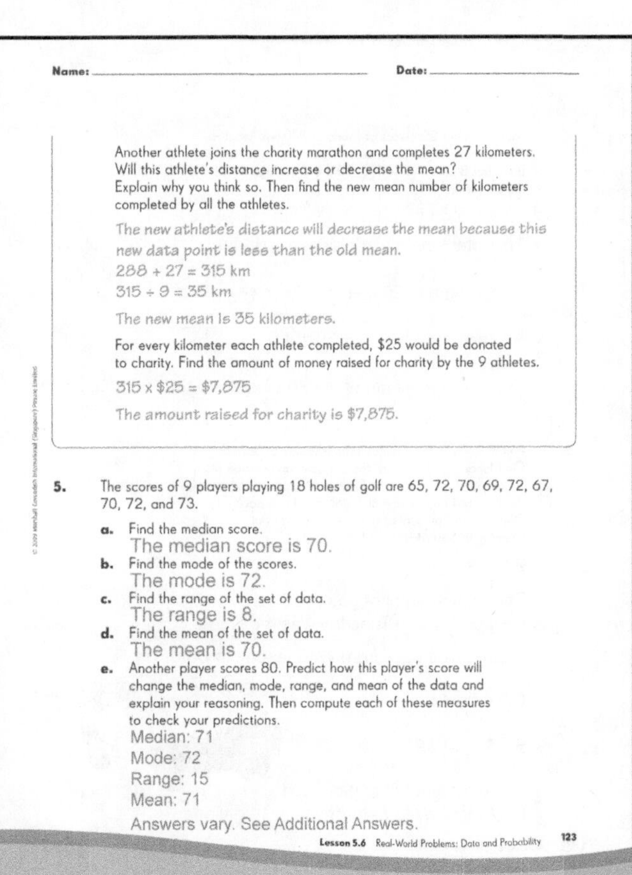

Name: ______________________ Date: ______________

Another athlete joins the charity marathon and completes 27 kilometers. Will this athlete's distance increase or decrease the mean? Explain why you think so. Then find the new mean number of kilometers completed by all the athletes.

The new athlete's distance will decrease the mean because this new data point is less than the old mean.
288 + 27 = 315 km
315 ÷ 9 = 35 km

The new mean is 35 kilometers.

For every kilometer each athlete completed, $25 would be donated to charity. Find the amount of money raised for charity by the 9 athletes.

315 x $25 = $7,875

The amount raised for charity is $7,875.

5. The scores of 9 players playing 18 holes of golf are 65, 72, 70, 69, 72, 67, 70, 72, and 73.

a. Find the median score.
The median score is 70.

b. Find the mode of the scores.
The mode is 72.

c. Find the range of the set of data.
The range is 8.

d. Find the mean of the set of data.
The mean is 70.

e. Another player scores 80. Predict how this player's score will change the median, mode, range, and mean of the data and explain your reasoning. Then compute each of these measures to check your predictions.
Median: 71
Mode: 72
Range: 15
Mean: 71
Answers vary. See Additional Answers.

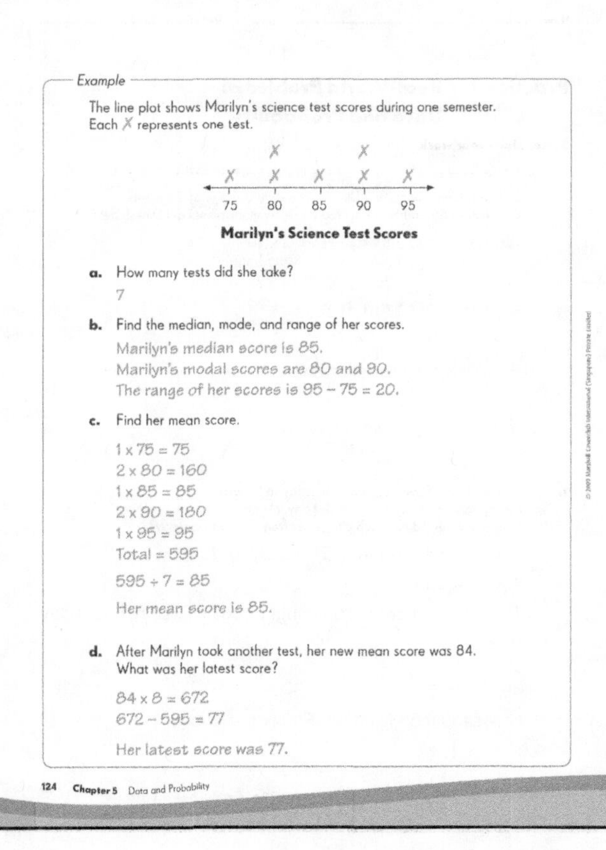

Example

The line plot shows Marilyn's science test scores during one semester. Each X represents one test.

Marilyn's Science Test Scores

a. How many tests did she take?
7

b. Find the median, mode, and range of her scores.
Marilyn's median score is 85.
Marilyn's modal scores are 80 and 90.
The range of her scores is 95 − 75 = 20.

c. Find her mean score.
1 x 75 = 75
2 x 80 = 160
1 x 85 = 85
2 x 90 = 180
1 x 95 = 95
Total = 595
595 ÷ 7 = 85
Her mean score is 85.

d. After Marilyn took another test, her new mean score was 84. What was her latest score?
84 x 8 = 672
672 − 595 = 77
Her latest score was 77.

Name: ______________________ Date: ______________

6. Kurt recorded the daily temperature highs for a science project. The results are shown in the line plot.

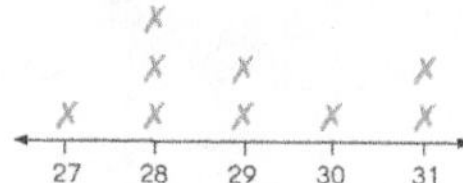

Daily Temperature Highs in °F

a. On how many days did he record the temperature?

9 days

b. What were the mean and median temperatures?

Mean: 29°F Median: 29°F

c. The temperature high on another day was included with the data. The new mean temperature changed to 30°F. What was this temperature?

39°F

d. Find the new median temperature.

29°F

© 2009 Marshall Cavendish International (Singapore) Private Limited

7. A restaurant pays its 9 employees these daily wages:
$90, $70, $100, $90, $90, $90, $100, $160, $200
Make a line plot to show the data.

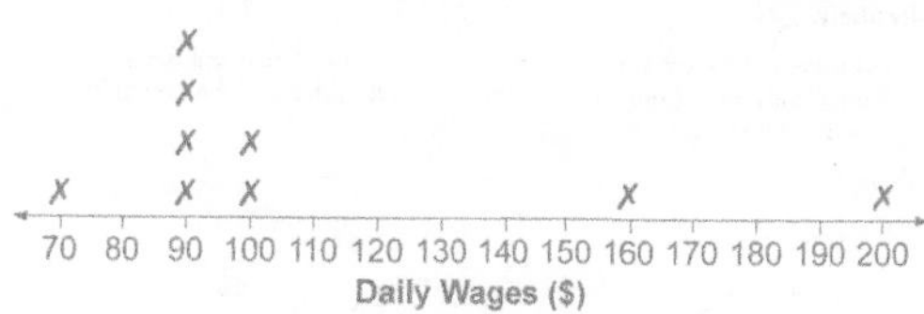

Daily Wages ($)

a. Find the mean and median of the set of wages.

$$\text{Mean} = \frac{70 + 90 + 90 + 90 + 90 + 100 + 100 + 160 + 200}{9}$$

$= \$110$

Median = $90

b. Does the mean or the median better describe what a new employee could expect to earn at this restaurant?

The median is a better description as most of the employees earn $90 or less.

c. Are there any outliers? If so, what are they?

The outliers are $160 and $200

d. How do the mean and median each change if you disregard the outliers? Now does the mean or median better represent what a new employee could expect to earn?

The outliers are $160 and $200. If these two data are not used, the new mean will be

$$\frac{70 + 90 + 90 + 90 + 90 + 100 + 100}{9} = \frac{630}{7}$$

$= 90$

The new median is 90.

If the outliers are disregarded, both the mean and the median can represent what a new employee could expect to earn.

© 2009 Marshall Cavendish International (Singapore) Private Limited

Name: ______________________ Date: ______________

Example

During a trip to the beach, 9 children collected seashells. The stem-and-leaf plot shows the number of shells each child collected.

Number of Seashells Collected	
Stem	Leaves
6	1 1 5
7	0 6 8
8	3 8
9	?

6 | 1 = 61

a. If the total number of seashells collected is 681, find the missing number. What is the outlier?

681 – 61 – 61 – 65 – 70 – 76 – 78 – 83 – 88 = 99

The missing number is 99. The outlier is 99 because it is farthest from the other numbers.

b. Find the median of the set of data.

The median is 76.

c. Find the mode of the set of data.

The mode is 61.

d. Find the range of the set of data.

99 – 61 = 38

The range is 38.

© 2009 Marshall Cavendish International (Singapore) Private Limited

8. The stem-and-leaf plot shows the weights of some bowling balls in pounds.

Weights of Bowling Balls (lb)	
Stem	Leaves
0	8 8 9
1	0 0 1 1 2 2 4 4 5 5 5 6 6 6 6

0 | 8 = 8

a. How many bowling balls are there?

18

b. Find the median, mode, and range.

The median is 13 pounds.

The mode is 16 pounds.

c. What is the least number of bowling balls needed to make the mode 14 pounds?

3

d. Find the total weight of the bowling balls in **Exercise 8.c**.

42 pounds

© 2009 Marshall Cavendish International (Singapore) Private Limited

Name: ______________________ Date: ______________

Find the probability of each outcome on a number line. Then describe the likelihood of each outcome as *more likely, less likely, certain, impossible,* or *equally likely.*

9. The weather forecast in a city is that for every week, 3 days are sunny, 2 are cloudy, and 2 are rainy. On any chosen day, describe the probability of each of these outcomes.

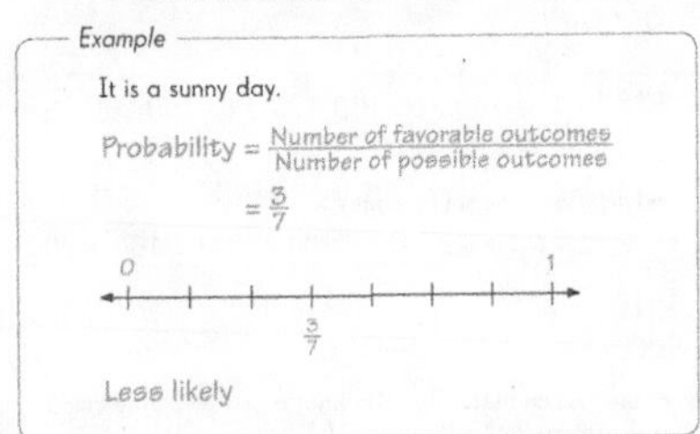

a. It is not a sunny day.

$$\text{Probability} = \frac{\text{Number of favorable outcomes}}{\text{Number of possible outcomes}}$$
$$= \frac{2+2}{7}$$
$$= \frac{4}{7}$$

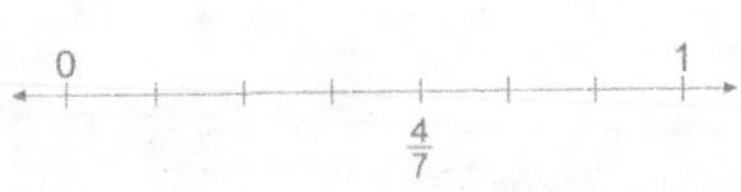

More likely

b. It is a rainy, sunny, or a cloudy day.

$$\text{Probability} = \frac{\text{Number of favorable outcomes}}{\text{Number of possible outcomes}}$$
$$= \frac{2+3+2}{7}$$
$$= \frac{7}{7}$$
$$= 1$$

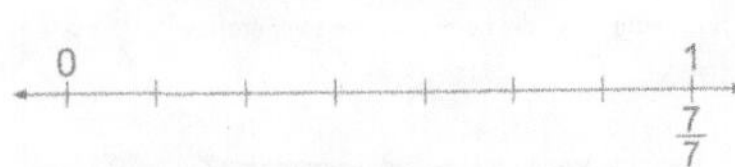

Certain

c. If today is sunny, tomorrow is rainy.

$$\text{Probability} = \frac{\text{Number of favorable outcomes}}{\text{Number of possible outcomes}}$$
$$= \frac{2}{7-1}$$
$$= \frac{2}{6}$$
$$= \frac{1}{3}$$

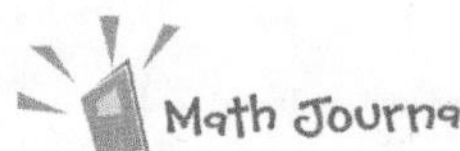

Less likely

Name: ______________________ Date: ______________

Solve.

10. In a class of 25 students, 10 are girls. The names of the students are written on cards and placed in a box. The names are chosen at random to win prizes donated by a local store.

a. What is the probability that the first student selected is a girl?

$$\text{Probability} = \frac{\text{Number of favorable outcomes}}{\text{Number of possible outcomes}}$$
$$= \frac{10}{25}$$
$$= \frac{2}{5}$$

b. What is the probability that the first student selected is a boy?

$$\text{Probability} = \frac{\text{Number of favorable outcomes}}{\text{Number of possible outcomes}}$$
$$= \frac{15}{25}$$
$$= \frac{3}{5}$$

c. If the first student selected is a girl, what is the probability that the second student selected is also a girl?

$$\text{Probability} = \frac{\text{Number of favorable outcomes}}{\text{Number of possible outcomes}}$$
$$= \frac{10-1}{25-1}$$
$$= \frac{9}{24}$$
$$= \frac{3}{8}$$

Math Journal

Write the steps to solve the problem.

Neil bought 5 books. The average price of 2 of the books is $5. The average price of the rest of the books is $4. Find the total amount of money Neil paid for the 5 books.

Step 1 Find the total cost of the first 2 books.

Step 2 Find the total cost of the remaining 3 books.

Step 3 Add the two totals to find the total amount paid for the 5 books.

Then, following your steps above, solve the problem.

Total cost of 2 books = 2 × 5
= $10

Total cost of the remaining books = 3 × 4
= $12

Total amount paid = 10 + 12
= $22

Neil paid $22 for the 5 books.

© 2009 Marshall Cavendish International (Singapore) Private Limited

Name: ______________________ Date: ______________

Put On Your Thinking Cap!

Challenging Practice

1. Michelle got an average score of 80 on two tests. What score must she get on the third test so that her average score for the three tests is the same as the average score for the first two tests?

Method 1:

Since the average score for the first two tests is 80, Michelle must score 80 on the third test to have the same average score.

Method 2:

Total score of two tests = 2 × 80
= 160

Total score of three tests = 3 × 80
= 240

240 – 160 = 80 marks

Michelle must score 80 on the third test.

Thinking skill: Identifying patterns and relationships

Strategy: Use a model

2. The line plot shows the shoe sizes of students in Ms. George's class.

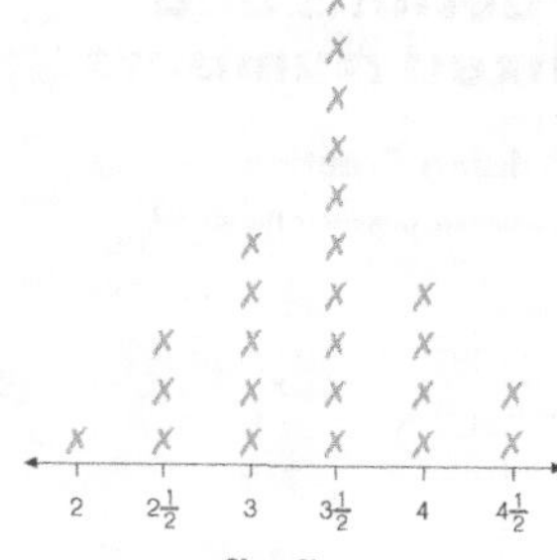

Shoe Sizes

a. How many students are in the class?
25

b. What is the mode of the set of data?
$3\frac{1}{2}$

c. How many students in the class wear a size $3\frac{1}{2}$ shoe?
10

d. Suppose you looked at 100 pairs of shoes for the grade, which includes 3 other classes. How many pairs of size $3\frac{1}{2}$ would there be? Explain your answer.

$\frac{10}{25} = \frac{40}{100}$.

There would probably be 40 pairs because there are ten students who wear size $3\frac{1}{2}$ in this class.

Thinking skill: Identifying relationships

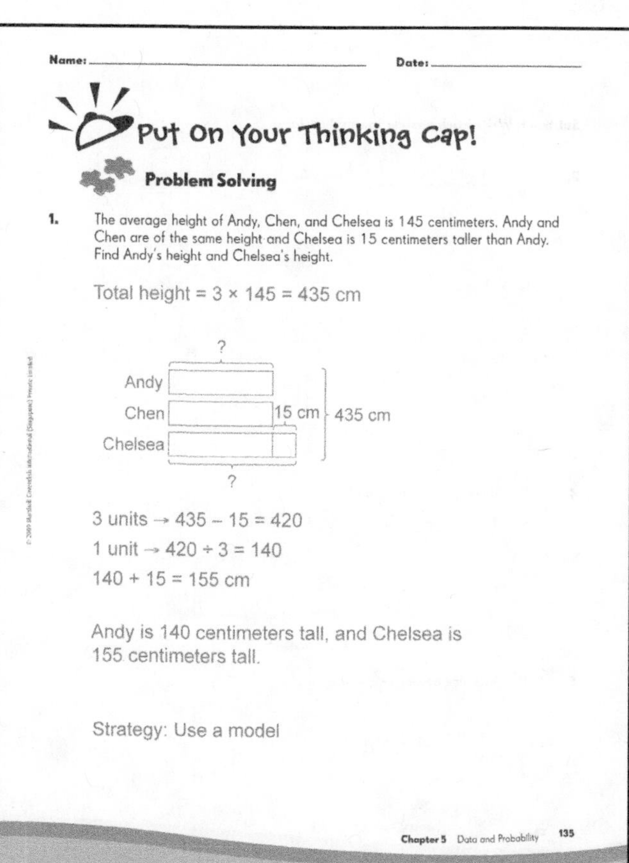

Name: ______________________ Date: ______________

Put On Your Thinking Cap!

Problem Solving

1. The average height of Andy, Chen, and Chelsea is 145 centimeters. Andy and Chen are of the same height and Chelsea is 15 centimeters taller than Andy. Find Andy's height and Chelsea's height.

Total height = 3 × 145 = 435 cm

3 units → 435 – 15 = 420

1 unit → 420 ÷ 3 = 140

140 + 15 = 155 cm

Andy is 140 centimeters tall, and Chelsea is 155 centimeters tall.

Strategy: Use a model

2. Eduardo has 3 times as many stamps as Sally. The average number of stamps they have is 450. How many more stamps does Eduardo have than Sally?

Total number of stamps = 2 × 450
= 900

Eduardo [| |] 900
Sally [ ]
?

4 units → 900

1 unit → 900 ÷ 4 = 225

2 units → 2 × 225 = 450

Eduardo owns 450 more stamps than Sally.

3. Bag A and Bag B each contain 2 marbles — 1 white and 1 red. Troy picks 1 marble from Bag A and 1 from Bag B. What is the probability that the following are picked?

a. 2 white marbles
$\frac{1}{4}$

b. 1 red and 1 white marble
$\frac{1}{2}$

Possible outcomes:
Red - White
Red - Red
White - Red
White - White

Strategy: Use a diagram / model,
Make a systematic list

© 2009 Marshall Cavendish International (Singapore) Private Limited

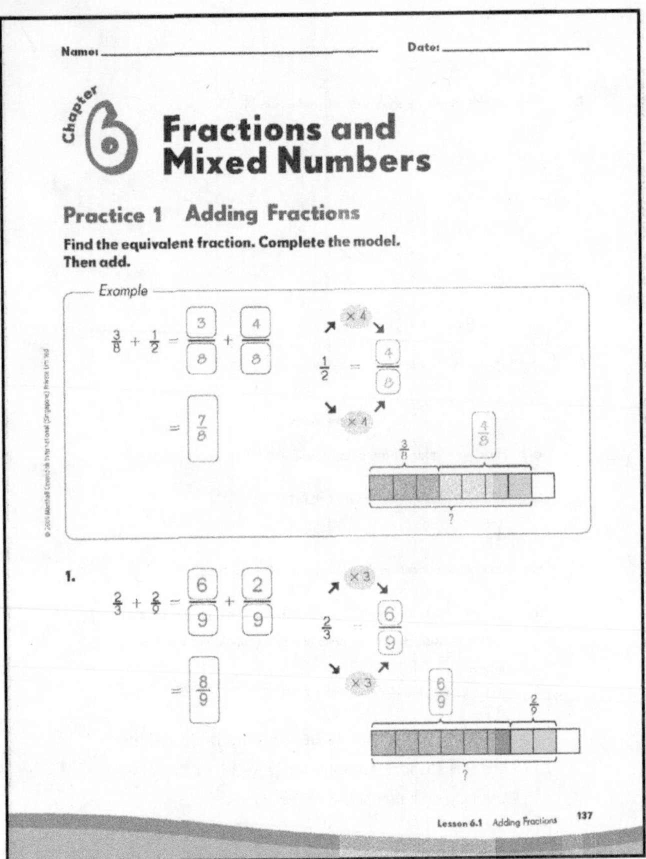

Name: ______________________ Date: ______________

Chapter 6
Fractions and Mixed Numbers

Practice 1 Adding Fractions

Find the equivalent fraction. Complete the model. Then add.

Example

$\frac{3}{8} + \frac{1}{2} = \frac{3}{8} + \frac{4}{8}$

$= \frac{7}{8}$

$\frac{1}{2} = \frac{4}{8}$ (×4)

1. $\frac{2}{3} + \frac{2}{9} = \frac{6}{9} + \frac{2}{9}$

$= \frac{8}{9}$

$\frac{2}{3} = \frac{6}{9}$ (×3)

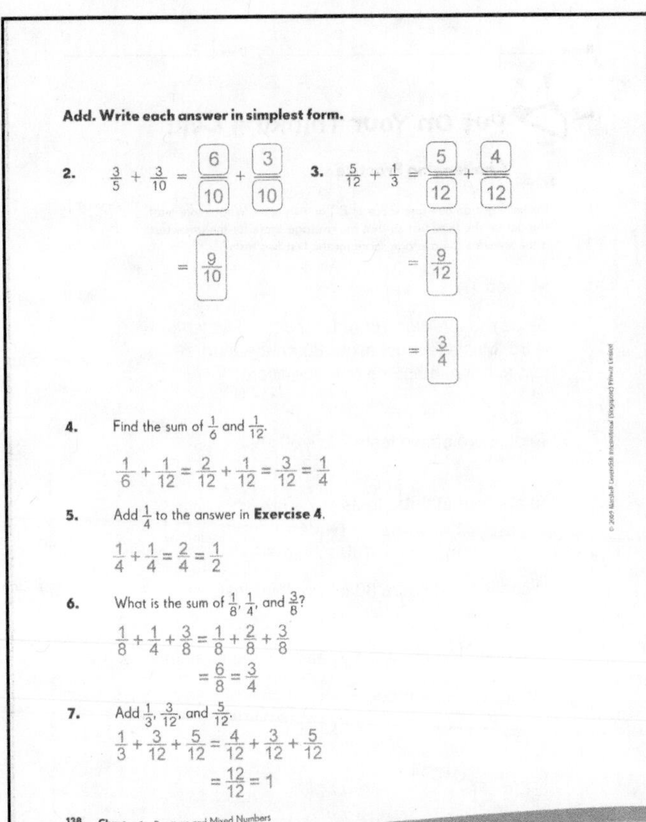

Add. Write each answer in simplest form.

2. $\frac{3}{5} + \frac{3}{10} = \frac{6}{10} + \frac{3}{10}$

$= \frac{9}{10}$

3. $\frac{5}{12} + \frac{1}{3} = \frac{5}{12} + \frac{4}{12}$

$= \frac{9}{12}$

$= \frac{3}{4}$

4. Find the sum of $\frac{1}{6}$ and $\frac{1}{12}$.

$\frac{1}{6} + \frac{1}{12} = \frac{2}{12} + \frac{1}{12} = \frac{3}{12} = \frac{1}{4}$

5. Add $\frac{1}{4}$ to the answer in **Exercise 4**.

$\frac{1}{4} + \frac{1}{4} = \frac{2}{4} = \frac{1}{2}$

6. What is the sum of $\frac{1}{8}$, $\frac{1}{4}$, and $\frac{3}{8}$?

$\frac{1}{8} + \frac{1}{4} + \frac{3}{8} = \frac{1}{8} + \frac{2}{8} + \frac{3}{8}$

$= \frac{6}{8} = \frac{3}{4}$

7. Add $\frac{1}{3}$, $\frac{3}{12}$, and $\frac{5}{12}$.

$\frac{1}{3} + \frac{3}{12} + \frac{5}{12} = \frac{4}{12} + \frac{3}{12} + \frac{5}{12}$

$= \frac{12}{12} = 1$

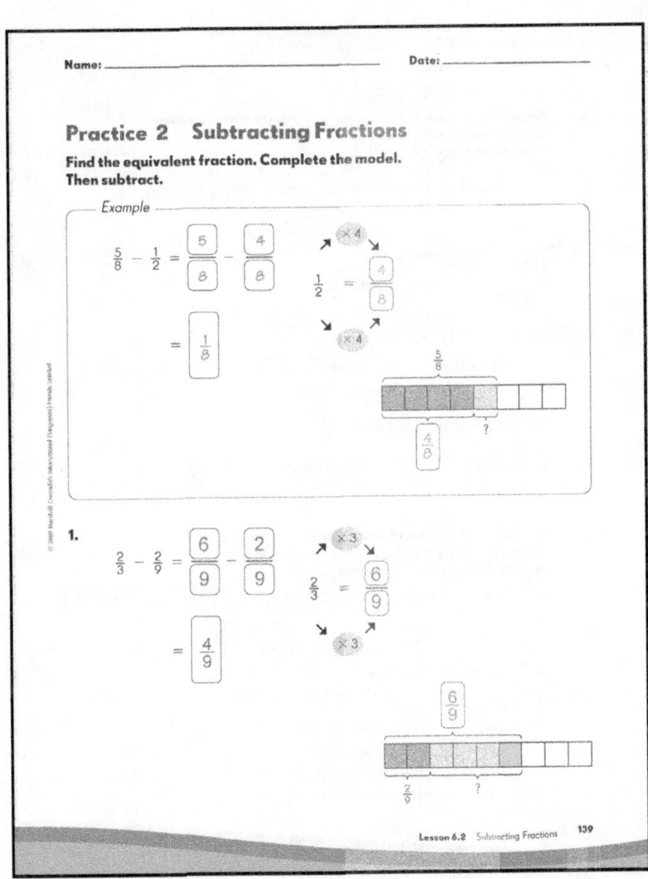

Name: ______________________ Date: ______________

Practice 2 Subtracting Fractions

Find the equivalent fraction. Complete the model. Then subtract.

Example

$\frac{5}{8} - \frac{1}{2} = \frac{5}{8} - \frac{4}{8}$

$= \frac{1}{8}$

$\frac{1}{2} = \frac{4}{8}$ (×4)

1. $\frac{2}{3} - \frac{2}{9} = \frac{6}{9} - \frac{2}{9}$

$= \frac{4}{9}$

$\frac{2}{3} = \frac{6}{9}$ (×3)

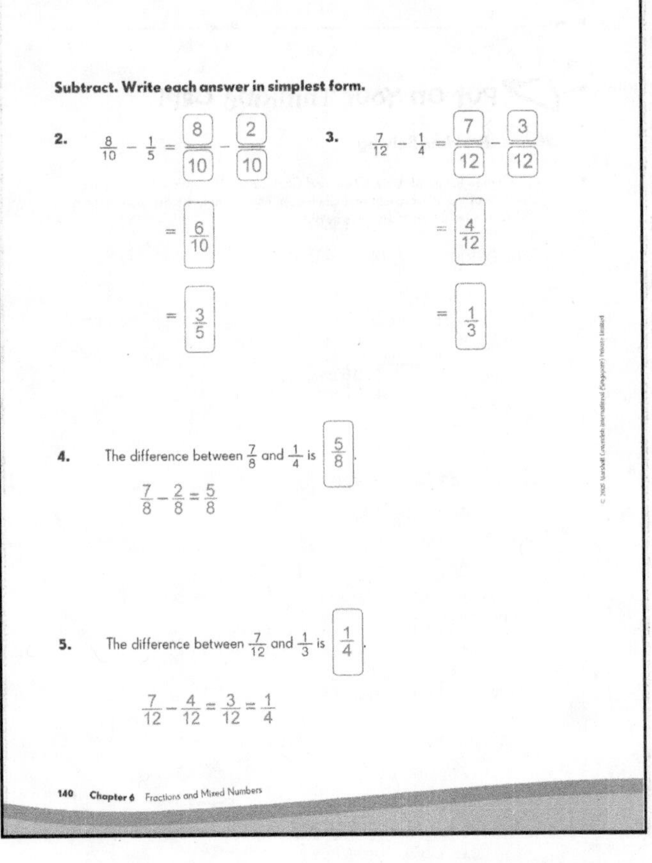

Subtract. Write each answer in simplest form.

2. $\frac{8}{10} - \frac{1}{5} = \frac{8}{10} - \frac{2}{10}$

$= \frac{6}{10}$

$= \frac{3}{5}$

3. $\frac{7}{12} - \frac{1}{4} = \frac{7}{12} - \frac{3}{12}$

$= \frac{4}{12}$

$= \frac{1}{3}$

4. The difference between $\frac{7}{8}$ and $\frac{1}{4}$ is $\frac{5}{8}$.

$\frac{7}{8} - \frac{2}{8} = \frac{5}{8}$

5. The difference between $\frac{7}{12}$ and $\frac{1}{3}$ is $\frac{1}{4}$.

$\frac{7}{12} - \frac{4}{12} = \frac{3}{12} = \frac{1}{4}$

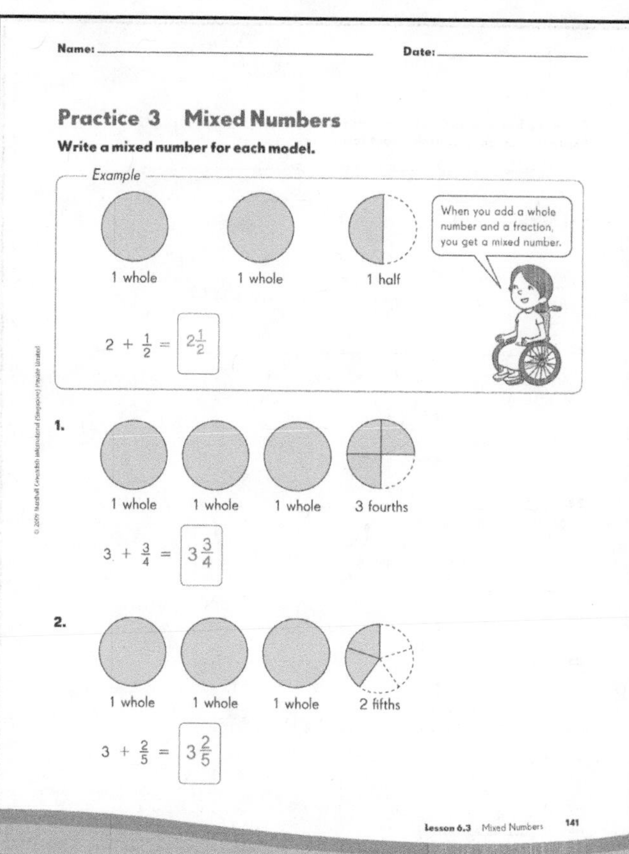

Name: ________________ Date: ________________

Practice 3 Mixed Numbers

Write a mixed number for each model.

Example

When you add a whole number and a fraction, you get a mixed number.

1 whole 1 whole 1 half

$2 + \frac{1}{2} = 2\frac{1}{2}$

1. 1 whole 1 whole 1 whole 3 fourths

$3 + \frac{3}{4} = 3\frac{3}{4}$

2. 1 whole 1 whole 1 whole 2 fifths

$3 + \frac{2}{5} = 3\frac{2}{5}$

© 2009 Marshall Cavendish International (Singapore) Private Limited

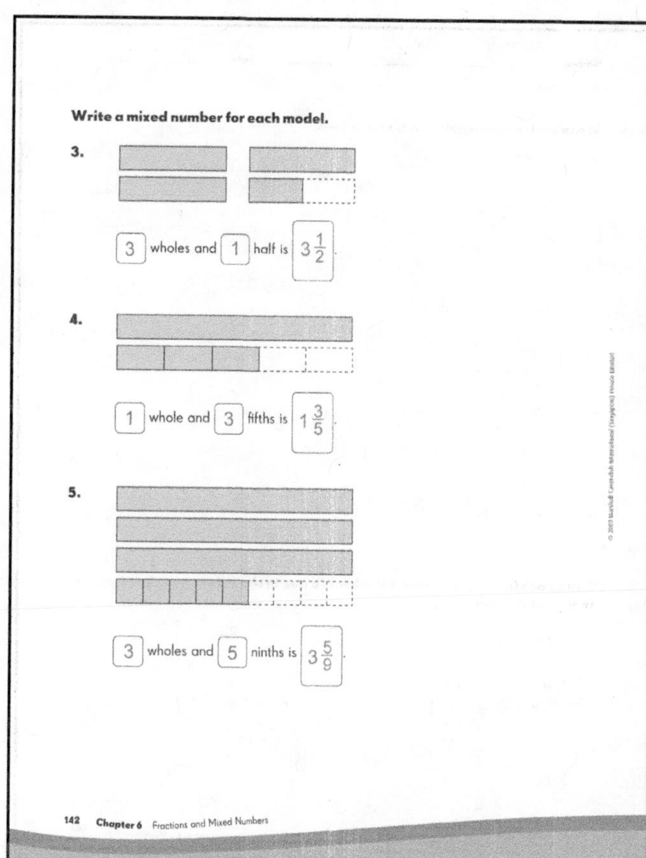

Write a mixed number for each model.

3. 3 wholes and 1 half is $3\frac{1}{2}$.

4. 1 whole and 3 fifths is $1\frac{3}{5}$.

5. 3 wholes and 5 ninths is $3\frac{5}{9}$.

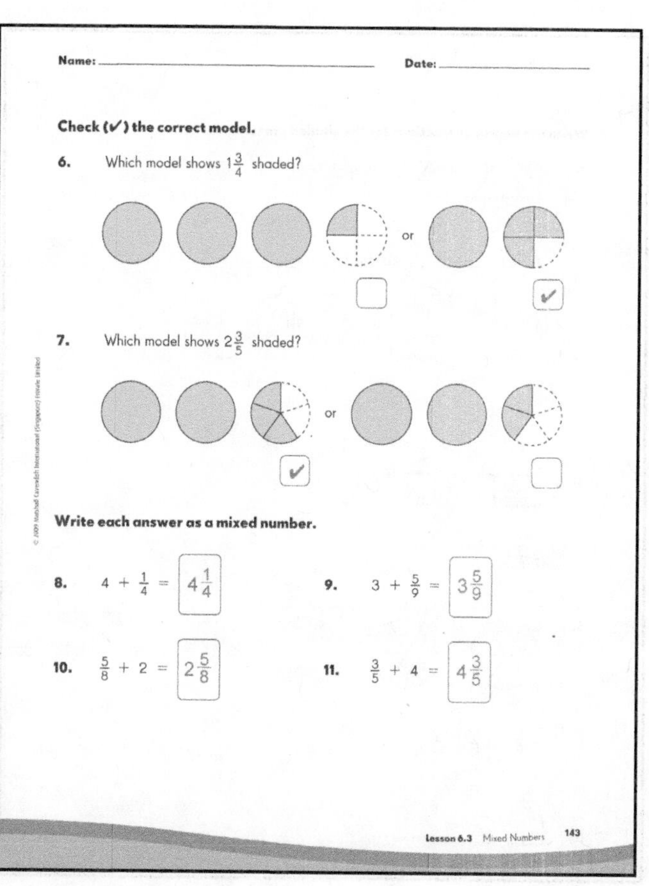

Name: ________________ Date: ________________

Check (✓) the correct model.

6. Which model shows $1\frac{3}{4}$ shaded?

☐ or ✓

7. Which model shows $2\frac{3}{5}$ shaded?

✓ or ☐

Write each answer as a mixed number.

8. $4 + \frac{1}{4} = 4\frac{1}{4}$

9. $3 + \frac{5}{9} = 3\frac{5}{9}$

10. $\frac{5}{8} + 2 = 2\frac{5}{8}$

11. $\frac{3}{5} + 4 = 4\frac{3}{5}$

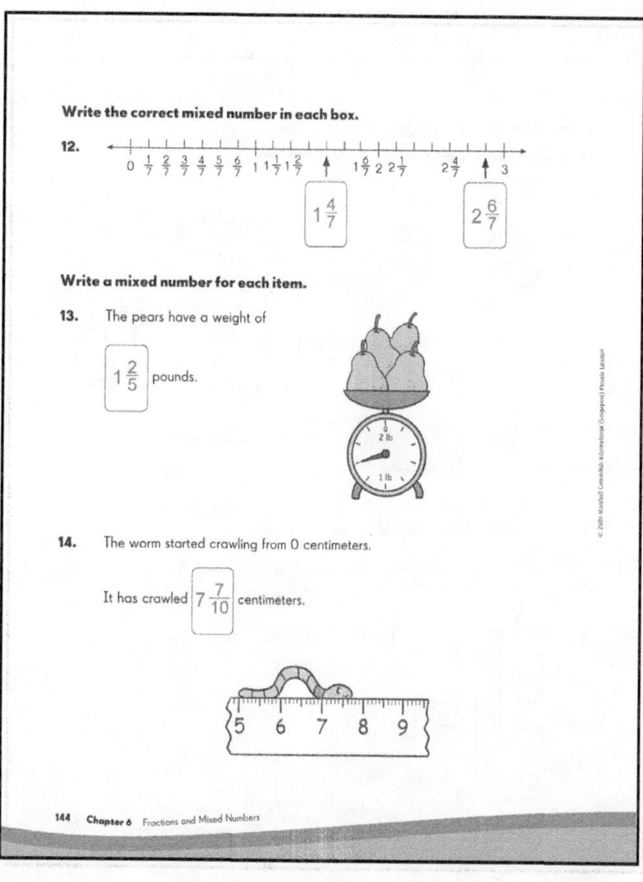

Write the correct mixed number in each box.

12.

$1\frac{4}{7}$ $2\frac{6}{7}$

Write a mixed number for each item.

13. The pears have a weight of $1\frac{2}{5}$ pounds.

14. The worm started crawling from 0 centimeters.

It has crawled $7\frac{7}{10}$ centimeters.

Name: ________________ Date: ________________

Write each mixed number in simplest form.

Example

$1\frac{2}{4} = \boxed{1\frac{1}{2}}$

15. $2\frac{4}{6} = \boxed{2\frac{2}{3}}$

16. $3\frac{4}{8} = \boxed{3\frac{1}{2}}$

17. $5\frac{6}{9} = \boxed{5\frac{2}{3}}$

18. $6\frac{4}{12} = \boxed{6\frac{1}{3}}$

19. $4\frac{3}{6} = \boxed{4\frac{1}{2}}$

Write each fraction and mixed number in a box to show its correct location on the number line.

20. $1\frac{1}{2}$ 21. $\frac{1}{2}$ 22. $1\frac{3}{4}$

Number line: 0, $\frac{1}{4}$, $\frac{3}{4}$, 1, $1\frac{1}{4}$, 2

$\boxed{\frac{1}{2}}$ $\boxed{1\frac{1}{2}}$ $\boxed{1\frac{3}{4}}$

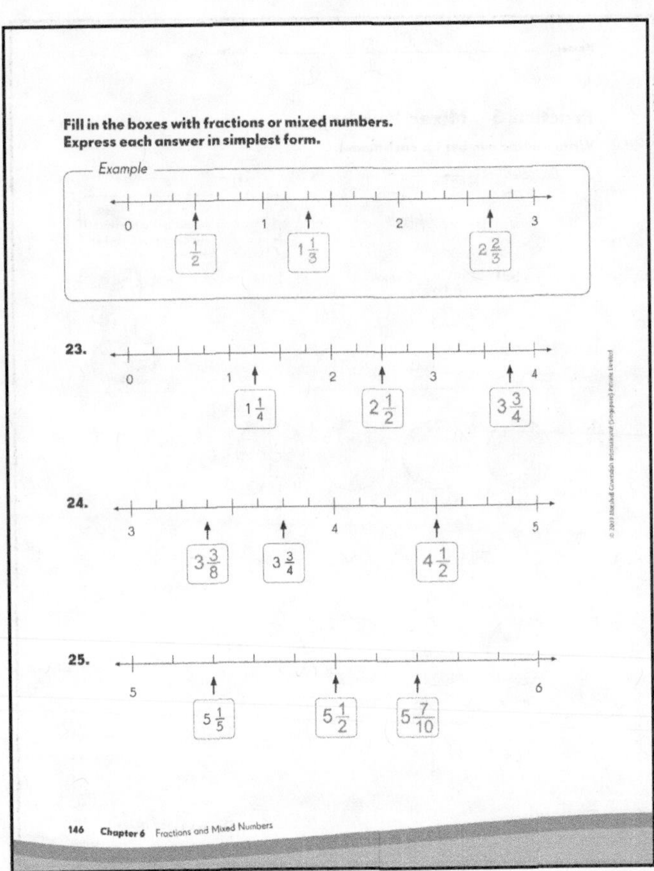

Fill in the boxes with fractions or mixed numbers. Express each answer in simplest form.

Example

0, 1, 2, 3: $\boxed{\frac{1}{2}}$ $\boxed{1\frac{1}{3}}$ $\boxed{2\frac{2}{3}}$

23. 0, 1, 2, 3, 4: $\boxed{1\frac{1}{4}}$ $\boxed{2\frac{1}{2}}$ $\boxed{3\frac{3}{4}}$

24. 3, 4, 5: $\boxed{3\frac{3}{8}}$ $\boxed{3\frac{3}{4}}$ $\boxed{4\frac{1}{2}}$

25. 5, 6: $\boxed{5\frac{1}{5}}$ $\boxed{5\frac{1}{2}}$ $\boxed{5\frac{7}{10}}$

146 Chapter 6 Fractions and Mixed Numbers

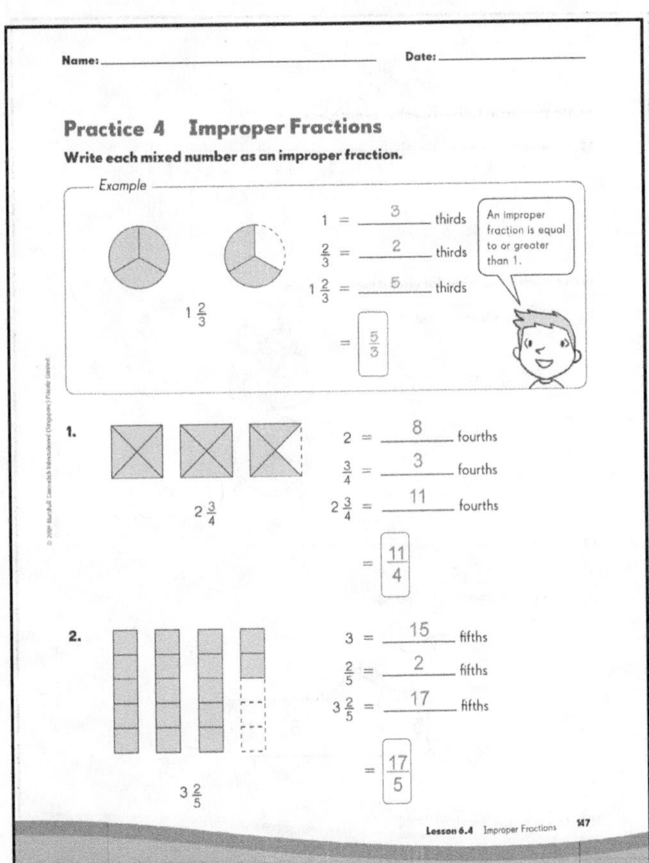

Name: ________________ Date: ________________

Practice 4 Improper Fractions

Write each mixed number as an improper fraction.

Example

$1\frac{2}{3}$

1 = 3 thirds

$\frac{2}{3}$ = 2 thirds

$1\frac{2}{3}$ = 5 thirds

$= \boxed{\frac{5}{3}}$

An improper fraction is equal to or greater than 1.

1. $2\frac{3}{4}$

2 = 8 fourths

$\frac{3}{4}$ = 3 fourths

$2\frac{3}{4}$ = 11 fourths

$= \boxed{\frac{11}{4}}$

2. $3\frac{2}{5}$

3 = 15 fifths

$\frac{2}{5}$ = 2 fifths

$3\frac{2}{5}$ = 17 fifths

$= \boxed{\frac{17}{5}}$

Lesson 6.4 Improper Fractions 147

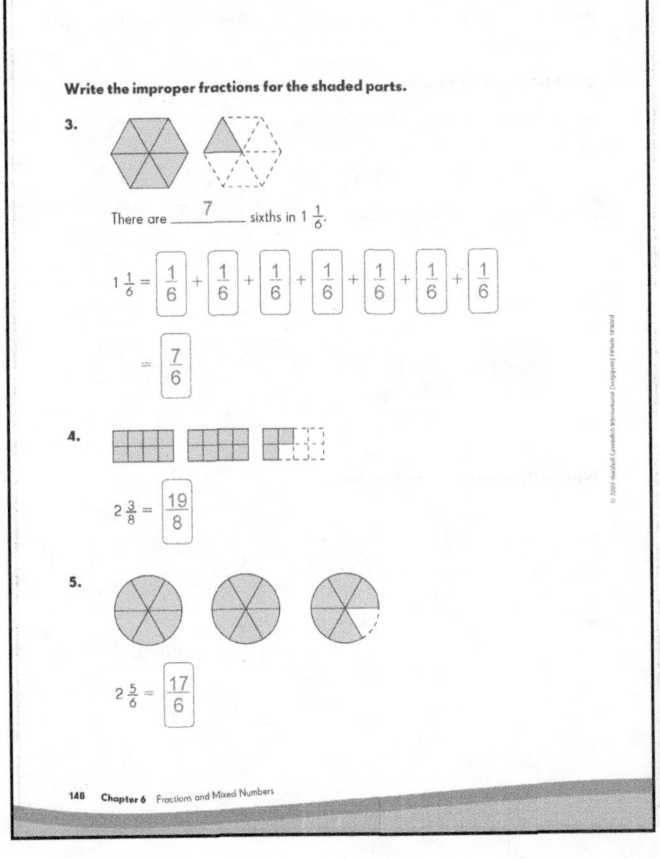

Write the improper fractions for the shaded parts.

3. There are 7 sixths in $1\frac{1}{6}$.

$1\frac{1}{6} = \boxed{\frac{1}{6}} + \boxed{\frac{1}{6}} + \boxed{\frac{1}{6}} + \boxed{\frac{1}{6}} + \boxed{\frac{1}{6}} + \boxed{\frac{1}{6}} + \boxed{\frac{1}{6}}$

$= \boxed{\frac{7}{6}}$

4. $2\frac{3}{8} = \boxed{\frac{19}{8}}$

5. $2\frac{5}{6} = \boxed{\frac{17}{6}}$

148 Chapter 6 Fractions and Mixed Numbers

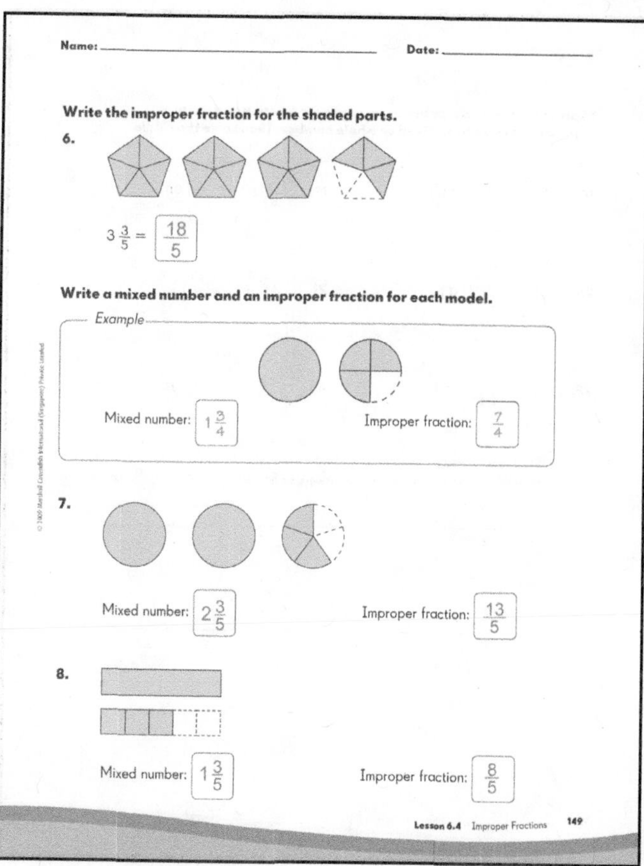

Name: ______________________ Date: ______________

Write the improper fraction for the shaded parts.

6. $3\frac{3}{5} = \boxed{\frac{18}{5}}$

Write a mixed number and an improper fraction for each model.

Example

Mixed number: $1\frac{3}{4}$ Improper fraction: $\frac{7}{4}$

7. Mixed number: $\boxed{2\frac{3}{5}}$ Improper fraction: $\boxed{\frac{13}{5}}$

8. Mixed number: $\boxed{1\frac{3}{5}}$ Improper fraction: $\boxed{\frac{8}{5}}$

© 2009 Marshall Cavendish International (Singapore) Private Limited

Lesson 6.4 Improper Fractions 149

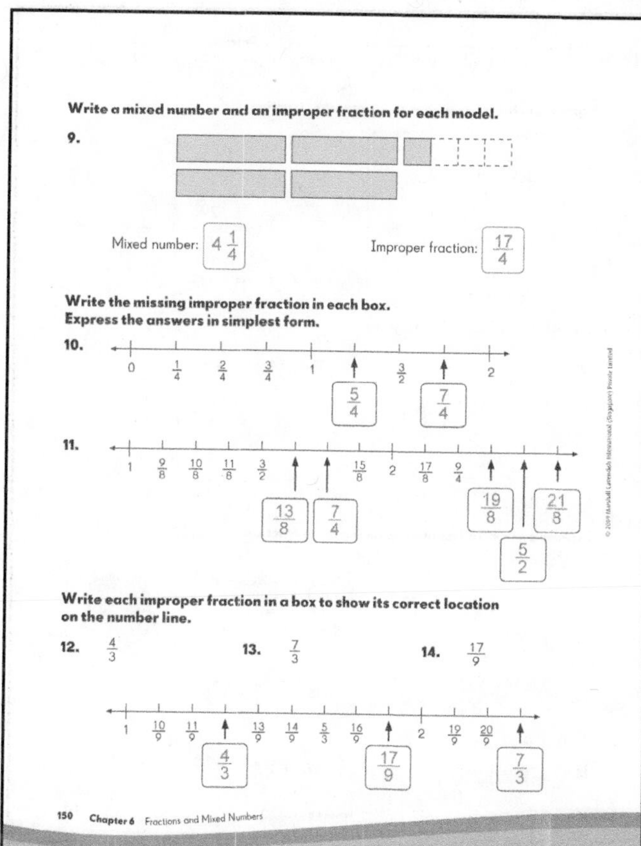

Write a mixed number and an improper fraction for each model.

9. Mixed number: $\boxed{4\frac{1}{4}}$ Improper fraction: $\boxed{\frac{17}{4}}$

Write the missing improper fraction in each box. Express the answers in simplest form.

10. 0, $\frac{1}{4}$, $\frac{2}{4}$, $\frac{3}{4}$, 1, $\boxed{\frac{5}{4}}$, $\frac{3}{2}$, $\boxed{\frac{7}{4}}$, 2

11. 1, $\frac{9}{8}$, $\frac{10}{8}$, $\frac{11}{8}$, $\frac{3}{2}$, $\boxed{\frac{13}{8}}$, $\boxed{\frac{7}{4}}$, $\frac{15}{8}$, 2, $\frac{17}{8}$, $\frac{9}{4}$, $\boxed{\frac{19}{8}}$, $\boxed{\frac{5}{2}}$, $\boxed{\frac{21}{8}}$

Write each improper fraction in a box to show its correct location on the number line.

12. $\frac{4}{3}$ 13. $\frac{7}{3}$ 14. $\frac{17}{9}$

1, $\frac{10}{9}$, $\frac{11}{9}$, $\boxed{\frac{4}{3}}$, $\frac{13}{9}$, $\frac{14}{9}$, $\frac{5}{3}$, $\frac{16}{9}$, $\boxed{\frac{17}{9}}$, 2, $\frac{19}{9}$, $\frac{20}{9}$, $\boxed{\frac{7}{3}}$

© 2009 Marshall Cavendish International (Singapore) Private Limited

150 Chapter 6 Fractions and Mixed Numbers

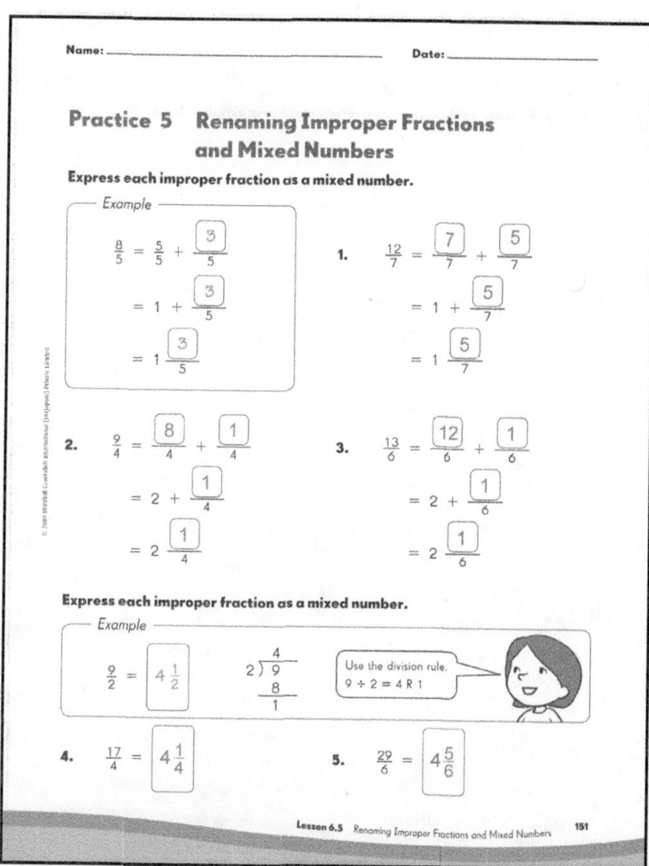

Name: ______________________ Date: ______________

Practice 5 Renaming Improper Fractions and Mixed Numbers

Express each improper fraction as a mixed number.

Example

$\frac{8}{5} = \frac{5}{5} + \frac{\boxed{3}}{5} = 1 + \frac{\boxed{3}}{5} = 1\frac{\boxed{3}}{5}$

1. $\frac{12}{7} = \frac{\boxed{7}}{7} + \frac{\boxed{5}}{7} = 1 + \frac{\boxed{5}}{7} = 1\frac{\boxed{5}}{7}$

2. $\frac{9}{4} = \frac{\boxed{8}}{4} + \frac{\boxed{1}}{4} = 2 + \frac{\boxed{1}}{4} = 2\frac{\boxed{1}}{4}$

3. $\frac{13}{6} = \frac{\boxed{12}}{6} + \frac{\boxed{1}}{6} = 2 + \frac{\boxed{1}}{6} = 2\frac{\boxed{1}}{6}$

Express each improper fraction as a mixed number.

Example

$\frac{9}{2} = \boxed{4\frac{1}{2}}$ $2\overline{)9}$ = 4, 8, 1

Use the division rule. 9 ÷ 2 = 4 R 1

4. $\frac{17}{4} = \boxed{4\frac{1}{4}}$ 5. $\frac{29}{6} = \boxed{4\frac{5}{6}}$

© 2009 Marshall Cavendish International (Singapore) Private Limited

Lesson 6.5 Renaming Improper Fractions and Mixed Numbers 151

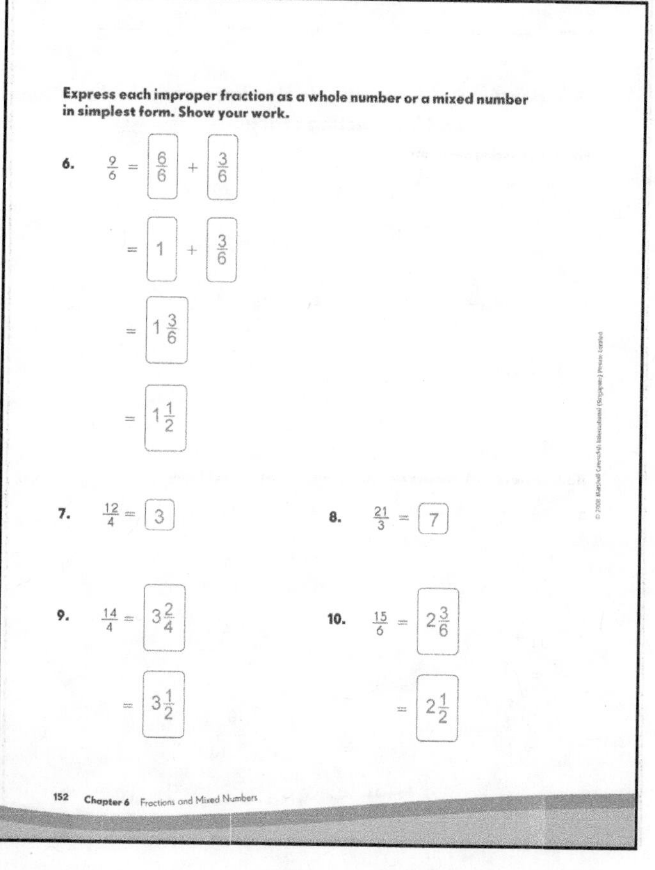

Express each improper fraction as a whole number or a mixed number in simplest form. Show your work.

6. $\frac{9}{6} = \boxed{\frac{6}{6}} + \boxed{\frac{3}{6}} = \boxed{1} + \boxed{\frac{3}{6}} = \boxed{1\frac{3}{6}} = \boxed{1\frac{1}{2}}$

7. $\frac{12}{4} = \boxed{3}$ 8. $\frac{21}{3} = \boxed{7}$

9. $\frac{14}{4} = \boxed{3\frac{2}{4}} = \boxed{3\frac{1}{2}}$ 10. $\frac{15}{6} = \boxed{2\frac{3}{6}} = \boxed{2\frac{1}{2}}$

© 2009 Marshall Cavendish International (Singapore) Private Limited

152 Chapter 6 Fractions and Mixed Numbers

Name: ______ Date: ______

Express each mixed number as an improper fraction.

Example

$2\frac{3}{5} = \frac{2}{} + \frac{3}{5}$

$= \frac{10}{5} + \frac{3}{5}$

$= \frac{13}{5}$

11. $3\frac{5}{9} = 3 + \frac{5}{9}$

$= \frac{27}{9} + \frac{5}{9}$

$= \frac{32}{9}$

12. $2\frac{5}{8} = 2 + \frac{5}{8}$

$= \frac{16}{8} + \frac{5}{8}$

$= \frac{21}{8}$

13. $4\frac{2}{7} = 4 + \frac{2}{7}$

$= \frac{28}{7} + \frac{2}{7}$

$= \frac{30}{7}$

Express each mixed number as an improper fraction.

Example

$2\frac{1}{5} = \frac{11}{5}$

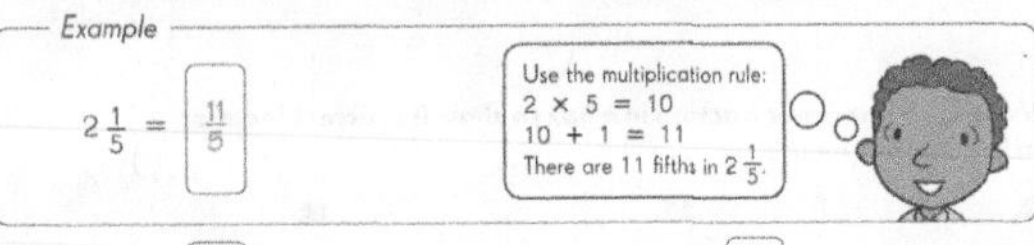

Use the multiplication rule:
2 × 5 = 10
10 + 1 = 11
There are 11 fifths in $2\frac{1}{5}$.

14. $2\frac{3}{8} = \frac{19}{8}$

15. $3\frac{3}{4} = \frac{15}{4}$

16. $6\frac{2}{5} = \frac{32}{5}$

17. $2\frac{4}{7} = \frac{18}{7}$

© 2009 Marshall Cavendish International (Singapore) Private Limited

Express each mixed number as an improper fraction and each improper fraction as a mixed or whole number. Then solve the riddle.

18. $\frac{9}{7} = 1\frac{2}{7}$ (b)

19. $\frac{15}{6} = 2\frac{1}{2}$ (o)

20. $\frac{14}{7} = 2$ (a)

21. $2\frac{2}{7} = \frac{16}{7}$ (i)

22. $3\frac{5}{8} = \frac{29}{8}$ (t)

23. $5\frac{3}{5} = \frac{28}{5}$ (r)

Which two animals can look behind without turning their heads?
Write the letters which match the answers to find out.

P A R R O T

A	R	R	O	T
2	$\frac{28}{5}$	$\frac{28}{5}$	$2\frac{1}{2}$	$\frac{29}{8}$

and

R	A	B	B	I	T
$\frac{28}{5}$	2	$1\frac{2}{7}$	$1\frac{2}{7}$	$\frac{16}{7}$	$\frac{29}{8}$

© 2009 Marshall Cavendish International (Singapore) Private Limited

Name: ______ Date: ______

Practice 6 Renaming Whole Numbers when Adding and Subtracting Fractions

Fill in the missing numerators.

Example

$3 = 2\frac{4}{4} = 1\frac{8}{4} = \frac{12}{4}$

1. $3 = 2\frac{6}{6}$

$= 1\frac{12}{6}$

$= \frac{18}{6}$

2. $2\frac{7}{9} = 1\frac{16}{9}$

$= \frac{25}{9}$

Add. Express each answer as a mixed number in simplest form.

3. $\frac{4}{9} + \frac{2}{3} = \frac{4}{9} + \frac{6}{9}$

$= \frac{10}{9}$

$= 1\frac{1}{9}$

4. $\frac{1}{6} + \frac{11}{12} = \frac{2}{12} + \frac{11}{12}$

$= \frac{13}{12}$

$= 1\frac{1}{12}$

5. $\frac{1}{4} + \frac{3}{8} + \frac{3}{4}$

$= \frac{2}{8} + \frac{3}{8} + \frac{6}{8}$

$= \frac{11}{8}$

$= 1\frac{3}{8}$

6. $\frac{4}{5} + \frac{7}{10} + \frac{9}{10}$

$= \frac{8}{10} + \frac{7}{10} + \frac{9}{10}$

$= \frac{24}{10}$

$= 2\frac{4}{10}$

$= 2\frac{2}{5}$

© 2009 Marshall Cavendish International (Singapore) Private Limited

Subtract. Express each answer as a mixed number in simplest form.

Example

$2 - \frac{1}{3}$

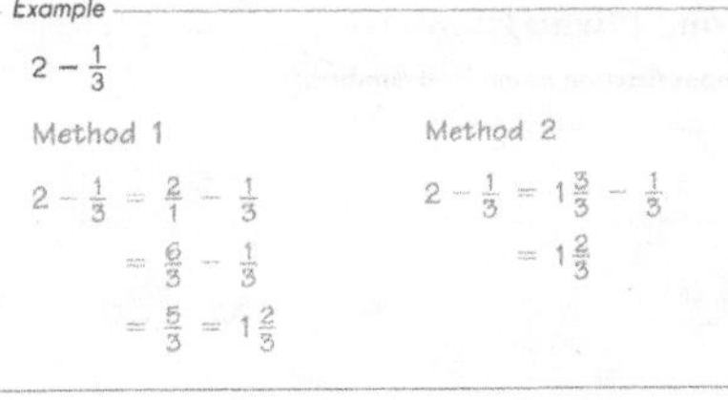

Method 1

$2 - \frac{1}{3} = \frac{2}{1} - \frac{1}{3}$

$= \frac{6}{3} - \frac{1}{3}$

$= \frac{5}{3} = 1\frac{2}{3}$

Method 2

$2 - \frac{1}{3} = 1\frac{3}{3} - \frac{1}{3}$

$= 1\frac{2}{3}$

7. $3 - \frac{5}{6} - \frac{1}{3}$

$= \frac{3}{1} - \frac{5}{6} - \frac{1}{3}$

$= \frac{18}{6} - \frac{5}{6} - \frac{2}{6}$

$= \frac{11}{6}$

$= 1\frac{5}{6}$

8. $2 - \frac{1}{4} - \frac{1}{4}$

$= \frac{2}{1} - \frac{1}{4} - \frac{1}{4}$

$= \frac{8}{4} - \frac{1}{4} - \frac{1}{4}$

$= \frac{6}{4} = \frac{3}{2}$

$= 1\frac{1}{2}$

9. $2 - \frac{2}{7} - \frac{3}{14}$

$= \frac{2}{1} - \frac{4}{14} - \frac{3}{14}$

$= \frac{28}{14} - \frac{4}{14} - \frac{3}{14}$

$= \frac{21}{14}$

$= 1\frac{1}{2}$

10. $3 - \frac{7}{10} - \frac{3}{5}$

$= \frac{3}{1} - \frac{7}{10} - \frac{6}{10}$

$= \frac{30}{10} - \frac{7}{10} - \frac{6}{10}$

$= \frac{17}{10}$

$= 1\frac{7}{10}$

© 2009 Marshall Cavendish International (Singapore) Private Limited

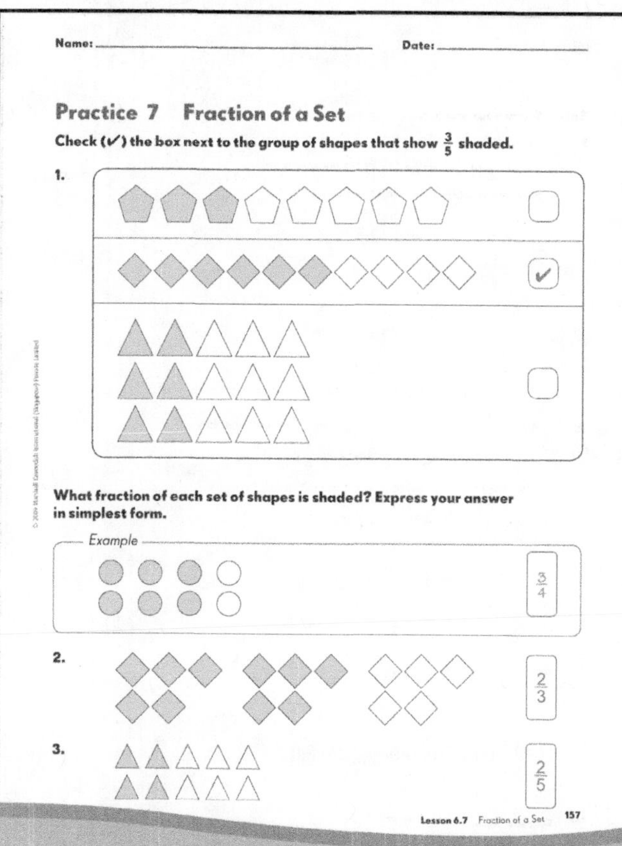

Name: ______________________ Date: ______________

Practice 7 Fraction of a Set

Check (✓) the box next to the group of shapes that show $\frac{3}{5}$ shaded.

1.

- 3 of 8 pentagons shaded ☐
- 6 of 10 diamonds shaded ☑
- 6 of 15 triangles shaded ☐

What fraction of each set of shapes is shaded? Express your answer in simplest form.

Example

6 of 8 circles shaded: $\frac{3}{4}$

2. $\frac{2}{3}$

3. $\frac{2}{5}$

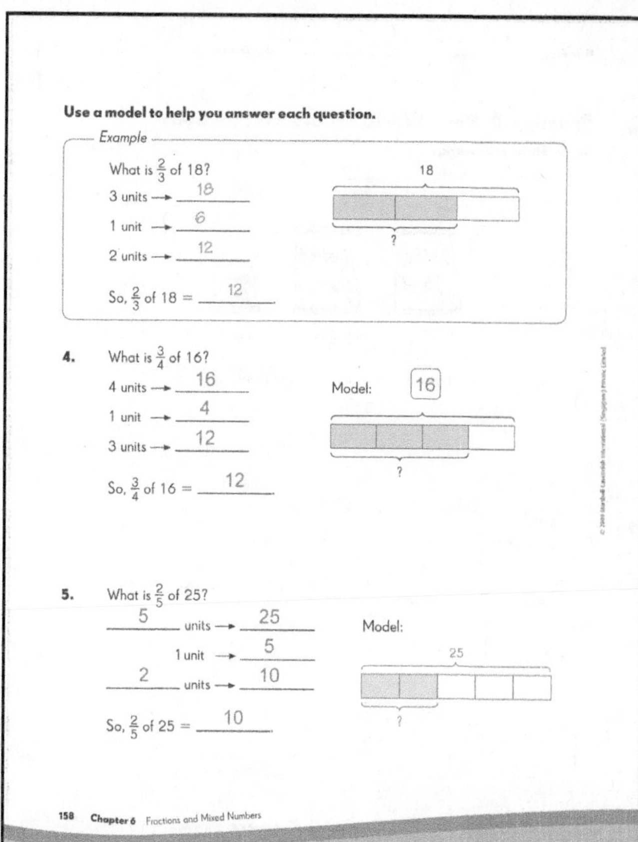

Use a model to help you answer each question.

Example

What is $\frac{2}{3}$ of 18?

3 units → 18

1 unit → 6

2 units → 12

So, $\frac{2}{3}$ of 18 = 12

4. What is $\frac{3}{4}$ of 16?

4 units → 16

1 unit → 4

3 units → 12

So, $\frac{3}{4}$ of 16 = 12

5. What is $\frac{2}{5}$ of 25?

5 units → 25

1 unit → 5

2 units → 10

So, $\frac{2}{5}$ of 25 = 10

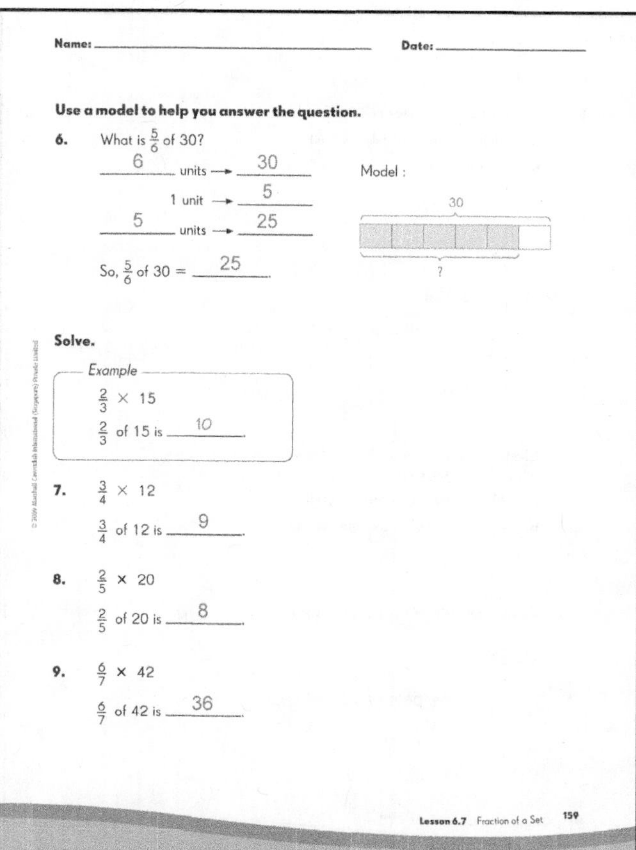

Name: ______________________ Date: ______________

Use a model to help you answer the question.

6. What is $\frac{5}{6}$ of 30?

6 units → 30

1 unit → 5

5 units → 25

So, $\frac{5}{6}$ of 30 = 25

Solve.

Example

$\frac{2}{3} \times 15$

$\frac{2}{3}$ of 15 is 10.

7. $\frac{3}{4} \times 12$

$\frac{3}{4}$ of 12 is 9.

8. $\frac{2}{5} \times 20$

$\frac{2}{5}$ of 20 is 8.

9. $\frac{6}{7} \times 42$

$\frac{6}{7}$ of 42 is 36.

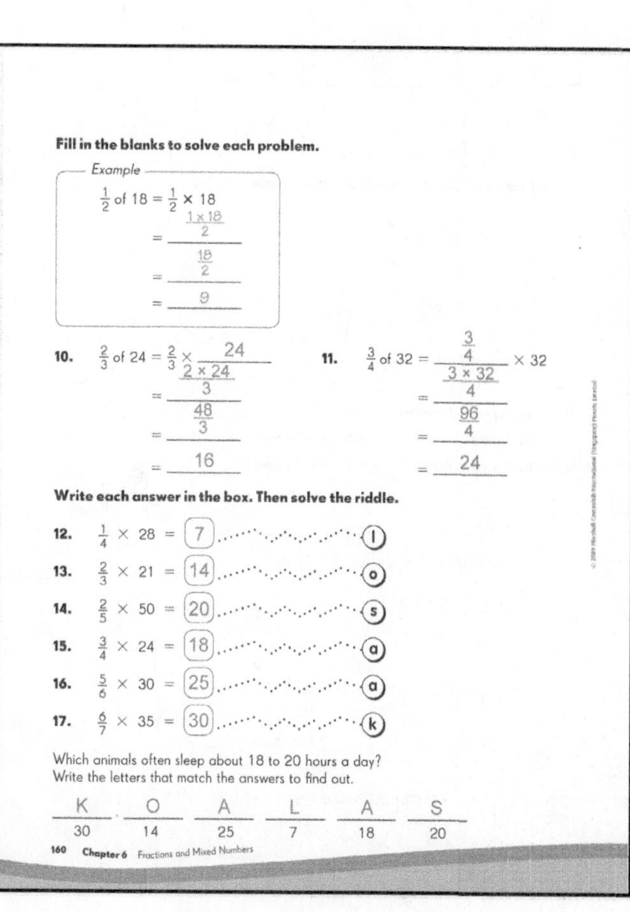

Fill in the blanks to solve each problem.

Example

$\frac{1}{2}$ of 18 = $\frac{1}{2} \times 18$

$= \frac{1 \times 18}{2}$

$= \frac{18}{2}$

$= 9$

10. $\frac{2}{3}$ of 24 = $\frac{2}{3} \times 24$

$= \frac{2 \times 24}{3}$

$= \frac{48}{3}$

$= 16$

11. $\frac{3}{4}$ of 32 = $\frac{3}{4} \times 32$

$= \frac{3 \times 32}{4}$

$= \frac{96}{4}$

$= 24$

Write each answer in the box. Then solve the riddle.

12. $\frac{1}{4} \times 28$ = 7 l

13. $\frac{2}{3} \times 21$ = 14 ...... o

14. $\frac{2}{5} \times 50$ = 20 ...... s

15. $\frac{3}{4} \times 24$ = 18 ...... a

16. $\frac{5}{6} \times 30$ = 25 ...... a

17. $\frac{6}{7} \times 35$ = 30 ...... k

Which animals often sleep about 18 to 20 hours a day?
Write the letters that match the answers to find out.

K	O	A	L	A	S
30	14	25	7	18	20

Name: ______________________ Date: ______________

Practice 8 Real-World Problems: Fractions

Solve. Show your work.

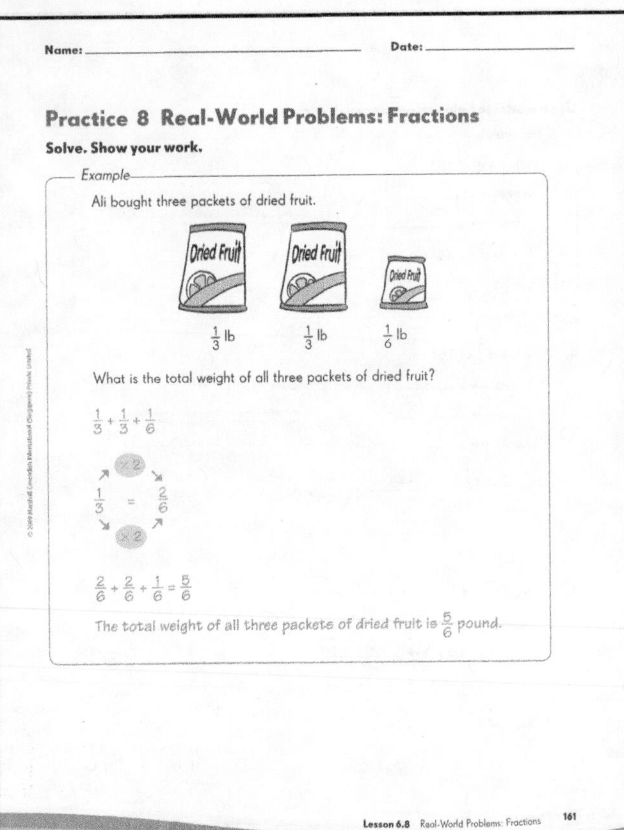

Example
Ali bought three packets of dried fruit.
Dried Fruit
Dried Fruit
Dried Fruit
$\frac{1}{3}$ lb
$\frac{1}{3}$ lb
$\frac{1}{6}$ lb
What is the total weight of all three packets of dried fruit?
$\frac{1}{3} + \frac{1}{3} + \frac{1}{6}$
×2
$\frac{1}{3} = \frac{2}{6}$
×2
$\frac{2}{6} + \frac{2}{6} + \frac{1}{6} = \frac{5}{6}$
The total weight of all three packets of dried fruit is $\frac{5}{6}$ pound.

© 2009 Marshall Cavendish International (Singapore) Private Limited

Solve. Show your work.

1. Jim had three waffles.
   He ate $\frac{1}{6}$ of one waffle, and $\frac{2}{3}$ of another waffle.
   How many waffles were left?

$$3 - \frac{1}{6} - \frac{2}{3} = \frac{3}{1} - \frac{1}{6} - \frac{2}{3}$$
$$= \frac{18}{6} - \frac{1}{6} - \frac{4}{6}$$
$$= \frac{13}{6} = 2\frac{1}{6}$$

$2\frac{1}{6}$ waffles were left.

2. A grocery store has 5 pounds of granola. One customer buys $\frac{2}{3}$ pound of granola and another buys $\frac{5}{6}$ pound.
   After these purchases, how much granola is left?

$$5 - \frac{2}{3} - \frac{5}{6} = \frac{5}{1} - \frac{2}{3} - \frac{5}{6}$$
$$= \frac{30}{6} - \frac{4}{6} - \frac{5}{6}$$
$$= \frac{21}{6}$$
$$= \frac{7}{2}$$
$$= 3\frac{1}{2}$$

$3\frac{1}{2}$ pounds of granola are left.

© 2009 Marshall Cavendish International (Singapore) Private Limited

Name: ______________________ Date: ______________

3. Karen jogs $\frac{1}{2}$ mile. Selma jogs $\frac{1}{4}$ mile more than Karen.
   Lena jogs $\frac{3}{4}$ mile more than Selma. How far does Lena jog?

$$\frac{1}{2} + \frac{1}{4} = \frac{2}{4} + \frac{1}{4} = \frac{3}{4}$$
$$\frac{3}{4} + \frac{3}{4} = \frac{6}{4}$$
$$= 1\frac{2}{4} = 1\frac{1}{2}$$

Lena jogs $1\frac{1}{2}$ miles.

4. Jeremy has 18 marbles. He loses 6 of them.
   a. What fraction of the marbles does he lose?
   b. What fraction of the marbles does he have left?

a. $\frac{6}{18} = \frac{1}{3}$

He loses $\frac{1}{3}$ of the marbles.

b. $18 - 6 = 12$

$\frac{12}{18} = \frac{2}{3}$

$\frac{2}{3}$ of the marbles are left.

or

$1 - \frac{1}{3} = \frac{2}{3}$

$\frac{2}{3}$ of the marbles are left.

© 2009 Marshall Cavendish International (Singapore) Private Limited

5. Mrs. Yan buys 4 red tulips and 5 yellow tulips.
   a. What fraction of the tulips are red?
   b. What fraction of the tulips are yellow?

a. $4 + 5 = 9$

$\frac{4}{9}$ of the tulips are red.

b. $1 - \frac{4}{9} = \frac{5}{9}$

$\frac{5}{9}$ of the tulips are yellow.

6. Charles owns 3 cats, 4 goldfish, and some parakeets.
   Altogether, he has 10 pets.
   a. What fraction of his pets are goldfish?
   b. What fraction of his pets are parakeets?

a. $\frac{4}{10} = \frac{2}{5}$

$\frac{2}{5}$ of his pets are goldfish.

b. $10 - 3 - 4 = 3$

$\frac{3}{10}$ of his pets are parakeets.

© 2009 Marshall Cavendish International (Singapore) Private Limited

Name: ______________ Date: ______________

7. Rick had $20. He spent $10 on food, $6 on a movie ticket and saved the rest.

a. How much money did he save?

b. What fraction of the total amount did he save?

a. $20 - 10 - 6 = 4$

Rick saved $4.

b. $\frac{4}{20} = \frac{1}{5}$

Rick saved $\frac{1}{5}$ of the amount of money he had at first.

8. There are 24 boys in a class, and $\frac{2}{3}$ of the students in the class are boys. How many students are girls?

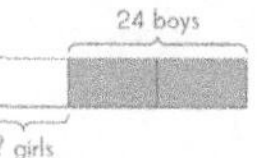

2 units → 24

1 unit → $24 \div 2 = 12$

There are 12 girls.

9. One morning, The Shirt Shop sold 15 T-shirts.
Of the T-shirts sold, $\frac{1}{5}$ were gray. The rest were white.
How many white T-shirts were sold?

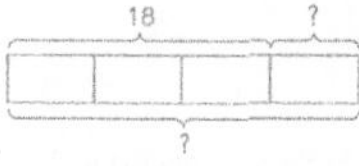

$\frac{1}{5} \times 15 = \frac{15}{5} = 3$

3 gray T-shirts were sold.

$15 - 3 = 12$

12 white T-shirts were sold.

10. A chef bought some green and red peppers. She bought 18 green peppers, which was $\frac{3}{4}$ of the total number.

a. How many red peppers did she buy?

b. How many peppers did she buy altogether?

18 ?
?

a. 3 units → 18

1 unit → 6

She bought 6 red peppers.

b. 4 units → 24

She bought 24 peppers altogether.

Name: ______________ Date: ______________

11. There were 25 melons in a box at the grocery store.
The store sold $\frac{3}{5}$ of the melons.
How many melons were sold?

$\frac{3}{5} \times 25 = \frac{3 \times 25}{5}$

$= \frac{75}{5}$

$= 15$

The store sold 15 melons.

12. Ava read $\frac{1}{4}$ of a book on Monday, and $\frac{1}{5}$ of it on Tuesday.
There are 80 pages in the book.
How many pages did she read altogether on both days?

$\frac{1}{4} + \frac{1}{5} = \frac{5}{20} + \frac{4}{20}$

$= \frac{9}{20}$

$\frac{9}{20} \times 80 = \frac{9 \times 80}{20}$

$= \frac{720}{20}$

$= 36$

She read 36 pages altogether on both days.

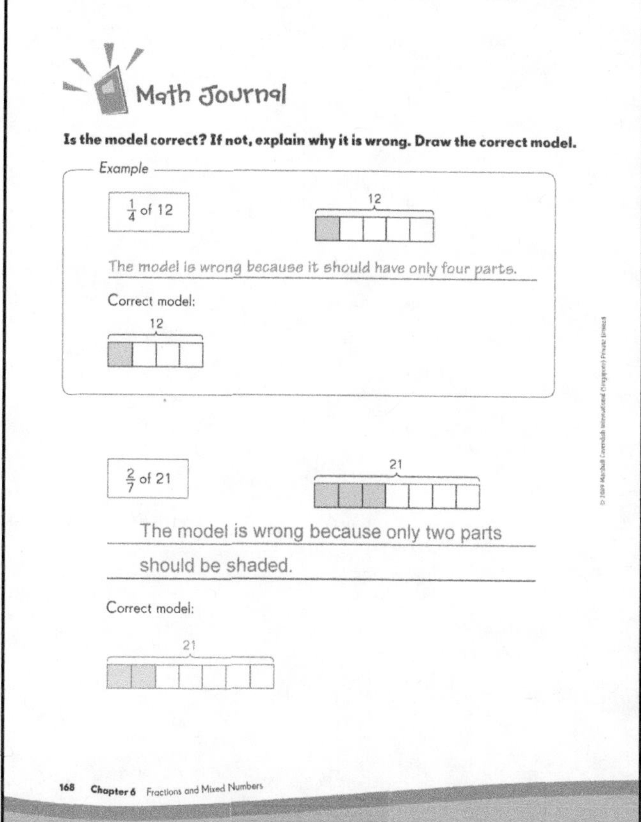

Math Journal
Is the model correct? If not, explain why it is wrong. Draw the correct model.
Example
$\frac{1}{4}$ of 12
12
The model is wrong because it should have only four parts.
Correct model:
12
$\frac{2}{7}$ of 21
21
The model is wrong because only two parts should be shaded.
Correct model:
21

Name: _______________ Date: _______________

Put On Your Thinking Cap!

Challenging Practice

1. Show $1\frac{1}{4}$ shaded, if 1 whole is made up of 4 squares.

   Some of the shading has been done for you.

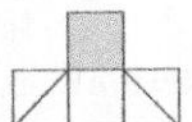

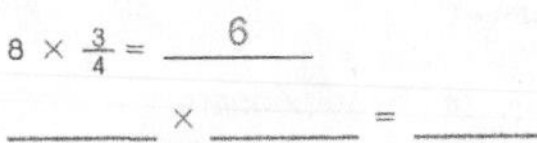

2. Is the answer of $21 \times \frac{2}{7}$ the same as that of $2 \times \frac{21}{7}$?
   Show your work.

$21 \times \frac{2}{7} = \frac{21 \times 2}{7} = \frac{42}{7} = 6$

$2 \times \frac{21}{7} = \frac{2 \times 21}{7} = \frac{42}{7} = 6$

Yes, they are the same.

3. Write a fraction and a whole number that have the same product as the problem below.

$8 \times \frac{3}{4} =$ 6

_______ × _______ = _______

Answers vary.

Thinking skill: Identifying relationships

© 2009 Marshall Cavendish International (Singapore) Private Limited

Put On Your Thinking Cap!

Problem Solving

Caroline places five poles A, B, C, D, and E in order along a straight line. The distance between poles A and D is 1 yard. The distance between poles B and C is the same as the distance between poles A and B.

Poles A and B are $\frac{1}{5}$ yard apart.

Strategy: Use a diagram

The distance between D and E is $\frac{7}{10}$ yard.

How far apart are poles B and E?

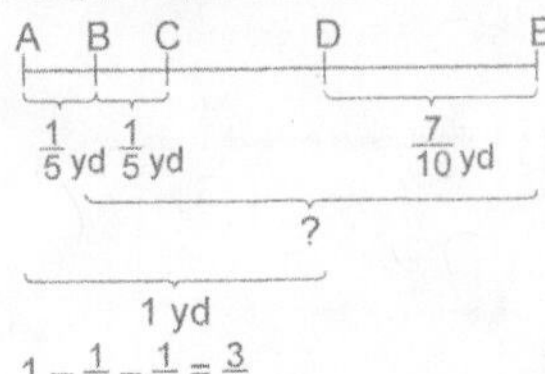

$1 - \frac{1}{5} - \frac{1}{5} = \frac{3}{5}$

Poles C and D are $\frac{3}{5}$ yard apart.

$\frac{1}{5} + \frac{3}{5} + \frac{7}{10} = \frac{15}{10}$

$= 1\frac{5}{10}$

$= 1\frac{1}{2}$

Poles B and E are $1\frac{1}{2}$ yards apart.

© 2009 Marshall Cavendish International (Singapore) Private Limited

Name: ______________________ Date: ______________

Cumulative Review

for Chapters 5 and 6

Concepts and Skills

Complete. Use the data in the table. *(Lesson 5.1)*

The ages of four cousins are shown.

8, 12, 10, 6

1. The sum of their ages is 36 years.
2. The mean age of the cousins is 9 years.

Answer each question. Use the data in the line plot. *(Lesson 5.2)*

A group of hikers made a line plot to show the number of mountains they climbed. Each X represents one hiker.

1	2	3	4	5	6
X X X	X	X X X X	X X	X X X	X X X X X

Number of Mountains Climbed

3. What is the median number of mountains climbed? 4
4. What is the range of the set of data? 5
5. What is the mode of the set of data? 6

Make a stem-and-leaf plot to show the data. *(Lesson 5.3)*

6. A group of friends went bowling and recorded these scores.

75 73 79 84 98 64 84 67

Bowling Scores

Stem	Leaves
6	4 7
7	3 5 9
8	4 4
9	8

9|8 = 98

Complete. Use the data in your stem-and-leaf plot.

7. 84 is the mode.
8. 77 is the median.
9. 34 is the range.
10. 98 is an outlier.
11. How do the mode and median each change if you disregard the outlier?
If the outlier is disregarded, the mode remains the same. The median changes to 75.

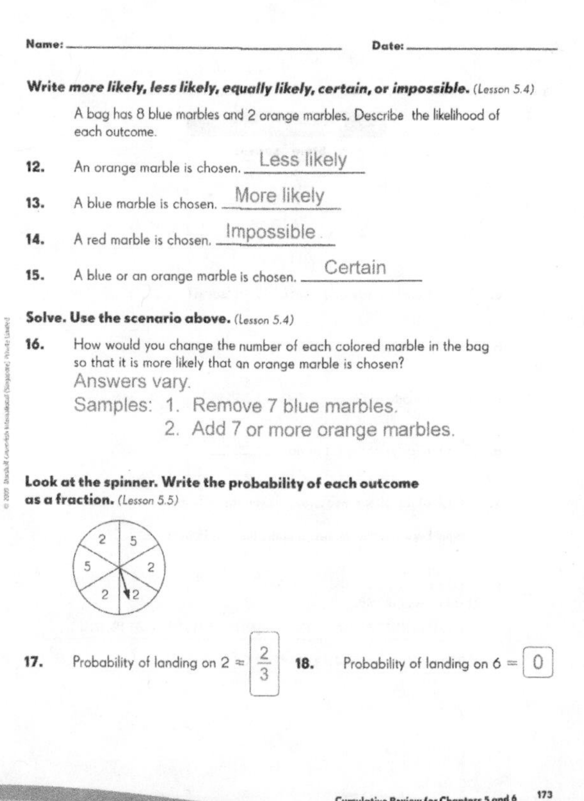
Name: ______________________ Date: ______________

Write *more likely, less likely, equally likely, certain,* or *impossible.* *(Lesson 5.4)*

A bag has 8 blue marbles and 2 orange marbles. Describe the likelihood of each outcome.

12. An orange marble is chosen. Less likely
13. A blue marble is chosen. More likely
14. A red marble is chosen. Impossible
15. A blue or an orange marble is chosen. Certain

Solve. Use the scenario above. *(Lesson 5.4)*

16. How would you change the number of each colored marble in the bag so that it is more likely that an orange marble is chosen?
Answers vary.
Samples: 1. Remove 7 blue marbles.
2. Add 7 or more orange marbles.

Look at the spinner. Write the probability of each outcome as a fraction. *(Lesson 5.5)*

17. Probability of landing on 2 = $\frac{2}{3}$
18. Probability of landing on 6 = 0

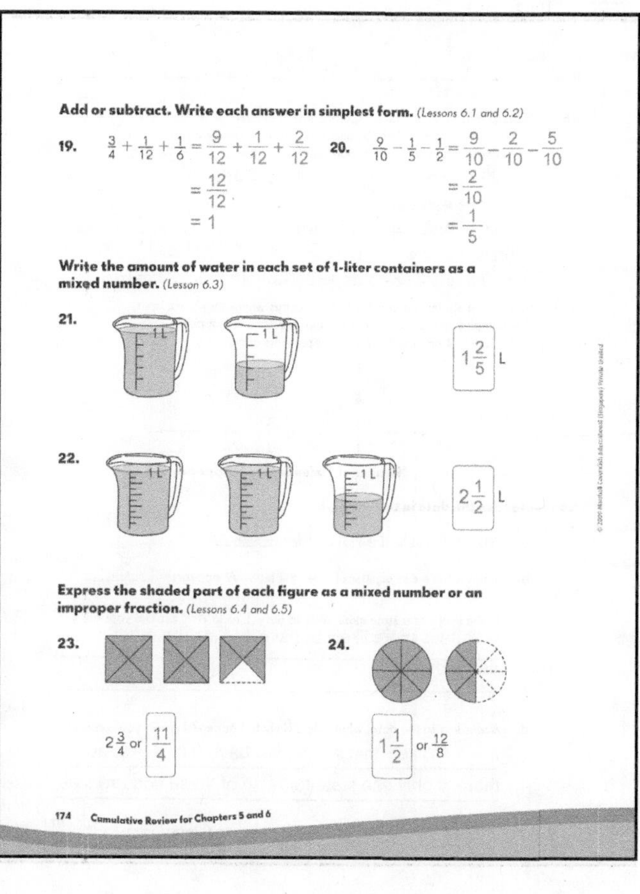
Add or subtract. Write each answer in simplest form. *(Lessons 6.1 and 6.2)*

19. $\frac{3}{4}+\frac{1}{12}+\frac{1}{6}=\frac{9}{12}+\frac{1}{12}+\frac{2}{12}=\frac{12}{12}=1$

20. $\frac{9}{10}-\frac{1}{5}-\frac{1}{2}=\frac{9}{10}-\frac{2}{10}-\frac{5}{10}=\frac{2}{10}=\frac{1}{5}$

Write the amount of water in each set of 1-liter containers as a mixed number. *(Lesson 6.3)*

21. $1\frac{2}{5}$ L

22. $2\frac{1}{2}$ L

Express the shaded part of each figure as a mixed number or an improper fraction. *(Lessons 6.4 and 6.5)*

23. $2\frac{3}{4}$ or $\frac{11}{4}$

24. $1\frac{1}{2}$ or $\frac{12}{8}$

Chapters 5-6 Review

Name: ______ Date: ______

Express each improper fraction as a mixed number. (Lesson 6.5)

25. $\frac{9}{7} = 1\frac{2}{7}$

26. $\frac{20}{9} = 2\frac{2}{9}$

Express each mixed number as an improper fraction. (Lesson 6.5)

27. $3\frac{2}{5} = \frac{17}{5}$

28. $2\frac{8}{9} = \frac{26}{9}$

Add or subtract. (Lesson 6.6)

29. $2 + \frac{2}{5} + \frac{1}{10} = 2\frac{1}{2}$

30. $3 - \frac{3}{4} - \frac{5}{8} = 1\frac{5}{8}$

Check (✓) each set in which $\frac{2}{5}$ of the figures are shaded. (Lesson 6.7)

31.

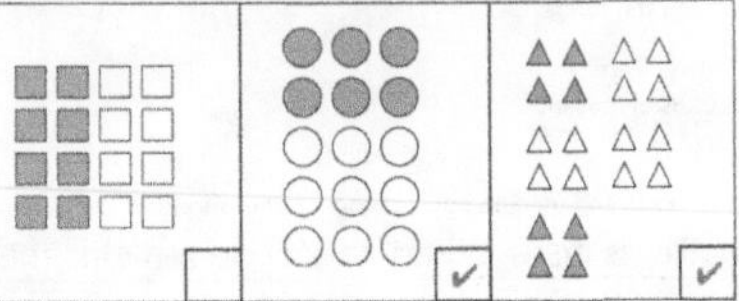

Solve. (Lesson 6.7)

32. $\frac{2}{3}$ of 15 = 10

33. $\frac{3}{5}$ of 40 = 24

Problem Solving

Solve. Show your work.

34. Teams A, B, C, and D were in a tournament. The average score of the 4 teams was 92. Team A scored 78 points, Team B scored 95 points, and Team C scored 88 points.

a. How many points did Team D score?

Total score = 92 × 4 = 368 points
368 – 78 – 95 – 88 = 107 points
Team D scored 107 points.

b. Find the range of the scores. Hence, state the difference in score between the winning team and the losing team.

Range = Greatest score – Least score = 107 – 78 = 29
The difference between the winning team and the losing team is 29 points.

35. Michael scored 15, 21, and 24 in the first three basketball games of the season.

a. What is his mean score?

15 + 21 + 24 = 60
Mean score = 60 ÷ 3 = 20

b. What is the range of his scores?

Range = 24 – 15 = 9

c. How many points must he score in the next game to achieve a mean score of 27?

27 × 4 = 108
108 – 60 = 48
He must score 48 points in the next game.

Name: ______ Date: ______

36. Samuel and Kenneth collect sports cards. The average number of cards they have is 248. Samuel has 3 times as many cards as Kenneth. How many cards does each boy have?

Total number of cards = 248 × 2 = 496
4 units = 496 cards
1 unit = 496 ÷ 4 = 124 cards
3 units = 124 × 3 = 372 cards
Samuel has 372 cards and Kenneth has 124 cards.

Samuel / Kenneth — 496

37. A group of students made a list of the states where they were born. The line plot shows the number of times the letter 'A' appears in the name of each state. Each ✗ represents one state.

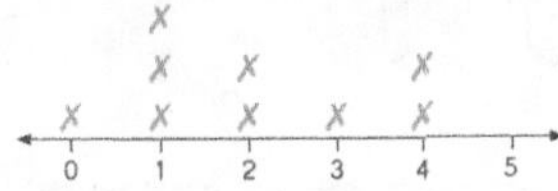

Number of Times Letter A Appears

Complete. Use the data in the line plot.

a. What is the mode of the set of data? 1

b. What is the mean number of times the letter 'A' appears? 2

c. Is the name of a state more likely to have 1 or 2 'A's? Explain your answer.

A state is more likely to have 1 'A' as the mode of the set of data is 1.

d. According to the data, what is less likely to happen? Explain your answer.

It is less likely that a state will have 0 or 3 'A's, as there is only one state for each of these occurrences.

38. The stem-and-leaf plot shows the number of pages in 8 books.

Number of Pages	
Stem	Leaves
2	1 5
3	0 5 5 7
4	3 6

2|1 = 21

a. Which stem has only odd numbers for its leaves? 2

b. Find the median of the set of data. 35

c. Find the mode of the set of data. 35

d. Find the range of the set of data. 25

e. Which of the above measures tells you the difference in the number of pages between the thickest and the thinnest books? Range

f. Is there an outlier in the set of data? Explain your answer.

No, because there is no item of data that is much farther away from the rest of the data.

Name: ______________________ Date: ______________

39. A cube is numbered from 1 to 6 and tossed once. What is the probability of tossing

a. a 5 or a 6? $\boxed{\frac{1}{3}}$

b. an odd number? $\boxed{\frac{1}{2}}$

40. Sasha has 40 stamps in her collection. 12 of them are from foreign countries.

a. What fraction of the stamps are foreign stamps?

$\frac{12}{40} = \frac{3}{10}$

$\frac{3}{10}$ of the stamps are foreign stamps.

b. What fraction of the stamps are U.S. stamps?

$1 - \frac{3}{10} = \frac{7}{10}$

$\frac{7}{10}$ of the stamps are U.S. stamps.

© 2009 Marshall Cavendish International (Singapore) Private Limited

41. A string is 1 foot long. Blake cuts off 3 inches of the string. What fraction of the string is left?

1 ft = 12 in.

12 – 3 = 9 in.

$\frac{9}{12} = \frac{3}{4}$

$\frac{3}{4}$ of the string is left.

42. Pedro scored $\frac{1}{4}$ of all the goals scored during a soccer game. He scored 2 goals. How many goals were not scored by Pedro?

1 unit = 2

4 units = 8

8 – 2 = 6

6 goals were not scored by Pedro.

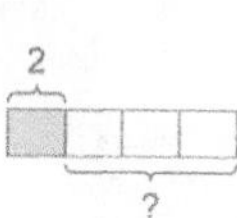

© 2009 Marshall Cavendish International (Singapore) Private Limited

Mid-Year Review

Name: ______________________ Date: ______________

Mid-Year Review

Test Prep

Multiple Choice

Fill in the circle next to the correct answer.

1. 13 thousands + 4 tens + 8 ones in standard form is ______. (Lesson 1.1)
   Ⓐ 1,348 Ⓑ 10,348
   Ⓒ 13,048 Ⓓ 13,480

2. In the number 83,415 the value of the digit 3 is ______. (Lesson 1.1)
   Ⓐ 30 Ⓑ 300
   Ⓒ 3,000 Ⓓ 30,000

3. 1,000 more than 37,568 is ______. (Lesson 1.2)
   Ⓐ 36,568 Ⓑ 37,468
   Ⓒ 37,668 Ⓓ 38,568

4. Estimate 681 − 307 by rounding to the nearest 100. (Lesson 2.1)
   Ⓐ 300 Ⓑ 370
   Ⓒ 374 Ⓓ 400

5. Which is the greatest common factor of 27 and 45? (Lesson 2.2)
   Ⓐ 1 Ⓑ 3
   Ⓒ 9 Ⓓ 45

6. Which pair of numbers has both a prime and a composite number? (Lesson 2.2)
   Ⓐ 4 and 7 Ⓑ 3 and 13
   Ⓒ 14 and 28 Ⓓ 6 and 8

7. What is the sum of the first two multiples of 6? (Lesson 2.3)
   Ⓐ 3 Ⓑ 6
   Ⓒ 12 Ⓓ 18

8. Mr. Finch exercises at the gym every two days. Mr. Chavez exercises at the gym every five days. When will they meet next if they first met on January 5? (Lesson 2.3)
   Ⓐ January 7 Ⓑ January 10
   Ⓒ January 15 Ⓓ January 25

9. Divide 5,613 by 7. The remainder is ______. (Lesson 3.4)
   Ⓐ 1 Ⓑ 6
   Ⓒ 18 Ⓓ 81

10. After using 35 jars to store 14 marbles each, Ali has 3 marbles left. How many marbles did he have at first? (Lesson 3.5)
    Ⓐ 52 Ⓑ 178
    Ⓒ 490 Ⓓ 493

11. The table shows the medals different teams won at a competition. (Lesson 4.2)

Number of Medals Won

Team	Gold	Silver	Bronze
Sandcastle	3	5	8
Coral Reef	6	1	5
Sunshine	2	4	3
Sea Horse	5	2	6

At which intersection was one medal won?
    Ⓐ Sandcastle and Gold Ⓑ Coral Reef and Silver
    Ⓒ Sunshine and Bronze Ⓓ Seahorse and Silver

Name: ______________________ Date: ______________

12. Find the mode. (Lesson 5.2)
    31 lb 36 lb 21 lb 40 lb 38 lb 40 lb
    Ⓐ 31 lb Ⓑ 36 lb
    Ⓒ 37 lb Ⓓ 40 lb

13. Jim ordered cans of fruit cocktail for his diner for 6 months. (Lesson 5.3)

Cans of Fruit Cocktail

Stem	Leaves
2	6 9
3	1 3 3
4	0

2|6 = 26

What is the median number of cans he ordered?
    Ⓐ 29 cans Ⓑ 32 cans
    Ⓒ 33 cans Ⓓ 40 cans

14. A bag contains 5 yellow balls and 3 green balls. Choose the correct word to describe the likelihood of drawing a yellow ball from the bag. (Lesson 5.4)
    Ⓐ Impossible Ⓑ Certain
    Ⓒ More likely Ⓓ Less likely

15. Stacy draws one of these number cards from a bag.

    12 8 5 16 10 3

    What is the probability that she draws a number less than 10? (Lesson 5.5)
    Ⓐ $\frac{1}{2}$ Ⓑ $\frac{1}{3}$
    Ⓒ $\frac{2}{3}$ Ⓓ $\frac{1}{6}$

16. Which two fractions have a sum of $\frac{9}{10}$? (Lesson 6.1)
    Ⓐ $\frac{1}{2}$ and $\frac{4}{10}$ Ⓑ $\frac{1}{2}$ and $\frac{1}{10}$
    Ⓒ $\frac{2}{5}$ and $\frac{1}{10}$ Ⓓ $\frac{3}{4}$ and $\frac{6}{6}$

17. Which mixed number is represented by **A** on the number line? (Lesson 6.3)

    3 — A — 4 — 5

    Ⓐ $3\frac{4}{5}$ Ⓑ $3\frac{2}{3}$
    Ⓒ $4\frac{1}{3}$ Ⓓ $4\frac{2}{3}$

18. How many fifths are in $2\frac{3}{5}$? (Lesson 6.4)
    Ⓐ 10 Ⓑ 11
    Ⓒ 13 Ⓓ 23

19. Express $\frac{14}{6}$ as a mixed number in simplest form. (Lesson 6.5)
    Ⓐ $1\frac{4}{6}$ Ⓑ $1\frac{2}{3}$
    Ⓒ $2\frac{2}{6}$ Ⓓ $2\frac{1}{3}$

20. Ms. Lee cut a piece of yarn into different fractional parts: $\frac{1}{12}$, $\frac{1}{4}$ and $\frac{5}{12}$. What fraction of the yarn is left? (Lesson 6.7)
    Ⓐ $\frac{1}{4}$ Ⓑ $\frac{5}{12}$
    Ⓒ $\frac{8}{12}$ Ⓓ $\frac{3}{4}$

[copyright TK]
© Houghton Mifflin Harcourt Publishing Company

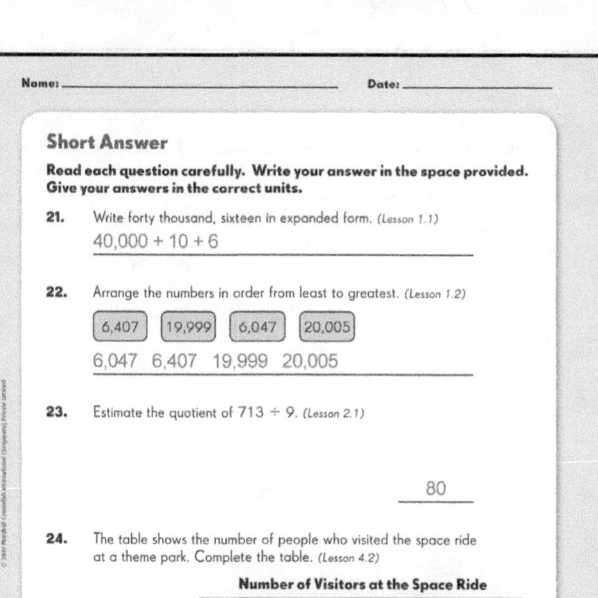

Name: ______________________ Date: __________

Short Answer

Read each question carefully. Write your answer in the space provided. Give your answers in the correct units.

21. Write forty thousand, sixteen in expanded form. *(Lesson 1.1)*

40,000 + 10 + 6

22. Arrange the numbers in order from least to greatest. *(Lesson 1.2)*

6,407 | 19,999 | 6,047 | 20,005

6,047 6,407 19,999 20,005

23. Estimate the quotient of 713 ÷ 9. *(Lesson 2.1)*

80

24. The table shows the number of people who visited the space ride at a theme park. Complete the table. *(Lesson 4.2)*

Number of Visitors at the Space Ride

	Male	Female	Total
Adults	18	32	50
Children	32	38	70

Use the table to answer Exercises 25 and 26.

25. How many people visited the space ride? *(Lesson 4.2)* 120

26. What fraction of the people who visited the space ride were children? *(Lesson 6.7)*

$\frac{7}{12}$

The line graph shows the number of visitors at a museum during the course of a day. *(Lesson 4.3)*

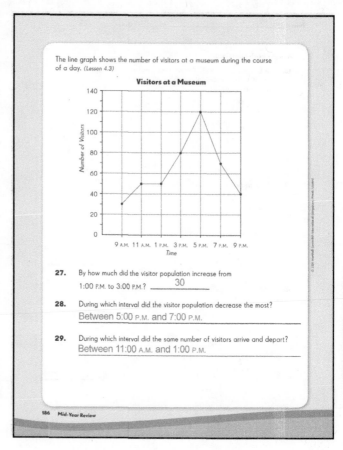

Visitors at a Museum

Number of Visitors: 0, 20, 40, 60, 80, 100, 120, 140

Time: 9 A.M., 11 A.M., 1 P.M., 3 P.M., 5 P.M., 7 P.M., 9 P.M.

27. By how much did the visitor population increase from 1:00 P.M. to 3:00 P.M.? 30

28. During which interval did the visitor population decrease the most?

Between 5:00 P.M. and 7:00 P.M.

29. During which interval did the same number of visitors arrive and depart?

Between 11:00 A.M. and 1:00 P.M.

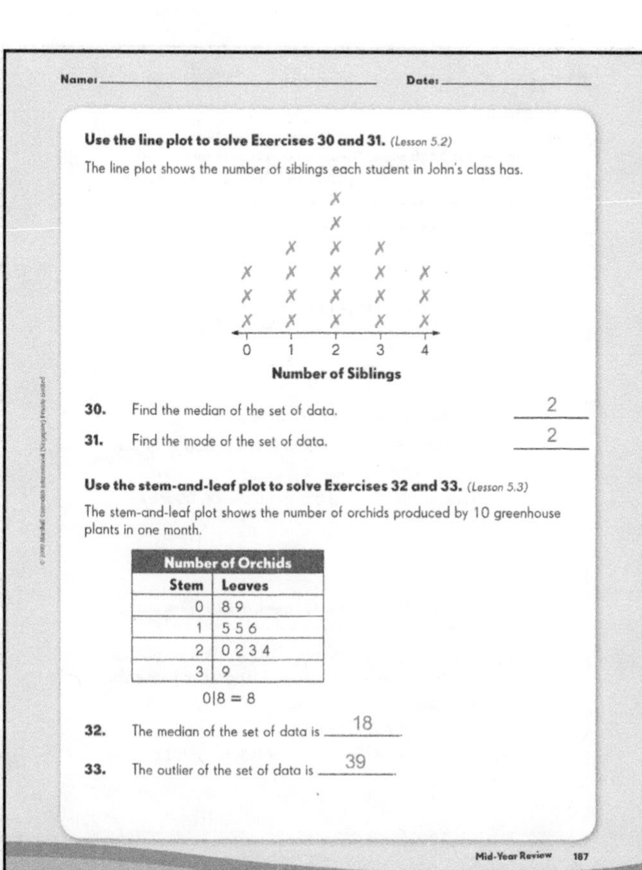

Name: ______________________ Date: __________

Use the line plot to solve Exercises 30 and 31. *(Lesson 5.2)*

The line plot shows the number of siblings each student in John's class has.

30. Find the median of the set of data. 2

31. Find the mode of the set of data. 2

Use the stem-and-leaf plot to solve Exercises 32 and 33. *(Lesson 5.3)*

The stem-and-leaf plot shows the number of orchids produced by 10 greenhouse plants in one month.

Number of Orchids

Stem	Leaves
0	8 9
1	5 5 6
2	0 2 3 4
3	9

0|8 = 8

32. The median of the set of data is 18.

33. The outlier of the set of data is 39.

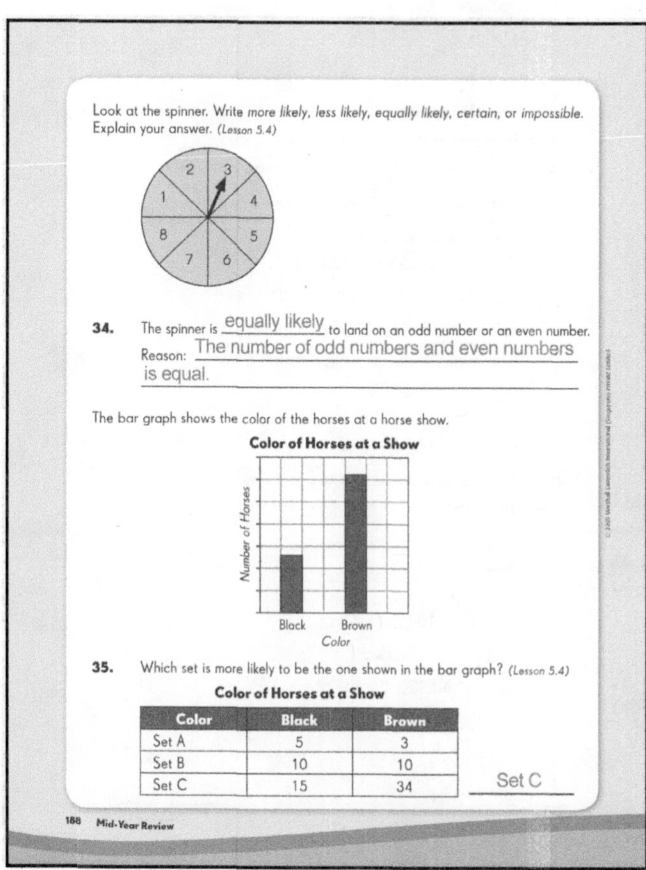

Look at the spinner. Write *more likely, less likely, equally likely, certain,* or *impossible.* Explain your answer. *(Lesson 5.4)*

34. The spinner is equally likely to land on an odd number or an even number.

Reason: The number of odd numbers and even numbers is equal.

The bar graph shows the color of the horses at a horse show.

Color of Horses at a Show

35. Which set is more likely to be the one shown in the bar graph? *(Lesson 5.4)*

Color of Horses at a Show

Color	Black	Brown
Set A	5	3
Set B	10	10
Set C	15	34

Set C

[copyright TK]
© Houghton Mifflin Harcourt Publishing Company

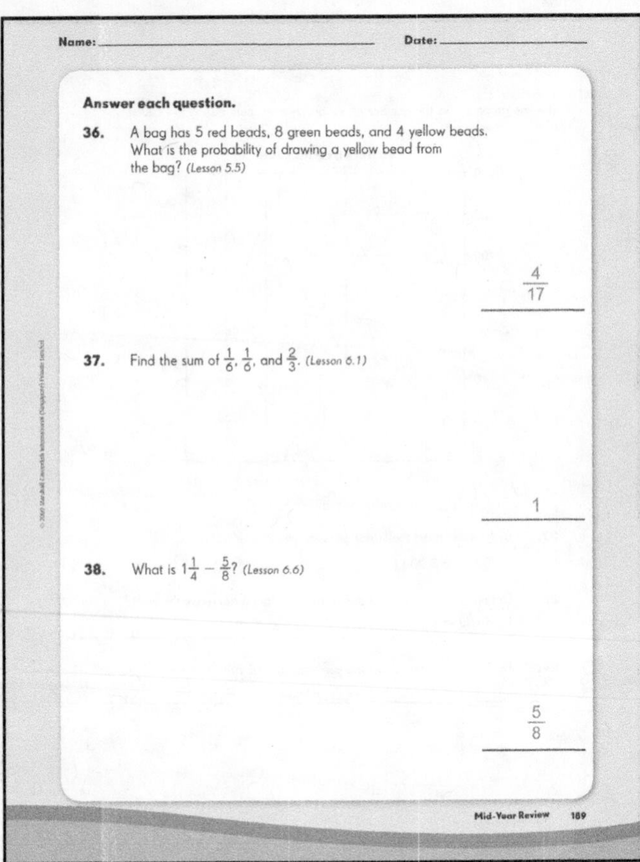

Name: ______________ Date: ______________

Answer each question.

36. A bag has 5 red beads, 8 green beads, and 4 yellow beads. What is the probability of drawing a yellow bead from the bag? *(Lesson 5.5)*

$\frac{4}{17}$

37. Find the sum of $\frac{1}{6}$, $\frac{1}{6}$, and $\frac{2}{3}$. *(Lesson 6.1)*

1

38. What is $1\frac{1}{4} - \frac{5}{8}$? *(Lesson 6.6)*

$\frac{5}{8}$

Mid-Year Review 189

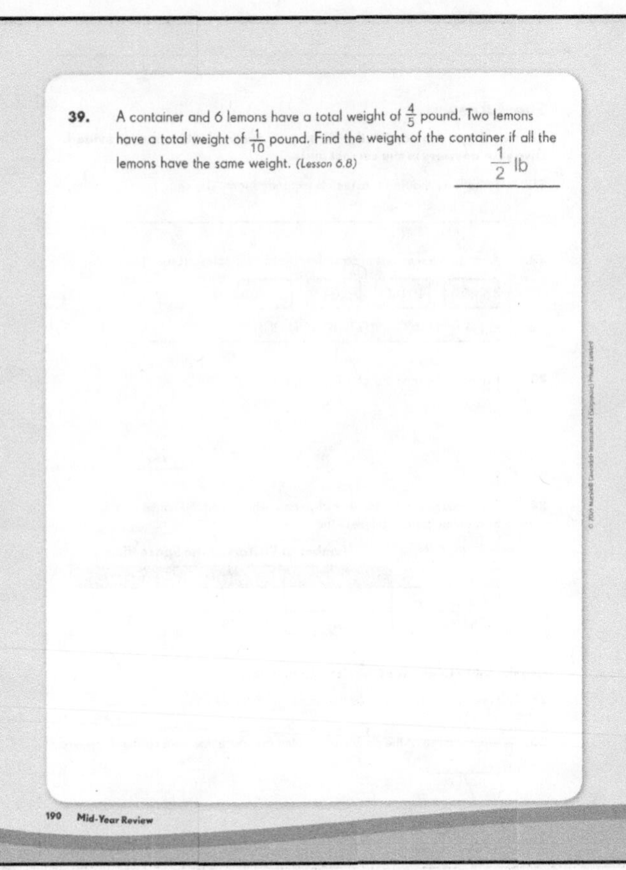

39. A container and 6 lemons have a total weight of $\frac{4}{5}$ pound. Two lemons have a total weight of $\frac{1}{10}$ pound. Find the weight of the container if all the lemons have the same weight. *(Lesson 6.8)*

$\frac{1}{2}$ lb

190 Mid-Year Review

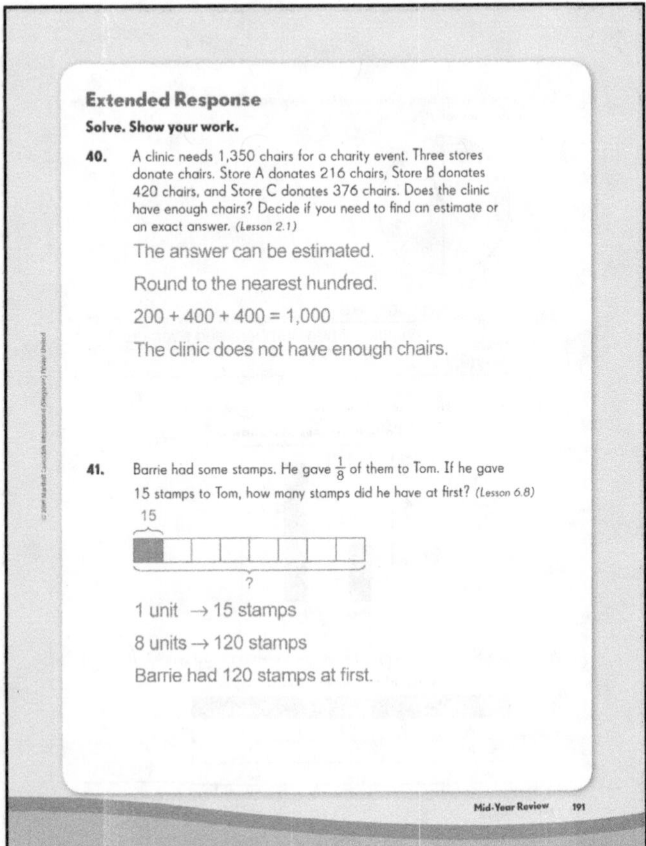

Extended Response

Solve. Show your work.

40. A clinic needs 1,350 chairs for a charity event. Three stores donate chairs. Store A donates 216 chairs, Store B donates 420 chairs, and Store C donates 376 chairs. Does the clinic have enough chairs? Decide if you need to find an estimate or an exact answer. *(Lesson 2.1)*

The answer can be estimated.

Round to the nearest hundred.

200 + 400 + 400 = 1,000

The clinic does not have enough chairs.

41. Barrie had some stamps. He gave $\frac{1}{8}$ of them to Tom. If he gave 15 stamps to Tom, how many stamps did he have at first? *(Lesson 6.8)*

1 unit → 15 stamps

8 units → 120 stamps

Barrie had 120 stamps at first.

Mid-Year Review 191

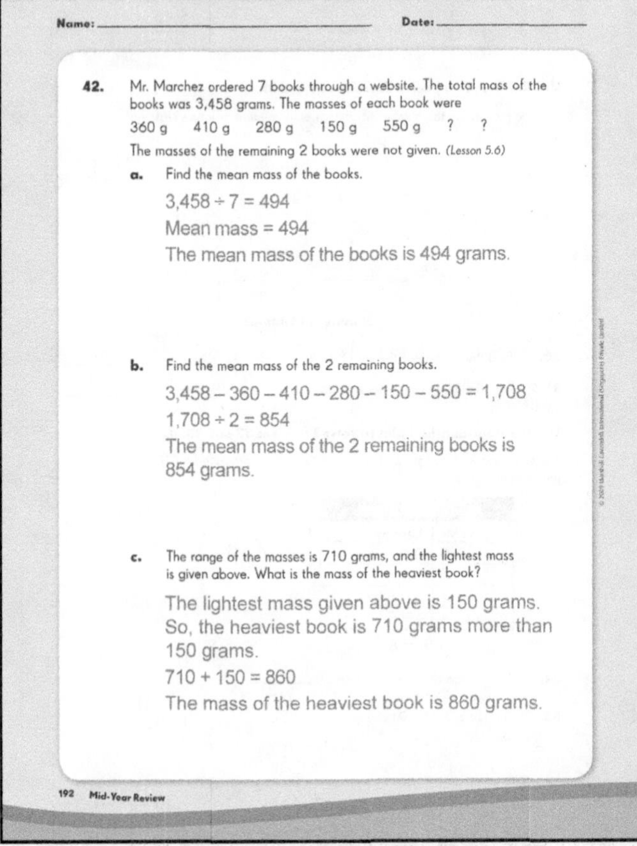

Name: ______________ Date: ______________

42. Mr. Marchez ordered 7 books through a website. The total mass of the books was 3,458 grams. The masses of each book were

360 g 410 g 280 g 150 g 550 g ? ?

The masses of the remaining 2 books were not given. *(Lesson 5.6)*

a. Find the mean mass of the books.

3,458 ÷ 7 = 494

Mean mass = 494

The mean mass of the books is 494 grams.

b. Find the mean mass of the 2 remaining books.

3,458 – 360 – 410 – 280 – 150 – 550 = 1,708

1,708 ÷ 2 = 854

The mean mass of the 2 remaining books is 854 grams.

c. The range of the masses is 710 grams, and the lightest mass is given above. What is the mass of the heaviest book?

The lightest mass given above is 150 grams. So, the heaviest book is 710 grams more than 150 grams.

710 + 150 = 860

The mass of the heaviest book is 860 grams.

192 Mid-Year Review

[copyright TK]
© Houghton Mifflin Harcourt Publishing Company

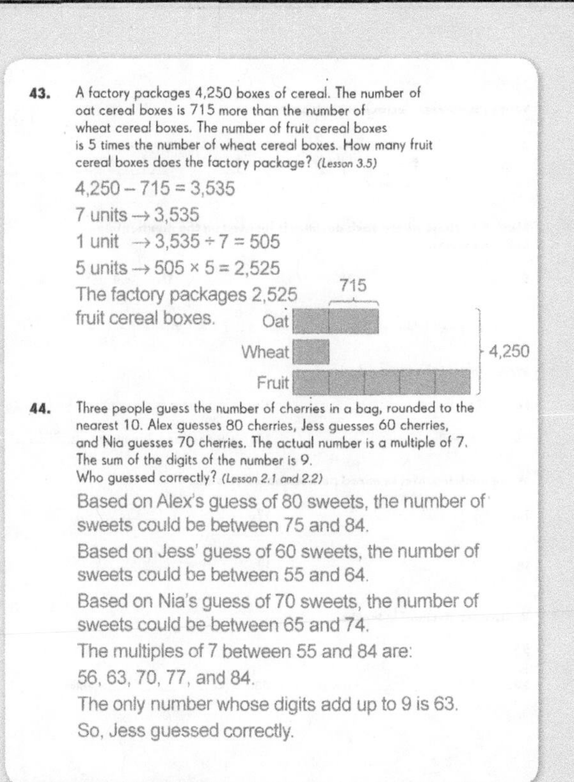

43. A factory packages 4,250 boxes of cereal. The number of oat cereal boxes is 715 more than the number of wheat cereal boxes. The number of fruit cereal boxes is 5 times the number of wheat cereal boxes. How many fruit cereal boxes does the factory package? *(Lesson 3.5)*

4,250 – 715 = 3,535

7 units → 3,535

1 unit → 3,535 ÷ 7 = 505

5 units → 505 × 5 = 2,525

The factory packages 2,525 fruit cereal boxes.

44. Three people guess the number of cherries in a bag, rounded to the nearest 10. Alex guesses 80 cherries, Jess guesses 60 cherries, and Nia guesses 70 cherries. The actual number is a multiple of 7. The sum of the digits of the number is 9. Who guessed correctly? *(Lesson 2.1 and 2.2)*

Based on Alex's guess of 80 sweets, the number of sweets could be between 75 and 84.

Based on Jess' guess of 60 sweets, the number of sweets could be between 55 and 64.

Based on Nia's guess of 70 sweets, the number of sweets could be between 65 and 74.

The multiples of 7 between 55 and 84 are:

56, 63, 70, 77, and 84.

The only number whose digits add up to 9 is 63.

So, Jess guessed correctly.

[copyright TK]
© Houghton Mifflin Harcourt Publishing Company

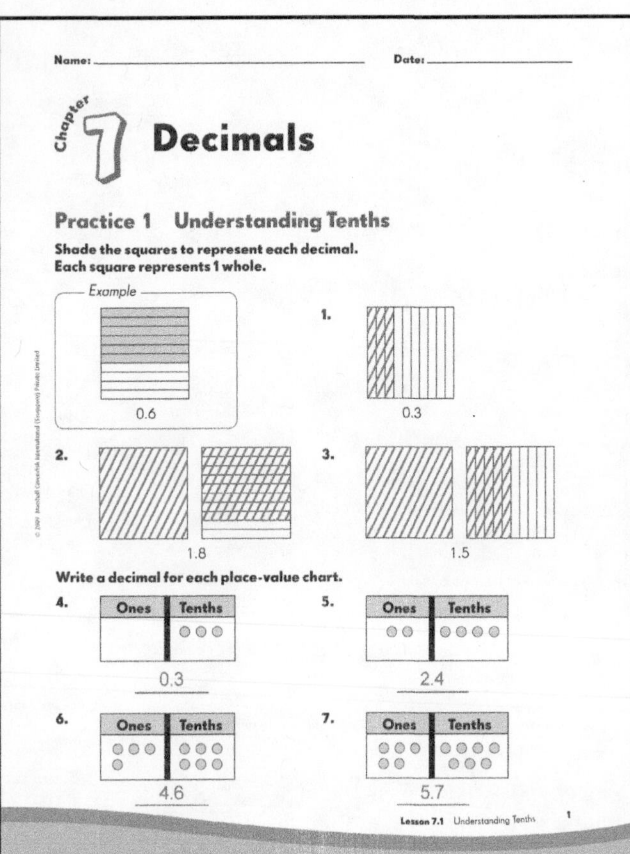

Name: ______ Date: ______

Chapter 7 Decimals

Practice 1 Understanding Tenths

Shade the squares to represent each decimal. Each square represents 1 whole.

Example: 0.6

1. 0.3

2. 1.8

3. 1.5

Write a decimal for each place-value chart.

4.

Ones	Tenths
	●●●

0.3

5.

Ones	Tenths
●●	●●●●

2.4

6.

Ones	Tenths
●●●●	●●●●●●

4.6

7.

Ones	Tenths
●●●●●	●●●●●●●

5.7

© 2009 Marshall Cavendish International (Singapore) Private Limited

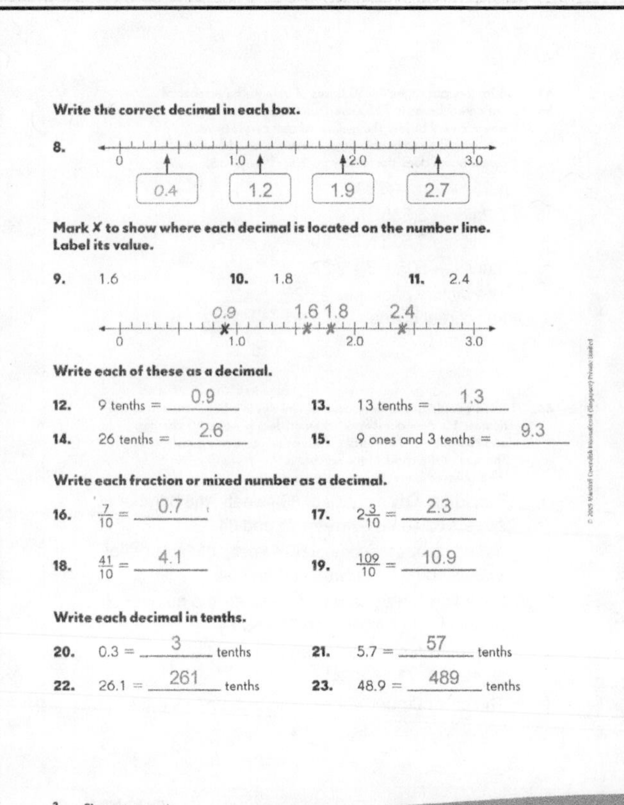

Write the correct decimal in each box.

8. 0.4, 1.2, 1.9, 2.7

Mark X to show where each decimal is located on the number line. Label its value.

9. 1.6 10. 1.8 11. 2.4

0.9, 1.6, 1.8, 2.4

Write each of these as a decimal.

12. 9 tenths = 0.9

13. 13 tenths = 1.3

14. 26 tenths = 2.6

15. 9 ones and 3 tenths = 9.3

Write each fraction or mixed number as a decimal.

16. $\frac{7}{10}$ = 0.7

17. $2\frac{3}{10}$ = 2.3

18. $\frac{41}{10}$ = 4.1

19. $\frac{109}{10}$ = 10.9

Write each decimal in tenths.

20. 0.3 = 3 tenths

21. 5.7 = 57 tenths

22. 26.1 = 261 tenths

23. 48.9 = 489 tenths

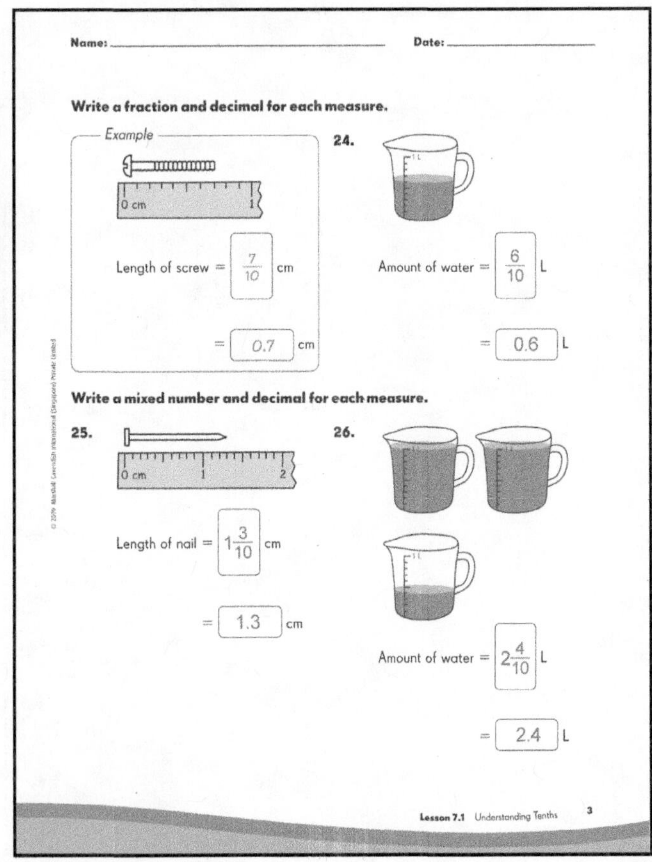

Name: ______ Date: ______

Write a fraction and decimal for each measure.

Example: Length of screw = $\frac{7}{10}$ cm = 0.7 cm

24. Amount of water = $\frac{6}{10}$ L = 0.6 L

Write a mixed number and decimal for each measure.

25. Length of nail = $1\frac{3}{10}$ cm = 1.3 cm

26. Amount of water = $2\frac{4}{10}$ L = 2.4 L

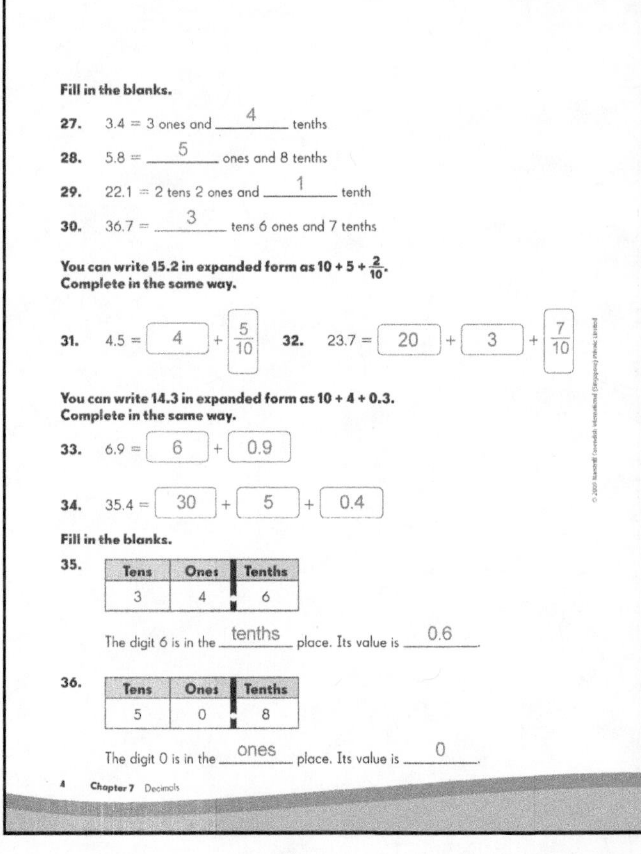

Fill in the blanks.

27. 3.4 = 3 ones and 4 tenths

28. 5.8 = 5 ones and 8 tenths

29. 22.1 = 2 tens 2 ones and 1 tenth

30. 36.7 = 3 tens 6 ones and 7 tenths

You can write 15.2 in expanded form as $10 + 5 + \frac{2}{10}$. Complete in the same way.

31. 4.5 = 4 + $\frac{5}{10}$

32. 23.7 = 20 + 3 + $\frac{7}{10}$

You can write 14.3 in expanded form as 10 + 4 + 0.3. Complete in the same way.

33. 6.9 = 6 + 0.9

34. 35.4 = 30 + 5 + 0.4

Fill in the blanks.

35.

Tens	Ones	Tenths
3	4	6

The digit 6 is in the tenths place. Its value is 0.6.

36.

Tens	Ones	Tenths
5	0	8

The digit 0 is in the ones place. Its value is 0.

Name: ______________ Date: ______________

Practice 2 Understanding Hundredths

Shade the squares to represent each decimal. Each large square represents 1 whole.

Example

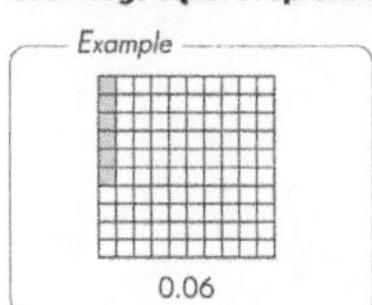

0.06

1. 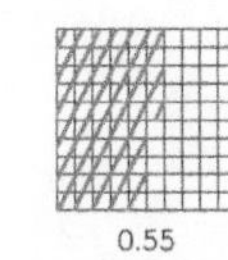

0.55

2. 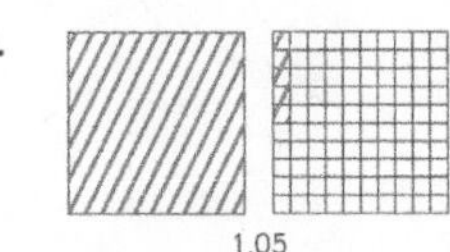

1.05

3. 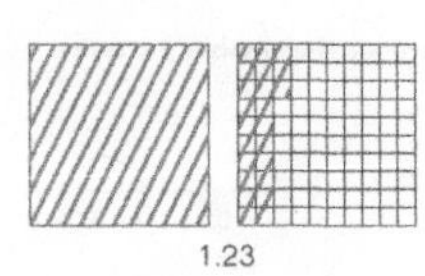

1.23

Write a decimal for each place-value chart.

4.

Ones	Tenths	Hundredths
	●●●	●●●●●●

0.36

5.

Ones	Tenths	Hundredths
●●●●●	●●●●●●	●●●●●●●●

5.68

6.

Ones	Tenths	Hundredths
●●●●	●●●●●	

4.50

7.

Ones	Tenths	Hundredths
●●		●●●●●

2.05

Write the correct decimal in each box.

8. 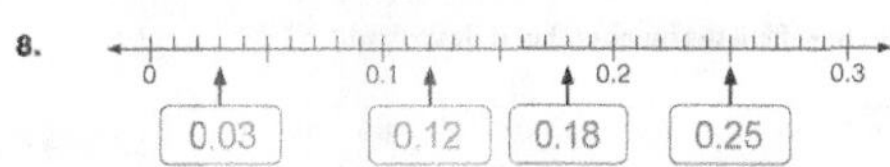

0.03 0.12 0.18 0.25

Mark X to show where each decimal is located on the number line. Label its value.

9. 0.14 10. 0.22 11. 0.27

0.02 0.14 0.22 0.27

Write each of these as a decimal.

12. 9 hundredths = 0.09

13. 23 hundredths = 0.23

14. 6 tenths 1 hundredth = 0.61

15. 7 ones and 90 hundredths = 7.90

Write each fraction as a decimal.

16. $\frac{5}{100}$ = 0.05

17. $\frac{19}{100}$ = 0.19

18. $\frac{83}{100}$ = 0.83

19. $\frac{70}{100}$ = 0.70

Write each fraction or mixed number as a decimal.

20. $3\frac{17}{100}$ = 3.17

21. $18\frac{9}{100}$ = 18.09

Name: ______________ Date: ______________

Write each fraction or mixed number as a decimal.

22. $\frac{233}{100}$ = 2.33

23. $\frac{104}{100}$ = 1.04

Write each decimal in hundredths.

24. 0.07 = 7 hundredths

25. 2.31 = 231 hundredths

26. 1.83 = 183 hundredths

27. 5.09 = 509 hundredths

Fill in the blanks.

28. 0.38 = 3 tenths 8 hundredths

29. 2.71 = 2 ones and 7 tenths 1 hundredth

30. 5.09 = 5 ones and 9 hundredths

31. 8.86 = 8 ones and 8 tenths 6 hundredths

You can write 6.13 in expanded form as $6 + \frac{1}{10} + \frac{3}{100}$. Complete in the same way.

32. 5.24 = 5 + $\frac{2}{10}$ + $\frac{4}{100}$

33. 8.96 = 8 + $\frac{9}{10}$ + $\frac{6}{100}$

You can write 7.45 in expanded form as 7 + 0.4 + 0.05. Complete in the same way.

34. 4.31 = 4 + 0.3 + 0.01

35. 9.57 = 9 + 0.5 + 0.07

Fill in the blanks.

36. In 0.38, the digit 8 is in the hundredths place.

37. In 12.67, the digit in the tenths place is 6.

38. In 3.45, the value of the digit 5 is 0.05.

39. In 5.02, the value of the digit 2 is 2 hundredths.

Write each amount in decimal form.

40. 75 cents = $0.75

41. 40 cents = $0.40

42. 5 cents = $0.05

43. 130 cents = $1.30

44. 10 dollars and 25 cents = $10.25

45. 28 dollars = $28.00

46. 1 dollar and 9 cents = $1.09

Name: ______________________ Date: ______________

Practice 3 Comparing Decimals

Use the number line. Find the number that is described.

0 0.1 0.2 0.3 0.4 0.5 0.6 0.7 0.8 0.9 1.0

1. 0.1 more than 0.2. 0.3
2. 0.3 more than 0.5. 0.8
3. 0.1 less than 0.6. 0.5
4. 0.2 less than 0.9. 0.7

Use the number line. Find the number that is described.

0.1 0.11 0.12 0.13 0.14 0.15 0.16 0.17 0.18 0.19 0.2

5. 0.01 more than 0.13. 0.14
6. 0.04 more than 0.16. 0.2
7. 0.01 less than 0.18. 0.17
8. 0.05 less than 0.17. 0.12

Fill in the missing numbers.

	Number	0.1 More Than the Number	0.1 Less Than the Number
9.	4.7	4.8	4.6
10.	2.05	2.15	1.95

	Number	0.01 More Than the Number	0.01 Less Than the Number
11.	0.94	0.95	0.93
12.	3.8	3.81	3.79

© 2009 Marshall Cavendish International (Singapore) Private Limited

Complete the number patterns. Use the number line to help you.

0 0.5 1.0 1.5 2.0

13. 0.2 0.4 0.6 0.8 1.0
14. 1.1 0.9 0.7 0.5 0.3
15. 0.1 0.4 0.7 1.0 1.3
16. 2.0 1.6 1.2 0.8 0.4

Continue the number patterns.

17. 0.03 0.06 0.09

0.03 0.06 0.09 0.12 0.15

18. 0.16 0.20 0.24

0.24 0.20 0.16 0.12 0.08

© 2009 Marshall Cavendish International (Singapore) Private Limited

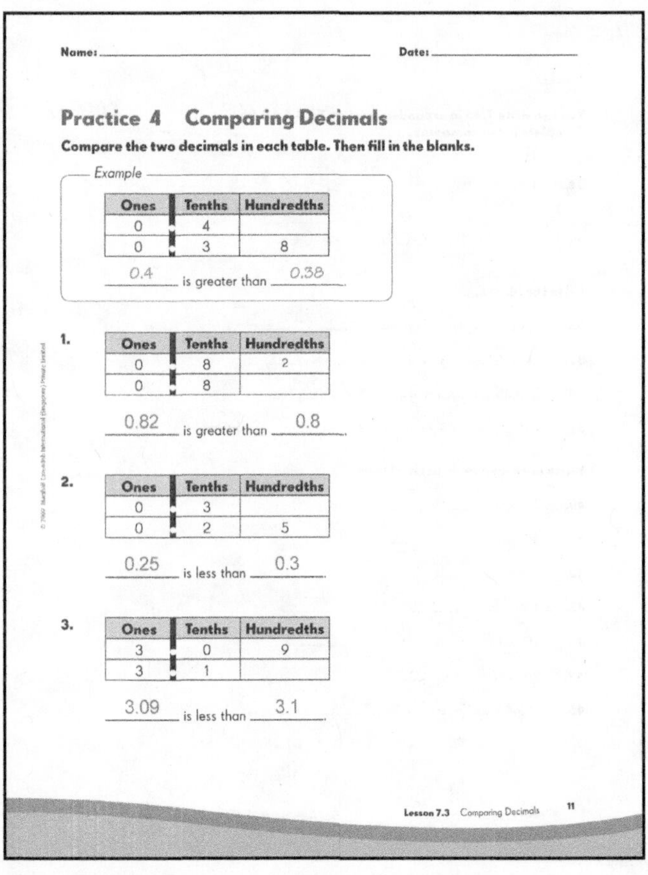

Name: ______________________ Date: ______________

Practice 4 Comparing Decimals

Compare the two decimals in each table. Then fill in the blanks.

Example

Ones	Tenths	Hundredths
0	4	
0	3	8

0.4 is greater than 0.38.

1.

Ones	Tenths	Hundredths
0	8	2
0	8	

0.82 is greater than 0.8.

2.

Ones	Tenths	Hundredths
0	3	
0	2	5

0.25 is less than 0.3.

3.

Ones	Tenths	Hundredths
3	0	9
3	1	

3.09 is less than 3.1.

© 2009 Marshall Cavendish International (Singapore) Private Limited

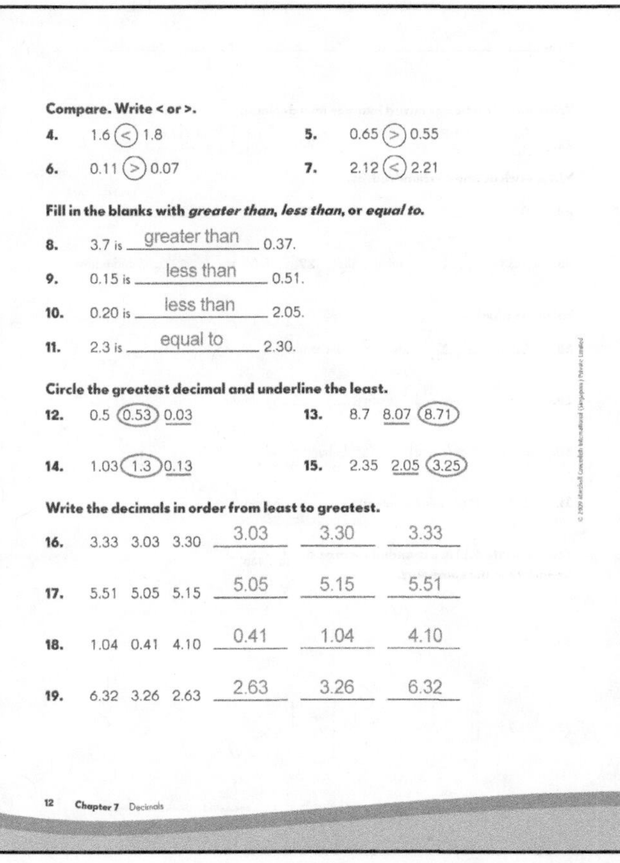

Compare. Write < or >.

4. 1.6 (<) 1.8
5. 0.65 (>) 0.55
6. 0.11 (>) 0.07
7. 2.12 (<) 2.21

Fill in the blanks with *greater than*, *less than*, or *equal to*.

8. 3.7 is greater than 0.37.
9. 0.15 is less than 0.51.
10. 0.20 is less than 2.05.
11. 2.3 is equal to 2.30.

Circle the greatest decimal and underline the least.

12. 0.5 (0.53) <u>0.03</u>
13. 8.7 <u>8.07</u> (8.71)
14. 1.03 (1.3) <u>0.13</u>
15. 2.35 <u>2.05</u> (3.25)

Write the decimals in order from least to greatest.

16. 3.33 3.03 3.30 3.03 3.30 3.33
17. 5.51 5.05 5.15 5.05 5.15 5.51
18. 1.04 0.41 4.10 0.41 1.04 4.10
19. 6.32 3.26 2.63 2.63 3.26 6.32

© 2009 Marshall Cavendish International (Singapore) Private Limited

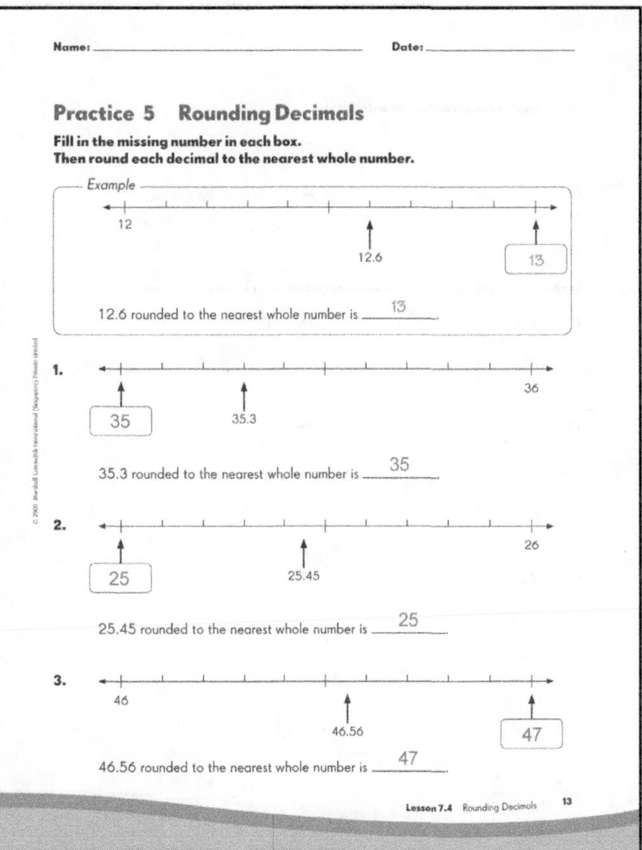

Name: ____________ Date: ____________

Practice 5 Rounding Decimals

Fill in the missing number in each box.
Then round each decimal to the nearest whole number.

Example

12 — 12.6 — 13

12.6 rounded to the nearest whole number is 13.

1. 35 — 35.3 — 36

35.3 rounded to the nearest whole number is 35.

2. 25 — 25.45 — 26

25.45 rounded to the nearest whole number is 25.

3. 46 — 46.56 — 47

46.56 rounded to the nearest whole number is 47.

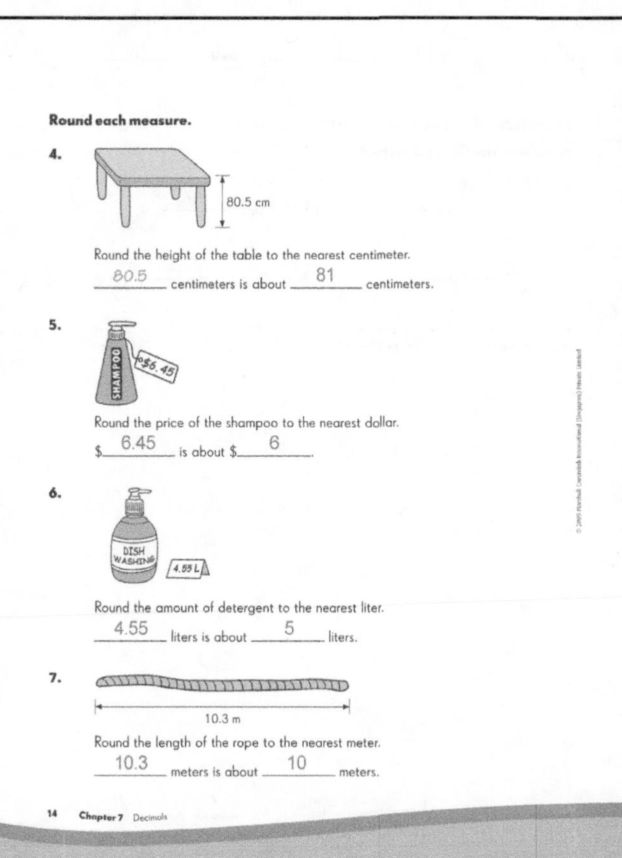

Round each measure.

4. 80.5 cm

Round the height of the table to the nearest centimeter.
80.5 centimeters is about 81 centimeters.

5.

Round the price of the shampoo to the nearest dollar.
$6.45 is about $6.

6.

Round the amount of detergent to the nearest liter.
4.55 liters is about 5 liters.

7. 10.3 m

Round the length of the rope to the nearest meter.
10.3 meters is about 10 meters.

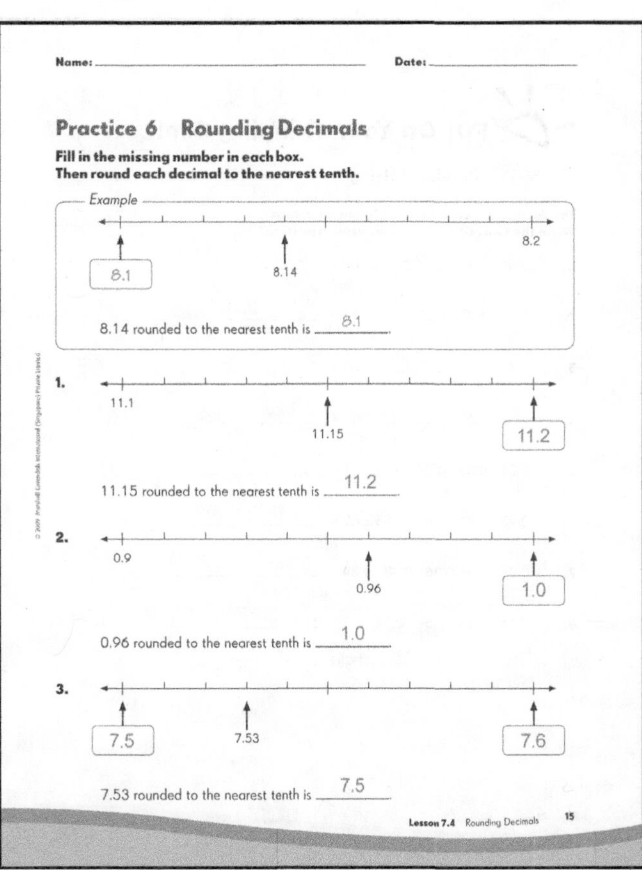

Name: ____________ Date: ____________

Practice 6 Rounding Decimals

Fill in the missing number in each box.
Then round each decimal to the nearest tenth.

Example

8.1 — 8.14 — 8.2

8.14 rounded to the nearest tenth is 8.1.

1. 11.1 — 11.15 — 11.2

11.15 rounded to the nearest tenth is 11.2.

2. 0.9 — 0.96 — 1.0

0.96 rounded to the nearest tenth is 1.0.

3. 7.5 — 7.53 — 7.6

7.53 rounded to the nearest tenth is 7.5.

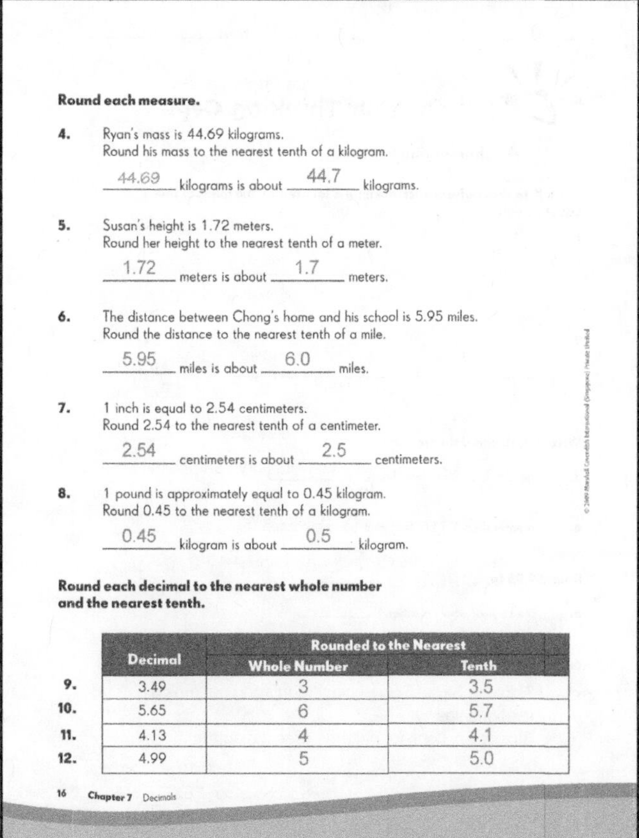

Round each measure.

4. Ryan's mass is 44.69 kilograms.
Round his mass to the nearest tenth of a kilogram.
44.69 kilograms is about 44.7 kilograms.

5. Susan's height is 1.72 meters.
Round her height to the nearest tenth of a meter.
1.72 meters is about 1.7 meters.

6. The distance between Chong's home and his school is 5.95 miles.
Round the distance to the nearest tenth of a mile.
5.95 miles is about 6.0 miles.

7. 1 inch is equal to 2.54 centimeters.
Round 2.54 to the nearest tenth of a centimeter.
2.54 centimeters is about 2.5 centimeters.

8. 1 pound is approximately equal to 0.45 kilogram.
Round 0.45 to the nearest tenth of a kilogram.
0.45 kilogram is about 0.5 kilogram.

Round each decimal to the nearest whole number and the nearest tenth.

	Decimal	Rounded to the Nearest	
		Whole Number	Tenth
9.	3.49	3	3.5
10.	5.65	6	5.7
11.	4.13	4	4.1
12.	4.99	5	5.0

Chapter 7

Name: ______________________ Date: ______________

Practice 7 Fractions and Decimals

Write each fraction as a decimal.

Example

$\frac{9}{10}$ = 0.9

1. $\frac{7}{10}$ = 0.7

2. $\frac{3}{100}$ = 0.03

3. $\frac{51}{100}$ = 0.51

Express each fraction as a decimal.
Hint: Make the denominator 10 or 100.

Example

$\frac{2}{5} = \frac{4}{10}$

$= 0.4$

4. $\frac{1}{2} = \frac{5}{10}$
$= 0.5$

5. $\frac{5}{2} = \frac{25}{10}$
$= 2.5$

6. $\frac{5}{4} = \frac{125}{100}$
$= 1.25$

7. $\frac{7}{20} = \frac{35}{100}$
$= 0.35$

8. $\frac{2}{25} = \frac{8}{100}$
$= 0.08$

© 2009 Marshall Cavendish International (Singapore) Private Limited

Write each mixed number as a decimal.

9. $3\frac{5}{10} = 3.5$

10. $6\frac{43}{100} = 6.43$

11. $8\frac{3}{5} = 8 + \frac{6}{10}$
$= 8 + 0.6$
$= 8.6$

12. $10\frac{3}{20} = 10 + \frac{15}{100}$
$= 10 + 0.15$
$= 10.15$

Write each decimal as a fraction or mixed number in simplest form.

13. $0.3 = \frac{3}{10}$

14. $0.5 = \frac{5}{10}$
$= \frac{1}{2}$

15. $5.2 = 5 + 0.2$
$= 5 + \frac{2}{10}$
$= 5 + \frac{1}{5}$
$= 5\frac{1}{5}$

16. $0.25 = \frac{25}{100}$
$= \frac{1}{4}$

17. $4.08 = 4 + \frac{8}{100}$
$= 4 + \frac{2}{25}$
$= 4\frac{2}{25}$

18. $3.45 = 3 + \frac{45}{100}$
$= 3 + \frac{9}{20}$
$= 3\frac{9}{20}$

© 2009 Marshall Cavendish International (Singapore) Private Limited

Name: ______________________ Date: ______________

Put On Your Thinking Cap!

Challenging Practice

Mark X to show where each decimal is located on the number line. Label its value.

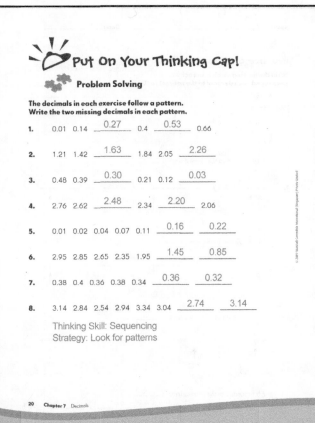

1. 1.2

Number line: 0, 0.4, 0.8, X marked at 1.2 (labelled 1.2)

2. 0.12

Number line: 0, 0.03, 0.06, X marked at 0.12 (labelled 0.12)

Write any decimal that is

3. greater than 2 but less than 2.1. Answers vary. Sample answer: 2.05

4. greater than 1.1 but less than 1.2. Answers vary. Sample answer: 1.18

Round 9.95 to

5. the nearest whole number. 10

6. the nearest tenth. 10.0

Thinking Skills: Sequencing, Identifying patterns & relationships
Strategies: Look for patterns, Use a diagram

© 2009 Marshall Cavendish International (Singapore) Private Limited

Put On Your Thinking Cap!

Problem Solving

The decimals in each exercise follow a pattern.
Write the two missing decimals in each pattern.

1. 0.01 0.14 0.27 0.4 0.53 0.66

2. 1.21 1.42 1.63 1.84 2.05 2.26

3. 0.48 0.39 0.30 0.21 0.12 0.03

4. 2.76 2.62 2.48 2.34 2.20 2.06

5. 0.01 0.02 0.04 0.07 0.11 0.16 0.22

6. 2.95 2.85 2.65 2.35 1.95 1.45 0.85

7. 0.38 0.4 0.36 0.38 0.34 0.36 0.32

8. 3.14 2.84 2.54 2.94 3.34 3.04 2.74 3.14

Thinking Skill: Sequencing
Strategy: Look for patterns

© 2009 Marshall Cavendish International (Singapore) Private Limited

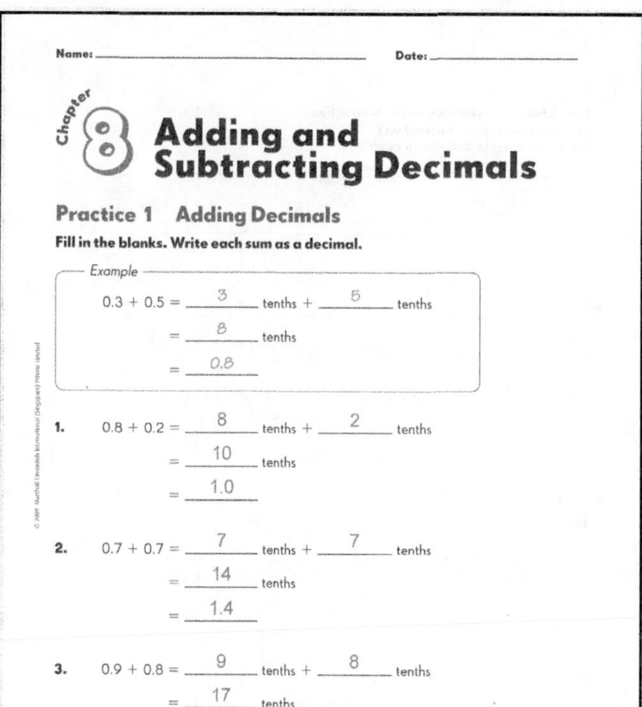

Name: ______ Date: ______

Chapter 8 Adding and Subtracting Decimals

Practice 1 Adding Decimals

Fill in the blanks. Write each sum as a decimal.

Example

0.3 + 0.5 = 3 tenths + 5 tenths
= 8 tenths
= 0.8

1. 0.8 + 0.2 = 8 tenths + 2 tenths
= 10 tenths
= 1.0

2. 0.7 + 0.7 = 7 tenths + 7 tenths
= 14 tenths
= 1.4

3. 0.9 + 0.8 = 9 tenths + 8 tenths
= 17 tenths
= 1.7

© 2009 Marshall Cavendish International (Singapore) Private Limited

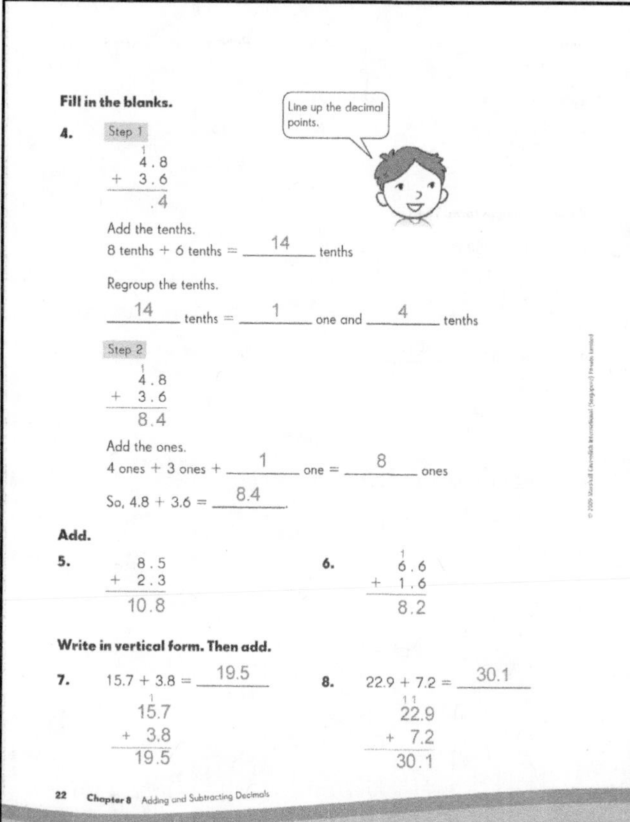

Fill in the blanks.

Line up the decimal points.

4. Step 1

$$\begin{array}{r} \overset{1}{4}.8 \\ +\ 3.6 \\ \hline .4 \end{array}$$

Add the tenths.
8 tenths + 6 tenths = 14 tenths

Regroup the tenths.
14 tenths = 1 one and 4 tenths

Step 2

$$\begin{array}{r} \overset{1}{4}.8 \\ +\ 3.6 \\ \hline 8.4 \end{array}$$

Add the ones.
4 ones + 3 ones + 1 one = 8 ones

So, 4.8 + 3.6 = 8.4.

Add.

5.
$$\begin{array}{r} 8.5 \\ +\ 2.3 \\ \hline 10.8 \end{array}$$

6.
$$\begin{array}{r} \overset{1}{6}.6 \\ +\ 1.6 \\ \hline 8.2 \end{array}$$

Write in vertical form. Then add.

7. 15.7 + 3.8 = 19.5

$$\begin{array}{r} 1\overset{1}{5}.7 \\ +\ 3.8 \\ \hline 19.5 \end{array}$$

8. 22.9 + 7.2 = 30.1

$$\begin{array}{r} \overset{1}{2}\overset{1}{2}.9 \\ +\ 7.2 \\ \hline 30.1 \end{array}$$

© 2009 Marshall Cavendish International (Singapore) Private Limited

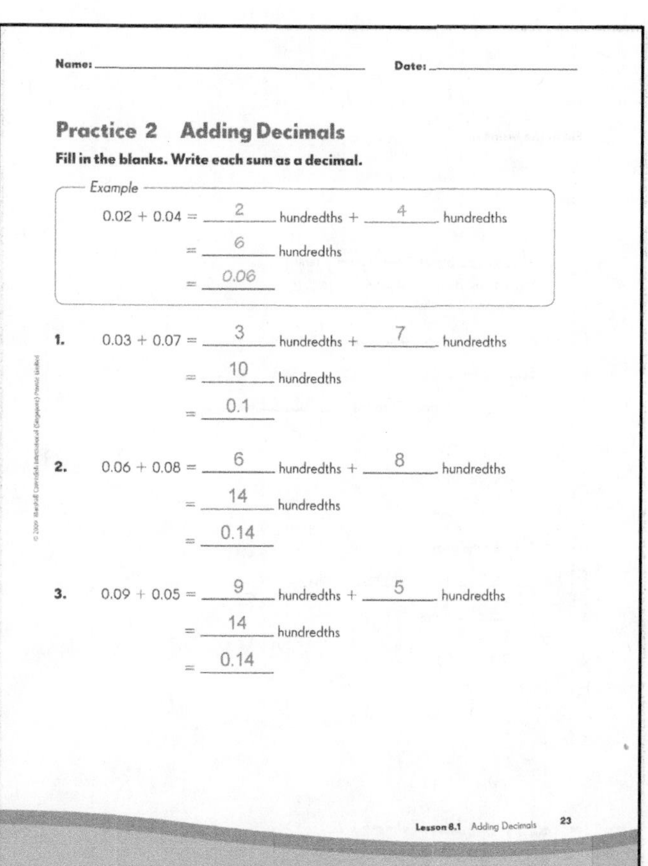

Name: ______ Date: ______

Practice 2 Adding Decimals

Fill in the blanks. Write each sum as a decimal.

Example

0.02 + 0.04 = 2 hundredths + 4 hundredths
= 6 hundredths
= 0.06

1. 0.03 + 0.07 = 3 hundredths + 7 hundredths
= 10 hundredths
= 0.1

2. 0.06 + 0.08 = 6 hundredths + 8 hundredths
= 14 hundredths
= 0.14

3. 0.09 + 0.05 = 9 hundredths + 5 hundredths
= 14 hundredths
= 0.14

© 2009 Marshall Cavendish International (Singapore) Private Limited

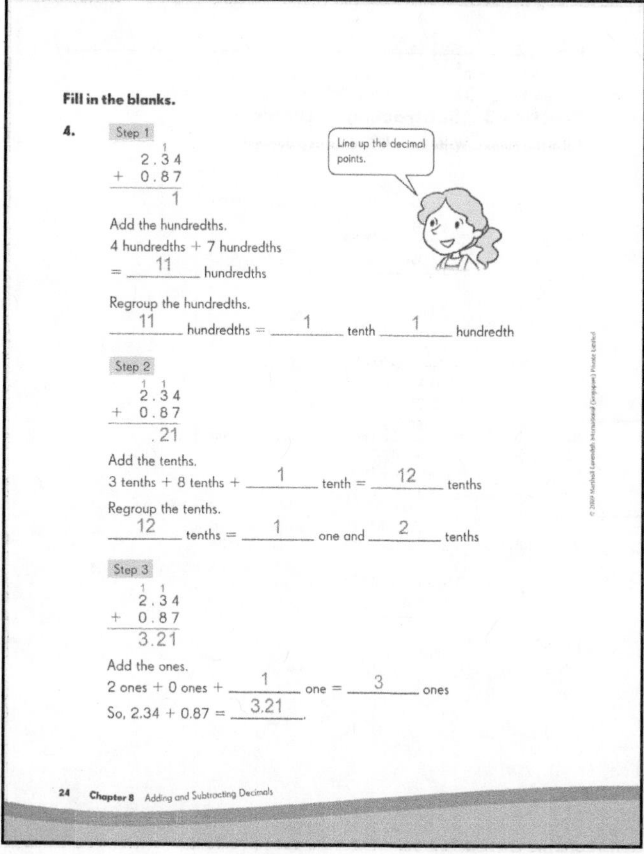

Fill in the blanks.

Line up the decimal points.

4. Step 1

$$\begin{array}{r} 2.\overset{1}{3}4 \\ +\ 0.87 \\ \hline 1 \end{array}$$

Add the hundredths.
4 hundredths + 7 hundredths
= 11 hundredths

Regroup the hundredths.
11 hundredths = 1 tenth 1 hundredth

Step 2

$$\begin{array}{r} \overset{1}{2}.\overset{1}{3}4 \\ +\ 0.87 \\ \hline .21 \end{array}$$

Add the tenths.
3 tenths + 8 tenths + 1 tenth = 12 tenths

Regroup the tenths.
12 tenths = 1 one and 2 tenths

Step 3

$$\begin{array}{r} \overset{1}{2}.\overset{1}{3}4 \\ +\ 0.87 \\ \hline 3.21 \end{array}$$

Add the ones.
2 ones + 0 ones + 1 one = 3 ones

So, 2.34 + 0.87 = 3.21.

© 2009 Marshall Cavendish International (Singapore) Private Limited

Name: ______________________ Date: ______________

Add.

5.
```
  0.02
+ 0.35
------
  0.37
```

6.
```
     1
  0.06
+ 0.46
------
  0.52
```

Write in vertical form. Then add.

7. $0.57 + $0.29 = $ 0.86
```
   1
  $0.57
+ $0.29
-------
  $0.86
```

8. 3.6 + 0.54 = 4.14
```
  1
  3.6
+ 0.54
------
  4.14
```

9. $0.78 + $0.88 = $ 1.66
```
   1 1
  $0.78
+ $0.88
-------
  $1.66
```

10. 7.25 + 1.78 = 9.03
```
  1 1
  7.25
+ 1.78
------
  9.03
```

© 2009 Marshall Cavendish International (Singapore) Private Limited

Derek hops two steps on each number line.
Which decimal does he land on?
Write the correct decimal in each box.

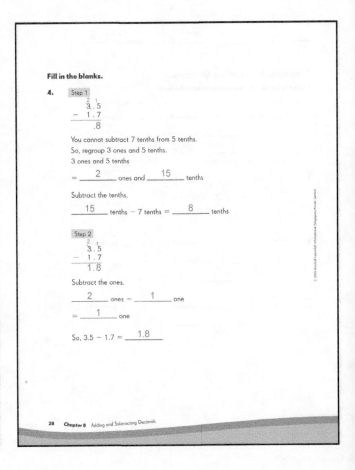

Example

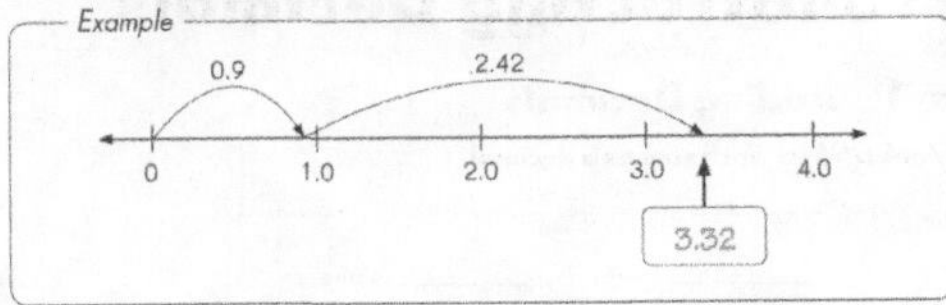

11.

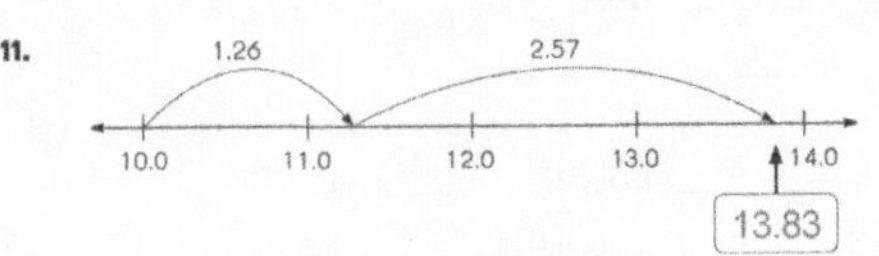

12.

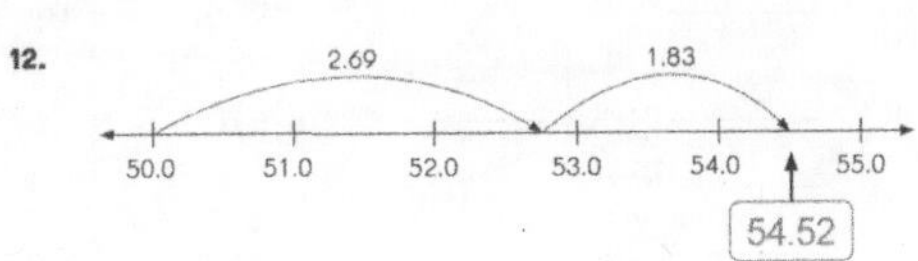

13.

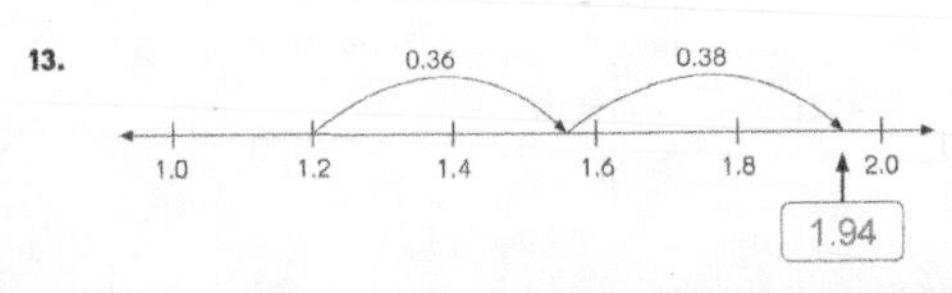

© 2009 Marshall Cavendish International (Singapore) Private Limited

Name: ______________________ Date: ______________

Practice 3 Subtracting Decimals

Fill in the blanks. Write each difference as a decimal.

Example

0.9 − 0.4 = 9 tenths − 4 tenths
= 5 tenths
= 0.5

1. 1 − 0.3 = 10 tenths − 3 tenths
= 7 tenths
= 0.7

2. 1.3 − 0.6 = 13 tenths − 6 tenths
= 7 tenths
= 0.7

3. 1.8 − 0.9 = 18 tenths − 9 tenths
= 9 tenths
= 0.9

© 2009 Marshall Cavendish International (Singapore) Private Limited

Fill in the blanks.

4. Step 1
```
  2 1
  3.5
- 1.7
-----
   .8
```

You cannot subtract 7 tenths from 5 tenths.
So, regroup 3 ones and 5 tenths.
3 ones and 5 tenths
= 2 ones and 15 tenths

Subtract the tenths.
15 tenths − 7 tenths = 8 tenths

Step 2
```
  2 1
  3.5
- 1.7
-----
  1.8
```

Subtract the ones.
2 ones − 1 one
= 1 one

So, 3.5 − 1.7 = 1.8.

© 2009 Marshall Cavendish International (Singapore) Private Limited

Name: ______________________ Date: ______________

Subtract.

5.
```
  4.6
− 2.2
  2.4
```

6.
```
  ⁶7.¹4
− 6.5
  0.9
```

Write in vertical form. Then subtract.

7. 6.7 − 2.4 = 4.3
```
  6.7
− 2.4
  4.3
```

8. 3 − 1.3 = 1.7
```
  ²3.¹0
− 1.3
  1.7
```

Fill in the blanks. Write each difference as a decimal.

Example

0.08 − 0.02 = 8 hundredths − 2 hundredths
= 6 hundredths
= 0.06

9. 0.23 − 0.19 = 23 hundredths − 19 hundredths
= 4 hundredths
= 0.04

10. 0.1 − 0.06 = 10 hundredths − 6 hundredths
= 4 hundredths
= 0.04

© 2009 Marshall Cavendish International (Singapore) Private Limited

Fill in the blanks.

11. Step 1
```
  4.¹2¹3
− 1.5 4
      9
```

You cannot subtract 4 hundredths from 3 hundredths.
So, regroup 2 tenths 3 hundredths.
2 tenths 3 hundredths
= 1 tenth 13 hundredths

Subtract the hundredths.
13 hundredths − 4 hundredths
= 9 hundredths

Step 2
```
  ³4.¹2¹3
− 1.5 4
   .6 9
```

You cannot subtract 5 tenths from 1 tenth.
So, regroup 4 ones and 1 tenth.
4 ones and 1 tenth
= 3 ones and 11 tenths

Subtract the tenths.
11 tenths − 5 tenths = 6 tenths

© 2009 Marshall Cavendish International (Singapore) Private Limited

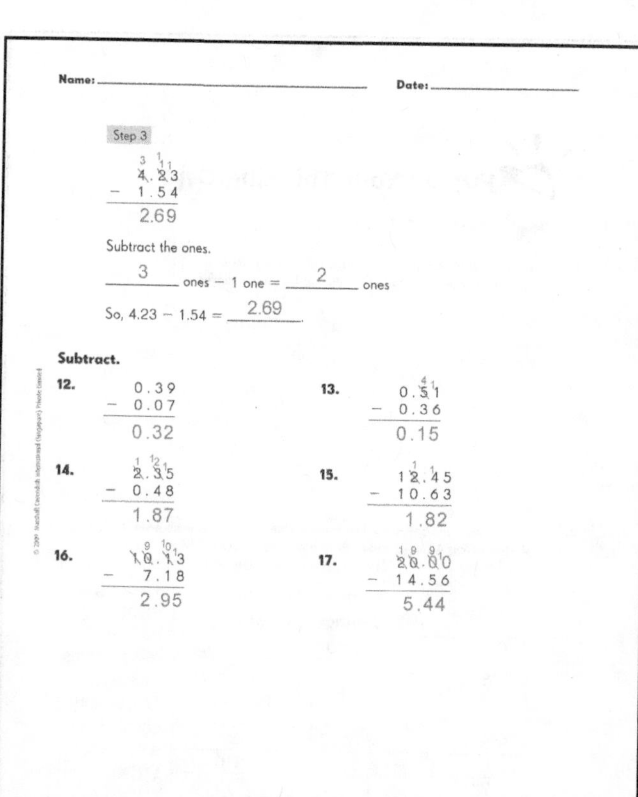

Name: ______________________ Date: ______________

Step 3
```
  ³4.¹²¹3
− 1.5 4
  2.6 9
```

Subtract the ones.
3 ones − 1 one = 2 ones

So, 4.23 − 1.54 = 2.69

Subtract.

12.
```
  0.39
− 0.07
  0.32
```

13.
```
  0.⁴5¹1
− 0.36
  0.15
```

14.
```
  ¹2.¹²3¹5
− 0.48
  1.87
```

15.
```
  1¹2.¹4 5
− 10.63
   1.82
```

16.
```
  ⁹1̸0.¹⁰1̸¹3
−  7.18
   2.95
```

17.
```
  ¹2⁹0.⁹0¹0
− 14.56
   5.44
```

© 2009 Marshall Cavendish International (Singapore) Private Limited

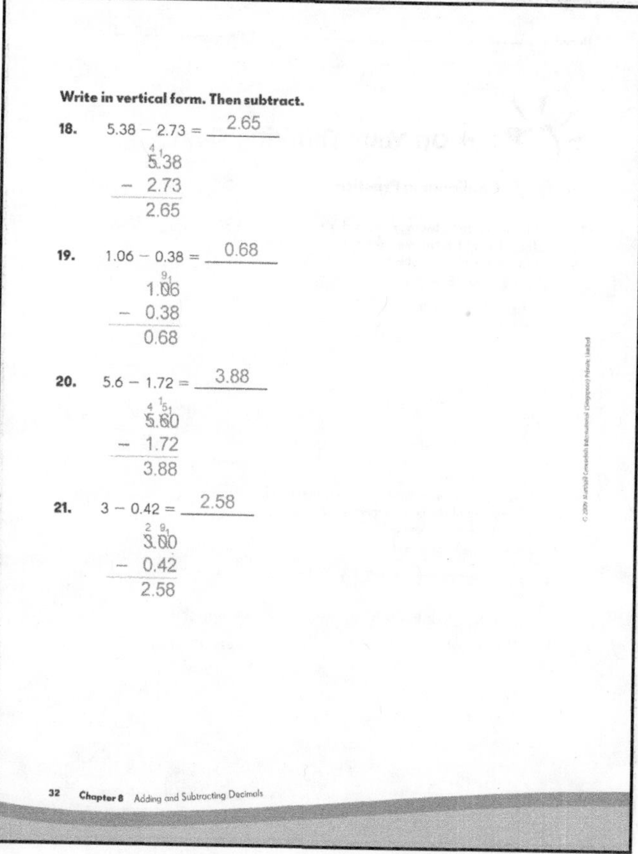

Write in vertical form. Then subtract.

18. 5.38 − 2.73 = 2.65
```
  ⁴5.¹38
− 2.73
  2.65
```

19. 1.06 − 0.38 = 0.68
```
  1.⁹0¹6
− 0.38
  0.68
```

20. 5.6 − 1.72 = 3.88
```
  ⁴5.¹⁵6¹0
− 1.72
  3.88
```

21. 3 − 0.42 = 2.58
```
  ²3.⁹0¹0
− 0.42
  2.58
```

© 2009 Marshall Cavendish International (Singapore) Private Limited

Chapter 8

Name: ______________________ Date: ______________

Practice 4 Real-World Problems: Decimals

Solve. Show your work.

Example

1 pound of grapes costs $1.79 and 1 pound of peaches costs $1.49. What is the total cost of 1 pound of grapes and 1 pound of peaches?

Cost of grapes + cost of peaches = total cost
$1.79 + $1.49 = $3.28
The total cost of 1 pound of grapes and 1 pound of peaches is $3.28.

1. A tank is full of water. After 16.5 liters of water are used, 8.75 liters of water are left. How much water was in the full tank?

Amount of water used + amount of water left = total amount of water
16.5 + 8.75 = 25.25
There were 25.25 liters of water in the tank at first.

2. A piece of fabric is 4.5 yards long. A customer buys 2.35 yards of the fabric. How many yards of fabric are left?

Total length of fabric – length of fabric sold = length of fabric left
4.5 – 2.35 = 2.15
2.15 yards of fabric are left.

3. Mr. Larson lives 8.7 miles from school. He was driving home from school and stopped 3.5 miles along the way at a supermarket. How much farther does he have to drive before he reaches home?

Distance from home – distance traveled = distance remaining
8.7 – 3.5 = 5.2
He has to drive 5.2 miles farther to reach home.

4. A grocery store is having a sale. A loaf of wheat bread regularly costs $2.29, but the sale price is $1.79. The store is also offering 50¢ off on a gallon of fresh milk. If Mrs. Larson buys a gallon of fresh milk and a loaf of wheat bread, how much does she save on her purchases?

Regular price of wheat bread – sale price of wheat bread = savings from the loaf of wheat bread
$2.29 – $1.79 = $0.50
Mrs. Larson saves $0.50 on the loaf of wheat bread.
Savings from the loaf of wheat bread + the gallon of fresh milk = total savings
$0.50 + $0.50 = $1
Mrs. Larson saves $1 on her purchases.

5. Lily bought a skirt for $25.90 and a shirt for $19.50. She paid the cashier $50. How much change did she receive?

Cost of skirt + cost of shirt = total amount spent
$25.90 + $19.50 = $45.40
Lily spent $45.40.
$50 – total amount spent = amount of change
$50 – $45.40 = $4.60
She received $4.60 change.

6. Shannon collects rainwater to water her flowers. She has one bucket with 3.4 gallons of water and another with 1.85 gallons less. She uses both buckets to water the flowers. How many gallons of water does she use?

Water in first bucket – 1.85 = water in second bucket
3.4 – 1.85 = 1.55
There are 1.55 gallons of water in the second bucket.
Water in first bucket + water in second bucket = total amount of water used
3.4 + 1.55 = 4.95
She uses 4.95 gallons of water.

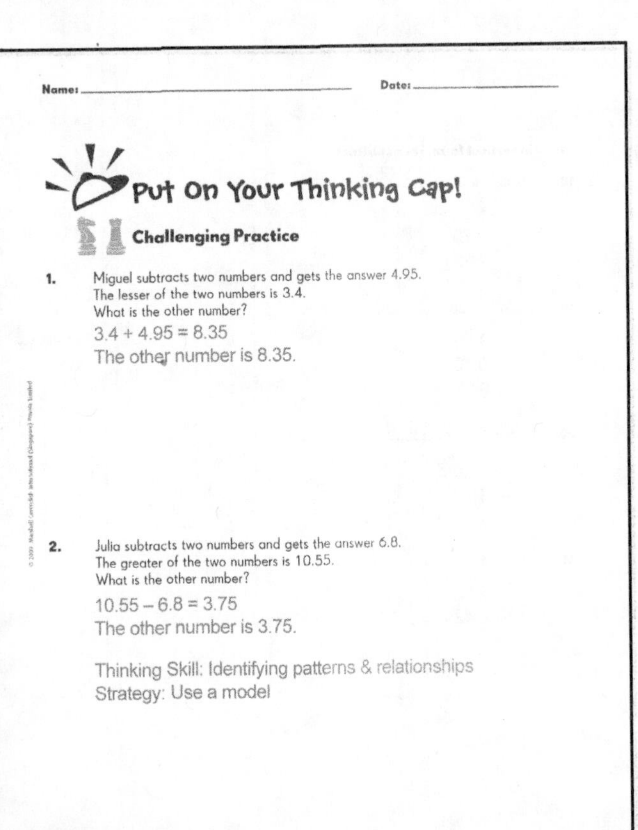

Name: ______________________ Date: ______________

Put On Your Thinking Cap!

Challenging Practice

1. Miguel subtracts two numbers and gets the answer 4.95. The lesser of the two numbers is 3.4. What is the other number?

3.4 + 4.95 = 8.35
The other number is 8.35.

2. Julia subtracts two numbers and gets the answer 6.8. The greater of the two numbers is 10.55. What is the other number?

10.55 – 6.8 = 3.75
The other number is 3.75.

Thinking Skill: Identifying patterns & relationships
Strategy: Use a model

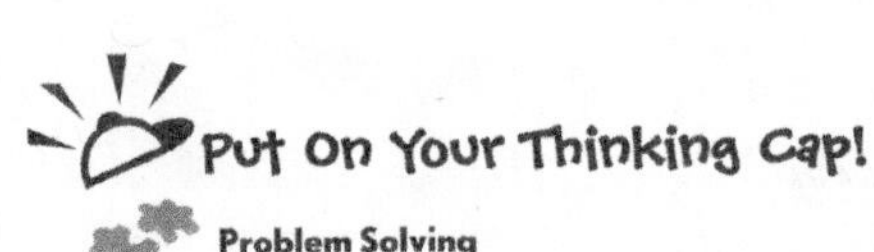

Put On Your Thinking Cap!

Problem Solving

1. The number in each rectangle is the sum of the numbers in the two circles next to it. Find the numbers in the circles.

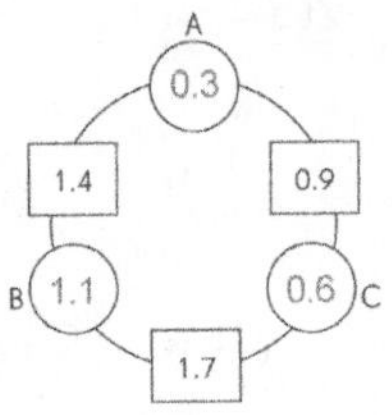

2. Each week, Rena saves $5. Her brother saves $2.50 less each week, but he started saving 4 weeks earlier. After how many weeks will Rena's savings be equal to her brother's? Their savings will be equal after eight weeks.

Week	Brother's Savings	Rena's Savings
1	$2.50	
2	$5	
3	$7.50	
4	$10	
5	$12.50	$5
6	$15	$10
7	$17.50	$15
8	$20	$20

Thinking Skill: Identifying patterns & relationships
Strategies: Guess and check, Make a systematic list

Name: ______________________ Date: ______________

Cumulative Review

for Chapters 7 and 8

Concepts and Skills

Write each fraction or mixed number as a decimal. *(Lesson 7.1)*

1. $\frac{4}{10}$ = 0.4
2. $3\frac{3}{10}$ = 3.3
3. $\frac{18}{10}$ = 1.8

Write each decimal in tenths. *(Lesson 7.1)*

4. 0.6 = 6 tenths
5. 1.7 = 17 tenths
6. 9.5 = 95 tenths
7. 4.2 = 42 tenths

Write each of these as a decimal. *(Lesson 7.1)*

8. 3 ones and 4 tenths = 3.4
9. 8 ones and 1 tenth = 8.1
10. 77 tenths = 7.7
11. 19 tenths = 1.9

Fill in the blanks. *(Lesson 7.1)*

12. 22 tenths = 2 ones and 2 tenths
13. 3.2 = 3 ones and 2 tenths

Write the correct decimal in each box. *(Lesson 7.1)*

14.

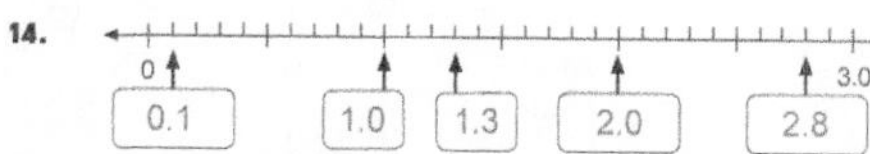

Complete the expanded form of each decimal. *(Lesson 7.1)*

15. 5.4 = 5 + 0.4
16. 7.1 = 7 + 0.1
17. 3.6 = 3 + 0.6
18. 10.2 = 10 + 0.2

Fill in the blanks. *(Lesson 7.1)*

19. In 22.3, the digit 3 is in the tenths place.

Its value is 0.3.

Write each fraction or mixed number as a decimal. *(Lesson 7.2)*

20. $\frac{9}{100}$ = 0.09
21. $2\frac{26}{100}$ = 2.26
22. $\frac{105}{100}$ = 1.05

Write each decimal in hundredths. *(Lesson 7.2)*

23. 0.06 = 6 hundredths
24. 1.33 = 133 hundredths
25. 2.5 = 250 hundredths

Write each of these as a decimal. *(Lesson 7.2)*

26. 2 ones and 6 hundredths = 2.06
27. 5 tenths 5 hundredths = 0.55
28. 7 ones and 3 tenths 4 hundredths = 7.34

Name: ______________________ Date: ______________

Fill in the blanks. *(Lesson 7.2)*

29. 16 hundredths = 1 tenth 6 hundredths
30. 0.45 = 4 tenths 5 hundredths

Mark X to show where each decimal is located on the number line. Label its value. *(Lesson 7.2)*

31. 0.04
32. 0.15
33. 0.26

0.04 0.15 0.26

0 0.1 0.2 0.3

Complete. *(Lesson 7.2)*

34. 5.2 = 5 ones and 2 tenths
35. 0.86 = 8 tenths 6 hundredths
36. 3.7 = 37 tenths
37. 0.93 = 93 hundredths

Write each sum as a decimal. *(Lesson 7.2)*

38. 7 + 0.6 + 0.02 = 7.62
39. 10 + 0.4 + 0.04 = 10.44
40. $5 + \frac{1}{10} + \frac{8}{100}$ = 5.18
41. $9 + \frac{3}{10} + \frac{7}{100}$ = 9.37

Fill in the blanks. *(Lesson 7.2)*

42. In 14.68, the digit 8 is in the hundredths place.

Its value is 0.08.

Fill in the blanks. *(Lesson 7.2)*

43. \$0.75 = 75 cents
44. \$12.25 = 1,225 cents
45. \$8.05 = 805 cents

Write each amount of money in decimal form. *(Lesson 7.2)*

46. 65 cents = \$0.65
47. 10 dollars and 90 cents = \$10.90
48. 2 dollars and 5 cents = \$2.05

Fill in the blanks. *(Lesson 7.3)*

49. 0.1 more than 1.1 is 1.2.
50. 0.2 less than 2 is 1.8.
51. 0.01 less than 0.1 is 0.09.
52. 0.03 more than 0.07 is 0.10.

Name: ______ Date: ______

Mark X to show where each decimal is located on the number line. Label its value. *(Lesson 7.3)*

53. 0.16 54. 0.24

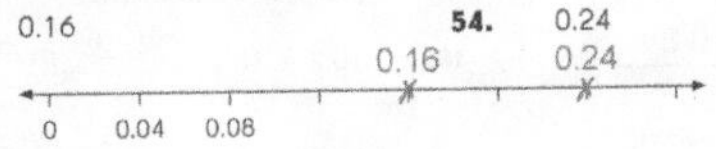

Number line: 0, 0.04, 0.08 — X at 0.16, X at 0.24

Compare. Write > or <. *(Lesson 7.3)*

55. 4.1 (>) 0.41 56. 0.73 (>) 0.70

Circle the greatest decimal and underline the least. *(Lesson 7.3)*

57. 3.04 (3.4) <u>0.34</u>

58. <u>0.6</u> 0.61 (0.65)

Fill in the blank. *(Lesson 7.3)*

59. Write a decimal that is greater than 0.9 but less than 1.0. Answers vary. Sample answer: 0.92

Round each decimal to the nearest whole number. *(Lesson 7.4)*

60. 4.36 = 4 61. 7.81 = 8 62. 5.07 = 5

Round each decimal to the nearest tenth. *(Lesson 7.4)*

63. 2.39 = 2.4 64. 6.63 = 6.6 65. 4.00 = 4.0

Write each decimal as a fraction in simplest form. *(Lesson 7.5)*

66. $0.6 = \frac{3}{5}$ 67. $0.55 = \frac{11}{20}$

Write each fraction or mixed number as a decimal. *(Lesson 7.5)*

68. $\frac{1}{5}$ = 0.2 69. $\frac{9}{20}$ = 0.45

70. $\frac{5}{2}$ = 2.5 71. $1\frac{3}{4}$ = 1.75

72. $4\frac{2}{5}$ = 4.4 73. $5\frac{1}{4}$ = 5.25

Find each sum or difference. *(Lessons 8.1 and 8.2)*

74. 6.74 + 2.17 = 8.91 75. 3.28 + 0.91 = 4.19

76. 5.76 + 4.26 = 10.02 77. 7.05 − 1.33 = 5.72

78. 8.72 − 3.43 = 5.29 79. 6.36 − 5.79 = 0.57

Name: ______ Date: ______

Problem Solving

Solve. Show your work. *(Lesson 8.3)*

80. Lina thinks of a number. When she adds 9.65 to it, she gets 20.7. What number is Lina thinking of?

20.7 − 9.65 = 11.05
The number is 11.05.

81. Suri bought a skirt for $25.90 and a sweatshirt for $19.90. She paid the cashier $50. How much change did she receive?

Cost of skirt + cost of sweatshirt = total cost
$25.90 + $19.90 = $45.80
The skirt and sweatshirt cost $45.80.
$50 − total cost = amount of change
$50 − $45.80 = $4.20
Suri received $4.20 change.

82. Jim bought a pen and a calculator. He paid the cashier $50 and received $20.45 change. If the pen cost $4.50, how much did the calculator cost?

$50 − amount of change = total cost
$50 − $20.45 = $29.55
The pen and calculator cost $29.55 altogether.
Total cost − cost of pen = cost of calculator
$29.55 − $4.50 = $25.05
The calculator cost $25.05.

83. A pole is painted white and red. The white part is 0.75 meter long and the red part is 1.45 meters longer. What is the length of the pole?

Length of white part + 1.45 m = length of red part
0.75 + 1.45 = 2.20
The length of the red part is 2.2 meters.
Length of red part + length of white part = length of pole
2.2 + 0.75 = 2.95
The length of the pole is 2.95 meters.

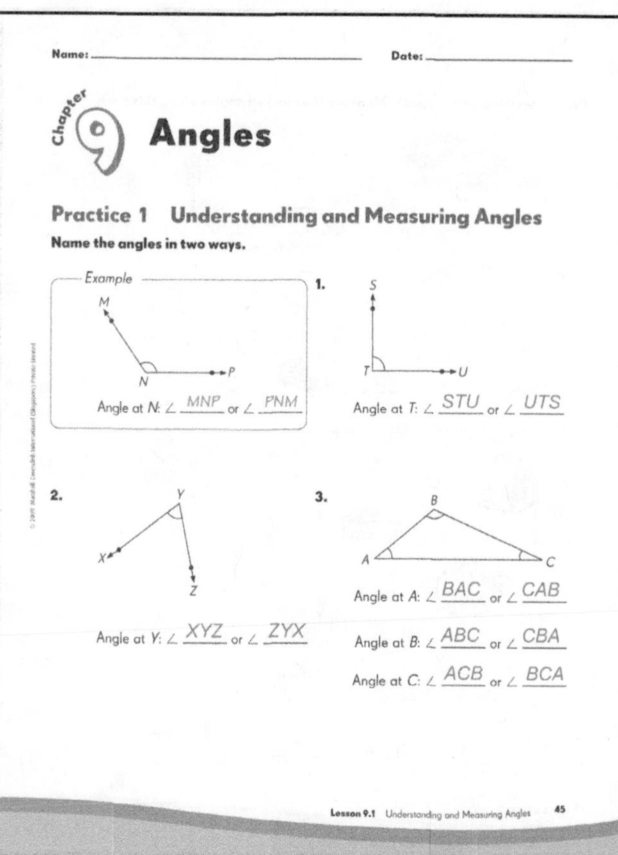

Name: ______________ Date: ______________

Chapter 9 Angles

Practice 1 Understanding and Measuring Angles

Name the angles in two ways.

Example

Angle at N: ∠ MNP or ∠ PNM

1. Angle at T: ∠ STU or ∠ UTS

2. Angle at Y: ∠ XYZ or ∠ ZYX

3. Angle at A: ∠ BAC or ∠ CAB

   Angle at B: ∠ ABC or ∠ CBA

   Angle at C: ∠ ACB or ∠ BCA

© 2009 Marshall Cavendish International (Singapore) Private Limited

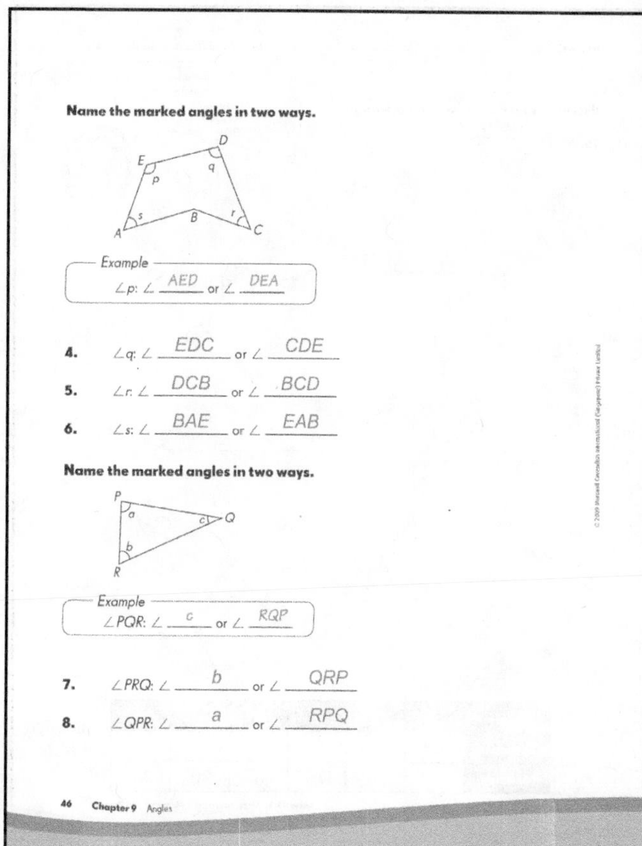

Name the marked angles in two ways.

Example

∠p: ∠ AED or ∠ DEA

4. ∠q: ∠ EDC or ∠ CDE
5. ∠r: ∠ DCB or ∠ BCD
6. ∠s: ∠ BAE or ∠ EAB

Name the marked angles in two ways.

Example

∠PQR: ∠ c or ∠ RQP

7. ∠PRQ: ∠ b or ∠ QRP
8. ∠QPR: ∠ a or ∠ RPQ

© 2009 Marshall Cavendish International (Singapore) Private Limited

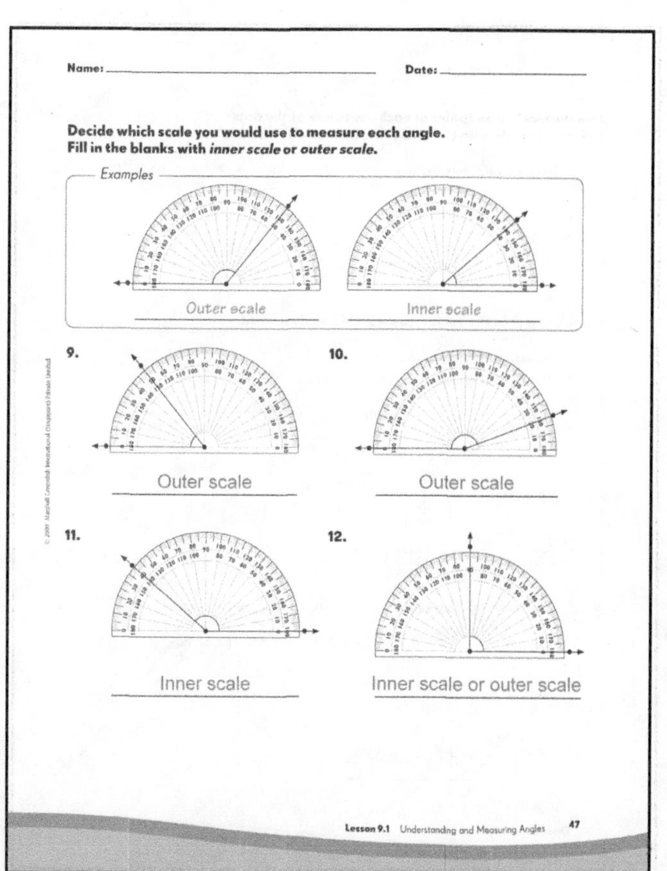

Name: ______________ Date: ______________

Decide which scale you would use to measure each angle.
Fill in the blanks with *inner scale* or *outer scale*.

Examples

Outer scale

Inner scale

9. Outer scale

10. Outer scale

11. Inner scale

12. Inner scale or outer scale

© 2009 Marshall Cavendish International (Singapore) Private Limited

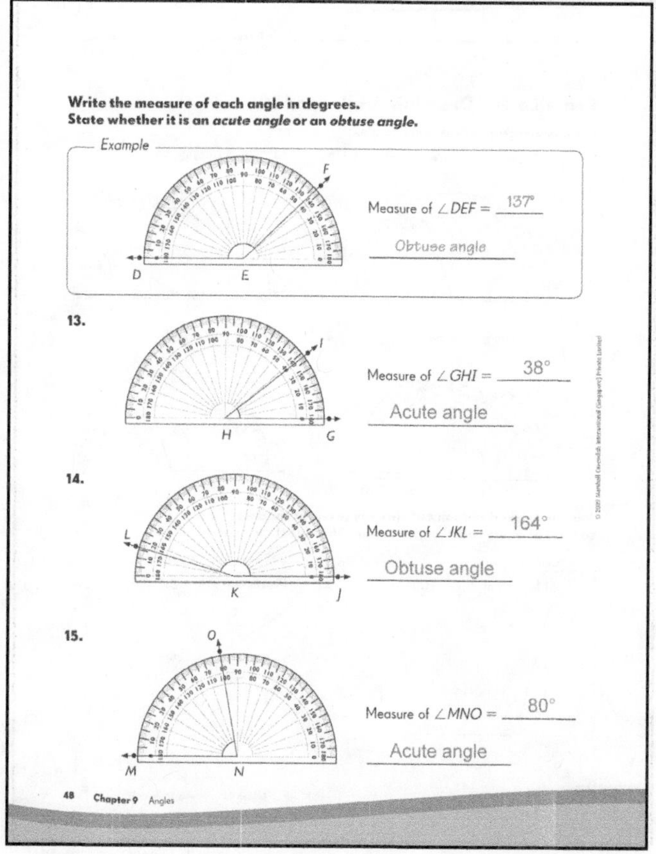

Write the measure of each angle in degrees.
State whether it is an *acute angle* or an *obtuse angle*.

Example

Measure of ∠DEF = 137°

Obtuse angle

13. Measure of ∠GHI = 38°

    Acute angle

14. Measure of ∠JKL = 164°

    Obtuse angle

15. Measure of ∠MNO = 80°

    Acute angle

© 2009 Marshall Cavendish International (Singapore) Private Limited

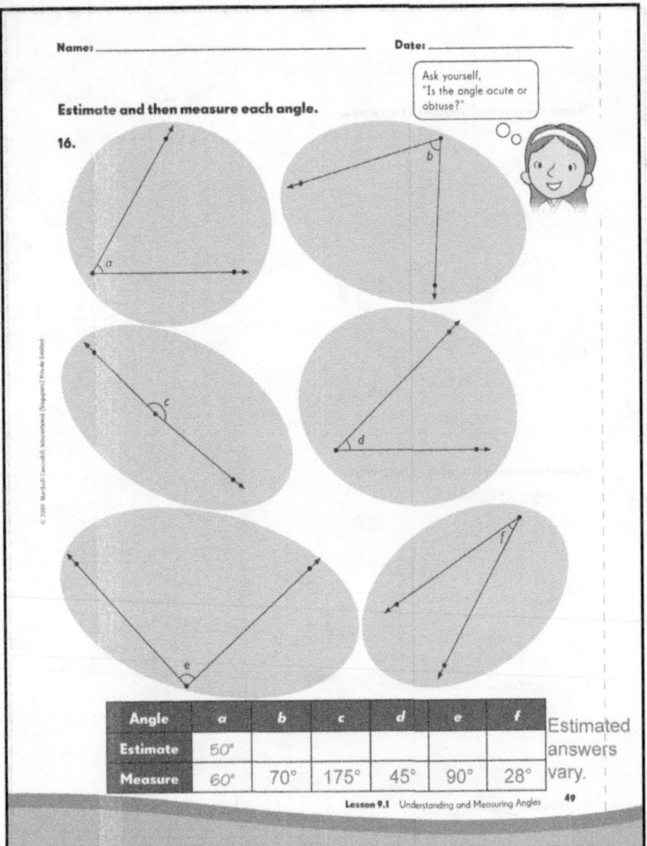

Name: ______________________ Date: ______________

Estimate and then measure each angle.

Ask yourself, "Is the angle acute or obtuse?"

16.

Angle	a	b	c	d	e	f
Estimate	50°					
Measure	60°	70°	175°	45°	90°	28°

Estimated answers vary.

Lesson 9.1 Understanding and Measuring Angles 49

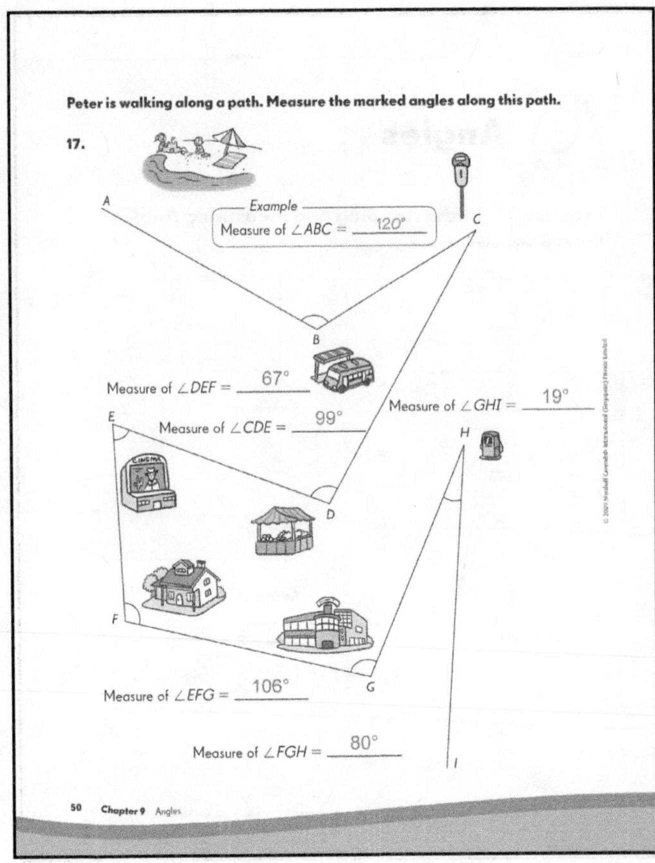

Peter is walking along a path. Measure the marked angles along this path.

17.

Example
Measure of ∠ABC = 120°

Measure of ∠DEF = 67°

Measure of ∠CDE = 99°

Measure of ∠GHI = 19°

Measure of ∠EFG = 106°

Measure of ∠FGH = 80°

50 Chapter 9 Angles

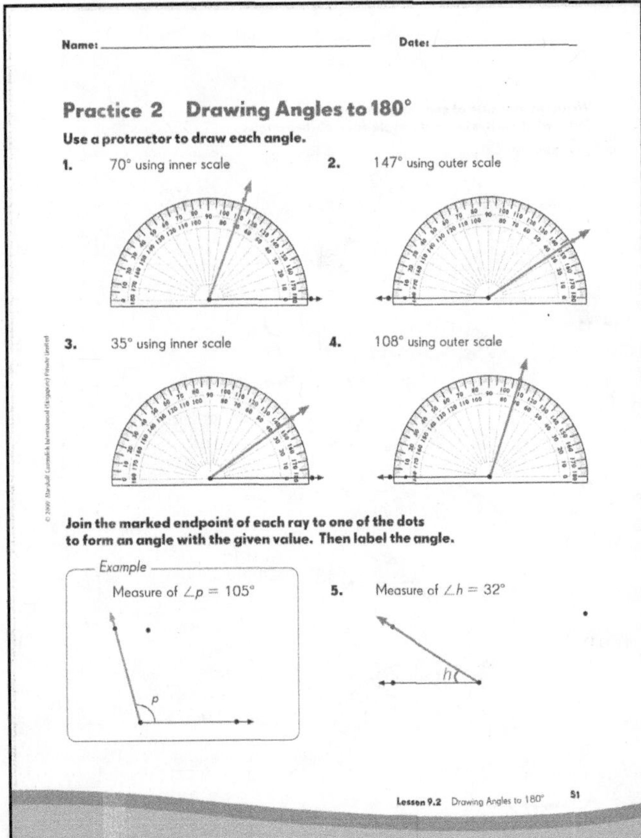

Name: ______________________ Date: ______________

Practice 2 Drawing Angles to 180°

Use a protractor to draw each angle.

1. 70° using inner scale
2. 147° using outer scale
3. 35° using inner scale
4. 108° using outer scale

Join the marked endpoint of each ray to one of the dots to form an angle with the given value. Then label the angle.

Example
Measure of ∠p = 105°

5. Measure of ∠h = 32°

Lesson 9.2 Drawing Angles to 180° 51

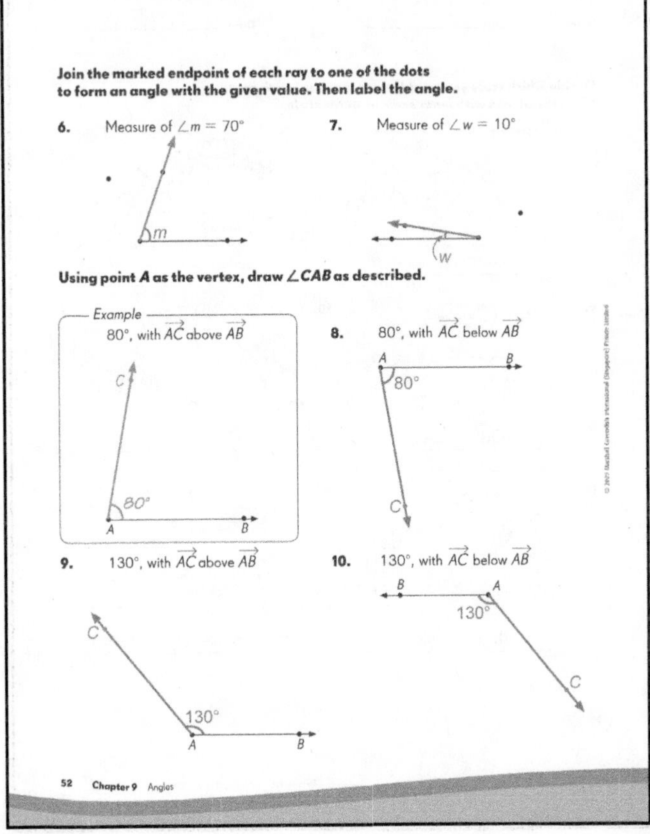

Join the marked endpoint of each ray to one of the dots to form an angle with the given value. Then label the angle.

6. Measure of ∠m = 70°
7. Measure of ∠w = 10°

Using point *A* as the vertex, draw ∠*CAB* as described.

Example
80°, with $\overrightarrow{AC}$ above $\overrightarrow{AB}$

8. 80°, with $\overrightarrow{AC}$ below $\overrightarrow{AB}$

9. 130°, with $\overrightarrow{AC}$ above $\overrightarrow{AB}$

10. 130°, with $\overrightarrow{AC}$ below $\overrightarrow{AB}$

52 Chapter 9 Angles

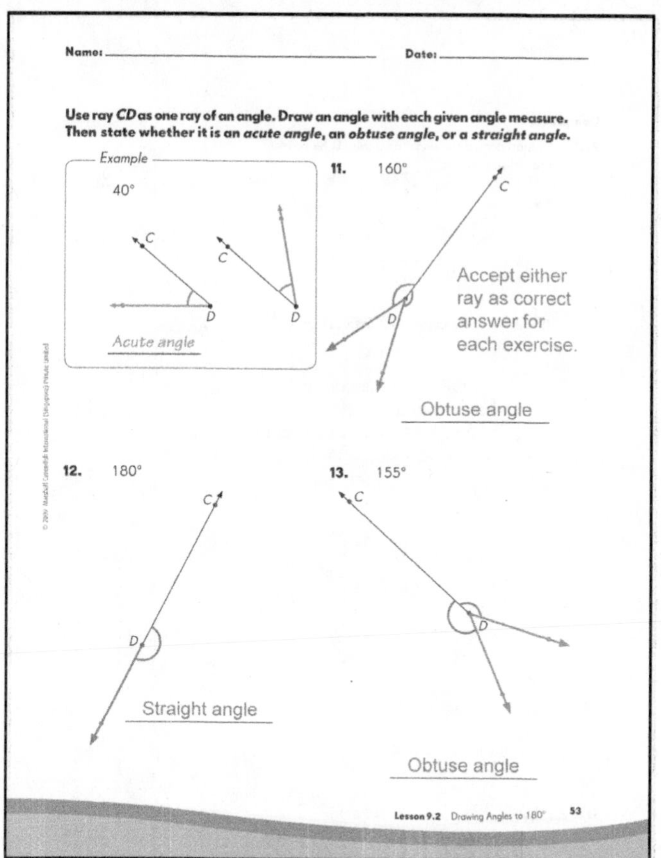

Name: ______________ Date: ______________

Use ray *CD* as one ray of an angle. Draw an angle with each given angle measure. Then state whether it is an *acute angle*, an *obtuse angle*, or a *straight angle*.

Example

40°

Acute angle

11. 160°

Accept either ray as correct answer for each exercise.

Obtuse angle

12. 180°

Straight angle

13. 155°

Obtuse angle

Lesson 9.2 Drawing Angles to 180° 53

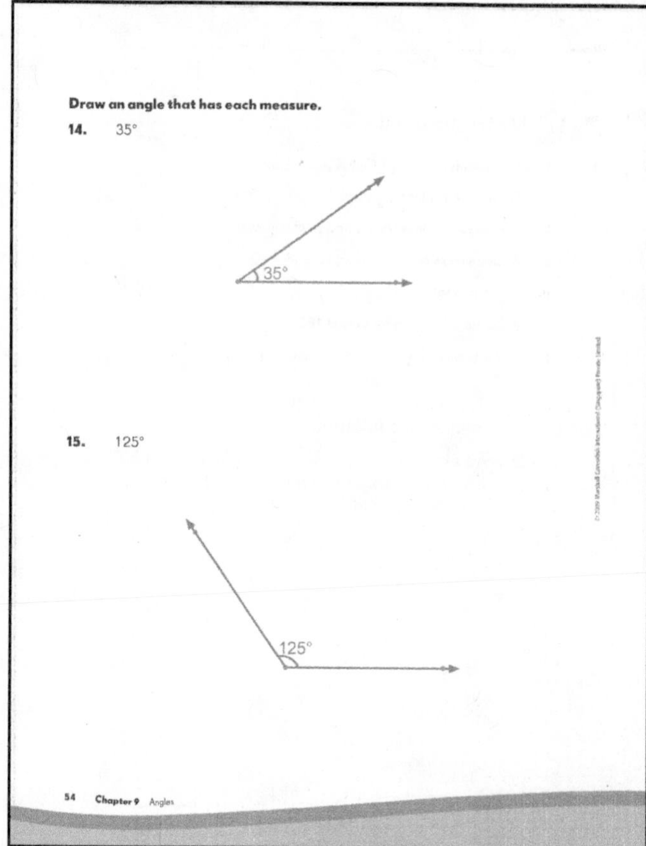

Draw an angle that has each measure.

14. 35°

15. 125°

54 Chapter 9 Angles

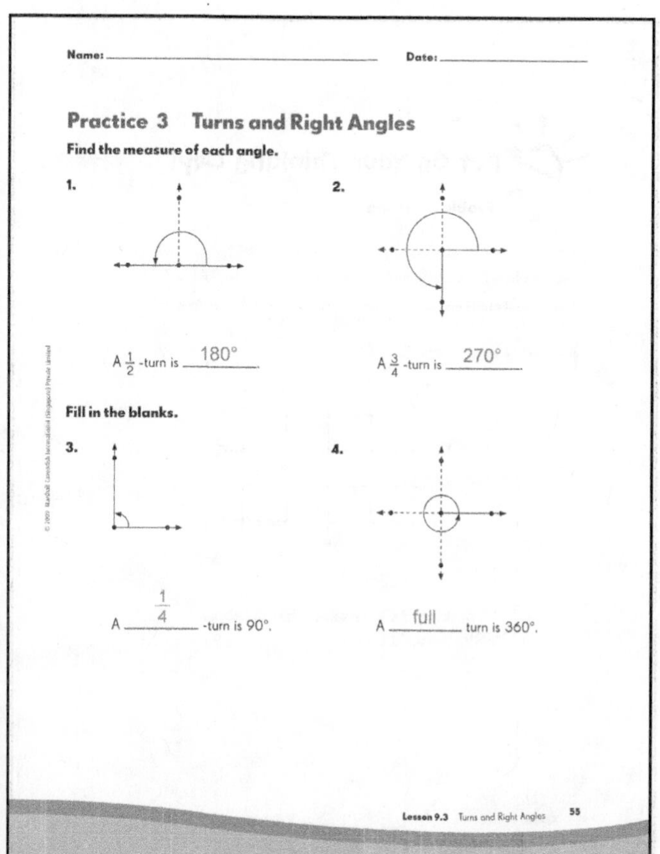

Name: ______________ Date: ______________

Practice 3 Turns and Right Angles

Find the measure of each angle.

1. A $\frac{1}{2}$-turn is 180°.

2. A $\frac{3}{4}$-turn is 270°.

Fill in the blanks.

3. A $\frac{1}{4}$ -turn is 90°.

4. A full turn is 360°.

Lesson 9.3 Turns and Right Angles 55

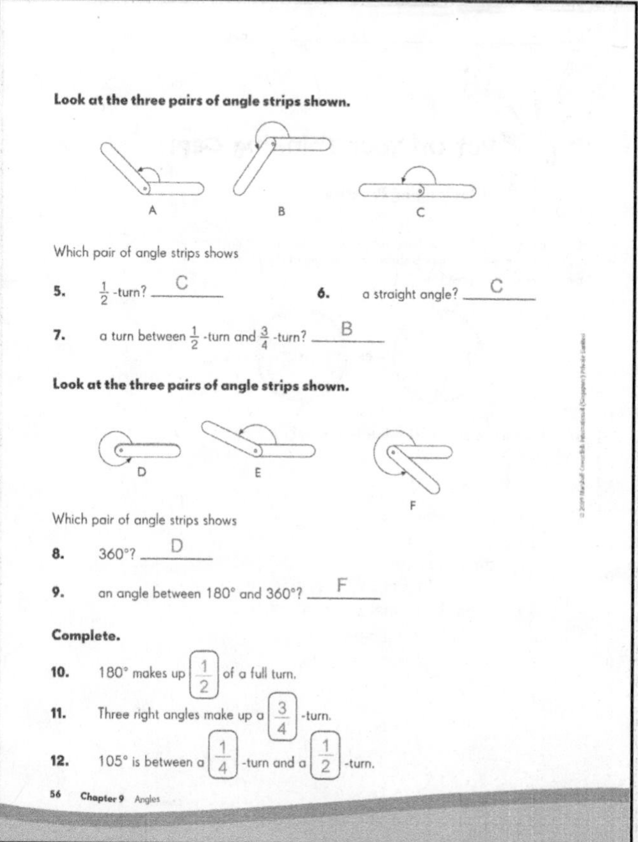

Look at the three pairs of angle strips shown.

Which pair of angle strips shows

5. $\frac{1}{2}$-turn? C

6. a straight angle? C

7. a turn between $\frac{1}{2}$-turn and $\frac{3}{4}$-turn? B

Look at the three pairs of angle strips shown.

Which pair of angle strips shows

8. 360°? D

9. an angle between 180° and 360°? F

Complete.

10. 180° makes up $\frac{1}{2}$ of a full turn.

11. Three right angles make up a $\frac{3}{4}$-turn.

12. 105° is between a $\frac{1}{4}$-turn and a $\frac{1}{2}$-turn.

56 Chapter 9 Angles

Name: ______________________ Date: ____________

Math Journal

1. Which statements are wrong? Explain your answer.

   a. Two right angles form a $\frac{1}{2}$-turn.

   b. The measure of an angle is a fraction of a $\frac{3}{4}$-turn.

   c. An acute angle has a measure greater than 90°.

   d. A $\frac{1}{4}$-turn is 90°.

   e. A straight angle has a measure of 180°.

   f. 150° is between a $\frac{1}{4}$-turn and a $\frac{1}{2}$-turn.

   b. The measure of an angle is a fraction of a **full turn**.

   c. An **acute angle** has a measure **less than** 90°. An **obtuse angle** has a measure greater than 90°, but less than 180°.

© 2009 Marshall Cavendish International (Singapore) Private Limited

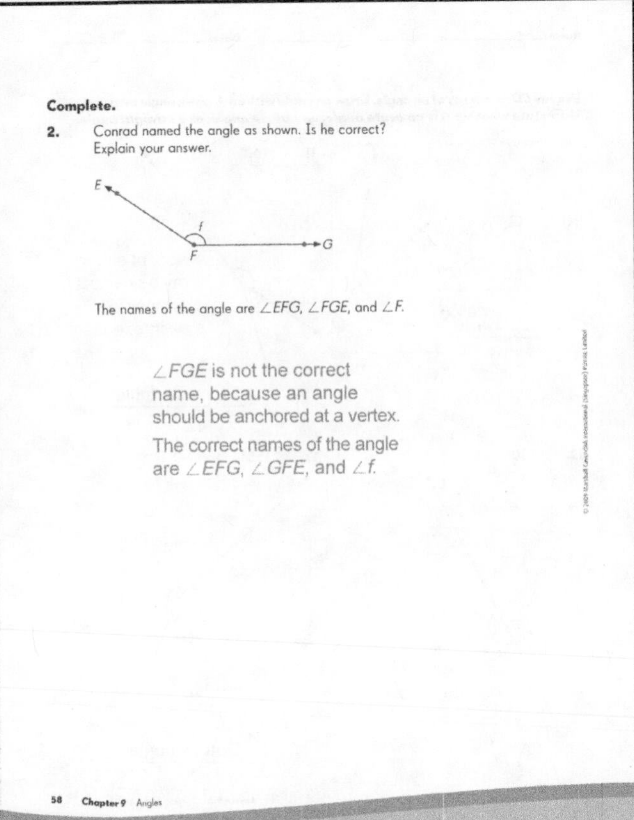

Complete.

2. Conrad named the angle as shown. Is he correct? Explain your answer.

The names of the angle are ∠EFG, ∠FGE, and ∠F.

∠FGE is not the correct name, because an angle should be anchored at a vertex.

The correct names of the angle are ∠EFG, ∠GFE, and ∠f.

© 2009 Marshall Cavendish International (Singapore) Private Limited

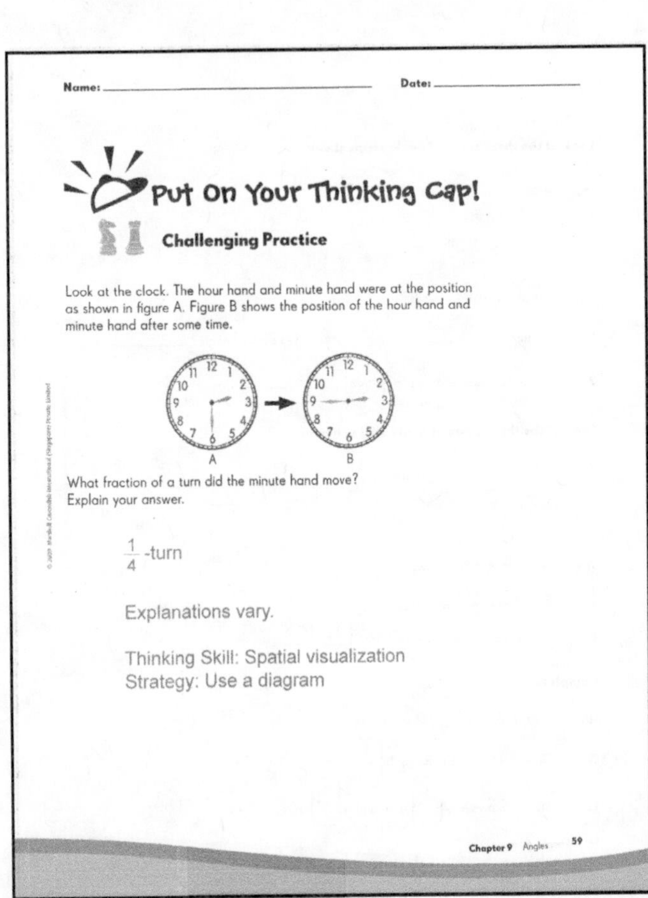

Name: ______________________ Date: ____________

Put On Your Thinking Cap!

Challenging Practice

Look at the clock. The hour hand and minute hand were at the position as shown in figure A. Figure B shows the position of the hour hand and minute hand after some time.

What fraction of a turn did the minute hand move? Explain your answer.

$\frac{1}{4}$-turn

Explanations vary.

Thinking Skill: Spatial visualization
Strategy: Use a diagram

© 2009 Marshall Cavendish International (Singapore) Private Limited

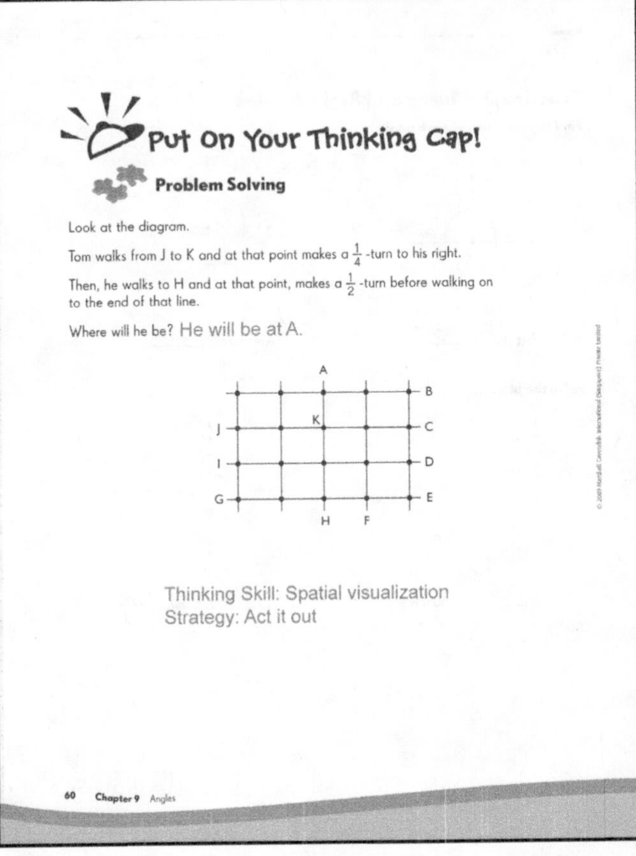

Put On Your Thinking Cap!

Problem Solving

Look at the diagram.

Tom walks from J to K and at that point makes a $\frac{1}{4}$-turn to his right.

Then, he walks to H and at that point, makes a $\frac{1}{2}$-turn before walking on to the end of that line.

Where will he be? He will be at A.

Thinking Skill: Spatial visualization
Strategy: Act it out

© 2009 Marshall Cavendish International (Singapore) Private Limited

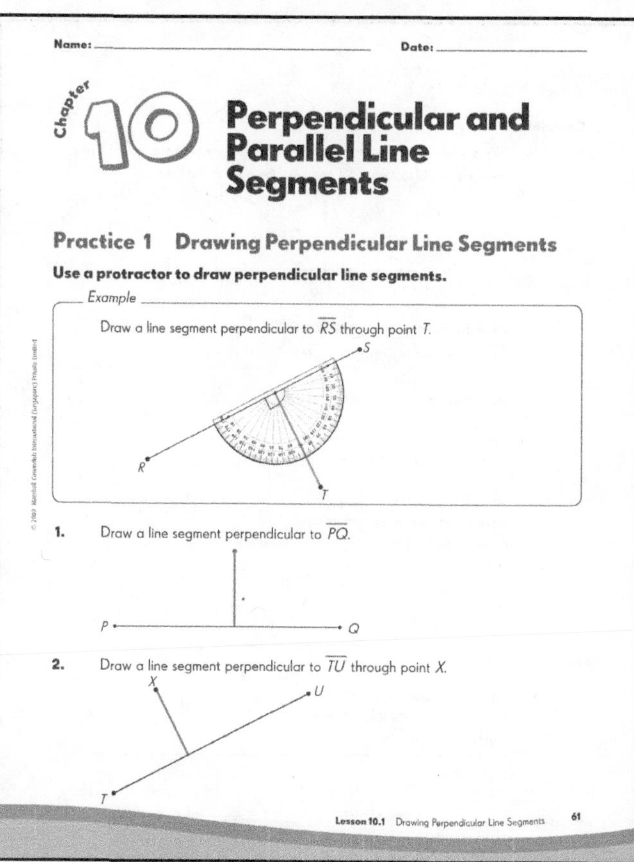

Name: __________ Date: __________

Chapter 10 **Perpendicular and Parallel Line Segments**

Practice 1 Drawing Perpendicular Line Segments

Use a protractor to draw perpendicular line segments.

Example

Draw a line segment perpendicular to $\overline{RS}$ through point T.

1. Draw a line segment perpendicular to $\overline{PQ}$.

2. Draw a line segment perpendicular to $\overline{TU}$ through point X.

© 2009 Marshall Cavendish International (Singapore) Private Limited

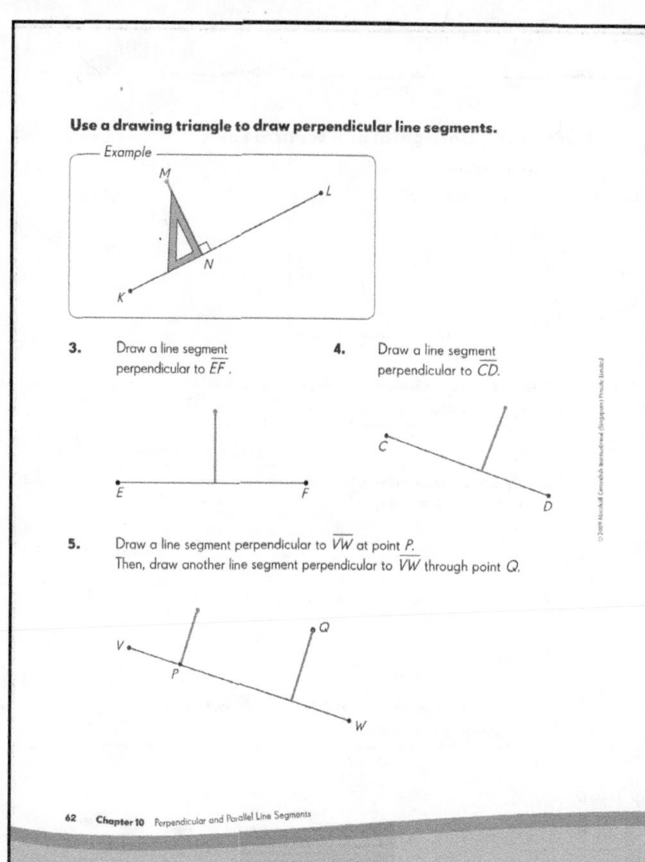

Use a drawing triangle to draw perpendicular line segments.

Example

3. Draw a line segment perpendicular to $\overline{EF}$.

4. Draw a line segment perpendicular to $\overline{CD}$.

5. Draw a line segment perpendicular to $\overline{VW}$ at point P. Then, draw another line segment perpendicular to $\overline{VW}$ through point Q.

© 2009 Marshall Cavendish International (Singapore) Private Limited

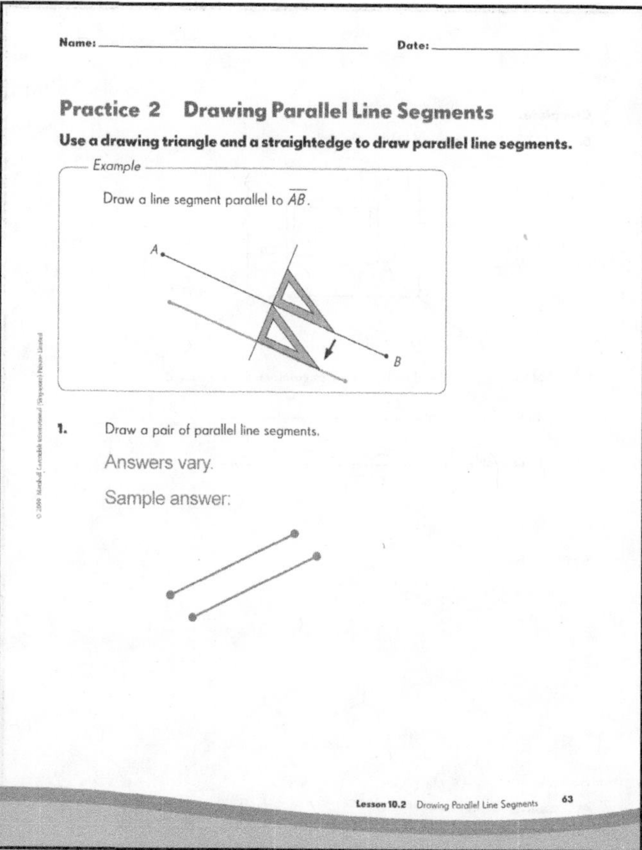

Name: __________ Date: __________

Practice 2 Drawing Parallel Line Segments

Use a drawing triangle and a straightedge to draw parallel line segments.

Example

Draw a line segment parallel to $\overline{AB}$.

1. Draw a pair of parallel line segments.

Answers vary.

Sample answer:

© 2009 Marshall Cavendish International (Singapore) Private Limited

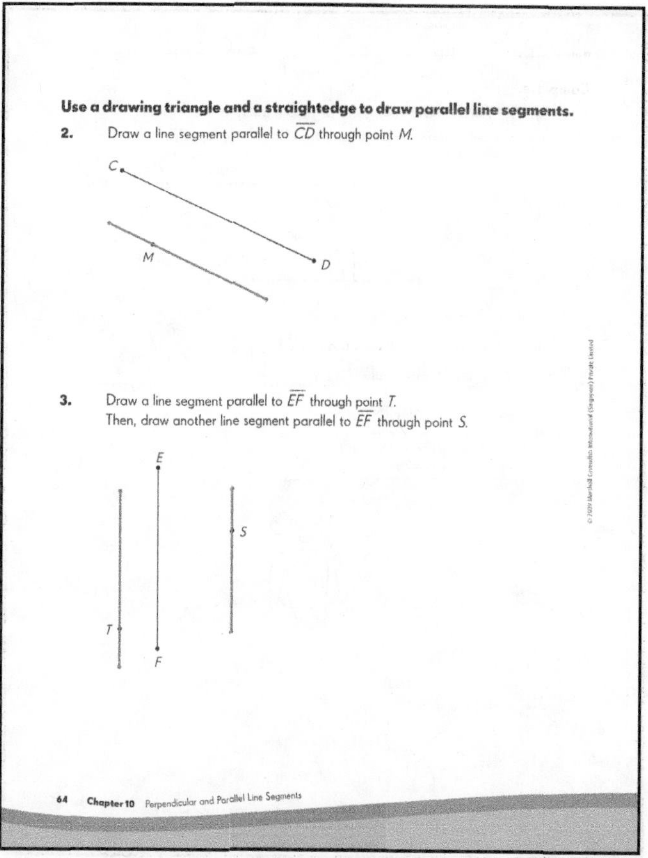

Use a drawing triangle and a straightedge to draw parallel line segments.

2. Draw a line segment parallel to $\overline{CD}$ through point M.

3. Draw a line segment parallel to $\overline{EF}$ through point T. Then, draw another line segment parallel to $\overline{EF}$ through point S.

© 2009 Marshall Cavendish International (Singapore) Private Limited

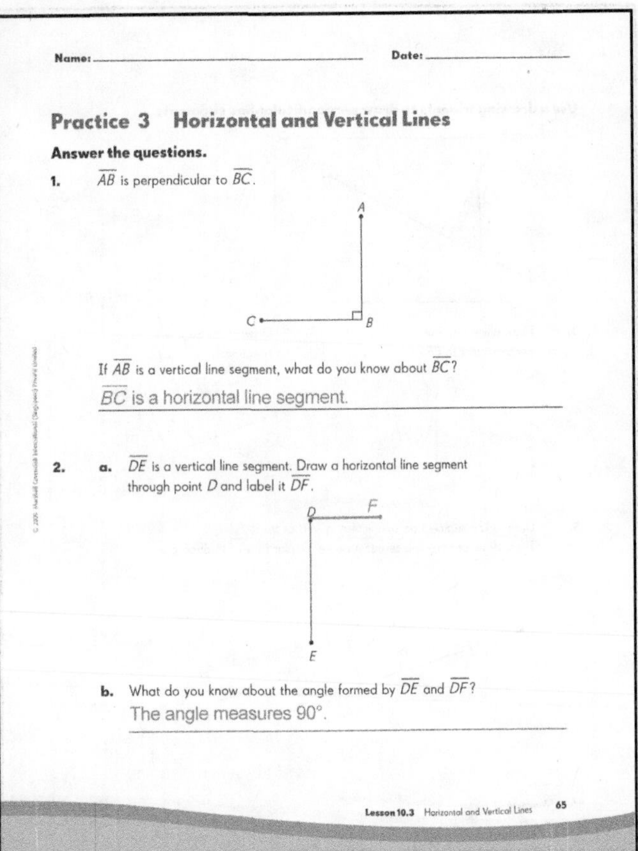

Name: ______________________ Date: ______________

Practice 3 Horizontal and Vertical Lines

Answer the questions.

1. $\overline{AB}$ is perpendicular to $\overline{BC}$.

If $\overline{AB}$ is a vertical line segment, what do you know about $\overline{BC}$?

$\overline{BC}$ is a horizontal line segment.

2. a. $\overline{DE}$ is a vertical line segment. Draw a horizontal line segment through point D and label it $\overline{DF}$.

b. What do you know about the angle formed by $\overline{DE}$ and $\overline{DF}$?

The angle measures 90°.

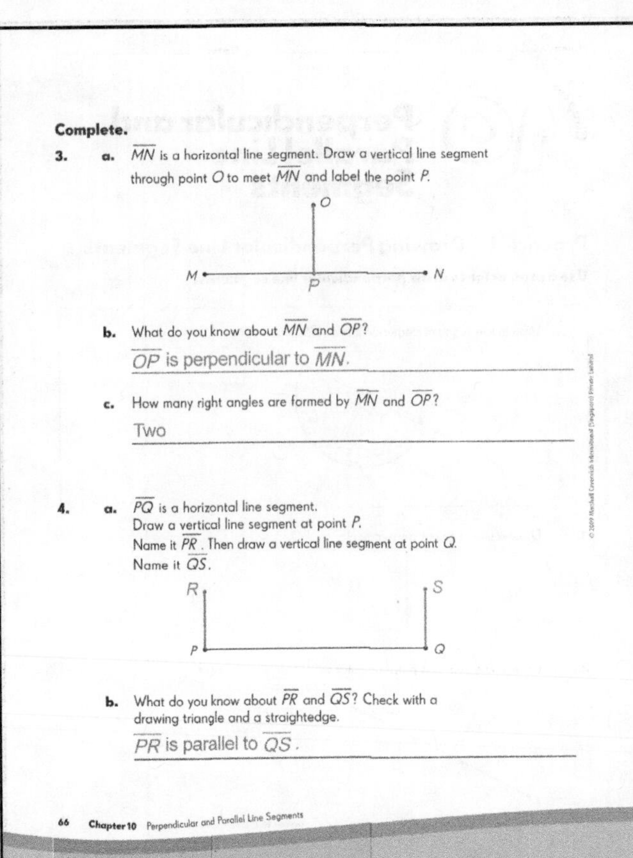

Complete.

3. a. $\overline{MN}$ is a horizontal line segment. Draw a vertical line segment through point O to meet $\overline{MN}$ and label the point P.

b. What do you know about $\overline{MN}$ and $\overline{OP}$?

$\overline{OP}$ is perpendicular to $\overline{MN}$.

c. How many right angles are formed by $\overline{MN}$ and $\overline{OP}$?

Two

4. a. $\overline{PQ}$ is a horizontal line segment. Draw a vertical line segment at point P. Name it $\overline{PR}$. Then draw a vertical line segment at point Q. Name it $\overline{QS}$.

b. What do you know about $\overline{PR}$ and $\overline{QS}$? Check with a drawing triangle and a straightedge.

$\overline{PR}$ is parallel to $\overline{QS}$.

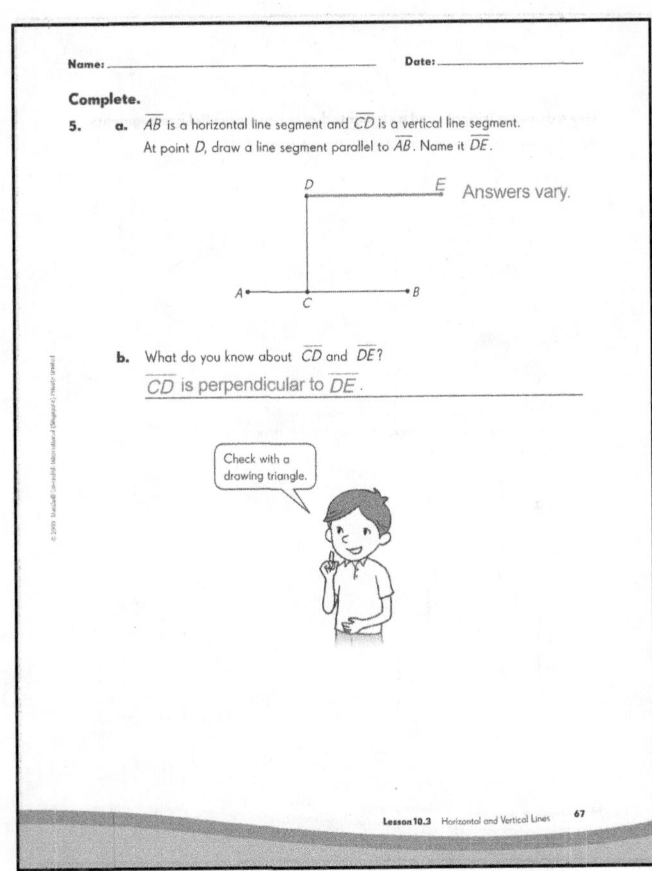

Name: ______________________ Date: ______________

Complete.

5. a. $\overline{AB}$ is a horizontal line segment and $\overline{CD}$ is a vertical line segment. At point D, draw a line segment parallel to $\overline{AB}$. Name it $\overline{DE}$.

b. What do you know about $\overline{CD}$ and $\overline{DE}$?

$\overline{CD}$ is perpendicular to $\overline{DE}$.

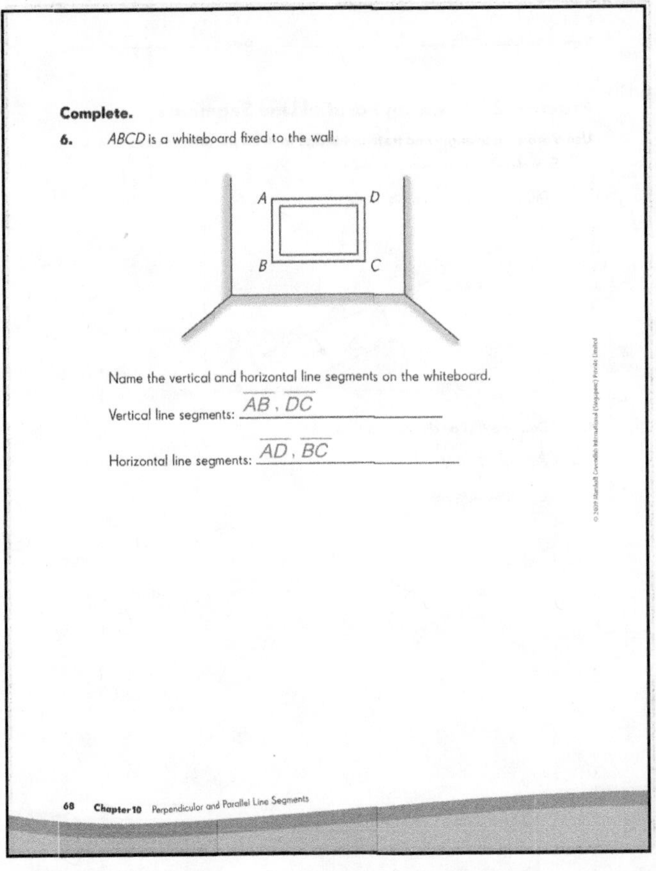

Complete.

6. $ABCD$ is a whiteboard fixed to the wall.

Name the vertical and horizontal line segments on the whiteboard.

Vertical line segments: $\overline{AB}$, $\overline{DC}$

Horizontal line segments: $\overline{AD}$, $\overline{BC}$

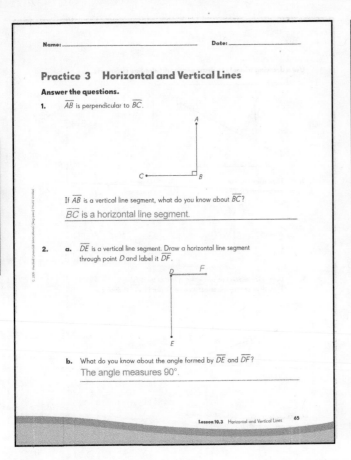

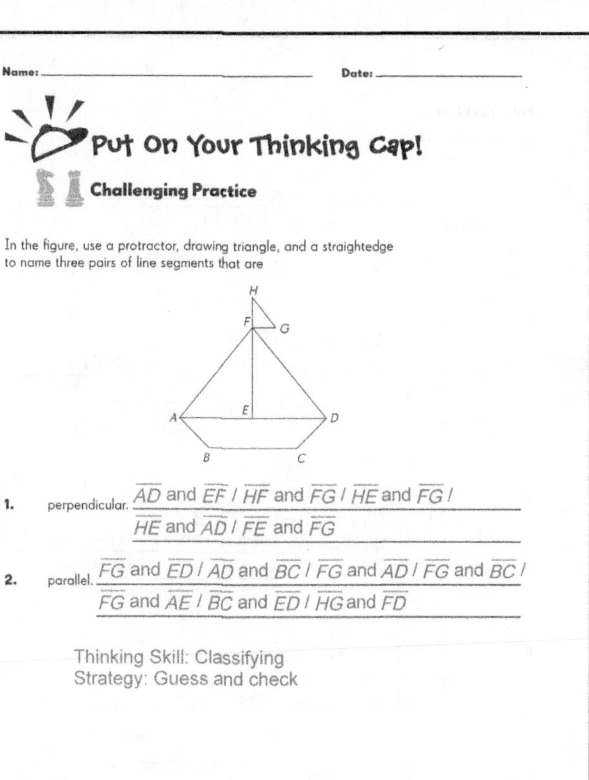

Name: ______________________ Date: ______________

Put On Your Thinking Cap!

Challenging Practice

In the figure, use a protractor, drawing triangle, and a straightedge to name three pairs of line segments that are

1. perpendicular. $\overline{AD}$ and $\overline{EF}$ / $\overline{HF}$ and $\overline{FG}$ / $\overline{HE}$ and $\overline{FG}$ / $\overline{HE}$ and $\overline{AD}$ / $\overline{FE}$ and $\overline{FG}$

2. parallel. $\overline{FG}$ and $\overline{ED}$ / $\overline{AD}$ and $\overline{BC}$ / $\overline{FG}$ and $\overline{AD}$ / $\overline{FG}$ and $\overline{BC}$ / $\overline{FG}$ and $\overline{AE}$ / $\overline{BC}$ and $\overline{ED}$ / $\overline{HG}$ and $\overline{FD}$

Thinking Skill: Classifying
Strategy: Guess and check

© 2009 Marshall Cavendish International (Singapore) Private Limited

Chapter 10 Perpendicular and Parallel Line Segments 69

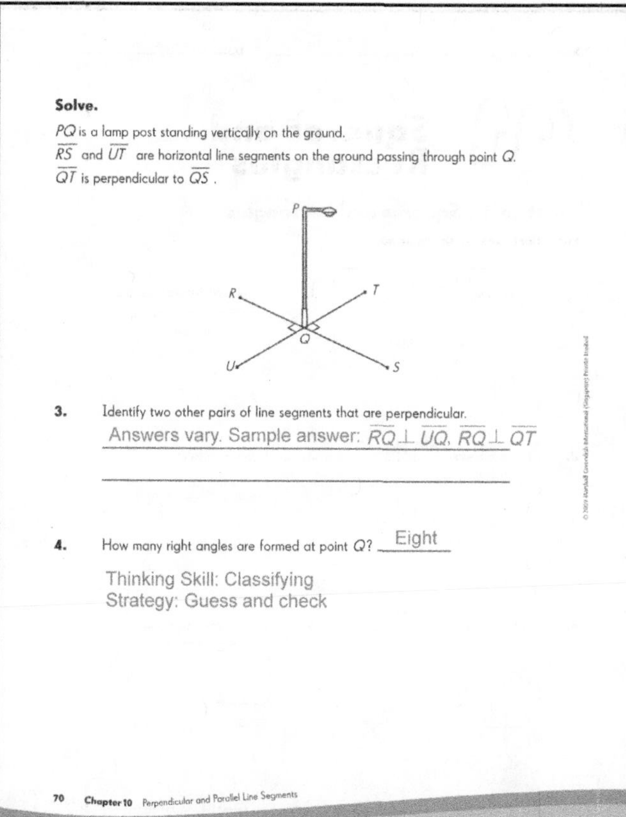

Solve.

$\overline{PQ}$ is a lamp post standing vertically on the ground.
$\overline{RS}$ and $\overline{UT}$ are horizontal line segments on the ground passing through point Q.
$\overline{QT}$ is perpendicular to $\overline{QS}$.

3. Identify two other pairs of line segments that are perpendicular.
Answers vary. Sample answer: $\overline{RQ} \perp \overline{UQ}$, $\overline{RQ} \perp \overline{QT}$

4. How many right angles are formed at point Q? Eight

Thinking Skill: Classifying
Strategy: Guess and check

70 Chapter 10 Perpendicular and Parallel Line Segments

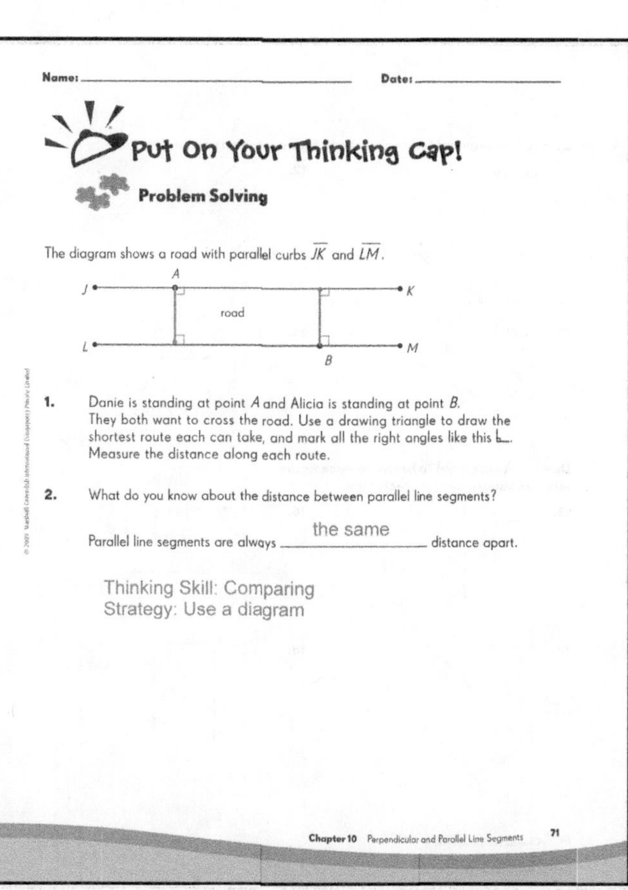

Name: ______________________ Date: ______________

Put On Your Thinking Cap!

Problem Solving

The diagram shows a road with parallel curbs $\overline{JK}$ and $\overline{LM}$.

1. Danie is standing at point A and Alicia is standing at point B. They both want to cross the road. Use a drawing triangle to draw the shortest route each can take, and mark all the right angles like this ∟. Measure the distance along each route.

2. What do you know about the distance between parallel line segments?
Parallel line segments are always the same distance apart.

Thinking Skill: Comparing
Strategy: Use a diagram

Chapter 10 Perpendicular and Parallel Line Segments 71

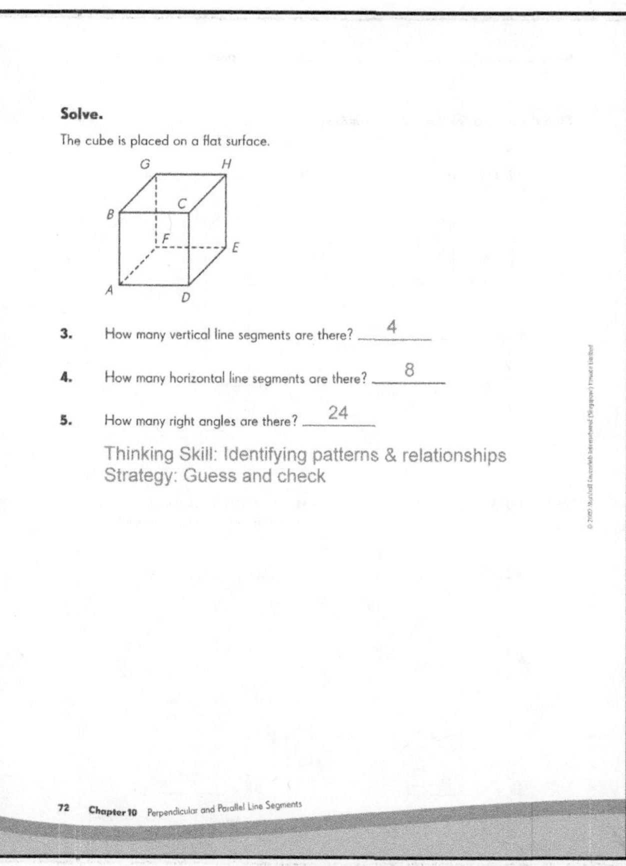

Solve.

The cube is placed on a flat surface.

3. How many vertical line segments are there? 4

4. How many horizontal line segments are there? 8

5. How many right angles are there? 24

Thinking Skill: Identifying patterns & relationships
Strategy: Guess and check

72 Chapter 10 Perpendicular and Parallel Line Segments

Chapter 11

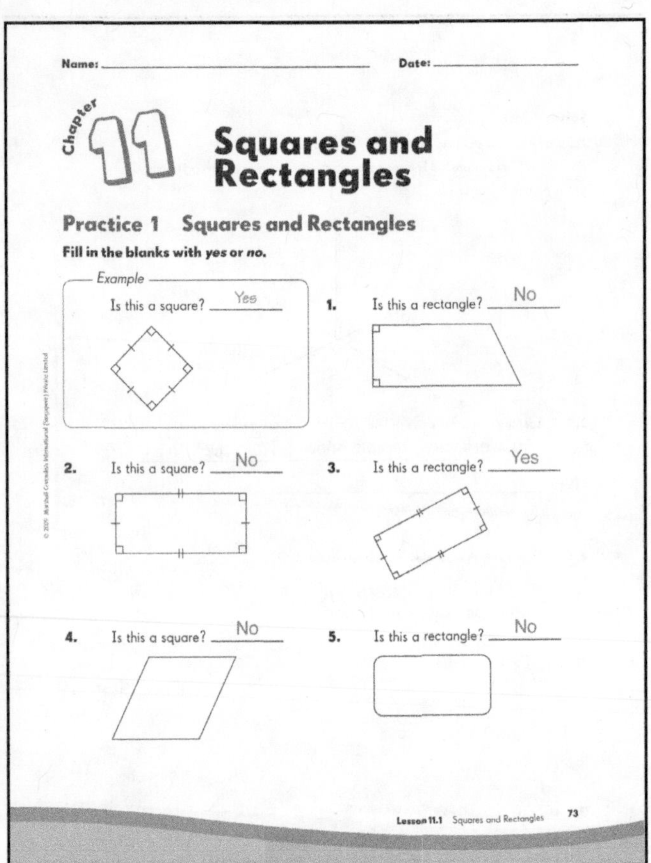
Name: ______________________ Date: ______________

Chapter 11 Squares and Rectangles

Practice 1 Squares and Rectangles

Fill in the blanks with *yes* or *no*.

Example

Is this a square? Yes

1. Is this a rectangle? No

2. Is this a square? No

3. Is this a rectangle? Yes

4. Is this a square? No

5. Is this a rectangle? No

© 2009 Marshall Cavendish International (Singapore) Private Limited

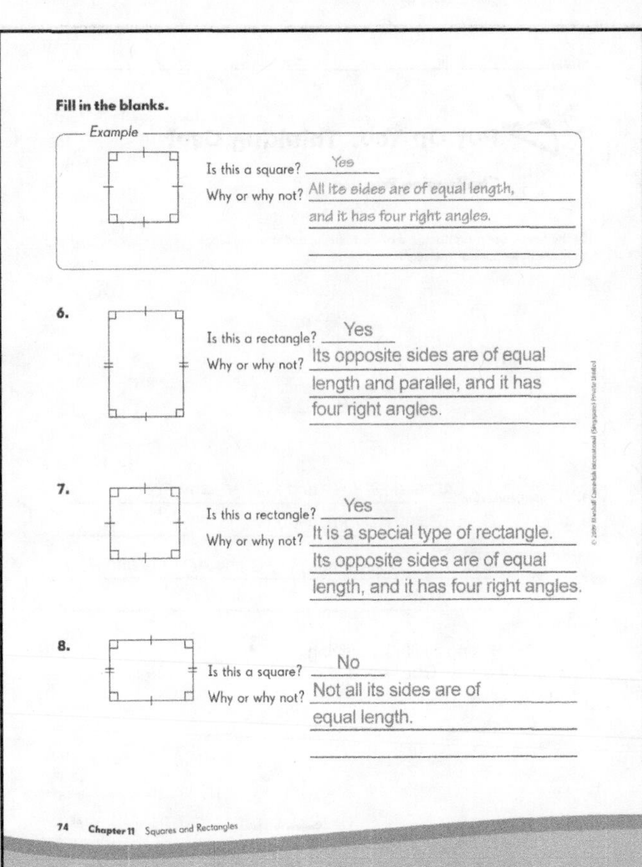
Fill in the blanks.

Example

Is this a square? Yes

Why or why not? All its sides are of equal length, and it has four right angles.

6. Is this a rectangle? Yes

Why or why not? Its opposite sides are of equal length and parallel, and it has four right angles.

7. Is this a rectangle? Yes

Why or why not? It is a special type of rectangle. Its opposite sides are of equal length, and it has four right angles.

8. Is this a square? No

Why or why not? Not all its sides are of equal length.

© 2009 Marshall Cavendish International (Singapore) Private Limited

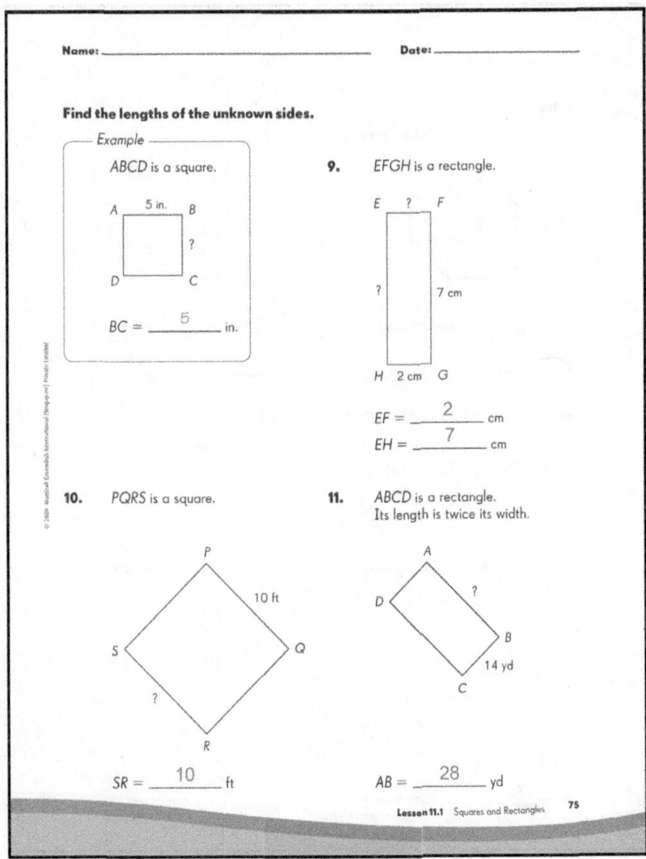
Name: ______________________ Date: ______________

Find the lengths of the unknown sides.

Example

ABCD is a square.

BC = 5 in.

9. *EFGH* is a rectangle.

EF = 2 cm

EH = 7 cm

10. *PQRS* is a square.

SR = 10 ft

11. *ABCD* is a rectangle. Its length is twice its width.

AB = 28 yd

© 2009 Marshall Cavendish International (Singapore) Private Limited

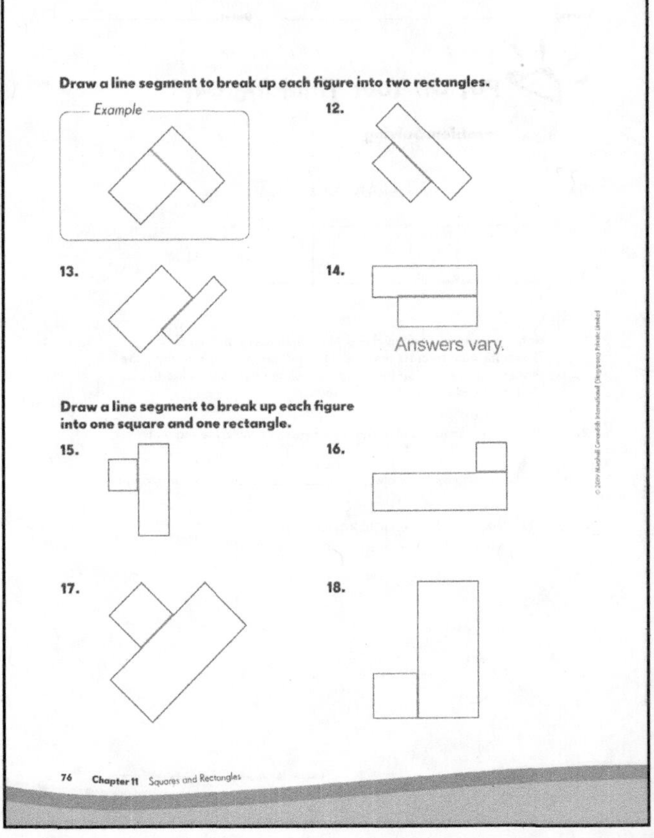
Draw a line segment to break up each figure into two rectangles.

Example

12.

13.

14.

Answers vary.

Draw a line segment to break up each figure into one square and one rectangle.

15.

16.

17.

18.

© 2009 Marshall Cavendish International (Singapore) Private Limited

Name: ______________________ Date: ______________

Practice 2 Properties of Squares and Rectangles

All the figures are rectangles. Find the measures of the unknown angles.

Example

Find the measure of ∠a.

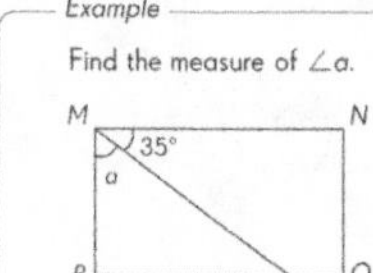

Measure of ∠a = 90° − 35°
= 55°

1. Find the measure of ∠b.

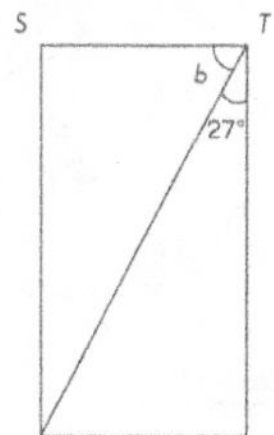

Measure of ∠b = 90° − 27°
= 63°

2. Find the measure of ∠c.

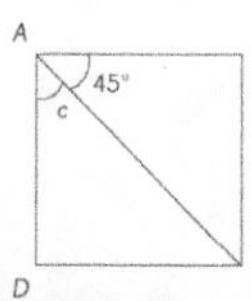

Measure of ∠c = 90° − 45°
= 45°

All the figures are rectangles. Find the measures of the unknown angles.

3. Find the measure of ∠p.

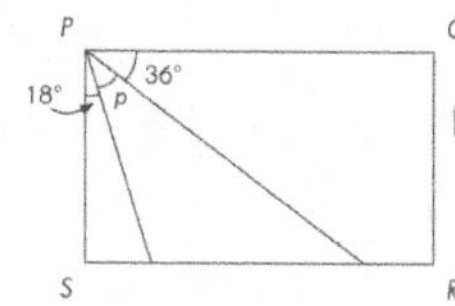

Measure of ∠p = 90° − 36° − 18°
= 36°

4. Find the measure of ∠m.

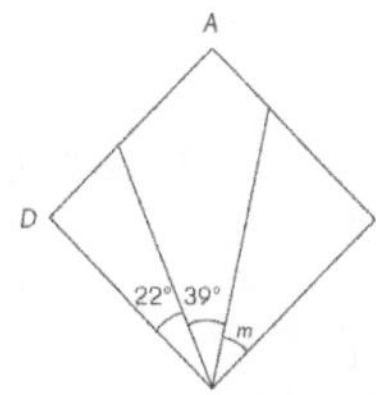

Measure of ∠m = 90° − 22° − 39°
= 29°

Chapter 11

Name: ______________________ Date: ______________

The figure is a rectangle. Find the measure of the unknown angle.

5. Find the measure of ∠s.

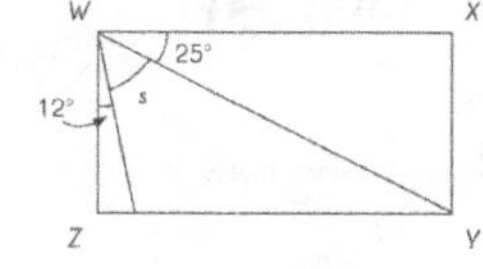

Measure of ∠s = 90° − 25° − 12°
= 53°

Find the lengths of the unknown sides.

6. The figure is made up of a rectangle and a square. Find BC and GE.

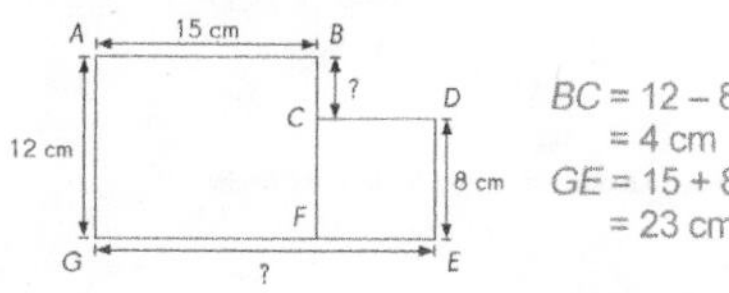

BC = 12 − 8
= 4 cm
GE = 15 + 8
= 23 cm

Find the lengths of the unknown sides.

7. The figure is made up of two rectangles. Find BD and FG.

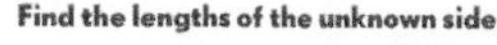

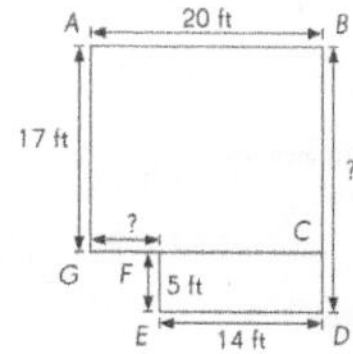

BD = 17 + 5
= 22 ft
FG = 20 − 14
= 6 ft

8. The figure is made up of two rectangles. Find QR and RT.

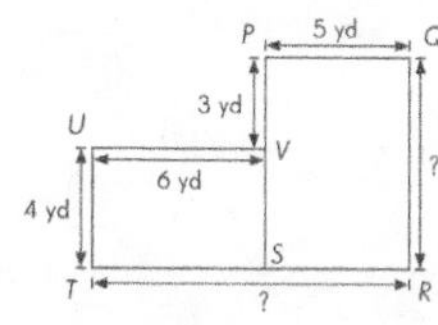

QR = 3 + 4
= 7 yd
RT = 5 + 6
= 11 yd

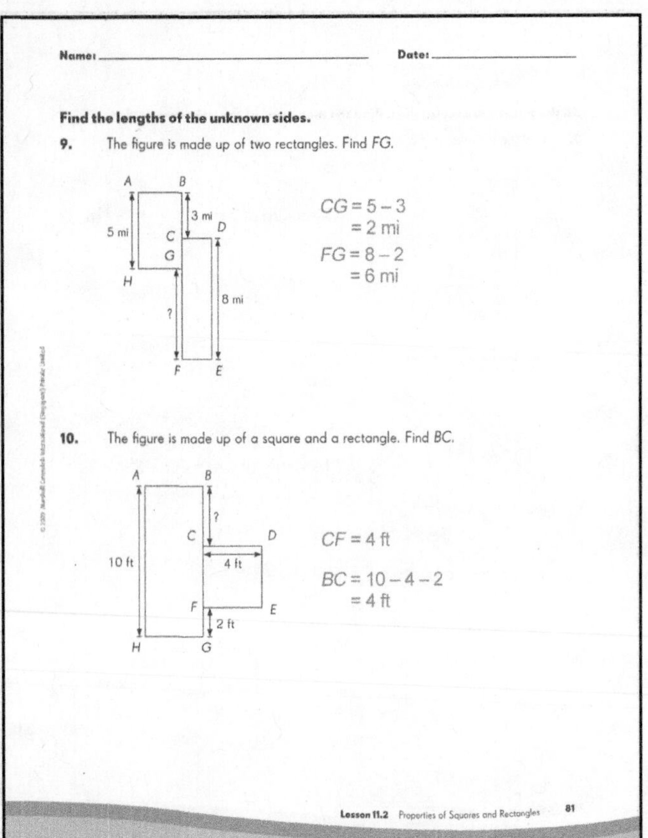
Name: ______ Date: ______

Find the lengths of the unknown sides.

9. The figure is made up of two rectangles. Find FG.

$CG = 5 - 3$
$= 2$ mi
$FG = 8 - 2$
$= 6$ mi

10. The figure is made up of a square and a rectangle. Find BC.

$CF = 4$ ft

$BC = 10 - 4 - 2$
$= 4$ ft

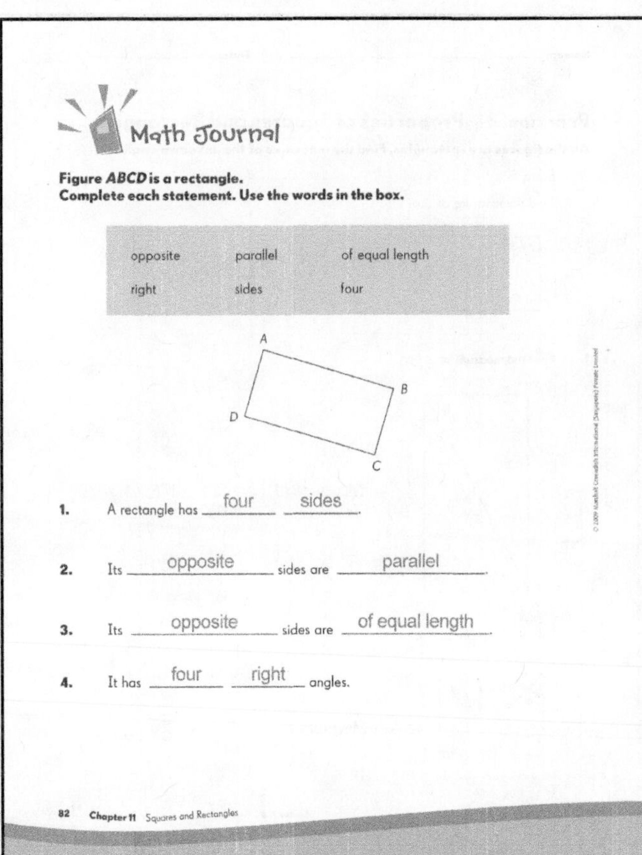
Math Journal

Figure *ABCD* is a rectangle.
Complete each statement. Use the words in the box.

opposite	parallel	of equal length
right	sides	four

1. A rectangle has four sides.
2. Its opposite sides are parallel.
3. Its opposite sides are of equal length.
4. It has four right angles.

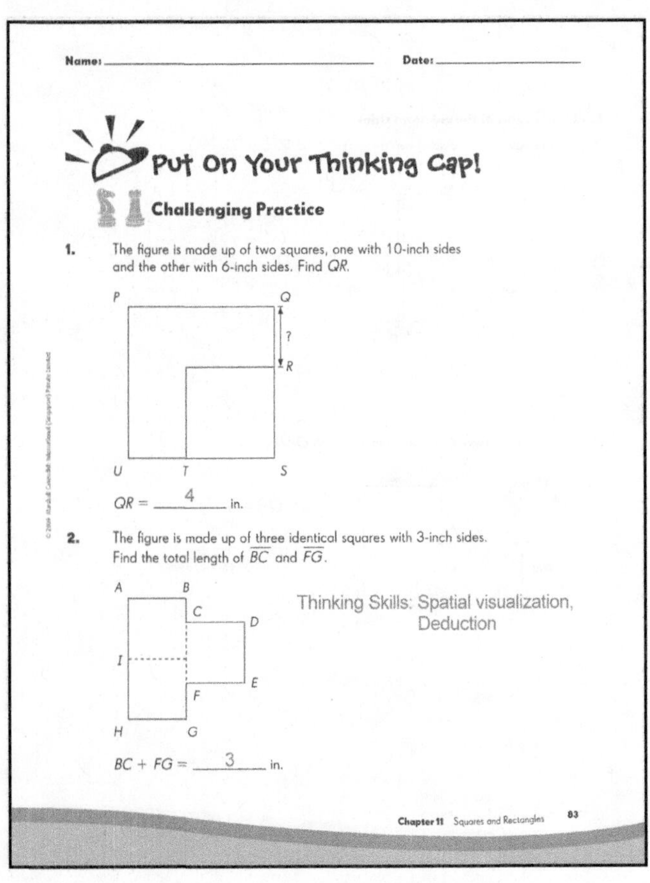
Name: ______ Date: ______

Put On Your Thinking Cap!

Challenging Practice

1. The figure is made up of two squares, one with 10-inch sides and the other with 6-inch sides. Find QR.

$QR =$ 4 in.

2. The figure is made up of three identical squares with 3-inch sides. Find the total length of $\overline{BC}$ and $\overline{FG}$.

Thinking Skills: Spatial visualization, Deduction

$BC + FG =$ 3 in.

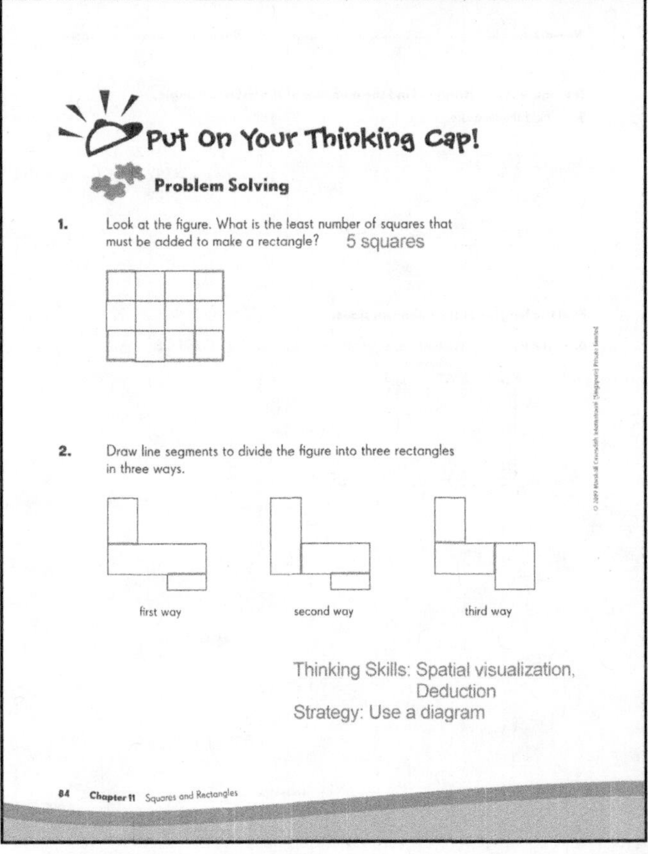
Put On Your Thinking Cap!

Problem Solving

1. Look at the figure. What is the least number of squares that must be added to make a rectangle? 5 squares

2. Draw line segments to divide the figure into three rectangles in three ways.

Thinking Skills: Spatial visualization, Deduction
Strategy: Use a diagram

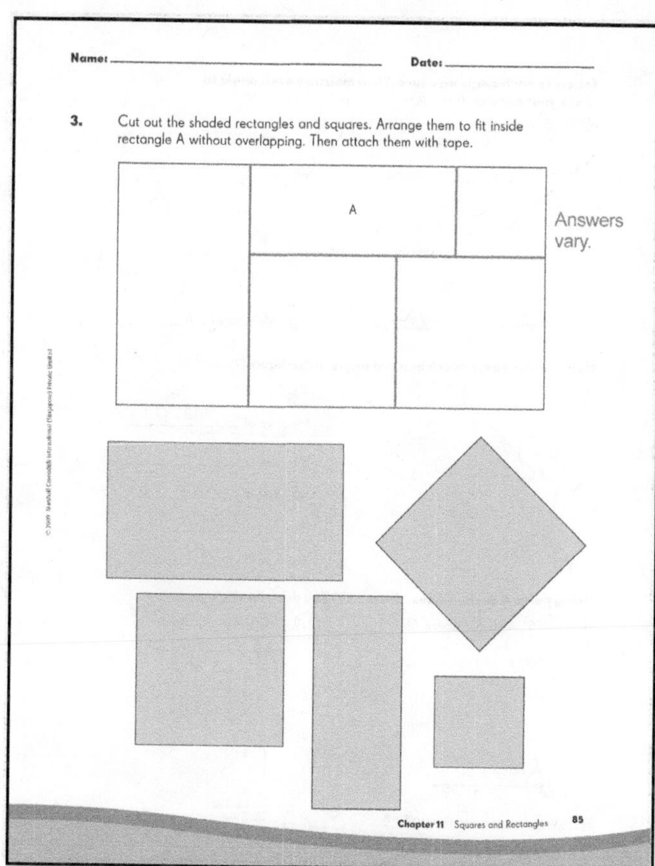
Name:
Date:
3. Cut out the shaded rectangles and squares. Arrange them to fit inside rectangle A without overlapping. Then attach them with tape.
A
Answers vary.
Chapter 11 Squares and Rectangles 85

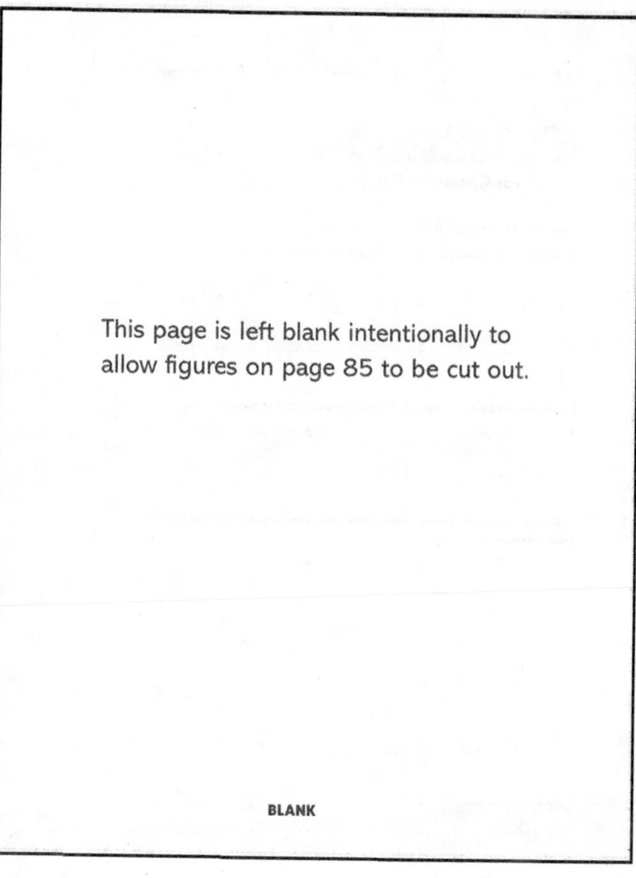
This page is left blank intentionally to allow figures on page 85 to be cut out.
BLANK

Chapter 11

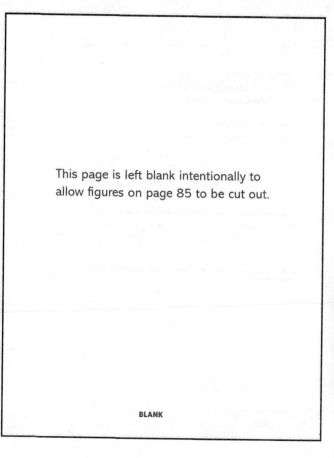

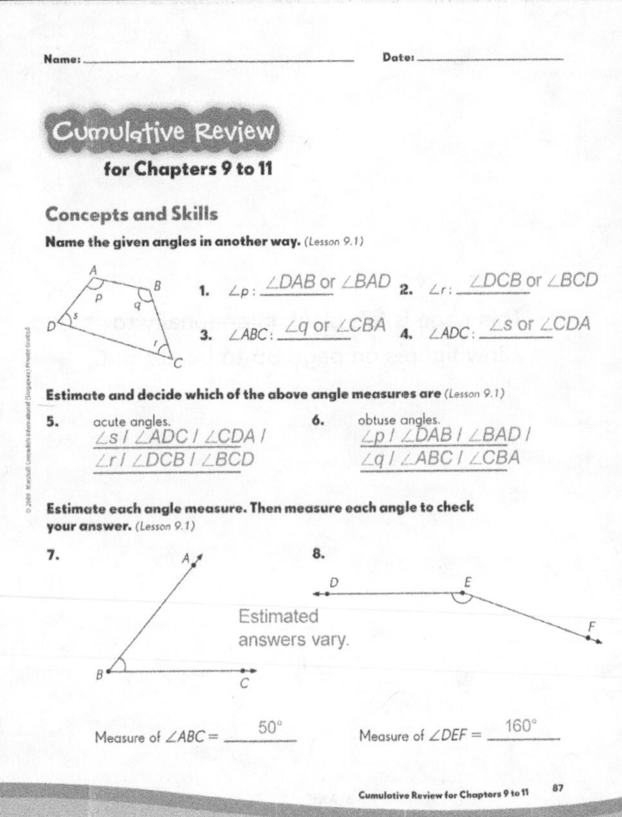

Name: ______________________ Date: ______________

Cumulative Review
for Chapters 9 to 11

Concepts and Skills

Name the given angles in another way. *(Lesson 9.1)*

1. $\angle p$: $\angle DAB$ or $\angle BAD$
2. $\angle r$: $\angle DCB$ or $\angle BCD$
3. $\angle ABC$: $\angle q$ or $\angle CBA$
4. $\angle ADC$: $\angle s$ or $\angle CDA$

Estimate and decide which of the above angle measures are *(Lesson 9.1)*

5. acute angles. $\angle s$ / $\angle ADC$ / $\angle CDA$ / $\angle r$ / $\angle DCB$ / $\angle BCD$
6. obtuse angles. $\angle p$ / $\angle DAB$ / $\angle BAD$ / $\angle q$ / $\angle ABC$ / $\angle CBA$

Estimate each angle measure. Then measure each angle to check your answer. *(Lesson 9.1)*

7.
8.

Estimated answers vary.

Measure of $\angle ABC$ = 50°

Measure of $\angle DEF$ = 160°

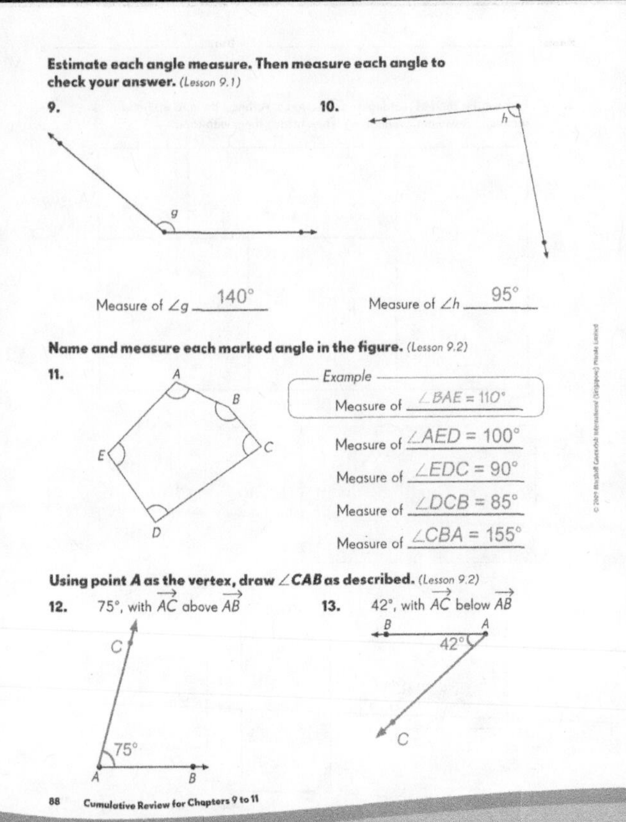

Estimate each angle measure. Then measure each angle to check your answer. *(Lesson 9.1)*

9.
10.

Measure of $\angle g$ 140°

Measure of $\angle h$ 95°

Name and measure each marked angle in the figure. *(Lesson 9.2)*

11.

Example
Measure of $\angle BAE = 110°$

Measure of $\angle AED = 100°$

Measure of $\angle EDC = 90°$

Measure of $\angle DCB = 85°$

Measure of $\angle CBA = 155°$

Using point *A* as the vertex, draw $\angle CAB$ as described. *(Lesson 9.2)*

12. 75°, with $\overrightarrow{AC}$ above $\overrightarrow{AB}$
13. 42°, with $\overrightarrow{AC}$ below $\overrightarrow{AB}$

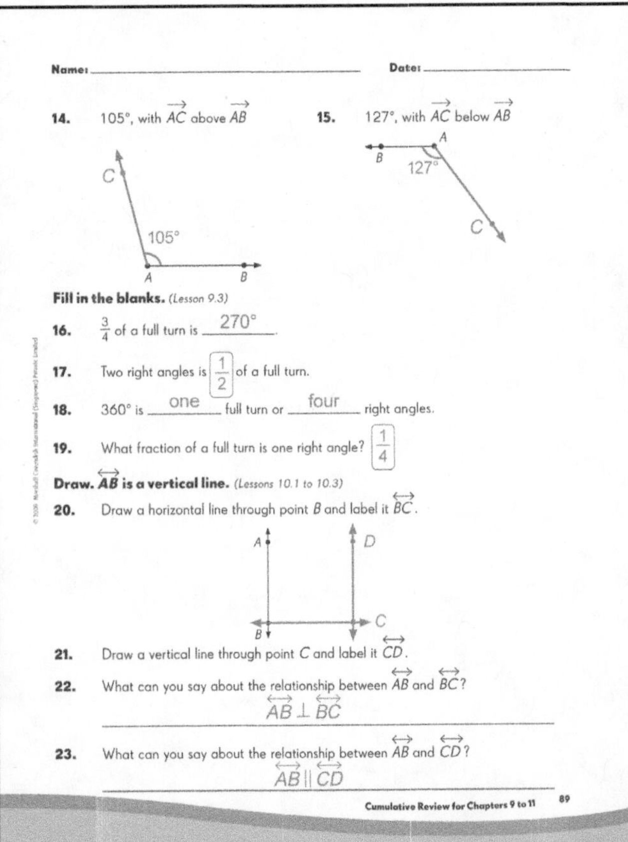

Name: ______________________ Date: ______________

14. 105°, with $\overrightarrow{AC}$ above $\overrightarrow{AB}$
15. 127°, with $\overrightarrow{AC}$ below $\overrightarrow{AB}$

Fill in the blanks. *(Lesson 9.3)*

16. $\frac{3}{4}$ of a full turn is 270°.
17. Two right angles is $\frac{1}{2}$ of a full turn.
18. 360° is one full turn or four right angles.
19. What fraction of a full turn is one right angle? $\frac{1}{4}$

Draw. $\overleftrightarrow{AB}$ is a vertical line. *(Lessons 10.1 to 10.3)*

20. Draw a horizontal line through point *B* and label it $\overleftrightarrow{BC}$.

21. Draw a vertical line through point *C* and label it $\overleftrightarrow{CD}$.
22. What can you say about the relationship between $\overleftrightarrow{AB}$ and $\overleftrightarrow{BC}$?
$\overleftrightarrow{AB} \perp \overleftrightarrow{BC}$
23. What can you say about the relationship between $\overleftrightarrow{AB}$ and $\overleftrightarrow{CD}$?
$\overleftrightarrow{AB} \parallel \overleftrightarrow{CD}$

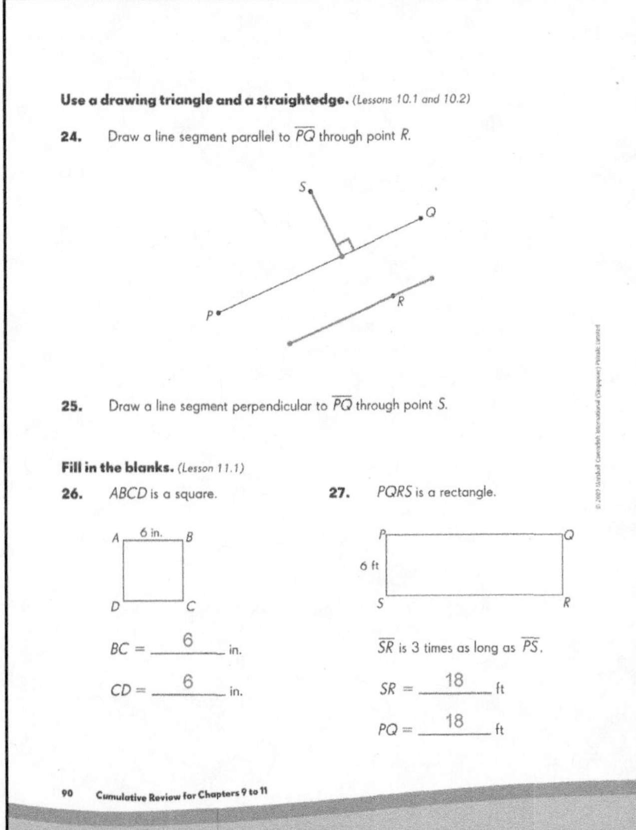

Use a drawing triangle and a straightedge. *(Lessons 10.1 and 10.2)*

24. Draw a line segment parallel to $\overline{PQ}$ through point *R*.

25. Draw a line segment perpendicular to $\overline{PQ}$ through point *S*.

Fill in the blanks. *(Lesson 11.1)*

26. *ABCD* is a square.

BC = 6 in.

CD = 6 in.

27. *PQRS* is a rectangle.

$\overline{SR}$ is 3 times as long as $\overline{PS}$.

SR = 18 ft

PQ = 18 ft

Name: _______________ Date: _______________

Find the measures of the unknown angles in the squares and rectangles. *(Lesson 11.2)*

28. *STUV* is a square.

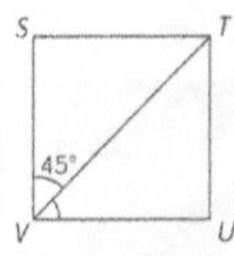

Measure of ∠*TVU* = 45°

29. *ABCD* is a rectangle.

Measure of ∠*BDC* = 67°

30. *MNOP* is a rectangle.

Measure of ∠*MNQ* = 54°

Measure of ∠*OMP* = 75°

31. *PQRS* is a square.

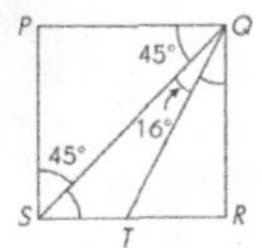

Measure of ∠*QSR* = 45°

Measure of ∠*RQT* = 29°

Solve. All sides in the figures meet at right angles.
Find the lengths of the unknown sides in each figure. *(Lesson 11.2)*

32.

EF = 8 cm

BC = 11 cm

33.

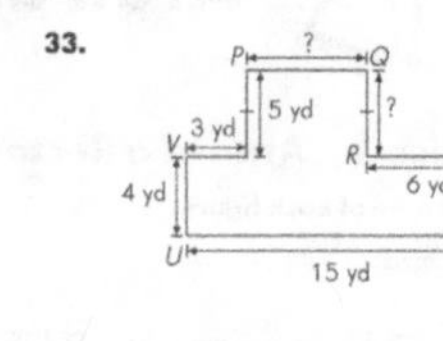

QR = 5 yd

PQ = 6 yd

34.

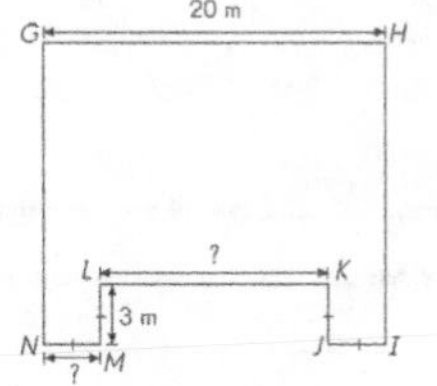

NM = 3 m

LK = 14 m

35.

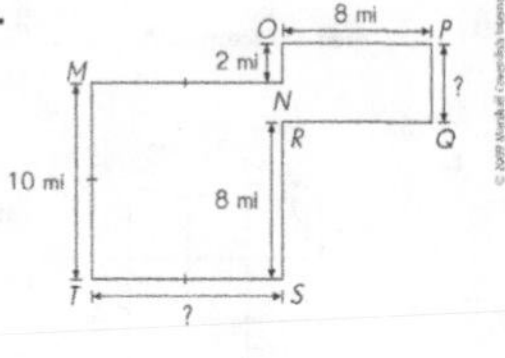

PQ = 4 mi

TS = 10 mi

Chapters 9-11 Review

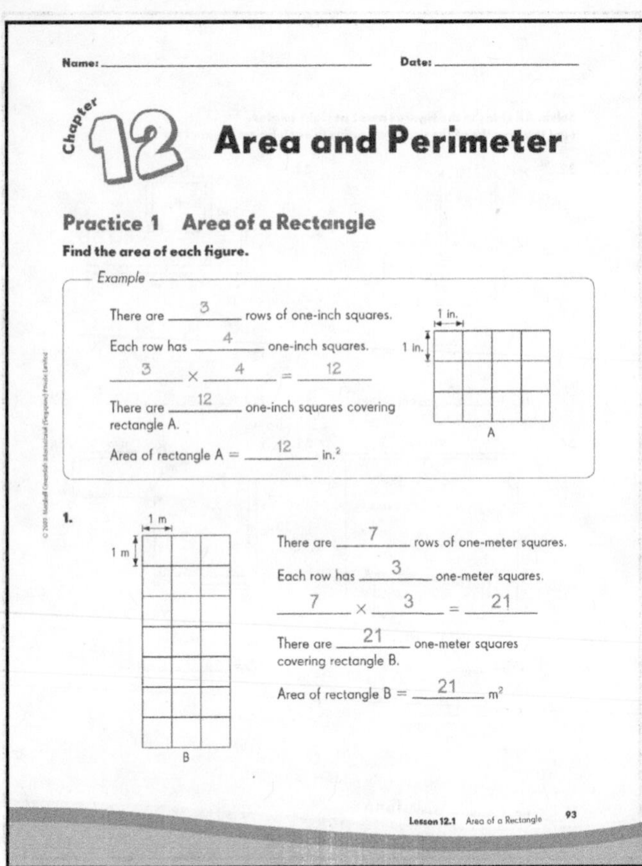

Name: ____________ Date: ____________

Chapter 12 Area and Perimeter

Practice 1 Area of a Rectangle

Find the area of each figure.

Example

There are 3 rows of one-inch squares.

Each row has 4 one-inch squares.

3 × 4 = 12

There are 12 one-inch squares covering rectangle A.

Area of rectangle A = 12 $in.^2$

1.

There are 7 rows of one-meter squares.

Each row has 3 one-meter squares.

7 × 3 = 21

There are 21 one-meter squares covering rectangle B.

Area of rectangle B = 21 m^2

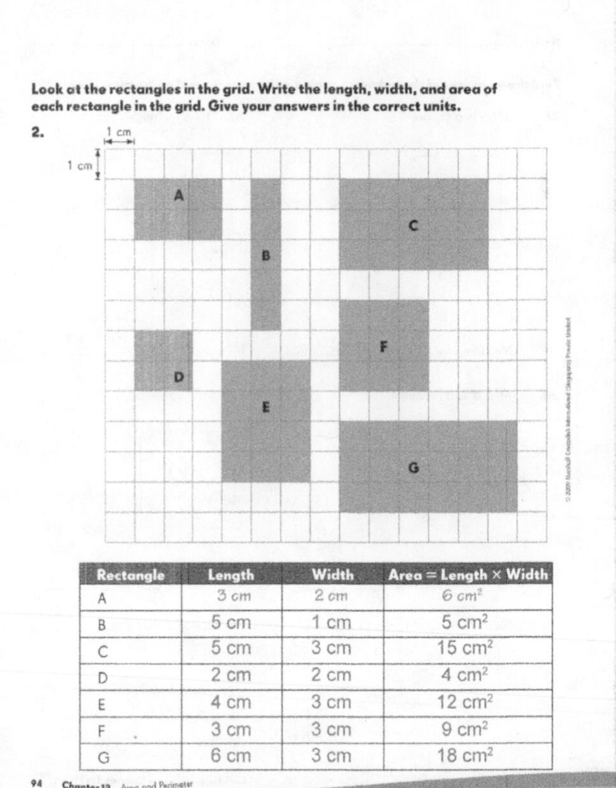

Look at the rectangles in the grid. Write the length, width, and area of each rectangle in the grid. Give your answers in the correct units.

2.

Rectangle	Length	Width	Area = Length × Width
A	3 cm	2 cm	6 cm^2
B	5 cm	1 cm	5 cm^2
C	5 cm	3 cm	15 cm^2
D	2 cm	2 cm	4 cm^2
E	4 cm	3 cm	12 cm^2
F	3 cm	3 cm	9 cm^2
G	6 cm	3 cm	18 cm^2

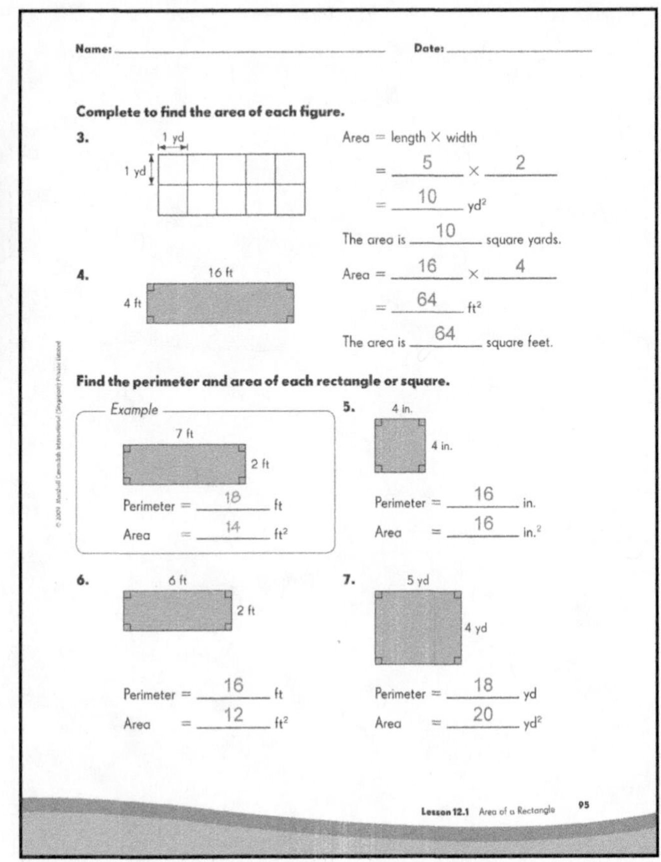

Name: ____________ Date: ____________

Complete to find the area of each figure.

3. Area = length × width

= 5 × 2

= 10 yd^2

The area is 10 square yards.

4. Area = 16 × 4

= 64 ft^2

The area is 64 square feet.

Find the perimeter and area of each rectangle or square.

Example

Perimeter = 18 ft

Area = 14 ft^2

5.

Perimeter = 16 in.

Area = 16 $in.^2$

6.

Perimeter = 16 ft

Area = 12 ft^2

7.

Perimeter = 18 yd

Area = 20 yd^2

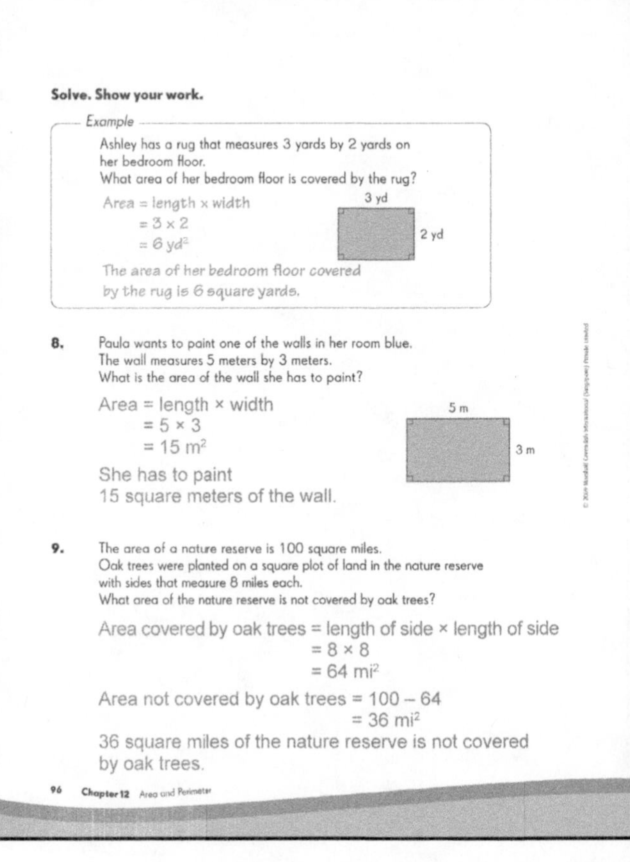

Solve. Show your work.

Example

Ashley has a rug that measures 3 yards by 2 yards on her bedroom floor.
What area of her bedroom floor is covered by the rug?

Area = length × width
= 3 × 2
= 6 yd^2

The area of her bedroom floor covered by the rug is 6 square yards.

8. Paula wants to paint one of the walls in her room blue.
The wall measures 5 meters by 3 meters.
What is the area of the wall she has to paint?

Area = length × width
= 5 × 3
= 15 m^2

She has to paint 15 square meters of the wall.

9. The area of a nature reserve is 100 square miles.
Oak trees were planted on a square plot of land in the nature reserve with sides that measure 8 miles each.
What area of the nature reserve is not covered by oak trees?

Area covered by oak trees = length of side × length of side
= 8 × 8
= 64 mi^2

Area not covered by oak trees = 100 – 64
= 36 mi^2

36 square miles of the nature reserve is not covered by oak trees.

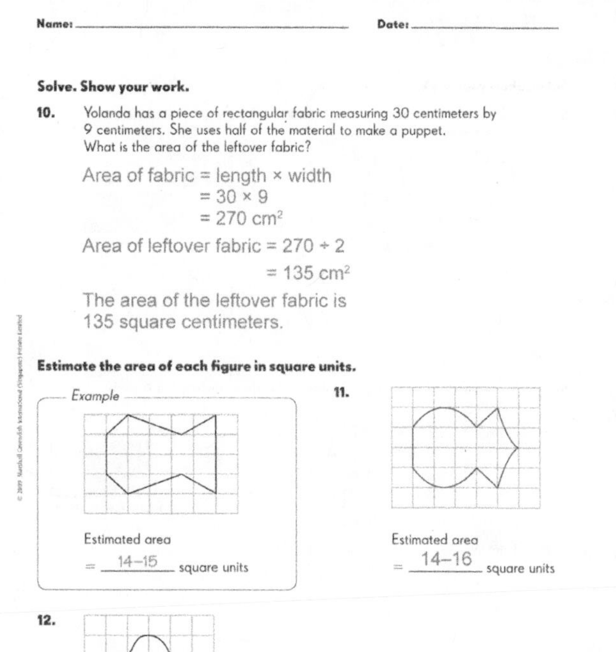

Name: ______ Date: ______

Solve. Show your work.

10. Yolanda has a piece of rectangular fabric measuring 30 centimeters by 9 centimeters. She uses half of the material to make a puppet. What is the area of the leftover fabric?

Area of fabric = length × width
= 30 × 9
= 270 cm^2

Area of leftover fabric = 270 ÷ 2
= 135 cm^2

The area of the leftover fabric is 135 square centimeters.

Estimate the area of each figure in square units.

Example

Estimated area = 14–15 square units

11. Estimated area = 14–16 square units

12. Estimated area = 7–8 square units

Lesson 12.1 Area of a Rectangle 97

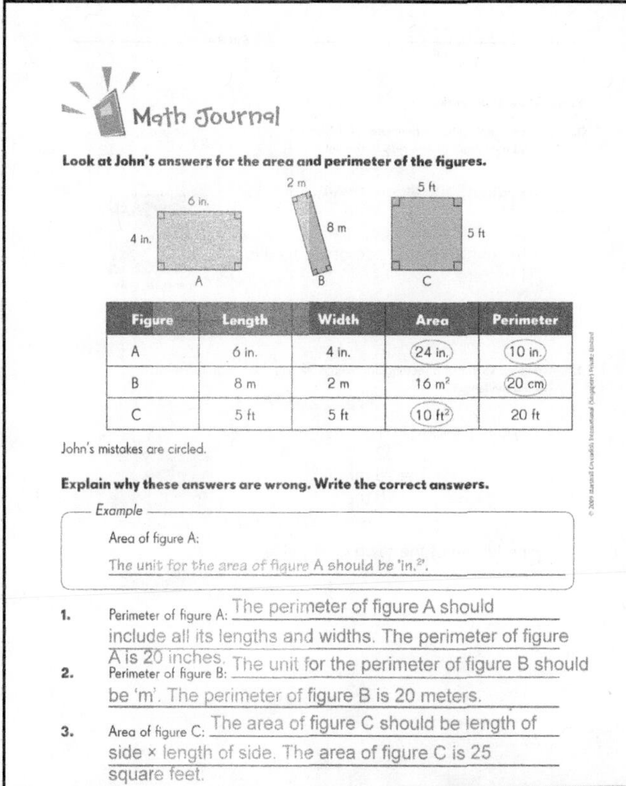

Math Journal

Look at John's answers for the area and perimeter of the figures.

Figure	Length	Width	Area	Perimeter
A	6 in.	4 in.	(24 in.)	(10 in.)
B	8 m	2 m	16 m^2	(20 cm)
C	5 ft	5 ft	(10 ft^2)	20 ft

John's mistakes are circled.

Explain why these answers are wrong. Write the correct answers.

Example

Area of figure A:
The unit for the area of figure A should be 'in.^{2}'.

1. Perimeter of figure A: The perimeter of figure A should include all its lengths and widths. The perimeter of figure A is 20 inches.

2. Perimeter of figure B: The unit for the perimeter of figure B should be 'm'. The perimeter of figure B is 20 meters.

3. Area of figure C: The area of figure C should be length of side × length of side. The area of figure C is 25 square feet.

98 Chapter 12 Area and Perimeter

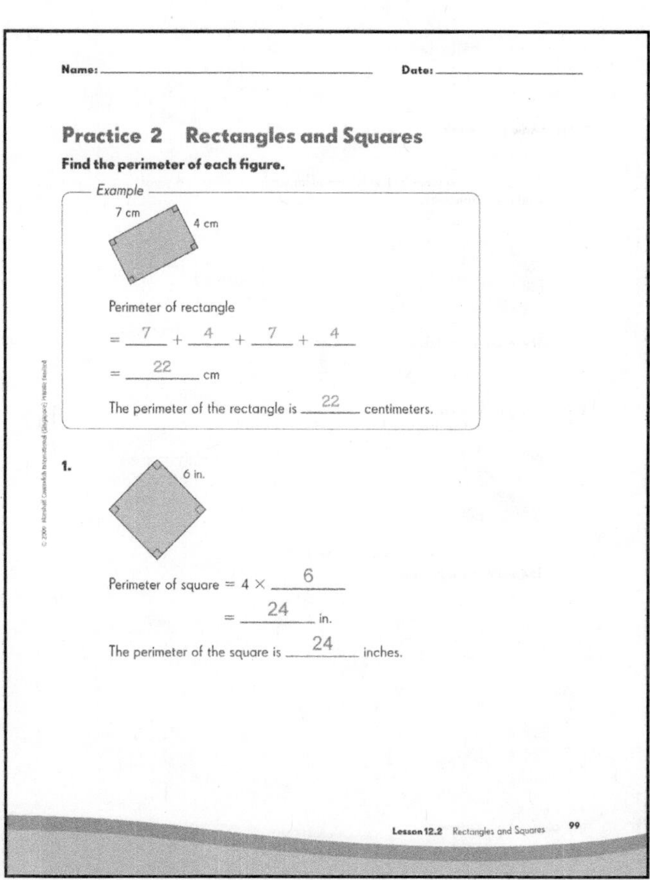

Name: ______ Date: ______

Practice 2 Rectangles and Squares

Find the perimeter of each figure.

Example

Perimeter of rectangle
= 7 + 4 + 7 + 4
= 22 cm

The perimeter of the rectangle is 22 centimeters.

1.

Perimeter of square = 4 × 6
= 24 in.

The perimeter of the square is 24 inches.

Lesson 12.2 Rectangles and Squares 99

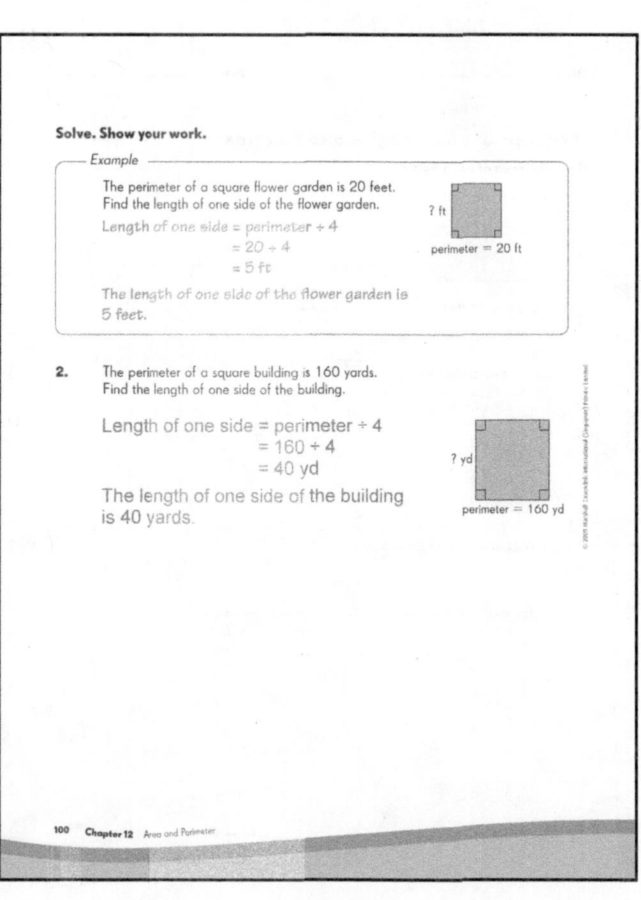

Solve. Show your work.

Example

The perimeter of a square flower garden is 20 feet. Find the length of one side of the flower garden.

Length of one side = perimeter ÷ 4
= 20 ÷ 4
= 5 ft

The length of one side of the flower garden is 5 feet.

2. The perimeter of a square building is 160 yards. Find the length of one side of the building.

Length of one side = perimeter ÷ 4
= 160 ÷ 4
= 40 yd

The length of one side of the building is 40 yards.

100 Chapter 12 Area and Perimeter

Chapter 12

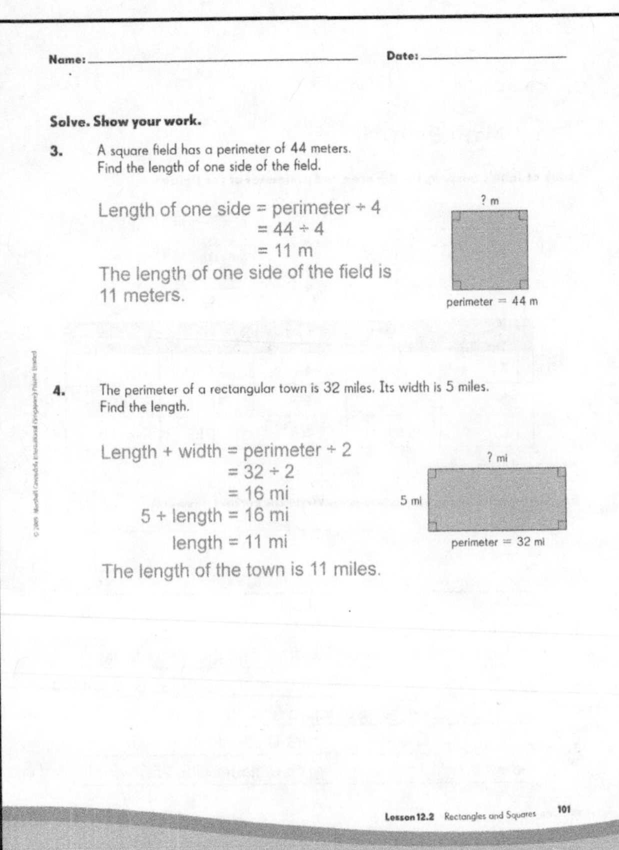
Name: ______ Date: ______

Solve. Show your work.

3. A square field has a perimeter of 44 meters. Find the length of one side of the field.

Length of one side = perimeter ÷ 4
= 44 ÷ 4
= 11 m

The length of one side of the field is 11 meters.

4. The perimeter of a rectangular town is 32 miles. Its width is 5 miles. Find the length.

Length + width = perimeter ÷ 2
= 32 ÷ 2
= 16 mi
5 + length = 16 mi
length = 11 mi

The length of the town is 11 miles.

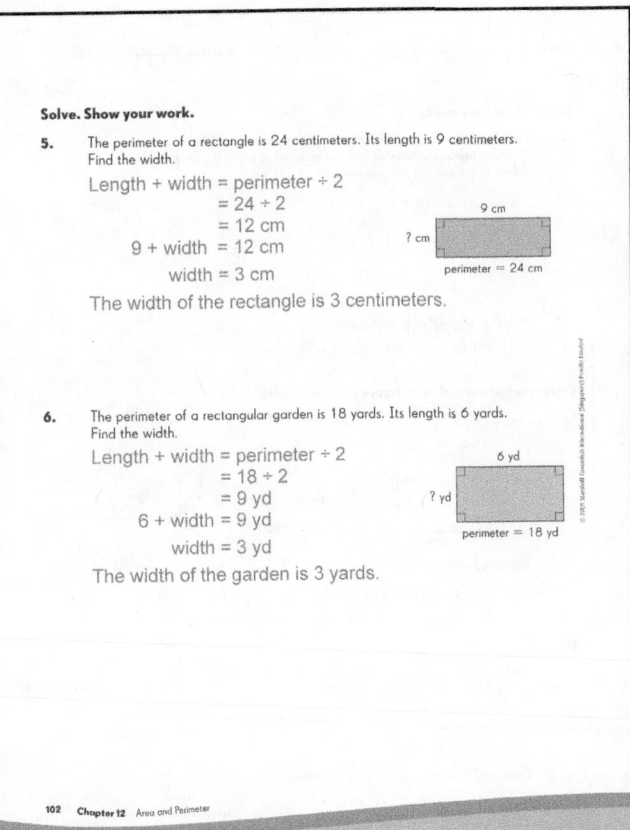
Solve. Show your work.

5. The perimeter of a rectangle is 24 centimeters. Its length is 9 centimeters. Find the width.

Length + width = perimeter ÷ 2
= 24 ÷ 2
= 12 cm
9 + width = 12 cm
width = 3 cm

The width of the rectangle is 3 centimeters.

6. The perimeter of a rectangular garden is 18 yards. Its length is 6 yards. Find the width.

Length + width = perimeter ÷ 2
= 18 ÷ 2
= 9 yd
6 + width = 9 yd
width = 3 yd

The width of the garden is 3 yards.

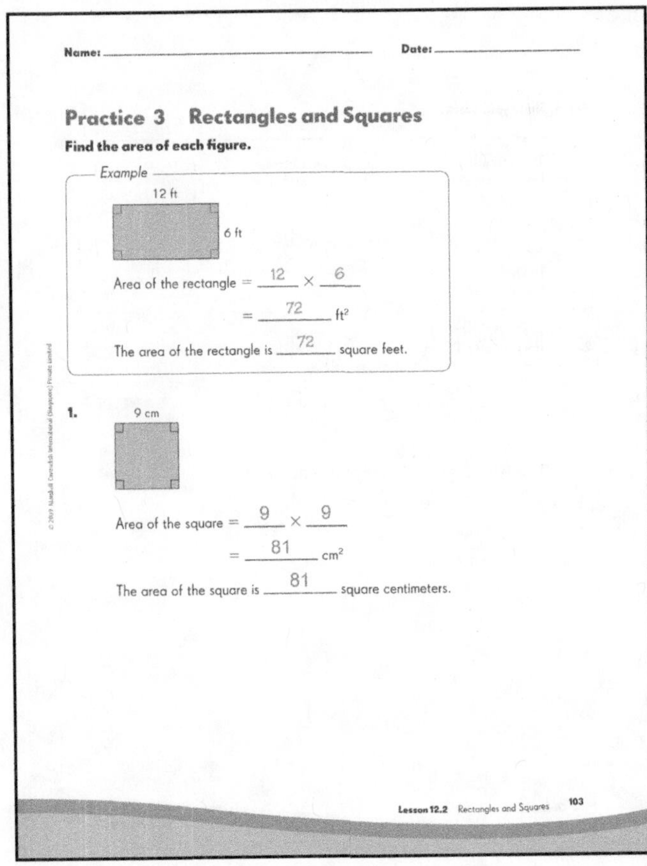
Name: ______ Date: ______

Practice 3 Rectangles and Squares

Find the area of each figure.

Example

Area of the rectangle = 12 × 6
= 72 ft^2

The area of the rectangle is 72 square feet.

1.

Area of the square = 9 × 9
= 81 cm^2

The area of the square is 81 square centimeters.

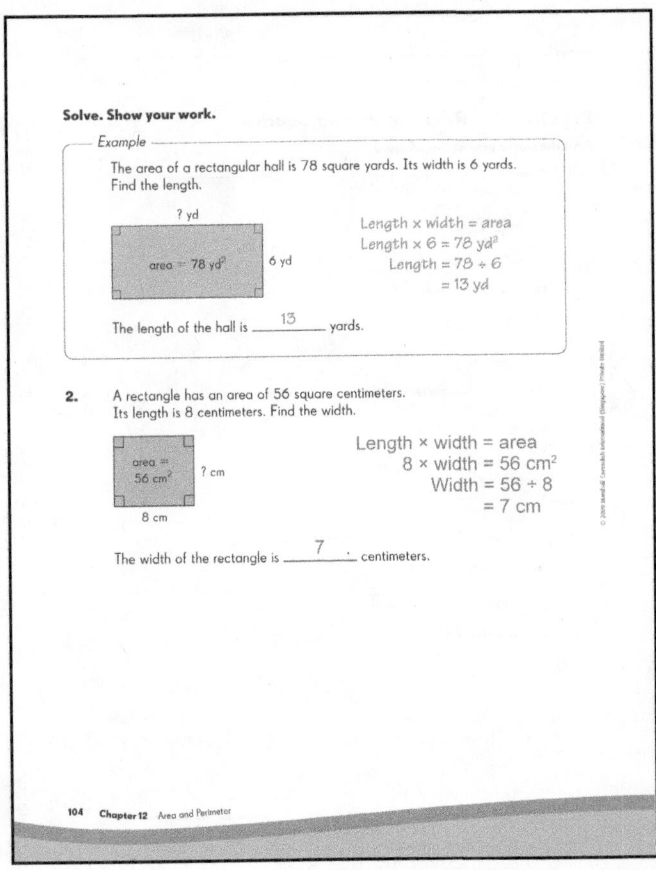
Solve. Show your work.

Example

The area of a rectangular hall is 78 square yards. Its width is 6 yards. Find the length.

Length × width = area
Length × 6 = 78 yd^2
Length = 78 ÷ 6
= 13 yd

The length of the hall is 13 yards.

2. A rectangle has an area of 56 square centimeters. Its length is 8 centimeters. Find the width.

Length × width = area
8 × width = 56 cm^2
Width = 56 ÷ 8
= 7 cm

The width of the rectangle is 7 centimeters.

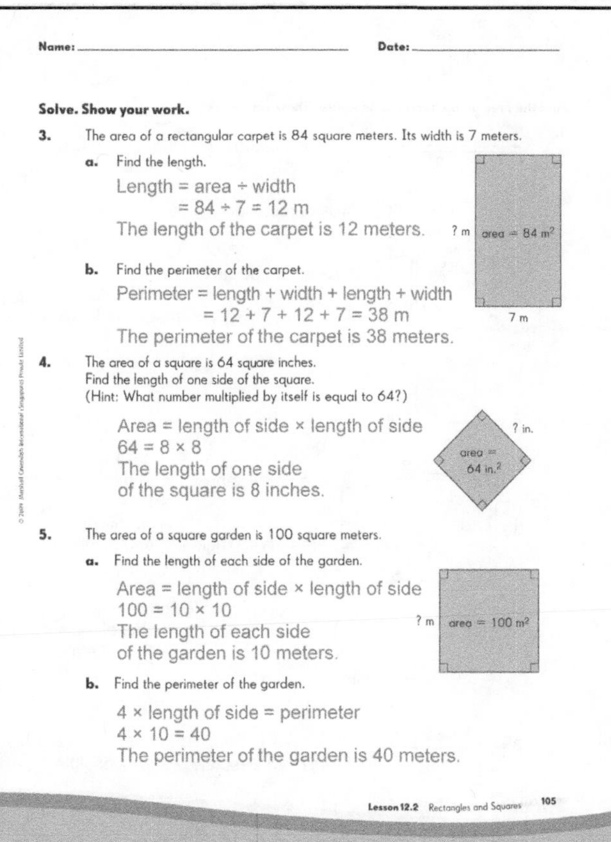

Name: ____________ Date: ____________

Solve. Show your work.

3. The area of a rectangular carpet is 84 square meters. Its width is 7 meters.

a. Find the length.

Length = area ÷ width
= 84 ÷ 7 = 12 m
The length of the carpet is 12 meters.

b. Find the perimeter of the carpet.

Perimeter = length + width + length + width
= 12 + 7 + 12 + 7 = 38 m
The perimeter of the carpet is 38 meters.

4. The area of a square is 64 square inches.
Find the length of one side of the square.
(Hint: What number multiplied by itself is equal to 64?)

Area = length of side × length of side
64 = 8 × 8
The length of one side of the square is 8 inches.

5. The area of a square garden is 100 square meters.

a. Find the length of each side of the garden.

Area = length of side × length of side
100 = 10 × 10
The length of each side of the garden is 10 meters.

b. Find the perimeter of the garden.

4 × length of side = perimeter
4 × 10 = 40
The perimeter of the garden is 40 meters.

© 2009 Marshall Cavendish International (Singapore) Private Limited

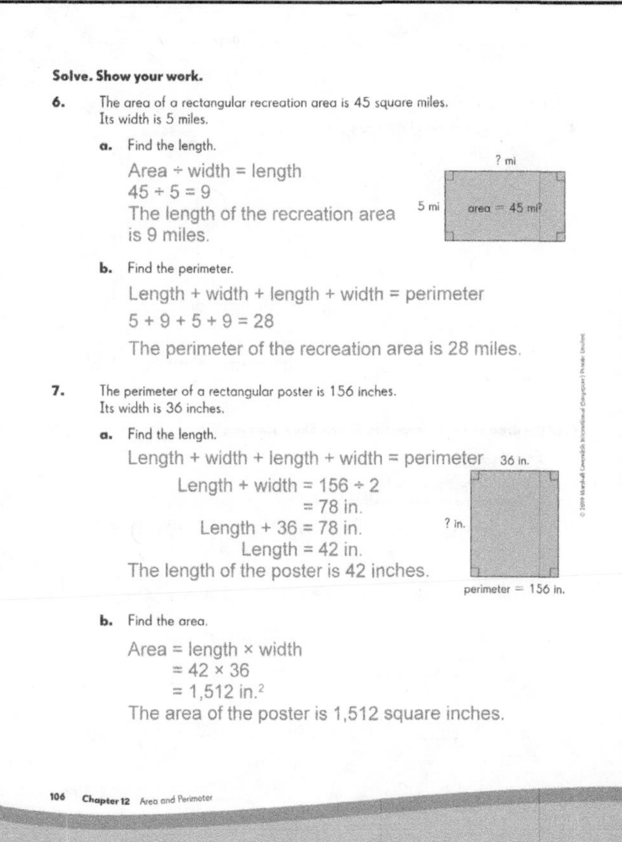

Solve. Show your work.

6. The area of a rectangular recreation area is 45 square miles.
Its width is 5 miles.

a. Find the length.

Area ÷ width = length
45 ÷ 5 = 9
The length of the recreation area is 9 miles.

b. Find the perimeter.

Length + width + length + width = perimeter
5 + 9 + 5 + 9 = 28
The perimeter of the recreation area is 28 miles.

7. The perimeter of a rectangular poster is 156 inches.
Its width is 36 inches.

a. Find the length.

Length + width + length + width = perimeter
Length + width = 156 ÷ 2
= 78 in.
Length + 36 = 78 in.
Length = 42 in.
The length of the poster is 42 inches.

b. Find the area.

Area = length × width
= 42 × 36
= 1,512 in.²
The area of the poster is 1,512 square inches.

© 2009 Marshall Cavendish International (Singapore) Private Limited

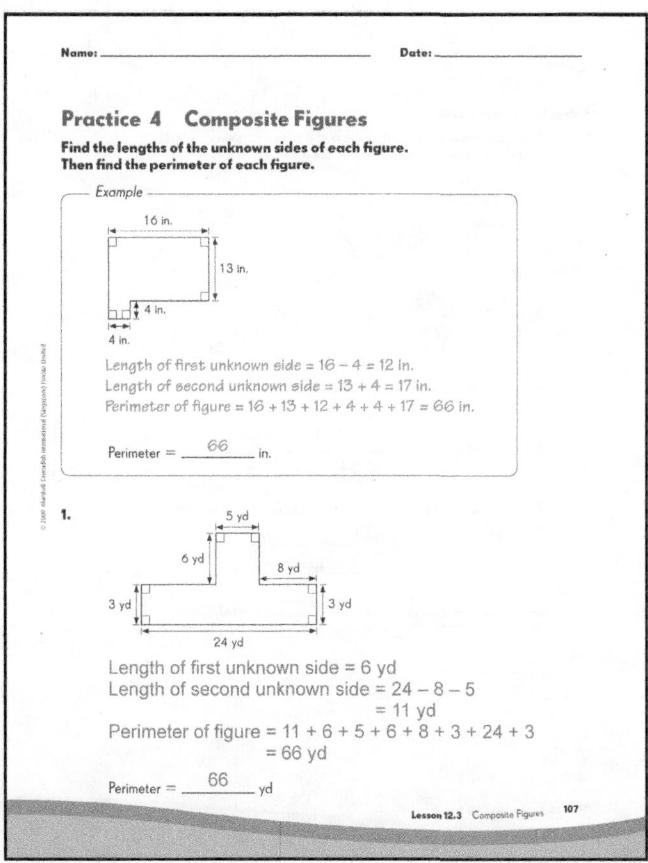

Name: ____________ Date: ____________

Practice 4 Composite Figures

**Find the lengths of the unknown sides of each figure.
Then find the perimeter of each figure.**

Example

Length of first unknown side = 16 – 4 = 12 in.
Length of second unknown side = 13 + 4 = 17 in.
Perimeter of figure = 16 + 13 + 12 + 4 + 4 + 17 = 66 in.

Perimeter = 66 in.

1.

Length of first unknown side = 6 yd
Length of second unknown side = 24 – 8 – 5
= 11 yd
Perimeter of figure = 11 + 6 + 5 + 6 + 8 + 3 + 24 + 3
= 66 yd

Perimeter = 66 yd

© 2009 Marshall Cavendish International (Singapore) Private Limited

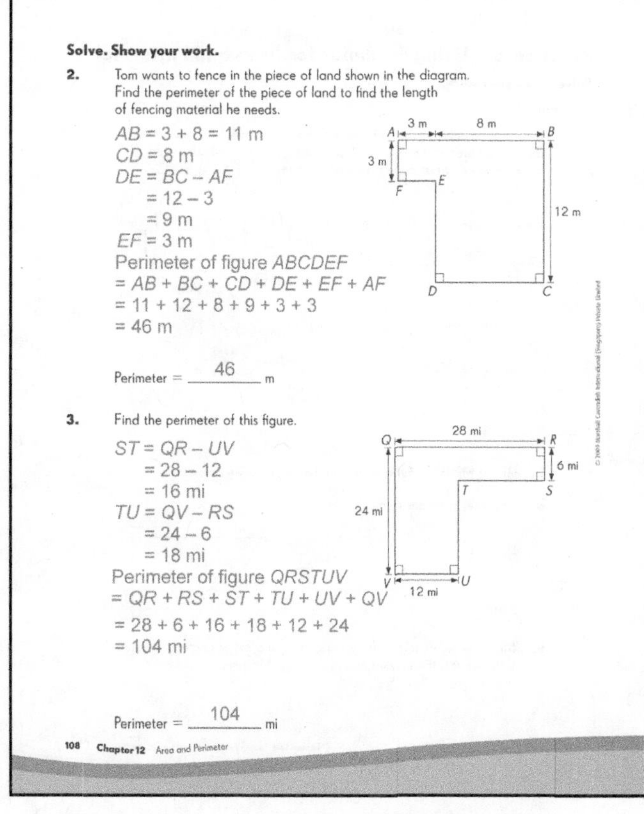

Solve. Show your work.

2. Tom wants to fence in the piece of land shown in the diagram.
Find the perimeter of the piece of land to find the length of fencing material he needs.

AB = 3 + 8 = 11 m
CD = 8 m
DE = *BC* – *AF*
= 12 – 3
= 9 m
EF = 3 m
Perimeter of figure *ABCDEF*
= *AB* + *BC* + *CD* + *DE* + *EF* + *AF*
= 11 + 12 + 8 + 9 + 3 + 3
= 46 m

Perimeter = 46 m

3. Find the perimeter of this figure.

ST = *QR* – *UV*
= 28 – 12
= 16 mi
TU = *QV* – *RS*
= 24 – 6
= 18 mi
Perimeter of figure *QRSTUV*
= *QR* + *RS* + *ST* + *TU* + *UV* + *QV*
= 28 + 6 + 16 + 18 + 12 + 24
= 104 mi

Perimeter = 104 mi

© 2009 Marshall Cavendish International (Singapore) Private Limited

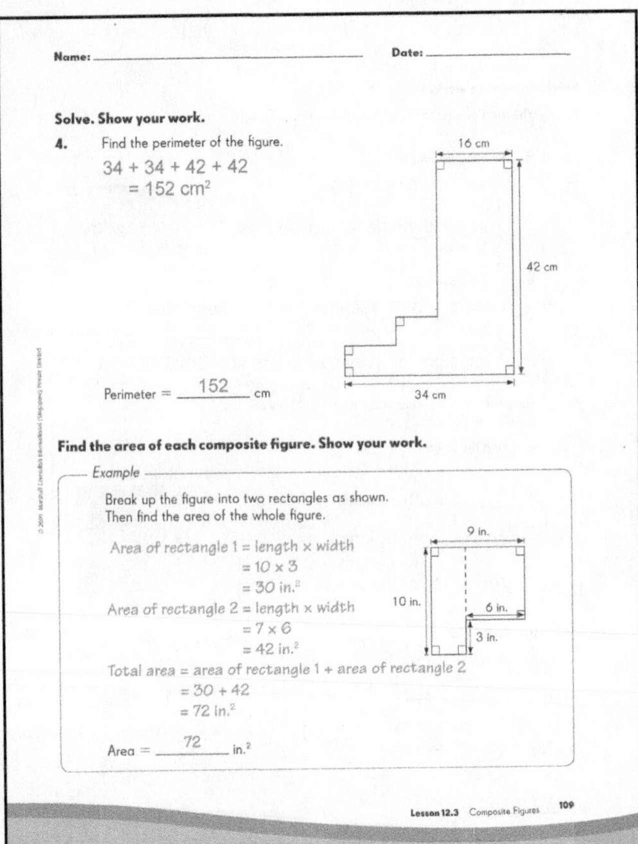

Name: ______________ Date: ______________

Solve. Show your work.

4. Find the perimeter of the figure.

34 + 34 + 42 + 42
= 152 cm^2

Perimeter = 152 cm

Find the area of each composite figure. Show your work.

Example

Break up the figure into two rectangles as shown.
Then find the area of the whole figure.

Area of rectangle 1 = length × width
= 10 × 3
= 30 $in.^2$

Area of rectangle 2 = length × width
= 7 × 6
= 42 $in.^2$

Total area = area of rectangle 1 + area of rectangle 2
= 30 + 42
= 72 $in.^2$

Area = 72 $in.^2$

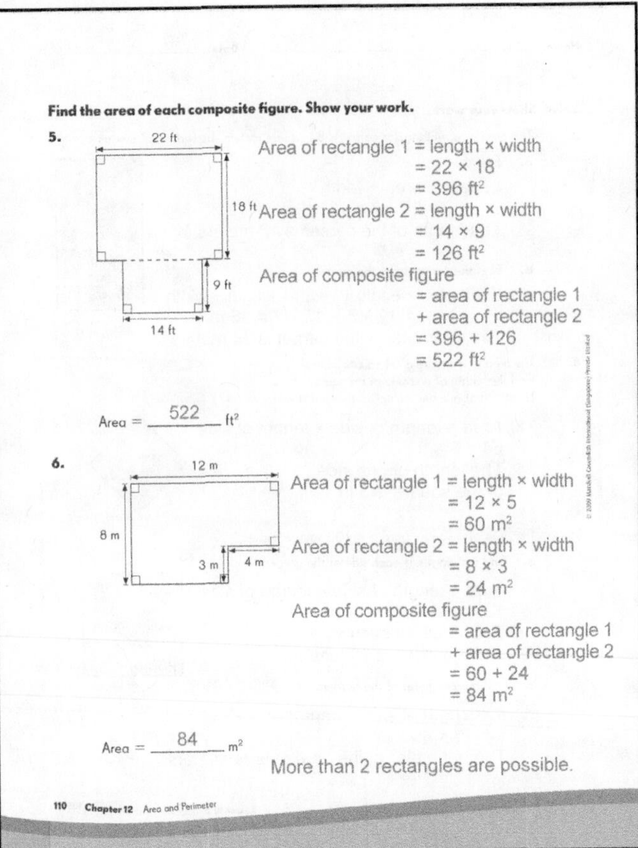

Find the area of each composite figure. Show your work.

5.

Area of rectangle 1 = length × width
= 22 × 18
= 396 ft^2

Area of rectangle 2 = length × width
= 14 × 9
= 126 ft^2

Area of composite figure
= area of rectangle 1
+ area of rectangle 2
= 396 + 126
= 522 ft^2

Area = 522 ft^2

6.

Area of rectangle 1 = length × width
= 12 × 5
= 60 m^2

Area of rectangle 2 = length × width
= 8 × 3
= 24 m^2

Area of composite figure
= area of rectangle 1
+ area of rectangle 2
= 60 + 24
= 84 m^2

Area = 84 m^2

More than 2 rectangles are possible.

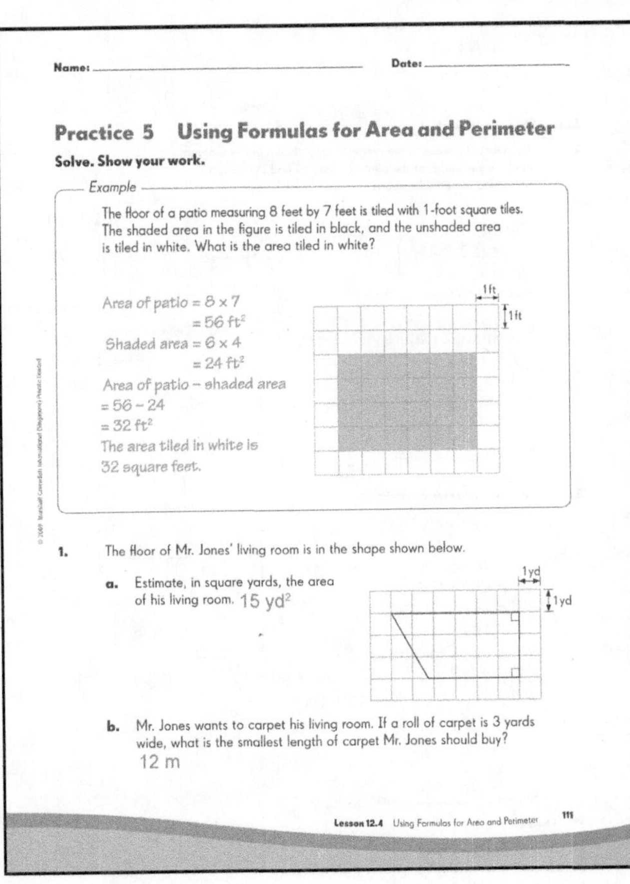

Name: ______________ Date: ______________

Practice 5 Using Formulas for Area and Perimeter

Solve. Show your work.

Example

The floor of a patio measuring 8 feet by 7 feet is tiled with 1-foot square tiles. The shaded area in the figure is tiled in black, and the unshaded area is tiled in white. What is the area tiled in white?

Area of patio = 8 × 7
= 56 ft^2

Shaded area = 6 × 4
= 24 ft^2

Area of patio − shaded area
= 56 − 24
= 32 ft^2

The area tiled in white is 32 square feet.

1. The floor of Mr. Jones' living room is in the shape shown below.

a. Estimate, in square yards, the area of his living room. 15 yd^2

b. Mr. Jones wants to carpet his living room. If a roll of carpet is 3 yards wide, what is the smallest length of carpet Mr. Jones should buy?
12 m

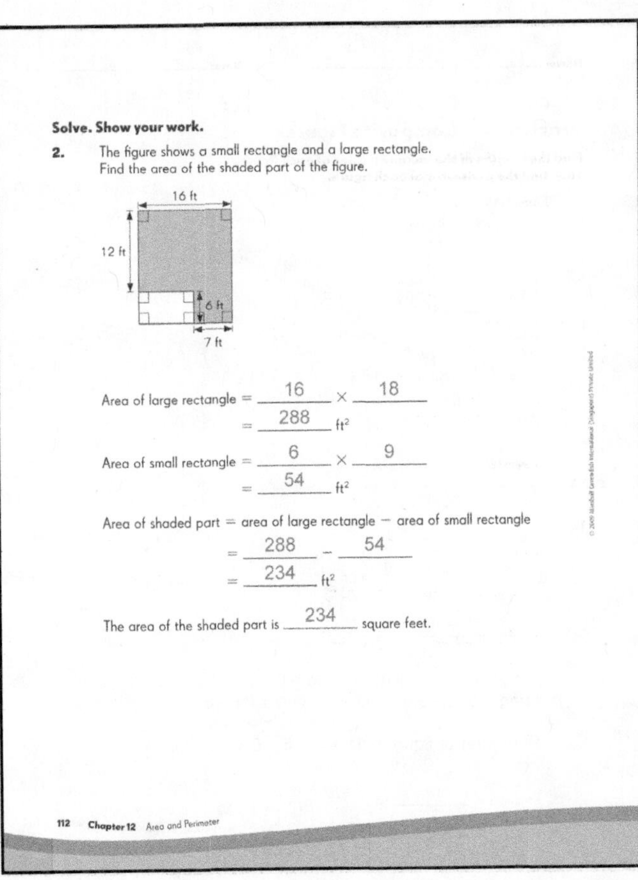

Solve. Show your work.

2. The figure shows a small rectangle and a large rectangle. Find the area of the shaded part of the figure.

Area of large rectangle = 16 × 18
= 288 ft^2

Area of small rectangle = 6 × 9
= 54 ft^2

Area of shaded part = area of large rectangle − area of small rectangle
= 288 − 54
= 234 ft^2

The area of the shaded part is 234 square feet.

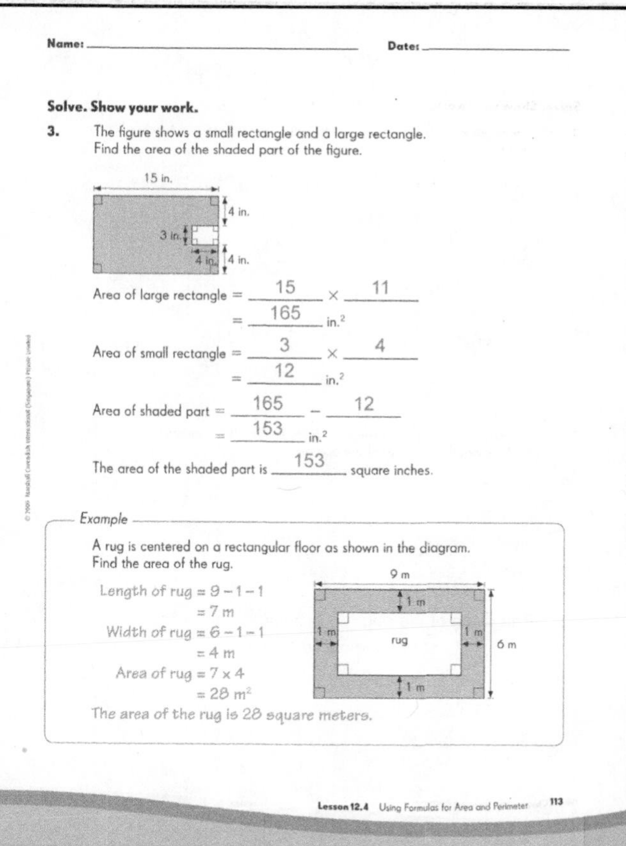

Name: ______ Date: ______

Solve. Show your work.

3. The figure shows a small rectangle and a large rectangle. Find the area of the shaded part of the figure.

Area of large rectangle = 15 × 11
= 165 in.^{2}

Area of small rectangle = 3 × 4
= 12 in.^{2}

Area of shaded part = 165 − 12
= 153 in.^{2}

The area of the shaded part is 153 square inches.

Example

A rug is centered on a rectangular floor as shown in the diagram. Find the area of the rug.

Length of rug = 9 − 1 − 1
= 7 m
Width of rug = 6 − 1 − 1
= 4 m
Area of rug = 7 × 4
= 28 m^2
The area of the rug is 28 square meters.

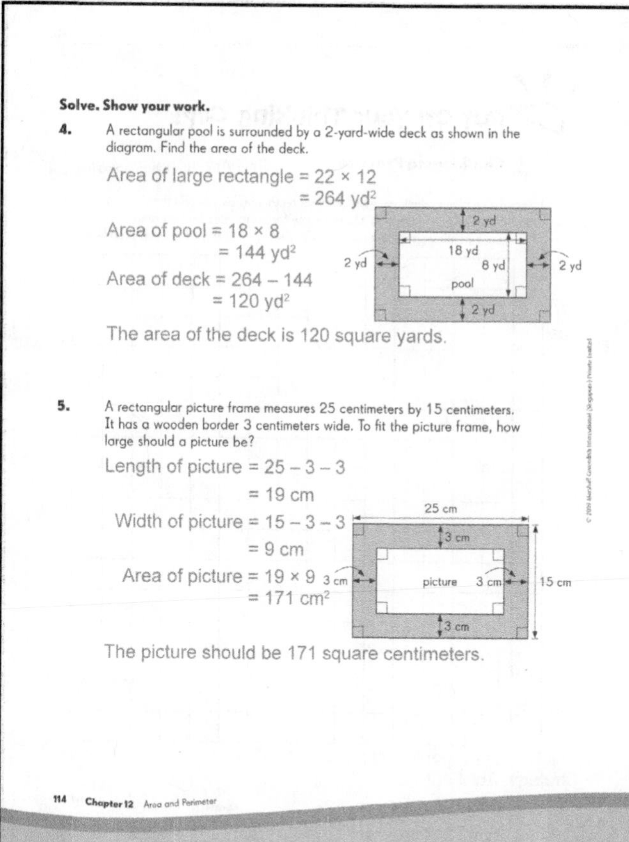

Solve. Show your work.

4. A rectangular pool is surrounded by a 2-yard-wide deck as shown in the diagram. Find the area of the deck.

Area of large rectangle = 22 × 12
= 264 yd^2

Area of pool = 18 × 8
= 144 yd^2

Area of deck = 264 − 144
= 120 yd^2

The area of the deck is 120 square yards.

5. A rectangular picture frame measures 25 centimeters by 15 centimeters. It has a wooden border 3 centimeters wide. To fit the picture frame, how large should a picture be?

Length of picture = 25 − 3 − 3
= 19 cm

Width of picture = 15 − 3 − 3
= 9 cm

Area of picture = 19 × 9
= 171 cm^2

The picture should be 171 square centimeters.

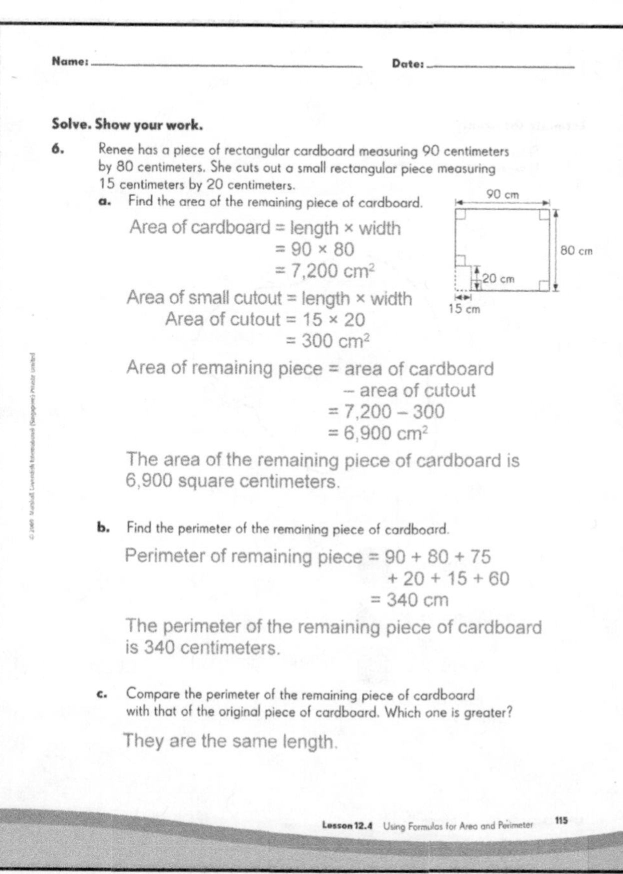

Name: ______ Date: ______

Solve. Show your work.

6. Renee has a piece of rectangular cardboard measuring 90 centimeters by 80 centimeters. She cuts out a small rectangular piece measuring 15 centimeters by 20 centimeters.

a. Find the area of the remaining piece of cardboard.

Area of cardboard = length × width
= 90 × 80
= 7,200 cm^2

Area of small cutout = length × width
Area of cutout = 15 × 20
= 300 cm^2

Area of remaining piece = area of cardboard − area of cutout
= 7,200 − 300
= 6,900 cm^2

The area of the remaining piece of cardboard is 6,900 square centimeters.

b. Find the perimeter of the remaining piece of cardboard.

Perimeter of remaining piece = 90 + 80 + 75 + 20 + 15 + 60
= 340 cm

The perimeter of the remaining piece of cardboard is 340 centimeters.

c. Compare the perimeter of the remaining piece of cardboard with that of the original piece of cardboard. Which one is greater?

They are the same length.

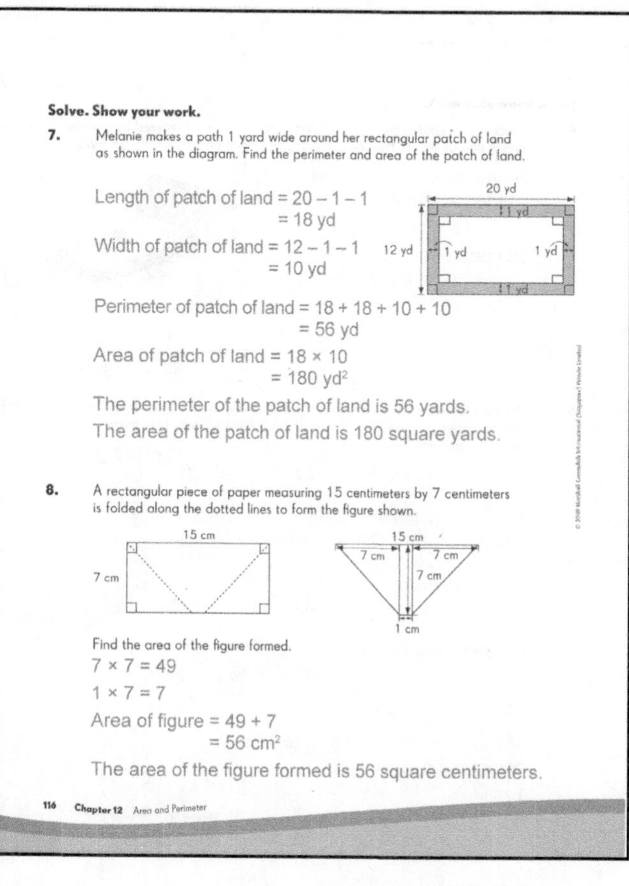

Solve. Show your work.

7. Melanie makes a path 1 yard wide around her rectangular patch of land as shown in the diagram. Find the perimeter and area of the patch of land.

Length of patch of land = 20 − 1 − 1
= 18 yd

Width of patch of land = 12 − 1 − 1
= 10 yd

Perimeter of patch of land = 18 + 18 + 10 + 10
= 56 yd

Area of patch of land = 18 × 10
= 180 yd^2

The perimeter of the patch of land is 56 yards.
The area of the patch of land is 180 square yards.

8. A rectangular piece of paper measuring 15 centimeters by 7 centimeters is folded along the dotted lines to form the figure shown.

Find the area of the figure formed.

7 × 7 = 49
1 × 7 = 7
Area of figure = 49 + 7
= 56 cm^2

The area of the figure formed is 56 square centimeters.

Chapter 12

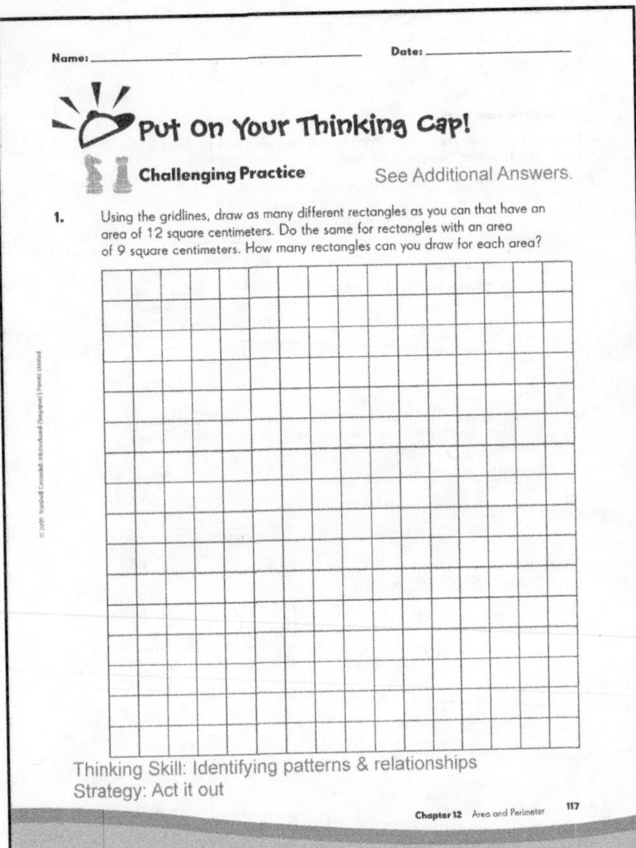
Name: ______ Date: ______

Put On Your Thinking Cap!

Challenging Practice

See Additional Answers.

1. Using the gridlines, draw as many different rectangles as you can that have an area of 12 square centimeters. Do the same for rectangles with an area of 9 square centimeters. How many rectangles can you draw for each area?

Thinking Skill: Identifying patterns & relationships
Strategy: Act it out

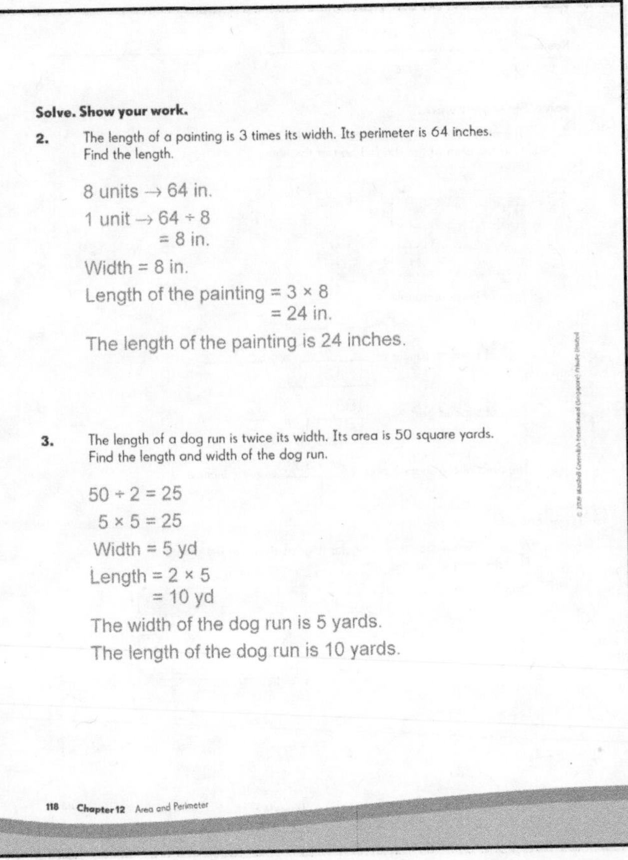
Solve. Show your work.

2. The length of a painting is 3 times its width. Its perimeter is 64 inches. Find the length.

8 units → 64 in.
1 unit → 64 ÷ 8
= 8 in.
Width = 8 in.
Length of the painting = 3 × 8
= 24 in.
The length of the painting is 24 inches.

3. The length of a dog run is twice its width. Its area is 50 square yards. Find the length and width of the dog run.

50 ÷ 2 = 25
5 × 5 = 25
Width = 5 yd
Length = 2 × 5
= 10 yd
The width of the dog run is 5 yards.
The length of the dog run is 10 yards.

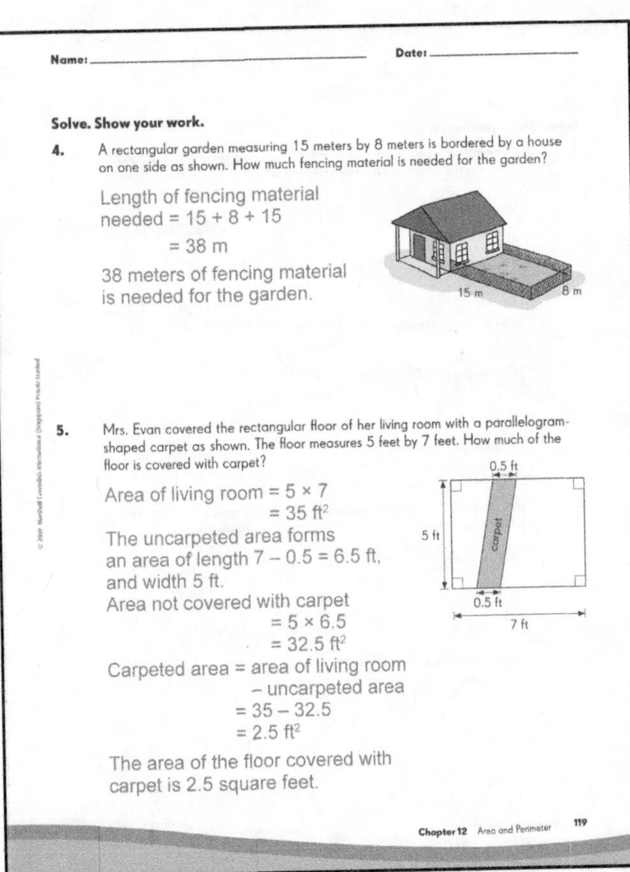
Name: ______ Date: ______

Solve. Show your work.

4. A rectangular garden measuring 15 meters by 8 meters is bordered by a house on one side as shown. How much fencing material is needed for the garden?

Length of fencing material needed = 15 + 8 + 15
= 38 m
38 meters of fencing material is needed for the garden.

5. Mrs. Evan covered the rectangular floor of her living room with a parallelogram-shaped carpet as shown. The floor measures 5 feet by 7 feet. How much of the floor is covered with carpet?

Area of living room = 5 × 7
= 35 ft^2
The uncarpeted area forms an area of length 7 – 0.5 = 6.5 ft, and width 5 ft.
Area not covered with carpet
= 5 × 6.5
= 32.5 ft^2
Carpeted area = area of living room – uncarpeted area
= 35 – 32.5
= 2.5 ft^2
The area of the floor covered with carpet is 2.5 square feet.

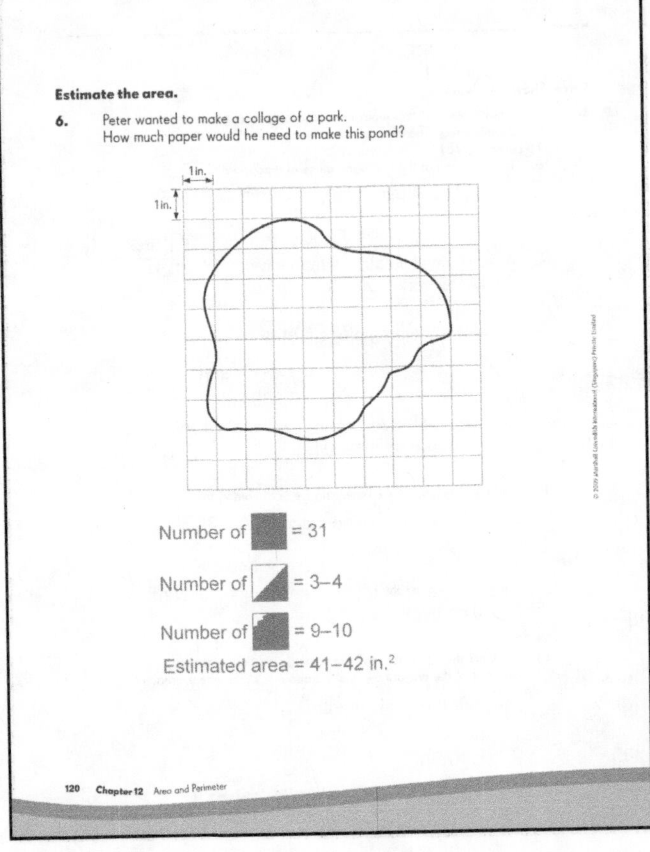
Estimate the area.

6. Peter wanted to make a collage of a park. How much paper would he need to make this pond?

Number of ■ = 31
Number of ◩ = 3–4
Number of ▟ = 9–10
Estimated area = 41–42 $in.^2$

Name: ______________________ Date: ______________

Put On Your Thinking Cap!

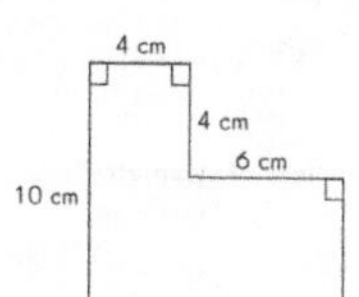
Problem Solving

1. Shawn has a piece of cardboard as shown in the diagram. He wants to cut out as many squares as possible from the cardboard. How many squares can he cut if each side of a square is

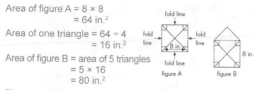

Strategy: Use a diagram

a. 2 centimeters long? 19

b. 3 centimeters long? 7

c. 4 centimeters long? 3

2. Figure A shows a piece of paper folded to form a square with 8-inch sides as shown in the diagram. Figure B shows one of the flaps opened. Find the area of figure B.

Area of figure A = 8 × 8
= 64 in.²

Area of one triangle = 64 ÷ 4
= 16 in.²

Area of figure B = area of 5 triangles
= 5 × 16
= 80 in.²

The area of figure B is 80 square inches.

© 2009 Marshall Cavendish International (Singapore) Private Limited

Solve. Show your work.

3. The figure shows two squares. The area of the unshaded part of the figure is 9 square feet. If the sides of both the squares are whole numbers, find the perimeter of the unshaded part.

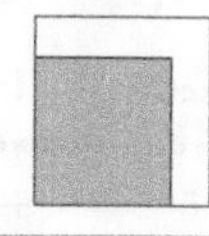

	1st Guess	2nd Guess	3rd Guess	4th Guess
Area of large square	2 × 2 = 4 ft²	3 × 3 = 9 ft²	4 × 4 = 16 ft²	5 × 5 = 25 ft²
Area of small square	1 × 1 = 1 ft²	1 × 1 = 1 ft²	2 × 2 = 4 ft²	4 × 4 = 16 ft²
Area of unshaded part	3 ft²	8 ft²	12 ft²	9 ft²

From the 4th guess, side of big square = 5 ft
side of small square = 4 ft.

Perimeter of the unshaded part
= 5 + 5 + 1 + 4 + 4 + 1
= 20 ft

The perimeter of the unshaded part is 20 feet.

© 2009 Marshall Cavendish International (Singapore) Private Limited

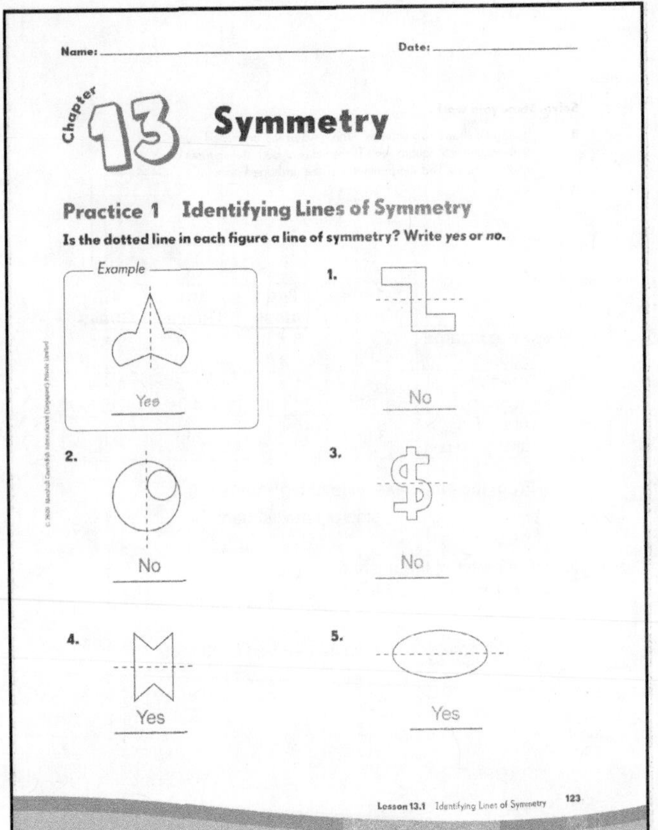

Name: ______________________ Date: ____________

Chapter 13 Symmetry

Practice 1 Identifying Lines of Symmetry

Is the dotted line in each figure a line of symmetry? Write *yes* or *no*.

Example: Yes

1. No

2. No

3. No

4. Yes

5. Yes

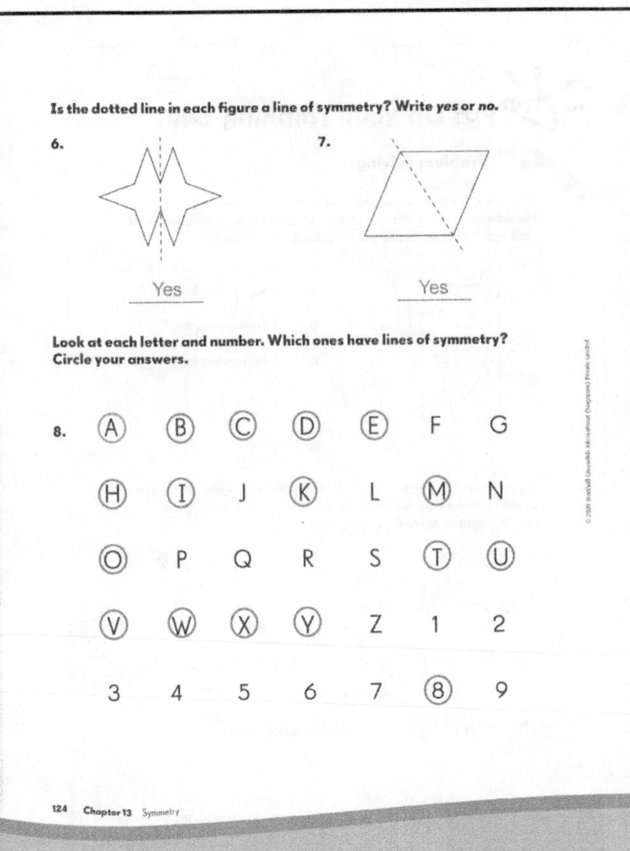

Is the dotted line in each figure a line of symmetry? Write *yes* or *no*.

6. Yes

7. Yes

Look at each letter and number. Which ones have lines of symmetry? Circle your answers.

8. (A) (B) (C) (D) (E) F G

(H) (I) J (K) L (M) N

(O) P Q R S (T) (U)

(V) (W) (X) (Y) Z 1 2

3 4 5 6 7 (8) 9

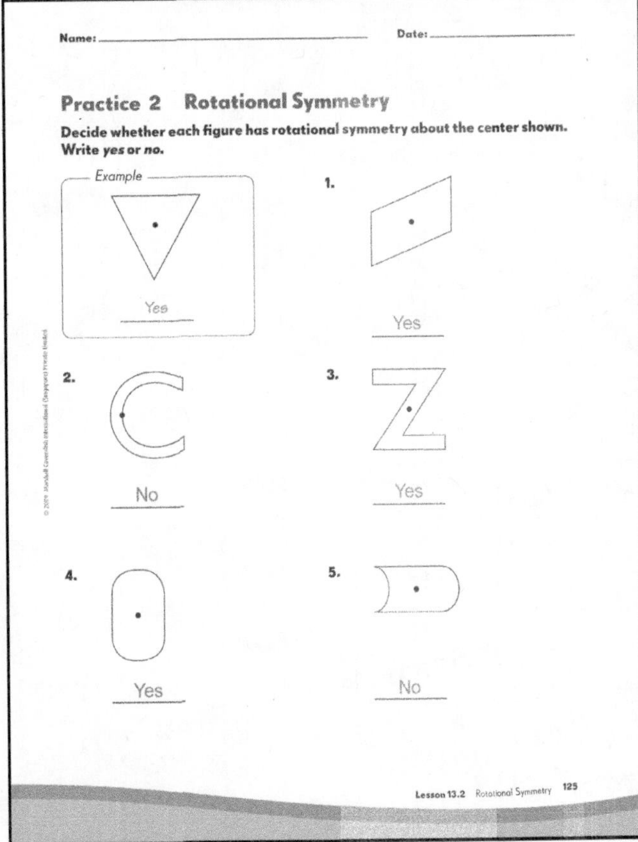

Name: ______________________ Date: ____________

Practice 2 Rotational Symmetry

Decide whether each figure has rotational symmetry about the center shown. Write *yes* or *no*.

Example: Yes

1. Yes

2. No

3. Yes

4. Yes

5. No

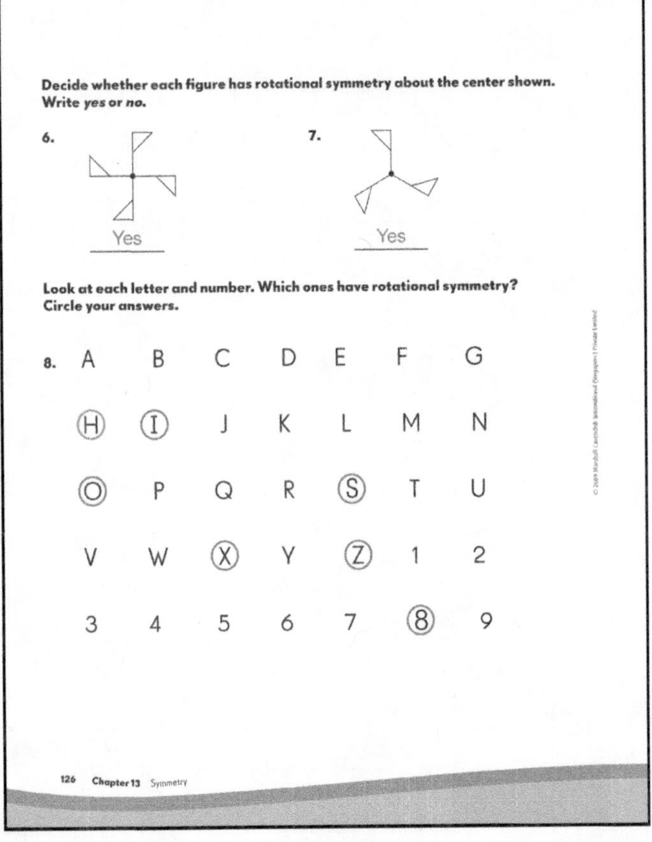

Decide whether each figure has rotational symmetry about the center shown. Write *yes* or *no*.

6. Yes

7. Yes

Look at each letter and number. Which ones have rotational symmetry? Circle your answers.

8. A B C D E F G

(H) (I) J K L M N

(O) P Q R (S) T U

V W (X) Y (Z) 1 2

3 4 5 6 7 (8) 9

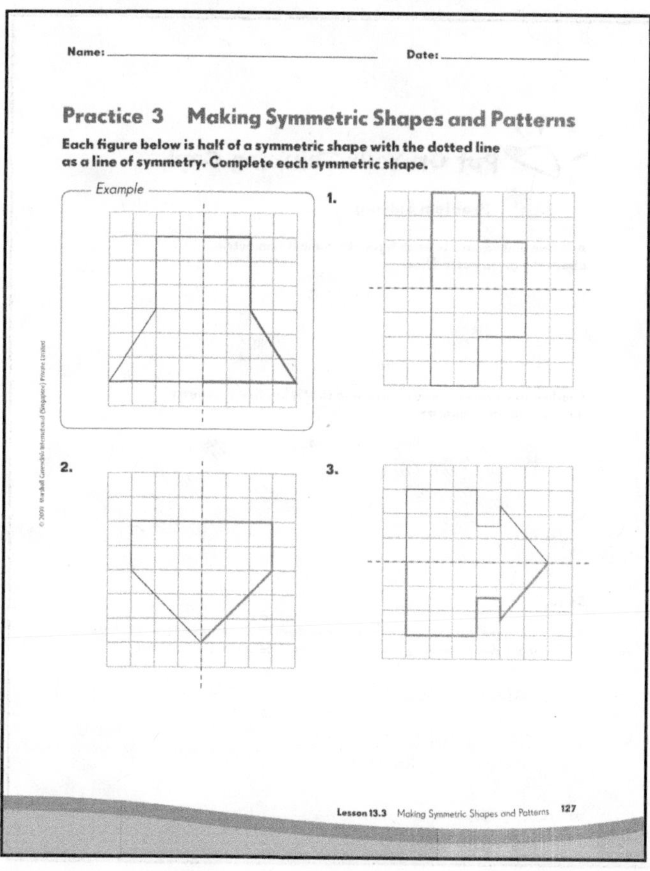
Name: ____________________ Date: ____________

Practice 3 Making Symmetric Shapes and Patterns

Each figure below is half of a symmetric shape with the dotted line as a line of symmetry. Complete each symmetric shape.

Example

1.

2.

3.

© 2009 Marshall Cavendish International (Singapore) Private Limited

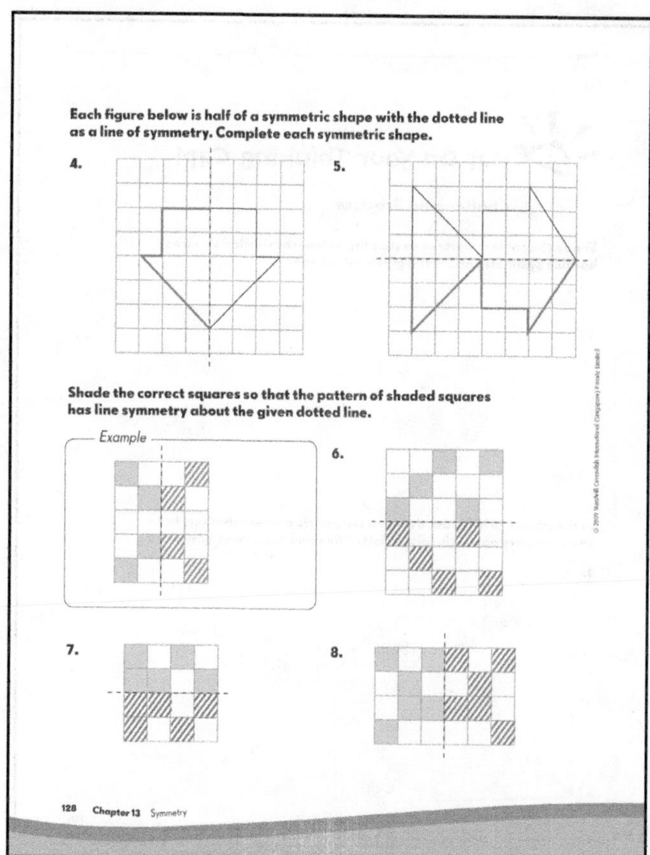
Each figure below is half of a symmetric shape with the dotted line as a line of symmetry. Complete each symmetric shape.

4.

5.

Shade the correct squares so that the pattern of shaded squares has line symmetry about the given dotted line.

Example

6.

7.

8.

© 2009 Marshall Cavendish International (Singapore) Private Limited

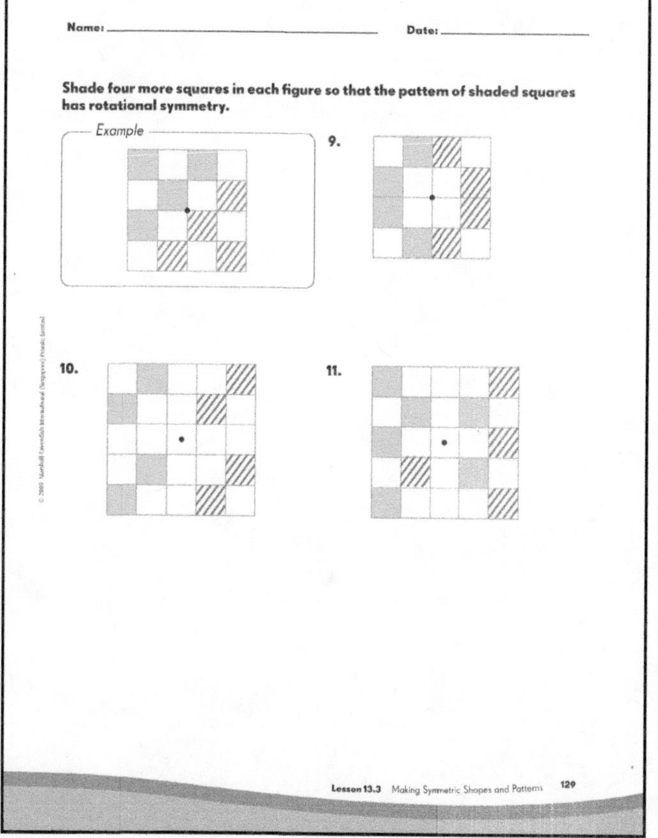
Name: ____________________ Date: ____________

Shade four more squares in each figure so that the pattern of shaded squares has rotational symmetry.

Example

9.

10.

11.

© 2009 Marshall Cavendish International (Singapore) Private Limited

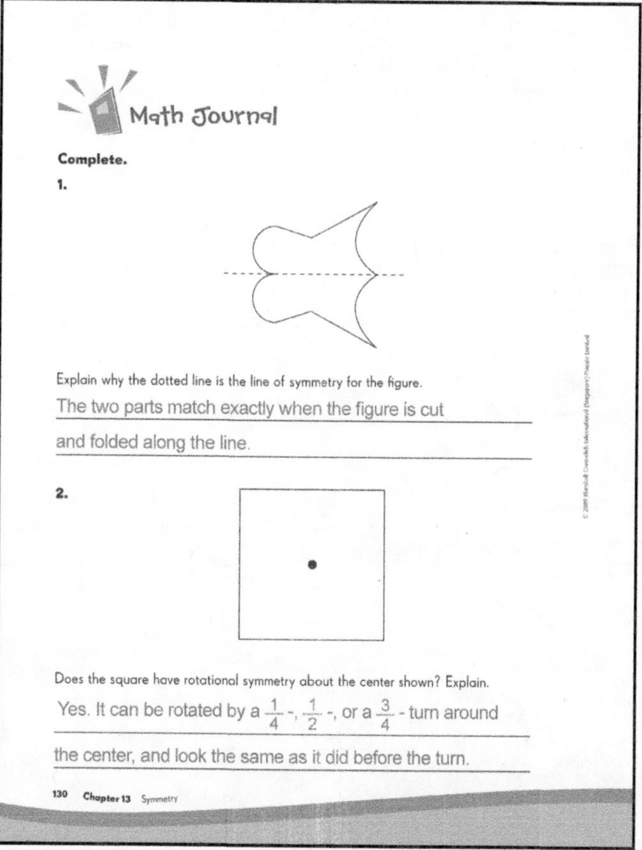
Math Journal

Complete.

1.

Explain why the dotted line is the line of symmetry for the figure.

The two parts match exactly when the figure is cut and folded along the line.

2.

Does the square have rotational symmetry about the center shown? Explain.

Yes. It can be rotated by a $\frac{1}{4}$-, $\frac{1}{2}$-, or a $\frac{3}{4}$- turn around the center, and look the same as it did before the turn.

© 2009 Marshall Cavendish International (Singapore) Private Limited

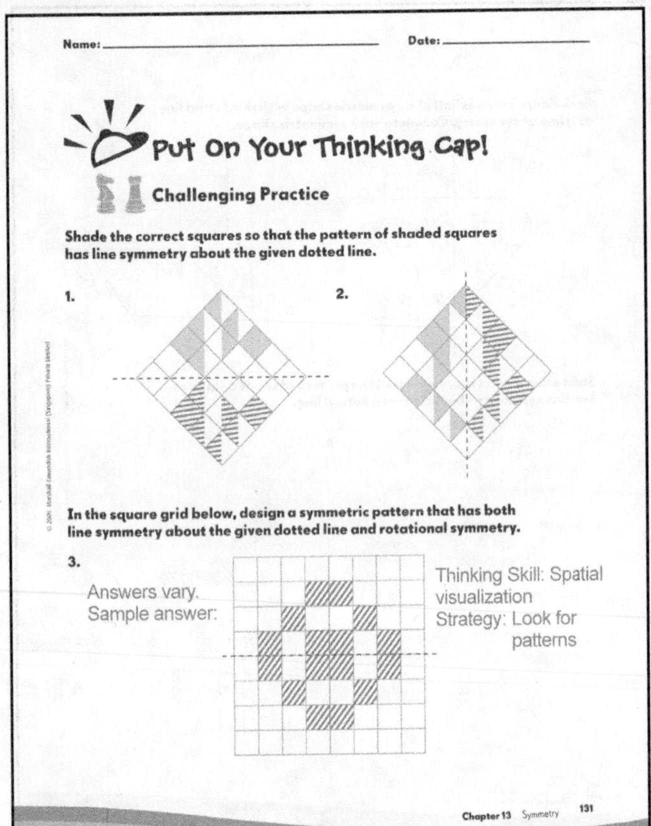

Name: ______________________ Date: ______________

Put On Your Thinking Cap!

Challenging Practice

Shade the correct squares so that the pattern of shaded squares has line symmetry about the given dotted line.

1.

2.

In the square grid below, design a symmetric pattern that has both line symmetry about the given dotted line and rotational symmetry.

3.

Answers vary.
Sample answer:

Thinking Skill: Spatial visualization
Strategy: Look for patterns

Chapter 13 Symmetry 131

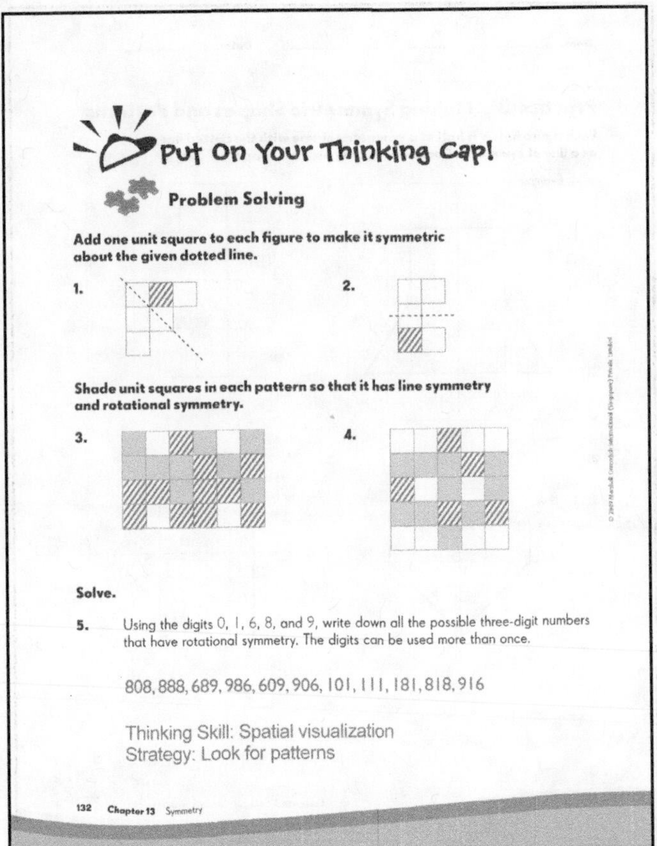

Put On Your Thinking Cap!

Problem Solving

Add one unit square to each figure to make it symmetric about the given dotted line.

1.

2.

Shade unit squares in each pattern so that it has line symmetry and rotational symmetry.

3.

4.

Solve.

5. Using the digits 0, 1, 6, 8, and 9, write down all the possible three-digit numbers that have rotational symmetry. The digits can be used more than once.

808, 888, 689, 986, 609, 906, 101, 111, 181, 818, 916

Thinking Skill: Spatial visualization
Strategy: Look for patterns

132 Chapter 13 Symmetry

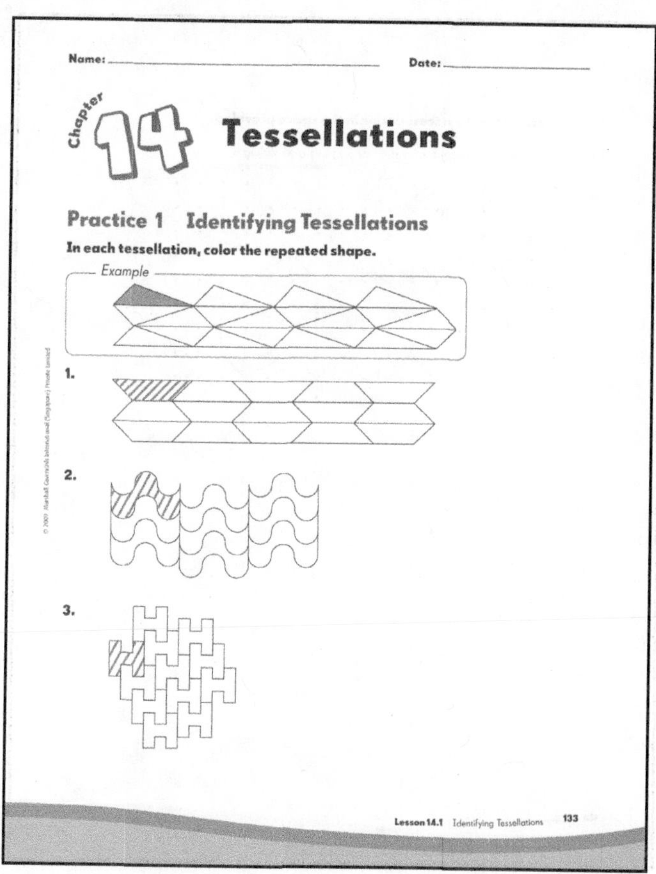

Name: ______________________ Date: ______________

Chapter 14 **Tessellations**

Practice 1 Identifying Tessellations

In each tessellation, color the repeated shape.

Example

1.

2.

3.

Lesson 14.1 Identifying Tessellations 133

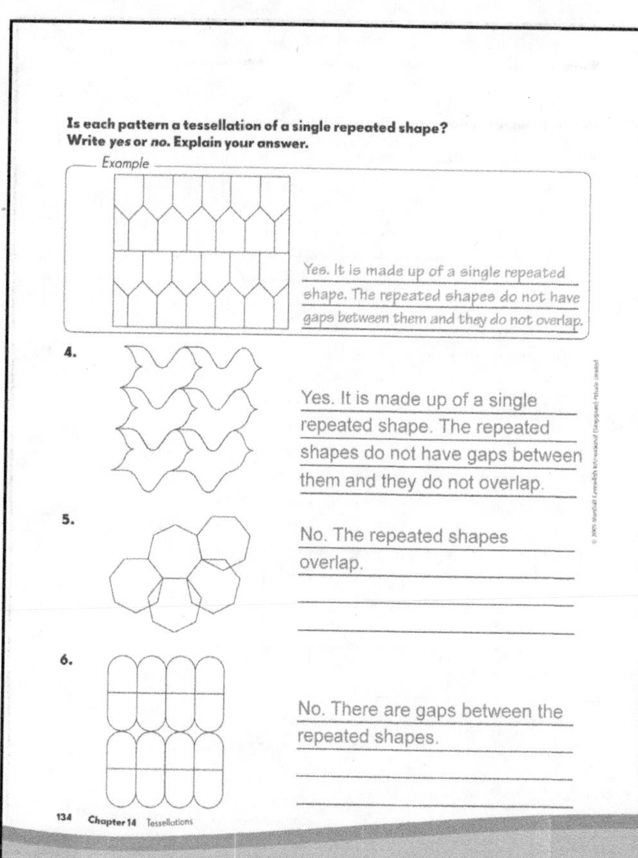

Is each pattern a tessellation of a single repeated shape? Write *yes* or *no*. Explain your answer.

Example

Yes. It is made up of a single repeated shape. The repeated shapes do not have gaps between them and they do not overlap.

4. Yes. It is made up of a single repeated shape. The repeated shapes do not have gaps between them and they do not overlap.

5. No. The repeated shapes overlap.

6. No. There are gaps between the repeated shapes.

134 Chapter 14 Tessellations

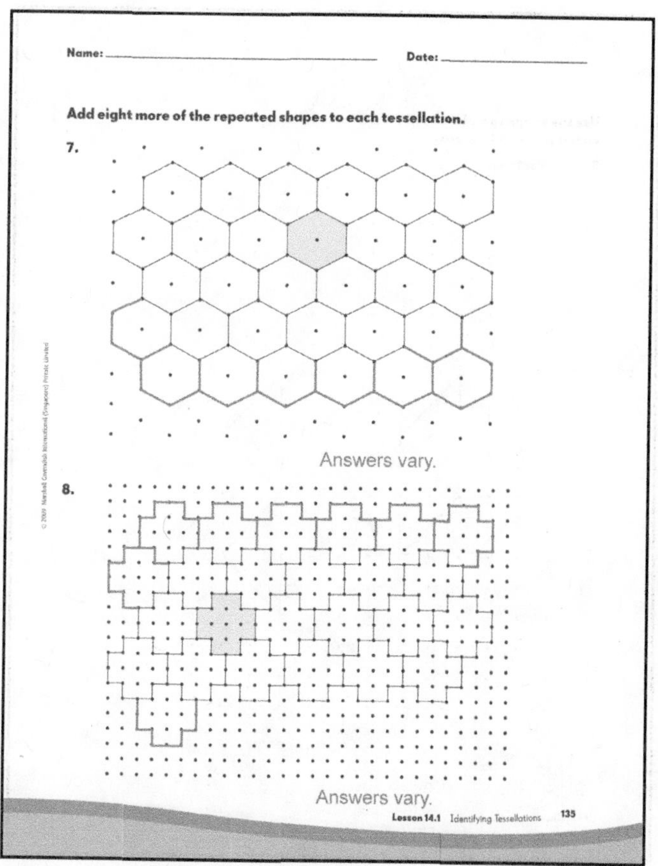

Name: ______________________ Date: ______________

Add eight more of the repeated shapes to each tessellation.

7.

Answers vary.

8.

Answers vary.

Lesson 14.1 Identifying Tessellations 135

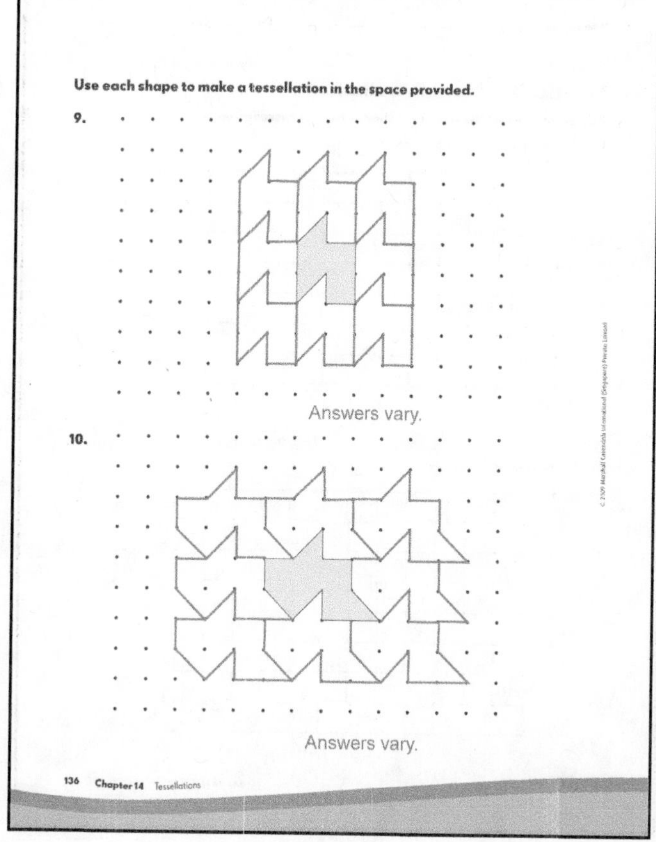

Use each shape to make a tessellation in the space provided.

9.

Answers vary.

10.

Answers vary.

136 Chapter 14 Tessellations

Chapter 14

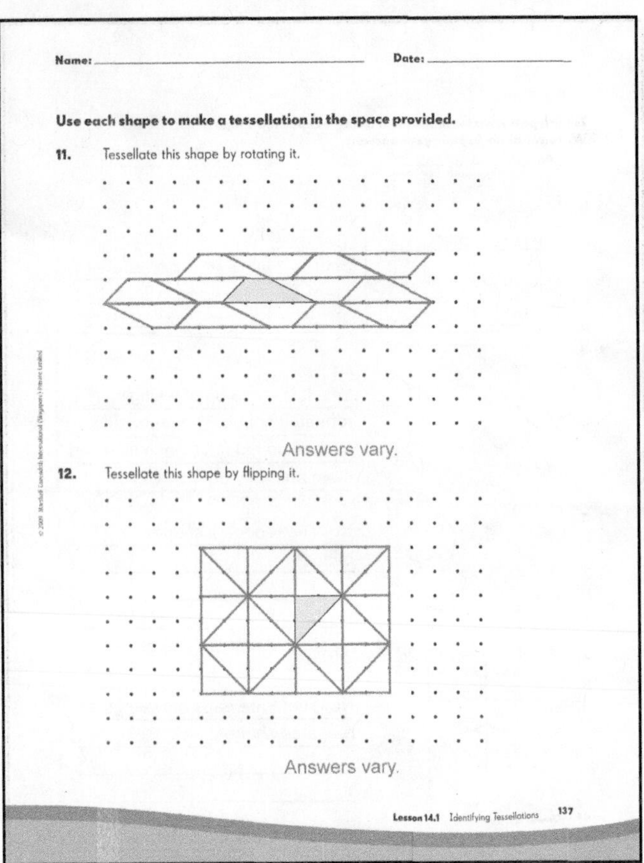

Name: ______________________ Date: ____________

Use each shape to make a tessellation in the space provided.

11. Tessellate this shape by rotating it.

Answers vary.

12. Tessellate this shape by flipping it.

Answers vary.

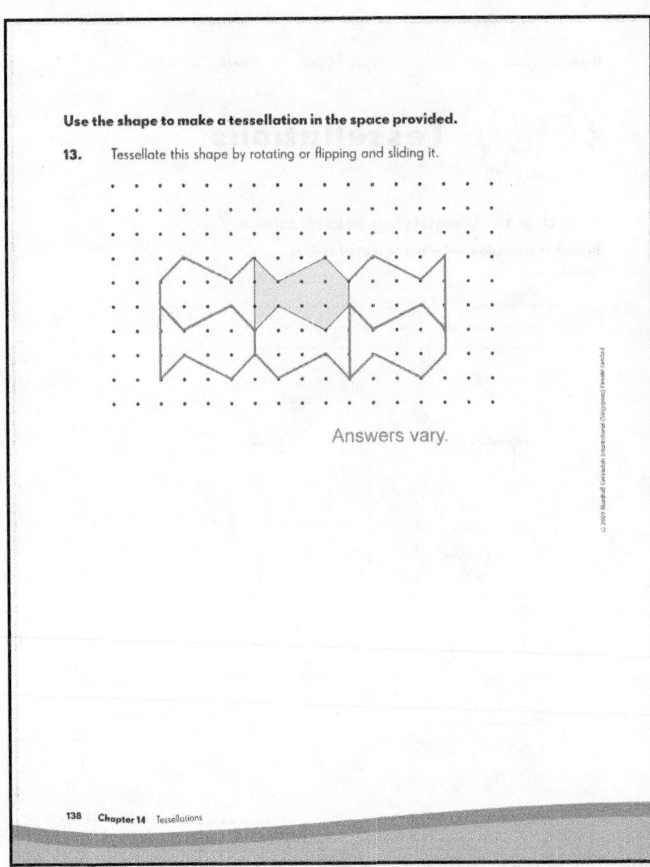

Use the shape to make a tessellation in the space provided.

13. Tessellate this shape by rotating or flipping and sliding it.

Answers vary.

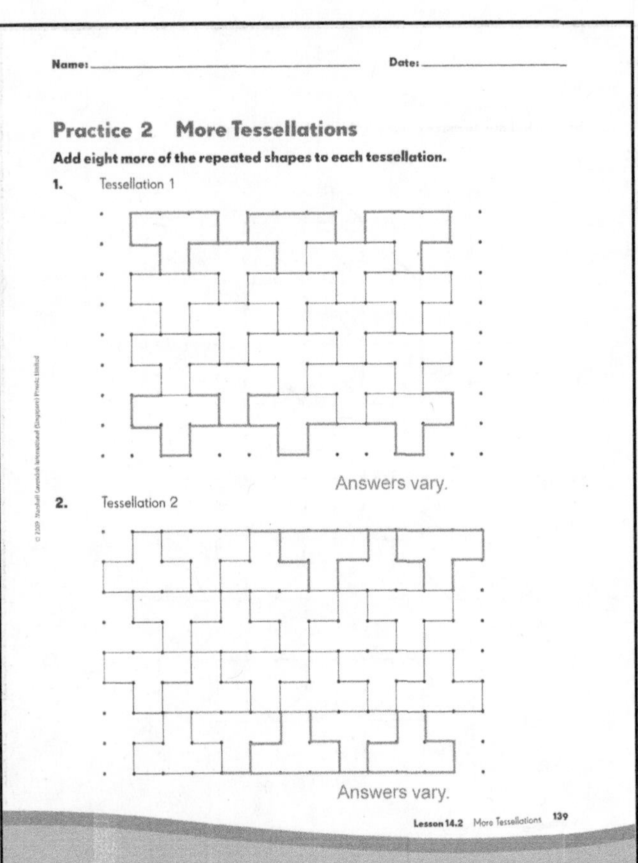

Name: ______________________ Date: ____________

Practice 2 More Tessellations

Add eight more of the repeated shapes to each tessellation.

1. Tessellation 1

Answers vary.

2. Tessellation 2

Answers vary.

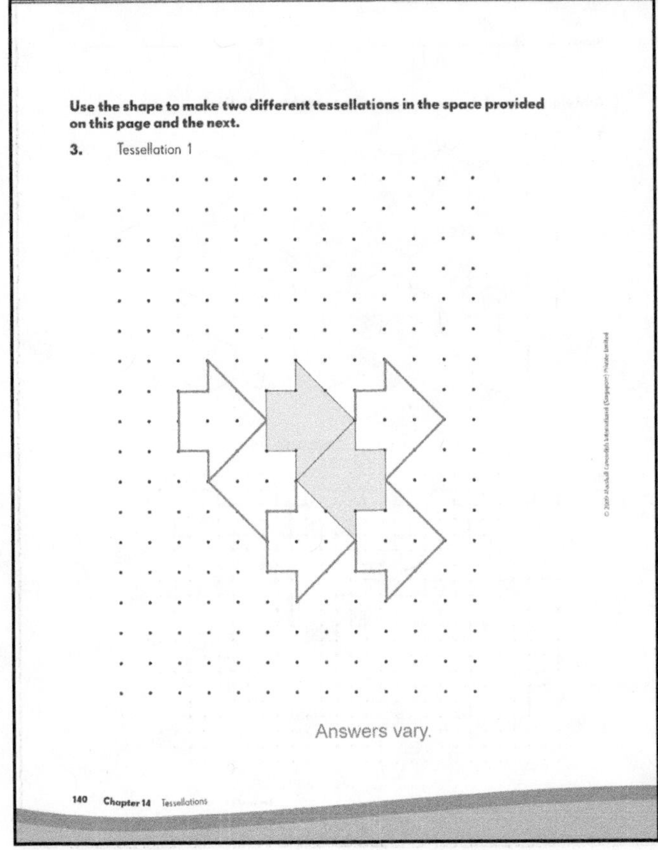

Use the shape to make two different tessellations in the space provided on this page and the next.

3. Tessellation 1

Answers vary.

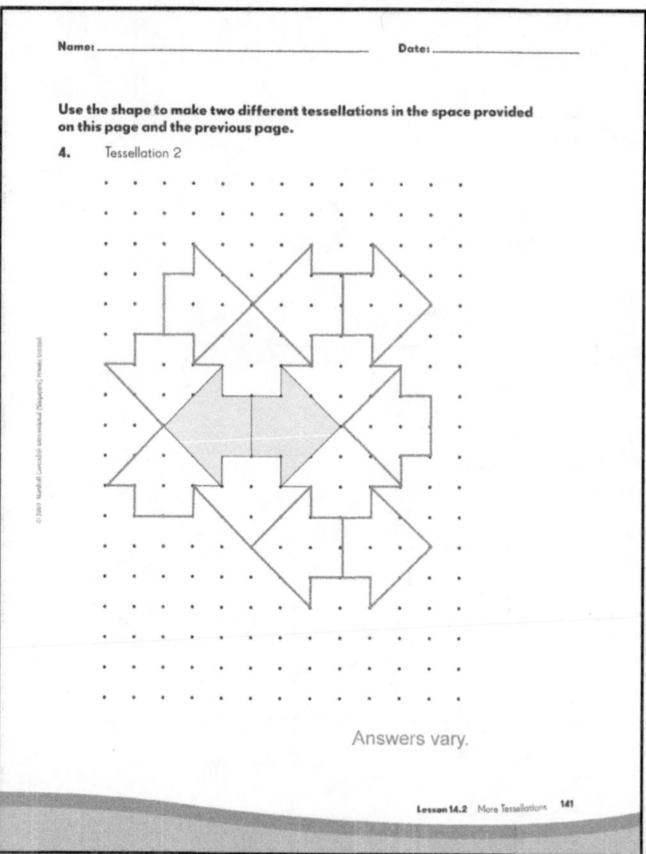
Name:
Date:
Use the shape to make two different tessellations in the space provided on this page and the previous page.
4. Tessellation 2
Answers vary.
Lesson 14.2 More Tessellations 141

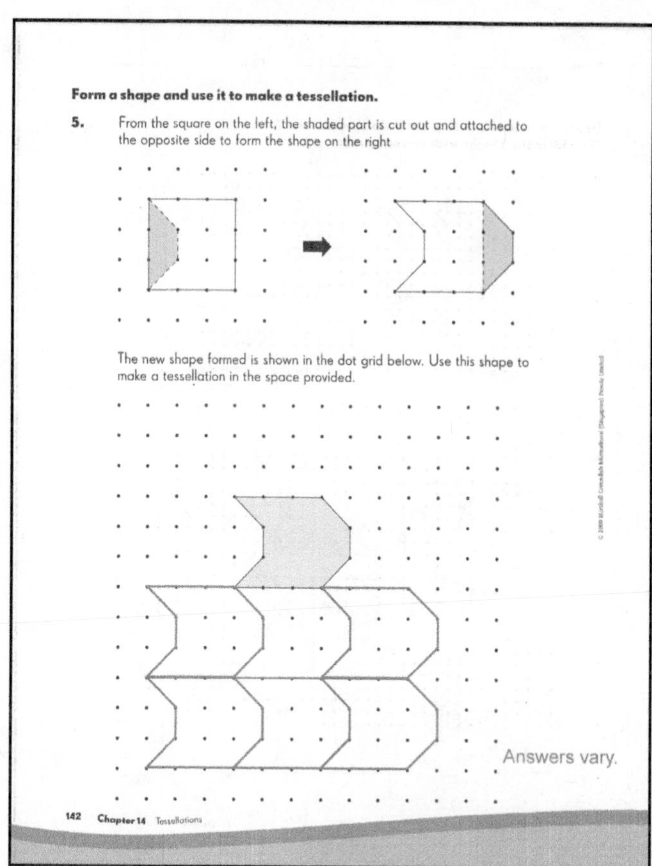
Form a shape and use it to make a tessellation.
5. From the square on the left, the shaded part is cut out and attached to the opposite side to form the shape on the right
The new shape formed is shown in the dot grid below. Use this shape to make a tessellation in the space provided.
Answers vary.
142 Chapter 14 Tessellations

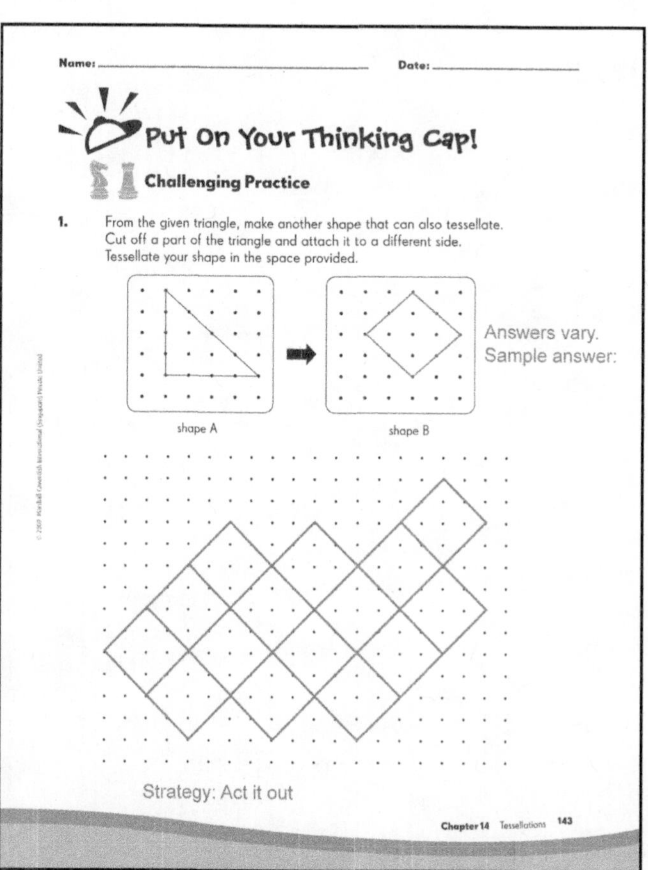
Name:
Date:
Put On Your Thinking Cap!
Challenging Practice
1. From the given triangle, make another shape that can also tessellate. Cut off a part of the triangle and attach it to a different side. Tessellate your shape in the space provided.
Answers vary.
Sample answer:
shape A
shape B
Strategy: Act it out
Chapter 14 Tessellations 143

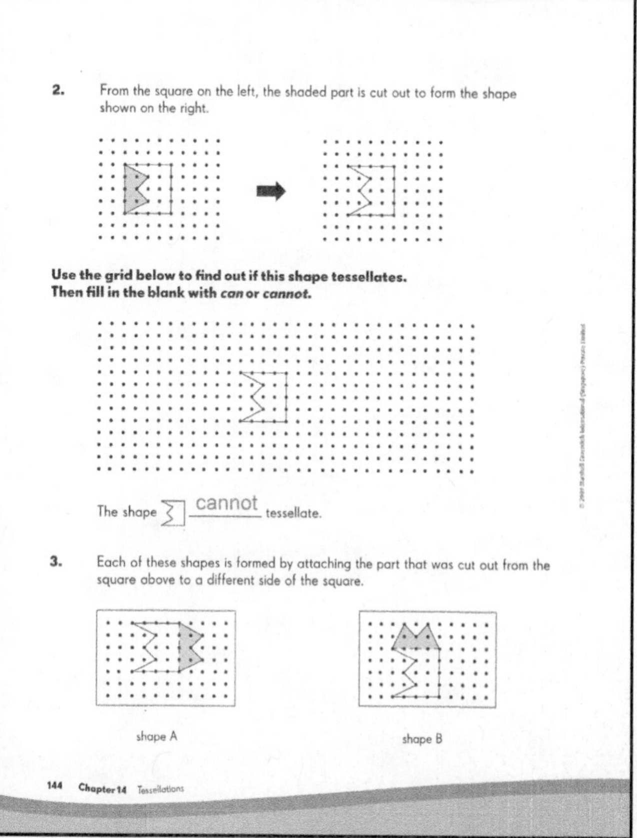
2. From the square on the left, the shaded part is cut out to form the shape shown on the right.
Use the grid below to find out if this shape tessellates.
Then fill in the blank with can or cannot.
The shape cannot tessellate.
3. Each of these shapes is formed by attaching the part that was cut out from the square above to a different side of the square.
shape A
shape B
144 Chapter 14 Tessellations

Chapter 14

Name: ____________________ Date: ____________________

Use the grid below to find out if the shapes tessellate.
Then fill in the blanks with *can* or *cannot.*

a.

The shape ____can____ tessellate.

b.

The shape ____can____ tessellate.

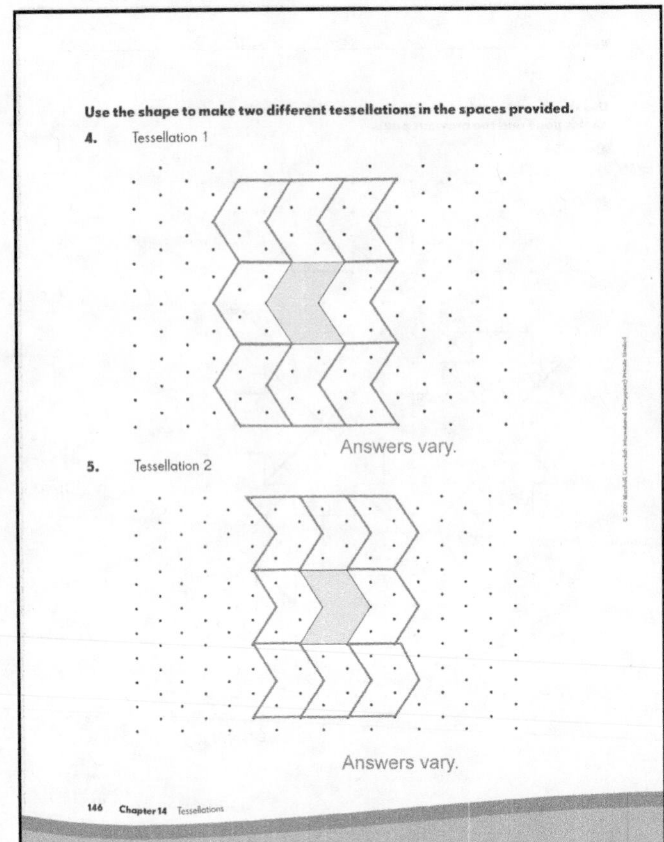

Use the shape to make two different tessellations in the spaces provided.

4. Tessellation 1

Answers vary.

5. Tessellation 2

Answers vary.

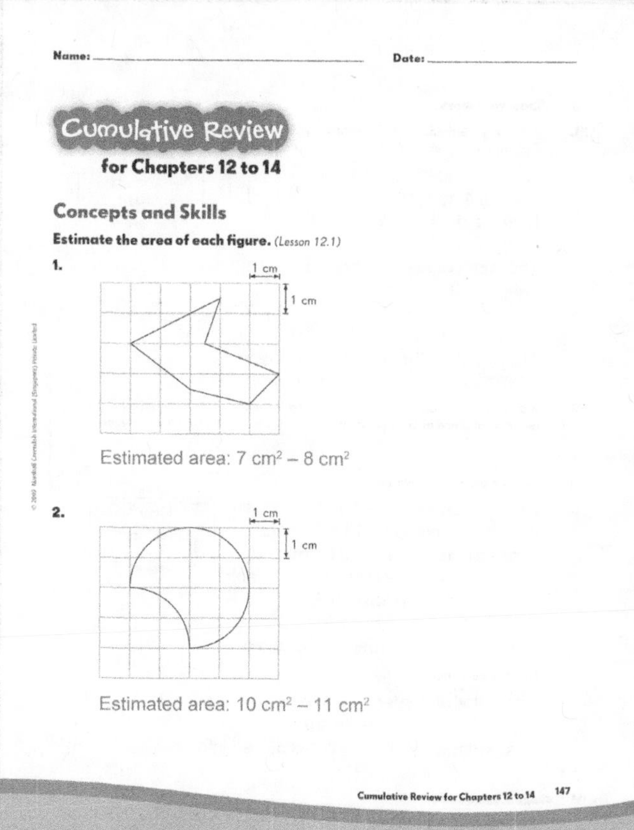

Name: ____________ Date: ____________

Cumulative Review for Chapters 12 to 14

Concepts and Skills

Estimate the area of each figure. *(Lesson 12.1)*

1\.

Estimated area: 7 cm² – 8 cm²

2\.

Estimated area: 10 cm² – 11 cm²

© 2009 Marshall Cavendish International (Singapore) Private Limited

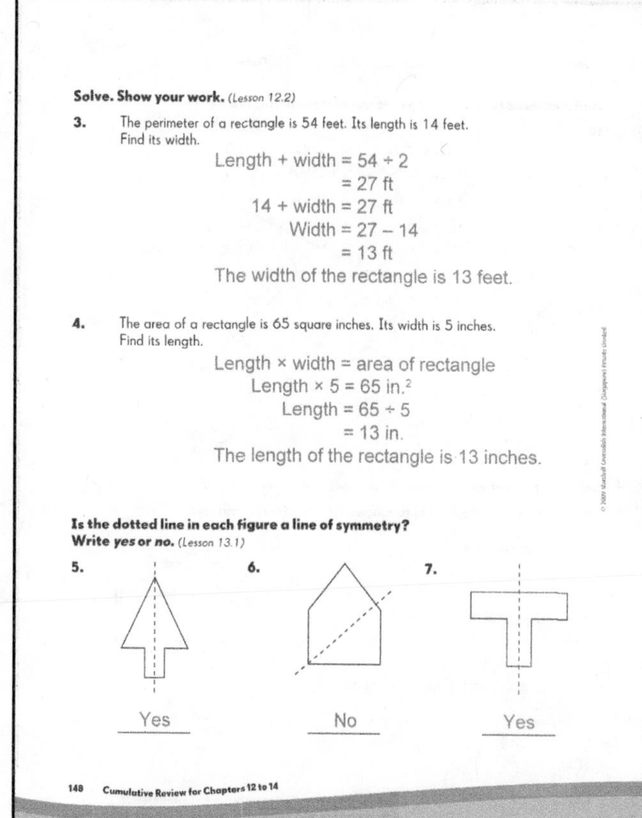

Solve. Show your work. *(Lesson 12.2)*

3\. The perimeter of a rectangle is 54 feet. Its length is 14 feet. Find its width.

$$\text{Length} + \text{width} = 54 \div 2$$
$$= 27 \text{ ft}$$
$$14 + \text{width} = 27 \text{ ft}$$
$$\text{Width} = 27 - 14$$
$$= 13 \text{ ft}$$

The width of the rectangle is 13 feet.

4\. The area of a rectangle is 65 square inches. Its width is 5 inches. Find its length.

$$\text{Length} \times \text{width} = \text{area of rectangle}$$
$$\text{Length} \times 5 = 65 \text{ in.}^2$$
$$\text{Length} = 65 \div 5$$
$$= 13 \text{ in.}$$

The length of the rectangle is 13 inches.

Is the dotted line in each figure a line of symmetry? Write *yes* or *no*. *(Lesson 13.1)*

5\. Yes

6\. No

7\. Yes

© 2009 Marshall Cavendish International (Singapore) Private Limited

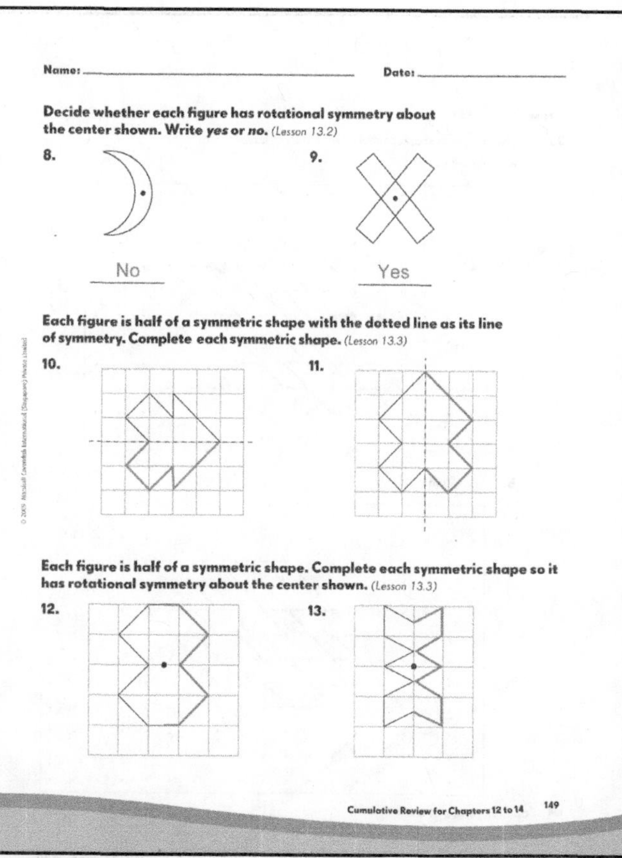

Name: ____________ Date: ____________

Decide whether each figure has rotational symmetry about the center shown. Write *yes* or *no*. *(Lesson 13.2)*

8\. No

9\. Yes

Each figure is half of a symmetric shape with the dotted line as its line of symmetry. Complete each symmetric shape. *(Lesson 13.3)*

10\.

11\.

Each figure is half of a symmetric shape. Complete each symmetric shape so it has rotational symmetry about the center shown. *(Lesson 13.3)*

12\.

13\.

© 2009 Marshall Cavendish International (Singapore) Private Limited

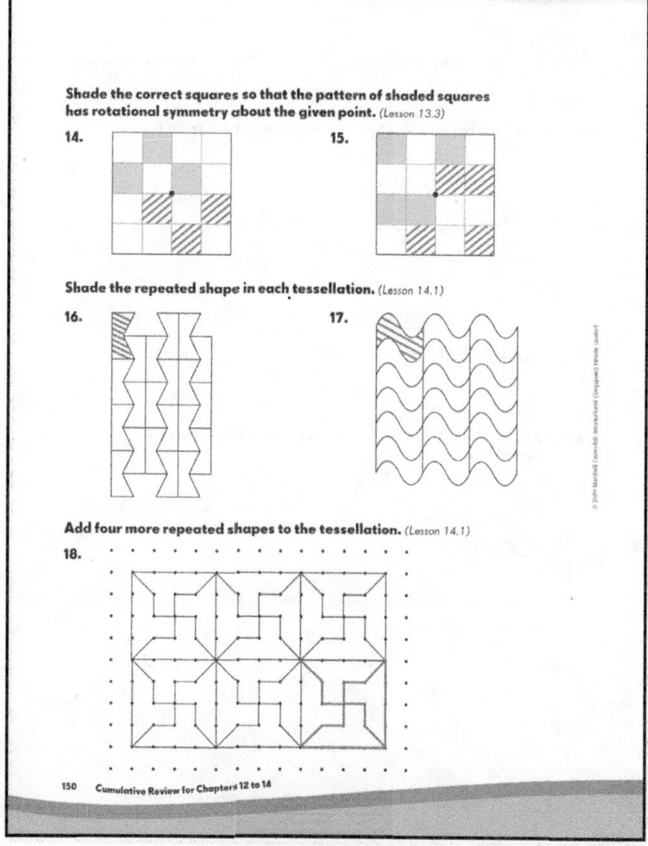

Shade the correct squares so that the pattern of shaded squares has rotational symmetry about the given point. *(Lesson 13.3)*

14\.

15\.

Shade the repeated shape in each tessellation. *(Lesson 14.1)*

16\.

17\.

Add four more repeated shapes to the tessellation. *(Lesson 14.1)*

18\.

© 2009 Marshall Cavendish International (Singapore) Private Limited

Name: ______________________ Date: ______________

Add nine more repeated shapes to the tessellation. *(Lesson 14.1)*

19.

Problem Solving

Solve. Show your work. *(Lessons 12.3 and 12.4)*

20. This figure is made up of rectangles. Find its perimeter and area.

Perimeter = 9 + 5 + 7 + 6 + 12 + 3
= 42 cm

Its perimeter is 42 centimeters.

Area = 7 × 6 + 9 × 5
= 42 + 45
= 87 cm^2

Its area is 87 square centimeters.

© 2020 Marshall Cavendish International (Singapore) Private Limited

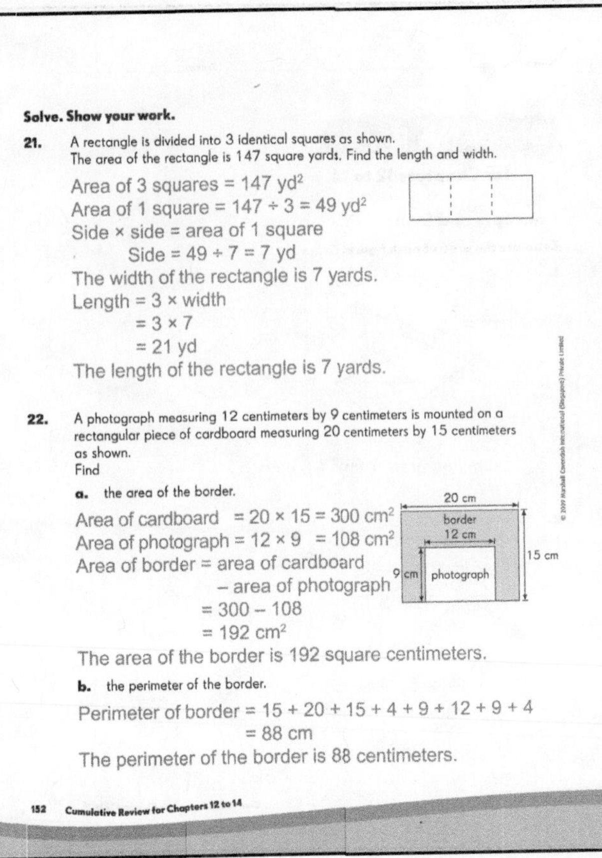

Solve. Show your work.

21. A rectangle is divided into 3 identical squares as shown. The area of the rectangle is 147 square yards. Find the length and width.

Area of 3 squares = 147 yd^2
Area of 1 square = 147 ÷ 3 = 49 yd^2
Side × side = area of 1 square
Side = 49 ÷ 7 = 7 yd
The width of the rectangle is 7 yards.
Length = 3 × width
= 3 × 7
= 21 yd
The length of the rectangle is 7 yards.

22. A photograph measuring 12 centimeters by 9 centimeters is mounted on a rectangular piece of cardboard measuring 20 centimeters by 15 centimeters as shown.
Find

a. the area of the border.

Area of cardboard = 20 × 15 = 300 cm^2
Area of photograph = 12 × 9 = 108 cm^2
Area of border = area of cardboard
– area of photograph
= 300 – 108
= 192 cm^2
The area of the border is 192 square centimeters.

b. the perimeter of the border.

Perimeter of border = 15 + 20 + 15 + 4 + 9 + 12 + 9 + 4
= 88 cm
The perimeter of the border is 88 centimeters.

© 2020 Marshall Cavendish International (Singapore) Private Limited

Name: ______________________ Date: ______________

Solve. *(Lesson 13.1)*

23. In the figure below, do joining points *A* and *B* form a line of symmetry? Explain your answer.

No. The two halves do not match exactly when the figure is folded about line *AB*.

Solve. *(Lessons 13.1 and 13.2)*

24. Using the letters H, I, M, O, S, and U, form a three-letter symmetrical pattern that has

a. only line symmetry. MUM

b. only rotational symmetry. SIS or SOS

c. both line and rotational symmetry. OHO

The letters may be used more than once.

© 2020 Marshall Cavendish International (Singapore) Private Limited

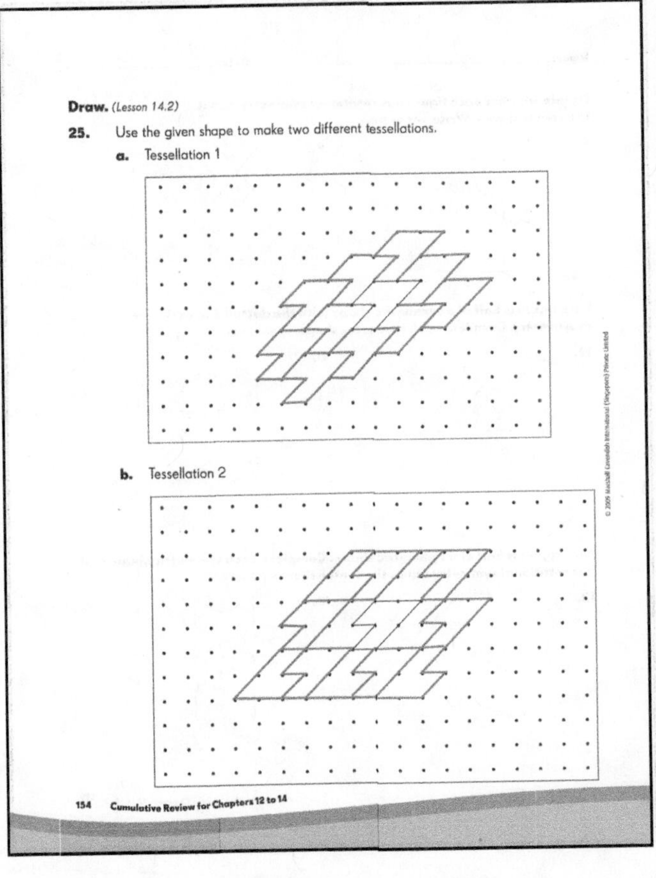

Draw. *(Lesson 14.2)*

25. Use the given shape to make two different tessellations.

a. Tessellation 1

b. Tessellation 2

© 2020 Marshall Cavendish International (Singapore) Private Limited

End-of-Year Review

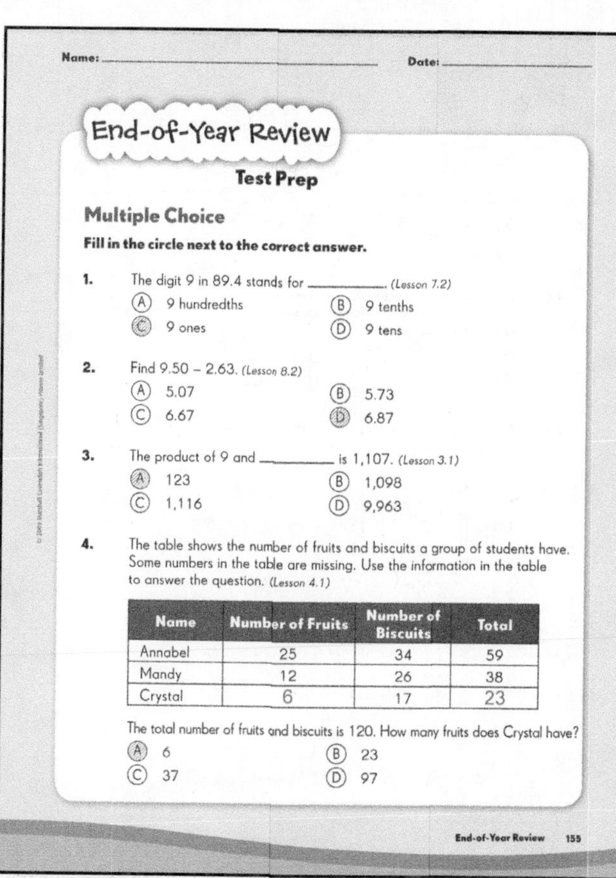

Name: ______________________ Date: ______________

End-of-Year Review

Test Prep

Multiple Choice

Fill in the circle next to the correct answer.

1. The digit 9 in 89.4 stands for ________. *(Lesson 7.2)*
   (A) 9 hundredths (B) 9 tenths
   (C) 9 ones (D) 9 tens

2. Find 9.50 – 2.63. *(Lesson 8.2)*
   (A) 5.07 (B) 5.73
   (C) 6.67 (D) 6.87

3. The product of 9 and ________ is 1,107. *(Lesson 3.1)*
   (A) 123 (B) 1,098
   (C) 1,116 (D) 9,963

4. The table shows the number of fruits and biscuits a group of students have. Some numbers in the table are missing. Use the information in the table to answer the question. *(Lesson 4.1)*

Name	Number of Fruits	Number of Biscuits	Total
Annabel	25	34	59
Mandy	12	26	38
Crystal	6	17	23

   The total number of fruits and biscuits is 120. How many fruits does Crystal have?
   (A) 6 (B) 23
   (C) 37 (D) 97

End-of-Year Review 155

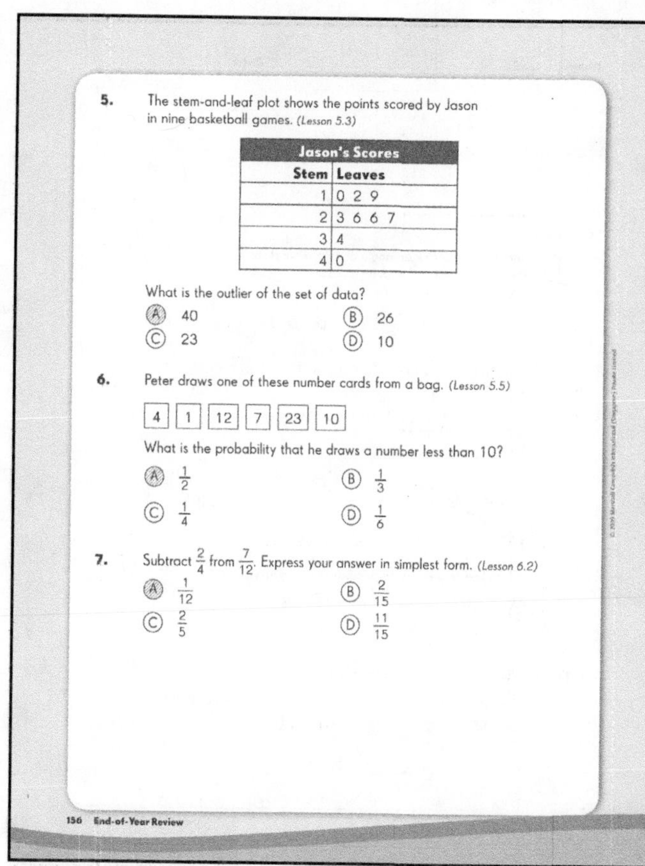

5. The stem-and-leaf plot shows the points scored by Jason in nine basketball games. *(Lesson 5.3)*

Jason's Scores

Stem	Leaves
1	0 2 9
2	3 6 6 7
3	4
4	0

   What is the outlier of the set of data?
   (A) 40 (B) 26
   (C) 23 (D) 10

6. Peter draws one of these number cards from a bag. *(Lesson 5.5)*

   4 1 12 7 23 10

   What is the probability that he draws a number less than 10?
   (A) $\frac{1}{2}$ (B) $\frac{1}{3}$
   (C) $\frac{1}{4}$ (D) $\frac{1}{6}$

7. Subtract $\frac{2}{4}$ from $\frac{7}{12}$. Express your answer in simplest form. *(Lesson 6.2)*
   (A) $\frac{1}{12}$ (B) $\frac{2}{15}$
   (C) $\frac{2}{5}$ (D) $\frac{11}{15}$

156 End-of-Year Review

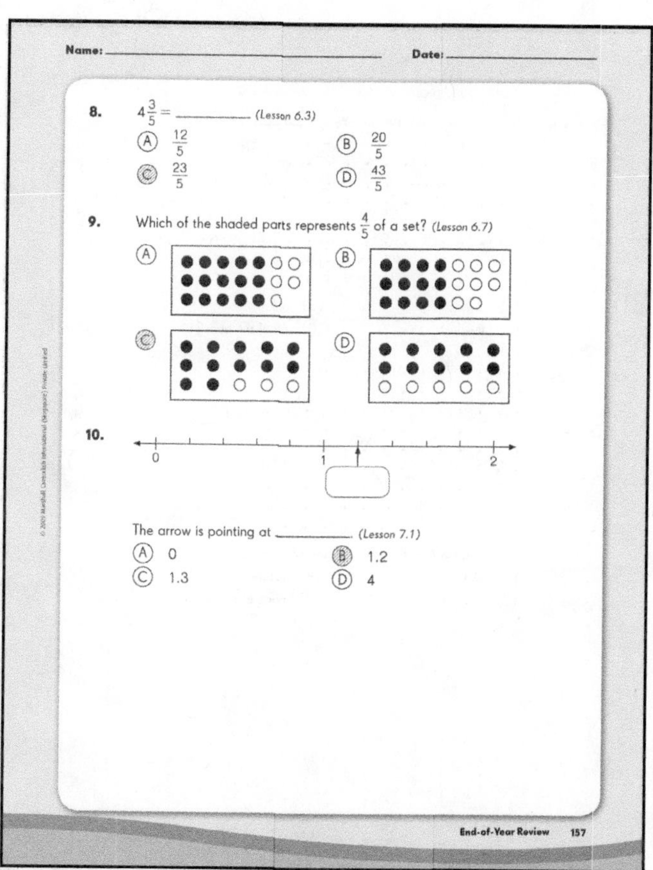

Name: ______________________ Date: ______________

8. $4\frac{3}{5}$ = ________ *(Lesson 6.3)*
   (A) $\frac{12}{5}$ (B) $\frac{20}{5}$
   (C) $\frac{23}{5}$ (D) $\frac{43}{5}$

9. Which of the shaded parts represents $\frac{4}{5}$ of a set? *(Lesson 6.7)*
   (A) (B)
   (C) (D)

10.

   The arrow is pointing at ________. *(Lesson 7.1)*
   (A) 0 (B) 1.2
   (C) 1.3 (D) 4

End-of-Year Review 157

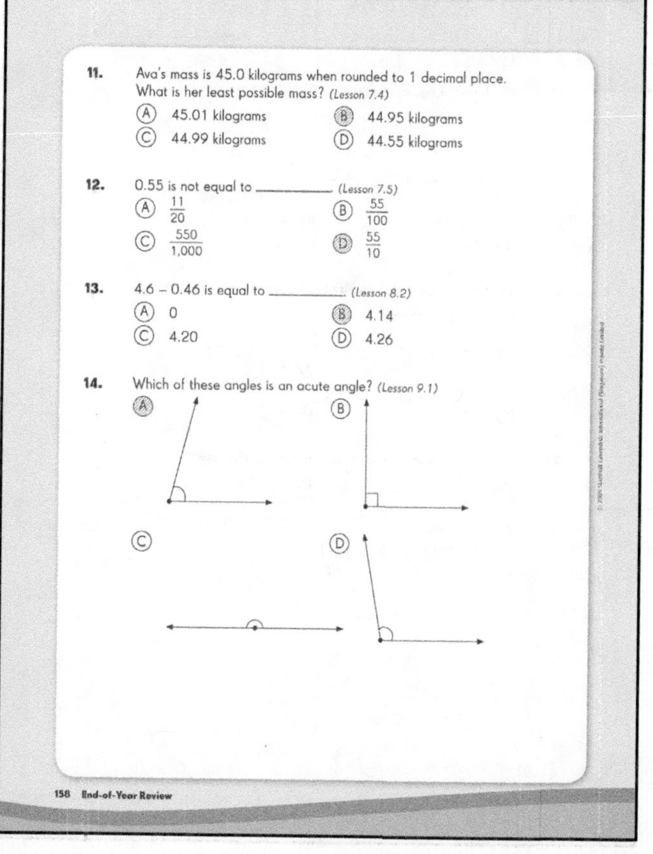

11. Ava's mass is 45.0 kilograms when rounded to 1 decimal place. What is her least possible mass? *(Lesson 7.4)*
   (A) 45.01 kilograms (B) 44.95 kilograms
   (C) 44.99 kilograms (D) 44.55 kilograms

12. 0.55 is not equal to ________. *(Lesson 7.5)*
   (A) $\frac{11}{20}$ (B) $\frac{55}{100}$
   (C) $\frac{550}{1,000}$ (D) $\frac{55}{10}$

13. 4.6 – 0.46 is equal to ________. *(Lesson 8.2)*
   (A) 0 (B) 4.14
   (C) 4.20 (D) 4.26

14. Which of these angles is an acute angle? *(Lesson 9.1)*
   (A) (B)
   (C) (D)

158 End-of-Year Review

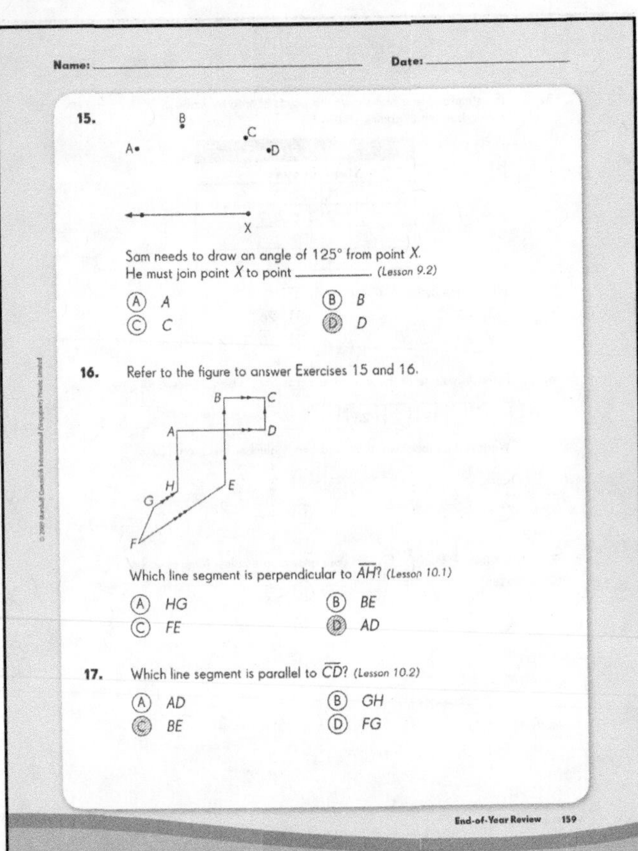

Name: ______________________ Date: ______________

15.

Sam needs to draw an angle of 125° from point *X*. He must join point *X* to point ________. *(Lesson 9.2)*

Ⓐ *A* Ⓑ *B*
Ⓒ *C* Ⓓ *D*

16. Refer to the figure to answer Exercises 15 and 16.

Which line segment is perpendicular to $\overline{AH}$? *(Lesson 10.1)*

Ⓐ *HG* Ⓑ *BE*
Ⓒ *FE* Ⓓ *AD*

17. Which line segment is parallel to $\overline{CD}$? *(Lesson 10.2)*

Ⓐ *AD* Ⓑ *GH*
Ⓒ *BE* Ⓓ *FG*

End-of-Year Review 159

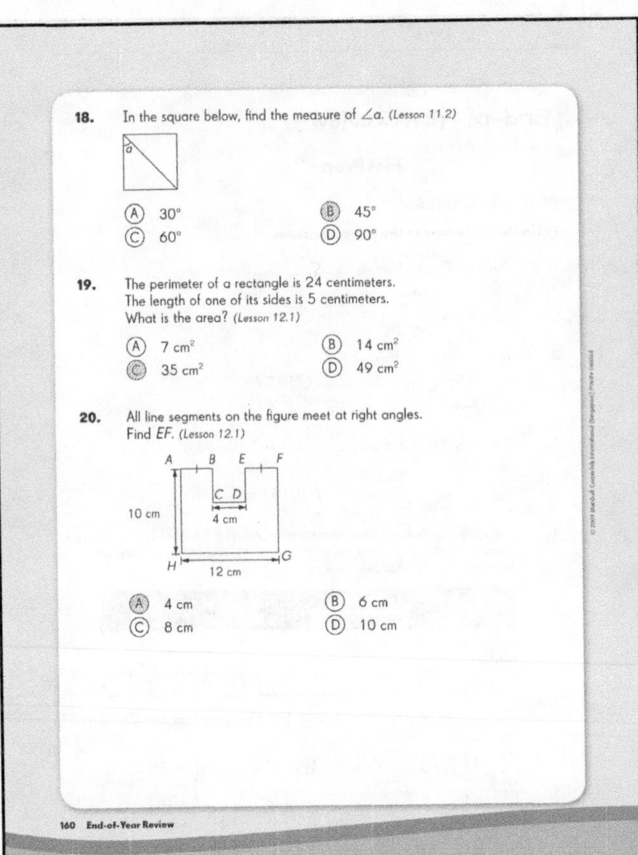

18. In the square below, find the measure of ∠*a*. *(Lesson 11.2)*

Ⓐ 30° Ⓑ 45°
Ⓒ 60° Ⓓ 90°

19. The perimeter of a rectangle is 24 centimeters. The length of one of its sides is 5 centimeters. What is the area? *(Lesson 12.1)*

Ⓐ 7 cm² Ⓑ 14 cm²
Ⓒ 35 cm² Ⓓ 49 cm²

20. All line segments on the figure meet at right angles. Find *EF*. *(Lesson 12.1)*

Ⓐ 4 cm Ⓑ 6 cm
Ⓒ 8 cm Ⓓ 10 cm

160 End-of-Year Review

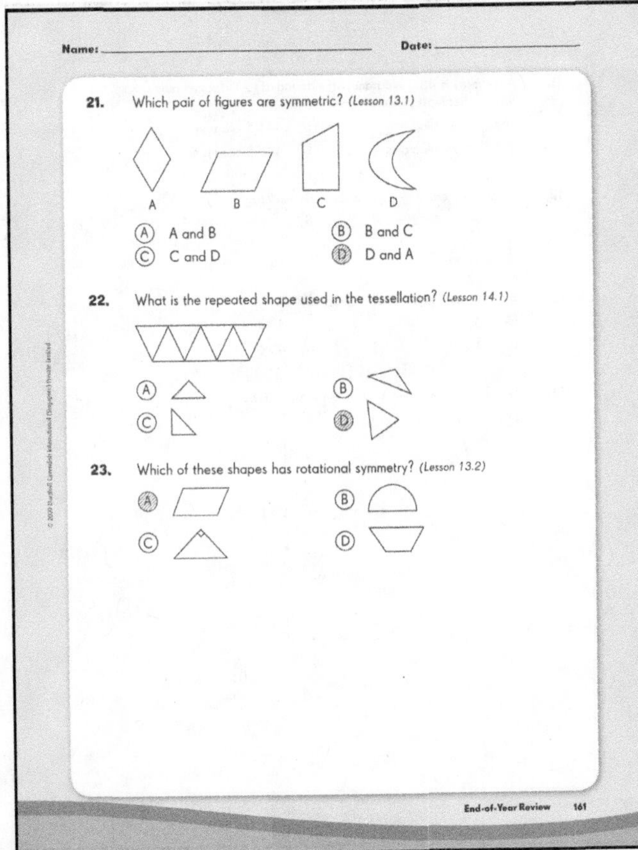

Name: ______________________ Date: ______________

21. Which pair of figures are symmetric? *(Lesson 13.1)*

Ⓐ A and B Ⓑ B and C
Ⓒ C and D Ⓓ D and A

22. What is the repeated shape used in the tessellation? *(Lesson 14.1)*

Ⓐ Ⓑ
Ⓒ Ⓓ

23. Which of these shapes has rotational symmetry? *(Lesson 13.2)*

Ⓐ Ⓑ
Ⓒ Ⓓ

End-of-Year Review 161

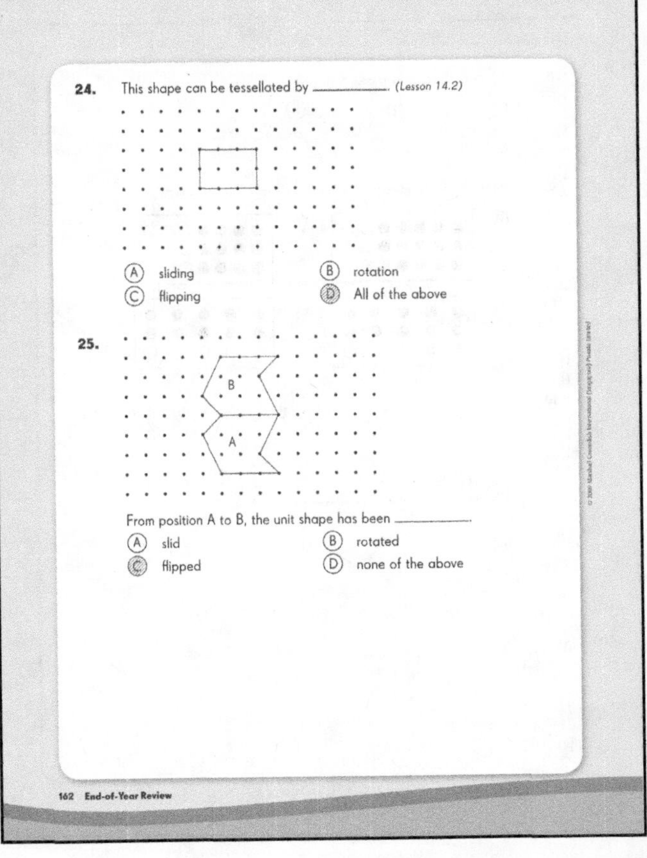

24. This shape can be tessellated by ________. *(Lesson 14.2)*

Ⓐ sliding Ⓑ rotation
Ⓒ flipping Ⓓ All of the above

25.

From position A to B, the unit shape has been ________.

Ⓐ slid Ⓑ rotated
Ⓒ flipped Ⓓ none of the above

162 End-of-Year Review

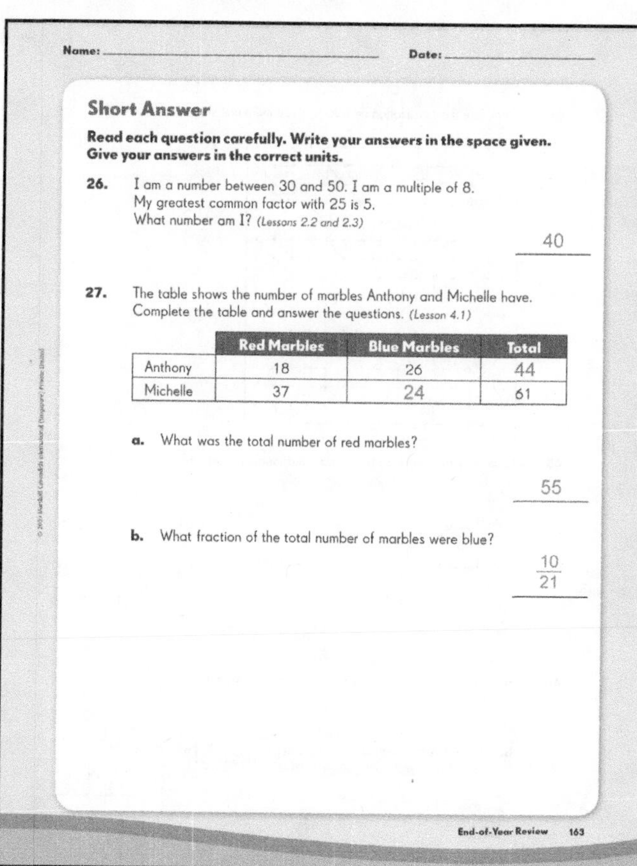

Name: Date:

Short Answer

Read each question carefully. Write your answers in the space given. Give your answers in the correct units.

26. I am a number between 30 and 50. I am a multiple of 8. My greatest common factor with 25 is 5. What number am I? *(Lessons 2.2 and 2.3)*

40

27. The table shows the number of marbles Anthony and Michelle have. Complete the table and answer the questions. *(Lesson 4.1)*

	Red Marbles	Blue Marbles	Total
Anthony	18	26	44
Michelle	37	24	61

a. What was the total number of red marbles?

55

b. What fraction of the total number of marbles were blue?

$\frac{10}{21}$

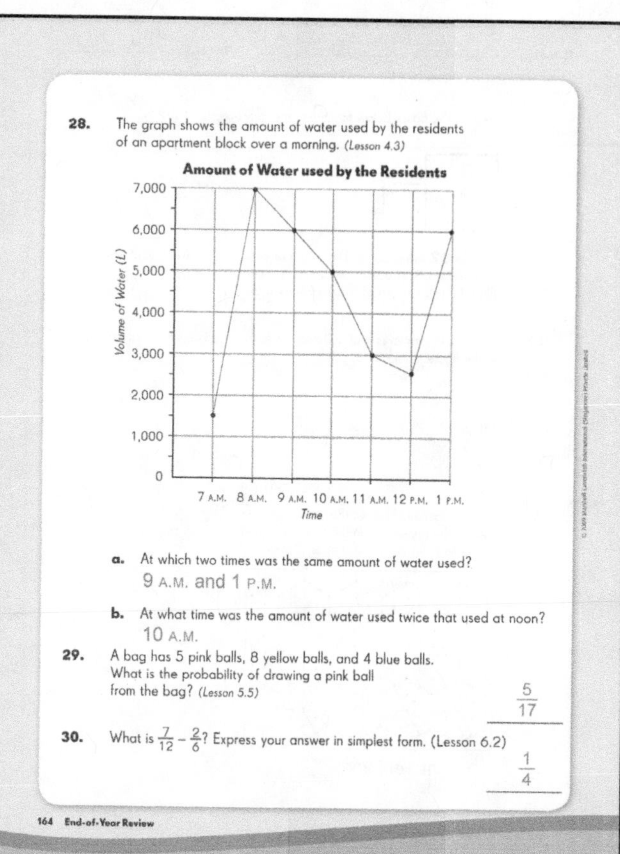

28. The graph shows the amount of water used by the residents of an apartment block over a morning. *(Lesson 4.3)*

a. At which two times was the same amount of water used?
9 A.M. and 1 P.M.

b. At what time was the amount of water used twice that used at noon?
10 A.M.

29. A bag has 5 pink balls, 8 yellow balls, and 4 blue balls. What is the probability of drawing a pink ball from the bag? *(Lesson 5.5)*

$\frac{5}{17}$

30. What is $\frac{7}{12} - \frac{2}{6}$? Express your answer in simplest form. (Lesson 6.2)

$\frac{1}{4}$

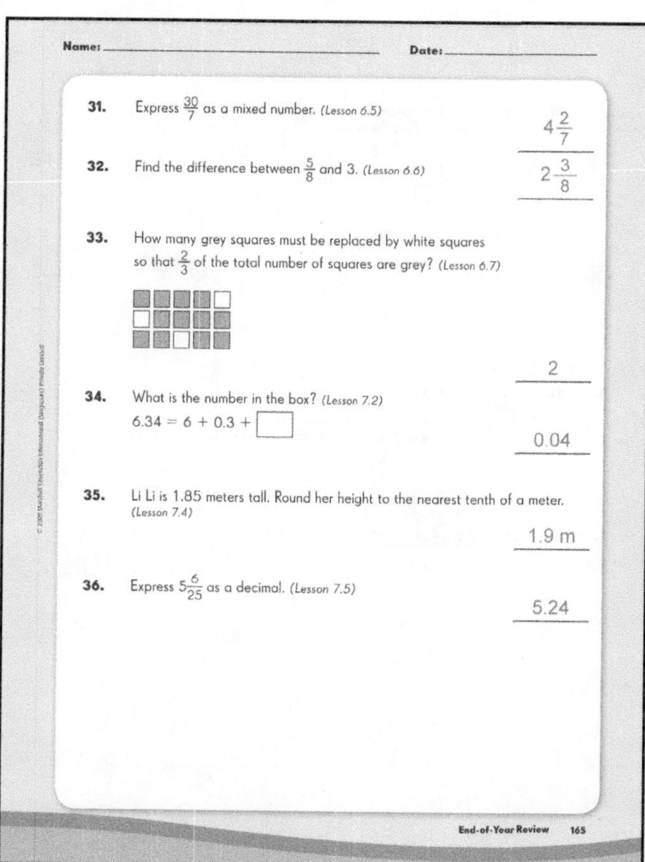

Name: Date:

31. Express $\frac{30}{7}$ as a mixed number. *(Lesson 6.5)*

$4\frac{2}{7}$

32. Find the difference between $\frac{5}{8}$ and 3. *(Lesson 6.6)*

$2\frac{3}{8}$

33. How many grey squares must be replaced by white squares so that $\frac{2}{3}$ of the total number of squares are grey? *(Lesson 6.7)*

2

34. What is the number in the box? *(Lesson 7.2)*
6.34 = 6 + 0.3 + ☐

0.04

35. Li Li is 1.85 meters tall. Round her height to the nearest tenth of a meter. *(Lesson 7.4)*

1.9 m

36. Express $5\frac{6}{25}$ as a decimal. *(Lesson 7.5)*

5.24

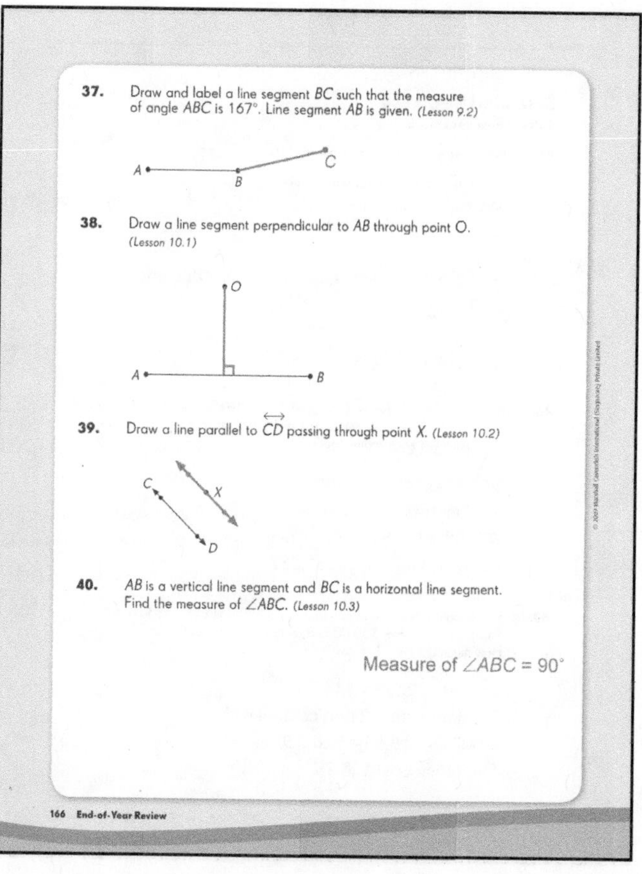

37. Draw and label a line segment *BC* such that the measure of angle *ABC* is 167°. Line segment *AB* is given. *(Lesson 9.2)*

38. Draw a line segment perpendicular to *AB* through point O. *(Lesson 10.1)*

39. Draw a line parallel to $\overleftrightarrow{CD}$ passing through point *X*. *(Lesson 10.2)*

40. *AB* is a vertical line segment and *BC* is a horizontal line segment. Find the measure of ∠*ABC*. *(Lesson 10.3)*

Measure of ∠*ABC* = 90°

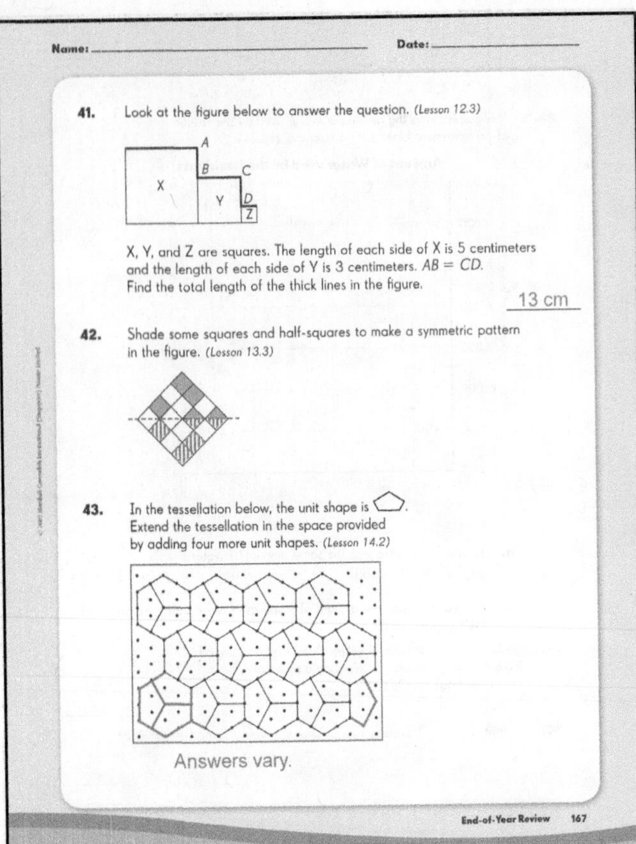
Name: ______ Date: ______

41. Look at the figure below to answer the question. *(Lesson 12.3)*

X, Y, and Z are squares. The length of each side of X is 5 centimeters and the length of each side of Y is 3 centimeters. AB = CD. Find the total length of the thick lines in the figure.

13 cm

42. Shade some squares and half-squares to make a symmetric pattern in the figure. *(Lesson 13.3)*

43. In the tessellation below, the unit shape is ⬠. Extend the tessellation in the space provided by adding four more unit shapes. *(Lesson 14.2)*

Answers vary.

End-of-Year Review 167

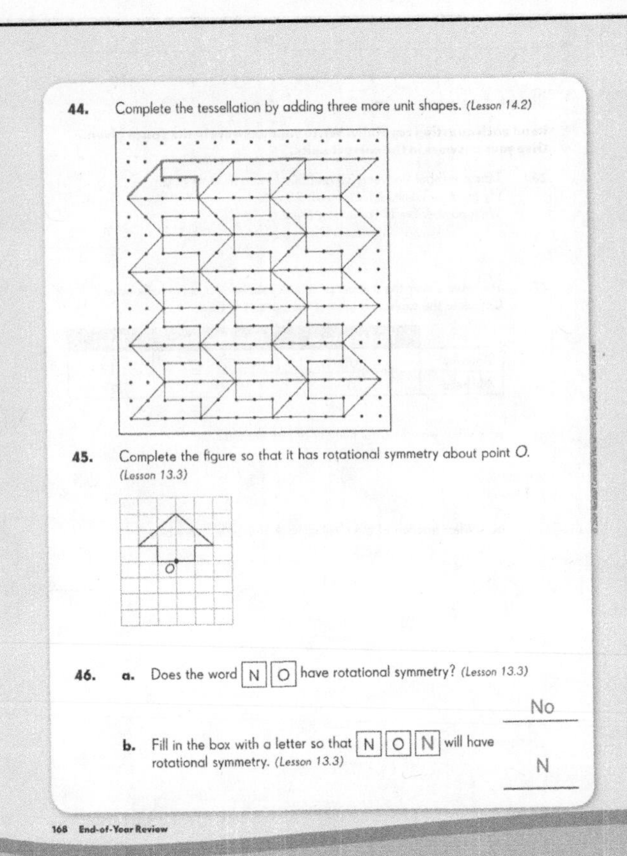
44. Complete the tessellation by adding three more unit shapes. *(Lesson 14.2)*

45. Complete the figure so that it has rotational symmetry about point *O*. *(Lesson 13.3)*

46. a. Does the word N O have rotational symmetry? *(Lesson 13.3)*

No

b. Fill in the box with a letter so that N O N will have rotational symmetry. *(Lesson 13.3)*

N

168 End-of-Year Review

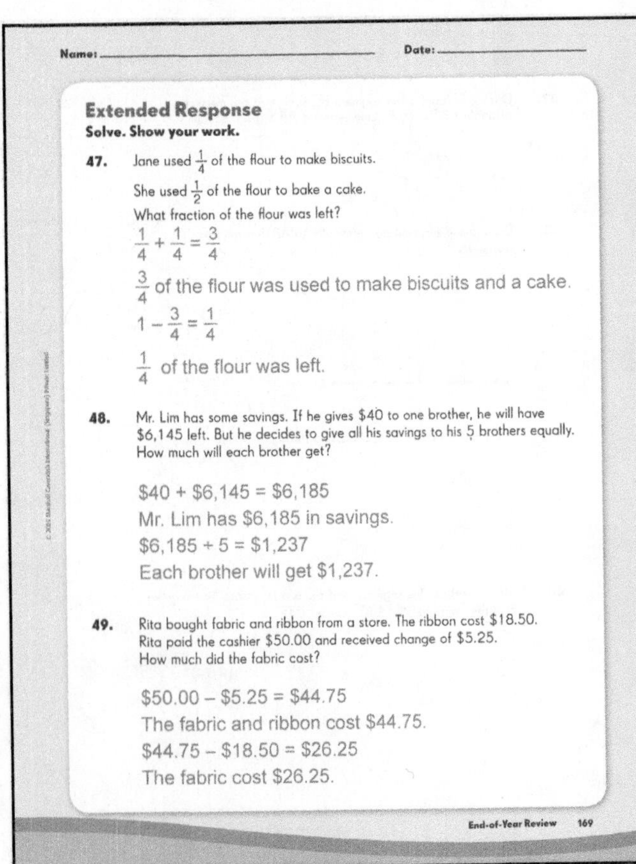
Name: ______ Date: ______

Extended Response

Solve. Show your work.

47. Jane used $\frac{1}{4}$ of the flour to make biscuits.
She used $\frac{1}{2}$ of the flour to bake a cake.
What fraction of the flour was left?

$\frac{1}{4} + \frac{1}{4} = \frac{3}{4}$

$\frac{3}{4}$ of the flour was used to make biscuits and a cake.

$1 - \frac{3}{4} = \frac{1}{4}$

$\frac{1}{4}$ of the flour was left.

48. Mr. Lim has some savings. If he gives $40 to one brother, he will have $6,145 left. But he decides to give all his savings to his 5 brothers equally. How much will each brother get?

$40 + $6,145 = $6,185
Mr. Lim has $6,185 in savings.
$6,185 ÷ 5 = $1,237
Each brother will get $1,237.

49. Rita bought fabric and ribbon from a store. The ribbon cost $18.50. Rita paid the cashier $50.00 and received change of $5.25. How much did the fabric cost?

$50.00 – $5.25 = $44.75
The fabric and ribbon cost $44.75.
$44.75 – $18.50 = $26.25
The fabric cost $26.25.

End-of-Year Review 169

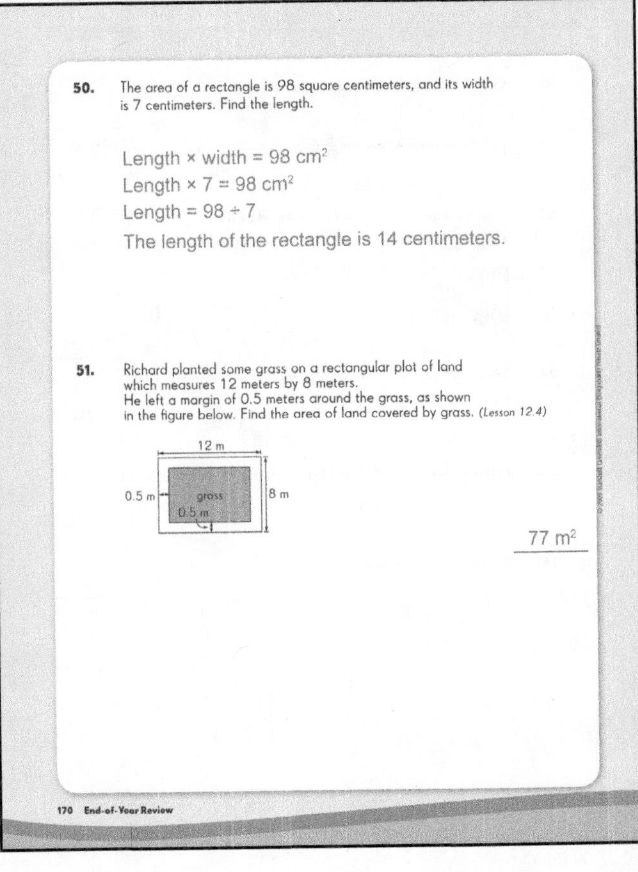
50. The area of a rectangle is 98 square centimeters, and its width is 7 centimeters. Find the length.

Length × width = 98 cm^2
Length × 7 = 98 cm^2
Length = 98 ÷ 7
The length of the rectangle is 14 centimeters.

51. Richard planted some grass on a rectangular plot of land which measures 12 meters by 8 meters. He left a margin of 0.5 meters around the grass, as shown in the figure below. Find the area of land covered by grass. *(Lesson 12.4)*

77 m^2

170 End-of-Year Review

End-of-Year Review

Additional Answers

Student Book

Chapter 1

Lesson 1.2, Let's Explore! (page 17)

1. The numbers increase by 1,000.
2. The numbers decrease by 10,000.
3. The numbers in the green and yellow boxes have the same number of hundreds, tens, and ones.
   30,432 – 21,432 = 9,000 and
   19,432 – 10,432 = 9,000.
   They have the same difference of 9,000.
4. The numbers in the red and blue boxes have the same number of hundreds, tens, and ones.
   40,432 – 22,432 = 18,000 and
   18,432 – 432 = 18,000.
   They have the same difference of 9,000.

Lesson 1.2, Put on Your Thinking Cap! (page 22)

4. 11,000 13,000 15,000 17,000 19,000
   10,000 12,000 14,000 16,000 18,000 20,000
   16,500

5. 16,510 16,530 16,550 16,570 16,590
   16,500 16,520 16,540 16,560 16,580 17,000
   16,575

Chapter 2

Lesson 2.3, Put on Your Thinking Cap! (page 62)

1. List the multiples of 3 and 5.
   Multiples of 3: 3, 6, 9, 12, 15, 18, 21, 24, 27, 30, 33
   Multiples of 5: 5, 10, 15, 20, 25, 30, 35
   - > 23 and < 32: 24, 25, 27, and 30
   - Divisible by 3: 24, 27, and 30
   - When 3 is added to the number, it can be divided by 5: 27 + 3 = 30, so the answer is 27.
2. Find the multiples of 20 and 5 that are less than 100.
   Multiples of 20: 20, 40, 60, 80, 100
   Multiples of 5: … 20, 25, 30, 35, 40, 45, 50, 55, 60, 65, 70, 75, 80, 85, 90, 95, 100
   So the possible prices are: $20, $40, $60, $80.

Chapter 3

Lesson 3.1, Math Journal (page 83)

1.
$$\begin{array}{r} \scriptsize{2\ 2\ 1} \\ 6,875 \\ \times\quad\ 3 \\ \hline 20,625 \end{array}$$

For each step, multiply the digit for each place by 3.

Step 1: 5 ones × 3 = 15 ones → Regroup the ones.
15 ones = 1 ten and 5 ones

Step 2: 7 tens × 3 = 21 tens → Add and regroup the tens. 1 ten + 21 tens = 22 tens = 2 hundreds and 2 tens

Step 3: 8 hundreds × 3 = 24 hundreds → Add and regroup the hundreds. 2 hundreds + 24 hundreds = 26 hundreds = 2 thousands and 6 hundreds

Step 4: 6 thousands × 3 = 18 thousands → Add and regroup the thousands → 2 thousands + 18 thousands = 20 thousands

So, 6,875 × 3 = 20,625.

Lesson 3.4, Let's Explore! (page 83)

Find the estimated quotient for 468 ÷ 5.
40 ÷ 5 = 8 → 400 ÷ 5 = 80
45 ÷ 5 = 9 → 450 ÷ 5 = 90
Only Carol's answer is reasonable.
Allen found the estimated product; Ben did not divide the estimated number; and Dawn divided 45 ones instead of 45 tens.

Chapter 4

Lesson 4.3, Let's Practice (page 150)

1. Use a bar graph to represent and compare data with larger numbers.
2. Use a picture graph to represent and compare data with smaller numbers.
3. Use a line graph to show how data changes over time.

Chapter 5

Lesson 5.2, Let's Explore! (page 177)

Step 3: The median is more typical based on this set of data. This is because the number of video games sold on Friday is an outlier, which is far greater than the rest of the data. It is likely that more video games were sold on Friday as it is the last day before the weekend.

Lesson 5.2, Guided Practice (page 182)

17. Yes; The number of Xs on either side of the line plot is the same, so the mean is the number in the middle, 7.

Lesson 5.2, Math Journal (page 183)

1. False; The median of this set of data is 12. If the set of numbers is even, we can find the median by finding the total of the two middle numbers and dividing it by 2.
2. False; The mean of this set of data is 13 R 2. The median is 12.

Lesson 5.2, Let's Practice (pages 184 and 185)

6. Yes
7. Yes
8. Yes
9. Mean = 16 yd; Median = 6 yd; Mode = 5 yd
   The median and mode are unchanged.
   The mean is not typical of the set of data.

Lesson 5.4, Let's Practice (page 197)

3. Draw 6 red marbles; Draw 6 marbles of any color but red.
4. Draw 6 marbles of which at least 4 are red;
   Draw 6 marbles of which less than 3 are red;
   Draw 6 marbles of which 3 are red.

Lesson 5.5, Let's Explore! (page 200)

The probability of each favorable outcome is the same as long as the number of cards is the same.

Lesson 5.6, Guided Practice (page 209)

6. c. Accept all reasonable answers; for example, change the numbers 28 to 26 and 56 to 58.

Lesson 5.6, Guided Practice (page 214)

12. b. Yes, the mode is typical of the set of data.

Lesson 5.6, Put on Your Thinking Cap! (page 215)

Since there are an equal number of students on each team, there are either 8, 6, 4, or 2 students altogether.
8 students: 4 × 48 = 192; 4 × 62 = 248, 248 – 192 = 56
6 students: 3 × 48 = 144; 3 × 62 = 186; 186 – 144 = 42
4 students: 2 × 48 = 96; 2 × 62 = 124; 124 – 96 = 28
2 students: 1 × 48 = 48; 1 × 62 = 62; 62 – 48 = 14
There are 6 students altogether, and 3 students on each team.

Workbook

Chapter 5

Practice 6 (page 123)

5. e. The additional score of 80 will increase the median and mean of the set of data to 71. Since there are 3 scores of 72, the mode will remain unchanged. The range of the set of data is most affected by the additional score; it will increase to more than double its original number, from 8 to 15.

Additional Answers

Additional Answers

Student Book

Chapter 9

Lesson 9.1, Let's Practice (page 93)

2. measure of $\angle AOC = 20°$, measure of $\angle AOD = 35°$, measure of $\angle COD = 15°$, measure of $\angle COE = 70°$, measure of $\angle DOE = 55°$, measure of $\angle EOF = 35°$, measure of $\angle EOG = 70°$, measure of $\angle FOG = 35°$, measure of $\angle FOB = 55°$, measure of $\angle GOB = 20°$
3. measure of $\angle AOF = 125°$, measure of $\angle AOG = 160°$, measure of $\angle AOB = 180°$, measure of $\angle COF = 105°$, measure of $\angle COG = 140°$, measure of $\angle COB = 160°$, measure of $\angle DOG = 125°$, measure of $\angle DOB = 145°$

Chapter 10

Quick Check (page 110)

12. $\overleftrightarrow{AD}$ is perpendicular to $\overleftrightarrow{DC}$.
    $\overleftrightarrow{BC}$ is perpendicular to $\overleftrightarrow{DC}$.
    $\overleftrightarrow{AD}$ is parallel to $\overleftrightarrow{BC}$.
13. $\overleftrightarrow{PQ}$ is perpendicular to $\overleftrightarrow{QR}$.
    $\overleftrightarrow{PQ}$ is parallel to $\overleftrightarrow{TS}$.

Chapter 12

Math Journal (page 188)

1. Step 1: Multiply the length by 2.
   Step 2: Subtract the product from the perimeter.
   Step 3: Divide the difference by 2 to get the width of the rectangle.
2. No, Alice is wrong. To find the length of one side of a square given its area, Alice should find a number which when multiplied by itself gives the area. This number is the length of one side of the square.

Chapter 13

Lesson 13.2, Guided Practice (page 206)

3. These figures have rotational symmetry.

They can be rotated less than a full turn (360°) about a point and look the same as they did before the turn.

Chapter 14

Math Journal (page 235)

This is how the second shape is created from the rectangle: Cut a triangle from the bottom of the rectangle, flip it, and put it at the top.

Yes, it matters how shapes are modified. Not all modified shapes can tessellate.

Modifications that involve flipping, rotating, and sliding will allow the shape to continue to tessellate.

Workbook

Chapter 12

Put on Your Thinking Cap! (page 117)

1. 21 rectangles with an area of 12 square centimeters

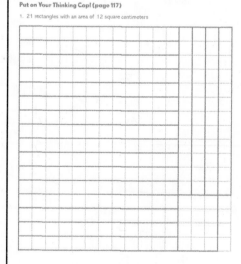

Additional Answers

27 rectangles with an area of 9 square centimeters